T5-DHA-611

THE OXFORD HANDBOOK OF

VIRTUALITY

THE OXFORD HANDBOOK OF

VIRTUALITY

EDITED BY MARK GRIMSHAW

OXFORD
UNIVERSITY PRESS

Library
Quest University Canada
3200 University Boulevard
Squamish, BC V8B 0N8

OXFORD
UNIVERSITY PRESS

Oxford University Press is a department of the University of Oxford.
It furthers the University's objective of excellence in research, scholarship,
and education by publishing worldwide.

Oxford   New York
Auckland   Cape Town   Dar es Salaam   Hong Kong   Karachi
Kuala Lumpur   Madrid   Melbourne   Mexico City   Nairobi
New Delhi   Shanghai   Taipei   Toronto

With offices in
Argentina   Austria   Brazil   Chile   Czech Republic   France   Greece
Guatemala   Hungary   Italy   Japan   Poland   Portugal   Singapore
South Korea   Switzerland   Thailand   Turkey   Ukraine   Vietnam

Oxford is a registered trademark of Oxford University Press
in the UK and certain other countries.

Published in the United States of America by
Oxford University Press
198 Madison Avenue, New York, NY 10016

© Oxford University Press 2014

All rights reserved. No part of this publication may be reproduced, stored in a
retrieval system, or transmitted, in any form or by any means, without the prior
permission in writing of Oxford University Press, or as expressly permitted by law,
by license, or under terms agreed with the appropriate reproduction rights organization.
Inquiries concerning reproduction outside the scope of the above should be sent to the
Rights Department, Oxford University Press, at the address above.

You must not circulate this work in any other form
and you must impose this same condition on any acquirer.

Library of Congress Cataloging-in-Publication Data
The Oxford handbook of virtuality / edited by Mark Grimshaw.
p. cm.
Includes bibliographical references and index.
ISBN 978-0-19-982616-2 (alk. paper)
1. Virtual reality—Social aspects. 2. Communication—Social aspects. 3. Avatars (Virtual reality)
I. Grimshaw, Mark, 1963-
HM1206.O94 2013
006.8—dc23
2013018114

1 3 5 7 9 8 6 4 2
Printed in the United States of America
on acid-free paper

CONTENTS

PART III.   CULTURE AND SOCIETY

PART IV. SOUND

PART V. IMAGE

PART VI. ECONOMY AND LAW

PART VII. A-LIFE AND ARTIFICIAL INTELLIGENCE

PART VIII. TECHNOLOGY AND APPLICATIONS

PART IX. UTOPIA AND DYSTOPIA

Acknowledgments

WHEN I first started this project in 2010, I proposed a modest anthology of 21 chapters almost all of which dealt with aspects of virtuality in online worlds. By the time the proposal had been through the hands of several reviewers, had been resubmitted to Oxford University Press, and had successfully solicited its contributors, the plan called for 44 chapters, excluding introduction and afterword, and this is the version you now have in your hands, a volume of approximately 330,000 words. My first thanks, therefore, go to these anonymous reviewers for pushing me to expand the ambitions of this book beyond its initial, lamentably limited horizons. Any book is ultimately dependent on the consistent high quality of its writing, a consistency you will find here, but an anthology is no less dependent upon the willingness of its many contributors to meet deadlines and to respond positively to the editor's suggestions. My thanks, therefore, to the many authors who have collaborated with me in bringing this project to life and expanding my own horizons; I set sail in 2010 intending to keep to those seas I was reasonably familiar with and have ended, in 2013, having navigated what are, for me, uncharted oceans of thinking on virtuality. In addition to an internal review process, there has also been an external reviewing process; my gratitude to the reviewers for their thorough work and thoughtful comments. Thanks are also due those staff and employees of Oxford University Press—Molly Davis, Sunoj Sankaran, and other anonymous persons—who have worked efficiently and tirelessly behind the scenes carrying out the important work of chapter collation, design, copy-editing, and a myriad other tasks I know little about. Finally, my heartfelt thanks must go to my commissioning editor Norman Hirschy for guiding my editorial efforts and displaying the rare talent of being able to furnish comments that flatter and burnish my ego while, at one and the same time, gently but firmly correcting my missteps.

Contributor Affiliations

Deborah Abdel Nabi: University of Bolton, United Kingdom

Paul C. Adams: University of Texas–Austin, United States

Julie M. Albright: University of Southern California, United States

Huidong Bai: University of Canterbury, New Zealand

Jeremy N. Bailenson: Stanford University, United States

Mark Billinghurst: University of Canterbury, New Zealand

Maria Beatrice Bittarello: Independent scholar, Italy

Tom Boellstorff: University of California–Irvine, United States

Philip Brey: University of Twente, Netherlands

Gordon Calleja: University of Malta, Malta/IT-University of Copenhagen, Denmark

Phil Carlisle: University of Bolton, United Kingdom

Elizabeth J. Carter: Carnegie Mellon University, United States

Alan Chalmers: University of Warwick, United Kingdom

Erik Champion: Curtin University, Australia

Tom Chandler: Monash University, Australia

John P. Charlton: University of Bolton, United Kingdom

William Cheng: Harvard University, United States

Karen Collins: University of Waterloo, Canada

Bruce Damer: DigitalSpace, Santa Cruz, United States

Charles M. Ess: University of Oslo, Norway

Patrice Flichy: Université Paris Est, France

Keysha I. Gamor: KG2 Consulting, United States

Tom A. Garner: Aalborg University, Denmark

Robert M. Geraci: Manhattan College, United States

David G. Green: Monash University, Australia

Mark Grimshaw: Aalborg University, Denmark

Simon J. Harris: University of Wolverhampton, United Kingdom

Trevor S. Harvey: University of Iowa, United States

Michael R. Heim: Mount St. Mary's College, Los Angeles, United States

Randy Hinrichs: 2b3d Studios, Seattle, United States

Andrea Hunter: Concordia University, Canada

Martin Knakkergaard: Aalborg University, Denmark

David Kreps: University of Salford, United Kingdom

Greg Lastowka: Rutgers School of Law, United States

Gun Lee: University of Canterbury, New Zealand

Vili Lehdonvirta: University of Oxford, United Kingdom

Patrick Lichty: University of Wisconsin, Milwaukee, United States

Robert Lindeman: Worcester Polytechnic Institute, United States

Jean-Claude Martin: LIMSI-CNRS/University of Paris South, France

Brian Massumi: University of Montreal, Canada

Vincent Mosco: Queen's University, Canada

André Nusselder: University of Amsterdam, The Netherlands

Frank E. Pollick: University of Glasgow, United Kingdom

Giuseppe Riva: Università Cattolica del Sacro Cuore, Italy

Gabriel Robles-De-La-Torre: International Society for Haptics

David Rudd: University of Bolton, United Kingdom

James K. Scarborough: Stanford University, United States

Eddie Simmens: University of Southern California, United States

Roger Smith: Florida Hospital, United States

Anthony Steed: University College London, United Kingdom

Ståle Stenslie: Aalborg University, Denmark

Tim Taylor: Goldsmiths, University of London, United Kingdom

Angela Tinwell: University of Bolton, United Kingdom

Eva L. Waterworth: Umeå University, Sweden

John A. Waterworth: Umeå University, Sweden

Gary Zabel: University of Massachusetts–Boston, United States

About the Companion Web Site

www.oup.com/us/ohov

A password-protected web site accompanies *The Oxford Handbook of Virtuality* where all images printed in the book are available in color. Material that cannot be made available in a book, such as music and videos, is also provided.

The reader is strongly encouraged to read the handbook in conjunction with viewing and listening to the media available on the website as examples available online are found throughout the text.

Username: Music5
Password: Book1745

INTRODUCTION

MARK GRIMSHAW

Ah, but a man's reach should exceed his grasp,
Or what's a heaven for?

—Robert Browning, *Andrea del Sarto*

THE nature of virtuality, and its relationship to reality and actuality, is one that has vexed the academy for many years. While a precise understanding of the concept remains elusive, the application of that concept, sometimes implicit, sometimes explicit, has profound implications for the public, particularly in one of its modern incarnations, that of a virtuality enabled by an increasing digitalization of society. As a brief perusal of the list of contents of *The Oxford Handbook of Virtuality* will show, the understanding of virtuality, its manifestation, its applications, and its effect on humanity, is a diverse and multifaceted one. Readers will be as hard-pressed to find a definitive answer to the question of what virtuality is—although several chapters here present definitions—as they will be to find common agreement as to the usage of the concept and its connection, or opposition, to reality and actuality (terms equally difficult to pin down). The 44 chapters do, however, agree that there is such a thing as virtuality, that there is a long history of debate on the subject and the meaning and theorization of the term, that it is a concept that has practical applications, that it has a wide-ranging effect on human society and culture, our relationship to and use of technology, our bodies, and our perception, and that it is a term and a concept coming increasingly to the fore with the advent of computers and computer networks.

This book had its genesis in 2010 when, following discussions with commissioning editor Norm Hirschy, I submitted the proposal for this handbook to Oxford University Press. At the time, I envisioned 21 chapters in six parts dealing almost exclusively with the virtuality of online worlds. Following feedback from reviewers, the final submitted proposal grew to over 50 chapters across 10 parts (which later settled down to 44 chapters across nine parts) and overflowed the boundaries of its original premise. This is illuminating for a number of reasons, not least because it demonstrates the wide and varying understanding of the concept and application of virtuality among the reviewers who helpfully suggested many, many other potential contributors and the inclusion of other areas of study. Indeed, this book might well have comprised over 100 chapters, so varied and wide-ranging were the suggestions, were it not for the limits imposed by book-binding technology.

But the tale of this book's evolution tells another story, one that has import for the reader attempting to navigate a path through the diverse opinions offered here. While their meanings may differ to some degree, terms such as *virtuality* and *the virtual* are common currency across many academic disciplines, and the growth of this book's proposal reflects the inclusion of contributions from many of those disciplines. Naturally, as with any anthology on such a broad subject, not everything can be included, but this anthology is certainly a very multidisciplinary one and a challenge for an editor who comes from one particular academic background, as I do, that of the humanities. The decision to make it so multidisciplinary allows many approaches to the theme of virtuality to be voiced, but it carries its risks too. The reader will therefore find a wide range of writing styles and differences in degree of objectivity or subjectivity; some chapters concentrate on application, whereas others are of a more philosophical bent, and there are different methodologies, approaches to essay structure, and discipline-specific jargon. As the editor, I have applied a light touch to these issues: where I might have imposed a single discipline's stylistic unity across all chapters, I have instead allowed discipline-based forms and terminology to stand (for example, the near synonyms: computer game, video game, and digital game), limiting myself to the occasional request to clarify particularly opaque jargon and concepts. Virtuality is not the domain of one field of study alone.

It is therefore an impossible task to give one concise account in this introduction of what virtuality is. I do not attempt to do so, preferring to let the chapters speak for themselves. However, this introduction does serve to introduce the varying definitions and approaches to virtuality that appear in each chapter; indeed, the contributors were encouraged to explicitly state their conception of virtuality from the start. Each illustrates varying approaches to and manifestations of virtuality as used by different theoretical and practical disciplines, and the reader will not find definitive answers that are uncontested across all chapters, merely more questions. This is as it should be. One thing should be noted, though: it is clear that the concept and the application of virtuality are not new and have not been born with the advent of digital computers. Terms such as "virtual world," "virtual environment," "virtual character," and "virtual reality" and their application and usage may well be ingrained in the modern digital consciousness, but thinking about virtuality has a history almost as long as that of Western civilization itself. Digital technology simply provides new ways to conceptualize, to use, and to experience that virtuality.

I have already noted that the book's contributors come from many disciplines. Another editorial decision was to ensure that those contributors comprised a wide age range. There were several reasons for this. The young, being young, are more likely to put forward provocative and contentious views, and, indeed, there are several such chapters balanced against the, dare I say it, more mature and experienced views of the older generation. I particularly wanted this friction. But the decision was also a nod to the influence of the digital revolution, and the latter network revolution, on virtuality; there are contributors here who, like myself, have seen these revolutions occurring and can remember a more leisurely, slow-paced world of courteous letter-writing and precise spelling, a time of more privacy and less digital intrusion, and there are contributors here who have known nothing else but a fast-paced, ready-to-hand, and very public digital world. Because digital artifacts figure heavily in the discussions here, each group brings different perspectives to bear on what it means to act and be in digital virtual domains.

Writing the proposal and editing this book over the last three years, it has become increasingly apparent that there is no monolithic approach to virtuality and, as previously noted here, that there is no one academic field with ownership of the term. Accordingly, I asked the anthropologist Tom Boellstorff to read all the chapters and to write a short afterword that would provide a meta-analysis, a more objective summing up of the *approaches* to virtuality in this book than any editor, with his nose buried deep in each chapter's dense thematic content, length, style and formatting issues, and the management of such a large project, could ever hope to undertake. The reader looking for such a summary of the many conflicting views arising from such approaches and a teasing out of any consensuses will find it in the afterword. It is another editorial decision to make such writing an afterword rather than place it in the introduction, where it might normally be expected to be; this allows the introduction to provide the editorial context, and to function properly as an introduction to the purpose and structure of the book, and the afterword to function as an analytical summing up of the use of the term "virtuality" to be read at the end.

THE STRUCTURE OF THE BOOK

This book has a carefully plotted trajectory across its 44 chapters and nine parts. It moves from philosophy and theoretical concerns to the technology and applications of virtuality before returning to philosophy again. This is not to say that each part is exclusive and that, for example, there is no dirtying of philosophers' hands with the grease of technology or that those who apply do not care to think. Precisely the opposite is true, and the reader will find what appear to be, prima facie, interlopers flaunting their charms in the wrong place. The development and use of technology in the context of the virtual is the art of the currently possible supported by the imaginings of philosophy, and such development spurs further considerations and speculations as well as new possibilities. As some of the chapters here make clear, language itself is a virtual technology, and an understanding of the implications and applications of virtuality requires contributions from both philosophy and technology, each prodding the other forward.

Part I: The Foundations of Virtuality

The opening part of the book explores the foundations of the existential concept of virtuality. These foundations are uncovered through six chapters dealing with the changing history of the usage of the term, its semantics and ethics, and modern interpretations both theoretical and practical. It becomes clear that, despite its recent connection to the digital domain, the virtual has a long bloodline concerning its relationship to the real and the actual and that ideas and applications of modern digital virtuality are merely late arrivals to the party.

In the opening chapter, two early implementers of digital virtual worlds, Bruce Damer and Randy Hinrichs, offer a history of the origins and development of such worlds before taking a look at what the future might hold. For the authors, virtual worlds have not yet achieved what was envisioned for them in both science fiction and the hype of start-up companies because of a lack of something meaningful to do coupled with a lack of rich situational feedback. The authors offer their thoughts on the challenges that must be met before that potential can be realized.

Philip Brey conducts an ontological analysis of digital virtual worlds as a means to question the mode of existence of virtual objects, events, and actions and to ask whether aspects of such virtuality can be considered part of the real world. In response to these questions, Brey defines a number of *uncertainties* in virtual environments: ontological, semantic, contributive, existential, and the role of the institution. Through this framework, it is shown that, while some aspects of virtuality exist only in the virtual, others occupy uncertain ground between the virtual and the real and shift between being imitations and simulations of reality to being real themselves.

From the starting point of the Deleuzian view of the virtual as potential, and thus an aspect of reality, Brian Massumi asks how such potential, never appearing as such because it is fundamentally abstract, can be perceived. To answer this philosophical conundrum, Massumi looks at the case of optical illusions, in particular the pop-out effect of the Kanizsa triangle. From this study, three types of virtuality are identified, forms, events, and values, leading Massumi to suggest that a theory of the virtual must be explicitly ethical as it deals with actions that lead to dynamic life differences.

André Nusselder's essay references the work of philosophers such as Kierkegaard and Badiou to argue for an ethical framework to regulate the excess of virtuality brought about by the computer and Internet revolution. Virtuality is approached from the perspective of the signs and tools that humans use. The instability of the self arises from the dimension of virtuality that is called *freedom*, and through this freedom, brought about by our use of symbolic representation, virtuality permeates the human world. Nusselder concludes by calling for a framework to protect humankind from the nihilism we are at risk of suffering through the excesses brought about by the freedom implicit in virtuality.

Rejecting the Platonic distinction between the world of simulacra and the world of ideas as the basis for a theory of virtuality, Maria Beatrice Bittarello instead focuses upon more recent ideas showing that virtuality is both dependent on and effective on reality. This conception is used to demonstrate the similarities in the imagination of virtual worlds across cultures and across ages. From the Epic of Gilgamesh to More and Shakespeare to digital virtual worlds, Bittarello finds shared structural elements demonstrating that our shared reality is constructed by a shared virtuality.

The paradox of virtuality, according to Michael R. Heim, is that it gradually falls victim to its own success. The more virtual something is, the weaker the meaning of virtuality becomes, and, over time, virtuality becomes absorbed in the reality of its culture. Reaching back to first-century Rome, Heim uses the technology of virtuality as a lens to analyze the shifting semantics of the term. Rather than construct theories of virtuality, the richer vein of research is to be found in the street use and normalization of the products of technology. Indeed, there is a pathology of virtuality, and the virtual aims at its own extinction.

Part II: Psychology and Perception

As human beings, we experience virtuality in many domains and thus have a conception of the virtual as being a part of reality, as forming a continuum with reality, or as opposing our notions of reality. These views are debated in the next part, comprising seven chapters, that uses concepts such as self and presence to explain how we perceive of our relationship(s) to virtuality and reality.

James K. Scarborough and Jeremy N. Bailenson discuss the psychological effects on humans of the use of avatars. Empirical research is provided to show that there are distinct psychological implications for humans as they interact in virtual societies as avatars; the use of avatars affects and alters human behavior outside virtuality. The chapter analyzes this use and both beneficial and negative effects of avatars through various debates on spatial presence, self-presence, and social presence, before concluding with a look to what the future might bring and where research in the area should head to.

In dealing with the question *Can virtual characters replace humans in experiments?* Elizabeth J. Carter and Frank E. Pollick's chapter on person perception relates how the development and use of virtual characters and improving animation techniques have advanced understanding in the fields of cognitive neuroscience and social perception. The chapter starts with a brief review of findings in behavioral research using virtual characters, particularly where such findings contribute to knowledge on psychological processes and virtual character design, before concluding with a look at the problems and limitations of conducting such research. In particular, the double-edged sword of improvements in technology necessitates the rerunning of experiments with better-realized virtual characters but also raises the specter of the Uncanny Valley.

Jean-Claude Martin's chapter is an exposition of the role of emotions in human-computer interfaces and concerns an assessment of real emotions versus virtual emotions and questions if there is indeed such a difference. The chapter takes a multidisciplinary approach that reviews theories of emotions from psychology to theater studies before addressing affective computing: the design of computational models of emotions and the development of affective agents and their applications. A number of questions are raised for future research: do users of virtual reality feel the same emotions as in real life? Should virtual agents be capable of expressing and, importantly, feeling emotions? And should these emotions be any different from those expressed by humans in real life?

In 1970, Masahiro Mori developed the Uncanny Valley theory to explain why, the more humanlike robots become, the more uncomfortable humans become when confronted with them. Angela Tinwell develops this theory in the context of virtual characters and psychological theories on the notion of the self to suggest that the cause of the Uncanny Valley phenomenon is a lack of empathy expressed by such characters. It derives from missing facial cues and the lack of expected mimicry responses to a human, and this leads to an inability to predict the behavior of the character; thus we become detached from the character and experience discomfort. For Tinwell, this theory of the Uncanny Valley explains why the boundary between the virtual and the real may never be crossed.

What is it about social networking systems such as Twitter that makes them, according to some studies, more difficult to give up than alcohol or nicotine? Virtual addiction, in the context of interactive, digital environments and activities having a real-world parallel, is the subject of Deborah Abdel Nabi and John P. Charlton's chapter. The authors review previous studies of virtual and Internet addiction, discuss the relationship between flow and immersion and escaping from negative moods, and conclude that, while virtual addiction bears similarity to substance-related addiction, online digital environments offer other conditions for addiction such as narcissistic self-reflection and the opportunity to present an idealized, new embodiment of self to an unseen audience.

Giuseppe Riva and John A. Waterworth also look at the issue of self in their chapter but from the perspective of presence. Inner presence is used as a means to explain the phenomenon of media presence whereby presence is mediated by technology. Inner presence is, according to the authors, a neurophysiological phenomenon that is related to the evolution of a conscious sense of self. Inner presence allows subjects the sense that they can act upon an external world and is intuitive, provides feedback to the self, and allows the self's evolution through the incorporation of tools. Particularly this last point helps to explain media presence; in digitally mediated environments, we have the potential to perceive and act as if unmediated.

Gordon Calleja continues the theme of presence by including the related term *immersion* and focusing the discussion on digital games. For Calleja, the two terms are confusingly used and are inadequate metaphors to describe the player-game relationship; their use assumes a division between the physical "here" and the virtual "there" rather than virtual worlds being a part of our consciousness and coextensive with our reality. Instead, *incorporation* is proposed as a term that is specific to games and that accounts for the assimilation of virtual environments to mind and for the embodiment of the player, an embodiment that, Calleja claims, is fundamental to our experience of such virtual worlds.

Part III: Culture and Society

The seven chapters of the third part of the book deal with forms of culture and structures of society as represented through technologies such as spoken and written language and computers and networks. Themes of imagination, proximity, distancing, and the uses of new technologies and old are used to explore the effects of virtuality on societal practices, our comprehension of cultural heritage, and our use of social media for the purposes of sex and religion.

A historical analysis of forms of communication allows Paul C. Adams to describe the virtual spaces of the word, writing, and printing and how these prior forms of virtuality remain fundamental to new media despite their claims for ownership of the concept. If virtuality can be understood as a system permitting communication without proximity of communicators, that is, *distanciation*, then language is a virtual technology. A language's grammar imposes a temporal and spatial virtuality of distanciation, writing reorganizes the space of the word, and printing incorporates the fixed word into society, allowing the creation of utopian spaces far removed from the control of the authority provided by proximity.

David Rudd takes a Lacanian perspective to argue that fantasy novels hint at deeper truths and are therefore not, as they ostensibly appear to be when they are compared to other forms of fiction, about the virtual. The Lacanian Real is mediated by the imaginary, by childhood experiences, and by the symbolic (when we become users of language), and we rarely experience the Real directly, only through this mediation. Using extraliterary examples such as trompe l'oeil and trompe l'oreille as well as examples from the writings of Tolkien and C. S. Lewis, Rudd's chapter shows that such mediation means that the Real is already virtual.

There is an increasing move toward the practice of "learning by doing" through digitally simulated means of history and cultural heritage, but, argues Erik Champion, technology often overwhelms content to the detriment of understanding one another's cultural heritage. Cultural heritage in a digital world is not just a question of spatial presence and ownership of cultural knowledge but also of the contexts of practices, expressions, skills, and the knowledge of that culture. Champion examines various forms of virtual heritage artifacts and suggests that existing forms are all too often context free and that, rather than replicate heritage facts as a means to demonstrate the latest technology, we should concentrate on understanding through context.

Recent research in America and Europe shows that online matchmaking has become the third most common way to meet a partner, and its many forms and techniques have evolved hand in hand with the development and proliferation of digital technology. Julie M. Albright and Eddie Simmens chart these changes in a chapter that ranges from predigital antecedents, such as letter-writing and the sending of photographs, to the impact of social networking on self-representation, and the influence of smartphone mobility on location-based and short-term dating and sexual relationships.

The interface and interplay between sex and digital technologies is the subject of Ståle Stenslie's chapter on cybersex. It raises a number of questions about the virtuality or reality of such sexual encounters as it charts the development and forms of cybersex, from its historical origins to current experimentation and future possibilities and from chat-based cybersex to teledildonics and cybersex machines. Stenslie critiques the allure of cybersex: that it promises a technologically enhanced and telematic body to sexually, but safely, experiment with in an environment where you can be anyone and anything you want.

Robert M. Geraci makes use of actor-network theory to investigate the place of virtual worlds in religion and the effect they have on religious practice and belief. For Geraci, a virtual world, as religion is, is an assemblage of the natural; the social and virtual worlds' constituents, human and nonhuman alike, are all actors. The simple fact of using virtual worlds to sustain religious life or, indeed, to create new religious forms will indelibly change our religious practices and beliefs: as objects, virtual worlds have as much power as religious objects, such as books, have to affect and effect religious life.

The recent introduction of voice-chat into virtual worlds such as video games is the topic of William Cheng's enquiry into the practices of assimilation, repression, deception, and revelation made possible by such technologies. Voice-chat can be seen as an unwelcome intrusion of reality and can militate against the suspension of disbelief that allows virtual worlds to function. The power of the voice to divulge, Wizard of Oz-like, that which game players may prefer to remain hidden reveals the voice as a prosthetic stamp of self; disembodied voices evoke real human bodies and affect ludic relationships as shown by the changing sexual politics when voice-chat is used in male-dominated games such as those involving a first-person shooter.

Part IV: Sound

Part IV deals with sound in the context of virtuality. The use of sound and music to separate spaces, to permeate boundaries between spaces, and to construct previously unheard and often ambiguous spaces is one of the main themes of the four chapters here, and it is explored through discussions about sound in computer games, music performance in *Second Life*, and the art of constructing music in the recording studio.

The constructed nature of theatrical space can be exposed by breaking down the fourth wall, the artificial boundary that exists between actors and audience. The concept of the fourth wall has recently been extended to the boundary between fictional and nonfictional spaces, and Karen Collins extends it further by examining how user-generated content, particularly sonic content, breaks down the fourth wall between virtual worlds and physical worlds. Sound is useful as a mediator between such spaces because, uniquely among the content of virtual worlds, it always penetrates our physical space. For Collins, when users can cocreate video games with their own sonic content, video games become participatory and performative art.

Tom A. Garner and Mark Grimshaw propose the notion of *acoustic virtuality* for digital games in a chapter that uses sound in games to explore the subjective nature of reality. Here, virtual reality is explained in the area of games as a subjective perception of reality. Sound in games blurs many of the supposed boundaries between the virtual and the real not merely through its context and its semantic associations but also because it exists in the same acoustic environment as that of the player sitting in front of the screen. The chapter uses *embodied cognition* as the theoretical glue with which to combine theories of acoustic ecology and virtual reality for the purposes of exploring our relationship to sound.

Ethnomusicology is a study of the relationship between music and culture, focusing on the processes of music-making, and Trevor S. Harvey uses this perspective to investigate the practice of live music performance in *Second Life*. Through the technology of music streaming, musicians are able to broadcast performances into the virtual spaces of *Second Life*, and this produces a discrepancy between what is heard and what is seen, between physical distance and virtual distance. For Harvey, such music-making mediates social interaction and contributes to meaning-making, thus actualizing social relationships in virtual worlds.

Martin Knakkergaard's chapter is an exposition of the transitory nature of music, its articulation of time through the medium of air, and an investigation into the creation of virtual acoustic spaces that can only be brought about by technological construction in the recording studio. The perception of space comes about through interaction between sound sources; recorded music is the primary musical reference for the public, and recording studios have a long history of constructing abstract auditory spaces with an ambiguity of location. The recent digitalization of the recording process creates, for Knakkergaard, a double virtuality where the digital mimics the analogue but imposes a further abstraction, where the recorded bits can be anything but what was originally performed.

Part V: Image

The following four chapters of the next part discuss visual art either as a form of virtuality itself or as virtuality mediated, in both practice and reception, through digital technologies. The subjects range across traditional practices and reception of visual art through painting, the various forms in which older art forms are transferred to new media platforms, the innovative art forms enabled by digital technologies, and the relationship between the virtual, the real, and the actual as perceived by artist and viewer.

In a chapter that traces ancient uses and understandings of the concept of virtuality to its incarnation in the art of virtual worlds, Gary Zabel makes the claim that such art is a unique medium of aesthetic expression and that the art of virtual worlds has a computer-generated virtuality with a form of worldhood. Zabel defines six dimensions of the art of virtual worlds that, in their comprehensive use, distinguish such art from earlier forms that, since the Renaissance, have steadily moved toward a process of artistic productivity without bodily production: immersion; interaction; ambiguity of identity; environmental fluidity; artificial agency; and networked collaboration.

Anthony Steed delivers an assessment of the technology required to create images in mixed reality systems and discusses how various technological possibilities and external drivers, such as industry needs, lead to new forms of mixed reality. Hardware and system architecture is discussed before an extended analysis of the virtuality continuum, the conceptual model that currently underlies much of the thinking behind mixed reality's image creation and processing. Here Steed extends the model with the notion of the primary environment and the concept of immediacy of representation before concluding with a look at the future possibilities of image presentation in mixed reality.

In his chapter on art in virtual worlds, Patrick Lichty tackles modes of representation that raise questions of modality, context, audience, and formalism. Concentrating on artistic practice in and around *Second Life*, Lichty identifies five modes of representation: transmediated, the translation of physical work into virtual space; remediated, where tangible performance art is represented in the virtual; virtual, where art derives from and exists only in-world; evergent, where art traverses the boundary from virtual to tangible; and cybrid, where art forms occupy both spaces. While artists initially tend to represent the tangible on taking their first steps into virtual worlds, in seeking an embodied conceptualism, practices soon diverge.

The relationship between viewer and painting, and how this relationship is attended to during the process of painting, is the subject of the painter Simon J. Harris's chapter. Harris views the virtual as an extension to the actual that is the surface of the painting. Viewer and painter have different perspectives on the painting as a result of their different encounters with the surface, the one subjective, the other the painter's objective relationship with that surface. Deleuze's *crystal image* is the unseen image that arises from the surface of the painting, a painting that continuously oscillates between virtual and actual.

Part VI: Economy and Law

The intersection between real-world economies and legal systems and virtual practices is the subject of the two chapters of Part VI. Ideas and effects travel in both directions: virtual economies affect real economies; the application of intellectual rights and property laws has impact upon virtual-world objects and avatars; and virtual law is expanding at the expense of the traditional laws that struggle to keep pace with developments in online worlds.

Through a variety of illustrative examples, Greg Lastowka demonstrates the many intersections between legal institutions and virtual worlds, shows how real law has been applied to the virtual, and asks how far real law should go in its attempts to regulate realms of representation and simulation. Lastowka presents two concurrent views of the present situation: that legal institutions enhance the technological power wielded by companies operating in the virtual sphere; and that the expansion of virtual law and private powers is paralleled by a decline in traditional legal institutions.

Vili Lehdonvirta exposes the illusory nature of the supposed dichotomy between virtual economy and real economy through a study that takes in examples from the negative view of the post-Soviet virtual economy to the gold farmers of today's online worlds. Where once virtual economies were a simulation of real economies, now virtual economies encroach onto real economies with tangible economic and political consequences. Practices of virtual consumption parallel the consumption of material goods and virtual money, and when they begin to have an influence outside of online worlds, they become a threat to governments.

Part VII: A-Life and Artificial Intelligence

The next four chapters concern practical questions of human interactions with digital virtual environments and the interactions and codependencies that take place between artifacts inside those environments. The topics in this part range across imbuing computer game characters with emotional responses to provide new experiences to players, new solutions to modeling virtual worlds with evolvable virtual organisms, understanding ancient civilizations through the combination of the simulation of ecologies with 3D modeling, and an analysis of how the brain learns the dynamics of body movements in the context of real environments as a means to model a mode of interaction with virtual environments. In their scope, these chapters explore how the virtuality inherent in new technologies provokes fundamental questions about the world we live in and the bodies we inhabit.

Phil Carlisle looks at the development of an emotional relationship to the player in video games; whereas this was previously attempted using noninteractive methods, the trend now is the development of interactive game characters who are behaviorally believable and are capable of responding with, for example, movement, emotion, and nonverbal cues to the actions of the player. Where games had been using passive narrative forms, similar to those used in other media such as films, the question now is what new narrative forms must be designed to account for the prototype emotive digital actors who are now appearing and what new experiences await the player.

The question Tim Taylor deals with in his chapter is whether virtual worlds can be programmed with the neo-Darwinist principles of reproduction, heritable variation, and competition for limited resources such that complex virtual organisms may then arise from evolutionary processes. This is a problem of open-ended evolution, and Taylor identifies a number of problems with past and current models that have meant that such a goal remains elusive. Rather than focus on individual organisms, Taylor argues, we should focus on the relationship between organism and environment. The organism must be fully embodied in the medium of the world; the greater the degree of embodiment, the greater the evolvability of the organism.

How can we solve the many puzzles about ancient civilizations? How can we predict the ecological consequences of genetic manipulation? The solutions, according to David G. Green and Tom Chandler, might be found in the recent combination of simulation and 3D modeling, creating virtual models of ecologies and environments that can reach into the past or see into the future. Such virtual models offer the potential to approach many problems in environmental science and create the opportunity for many disciplines to work together. However, many challenges remain, such as integration, complexity, and scale, before environmental virtual models can realize this potential.

Touch and other haptic processes are understudied when compared to vision and hearing, yet such a focus can offer a unique window onto our interaction with real and virtual environments. Gabriel Robles-De-La-Torre proposes a new computational model for how the brain learns the dynamics of the body within an environment; apparently random neural spiking follows a Poisson point process that can be used to learn internal models and which, in turn, can be used to predict the body's spiking response to motor commands. Robles-De-La-Torre presents the model within a larger framework that asks how such models are used for interaction and how and why the brain responds to virtual environments as if they were real.

Part VIII: Technology and Applications

The six chapters of the penultimate part begin with an assessment of the role digital technologies have in our evolving conception of self before looking at the application of such technologies, and their potential, in a diverse set of fields. These fields include the military, health, and education and cover topics such as augmented reality and the use in virtual worlds of sensory stimuli beyond sight and sound in order to create not a virtual reality but a real virtuality.

Distributed embodiment is the subject of the first chapter, where John A. Waterworth and Eva L. Waterworth suggest that new technologies have the potential to give us an embodied sense of presence in a physical-virtual world where our sense of self is transferred to one or more other bodies. To this end, they map out a research agenda that takes account of the notion that the increase in forms of virtuality that we are witnessing is a part of the evolution of the human sense of self and nonself. As the virtual body is incorporated into our sense of self, and as technology becomes part of the self, presence coevolves with virtual forms of self.

For Alan Chalmers, virtual reality systems have a low level of realism because they typically work only with sight and hearing and because scarce computing power is given over to the required interaction. Real virtuality systems, on the other hand, supply a greater range of sensory stimuli, including feel, smell, and taste, and they also work to provide a perceptual equivalence to the experience of the physical world. Such systems take account of the individual's context, work cross-modally, and selectively prioritize stimuli in a similar manner to how the brain attends to the most salient stimuli. Real virtuality systems thus potentially have a greater level of realism than virtual reality systems.

Mark Billinghurst, Huidong Bai, Gun Lee, and Robert Lindeman provide an overview of augmented reality applications on handheld devices; interactable virtual imagery overlaid onto the user's real surroundings within a device such as a smartphone. In providing a set of design guidelines illustrated through three case studies of such applications, the authors also provide some of the history of augmented reality applications and discuss concepts including a variety of interaction metaphors for viewing images and the manipulation of objects.

Almost since their inception, virtual worlds have been touted as a medium for training, learning, and education, but, as Keysha I. Gamor shows, the history of learning applications in virtual worlds has had mixed results, and debate continues over their instructional merits. There are aspects of virtual-world learning design that can be mapped transparently from real-world learning scenarios, and there are other aspects that offer possibilities otherwise unavailable. Virtual worlds have the potential to provide memorable experiences, contextually authentic representations, and social interaction—all of which point to the possibility of rich experiential learning—and Gamor presents a set of design guidelines to take advantage of this potential.

Using the current state of research and technology in the field, Giuseppe Riva presents a view of the principles, concepts, and outstanding issues in the use of virtual reality and virtual worlds for medical clinical uses. Their application has grown dramatically since the early 1990s and now includes uses in surgery (both planning and operational), neuropsychology, and rehabilitation. However, there remain many technology challenges and outstanding safety issues, in addition to which Riva outlines a number of concerns about the state of research in the area (such as the paucity of controlled trials).

Roger Smith's chapter starts with a look at the history of military simulations, from sand tables and board war games to mechanical devices, before turning its attention to the use of virtual worlds for such purposes. Smith identifies the close relationship between computer game technology and modern military simulations and discusses how changes in computing technologies and networks lead to new possibilities. Questions of degree of emulation are dealt with, as is the potential for virtual worlds to move beyond their use solely for training to their use in logistical, intelligence, and even operational roles.

Part IX: Utopia and Dystopia

The last part, comprising four chapters, returns to questions of philosophy in order to explore aspects of utopia and dystopia in the context of virtuality. The part covers topics including the ethics of the use of networked digital technologies for the purposes of adultery and the distribution of child pornography, the utopian and the ideological bases of the contemporary social imaginary, the effects on our humanity of the increase in use of digital virtuality, and the sublime nature of virtual dystopias as realized in literature, film, and computer games.

If virtuality is disparate from our everyday practices, our common reality, new ethical frameworks are required; if not, then current ethical considerations continue to hold. Charles M. Ess takes the latter view and shows that real-world practices remain the touchstone of ethical consideration despite the potential of virtual technologies. The potential for adultery and child pornography in virtual worlds is used as an example to explicate a *virtue ethics*; we ineluctably embrace the novelty offered by new technologies within existing ethical frameworks because we cannot but help bring an embodied sense of self into our experiences of virtual worlds.

Patrice Flichy examines the roles of common social representations and the imaginatively created common world that give birth to new technologies such as virtual reality. This contemporary social imaginary is not the creation of an individual but a shared understanding that combines utopian imagination and ideological views. The notion of a utopia stands opposed to ideology, as it allows the exploration of alternatives rather than seeking to preserve social order; yet ideology can mobilize, and it can legitimize choices and provide social cohesion. Flichy shows how the imaginary is a shared constituent of social identity that is present in mass culture and that utilizes and combines forms of utopia and ideology; this is what leads to the development of new technologies of the virtual.

Is there a cost to be borne by humanity in the encroachment of digital virtuality? Does it offer more scope to express our humanity, or does it lead to an overload of engagement that exhausts our limited faculties? Does its use lead to our ideal or instead further entrench existing power structures? David Kreps addresses these concerns in a chapter that explores the nature of virtuality, humanity, and reality through the philosophies of Bergson and Foucault, among others. Digital virtuality, Kreps argues, is a continuation of human consciousness, and designers of virtual worlds should take heed that such spaces are as real and replete with knowledge and power as any other space.

Andrea Hunter and Vincent Mosco, using three modern examples drawn from literature, film, and computer games, explore the attraction of virtual dystopias. In this, they link such dystopian visions to historical understandings of the sublime; dystopian virtual worlds have the allure of the sublime and are compelling because they offer an experience of horror without the necessity of actually experiencing that horror. Such experiences provide distance and therefore safety while still allowing us to undergo the astonishment, awe, and terror that are the hallmarks of the sublime.

The Companion Website

Oxford University Press provides a companion website to this handbook at www.oup .com/us/ohov. Here the reader can find color versions of the images and diagrams given in the book as well as links to other media such as the videos and music that are referred to in some chapters. Individual chapters can be accessed and downloaded, and the intention is that this online, virtual version will, from time to time, be updated both with updated versions of the current chapters and with new chapters as the story of virtuality unfolds.

PART I

THE FOUNDATIONS OF VIRTUALITY

CHAPTER 1

··

THE VIRTUALITY AND
REALITY OF AVATAR
CYBERSPACE

··

BRUCE DAMER AND RANDY HINRICHS

THIS chapter takes on key questions surrounding the *virtuality and reality of avatar cyberspace* by first plumbing the prehistory and recent emergence of the young medium of virtual worlds and then peering into a crystal ball view of its possible future. The authors foresee a time when virtual worlds will converge with the data of the real world and produce a hybrid reality that could be *stranger than we can suppose*. Our particular vision for avatar cyberspace emerged from a series of interviews of coauthor Bruce Damer conducted by Henry Lowood at Stanford, the news organization CNET (Damer 2006; 2010), and nearly a decade of research and real-world virtual applications by coauthor Randy Hinrichs. We will begin with definitions of virtuality, offer a brief historical contextualization, and continue with Damer describing the birth of the virtual world in concept and reality from the 1950s through to the 1990s emergence of Internet-based virtual worlds. Damer will conclude with a vision for where the medium may be headed and then pass it over to Hinrichs, who will take on some of the opportunities and challenges that remain to enable the medium to reach its full promise as a ubiquitous tool of interaction, especially in education, where we discover the formation of "avatar psychology," the role of virtuality, the relationship to avatars, and the role of imagination in learning

Let us begin by offing Heim's (1998, 221) definition of virtual worlds' virtuality: "Virtual reality is a technology that convinces the participant that he or she is actually in another place by substituting the primary sensory input with data received produced by a computer...when the virtual world becomes a workspace and the user identifies with the virtual body and feels a sense of belonging to a virtual community." Ropolyi (2001, 178) contends that "some kind of presence is a necessary condition for any kind of reality and virtuality," but claims it is not enough to just be present in a virtual world. He adds *worldliness* as another prerequisite to be immersed in virtuality. Worldliness would require, for instance, that in order for any representation to be internalized as an embodiment of a person, other users' representations must also be present and engaged in explicit shared activities. Virtuality seeks to create a synthetic view of reality but also to imbue it with this concept of worldliness. Concluding our introductory thoughts, the medium of virtual worlds is most certainly a work in progress. Lauria (1997) suggests that although we do not know exactly where the technology is taking us, it certainly is a great "metaphysical test bed."

The use of *avatars*, the digital representation of a human being in a virtual world, must be able to replicate human experience wherever it embodies its worldliness. In short, it needs to offer more value than a blinking cursor. The avatar is a key element of immersion and represents the individual as the interface appearing as a body in context, whether it is an exact replica or a metaphoric transformation of what the individual wants to project either consciously or subconsciously. Personalization of the avatar can be a significant part of a user's reality, or it can be as simple as a fixed object on the screen, with just the user's dialogue providing his or her presence. However the representation, an avatar can ably embody the user's identity and be used to powerfully influence others. Along these lines, this chapter will therefore also look at the virtuality and the reality of life as an avatar. We will explore presence, permanence, performance, identity, and community to help frame how an avatar exists in the virtual world and how this can augment the real world of the person behind the avatar.

A Brief History of Immersive Virtuality

Virtual worlds, or as we will now more broadly define them, immersive experiences delivered through the human imagination, have their origins in deep prehistory. Whether these varieties of nonphysical, dreamlike realities were communicated by our ancestors through the imitation of animals, the incarnation of spirits, the painting of scenes on the stone canvasses of caves, the holding of ceremonial rites in temples, or the elaboration of the human story through the fount of theater, humans have craved and crafted virtual-world experiences from the dawn of artistic and linguistic expression (see also Bittarello, chapter 5 in this volume).

A substantial proportion of human toolmaking and expressive technique has been dedicated to manifesting imaginative virtualities in sharable artifacts. A revolution in thought, science, the arts, and architecture occurred in the fifteenth through eighteenth centuries. One of the inventions factoring into this revolution was the camera obscura. This device allowed light to enter through a pinhole into a darkened enclosure within which was cast a sharp inverted image of the scene outside. Geometers, artists, architects, and scientists alike used these projections to develop new understanding of perspective, derive mathematical coordinate systems, illustrate remarkable new depictions of reality, and begin to ponder key scientific questions about the duality of matter and energy.

In the late 1950s Morton Heilig created the first multisensory virtual experience. The Sensorama introduced immersive virtual spaces into public consciousness. With diminished sensory input from the world outside, users ensconced in the enclosure of the Sensorama had their senses replaced by media that included film, sound, vibration, wind, and even odor. The user thus became immersed as an inner voyeur.

From the 1960s to the 1980s research into computer graphics and animation grew rapidly, generating numerous practical applications, including image processing, computer animation, CAD software, fly-by simulations, key-frame animation, embodied agents, digital film, raster graphics, flight simulators, CGI filmmaking and geometry engine hardware, and virtual reality displays and software. Walt Disney's *Tron*, created in CGI, visualized immersion as the user pulled inside the game and competing with the programmer. In this case, the user was immersed as an imaginary adversary.

Real-time rendering of 2D and 3D graphics on personal computers evolved through the powerful economic driver of the videogame industry. Meanwhile, textual interfaces connecting users through e-mail, bulletin boards, threaded forums, and early forms of real-time text messaging were setting the stage by the 1990s for the rise of shared, immersive multiuser virtuality. In this last example, the user is immersed as a textual conversation stream.

My involvement in some of the early pioneering work in the medium of virtual worlds came about almost by accident. In the early 1990s I was working in Prague, Czechoslovakia, leading a team designing early graphical user interface systems when I happened to meet a student user of a MUD (Multi User Dungeon) called *SolSys* run by anthropologist Dr. Reed Riner at Northern Arizona University (NAU) (Reed & Clodius 1995). This MUD had been used for years as a class teaching tool between NAU and several universities and high schools. I was fascinated by users' descriptions of the spaces (an L5 colony, Lunar and Mars bases), and the rich and deeply immersed roles of participants in this "virtual world." I assumed that these worlds were somehow rendered visually and was surprised to discover that they were entirely described through text. I later joined *SolSys* as the bartender in the L5 colony to experience this for myself. I felt a calling and left Prague to first visit Dr. Riner and then drive around North America seeking out any person or group working on the realization of visual multiuser graphical worlds. When I set out on this quest in August 1994 the growth of the new World Wide Web was underway, but it took me twelve thousand real road miles to identify groups and companies engaged in the nascent enterprise of multiuser virtual worlds. Having had years working on pedestrian 2D user interfaces derived from Xerox and its research groups, including the Palo Alto Research Center (PARC), I was intent on finding ways through which cyberspace might become a *place*, not just an *interface*. I settled in the redwood forest next to the San Francisco Bay Area to continue this research and establish a not-for-profit organization, the Contact Consortium, which would be ready to serve as a community and innovative force for when the medium of virtual worlds eventually came to life.

SolSys itself was an outgrowth of the CONTACT Conference, where, since 1983 anthropologists, planetary scientists, science fiction writers, artists, and futurists had met and exchanged interdisciplinary ideas about hypothetical alien civilizations and the "first contact" challenges humanity might one day face. I attended the March 1995 meeting to present a vision for graphically realized virtual worlds on the Internet. After an all-night marathon exploratory conversation with science fiction writer Larry Niven, anthropologists Jim Funaro, Reed Riner, and others, the Contact Consortium was formed. The consortium went on to become the vehicle for many seminal projects, including the Avatars conference series.

Of course, by the early 1990s Hollywood films such as *Tron* and *Lawnmower Man*, and books such as *Neuromancer* and *Snow Crash*, had already given the popular imagination a view of what cyberspace could be like: fantastical 3D worlds populated by users represented as some sort of graphical entities. In the 1980s, the term *virtual reality* (VR) had been coined (Lauria 1997). By 1993 real-time 3D experiences could be rendered by expensive graphics workstations and projected in head-mounted displays, but they also could be delivered on personal computers through the less encumbered experience of first-person shooter games like DOOM. In 1985 Lucasfilm had developed *Habitat* in which platform creators Morningstar and Farmer (1991) coined the term *avatar* to name the visual representation of a user inhabiting a graphical virtual landscape (Smith 2008). They described interactions in the *Habitat* worlds as far from being a simple online chat room, instead being "more like governing an actual nation" (Morningstar and Farmer 1991). In *Habitat*, users running Commodore 64 personal computers could interact through the Quantum Link dial-up service with other players, connected in a massive online world composed of twenty thousand "regions." By 1995 an explosion of virtual worlds on the Internet was about to occur, this time supported by faster, ubiquitous networks connecting personal computers just capable enough to support a wider range of visual experience. With the advent of online avatar spaces, users were immersed in a persistent environment in which their social performance and effect upon virtual objects was observable in real time by other users.

The first commercially developed, public, multiuser Internet virtual-world platform was *Worlds Chat* created by a San Francisco startup company called Worlds Incorporated (Damer 1996). Worlds Chat launched online without much fanfare in the spring of 1995, and a screen capture taken by the author is shown in figure 1.1. Entering the beautifully designed 3D space station was a compelling experience. Because *Worlds Chat* was online and inhabited by other users, it was somehow elevated over the typically solo experiences of VR and single-player games. The first few users to step into this new space wandered around entranced, not yet understanding social norms, such as *Is it polite to simply pass through other people's avatars?* While *Habitat* had established a vibrant history of avatar experience in the late 1980s, at the time this was unknown to most Internet users.

In the late summer of 1995, Worlds Incorporated launched an alpha version of *AlphaWorld*, the first 3D shared Internet avatar environment that permitted users to assemble groups of persistent objects and thereby "build." Our newly formed Contact

FIGURE 1.1 Worlds Chat in May 1995.

Consortium organization adopted *AlphaWorld* as our experimental space, using it to pioneer many "firsts" in virtual worlds. In fact, we helped many virtual-world platform software developers design user affordances that later became standard. Henry Lowood, curator for History of Science and Technology Collections and Film and Media Collections in the Stanford University Libraries, has been researching the early history and terminology used in virtual worlds and multiuser game environments and interviewed me in 2009. I recounted how early-adopter users of avatars were struggling to find words to describe their spaces, each other, and their activities. I recalled standing among other avatars near the *AlphaWorld* "ground zero" (its entry portal) asking them, "What are we doing, I mean how do we describe the state of being together here in this world?" I thought for a moment and then offered up the term "in-world" (or "inworld" for typing brevity) to describe our experience of being there. We may well have been the first to use this now common term. What is key to immersion is the use of the word "we" to describe "our shared experience." In *AlphaWorld*, where users can also create content, the user is immersed with an identity that expands as the user commits to objects the user places in the environment, especially those with context and shared meaning. "This building, garden or street, was built by me under my property rights," users might indicate to others, and so their identity within the world grows.

Pioneering *AlphaWorld* citizens had truly entered a "new world" and the term "world" began to find a footing. *AlphaWorld* was not a game; it was a literal tabula rasa, where the users themselves created content through virtual building and found meaning through social interactions. So "virtual world" seemed to ring true for myself and others as a viable term for the medium. From that point on I promoted the term virtual world. Throughout the 1990s many terms were offered in place of virtual worlds, including *desktop VR, metaverses, metaworlds,* and the rather ponderous academic term *multiuser virtual environment.* For me virtual world rang truest and purest in describing this experience of virtuality. In arguing against using the earlier term *virtual reality,* I often stated, "There is nothing virtual about the reality of being in-world with other people." I felt that the cognitive immersion experienced in these spaces was as compelling as that created by the storytelling shaman in the caves of Lascaux, by the actors in classical Greek theater, by great novelists and filmmakers, or by the wizards in textual worlds of MUD predecessors. Continuing along the terminology vein, I built into my book *Avatars! Exploring and Building Virtual Worlds on the Internet* (Damer 1997) a large glossary of observed words along with many stories contributed by early-adopter users.

At this time I also began to ponder the cognitive differences between being in-world (virtual) and being in the real (physical) world. While researching early virtual worlds antecedents I came across a fascinating cartoon by computer scientist Ted Kaehler showing a user in the *Maze War* 3D first-person shooter on an Alto computer at Xerox PARC around 1980 (see figure 1.2). It clearly depicts someone *in-world* voicing a confusing response to someone *in the real world.* This is perhaps the first avatar-centric reference to this kind of virtuality/reality divide. Despite the competitive fast action of *Maze War,* users were beginning to experience a sense of community, both virtual and physical.

Fast on the heels of *AlphaWorld,* several other platforms such as *The Palace,* the innovative voice and lip synch-enabled *Onlive Traveler, WorldsAway* (the successor to *Habitat*), as well as *Blaxxun, Virtual Places,* and *Comic Chat* all emerged in the three years between 1995 and 1997. By 2000 many of these early virtual worlds and their sponsoring companies had fallen by the wayside, largely due to lack of revenue and curtailed

FIGURE 1.2   In-world in Maze War, by Ted Kaehler circa 1980. Cartoon by Ted Kaehler, reprinted with permission.

investor dollars. In 2002 I met with Philip Rosedale, founder of Linden Lab, who was developing a next-generation virtual world called *Second Life*. I was grateful that *virtual world* and *avatar* were being used by the *Second Life* developers and that these themes would be carried forward into a new era.

To bring the community of early virtual worlds developers and users together, the Contact Consortium held two in-person conferences in San Francisco in 1996 and 1997. In 1998 we carried out the most ambitious of many consortium experimental projects: to hold a full "cyber-conference" held entirely in-world. Called "Avatars98: Inside Cyberspace," it hosted nearly a thousand users simultaneously navigating and interacting in a 3D trade-show floor, speaker "pods," an art gallery, a webcam wall, a worlds portal tour, and a grand finale event (Damer 2008). The main conference world was built using *Active Worlds* and featured many innovations including Web-based database construction of the exhibit hall, customized individual speaker areas with a voice interface, "bots" (nonplayer automata) for performances and a public address system, a "big board" schedule wall for teleporting users to events, and a team of volunteers for event management. We followed the success of "Avatars98" with five more years of cyber-conferences across multiple platforms, one of which, "Avatars99," is shown in figure 1.3. For each of these events we made an effort to bridge virtuality and reality by promoting local in-person gatherings at locations as diverse as an electronic café in California, university campuses, and an art museum in Finland, all connecting into a

FIGURE 1.3 "Avatars99," a conference held within virtual worlds.

common virtual-world event space for the 24-hour period of the event. These events and many other consortium projects helped bring the virtual-world medium to birth and mature its uses and interfaces. The consortium pioneered pedagogical applications of worlds through its VLearn special interest group that had its own annual multicampus cyber-conference. The consortium also initiated the Biota project and conference series with a focus on generative and biological artificial life themes in virtual worlds. At that time I also founded a company called DigitalSpace, which from 1999 to 2009 focused on deploying virtual meeting rooms and developed 3D virtual environments to help NASA visualize and design space missions (Damer et al. 2006). Today DigitalSpace is using virtual environments scientifically in molecular simulations for research into the origins of life (Damer et al. 2011). In the NASA virtual spaces, high-fidelity representations of real environments were put at a premium as astronauts in training were themselves a kind of richly afforded avatar both on the earthly and the heavenly plane. Scientific simulations immerse the investigator's intellect as an avatar on the scale of the very small and the very large, especially as an intellectual place of learning, or a "home base" as the users return with others to master their expertise in the simulated scenario.

Unexpectedly for me, virtual worlds experienced limited adoption outside of social, creative, and educational purposes. In this era, the rise of company-designed multiuser online gaming platforms such as *EverQuest* provided a viable economic model in stark contrast to user-built, primarily social avatar environments. In the late 1990s at DigitalSpace we used virtual worlds frequently for globally distributed business meetings. The company designed and deployed many virtual discussion rooms containing relevant graphics, web cameras, and controls for presenting slides. At the time we felt that virtual worlds afforded ourselves and others a genuine sense of presence with team members and clients, as we had experienced with "Avatars98" and the other cyber-events. However, over time we used these spaces less and less, defaulting to Skype chat and WebEx for business meetings. I asked myself why this was, and the answer came in two concepts: "capture of gaze" and "cognitive overload." Virtual worlds tend to require users to continuously focus their gaze on other avatars at the same time as situating themselves within the virtual world itself. In an increasing era of multitasking, users tended to prefer their gaze to freely wander between e-mail, text, the Web, mobile devices, and other interfaces while engaged in an online meeting. Unless immersed in big visual experiences such as multiplayer gaming or watching video, most users were beginning to prefer information in increasingly short-attention-span packages, especially when on the move or at work. As a result of this trend, many cumbersome, screen-hogging virtual worlds applications were outcompeted for precious attention span resources.

Over a decade of work with NASA I learned that the cognitive fatigue and overload experienced by astronauts navigating and working in the 3D microgravity environment outside spacecraft is a major factor in the length of time they can be engaged in any task. So, as with astronauts, the constant movement of a user's avatar in relation to a 3D virtual world could place a higher tax on cognitive functions than simple rapid eye movement around more static 2D objects such as documents and text chat windows. I found this tax becoming greater as I grew older and research reported that users can experience a full sense of vertigo in virtual worlds as well as 3D movies, as seen in the work of Merhi (2009). Today I only occasionally venture in-world, preferring the less stressing 2D interfaces of the Web, chat, and voice interfaces to get work done and connect with my community. One might expect that such multitasking would contribute to cognitive overload as much as the use of avatars and virtual worlds, but anecdotally there does seem to be a qualitative difference. While outside the scope of this chapter, research on the cognitive cost versus benefits of using virtual-world spaces over other modes of interaction would be a valuable part of future studies of avatar virtuality. As my coauthor will point out later, he and many other users regularly "live" in virtual worlds, socializing, collaborating, and full-time teaching weekly, accredited college courses. For those dedicated users, their avatar has become a central part of their reality, and they employ it as a full agency of self when dealing with colleagues, friends, and students or, in some applications, patients.

In 2006 I started a project to chronicle the first-generation virtual worlds from the perspectives of both history and utility. I was asked to engage in a number of press interviews, and one of the most thought provoking was by Daniel Terdiman at CNET (Damer 2010) about how James Cameron's film *Avatar* presaged the future of 3D virtual worlds. Cameron and his team developed a "virtual camera" with which the director could walk through the physical set and view a rendering of the virtual terrain and characters representing avatars of the actors captured in real time. This was one of the first high-resolution, 3D, walkable augmented reality (AR) virtual worlds. What Cameron achieved on the set of *Avatar* is a glimpse into the possible future of all avatar worlds. Even today, artfully combining consumer motion capture devices such as the Nintendo Wii or the Microsoft Avatar Kinect system with an AR glasses retinal display or by simply holding up a GPS-equipped smartphone, one could potentially imitate Cameron and walk one's avatar self into a virtual world projected onto the surrounding real world.

In Vernor Vinge's near-future novel *Rainbows End* (Vinge 2006), people use a surgically implanted virtual retinal display called the "Epiphany system" that gives them a view of a composite computer-generated landscape overlain onto their view of the physical landscape. It is a breathtaking vision for the late 2020s and may hold clues as to where avatars may be by then. To bring this sort of virtuality to the world at large, Vinge envisions untold numbers of sensors floating in the air and on every surface constantly communicating and giving Epiphany users a truly high-resolution reality to map onto. Wearing your Epiphany system, you would see avatars and fantastical game characters walking down the street next to you and reams of weather data infused into the sky, and peer through real hills at a virtual rendering of an approaching physical Sherman tank.

In order for these far future worlds to provide such a rich experience, a company or government would have to program the entire cyber infrastructure of the real world first and then allow users to add to it virtually. For example, Google could build out a global 3D SketchUp version of its Street View maps, permitting local residents and businesses to enhance these views, overlaying their social networking photos and other location-based content. Users would likely go beyond realistic metaphors and add fantastic otherworldly virtual worlds. Such a planet-wide virtual world might be inhabited by millions, or even billions of users, and at long last, Stephenson's *metaverse* might finally have become our reality.

In an example illustrating this possible future: picture attending the Burning Man festival (Burning Man 2012) in the year 2029 carrying your nth-generation iPhone, or possibly your Apple iEpiphany system. While strolling along you would not only see the normal cast of costumed *in-real-life (IRL) burners* (festival attendees) and their vehicles but you would also see a virtual parade of truly bizarre contraptions and avatars representing remotely connecting *virtual burners* trying to outdo the IRL festival celebrants. Entering a theme camp might switch your iEpiphany system over to an alternate rendition of the physical camp you are standing in as each tries to outdo the other. The infrastructure to make all this possible would be very costly, especially for high-resolution, centimeter-scale, 3D global-positioning data, so investment might start in gated, experimental location-based entertainment theme parks modeled after successful multiplayer game franchises such as *World of Warcraft*.

Such visions stimulate concern about the potential human cost borne by our society in this all-inclusive virtuality (Introna 2011). Our moral obligations on how we might interact in a fully blended physical and virtual lifestyle may also be stretched. Our reactions to others have traditionally been situated in our embodied selves. If we become so totally virtualized that reacting to user's avatars gains primacy over physically present people, this may cause us to reconsider our authenticity (Turkle 1996), and our behavior in either sphere may slowly become devoid of real consequence (Borgmann 1999). Without a doubt, by 2029 today's virtual worlds will seem like the Keystone Kops in comparison to a modern Hollywood feature film. Except as a museum display, worlds like *Second Life* might not make the jump to this future. It may well be that entire generations of walled-off virtual-world platforms will continue to be created and die before a ubiquitous AR-centric *Third Life* virtual world arises. Experience is hard to migrate, but the ideas and processes that have helped evolve generations of virtuality will certainly inform that strange future.

In conclusion, I put forth that we are entering a "connect the dots" period. The development of cinema took decades from the first experience of film, as one peered into Edison's Kinetoscope in the 1890s. Cinema matured and became mainstream only in the 1930s with the rise of the stars and studio system powered by well-crafted stories projected with sound and color. The biggest clue we can draw from the success of cinema is *production values create human value*. If the experience of virtual worlds might be considered somewhat underwhelming today, we may yet wake up to a defining moment when it is crystal clear that "the medium has made it."

LOOKING THROUGH A CRYSTAL BALL INTO THE FUTURE OF VIRTUAL WORLDS

From the vantage point of the twenty-first century's early years, we need a lot of innovation and commercialization to put Vinge's vision into place. For example, we need to achieve real, working artificial intelligence to support virtual worlds that are not just filled with human users. Even more, we need human characteristics integrated into virtual worlds to enable effective, natural interfaces to manage cognitive overload, enhance fixed gaze, and ensure body language conversation is taking place. The absence of vitality is seen explicitly in a World Wide Web that is largely a very lonely experience. No one knows when another user is on his or her web page, and no one really believes a "bot" can create meaningful interactions, although bots help to bring a sense of others in the same virtual space. So supporting natural action and intuitive presence is essential for creating vital virtual worlds. When humans are interacting using the natural synchronicity of human emotion and response, magic happens. But when the communication is lacking, avatars seem isolated and nonhuman. Users need to enter worlds that are *alive*: where questions are answered by real people, where meaningful social and intellectual knowledge can be gained, where synchronicity happens, and where the environment is so well designed that it senses your presence and addresses what you want. Similarly we need to build intelligent databases of objects that interact with each other and interoperate across worlds. We need system-wide functions and *interfunctions* of other objects (Dionisio, Burns, and Gilbert 2011) that need to be automatically paired with physics, chemistry, and biology producing a fluid sense of natural interaction.

To complete this picture, we also need to experiment with implementing the representation of avatars in uncanny human likeness, able to more fully embody our emotions, our culture, and other psychological subtleties that define who we are and how we interact with other biological organisms. We also need to populate databases storing human behaviors and social patterns representing a rich variety of potential avatar personalities. No less important is that the future of virtual worlds requires a natural understanding of how to be a resident in a virtual world and how to learn not only content effectively, but culture as well. Learning in the physical world requires cognitive and emotional engagement with the external world, and we need seamless flow between the virtual and the physical so that we do not differentiate between them. Virtual-world objects and avatars that aid our learning about the physical world will increase engagement significantly (Reeves 2009). As we move into global interaction models, our technology must enable us to be natural, adapting to communication, navigating with our physical bodies, and interacting effortlessly with objects that self-assemble and allow us to easily create them using our imagination as the technology.

From the vantage point of today, we need to see defining moments in computing technology to achieve Stephenson's vision of the *metaverse*. For example, we might ensure that computing and the interface are able to perceive and communicate with all five senses naturally. This would be a single defining moment. Our interfaces today are pretty awkward comparatively. Broadly, we have been using the sole perceptory sense of vision to peer into a 2D screen, perhaps aided by 3D goggles and head-mounted displays. We then interact with computers solely using finger touch via keyboards, mice, or tapping and pinching the screen of a multitouch device. We use voice to activate a few commands. But we do not employ other feeling senses, smell or taste, at least not in widely available commercial applications. Developing computer interfaces able to perceive and communicate with all five senses equally will likely move us toward the first defining epiphany for virtual worlds.

In a fully enabled sensory virtual world, the avatar experience will truly come of age. In the last few years, research has made some discoveries about both the psychology and the sociology of the users of avatars indicating that sensing avatar presence and interacting with others in ways that simulate our physical experience influences our behavior significantly (Blascovich and Bailenson 2011). These findings suggest the following cycle of betterment: the more users engage routinely with avatars, the more they will employ them effectively to focus attention, increase recall, and organize information in-world in ways that produce meaningful interactions.

Immersion in the content of today's virtual worlds is different than in 1995, when interaction and virtual-world content was just emerging. Inspired by gaming, in today's virtual worlds, cues exist that make it more obvious who has skills and who does not, who has reputation and who does not, and who is safe and who is not. In addition, good world design makes it more obvious what the intent is and what the goals are, how to score and how to win, how to both learn from and teach experiences. In today's virtual worlds, increasingly sophisticated avatar users are concerned with privacy, anonymity, security, interpersonal distance, and agency from the first few minutes after landing in a new environment. Avatar users exceed or fail, just as the physical world. Avatar users' relationships either flourish or diminish.

In order to create a deep sense of immersion, good design in virtual environments is paramount. For example, either the designers know the world is active and that it requires skills, socialization, and community or they do not. Either the designers paint an environment that precisely imitates the physical and psychological or they do not. Either the designers understand fundamental neurological factors active in the human brain as we actively participate with others in virtual worlds, or they do not. Designers of worlds can rely on these factors to spur action, imbuing users with scenarios that require a sudden decision to fight or flee. In virtual worlds, designers can intensify the focus of attention with story. They can distort the sense of time through teleportation. They can make us concentrate on discovery, success, or rewards for participating in communities. They can capture our attention and engage us in activities that make us learn, that make us adapt to what we are experiencing. The future of virtual worlds requires a whole new level of designer literacy, where immersion and interactivity and the affordances of being in 3D make a difference. These are characteristics of successful virtual worlds that have achieved real meaning and that are far beyond simple chat rooms. In the future renditions of virtual worlds, the user will be pulled into more enveloping augmented realities that may not let their sense of immersion be interrupted as easily.

Blascovich and Bailenson (2011) underscore both the positive and negative effects on users immersed within their avatars. They have recently reported on several sociopsychological studies that indicate "humans are neurophysiologically wired to subjectively 'right' sensory stimulus according to previously established expectations." We interpret these results to mean that correctly cued social influences work in virtual worlds. This can be seen in studies that show ostracism, startle response, stigma, reactions to mimicry, body positioning, effects of appearance (clothing, stature, age, weight, etc.), and *proxemic* distance all potentially influence the way users interact with each other, which corresponds to how people interact with each other in physical spaces (Llobera & Juan 2010). The term *proxemics* was first used by Edward Hall in his study of how people manage interpersonal space. The distances between people can make us feel more relaxed or more anxious and vary with culture, gender, and age.

Leveraging this research, today's designers address how people "live" inside virtual worlds for both intense short bursts and for extended periods of time. In either case, users need something meaningful to do in-world both immediately and consistently over longer time frames. Meaningful experiences are the single greatest mechanism to attract users globally and support their social needs persistently. Gaming techniques are consistently incorporated into virtual worlds to increase user engagement (Kapp 2012). For example, Marriott International created a game similar to *The Sims* in which the player practices being a hotel kitchen manager, guaranteed to be a constantly engaging experience. Such experiences, sometimes referred to as *serious games*, are emerging as a new training environment. Experiencing content is only part of the equation, however. Leveraging content creation abilities provides cocreation and collaborative techniques that intensify user experiences even more (Sanchez 2009). Users may not only participate as hotel kitchen managers, but in the future of content creation, recreate the kitchen to work in the way that makes sense to them, the users of the space. Users who create things together have deeper learning experiences. Deeper learning experiences are only part of the compensation for the next generation of avatar user. Increased performance among coworkers based on collaborative designs, and management-building spaces to suit the needs of the user are other potential gains.

Successful virtual worlds often use reward systems where feedback is continuous as users seek to continuously increase outcomes. In virtual worlds employing scripting, coding every virtual object to respond and collect information about users adds another layer of utility and takes virtual interactivity up a notch. Even more powerful applications emerge in virtual worlds that are directly embedded into the World Wide Web or any other device that has an IP address in order to provide increased access to data and web services. This level of content integration and programmability of every object in every virtual-world environment was unanticipated in early versions of virtual worlds.

Recognizing avatar presence and immediately responding to it when the users are engaged in procedural activities is common. Inspired by *gamification* literature (Kapp 2012), imagine an in-world exercise involving learning how to properly prepare food in a virtual fast-food restaurant. You (or your avatar) are tasked with cooking a hamburger the right way. First, you start by taking a hamburger from a refrigerator, making sure it has maintained a certain temperature before slapping it on the stove. If it is not the right temperature, the virtual refrigerator unemotionally reminds you to set the temperature correctly. Everything you do in the kitchen is enhanced through virtual imagery on your in-world interface, perhaps a set of 3D glasses, or large screen displays on all sides, or even holodecks. As you place the hamburger on the stove, you get another reminder from the stove that you must make sure you are using a standard regulated temperature.

The pressure mounts. As you cook the hamburger for a designated period of time as required by health standards, turning it just at the right time, the hamburger itself tells you, "Wait, I am not done on this side yet." If you take it off the heat too soon, both the stove and the hamburger direct concerned audio and text messages at you, connecting you to your AI virtual assistance, so you can do real-time Q and A seeking answers to questions you don't know. The virtual world AI accesses every instance of anyone in your situation that has engaged in this very conversation, so the answers are all crowd sourced. If that is not enough, a video begins playing over the stove to remind you how the process actually should work. A few minutes later, the condiments and the vegetables may also argue with you, reminding you customers are watching their carbohydrates and the amount you are putting on the hamburger as a condiment exceeds their dietary limits. The customer who buys your virtual burger tells you to provide nutritional information, and your virtual agent incorporates that information and recommends what other users ordered with it to get the same level of satisfaction without the extra calories. This fanciful and highly compressed learning experience would likely be much more impactful than cooking in a real restaurant with a manager watching over your shoulder.

Rich situational feedback is essential for creating a vibrant future of interaction in virtuality. Training and education are daily activities for lifelong learning. Seeking a virtual world that is constantly informing us, managing our experience, and helping us gain a better understanding of our world around us is why looking at virtual worlds as training environments is likely the most immediate step toward the defining the future. The utility of virtual worlds will scale as the number of virtual worlds are digitized. The more learning algorithms are incorporated into how our virtual world and our physical world interact, the more the implications reach back directly into even more relevant functions such as job performance, product sales, and personalized entertainment and are incorporated into everything we do: business, entertainment, education, health care, and science, just to name a few.

This sort of training in-world might lead directly to mirroring reality in actual food-provisioning processes. With sensors embedded in many kinds of apparatus in the next decade, what we would be able to model in virtual worlds may be directly mirrored in reality as well. We can see after our analysis here that virtuality designers must purposefully blur their conceptions of virtual worlds, games, shared community spaces, education, job performance, and the physical world to heighten user experiences. What we have observed in this past decade of rapid virtual-world development is an emphasis on avatar/avatar interaction combined with avatar/object compatibility, fusing physics and psychology in a way that defines action and agency. What we should expect to see next is an upswing in effective immersive design that laces the technology to the user's psychology and sociology in inextricable ways.

We are seeing improvement in people's lives because of rich varieties of psychological contact when they meet as avatars. Norris (2009) reported on 10,000 members in virtual health-related support groups. The groups identified were dealing with various types of mental conditions including bereavement, grief, stigma, and social isolation.

Key groups represented included people with self-diagnosed health issues, transgender issues, people who had wheelchair-bound disabilities, and people in depression support groups. The analysis of these groups found psychological well-being improved through online support groups. We observed evidence of physical transformations as well as a result of health-related programs and support groups. In a virtual weight loss program, Johnston et al. (2011) observed that real people lost weight through in-world counseling as effectively as the in-person program taught in a health club (see also Riva, chapter 39 in this volume). But what is even more revealing is that the research also suggested that the virtual world-based program might be even more effective in influencing "meaningful behavioral changes and increased self efficacy" (1). To many, behavior change in virtual-world weight loss sounds counterintuitive. Yet at the University of Washington, we studied an early example of burn victims immersed in a virtual world of snow and ice. Sharar and colleagues (2008) reported a significant impact after examining the psychological state of users in their Snow Globe study. They reported a decrease in the pain and anxiety among postburn victims undergoing physical treatment while immersed in a virtual snowy winter world, suggesting that the blending of appropriate suggestive environments produces a beneficial psychological effect. We can only imagine what might be possible combining such worlds with the wealth of content on the Internet.

Stanford's Reeves and Read (2009) predict that certain factors will influence our next steps in total engagement over the Internet. They predict business will take on virtual worlds to change the way we work and compete. The elements of successful games can also be easily extended into the virtual-world genre. Principal among these elements is the use of a narrative. Well-crafted storytelling is at the heart of every good multimedia product and at the soul of all human culture. The more we create places that bring together good production values and characters in a narrative with a beginning, middle, and end, adding a little emotional music, suspense, or humor, the more we will believe in where we are and why we are there. This is especially true if we as users have some control over the unfolding of the story.

The balance between work, learning, and play is a natural outgrowth of this convergence of 2D and 3D storytelling and ubiquitous technology. Having fun, or simply being truly engaged and caring about the outcomes as they relate both to you and others, is the greatest element of gaming that will influence virtuality in the long run. As any well-designed 3D environment provides iterative types of feedback, making the environment fun is essential for successful virtual-world development. Users report that fun in games can be characterized as having a sense of control, exploring solutions, and getting rewards for winning. Jane McGonigal in her TED talk refers to this as the *epic win* (McGonigal 2010), that moment when the person playing is so engrossed in the outcome that every last detail of action seems to create an emotional experience so intense that the actual physiology of the player is altered. These physiological changes are not merely limited to acceleration of heart rate and sharpening of visual focus on details key to accomplishing the goal. These changes are experiential and provide the user with a desire to be there more often; in essence they form a habit of being immersed (see also Abdel Nabi and Charlton, chapter 11 in this volume). The implication of digital habituation is to create long-term meaningful activity that provides a value not only to the individual, but to the society around the individual, codependent upon their unique participation and role. The key is to make meaningful worlds that serve as value chains.

One key gain resulting from using virtual worlds can be acquiring leadership skills and learning how to manage both the positive and negative effects of technology value entering our lives so deeply. The more the user experiences team leadership feedback in an interactive environment, the more behavioral change on the job might be anticipated. We live in an era when our performance-standing in a virtual world can indirectly or directly affect a promotion in management at work. Brown and Thomas (2006) write that "the process of becoming an effective *World of Warcraft* guild master amounts to a total-immersion course in leadership. A guild is a collection of players who come together to share knowledge, resources, and manpower. To run a large one, a guild master must be adept at many skills: attracting, evaluating, and recruiting new members; creating apprenticeship programs; orchestrating group strategy; and adjudicating disputes." Since the rules are explicit and enforced, it is anticipated that game rules in virtual worlds may likely help develop an internal sense of control. This should be explored more deeply in the creation and evaluation of teams working together in virtual worlds. The identification of a team member's emotional state is still primitive, however, but as facial recognition and emotional state detection use increases rapidly in the future, virtual teams will start to rely on the expressed avatar state and work more seamlessly across digital boundaries, allowing virtual leaders to arise and guide such teams effectively.

The promise of immersion and having a meaningful impact is seen in the last decade of research on learning environments that we discuss here to help put the future of cognitive engagement into perspective (see also Gamor, chapter 38 in this volume). How does technology impact us as learners? Learners are those people who adapt to and change their environment to benefit themselves and others. Dede (1996) guides us in looking at virtual worlds as constructivist learning environments. You have to teach your students to "think in 3D" and not simply transfer the current classroom into the virtual world—a warning for every technology and how it impacts the user's initial perceptions of the environment. The best way to do that is by engaging the user to experience the virtual world, to do something that has consequences, and to record and observe those outcomes while remaining actively involved. For example, we created a virtual world for Ernst & Young in which the students had to conduct inventory audit observations (see figure 1.4). Students were required to conduct the inventory in a warehouse in which they had to count boxes, get help to open up boxes, discern items on a loading dock, calculate various kinds of material, and reconcile compilations that had previously recorded all of their touches and investigations in the warehouse. This activity led users to discover that doing real-time inventory observations was something that required experience, more than succeeding in simply answering questions on a test. The fluidity of identity in solving problems in situ is different than in the classroom. So for these learners, being in a warehouse in which everything is a variable causes more thought process to occur. The reason is apparent: many things happen in the active environment

FIGURE 1.4 Ernst & Young Inventory Observation.

that cannot be anticipated. Each location is different, each group of people is different, and coursing through the differences requires the learners to quickly become proficient.

In another example, teaching the causes, effects, and next steps to seek assessment, diagnosis, and treatment of PTSD (post-traumatic stress disorder) in a game-based PTSD experience based in Second Life encouraged anonymous visitors to experience an IED explosion and identify the triggers carried over from the incident into a mall in which they gather health points by lowering their anxiety while increasing their health (see figure 1.5). They do this by immersing their avatars in experiential learning rather than experiencing the IED explosion directly. With the use of realism, such an experience will be unquestionably impactful. There is really no substitute for creating learning experiences in which students are at the center of learning, constructing their own solutions to problems that are part of the environment. The more immersion, the more identity, the more believability, the more change to the user. The immersion factor leads to compelling outcomes. Think of this by imagining the best way to learn a foreign language. Going to the country that speaks the language and being surrounded constantly by everything in that language in context pushes you to levels of adaptation you cannot possibly recreate in a classroom setting. Living through a traumatic event and using exposure therapy in a virtual world is one of the serious applications of these technologies that focuses on immersive learning. These examples are meant to visualize the impact of taking virtual worlds to the next level.

Putting the student in the center of learning has taken a foothold in virtual worlds. In two books edited by Hinrichs and Wankel, *Transforming Virtual World Learning* (2011) and *Engaging the Avatar* (2012), we examined longtime users of virtual worlds for education. We found that social constructivism, experiential learning, and problem-based

FIGURE 1.5: PTSD experience reinforces trigger effects of an IED explosion.

learning challenged students as actors and participants in adapting to the culture of the virtual world. Students learned how to research marshland erosion, develop faculty in simulated schools, known as *sim escuelas* (Santos 2012), understand the world of stutterers, and conduct experiments in genetics labs. Forming hypotheses by doing, and then testing the environment while learning and interpreting evidence over time, leads students to become problem solvers and learn with a purpose. Kapp and O'Driscoll (2010, convergence point 4) describe the transformation in education because of these affordances: "With the infusion of three-dimensional (3D) technology platforms, it is only a matter of time before 3D social networking takes off. When this happens, *Facebook* will truly become the Faces of the User."

Given all of this optimism there still is some adaptation that must take place. The technology of interactivity for this generation of learning virtual worlds requires assessment to be the underbelly of any design. Anything a user or student does in the virtual world must provide effective feedback and allow for both individual and group reflection. Testing is simply inefficient, and adaptation to a real-time environment is optimal (see also Gamor, chapter 38 in this volume). However, there is much ground to be gained in virtual worlds. In a study conducted at Moscow State University by Alexander Voiskounsky (2011), university students in two studies were surveyed to discover what they knew about virtual realities. The first study was administered before showing the movie *Avatar* (2009). Voiskounsky found that

> while students believed that activities such as social networking and online
> gaming represent virtual realities, some other examples provided by the students

in the two studies differed: in the second study the participants expressed a better understanding of the items related to virtual realities . . . at the same time, not a single participant reported particular psychological states (either regular or altered) as examples of virtual realities.

It is not surprising that many students cannot distinguish between virtual worlds and video gaming. Pew Research in 2008 reports 97 percent of American teens play computer, web, portable, or console games. It cannot be assumed that if you were born in the digital era, you differentiate between games, simulations, and virtual worlds. The reward systems for learning are scores on tests, not performance in simulations. However, as the population grows more mobile in their computing, the need to create technologies that support ongoing, cumulative learning will become standard, and we believe that the interfaces to enable deep learning will leverage the power of 3D. One area of differentiation is movement awareness in ubiquitous computing. Movement augments experiential interaction among avatars and creates a somatic awareness that is unparalleled in other forms of online learning or collaboration software (Levisohn 2011).

For me (Randy Hinrichs), it has been highly gratifying to participate in a pioneering first decade of early twenty-first century virtual worlds research and development following along in the tradition that Damer and others created in the 1990s. Simulating large-scale virtual worlds with "real world" high fidelity is likely to remain a long way off. In this era, research is critically important to strengthen our understanding of how this new medium actually functions and can best serve humanity. While it is insightful to be informed and emboldened by science fiction visions such as those of William Gibson, Neal Stephenson, and Vernon Vinge, the enthusiasm and hard work of first adopters is what is truly needed. Last, some of the solid research results of the past decade need to be faithfully applied and tested with commercialization of new virtual-world experiences.

In the end, there is no better recourse for researchers than immersing themselves in a variety of virtual worlds and learning their languages and cultures. In this book, you will enter into various readers' experiences in virtuality and learn of those experiences as they take on a wide variety of aspects of virtuality; tantamount among these varieties: defining virtuality in a collective way. There is no substitute to entering into virtuality yourself, carrying with you this book as your guide.

A Virtual-World Benchmark

In June 1995, the members of the Contact Consortium engaged in a brainstorming and white paper writing exercise on what virtual worlds might become in the coming decades. This document gives us a benchmark to measure the actual emergence of avatar virtuality. At that time, Worlds Chat was the sole graphical virtual world available on the Internet, and there were few multiuser games and no social networks. The consortium membership posed and addressed questions about prospective virtual-world

Table 1.1 Mapping of 1995 Contact Consortium Virtual World Projections White Paper to Today's Outcomes in 2013

Virtuality then (1995)	Reality (2013)	Realization challenges	Trajectory
Will we see useful virtual meeting rooms within virtual worlds?	Virtual worlds have been used for business meetings providing integration with standard office tools such as documents and presentations. Embedded virtual world communities are also used in teamwork and role-playing for project management, collaboration, and tele-working.	Enterprise-ready systems require security, privacy, and scalability. Interoperable assets with a minimum of required training time. Virtual worlds currently do not tightly integrate into enterprise information systems.	Immersive "holodeck" realistic reproduction of the physical office or classroom setting may appear and also support the visualization of more abstract "data spaces."
Will we see the development of shared virtual learning spaces?	Simulations used in virtual worlds are now commonly used as learning tools (Second Life, SLoodle, Active Worlds, EdHeads). Virtual classrooms are utilized in a growing number of schools and universities to provide e-learning, tracking active performance and cognitive behavior. Context-specific active-based learning standards are emerging.	With the lack of standard platforms and objects for virtual worlds, the cost of deploying virtual learning spaces is high. With schools largely using 2D document content there are challenges to mapping this onto a learning space in 3D. Testing learning performance in virtual worlds is still at a nascent stage.	Game-based learning is making advances. Virtual worlds may benefit from Net Central personalized learning points, competency-based uses of avatars, and mentor-based learning supporting individualized student programs for accredited degrees.
Will we be able to implement biologically inspired behavior in a virtual world?	Facilities within virtual worlds can be scripted to sense users' avatars in action and engage in increasingly sophisticated procedural responses. Simple forms of artificial intelligence (AI) and artificial life (AL) may be embodied in-world as "bots" for entertainment and in the management of world infrastructure.	Human behavior is complex, and AI is often insufficient to provide meaningful responses to users' needs. Simulating biological systems including plants and animals is a major challenge for science and even more difficult to fit into the limited computational capacity of virtual worlds.	Fast voice-based mobile phone interfaces such as Apple's Siri show the way for conversational bots interacting with human users. Generative worlds based upon genetic algorithms or using other natural dynamical systems even at the level of molecules may support the realistic simulation of lifelike behaviors.
Will virtual worlds be equipped with voice and video?	Voice over IP now enables many-to-many, ad hoc chat, group meetings, and textual back-chatting. Video playback within virtual worlds is feasible and an important addition to human presence and content in virtual spaces.	Bandwidth and rendering performance put limits on the number of users able to use voice and video in a shared virtual environment.	Voice recognition tied to navigating and affecting the content of virtual worlds could improve usability. The merger of live performance and avatar interaction could be enabled by rapid detection and extraction of objects or people within video streams.

Question			
Will we understand how virtual world communities work?	Numerous university research programs are actively investigating the workings of virtual world communities.	Virtual communities are bound to their particular virtual world platform, and users cannot easily cross over between worlds. Therefore these communities will remain small and circumscribed in their development.	Similar to the Web, once a ubiquitous, standard, and open virtual world platform emerges, so will understanding of the function and best practices around virtual world communities.
Will virtual worlds be able to track users' avatar motion, provide multiple points of view, utilize navigational aids, and represent real-world spaces like cities?	Virtual world platforms have been developed where users' avatars are connected to virtual and physical sensors that track movement and body and facial gestures. First- and third-person points of view, maps, and way-finding methods are all commonplace in virtual worlds. A great deal of geoinformational content such as 3D city models, terrain, and even planetary surfaces has been modeled within virtual worlds.	Data rates from motion tracking and image recognition such as facial expressions are still short of real-time responsiveness and fall short of realism. The lack of ubiquitous real-time data about the physical world prevents high-fidelity, believable landscapes and built environments from being represented in virtual worlds. Ubiquitous computing including wearables and technology integrated into the human body will serve to transfer information across the digital and the corporeal.	Rapid progress in 3D sensing and rendering hardware will enable new frontiers of real-time interaction. Face and motion tracking, high-fidelity physics including fluid dynamics, and real-time capture of data from landscapes and geographical information databases will produce virtual worlds with high realism and fine granularity of detail.
Will the user interfaces employed in virtual worlds be limited to mouse, keyboard, and screen or branch out allowing more "natural" interaction?	Current interfaces to virtual worlds are still largely based on the mouse, keyboard, and joystick and require a large number of 2D on-screen menus. Real-time motion capture systems have just entered the market and allow full-body interaction with virtual worlds.	User affordances for virtual worlds are not standardized and ubiquitous high-performance devices to enable more natural interaction are years in the future. Not all human senses are incorporated into the experience (haptics or smell, for example).	Wearable computing within clothing and even implants will enable unencumbered full-body interaction with virtual worlds. As more senses are added to the user's experience, increased emotional expressiveness and autonomy will be embedded into avatars, enabling them to serve as more full prostheses of the self.

technologies, user affordances, social norms, applications, and more. It is valuable now to look back at the virtuality and reality of what was accomplished over seventeen years. Table 1.1 lists some of the key questions from the 1995 white paper, looks at today's reality, addresses why the concepts may not have been fully realized, and makes some predictions about the trajectory that virtual worlds are taking.

CONCLUSION

The benchmark in table 1.1 provides a mere snapshot of the ongoing evolution of avatar cyberspace. Dourish and Bell (2011) guides us in our understanding of how information technology shapes our daily experience, especially as ubiquitous computing interlaces our physical lives ever more tightly with our virtual experience. We are confident that the compelling spatiality of virtual worlds coupled with human presence through expressive avatars and world designs that depict both realistic and fantastical realities will combine to become major tools for the human enterprise. When we sense objects around us, we develop a narrative and meaning for them. We then leverage this context for communication, role-playing, creativity, learning, task accomplishment, and relationship building. We believe that sensing each other online as avatars has far more emotive and cognitive power than a cursor, a web page, a chat message, a photo, or a movie. These artifacts serve their purpose well, but it is the human being embodied as an avatar in a virtual space that we believe will allow us to truly evolve ourselves and our cultural practices. Virtual worlds may be humanity's new caves of Lascaux: we shape their stone surfaces in polygons, we paint their petroglyphs with textures, and our voices echo within their walls and give meaning to our avatar's hero's journey.

In this chapter, we peered into the prehistory and brief recent emergence of the medium of virtual worlds, pondered its present state, and then presented one crystal ball view of its possible future. As a consequence of our exploration it became clear to us that the virtual world is actually a camera obscura for the twenty-first century. Through its lens we shall behold a new projection of ourselves and our society, discover novel ways to communicate, develop profound insights into science and nature, take up fresh tools for art, and come to an expanded sense of our place in the universe. We choose to take up this form of *virtuality* precisely because it stands at the crux of so much of what it means to be human and what it might mean to all of humanity in the future. We believe that, in the evolution of virtual worlds, the best is yet to come.

REFERENCES

Avatar. 2009. Directed by James Cameron. Distributed by 20th Century Fox. Los Angeles, CA.
Blascovich, J., and J. Bailenson. 2011. *Infinite Reality*. New York: William Morrow.
Borgmann, A. 1999. *Holding On to Reality*. Chicago/London: University of Chicago Press.

Brown, J. S., and D. Thomas. 2006. You Play World of Warcraft? You're Hired! *Wired Magazine* 14 (4), April. http://www.wired.com/wired/archive/14.04/learn.html. Accessed June 12, 2013.

Burning Man Website. *Afterburn Report 2012: Introduction.* http://afterburn.burningman. com/12/. Accessed April 5, 2013.

Damer, B. 1996. Inhabited Virtual Worlds: A New Frontier for Interaction Design. *ACM Interactions.* New York: ACM Press.

Damer, B. 1997. *Avatars! Exploring and Building Virtual Worlds on the Internet.* Berkeley, CA: Peachpit Press.

Damer, B. 2006. Newsmaker: A Brief History of the Virtual World. Interview by Daniel Terdiman. *CNET.* November 9. http://news.cnet.com/A-brief-history-of-the-virtual-world/2008-1043_3-6134110.html?tag=nefd.lede. Accessed June 12, 2013.

Damer, B. 2008. Meeting in the Ether: A Brief History of Virtual Worlds as a Medium for User-Created Events. *Journal of Virtual Worlds Research* 1 (1). https://journals.tdl.org/jvwr/article/view/285. Accessed June 12, 2013.

Damer, B. 2010. Full CNET Avatar Interview with Daniel Terdiman. *Terra Nova, Simulation + Society + Play.* January 29. http://terranova.blogs.com/terra_nova/2010/01/full-cnet-avatar-interview-with-daniel-terdiman.html. Accessed June 12, 2013.

Damer, B., P. Newman, R. Norkus, J. Graham, R. Gordon, and T. Barbalet. 2011. Cyberbiogenesis and the EvoGrid: A 21st Century Grand Challenge. In *Genesis—In the Beginning: Precursors of Life, Chemical Models and Early Biological Evolution,* edited by J. G. Seckbach. Dordrecht: Springer. 267–288.

Damer, B., D. Rasmussen, P. Newman, R. Norkus, and B. Blair. 2006. Design Simulation in Support of NASA's Robotic and Human Lunar Exploration Program. *Proceedings of AIAA Space 2006.* July 15. http://www.digitalspace.com/presentations/aiaa-2006/DSLunarExplorationPaper.html. Accessed June 12, 2013.

Dede, C. 1996. The Evolution of Constructivist Learning Environments: Immersion in Distributed, Virtual Worlds. In *Constructivist Learning Environments: Case Studies in Instructional Design,* edited by Brent Wilson. Englewood Cliffs, NJ: Educational Technology Publications. 165–176.

Dionisio, J. D., W. Burns, and R. Gilbert. 2011. 3D Virtual Worlds and the Metaverse: Current Status and Future Possibilities. *ACM Computing Surveys* 5 (N), June. http://www.scribd.com/doc/6 6926500/3D-Virtual-Worlds-and-the-Metaverse-Current-Status-and-Future-Possibilities. Accessed June 12, 2013.

Dourish, P., and G. Bell. 2011. *Divining a Digital Future: Mess and Mythology in Ubiquitous Computing.* Cambridge, MA: MIT Press.

Heim, M. 1998. *Virtual Realism.* New York: Oxford University Press.

Hinrichs, R., and C. Wankel, eds. 2011. *Transforming Virtual World Learning: Cutting-Edge Technologies in Higher Education.* Bingley, UK: Emerald Group Publishing.

Hinrichs, R., and C. Wankel, eds. 2012. *Engaging the Avatar: New Frontiers in Immersive Education.* Charlotte, NC: Information Age Publishing.

Introna, L. 2011. Phenomenological Approaches to Ethics and Information Technology. In *The Stanford Encyclopedia of Philosophy,* edited by Edward N. Zalta. Summer 2011 Edition http://plato.stanford.edu/archives/sum2011/entries/ethics-it-phenomenology/. Accessed June 12, 2013.

Johnston, J., A. Massey, and C. DeVaneaux. 2011. Innovation in Weight Loss Intervention Programs: An Examination of a 3D Virtual World Approach. In *Proceedings from the Hawaii International Conference on Systems Sciences.* http://www.cluboneisland.com/assets/research/HICSS12_formatted_FINAL_sept.pdf. Accessed June 12, 2013.

Kapp, K. M. 2012. *The Gamification of Learning and Instruction: Game-Based Methods and Strategies for Training and Education*. San Francisco: Pfeiffer.

Kapp, K. M., and T. O'Driscoll. 2010. *Learning in 3D*. San Francisco: Pfeiffer.

Lauria, R. 1997. Virtual Reality: An Empirical-Metaphysical Testbed. *Journal of Computer-Mediated Communication* 3 (2). http://www.ascusc.org/jcmc/vol3/issue2/lauria.html. Accessed May 28, 2013.

Levisohn, A., and T. Schiphorst. 2011. Embodied Engagement: Supporting Movement Awareness in Ubiquitous Computing Systems. *Ubiquitous Learning* 3 (4): 97–112.

Llobera, J., B. Spanlang, G. Ruffini, and M. Slater. 2010. Proxemics with Multiple Dynamic Characters in an Immersive Virtual Environment. *ACM Transactions on Applied Perception* 8 (1): 3.

McGonigal, J. 2010. Gaming Can Make a Better World. *Ted Talk Video*. February. http://www.ted.com/talks/jane_mcgonigal_gaming_can_make_a_better_world.html. Accessed June 12, 2013.

Merhi, O. A. 2009. Motion Sickness, Virtual Reality and Postural Stability. Ph.D. diss., University of Minnesota. December. http://conservancy.umn.edu/handle/58646. Accessed June 12, 2013.

Morningstar, C., and F. R. Farmer. (n.d.). *The Lessons of Lucasfilm's Habitat*. http://www.fudco.com/chip/lessons.html. Accessed June 12, 2013.

Morningstar, C., and R. R. Farmer. 1991. The Lessons of Lucasfilm's Habitat. In *Cyberspace: First Steps*, edited by Michael Benedikt. London: MIT Press. 273–300.

Norris, J. 2009. The Growth and Direction of Healthcare Support Groups in Virtual Worlds. *Journal of Virtual Worlds Research* 2 (2): 3–20.

Pew Research. 2008. *Teens, Video Games and Civics*. http://pewresearch.org/pubs/953/. Accessed May 27, 2013.

Reeves, B., and J. Leighton Read. 2009. *Total Engagement: Using Games and Virtual Worlds to Change the Way People Work and Businesses Compete*. Boston: Harvard Business Press.

Riner, R., and J. Clodius. 1995. Simulating Future Histories: The Nau Solar System Simulation & Mars Settlement. *Anthropology & Education Quarterly* 26 (1): 95–104. http://dragonmud.com/people/jen/solsys.html. Accessed March 15, 2012.

Ropolyi, L. 2001. Virtuality and Plurality. In *Virtual Reality: Cognitive Foundations, Technological Issues and Philosophical Implications*, edited by Alexander Riegler, Markus F. Peschl, Karl Edlinger, Gunther Fleck, and Walter Feigl. Frankfurt am Main: Peter Lang Publishing. 167–187.

Sanchez, A. 2009. Games for Good: How DAU Is Using Games to Enhance Learning. *A Publication of the Defense Acquisition University*. http://www.dau.mil/pubscats/PubsCats/Sanchez.pdf. Accessed May 27, 2013.

Santos, A. 2012. The Simescuela: An Innovative Virtual Environment for Teacher Training. In *Engaging the Avatar*, edited by Randy Hinrichs and Charles Wankel. Charlotte, NC: Information Age Publishing. 365–390.

Sharar, S., W. Miller, A. Teeley, M. Soltani, H. Hoffman, M. Jensen, and D. Patterson. 2008. Applications of Virtual Reality for Pain Management in Burn-Injured Patients. *Expert Rev Neurother* 8 (11): 1667–1674. http://www.ncbi.nlm.nih.gov/pmc/articles/PMC2634811/. Accessed June 12, 2013.

Smith, R. 2008. *Rogue Leaders: The Story of LucasArts*. London: Titan.

Turkle, S. 1996. Parallel Lives: Working on Identity in Virtual Space. In *Constructing the Self in a Mediated World*, edited by Debra Grodin and Thomas R. Lindlof. London: Sage. 156–175.

Vinge, V. 2006. *Rainbows End*. New York: Tor Science Fiction.

Voiskounsky, A. 2011. Interpretations of Virtual Reality. Studies in Health Technology and Informatics. Student Health Technology Information. Annual Review of Cybertherapy and Telemedicine 2011. *Advanced Technologies in Behavioral, Social and Neurosciences* 167: 26–31.

CHAPTER 2

THE PHYSICAL AND SOCIAL REALITY OF VIRTUAL WORLDS

PHILIP BREY

INTRODUCTION: A QUESTION OF ONTOLOGY

IT is a common belief that objects in virtual environments are not real but are mere imitations or simulations of real objects. A virtual apple, for example, has the appearance of an apple but by no means qualifies as real. A real apple has weight, mass, a physical location in space, and physical and chemical capabilities by which it can interact with objects in the real world. These are the kinds of properties by which we hold it to actually exist, instead of just being imagined or represented. A virtual apple, in contrast, has no such properties. Instead, it seems to be a make-believe object, a mere visual projection that responds to computer inputs but not to anything else. But if virtual objects are not real, physical objects, then what kinds of objects are they? Are they nonphysical objects or are they still reducible to something physical? And could it be the case that some virtual objects are real after all? Isn't a virtual chess game that allows one to play chess with an opponent, also in a way a real chess game? Cannot virtual money qualify as real money, if it can be exchanged for dollars or other currencies, as is the case for virtual money in certain virtual worlds like *Second Life*? Aren't virtual insults real insults, if they are intended and taken personally by users of a virtual world?

These kinds of questions have been central to philosophical and social studies of virtual reality since its early beginnings (Rheingold 1991; Heim 1993; Zhai 1998). They belong to the field of *ontology*, the study of being, which is a branch of philosophy concerned with the question of what kinds of entities exist and how different kinds of existing things relate to each other. Ontology asks questions like these: What is a physical object? Are there objects that are nonphysical? What is a property and how do properties relate to objects? How do we distinguish essential from contingent properties of objects? Are there different kinds of existence or being for objects? What is the mode of existence of a number? Of a set? Of an event? Of a fictional object? And so forth.[1]

In this chapter, I will perform an ontological analysis of virtual objects, actions, and events. My focus will be on two ontological questions: (1) What is the mode of existence of virtual objects, actions, and events? (2) Can any virtual objects, actions, or events be claimed to be part of the real world as opposed to being unreal, a merely simulated reality, and if so, how does this fact problematize the distinction between reality and virtuality? Currently, there is widespread ontological confusion about virtual reality and its relation to the real world, which contributes to a flawed understanding of virtual reality and its potential. A better understanding of the ontology of the virtual can contribute to a better design and use of virtual environments and virtual reality systems.

In the next section of this chapter, I aim to give an answer to the first of these two questions. I will study how virtual objects relate ontologically to physical objects, and will attempt to determine their ontological status. In the third section, I will focus on the second question, and will study under which circumstances a virtual object may qualify as real. This will move me into the domain of social ontology. In the fourth section, my focus will be on virtual actions, which are ontologically different from virtual objects and require a separate analysis. In the fifth section, I will investigate the various ways in which virtual entities create ontological confusion or uncertainty, and hence muddy the distinction between reality and fiction. In a concluding section, I summarize my findings and briefly discuss their significance.

General Ontology of Virtual Reality

This section is devoted to answering the first question of this chapter, concerning the mode of existence of virtual objects (and actions and events). We have already seen that many, if not all, objects in virtual worlds do not have real existence. That is, they are not part of the real world. But is this to say that virtual objects have no existence at all? This seems clearly false. Virtual objects do exist, they populate the virtual environments used by millions of users all over the world, and they are things we refer to and interact with. But how can we then say that something exists and at the same time is not real?

By speaking about virtual objects (not) existing or being (un)real, we get confused by our language. So let us try to be more precise in our use of it. It is true that virtual apples exist, or are real, *as virtual apples*. However, it is false that virtual apples exist, or are real, *as real apples*. This is the confusion: virtual apples simulate or imitate real apples. To say that they are not real is ambiguous between saying that they are not real apples and that they do not exist (not even as virtual apples). But they do exist as virtual apples, just like imitation apples made out of clay or plastic exist as imitation apples but not as real apples. A virtual apple is a real entity, just not a real apple. It is, as Dilworth (2010) calls it, a concrete model, just like a physical imitation apple.

At this point, an objection may be in order. While it is true that fake apples are real (physical) objects, can we genuinely say that virtual apples are real objects? Isn't it a necessary condition for something to be a real object that it exists in space and time in the physical world and has mass and weight? Virtual objects, it would seem, are immaterial and usually are not clearly located in the physical world. In short, they seem to have no physical existence, and therefore do not really exist, not even as virtual objects.

In reply to this objection, it may be pointed out that virtual objects do have an underlying physical basis, and that they resemble physical objects in significant ways. To see this, some more detail is in order as to how they are generated by computers and what properties they have. Virtual objects are generated by computer systems. Computer systems are devices that are characterized by their ability to perform logical operations over *symbolical representations*, or symbol structures, or symbols in short. The software that runs on a computer and the data structures used by software programs consists of strings of symbols that ultimately are represented in the form of bits and bytes. Many of these symbols remain invisible to users, as they are "machine code" that is interpreted by the machine. Larger symbolical structures, which rely on these lower-level symbols, may, however, be made accessible to users as objects that they can manipulate. They are usually made visible on the screen, where they are represented by an icon (e.g., one that depicts a folder) or a symbol string (e.g., "prog.exe" representing a program). Such symbolical structures I will call *digital objects*.

Although digital objects do not appear to have an identifiable mass and region in physical space, unlike (ordinary) physical objects, they have other features in virtue of which they may be defined as an object of some sort. Digital objects qualify as objects because they are persistent, unified, stable structures with attributes and relations to other objects, and agents can use and interact with them. It appears that computers can generate complex phenomena that imitate real objects, offer possibilities for interaction, and manifest themselves in an object-like manner. Because of their object-like behavior we may pragmatically define them as objects of some sort. Their unity and behavioral consistency is guaranteed by the underlying hardware and software.

A *virtual object* is a digital object that is represented by a computer, usually graphically as an object or region in a two- or three-dimensional space, and that can be interacted with or used through a computer interface.[2] Virtual objects are digital objects that appear to us as physical objects and that we interact with in a manner similar to physical objects. An example of a virtual object is a folder on the desktop of a PC. Such a folder looks like a real folder and functions and behaves in many ways like a real folder: it can be opened, documents or items can be put into it or removed from it, we can label it, move it, discard it, and so forth.

In addition to being physical phenomena that have a physical basis, virtual objects are also *artifacts*, designed by human beings to serve particular functions in a virtual world or environment. Thus, they usually have a specific functionality and specific (scripted) interactive possibilities tailored to the aim of the application. Moreover, virtual objects have features in common with *fictional objects*: objects and characters that appear in products of the imagination, such as novels and movies, and which do not have real existence. Virtual objects resemble fictional objects in requiring a suspension of disbelief: just as immersing oneself in a movie or novel requires one to experience or perceive depicted events as if they are actually happening, immersion in a virtual world requires one to act as if it is real. In addition, just like fictional objects, virtual objects depend on authorship, and this sometimes implies that facts concerning virtual objects are made true by fiat of their creator, in the interest of a narrative of which these objects are a part. For instance, a building in a virtual environment may be introduced as being very old, made of granite, being formerly owned by a wealthy family, and so on, without there being an independent way within the context of the simulation to verify these claims: they are made true, as with fictional objects, by fiat of the author or narrator.

THE SOCIAL ONTOLOGY OF VIRTUAL REALITY

Let us now turn to our second question, whether virtual objects, events, or actions can ever be said to be real rather than merely simulated. We have already seen that virtual objects are real *as* virtual objects, but this is obviously not the kind of answer we are looking for. So let us rephrase it to clarify what we are after. We want to know whether a virtual X (apple, rock, automobile, etc.) can in some cases be an instance of a real X. By a real X, I mean an X that actually exists or occurs, instead of merely being supposed, imagined, or represented. Let us say that when a virtual X merely succeeds in imitating a real X, but is not a real X itself, it is a (computer) *simulation*. A virtual apple, for example, is a simulation of a real apple. When a virtual X instead manages to qualify as a real X, it will be called an *ontological reproduction* (Brey 2003). Ontological reproductions are actual members of the class that they simulate. They share essential properties with a physical X in the real world by which they themselves qualify as a real X.

So are there any virtual X that can qualify as real X? Let us first consider ordinary physical objects, like apples, rocks, and trees. I claim that virtual versions of ordinary physical objects can never qualify as real instances of these objects. The reason is that their having physical mass as well as a certain physical composition is an essential part of their definition of a real object. Virtual objects do not have mass, nor do they have a physical composition, and therefore ordinary physical objects cannot be ontologically reproduced in virtual environment.

While physical *objects* cannot be ontologically reproduced in virtual environments, some physical *phenomena* can be. A phenomenon is an observable event or pattern, like a thunder flash or a repeating high-pitched sound. While computers do not have the causal power to produce physical objects, they do have the causal powers to produce certain types of physical phenomena, specifically phenomena that are composed of light or sound. They can do so because computer systems equipped with adequate output devices (monitors and speakers) have the causal powers of producing a wide variety of visual and auditory phenomena. Hence, they are able to ontologically reproduce certain "weightless" physical entities like images, sounds, shapes, and colors. Consequently, when in a virtual environment an orchestra plays Bach's Toccata and Fugue in D minor, a real performance of Toccata and Fugue in D minor is actually produced. Similarly, when in a virtual environment a circle is drawn, the result is a real circle, since a circle is mathematically defined as a phenomenon consisting of points in a plane, and is not by definition a physical object with weight and mass.

Computers are also capable of ontologically reproducing Xs that normally exist as physical objects but that do not *essentially* exist in physical form. Money, for example, traditionally exists in the form of physical coins and bills. But that it exists as such is mere convention. And conventions are changing. More and more, money exists as digital objects. A smart money card contains a code (a series of zeroes and ones) that defines how much money is present on the card. Money here has become a digital object. Money, it seems, does not essentially exist in physical form but may exist in digital or virtual form as well. Money is hence not essentially but only contingently physical.

John Searle (1995) has developed an ontological theory that can answer in a principled way which kinds of objects, actions, and events are essentially physical and which ones are only contingently so. I have used his theory to analyze which kinds of things can be ontologically reproduced in virtual form (Brey 2003). Searle holds that within what we call reality, a fundamental distinction can be made between physical and social reality. *Physical reality* consists of entities and facts that are genuinely objective and that exist independently of our representations of them. *Social reality* consists of all those entities and facts that are not genuinely objective but are the outcome of a process of social interpretation or construction.

Physical facts includes such truths as that there are snow and ice near the summit of Mt. Everest, that apples grow on apple trees, and that there is electric lighting in many houses on the Western Hemisphere. Searle is willing to admit that the *concepts* used in expressing physical facts are socially constructed. Yet Searle denies that their *referents* are also socially constructed. Rather, they are held to exist independently of our representations of them. Even if no humans existed there would be snow and ice near the summit of Mt. Everest. In contrast, *social facts* are also themselves socially constructed. The class of social facts includes such facts as that a bar of gold is worth a lot of money, that Harvard University offers a graduate degree program in physics, and that the curved object in my kitchen drawer is a corkscrew. These facts, Searle claims, seem to be objective in that there is (near-)universal agreement on them. Yet, Searle argues, these social facts and entities seem to be dependent on human representation or intentionality in a way that physical facts and entities are not. There is nothing intrinsic about the green paper bills that are used as money that determines their nature as money. Only when people start representing (intentionally using, accepting, believing in) such bills as money, intuitively, does it become a fact that these bills are money.

Searle argues that social facts come into existence through the *collective imposition of a function* on some object, event, or action. For instance, it is now a fact that the Dutch Delta works constitute a barrier against floods, because this function has in the past been collectively imposed on them in Dutch society. Searle claims that the collective imposition of function is a *collective intentional act*, which is an act that is intentionally performed by a collective (e.g., Dutch society). Searle distinguishes between two kinds of collectively imposed functions, which give rise to two different kinds of social facts. The first kind, consisting of ordinary collectively imposed functions, leads to *ordinary social facts*, which seem to apply mainly to *(material) artifacts*. Examples of such facts include the fact that devices of a certain form are screwdrivers, or the fact that the Delta works are a barrier against floods. The second kind, called *status functions*, leads to *institutional facts* that constitute *institutional reality*. Such facts are normally created within the context of previously created human institutions, like marriage, higher education, and the economy. Examples include the fact that the pope is not married, that dollar bills exist, that some people possess real estate, and that Paul McCartney is a former member of the Beatles.

An important difference between ordinary social facts and institutional facts is that the creation of institutional facts does not require any (physical) capabilities in objects, whereas the creation of ordinary social facts requires objects to be able to perform a physical function. For an object to be a screwdriver, it must be physically capable of driving screws. However, for an object to function as money, the only requirement is that people start *treating* it as money. The imposition of a status function brings with it an agreement to consider or treat this entity *as if* it had inherent causal powers to perform this function. Such agreement, Searle claims, takes the form of a *constitutive rule*, which has the form "X counts as Y (in C)," where X defines the class of objects that qualify to be assigned a status, Y defines the status that is assigned, and C is any context that must be present for this status to hold. Thus, for example, undergoing the marriage ceremony (C) has made Barack Obama (X) into a married man (Y). That this happened is because in American society, this constitutive rule exists by collective agreement.

Many entities in the real world are institutional in nature. They include people (e.g., janitors, professors), physical objects (e.g., dollar bills, wedding rings, contracts, chess games), properties (e.g., being licensed, being under probation), events (e.g., weddings, parties, elections), and actions (e.g., trespassing, scoring, prohibiting). Importantly, language is also an institutional phenomenon. The marks that read "tree" can only refer to trees because it is collectively accepted that these marks have this meaning. Nonlinguistic symbols similarly derive their meaning from a collective imposition of a symbolizing function to them.

Interestingly, the distinction between physical, ordinary social, and institutional reality corresponds in large part with the previously made distinction between simulation and ontological reproduction in virtual environments. Physical reality and ordinary social reality can usually only be *simulated* in virtual environments, whereas institutional reality can in large part be *ontologically reproduced* in virtual environments. For example, rocks and trees (physical objects) and screwdrivers and chairs (ordinary social objects) can only be simulated in virtual reality. The reason is that their simulations are not capable of reproducing the actual physical capabilities of physical and ordinary social objects. On the other hand, money and private property (institutional objects) can literally exist in virtual reality. This is possible because institutional entities are ontologically constituted through the assignment of a status function, of the form "X counts as Y (in context C)."

In principle, any status function can be assigned to anything, if only there is the collective will to do it. For example, it is possible in principle to collectively grant telephones the right to marry, which means there can be married telephones. Therefore, if an institutional entity can exist in the real world, it can also exist in a virtual environment. In practice, of course, status functions are only assigned to entities that have certain features that make it sensible to assign the status function to them. As it turns out, many virtual entities lend themselves well to the meaningful assignment of status functions. The consequence is that a large part of institutional reality is currently being reproduced in virtual environments, where real institutional activities are taking place like buying, selling, voting, owning, chatting, playing chess, gambling, stealing, trespassing, taking a test, and joining a club, and one can find corresponding objects like contracts, money, letters, and chess pieces. This is not to say that a virtual institutional object or action is always real. On the contrary, many of them only exist within the context of the simulation. For virtual institutional objects and actions to be real, they must be part of an institution in the real world, rather than a simulated one. For example, virtual money is only real money if it can be transferred to one's bank account or be used to make real purchases.

Institutional entities in virtual environments come into existence in ways similar to institutional entities in the real world. They are assigned a status function either by some recognized authority who is held to assign this status, or because this status has been proposed in a nonauthoritative way and members of the community of users have come to accept it as useful. For example, a virtual room may become a women-only chat room either because a provider has labeled it that way from the beginning and it is granted this authority by its customers, or because this status has gradually emerged and come to be accepted within the collective of users. For virtual environments, relevant authorities will usually be producers, providers, system operators, moderators, or certifying agencies. However, users frequently reject impositions of status functions on virtual entities by authorities and often come to assign their own status functions.

Because a large part of our reality is institutional in nature, it is possible in principle to transfer large parts of our institutions and social life to the digital and virtual realm (Mitchell 1995; Brey 1998). This is already occurring. Banking, trading, and selling, for example, more and more take place in the digital realm. So do communicating, playing, working, learning, teaching, and organizing. Only a small part of the institutional reality in the digital realm is realized in graphical, interactive environments. But most of it involves virtual objects like graphically represented folders and files, and all of it is virtual in a wider sense, in that it is defined over mass-less digital objects and events in cyberspace. Yet even in 3D virtual environments one can find real institutional objects, actions, and events. For example, the societies in virtual worlds like *Second Life*, and in massively multiplayer online role-playing games (MMORPGs) like *Entropia Universe* and *World of Warcraft*, have economies that are not merely simulated but real, in that money is used that can be exchanged for real dollars or euros, and users set up businesses in which virtual objects and services are sold for money (see also Brey 2008; and Lehdonvirta, chapter 30 in this volume). In addition, real friendships sometimes develop in these worlds, and real conflicts occur.

THE ONTOLOGY OF VIRTUAL ACTIONS

Actions in virtual environments have ontological properties that are different from that of virtual objects, and are for this reason discussed separately in this section. The question I aim to investigate is under which circumstances, if any, actions performed in virtual environments qualify as actions in the real world. Actions are intentional behaviors by persons (Davidson 1980). A person performing an action is called an agent. Actions frequently involve, next to the agent, other persons or objects over which they are defined. Most importantly, many actions have one or more *patients*, which are objects or persons upon which an action is carried out (e.g., "Mary laughed at John," "Luis took the book"). Actions may, however, also lack a patient (e.g., "John waved").

We can define a *virtual action* as an action initiated by a user within a virtual environment and involving (only) objects and persons within the virtual environment. In virtual environments, users are normally represented by *avatars*, which are a graphical representation of the user or the user's character. The avatar is then the means by which an agent performs virtual actions. Virtual actions may involve as their patients virtual objects, simulated persons (so-called nonplayer characters or bots), and the avatars of other human users. Examples of virtual actions are lifting a crate, killing a zombie, or lecturing to students in a virtual environment.

Virtual actions have, by definition, effects within the virtual world in which they are performed. For example, a crate is lifted or a zombie is killed. Such effects within the virtual realm are called *intravirtual effects* by Søraker (2010). A virtual action is defined over virtual objects, and intravirtual effects should not be understood as really occurring. When a user kills a character in a virtual world, for example, no real act of killing has occurred. Virtual actions may, however, also have *extravirtual effects*, as Søraker calls them. These are effects on the real world outside the simulation. I wish to argue that a virtual act, *described in reference to its extravirtual effects*, qualifies as a real act.

Virtual actions, I claim, can have two types of extravirtual consequences: institutional and physical ones. Thus, there are two ways in which virtual actions may qualify as real actions. The first applies when virtual actions have an institutional status or significance in the real world. Killing a zombie in a computer game may *count as* winning an online game tournament. The tournament is an institutional object in the real world, and winning it is a real institutional action. Similarly, acquiring gold coins in a virtual simulation may *count as* putting real dollars into one's real bank account. Making a promise to another user of a virtual world *counts as* making a real promise. And taking virtual objects away that are in someone's possession in a virtual world may *count as* stealing in the real world (discussed in Lastowka, chapter 29 in this volume, on virtuality and law).

A second way in which virtual actions may qualify as real actions is by causing extravirtual physical effects on persons and things. I use the term "physical" broadly, as does Searle, to mean "physical and mental"; physical effects, as defined here, thus include effects on physical objects and effects on the bodily and mental states and behaviors of persons. Virtual actions are capable of causing extravirtual physical effects on things and human bodies because they may cause output devices to transmit real light, sound, and force (through force-feedback devices). For example, lighting a virtual flashlight in a virtual environment may—accidentally or intentionally—cause an actual room to light up because of the additional light coming from the screen. Thus, the virtual action of switching on a virtual flashlight may correspond to a real action of lighting up a room. More importantly, virtual actions by a user may cause mental and physiological responses in other users. They may cause real feelings, emotions, sensory impressions, beliefs, desires, bodily states, and behaviors. A sudden action in a virtual world may cause another user to blink or move backward. A kind gesture may make another user smile and feel good. Disgusting behavior may cause repulsion and anger in another user.

While some physical actions therefore can be performed by means of virtual actions, most cannot be. Actions that cannot be so performed include any action that essentially requires physical contact between the agent and a real object or person. For example, it is not possible to hug or hit a real person through a virtual act. Also excluded are actions necessarily mediated by real physical objects and tools, like carving and baking. However, some actions that are currently impossible may become possible as input and output devices of computer systems become more sophisticated. Virtual environments may receive user input through motion detection and may include haptic devices, which use tactile feedback to apply forces, vibrations, or motions to users. In such immersive environments, it may be quite literally possible to kiss or hit another user, since the physical behavior that is performed and the effect it has on others (and on the agent herself) will be essentially the same as they are in their nonvirtual version.

Ontological Uncertainty in Virtual Environments

It is a characteristic feature of virtuality that it causes puzzlement regarding its relation to reality. We have seen that virtual objects and actions imitate real objects and actions, but they sometimes also constitute real objects and actions. The objects and actions constituted by them are sometimes the objects and actions that they imitate, but are at other times different from them. Virtual objects, actions, and events are the subject of what I call *ontological uncertainty*: uncertainty regarding their mode of existence and their relation to reality. In this section I analyze different ways in which ontological uncertainty may emerge in relation to the virtual.

For virtual physical objects and artifacts like apples, rocks, screwdrivers, and automobiles, it is usually clear that they do not have real existence because it is obvious that their causal powers and functional properties are only simulated and have no impact outside the simulation. For virtual physical actions, like kicking and eating, it is also usually evident that they are not real, because they do not involve the appropriate physical motions of the body and have no effects on real persons or objects. However, virtual physical actions may have extravirtual physical or institutional effects, in which case they may also qualify as real actions *under the appropriate description*. This description is usually different from its description in the virtual realm (e.g., the virtual act of killing John's avatar can correspond with the real act of angering John or of winning the game).

For some physical actions, it is unclear whether they can be performed through virtual actions because there is a *semantic uncertainty* (ambiguity or vagueness) whether they necessarily involve physical contact between the agent and an object or other person. Such uncertainly particularly applies to actions performed in relation to another person. Consider, for example, the acts of assault and sexual assault. By most definitions, assault need not involve physical harm, but can also result from verbal abuse and threats. Thus, by most definitions, assault can literally occur in the virtual realm. Sexual assault, however, is usually defined as involving sexual acts that are performed without consent. Verbal sexual abuse or threats of unwanted sexual acts usually do not qualify as sexual assault. It therefore seems that sexual assault cannot be performed by virtual means because it necessarily involves sex acts. However, do sex acts necessarily require physical contact between real bodies? Or could a virtual sex act performed on someone else's avatar also qualify as a kind of sexual activity with that person, just like phone sex is sometimes seen as sexual activity (see Stenslie, chapter 18 in this volume)?

This is just one example of many in which different opinions may exist on how far language may be stretched that describes actions that normally involve physical contact or copresence to include acts that do not involve it. Language itself, as Searle argues, is an institution, and the meanings of words are defined through constitutive rules that may differ from person to person and that may be altered and stretched for pragmatic reasons when people try to use existing words to describe new phenomena.[3]

For institutional objects and actions, ontological uncertainty arises when it is not clear whether they have a status within real institutions (including institutions that regulate online behavior). Such uncertainty may arise in several ways. First, it may be an instance of what I call *constitutive uncertainty*, which is uncertainty regarding the existence of a constitutive rule (of the form X counts as Y in C) or regarding the conditions under which it applies (which depends on the interpretations given to the X and C terms). Different opinions on the existence or applicability of constitutive rules may occur because there are different beliefs on whether a constitutive rule has been instituted, on whether those who instituted it had the authority to do so, or whether instituting it was the right thing to do. Disagreement may also concern the proper scope of X or the proper definition of C. The opinion whether a constitutive rule should be instituted normally depends on whether Xs are seen as a good candidate for fulfilling the role of Y, and whether giving Xs the status of Ys would bring benefits. As a result of constitutive uncertainty, it can be unclear whether a certain virtual entity has a particular institutional status. For instance, some users of a virtual environment may hold that a certain room counts as a classroom, while others hold it is a party room, because they disagree about the relevant constitutive rules. Similarly, some users may hold that certain virtual objects qualify as individual property, whereas others hold it to be communal property.

Constitutive uncertainty can occur in relation to any type of institutional object or action, both virtual and nonvirtual. A specific type of constitutive uncertainty, which I call *existential uncertainty*, applies exclusively to virtual institutional items. This uncertainty applies to virtual items for which it is clear that they have an institutional status in the virtual world but unclear whether this institutional status also carries over to the real world. It may be unclear, for example, whether a dollar bill in a virtual world is also worth a dollar in the real world, or whether theft of virtual objects should also qualify as theft in the real world. Thus, existential uncertainty arises when it is unclear whether only the rule X counts as Y in V applies (where X is a virtual object, Y is an institutional status, and V is the virtual world, or an institution defined within it) or whether in addition the rule applies that X counts as Y in R, where R is (an institution in) the real world.[4]

Another type is *epistemic uncertainty*, which results from a lack of information about the object to which a constitutive rule is believed to apply or the context in which it is to be applied, so that it cannot be properly determined whether the object or context meets the criteria specified by the constitutive rule. The problem here is not with the constitutive rules themselves, but with the information needed for their proper application. For example, it may be agreed within a society that real marriages may be contracted online if officiated by a real priest or state official. In a certain circumstance, it may, however, be unclear whether the person who officiated the wedding was in fact authorized to do so (and hence contributes to the appropriate context C), and hence it is unclear whether the two persons (X) who wished to marry now qualify as married (Y).

Institutional role uncertainty is yet another type of ontological uncertainty that may occur in virtual environments. It concerns uncertainty about what a particular institutional status means. In this kind of uncertainty, there is agreement that X counts as Y in C, and that X occurs in C, and therefore that Y occurs, but it is unclear what it means to be a Y. Specifically, there is uncertainty about the institutional role of a Y, including what Searle calls the deontic powers conferred by an institutional role: the powers or potentialities something or someone acquires by virtue of fulfilling this role. For example, a person (X) may be appointed as associate director (Y) within a firm (C), but it may be unclear what the role of an associate director is within the organization. It may be argued that institutional role uncertainty is not a type of ontological uncertainty, since there is agreement that a Y exists. However, if there are substantially different opinions on what "Y" means, it could be argued that different parties are in fact referring to different institutional objects, thus creating ontological uncertainty.

CONCLUSION

In this chapter, I have performed an ontological investigation of two ontological questions: what the mode of existence is of virtual objects, actions, and events, and whether any of them can be claimed to be part of the real world rather than of a simulated reality. My answer to the first question has been that virtual objects are a special class of digital objects that are represented graphically as objects and can be interacted with through a computer interface. They are complex, systematically generated physical phenomena that imitate real objects and can do so successfully by virtue of the underlying computer hardware. Virtual actions are actions initiated by human agents that are defined over virtual objects. Virtual events can likewise be defined as events defined over virtual objects.

In answer to the second question, I have argued that certain types of virtual objects, actions, and events qualify as real, in the sense that they do not just simulate but ontologically reproduce the entity that they are an imitation of. Virtual objects can ontologically reproduce those phenomena that computer systems and their output devices have the causal powers to reproduce, such as light, sound, and resulting structures like images and tunes. More importantly, virtual objects and actions can ontologically reproduce institutional objects and actions, objects like money and chess games and actions like selling and promising. In addition, virtual actions often have extravirtual (physical) effects next to intravirtual ones, by which they qualify as actions in the real world under the appropriate description.

I also considered a variety of ways in which virtual entities can be the object of ontological uncertainty, which is uncertainty regarding their ontological status. Virtual environments, and the digital realm more generally, create ontological confusion and challenge us to draw and redraw the boundaries between reality and fiction, and truth and falsehood. Understanding the sources of our ontological confusion, and the ways in which it can be overcome, can help us better understand the potentiality and pitfalls of virtual worlds, and of digital realities in general. It can ultimately help us to design better virtual worlds and to interpret and use them in better ways.

NOTES

1. Philosophical ontology is not to be confused with ontology in computer science, or computational ontology, which is a formal description of basic categories and relations between them that is used to model a knowledge domain or discourse. In this chapter, I will not be concerned with ontologies in this sense.
2. Virtual objects may also be represented by means of other types of sensory representations, such as tactile and sonic ones, but their visual mode of representation is usually the dominant mode.
3. To add to ontological uncertainty, certain terms, like "assault," have both an everyday meaning and an institutional meaning, in this case within the context of law. These different meanings may result in different ontological readings of virtual actions and objects.

4. One factor that sometimes contributes to existential uncertainty in virtual worlds is that different interpretations exist of their seriousness: some see virtual interactions as a kind of role-playing that does not involve real interactions and therefore no real harms, whereas others perceive it more like real interactions between real persons in which real psychological and emotional harm can result.

References

Brey, P. 1998. Space-Shaping Technologies and the Geographical Disembedding of Place. In *Philosophy and Geography*, vol. 3: *Philosophies of Place*, ed. Andrew Light and Jonathan B. Smith, 239–263. New York: Rowman & Littlefield.

Brey, P. 2003. The Social Ontology of Virtual Environments. *American Journal of Economics and Sociology* 62 (1): 269–282.

Brey, P. 2008. Virtual Reality and Computer Simulation. In *Handbook of Information and Computer Ethics*, ed. K. Himma and H. Tavani, 361–384. New York: John Wiley & Sons.

Davidson, D. 1980. *Essays on Actions and Events*. New York: Oxford University Press.

Dilworth, J. 2010. Realistic Virtual Reality and Perception. *Philosophical Psychology* 23 (1): 23–42.

Heim, M. 1993. *The Metaphysics of Virtual Reality*. New York: Oxford University Press.

Mitchell, W. 1995. *City of Bits: Space, Place, and the Infobahn*. Cambridge, MA: MIT Press.

Rheingold, H. 1991. *Virtual Reality*. New York: Touchstone.

Searle, J. 1995. *The Construction of Social Reality*. Cambridge, MA: MIT Press.

Søraker, J. 2010. The Value of Virtual Worlds and Entities: A Philosophical Analysis of Virtual Worlds and Their Potential Impact on Well-Being. Ph.D. diss., Proefschrift Universiteit Twente, Enschede.

Zhai, P. 1998. *Get Real: A Philosophical Adventure in Virtual Reality*. Lanham, MD: Roman & Littlefield.

CHAPTER 3

···

ENVISIONING THE
VIRTUAL

···

BRIAN MASSUMI

THE word "virtual" came into everyday use in the 1990s, as a rider on "reality." The rider overrode: the connotation was *unreality*. In the phrase "virtual reality," the adjective virtual stood as a synonym for artificial. Artificial, in this context, meant illusionary. The context, of course, was the dramatic registering in the popular imaginary that enormous changes were on the horizon with the dawning of the digital age. The first tentative steps toward the construction of interactive immersive environments had triggered hyperbolic worries—or hopes—that the fabled "cyberspace" of 1980s futurist fiction was on its way to supplanting "actual" reality. The world would be swallowed in its own artifice. Synthetic imagery, animated with simulated events, would morph into an all-encompassing virtual habitat, somnabulist Matrix of the illusion of life.

The word virtual had a prehistory before its apocalyptic coming out into popular use. It had long existed as a specialist term in philosophy, where the noun form took precedence: *the* virtual. Almost synchronously with the sudden popularity of its adjectival incarnation, efforts began to bring the philosophical force of the virtual into evidence. These efforts built in particular on Gilles Deleuze's late-twentieth-century reinvention of the concept, working in the lineage of Henri Bergson.[1] As a philosophical concept, the virtual has precisely to do with force. Derived from the Latin word for strength or potency, the base definition of the virtual in philosophy is "potentiality." What is in potentiality may come to be; and what has been, already was in potential. The virtual must thus be understood as a *dimension of* reality, not its illusionary opponent or artificial overcoming. The virtual, as allied to potential, belongs specifically to the *formative* dimension of the real. It concerns the potency in what is, by virtue of which it really comes to be. In other words, it connotes a *force* of existence: the press of the next, coming to pass. The virtual pertains to the power to be, pressing, passing, eventuating into ever new forms, in a cavalcade of emergence. For Deleuze, the question is then not "virtual reality," but *the reality of the virtual*. Far from designating a sterile replica of the real, the virtual is the very motor of its continued becoming. Attributing such a moving charge of reality to the virtual leads to a conundrum, but also to an opportunity.

The conundrum is that potential never appears as such. What appears is that to which it gives rise—which is precisely not it, but its fulfillment. Potential's fulfillment is unlike it: newly arisen but fully determined; a closed case. The openness of potential's coming to pass passes into the over-and-doneness of what comes. Potential effectively disappears into what determinately emerges from its movement. It is recessive. And re-arising: no sooner has it disappeared into its own fulfillment than it makes itself felt again in the press toward a next. Potential is abstract: never actually present as such. It is as evasive of the present as it is effective in its formation. The question of the reality of the virtual is that of the *reality of the abstract*, as force of existence that never *is* itself; as formative movement with no proper form of its own. But then what can it mean to say that it "makes itself felt"? It is no accident that Deleuze reinvents the concept of the virtual working from Bergson, whose philosophy revolved around the rethinking of perception. The virtual cannot be separated from the question of perception. If the virtual is real as charged, then it must in some way bear witness to its own force. For it is the very definition of "real" to make a forceful difference. That which is real is *effectively* real. The difference made cannot but be apparent, somewhere, somehow, really, in effect. But how does an abstract reality effectively appear? How does what cannot appear by nature nevertheless appear, in effect? In what way is the imperceptible force of the virtual still really perceived?

The opportunity is that the question of the virtual, connected in this way to the question of perception, encourages a reconsideration of the place of abstraction in our lives. It forbids placing the abstract in simple opposition to the concreteness of experience, or plotting it mechanically into an alternative between the artificial and the real—as if the artificial did not have its own mode of reality. The issue becomes, not an epochal struggle between the artificial and the real, but more positively the formative relation between the virtual and what actually appears. The issue becomes the relation of the virtual to the *actual*, as pertains to perception. This question addresses itself as much to natural perception as it does to synthetic images or simulated events in a crafted domain such as that of the digital. It raises the possibility that we might find no less artifice in "natural" perception as reality on-screen. The question of perception is no longer one of truth or illusion, but of differing modes of reality, in the movement of emergence through which the forms of experience come to pass.

The answer to the question of the reality of the virtual—or how that which is abstract really appears—will necessarily remain as paradoxical as the question itself. If potential is about-to-be or already-fulfilled, still-to-come or just-past, then however it appears, it will always come *too early* or *too late* (perhaps even both at once). As a function of this untimeliness, it will always also come across as *too little* or *too much*: in excess of or superfluous to the being of the actual whose force of existence it always still will have been.

The only way to proceed is by example, catching the virtual in the act, then looking closely at how it works, and working from there to press its paradox into conceptual service in order to see what difference might be made in how we think about perception. In other words: to realize the virtual in thought, from and for experience, through exemplification.

What better place to begin than the species of example that would seem least amenable: optical "illusions." The very name militates against taking what appears under the perceptual conditions in question as real. Take the classic case of the Kanizsa triangle. In its simplest presentation, it consists of three black circles out of each of which an angular bite has been taken, yielding a little company of what look like Pac-Man figures. But what grabs your attention is not the Pac-Mans. The bites face each other in a configuration that suggests the three apices of a triangle. What grabs you is that, although the triangle is not filled in by actually drawn lines, you see it as clearly as the Pac-Mans. To say that the triangle is "suggested" is an understatement. You not only see it—you cannot not see it. It jumps out at you so vividly that it backgrounds the figures that are "actually" there. It shimmers forth from their configuration to take center stage. It is what this occasion of perception is all about. It is what gives the experience its dominant character.

Now it may seem reasonable to call seeing something that isn't actually there an illusion. But what do you call an illusion that you cannot *not* see? And not just you, but anyone who cares to look? What do you call an illusion that insistently refuses *not* to appear? Something that jumps out unrefusably is certainly exhibiting an effectiveness. The triangle appears, in effect. And it makes a difference. Its effectively appearing in this way determines what this experience is actually felt to be about. Looked at this way, the "illusion" robustly satisfies the criteria for being real. The question is, what mode of reality are we, seers of triangles that are not there, commonly engaged in unrefusing?

An immediate response is: a *relational* reality. The triangle emerges from the way in which the Pac-Man figures come together, separated from each other just so. Had the figures been too close or farther apart, the effect would have failed to take. Neither would the effect have come about had their configuration been skewed. There are conditions: a critical distance and a requisite configuration. When the three figures appear together under these conditions, the triangle appears, filling the *distance* between them.

The figures are actually separated and remain so. No actual lines ever join them. They are and remain disjunctive: countable one by one, no one accountable to any other. They are a disjunctive plurality, together in the mutual separation of their indifference to each other, just being what they are, where they are, in their individual Pac-Manliness. When the triangle comes to take the angle of their open mouths for its own corners, all of that changes. The figures instantly enter into relation, across their separation, because their *separation* has fulfilled certain conditions. The triangle *takes* them up separately-together into its own ability to appear. The Pac-Men now figure conjointly as requisite elements for the triangle's emergence. They count for the triangle, conjunctively. But still at a distance. In virtue of their conjunctively concerning the triangle, they remotely but effectively concern each other. They concern each other *through* it, *across* their separation, as a taken *effect* of their disjunctive plurality. The effected triangle *is* their concern for each other. It is their coming to be in relation, in visible form.

The triangle is a coming into relation coming into sight—a *being of relation* taking perceptible effect. The effective seeing of the being of the relation does not replace or contradict the disjunctive plurality of the elements providing the conditions for its appearance. It comes in addition to their plurality. The oneness of the triangle superadds itself to the Pac-Men's being just what they are individually, plurally one-by-one, each in its own disjunctive corner. The supervening triangle is the emergent unity *of* its requisite elements' diversity. It unitarily occupies their disjunctive in-between, taking their distance from each other as its own locus.

Of course, it is artificial to speak as if the Pac-Men came first and then in a second moment a triangle took advantage of their separateness to add its alien unity to them. The triangle and the elements conditioning its appearance come strictly at the same time. They enjoy equal immediacy. They are equally insistent in their refusal not to be seen. But of course, there is a difference. The company of Pac-Men are "actually" seen: they correspond to regions of ink on the page, or arrays of pixels on the screen, whose presence strikes our eyes in the form of reflected rays of light.[2] The triangle per se, however, corresponds to no such sensuous input. It corresponds, as such, to no material presence. And yet it shimmers. It is really seen, without "actually" being seen. It appears nonsensuously, in excess over the actual conditions of its appearance. It is a visibly real, virtual triangle.

This way of expressing the difference between the triangle and its material conditions creates a vocabulary problem. If we call something we really see without "actually" seeing it virtual, it sounds as if we are defining the virtual as the *opposite* of the actual, when we have just established that in this case the virtual effect and the actual elements conditioning its appearance come to perception strictly at the same time, with equal immediacy, and are equally insistent in their really being seen. A shift in vocabulary resolves this problem. If we work in the distinction between *sensuous* and *nonsensuous* (Whitehead 1967, 180–183), it becomes easier to articulate how the Pac-Men and the triangle through which they relate are equally real, in different *modes*. The distinction between the actual and virtual shifts accordingly.

We already have the basis on which to build an understanding of the difference in their mode of reality: the individual Pac-Men, as such, figure as a disjunctive plurality. This means you can count them singly, taking each separately from the others in turn, without it making any difference in what they are understood to be. Each is still a Pac-Man. A disjunctive plurality is a set whose members come separately together, countable one by one. They count singly. Together, they are an aggregate of singles. The triangle, for its part, appears as a unitary figure, directly and in all immediacy. It doesn't count one by one. It counts, in all immediacy, *as* one. It is a *singularity*. Since this singularity corresponds to nothing outside itself on a material plane where elements of sets can be understood to figure separately, strictly speaking it has *no parts*. It comes as a unity *in addition to* the diversity of the elements conditioning it. It is a whole apart from that diversity, singularly occupying the distance between the elements. It dodges their plurality, making its locus precisely where they are *not*. Yes, a triangle has three sides. This is undeniable. Just count them. But: in counting, you are no longer dealing directly with the triangle as the unitary figure it is in all immediacy. You are dealing with a set of lines, taken individually one after the other. You cannot analyze the unity of the triangle into constituent parts without *changing its nature*: without resolving it into a plurality that it singularly isn't in the immediacy of its effective appearance.

There is a mode of reality that is *countable* one by one, and there is a mode of reality that *counts-as-one*. These modes come together, as coincident dimensions of the same occasion of experience, with equal immediacy and insistence. What we *actually* experience is this insistent coincidence. What we actually see is the concernful binding of the different modes, effectively expressed in the appearance of a unitary form taking singular effect as the visible being of a relation. The relation is the taking-up of the disjunct elements in emergent form. What we see most saliently is that supervening form. The salience of the form is the product of the different modes' coinciding. It is also *their* relation, made visible. The emergent triangle is what singularly comes of the modal difference between disjunctive plurality and singularity.

We can now take the word "actual" in its etymological sense: "*in act*." The salient unity of the triangle and the disjunctive plurality of its conditions of emergence are in on the act of perception. They are constitutive dimensions of its coming to pass. They belong equally to the event that is this occasion of experience. From this point of view, they are dimensions of the actual.

This might seem like a counterproductive move. It now seems as if the virtual has been swallowed by the actual, when the whole point was to respect the reality of their difference. But progress has been made. We now can understand their difference differently, by returning to the distinction between the sensuous and the nonsensuous. We can understand it, precisely, in modal terms. Not as different "spaces" that are in opposition to each other. Not as real versus unreal. But as different manners of really belonging to the same *event*: different ways of being in the act, effectively bound in a relation of concern, to saliently figural effect.

The sensuous elements in the event do involve a necessary reference to space. To say that they are countable is to say that we can point to them "over there" one by one. The sequence of the counting corresponds to the sequential progression of our pointing from one "over there" to another. The demonstrative over-thereness of the countable elements locates them as *projective* space. It is important to be clear that it is not the space that is projected; rather, it is our *counting* that projects itself. Our *activity* projects itself. It is executed here, for counting over there. Stretching from here to there, it is *self-distancing*. This stretch of activity *constitutes* the "space" of our experience. Space is now in scare quotes because a "space" of experience is not just made of over-thereness. It is also made of a sequential *progression* that takes time to unfold. In other words, the space of experience includes a time factor. It is a *space-time* of experience. That which is sensuously real (i.e., the reality of which corresponds to physical impingements upon our body, as for example, and it is just one example, light upon the retina) belongs to a projective space-time of experience actively constituted by a counting of—or more generally and significantly, an *accounting for*—a plurality of disjunct elements.[3]

Compare this to the triangle. It jumps out at us, into our vision, bypassing any corresponding physical impingement upon our eyes. It dodges the plurality of the sensuous elements in play in eager display of its own nondecomposable unity, in all immediacy. If we treat it as though it were "over there" in the same mode as the Pac-Men and try to straddle it with our activity, the singularity of its appearance evaporates. For example, if we trace its nonsensuous form by passing our fingers along one side, then another, we have replaced the singularity of the triangle by a set of lines counting one by one. We have accounted for it by transposing it into another mode of existence, translating it in terms of figures it is not. Caress it with your well-considered thoughts, and you've done it again. Judge its geometry; likewise.

The triangle only appears as the singular figure it is as a unitary pop-out effect, in immediate offset from its conditioning elements' disjunctive plurality. To experience it as it is, and for what it is, we must simply leave it be. There is nothing to be done with it that won't change its nature. In its simplicity, it has a strangely compelling, shimmering sterility. It is simply there *in excess over* the disjunctive plurality that sensuously conditions its appearance—as well as any actively constituted space-time of experiential accounting for that plurality. The visibly appearing being of the relation that it is, is a dodge of sensuous experience. It is unitarily all and only a nonsensuous appearance. Lacking sensuous correlates, it has a spectral quality to it. It is a *pure appearance*. But once again appearance is used here in the strong sense: as that which effectively appears, regardless. The triangle effectively appears, in a dodgy, unrefusably nonsensuous mode of offset, pop-out reality. The mode of reality of the triangle is not projective but *superjective*, in the etymological sense of that word: "thrown over," "going beyond," "exceeding." The virtual is the pop-out dimension *of the actual* whereby it really, appearingly, exceeds itself. The virtual is the excessive dimension of the in-act as it throws itself into experience over and above its sensuous conditions. It is the dodgy, supervenient manner in which the actual effectively appears to include *more than* can be sensuously accounted for: a reality of the abstract. The appearance of an abstract locus nonsensuously filled with a spectral being of relation.

Time is a factor in a much more primordial way than the discussion of counting let on. We don't have to start counting the Pac-Men to constitute the space of projective experience to which they belong. Too late—we already have an intuition of their number and their mode of spatiotemporal existence before it even occurs to us to count them or ask ourselves about their status. This is because we have encountered many sets of sensuous elements in the past, counted many an element, actively accounted for many a configuration. The "intuition" we have of what might be done with their plurality and spatiotemporality is a habit we have contracted. The experience comes with the *potential* for us to account for them disjunctively in the same mode we have countless times before. This potential experience presents itself in the immediacy of experience, flush with the just-occurring of this event of vision. We already *see the potential* without having to actively plumb it, *as if* we had *already* gone through the motions—it has come too early for that. *The unfolding of sensuous experience precedes itself in potential as a directly lived hypothesis*—an "as if" directly experienced in an immediacy of seeing, too early

for the hypothetical judgment to have actually occurred. That is why there was a certain circularity in our explanation. We began by remarking the distance separating the
Pac-Men as a *given*, when in the theoretical terms set in place here that distance can only
figure as *constituted* by activity in a spatiotemporal thickness of experience coming too
early *and* too late. The circularity is real: what is given is a *recursiveness* of actual experience whereby it precedes itself in potential, already giving itself for the future.

Fundamentally, what is given is the thickness of potential. The given potential that
the event is thick with is past activity making itself present in visible form, for the future.
Neither the future, nor the past thickening the present for it, is sensuous. The sensuous elements in play *envelop the nonsensuous* past and future in the materiality of their
impinging on the body. They are the leading edge of the forming event, bringing past
and future together in the present of their bodily impingement (Whitehead 1967, 189). At
the dawning of a perception, in the flush of its first occurring, we already *find ourselves*,
too early, too late, in a being of relation in which sensuous and nonsensuous, material
and immaterial realities, past and future, presently coincide, *in act*.

When we say that the presence of the Pac-Men is "sensuous" we really mean that the
nonsensuous dimension of future-past recursivity is *recessive*. It is enveloped in the
material activity of impingement that strikes as the leading edge of the event's occurrence. The event is finally characterized at a second nonsensuous level: that of the
supervening appearance of an abstract and immaterial pop-out reality, in this case an
all-too-present triangle-form. That which is recessive in the act, enveloped in its taking
effect, is "infra" to it. The enveloped nonsensuous reality of the past and future is *infraceptive* (etymologically, "seized within"). The sensuous is thus sandwiched between two
virtualities, two ways in which sensuous experience exceeds itself. One is recessive, the
other pop-out. One is infraceptive, the other superjective. One hits with the present of
appearance, seized recursively within; the other doubles that sensuous impact, show-
ily jumping out. One is enveloped, the other supervenient. One is thick with potential,
the other superfluously ashimmer with sterile impassivity. Both aspects of virtuality are
"immanent" (to the in-act; to the event of perception's occurring). They come together
in the recursivity of that event, across their infra-super difference.

All of this invites the introduction of a further term. There is a *tension* between the
unrefusable just being-there of the Pac-Men on the one hand, and on the other the as-if
of their appearing in all immediacy as a countable plurality, without actually having
been counted. There is tension between the disjunctive plurality of the elements countable one by one, and the nondecomposability of the emergent figure that dodges them
to count-as-one. There is a tension between the single and singular. There is a tension
between the backgrounded impact of sensuous impingement and the impassivity of
nonsensuous salience. There is a tension between the splay of space given "out there,"
and the dynamic stretch of experiential space-time constitutive of it. There is a tension
between the infraception and supervention.

The tensions are between modes of existence proposing themselves to the experience. The tensions come with the simultaneous contrast between the sensuous and
the nonsensuous (Pac-Men/triangle, coinciding in vision). And they come recursively

between aspects of the nonsensuous in contrast with itself (infraceptive/superjective in different tenses, future-past and present). The modes do not add up to a form. They are tensely, incommensurably different. Their incommensurability exerts a differential pressure. The pressure is unsustainable. Something has to give. What gives is a triangle. The appearance of the triangle resolves the tensions into its own emergence. And it *is* an "emergence," even if we cannot place the triangle's appearance after that of the plurality of elements conditioning it in chronological time. The order is logical, not chronological.[4] The superjective figure of the triangle pops out from the tensional field, refusing to restrict itself to its sensuous dimensions. The dodgy superject is "new" vis-à-vis the sensuous elements in play in the sense of being beyond them, in excess of their figuring, singularly superadded to their plurality. By their sensuous logic, it is a supervening alien being (the being of a relation that does not concern them individually, but only as *taken* together, abducted, in the emergent interests of an added appearance "thrown over" their disjunctive plurality).

If we ask what the "cause" of the experience is, the only answer is: the nonform of the differential tensions between modes. Although without form, this is not nothing. The pressure is intense. This is a *field* of intensity for something to give. The pressure for resolution is a formative *force*. The "cause" is a force field of emergence resolving itself into the appearance of a superject.[5] The Pac-Man configuration does not *cause* that event in any linear sense: the superjective appearance of the nonsensuous figure of the triangle dodgily *lifts off* from them. It throws itself over their distance, rather than following closely upon them. It does not follow through with them in like manner, as in continuity with their mode of existence. It supervenes upon them, jumping singularly out into its own mode. At the same time, the Pac-Men are required for the triangle's appearance. Without them, it would not occur. They provide it the propitious conditions. That is exactly what these sensuous elements are: not causes, but *conditions*. Leading-edge conditions for an event that exceeds them.

Causes subordinate (the what-may-come to their own mode, asserting itself in the imperative). Conditions are jumping-off points (for the emergence of the new). Causes command follow-through in their own mode: they are *conformal*. To take a classic Newtonian example, if the impetus is a collision, the causal impact will govern an equal if opposite movement, accountable in like terms. Conditions do not command follow-through. They propitiate liftoff. The impetus is a disjunctive plurality, and what gives is a supernumerary unity counting immediately as one in its own singular way. Conditions are not conformal. They are *formative* field factors, giving figure to the new. Formation, in this emergent sense, is a conditional field phenomenon, energized by differential intensity. "Energy" here does not refer to matter alone. It refers to the tension between on the one hand the sensuous reality we associate with materiality, and on the other the nonsensuous reality of the abstract that sensuous reality envelops and by which, with equal immediacy, it is supervened (Whitehead 1967, 182–183).

There is one more term that needs to be added to tension: *tendency*. The role of acquired habit in the immediacy of experience was discussed earlier. Habit brought the future-past of potential intraceptively into the occasion of experience as a perceptual "judgment" occurring flush with the event. The "judgment" comes "as if"—as if an act of judgment, like counting, had actually been performed when the knowing comes so flush that there is no way that it could have been. Perceptual judgments are neither deductions nor inferences, but deserve a logical category all their own: "abductions" (Peirce 1997, 93–94, 242–247). In addition to acquired habits, there are also arguably innate "habits," arriving from the genetic past of the species, that predispose perception toward the isolation of Platonic forms like the triangle. However they are contracted, at whatever scale of the past, habits are formative vectors: they exert a formative pressure in a certain direction, toward a certain outcome. They are one of the formative factors that give *aim* to the experience (Whitehead 1978, 25, 27, 69). Of course, the field conditions have everything to say about this. If they are propitious, the aim will culminate in a "new" emergence along habitual lines. Some conditions might throw the aim off, so that it will not reach its end. In still other conditions, the field may resolve itself in the direction of an emergence in a stronger sense of "new": not a new iteration along the same lines, but a supervening appearance of something unprefigured that has never been seen before.

It is all a question of *technique*. The element of technique is how the experiential leading edge of the sensuous elements are disposed toward a nonsensuous outcome, how the conditions configure. This dispositional configuring of conditions may occur in a way we tend to call "natural." Or they may be "artificial," as in the setting in place of the conditions for an optical "illusion" to appear. In fact, it is always both. Producing an optical illusion depends as much on the human body's "natural" propensities (its innate predispositions) as it does on artifice (such as the body's acquired predispositions and the craft of configuring Pac-Men). It is entirely conceivable that under certain conditions a pop-out nonsensuous triangle might occur entirely "naturally." There is nothing to say that a nonsensuous triangle could not pop out from a disjunctive plurality encountered in the woods, just as well as from a sheet of paper or a computer screen. Everything about the virtual is a question of technique. But the question of technique is not limitative, in the sense of being restricted to a given domain of activity. Nor is it categorical, in the sense of pertaining to the artificial as opposed to the natural. Techniques lending themselves to nonsensuous emergences are *transducible* to different domains of activity (Simondon 2005), where they come to operate to new effect. In whatever domain, they always involve a mixed regime of factors categorizable as natural and artificial.

If this is the case, then nonsensuous "artifice" must be found in even the most "natural" of experiences. Take the experience of depth in everyday life. There is a disjunctive plurality built into the human body: our two offset eyes. The offset creates a tension— the binocular disparity of two images that do not coincide. The tension is unsustainable. Something has to give. From the differential between the two, a singular image emerges to resolve the tension. What arises is not only a new image over and above the two built into our sensuous body's apparatus. An entirely new quality of experience emerges: depth. Depth is an emergent property possessed by neither of the images conditioning its appearance. A new dimension, a third dimension, is thrown over binocular disparity. People who lack depth perception then have it restored describe the incredible novelty of seeing objects "pop out" into a shimmering salience of stereoscopic relief

(Sacks 2011, 130). The objects of our experience as we "naturally" perceive them in all their 3D glory is a really appearing optical "illusion": a really abstract, superjective emergence conditioned by our body's innate "habit" of growing two offset eyes.

Acquired predispositions also play an essential role. It is well known that even with a well-functioning visual apparatus, depth perception cannot develop without movement. Movement indexes the reaching of our hands for things "over there" with our accounting for them visually "here." It similarly indexes the experience of the steps we may take to reach them. We are seeing "as if" we were moving. Seeing an object's three-dimensionality is seeing the movement without its actually having occurred. We are seeing in the "as if" of movement. In other words, we are seeing the potential stretch of our experience, in all the immediacy of an event of vision. We are seeing the stretch of our bodily potential in the pop-out form of the object. The differential tension between vision, touch, and proprioception (the disjunctive plurality of our separate sense channels) is resolved into the superjective unity of the object.[6] Such is our perceptual tendency: to aim for the superaddition of objects to our lives.

The natural *objects of our perception are virtual* appearances (Noë 2004). Their arising is conditioned by the cofunctioning of the separate senses, and of innate and acquired predispositions, taking aim. The bodily artifice of binocular disparity is just the most proximate conditioning factor (being right in front of our nose). Other techniques involved in making objects appear may be artistic, craftsman-like, or technological. When innovations in art or craft or technology elaborate upon our "natural" talents for object perception to invent new experiential effects that have never seen before, they are not "extending" our bodies away from its natural conditions into the realm of the artificial (the "prosthetic" theory inherited from Marshall McLuhan). Our experience is already a stretch of potential. It is self-prosthetic. What art and technology do is extend the body's existing regime of natural and acquired *artifice*, already long in active duty in producing the "virtual reality" of our everyday lives. The life of the body is naturally crafty.

There is an oddity in the emergence of 3D vision that adds an important lesson to how we understand the concept of the virtual. If the two images belonging to our respective offset eyes were *actually* seen, then there would be no pop-out stereoscopic vision. The disparity of the images would interfere with the emergence of the resolving image. They would conspire plurally against its unity, in competition with it. We are in the as-if again: it is *as if* the images were actually produced, when they can't have been. The emergence of the 3D vision does not just resolve the disparity between the disjunct images. It makes as if they never happened. It offers its own emergence in their stead. It takes their place for its own locus, throwing itself over their conditioning differential. The contributory images are *virtualized* by the emergence of depth perception. They are recursively determined by the emergence of the new image never actually to have occurred.

But at the same time, the disparate images and their interference cannot not have occurred, being requisite conditions for the experience that did effectively came to pass. If the images cannot not have occurred, but didn't actually occur, the only option is that they occurred *virtually*. They contributed their potential interference to the 3D image.[7]

The emergence of the 3D image resolved the *potential* conflict into its own effective appearance. The interference of the two ingredient images that did not occur figures, in 3D effect, as a *virtual event*.

The oddity is that events that do not actually occur can be requisite conditions for what does eventuate. To translate this example back into the distinction between the sensuous and the nonsensuous, in this case the sensuous elements (the images corresponding to the disparate physical impingement of light rays upon two retinas) are resolved by the superjective experience to have been virtual. They are, in effect, rendered nonsensuous. They are *infracepted*. This happens recursively. The superjective emergence backcasts its resolve into an imperative for its own conditions to have been otherwise. (Parenthetically, this could form the basis of a superjective theory of the *will*: an effective resolve lacking a subject separate from its own emergent pop-out effect, appearing as superject; the will as a really appearing "optical illusion" of abstract agency; in the terms of the concepts developed here, this amounts to a formative *fielding* of the will.)[8]

Nonsensuous rendering—the infraception of sensuous elements—is a necessary part of any theory of the virtual. The reality of the virtual is not only coextensive with the potential stretch and superjective resolve of our lives. The formative factors of that reality vary widely, even wildly. There is no once-and-for-all, jack-of-all-trades description of their role. They remobilize under continual transformation. The roles they play effectively vary, especially as techniques for the emergence of virtual realities transduce from field to field. Not only can they vary. As nonsensuous rendering shows, they can *transmute*, changing their very natures, as if by an alchemy of experience. This means that the account of the virtual, and the role it itself plays, must be continually renegotiated for every example considered. The virtual is all about creativity: potential and the emergence of the new. Its conceptualization cannot fail to be equally creative, at the price of failing to be true to the protean reality of nature's artifice (and the nature of the artificial).

In the course of this account, we have "seen" the emergence of virtual *figures*, strenuously exemplified by a now very tired triangle. We have seen, more briefly but also more suggestively, that *objects* themselves are similarly emergent virtual forms (Massumi 2011, 6, 41–43). We have also seen that there are virtual *events* upon which perception depends (no relation to the cyberspatial notion of simulated events; or rather, related, but in ways we can only really understand thorough an exemplary rethinking of the artificial and of abstraction in terms of nonsensuous reality and its sensuous conditions).

One last form of virtuality must be mentioned to do justice to the full stretch of the virtual's reality: *value*. A crawling baby, whose predisposition to continue in existence is not yet finely honed, advances wormlike toward a cliff edge.[9] Its deficit of depth perception, and its lack of ability to "judge" with all immediacy, flush with perception, the hypothetical outcomes enveloped in locomotor experience, conspire to endanger its life. Not yet proficient in the perceptual judgment of the "as if," it fails to register the "what if" of its crawl. Not so the distracted parent. No sooner has attention turned back to the child than the parent is launched into action, without pausing to think, too fast to have actually sized up the danger. The "what if" came immediately, in a blink, and was directly transduced into action. What the parent "saw" was not just a baby crawling.

The parent saw a set of *differentials*: a gravitational differential between the top of the cliff and the bottom, coincident with the existential differential between life and death. The interference pattern of these differentials produced an unsustainable tension that resolved itself into immediate action.

Here, the experiential pop-out effect is not a figure or an object, although these also appear (the baby's advance is perceived nonsensuously as an abstract line [Massumi 2011, 17, 106] of future-pastness; 3D objects of all manner populate the field). The launching-into-action effect may be conditioned by virtual events (including the usual tricks of our two not always watchful enough eyes), but these were back-grounded. What singularly came into salience, thrown over the plurality of the ingre-dient figural, objective, and evental factors, characterizing what this experience is all about, was a *value*. A life value. An existential value. What the parent "saw," in the blink of the forming experience, was the life value of the child's continued existence. This is a maximally abstract virtual reality. There is nothing "over there" to which it corresponds. The great "out there" is utterly indifferent to one infant more or less. It is only out of the tensional field of the parent's love and desires, stretching their salva-tional potential over to the child's oblivious locomotion, taking into that stretch the energizing motive force of the differential between up and down, life and death, that this singular experiencing of existential value emerges. Existential value is a virtu-ally occurring added-value: a *surplus value of perception* (as are figures and objects, in their own virtual way). It is a really appearing, abstractly real superaddition of and to experience. Unlike the virtual figure of the triangle and the virtual forms objects, value is invisible. It is imperceptible by nature.[10] Even so, like them its superaddition *really makes a difference*. It is what transmutes the world's *in*difference into concern, for this event. As this happens, nothing of indifference subsists. The ingredient ele-ments of the event, of whatever nature, are integrally bound together in the form of the emergent concern. The conditioning differentials and disjunctive pluralities are thrown over into this value integration (in much the same way our Pac-Men came to concern each other in the figure of the triangle, overcoming the separateness of their counting one by one in its relational counting-as-one). Value is the ultimate way in which the world's actuality includes that which exceeds the just-being-there of the disjunctive plurality of its elements.

The virtual reality of the superadded value is immediately *doubled* by an action path. The perception of value and the path of action are in the closest of eventful embraces, but occur as on parallel tracks. The perception of value is nonsensuous and impassive, in the sense that it figures as something that will not change, and cannot change if it really be what it is (once a value, always a value). The perception of value is nondecom-posable. This time, for all time, it is an existential value enveloping love and desire. Its nondecomposable once-and-for-all does not make it simple. It is singular, yet complexly conditioned: not simple, *simplex*. The other track, the causal path of action, is also com-plex, but in a different mode. It is sensuous, physically charged, and decomposable into separate steps: *composite*, emphasizing that word's base connotation of disjunctive plu-rality ("made up of distinct parts"). In more inclusive examples, where virtual figures, objects, events, and values co-occur, the situation is always marked by this doubleness of conditioning and causality (of conditioned nonsensuous emergence and the conformal physical/sensuous causality; Deleuze 1990a, 4–11, 94–99). The sensuous and the nonsensuous, the simplex and the complex, the actual and the surplus values of its various ways of exceeding itself, are everywhere in the closest of embrace, and interlace (Deleuze 2002; Massumi 2002, 133–143). Even the run to the edge of the cliff takes effect in its pop-out way, as a dynamic unity of forward rush across the steps, filling the distance between them with its overarching of their separateness.

The reality of the matter is: virtual forms (figures, objects), events, and values *always* co-occur. Life comes in situations, and situations are complex—which is to say, simplex too. The different species of virtuality always occur together as part of a *virtual ecology* of sensuous and nonsensuous embracings and interlacings (Guattari 1995, 88–97, 109–110).

The point of this final example with which this account is crawling to its end is that the *axiological dimension* of our immediate experience—the value dimension—cannot be adequately described without recourse to a theory of the virtual. At its farthest stretch, as Félix Guattari reminds us (1989; 1995), the ultimate significance of the virtual resides in "universes of value" that are "incorporeal" in nature (nonsensuously real). In this axiological dimension, as relating to universes of value, the theory of the virtual is directly *ethical*: it immediately pertains to courses of action that make a dynamic life difference. What qualifies action as ethical is the doubling of its causal efficacy by a virtual transmutation of indifference into real concern for the event. The transmutation runs parallel to the action, in another mode of being, effectively on another track. It is singularly conditioned, arising as a simplexity of immediate experience superveniently overstretching the compositing of causes. Where we come to is a situational ethics—redefined as the axiological alchemy of the virtual.

NOTES

1. More recently, this Bergsonian/Deleuzian line of thinking on the virtual has cross-fertilized with Alfred North Whitehead's work, in particular his concept of "pure potentiality" (Massumi 2011). What follows is strongly accented by this encounter. Deleuze's sometime coauthor, Félix Guattari, develops in his solo writing his own account of the virtual, whose influence is also strongly felt here, particularly in the final sections. The key texts are Bergson (2004), Deleuze (1986, 1989, 1990a, 1994, 2002), Deleuze and Guattari (1987), Guattari (1989, 1995), and Whitehead (1978).

2. Although black is defined in optics as the absorption of all light waves, under real-world conditions there is never complete absorption. To be precise, "being colored black or white depends on the contrasts in the light intensity between adjacent areas. . . . An increase in the brightness of the surround can drive a white area to grey or black" (Thompson 2005, 46–47). This relational fact of perception is of fundamental importance, but is not essential to emphasize for the purposes of this stage of the current account, where the operative distinction is between perceptual effects that are objectively plottable to the optical array and those that are not (developed below into the distinction between "sensuous" and "nonsensuous" perception).

3. On counting, space, and the space-time experience, and the relation between multiplicity and its unification, see Bergson 2001, 73–87. Bergson captures the "stretch" of the projective space-time of experience in the phrase "the object is where it is perceived" (2004, 311).

4. See Deleuze on "static logical genesis" (1990b, 118–126).

5. The field intensity of the sensuous array—the relational nature of its elements as discussed in note 2—is what links the level of physical causality to the emergent liftoffs it conditions. *Intensity* is the only common factor between the sensuous and the nonsensuous. Its transverality—its double featuring in both dimensions—is what binds them together as belonging to the same event. Of course, intensity features differently in each dimension. This difference marks the tension that registers the differential between them. This differential is discussed below as itself being the condition of emergence of value.

6. On stereoscopic vision interpreted along lines similar to this account (in terms of a integrative emergence resolving a constitutive tension of a differential field), see Simondon 2005, 208–209, 223–224.

7. In other words, the offset "images" contributed their *differential*—their disparity—as potential. They figure purely as nonsensuous differentials. This is an example of why the intertwining of the sensuous and the nonsensuous discussed below is necessary to the theory of perception. That intertwining can be carried to the sensuous level below that of the eyes as a whole. The retina, composed of a disjunctive plurality of rods and cones, is riddled with resident disparities. This all-the-way-down gappiness of the perception apparatus is what led cognitive scientist Alva Noë (2004) to argue that all vision is actually virtual. See also Massumi 2011, 94–97. On generative force of pure differentials, see Deleuze 1994, 170–182.

8. This requires a thorough rethinking of what constitutes the subject of experience. As Nietzsche famously stated, there is no doer separate from the deed (1967, 45). There is a multimodal fielding of activity culminating in the appearance of a superject. The arc of the fielding resolving itself in the superject is the subject of the experience (Whitehead 1978, 27–28, 166). In the triangle example, the *triangle* is finally the subject of the experience. "We" who come to claim it—that is, our bodies, our senses, our habits, our inheritances, our tendencies—are a plurally disjunctive set of *formative elements* in differential tension, whose roles are not so fundamentally different from that of the Pac-Men. The conventions of language make it difficult to speak without smudging this fact: "we" are the superjective perspective of the event's culmination, recursively throwing itself back over to the cusp of its beginning, to claim the arising as all its own. It is more of a stretch to say "I" than one likes to acknowledge. The sense of self is an emergent nonsensuous effect whose reiterative rearising in the stream of experience is a renewed achievement, full of artifice and high craft. It is only the habit of saying "I" that makes it come as natural.

9. I have to say that this sadistic example is not my own (only the worm is mine). It comes from Raymond Ruyer (1956).

10. The really imperceptibly-abstract is a mode of the reality of the virtual that is of utmost importance. All virtualities that appear, as if in vision or other sense modes, whether they be figures, objects, or events (the kind that are not recessive but which we feel we directly perceive), are seized with *relation* (as we saw in the case of the virtual figures of the triangle as well as that of the object). Relation is by nature imperceptible. It is the ultimate really abstract mode of reality. It comes infraceptively in all experience. Value is imperceptible relation with the element of concern in relief, marked by a salient affective tonality that makes itself what the occasion is actually all about.

REFERENCES

Bergson, H. 2001. *Time and Free Will: An Essay on the Immediate Data of Consciousness.* Translated by F. L. Pogman. Mineola, New York: Dover.

Bergson, H. 2004. *Matter and Memory.* Translated by N. M. Paul and W. S. Palmer. New York: Dover.

Deleuze, G. 1986. *Cinema 1. The Movement-Image.* Translated by H. Tomlinson and B. Habberjam. Minneapolis: University of Minnesota Press.

Deleuze, G. 1989. *Cinema 2. The Time-Image.* Translated by Hugh. Tomlinson and R.t Galeta. Minneapolis: University of Minnesota Press.

Deleuze, G. 1990a. *Bergsonism.* Translated by H. Tomlinson and B. Habberjam. New York: Zone Books.

Deleuze, G. 1990b. *Logic of Sense.* Translated by M. Lester with C. Stivale. Ed. C. V. Boundas. New York: Columbia University Press.

Deleuze, G. 1994. *Difference and Repetition.* Translated by P. Patton. New York: Columbia University Press.

Deleuze, G. 2002. The Actual and the Virtual. Translated by E. R. Albert. In *Dialogues II,* by G. Deleuze and C. Parnet, 148–152. New York: Columbia University Press.

Deleuze, G., and F. Guattari. 1987. *A Thousand Plateaus.* Translated by B. Massumi. Minneapolis: University of Minneapolis Press.

Guattari, F. 1989. *Cartographies schizoanalytiques.* Paris: Galilée.

Guattari, F. 1995. *Chaosmosis: An Ethico-Aesthetic Paradigm.* Translated by P. Bains and J. Pefanis. Bloomington: Indiana University Press.

Massumi, B. 2011. *Semblance and Event: Activist Philosophy and the Occurrent Arts.* Cambridge, MA: MIT Press.

Nietzsche, F. 1967. *On the Genealogy of Morals.* Translated by W. Kaufmann and R. J. Hollingdale. New York: Vintage.

Noë, A. 2004. *Action in Perception.* Cambridge, MA: MIT Press.

Peirce, C. S. 1997. *Pragmatism as a Principle and Method of Right Thinking: The 1903 Lectures on Pragmatism.* Albany: State University of New York Press.

Ruyer, R. 1956. Le relief axiologique et le sentiment de profondeur. *Revue de métaphysique et de la morale* (3–4): 242–258.

Sacks, O. 2011. "Stereo Sue." In *The Mind's Eye,* 111–143. New York: Vintage.

Simondon, G. 2005. *L'individuation à la lumière des notions de forme et d'information.* Grenoble: Millon.

Thompson, E. 2005. *Colour Vision: A Study in Cognitive Science and the Philosophy of Perception.* London: Routledge.

Whitehead, A. N. 1967. *Adventures of Ideas.* New York: Free Press.

Whitehead, A. N. 1978. *Process and Reality.* New York: Free Press.

Further Reading

Ansell-Pearson, K. 2002. *Philosophy and the Adventure of the Virtual: Bergson and the Time of Life.* London: Routledge.

Gaffey, P., ed. 2009. *The Force of the Virtual: Deleuze, Science, and Philosophy.* Minneapolis: University of Minnesota Press.

Lévy, P. 1998. *Becoming Virtual.* New York: Basic Books.

Manning, E. 2009. *Relationscapes: Movement, Art, Philosophy*. Cambridge, MA: MIT Press.

Massumi, B. 2002. *Parables for the Virtual: Movement, Affect, Sensation*. Durham, NC: Duke University Press.

Munster, A. 2006. *Materializing the New Media: Embodiment in Information Aesthetics*. Hanover, NH: University Press of New England.

Murphie, A. 2002. Putting the Virtual Back into VR. In *A Shock to Thought: Expression after Deleuze and Guattari*, edited by B. Massumi, 188–214. London: Routledge.

Shields, R. 2002. *The Virtual*. London: Routledge.

CHAPTER 4

BEING MORE THAN YOURSELF: VIRTUALITY AND HUMAN SPIRIT

ANDRÉ NUSSELDER

THIS chapter discusses virtualization from the perspective of the fundamental processes that make us human: the use of signs and of tools. It points out the virtual dimension of freedom as specific to the human spirit. The virtual introduces an openness and with that an imbalance to human existence. The chapter discusses cases of the current instable self that hovers between creative freedom and excess. It uses the thoughts of Søren Kierkegaard and Alain Badiou to introduce a broader ethical perspective on this instable self. Thus it makes the point that at the horizon of humanity is freedom, which calls upon us to reinvent our self and not slip down into complacency. The virtuality of human existence is a condition both for its deepening and for its superficiality.

THE ORIGIN OF MAN AND THE EMERGENCE OF A VIRTUAL WORLD

> Cannot consciousness then remain in immediacy? This is a foolish question, for if it could, no consciousness would exist.... Man would be an animal, or in other words, he would be dumb. That which annuls immediacy, therefore is language. If man could not speak, he would remain in immediacy (Kierkegaard 1976, 148).

As symbolic anthropology has taught us, being human is intricately connected to the symbolic capacity and the use of signs (Geertz 1974; Turner 1974). The first genus of hominids (the *Australopithecus*) did not have this symbolic capacity to detach itself from its environment and therefore did not differ substantially from the monkeys and other animals that surrounded it. Those hominids only used signals when the object that the signals gave evidence of was perceptibly present. So sounds were used to indicate the presence of a predator, but those sounds did not function yet as a symbolic language. This would only be the case when sounds were also made without the direct presence of a predator. The early modern man *Homo sapiens* did develop this ability to communicate with other members of the group about a nonvisible prey or predator, or even the threat of a possible predator. The ability evolved to connect to *absent* objects. With the development of the linguistic ability to also symbolize absent things, modern humans were able to multiply and change sounds in order to refer to an ever-increasing amount of things. In this way they discovered the symbolic capacity for communication, and it generated the (almost magical) power to master their expanding world. This changed their behavior, made them more conscious of their actions and of themselves, and allowed them to repeat past actions and think ahead to future ones (Noble and Davidson 1991; 1996). Parallel to *Homo sapiens'* use of signs in order to organize and transcend the immediate environment, his world became a human world defined by the mental capacities for introspection, abstract reasoning, and problem solving (by means of tools).

Another piece of consciousness evolved around 100,000 years ago when *Homo sapiens* transcended the preceding "indifference" toward dead tribe members. They were no longer left aside, but their corpse became a special thing to be treated differently than other lifeless objects. With the emerging capacity to remember the actions that surrounded death (with the use of signs as a condition for remembrance and future projections), the deceased did not slip away into meaninglessness but became dear kin as remembered ancestors (Fletcher 1993). When around 60,000 years ago the Neanderthals (*Homo sapiens neanderthalensis*) also started to instinctively bury their dead with ritual and ceremony, human self-consciousness had apparently so evolved that death was conceived of as a violence that had to be concealed. The human being became conscious of itself as a mortal being; also the earliest forms of art show that man's capacity for symbolic expression is penetrated by an awareness of death (Bataille 1989). This suggests that human consciousness and absence are intricately connected. Later on in its development, at about 50,000 years ago, *Homo sapiens* not merely was able to make gestures and sounds, but developed the capacity to also leave traces of it in loam or sand. Signs became independent entities in the outside world that could transmit information independently. The use of signs evolved into the construction of complex sign systems. The ability to make (complex) connections and to retain and develop mental images gave man the ability to express his world and thoughts. This is best visible in the development of art, which started about 35,000 years ago, and which initially took place in a ritual context dedicated to the divine dimension: "Ice Age art" (Bahn and Vertut 1997). By transferring (moral) values, knowledge, and beliefs, these sign systems expressed and transmitted what it meant to be human (Geertz 1973).

Being human is not only intricately connected to the use of signs, but also to the use of tools and technology. Anthropogenesis might even correspond to technogenesis (Leroi-Gourhan 1993; Stiegler 1998). Through the development of symbolic representation and of tools, the human world became a world permeated by virtuality; another world than that of immediate presence appeared. Underlying this virtual presence is man's relation to *absence*, that is, distance in space or time, or even a distance beyond the horizon of life: death. The "inventory of the imaginary" (in myth, art…) would be motivated by a desire to deal with and escape from "absence," that is, death and decay (Durand 1999, 391). It is even argued that, on a psychical level, all technologies revolve around man's struggle with "absence, leave, separation, disappearance, interruption, withdrawal, or loss. By overcoming or shutting off the negative horizon of absence, the technical media become technologies of care and presence" (Weibel 1992, 75). The effort to escape death and decay would be the ultimate goal of virtualization. "In general, virtualization is a war against fragility, pain, wear. In search of safety and control, we pursue the virtual because it leads us towards ontological regions that ordinary dangers never reach" (Lévy 1998, 99).

HUMANIZATION AS VIRTUALIZATION

> Freedom … is the one sole and original right belonging to every person by virtue of his humanity (Kant 1999, 38).

Not only archaeological studies on the history of the human species (phylogenesis) show that human consciousness emerges as a transcendence of nature, but this is also a central theme in philosophical anthropology. The idealistic tradition in philosophy, as represented by philosophers such as Fichte, Schelling, and Hegel, makes the decisive point that consciousness ("Spirit") emerges as a result of the human being breaking its association with its natural environment (Pinkard 2002). Human consciousness introduces a rupture between itself and nature (Schelling 1985 Vol. 1, 400).[1]

This German transcendental idealism builds upon the revolutionary work of Kantian transcendental philosophy. Kant defined this division of planes (nature/culture; matter/consciousness) in a useful way. According to Kant the human being exists on two planes: natural and moral. On the natural plane man is subjected to the laws of causality, which implies that everything is the result of something else that preceded it in time. At this level the (natural) sciences explain events from their (preceding) conditions—for example, in the current scientific paradigm we are inclined to explain the habit of smoking from its neurocognitive conditions. This would explain why the act *had to* occur. At the same time, at the moral plane, there is the awareness that the act *could have been* omitted (it was our choice to light a cigarette); this is what our conscience tells us. So the human being exists not only at the plane of (natural) necessity, but also at the plane of (virtual) freedom: at this plane there would have been *other possibilities*. This (virtual) domain of freedom, states Kant, is the domain of morality, religion, and art.

The Hegelian tradition of thought extends the above insights, which are Kantian in origin, and is an intellectual enterprise aimed at the "realization of freedom." This tradition connects the breaking free from natural causality to man's use of language.

Language is a "murder of the thing," as Hegel scholar Alexandre Kojève explained in the 1930s to a whole generation of French intellectuals (Kojève 1980). Language is an annulment of immediate presence, so that presence becomes *presence for a human consciousness*. This consciousness is not "full" anymore like the supposed "natural consciousness" (exemplified by the spontaneity of the child): it is always relational and as much referring to other signs as to the "natural thing."[2] Human consciousness contains an emptiness or negativity so that the mind is a virtual entity (cf. Nusselder 2009, ch. 3). Sartre distinguishes this ontological domain of the "for-itself" (the subject of consciousness) from the plenitude of the "in-itself," which is the object of consciousness (Sartre 1958).

Man is an animal without steady *Umwelt* and because of this (organic) lack he must build a "second nature" that we name culture (Arnold Gehlen). Nowadays the Slovenian philosopher Slavoj Žižek (b. 1949) pursues the Kantian-Hegelian line of thinking by articulating a philosophy in which man's "withdrawal" from the outer world (the arising of interiority or subjectivity), the severing of ties with the *Umwelt*, or the rupture of the immersion in the natural environment, is exactly the foundation of "humanization" (Žižek 1998, 258).

Also in the analysis of individual development (ontogenesis) there are significant theories that consider human consciousness a result from the break with the natural environment. The psychoanalytic tradition thinks the development of individual consciousness derives from the child's separation from the "original plenitude" (the mother-child unity). The British psychoanalyst Donald Winnicott (1896–1971) considers a "potential space" the result of the child's separation from the mother: an interpersonal space in which the child can playfully explore its identity (Winnicott 1971). Before this adaptation of Freudian ideas into British psychiatry, the work of the French psychiatrist Jacques Lacan (1901–1981) uses the same Freudian inspiration to conceptualize how human identity arises as a result of departing from the real by means of images and symbols (Lacan 2006). As a consequence, man's basic desire for self-exploration and self-knowledge can, according to Lacan, only take shape by means of speculation and language: for humans there is no "real reality" stripped of these imaginary and symbolical constructions. Images and symbols represent us in the second world we name *human* reality—as a mirror image represents our physical self in an objectified (though imaginary) form.

Under the right psychological conditions, this second world of potentiality is the domain for the creative expression of humanity. Winnicott: "Here where there is trust and reliability is a potential space, one that can become an infinite area of separation, which the baby, child, adolescent, adult, may creatively fill with playing, which in times becomes the enjoyment of the cultural heritage" (Winnicott 1971, 108). This process nevertheless remains tricky as it involves the loss of security and of adaptation, the loss of the merging in with the other, "so that disaster threatens" (Winnicott 1971, 107). The human being hovers between (creative) freedom and destruction/excess. "Desire's excess shows a break with immediacy. Desire is excessive because it is free" (Desmond 1990, 172).

THE VIRTUAL: FROM ESSENCE TO "ENTWURF"

When humanization and virtualization are so closely connected, an important philosophical question is how we should think of notions like "man," "reality," or "truth." This intricate connection of the human and the virtual prevents thinking in terms of "essences," an essentialism as can be found in the influential Platonic philosophy that dominated the Western intellectual landscape for centuries. Platonism considers the ideal world (a "virtual reality") as the fundamentals of our everyday, shadowlike reality. The ideal form virtually contains the essence of the real. Thus for Plato truly knowing a thing like a chair is contemplating its ideal form, and truly knowing all differently shaped triangles is knowing the general form of a triangle: mathematics is at the forefront of knowledge. Nowadays we can again find this Platonic thinking in "idealistic" understandings of the Internet as the realm of "timeless data" where the cybercast can wander around as a free spirit detached from its physical condition. It would thus allow a person to be as she "really is" and not being evaluated by all sorts of physical characteristics (being female, colored, disabled) (Turkle 1995; Stone 1995; Plant 1997). In such views, "cyberspace is Platonism as a working product" (Heim 1993, 89).

Platonic thought is thinking in terms of opposites; "the real" versus "the imaginary," being versus appearance, reality versus illusion. The "deconstruction" of this thinking is especially visible in twentieth-century philosophy. Martin Heidegger (1889–1976) defined man's existence as time, as openness for the future: being-in-the-world is a "projection" into the future, an "Entwurf" (Heidegger 1962, 185). In the philosophy of Gilles Deleuze (1925–1995) too, man is characterized by its "exceptional opening," by the "power of going beyond his 'plane' and his condition" (Deleuze 1991, 109). For Deleuze there is not one "true reality" that should be distinguished from "false appearances," but there are different kinds of reality. The notion of the virtual is pivotal to this philosophy, for the virtual indicates that which does have a kind of reality but is not yet actual, as a task that is virtually completed indicates that the completion is just about *upon* us (cf. Lister, Dovey, and Giddens 2009, 389).

In the classical (Platonist) conception of the virtual, human desire finds completion in the contemplation of the virtual "other world" (God, true knowledge); it depends on a "metaphysics of presence" wherein the original presence is allied with Logos, God, and teleology (Derrida 1976). However, when thinking in terms of ideal forms or essences is no longer tenable, as in much of twentieth-century philosophy, the status of the virtual changes. Then the virtual is no longer able to harmonize and unify our strivings and instead becomes a field of forces that tears the unified subject apart, driving it ever further away from its home and its self-identity—without the promise of finding it again at the end of the journey.[3] This is the condition of the virtual that we are in nowadays: a condition of dissemination and dispersion, of diversion and distraction (and maybe even an absence of mind?). This virtual condition needs an ethical orientation. Some examples of current virtual experiences may show this.

The Uneasiness of the Virtual Experience and the Instable Self

Digital technologies with their specific hardware and software configurations impose constraints upon virtuality and thus define the virtual experience. They provide us with powerful abilities for communication, for instance, of communicating with people at the other end of the world. But at the same time they destabilize selfhood, as illustrated by the feeling of disorientation and the loss of homeland and of security that accompanies processes of global communication. The current virtual experience puts us in the uncanny situation of both a strong (excessive) need and desire for communication and extreme vulnerability or instability. On one level the virtual seduces us by the many possibilities it opens up, and on another level it gravitates around a feeling of anxiety or sense of loss (see also Tinwell, chapter 10 in this volume).

The analysis of the function of information and communication technologies (ICT) among the younger generation testifies to this situation of hardly being able to live outside this virtual condition: for when the opportunities for communication are not there, we feel lost; anxiety is the missing concept for understanding the current human condition (Turkle 2011). The fundamental anxiety that Turkle diagnoses among youngsters is most visible in the treatment of computer addiction (thus we follow Freud's "crystal principle" wherein pathology shows the fracture lines of "normal" human existence). For the patient the expectation of having no "access" is almost unbearable, and therapists use moments of being "disconnected" (like having to sit at a dinner table with parents and having a conversation with them) as one of the first steps in therapy (cf. Aboujaoude 2011, 27). These examples indicate that the initial euphoric approaches to the influence of new media and the Internet, of which the earlier work of Sherry Turkle was exemplary, now must also acknowledge the fundamental discontent that lies beneath it. In the approach of this chapter these discontents indicate the excessive, destabilizing side of the virtual. Virtualization drives us ever further away from our "intimacy" or "wholeness" (our self, community, home…) without there ever being an end to this journey. It is the underlying principle of both the human quest for freedom and of anxiety and uncertainty—phenomena we can nowadays observe so strongly.

The phenomenon of "information overload" shows that the individual person finds it difficult to make sense of all this information and to find (personal) relevance in it. In his best-selling book *The Shallows: What the Internet Is Doing to our Brains* Nicholas Carr analyzes how through the centuries human thought has been shaped by so-called "tools of the mind"—from the alphabet, to maps, to the printing press, the clock, and the computer (also Ong 1982). Carr uses recent discoveries in neuroscience to put forward the thesis that our brain is actually changing because of the experiences that new media provide us with, and he finds that the Internet encourages the rapid, distracted sampling of small bits of information from many sources. The resulting information overload is for Carr, as he explained in a blog post, not a question of finding the "needle in the haystack." What he names "ambient overload" concerns the problem that there are "too many needles": "We experience ambient overload when we're surrounded by so much information *that is of immediate interest to us* that we feel overwhelmed by the never-ending pressure of trying to keep up with it all. We keep clicking links, keep hitting the refresh key, keep opening new tabs, keep checking email in-boxes and RSS feeds, keep scanning Amazon and Netflix recommendations—and yet the pile of interesting information never shrinks" (Carr 2011). The use of filters, which is supposedly a technical means to regulate or "frame" the abundance of information, for him actually makes the problem worse, as it is a sophisticated way of providing us with exactly all the information that we are interested in, and thus with more information. Also, political scientist Jodi Dean puts forward that the Internet put us in the never-ending circuit of the drive. We enjoy our participation in affective networks; we can't get enough of the communication technologies that make us participate. "We contribute to the networks as creative producers and vulnerable consumers because we enjoy it. In fact, the open architecture of the internet enables and requires the capture of enjoyment insofar as it is premised on users' contributions, alterations, and engagement" (Dean 2010, 114). These analyses may contribute to Carr's larger thesis that the Internet is remaking us in its own image: it increases our capacity for scanning and skimming, but decreases the capacity for concentration, contemplation, and reflection.

The current trend of personalizing information, of adjusting it to the registered preferences of the user/consumer ("content in context"), can be considered an attempt to reintroduce some sort of "personal measure" into the information overload and transform the abundance of information into meaningful information (but we must question whether it succeeds in doing so or is actually stimulating the excess). And in the current development of the Internet, trusted sites and portals must provide the user some sort of grip upon the almost infinite amount of options and choices available. Also, the phenomenon of online recommendation shows that we need guidelines and other people for orientation. At the subjective level the current human condition, as brought together here in the experience of the Internet, confronts us with the question of responsibility, meaning, and "authentic subjectivity."

THE CHALLENGE FOR THOUGHT

What characterizes the human subject in the current mode of the superabundance or redundancy of information available through ICTs is, on one level, excessive stimulation and, on another level, insecurity and a lack of orientation. The result is that people find themselves left to the mercy of the flows of information, with all the uneasiness that accompanies this position. Carr, for instance, acknowledges the danger that within the field of ICT all that is left is an industrialist ethic of speed and efficiency, of optimized production and consumption (Carr 2010).

The examples mentioned occur within a social context where individualization and globalization further dissolve the securities of man's socio-symbolic environment (state, family, tradition). There is an individualization of social life (Bauman 2001). The German sociologist Beck characterizes the current society as a "risk society" (Beck 1992). Without us being aware of it we have entered a new type of society in which former mechanisms of control (through politics and science) no longer function adequately. However, the greatest danger is not in physical but in social "explosiveness" due to a loss of trust in all sorts of institutions. What is required to deal with this situation, states Beck, are new frameworks for responsibility and for giving meaning to the world (Beck 1996).

As a result of the decline of symbolic authority in the contemporary Western world, subjectivity lacks consistent (symbolic) frameworks. Where this decline of symbolic authority is often celebrated as liberation, there is also a "darker" side to it. It also leads to an instable self that is an easy prey for manipulating techniques stimulating the pursuit of infinite possibilities, thus reducing the human subject to an object, deprived of freedom, in the chain of production and consumption. With its focus on notions such as "free will," philosophy thinks the human subject as being more than an object—as in current debates whether or not the human subject is nothing but an object determined by "genes" or neurobiological laws. The major quest for contemporary philosophy is therefore to "rethink the subject" in a manner that cannot be content with (will not accept) the reduction of subjectivity to an object. The task of philosophy is to transcend the uneasiness (or spiritual lack) that defines current times (and which is at the basis of all sorts of reactions and countermovements against globalization). It should answer Nietzsche's call that man after the "death of God" must formulate new goals (perform his existence as "Entwurf") in order to give meaning to his life. This chapter seeks to "rethink the subject" by referring to the philosophies of Kierkegaard and Badiou.

The challenge for current thought concerns ethics—and it is not without reason that Badiou names one of his central works simply "Ethics." The (ethical) challenge in the field of ICT is to process the abundance of information within our own meaningful goals, and not be carried away by the seductiveness of the "many possibilities." What Kierkegaard and Badiou teach us is that with the truthful realization of certain possibilities the subject is guided toward a higher level of being. Then it is not about providing the largest amount of information possible for a subject that is endlessly striving for more (we will get to know this as "aesthetic subjectivity").[4] It is about information for a subject with a specific "ethical" interest (ethical subjectivity). This second position would be the ideal world of Wikileaks[5] and other (progressive) movements wherein the transparency of information leads to (social) invention. This subject position is motivated by (an almost religious) hope for the emergence of something New (and this may also explain why Wikileaks leader Julian Assange was perceived in certain circles as the messiah of a new world).

Ethical Subjectivity: From Kierkegaard to Badiou

> You cannot get the truth by capturing it, only by its capturing you.
> (Kierkegaard 1967–1978 Vol. 11, A 355).

The thought of Søren Kierkegaard, certainly one of the sharpest thinkers on subjectivity, is also useful for understanding human subjectivity in the current "era of information" to which the work of Hubert Dreyfus testifies (Dreyfus 2001). Kierkegaard in his times turned himself against the superabundance/triviality of information of the press. For him the press exemplified a public sphere of individuals having an opinion about public matters without taking personal responsibility, a sphere of readers disengaged from their local situation and personal "concreteness" (Dreyfus 2001, 76). The subject captivated by this kind of infinity of "news facts" without genuine consequences was to him typical of the aesthetic lifestyle. According to Kierkegaard the basic motivations of the aesthetic positions are a desire to see, try, and do everything, explore all the opportunities, without a genuine engagement that makes one of the many possibilities an emphatic reality. The aesthete is the person who is constantly in love but refuses to be bound to one person. The aesthetic domain is that of seduction and of seducing—as embodied by Kierkegaard's character Johannes Climacus in the *Journal of the Seducer*. The aesthete considers existence and its contradictions as imaginary and contingent possibilities, and lives a fantastic eternity in which everything is possible but nothing is real. It is the subject of the spectacle (Debord 2004); the subject of the screen who is endlessly surfing the Internet in order to find spectacle, sensation, and pleasure (Dreyfus 2001, ch 4).

However, despite the "fun," there is something lacking in this aesthetic position, and it is here that we touch again upon the fundamental discontent of the virtual subject. Kierkegaard calls this despair: a summit of anxiety and melancholy.[6] Nevertheless, it is from this despair that the aesthete gains intuitive knowledge of his lack of freedom and thereby of his true, infinite destination. For despair opens up the opportunity to transform his relationship to the endless possibilities and to let some sort of "eternity" enter the sequence of moments of satisfaction, disappointment, and the greed of conquest. This ethical decision, which is more passivity than a conscious activity, introduces eternity in time.[7] What Kierkegaard names the Moment synthesizes the contradictions of existence (the somatic and the psychical: body and soul) into a third element: Spirit, which is eternity-in-time. Spirit expresses the transubstantiation of the self into a new way of becoming (Podmore 2011, 62). In the ethical stage of subjectivity, a person transforms from a "being-in-between" (an "inter-esse") into a new subject: as in a religious context, an act of faith transforms someone into a new subject.[8] The ethical individual does not merely consider his existence an abstract possibility but a *question* that requires *personal engagement*. In ethical engagement a new subject appears that forms the horizon or framework for the subject to pursue its trajectory.[9]

How new forms of subjectivity may appear, other than that of postmodern multiplicity, is also developed by the French philosopher Alain Badiou (b. 1937) in his *Ethics* (Badiou 2000). Badiou devoted his philosophical life to developing a theory of the human aspiration for "the good" in postmodern times. He discusses the theme not so much in a religious context (as Kierkegaard does) but rather in a revolutionary context. Nevertheless, for Badiou, St. Paul's conversion on the road to Damascus is the paradigmatic example of the transformative power of a moment when eternity hits us (Badiou 2003). For him the human being is not just an *object* as studied by all sorts of positive sciences (we are our body, our brain . . .) but is also a *subject* that is the carrier of a higher truth. The human being is both itself and something that transcends itself (Badiou 2000, 45), as lovers at the moment that they declare their love enter into the composition of one loving subject (or Spirit) that exceeds them both and makes them participate in Eternity (Badiou 2000, 43). For Badiou, there are four domains in which the formation of a subject of truth is possible: science, art, love, and politics (cf. Hallward 2003). Inventions occur when, in these domains, something radically new occurs: the transcendence of love, a new scientific paradigm or political configuration, or truly great art. What appears in such "events" is the surplus of the natural, the excess of necessity, in short: that which is "more" than the object (and it is this surplus, of freedom, that is in my story defining the virtual). In an invention this "surplus" leads to something New, and it is carried by a subject that is devoted and loyal to another or new truth. To put it in the words of Kierkegaard: "What is truth but to live for an idea" (Kierkegaard 1967–1978, Vol. 5 JP 5, 34). Also, for Kierkegaard the way to pass beyond self-alienation is that of becoming subject of a "higher truth": a risky enterprise through which man establishes in his interiority a relation to the absolute and thus becomes himself infinite.

Virtuality and Invention

> To be a person is to be an appeal—an ethical appeal for dignity (Desmond 1990, 187).

Virtuality introduces an "openness" (otherness) in human existence: the dimension of infinity and freedom. Because of this "openness" human existence cannot entirely be grasped on an objective level (as an object). On the ontological plane, this openness or "wound" of the human subject is the *condition of possibility* of new configurations of humanity (of human existence as "Entwurf"). On the ethical plane, the human subject is the carrier of the appeal for dignity (recalling the crucial Kantian division of planes). Anthropology or even ontology is in the end inseparable from ethics (Peperzak 2004). It is therefore not by chance that this chapter provides a philosophical-anthropological perspective on virtuality that results in ethics, an ethics that centers on freedom and invention. From this perspective the human condition is guided by the appeal to show human grandeur or dignity, to aspire for a higher good.

The philosophies of Kierkegaard and Badiou of the transformative capacity of "moments of truth" can teach us that a use of the superabundance of information other than that of "seduction" is possible: it is exactly this condition that shows our freedom and "spirit." Information then is intricately connected to meaning: it is meaningful in relation to the (ethical) goal that the subject pursues, or as Dreyfus puts it: "Information is not played with, but is sought and used for serious purposes" (Dreyfus 2001, 83). As in the Arab Spring, the electronic exchange of information ("Twitter revolution") is taking place within the larger political framework of the quest for freedom, of getting rid of authoritarian leaders and dictators. In a similar way, the revealing of information by Wikileaks took place within the larger framework of creating a (more) transparent society, and establishing equality. On a more daily level, Dreyfus uses the same line of Kierkegaardian thinking to propose that a genuine use of the potentials of information technologies requires that they be brought into action for improved quality of life, for example, using distance learning for education. We then see that the increased opportunities for information and communication have the potential to (re)invent the circumstances and the conditions of human existence.

So when we use this perspective, can we say then that Wikileaks is an invention, a new configuration of our (political) reality? Or is it nothing more than some mischief by some rebel youngsters, as its strongest critics would have it? And is the Internet, as a technological formation of the virtual, an invention? For instance, because it offers people the opportunity to relate to others while released from the physical situation or physical characteristics (so that persons can appear in their "true," eternal dimension)? Is the use of social media by youngsters in the Arab world who dream of living in a free country an invention? The key to an answer from the perspective in this chapter lies in the notion of subjective involvement: we can only speak of an invention when there is a *new subjective relation* to the object. So it is not the object that is new (for that would be the aesthetic subjectivity in the Kierkegaardian sense wherein the object is only interesting when it is constantly "new" or "different") but our relation to it (cf. Desmond 1990).

Wikileaks allows people to take direct notice of political documents without getting biased information via institutions (political parties, newspapers...) that have their own agenda. Thus, Wikileaks can radically change the political landscape and is a reinvention of politics (and it was, of course, because of this enormous potential that it was attacked so fiercely by the existing powers: Hillary Clinton called the Wikileaks releases an "attack on America's foreign policy interests" and on the international community). But contrary to these transformative powers offered to us, we are quickly diverted (distracted, entertained) by all sorts of personal motives (see the turbulence within the organization of Wikileaks itself), or may find it too hard to interpret the enormous amount of information ourselves. Because of a decline into lazy habits, we develop a kind of general casualness and fall back into older methods. People find it very difficult (or too difficult) to stay loyal to their initial ideals, so that decisive "events" will not fully deliver their truth. Similarly, the Internet did have the potential of reinventing human relations and of liberation (as the early euphoric reception of it had it), as it does allow for a communication of kindred spirits throughout the world. Nevertheless all sorts of restricting social and businesslike patterns (stereotypes, profits...) very soon again came to dominate this communication. It shows how the ethics of invention is constantly threatened by decline; there is a "permanent temptation of giving up, of returning to the mere belonging to the 'ordinary' situation, of erasing the effects of the not-known" (Badiou 2000, 48).

CONCLUSION: EXISTENCE AS CHANCE

> The noble man wants to create new things and a new virtue.... But, by my love and hope I entreat you: do not reject the hero in *your* soul! Keep holy your highest hope! (Nietzsche 1969, 71)

Man is an "inter-esse," a being-in-between here and there, now and later, body and mind, necessity and freedom: between the real and the virtual. Human reality is exactly the result of the interplay between those two dimensions. The notion of virtuality should teach us that this reality always has the potential of being radically different from what it actually is. Man remains human, he remains faithful to his uttermost dignity or intention (and is this not the meaning of Nietzsche's ideal of the *Übermensch*?), as long as this virtual dimension keeps the promise of (radical) invention and is not ruined by seductions. Earthly reality with all its physical pleasures, conditions, habits, and limitations is a drag that we cannot easily leave behind. The new configuration is almost never as good as when perceived from a distance, or as dreamed of. The (almost) religiously inspired notion of the (advent of the) New is always corrupted by some sort of disloyalty. Therefore, the virtuality of the human condition places us at the limit: it promises a lot, but also requires an enormous effort. For Heidegger (1962), an "authentic" "Entwurf" of existence must face the absence of death (an absence that is brought forward in this chapter as being at the heart of the virtual condition).

The lesson of many great philosophers therefore is that human "potential space" is constantly at risk from phenomena like boredom, disinterestedness, complacency, fatigue, banality, and triviality. Nevertheless, they tell us what the human being *can be*. Nietzsche tells us his grand story of the *Übermensch*, which is not the fascist superman but the man who seeks to establish new goals in a meaningless world without orientation. Derrida's work develops toward a philosophy that revolves around notions like responsibility and an "ethics of the future" (Beardsworth 1996). Despite the fact that our virtual condition may have "disengaged" us from our natural condition, and will continue to perform this insecure operation, it still requires some sort of "subjective engagement" to lead us into the future. In the realm of transcendence, infinity, and freedom—that is, the world of the Spirit that is the virtual world—there needs to be an ideal that guides us in order to prevent us from disorientation and nihilism. We may call this the question of love.

NOTES

1. With this movement toward freedom there is also violence (violation) inherent to the human being as it bursts its natural chains.
2. Eventually leading to the challenging and provocative thesis of the French sociologist Jean Baudrillard (1929–2007) that the excessive use of these mechanisms (due to media, advertising) might even lead to a loss of reality itself (Baudrillard 1994).
3. It is therefore not without reason that Deleuze discusses the painter Francis Bacon, whose work shows the human body in all sorts of distorted and affected states and is thus at the opposite of the classical ideal of the human body as a perfect form.
4. The work of Jean Baudrillard describes, in its extreme conditions, this subject position of a (postmodern) "world without depths"; an aesthetic position of a "world of surfaces," where symbolic frameworks delivered by tradition or reason have lost their structuring function. Subjectivity then is nothing but an effect of the flows of information and of production that dominate it, without some sort of "critical center" (a situation that is not even felt anymore as a loss—and is that not the extreme form of nihilism as predicted by Nietzsche?). Nevertheless, Baudrillard tried to formulate an alternative to the all-encompassing mode of production by a theory of seduction advocating artifice, appearance, and play—which can be named a neo-aristocratic form of aestheticism (cf. Baudrillard 1990).
5. Wikileaks is an international nonprofit organization whose website, launched in 2006, publishes large amounts of secret and classified information in order to address abuses and irregularities. Important "leaks" were on the US-led wars in Afghanistan and Iraq, on the US prison camp Guantánamo Bay, and on international diplomatic cables ("Cablegate").
6. Despair and depression were for Kierkegaard characteristic of his time; maybe they are no less a characteristic of our society and its crisis in giving meaning to the world.
7. For Kierkegaard the sinner is at the threshold of discovering what he has lost, the eternal dimension of his freedom. His "duty" is to "repeat" his eternal value; he must realize the most concrete assignment or question of life: that of love.
8. For Kierkegaard, the religious stage is the highest stage of interiorization and expresses a "choice" grounded in devotion. As I am primarily focused here on the transformative power of ethical engagement I will only discuss this stage shortly here. The religious person, according to Kierkegaard, genuinely founds his existence, his choices, and his truth in (a conception of) God. In the religious self-relation, all relativity and finitude of the self melt away. The "paradox" is that, in this breaking with the finite self and "natural immediacy," the religious subject receives a new self and a new immediacy.
9. The emergence of a new subject is exactly possible because, through processes of virtualization, human subjectivity is not something fixed and finished ("full"), but is founded on absence, emptiness, negativity (as discussed in the first two sections of this chapter).

REFERENCES

Aboujaoude, E. 2011. *Virtually You. The Dangerous Powers of the E-Personality*. New York/London: Norton.

Badiou, A. 2000. *Ethics: An Essay on the Understanding of Evil*. Translated by P. Hallward. New York: Verso.

Badiou, A. 2003. *Saint Paul: The Foundation of Universalism*. Translated by R. Brassier. Stanford: Stanford University Press.

Bahn, P. G., and J. Vertut. 1997. *Journey Through the Ice Age*. Berkeley: University of California Press.

Bataille, G. 1989. *The Tears of Eros*. Translated by P. Connor. San Francisco: City Lights Books.

Baudrillard, J. 1990. *Seduction*. Translated by B. Singer. Montreal: New World Perspective.

Baudrillard, J. 1994. *Simulacra and Simulations* Translated by S. F. Glaser. Ann Arbor: Michigan University Press.

Bauman, Z. 2001. *The Individualized Society*. Cambridge: Polity Press.

Beardsworth, R. 1996. *Derrida and the Political*. London: Routledge.

Beck, U. 1992. *Risk Society: Towards a New Modernity*. London: Sage.

Beck, U. 1996. *The Reinvention of Politics: Rethinking Modernity in the Global Social Order*. Cambridge: Polity Press.

Carr, N. 2010. *The Shallows: What the Internet Is Doing to Our Brains*. New York: Atlantic Books.

Carr, N. 2011. Situational Overload and Ambient Overload. March 7. http://www.roughtype.com/archives/2011/03/situational_ove.php. Accessed June 13, 2013.

Dean, J. 2010. *Blog Theory: Feedback and Capture in the Circuits of Drive*. Cambridge/Malden: Polity Press.

Debord, G. 2004. *The Society of the Spectacle*. London: Rebel Press.

Deleuze, G. 1991. *Bergsonism*. New York: Zone Books.

Derrida, J. 1976. *Of Grammatology*. Translated by G. C. Spivak. Baltimore: Johns Hopkins University Press.

Desmond, W. 1990. *Philosophy and its Others*. Albany: SUNY Press.

Dreyfus, H. 2001. *On the Internet*. London/New York: Routledge.

Durand, G. 1999. *The Anthropological Structures of the Imaginary*. Translated by M. Sankey and J. Hatten. Brisbane: Boombana Publications.

Fletcher, R. J. 1993. The Evolution of Human Behaviour. In *The Illustrated History of Humankind*, vol. 1: *The First Humans*, edited by G. Burenhult, 17–25. St. Lucia: University of Queensland Press.

Geertz, C. 1973. *The Interpretation of Cultures: Selected Essays*. New York: Basic.

Geertz, C., ed. 1974. *Myth, Symbol, and Culture*. New York: Norton.

Hallward, P. 2003. *Badiou: A Subject to Truth*. Minneapolis: University of Minnesota Press.

Heidegger, M. 1962. *Being and Time*. Translated by J. MacQuarrie and E. Robinson. Malden, MA: Blackwell.

Heim, M. 1993. *The Metaphysics of Virtual Reality*. Oxford: Oxford University Press.

Kant, I. 1999. *The Metaphysical Elements of Justice*. Translated by J. Ladd. Indianapolis: Hackett.

Kierkegaard, S. 1967–1978. *Journals and Papers Vol. 1–11*. Edited and translated by H. V. Hong and E. H. Hong. Bloomington: Indiana University Press.

Kierkegaard, S. 1976. *Johannes Climacus, or De omnibus dubitandum est*. Translated by T. H. Croxall. Stanford, CA: Stanford University Press.

Kojève, A. 1980. *Introduction to the Reading of Hegel: Lectures on the Phenomenology of Spirit*. Assembled by R. Queneau. Edited by A. Bloom. Translated by J. H. Nichols Jr. Ithaca, NY: Cornell University Press.

Lacan, J. 2006. *Écrits*. Translated by B. Fink. New York: Norton.

Leroi-Gourhan, A. 1993. *Gesture and Speech*. Translated by A. B. Berger. Cambridge: MIT Press.

Lévy, P. 1998. *Becoming Virtual: Reality in a Digital Age*. New York: Plenum Trade.

Lister, M., J. Dovey, and S. Giddens. 2009. *New Media: A Critical Introduction*. New York: Routledge.

Nietzsche, F. 1969. *Thus Spoke Zarathustra*. Translated by R. J. Hollingdale. New York: Penguin.

Noble, W., and I. Davidson. 1991. The Evolutionary Emergence of Modern Human Behaviour: Language and Its Archaeology. *Man* 26: 223–253.

Noble, W., and I. Davidson. 1996. *Human Evolution, Language and Mind: A Psychological and Archaeological Inquiry*. Cambridge: Cambridge University Press.

Nusselder, A. 2009. *Interface Fantasy: A Lacanian Cyborg Ontology*. Cambridge, MA: MIT Press.

Ong, W. 1982. *Orality and Literacy: The Technologizing of the Word*. New York: Methuen.

Peperzak, A. 2004. *Elements of Ethics*. Stanford, CA: Stanford University Press.

Pinkard, T. 2002. *German Philosophy, 1760–1860: The Legacy of Idealism*. Cambridge: Cambridge University Press.

Plant, S. 1997. *Zeroes and Ones: Digital Women and the New Technoculture*. New York: Doubleday.

Podmore, S. D. 2011. *Kierkegaard and the Self before God: Anatomy of the Abyss*. Bloomington: Indiana University Press.

Sartre, J.-P. 1958. *Being and Nothingness: An Essay on Phenomenological Ontology*. Translated by H. E. Barnes. London: Methuen.

von Schelling, F. W. J. 1985. *Ausgewählte Schriften*. Edited by M. Frank. 6 vols. Frankfurt am Main: Suhrkamp.

Stiegler, B. 1998. *Technics and Time*, vol. 1: *The Fault of Epimetheus*. Translated by R. Beardsworth and G. Collins. Stanford, CA: Stanford University Press.

Stone, A. R. 1995. *The War of Desire and Technology*. Cambridge, MA: MIT Press.

Turkle, S. 1995. *Life on the Screen: Identity in the Age of Internet*. New York: Simon and Schuster.

Turkle, S. 2011. *Alone Together: Why We Expect More from Technology and Less from Each Other*. New York: Basic Books.

Turner, V. 1974. *Dramas, Fields and Metaphors: Symbolic Action in Human Society*. Ithaca, NY: Cornell University Press.

Weibel, P. 1992. New Space in the Electronic Age. In *Book for the Instable Media*, edited by E. Bolle, 65–75. Den Bosch: V2 Publishing.

Winnicott, D. W. 1971. *Playing and Reality*. New York: Routledge.

Žižek, S. 1998. Cartesian Subject versus Cartesian Theatre. In *Cogito and the Unconscious*, edited by S. Žižek, 247–274. Durham, NC: Duke University Press.

CHAPTER 5

MYTHOLOGIES OF VIRTUALITY: "OTHER SPACE" AND "SHARED DIMENSION" FROM ANCIENT MYTHS TO CYBERSPACE

MARIA BEATRICE BITTARELLO

THIS chapter explores the concept of virtuality in relation to "virtual worlds"; it is an attempt to outline how there are certain elements of continuity in the way virtual worlds are imagined cross-culturally. In particular, the chapter shows how, from mythical narrations to contemporary conceptualizations of digital communications, virtual worlds are described either as separate distant spaces or as different but interconnected planes of reality. Both conceptions of imaginary spaces coexisted in ancient myths, literature, and art as they coexist in contemporary conceptualizations of digital technologies.

The expression "virtual worlds" indicates fully fledged imaginary worlds that, according to some scholars (Wertheim 1999; Ward 2000) have always been described in myths, literature, and religion, and represented on stage and in art. Also, Marie Laure Ryan (2001, 14–15) has highlighted how novels, movies, drama, and representational paintings, as well as certain computer games (those casting the user as one of the characters of a story), manage to create a space to which readers/spectators/users can relate and that can potentially function as a setting or habitat for (narrative) action as it can be populated with objects and characters. Ryan (2001, 15–16), referring to a relevant body of literary studies, talks of textual worlds as "immersive"—in her work, immersion presupposes an active imaginative engagement with the text, and it is therefore far from a passive attitude.

"Digital virtual worlds" indicates imaginary worlds digitally constructed (or coconstructed) by users on commercial digital platforms such as *Active Worlds* or *Second Life*. The key feature of digital virtual worlds is that through digital technology users can participate in the story, add to the content, modify the settings, and interact with other users, whereas in literary or "visual" virtual worlds, or in other technologies that just show alternate realities, such as cinema, readers/viewers do not have this possibility. As we shall see in this chapter's third section, digital virtual worlds can be either textual, or graphical, or 3D. In immersive 3D virtual environments, users experience the virtual world through immersion in a digital simulation, by using specific technological devices (such as head-mounted display and data-gloves) ("virtual reality" environments).

In sum, the medium that allows for the fruition of a virtual world can vary, but in any case, each medium necessitates the active use of the imagination. The definition of virtual worlds adopted in this chapter is grounded in a rejection of the Platonic distinction between the actual world of simulacra and the Empyrean world of "Ideas." Two interpretations, which both reject this Platonic distinction, are of particular interest in relation to this chapter's exploration of virtual worlds. The first is Jeff Malpas's argument (2008) that the virtual is "nonautonomous"; rather it depends on the "nonvirtual" (the everyday). Malpas notes that the virtual depends on the everyday both causally (i.e., it depends on an infrastructure—for instance, on equipment—and on socioeconomic and sociocultural processes existing in the everyday world) and content-wise (i.e., its narratives, significance, and meanings always depend "on the everyday world in which the virtual is embedded"). Malpas's point is valid for predigital and digital virtual worlds: a book, a painting, stage scenery, a DVD reader, a PC are all forms of equipment; the voice of a storyteller or the gestures of an actor are also "material supports" that allow for the communication within a virtual world. In sum, the virtual is nonautonomous but "embedded within" (and extending) everyday reality. However, Malpas adds that the virtual is just a part or aspect of the everyday world; hence, there are not two worlds, but "the one world," of which the virtual is a part. Malpas further notes that the virtual is constructed or "fictional," as well as real—it is at once dependent and effective on the everyday.

Doel and Clarke (1999, 279) examine different conceptions of the relationship between virtuality and conclude (mainly drawing on and discussing Deleuze) that the virtual and the real are not separable, either by imagining the virtual as a false approximation of reality (a mere simulation) or as a resolution, a hyperrealization of the real (as the actualization of infinite potential). Reality cannot be reduced to actuality: "The real is always already virtual" that is, "disadjusted and untimely" and reality is "the immanent twofold of actuality-virtuality." Doel and Clarke manage to capture the dialectical aspect of the actual/virtual dynamic to a greater extent than Malpas, and show how the virtual is at once dependent on and effective on reality. Nonetheless, Malpas's work also offers some practical means to understand virtual worlds. Both interpretations of virtuality show that virtual worlds can be useful, as they both imply that these are not futile creations, but are integral to the construction of culture. The key point, in my view, is that the virtual (e.g., utopias) can shape reality (as Malpas would argue), though this fully depends on everyday reality—and that, borrowing on Doel and Clarke's theory, reality itself is the unfolding of the actual (e.g., everyday reality) and the virtual (e.g., how utopias affect the everyday).

This chapter will show that these two perspectives can both offer useful elements to read predigital and digital virtual worlds. The survey of virtual worlds will be, by necessity, selective and limited to significant examples, rather than exhaustive. Also, even if extra-European literary and religious traditions, not to mention figurative arts, offer an impressive wealth of imaginary worlds—which are described in ways substantially *analogous* to those adopted in the West—this survey focuses mostly on Western traditions describing virtual worlds because digital virtual worlds seem to bear (so far) a strong (though by no means exclusive) Western mark. Hence, it is likely that the ideas inspiring their creators have been drawn principally from Western traditions.[1]

MYTHS AND VIRTUAL WORLDS, OR WHAT ARE VIRTUAL WORLDS FOR?

Different academic schools define myth in different ways. However, if we look at the key ideas in their theories, we see that each school or scholar has highlighted specific aspects of the complex reality described by the term "myth" and that different theories are not fully mutually exclusive. First, we can say that myths are "traditional tales," a definition by Jan Bremmer (1990) that points to the narrative structure of myth (i.e., there is a plot) and to its being *traditum*—that is, transmitted through the years. Several scholars have shown that myths are stories dealing with issues such as the shaping of the cosmos, the birth of the gods, and of humankind, the destruction of monsters menacing the existence of the cosmos, the foundation of mortality, material (techniques), and "moral" human culture (e.g., institutions, rules of conduct, good/evil); that is, concerned with all the issues that are important for a society (Eliade 1963, 5–6; Brelich 1958). Myths express and shape a society's symbolic order, which justifies a culture's activities and structure—and a culture is thought of as the result of the actions that take place in myths (Dumézil 1968–1971; Brelich 1958; Vernant 1983). Hence, they are not "neutral" stories, since they express and give form to power relations by establishing structures and systems of oppositions and similarities according to class—and the function of each class in society (Dumézil 1968–1971)—and gender (Christ 1982, 72–78). Myths indeed describe other-worlds: mythic space is intrinsically different from that of everyday life (for example, it is a desert); time is different (myths are either set in a different time or time is different there); it is located far away; it is inhabited by strange creatures (gods, monsters, heroes) and prodigies occur there; and it is the opposite or reversal of the real world, though in several cases differences are minimal (Jouan and Deforge 1988). Table 5.1 shows how these five aspects are found in the mythic spaces described in the Mesopotamian epic cycle of Gilgamesh and in the Greek *Odyssey*.

Table 5.1 Virtual Worlds (Mythic Spaces) in the Gilgamesh Cycle and the *Odyssey*

	Mythic space	Location	Inhabitants	Peculiarities	Source
			Gilgamesh Cycle		
Divine space	Masu mountain	Faraway Twin peaks	The Scorpion men and women, Guardians of Masu mountain	Scorpion men and Scorpion women are sage half-human, half-dragon beings No light	Tablet 9
Divine space	Land of Dilmun	Across the Ocean There transits the Sun.	Utnapishti and his wife	Deathless land Utnapishti is the builder of the ark and guards the secret of immortality.	Tablets 10–11
Divine space	Garden of the Gods	Distant Desert	No human inhabitants	Fruits and leaves made of precious stones	Tablet 9
			Odyssey		
Divine space	Aeolia (Aeolus's island)	Somewhere in the Mediterranean Sea	Aeolus, King of Winds His family	Aeolus's twelve sons married to his twelve daughters Perennial banquets Floating island surrounded by bronze wall	Odyssey 10.1–76
Divine space	Aiaie (Circe's island)	Somewhere in the Mediterranean Sea	Circe Thea (= goddess), daughter of the god Helios, the sun, and a daughter of Oceanus Magician who prepares evil potions, weaves immortal cloth Four nymphs (daughters of rivers) serve her.	No farmlands and no smoke (= no human beings) Magic Oak trees Deer House built with polished stones The god Hermes her guest	Odyssey 10.133–487

(Continued)

Table 5.1 (Continued)

	Mythic space	Location	Inhabitants	Peculiarities	Source
Divine space	Hades	In the north across Oceanus where rivers cross	The Dead	The Dead have no memory till they drink blood.	Odyssey 10.508; 11.13
Divine space	Thrinachia (Sun's cattle island)	Island near Scylla and Charybdis	Herds of immortal cows The nymphs Phaetusa and Lampetie, daughters of Helios (guardians of the cattle)	No human beings	Odyssey 12.129–131
Divine space	Ogygie (Calypso's island)	Island across the sea, near the end of the world	Calypso (nymph, daughter of Atlas)	Cave Garden No cities, no signs of human presence	Odyssey 5.101–102
Divine space	Land of the Lotus-eaters	Unknown (thought to be Libya)	Lotophagi (Lotus-eaters)	Eat flowery foods Live in a perennial lotus-induced contentment No pain, no anxiety, no memory	Odyssey 9.84–99
Inhospitable space	Island of the Cyclopes	Somewhere in the Mediterranean Sea	The Cyclopes (giants with one eye)	Athemistoi (= do not respect the divine law) Inhospitable No laws, no assembly Live in caves No farmlands and no smoke (= no human presence) Wheat, barley, vines grow spontaneously No ships	Odyssey 9.106–540

Inhospitable space	Lamos Telepylos	Somewhere in the Mediterranean Sea Palace of the king	The Laestrygonians	Days last 24 hours Man-eating giants No farmlands and no smoke (= no human presence)	*Odyssey* 10.81–132
Inhospitable space	Land of the Cimmerians	At the borders of the river Oceanus	The Cimmerians	"Unhappy" Mist and clouds No sun	*Odyssey* 1.14–19
Inhospitable space	Sirens' island	Unknown island	Sirens	Sirens Monsters Charming singers	*Odyssey* 11.70–72
Inhospitable space	Charybdis	Faces Scylla	Charybdis	The whirlpool Charybdis is "*dia*" (divine), terrible	*Odyssey* 12.235–243
Inhospitable space	Scylla	Faces Charybdis	Scylla	Scylla: immortal, 'wild, monster with 6 arms	*Odyssey* 12.245–250
Ideal space	Scheria	Unknown island	The Phaeacians	Descend from giants Cyclopes their kin "Close" to the gods, who meet with the Phaeacians Prodigious self-directing ships Fertile soil	*Odyssey* 6.4

Those who are said to have reached mythic spaces were said to do this by travel, dream, vision, by some inexplicable accident, or by crossing a threshold (Bittarello 2008). In some cases, mythic spaces are invisible, which suggests the existence of multidimensional realities that can be accessed through various means; in this case, the visible and the invisible appear to be more closely intertwined (Bittarello 2008). Some examples are the ghost's space, which is not normally visible, or the enchanted islands and "fairylands" in European traditions, which are always "out there," but can be visible only under special circumstances.

In 1999 Childress attempted to draw (from a deep psychology perspective) a comparison between a mythic space (the Celtic other-world) and early descriptions of the Internet, noting that both were presented as being outside normal space and time, populated by disembodied beings, full of wonders, and with both monsters/horrors and beauty. Indeed, new technological media have often been described as "new space"; Flichy's 2007 study shows that several actors, with specific agendas, have described a communication tool such as the Internet as a new virtual space. This new space has therefore been presented as a sacred, as a mythic, or as a religious space (Bittarello 2008; 2009a). Once a communication tool (the Internet) is conceptualized as a virtual space, it can also be imagined as a self-contained virtual-world hosting an (infinite) number of virtual places (Bittarello 2009a).

But why is this comparison between mythic space and virtual worlds (digital and predigital) relevant? The reason is that across the ages mythic spaces and imaginary worlds—those imagined as distant as well as those believed to be coexisting with everyday life—have had a variety of functions, for example by constituting the other through constructing distorted images of one's society (us versus them), as we shall see in this chapter. Imaginary worlds can be used to control possible subversion and eradication of the dominant social order and establish one society's identity in favor of one or more dominant groups; but they can also serve to play the opposite function: to express the longing for alternatives. Finally, virtual worlds can also be used to experiment with social roles and with identities, though ancient myths, shared by the whole society, have a function quite different from contemporary virtual worlds, which are frequented today only by a limited portion of the populace.

The Ancient World

In the literature and religions of the ancient world we find two ways of constructing virtual worlds. The first way seems to be consistent with Malpas's interpretation of the virtual; the second has analogies with Doel and Clarke's reading of virtuality. On the one hand, we find descriptions of either paradisiacal places, usually located far away in space or time, and sometimes inhabited by the deserving dead, or scary places where either monsters or the dead reside. On the other hand, we find descriptions of real places located in the known world whose customs are, however, portrayed as peculiar (either as extraordinarily perfect or extraordinarily savage, or as the reversal of customs presented as "normal").

Paradisiacal Lands and the Nether World

Besides the paradisiacal, unreachable lands listed in table 5.1—such as the land of Dilmun, the land of the Phaeacians, or Circe's and Calypso's islands—many other examples taken from the literature of the ancient world can be found. The ancient Near East knew of places rich in forests, exotic animals, and desirable goods, such as the fabulous Land of Punt of the Egyptians, and of temporal utopias such as the original dwelling place of humankind, the Garden of Eden, a plentiful place where the desired but dangerous trees of knowledge of good and evil and the tree of life grow (Genesis 2:8), or the New Testament's imagination of the New Jerusalem (Apocalypse 21). Greek myths describe a number of wonderful, happy places all located far away and inhabited by gods and goddesses, such as Olympus, the Garden of the Hesperides, and the land of the Hyperboreans, as well as utopian places imagined as existing in a remote past, such as the Golden Age, or the island of Atlantis invented by Plato (table 5.2). Some European traditions also describe the happy places inhabited by the deserving dead, from the Greek Elysion island, which the Romans either identified with the Islands of the Blessed and the Western Fortunate islands (table 5.2), or located in the Underworld (Ogden 2002, 146–172), to the Germanic Valhöll/Walhalla, where the souls of dead warriors dwell. Though apparently attractive, these places are dangerous and disturbing in various respects—for example, the inhabitants are either the gods, the dead, monsters, or heroes. Although these ideal worlds are located in a separate space beyond the reach of normal human beings, they do not dramatically differ from the cultures that imagined them—for example, the Greek gods use objects similar to those used by human beings but made of gold.

The ancient world also imagined the existence of several inhospitable and scary places where the dead and/or monsters reside; these places too are located at a remote distance, for example, somewhere west of the Nile Valley for the Egyptians, or in the underworld for the Mesopotamian culture. In the *Odyssey*, the dead (evanescent and deprived of memory) reside in the Land of the Dead, situated at the farthest limits of the earth (table 5.1), whereas in Hesiod the dead share the Underworld with the older generation of gods and with monsters like Cerberus (table 5.2). A similar idea (i.e., that of virtual worlds existing in this space but in places not normally inhabited by human beings) is also found in different cultural contexts. For example, Japanese traditions describe the ocean, the sky, or the top of mountains as the dwelling place of the dead and of supernatural beings (Bonnefoy and Doniger 1989, 25–28).

In all the examples examined, the lack of autonomy and the constructed nature of virtual worlds is evident—they are presented as wholly detached from the everyday world—that is, as being part of a different reality—but they depend, content-wise, entirely on the socioeconomic and cultural reality that produced them. Nonetheless, they have effects on the everyday, as Malpas argued for online virtual worlds, since, for example, they can orient cultic practices, political actions, and behaviors.

Table 5.2 Examples of Virtual Worlds (Mythic Spaces) in the Greek and Roman World

Mythic Space	Location	Features	Inhabitants	Main Sources
Atlantis	Island destroyed by earthquakes in ancient times	Earthly paradise	Descendants of Poseidon destroyed by the gods because of their arrogance	Plato, *Critias*, *Timaeus*
Land of the Hyperboreans	Unreachable land Fertile northern island	Mild climate Close association with Apollo	Pious No sickness, neither old age nor toil nor warfare Peculiar rites and temples Imaginary people	Herodotus Pindar *Pythica* 10 Pausanias Diodorus Siculus
Golden Age	The earth before Zeus became king of the gods	Earthly paradise No toil, no pain, no old age	Heroic races	Hesiod, *Erga*
Fortunate Isles (Islands of the Blessed)	Island in the Western Ocean near river Oceanus Ends of Libya	Salubrious air Fruits and birds of all kinds	Later identified with the dwelling place of the deserving Dead	Plutarch, *Sertorius* Pliny, *Naturalis Historia*
Elysium	Island in the West	Earthly paradise	Deserving souls of heroes	Homer, *Odyssey* Virgil, *Aeneid*
Garden of the Hesperides	At earth's farthest limits, across the stream of Oceanus (Hesiod) Far (Ovid) Near the limit of the Sky	Streams flow with ambrosia. Earth yields to the gods trees with golden boughs, leaves, and apples Fruit-bearing orchards	The three nymphs Hesperides	Hesiod, *Theogony* Euripides,*Hippolytus* Apollonius, *Argonautica* Ovid, *Metamorphoses*
Olympus	Dwelling place of the Greek deities	Beautiful palaces made in precious metals, especially gold Mechanical servants	Gods and goddesses	Homer, *Iliad* Virgil, *Aeneid*
Tartarus (the Underworld)	Below the earth		Titans, Hecatoncheires (one-hundred hands giants), Night, her daughter Day, and her sons Morpheus (Sleep) and Thanatos (Death)	Hesiod, *Theogony*
House of Hades (in Tartarus)	In Tartarus		Monstrous dog Cerberus, Styx, the goddess invoked by the immortals when they pronounce an oath The dead	Hesiod, *Theogony*

The Construction of Otherness

The second way of imagining a virtual world was the construction of a virtual image of real peoples and places both in myths (e.g. the *Iliad* describes the Trojans as "others"; the peoples met by Odysseus are also presented as "others"—see table 5.1) and in ethnographic accounts. Even apparently neutral portrayals of other peoples had the function of transforming their customs into the reversal of the Greek way of life (Hartog 1988). Both the Greeks and the Romans (from Herodotus to Caesar and Tacitus) constructed virtual images of real peoples, portrayals that were neither faithful accounts of these countries' realities nor entirely an invention, but rather created a virtual Egypt, Scythia, or Babylonia, giving a biased interpretation of the history, geography, religion, and customs of these countries.[2]

Transforming a real place into an imaginary space, into a virtual world, had effects on the actuality of the Greek and Roman world—the rejection of possible alternatives (i.e., of the virtual images of other countries) established the actual reality of the Greek world. Eastern traditions also adopted the strategy of describing foreign countries as "spaces of otherness": for instance, Hindu traditions described Tibet as a magic land, inhabited by demons, as well as a paradisiacal land; Arab and Persian stories (e.g., in *The Thousand and One Nights*) describe real places as exotic imaginary worlds visited by supernatural beings such as the jinn.

Alternative Realities on Stage and Visual Representation of Virtual Worlds

The ancient Greek and Roman literary texts evoked imaginary worlds. On stage, virtual worlds were made visible and literally brought into the real world through the use of a series of devices (exotic robes, high-heeled shoes, and voice-altering masks) and "special effects" (such as machines that brought the gods on stage). Such devices served to materialize alien, supernatural worlds. Otherness could also be portrayed, as in the Old Athenian Comedy—which aimed to show that when human beings behave in a grotesque, animal-like, subhuman way, the consequences for society are devastating (Brelich 1965)—by staging extravagant characters (including distorted images of the gods), situations impossible in the real world, and paradoxical reversals of the Athenian reality (table 5.3).

Virtual worlds were made visible not only on stage, but also through visual representation. A great number of paintings, frescoes, and mosaics portray imaginary spaces and often imaginary characters located in imaginary spaces. Some of the examples range from painted vases and frescoes in Hellenistic palaces and in the imperial palaces on the Palatine Hill and in the Domus Aurea, to the mosaics and statues of monsters, heroes, and imaginary creatures found all over the eastern Mediterranean lands and the Roman Empire in public edifices and in a number of countryside residences.

Table 5.3 Old Athenian Comedy: Aristophanes (5th Century BCE)

Aristophanes

Play	Location	Story
The Acharnians	Athens	An Athenian citizen makes a separate peace with Sparta.
The Birds	Athens Nephelokokkygia	New gods are created in the image of birds.
The Clouds	Athens	Satire of Socrates and his teachings
The Frogs	The Underworld	Dionysus tries to bring Euripides back from the underworld
The Knights	Athens	Political attack on the demagogue Cleon
Thesmophoriazusae	Athens—temple	Women want to punish Euripides because of his misogyny.
The Wasps	Athens	The demagogue Cleon divides the older and younger generations.
Lysistrata	Athens	Women manage to end the war with Sparta.
Ecclesiazusae	Athens	Athenian women change the constitution and the structure of Athenian society.
Plutus	Delphic oracle Athens	When the blind god of wealth, Plutus, regains the use of his eyes, prosperity and equity dominate the earth.
Peace	Athens Olympus	An Athenian countryman reaches Olympus and manages to end the war with Sparta by freeing the goddess Peace.

Alterity in Everyday Life: A World Full of . . .

For the civilizations of the ancient world, the world was "full of gods" (any river, tree, cave, mountain was thought to be inhabited by divine beings), of nightly dangerous supernatural creatures, and of portents all considered part of the natural world not as a separate realm (Felton 1999). There was also a belief that the souls of those whose death had been untimely or violent, or who had not received proper final honors remained nearby their bodies or gravitated near the place where they had died until certain conditions had been fulfilled by those left behind (Ogden 2002, 146–152). The reality normally experienced by human beings could come into contact with the coexisting and unseen nonhuman realities through appropriate channels. Dreaming was considered the normal channel through which the living could encounter the dead, but on some occasions human beings could also come into direct contact with ghosts and divine beings through rituals of various kinds, oracles, visions, illnesses, possession, and prodigies (Ogden 2002). In other words, the ancient world had developed the idea of an always present but invisible dimension, which could be accessed through appropriate means. This was a concept developed also in other cultural contexts—for example, the souls of Siberian shamans were thought to travel to intercommunicating worlds whose topography could be drawn on a map (Bonnefoy and Doniger 1989, 1731). For the Greeks this invisible dimension could at any time break into everyday reality, with terrifying consequences for those involved. In terms of virtuality, we find here the idea that the (invisible) virtual world is as real as the visible "real" one. Also, the virtual world is not parallel to the visible world, but *coexisting* in the same space: both are just one world. The invisible world has tangible effects on the real world. There is here a reversal of Malpas's point about the dependence of the virtual on the real, since, in this case, the visible reality depends on the invisible reality (e.g., on the divine immanent powers in nature).

The Middle Ages: From Fairies and Ghosts to Meditative Imagination

In the medieval age, virtual worlds could be imagined as separate unreachable spaces; real spaces of otherness; transcendental realms; invisible parallel worlds coexisting with the visible reality; and virtual worlds of imagination.

Into the first group (unreachable, separate—or past—spaces, either paradisiacal or not) fall stories of the Islands of the Blessed, Celtic tales of fairylands (in the Welsh *Mabinogi*, and the Irish cycles of Cu-Chulainn and the Fianna), and of many magical places such as Avalon in the Round Table romances and references to the snowy land of the giants in Norse sagas and to lands inhabited by monsters and dragons (*Beowulf*; *Nibelungenlied*).

Accounts of travels to faraway lands construct, instead, imaginary worlds along the classical tradition of the marginalization of the periphery of the world (as in Marco Polo's description of the otherness of customs of the Far Eastern countries he visited).

Accounts of journeys by living persons to the transcendental realms of heaven, hell, and purgatory, imagined as existing in separate spaces linked to *this* world, characterize medieval Christian traditions that claimed that these places could either be entered by visiting specific locations in *this* world (Walters Adams 2007, 45), or in vision, or in mysterious ways (as in the case of Dante's travel to the other world).

The idea of an alternative and generally invisible reality that coexists with the reality of everyday life is found in both medieval romances and ghost stories. Medieval romances, a literary genre based on popular traditions about visits to fairyland, but specifically aimed at the aristocratic elites, frequently describe the realm of fairies imagined as a parallel world where time has no meaning and whose inhabitants interact, on occasion, with human beings. The Christian medieval age inherited the belief in ghosts who inhabit the world of the living from both Greco-Roman culture (with its idea of the ghost as "image") and the ancient Germanic cultures (who believed in the ghost's corporeality [Schmitt 1998, 26]). These two sets of ideas coexisted, so that ghosts, as well as angels and demons, could be seen in visions or dreams, but could also be met face to face.

An element of novelty in the conception of virtual worlds is found in Margery Kempe's visionary pilgrimages to the world of the biblical past. By means of meditative imagination, which was based on a peculiar theological elaboration of the followers of Saint Bonaventure, Margery imagined herself as a character in the New Testament, "virtually" *entering* into the story, and interacting with the biblical characters (Walters Adams 2007, 48).

THE MODERN AGE

Shakespeare's Two Varieties of Virtual Worlds

Two types of imaginary worlds can be identified in Shakespeare's tragedies and comedies: a world of fairies, spirits, and magic, which is described as coexisting and occasionally overlapping with the reality experienced by human beings; and a world of reversal, deception, and excess comparable to the worlds of the Old Athenian Comedy and to the heroic myths developed in Greek tragedies.

As table 5.4 illustrates, though the invisible world of magic, spirits, witches, and ghosts features in several plays, in three of them it takes center stage. In *A Midsummer Night's Dream*, the world of the fairies coexists with the world inhabited by the ancient Athenians. In the play, nighttime, dreams, and wild (nonurban) spaces are the domain of fairies, who enjoy altering the course of human existence by using magic herbs and spells. Shakespeare's fairies can shrink and change dimension at will (an aspect reminiscent of the popular fairy-lore on the "little people" of Celtic traditions) and possess magical powers. What is more, their actions lead to a disruption of the cosmic order on earth, alter the right course of seasons, and influence the fertility of the soil and of cattle. In *Macbeth*, ancient Scotland is portrayed as a country haunted by witches, ghosts, and devils who actively shape the course of events. *The Tempest* takes place on an unnamed island in the Mediterranean Sea where the magician Prospero holds sway over ethereal spirits and nymphs and uses their powers to shape reality at will. In the three plays, the visible (human) reality depends on the coexisting invisible (nonhuman) reality, but the invisible supernatural reality is experienced as dream, which yet again reaffirms the reality of the visible world.

As Gillies (1994) has shown, Shakespeare adopts the same strategies as ancient writers in describing real places as imaginary worlds, by ascribing to real spaces different customs and a dramatic reversal of his own society's rules. Three main themes run throughout the tragedies and comedies: deception; subversion of society's rules; and excess.[3] This functions as a reinforcement of Elizabethan England as the only valid (and possible) actual reality. It is not surprising that such strategic positioning is also adopted

Table 5.4 Virtual Worlds (Mythic Spaces) in Shakespeare

	Events/characters	Space	Continent	Play
Supernatural	Fairies	Athens	Europe	*A Midsummer Night's Dream*
	Spirits	Britain (pre-Christian)	Europe	*King Lear*
	Apparitions Jupiter	Britain (time of Augustus)	Europe	*Cymbeline*
	Spirits Magic	Prospero's island	Europe	*The Tempest*
	Witches, Hecate, devils Prophecies Ghosts	Royal palace of Forres, Inverness, Fife, Dunsinane (Scotland) England (time of the Saxons)	Europe	*Macbeth*
	Ghost	Philippi (Epyrus)	Europe	*Julius Caesar*
	Ghost	Elsinore (Denmark)	Europe	*Hamlet*
	(False) Ghost of the hunter	England (reign of Henry V)	Europe	*The Merry Wives of Windsor*
	Dead brought back to life	Ephesus	Asia	*Pericles*
	Prophecy (letter G dangerous for Edward IV) The ghosts of the victims of Richard III	Britain (Wars of the Roses)	Europe	*Richard III*
	Prophecy: Richmond's destiny	Britain (Wars of the Roses)	Europe	*Henry VI*
	Prophecy: death in Jerusalem of Henry IV	Britain (Wars of the Roses)	Europe	*Henry IV*
	Witchcraft and demons (Eleanor Cobham and Joan of Arc)	Britain (Wars of the Roses)	Europe	*Henry VI*
	Owen Glendower conjures up spirits and demons from the abyss. He is deceived and destroyed by his superhuman allies.	Britain (Wars of the Roses)	Europe	*Henry IV*

(Continued)

Table 5.4 (Continued)

	Events/characters	Space	Continent	Play
Deception	False death Substitution Deception of lover	Florence (Italy)	Europe	*All's Well That Ends Well*
	Lover's deception	Troy	Asia	*Troilus and Cressida*
	Physical appearance deceptive	Ephesus	Asia	*The Comedy of Errors*
	Perjury	Milan (Italy)	Europe	*The Two Gentlemen of Verona*
	False deaths Lover's deception	Messina in Sicily (Italy)	Europe	*The Winter's Tale* *Much Ado about Nothing*
	Deception False stories	Britain (reign of Henry V)	Europe	*The Merry Wives of Windsor*
Subversion of rules	Subversion of gender, rank, family values	Forest of Arden (France)	Europe	*As You Like It*
	Subversion of rank	Paris, Marseilles, Roussillon (France)	Europe	*All's Well That Ends Well*
	Subversion of rank ignorance of the world (*Cymbeline*, III, 3)	Wales	Europe	*Cymbeline*
	Subversion of family relationships	Britain (pre-Christian)	Europe	*King Lear*
	Temporary subversion of gender and rank	Royal residence in Navarre	Europe	*Love's Labour's Lost*
	Rank swap	Bohemia	Europe	*The Winter's Tale*
	Women's disobedience to men's rule	Padua (Italy)	Europe	*Taming of the Shrew*
	Gender swap	Illyria	Europe	*Twelfth Night*
	Courtesy ignores rank distinction	Pentapolis	Asia	*Pericles*
	Refuge for bandits Plague	Mantua (Italy)	Europe	*The Two Gentlemen of Verona* *Romeo and Juliet*
	Intelligence vs rules and laws	Venice (Italy)	Europe	*The Merchant of Venice* *Othello*

(Continued)

Table 5.4 (Continued)

	Events/characters	Space	Continent	Play
Excess	Corruption	Vienna	Europe	*Measure for Measure*
	Corruption, ingratitude, reversal of moral law	Athens	Europe	*Timon of Athens*
	Incest	Antioch	Asia	*Pericles*
	Ingratitude, cruelty	Tarsus	Asia	*Pericles*
	Lust	Mytilene	Asia	*Pericles*
	Luxury	Egypt	Africa	*Antony and Cleopatra*
	Folly	Britain (pre-Christian)	Europe	*King Lear*
	Unrestrained passions Violence Inconstancy	Verona (Italy)	Europe	*Romeo and Juliet* *The Two Gentlemen of Verona*
	Violence Civil wars Romans attacking Rome Inhuman space	(Ancient) Rome (Italy)	Europe	*Coriolanus* *Julius Caesar* *Antony and Cleopatra* *Titus Andronicus*

by the *Journey to the West*, a masterpiece of Chinese literature, probably written in the sixteenth century, which describes the lands to the west of China, especially India, as fabulous lands, full of prodigies and heroic characters.

Utopian and Satirical Writings

Throughout the Middle Ages and the Renaissance, imaginary worlds were constructed by drawing on either the literature of the ancient world, medieval sagas, and romances, or the Christian heaven, hell, and purgatory. For example, Ludovico Ariosto's *Orlando Furioso* revisited the world of Charlemagne and his knights, enriching the story with marvels, magic, fantastic creatures, and imaginary spaces such as the Moon, which is described as an immense lost-and-found office of mostly immaterial things (such as Astolfo's and Orlando's wisdom). The "sacred wood," built in the sixteenth century at Bomarzo (Viterbo, Italy), with its sculptures of dragons and giants, exemplifies the late Renaissance aristocratic wish to bring to life other-worlds not only in literature, but also in art.

Utopian writers such as Thomas More (*Utopia*), Tommaso Campanella (*City of the Sun*), and, later, Francis Bacon (*New Atlantis*) created ideal cities in the tradition of Plato's ideal *Republic*. The literary, elitist, and immensely successful utopia of Arcadia, introduced by the courtier poet Philip Sidney (*Old Arcadia*, 1580), who drew on Jacopo Sannazaro's *Arcadia* (1504), idealized pastoral life. Extraordinary wealth characterized the golden cities, such as Eldorado, that attracted the European colonizers of the Americas. The popular imagination drew, instead, on ancient traditions about a Golden Age free of labor and characterized by a hedonistic license to imagine the proverbial land of Cokaygne, an idea that still survives, with considerable adaptations, in the imagination of the dispossessed (for example, in the North American ballad "Big Rock Candy Mountain"). Similarly, the Tibetan "Pure Land" of Shambhala, an imaginary happy kingdom in Central Asia, which later contributed to the literary construction of Shangri-la, is thought to be hidden somewhere in this world.

Often writers who describe imaginary worlds have a parodic or satirical intent and aim at criticizing the present by emphasizing exaggerated behaviors. In this tradition, which marks a progressive distancing from the sense of wonder that characterized previous ages, can be found, for example, François Rabelais's *Gargantua and Pantagruel* and, later, Johnathan Swift's *Gulliver's Travels* and Voltaire's *Micromegas* (1752) and *Candide* (1759)—in these cases, as in utopian writing, creating virtual worlds aimed at modifying the present.

Ghost Stories, Science Fiction, and Fantasy

The Victorian age did not conceive the supernatural itself in terms of other-world; rather, the supernatural was considered a natural phenomenon to be studied and understood. In Victorian ghost stories, the invisible reality is interconnected and often overlaps with the actual reality of everyday life. For example, in Henry James's short story "The Others," the two realities (of the living and of the ghosts) are parallel but connected through peculiar (technical) tools (the medium's table and the medium's body) that can provoke the sudden disappearance of the tenuous barrier between realities. Victorian scientists developed this idea of parallel but interconnected spaces; for example, the notion of a fourth dimension as a "place, or demarcated region of space," which started to be formulated at the time, is directly linked to the twentieth-century conceptualization of the spaces of information (Connor 2004, 270). Genre literature, in particular science fiction and fantasy, follows on and develops the two main conceptions outlined so far (separate/coexisting). The imaginary worlds of science fiction can be located in an unexplored section of planet Earth, on other planets, as well as in the past or in the future, and can be reached by means of sophisticated technologies, such as spaceships and transporters. The possibility of the existence of multiple dimensions, of parallel worlds and intercommunicating realities, likewise to be reached through a variety of complex tools, is also explored (table 5.5).

Table 5.5 Examples of Virtual Worlds in Science Fiction

	Text	Space
VW as separate spaces	Arthur Conan Doyle, *The Lost World*	Unknown space on the earth
	A. Van Vogt, *The Voyage of the Space Beagle*	Interstellar space
VW as past/future realities	H. G. Wells, *The Time Machine*	The earth in the future
	Isaac Asimov, *The End of Eternity* (1955)	Out of time space
VW as coexisting realities	Jack Williamson, *Wolves of Darkness* (1932)	Parallel dimension
	Murray Leinster, *Sidewise in Time* (1934)	Alternate realities
	Frederic Brown, *What Mad Universe* (1948)	Infinite coexisting realities
	Isaac Asimov, *The Gods Themselves* (1972)	Parallel dimension

Table 5.6 Examples of Virtual Worlds in the Fantasy Genre

	Text	Space
VW as separate spaces (on this plane of reality)	Ryder Haggard, *King Solomon's mines* (1892); *She* (1896)	Remote African places
	James Barrie, *Peter Pan* (1904)	Neverland (island far away)
VW aspast/future realities	J. R. R. Tolkien, *The Lord of the Rings* (1954–55)	Middle Earth
	Robert E. Howard, *Conan the Barbarian* (1935)	Imaginary prehistory
	Mark Twain, *A Connecticut Yankee in King Arthur's Court* (1889)	Imaginary earth space (and temporal paradox)
	Marion Zimmer Bradley, *The Mists of Avalon* (1983)	Imaginary matriarchal past
	Terry Brooks, *The Sword of Shannara* (1977)	Future earth
VW as coexisting realities (parallel universes or invisible dimensions)	C. S. Lewis, *Chronicles of Narnia* (1950–1956)	Narnia (parallel world)
	Michael Ende, *The Never ending Story* (1979)	Parallel universe

According to Timmerman (1983, 48–54), fantasy other-worlds are not dreamworlds, neither are they escapist worlds, since these other-worlds focus on fears, choices, dilemmas, and truths proper to the human condition. Fantasy worlds must have internal consistency—that is, they have to be fully fledged imaginary worlds—and are usually connoted by magic or by peculiar customs, often inspired by elements of medieval age stories and sagas, or by an imagined prehistory (table 5.6).

Baroque and Neobaroque: Calderón, Borges, and Calvino

The baroque marked a fundamental turning point in the way the virtual is conceived, by developing the idea that life is a dream. According to Egginton (2009, 85), the baroque drama of Calderón de la Barca, entitled *Life Is a Dream*, did not question the existence of the real, but rather our ability to gain concrete knowledge about the world. In other words, it questioned the reality of the real. Developing Egginton's point further in relation to virtuality, we can conclude that the alternate dimension could—at any moment—turn out to be *this* world, the one we experience daily. This intuition was reshaped and developed in the twentieth century, by writers such as Borges and Calvino. Egginton (2009, 94) compares Calderón's strategy with Borges's idea of the "dreamlike" nature of the world. For Borges, "we have dreamt the world" and there is no escape out of the dream because the base reality is yet another dream. Whereas the baroque did not deny the existence of a reality (that we can never know), in Borges's (neobaroque) conception, deciphering the code, the structure of reality, would be to destroy the world—the dream can have no end.

Borges's work had a remarkable influence on Italo Calvino, whose rewriting of canonical texts (such as *il Milione*, Ariosto's *Orlando Furioso*, and More's *Utopia*) involves a recreation/rewriting of the imaginary worlds described or alluded to in those works. Calvino's imaginary cities are *Invisible Cities* (1972); they could hardly be "seen," as they are mere signs on a map. These cities are constructed/made up/formed by the "words" (and "gestures") of Marco Polo. In a way, both Borges (for example in *The Library of Babel*) and Calvino come close to comparing language (and communication) to the spaces it creates. Hence from the point of view of digital virtual worlds, their work alludes to contemporary metaphorical conceptualizations of new media as spaces. Calvino, a self-reflexive writer influenced by structuralist and poststructuralist theories in works such as *If on a Winter's Night a Traveler* (1979), also takes to extremes the Chinese box game that characterizes most literary works dealings with virtual worlds. In many of the works examined so far we have seen imaginary characters living in the central fictive world enter other imaginary worlds. The journeys of Odysseus throughout a series of imaginary lands, Astolfo's visit to the Moon in *Orlando Furioso*, and the *Never ending Story* (table 5.6) require of readers a double immersion into other realities, as they propose a series of worlds within worlds that implicitly question the reality of the world experienced by the reader. This theme is a favorite in contemporary cinema, with examples as different as *The Icicle Thief* (1989), *eXistenZ* (1999), and *Pleasantville* (1998).

MYTHOLOGIES OF DIGITAL
VIRTUAL WORLDS

This section examines first the path of development of digital virtual worlds, and then compares historical virtual worlds and contemporary digital virtual worlds, in order to highlight any similarity and any difference. Digital virtual worlds started with the introduction of the first MUD (Multi User Dungeon), a text-based (interactive) chat. MUD textual virtual worlds were a translation into electronic form of popular fantasy role-playing games and text-based adventures (Stam and Scialdone 2008; Calleja 2008). MUDs required of users a shared mental visualization of the room's inhabitants (Calleja 2008, 18); thus they are comparable to virtual worlds in books. The second step in the development of digital virtual worlds was the introduction, in 1996, of visual aspects, in the MMORPGs (massively multiplayer online role-playing games) *Meridian 59* (Stam and Scialdone 2008). MMORPGs are interactive and use text-based windows for communication; because of the addition of visual aspects and the introduction of the avatar, initially a 2D cartoon-like character representing the user in the virtual world, MMORPGs are comparable to both videogames and graphic novels, as well as to the virtual worlds in frescoes and miniatures simulating other space.

The next step was the introduction of 3D virtual worlds. For now, 3D, immersive, holographic worlds or desktop-based "immersive virtual environments" (desktop virtual reality), which need specialized hardware, are still at an experimental stage (Dalgarno 2010, 10). Academic debate on the characteristics of 3D virtual worlds is fervent, with a focus on the attempt to define their main characteristics, which appear to be the chat (sometimes also audio) tools that allow for interaction in the 3D space, the presence of avatars representing users, and the ability of a user to act on the online space (Dalgarno 2010).

At this point, two questions must be answered: The first is, are all the digital virtual worlds available online virtual worlds in the sense used in this chapter? And the second is, what are the novel elements that distinguish digital virtual worlds from predigital virtual worlds?

Calleja, following Klastrup, makes a distinction between "game worlds" (such as *World of Warcraft* or *EverQuest*) and "social virtual worlds," from *Habitat* (1985) and *TinyMUD* (1989), to 3D virtual worlds, such as *Active Worlds* or *Second Life*. We can hardly consider as virtual worlds, in the sense used in this chapter (i.e., an alternative, different space, with internal consistency, and an implicit or an explicit "plot," peculiar features, e.g., abundance, excess, otherness, monsters, magic, which appears as a fully fledged universe), environments devoted to collaborative teamwork online, business websites, and educational environments (although some examples of educational virtual worlds may indeed be included, such as some examples in dos Santos 2009).

Fantasy role-playing games—whether free or commercial—can be considered virtual worlds. The case of videogames is peculiar, as there is a debate on the nature of videogames; scholars discuss whether these are narratives, games, simulation, or interactivity (Miller 2011, 41–43). In this context we should ask: are videogames fully fledged, internally consistent "worlds" rather than focused on the issue of rules, on open-ended situations, and on the presence of complex plots (Miller 2011)? Players engage in simulated play (Miller 2011), but this play takes place in the spatiotemporal-historical context established by the specific videogame. Hence, within this perspective, videogames could be considered virtual worlds.

The same considerations apply to virtual worlds hosted on platforms such as *Habitat* or *Second Life*, insofar as they are conceptualized as spatially localized fully fledged worlds, around which a consistent narrative is constructed that explicitly or implicitly ascribes to them the features of mythic space, and where users pursue the creation of, for example, alternative cultures; these too are fully fledged worlds, with internal consistency and developments. These considerations find support in interpretations of cinematic 3D films as a "genre" more apt to certain spectacular genres, such as fantasy, science fiction, horror, and musical, because it offers the chance to create unreal worlds (Jockenhövel 2011).

It is worth noting that social networks such as Twitter, Facebook, or MySpace, or networks that aim at sharing multimedia materials produced by users (such as YouTube or Flickr) can hardly be considered "virtual worlds."

Although some of these websites may encourage creativity and the learning of basic technological skills by enabling users to easily create multimedia artifacts, this encouragement of creativity hides the bleak reality of the economic exploitation of the users of social networks and their data: without the immaterial (= free) labor of users, no content would be produced, and, thus, there would be no profit for the Web 2.0 business companies (Cohen 2008, 9–10; Turner 2010, 148–149)—a consideration, of course, that is valid also for social virtual worlds and videogames, although exploitation mechanisms may vary. Also, even if, for example, on Facebook, users are creative in the way they present themselves, for example by presenting their Self in the best light, or telling lies about their lives, most users seem to play on variations in the presentation of a monolithic Self—they play with just *one* identity, which is a way of producing a mono-dimensional flattening of offline and online identities and of flattening the complexity of each person's life.

Two connected allegations have been attributed to virtual worlds: the users' lack of critical engagement; and escapism. The fictive worlds of literature and myth may allow for a reflective distancing from one's reality, according to, for instance, Timmerman's (1983) argument that fantasy virtual worlds allow critical distancing or to Rider's (2000, 125) point that medieval other-worlds portrayed in romances allowed the ruling elites to view their own real world "critically." Is critical distancing from one's reality allowed in digital technologies described as virtual worlds? We should go back to the studies on the early mythologization of the Internet and of the World Wide Web as virtual worlds mentioned above. Arguably the dialectical opposition between two ways of imagining virtual worlds is still operative. In social networks like Facebook we can see the inter-communicating realities model, with the invisible online reality intruding into real life, and eroding private space (by eroding any barrier between real and virtual identities). In "game virtual worlds," in religious uses of the Internet (e.g., in interactive virtual temples; see also Geraci, chapter 19 in this volume), and in certain instances of social virtual worlds (for example, those imagining alternative cultures and places), we see the distant and separate other-world model. As for the allegation of escapism, the argument applied by Calleja (2010) to (digital) games can be applied to social virtual worlds. Calleja (2010, 345) shows that playing games should not be seen as an escapist activity "per se," as play-ers engage in the exercise of important skills such as pattern seeking, problem solving, or decision making. Also, recent studies on MMORPGS have shown that game playing is not isolating, but, rather, is a social activity (Stam and Scialdone 2008, 63).

As for the new elements introduced by digital virtual worlds, three outstanding similarities and two key differences emerge from a comparison with the virtual worlds examined in this chapter (which are described as "separate distant spaces" and "inter-connected planes of reality"). The first similarity is that virtual worlds can be accessed through a medium, and this medium is generally (with the possible exception of dreams), a technology. Digital technologies are the latest in a series of technological sup-ports and media that include voice technology (i.e., storytelling uses as a technological support and medium the trained voice of the poet/actor/singer); visual technologies, such as frescoes, miniatures, and paintings, particularly those that use techniques such as "perspective" and trompe l'oeil; stage technologies that combine audio and visual technologies (with the body and voice of the actor and the scenery both bringing to life other-worlds); book technology; radio; and cinema. The second similarity is that both digital and predigital virtual worlds are always located in a space that is never normal (whether because it is not visible, or because time runs differently there, or because cus-toms are different or the rules valid in "normal" space are different). The third similar-ity is that both predigital and digital virtual worlds are immersive, an immersion that requires active engagement and enlarges readers', listeners', viewers', and users' experi-ence: they learn skills and social rules and test one's limits and abilities through play.

The two main differences are the presence of avatars and the strong interactivity allowed to users. Virtual worlds where users are represented by avatars are an example of a digital virtual world that is both a "separate distant space" and an "interconnected plane of reality." The user sitting at a PC and controlling an avatar is at once remote and separate (for example, the avatar stays in the virtual space, even if the user is not sitting in front of a PC) and interconnected (users move their avatar around; these represent them and, as recent studies such as that by Merola and Peña [2010] have pointed out, avatars can even influence the behavior of the user and the reactions of others to the user). Also, the virtual world can be compared to the irruption of other interconnected dimensions into the everyday space of daily life.

In conclusion, this broad outline of virtual worlds from antiquity to the digital age has shown that the main points made by Malpas in relation to digital virtual worlds—such as their being an aspect or part of the real, their being both effective on and dependant on the everyday—are also valid for predigital virtual worlds. The constant interplay between the imagination of other spaces (seen as possibilities) and historical developments (seen as actuality) from Athenian drama, to Shakespeare's plays, to Utopian thinking and genre literature has given a peculiar application of Doel and Clarke's argument that the real is the immanent twofold of actuality and virtuality—in a way, we make sense of actuality through virtuality (or rather, we construct our agreed reality by means of virtuality). In such a context, however, the baroque and neobaroque strategy of questioning the reality of "reality" is the novel element that undermines any theorizing on the duality between virtual and real—if the real is unknowable or virtual, then virtual and real are one and the same.

Notes

1. Digital virtual worlds have been largely developed in the United States and Europe, though Japanese and Korean contributions are not secondary, as emerges from the outline in Calleja 2008. Most companies producing digital virtual worlds platforms are from the United States.

2. For the rich scholarly literature on the construction of foreign lands as imaginary "other" worlds in Greece and Rome and for debates on the issue of "otherness" in the ancient world, see the literature in Bittarello 2009b. The concept of otherness originally developed in classical studies has been successfully applied to modern labeling mechanisms by Said (1978).

3. Sometimes temporal distance establishes the otherness of the place, for example when the action is set in the England of the past (see table 5.4).

References

Bittarello, M. B. 2008. Another Time, Another Space: Virtual Worlds, Myths and Imagination. *Journal of Virtual Worlds Research* 1 (1): 1–10. http://journals.tdl.org/jvwr/article/view/282. Accessed June 14, 2013.

Bittarello, M. B. 2009a. Spatial Metaphors Describing the Internet and Religious Websites: Sacred Space and Sacred Place. *Observatorio (OBS*)* 3 (4): 1–12. http://www.obs.obercom.pt/index.php/obs/article/view/237. Accessed June 14, 2013.

Bittarello, M. B. 2009b. The Construction of Etruscan "Otherness" in Latin Literature. *Greece & Rome* 56 (2): 211–233.

Bonnefoy, Y., and W. Doniger, eds. 1989. *Dizionariodellemitologie e dellereligioni*. Milan: Rizzoli.

Brelich, A. 1958. *Glieroigreci*. Rome: Edizionidell'Ateneo.

Brelich, A. 1965. Aspettireligiosi del drammagreco. *Dioniso* 39: 82–94.

Bremmer, J. 1990. What Is a Greek Myth? In *Interpretations of Greek Mythology*, edited by Jan Bremmer, 1–9. London: Routledge.

Calleja, G. 2008. Virtual Worlds Today: Gaming and Online Sociality. *Online—Heidelberg Journal of Religions on the Internet* 3.1: 7–42. http://www.ub.uni-heidelberg.de/archiv/8288. Accessed June 14, 2013.

Calleja, G. 2010. Digital Games and Escapism. *Games and Culture* 5: 335–353.

Calvino, I. 1997. *Invisible Cities*. Translated by William Weaver. New York: Vintage.

Childress, C. 1999. Archetypal Conceptualization of Cyberspace as the Celtic Otherworld. *Cyberpsychology & Behavior* 2 (3): 261–265.

Christ, C. 1982. "Why Women Need the Goddess: Phenomenological, Psychological, and Political Reflections." In *The Politics of Women's Spirituality*, edited by Charlene Spretnak, 71–86. New York: Doubleday.

Cohen, N. S. 2008. The Valorization of Surveillance: Towards a Political Economy of Facebook. *Democratic Communiqué* 22 (1): 5–22.

Connor, S. 2004. Afterword. In *The Victorian Supernatural*, edited by N. Bown, C. Burdett, and P. Thurschwell, 258–275. Cambridge: Cambridge University Press.

Dalgarno, B., and M. J. W. Lee. 2010. What Are the Learning Affordances of 3-D Virtual Environments? *British Journal of Educational Technology* 41 (1): 10–32.

Doel, M. A., and D. Clarke. 1999. Simulations, Suppletion, S(ed)uction and Simulacra. In *Virtual Geographies: Bodies, Space, and Relations*, edited by Mike Crang, Phil Crang, and John May, 261–280. London: Routledge.

dos Santos, R. P. 2009. Pedagogy, Education and Innovation in 3-D Virtual Worlds. *Journal of Virtual Worlds Research* 2 (1): 1–21. https://journals.tdl.org/jvwr/article/view/383/455. Accessed June 14, 2013.

Dumézil, G. 1968–1971. *Mythe et épopée: L'idéologie des trois fonctions dans les épopées des peuples indo-européens*. 3 vols. Paris: Editions Gallimard.

Egginton, W. 2009. *The Theater of Truth: The Ideology of (Neo)Baroque Aesthetics*, Stanford, CA: Stanford University Press.

Eliade, M. 1963. *Myth and Reality*. Translated by Willard R. Trask. New York: HarperCollins.

Felton, D. 1999. *Haunted Greece and Rome: Ghost Stories from Classical Antiquity*. Austin: University of Texas Press.

Flichy, P. 2007. *The Internet Imaginaire*. Cambridge, CA: MIT Press.

George, A. R., trans. and ed. 2003. *The Babylonian Gilgamesh Epic: Critical Edition and Cuneiform Texts*. New York: Oxford University Press.

Gillies, J. 1994. *Shakespeare and the Geography of Difference*. Cambridge: Cambridge University Press.

Hartog, F. 1988. *The Mirror of Herodotus: The Representation of the Other in the Writing of History*. Berkeley: University of California Press.

Jockenhövel, J. 2011. What Is It If It's Not Real? It's Genre—Early Color Film and Digital 3D. *Cinemascope* 7 (15): 1–14. http://www.cinemascope.it/Issue%2015/PDF/jockenhovel.pdf. Accessed August 5, 2013.

Jouan, F., and B. Deforge, eds. 1988. *Peuples et pays mythiques: Actes du Ve Colloque du Centre de Recherchesmythologiques de l'Université de Paris X, Chantilly, 18–20 septembre 1986*. Paris: Belles Lettres.

Malpas, J. 2008. The Non-autonomy of the Virtual: Philosophical Reflections on Contemporary Virtuality. *Ubiquity* 9 (18). http://ubiquity.acm.org/article.cfm?id=1378359. Accessed June 13, 2013.

Merola, N., and J. Peña. 2010. The Effects of Avatar Appearance in Virtual Worlds. *Journal of Virtual Worlds Research* 2 (5). http://journals.tdl.org/jvwr/article/view/843/706. Accessed June 14, 2013.

Miller, V. 2011. *Understanding Digital Culture*. Los Angeles: Sage.

Ogden, D. 2002. *Magic, Witchcraft, and Ghosts in the Greek and Roman Worlds*. New York: Oxford University Press.

Rider, J. 2000. The Other Worlds of Romance. In *The Cambridge Companion to Medieval Romance*, edited by Roberta L. Krueger, 115–127. Cambridge: Cambridge University Press.

Ryan, M.-L. 2001. *Narrative as Virtual Reality: Immersion and Interactivity in Literature and Electronic Media*. Baltimore: Johns Hopkins University Press.

Said, E. W. 1978. *Orientalism*. London: Routledge and Kegan Paul.

Sannazaro, I. 1961. Opere Volgari. Edited by Alfredo Mauro. Bari: Laterza.

Schmitt, J.-C. 1998. *Ghosts in the Middle Ages: The Living and the Dead in Medieval Society*. Translated by Teresa Lavender Fagan. Chicago: University of Chicago Press.

Shakespeare, W. 1914. *The Complete Works of William Shakespeare*. Edited by William J. Craig. London: Oxford University Press.

Stam, K., and M. Scialdone. 2008. Where Dreams and Dragons Meet: An Ethnographic Analysis of Two Examples of Massive Multiplayer Online Role-Playing Games (MMORPGs). *Online— Heidelberg Journal of Religions on the Internet* 3 (1): 61–95. http://www.ub.uni-heidelberg.de/archiv/8290. Accessed June 14, 2013.

Timmerman, J. H. 1983. *Other Worlds: The Fantasy Genre*. Bowling Green, OH: Bowling Green University Popular Press.

Turner, G. 2010. *Ordinary People and the Media: The Demotic Turn*. Los Angeles: Sage.

Vernant, J.-P. 1983. *Myth and Thought among the Greeks*. London: Routledge and Kegan Paul.

Walters Adams, G. 2007. *Visions in Late Medieval England: Lay Spirituality and Sacred Glimpses of the Hidden Worlds of Faith*. Leiden: Brill.

Ward, G. 2000. *Cities of God*. London: Routledge.

Wertheim, M. 1999. *The Pearly Gates of Cyberspace: A History of Space from Dante to the Internet*. London: Virago Press.

CHAPTER 6

....

THE PARADOX OF
VIRTUALITY

....

MICHAEL R. HEIM

VIRTUALITY vanishes with its own success. When successful, virtual reality fades into the background. As a transparent platform for activities, virtuality attains invisibility in the culture that adopts it. When its functions square perfectly with human desires and gestures, virtuality is absorbed, and something virtualized becomes a reality within the culture that constructs it. Having found a proper niche within the cultural media ecology (Levinson 1997), a virtual reality slips over the horizon of consciousness and becomes invisible. Over time, the gap closes entirely between the virtual and the real. Embedded in cultural reality, the semantics of naming "virtuality" yields to the things themselves, and previously awkward techno-references fall away. The more virtual things become, the weaker the meaning of "virtuality."

The phase fluctuations in the semantics of "virtuality" have a long history. These macro phases in the history of language alert us to what has been transpiring on a micro scale over the past 30 years of technological change. The semantic fluctuations begin with the first-century Romans, for whom the "virtual" suggested manly strength and straightforward power (Latin *vir*). Later Christian thinkers downshifted the Roman meaning of the word as scholastics like Thomas Aquinas (circa 1250) distinguished a power existing in something "inherently" or *virtualiter* as opposed to essentially (*essentialiter*) or actually (*actualiter*). Here the virtuality of a thing is no longer its power to be present straightforwardly with strength. Italian Renaissance courtiers would later seek to retrieve the ancient Roman meaning but would sculpt it into a more refined and courteous Christian *virtu*. The strong but now less visibly intrinsic power fades in the fourteenth-century English term, which was borrowed from the French *virtuel*, by which "virtual" came to mean something implicit but not formally recognized, something that is indeed present but not openly admitted—something there "virtually" but not really or actually present. This weaker, nearly invisible virtuality would bloom a new semantic branch as the need for a computer-based aesthetics arose in the 1980s. Computers began to simulate digitized objects as recognizably vivid phenomena. The newly digitized phenomena were visible with many of the characteristics of primary realities and needed a new descriptive term. The virtual object was now a functional object—even reproduced as a three-dimensional object—but now generated in a digital environment. The historical linguistic paradox—strong presence dimmed to near invisibility followed by subtle presence—parallels the general paradox of contemporary virtuality.

In early phases of development, virtuality is highly visible. Prior to the routine digitization of culture, there is a Platonic yearning to carve out a separate uncontaminated space, an independent realm fully controlled by computer. Such an idealized and highlighted VR (virtual reality) enjoys hermetic properties as a separate environment. For Ivan Sutherland (1968) virtuality is a set of three-dimensional artificial light cubes seen through a monitor. For Jaron Lanier (1989) VR includes a data glove and a nearly instantaneous wellspring of 3D objects that promise to supersede spoken symbols. Decades later, mobile smartphones and networked computers push the holy grail of "full-blown" virtual reality off the table. Virtuality recedes as it becomes a ubiquitous subconscious component of everyday life, no longer a distant goal to be achieved somewhere special. A once stand-alone research vision gradually merges with everyday activities on computers. Such a blending process dissolves the specialized vocabulary that isolates and separates "virtual worlds," "avatars," and "telepresence": these phenomena now scatter across many fields of routine activities.

Paradoxically, the virtual aims at its gradual evaporation and eventual extinction. By successfully disseminating its goals, virtuality dissipates the virtual. What was formerly "content" to be digitized and framed by information systems now becomes inseparable and even identical with information. Merging with cultural conventions, a vapor trail may still hover long after VR made its first traces in the semantics of the English language, and the aging vocabulary still registers the disappearing act.

SHIFTING SEMANTICS

These days, the term "virtual" frequently functions as an adjective to modify specific phenomena, much as the general idea of "cyberspace" appears in *cybercafé* or *cyber warfare* or *cybersex*. The shift from the radically ontological noun "virtual reality" to an adjectival modifier parallels the path of software development as it migrated from utopian and transhumanist agendas to more pragmatic implementations in entertainment and the workplace. If it is even mentioned at all, the "virtual" functions around a multifaceted, richly nuanced node of meanings. Contrast this everyday familiarity with the early 1990s, when virtual reality became the realm of the visionary, the mantic, and the *mondo fantastico*. In the 1990s, Timothy Leary would exchange his robes as LSD hierophant to VR software designer as he pitched an electronic simulacrum of psychedelic experience. Magazines and journals addressed technology as a sensation of transcendence.

From its birth in the late 1980s to the second decade of the twenty-first century, the semantics of VR shed its skin several times. The breathless pace of technological innovation brought virtual reality as a technological specialty tool, as a specific disciplinary focus. Then gradually the virtual settled into a more generalized layer of everyday activities where most cultural items appear online in some form of electronic commerce and where everything is reflected in some form of digital data. Was scaling down the ambition already implicit in the paradoxical and/or hubristic term "virtual reality"? If already a "reality," why qualify something as "virtual"? Hyperbolic ambiguity can serve nicely as a shell for technological overpromise, but at the same time the term's multivalent semantics toggles an array of flickering, pulsating possibilities. Eventually those possibilities would be swept into a whirlwind of commercial, political, and entertainment activities.

Early speculation about cyberspace, virtual reality, and their connections still haunts the general cultural in the form of many unresolved and as yet unsettled questions. One early conference brought some degree of organization into the discussion. A study of the evolving semantics of virtuality might begin with a look at the First Conference on Cyberspace (May 1990), which later became a seminal collection of papers that is still a bounty for in-depth readers (Benedikt 1991).

FIRST CONFERENCE ON CYBERSPACE

The conference began with a bewildering conceptual variety, with a chaos of the kind that spins multiple threads that were just branching into fruitful directions, all tangents radiating from the single buzzword "cyberspace" coined by fiction writer William Ford Gibson. Gibson's own fictional contribution to the proceedings, "Academy Leader," (Gibson 1989) is itself very much like the countdown numbers it refers to in the title. The academy leader is the countdown at the beginning of films used by cinema labs to coordinate a soundtrack with film and to remind projectionists to adjust the lens as the start of the film. The ciphers from 10 to 1 flash in the darkened theater and lead hypnotically to an hour or two of collective dreaming. The text of "Academy Leader" exemplifies the literary "cut-up" technique Gibson used to create the term "cyberspace," the term that brings together the subsequent collection of papers:

> Assembled word *cyberspace* from small and readily available components of language. Neologic spasm: the primal act of pop poetics. Preceded any concept whatever. Slick and hollow—awaiting received meaning. All I did: folded words as taught. Now other words accrete in the interstices. (Benedikt 1991, 27)

The search for semantic content to fill the hollow word "cyberspace" begins in earnest when Michael Benedikt, the conference organizer at the University of Texas in Austin, opens his paper describing

> Physical space—the space of the everyday world—in relation to what can be said about the nature of the artificial or illusory space(s) of computer-sustained *virtual*

worlds. Because virtual worlds—of which *cyberspace* will be one—are not real in the material sense, many of the axioms of topology and geometry...can be violated or re-invented, as can many of the laws of physics. (Benedikt 1991, 119)

Benedikt uses his architect's imagination to envision a cyberspace that can defy the laws of terrestrial physics and perhaps even recast modern geometries. In his introduction to the printed papers, Benedikt also refers to a "pure VR" as he describes Jaron Lanier's virtual reality project that seeks its own "post-symbolic communication." In Lanier's shared world, digital objects are summoned to present meanings that supersede textual or ideational communication. Benedikt suggests a further additive rather than media-transcending dimension: "While pure VR [in Lanier's sense] will find its unique uses, it seems likely that cyberspace, in full flower, will employ all modes" (Benedikt 1991, 13).

This conference's 1990 point of departure—the most popular collection of papers printed by MIT Press—launched prior to the Mosaic browser's blend of images and text, prior to the era of Netscape, the 1990 "browser wars" with their Internet portals, long before software engines like Google or AltaVista wormed their way through the Internet. Here Michael Benedikt conceptually distinguishes a quasi-physical simulation called "virtual reality" from a more general "cyberspace." Benedikt appreciates the more generic cyberspace as a sharing of worlds that incorporates text and images in ways that require rethinking spatial geometry and topology. Here is a "space" that can contain new dimensions of connectivity or hyperlinks. Even at the time of the conference, the temptation is strong to conceive cyberspace according to existing models of physical space, however much the models might need adjustment. Benedikt's leap is imaginative but still tends to construct objects outside the disengaged psyche in ways much like a Cartesian cartographer who imposes a measurement grid over physical space. Even decades later, with Net interaction continually beneath the culture's fingertips, Benedikt's brainstorming launch in Austin seems daring for its time.

The collected papers from the First Conference on Cyberspace show semantic diversity in speaking about "virtual worlds" and the various ways they might be construed. The variety was assembled under the empty fictional "cyberspace" placeholder of Gibson's pop poetics. The cyberpunk notion functions as umbrella for an interdisciplinary conference that entertains a wide range of vaguely imagined phenomena. Like the proverbial elephant and the blind men, futuristic shots in the dark could point to an open-ended, blank canvas as the first phase of implementing virtuality begins. A fictional vocabulary offers a neologism as a springboard for the conceptual foundations of several adjacent disciplines. Engineering, human interface design, psychology of perception, phenomenology of software interaction, computer architecture, and several other disciplines could glom onto an open concept. The semantic struggle that grows out of fictional entertainment was to emanate nonfictional projects that gather manifold meanings under the shared roof of "virtuality." Although representatives from American Express Corporation were in attendance at the First Conference on Cyberspace, the discourse of the conference lacked the shape and definition that was to emerge later, when in following decades, the floodgates of commercial interest would open and practical applications of Internet culture and the "street language" of universal usage would pour in and normalize to near banality the cultural perception of virtuality. At the time, this blank conceptual canvas invited the projection of desires and dreams, inventions and fantasies. One projection was the utopian VR visionary Jaron Lanier.

Two Senses of Virtual

If Benedikt's *Cyberspace: First Steps* had a placeholder for utopian VR, it was Lanier's concept of a nonverbal, pretextual "virtual reality." Virtual reality, in this strong utopian sense, aimed to displace, replace, or, at the very least, challenge mundane reality. The new technological art-form was to upend communication as practiced in contemporary print, film, and television media. An immersive three-dimensional interactive world would sequester a shared space where the limitations of physics and personal identity no longer apply. Slip on goggles, choose or build your avatar, and you move into a superreal hyperspace. Cyberspace in this sense provides an esoteric environment that eventually revolutionizes modern culture as seen in popular magazines like *Mondo 2000*, the predecessor to *Wired* magazine. By absorbing the energy of cyberpunk, the syncretic postmodern VR culture inaugurated "virtual reality parties" for discussing products that did not exist yet. Timothy Leary entered the scene to endorse VR as a psychedelic panacea. Raves pulsated with interactive light shows on walls radiating hallucinatory graphics. Virtual reality gained cultural momentum first as a zeitgeist of the imagination, not as an existing technology. The buzz surrounding VR in the 1990s arrived prior to the new millennium with its greater emphasis on actual distribution, on multiple independent variations, on decentralized microcultures with no single overarching narrative.

The First Conference on Cyberspace was recorded by an early promoter of socializing virtual communities, journalist Howard Rheingold. Rheingold described activities on the Well, one of the oldest continuous virtual communities to sustain online contacts through vigorous discussion of a vast array of topics. Like the Usenet and CompuServe forums, the Well was text-based and became a model for how personal computers implemented "tools for thought" in support of extra-academic and extra-military communication. Rheingold's study of the DARPA (Defense Advanced Research Projects Agency) origins of networked computer communication would later apply to large-scale networks crossing the globe much like the telephone dial-up lines that fed the Well's rich conversational environment (Rheingold 2000). Like a semantic detective, Rheingold traces the origins of virtuality to the human interface workgroups at DARPA and then sees these experiments reach a general public that now possesses personal computers. The virtual community was to spread rapidly beyond the military workgroups and beyond the Unix-based communities of academic computing. Virtualization expanded into the domain of everyday text entry as word processing became a fixture on personal computers and permanently altered the writing procedures for many kinds of writing (Heim 1987, Rheingold 1991).

The cultural stream of VR moved toward ever-evolving and expanding kinds of community. Virtual communities often began as extensions of older dial-up networks like Usenet, the Well, and CompuServe, but they also incorporate playful interactions that include games and wildly imaginative scenes fabricated by using text to visualize three-dimensional space: MUDs (Multi-User Dungeons), where a single player chases adventures through a densely described text environment; and MOOs (Multi-Object Orientation), where multiple simultaneous players use text to establish and share a world of objects they manipulate and scenes they traverse. In the mid-1990s, such text-based environments morphed into graphical animation platforms such as *Active Worlds*, *Atmosphere*, *Croquet*, *OLIVE*, and *Teleplace*, to name a few. *Second Life* in 2003 ushered in a wave of educators who sought to supplement web-based education with interactive social learning experiences. Platforms like *Opensim*, and other virtual-world-based learning initiatives introduced education software in areas like medicine, government, military, museum, and higher education.

SIMULATION/IMMERSION/ COMMUNICATION

The First Conference on Cyberspace exhibited a certain polarity:

- VR as portal to a private world of simulation where physical senses are immersed by prosthetics, where users temporarily "forget" the primary sensory world
- VR as a communication tool where human contact transcends the constrictions imposed by limited sensory data passing through the electronic network

Both polar concepts vie for dominance early on in the narrative of virtuality. The second pole relies on the drive to make human contact and sustain shared connectivity despite sensory limitations. Straddling both threads was the computer-gaming industry, where compelling action can reduce the need for full-scale visualization and where commercial design continually pushes the envelope toward richer graphics and cinematic production values.

To some, virtuality was an alternate universe; to others, it was merely an additional layer in the given concourse of human interaction. The first thread of immersive VR took the holy grail of realism to metaphysical heights (Coyne 2001). The pursuit of realism would fly beyond the aesthetic trompe l'oeil to envision a new mission for humanity. Given the rapid growth of technology, humans might plan to recast reality entirely and place their hopes in virtuality. Since virtuality is of human design and implementation, some conclude that reality is ultimately to be manipulated and recast entirely.

With no limitations imposed by nature, this line of thinking invites a utopian or trans-humanist teleology. Transhumanism takes seriously the reduction of all reality to data (Hayles 1999). The final stop for this line of thinking is to release the human body-mind from carbon-based forms and to inject it into a silicon format that removes most tem-poral and spatial limitations. Humans thereby transform themselves into virtual enti-ties capable of new freedoms. Some transhumanists imagine liberation so complete that transformed human entities might flee planet Earth in search of more habitable grounds in other solar systems. VR then becomes the Promethean power to recreate selfhood according to newly designed specifications. The Nietzschean exhilaration of this kind of superman depends on the isomorphic assimilation of data to "reality," making this version of virtual reality the strongest and most literal interpretation of the phrase. The virtual does not create an illusory reality but literally replaces reality.

Leaning more toward the aesthetic illusion are those who interpret the holy grail of VR to be precise mimesis. The imitation of reality in this view proceeds farther down the path of illusion than traditional arts like painting. Because all or most of the senses are involved by a prosthetic type of VR, which includes kinesthetic positioning, such a technological goal aims at fabricating for first-person users the "you are there" illusion (Ellis, Kaiser, and Grunwald 1991; Kalawsky 1993; Barfield and Furness 1995; Burdea and Coiffet 2003; Bracken and Skalsi 2010). Like lucid dreams, such virtual experiences are difficult to distinguish from actual experiences until the laws of physics are suspended. The less cumbersome the technological interface, the smoother the mimetic power of such experience. This leads some proponents to envision neural implants that input data for raw aesthetic experience without the burden of the typical prosthetic interface. With neural implants, the agent can "jack in" directly to the computer much like the protag-onists in cyberpunk science fiction novels. While the surgically intrusive VR implant remains largely, though not entirely, speculative, the teleology behind the concept con-tinues to guide some research directions and presents a distinct shade in the semantics of virtuality.

Substituting or replacing primary sensory input, whether through neural implants or through prosthetic devices, creates a break. The break opens between subjective experiences that are private and subjective experiences that are normally linked to the intersubjective sense of a shared world. This "common sense," the medieval *sen-sus communis*, provides a basis for interpersonal empathy, for shared fellow feeling. Phenomenologically, the human somatic experience, as lived and felt in first person, connects individual awareness with the awareness of others. Everyday experiences, like walking on the beach or watching a sunset, can be shared phenomena: seeing the sun move across the sky. Humanistic learning, literature, poetry, and the arts depend on such elemental intersubjectivity. What distinguishes the strong sense of VR, whether as neural implant or as prosthetic system, is the rupture of intersubjective experience or at least the fully controlled mediation of intersubjective experience (Ommeln 2005). There are, of course, many cases where normal people go off each "into their own world," but usually one assumes that others have access to a shared world from which the indi-vidual perspective unfolds. The strictest meaning of "hard" virtuality hovers around the rupture of primary experience and intersubjective sharing. Philosophically, this is an issue that perennially plagues radical skepticism. Once challenged by thoroughgoing doubt, the common feeling of a shared world is not easily restored. Sensory isolation provides a powerful controlled experience but often suffers from the psychological rupture. And the rupture can include the disruption of internal somatic experience as well, where bodily awareness splits from mental-perceptual awareness and the mind's eye watches something out of sync with felt bodily awareness (Heim 1998).

ARTIFICIAL REALITY

One VR artist who rejects sensory isolation is the "artificial reality" artist and installation theorist Myron Krueger. Beginning in the early 1970s, Krueger spearheaded the creation of virtual environments that incorporate human bodily actions without sensory isolation (Krueger 1991). As computers monitor gestures and whole body movements, Krueger's artificially generated environments respond smartly in real time to intersubjective activities. Multiple users share real space together and interact with artificially projected objects. A wide variety of ingenious devices—from shared desktops to entire buildings that respond to gestures—invite human interactivity without prosthetic sensory immersion. Krueger's "smart environments" blend interactivity with multiple synchronic subjectivities. The players in his installations share the same real-time computer-generated objects that range from physically triggered props to full-scale holograms. Although Krueger's work was not included in the First Conference on Cyberspace, Myron Krueger quickly promoted his "no goggles or gloves" line of VR design at several subsequent conferences.

Much of the later VR vapor trail shows the influence of Myron Krueger's designs. Contemporary adaptations of virtuality tend to avoid prosthetic interfaces. The preference is for handheld devices that feel comfortable to users and do not block or encumber the physical senses. The successful design leadership of Apple Computer's Steve Jobs brought the "look and feel" aesthetic to the forefront. The "at-hand" quality of the interface of virtuality plays an important role in cultural adaptation. The gap between the virtual and the mundane closes with the sensuous adaptation of the device. Instead of sensory input via prosthetics, the focus is on how to enter smoothly *through the physical device* into the computerized world. The line of invention from Steve Jobs tended to blur the line between "through" and "into" the device so that entry into virtuality moves smoothly from and back to the physical world. The sense of encumbrance or special portal falls away when the delivery device develops an integral aesthetic.

Another feature of this smooth access to virtuality is the avoidance of proxy identifiers for acting inside the virtual environment. Instead of projecting oneself into the artificial world, the player participates directly and bodily in the construction of virtual activities. Direct user movement becomes the central focus of the experience—as the touch-panel, trackball, or mouse becomes the pivot point of an interface design. Players who enter with their own bodies into Krueger's artificial reality contrast notably with the self-presentations of the users who enter *into* the virtual world as a distinct incarnation or avatar of the actual person.

ARRIVAL OF AVATARS

Also present at the First Conference on Cyberspace were the game designers Chip Morningstar and Randy Farmer (Benedikt 1991, 273). These pioneers applied the ancient Sanskrit term "avatar"—the earthly incarnation of godly powers according to the mystical scriptures of the Hindu Upanishads—to the visual embodiments of users. The Hindu concept is the descent (*ava* = down) to earth of a deity, particularly Vishnu, in human, superhuman, or animal form. Morningstar and Farmer envisioned a similar descent of a human identity into a graphic representation in a virtual world. This notion evolved in their experimental *Habitat* virtual world run in the mid-1980s on Commodore 64 computers at Lucasfilm. The graphic embodiments of human spirits, descendants of the puppet theaters of medieval Europe and Asia, were to make their way from the dial-up days of the World Wide Web in the mid-1990s to the present. In the early 1990s, avatars appeared in over a dozen new virtual-world platforms ranging from enormous citizen-built 3D cityscapes (*Active Worlds*) to cocktail party worlds where users conversed in their own voices through lip-synching heads (*Digital Space Traveler*). The avatar would become a new component of self-identification on computer networks and would later play a key role in distinguishing computer communication from previous media where readers or viewers assume the role of spectators who are less involved in the participatory agency of virtual events. Users of previous media do initiate internal dialogues within themselves but remain more private receivers than social agents who band together for action. By contrast, the avatar is inherently social. The graphic acknowledgment of spirited human presence tends to distinguish virtual communication from other types and distinguishes one type of virtual world from another.

The avatar paradox is another facet of the larger paradox of virtuality. The avatar appears to project or represent the self of the human agent or player. The player makes an appearance that offers to break the illusion of absence or withdrawal behind a screen. The player offers a proxy presence to act "as if" the self were actually—though virtually—present. The virtual self that presents itself, however, is not identical to the self that presents itself. The virtual self or avatar derives from a set of choices either made by the avatar system or by the deliberate agency of the player. The avatar results from the combination of software capabilities and choices made by interacting with the software. The details that are involved in choosing an avatar or virtual profile differ with the specific software platforms. Variations can range widely from aesthetic features to gender differences to ontological predilections of the graphical environment. Many situations, for example, in the contemporary virtual workplace require realistic elements in avatar creation, such as photographic elements, instant message icons, or unmodified telephonic voice presence. Fashioning the most appropriate avatar in the contemporary world may invoke all the complexity of classical rhetoric as considerations arise concerning the audience, social timing, authentication, and the venue or online meeting place. The image of the user's desktop at a Net meeting can be as important as the facial makeup and body language used in a webcast sent to hundreds of thousands of corporate colleagues. An avatar can be as simple as a Facebook composition or as complex as a work environment where individual identities develop over weeks or months through a parade of subtly revealing choices.

The styles of self-presentation in the earliest avatars offer lessons in the self-construction process (Jakobsson 2003). Contemporary virtuality tends to be sophisticated, subtle, and multimedia, hence more difficult to analyze. The first avatar worlds showed that human agents are reluctant to reveal their primary identity. Photographic realism was not intrinsic to avatar construction. Avatars only reluctantly provided realistic photographs of themselves. Of 20 avatars asked to identify themselves photographically, only two or three would typically agree, preferring perhaps a degree of distance, freedom, unpredictability, and leeway for surprise, humor, and whimsical behavior. While the first avatar worlds were primarily game-related, the need for personal distance or self-withholding surfaces even in more serious workaday contexts where accountability is required and ludic elusiveness is discouraged (Pearce 2009; Papacharissi 2011). The ironic stance of the avatar seems related to protecting an individual aura of freedom. Some preferences seem connected to personal privacy. Tracking avatar choices can reveal much of avatar-human identities, but withholding choices preserves the privacy of a more intimate identity. Stereotypes and prejudices remain as problematic in the online as in the primary world.

The smartphone, when linked to avatar behavior, supplies much information about identity. Identities can be tracked by global positioning satellites (GPS), which adds yet another source of data reconnaissance. Tilting toward mobility over immersion, the smartphone provides a new resource for augmenting reality. Augmented reality (AR) overlays the sensory field with data points so that, for example, a building seen through a smartphone camera can show the history of ownership, market value, and number of occupants of a building. The smartphone pointed at the night sky can reveal constellations or other astronomical bodies that are barely visible to the naked eye. The virtual city or augmented sky becomes data rich as the mobile phone user assumes a first-person position that reveals scenic information through virtual filtering. In a similar way, telepresent medical practitioners can address the patient ailments through the virtual viewer and not from inside the virtual world. The patient in view can be data rich but at the same time remain an actual physical object at a distance. Although a face-to-face meeting may yield more primary sensory information, the tools of telepresent medicine offer enhancements that can even improve face-to-face examinations.

CRITIQUE OF COLLECTIVE ILLUSION

As soon as virtuality involves the avatar, which involves an act of conscious self-presentation, the complex paradoxes of virtuality multiply. The avatar is the pivot point where the psyche of psyche-ology introduces critical issues that go beyond sense perception, visual accuracy, sensory feedback, and the other issues typical of human-machine interaction. Avatar self-perception involves social awareness and social role-playing (Schroeder and Axelsson 1996; 2010). The avatar self-construct involves personal choices that include an awareness of social perception at a certain historical moment. Social perception imposes fashions, conventions, and even perceptual conditions on how human beings—each avatar-choosing individual—can or should appear to others in society. Such complexity invites a depth-psychological analysis. The analysis addresses questions about human selves in their virtual identities and what virtual identities reveal about human selves.

Criticisms of virtuality by psychologists are too numerous to mention, but the broadest critique of the avatar as a universal trend comes from analytic or depth psychology. This critique of virtuality argues that the virtual world both enables and reinforces emotional distancing or affective disengagement. Seen through the method of phenomenological psychopathology (Romanyshyn 1989), the computer avatar symptomizes and culminates a centuries-old cultural trajectory begun during the Renaissance. The trajectory was later consolidated in a dream (Descartes) that envisions an emotional security achieved by opening a felt distance from the confusing entanglements of everyday life. The dream, in this critique, culminates in the Cartesian fantasy of total objectivity and certainty, of greater control through an ever-increasing distance from immediate experience. Finally, through the computer implementation of the objective viewpoint, the human subject no longer has a fully responsive emotional role to play in the dreamscape. The psyche comes to prefer disengagement. This critique of virtuality sees cyberspace emerging from a "collective illusion"—or even delusion. Like the antiheroes of cyberpunk fiction, the victims of this pathology suffer a spreading emotional numbness and an inclination toward ethical irresponsibility as experience loses its affective edge and as human agency hides in general behind a screen.

The depth-psychological critique of virtuality gains cogency from its application to the early evolution of avatars. The fifteenth-century trajectory begins with the discovery of linear perspective by Renaissance artists, who used an array of visual techniques to frame space and thereby prepared the way for Descartes's dream of a complete system of linear coordinates (Edgerton 1975). Linear perspective projects three dimensions onto a two-dimensional surface. The projection opens the depth of the Z-axis by assigning spatial coordinates to the body of the spectator who is presumed to be at the center of the projection. This center or virtual body then becomes the point of view that looks toward an imagined horizon extending beyond the two-dimensional surface of the canvas. The perspectival gaze of the virtual spectator's eyes then sees depicted objects as in their substantial dimensionality on the flat canvas of the painting. While the invisible "wall" of the flat canvas prevents physical interaction with the painted objects, the things in the painting appear fully present rather than flatly "iconic" as in pre-Renaissance art. A further use of the grid makes possible the trompe l'oeil of ceiling frescoes in baroque-era churches where the distinction between physical and pictorial space is blurred by blending the painting of heavenly space of the sky so it appears seamlessly continuous with physical space. A grid of perspectival coordinates allows the painting to fit properly onto the physical dome.

Computer game players will recognize the Cartesian grid as the underlying structure of the faux 3D used in their virtual worlds, and software designers who build in software tools like *Maya* or *3D Studio* will be all too familiar with this grid and its multiple viewing perspectives. The perspectives of computer gaming further strengthen the virtuality of avatars and objects through instantaneous feedback mechanisms and through interactivity, but the overall design relies on variants of Renaissance perspective. The setup implies two main viewpoints for avatars: first-person users and third-person overhead points of view. Either I peer out from my virtual eyes to the infinite vanishing point of the horizon, or I can choose, from a god's-eye point of view, to see my virtual body from any 360-degree angle on a spherical pivot. I either see in first person or I become an object seen from outside. The blend of inside and outside, their mutual interpenetration, is not a feature of in-world perception. In avatar, I am either a spectator or a corpse. Absent is the everyday experience of the constant interchange with things and persons that make up the activities of life. The virtual body is enmeshed in a grid that removes empathic responses and that replaces empathy with the manipulation of objects that are confronted.

Depth psychology suggests that Renaissance cultural perception has penetrated the groundwater of the collective unconscious. Emotional distancing has seeped into and permeates modern conscious experience. The eyes dominate sensory input and the world becomes a spectacle of controllable objects. The body becomes a specimen to be examined like a corpse. The tendency to objectify and impose measurable geometrical grids over modern experience opened for publishers the floodgates of maps, charts, schematics, and all manner of diagrams made possible by modern printing and linear perspective. Linear perspective supported the development of movable type and the printing press (McLuhan [1962] 2011). Modern consciousness moved further from unmediated experience and assumed the posture of an observer at a distance, even to the point where the observing consciousness appears to inhabit an anatomical rack of "meat." As representing the anatomical body of the player, the avatar is then the final step toward an objectifying self-suspension inside a fully controlled software environment. As such, the avatar delivers the ultimate paradox of virtuality: Realizing the limits of the avatar, the Renaissance trajectory comes up against its own dark side. The postmodern psyche now needs therapy to recover from modernity.

The collective pathology of virtuality deserves further research. The contemporary workplace, where most people spend much of their time, shows a reluctance to adopt certain aspects of full-blown virtual reality. An instinctive resistance to some forms of virtuality may signal a healthy internal need to counterbalance the cultural trends observed by the critique of psychopathology. Office workers today who work, paradoxically, from home, tend to develop mixed versions of telepresence rather than use integrated virtual worlds. They tend to use

- mobile access to shared data on the Web
- avatars composed of selected photo fragments
- instant messaging and shared desktops
- webcasts for company meetings rather than in-world events
- telephone voice conferences with shared desktops

A loose and inventive approach to using the computer grid somewhat dampens the criticism of the collective dream as a pathological extension of the single-minded drive of modernity.

CONCLUSION

The paradox of virtuality prompts a look at the speculative trends of the past, how they change, and how things in the present are now unfolding toward possible futures. The terms that once held a numinous radiance are stamped into the coins of everyday commerce. "Avatars" can suggest a wide range of composited elements. The terms "virtual world" and "virtual reality" are spread tenuously and used loosely. Social adoption brings new uses for old things. Something once held strange and wonderful becomes the new normal. "The Street," as cyberpunk Gibson puts it, "finds its own uses for things—uses the manufacturers never imagined" (Benedikt 1991, 29).

The idealizations of technological innovators limn abstract artifacts that change under conditions of actual usage. Twentieth-century philosophy, led by Heidegger and Wittgenstein, critically assessed the modern tendency to disengage models or paradigms from their at-hand applications. The disengaged and external vantage point is a modern abstraction lacking the give-and-take of applied experience. Both Heidegger's *Lichtung* and Wittgenstein's *Lebensform* point to the need for the repeated regrounding of ideals in the grit of human activity where things are "defined" more by existential practice than by the imaginings of a disengaged speculative mind (Taylor 1995, 61). The normalization of technology, its "street use," suggests that, rather than construct theories about virtuality, it is more fruitful to attend to the many very particular practices that currently infiltrate everyday activities. Contemporary life is replete with virtual reality in different shapes and forms, and there is no need to construct a special model to understand virtuality. The "Street" continues to surprise any and all ideas of what virtual reality is or can be (Heim 1993; Schroeder and Axelsson 1996; Rossi 2010). The normalization of technology is the other side of Wittgenstein's motto: "Progress always seems larger than it really is" (Cahill 2006). A careful look at past speculation can help adjust the illusions that appear in the rearview mirror as the drive to progress steers ever forward.

REFERENCES

Barfield, W., and T. A. Furness, eds. 1995. *Virtual Environments and Advanced Interface Design.* New York: Oxford University Press.

Benedikt, M. L., ed. 1991. *Cyberspace: First Steps.* Cambridge, MA: MIT Press.

Bracken, C. C., and P. D. Skalsi, eds. 2010. *Immersed in Media: Telepresence in Everyday Life.* New York: Taylor & Francis.

Burdea, G., and P. Coiffet, eds. 2003. *Virtual Reality Technology.* 2nd ed. New York: John Wiley & Sons.

Cahill, K. 2006. The Concept of Progress in Wittgenstein's Thought. *Review of Metaphysics* 60 (September): 71–100.

Coyne, R. 2001. *Technoromanticism: Digital Narrative, Holism, and the Romance of the Real.* Cambridge, MA: MIT Press.

Edgerton, S. Y. 1975. *The Renaissance Rediscovery of Linear Perspective.* New York: Basic Books.

Ellis, S. R., M. K. K., and A. C. Grunwald, eds. 1991. *Pictorial Communication in Virtual and Real Environments.* New York: Taylor & Francis.

Gibson, W. 1989. Rocket Radio. *Rolling Stone,* 84–86, June 15.

Hayles, K. 1999. *How We Became Posthuman: Virtual Bodies in Cybernetics, Literature, and Informatics.* Chicago: University of Chicago Press.

Heim, M. 1993. *The Metaphysics of Virtual Reality.* New York: Oxford University Press.

Heim, M. 1998. *Virtual Realism.* New York: Oxford University Press.

Heim, M. 1987, 1999. *Electric Language: A Philosophical Study of Word Processing.* 2nd ed. New Haven: Yale University Press.

Jakobsson, M. 2003. A Virtual Realist Primer to Virtual World Design. In *Searching Voices: Towards a Canon for Interaction Design,* edited by P. Ehn and J. Löwgren. Malmö, Sweden: Malmö University Press.

Kalawsky, R. S. 1993. *The Science of Virtual Reality and Virtual Environments: A Technical, Scientific and Engineering Reference on Virtual Environments.* Reading, MA: Addison-Wesley.

Krueger, M. 1991. *Artificial Reality II.* Reading, MA: Addison-Wesley.

Lanier, J. 1989. "Data Glove," patented (US Patent 4988981).

Levinson, P. 1997. *The Soft Edge: A Natural History and Future of the Information Revolution.* New York: Routledge.

Lunenfeld, P., ed. 2000. *The Digital Dialectic: New Essays on New Media.* Cambridge, MA: MIT Press.

McLuhan, H. M. (1962) 2011. *The Gutenberg Galaxy: The Making of Typographic Man.* Toronto: University of Toronto Press.

Ommeln, M. 2005. *Die Technologie der Virtuellen Realitaet.* Frankfurt am Main: Peter Lang.

Papacharissi, Z. A., ed. 2011. *A Networked Self: Identity, Community and Culture on Social Network Sites.* New York: Taylor & Francis.

Pearce, C., and Artemesia. 2009. *Communities of Play: Emergent Cultures in Multiplayer Games and Virtual Worlds.* Cambridge, MA: MIT Press.

Rheingold, H. 1991. *Virtual Reality*. New York: Summit Books.

Rheingold, H. 2000. *Tools for Thought: The History and Future of Mind-Expanding Technology*. 2nd ed. Cambridge, MA: MIT Press.

Romanyshyn, R. 1989. *Technology as Symptom and Dream*. New York: Routledge and Kegan Paul.

Rossi, D. 2010. *L'estasi dell'uomo sperimentale*. Rome: Aracne Publishing.

Schroeder, R., and A.-S. Axelsson. 1996. *Possible Worlds: The Social Dynamic of Virtual Reality Technology*. Boulder, CO: Westview Press.

Schroeder, R., and A.-S. Axelsson, eds. 2010. *Avatars at Work and Play: Collaboration and Interaction in Shared Virtual Environments*. Dordrecht, Netherlands: Springer.

Stanney, K. M., ed. 2002. *The Handbook of Virtual Environments: Design, Implementation, and Applications*. Mahwah, NJ: Lawrence Erlbaum Associates.

Sutherland, I. A Head-Mounted Three Dimensional Display. In *Proceedings of Fall Joint Computer Conference*, 1968, 757–764. http://portal.acm.org/citation.cfm?id=1476686. Accessed July 20, 2013.

Taylor, C. 1995. *Lichtung* or *Lebensform*: Parallels between Heidegger and Wittgenstein. In *Philosophical Arguments*. Cambridge, MA: Harvard University Press. 61–78.

Zudilova-Seinstra, E., T. Adriaansen, and R. van Liere, eds. 2009. *Trends in Interactive Visualization: State-of-the-Art*. London: Springer-Verlag.

PART II

PSYCHOLOGY AND
PERCEPTION

CHAPTER 7

AVATAR PSYCHOLOGY

JAMES K. SCARBOROUGH AND JEREMY N.
BAILENSON

Avatar Psychology

Avatar Psychology

THE digital information age has arrived. In the year of this publication, the population of planet earth is projected to hit 7 billion.[1] At the same time, the number of Internet users is estimated to be well over 2 billion.[2] The percentage of the total population on the Internet varies from region to region, with Africa around 11 percent penetration and North America just below 80 percent penetration. Yet these numbers suggest significant portions of the planet's population (somewhere around 30 percent) are Internet users. The variety of internetworking applications in use is difficult to quantify, but one thing is clear: For many, the Internet has become a primary mode of communication internationally.

The explosive growth and dissemination of internetworking technology has changed the commonly accepted definition of *community*. In 1993, Rheingold wrote about how electronically mediated social interactions had very real effects on his life (Rheingold 1993). Rheingold reflects on his experience: "My mind, however, is linked with a worldwide collection of like-minded (and not so like-minded) souls: My virtual community" (57). Rheingold went further, suggesting that participation in a virtual community had a very real psychological effect. He states: "We do everything people do when people get together, but we do it with words on computer screens, leaving our bodies behind" (58). Sánchez-Segura and colleagues later extended the idea of virtual community to a far more inclusive virtual society:

> Now there are groups which are joined across the distance with the aim of "interacting," groups formed by people born within different environments, but now joined in another one in which they form a new society called "virtual society," where they can develop a new and different lifestyle. (Sánchez-Segura et al. 1998, 1)

Combine this with the fact that media use in younger populations has far exceeded any previous generation (Rideout, Foehr, and Roberts 2010) and it becomes clear that the culture of Internet use is spreading irrepressibly.

As more and more people have begun using digital media to meet their need for social interaction, an increasing number of new applications has been designed to keep up with the generated demand. This has led to the creation of a variety of novel ways to represent oneself during the ensuing social interactions that take place in virtual places. The challenge of unique digital representation has led to the proliferation of particular forms of individual embodiment. Graphical forms of online representation have become known as *avatars*. Avatars can range from very simple images, to still-frame photos (aka profile picture), to complex animated 3D forms frequently *anthropomorphized*, that is, made to appear roughly human. The anthropomorphized avatar will be the subject of focus for this chapter.

It has become clear that the use of avatars in everyday life and in the workplace will continue to expand as the global network is built out. In the book *Infinite Reality*, Blascovich and Bailenson also describe this trend as "spreading virally":

> People interact via digital stimuli more and more. According to a recent study by the Kaiser Family Foundation, kids spend eight hours per day on average outside of the classroom using digital media. This translates to billions of hours per week.... In the world of online games and virtual worlds, millions of players spend over twenty hours each week "wearing" avatars, digital representations of themselves.... Household "console" video arenas, especially games, in which people control and occupy avatars, consume more hours per day for kids than movies and print media combined. To borrow a term from the new vernacular, virtual experiences are spreading virally. (Blascovich and Bailenson 2011, 2)

Studies have demonstrated that interactions between humans while they are embodied in avatars have distinct psychological implications. Academic research is increasingly focused on exploring these effects because evidence suggests that the use of avatars could profoundly alter our social behaviors and work performance—for better or worse (Bailenson and Blascovich 2011). Behavioral changes that are caused by avatars have been demonstrated to include both immediate adaptive changes (Yee and Bailenson 2007) and longitudinal changes that can be measured over time (Fox and Bailenson 2009).

Using technology to mediate social communication has been theorized to change the way we perceive our own identity and the identity of others. In the book *Identity Shift: Where Identity Meets Technology in the Networked-Community Age*, Cerra and James (2011) explore how the proliferation of networking technology has impacted both an individual's perception of his or her own identity and the perception of others' identities. One particularly relevant thesis discussed in the book is the closing of the gap between personal life and professional life. In one example, the authors demonstrate how having a Facebook account can affect the chances of getting a job. Facebook activity has traditionally been considered a personal space. Yet employers now routinely research job applicants' Internet presence to get a feel for what type of person an applicant might be in the workplace.

Research has also established the effect of digital representation on the individual. In one series of studies, the appearance and behavior of an avatar has been demonstrated to have immediate effects on the behavior of the user. Deeming it the *Proteus effect*, Yee and Bailenson (2007) produced a variety of behavioral effects by altering the height and attractiveness of a user's avatar. This is but one example of the growing body of research on the effect of virtual identity on physical behaviors.

What Does It Mean to Have an Avatar?

Avatars, a word once uttered only by hardcore gamers and science fiction fans, have begun to make their way into living rooms across the world. Their infiltration into our everyday lives has grown from a subtle trend to a suddenly marked phenomenon (Ahn, Fox, and Bailenson 2011).

In mythology, the term "avatar" is used to describe what happens when an ethereal deity embodies its heavenly essence to visit the material world. When deities had a desire to walk among the people or visit a world they had created, they would instantiate their essence into a physical body. In order to experience life from the perspective of the local inhabitants, the received avatar would typically look and act very similar to the people who populated the world. Doing so would allow the deity to experience life as it was for mortal man.

James Cameron's movie *Avatar* features a type of avatar similar to the mythological definition. In the film, a military veteran (Jake Sully) has suffered a combat injury limiting the use of his legs. By transferring his consciousness to the avatar body, Jake becomes captivated by the renewed ability to use "his legs" again. Yet in the process of learning to use the avatar body, Jake gradually becomes the avatar in essence. In this narrative, the more Jake experiences the world through his avatar, the stronger his emotional connection with the avatar body becomes. At the same time, his cognitive connection with his own body begins to deteriorate. While merely a fictional illustration of the user-avatar relationship, this example illuminates potential effects on cognition, emotion, and perception that continued development of avatar technology may have on humans.

It is important to note that effects generated by digital representation vary significantly between the human-controlled avatar and the programmatically controlled embodied computer *agent*. In both instances, the graphical display a user sees may be identical. Both avatars and agents have become very anthropomorphically human. Both versions feature highly realistic behaviors. Each has the ability to respond to their environment and to the user. Yet people respond very differently to representations they know to be avatars than to agents, even when the difference is based entirely on the subject's perception. In a series of studies comparing subjects' responses to other virtual people, it was found that "players exhibited greater physiological arousal to otherwise identical interactions when other characters were introduced as an avatar rather than an agent" (Lim and Reeves 2010, 57). The net result of this finding is that avatars that represent humans are more emotionally and psychologically interesting to other people than automated agents appear to be. While the cognitive and emotional implications of interacting with automatons and embodied agents are of great interest psychologically, this chapter will focus on the relationship and effects that occur between humans and avatars.

Social scientists are beginning to study avatars as a way of understanding people. There are now several academic research institutes and departments that are dedicated to the study of human interaction with the virtual. Universities all over the world, including Oxford, Stanford, Cypress, and Toronto, have groups dedicated to exploring the psychological effects of virtual reality on humans. Their collective hope is to leverage emerging technology to improve research methods and to study phenomena, such as nonverbal behavior and social interaction, that have traditionally been difficult to study in a physical setting (Fox, Arena, and Bailenson 2009).

With the massive increase in virtual-world use and immersive gaming, academic and commercial interest in VR research continues to grow. Virtual reality researchers have demonstrated the utility of virtual reality for social science and the inherent benefits of VR technology for doing laboratory research in general. Immersive virtual environment technology (IVET) uses technology to perceptually surround a person with a digital environment such that the subject feels "inside" a virtual world with avatars. IVET has been advocated to ameliorate, if not solve, methodological research problems and, thus, holds promise as the new social psychological research tool (Blascovich et al. 2002). Among the motivations for developing VR technology is the ability for humans to interact without the constraints of the physical world, for example being able to change body shape, color, and even species (Lanier 1992). At the time of Lanier's original publication, practical VR existed only in the laboratories of a few scientific visionaries. Today, the application of VR technology to everyday problems in business (e.g., distributed team coordination) and medicine (e.g., physical rehabilitation) has become increasingly commonplace. A few practical applications are detailed at the end of this chapter.

Historically, advancements in communication media technology have expanded humans' ability to make contact with others, physically or virtually, in ever more ways (Turkle 1985; Turkle 1995; Rheingold 1993). As virtual representation increases in popularity and utility, it has become important to understand how using avatars changes people. Today, both scientists and citizens, for example concerned parents, question how virtual reality is affecting life as we know it.

The question remains: exactly how does use of an avatar as a representation of the self during increasingly real social interactions in virtual spaces affect the individual and one's perception of selfhood? The emerging answer is surprisingly complex and frequently contrary to intuition. For example, one study suggests that in high-use situations, users' neural activation patterns indicating emotional connection with their avatars have been measured as roughly equal to the neural patterns indicating emotional connection with their biological selves (Ganesh et al. 2012). While this is merely one example of a specific effect, a growing body of research has begun to reveal a range of very real psychological and physiological implications of avatar use. This chapter will explore research on the effects of human-avatar interaction as well as effects found to occur when people interact via technology-mediated environments. The following sections will outline effects on individuals, social interactions, and then provide several exemplars of beneficial avatar use.

INDIVIDUAL EFFECTS: SPATIAL PRESENCE AND SELF-PRESENCE

Spatial Presence

Spatial presence is the feeling of being *there*.

Emerging technologies including virtual reality, simulation rides, videoconferencing, home theater, and high-definition television are designed to provide media users with an illusion that a mediated experience is not mediated (Lombard and Ditton 1997). These technologies are designed for both distraction and practical utility. Most popular examples are of the entertainment variety. For example, riding an immersive ride such as Disneyland's Pirates of the Caribbean, at a popular amusement park provides stimulation to the physiological senses. There are visuals in the form of pirates doing what pirates do best (looting and pillaging), audible music and singing ("Yo ho, yo ho, a pirate's life for me!"), olfactory simulation of gunpowder and burning buildings, and the feel of water splashing on one's face as the floating carriage moves from one display to another. Yet physical simulation is not the only method for immersion. In an article for the *American Journal of Bioethics*, Schaefer writes, "James Cameron's new film *Avatar* is, at its core, a visual experience. It engages audiences with swooping shots of luscious vegetation from an imaginary world, its characters confront and are confounded by all manner of wondrous beasts and it culminates in rousing battle scenes which are meant to thrill and delight—and in 3D, to boot" (Schaefer 2010, 68). These effects in general have become known as *presence* or the feeling of "being there" (see also Riva and Waterworth, chapter 12, and Calleja, chapter 13, both in this volume).

The idea of presence can be thought of as the experience of one's physical environment; it refers not to one's surroundings as they exist in the physical world, but to the perception of those surroundings as mediated by both automatic and controlled mental processes (Gibson 1986). This description refers to the focus of one's perception and cognition during virtual experiences. When one enters a virtual environment by donning a head-mounted display or starting up a favorite immersive video game, one's senses become focused on the virtual environment. When perception is mediated by a communication technology, one is forced to perceive two separate environments simultaneously: the physical environment in which one is actually present; and the environment presented via the medium (Steuer 1992).

Elements that define virtual reality such as vividness and interactivity influence the degree of spatial presence (Steuer 1992). *Vividness* refers to the ability of a technology to produce a sensorially rich mediated environment. This includes stimulation of any combination of the perceptual senses, as well as elements such as range and vibrancy of colors, depth of audio or music, and the ability to draw one into the presented environment. *Interactivity* refers to the degree to which users of a medium can influence the form or content of the mediated environment. This includes both the ability of the environment to respond to user input (responsiveness) and the ability of the user to respond to the environment (interaction). Interactivity has also been defined by other scholars with reference to *functionality*, or the degree of multimodality, and *contingency*, or the degree to which interactions are based on previous interactions (Sundar, Kalyanaraman, and Brown 2003). Higher degrees of vividness and interactivity can cause users to become more involved in the delivered content, provided the content is of relevance to the user.

There are several other key factors affecting the level of spatial presence virtual environments can produce. Elements such as the ability to represent oneself within the environment, ease of use, engaging narrative, and frequent real-time feedback rank high among the many factors that can affect presence. Each of these elements can add depth to virtual experiences, making them increasingly engaging.

The ability to represent oneself within the media makes the experience more personally relevant (Reeves and Read 2010). Additionally, the ability to customize one's avatar can affect both subjective feelings of presence and psychophysiological indicators of emotion during the virtual experience (Bailey, Wise, and Bolls 2009).

Ease of use can reduce the barriers to entry for a virtual environment, making it feel more "user friendly." Natural mapping of form to function makes avatar use in 3D environments easy and familiar (Norman 2002). For instance, using a joystick to "drive" an avatar represents a far lower cognitive load than mapping movement to keys on a crowded keyboard. Presumably, as the ability to track avatars more naturally increases, for example using computer vision algorithms that can track body movements, the naturalness will improve considerably.

Leveraging a compelling narrative can also increase levels of spatial presence. The ability to interact with a vivid narrative, unconstrained by ordinary life, can increase engagement in presented content (Crawford 2004). This technique was applied to help children learn about ecosystems in the NICE project (Roussos et al. 1997). In this project, children constructed and cultivated simple virtual ecosystems, collaborated via networks with other remotely located children, and created stories from their interactions in the real and virtual worlds. The element of narrative construction helped children become engaged in a topic that would otherwise be uninteresting to them. In her book on the power of storytelling, Simmons states: "When you want to influence others, there is no tool more powerful than story" (Simmons 2006, 29).

High levels of feedback, especially in real time, provide a powerful mechanism for behavior change. The concept of feedback has a long history in the study of psychology and behavior change (Skinner 1958). Real-time feedback causes the human brain to adapt to changing circumstances more rapidly and with increased precision. For example, Welch and colleagues demonstrated that providing high levels of feedback via computer while teaching children to sing improved speed and accuracy of vocal pitch production (Welch, Howard, and Rush 1989).

When spatial presence is achieved, it mediates the effects generated by virtual experiences. Biocca and colleagues conducted a series of studies evaluating the effects of 3D advertising. In one study, subjects were either shown a normal product video or were allowed to interact with 3D images of the featured product. Interaction with 3D versions of a product was hypothesized to increase subject presence. The results of the study demonstrated that increasing the level of interaction increased self-reported presence and enhanced product knowledge, brand attitude, and purchase intention (Li, Daugherty, and Biocca 2002). Hence, personal involvement in virtual experiences can amplify the effectiveness of a simulation.

Self-Presence

Self-presence is the feeling that my avatar is *me*.

Using an interactive virtual environment (IVE) or playing an interactive video game that requires the use of avatars adds the element of self-presence. *Self-presence* is defined as "a psychological state in which virtual (para-authentic or artificial) self/selves are experienced as the actual self in either sensory or nonsensory ways" (Lee 2004, 37). In essence, self-presence is the feeling that one's avatar is more than a mechanism to interact with the virtual environment. It is an extension of the self.

Avatars are not all created equal. Research has shown that many factors affect the cognitive connection or sense of identification between user and avatar. The ability to personalize an avatar can cause a significant bond between users and their representation (Ratan 2012). In one study, it was found that customizing an avatar caused users' heart rate to increase as much as 10 percent over avatars that were assigned (Lim and Reeves 2009).

Higher levels of self-presence will increase engagement in virtual experiences, but there are other more subtle effects that can occur as well. A number of additional consequences of using avatars have been identified through laboratory research. Yee and colleagues conducted a series of experiments designed to explore the effects of avatar appearance and behavior on their users. The result has become known as the Proteus effect (Yee and Bailenson 2007).

The Proteus effect suggests that an individual's behavior conforms to his or her digital self-representation. In laboratory studies, subjects who used more attractive avatars were more intimate with confederates than those who used less attractive avatars, and those who used tall avatars negotiated more aggressively than those who used short ones. In a similar line of research, Groom and colleagues found that people embodied by black avatars in a laboratory VR environment demonstrated greater implicit racial bias outside the virtual environment than people embodied by white avatars (Groom, Bailenson, and Nass 2009).

Other lines of avatar study have extended effects identified in this research. Fox and colleagues found that simulating positive health results through an avatar similar in appearance to the user increased healthy exercise behaviors over time (Fox and Bailenson 2009). In a study designed to explore the psychological impact of avatar appearance, Nowak and Rauh identified several important implications of avatar appearance by having subjects evaluate images of avatars. Through the evaluation process, it was found that gender, attractiveness, and level of anthropomorphism significantly influenced subjects' perception of avatars. Avatars that appeared more human were perceived to be more credible and attractive, and subjects were more likely to choose to be represented by them (Nowak and Rauh 2005). However, as described by the hypothetical "Uncanny Valley" (Mori 1970), extreme levels of avatar realism can heighten sensitivity to cues of falsehood (Brenton et al. 2005) and can cause users to become uncomfortable when interacting with the representation (MacDorman et al. 2009; see also Tinwell, chapter 10 in this volume). Taken together, results suggest that a user's perception of an avatar extends well beyond the avatar itself.

Gaming experts have theorized that maintaining personal relationships through avatar use can also intensify the effects. In a book dedicated to the effects of avatar use on real life, T. L. Taylor (2006) suggests, *when things happen to my avatar they also happen to me* (4–5). Taylor reports, through multiple examples and anecdotes, the effects of "having an avatar" extend well outside the virtual environment. For example, *EverQuest* and *World of Warcraft* players who attend player "meet-ups" tend to identify themselves using their avatar names rather than their given names. Instead of informing virtual friends and acquaintances of their real identity ("Hi, my name is Fred, I play an elf"), players tend to extend the role-play aspects of their favorite game to real interactions ("Hi, Mordock! I'm Farkle, the elf!"). This is one of many real-life experiences detailed by Taylor that have been echoed throughout the MMORPG community. As the use of avatars alters the individual, it also mediates social interaction.

SOCIAL EFFECTS: SOCIAL PRESENCE, THE SOCIAL INFLUENCE MODEL, AND TRANSFORMED SOCIAL INTERACTION

Social Presence

Social presence is the degree to which users feel that *others are there* as well.

As virtual experiences and avatar use cause a variety of effects on individual users, they affect social experiences mediated by virtual environments as well. The perception of other users as being present in the virtual environment has become known as *social presence*. Social presence occurs when technology users successfully simulate other humans or nonhuman intelligences (Lee 2004; Biocca 1997; Biocca 1999). Successful simulation of other intelligences occurs when technology users do not notice the artificiality of social actors (both human and nonhuman intelligences) (Lee 2004).

The social influence model identifies several characteristics of avatars and virtual environments that impact computer mediated social interactions and increase the utility of collaborative virtual environments (CVEs) (Blascovich 2002). The key factor affecting social influence in the Blascovich model is social verification or copresence. Social verification is the result of the interaction between agency and behavioral realism. In this case, agency is defined as the perception of a virtual representation being associated with a real human. Behavioral realism is defined as the level of realism exhibited in the perceived behavior of a virtual representation.

Other factors that affect social verification are the self-relevance of interactions that occur, the context in which the interaction occurs, and the behavioral response level of the system. Blascovich discusses each of these in some depth in his work on social influence within immersive virtual environments. Self-relevance describes the degree to which interactions are meaningful or important to a particular user. Context refers to the circumstances of the virtual experience and whether there are real consequences such as a virtual job interview versus a simple game. Behavioral response level describes the manner in which social presence is instantiated. For example, if one is measuring a flinch response, then both agents and avatars elicit presence if they charge right at a user in virtual reality (Mennecke et al. 2011). However, if one is measuring a higher-level behavior, such as romantic interest, then avatars are more likely to elicit a response than agents (Lim and Reeves 2010).

Research has illustrated several consequences of avatar use in social interactions. Building on the Proteus effect on individuals, social interactions are also impacted by avatar appearance (Yee and Bailenson 2007). In a series of studies in perceptual psychology, social psychologists Snyder, Tanke, and Berscheid established that unconfirmed perception of appearance in social situations (e.g., neither participant knows what the other truly looks like) can cause significant changes in the behavior of both participants. In one study, subjects participated in a blind social interaction where one of the subjects was shown an arbitrary attractive image and told it was the other subject. In the ensuing conversation, both participants began behaving more flirtatiously. This effect even lasted after the conclusion of the experiment when subjects met in person and were informed of the deception (Snyder, Tanke, and Berscheid 1977). According to this hypothesis, social stereotypes applied to avatars will elicit behavior change in users depending on the appearance of each user's avatar.

The flexibility of virtual environments to present "reality" in an unconstrained manner brings up an interesting psychological dilemma. The perceptions of individuals involved in social interactions might be entirely different depending on their own perception of events. There is no requirement for each participant to receive the same version of events. While potentially problematic if left to chance, social interactions intentionally transformed represent a powerful mechanism for social influence

(Bailenson et al. 2005). This concept has become known as transformed social interaction, or TSI.

The theory behind TSI suggests the imminent flexibility of virtual reality is the perfect medium for leveraging known psychological concepts to enhance both individual and group performance (Bailenson et al. 2008). For example, there is evidence for potential benefits of specific seating locations in a classroom (Montello 1988; Stires 1980). Yet physical reality dictates that only one individual can occupy the "sweet spot" in any given classroom. With the unconstrained nature of the virtual, each participant can be shown his or her avatar occupying that spot in a virtual classroom while simultaneously being shown others' avatars distributed throughout unoccupied seats and be none the wiser. Further, directed eye gaze from an instructor has proven to increase compliance as well as perception of individual attention (Segrin 1993). The same TSI approach can be applied to allow every participant in a virtual classroom to receive the virtual gaze of the instructor a majority of the time, eliciting performance improvement as well as improving classroom management significantly.

Applications of the Virtual to Affect the Actual

Current Applications

Many fields have begun to exploit VR and immersive video games to achieve results that would otherwise be unavailable or costly. Here are just a few examples of how avatar psychology has been leveraged for commercial applications.

Corporate giants such as Intel, Raytheon, BP, and Hewlett-Packard are now using virtual meeting spaces to reduce costs, allow multiple team interactions in compressed time frames, and foster individual creativity (Reeves, Malone, and O'Driscoll 2008). Providing a level of plasticity in how workers can represent themselves in virtual spaces has resulted in a positive effect on worker productivity rather than suppressing it. Companies are finding that leveraging virtual worlds to affect day-to-day operations offers a level of interaction, both personal and professional, that is not possible over the phone or via videoconferencing, particularly when team members are distributed internationally.[3]

Facebook has leveraged a simple version of avatars (vivid user profiles) to affect massive changes in social networks. Elements of a typical Facebook user profile are demonstrated to predict both the number of Facebook friends as well as frequency of contact from friends associated with relevant user groups (Lampe, Ellison, and Steinfield 2007). This means that descriptive details of an avatar can also have a significant impact on how the person represented by the avatar is perceived by others.

MMO game companies like Sony Online Entertainment (SOE) and Activision Blizzard (Vivendi SA) have designed a variety of games and virtual worlds like *EverQuest* and *World of Warcraft* that allow players to coordinate massively compli- cated events (Williams et al. 2006). While some of these events feature highly fan- tastical activities such as killing gigantic virtual dragons or fighting massive virtual armies of enemies, the positive effects on shared attentional focus (the ability to focus on a single shared task for extended periods of time), multiple simultaneous cog- nition (the ability to track and manage multiple objects on screen simultaneously), and audio-spatial tracking (the ability to identify where a specific noise is coming from in 3D) have been well documented (Dye, Green, and Bavelier 2009; Honda et al. 2007). Additionally, experiences in these highly social, time-sensitive environ- ments are reported to cultivate and improve real-world leadership abilities (Reeves, Malone, and O'Driscoll 2008). Many of the leadership skills and people management tasks required to successfully manage a virtual team are analogous to the real-world demands faced by small group leaders in modern business. Some forward-thinking companies, like IBM, have now begun to inquire about employee's online video game experience as a measure of future leadership potential (Reeves, Malone, and O'Driscoll 2008).

Health care and related fields have also begun to explore the virtual to extend the ben- efits of modern medicine and reduce the risks of medical procedures, especially on chil- dren (see also Riva, chapter 39 in this volume). MDNationwide has created a robotic assisted surgery system that allows expert surgeons to provide real-time surgical sup- port across any distance using a high-definition avatar of the patient created using mag- netic resonance imaging (MRI) and computed tomography (CT) scans.[4] This approach to sharing real medical expertise through virtual reality extends the potential benefit of modern medicine well beyond historical limitations of regional access. Physical reha- bilitation techniques using avatars and VR have been demonstrated to improve patient recovery time and their feelings of self-efficacy (Keshner 2004; Kim et al. 2007; Kurillo et al. 2011). Pediatric anesthesiology has effectively used immersive games to reduce pain in young patients for whom traditional anesthesia is too dangerous (Gold et al. 2006; Furman et al. 2009; Dahlquist et al. 2009). This innovative approach to pain man- agement has also been applied to reduce experienced pain in treatment for burn victims (Hoffman et al. 2008). Taken together, these applications are nothing short of a virtual revolution in commerce, learning, and modern medicine.

Future Applications

With the introduction of wearable technologies, it is possible that avatars could be used to perceive daily life moment by moment through pervasive mobile sensors and ubiquitous computing (Reeves and Read 2010). A forward-looking group known as The Quantified Self has begun measuring and reporting data on nearly every aspect of life from exercise and eating behaviors to priority optimization of tasks and tracking of health issues.[5] It is not difficult to imagine a world where one's every action is measured and reported. In a paper written for the US government, serious game researchers identified applications of the principles outlined in this chapter to optimize choices for citizens and government workers in the areas of energy efficiency, educational assessment, worker productivity, safety and health, and the quality of information exchanges (Reeves et al. 2011). While there are no guarantees that governments and large organizations will adopt the particular applications, it is certain that avatar use and immersive environments will continue to grow and evolve in ways that are merely beginning to be imagined.

Conclusion and Directions for Future Research

The next step for research is to apply lessons learned from laboratory work to large-scale use environments "in the wild." More research is needed on longitudinal effects of using a unique avatar over time, for example, study of gender-based effects and the effects of gender-bending over extended periods of time. Continued development of casual VEs and avatar use in everyday life will warrant continual evaluation and extension of the principles outlined in this chapter.

In sum, the notion of an avatar has been around long before the computer in literature, religion, and mythology. Since the advent of personal computers in the late seventies, avatars have received a more rigorous treatment by scholars as they predicted when and how the revolution of virtual representation would proceed. It is only in the past decade that avatars have become commonplace enough in the world for social scientists to engage in rigorous study of the psychological effects of avatars. At the time this chapter is published, avatars have migrated from academic laboratories to the world at large. As such, understanding the psychological implications—both positive and negative—is critical.

Notes

1. World population projection. http://www.census.gov/population/international/. Accessed December 17, 2011.
2. Internet use estimates. http://www.internetworldstats.com/stats.htm. Accessed December 17, 2011.
3. The Virtual Meeting Room in Bloomberg Businessweek, April 16, 2007. http://www.businessweek.com/technology/content/apr2007/tc20070416_445840.htm.   Accessed April 30, 2012.

4. The DaVinci Surgery System is a robotic-assisted surgery system with a wide array of available surgical procedures. http://www.mdnationwide.org/robotic_surgery.htm. Accessed August 31, 2011.

5. The Quantified Self movement. http://quantifiedself.com/. Accessed December 23, 2011.

REFERENCES

Ahn, S. J., J. Fox, and J. N. Bailenson. 2011. Avatars. In *Leadership in Science and Technology: A Reference Handbook,* edited by W. S. Bainbridge. London: Sage: 695–702.

Bailenson, J. N., A. C. Beall, J. Loomis, J. Blascovich, and M. Turk. 2005. Transformed Social Interaction, Augmented Gaze, and Social Influence in Immersive Virtual Environments. *Human Communication Research* 31 (4): 511–537.

Bailenson, J. N., and J. Blascovich. 2011. This is your Mind Online. *IEEE Spectrum* 48 (6): 78–83.

Bailenson, J. N., N. Yee, J. Blascovich, A. C. Beall, N. Lundblad, and M. Jin. 2008. The Use of Immersive Virtual Reality in the Learning Sciences: Digital Transformations of Teachers, Students, and Social Context. *Journal of the Learning Sciences* 17 (1): 102–141.

Bailey, R., K. Wise, and P. Bolls. 2009. How Avatar Customizability Affects Children's Arousal and Subjective Presence during Junk Food–Sponsored Online Video Games. *CyberPsychology and Behavior* 12 (3): 277–283.

Biocca, F. 1997. The Cyborg's Dilemma: Embodiment in Virtual Environments. In *Cognitive Technology, 1997. Proceedings of the Second International Conference on "Humanizing the Information Age,"* 12–26. IEEE.

Biocca, F. 1999. The Cyborg's Dilemma: Progressive Embodiment in Virtual Environments. *Human Factors in Information Technology* 13: 113–144.

Blascovich, J. 2002. Social Influence within Immersive Virtual Environments. In *The Social Life of Avatars: Presence and Interaction in Shared Virtual Environments,* edited by R. Schroeder, 127–145. London: Springer-Verlag.

Blascovich, J., and J. N. Bailenson. 2011. *Infinite Reality: Avatars, Eternal Life, New Worlds, and the Dawn of the Virtual Revolution.* New York: HarperCollins.

Blascovich, J., J. Loomis, A. C. Beall, K. R. Swinth, C. L. Hoyt, and J. N. Bailenson. 2002. Immersive Virtual Environment Technology as a Methodological Tool for Social Psychology. *Psychological Inquiry* 13 (2): 103–124.

Brenton, H., M. Gillies, D. Ballin, and D. Chatting. 2005. The Uncanny Valley: Does It Exist? *HCI Annual Conference: Workshop on Human-Animated Character Interaction, Edinburgh,* September 2005.

Cerra, A., and C. James. 2011. *Identity Shift: Where Identity Meets Technology in the Networked-Community Age.* Indianapolis, IN: Wiley.

Crawford, C. 2004. *Chris Crawford on Interactive Storytelling.* Indianapolis, IN: New Riders Games.

Dahlquist, L. M., K. E. Weiss, L. D. Clendaniel, E. F. Law, C. S. Ackerman, and K. D. McKenna. 2009. Effects of Videogame Distraction Using a Virtual Reality Type Head-Mounted Display Helmet on Cold Pressor Pain in Children. *Journal of Pediatric Psychology* 34 (5): 574–584.

Dye, M. W. G., C. S. Green, and D. Bavelier. 2009. Increasing Speed of Processing with Action Video Games. *Current Directions in Psychological Science* 18 (6): 321–326.

Fox, J., D. Arena, and J. N. Bailenson. 2009. Virtual Reality: A Survival Guide for the Social Scientist. *Journal of Media Psychology: Theories, Methods, and Applications* 21 (3): 95–113.

Fox, J., and J. N. Bailenson. 2009. Virtual Self-Modeling: The Effects of Vicarious Reinforcement and Identification on Exercise Behaviors. *Media Psychology* 12 (1): 1–25.

Furman, E., T. Jasinevicius, N. F. Bissada, K. Z. Victoroff, R. Skillicorn, and M. Buchner. 2009. Virtual Reality Distraction for Pain Control during Periodontal Scaling and Root Planing Procedures. *Journal of the American Dental Association* 140 (12): 1508–1516.

Ganesh, S., H. T. Van Schie, F. P. de Lange, E. Thompson, and D. H. J. Wigboldus. 2012. How the Human Brain Goes Virtual: Distinct Cortical Regions of the Person-Processing Network are Involved in Self-identification with Virtual Agents. *Cerebral Cortex* 22 (7): 1577–1585.

Gibson, J. J. 1986. *The Ecological Approach to Visual Perception.* Hillsdale, NJ: Lawrence Erlbaum.

Gold, J. I., S. H. Kim, A. J. Kant, M. H. Joseph, and A. S. Rizzo. 2006. Effectiveness of Virtual Reality for Pediatric Pain Distraction during IV Placement. *CyberPsychology and Behavior* 9 (2): 207–212.

Groom, V., J. N. Bailenson, and C. Nass. 2009. The Influence of Racial Embodiment on Racial Bias in Immersive Virtual Environments. *Social Influence* 4 (1): 1–18.

Hoffman, H. G., D. R. Patterson, E. Seibel, M. Soltani, L. Jewett-Leahy, and S. R. Sharar. 2008. Virtual Reality Pain Control during Burn Wound Debridement in the Hydrotank. *Clinical Journal of Pain* 24 (4): 299–304.

Honda, A., H. Shibata, J. Gyoba, K. Saitou, Y. Iwaya, and Y. Suzuki. 2007. Transfer Effects on Sound Localization Performances from Playing a Virtual Three-Dimensional Auditory Game. *Applied Acoustics* 68 (8): 885–896.

Keshner, E. A. 2004. Virtual Reality and Physical Rehabilitation: A New Toy or a New Research and Rehabilitation Tool? *Journal of Neuroengineering and Rehabilitation* (1): 8.

Kim, J., K. Kim, D. Y. Kim, W. H. Chang, C. I. Park, S. H. Ohn, K. Han, J. Ku, S. W. Nam, and I. Y. Kim. 2007. Virtual Environment Training System for Rehabilitation of Stroke Patients with Unilateral Neglect: Crossing the Virtual Street. *Cyberpsychology and Behavior* 10 (1): 7–15.

Kurillo, G., T. Koritnik, T. Bajd, and R. Bajcsy. 2011. Real-Time 3d Avatars for Tele-rehabilitation in Virtual Reality. In *Proc. 18th Medicine Meets Virtual Reality (MMVR) Conf,* 290–296.

Lampe, C. A. C., N. Ellison, and C. Steinfield. 2007. A Familiar Face(book): Profile Elements as Signals in an Online Social Network. In *Proceedings of the SIGCHI Conference on Human Factors in Computing Systems,* 435–444. ACM. doi:http://dx.doi.org/10.1145/1240624.1240695.

Lanier, J. 1992. Virtual Reality: The Promise of the Future. *Interactive Learning International* 8 (4): 275–279.

Lee, K. M. 2004. Presence, Explicated. *Communication Theory* 14 (1): 27–50.

Li, H., T. Daugherty, and F. Biocca. 2002. Impact of 3-D Advertising on Product Knowledge, Brand Attitude, and Purchase Intention: The Mediating Role of Presence. *Journal of Advertising* 31 (3): 43–57.

Lim, S., and B. Reeves. 2009. Being in the Game: Effects of Avatar Choice and Point of View on Psychophysiological Responses during Play. *Media Psychology* 12 (4): 348–370.

Lim, S., and B. Reeves. 2010. Computer Agents versus Avatars: Responses to Interactive Game Characters Controlled by a Computer or Other Player. *International Journal of Human-Computer Studies* 68 (1–2): 57–68.

Lombard, M., and T. Ditton. 1997. At the Heart of It All: The Concept of Presence. *Journal of Computer-Mediated Communication* 3 (2). http://www.ascusc.org/jcmc/vol3/issue2/lombard.html. Accessed July 31, 2013.

MacDorman, K. F., R. D. Green, C. C. Ho, and C. T. Koch. 2009. Too Real for Comfort? Uncanny Responses to Computer Generated Faces. *Computers in Human Behavior* 25 (3): 695–710.

Mennecke, B. E., J. L. Triplett, L. M. Hassall, Z. J. Conde, and R. Heer. 2011. An Examination of a Theory of Embodied Social Presence in Virtual Worlds. *Decision Sciences* 42 (2): 413–450.

Montello, D. R. 1988. Classroom Seating Location and Its Effect on Course Achievement, Participation, and Attitudes. *Journal of Environmental Psychology* 8 (2): 149–157.

Mori, M. 1970. The Uncanny Valley. *Energy* 7 (4): 33–35.

Norman, D. A. 2002. *The Design of Everyday Things*. New York: Basic Books.

Nowak, K. L., and C. Rauh. 2005. The Influence of the Avatar on Online Perceptions of Anthropomorphism, Androgyny, Credibility, Homophily, and Attraction. *Journal of Computer-Mediated Communication* 11 (1): 153–178.

Ratan, R. A. 2012. Self-Presence: Body, Emotion, and Identity Extension into the Virtual Self. Ph.D. diss., University of Southern California.

Reeves, B., T. W. Malone, and T. O'Driscoll. 2008. Leadership's Online Labs. *Harvard Business Review* 86 (5): 58–66.

Reeves, B., and J. L. Read. 2010. *Total Engagement: Using Games and Virtual Worlds to Change the Way People Work and Businesses Compete*. Boston, MA: Harvard Business Press.

Reeves, B., J. L. Read, J. J. Cummings, and J. K. Scarborough. 2011. Government Uses for Games and Virtual Worlds. Institute for Defense Analysis.

Rheingold, H. 1993. A Slice of Life in My Virtual Community. In *Global Networks: Computers and International Communication*, edited by Linda M. Harasim, 57–80. Cambridge, MA: MIT Press.

Rideout, V. J., U. G. Foehr, and D. F. Roberts. 2010. Generation M2: Media in the Lives of 8-to 18-Year-Olds. Kaiser Family Foundation report. http://kff.org/other/report/generation-m2-media-in-the-lives-of-8-to-18-year-olds/. Accessed July 31, 2013.

Roussos, M., A. Johnson, J. Leigh, C. R. Barnes, C. A. Vasilakis, and T. G. Moher. 1997. The NICE Project: Narrative, Immersive, Constructionist/Collaborative Environments for Learning in Virtual Reality. In *Proceedings of ED-MEDIA/ED-TELECOM 97*: 917–922.

Sánchez-Segura, M. I., R. Imbert, A. de Antonio, and J. Segovia. 1998. Modeling and Evolution of Social Trends in Virtual Environments. *Workshop in Socially Situated Intelligence*, SAB '98, University of Zürich, August.

Schaefer, G. O. 2010. Review of James Cameron's *Avatar*. *American Journal of Bioethics* 10 (2): 68–69.

Segrin, C. 1993. The Effects of Nonverbal Behavior on Outcomes of Compliance Gaining Attempts. *Communication Studies* 44 (3–4): 169–187.

Simmons, A. 2006. *The Story Factor: Inspiration, Influence, and Persuasion through the Art of Storytelling*. New York: Basic Books.

Skinner, B. F. 1958. Teaching Machines. *Science* 128 (3330): 969–977.

Snyder, M., E. D. Tanke, and E. Berscheid. 1977. Social Perception and Interpersonal Behavior: On the Self-Fulfilling Nature of Social Stereotypes. *Journal of Personality and Social Psychology* 35 (9): 656–666.

Steuer, J. 1992. Defining Virtual Reality: Dimensions Determining Telepresence. *Journal of Communication* 4 (2): 73–93.

Stires, L. 1980. Classroom Seating Location, Student Grades, and Attitudes. *Environment and Behavior* 12 (2): 241–254.

Sundar, S. S., S. Kalyanaraman, and J. Brown. 2003. Explicating Web Site Interactivity. *Communication Research* 30 (1): 30–59.

Taylor, T. L. 2006. *Play between Worlds: Exploring Online Game Culture*. Cambridge, MA: MIT Press.

Turkle, S. 1985. *The Second Self: Computers and the Human Spirit*. New York: Simon and Schuster.

Turkle, S. 1995. *Life on the Screen: Identity in the Age of the Internet*. New York: Simon and Schuster.

Welch, G. F., D. M. Howard, and C. Rush. 1989. Real-Time Visual Feedback in the Development of Vocal Pitch Accuracy in Singing. *Psychology of Music* 17 (2): 146–157.

Williams, D., N. Ducheneaut, L. Xiong, Y. Zhang, N. Yee, and E. Nickell. 2006. From Tree House to Barracks: The Social Life of Guilds in *World of Warcraft*. *Games and Culture* 1 (4): 338–361.

Yee, N., and J. N. Bailenson. 2007. The Proteus Effect: The Effect of Transformed Self-Representation on Behavior. *Human Communication Research* 33 (3): 271–290.

CHAPTER 8

NOT QUITE HUMAN: WHAT VIRTUAL CHARACTERS HAVE TAUGHT US ABOUT PERSON PERCEPTION

ELIZABETH J. CARTER AND FRANK E. POLLICK

BACKGROUND

RESEARCH into person perception is a broad field that can be characterized along two dimensions: the complexity of the representation of individuals and the nature of their interpersonal interactions. The first dimension spans from minimal, possibly degraded displays of another individual to full views of realistic human stimuli. Because of variability in the environment, observers often have distant or partially occluded views of others; however, they are still able to locate, identify, and discern various properties of other humans even from these degraded representations. In the second dimension, social perception and cognition can range from attributing person properties to a passively viewed representation of another individual, such as a photograph, to engaging with others in complex social interactions, including conversation and cooperative team behaviors.

In order to examine person perception along these dimensions, researchers need precise control over stimuli and the ability to produce systematic, measurable variations. Access to animation methods has provided a means for generating stimuli that can be manipulated on appearance and motion appearance dimensions in ways that video recorded or live stimuli cannot. As rapid technological advances have been made in computer graphics over the past 20 years, animation has become more practical and easy to perform. For example, the use of motion capture recording methods to generate motions for animated characters rather than creating each movement by hand has reduced production times dramatically. Additionally, models for animated characters can be reused with ease and even purchased in complete form, reducing time for model design. These achievements have made animation methods and the use of virtual worlds more widespread and have been a boon for research in psychology and cognitive neuroscience. Thus, experiments have used these methods with increasing frequency over the past decade to perform systematic examinations of person perception.

Moreover, animation methods have allowed researchers to manipulate stimulus characteristics that would be impossible in real life. Before animation went beyond hand-drawn, two-dimensional methods to faster techniques like motion capture and visually rich three-dimensional rendering, person perception research was largely limited to the use of photographs, drawings, videos, and live presentations. One early venture into the use of technology to examine person perception included the development of point-light displays. By placing lights on an actor's major joints and recording motions in a dark room, Johansson (1973) created two-dimensional video recordings to examine the role of human motion in person perception independent of human form. These point-light displays lie on the extreme end of the complexity dimension in person perception research by providing visually simple displays of movement. Motion capture systems have since been developed that use markers placed on the body in conjunction with cameras that record the movement of the markers in three dimensions. The recorded marker motion can then be used to create point-light displays as well as to map motion from a live human onto an animated character. In this fashion, real human motion can be reproduced on a variety of forms to examine precisely the interactions between movement and form. As the quality of animated characters has advanced, there have been increased opportunities to examine the perceptual effects of the level of detail available in the human form presented without concerns about movement differences.

In this chapter, we will describe how virtual characters and animation techniques have expanded and informed person perception research. First, we review findings in behavioral research and their implications both in knowledge of psychological processes and in designing virtual characters and worlds. Next, we present research in cognitive neuroscience that has advanced understanding of social perception and cognitive processes in the human brain. Finally, we discuss open questions in the field and potential future directions for virtual character research.

Behavioral Studies of Person Perception and Virtual Characters

By examining the complexity dimension of person perception, researchers have discovered several properties that can be determined from point-light and virtual characters, including gender, emotion, identity, and personal characteristics (Blake and Shiffrar 2007). Recently, studies of this domain have expanded beyond passive viewing of others to include interpersonal interactions, expanding the ability to examine multiple aspects of the dimension for the nature of the social interaction.

Gender

There is a long tradition of using point-light displays to study the recognition of gender that originates in some of the first experiments using point-light displays. Viewers were found to be able to identify the gender of walkers from full motion displays but not single frames (Kozlowski and Cutting 1977), and it was suggested that this discrimination could rely on shoulder and hip motion data (Barclay et al. 1978). Further research demonstrated that lateral movement of the shoulders and hips provided important gender information in addition to structural cues (Mather and Murdoch 1994; Troje 2002). Additionally, gender was recognizable from more complex displays than walking that also included carrying, grabbing, lifting, running, jumping, and sitting (Runeson and Frykholm 1983). A review of this literature showed that accuracy in gender identification for walking was only 66 percent correct from a side view and 71 percent from a front view (Pollick et al. 2005). However, this level of performance was shown to be very efficient when compared to a center-of-moment model of gender determination based on only structural information.

While studies using point-light displays have emphasized the role of motion in determining gender, body form is also, of course, a powerful cue to determining gender (Johnson and Tassinary 2005). An animated human of ambiguous sex was created with multiple waist-to-hip ratios and was presented with gait patterns that varied in hip and shoulder sway, both cues that influence gender perception. The authors reported that both factors influenced gender discrimination, but shape cues appeared to have primacy (Johnson and Tassinary 2005). When viewing gender-neutral walks, character appearance determines perceived gender, whereas the use of motion recorded from actual people of each gender biases gender perception for both gendered and gender-neutral characters (McDonnell et al. 2009a). Together, the point-light and virtual character research has expanded our understanding of gender cues during visual person perception in a way that was previously impossible.

Emotion

Simple point-light displays have revealed sensitivity to emotion from full body point-light dance movements (Dittrich et al. 1996) as well as point-light arm movements performing basic actions such as drinking and knocking (Pollick et al. 2001). Animated characters have allowed novel manipulations of motion and emotional displays for behavioral research. For example, viewers are able to similarly perceive emotion information from body motion when displayed by a variety of characters, regardless of body type (McDonnell et al. 2008; 2009b), but this is most robust when form information is present along with the motion rather than only displaying point lights (McDonnell et al. 2009b). Similarly, facial expressions of basic emotions presented in images of virtual characters can be recognized at a rate comparable to photographs of real people, with higher recognition rates for fear and sadness, similar rates for angry, happy, and neutral faces, and a lower rate for disgust (Dyck et al. 2008). These findings suggest that virtual characters can be employed in behavioral emotion research, at least involving basic emotions, in scenarios when careful stimulus control is necessary with relatively little disturbance of viewer experience.

Identity

Observing only point-light display videos showing joint movements, people can identify themselves and known others (Cutting and Kozlowski 1977; Beardsworth and Buckner 1981; Loula et al. 2005; Troje, Westhoff, and Lavrov 2005). A role for timing in identity recognition has been previously suggested in experiments that exaggerated temporal differences between how different point-light actors took a sip of water from a cup (Hill and Pollick 2000). Further research on identity recognition that expanded to the role that avatar form plays has shown that people are capable of recognizing their own body movement patterns mapped onto virtual characters (Mazalek et al. 2010). Moreover, avatar faces have been used to examine people's ability to discriminate between the motion of themselves and others during inversion and motion irregularities (Cook, Johnston, and Heyes 2012). Interestingly, there was a face inversion effect that negatively affected recognition of others' movements but not one's own, suggesting that perception of motion is mediated by different systems depending on whether it is produced by others or oneself. Moreover, recognition of self and other when timing irregularities were introduced suggested the use of a temporal strategy for recognition (Cook, Johnston, and Heyes 2012).

Personal Characteristics

Research has examined the effects of consistent and inconsistent characteristics in avatar perception, including face and voice matching as well as form and motion matching. When the face and voice style do not match (i.e., humanoid face with human voice or human face with humanoid voice), the inconsistency resulted in lower ratings of trust (Gong and Nass 2007). Other research examining mismatches in gender information using mannequin-style animations and outlines of recorded human walkers suggested that when gender information from form and motion conflicted such that the motion was atypical for the gender form, viewers were more likely to identify the actors as homosexual (Johnson et al. 2007). Together, these findings have implications for virtual character design in addition to informing typical person perception.

Interactions

Recently, research has expanded beyond passive viewing of others on a television or computer screen to include more interactive settings. One of the most basic examinations of these settings uses the avatar as an audience. When people were asked to perform a complex task in a laboratory setting, the presence of a real human, a head-mounted display showing a virtual human, and a virtual human projected on a wall inhibited performance equivalently, indicating that a virtual audience can be as intimidating as a human one (Zanbaka et al. 2007). Avatars can also be more active communication partners. During interpersonal interactions, humans synchronize nonverbal cues (e.g., Kendon 1970; LaFrance 1982; LaFrance and Broadbent 1976), and people prefer when their conversation partners engage in mimicry relative to when they do not (Chartrand and Bargh 1999). In collaborative virtual environments (CVEs), participants' activities are measured and can be used to drive digital avatars. The use of avatars allows research- ers to systematically vary components of social interactions in a way that is impossible with humans. For example, Bailenson and Yee used an avatar either to systematically mimic a human conversation partner's head movements with a four-second delay or to display another user's head movements from a different conversation. The mimicking avatar was assigned more positive character traits, and participants were more easily persuaded by it, showing that the previous human findings were robust and replicable even with a nonverbal, nonhuman conversation partner (Bailenson and Yee 2005).

Virtual characters have also been used to examine the effects of anthropomorphism and perceived agency on social response behaviors. Participants reported that virtual characters with low anthropomorphism resulted in more social presence and copres- ence relative to no visual feedback or a highly anthropomorphic character regardless of whether viewers believed the virtual character was controlled by a human or a com- puter. It was suggested that high degrees of anthropomorphism in appearance resulted in higher expectations for character behaviors (Nowak and Biocca 2003), and it is pos- sible that the stimuli were perceived as uncanny. Follow-up research using more levels of anthropomorphism and higher quality stimuli reported instead that there was in fact a linear relationship between the degree of anthropomorphism and positive social judg- ment, higher competency ratings, higher perceived trustworthiness, and homophily (Gong 2008). Later research further examined the role of agency by examining its inter- action with behavioral realism (as demonstrated by feedback behaviors). Again, agency did not affect assessments of the virtual characters; however, higher behavioral realism affected evaluations and reactions (von der Putten et al. 2010).

Neuroimaging Studies of Person Perception and Virtual Characters

Using virtual characters and animated stimuli has also opened up possibilities for cogni- tive neuroscientists to more clearly delineate the roles of social brain regions and net- works. Over the past two decades, neuroimaging research has implicated various brain regions in social processing, including the posterior superior temporal sulcus (pSTS), the fusiform face area (FFA), the amygdala, the mentalizing network, and the mir- ror neuron system. This work has largely focused on using technology to manipulate stimulus characteristics such as visual complexity and motion, as it is still difficult to engage in social interactions in the neuroimaging environment. In addition to using virtual characters to examine the basic functions of the social brain, neuroimaging also introduces the possibility of determining whether the behavioral responses to social partners of varying complexity result from correlated neural processing.

The pSTS

The pSTS is a category-selective region that processes human actions on multiple levels (for review, see Grosbras et al. 2012). The area was originally implicated in biological motion perception in studies using point-light displays for motion displays and randomized or otherwise not obviously organized point movement as a control condition (e.g., Bonda et al. 1996; Grossman et al. 2000; Vaina et al. 2001). Unfortunately, this method made it difficult to assess the role of motion organization and body structure. A study using videos that showed point-light animations of humans as well as full-body displays of humans determined that the pSTS was more active to the full-body stimuli than to point-light humans, and more active to both biological motion conditions than to coherent, nonbiological point-light displays (Grossman and Blake 2001). In order to compare biological and nonbiological motion in the presence of form information, Pelphrey and colleagues (2003a) created a set of four characters that moved over the course of various animated sequences, including a human that walked, a robot that walked, a grandfather clock that ticked, and a mechanical figure that consisted of the robot parts organized such that the pieces moved an equivalent amount to the robot but did not demonstrate biological motion. By using this set of animations rather than the previously popular point-light walkers and random-motion control conditions, it was determined that the pSTS is specifically sensitive to biological motion rather than meaningful coherent motion. A follow-up study demonstrated that this sensitivity is present during middle childhood and increases with age (Carter and Pelphrey 2006). Interestingly, the realism of animated characters has been found to correlate with the response bias to identify motion as biological in nature, independent of the motion properties themselves, which in turn correlates with activity in the left pSTS (Chaminade et al. 2007). Therefore, it is likely that this region is modulated by both motion and appearance.

Further research using virtual characters clarified the role of the pSTS in goal-directed action and intention understanding. Animated characters have been used to carefully control stimuli to examine the effects of violation of goal-directed action expectations for looking (Pelphrey et al. 2003b) and grasping (e.g., Pelphrey et al. 2004). The effects of the interaction of appearance and motion on brain responses to goal-directed action and intention expectations have also been examined. Using four characters, three of which performed identical biological motion while exhibiting various degrees of human likeness and one of which was clearly nonhuman and performed biological motion, it was again demonstrated that the pSTS is sensitive to biological motion (Carter et al. 2011). However, modulation of pSTS by goal-directed action and intention understanding only occurred for the two biological motion characters that had human characteristics, an animated human, and a humanoid robot with eyes.

The FFA

The fusiform gyrus (FFG) contains a category-selective region for faces that is commonly referred to as the fusiform face area (FFA) (e.g., Puce et al. 1995; 1996; Kanwisher et al. 1997). Given that newborn infants only minutes after birth preferentially attend to basic, schematic faces (Goren, Sarty, and Wu 1975; Johnson et al. 1991), it is possible that processing in this region occurs even when the face stimuli have a low level of visual detail. Neuroimaging research on adults has examined this issue to determine the level of detail necessary to engage this brain region. Yuasa and colleagues performed a series of studies in which they reported that graphic, stylized emoticons elicited activity in the FFG (Yuasa et al. 2011), although regular text-based emoticons did not (Yuasa et al. 2007). These findings suggest a threshold for level of detail in eliciting FFA activity. Additional research has found similar response patterns to face photographs and schematic drawings (Britton et al. 2008). However, these findings have not gone uncontested. When directly comparing human and avatar faces displaying emotions, subjects showed a higher response level in the FFA to the human than to the avatar stimuli (Moser et al. 2007). This finding is in contrast to research with event-related potential (ERP) measurements that found that avatar faces with emotional expressions elicited stronger N170 and P100 responses than did equivalent photographs of humans (Mühlberger et al. 2009). Studies performed using intracranial recordings (e.g., Allison et al. 1999) and source localization methods (Herrmann et al. 2005) have suggested that the source of these signals is the FFA. Thus, though experiments have demonstrated that faces of varying level of detail can engage the FFA, the degree to which they do so relative to real faces remains uncertain. The results suggest that future virtual character research, particularly during child development, could be highly informative in explaining how the brain identifies faces in the environment.

The Amygdala

The amygdala has long been implicated by neuroimaging studies in processing fearful facial expressions (e.g., Adolphs et al. 1995; Morris et al. 1996; 1998; Whalen et al. 1998). One meta-analysis found that any emotion elicited amygdala activity more than did neutral stimuli, but activity was particularly strong in response to displays of negative emotions, including fear and disgust (Costafreda et al. 2008). One difficulty faced in research on emotional displays is that the stimuli, particularly when dynamic, are very challenging to control. For example, manipulating intensity and ensuring that there are no other cues for emotions, nonverbal signals, or interstimulus differences is nearly impossible with live actors. Researchers have tried to address these issues by using morphs of multiple photographs of facial expressions to generate static (e.g., Sato et al. 2002) or dynamic stimuli (e.g., LaBar et al. 2003). However, these methods can create artifacts that result in abnormal-looking stimuli. Virtual characters provide control of stimuli while reducing the risk of these negative side effects occurring. Moreover, they allow the use of combined face and full-body stimuli, an option unavailable when using morphs. For example, both the amygdala and the pSTS were more active when an approaching figure made an angry face than when he made a happy face, showing an interaction between emotion and motion processing (Carter and Pelphrey 2008).

Unfortunately, little research has been done using virtual characters to explore amygdala response. Behavioral studies have found that emotion recognition can be as good for face and body expressions of emotions performed by avatars as it is for video recordings of humans; neuroimaging has the potential to further examine the equivalence of these two types of stimuli and determine whether avatars, with their beneficial features, can be used in place of video or morphed stimuli to examine the amygdala. Moser and colleagues (2007) reported superior emotion recognition for human rather than avatar facial expressions of emotions, but both types of stimuli elicited bilateral amygdala activity, although the number of active voxels in response to the human was higher. It is unknown, however, whether this is due to the quality of the stimuli themselves; the differences in behavioral performance indicate that the facial expressions were not equivalent across stimulus types. As virtual characters improve in quality, it will be increasingly possible to determine the roles of visual complexity and humanlike appearance in amygdala engagement.

The Mentalizing Network

Mentalizing, the understanding that other people have beliefs, desires, and knowledge of their own, is believed to rely on a network of regions that includes the temporoparietal junction (TPJ) and the medial prefrontal cortex (mPFC). Early neuroimaging research suggested that the TPJ and mPFC responded more to stories (Fletcher et al. 1995; Gallagher et al. 2000) and cartoons that involved mentalizing (Gallagher et al. 2000) than to those that involved only physical information. In order to clarify the role of perceptual information and identity in eliciting mentalizing network activity, Castelli and colleagues (2000) used animated shapes that moved in ways evoking either mental state attribution or action description and found that mental state attribution, even for these unusual characters and motion patterns, elicited social brain activity in the mPFC, the TPJ, basal temporal regions, and extrastriate cortex.

The mPFC also plays a role in perspective taking and determining similarities between the viewer and another individual and monitoring the actions of others (for review, see Amodio and Frith 2006). Vogeley and colleagues performed a series of studies to investigate the neural correlates of perspective-taking and actions using virtual characters (Vogeley et al. 2004; David et al. 2006). They reported overlapping brain activity in the mPFC for only one's own perspective and actions (Vogeley et al. 2004; David et al. 2006). The use of avatars allowed participants to control first-person interactions despite being immobile in an MRI scanner. Virtual characters also have been used during passive viewing to examine the role of self-similarity in this region. In addition to determining that pSTS activity was modulated by identity, Carter and colleagues (2011) found that the level of mPFC activity corresponded to the humanness of characters even when biological motion was equivalent, providing additional evidence for its importance in person identification and monitoring.

The Mirror Neuron System

In humans, the mirror neuron system has been proposed to include right inferior frontal gyrus (IFG) and inferior parietal lobule (IPL). This system has been suggested to be complementary to the mentalizing system (Van Overwalle and Baetens 2009) and responds during both observation and performance of actions (for review, see Rizzolatti and Craighero 2004). In numerous studies using live-action video recordings and photographic stimuli, these regions have been implicated in processing hand movements (e.g., Chaminade and Decety 2002; Iacoboni et al. 1999), and goal-directed actions on objects and communicative hand gestures (e.g., Montgomery et al. 2007; Grèzes et al. 2003). Additionally, the mirror neuron system is modulated if an action is presented within a context that confers intentional information on the movement, such as reaching to grasp a mug to drink from it or clean up after a meal (Iacoboni et al. 2005).

One challenge in examining this system using virtual characters is its inconsistent engagement by these stimuli. In a near-infrared spectroscopy (NIRS) study that sought to clarify the roles of appearance and kinematics, videos were shown of the bodies of an animated human and robot as they performed grasping actions in humanlike and robotic styles (Shimada 2010). The mirror neuron system, thought to be involved in motor observation and performance, was modulated by motion style for the human character, but not for the robot character. However, fMRI studies that have addressed goal-directed action and intention using animated stimuli have not always found mirror neuron system responses, even during grasping behaviors similar to those that elicited activity with live-action recordings (e.g., Pelphrey et al. 2004; Carter et al. 2011). Although it is possible that this is due to subtle differences in the actions performed in the different types of stimuli, it is also a potential side effect of using animated stimuli rather than live-action video recordings to study the mirror neuron system. There are also possible roles of identity and of action repetition and the presence of the faces of the animated characters. A few studies have used robot actions for comparison with human movements and also found conflicting results for elicitation of the mirror neuron system (Tai et al. 2004; Gazzola et al. 2007; Oberman et al. 2007). Together, these findings suggest that virtual and robotic stimuli might not enhance the ability to study this neural system.

Virtual versus Real: Preliminary Research in Neural Processes Using Moving Stimuli

Research using animated characters has been very beneficial in expanding our knowledge of the social brain; however, relatively little research has been performed to directly compare animated and veridical moving stimuli. Perani and colleagues (2001) examined whether live and virtual stimuli elicited similar neural responses by comparing object grasping by a real hand, by a high-quality virtual reality hand, and by a low-quality virtual reality hand in 3D and 2D presentations. Although a subset of regions was similar for all conditions, the right posterior parietal cortex only showed an increased response for the real actions performed in a natural environment. The high-quality virtual hand

and real hand elicited higher activity in the mesial premotor cortex and superior parietal lobule (SPL) than did the low-quality virtual hand, suggesting that animation quality also plays a role in brain response. Also, brain responses to movie clips that include live-action videos and cartoons of human and nonhuman characters have been examined in adults and children (Han et al. 2005; 2007). In adults, the mPFC was only active for the live-action video clips of other humans, whereas cartoons of humans and nonhumans and videos of animals elicited activity in the SPL (Han et al. 2005). In 10-year-old children, the mPFC did not show this differentiation, and was instead active in response to human and nonhuman agents in live-action videos and cartoons (Han et al. 2007). For these two studies, however, the cartoon and video clips were not matched for the amount, type, or content of motion. In order to address these issues, Mar and colleagues (2007) showed participants live-action videos and their rotoscoped cartoon counterparts. The rSTS, rTPJ, right middle frontal gyrus, and some areas of occipital cortex showed a higher level of activity in response to the live-action videos than the rotoscoped cartoons; the left intraparietal sulcus, right premotor cortex, right orbitofrontal cortex, right superior frontal gyrus, and right anterior IFG showed the reverse pattern of effects.

Unfortunately, it is difficult to tease apart what aspects of the results of these studies are driven by the differences between real and artificial characters versus the role of visual complexity in the stimuli. The cartoon-style and virtual stimuli did not have the same degree of color variation, shading, small detail, and other complex visual features present in the live-action video recordings. As animation techniques improve, it is important to continue to examine neural differentiation between virtual and live-action and carefully assess which stimuli are appropriate to specific lines of research.

Considerations for Future Research

Although the use of virtual characters has proven to expand our knowledge of person perception processes in behavior and the brain, this method still suffers from various limitations. One major concern is that research comparing real and animated humans must constantly be replicated and updated in order to address improvements in technology. As virtual characters increase in quality, they will presumably be less differentiable from real humans and therefore elicit more similar behavioral and brain responses. This convergence could result in a more widespread use of animated stimuli, as researchers would see less of a trade-off between stimulus realism and manipulability and control.

Another issue raised by improvement in animation quality is the possibility of virtual characters being perceived as uncanny. The Uncanny Valley hypothesis suggests that as human replicas (in our case, animated characters) become increasingly human-like, there is a point at which they cause a sense of revulsion in the viewer (Mori [1970] 2005) (fig. 8.1).

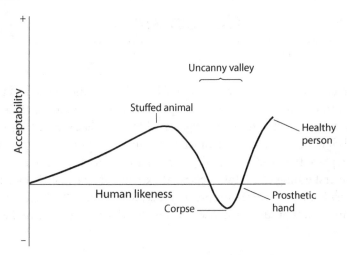

FIGURE 8.1. Adapted representation of Mori's Uncanny Valley: plot comparing acceptability and human likeness.

It is possible that as a virtual character becomes closer to a human, viewers are more prone to compare it to real humans and are repulsed by the numerous shortcomings and violations of human norms (e.g., MacDorman and Ishiguro 2006; Pollick 2010). Popular films that have attempted to achieve photorealistic, lifelike animated characters have fallen into the Uncanny Valley, eliciting critic descriptions such as that characters lack "the spark of true life" (Dargis 2007). Moreover, systematic research on animated characters suggests that the phenomenon is real and quantifiable. High-fidelity virtual characters have been consistently rated as uncanny (e.g., Seyama and Nagayama 2007; Tinwell et al. 2011), an effect that is exaggerated when upper facial movement is limited during emotional expressions (Tinwell et al. 2011). Additionally, uncanny video recordings of robots have been found to elicit different patterns of brain activity than actual humans or less humanlike robots (e.g., Saygin et al. 2012), providing further evidence for this phenomenon. Thus, future behavioral and brain research using realistic virtual characters must ensure that the characters are not uncanny in order to avoid the introduction of a potential confound: the visceral response of the viewer.

Finally, it is important not to overlook the role that person perception research involving real humans can play in informing social interactions with virtual characters. As virtual characters increase in quality, it will be possible to introduce increasingly human-like characteristics into avatar-mediated conversations. Past research investigating behavioral issues such as communication posture (Kendon 1970) and mimicry (Chartrand and Bargh 1999) as well as conversational head nodding (e.g., Boker et al. 2011) and facial expression dampening (Boker et al. 2011) can target areas for development in avatars. Moreover, these characters can then be compared to humans in behavioral and neuroimaging studies to systematically measure gains in realism and presence.

CONCLUSIONS

Virtual characters have proven to be a valuable tool in psychological and neuroscientific research into how human actions are perceived and recognized. This knowledge has fed back to studies that have investigated what parameters are effective for visualizing virtual characters. There is still much to be known before either a virtual character could fully replace the need for a real human character in an experiment or a precise scientific understanding could fully specify the design of a virtual character. However, much progress has been made in the previous decades, and this has begun to inform our understanding of important brain mechanisms and visual properties in the perception of virtual characters.

REFERENCES

Adolphs, R., D. Tranel, H. Damasio, and A. R. Damasio. 1995. Fear and the Human Amygdala. *Journal of Neuroscience* 15 (9): 5879–5891.

Allison, T., A. Puce, D. D. Spencer, and G. McCarthy. 1999. Electrophysiological Studies of Human Face Perception. http://www.ncbi.nlm.nih.gov/pubmed/10450888 1: Potentials Generated in Occipitotemporal Cortex by Face and Non-face Stimuli. *Cerebral Cortex* 9 (5): 415–430.

Amodio, D. M., and C. D. Frith. 2006. Meeting of Minds: The Medial Frontal Cortex and Social Cognition. *Nature Reviews Neuroscience* 7: 268–277.

Bailenson, J. N., and N. Yee. 2005. Digital Chameleons: Automatic Assimilation of Nonverbal Gestures in Immersive Virtual Environments. *Psychological Science* 16 (10): 814–819.

Barclay, C. D., J. E. Cutting, and L. T. Kozlowski. 1978. Temporal and Spatial Factors in Gait Perception That Influence Gender Recognition. *Perception and Psychophysics* 23 (2): 145–152.

Beardsworth, T., and T. Buckner. 1981. The Ability to Recognize Oneself from a Video Recording of One's Movements without Seeing One's Body. *Bulletin of the Psychonomic Society* 18 (1): 19–22.

Blake, R., and M. Shiffrar. 2007. Perception of Human Motion. *Annual Review of Psychology* 58: 47–73.

Boker, S. M., J. F. Cohn, B. J. Theobald, I. Matthews, J. R. Spies, and T. R. Brick. 2011. Something in the Way We Move: Motion Dynamics, Not Perceived Sex, Influence Head Movements in Conversation. *Journal of Experimental Psychology: Human Perception and Performance* 37 (3): 874–891.

Bonda, E., D. Ostry, and A. Evans. 1996. Specific Involvement of Human Parietal Systems in the Perception of Biological Motion and the Amygdala. *Perception and Psychophysics* 76 (11): 3737–3744.

Britton, J. C., L. M., Shin L. F. Barrett, S. L. Rauch, and C. I. Wright 2008. Amygdala and Fusiform Gyrus Temporal Dynamics: Responses to Negative Facial Expressions. *BMC Neuroscience* 9 (44): 1–6.

Carter, E. J., and K. A. Pelphrey. 2006. School-Aged Children Exhibit Domain-Specific Responses to Biological Motion. *Social Neuroscience* 1 (3–4): 396–411.

Carter, E. J., and K. A. Pelphrey. 2008. Friend or Foe? Brain Systems Involved in the Perception of Dynamic Signals of Menacing and Friendly Social Approaches. *Social Neuroscience* 3 (2): 151–163.

Carter, E. J., J. K. Hodgins, and D. H. Rakison. 2011. Exploring the Neural Correlates of Goal-Directed Action and Intention Understanding. *NeuroImage* 54 (2): 1634–1642.

Castelli, F., F. Happé, U. Frith, and C. Frith. 2000. Movement and Mind: A Functional Imaging Study of Perception and Interpretation of Complex Intentional Movement Patterns. *NeuroImage* 12: 314–325.

Chaminade, T., and J. Decety. 2002. Leader or Follower? Involvement of the Inferior Parietal Lobule in Agency. *NeuroReport* 13 (15): 1975–1978.

Chaminade, T., J. K. Hodgins, and M. Kawato. 2007. Anthropomorphism Influences Perception of Computer-Animated Characters' Actions. *Social Cognitive and Affective Neuroscience* 2 (3): 206–216.

Chartrand, T. L., and J. A. Bargh 1999. The Chameleon Effect: The Perception-Behavior Link and Social Interaction. *Journal of Personality and Social Psychology* 76 (6): 893–910.

Cook, R., A. Johnston, and C. Heyes. 2012. Self-Recognition of Avatar Motion: How Do I Know It's Me? *Proceedings of the Royal Society B: Biological Sciences* 279 (1729): 669–674.

Costafreda, S. G., M. J. Brammer, A. S. David, and C. H. Y. Fu. 2008. Predictors of Amygdala Activation during the Processing of Emotional Stimuli: A Meta-analysis of 385 PET and fMRI Studies. *Brain Research Reviews* 58: 57–70.

Cutting, James E., and L. T. Kozlowski. 1977. Recognizing Friends by Their Walk: Gait Perception without Familiarity Cues. *Bulletin of the Psychonomic Society* 9 (5): 353–356.

Dargis, M. 2007. Confronting the Fabled Monster, Not to Mention His Naked Mom. *New York Times*, November 16, E1.

David, N., B. H. Bewernick, M. X. Cohen, A. Newen, S. Lux, G. R. Fink, N. J. Shah, et al. 2006. Neural Representations of Self versus Other: Visual-Spatial Perspective Taking and Agency in a Virtual Ball-Tossing Game. *Journal of Cognitive Neuroscience* 18 (6): 898–910.

Dittrich, W. H., T. Troscianko, S. E. G. Lea, and D. Morgan. 1996. Perception of Emotion from Dynamic Point-Light Displays Represented in Dance. *Perception* 25 (6): 727–739.

Dyck, M., M. Winbeck, S. Leiberg, Y. Chen, R. C. Gur, R. C. Gur, and K. Mathiak. 2008. Recognition Profile of Emotions in Natural and Virtual Faces. *PloS One* 3 (11): e3628.

Fletcher, Paul C., F. Happe, U. Frith, S. C. Baker, R. J. Dolan, R. S. J. Frackowiak, and C. D. Frith. 1995. Other Minds in the Brain: A Functional Imaging Study of "Theory of Mind" in Story Comprehension. *Cognition* 57: 109–128.

Gallagher, H. L., F. Happé, N. Brunswick, P. C. Fletcher, U. Frith, and C. D. Frith 2000. Reading the Mind in Cartoons and Stories: An fMRI Study of "Theory of Mind" in Verbal and Nonverbal Tasks. *Neuropsychologia* 38: 11–21.

Gazzola, V., G. Rizzolatti, B. Wicker, and C. Keysers. 2007. The Anthropomorphic Brain: The Mirror Neuron System Responds to Human and Robotic Actions. *NeuroImage* 35 (4): 1674–1684.

Gong, L. 2008. How Social Is Social Responses to Computers? The Function of the Degree of Anthropomorphism in Computer Representations. *Computers in Human Behavior* 24: 1494–1509.

Gong, L., and C. Nass, 2007. When a Talking-Face Computer Agent Is Half-Human and Half-Humanoid: Human Identity and Consistency Preference. *Human Communication Research* 33 (2): 163–193.

Goren, C. C., M. Sarty, and P. Y. K. Wu. 1975. Visual Following and Pattern Discrimination of Face-Like Stimuli by Newborn Infants. *Pediatrics* 56 (4): 544–549.

Grèzes, J., J. Armony, J. Rowe, and R. Passingham. 2003. Activations Related to "Mirror" and "Canonical" Neurones in the Human Brain: An fMRI Study. *NeuroImage* 18: 928–937.

Grosbras, M.-H., S. Beaton, and S. B. Eickhoff. 2012. Brain Regions Involved in Human Movement Perception: A Quantitative Voxel-Based Meta-analysis. *Human Brain Mapping* 33: 431–454.

Grossman, E. D., and R. Blake 2001. Brain Activity Evoked by Inverted and Imagined Biological Motion. *Vision Research* 41: 1475–1482.

Grossman, E., M. Donnelly, R. Price, D. Pickens, V. Morgan, G. Neighbor, and R. Blake. 2000. Brain Areas Involved in Perception of Biological Motion. *Journal of Cognitive Neuroscience* 12 (5): 711–720.

Han, S., Y. Jiang, and G. W. Humphreys. 2007. Watching Cartoons Activates the Medial Prefrontal Cortex in Children. *Chinese Science Bulletin* 52 (24): 3371–3375.

Han, S., Y. Jiang, G. W. Humphreys, T. Zhou, and P. Cai. 2005. Distinct Neural Substrates for the Perception of Real and Virtual Visual Worlds. *NeuroImage* 24 (3): 928–935.

Herrmann, M. J., A.-C. Ehlis, A. Muehlberger, and A. J. Fallgatter. 2005. Source Localization of Early Stages of Face Processing. *Brain Topography* 18 (2): 77–85.

Hill, H., and F. E. Pollick. 2000. Exaggerating Temporal Differences Enhances Recognition of Individuals from Point Light Displays. *Psychological Science* 11 (3): 223–228.

Iacoboni, M., I. Molnar-Szakacs, V. Gallese, G. Buccino, J. C. Mazziotta, and G. Rizzolatti. 2005. Grasping the Intentions of Others with One's Own Mirror Neuron System. *PLoS Biology* 3 (3): e79.

Iacoboni, M., R. P. Woods, M. Brass, H. Bekkering, J. C. Mazziotta, and G. Rizzolatti. 1999. Cortical Mechanisms of Human Imitation. *Science* 286: 2526–2528.

Johansson, G. 1973. Visual Perception of Biological Motion and a Model for Its Analysis. *Perception and Psychophysics* 14: 201–211.

Johnson, K. L., S. Gill, V. Reichman, and L. G. Tassinary. 2007. Swagger, Sway, and Sexuality: Judging Sexual Orientation from Body Motion and Morphology. *Journal of Personality and Social Psychology* 93 (3): 321–334.

Johnson, K. L., and L. G. Tassinary. 2005. Perceiving Sex Directly and Indirectly: Meaning in Motion and Morphology. *Psychological Science* 16 (11): 890–897.

Johnson, M. H., S. Dziurawiec, H. Ellis, and J. Morton. 1991. Newborns' Preferential Tracking of Face-Like Stimuli and Its Subsequent Decline. *Cognition* 40 (1-2): 1–19.

Kanwisher, N., J. McDermott, and M. M. Chun. 1997. The Fusiform Face Area: A Module in Human Extrastriate Cortex Specialized for Face Perception. *Journal of Neuroscience* 17 (11): 4302–4311.

Kendon, A. 1970. Movement Coordination in Social Interaction: Some Examples Described. *Acta Psychologica* 32: 100–125.

Kozlowski, L. T., and J. E. Cutting. 1977. Recognizing the Sex of a Walker from a Dynamic Point-Light Display. *Perception and Psychophysics* 21 (6): 575–580.

LaBar, K. S., M. J. Crupain, J. T. Voyvodic, and G. McCarthy. 2003. Dynamic Perception of Facial Affect and Identity in the Human Brain. *Cerebral Cortex* 13: 1023–1033.

LaFrance, M. 1982. Posture Mirroring and Rapport. *Interaction Rhythms: Periodicity in Communicative Behavior*: 279-298.

LaFrance, M., and M. Broadbent. 1976. Group Rapport: Posture Sharing as a Nonverbal Indicator. *Group and Organization Studies* 1 (3): 328–333.

Loula, F., S. Prasad, K. Harber, and M. Shiffrar. 2005. Recognizing People from Their Movement. *Journal of Experimental Psychology-Human Perception and Performance* 31 (1): 210–220.

MacDorman, K. F., and H. Ishiguro. 2006. The Uncanny Advantage of Using Androids in Cognitive and Social Science Research. *Interaction Studies* 7 (3): 297–337.

Mar, R. A., W. M. Kelley, T. F. Heatherton, and C. N. Macrae. 2007. Detecting Agency from the Biological Motion of Veridical vs Animated Agents. *Social Cognitive and Affective Neuroscience* 2: 199–205.

Mather, G., and L. Murdoch. 1994. Gender Discrimination in Biological Motion Displays Based on Dynamic Cues. *Proceedings of the Royal Society B: Biological Sciences* 258 (1353): 273–279.

Mazalek, A., M. Nitsche, S. Chandrasekharan, T. Welsh, P. Clifton, A. Quitmeyer, F. Peer, et al. 2010. Recognizing Self in Puppet Controlled Virtual Avatars. *Fun and Games* September: 1–8.

McDonnell, R., S. Jörg, J. K. Hodgins, F. Newell, and C. O'Sullivan. 2009a. Evaluating the Effect of Motion and Body Shape on the Perceived Sex of Virtual Characters. *ACM Transactions on Applied Perception* 5 (4): 1–14.

McDonnell, R., S. Jörg, J. McHugh, F. Newell, and C. O'Sullivan. 2008. Evaluating the Emotional Content of Human Motions on Real and Virtual Characters. *Applied Perception in Graphics and Visualization* 1 (212): 67–74.

McDonnell, R., S. Jörg, J. McHugh, F. N. Newell, and C. O'Sullivan. 2009b. Investigating the Role of Body Shape on the Perception of Emotion. *ACM Transactions on Applied Perception* 6 (3): 1–11.

Montgomery, K. J., N. Isenberg, and J. V. Haxby. 2007. Communicative Hand Gestures and Object-Directed Hand Movements Activated the Mirror Neuron System. *Social Cognitive and Affective Neuroscience* 2: 114–122.

Mori, M. (1970) 2005. Bukimi no tani [The Uncanny Valley]. Translated by K. F. MacDorman and T. Minato. *Energy* 7: 33–35.

Morris, J. S., K. J. Friston, C. Büchel, C. D. Frith, A. W. Young, A. J. Calder, and R. J. Dolan. 1998. A Neuromodulatory Role for the Human Amygdala in Processing Emotional Facial Expressions. *Brain* 121: 47–57.

Morris, J. S., C. D. Frith, D. I. Perrett, D. Roland, A. W. Young, A. J. Calder, and R. J. Dolan. 1996. A Differential Neural Response in the Human Amygdala to Fearful and Happy Facial Expressions. *Nature* 383: 812–815.

Moser, E., B. Derntl, S. Robinson, B. Fink, R. C. Gur, and K. Grammer. 2007. Amygdala Activation at 3T in Response to Human and Avatar Facial Expressions of Emotions. *Journal of Neuroscience Methods* 161: 126–133.

Mühlberger, A., M. J. Wieser, M. J. Herrmann, P. Weyers, C. Tröger, and P. Pauli. 2009. Early Cortical Processing of Natural and Artificial Emotional Faces Differs between Lower and Higher Socially Anxious Persons. *Journal of Neural Transmission* 116: 735–746.

Nowak, K. L., and F. Biocca. 2003. The Effect of the Agency and Anthropomorphism on Users' Sense of Telepresence, Copresence, and Social Presence. *Presence* 12 (5): 481–494.

Oberman, L., J. McCleery, V. Ramachandran, and J. Pineda. 2007. EEG Evidence for Mirror Neuron Activity during the Observation of Human and Robot Actions: Toward an Analysis of the Human Qualities of Interactive Robots. *Neurocomputing* 70: 2194–2203.

Pelphrey, K. A., T. V. Mitchell, M. J. McKeown, J. Goldstein, T. Allison, and G. McCarthy. 2003a. Brain Activity Evoked by the Perception of Human Walking: Controlling for Meaningful Coherent Motion. *Journal of Neuroscience* 23 (17): 6819–6825.

Pelphrey, K. A., Morris, J. P., and McCarthy, G. 2004. Grasping the Intentions of Others: The Perceived Intentionality of an Action Influences Activity in the Superior Temporal Sulcus during Social Perception. *Journal of Cognitive Neuroscience* 16 (10): 1706–1716.

Pelphrey, K. A., J. D. Singerman, T. Allison, and G. McCarthy. 2003b. Brain Activation Evoked by Perception of Gaze Shifts: The Influence of Context. *Neuropsychologia* 41: 156–170.

Perani, D., F. Fazio, N. A. Borghese, M. Tettamanti, S. Ferrari, J. Decety, and M. C. Gilardi. 2001. Different Brain Correlates for Watching Real and Virtual Hand Actions. *NeuroImage* 14: 749–758.

Pollick, F. E. 2010. In Search of the Uncanny Valley. In *User Centric Media: First Internatonal Conference, UCMedia 2009*, edited by P. Daras and O. Mayora, 69–78. New York: Springer.

Pollick, F. E., J. W. Kay, K. Heim, and R. Stringer. 2005. Gender Recognition from Point-Light Walkers. *Journal of Experimental Psychology: Human Perception and Performance* 31 (6): 1247–1265.

Pollick, F. E., H. M. Paterson, A. Bruderlin, and A. J. Sanford. 2001. Perceiving Affect from Arm Movement. *Cognition* 82 (2): B51-B61.

Puce, A., T. Allison, M. Asgari, J. C. Gore, and G. McCarthy. 1996. Differential Sensitivity of Human Visual Cortex to Faces, Letterstrings, and Textures: A Functional Magnetic Resonance Imaging Study. *Journal of Neuroscience* 16 (16): 5205–5215.

Puce, A., T. Allison, J. C. Gore, and G. McCarthy. 1995. Face-Sensitive Regions in Human Extrastriate Cortex Studied by Functional MRI. *Journal of Neurophysiology* 74 (3): 1192–1199.

Rizzolatti, G., and L. Craighero. 2004. The Mirror-Neuron System. *Annual Review of Neuroscience* 27: 169–192.

Runeson, S., and G. Frykholm. 1983. Kinematic Specification of Dynamics as an Informational Basis for Person-and-Action Perception: Expectation, Gender Recognition, and Deceptive Intention. *Journal of Experimental Psychology: General* 112 (4): 585–615.

Sato, W., Y. Kubota, T. Okata, T. Murai, S. Yoshikawa, and A. Sengoku. 2002. Seeing Happy Emotion in Fearful and Angry Faces: Qualitative Analysis of Facial Expression Recognition in a Bilateral Amygdala-Damaged Patient. *Cortex* 38 (5): 727–742.

Saygin, A. P., T. Chaminade, H. Ishiguro, J. Driver, and C. Frith. 2012. The Thing That Should Not Be: Predictive Coding and the Uncanny Valley in Perceiving Human and Humanoid Robot Actions. *Social Cognitive and Affective Neuroscience* 7 (4): 413–422.

Seyama, J., and R. S. Nagayama. 2007. The Uncanny Valley: Effect of Realism on the Impression of Artificial Human Faces. *Presence: Teleoperators and Virtual Environments* 16(4): 337–351.

Shimada, S. 2010. Deactivation in the Sensorimotor Area during Observation of a Human Agent Performing Robotic Actions. *Brain and Cognition* 72 (3): 394–399.

Tai, Y. F., C. Scherfler, D. J. Brooks, N. Sawamoto, and U. Castiello. 2004. The Human Premotor Cortex Is "Mirror" Only for Biological Actions. *Current Biology* 14 (2): 117–120.

Tinwell, A., M. Grimshaw, D. Abdel Nabi, and A. Williams. 2011. Facial Expression of Emotion and Perception of the Uncanny Valley in Virtual Characters. *Computers in Human Behavior* 27 (741–749): 1–34.

Troje, N. 2002. Decomposing Biological Motion: A Framework for Analysis and Synthesis of Human Gait Patterns. *Journal of Vision* 2: 371–387.

Troje, N., C. Westhoff, and M. Lavrov. 2005. Person Identification from Biological Motion: Effects of Structural and Kinematic Cues. *Perception and Psychophysics* 67 (4): 667–675.

Vaina, L. M., J. Solomon, S. Chowdhury, P. Sinha, and J. W. Belliveau. 2001. Functional Neuroanatomy of Biological Motion Perception in Humans. *Proceedings of the National Academy of Sciences* 98 (20): 11656–11661.

Van Overwalle, F., and K. Baetens. 2009. Understanding Others' Actions and Goals by Mirror and Mentalizing Systems: A Meta-analysis. *NeuroImage* 48 (3): 564–584.

Vogeley, K., M. May, A. Ritzl, P. Falkai, K. Zilles, and G. R. Fink. 2004. Neural Correlates of First-Person Perspective as One Constituent of Human Self-Consciousness. *Journal of Cognitive Neuroscience* 16 (5): 817–827.

von der Pütten, A. M., N. C. Krämer, J. Gratch, and S. H. Kang. (2010). "It doesn't matter what you are!" Explaining social effects of agents and avatars. *Computers in Human Behavior* 26 (6): 1641–1650.Whalen, P. J., S. L. Rauch, N. L. Etcoff, S. C. McInerney, M. B. Lee, and M. A. Jenike. 1998. Masked Presentations of Emotional Facial Expressions Modulate Amygdala Activity without Explicit Knowledge. *Journal of Neuroscience* 18 (1): 411–418.

Yuasa, M., K. Saito, and N. Mukawa. 2007. Brain Activity Associated with Emoticons: An fMRI Study. *IEEJ Transactions on Electronics, Information and Systems* 127 (11): 1865–1870.

Yuasa, M., K. Saito, and N. Mukawa. 2011. Brain Activity Associated with Graphic Emoticons: The Effect of Abstract Faces in Communication over a Computer Network. *Electrical Engineering in Japan* 177 (3): 36–45.

Zanbaka, C., A. Ulinski, P. Goolkasian, and L. F. Hodges. 2007. Social Responses to Virtual Humans: Implications for Future Interface Design. In *Proceedings of the SIGCHI Conference on Human Factors in Computing Systems*, 1561–1570. San Jose, CA.

CHAPTER 9

EMOTIONS AND ALTERED STATES OF AWARENESS: THE VIRTUALITY OF REALITY AND THE REALITY OF VIRTUALITY

JEAN-CLAUDE MARTIN

WITH recent advances in graphical realism and immersive technologies, one may wonder if a user's experience when interacting with a virtual agent is almost indistinguishable from real-life interaction. In this chapter, I discuss the differences between virtuality and reality from the point of view of emotions. Emotion has long been considered to be key to human-human social interaction, but also more recently to human-computer interaction. Affective computing is the study and development of systems and devices that can recognize, interpret, process, and simulate human affects (Picard 1997).

But what defines the reality versus the virtuality of an emotion? One may define a real emotion as an emotion that happens in a real-life setting (e.g., you have a car accident). Virtual emotions occur when human participants are presented with virtual stimuli, or during interaction in a virtual reality setting (thus participants are aware of the virtuality of the setting), or any artificial setup that involves a kind of acting. This chapter thus also investigates the possible differences between the manifestations and experiences of emotions across this variety of situations.

Several studies have investigated how the use of virtual stimuli impacts social behaviors in real life. For example, Hershfield and colleagues (2011) observed that the use of a virtual representation of the future self of users causes them to allocate more resources to the future. Researchers also explored the possibility of placing socially anxious participants in a virtual reality where they can gain experience of how to act in a stressful

situation (Pan et al. 2012). The notion of presence is also addressed in terms of analogy between reactions in the virtual world and reactions to a similar situation in the
real world (e.g., fire) or by simulating a virtual environment within a virtual environment (Slater et al. 2010; Fox et al. 2009). Yet few studies explore if users of virtual reality
devices feel the same *emotions* as they do in real life.

The consideration of what might be a continuum between virtual and real emotions
raises several questions: Are there differences between real and virtual emotions? Does
virtual interaction elicit a blend of real and virtual emotions? Do users feel real emotions or do they pretend to feel real emotions? Do they keep and manage parallel social/
spatial representations of the virtual and the real world? Do users have the same level of
consciousness of their real and virtual emotions? Should computational models of emotion represent both the virtuality and reality of emotions?

As I explain in this chapter, these questions touch upon several theories from psychology and theater studies (e.g., cognitive theories of emotions, emotion regulation,
acting theories), concern several methodological issues (e.g. experimental protocol,
multimodal corpora), and have import for the design and evaluation of interactive systems (e.g., computational models of emotion, affective agents) and various applications
areas (e.g., therapy).

This chapter does not pretend to be an exhaustive survey of affective computing
research but rather points to several research areas that, brought together, suggest a
body of questions having to do with the differences between virtual and real emotions,
or more generally speaking between different levels of abstraction, and altered states of
emotion reality.

The first two sections are about theories of emotions. The first introduces some definitions and theories of emotion borrowed from psychology as well as some experimental
protocols that have been proposed for studying emotions of various natures. The second
section surveys theater studies with a focus on the actor's paradox and the double, parallel management of actors' emotions and characters' emotions.

The following two sections present computer approaches to emotions. The section on
corpora summarizes corpus-based research about the recording and evaluation of multimodal expressions of emotions, from so-called acted emotions to spontaneous emotions. The computational models section also considers the design and evaluation of
computational models of emotions and of virtual agents and how they impact the reality
of users' emotions in various applications.

The chapter concludes by outlining open questions and their impact on artificial intelligence techniques that have to manage emotions at multiple levels of reality/virtuality.

PSYCHOLOGICAL THEORIES OF EMOTIONS

An *emotion* can be seen as an episode of interrelated, synchronized changes in five components in response to an event of major significance to the organism (Scherer 2000).

These five components are cognitive processing, subjective feeling, action tendencies, physiological changes, and motor expression. Emotions are also defined as whole-body responses that signal personally relevant, motivationally significant events (Frijda 1994). There are multiple definitions of emotions but also multiple approaches to the study of emotion. In their survey, Gross and Barrett (2011) arrange perspectives on emotion along a continuum including the following approaches to emotion: basic emotion, appraisal, psychological construction, and social construction. Scherer represents these different models of emotions using a table describing how these models involve (*a*) the different components of emotions (cognitive, physiological, expressive, motivational/ action tendency, feeling), and (*b*) the different phases of cognitive evaluation (low-level evaluation, high-level evaluation, goal/need priority setting, examining action alternatives, behavior preparation, behavior execution, and communication and social sharing) (Scherer 2010).

Appraisal theories of emotion (e.g., Smith and Lazarus 1993; Scherer 2001) focus on the cognitive component of emotion. They attempt to specify the determinants of different emotions. For example, in the Smith and Lazarus model it is said that a person experiences anger when an event is motivationally important to the individual, is motivationally incongruent, and the subject considers that someone else is to blame. Such theories might have implications for the real emotion/virtual emotion distinction (e.g., do people see events as being just as motivationally important in virtual environments as in real-life environments?).

Affect generally stands for a larger variety of states with different features such as their duration (for example, moods that last longer than emotions and are not event-focused). Researchers also make a distinction between so-called *utilitarian* emotions and *aesthetic* emotions (Scherer 2000). The relation between aesthetic emotions and utilitarian emotions is traditionally said to rely on the disinterestedness of the aesthetic experience. Aesthetic emotions do not motivate practical behaviors in the way that utilitarian emotions do (such as fear motivating avoidance behaviors). Utilitarian emotions correspond to the common or variety of emotions usually studied in emotion research such as anger, fear, joy, disgust, sadness, shame, and guilt. These types of emotions can be considered utilitarian in the sense of facilitating our adaptation to events that have important consequences for our well-being (Scherer 2005). Such adaptive functions are the preparation of action tendencies (fight, flight), recovery and reorientation (grief, work), motivational enhancement (joy, pride), or the creation of social obligations (reparation). Because of their importance for survival and well-being, many utilitarian emotions are high-intensity emergency reactions, involving the synchronization of many organismic subsystems.

In order to investigate the various emotion theories, multiple elicitation and assessment procedures have been proposed and applied using pictures (such as the International Affective Picture System), films, music, voluntary facial actions, dyadic tasks, and recalling procedures (Coan and Allen 2007). More recently virtual stimuli have been involved, for example to study social phobia during real-time interaction with a virtual agent (Vanhala et al. 2012). These various procedures might be used to elicit emotions in a range of environments in order to ascertain if virtual emotions are distinct from real emotions.

Emotion skills, like coping behaviors, are central to human communication. They involve implicit/explicit and conscious/unconscious processes. If virtual and real emotions involve some kind of differences, it might be due to different underlying cognitive processes. In fact, many of the cognitive processes are interdependent, and they rarely occur in isolation (Marsella et al. 2010); emotions are known to affect judgment, especially of a social kind, and are used in persuasion. One can thus convey positive feelings with a conscious communicative purpose by smiling, frowning, or winking.

Regulation is another important skill related to emotion. People might regulate virtual and real emotions in a different way. Indeed, researchers have identified differences between explicit and implicit regulation mechanisms. Gyurak, Gross, and Etkin (2011) define *explicit emotion regulation* as those processes that require conscious effort for initiation and demand some level of monitoring during implementation, and that are associated with some level of insight and awareness. The same authors define *implicit emotion regulation* as a process evoked automatically by the stimulus itself, running to completion without monitoring, and capable of happening without insight and awareness. Explicit/implicit regulations are not considered to be mutually exclusive categories, but rather to have porous boundaries. Some studies about regulation instruct participants to use reappraisal by changing the way they think about the stimuli in order to reduce negative feelings, by distracting themselves, by employing attentional control, by realistically evaluating the stimuli, by distancing themselves from the negative stimuli, by using suppression, and by hiding their emotions so that someone watching them would not know what they are feeling (Gyurak, Gross, and Etkin 2011). All these studies possibly involve emotions at different levels of reality and virtuality.

Virtual and real emotions might also differ in terms of the conscious awareness that people have of their own emotions. The difference between a virtual and a real emotional situation may or may not be noticed by people and may be processed differently at several cognitive levels. Wiens and Öhman (2007) propose an information-processing model of emotion to illustrate different approaches to the study of unconscious emotion. In their model, emotion is inferred from the stimulus, emotional experience (feeling), behavior, and psychophysiology. They propose, for example, that in an experience-focused approach, unconscious emotion is conceptualized as emotional processing without any effects on emotional experience.

Of relevance to the user experience of emotions in virtual environments and the implementation and expression of emotions in virtual characters is the domain of acting and the various theories, systems, and methods that actors utilize both when portraying their emotions on stage and screen and when dealing with their own emotions during performance. This next section surveys these theories and techniques, particularly with a view to assessing those that might be useful when it comes to designing the emotional behavior of virtual characters and assessing the emotional effect upon users.

ACTING EMOTIONS

Several movies feature multiple and nested levels of reality and/or virtuality (e.g. *Inception, Matrix, eXistenZ, Avatar*). Several theater studies and well-known improvisation techniques (status, spontaneity, narrative skills, masks, and trance) inspire research in virtual characters (Johnstone 1979). Researchers in affective computing and expressive agents are thus interested in acting theories and theater studies (Marsella et al. 2006; Rousseau and Hayes-Roth 1998). The reason for this is that researchers and teachers in the acting area are experts in (*a*) inducing emotions in an audience without a real-life context, and (*b*) having actors express emotions using multimodal cues that may inspire the design of believable expressive characters. But how to assess an actor's quality of play? Do actors feel both virtual and real emotions (should there be a difference)? Do actors experience any differences in terms of emotion processing between rehearsals and performances in front of an audience?

These issues about the styling of emotions in the theater have been the subjects of heated debate for centuries (Konijn 2000). Should the emotions of the actor coincide with the emotions of the character, or should they not? Can they coincide? Diderot, in his *Paradoxe sur le comédien* (Diderot 1830), insisted that most brilliant actors do not feel anything onstage. Diderot took an extreme stance in the solution of the actor's dilemma, claiming that a great actor should feel nothing at all during his performance, because only then is he able to elicit the strongest emotions from the audience. On the contrary, acting styles tending toward emotional involvement are generally associated with Lee Strasberg and the Actors Studio and Konstantin Stanislavski's system. This system is a progression of techniques used to train actors to draw believable emotions to their performances. The method that was originally created and used by Stanislavski was based on the concept of emotional memory, with which an actor focuses internally to portray a character's emotions onstage.

In her book entitled *Acting Emotions*, Elly Konijn (2000) raises the issue of double consciousness, the paradox of the actor who must express emotions while creating the illusion of spontaneity. Her approach is useful in exploring any differences between virtual and real emotions, and she suggests that the emotional processes of an actor do differ between rehearsals and performances. During a performance in front of an audience, the actor transforms his real emotions (threat of loosing face by acting badly) into the virtual emotions to be displayed by the character he is acting. Konijn takes into account the emotions that actors experience as a result of performing their acting task in front of a critical audience or with the demands arising from the theater situation. She calls these emotions *task-emotions*. Her hypothesis is that these task-emotions play an important role in making character-emotions believable and convincing to an audience. These task-based emotions can be seen as real emotions, whereas the character's emotions that the actor has to express can be seen as virtual emotions or at least corresponding to another state of reality.

In an attempt to integrate emotions into virtual environments and to study the effects of the application of emotions in such environments on their users, several projects have recently arisen with the aim of studying the links between emotions and multimodality. Such an approach, and the data sets that are derived, are the subject of the following section.

CORPORA OF MULTIMODAL EXPRESSIONS OF EMOTIONS

Analogue video has been used for a long time to observe and manually annotate nonverbal behaviors (Bakeman and Gottman 1997). A multimodal corpus is characterized by a series of audio-video recordings of interaction between humans in which several modalities are available (e.g., speech, facial expressions, gestures, body postures). The goal is to study several expressive modalities and various affective and social constructs, and to explain the links among them. In the last 10 years, several studies using a multimodal corpora approach have been conducted in a variety of contexts (laboratory, meetings, TV material, field studies) (Kipp and Martin 2009; Kipp et al. 2009). Digital, corpus-based studies aim at defining computational models of multimodal behavior including details of individual behaviors that can be useful for the design of affective agents with individual profiles (Kipp 2004).

Multimodal emotional corpora are used for two main goals: experimental studies and computational models. Corpora-based approaches raise the question of the spontaneity of the collected emotional behaviors. A key issue of multimodal and emotional corpora is thus the availability of so-called "real-life" expressions of emotions (Cowie et al. 2010). Emotional data can be acted (e.g., in lab or in TV series, movies, theater plays), spontaneous, or induced using real or in-lab protocols, and can be recorded during human-computer interaction using virtual stimuli. The Geneva Multimodal Emotion Portrayal database represents more than 7,000 videos portraying 18 emotions produced by 10 professional actors via facial expressions, speech, and body movements (Bänziger and Scherer 2007). The HUMAINE database illustrates different approaches for collecting and annotating expressions of emotions (Douglas-Cowie et al. 2007). People are not only recorded in real-life situations or when acting emotions; they can be recorded when interacting with virtual agents or e-learning systems (Afzal and Robinson 2009; Eyharabide et al. 2011).

These data sets can potentially provide information relevant for studying individual differences with respect to age, gender, culture, learning style, preference, and personality. Such data can also be used to inform the specification of affective agents (Buisine et al. 2006).

Emotional corpora raise multiple methodological questions about the state of reality of the collected expressions of emotions; the quality and spontaneity of the collected data (that can be assessed experimentally) and the awareness that recorded participants have of their own emotions (e.g., if they can reliably report the emotions they feel using self-report methods). This is the reason why researchers combine several types of exper-imental protocols inspired by psychology and acting theories (Metallinou et al. 2012).

The penultimate section examines the application of the theories and approaches out-lined above to the development of affective agents and the applications they might be effectively used for. In particular, the effects of interacting on an emotional level with these virtual humans in a range of situations are examined.

COMPUTATIONAL MODELS OF EMOTIONS AND AFFECTIVE AGENTS AND THEIR APPLICATIONS

Recent years have seen a significant expansion of research on computational models of human emotional processes, driven both by their potential for furthering basic research on emotion and cognition and by their promise for an ever-increasing range of applica-tions (Marsella et al. 2010). The more recent models aim at representing various states of emotion reality, such as the use of recalled emotions using an autobiographical memory or the simulation of reappraisal mechanism.

Interactive virtual agents are a natural computer interface for humans that lever-age natural aspects of human social communication (Cassell et al. 2000). These agents build on anthropomorphic form and potential functionalities ranging from expressive abilities to dialogue possibilities. Such virtual humans aim at being socially believable, meaning that they can be endowed with autonomous behavioral and emotional abilities using multiple modalities for their expression: facial display, gesture, intonation, gaze, and so on. For instance, the affective state of an agent might be dynamically controlled to purposely express different emotional states, for example during a game (Courgeon et al. 2009). They can have a persuasive impact on behavioral change by being dynami-cally tailored to individuals' preferences and actual interaction.

Virtual humans might be perceived as more engaging and challenging characters than cartoon-like characters (Johnson, Rickel, and Lester 2000). This is a framework for believability where the degree of realism might be reflected at several levels, including user involvement. However, virtual agents can be quickly distrusted or elicit disillusion-ment if they do not behave in a coherent way in a specific scenario, or if there is a mis-match between the level of realism of their appearance and the level of realism of their behaviors (e.g., Uncanny Valley; see also Tinwell, chapter 10 in this volume). They must comply with social conventions inherent to the trustworthiness of the specific situation/scenario. Research has shown that individual learning styles and cultural background have an impact on how users look upon and benefit from intelligent agents in a collab-orative learning environment (Kim and Baylor 2006).

Virtual agents raise multiple questions with respect to reality and virtuality. Should a virtual agent be able to feel and express emotions at several levels of reality/spontaneity? When used in a training or therapy application, can the emotional capacities that users learn in a virtual context be generalized to real situations? Are emotions more real when expressed by physical agents such as robots? Experimental studies are required to understand how emotions expressed by different levels of embodiment are perceived by users (e.g., robots, virtual agents, and videos of real humans) (Riek and Watson 2012) to test if the greater the embodiment, the more real the emotion.

Researchers in multiple application areas are tackling the reality of emotions, for example how the training of emotional skill using virtual stimuli can scale up to the management of real emotions in real-life situations (Cobb and Sharkey 2006; Parsons and Rizzo 2008; Riva 2005).

Conclusions

With the recent interest about emotions in human-computer interaction research and virtual reality, there is a need for a better understanding of the different theories of emotions. What are the differences between emotions in real life and emotions in virtual reality interactions? Are the emotions felt by users different? Should the emotions displayed by virtual characters be different from those in real life? Are users conscious of these differences?

In this chapter, I have considered the continuum between real and virtual emotions in several disciplines—psychology, theater studies, multimodal corpora, computational models, virtual characters—and their applications. I believe that such a multidisciplinary approach is necessary for assessing the realness and virtuality of emotions. Such an approach enables us to identify the key concepts that will have a role to play in future investigations about these questions: the realness of the events eliciting the emotions; the possibly parallel cognitive processing of various levels of reality; the internal mechanisms that enable someone to reappraise the emotional situation; the consciousness that someone has of her own emotions; and the spontaneity of someone's emotional expressions. Further experimental studies using virtual reality interfaces should be investigated to provide experimental data about the differences between real and virtual emotions.

References

Afzal, S., and P. Robinson. 2009. Natural Affect Data-Collection and Annotation in a Learning Context. In *International Conference on Affective Computing and Intelligent Interaction (ACII '09)*, Vol. 1, 22–28, edited by J. F. Cohn, A. Nijholt, and M. Pantic. Amsterdam, The Netherlands: IEEE.

Bakeman, R., and J. M. Gottman. 1997. *Observing Interaction: An Introduction to Sequential Analysis.* 2nd ed. New York: Cambridge University Press.

Bänziger, T., and K. Scherer. 2007. Using Actor Portrayals to Systematically Study Multimodal Emotion Expression: The Gemep Corpus. In *2nd International Conference on Affective Computing and Intelligent Interaction (ACII 2007)*, edited by A. Paiva, R. Prada, and R. Picard, 476–487. LNCS vol. 4738. Lisbon, Portugal: Springer.

Buisine, S., S. Abrilian, R. Niewiadomski, J.-C. Martin, L. Devillers, and C. Pelachaud. 2006. Perception of Blended Emotions: From Video Corpus to Expressive Agent. In *Intelligent Virtual Agents: 6th International Conference, IVA 2006*, edited by J. Gratch, M. Young, R. Aylett, D. Ballin, and P. Olivier, 93–106. Berlin: Springer.

Cameron, J., dir. 2009. *Avatar.*

Cassell, J., J. Sullivan, S. Prevost, and E. Churchill. 2000. *Embodied Conversational Agents.* Cambridge, MA: MIT Press.

Coan, J. A., and J. B. Allen, eds. 2007. *The Handbook of Emotion Elicitation and Assessment.* New York: Oxford University Press.

Cobb, S. V., and P. M. Sharkey. 2006. A Decade of Research and Development in Disability, Virtual Reality and Associated Technologies: Promise or Practice? Paper prepared for the 6th Conference on Disability, Virtual Reality, and Associated Technologies, Esbjerg, Denmark.

Courgeon, M., C. Clavel, and J.-C. Martin. 2009. Appraising Emotional Events during a Real-Time Interactive Game. In *International Workshop on Affective-Aware Virtual Agents and Social Robots (AFFINE '09) Held during the ICMI-MLMI '09 Conference*, edited by G. Castellano, J. C. Martin, J. Murray, K. Karpouzis, and C. Peters, C. Boston, MA: ACM.

Cowie, R., E. Douglas-Cowie, J.-C. Martin, and L. Devillers. 2010. The Essential Role of Human Databases for Learning in and Validation of Affectively Competent Agents. In *Blueprint for Affective Computing: A Sourcebook*, edited by K. R. Scherer, T. Banziger, and E. Roesch, 151–165. New York: Oxford University Press.

Cronenberg, D., dir. 1999. *eXistenZ.*

Diderot, D. 1830. *Paradoxe sur le comédien.* Paris: Sautelet.

Douglas-Cowie, E., R. Cowie, I. Sneddon, C. Cox, L. Lowry, M. McRorie, L. J.-C. Martin, et al. 2007. The Humaine Database: Addressing the Needs of the Affective Computing Community. In *2nd International Conference on Affective Computing and Intelligent Interaction (ACII 2007)*, edited by A. Paiva, R. Prada, and R. Picard, 488–500. LNCS vol. 4738. Lisbon, Portugal: Springer.

Eyharabide, V., A. Amandi, M. Courgeon, C. Clavel, C. Zakaria, and J.-C. Martin. 2011. An Ontology for Predicting Students' Emotions during a Quiz: Comparison with Self-Reported Emotions. Paper prepared for IEEE Symposium Series on Computational Intelligence 2011 (SSCI '11)—Workshop on Affective Computational Intelligence (WACI), April 11–15, Paris, France.

Fox, J., J. N. Bailenson, and J. Binney. 2009. Virtual Experiences, Physical Behaviors: The Effect of Presence on Imitation of an Eating Avatar. *Presence: Teleoperators & Virtual Environments* 18 (4): 294–303.

Frijda, N. H. 1994. Varieties of Affect: Emotions and Episodes, Moods and Sentiments. In *The Nature of Emotion: Fundamental Questions*, edited by P. Ekman and R. J. Davidson, 59–67. Oxford: Oxford University Press.

Gross, J. J., and L. F. Barrett. 2011. Emotion Generation and Emotion Regulation: One or Two Depends on Your Point of View. *Emotion Review* 3 (8): 8–16.

Gyurak, A., J. J. Gross, and A. Etkin. 2011. Explicit and Implicit Emotion Regulation: A Dual-Process Framework. *Cognition and Emotion* 25(3): 400–412.

Hershfield, H. E., D. G. Goldstein, W. F. Sharpe, J. Fox, L. Yeykelis, L. L. Carstensen, and J. N. Bailenson. 2011. Increasing Saving Behavior through Age-Progressed Renderings of the Future Self. *Journal of Marketing Research* 48: 23–37.

Johnson, W. L., J. W. Rickel, and J. C. Lester. 2000. Animated Pedagogical Agents: Face-to-Face Interaction in Interactive Learning Environments. *International Journal of Artificial Intelligence in Education* 11: 47–78.

Johnstone, K. 1979. *Impro: Improvisation and the Theatre*. New York: Routledge / Theatre Arts Books.

Kim, Y., and A. L. Baylor. 2006. A Social-Cognitive Framework for Pedagogical Agents as Learning Companions. *Educational Technology Research & Development* 54 (6): 569–590.

Kipp, M. 2003. Gesture Generation by Imitation: From Human Behavior to Computer Character Animation. Ph.D. diss., Saarland University. http://www.dfki.de/~kipp/dissertation.html. Accessed June 15, 2013.

Kipp, M., and J.-C. Martin. 2009. Gesture and Emotion: Can Basic Gestural Form Features Discriminate Emotions? In *International Conference on Affective Computing and Intelligent Interaction (ACII-09)*, 1–8, edited by J. F. Cohn, A. Nijholt, and M. Pantic. Amsterdam: The Netherlands: IEEE Press.

Kipp, M., J. C. Martin, P. Paggio, and D. Heylen, eds. 2009. *Multimodal Corpora: From Models of Natural Interaction to Systems and Applications*. New York: Springer.

Konijn, E. 2000. *Acting Emotions: Shaping Emotions on Stage*. Amsterdam: Amsterdam University Press.

Marsella, S., S. Carnicke, J. Gratch, A. Okhmatovskaia, and A. Rizzo. 2006. An Exploration of Delsarte's Structural Acting System. In *Intelligent Virtual Agents: 6th International Conference, IVA 2006*, edited by J. Gratch, M. Young, R. Aylett, D. Ballin, and P. Olivier, 80–92. Berlin: Springer.

Marsella, S., J. Gratch, and P. Petta. 2010. Computational Models of Emotion. In *Blueprint for Affective Computing*, edited by K. R. Scherer, T. Banziger, and E. Roesch, 21–41. New York: Oxford University Press.

Metallinou, A., C. C. Lee, C. Busso, S. Carnicke, and S. S. Narayanan. 2012. The USC Creative IT Database: A Multimodal Database of Theatrical Improvisation. In *Multimodal Corpora: Advances in Capturing, Coding and Analyzing Multimodality*, 55–58, edited by M. Kipp, J.-C. Martin, P. Paggio, and D. Heylen. Valletta, Malta, http://embots.dfki.de/doc/MMC2010-Proceedings.pdf.

Nolan, C., dir. 2010. *Inception*. Warner Brothers Pictures.

Pan, X., M. Gillies, C. Barker, D. M. Clark, and M. Slater. 2012. Socially Anxious and Confident Men Interact with a Forward Virtual Woman: An Experimental Study. *PLoS ONE* 7 (4): e32931.

Parsons, T. D., and A. A. Rizzo. 2008. Affective Outcomes of Virtual Reality Exposure Therapy for Anxiety and Specific Phobias: A Meta-analysis. *Journal of Behavior Therapy and Experimental Pyschiatry* 39: 250–261.

Picard, R. 1997. *Affective Computing*. Cambridge, MA: MIT Press.

Riek, L. D., and R. N. M. Watson. 2012. The Age of Avatar Realism: When Seeing Shouldn't Be Believing. *IEEE Robotics and Automation* 17 (4): 37–42.

Riva, G. 2005. Virtual Reality in Psychotherapy: Review. *CyberPsychology & Behavior* 8: 220–230.

Rousseau, D., and B. Hayes-Roth. 1998. A Social-Psychological Model for Synthetic Actors. In *Second International Conference on Autonomous Agents*, edited by K. Sycara and M. J. Wooldridge, 165–172. Minneapolis, MN: ACM Press.

Scherer, K. R. 2000. Emotion. In *Introduction to Social Psychology: A European Perspective*, edited by M. H. W. Stroebe, 151–191. Oxford: Blackwell.

Scherer, K. R. 2001. Appraisal Considered as a Process of Multilevel Sequential Checking. In *Appraisal Processes in Emotion: Theory, Methods, Research*, edited by K. R. Scherer, A. Schorr, and T. Johnstone, 92–120. New York: Oxford University Press.

Scherer, K. R. 2005. What Are Emotions? And How Can They Be Measured? *Social Science Information* 44 (4): 693–727.

Scherer, K. R. 2010. Emotion and Emotional Competence: Conceptual and Theoretical Issues for Modelling Agents. In *Blueprint for Affective Computing*, edited by K. R. Scherer, T. Banziger, and E. Roesch, 3–20. New York: Oxford University Press.

Slater, M., B. Spanlang, and D. Corominas. 2010. Simulating Virtual Environments within Virtual Environments as the Basis for a Psychophysics of Presence. *ACM Transactions on Graphics (SIGGRAPH) (TOG)* 29 (3): 92.

Smith, C. A., and R. S. Lazarus. 1993. Appraisal Components, Core Relational Themes, and the Emotions. *Cognition and Emotion* 7: 233–269.

Vanhala, T., V. Surakka, M. Courgeon, and J.-C. Martin. 2012. Voluntary Facial Activations Regulate Physiological Arousal and Subjective Experiences during Virtual Social Stimulation. *ACM Transactions on Applied Perception* 9 (1): 1–21.

Wachowski, A., and L. Wachowski. 1999. *Matrix*.

Wiens, S., and A. Öhman. 2007. Probing Unconscious Emotional Processes: On Becoming a Successful Masketeer. In *The Handbook of Emotion Elicitation and Assessment*, edited by J. A. Coan and J. B. Allen, 65–90. New York: Oxford University Press.

CHAPTER 10

APPLYING PSYCHOLOGICAL PLAUSIBILITY TO THE UNCANNY VALLEY PHENOMENON

ANGELA TINWELL

THE concept of the uncanny was first introduced into contemporary thought by the psychologist Jentsch (1906), who combined a study of culture and psychological reasoning in his essay "On the Psychology of the Uncanny." Jentsch described the uncanny as a state of cognitive dissonance when one cannot decide what is real or unreal or alive or dead. Freud (1919) observed that, hitherto, with Jentsch's essay as the exception, earlier psychoanalytic writings on aesthetics had focused purely on why an object may be regarded as beautiful or pleasing, neglecting why objects may be regarded as ugly, repulsive, or frightening. Freud characterized the uncanny as a seemingly familiar object behaving in an unfamiliar and strange manner, raising alarm for the viewer. As a way to define why objects may be regarded as abhorrent or repulsive, Freud attributed the uncanny to an exposure of what should otherwise be concealed; the uncanny occurs as a revelation of the repressed, not only that which should be kept hidden in others, but also in one's self.

In the latter half of the twentieth century, the notion of the uncanny was revisited by the Japanese roboticist Masahiro Mori (1970) when observing people's typically negative reaction to android designs. Mori's theory hypothesizes that humans will be less accepting of robots as they become more human-like in their visual appearance and behavior. Mori created a hypothetical graph that showed a valley-shaped dip, as the otherwise positive emotional response to anthropomorphic robots decreased sharply as the robot's appearance approached full human-likeness. Objects such as corpses, prosthetic limbs, and zombie characters were placed in the valley with a human on the other side, escaping the valley.

A lack of congruency between the robot's behavioral fidelity and its realistic, human-like appearance was regarded as eerie or strange. When a robot appears close to being human, but not fully, the viewer experiences a sense of strangeness related to that robot, leading to feelings of unease and lack of engagement. This effect is referred to as the Uncanny Valley.

Given these examples and that movement is fundamental to humans, Mori predicted that the uncanny would be intensified with object movement. Thematically, an electronic prosthetic hand may appear similar to that of a human. For example, the skin tone and fingers may resemble closely that of a human hand. However, when it is moved, one may be shocked by the jerky, mechanical movements of the hand's joints, which evoke a sense of the uncanny (Mori 1970).

Since Mori's seminal work, the Uncanny Valley has also been associated with realistic, human-like characters (which are intended to be empathetic) featured in animation and video games, and various notions have been put forward as to the cause of the uncanny effect. It has been suggested that synthetic agents viewed as uncanny may provoke a reminder of one's own death (MacDorman and Ishiguro 2006; Mori 1970). Alternatively, uncanny, man-made objects such as realistic, human-like, virtual characters or humanoid robots may cause a disruption to one's predefined worldview, and, as a consequence, one perceives the object as a potential threat (Kang 2009). One's inability to empathize with a character has also been considered a possible explanation of the uncanny (Misselhorn 2009).

However, recent empirical evidence suggests that the potential adverse effect of a perceived lack of empathy *from* a realistic, human-like, virtual character may have greater uncanny consequences for the viewer (Tinwell et al. 2011). A study was conducted in which movement was disabled in the upper face region (including the eyelids, brows, and forehead) of realistic, human-like characters, limiting the amount of affective signals and the character's ability to indicate empathetic social interaction. The results showed that viewers rated these virtual characters as more uncanny than humans and fully animated, virtual characters (Tinwell et al. 2011). A meta-analysis of this empirical evidence on perception of the uncanny and emotional response in virtual characters, combined with psychoanalytic literature and findings in neuroscience, provides a new standpoint on Uncanny Valley theory and suggests a conceptual shift.

One's ability to empathize with others and understand the cognitive and emotive processes of another has been claimed as the unique quality that defines one as human (Azar 2005; Blakesee 2006; Gallese et al. 1996; Hogan 1969; Iacoboni et al. 2005; Winerman 2005). As such, I propose that the essence or cause of the Uncanny Valley lies in the perception of a lack of empathy in another. I discuss how the social brain interprets perceptual cues provided via facial expression and how a perceived lack of facial cues may cause the Uncanny Valley effect in synthetic agents. Given the importance of facial expression (especially in the upper face) as a primary, nonverbal communication mechanism to interpret the emotional state of another (Darwin [1872] 1965; Ekman

1992; 2004), my discussion is not based upon one unique concept, but on three possible cognitive scenarios in the context of human behavior and social cognition. In the following sections, consideration is given to these possible (hypothetical) scenarios: first, a perception of psychopathic traits in another; second, a lack of observed facial mimicry response to one's self from a character; and, last, a lack of affective reciprocity from a character that instigates a detachment reaction and doubt as to one's own very existence.

Historically, Aristotle's explanation of virtuality is the potential of an essence to exist as an entity in the real world (Pierce 1902). Influenced by television and technologies such as immersive three-dimensional environments, modern explanations of virtuality suggest a lack of distinction between the real and the virtual (Baudrillard 1994). Indeed, this ontological argument defines what designers of realistic, human-like characters hope to achieve in that, interaction with such a character is indistinguishable from that of a human. The notion of the Uncanny Valley has set a goal for designers to overcome to achieve realism that suspends disbelief for the viewer. While my new theory provides a plausible, operational definition of the uncanny that may be related back to the real world, it works against the modern usage of virtuality in that the boundaries between what is perceived as real or virtual may never be crossed. Set in the context of human behavior and social cognition, the actualization of the Uncanny Valley implies that viewers will fail to suspend disbelief and, in the case of virtual characters, the real and virtual may continue to remain as separate entities.

PERCEPTION OF PSYCHOPATHY

The ability to empathize with another is a critical component of effective and fluid social interaction (Caruso and Mayer 1998; Davis 1983; Hogan 1969; Mehrabian and Epstein 1972; Thornton and Thornton 1995), and a deficit in such is commonly associated with personality disorders, such as antisocial personality disorder (ASPD), also referred to as psychopathy (Hart and Hare 1996; Herpertz et al. 2001). One known visual (facial) marker for those diagnosed with psychopathy is an inherent lack of the startle reflex (including widening of the eyes, raising of the eyebrows and forehead) in response to fearful or aversive stimuli (Herpertz et al. 2001). As stated, the results of a recent study conducted by myself and colleagues showed that a perceived lack of emotional expressivity in the upper facial region around the eyes in realistic, human-like, virtual characters most strongly evokes the uncanny (Tinwell et al. 2011). Therefore, based on these previous findings I suggested that uncanniness may have occurred because it triggers, in human viewers, an innate recognition of the potential danger and unpredictability associated with a psychopathic personality (Tinwell et al. forthcoming).

Other researchers have suggested that those members of the population with personality disorders or psychopathic traits may resort to more violent and aggressive tactics to make themselves understood (Hare 1970; Hart and Hare 1996; Herpertz et al. 2001; Lynam et al. 2011). Emotions that normally regulate one's behavior in order to avoid acting on such impulses are lacking in psychopaths, making them more prone to violent outbursts. Based on the above, I propose that when one perceives an atypical diminished degree of emotional responsiveness from a virtual character, it may instill fear and panic as one cannot be aware of that character's intentions; the uncanny may be exaggerated because of the perceived potential threat of violent behavior or harm (Tinwell et al. forthcoming). Furthermore, this notion also might be considered consistent with Kang's (2009) previous interpretation of the uncanny; the anomalous, uncanny virtual agent that demonstrates a lack of empathy contradicts our predefined worldview in terms of human response and interaction. Most would expect to be able to predict another's intended behavior from their verbal and nonverbal cues. However, an atypical response bordering on that of the psychopathological, such as a lack of fear in response to an aversive stimulus, invalidates this assumption.

A comparison of verbal descriptors used to measure the uncanny effect and personality traits associated with psychopathy seems to lend some support for this proposed relationship between perception of psychopathy and the uncanny. Mori (1970) originally used the Japanese neologism *Shinwakan* to describe the eerie sensation that synthetic agents can evoke with increasing human-likeness in their appearance and behavior. The common translation for this neologism is "familiarity." However, previous authors have questioned the appropriateness and reliability of using familiarity as a variable to measure perception of the uncanny (see, e.g., Tinwell et al. 2011; Tinwell and Grimshaw 2009; Ho and MacDorman 2010; Bartnek et al. 2009; MacDorman 2006). Participants may risk missing the essence of what the Uncanny Valley stands for through a misinterpretation of "perceived familiarity." One might construe it to represent how well known or popular a character is personally or in mainstream culture (Tinwell and Grimshaw 2009), while another may believe the character should be rated on how often it, or someone or something of that type, has been encountered (Tinwell et al. 2011). As a solution, alternative semantic differential items have been suggested to measure the perceived human-likeness of a synthetic agent. In 2009, Bartnek and colleagues developed the Godspeed Indices (2009, 79), items used to measure the perceived human-likeness of android robot designs. The scale included various descriptions with a positive and negative effect: "Dead or Alive"; "Dislike or Like"; "Unfriendly or Friendly"; "Unkind or Kind"; and "Apathetic or Responsive" (Bartnek et al. 2009, 79). Building on the Godspeed Indices, in 2010, Ho and MacDorman empirically tested a new set of indices to assess *Shinwakan* (i.e., a new set of items to measure the Uncanny Valley) that applied to both animated, realistic, human-like characters and robots. It included the indices: "Eeriness"; "Attractiveness"; and "Humanness" with synonyms used to describe each dimension (Ho and MacDorman 2010, 1515).

Interestingly, many of the items in these "uncanniness scales" (developed to measure perception of human-likeness and the uncanny in synthetic agents) semantically or thematically mirror the items used within measures of psychopathy such as the Elemental Psychopathy Assessment (EPA). The EPA was developed in 2011 by Lynam and colleagues as a self-report inventory for assessment of psychopathy based on the five-factor model of personality traits (e.g., Digman 1981). The scale assesses the presence of traits such as "Anger or Hostility," "Unconcern," "Coldness," "Callousness," and "Distrust" (Lynam et al. 2011, 113), traits synonymous with those used to describe the uncanny in synthetic agents. For example, "Anger or Hostility" in the EPA maps directly onto "Unfriendly," "Unkind" (Bartnek et al. 2009, 79), or "Less Agreeable" (Ho and MacDorman 2010, 1515) in uncanniness scales. "Unconcern," an item in the EPA, relates to "Perceived Apathy" or "Unresponsiveness" from a synthetic agent, items in Bartnek and colleague's measure of the uncanny. "Perceived Distrust," another EPA item, semantically equates to "Less Predictable" (Ho and MacDorman 2010, 1515) and "Dislike" for that character (Bartnek et al. 2009), both uncanny characteristics. Last, a sense of "Coldness" from the EPA is thematically close to "Eerie" or "Spine-Chilling," both items in the Ho and MacDorman scale (2010, 1515). In other words, it may be that when researchers are attempting to measure perceived uncanniness in virtual characters, they are assessing the perceived presence of psychopathic traits.

MIMICRY, COGNITION, AND EMOTIONAL REACTIVITY

As a highly social creature, a human's survival is dependent on the comprehension of other's feelings, intentions, and actions (Iacoboni et al. 2005; Frith and Frith 1999). Accordingly, significant time and energy is being spent in the attempt to gain a better understanding of the neural and functional (cognitive and affective) mechanisms involved in this process in both humans and nonhuman primates (see e.g., Iacoboni et al. 2005; Rizzolatti, Fogassi, and Gallese 2001; Gallese et al. 1996). One interesting finding to emerge thus far is that mirror neuron activity helps us to fathom the "why" of an action observed in others (Di Pellegrino et al. 1992; Iacoboni 2008; Iacoboni et al. 2005; Iacoboni and Dapretto 2006) and to appraise and predict the possible events that could follow. For example, if one observes another grasp a ball, one might suppose the person will tidy the ball away. The context in which an action takes place also heightens our ability (and brain activity) to ascertain why a particular action was carried out and what is likely to happen next (Iacoboni et al. 2005). For example, if the person observed picking up a ball is on a sports field, the observer may be more confident of the person's likely action and intent (i.e., that the person is likely to throw the ball as part of play rather than tidy the ball away). This is where mirror neurons play a critical role; observing the actions and behavior of another stimulates the same brain cells in the observer that the other person (or agent) used for the original action (Iacoboni et al. 2005; Rizzolatti et al. 2001; Gallese et al. 1996). By reference to neurological templates set in the brain for our own actions, we can comprehend the actions of another (Iacoboni et al. 2005). The work of Keysers (2010) supports this notion with the finding of a causal link between mirror neuron activity and the ability for one to empathize with another. One typically automatically cringes in sympathy if one witnesses another being struck in the face by a fast-paced ball as mirror neuron activity is elicited that allows us to understand and empathize with the feelings and thoughts experienced by the person injured (Gallese et al. 1996; Iacoboni 2009; Keysers 2010). When one sees pain inflicted in another, one's own "templates for pain" are fired. Compelling support-ing evidence for this theory comes from the finding that those who measure high on a scale for empathy levels also have high levels of mirror neuron activity (Blakeslee 2006; Keysers 2010).

This automatic neurological process, referred to as "humaning" (Azar 2005, 54), allows us to appreciate another's given circumstance and interpret the individual's inten-tions (based on our ability to imitate the actions and behavior of others), and is claimed as the distinct feature that defines us as "human." This is possibly because it is an abil-ity that is paramount in effective face-to-face communications (Keysers 2010). In social situations, people, largely unconsciously, establish mutuality with, and signify trust and liking of, another by mimicking characteristics of the person's speech and facial expres-sion (Blakeslee 2006; Giles, Coupland, and Coupland 1991; Keysers 2010). For example, one may (consciously or unconsciously) mimic another's laughter (Provine 1992) or use a similar conversational tone, prosody, or articulation of mouth movement (Cappella and Panalp 1981; Giles 1973). Furthermore, it has been proposed that the facial nerves and muscles used in these overt behaviors may, involuntarily, stimulate the concomi-tant emotions as a useful part of the cognitive processes involved in comprehending the emotive qualities of another's speech or facial expression (Havas et al. 2010; Keysers 2010). In this way, we come to social situations with the unconscious expectation that we will be able to mimic, and thus cognitively and affectively empathize.

So what happens when we encounter a social interactant whose human behavioral fidelity is lower than expectation, such as a realistic, human-like, conversational agent in a virtual environment? One enters the social situation expecting to see similarities between one's own behavior and that of the agent, but if a disparity is detected in the ver-bal and nonverbal behavior of the speaker (e.g., the virtual character) and listener (you), the uncanny may be elicited and one may simply disengage with the virtual character.

The mirror neuron limitations and negative affective consequences of interacting with realistic, human-like characters are recognized by Iacoboni, a pioneer in research on mirror neuron activity: "Mirror neurons work best in real life, when people are face to face. Virtual reality and videos are shadowy substitutes" (Iacoboni, quoted in Blakeslee 2006). Mimicry not only allows one to empathize both emotionally and cognitively with another, but to identify similarities between oneself and others. As Gallese (2005) states, we instinctively mimic other's facial expression as we seek to gain a better understand-ing of not only the person's thoughts and emotions, but of one's *self*.

> This neural mechanism is involuntary and automatic, with it we don't have to think about what other people are doing or feeling, we simply know. It seems we're wired to see other people as similar to us, rather than different. At the root, as humans we identify the person we're facing as someone like ourselves. (Gallese, quoted in Winerman 2005)

To paraphrase, we empathize and seek empathy from others as a way to better understand ourselves, to evolve or consolidate our self-concept. If the process of mimicry is deficient when we are presented with a virtual character, because of a lack of facial expression in that character, the character may be unfathomable or inscrutable and thus rejected. In such circumstances, the receiver might fail to understand the emotive state of that character (the sender), as there is no facial expression that the receiver can mimic. Moreover, a person may perceive that he or she is not receiving appropriate adaptive feedback from the character, or being recognized or understood as would be expected in a typical social situation.

The critical role of mimicry in empathy has been recently demonstrated in a study conducted by Havas and colleagues (2010). The results showed that the ability to understand angry and sad sentences (empathize with negative emotional situations) was impaired in subjects who had received botulinum toxin-A (BTX) injections to disable muscles involved with the frown action. This implies that those who cannot mimic another's facial expression (e.g., those who have had BTX for cosmetic effect) may lose the ability to empathize with others as they themselves become less adept at reading other's emotions (Havas et al. 2010). The above evidence suggests that the kinesthetic (neurological) feedback we receive when facially expressing emotion or mimicking that of another is crucial for sensitivity and reactivity to emotive stimuli. If facial emotional expressivity is disabled in a virtual character (through inadequate facial animation) then one is denied the opportunity to mimic another because of the other's lack of expressivity. Hence, our ability to cognitively process and understand the character's emotion and to empathize with the person is limited or even eradicated, and that is when we enter optimal conditions for perception of the uncanny.

ATTACHMENT THEORY AND NOTION OF THE SELF

It has long been proposed that the concept of the self draws upon the cognitive, affective, and social behavior that represents one's personality and that, within the self-concept, there is a distinction between "I" (based on one's subjective account and experience) and "me" (as an *objective*, physical object) (James 1890). The complexities of the dynamics between the social, cognitive, and affective facets of the self that contribute to "identity" (and their underlying neural substrates) attract continued study, both empirically and theoretically; but long established is a line of evidence suggesting that recognition from others provided via facial expression reinforces the recognition of one's own identity and the model of one's self (Bowlby 1969; Tronick et al. 1975). Furthermore, actualization/confirmation of our own *existence* may be affirmed by other's facial actions in response to us (Bowlby 1969).

Influenced by observations made in ethology based on imprinting behaviors in early postnatal life (Lorenz 1952), Bowlby put forward a theory of attachment that emphasizes its critical role in how one perceives oneself and others (Bowlby 1969). The basic tenets of Bowlby's theory are that, born with an innate survival instinct, infants seek to form attachments with others. Instinctive behaviors such as crying, smiling, and babbling are used to gain the attention of the caregiver and achieve closer proximity with others. According to Bowlby, optimal development occurs in infancy, when an "affect harmony" and affinity is forged between the caregiver and child (Bowlby 1969; Prior and Glaser 2006). Such kinship inspires social responsiveness in that child, hence improving their future prospects in relationships and, thus, survival. Interestingly, it has been observed that attachment patterns acquired in infancy can remain intact through to adulthood (Fonagy, Steele, and Steele 1991; Hesse 1996).

If a child perceives a lack of mutuality with a caregiver and is unable to achieve affect harmony and affinity, then a pattern of behavior starts with a protest to the caregiver, then overt sadness, and then detachment from the caregiver (Ainsworth et al. 1978; Holmes 2001). I suggest that such a "protest-despair-detachment" pattern may occur when adults experience the Uncanny Valley phenomenon. When one cannot establish closeness or affinity with a character because of a perceived lack of response (as with poorly animated characters), one may feel uncomfortable or panicked, as one is in "dispute" (affect disharmony) with that character. The result is that one refers to the learned response pattern of detachment and the character is rejected and regarded, psychologically adaptively, as strange or uncanny. Anything else would constitute admission of something wrong with one's "self."

This notion is consistent with the propositions of Nakashima (2011), who suggested that infants may experience the Uncanny Valley when they perceive a lack of facial emotional expressivity from their caregiver. Nakashima's theory was based on an experiment conducted by Edward Tronick and colleagues in 1975 in which an infant clearly demonstrates a protest-despair-detachment pattern of behavior (Ainsworth et al. 1978; Holmes 2001) when the mother faces the infant with a blank, emotionless expression.[1] Nakashima postulated that, under these conditions, the infant falls into the Uncanny Valley and implied that if an infant has that experience (if emotional interaction with others in infancy is inhibited to a great extent), it could be self-destructive. I suggest that, with no facial expression from the mother, the infant cannot perceive any mimicry of self in the mother, nor experience the opportunity to mimic the facial actions of the mother, hence eliciting the uncanny. Tronick and colleagues (1975) coined a term for the situation in which an infant experiences prolonged, uninterrupted periods of a lack of attention as "ugly" and declared that such circumstances may result in potentially irreversible bad socialization behavior. While an infant can be moved from bad to good socialization with periods of full attention from a caregiver, there remains the risk of negative social traits being developed with no opportunity of positive interaction. In these circumstances, prolonged engagement with emotionally unexpressive virtual characters may be perceived as a threat to self, and thus evocation of a sense of the uncanny may serve as an adaptive alarm for disengagement in order to restore effective equilibrium and preserve self.

This "attachment" framework for understanding the uncanny is supported by the findings of an experiment by Minato and colleagues (2004) where participants of various age groups interacted with an android. When presented with an android as an interlocutor, the reported uncanniness of the android was stronger for preschool children between three and five years old than for the adults. Minato and colleagues suggested this may be due to the effect of habituation to android uncanniness in adults as they become comparatively more familiar and accepting of androids over time. However, I suggest a possible alternative explanation in that the children were more alarmed and scared because of a perceived lack of emotional empathy from the android, eliciting a protest-despair-detachment (uncanniness) pattern of behavior. While adults may still have been aware of the robot's uncanniness, the sensation was stronger for children because of their greater drive to forge attachments with others as part of cognitive and emotional development processes (Bowlby 1969).

This evidence suggests that one's interpretation of the world, oneself, and others is based on a working mental model that is, at least in part, the product of an infant's attachment relationship with their main caregiver (Bretherton and Munholland 1999) and that people will look to others to establish a sense of their own identity and sense of being (Prior and Glaser 2006). When presented with the opportunity to interact with a realistic, human-like character, an individual may recognize the potential of forging an attachment with that character. Based on the character's seemingly realistic, human-like appearance, one may expect it to respond in the same way that a human would. When this behavior is not demonstrated in virtual agents, who otherwise look and behave as a human, doubts are raised as to one's self and one's own existence. I put forward that if, as an adult, an individual interacts with a synthetic agent that demonstrates a lack of facial expressivity that inhibits the opportunity for reciprocal facial mimicry, one may be reminded of the panic and uncomfortable feeling that was experienced during infancy if confronted with a caregiver with little or no emotive response. This is alarming given the risk of developing bad socialization skills and the potential detrimental effect this may have on developing one's own identity and "sense of self." Without this affirming exchange of interplay and communication, either verbal or nonverbal, the certainty of one's own existence may be questioned (Bowlby 1969). If the physical me is not demonstrably recognized by another via facial expressions, despite my attempts to communicate, this goes against expectations raised from subjective experience. The conclusion may be drawn that "I" (James 1890, 291) does not exist, or is in some way less than effective, as one's "I" has failed to procure a reaction from another. Furthermore, this exacerbates abnegation of self, with the apparent loss of ability to mimic and to cognitively and affectively process the emotive state of another, crucial for survival, without which one infers the destruction or death of self.

In this sense, the uncanny is related to issues of survival, not inasmuch as it is a reminder that one's own death is inevitable (as stipulated by previous authors, e.g., MacDorman and Ishiguro 2006; Mori 1970), but rather because it acts as an adaptive alarm bell to remind the person of the importance of being able to form attachments with others, a necessary survival technique to avoid death. The perception of a lack of response and facial mimicry from a character may instill an innate panic with the realization that one is not being recognized as human, a circumstance that can distort or damage the sense of self. A lack of animation (i.e., emotional expressivity) in the upper facial region is a feature that prompts the viewer to conclude that the character may be apathetic, or may not respond to the viewer as expected, promoting the possibility of psychopathological or dysfunctional behavior in oneself.

Conclusion

The Uncanny Valley phenomenon may be caused by a perception of a lack of empathy from another, whether that be a human or a realistic, human-like, virtual character. Specifically, I suggest that the cause of the Uncanny Valley phenomenon may be attributable to any one of three things:

1. A perceived lack of emotional response in a synthetic agent, which may be reminiscent of human psychopathy that elicits a threat response, may inhibit the viewer's ability to mimic and interpret the emotional state of that agent.
2. In virtual characters, we do not observe the expected mimicry response to one's own emotions; hence there is no reflection of self in the character's face, perhaps leading to fear of destruction of self.
3. The lack of emotional expressivity in the face of the character we interact with may evoke negative autobiological memories of (even momentary or periodic or even perceived) lack of affective reciprocity with our childhood caregivers, thus prompting a detachment reaction.

Collectively all of the above lead to a state of confusion in the viewer. If one cannot predict another's behavior, one is unsure oneself what to do next, so this uncertainty and state of confusion may contribute to the uncanny. The importance of empathy (one's ability to recognize, imitate, and respond to another's feelings and actions) is regarded as a rudimentary aspect of what defines humanness. Arguably, it is these distinct qualities that are difficult to portray; perceived as lacking in human-like, virtual characters, they may account for the Uncanny Valley phenomenon. Moreover, we are predisposed to identify similarities (facilitated reciprocal mimicry) between ourselves and others (Blakeslee 2006), and a distinct lack of such in the characters might raise alarm in the viewer. A perceived lack of empathy from another (verging on the possibility of psychopathological in terms of human interaction) may induce annoyance, distress, and ultimately rejection for those seeking a human response. This uncanny effect may be caused by a perception of a lack of mirror-recognition of one's self in a virtual character that may escalate to extreme fear and dread at the potential (even momentary) suggestion of death of self.

As yet, there have been no experiments to test if the uncanny is significantly exaggerated during adult encounters with infant virtual characters. It may be that one's expectations of that character's behavior are reduced because an infant is expected to have less sophisticated social communication skills than an adult. Furthermore, one may consider that adult characters may intentionally attempt to be less empathetic toward others because of a more stoic disposition. Also, it is important to consider the implications of a perceived lack of empathic response across cultures; for example, less emphasis may be placed on nonverbal facial communication in other cultures, so characters with a lack of upper facial movement may not be regarded as uncanny. These alternative situations require further investigation to help establish how robust the possible causes of the uncanny that I have proposed in this chapter may be.

The notion of the Uncanny Valley has set a frontier for designers to overcome, in achieving authentic realism that is believable for virtual characters. Using psychological principles as a predictor of the Uncanny Valley may help shift this process from a virtual to a tangible concept. Experimental methods used to measure psychophysiological (and neurophysiological) feedback from participants in response to uncanny stimuli (e.g., recording facial electromyography [EMG] data) may provide a way of quantifying this phenomenon as an actual, objective, physical reaction in humans, not simply a vague, subjective argument as to why simulacra of the human form may elicit such a negative reaction. However, the actualization of the Uncanny Valley militates against the modern usage of virtuality in that the virtual is indistinguishable from reality (Baudrillard 1994). The appearance and behavior of a virtual character might never be sufficient to suspend disbelief for the viewer. Instead, the usage of modern virtuality in relation to human-like, virtual characters may remain set in Aristotelian thought, as the mere potentiality of actualization.

Identification of key factors in our perceptual and cognitive discrimination of what causes the uncanny effect can be extended to synthetic, human-like agents in a wider context, such as e-tutors used in training and assessment applications and androids designed to help care for an aging population. Importantly, given the potential confounding impact of the uncanny effect, this approach may help us decipher if it is appropriate to use human-like characters for such purposes, or, conversely, how uncanny characters may enhance viewers' experiences in the horror genre.

Note

1. Video footage and a full description of Tronik et al.'s (1975) experiment can be found at the URL   http://fhlfound.securesites.net/wordpress/2011/04/13/quick-look-at-too-real-means-too-creepy-in-new-disney-animation-usa-today-news/#more-1261   (accessed   June 16, 2013).

References

Ainsworth, M., M. Blehar, E. Waters, and S. Wall. 1978. *Patterns of Attachment*. Hillsdale, NJ: Erlbaum.

Azar, B. 2005. How Mimicry Begat Culture. *Monitor on Psychology* 36 (9): 54.

Bartnek, C., D. Kulic, E. Croft, and S. Zoghbi. 2009. Measurement Instruments for the Anthropomorphism, Animacy, Likeability, Perceived Intelligence, and Perceived Safety of Robots. *International Journal of Social Robotics* 1 (1): 71–81.

Baudrillard, J. 1994. *Simulacra and Simulation.* Translated by S. F. Glaser. Ann Arbor: University of Michigan Press.

Blakeslee, S. 2006. Cells That Read Minds. *New York Times*, January 10, http://www.nytimes.com/2006/01/10/science/10mirr.html. Accessed June 16, 2013.

Bowlby, J. 1969. *Attachment and Loss.* 3 vols. London: Hogarth Press.

Bretherton, I., and K. Munholland. 1999. Internal Working Models in Attachment Relationships: A Construct Revisited. In *Handbook of Attachment: Theory, Research, and Clinical Applications,* edited by J. Cassidy and P. R. Shaver, 89–111. New York: Guilford Press.

Cappella, J. N., and S. Panalp. 1981. Talk and Silence Sequences in Informal Conversations: III. Interspeaker Influence. *Human Communication Research* 7 (2): 117–132.

Caruso, D. R., and J. D. Mayer. 1998. A Measure of Emotional Empathy for Adolescents and Adults. Unpublished manuscript.

Darwin, C. (1872) 1965. *The Expression of the Emotions in Man and Animals.* Chicago: University of Chicago Press.

Davis, M. H. 1983. Measuring Individual Differences in Empathy: Evidence for a Multidimensional Approach. *Journal of Personality and Social Psychology* 44: 113–126.

Di Pellegrino, G., L. Fadiga, L. Fogassi, V.o Gallese, and G. Rizzolatti. 1992. Understanding Motor Events: A Neurophysiological Study. *Experimental Brain Research* 91: 176–180

Digman, J. M., and N. K. Takemoto-Chock. 1981. Factors in the Natural Language of Personality: Re-analysis, Comparison, and Interpretation of Six Major Studies. *Multivariate Behavioral Research* 16 (2): 149–170.

Ekman, P. 1992. An Argument for Basic Emotions. *Cognition and Emotion* 6: 169–200.

Ekman, P. 2004. Emotional and Conversational Nonverbal Signals. In *Language, Knowledge, and Representation*, edited by M. Larrazabal and L. Miranda, 39–50. Boston, MA: Kluwer Academic Publishers.

Fonagy, P., M. Steele, and H. Steele. 1991. Intergenerational Patterns of Attachment: Maternal Representations during Pregnancy and Subsequent Infant-Mother Attachments. *Child Development* 62 (5): 891–905.

Freud, S. 1919. The Uncanny. In *The Standard Edition of the Complete Psychological Works of Sigmund Freud*, edited by J. Strachey and A. Freud, 217–256. London: Hogarth Press.

Frith, C. D., and U. Frith. 1999. Interacting Minds: A Biological Basis. *Science* 286 (5445): 1692–1695.

Gallese, V., L. Fadiga, L. Fogassi, and G. Rizzolatti. 1996. Action Recognition in the Premotor Cortex. *Brain* 119 (2): 593–609.

Giles, H. 1973. Communicative Effectiveness as a Function of Accented Speech. *Speech Monographs* 40 (4): 330–331.

Giles, H., J. Coupland, and N. Coupland. 1991. Accommodation Theory: Communication, Context, and Consequence. In *Contexts of Accommodation: Developments in Applied Sociolinguistics*, edited by H. Giles, J. Coupland, and N. Coupland, 1–68. Cambridge: Cambridge University Press.

Hare, R. D. 1970. *Psychopathy: Theory and Research.* New York: Wiley and Sons.

Hart, S. D., and R. D. Hare. 1996. Psychopathy and Risk Assessment. *Current Opinion in Psychiatry* 9 (6): 380–383.

Havas, D. A., A. M. Glenberg, K. A. Gutowski, M. J. Lucarelli, and R. J. Davidson. 2010. Cosmetic Use of Botulinum Toxin-A Affects Processing of Emotional Language. *Psychological Science* 21 (7): 895–900.

Herpertz, S. C., U. Werth, G. Lukas, M. Qunaibi, A. Schuerkens, H. J. Kunert, et al. 2001. Emotion in Criminal Offenders with Psychopathy and Borderline Personality Disorder. *Archives of General Psychiatry* 58 (8): 737–745.

Hesse, E. 1996. Discourse, Memory and the Adult Attachment Interview: A Note with Emphasis on the Emerging Cannot Classify Category. *Infant Mental Health Journal* 17 (1): 4–11.

Ho, C.-C., and K. F. MacDorman. 2010. Revisiting the Uncanny Valley Theory: Developing and Validating an Alternative to the Godspeed Indices. *Computers in Human Behavior* 26 (6): 1508–1518.

Hogan, R. 1969. Development of an Empathy Scale. *Journal of Consulting and Clinical Psychology* 33: 307–316.

Holmes, J. 2001. *The Search for the Secure Base: Attachment Theory and Psychotherapy*. London: Routledge.

Iacoboni, M. 2008. *Mirroring People: The New Science of How We Connect with Others*. New York: Farrar, Straus and Giroux.

Iacoboni, M. 2009. Imitation, Empathy, and Mirror Neurons. *Annual Review of Psychology* 60: 653–670.

Iacoboni, M., and M. Dapretto. 2006. The Mirror Neuron System and the Consequences of its Dysfunction. *Nature Reviews Neuroscience* 7 (12): 942–951.

Iacoboni, M., I. Molnar-Szakacs, V. Gallese, G. Buccino, J. C. Mazziotta, and G. Rizzolatti. 2005. Grasping the Intentions of Others with One's Own Mirror Neuron System. *PLoS Biology* 3 (3): 529–535.

James, W. 1890. *The Principles of Psychology*. 2 vols. Cambridge, MA: Harvard University Press.

Jentsch, E. 1906. On the Psychology of the Uncanny. Translated by R. Sellars. *Angelaki* 2: 7–16.

Kang, M. 2009. The Ambivalent Power of the Robot. *Antennae* 1 (9): 47–58.

Keysers, C. 2010. Mirror Neurons. *Current Biology* 19 (21): R971–973.

Lorenz, K Z. 1952. *King Solomon's Ring*. New York: Crowell.

Lynam, D. R., E. T. Gaughan, J. D. Miller, D. J. Miller, S. Mullins-Sweatt, and T. A. Widiger. 2011. Assessing the Basic Traits Associated with Psychopathy: Development and Validation of the Elemental Psychopathy Assessment. *Psychological Assessment* 23 (1): 108–124.

MacDorman, K. F. 2006. Subjective Ratings of Robot Video Clips for Human Likeness, Familiarity, and Eeriness: An Exploration of the Uncanny Valley. In *Proceedings of the ICCS/CogSci-2006 Long Symposium: Toward Social Mechanisms of Android Science*, 26–29, http://www.androidscience.com/. Accessed September 28, 2013.

MacDorman, K. F., and H. Ishiguro. 2006. The Uncanny Advantage of Using Androids in Cognitive and Social Science Research. *Interaction Studies* 7 (3): 297–337.

Mehrabian, A., and N. Epstein. 1972. A Measure of Emotional Empathy. *Journal of Personality* 40 (4): 525–543.

Minato, T., M. Shimada, H. Ishiguro, and S. Itakura. 2004. Development of an Android Robot for Studying Human-Robot Interaction. In *Proceedings of the 17th International Conference on Industrial and Engineering Applications of Artificial Intelligence and Expert Systems*, edited by R. Orchard, C. Yang, and M. Ali, 424–434. Heidelberg: Springer.

Misselhorn, C. 2009. Empathy with Inanimate Objects and the Uncanny Valley. *Minds and Machines* 19 (3): 345–359.

Mori, M. (1970) 2012. The Uncanny Valley. Translated by K.l F. MacDorman and N. Kageki. *IEEE Robotics and Automation* 19 (2): 98–100.

Nakashima, R. 2011. Too Real Means Too Creepy in New Disney Animation. *Bowlby Less Traveled (BLT).* April 13. http://fhlfound.securesites.net/wordpress/2011/04/13/quick-look-at-too-real-means-too-creepy-in-new-disney-animation-usa-today-news/#more-1261. Accessed June 16, 2013.

Peirce, C. S. 1902. Virtual. In *Dictionary of Philosophy and Psychology*, edited by J. M. Baldwin. New York: Macmillan.

Prior, V., and D. Glaser. 2006. *Understanding Attachment and Attachment Disorders: Theory, Evidence and Practice.* London: Jessica Kingsley Publishers.

Provine, R. R. 1992. Contagious Laughter: Laughter Is Sufficient Stimulus for Laughs and Smiles. *Bulletin of the Psychonomic Society* 30 (1): 1–4.

Rizzolatti, G., L. Fogassi, and V. Gallese. 2001. Neurophysiological Mechanisms Underlying Action Understanding and Imitation. *Nature Reviews Neuroscience* 2 (9): 661–670.

Thornton, S., and D.d Thornton. 1995. Facets of Empathy. *Personality and Individual Differences* 19 (5): 765–767.

Tinwell, A., and M. Grimshaw. 2009. Bridging the Uncanny: An Impossible Traverse? In *Proceedings of the 13th International MindTrek Conference: Everyday Life in the Ubiquitous Era,* edited by O. Sotamaa, A. Lugmayr, H. Franssila, P. Näränen, and J. Vanhala, 66–73. New York: ACM.

Tinwell, A., M. Grimshaw, and D. Abdel-Nabi. In press. Nonverbal Communication in Virtual Characters and the Uncanny Valley. In *Non Verbal Communication in Virtual Worlds,* edited by J. Tanembaum, M. S. el-Nasr, and M. Nixon. Pittsburgh, PA: ETC Press.

Tinwell, A., M. Grimshaw, D. Abdel-Nabi, and A. Williams. 2011. Facial Expression of Emotion and Perception of the Uncanny Valley in Virtual Characters. *Computers in Human Behavior* 27 (2): 741–749.

Tronick, E., L. Adamson, H. Als, and T. B. Brazelton. 1975. Infant Emotions in Normal and Perturbated Interactions. Presentation at the Biennial Meeting of the Society for Research in Child Development, Denver, CO, April.

Winerman, L. 2005. The Mind's Mirror. *Monitor on Psychology* 36 (9): 49–50.

....

CHAPTER 11

THE PSYCHOLOGY OF ADDICTION TO VIRTUAL ENVIRONMENTS: THE ALLURE OF THE VIRTUAL SELF

....

DEBORAH ABDEL NABI AND JOHN P. CHARLTON

WHEN pondering the very idea of addictions involving virtual environments, a number of issues immediately come to the fore: Is it reasonable to talk of such addictions? How should such addictions be defined? Are such addictions likely to be phenomenologically and neurochemically the same as other addictions that psychologists talk about? What are the addictive properties of virtual environments? In the first part of this chapter we provide brief answers to such questions, noting that psychological escape and mood modification are central motivational drivers of addictions involving virtual environments. This lays the ground for the second part of the chapter, in which we examine comparatively less considered drivers of addictions that might work via escape and mood modification effects: exploration of the self, facilitated by social network sites (SNSs) and graphical worlds.

THE CONCEPT OF ADDICTION AND ITS APPLICATION TO VIRTUAL ENVIRONMENTS

....

There has been a considerable amount of research into the broad phenomenon of Internet addiction, one review of the literature concluding that 4.6 percent to 4.7 percent of adolescents, 6 percent to 15 percent of general populations, and 13 percent to 18.4 percent of college students are addicted to Internet-related activities (Young, Yue, and Ying 2011). However, Internet-related activities are large in number and highly diverse, not all such activities involving highly interactive virtual environments. For the purposes of this chapter, we define addictions to virtual environments as involving any type of interactive, electronically mediated activity or environment that could (in principle) have a real-world analogue. This encompasses most types of online activities; for example, SNSs and microblogs (which constitute virtual communities), both 3D and 2D games (played in virtual environments that could in principle be rendered physical), e-mail (virtual post), and websites (virtual books, brochures, etc.). Nevertheless, because much of the formative work conceptualizing and examining addictions to new technologies has been done with respect to Internet-related addictions in general, in referring to the relevant literature in the first part of this chapter we use the term "Internet addiction" in the interests of consistency.

Studies of the prevalence of addictions involving virtual environments show that they are not uncommon. For example, figures of 44.2 percent, 32.6 percent, and 27.5 percent, depending upon the screening instrument used, have been reported in one study of adult French massively multiplayer online role-playing game (MMORPG) users (Achab et al. 2011) and figures of 4.2 percent (severe addiction) and 29.1 percent (moderate addiction or at risk of addiction) have been reported for a study of users of the *Second Life* virtual environment (Gilbert, Murphy, and McNally 2011). Also, as we will see in the second part of the chapter, SNSs have high addictive potential.

Historically, when psychologists have used the term "addiction" such usage has usually been with reference to a person's physiological dependence on a stimulus (Davis 2001). Usage in connection with non-chemically related behaviors has sometimes been frowned upon (Jaffe 1990; Miele et al. 1990). For example, Jaffe (1990) expressed the opinion that using the term "addiction" in connection with non-drug-related behaviors may be seen to trivialize drug addictions and hamper research into identifying different underlying mechanisms and treatments. Also, the term "sexual addiction" was removed from the fourth edition of the American Psychiatric Association's *Diagnostic and Statistical Manual for Mental Disorders* (DSM-IV; APA 2000) because using the term "addiction" implied "a shared phenomenology, etiology and/or pathology with substance dependence" (Widiger and Smith 1994, 273–274). In fact, the DSM-IV, which is probably the single most authoritative global reference work for diagnosing psychiatric disorders, does not refer to "addiction" in any respect (nor does it refer to pathological technology use in any guise, although there is ongoing debate as to whether the next edition should do). Nevertheless, if we consider the neurophysiological and neurochemical evidence, brain-scanning techniques have revealed that increases in dopamine release affect the neural "reward system"[1] irrespective of whether this stems from ingesting substances or other behaviors (Holden 2001). Thus, there are similarities in the way in which addictive drugs and addictive behaviors act on the brain. Therefore, as far as the underlying biological mechanisms go, it is not necessarily incorrect to use the same term for drug-related and non-drug-related behaviors.

Rather than referring to "addiction," the DSM-IV's preferred diagnostic labels are "dependence" for drug use and "pathological" for gambling disorders, and excessive technology use has been said to display many similarities with pathological gambling (Griffiths 1995). The DSM-IV classifies pathological gambling as a type of impulse control disorder. Such disorders are said to exist where people have difficulty in limiting behaviors that result in harm to themselves or others, but where the behaviors in question do not involve the taking of substances. In the present context then, it might seem reasonable to refer to pathological involvement with virtual environments in referring to the behaviors under discussion. Such a label would mirror Davis's (2001) use of the term "pathological Internet use" in connection with excessive (i.e., problematic) Internet usage. However, in the remainder of this chapter we use the term addiction for brevity.

At its broadest, the concept of addiction involves a person engaging in a behavior that has important negative consequences for that person, but finding it difficult to desist from the behavior despite these consequences. However, psychologists have developed more stringent criteria and, when considering the criteria that should be used to classify someone as suffering from addiction to a virtual environment, these need to be considered. Although criteria have differed slightly across authors, those adopted by Griffiths (e.g., Griffiths and Davies 2005) are highly representative of those that are commonly used: salience (the tendency to be highly preoccupied with an activity), tolerance (spending increasingly greater amounts of time performing an activity), withdrawal symptoms (the occurrence of unpleasant emotions or physical effects upon cessation of an activity), conflict (conflict with others or self-conflict because of the extended amount of time spent engaging in an activity), relapse and reinstatement (recommencement of an activity to just the same extent after attempts to abstain), and mood modification (the gaining of either a buzz of excitement / a high from an activity or a feeling of psychological numbing or escape when engaging in an activity). The latter criterion, which involves the manipulation of psychological arousal, has been cited as a central motivational driver of all types of addictions, whether these involve chemicals such as alcohol, cocaine, heroin, and tobacco, or behaviors such as gambling (Brown 1997). It is not surprising then, that the need for psychological escape has been said to be the most common motivational driver of social networking addictions (Young 1998) and, indeed, of the above behavioral addiction criteria, mood modification is of particular interest when considering the nature of addictions involving virtual environments. It will be noted from the above that mood modification might be considered to take two different forms: changing a negative mood to a positive mood and escaping a negative mood by altering one's state of consciousness so that one's mood state is no longer phenomenologically present. Two concepts that are central to the latter possibility, which is likely to be the most pertinent with respect to virtual environments, are immersion and flow.

Several authors have attempted to define the concept of immersion. For example, in the context of computer games, Ermi and Mäyrä (2005, 4) considered immersion as "becoming physically or virtually a part of the (gaming) experience itself," and differentiated between sensory, challenge-based, and imaginative immersion. Similarly, Carr (2006, 69) distinguished psychological immersion ("becoming engrossed through...imaginative or mental absorption") from sensory immersion (one's senses being monopolized by the virtual gaming environment). In considering aspects of gaming that foster immersion (and which are likely to foster immersion in virtual environments in general), McMahan (2003) singles out high levels of interactivity between a player and the virtual environment along with physical and social realism, and realism, or at least plausibility, of the game's theme (see Calleja, chapter 13 in this volume, for more on immersion).

A phenomenon highly similar to immersion is Csíkszentmihályi's (e.g., 1992) concept of flow, although Nacke and Lindley (2008, 82) point out that immersion should be seen "as a precondition for flow, since immersion involves a loss of a sense of context, while flow describes a level of complete involvement." Flow is a phenemonological state where people's experiences occur in a continual stream; in which the self and environment, stimulus and response, and past, present, and future are blended together; and self-consciousness and sense of time are lost. It occurs in situations where one performs an activity as an end in itself; the activity is challenging and demands a high degree of concentration; one's abilities and the demands of the activity are well matched; one has a high degree of control; one's actions receive instantaneous feedback; and the activity is highly satisfying (Voiskounsky, Mitina, and Avetisova 2004). These situational characteristics are often likely to be in play when people are engaged with virtual environments, and, as discussed above in connection with the mood modification criterion for addiction, psychologically absenting one's self from one's nonvirtual physical environment is a possible factor in addictions. However, in a study of online games players, Wan and Chiou (2006) found a negative relationship between experience of flow states and addiction, and found that addicts experienced less flow than nonaddicts. They therefore concluded that a state of flow may not be the main psychological mechanism responsible for the addiction of game players. Wan and Chiou also collected needs gratification data and found that, while addicted players play to relieve dissatisfaction (rather than achieve satisfaction), nonaddicted players play for satisfaction. Superficially at least, this has parallels with substance addictions where, once an addiction is established, an addict's focus is upon relieving the dissatisfaction experienced in the presence of withdrawal symptoms rather than experiencing the satisfaction obtained from the feelings of euphoria or the easing of dysphoria that led to the person's repeated dalliance with the substance after the initial experience with it. However, although the presence of withdrawal symptoms is one of the criteria for addiction (Griffiths and Davies 2005), it seems plausible to suggest that any physical withdrawal symptoms will be milder than those experienced by substance addicts and that using virtuality for the relief of dysphoria is likely to be a key motivator for the addict once the addiction is established.

The above implies that dissatisfaction with one's life is likely to be a major risk factor for addiction, some people being so dissatisfied with their life that they seek a sense of oblivion in virtual environments. Research is consistent with this view. For example, greater likelihood of MMORPG addiction has been shown to be related to self-esteem-related personality characteristics such as lower emotional stability, lesser psychological attractiveness (feelings of being unimportant, not caring about appearance, and lack of motivation), and high negative valence (being demanding, needy, and eager to impress [Charlton and Danforth 2010]). Factors associated with social isolation such as introversion, shyness, and loneliness have also been associated with greater Internet use and addiction (see Charlton and Danforth 2010 for a brief review of the literature). Not surprisingly then, offline social isolation was included as one driver of addiction in Davis's (2001) model of pathological Internet use, and the aforementioned personality and circumstantial factors can interact with the characteristics of certain virtual activities to produce a potently addictive cocktail.

Where addictions arise from underlying causes such as some of those mentioned above, they are considered to be secondary addictions, and if the underlying problem (social isolation, relationship/work problems, etc.) is resolved, the addictive behavior disappears (Griffiths 1995). The idea that such underlying factors can cause addictions explains the fact that comorbidity across a number of addictions often arises (Wood 2008). In the broad Internet addiction literature, the term "secondary addiction" has also been used to refer to the idea that the Internet can be used as a medium for engaging in an addictive behavior that is not intrinsically Internet-related (Griffiths 1998). For example, some types of gambling or pornography viewing are just as addictive whether done online or offline: it is just that the Internet provides people with the opportunity to readily engage in these activities. Here then, the Internet might simply enhance the availability of the object of addiction. Both of these secondary types of addiction have been contrasted with primary Internet addictions—where pathological behaviors are related to features that are specific to the Internet-related activity engaged in; these behaviors would not be engaged in if the Internet did not exist (Griffiths 1995; Griffiths and Delfabbro 2001). With respect to virtual environments as previously defined, examples of these latter types of activity include use of SNSs, e-mail checking, and web surfing.

As previously discussed, the immersive and flow-inducing properties of activities are one important ingredient of addictions involving virtual environments. Another ingredient is the capacity of an activity to provide psychological rewards according to a variable-ratio (V-R) reinforcement schedule (Greenfield 2011). Here, the uncertainty of the timing of the next reward acts as a powerful incentive to persist with an activity. V-R reinforcement schedules are likely to contribute to the addictive potential of both online and offline 3D virtual worlds in instances where these are characterized by almost limitless geographical boundaries, and the possibilities for encountering differing agents (often avatars representing other people with whom a person can form friendships), artifacts, and landmarks within them are also virtually limitless. Particularly if persons are able to dissociate themselves from their real-life environment, roaming these worlds offers a huge potential for encountering hitherto unexperienced situations (rewards) without all of the attendant limitations and dangers that would exist if they were to roam unfamiliar places with equal abandon in the real world: the fact that such environments are accessible without stepping outside one's own front door—that is one can become a virtual tourist—makes them all the more attractive. V-R reinforcement schedules can also lead to repeated checking behavior for the appearance of avatars representing online acquaintances in virtual worlds such as *Second Life*, the receipt of e-mail messages in one's inbox, and the receipt of postings on social networking pages.

The first part of this chapter has provided an introduction to the concept of addictions in the context of virtual environments, has demonstrated these addictions' similarity to substance-related addictions, and has summarized many of the ideas that have previously been forwarded to explain them: V-R reinforcement schedules, the use of immersion as a means of psychological escape and mood modification, and how people with specific psychological characteristics or specific life-circumstances may be particularly inclined to such usage, and hence addiction. Finally we have discussed the distinction between primary and secondary addictions. In the next part of the chapter we concentrate on one type of primary addiction, examining the possible psychological substrates of addictions involving virtual environments by reviewing new perspectives on the issue. In particular, we examine the possibility that, in some cases, identity and self-presentation agendas motivate addiction. Given this context, the discussion focuses on SNSs since this medium of virtual communication, known to be highly gratifying and effective in allowing the manipulation of mood states (Blumer 2010; Nadkarni and Hofmann 2011) and implicated in many instances of Internet addiction (Caplan and High 2011) involves interpersonal, social, and *self-presentation* uses of the Internet.

NEW PERSPECTIVES ON ADDICTION TO VIRTUAL ENVIRONMENTS

Riding on the back of early (1970s/1980s) chat-based computer-mediated communities, the past 10–15 years have seen the emergence of a new means of interacting with others online: SNSs such as the highly familiar and popular MySpace, Bebo, and Facebook. Generically, the term "social network" is used to refer to social structures made up of individuals, or organizations, called "nodes," tied or connected by one or more specific types of interdependency such as friendship, kinship, or common interests. *Online* social network sites are web-based platforms that focus on building, supporting, and reflecting social networks or social relations among people. The backbone of all SNSs consists of visible user profiles; these are unique user-authored pages, typically generated by answers to questions on age, location, interests, and so on. The opportunity to graphically represent oneself with an image or photo is also typical. In addition, most sites allow multimedia content and contain various communication features, such as comment walls and chat rooms that allow both asynchronous and synchronous messaging. The public display of established connections via a friends list is a crucial component of SNSs as these lists contain hyperlinks to each friend's profile, enabling viewers to traverse networks and form new connections (see Adams, chapter 14 in this volume, for a general discussion of communication in virtual worlds).

Because of exponential growth in usage (Nielsen Company 2009) and the global impact of SNSs on social and cultural life, much attention has been invested on understanding their appeal and motivations for their use, with one line of research focused upon establishing if inherently maladaptive consequences, such as addiction, necessarily ensue. As Rosen (2011), states: "A big chunk of the world is 'on Facebook.' Is it a new lifestyle? A tool? A 'drug'?" That is, is there a cause for concern and, if so, what drives the fascination? Numerous studies have revealed evidence of heavy SNS use being associated with disruption of relationships (Elphinston and Noller 2011), poorer academic performance (Kirschner and Karpinski 2010), job dismissal, anxiety, and insomnia symptoms (Karaiskos et al. 2010), all of which suggests that, sometimes, the compulsion to engage with such media may represent a nascent social and/or mental health problem. Based on such findings, Young (2009) proposes that it is valid to refer to a new phenomenon of "Facebook Addiction Disorder" (or, perhaps more appropriately, "SNS Addiction Disorder"), because the previously mentioned criteria commonly used to diagnose addiction appear to be present in at least some people who use SNSs.

Researchers seeking to identify the cause of pathological SNS engagement began, quite reasonably, by examining the types of activities for which SNSs are used. The rationale for this is that the primary functions the platforms serve give a clue as to the motivations for using the medium and the mechanisms by which addiction might evolve. Studies (e.g., Lenhart and Madden 2007; Subrahmanyam et al. 2008) have revealed that the most common usages are to keep in touch with offline friends, make new friends, and monitor and respond to comments by others, which has led to the conclusion that one specific form of SNS addiction may be, as Young (1999) terms it, "cyber-relationship addiction"—an addiction to online relationships and community.

In one sense, these findings demonstrate that user activity generally matches the fundamental aims of SNSs, quite gratifyingly for their creators: to provide the opportunity for social connectivity. It is the transparency of the friends list that is the key to such connectivity. However, the opportunity to capitalize on the latent ties in the social network and increase one's own network size also provides something more than a chance to form new friendships and chat; it presents a potentially rich source of *social capital.* Although there are a number of definitions of this term, all of them share the core proposition that social networks have value for both the individual and society. As Putnam (2000) states: "Just as a screwdriver (physical capital) or a university education (human capital) can increase productivity (both individual and collective), so do social contacts affect the productivity of individuals and groups." Putnam proposes that social capital takes two forms: bridging social capital and bonding social capital, the former being linked to what network researchers refer to as "weak ties," implying loose connections between individuals who may provide useful information or new perspectives for one another but typically not emotional support. Alternatively, bonding social capital is found between individuals in tightly knit, emotionally close relationships.

Given that, as evidence indicates, friends on users' SNSs tend to be real-life social connections and support systems, it's easy to appreciate how such a virtual communication space might expediently increase bonding social capital and how gratifying this might be. Transfer of such is smoothly assisted by the medium and this may be an attractive and, understandably, potentially influential driver of repeated engagement. Furthermore, it appears that even the (initially) weak ties formed via SNSs present a means of accruing useful, adaptive bridging and even bonding capital, especially for those with low self-esteem (Ellison 2007); those who face psychological barriers to forming such large, heterogeneous networks of relationships outside the anonymous, invisible arena of an SNS. Some theorists have argued that the outcomes of weak ties are friendships that are satisfying and pleasurable and serve to positively modify self-concept and mood (Bargh and McKenna 2004), and that furthermore they meet not just emotional but also status needs via the number of friends on one's friends list. In such an environment, individuals may increasingly rely on SNS use as a strategy to positively modify mood, which, as previously discussed, is a powerful precipitator of addiction to virtual environments. However, others have questioned whether the seeming emotional gains to be had from weak SNS ties are always necessarily lasting or healthy. The observed increase in sense of well-being associated with SNS use in the Ellison study offers a compelling explanation for chronic, intensive use, and is consistent with Armstrong, Phillips, and Saling's (2000) and Charlton and Danforth's (2010) data that demonstrated those with low emotional stability become addicted to Internet-based activities and communities and relationships.

Pursuing an alternative perspective, some researchers have considered whether the unique affordances of these media may provide an additional condition for addiction; for example, the opportunity for self-reflection, self-presentation, and self-adaptation/evolution. For example, Joinson (2008) identified seven core reasons for Facebook usage that he grouped into two broad categories: (1) the previously discussed "social connectivity and opportunity for group membership" and (2) "people watching and social surveillance." He drew on uses-and-gratifications theory (e.g., Herzog 1944) to help explain the seven core activities, the basic tenet of which is that people proactively search for, and integrate into their lives, media that will not only meet (gratify) a given need but also enhance knowledge, social interactions, and entertainment or diversion. Many of the uses-and-gratifications theories on media use emanated from early 1970s research on why people use TV and radio. Two influential explanations to emerge at this period were those of McQuail, Blumler, and Brown (1972) and of Katz, Haas, and Gurevitch (1973). McQuail and colleagues identified four motivations for media use that were related to (1) formation of personal relationships; (2) diversion; (3) social surveillance; and (4) personal identity. A somewhat more psychologically elaborate model was articulated by Katz and colleagues (1973), who suggested that tension release, cognitive needs, affective needs, and social and personal integrative needs were the motivators for media engagement. Inclusion of diversion and tension release (from present, real-life conditions) in these theories indicates that the authors recognized that media are often used as a means of mood modification. The theme of community or relationship-based drivers is also still apparent, but the inclusion of "self"-related motivators for use, that is, personal identity integration, offers the possibility that a significant catalyst for media use, and therefore SNS use and addiction, may be more *egocentric*, possibly symptomatic of contemporary Western society's culture of individuality. As Boyd and Ellison (2008) suggest: "It is the individual rather than the community that is the focus of attention."

McQuail, Blumler, and Brown (1972) propose that a personal identity use of media is possibly an attempt at value reinforcement or reassurance, self-understanding, or reality exploration. Katz, Haas, and Gurevitch (1973) explain the personal integrative function of media use as reflecting a need for credibility, stability, and status. The generic affordances of cyberspace (anonymity, invisibility, lack of accountability, etc.—still inherently available properties of social network sites), in conjunction with the specific functional features of SNSs, conveniently meet these needs. In fact, some features of SNSs seem to provide a perfect vehicle for personal identity evaluation, verification, construction, and experimentation. For example, the user profile offers the individual the chance of engaging not only in self-reflection, evaluation, and presentation but also "identity lab play": self-exploration, elaboration, and promotion. "Ideal self" (Rogers 1951; 1961) or "aspirational or fantasy selves" (Turkle 1994) might be wheeled out into the "virtual display case" for the purposes of appraisal and feedback or gratification and catharsis. As Sundén (2003) states, SNSs allow one to "write oneself into being" and, depending on agenda, craft a persona that is attractive and popular. This meets both *psychogenic* needs (needs that reflect the priorities of a culture such as affiliation, status, and power) and *hedonic* needs (need for excitement, self-confidence, and fantasy [McClelland 1978]), both potentially addictive states because of their capacity to modify mood state.

If, however, online impression management processes and strategies (and self-concept development) mirror those of the real world, the virtual online self is unlikely to be authored *solely* by the user or be static and unaffected by the influence of others who encounter the user on SNSs. Just as in real life we observe and learn from the self-accounts or portrayals of others and monitor others' reactions to the persona we present to the world (Cooley 1902), it is likely that we use this information to reconsider, revise, reconstruct, and socially reposition our cyber, SNS "selves" with the aim of increasing popularity, self-confidence, and esteem and, concomitantly, enhancing mood state. Furthermore, as is the case in the real world, these processes are subject to variable-ratio reinforcement. The personal feedback we get from those we meet on SNSs is sometimes positive and consistent with the impression we intend to convey (a rewarding experience) but, intermittently, is negative and incongruent with impression management agendas and scripts. Such variable reinforcement goes some way to explaining the repeated checking behavior noted in one instance of SNS addiction by Karaiskos and colleagues (2010) and so prevalent in SNS users more widely (a constant need to seek reward in the form of high-regard comments). As Greenfield (2011) proposed, such intermittent rewards are highly psychologically gratifying and might be a significant contributor to addictive engagement with the platform.

One might be tempted to rely on traditional "affordance" (e.g., invisibility, lack of accountability) explanations to account for the seeming lack of restraint in identity-play, and there is certainly evidence to support this approach. For example, according to Markus and Nurius (1986), the actualization of the possible self can be blocked by the presence of physical gating features, such as an unattractive physical appearance or excessive shyness. This prompted Zhao, Grasmuck, and Martin (2008) to suggest that anonymous online venues (as all SNSs *can* be if one chooses) provide "a fertile ground for these 'gated' individuals to actualize the identities they hope to establish but are unable to achieve in face-to-face situations"—again, emotionally rewarding and conducive conditions for development of addiction. However, we suggest that another, rarely considered, factor may be at work here: the inherently emancipatory quality of the (current) primary method of online communication online—the written word. For centuries, humans have utilized words to make manifest the products of their creativity and imagination; fictional tales, myth and fantasy are brought to life via words, and man's innermost, private thoughts, desires, and possibilities (perhaps aspects of true self guarded from the world) have been vitalized by text in journals or diaries. Hence, exploration of possibilities and identities via text, however fantastical and distant from actuality the constructed identity may be, is not only a familiar and accepted means of expressing creativity, but one we may feel licensed to use. It may be perceived as a fun, exciting, certainly "harmless," and even, it could be argued, developmentally adaptive activity to engage in. Whatever the specific affective outcome, for those who feel a need for it, online identity experimentation via text could be, and could always have been since the dawn of computer-mediated communication, insidiously addictive because of its inherently hedonistic, mood-modifying qualities.

Suler's (2004) theory of the factors underlying online disinhibition also lends weight to this argument. Two of the concepts he puts forward, solipsistic introjection and dissociative imagination, may be used to help explain why an individual often feels little concern or guilt (or even awareness) that the identity insignia of the online self is somewhat inconsistent with the real-world or "real" self (Rogers 1951). Solipsistic introjection is the phenomenon whereby reading messages or information in text-based computer-mediated communications can lead to an experience akin to that we have when reading about a character in a book, a merging-of-minds sensation. Dissociative imagination proposes a similar thing, that is, the feeling that characters encountered in cyberspace or those that the user has created (a virtual self) are valid products of the imagination and exist in a different realm altogether, *not* the real world. Both of these experiences appear to be perfect precursors for development of the belief that once the computer is turned off and individuals return to their daily routine, they leave the "game" and their game-identity behind. Furthermore, both, according to Suler, have the potential to disrupt the ego boundary and evoke primary process thinking, a state dominated by the potentially addictive "pleasure principle" (e.g., Foddy and Savulescu 2007). Moreover, this disruption catapults the psychologically immersive properties of SNSs to a far higher level; a level that may, as previously discussed, be addictive to people with certain characteristics.

Perhaps the most significant difference between real-world works of fiction and the creative expression involved in scripting the virtual self is that online we position *ourselves*, and not some third party, as the eponymous, central character. Moreover, unlike real life, in cyberspace venues we are almost guaranteed an enthusiastic (and constantly expanding) global audience to appreciate or critique our product. It has been argued that the presence of an audience, in and of itself, may serve to fuel addiction. "Once one has a taste of externalizing one's thoughts and imagining that others care to ponder them, thinking that is not externalized seems kind of pointless, perhaps like singing in the shower after performing in front of a large audience" (Gibson 2009). In other words, one acquires the cognitive habit of thinking and experiencing on behalf of an audience for *their* satisfaction, leading to significant personal satisfaction, again a potent driver for repeated return.

Just how performing to an unseen, online audience might contribute to addiction can be better understood if we consider the noted relationship between intensity of Facebook use and narcissism (Buffardi and Campbell 2008; Mehdizadeh 2010). In both of these studies, the higher the self-reported (and other-rated) Narcissistic Personality Inventory score, the more intense the SNS use. Interestingly, intensity of use was also, somewhat counterintuitively, negatively correlated with self-esteem. Collectively, these findings indicate that, for those with narcissistic traits or low self-esteem or both, SNSs provide an ideal platform for showcasing and promotion of the virtual self via the content included on their user page, and present the opportunity to receive the desired positive feedback to support an inflated self-view (or modify fragile self-esteem) in real life. An obvious question to arise from these findings is, are narcissists naturally drawn to SNSs or do SNSs cultivate embryonic narcissism? Either way, a place that offers the chance to revel in ego-salving or ego-boosting narcissism may be too tempting to resist.

In 2006, a structurally and functionally different form of online social networking was introduced, Twitter, best described as a hybrid between a virtual social network and a blog. It is like a blog because users write and read largely public 140-character posts. The social networking part refers to the capacity to allow people to "follow" other users and their conversations and retransmit messages to their own followers. Early network analysis of uses and motivations for joining indicates that, at least initially, most people create an account because their offline friends are there (a similar motivation encourages people to join SNSs), and that the most popular types of posts can be classified as "conversational" rather than news-related or self-promotional (Java et al. 2007). However, comparatively few studies have yet been conducted. Those that have suggest, intriguingly, that engagement with the platform is, in psychological terms, unlike any social network that has come before. For example, users report that the experience of these hybrid SNSs is even more immersive with a real-time feel; a kind of Instant Messaging except that one is talking to the world rather than a single person. But is it addictive? The fact that in just six years Twitter has gained 100 million active users (50 million of whom use it every day), and that its use may be harder to resist than cigarettes and alcohol (Hoffman, Vohs, and Baumeister 2012), would suggest that it can be.

Data such as these have yielded a number of rather speculative but interesting explanations of why some people are intensely engaged with this particular medium to the point of addiction. One such theory is that of ambient intimacy (Reichelt 2007), the essence of which is that platforms such as Twitter allow individuals to "keep in touch with people with a level of regularity and intimacy that you wouldn't usually have access to, because time and space conspire to make it impossible." As Reichelt states, photo-sharing sites "let me see what friends are eating for lunch, how they've redecorated their bedroom, their latest haircut," whereas an SNS/microblog "tells me when they're hungry, what technology is currently frustrating them, who they're having drinks with tonight." One might be tempted to question, as Reichelt herself does, why anyone could possibly perceive this to be important or even interesting. Isn't this amount of detail about the lives of others simply useless, distracting noise in a world in which we already suffer information overload? In response, Reichelt acknowledges that for some it is, but for many individuals it is a means of creating an intimacy with people they would not otherwise be allowed to (or have to the time to) get to know well. Her theory works on the premise that "detail creates intimacy" and that it's not really about the capital conveyed by the detail but the fact that we share it, and regularly share it, that promotes a closeness with distant others. Reichelt also reminds us of the flip side of ambient connectedness: the opportunity for *ambient exposure* and its concomitant lure. The idea behind this concept is that disseminating the minutiae of one's life on SNSs or microblog sites such as Twitter allows the user to expose the self in a way that leads to vulnerability and risk, but that this risk is rewarded by developmentally adaptive feedback. It is, perhaps, analogous to placing oneself in a (virtual) shop window in a (cyber) High Street for appraisal by random passers-by. The implication is that sheer curiosity about the attractiveness of one's persona and life may be enough, in itself, to prompt the activity.

Both intimacy and exposure might be conceived as the positive consequences of ambient connectedness, but there is a price to pay—both states nurture a situation where the constant ability to connect with others, to observe, give, and receive feedback, compels us to want to do it more and more. We reside in a state of "desired hyperconnectivity." The more we do it, the more we feel the need to do it even though this repetition incapacitates the "informational pause button" and we risk the death of socioemotional and cognitive downtime, that is, periods within the day or night when we are *not* processing information, a time that allows us to reflect, consolidate, purge, and mentally reposition ourselves and recuperate. The addictive pull of the bidirectional information flow may far outweigh the acknowledged investment costs.

Following a similar notion, others have suggested that the drive for hyperconnectivity, an implicit criterion for online addiction, is so strong because we perceive, or have learned, that advances in technology have facilitated meeting a very basic and universal human need, the need for self-actualization (Maslow 1943). Ma (2009) postulates that microblogs such as Twitter not only help us meet social needs, a sense of being cared about and belonging as part of a Twitterverse family, evidenced by the sharing of highly intimate life events ("My waters broke... now timing contractions on an iPhone app"), and help leverage higher esteem (via positive feedback on posts and the opportunity to be distantly affiliated with celebrities), but also assist in us achieving authentic being or "eigenwelt" (Binswanger 1963) through the reactions of others to our presented virtual self. How this might occur can be explained in the context of findings by researchers such as Joinson (2001), Matheson, and Zanna (1988), and Sassenberg (2005), who have demonstrated that participating in computer-mediated social interactions provides increased mental space for self-reflection and monitoring and leads to an increase in *private self-awareness*, all of which are prerequisite states for realization of a "true self" (core and stable traits, beliefs, morality, etc). This possibility is supported by data suggesting that, regardless of the appeal of portraying aspirational or idealized selves, much of what people detail about themselves in SNS or Twitter user profiles is an authentic reflection of their real self and not idealization, and is thus ripe for useful, self-actualizing feedback (Back et al. 2010). From this perspective, it might appear that the affordances that social network sites offer to explore the self can serve nothing but good, but some have argued that SNSs may represent "narcissism unleashed," or even an existential anxiety ("I Twitter, therefore I am"), prompting the constant need to self-verify and affirm via recognition by others online (Lewis, cited by Pemberton 2009).

Narcissism is a recurring theme in recent SNS literature. It is possible that "luxuriating in being you," however close to the usual "you" that cyber you is, in that safe playground where there are few real-life repercussions, may be, for many, difficult to refuse, a case of "Narcisssus in Wonderland" (Ulman and Paul 2006). Undoubtedly, the relative quiet and solitude of this atypical social experience provides a perfect zone for self-reflection and, uniquely, allows imaginative, dissociative immersion and an ego-centrism and expression of aspects of self that are usually constrained by physical realities and cultural norms.

We can learn much about the dissociative processes implicit in virtual self construction from the course of events identified as inherent to avatar identity creation and evolution in MMORPGs such as *Second Life* and *World of Warcraft*. Warburton (2008) noted that, a period of time after spawning an avatar and drafting and consolidating its identity (achieved by strategically building friendships and connections, becoming part of a community, purchasing possessions that increase its aesthetic appeal, etc.), people begin to form complex relationships with their avatars. They start to empathize with, and even come to like or love their virtual, avatar-vesseled selves, almost as if they were distinct, external entities. Warburton refers to such figures as "alter-ego avatars." This terminology suggests the intriguing possibility that an addictive aspect of the virtual self may originate in a need for affiliation and socialization, the repeated desire to go online to visit a friend whom one quite likes (and certainly understands)—your digital self.

Warburton points out that the diversity of personal definitions we encounter in the process of avatar identity articulation and elaboration can lead to a dissonance and incidences of ego instability. He proposes that it is this experience (essentially a fractionation and compartmentalization of aspects of self) that often necessitates development of multiple avatars to embody these other "selves," which offer "multiple channels for reflecting the range of roles and identities that we take for granted in our everyday existence." Such a notion beckons us into penumbral landscapes of possibility in which the crafted virtual self acts as a source of inspiration (or at least a comparative reference point) for the genesis of other digital progeny. One might consider this a gestalt process in reverse whereby the sum of the digital "parts" appears to be distinctly different from the manifest offline "whole" (see Scarborough and Bailenson, chapter 7 in this volume, for discussion of avatar psychology).

The word "avatar," first used to indicate a virtual representation of self in the computer game *Ultima IV* (Origin Systems 1985), is originally a Sanskrit word meaning the deliberate descent to or incarnation of a deity on earth (Partridge, 2005). The implicit suggestion of these descriptions is that "avatars" are associated with a process of appearance in an alternative form; a new embodiment. This definition also perfectly captures the essence of what we propose to be a powerful motivator for heavy use of online social venues whether they be graphical or text-based, that is, that cyberspace presents an unparalleled opportunity for a psychologically revitalising and enriching, new embodiment of self. Whether this is, ultimately, ontologically healthy (hedonistic but harmless and possibly adaptively cathartic escapism) or instills an essentially maladaptive, sense of identity freedom that cannot be matched in the real world and thus triggers a cycle of need to continually retreat to that "happier place," is yet to be decided. Certainly, evidence suggests that the functional architecture of such virtual environments, in conjunction with the generic affordances of cyberspace, is endowed with powerful addiction triggers (interactivity, social realism, almost instant feedback on actions with intermittent reinforcement plus a loss of sense of time), but it is, perhaps, the ability to dissociate from the corporeal, reality-constrained "you" and the allure of the virtual self that may be, for many, *most* irresistible. Social network sites, and other online interaction venues such as 3D graphical worlds, provide us with a freely available, culturally sanctioned and psychologically secure "identity sandbox" that has reliably effective mood modification properties. It may prove to be that this is *the* most catalytic causal component in the complex mechanism of factors contributing to online addictions.

NOTE

1. Involving the ventral tegmental area, nucleus acumbens, and parts of the frontal lobe involved in impulsiveness and planning.

REFERENCES

Achab, S., M. Nicolier, F. Mauny, J. Monnin, B. Trojak, P. Vandel, D. Sechter, P. Gorwood, and E. Haffen. 2011. Massively Multiplayer Online Role-Playing Games: Comparing Characteristics of Addict vs Non-Addict Online Recruited Gamers in a French Adult Population. *BMC Psychiatry* 11: 144.

American Psychiatric Association. 2000. *Diagnostic and Statistical Manual of Mental Disorders.* 4th ed., Text Revision. Washington, DC: American Psychiatric Association.

Armstrong, L., J. G. Phillips, and L. L. Saling. 2000. Potential Determinants of Heavier Internet Usage. *International Journal of Human-Computer Studies* 53 (4): 537–550.

Back, M. D., J. M. Stopfer, S. Vazire, S. Gaddi, S. C. Schmukle, B. Egloff, and S. D. Gosling. 2010. Facebook Profiles Reflect Actual Personality, Not Self-Idealization. *Psychological Science* 21 (3): 372–374.

Bargh, J. A., and K. Y. A. McKenna. 2004. The Internet and Social Life. *Annual Review of Psychology* 55 (1): 573–590.

Binswanger, L. 1963. *Being-in-the-World: Selected Papers of Ludwig Binswanger.* Translated by Jacob Needleman. New York: Basic Books.

Blumer, T. 2010. Face-to-Face or Facebook: Are Shy People More Outgoing on Social Networking Sites? In *Media and Communication Studies, Interventions and Intersections: The Intellectual Work of the 2010 ECREA European Media and Communication Doctoral Summer School,* edited by N. Carpentier, I. T. Trivundza, P. Pruulmann-Vengerfeldt, E. Sundin, T. Olsson, R. Kilborn, H. Nieminen, and B. Cammaerts, 201–212. Tartu: Tartu University Press. http://www.researchingcommunication.eu/reco_book6.pdf#page=201. Accessed May 18, 2012.

Boyd, D. M., and N. B. Ellison. 2008. Social Network Sites: Definition, History, and Scholarship. *Journal of Computer Mediated Communication* 13 (1): 210–230.

Brown, I. 1997. A Theoretical Model of the Behavioural Addictions—Applied to Offending. In *Addicted to Crime?* edited by J. E. Hodge, M. McMurran, and C. R. Hollin, 13–65. Chichester: John Wiley.

Buffardi, L. E., and W. K. Campbell. 2008. Narcissism and Social Networking Web Sites. *Personality and Social Psychology Bulletin* 34 (10): 1303–1314.

Caplan, S. E., and A. C. High. 2011. Online Social Interaction, Psychosocial Well-Being, and Problematic Internet Use. In *Internet Addiction: A Handbook and Guide to Evaluation and Treatment,* edited by K. S. Young and C. N. de Abreu, 35–53. Hoboken, NJ: Wiley.

Carr, D. 2006. Space, Navigation and Affect. In *Computer Games: Text, Narrative and Play,* edited by Diane Carr, David Buckingham, Andrew Burn, and Gareth Schott, 59–71. Cambridge: Polity Press.

Charlton, J. P., and I. D. W. Danforth. 2010. Validating the Distinction between Computer Addiction and Engagement: Online Game Playing and Personality. *Behaviour and Information Technology* 29 (6): 601–613.

Cooley, C. H. 1902. *Human Nature and the Social Order.* New York: C. Scribner's Son's.

Csíkszentmihályi, M. 1990. *Flow: The Psychology of Optimal Experience.* New York: Harper Perennial.

Davis, R. A. 2001. A Cognitive Behavioral Model of Pathological Internet Use. *Computers in Human Behavior* 17 (2): 187–195.

Ellison, N. B., C. Steinfield, and C. Lampe. 2007. The Benefits of Facebook "Friends": Social Capital and College Students' Use of Online Social Network Sites. *Journal of Computer-Mediated Communication* 12 (4): 1143–1168.

Elphinston, R. A., and P. Noller. 2011. Time to Face It! Facebook Intrusion and the Implications for Romantic Jealousy and Relationship Satisfaction. *Cyberpsychology, Behavior, and Social Networking* 14 (11): 631–635.

Ermi, L., and F. Mäyrä. 2005. Fundamental Components of the Gameplay Experience: Analysing Immersion. In *Changing Views: Worlds in Play. Selected Papers of the 2005 DiGRA's Second International Conference,* edited by S. de Castell and J. Jenson, 15–27. Toronto: DiGRA. http://www.uta.fi/~tlilma/gameplay_experience.pdf. Accessed July 18, 2012.

Foddy, B., and J. Savulescu. 2007. Addiction Is Not an Affliction: Addictive Desires Are Merely Pleasure-Oriented Desires. *American Journal of Bioethics* 7 (1): 29–32

Gibson, D. 2009. [The social psychology of Facebook, etc.] *Complexity and Social Networks Blog.* March 23. http://www.iq.harvard.edu/blog/netgov/2009/03/the_social_psychology_of_faceb.html. Accessed March 27, 2012.

Gilbert, R. L., N. A. Murphy, and T. McNally. 2011. Addiction to the 3-Dimensional Internet: Estimated Prevalence and Relationship to Real World Addiction. *Addiction Research and Theory* 19 (4): 380–390.

Greenfield, D. 2011. The Addictive Properties of Internet Usage. In *Internet Addiction: A Handbook and Guide to Evaluation and Treatment,* edited by Kimberly S. Young and Cristiano Nabuco de Abreu, 135–153. Hoboken, NJ: Wiley.

Griffiths, M. 1995. Technological Addictions. *Clinical Psychology Forum* 76: 14–19.

Griffiths, M. 1998. Internet Addiction: Does It Really Exist? In *Psychology and the Internet,* edited by Jayne Gackenbach, 61–75. San Diego: Academic Press.

Griffiths, M., and M. N. O. Davies. 2005. Does Video Game Addiction Exist? In *Handbook of Computer Game Studies,* edited by Joost Raessens and Jeffrey Goldstein, 359–369. Cambridge, MA: MIT Press.

Griffiths, M., and P. Delfabbro. 2001. The Biopsychosocial Approach to Gambling: Contextual Factors in Research and Clinical Interventions. *Electronic Journal of Gambling Issues* 6(5). http://epe.lac-bac.gc.ca/100/202/300/e-gambling/html/2002/no6/issue5/feature/. Accessed June 17, 2013.

Herzog, H. 1944. What Do We Really Know about Daytime Serial Listeners? In *Radio Research, 1942–1943,* edited by P. F. Lazarsfeld, 2–23. London: Sage.

Hofmann, W., K. D. Vohs, and R. F. Baumeister. 2012. What People Desire, Feel Conflicted About and Try to Resist in Everyday Life. *Psychological Science.* doi:10.1177/0956797612437426.

Holden, C. 2001. "Behavioral" Addictions: Do They Exist? *Science* 294: 980–982.

Jaffe, J. H. 1990. Trivializing Dependence. *British Journal of Addiction* 85: 1425–1427.

Java, A., X. Song, T. Finnin, and B. Tseng. 2007. Why We Twitter: Understanding Microblogging Usage and Communities. *Proceedings of the 9th WebKDD and 1st SNA-KDD 2007 Workshop on Web Mining and Social Network Analysis.* New York: ACM. http://ebiquity.umbc.edu/paper/html/id/367. Accessed July 24, 2013.

Joinson, A. N. 2001. Self-Disclosure in Computer-Mediated Communication: The Role of Self-Awareness and Visual Anonymity. *European Journal of Social Psychology* 31 (2): 177–192.

Joinson, A. N. 2008. Looking At, Looking Up or Keeping Up with People? Motives and Use of Facebook. *Proceedings of the Twenty-Sixth Annual SIGCHI Conference on Human Factors in Computer Systems,* 1027–1036. New York: ACM.

Karaiskos, D., E. Tzavellas, G. Balta, and T. Paparrigopoulos. 2010. Social Network Addiction: A New Clinical Disorder? *European Psychiatry* 25 (Supplement 1): 855.

Katz, E., H. Haas, and M. Gurevitch. 1973. On the Use of the Mass Media for Important Things. *American Sociological Review* 38 (2): 164–181.

Kirschner, P. A., and A. C. Karpinski. 2010. Facebook® and Academic Performance. *Computers in Human Behavior* 26 (6): 1237–1245.

Lenhart, A., and M. Madden. 2007. *Social Networking Websites and Teens: An Overview.* Washington, DC: Pew Research Center. http://www.pewinternet.org/Reports/2007/Social-Networking-Websites-and-Teens/Data-Memo.aspx. Accessed March 27, 2012.

Ma, M. 2009. Understanding the Psychology of Twitter: The Tao of Innovation. *Psychology Today.* http://www.psychologytoday.com/blog/the-tao-innovation/200903/understanding-the-psychology-twitter. Accessed March 27, 2012.

Markus, H., and P. Nurius. 1986. Possible Selves. *American Psychologist* 41 (9): 954–969.

Maslow, A. H. 1943. A Theory of Human Motivation. *Psychological Review* 50 (4): 370–396.

Matheson, K., and M. P. Zanna. 1988. The Impact of Computer-Mediated Communication on Self-Awareness. *Computers in Human Behavior* 4 (3): 221–233.

McClelland, D. C. 1978. Managing Motivation to Expand Human Freedom. *American Psychologist* 33 (3): 201–210.

McMahan, A. 2003. Immersion, Engagement, and Presence: A New Method for Analyzing 3-D Video Games. In *The Video Game Theory Reader*, edited by M. J. P. Wolf and B. Perron, 67–87. London: Routledge.

McQuail, D., J. G. Blumler, and J. R. Brown. 1972. The Television Audience: A Revised Perspective. In *Sociology of Mass Communication*, edited by Denis McQuail, 135–165. Harmondsworth: Penguin.

Mehdizadeh, S. 2010. Self-Presentation 2.0: Narcissism and Self-Esteem on Facebook. *Cyberpsychology, Behavior and Social Networking* 13 (4): 357–364.

Miele, G. M., S. M. Tilly, M. First, and A. Frances. 1990. The Definition of Dependence and Behavioural Addictions. *British Journal of Addiction* 85 (11): 1421–1423.

Nacke, L., and C. A. Lindley. 2008. Flow and Immersion in First-Person Shooters: Measuring the Player's Gameplay Experience. In *Proceedings of the 2008 Conference on Future Play: Research, Play, Share*, 81–88. New York: ACM.

Nadkarni, A., and S. G. Hofmann. 2011. Why Do People Use Facebook? *Personality and Individual Differences* 52: 243–249.

Partridge, C. H. 2005. *Introduction to World Religions.* Minneapolis: Augsburg Fortress.

Pemberton, A. 2009. A Load of Twitter. *The Sunday Times*, February 22. http://www.thesundaytimes.co.uk/sto/style/fashion/trends/article150880.ece. Accessed July 23, 2013.

Putnam, R. D. 2000. *Bowling Alone: The Collapse and Revival of American Community.* New York: Simon and Schuster.

Reichelt, L. 2007. Ambient Intimacy. http://www.disambiguity.com/ambient-intimacy/. Accessed March 27, 2012.

Rogers, C. 1951. *Client-Centered Therapy: Its Current Practice, Implications and Theory.* London: Constable.

Rogers, C. 1961. *On Becoming a Person: A Therapist's View of Psychotherapy.* London: Constable.

Rosen, L. D. 2011. Poke Me: How Social Networks Can Both Help and Harm Our Kids. Invited Address No. 3378, 119th Annual Convention, American Psychological Association, Washington, DC, August 4–7. http://www.fenichel.com/pokeme.shtml. Accessed March 27, 2012.

Sassenberg, K., M. Boos, and S. Rabung. 2005. Attitude Change in Face-to-Face and Computer-Mediated Communication: Private Self-Awareness as Mediator and Moderator. *European Journal of Social Psychology* 35 (3): 361–374.

Subrahmanyam, K., S. M. Reich, N. Waechter, and G. Espinoza. 2008. Online and Offline Social Networks: Use of Social Networking Sites by Emerging Adults. *Journal of Applied Developmental Psychology* 29 (6): 420–433.

Suler, J. 2004. The Online Disinhibition Effect. *CyberPsychology and Behavior* 7 (3): 321–326.

Sundén, J. 2003. *Material Virtualities: Approaching Online Textual Embodiment.* New York: Peter Lang.

Nielsen Company. 2009. *Global Faces and Networked Places*. The Nielsen Company, New York. http://blog.nielsen.com/nielsenwire/wp-content/uploads/2009/03/nielsen_globalfaces_mar09.pdf. Accessed March 27, 2012.

Turkle, S. 1994. Constructions and Reconstructions of Self in Virtual Reality. *Mind, Culture, and Activity* 1 (3): 159–167.

Ulman, R. B., and H. Paul. 2006. *The Self Psychology of Addiction and Its Treatment: Narcissus in Wonderland*. New York: Routledge.

Ultima IV. 1985. Computer game. Manchester, NH: Origin Systems.

Voiskounsky, A. E., O V. Mitina, and A. A. Avetisova. 2004. Playing Online Games: Flow Experience. *PsychNology Journal* 2 (3): 259–281.

Wan, C.-S., and W.-B. Chiou. 2006. Psychological Motives and Online Games Addiction: A Test of Flow Theory and Humanistic Needs Theory for Taiwanese Adolescents. *CyberPsychology and Behavior* 9 (3): 317–324.

Warburton, S. 2008. Loving Your Avatar: Identity, Immersion and Empathy. *Liquid Learning*. http://warburton.typepad.com/liquidlearning/2008/01/loving-your-ava.html. Accessed May 18, 2012.

Widiger, T. A., and G. T. Smith. 1994. Substance Use Disorder: Abuse, Dependence and Dyscontrol. *Addiction* 89 (3): 267–282.

Wood, R. T. A. 2008. Problems with the Concept of Video Game "Addiction": Some Case Study Examples. *International Journal of Mental Health and Addiction* 6 (2): 169–178.

Young, K. S. 1998. *Caught in the Net*. New York: Wiley.

Young, K. S. 1999. Internet Addiction: Evaluation and Treatment. *Student BMJ* 7: 351–352.

Young, K. S. 2009. *Facebook Addiction Disorder?* The Center for Online Addiction: Bradford, PA http://www.netaddiction.com/index.php?option=com_blog&view=comments&pid=5&Itemid=0. Accessed March 27, 2012.

Young, K. S., X. D. Yue, and L. Ying. 2011. Prevalence Estimates and Etiologic Models of Internet Addiction. In *Internet Addiction: A Handbook and Guide to Evaluation and Treatment*, edited by K. S. Young and C. N. de Abreu, pp. 3–17. Hoboken, NJ: Wiley.

Zhao, S., S. Grasmuck, and J. Martin. 2008. Identity Construction on Facebook: Digital Empowerment in Anchored Relationships. *Computers in Human Behavior* 24 (5): 1816–1836.

CHAPTER 12

....

BEING PRESENT IN
A VIRTUAL WORLD

....

GIUSEPPE RIVA AND JOHN A. WATERWORTH

VIRTUAL reality (VR) literature includes many descriptions of users reacting to a virtual environment in instinctual ways that suggest they believe, at least for a short time, that they are "immersed" and even "present" in the synthetic experience. In the field of computer graphics "immersion" is generally understood to be a product of technology that facilitates the production of the multimodal sensory "input" to the user, while presence is defined as the psychological perception of being "there," within a virtual environment (Waterworth et al. 2012).

However, as commented by Biocca (1997), and agreed with by most researchers in the area, "while the design of virtual reality technology has brought the theoretical issue of presence to the fore, few theorists argue that the experience of presence suddenly emerged with the arrival of virtual reality." Rather, as suggested by Loomis (1992), presence may be described as a basic state of consciousness: the attribution of sensation to some distal stimulus, or more broadly to some environment. Because of the complexity of the topic and the interest in it, different attempts to define presence and to explain its role are available in the literature (Coelho et al. 2006). In general, as underlined by Lombard and Jones (2006, 25): "the first and most basic distinction among definitions of presence concerns the role of technology." In other words, do we need technology to experience presence?

One group of researchers describes the sense of presence as "media presence," a function of our experience of a given medium (Schloerb 1995; Sadowski and Stanney 2002; IJsselsteijn et al. 2000; Lombard and Ditton 1997; Loomis 1992; Sheridan 1992; 1996; Marsh, Wright, and Smith 2001). The main result of this approach is definitions of presence such as the "perceptual illusion of non-mediation" (Lombard and Ditton 1997) produced by means of the disappearance of the medium from the conscious attention of the subject. The main advantage of this approach is its predictive value: the level of presence is reduced by the experience of mediation during the action. The main limitation of this vision is what is not said. What is presence for? Is it a specific cognitive process? What is its role in our daily experience? It is important to note that these questions are unanswered even for the relationship between presence and media. As underlined by Lee (2004b, 496): "Presence scholars may find it surprising and even disturbing that there have been limited attempts to explain the fundamental reason *why* human beings can feel presence when they use media and/or simulation technologies."

To address these questions, a second group of researchers considers presence as "inner presence," a broad psychological phenomenon, not necessarily linked to the experience of a medium, the effect of which is the control of the individual and social activity (Riva, Davide, and IJsselsteijn 2003; Moore et al. 2002; Waterworth and Waterworth 2001; Mantovani and Riva 1999; Schubert, Friedman, and Regenbrecht 2001; Zahoric and Jenison 1998; Riva and Davide 2001; Waterworth and Waterworth 2003; Baños et al. 2000; Baños, Botella, and Perpiña 1999; Spagnolli, Gamberini, and Gasparini 2003; Spagnolli and Gamberini 2002; Lee 2004a; 2004b; Marsh, Wright, and Smith 2001; Waterworth et al. 2010; Riva et al. 2011). In this chapter we will present and discuss this second theoretical vision, starting from the following four pillars emerging from the recent work of cognitive sciences:

- The content of consciousness is the content of a simulated world in our brain (Metzinger 2009; Revonsuo 2006; Riva 2011).
- Presence is an evolved process related to the understanding and management of the causal texture of both the physical and social worlds (Waterworth and Waterworth 2001; Lee 2004a; 2004b).
- The psychology of presence is related to human action and its organization in the environment (Riva et al. 2003; Mantovani and Riva 1999; Marsh 2003).
- The feeling of presence is not the same in all situations (virtual or real) but differs in relation to the characteristics of the physical, social, and cultural space the subject is in (Mantovani and Riva 1999; 2001; Mantovani and Spagnolli 2000).

PRESENCE AND THE SELF

In this chapter we will draw on the recent findings of cognitive sciences to offer a broader definition of presence, not related to technology only. Specifically, presence is described here as a core neuropsychological phenomenon the effect of which is to produce a sense of agency and control: subjects are "present" if they feel themselves able to enact their intentions in an external world (see table 12.1). In this view, the basic evolutionary function of presence is to allow the organism to differentiate between the internal (the self/imagination) and the external (the world/perception). Moreover, we relate presence to the evolution of the conscious sense of self—borrowing heavily from Damasio (1999; 2010)—and suggest that the three levels of self he identified, emerging over the course of human evolution, correspond directly to three distinct *layers of presence* (Riva, Waterworth, and Waterworth 2004).

Table 12.1 The Presence Model

Concept	Definition
Presence	The intuitive (nonreflective) perception of successfully transforming our own intentions in action. Although presence is a unitary feeling, on the process side it can be divided into three different layers or subprocesses, phylogenetically different and strictly related to the evolution of self.
Proto-presence	The first subprocess of presence is related to the emergence of the proto-self: the intuitive perception of successfully differentiating the self from the external world through action. It depends on the level of perception-action coupling (self vs. nonself).
Core presence	The second subprocess of presence is related to the emergence of the core self: the intuitive perception of successfully acting in the external world toward a present object. It depends on the level of vividness (self vs. present external world).
Extended presence	The third subprocess of presence is related to the emergence of extended self: the intuitive perception of successfully acting in the external world toward a possible object. It depends on the level of relevance (self vs. possible external world).
Object	The person, condition, thing, or event at which an action is directed. An object is a psychological representation, and therefore actions can be directed either at objects of the world (present objects) or fictions, the future, and other forms of virtuality (possible objects).
Flow	There are exceptional situations—e.g., a tennis player who goes to the right (proto-presence) before the ball bounces on the court to swing a winning forehand groundstroke (core presence) on a second set-point at the Wimbledon final (extended presence)—in which the activity of the subject is characterized by a high level of presence in all the three different subprocesses (maximal presence). When this experience is associated with a positive emotional state, it constitutes a flow state.

Source: Adapted from Riva et al. 2011.

The Evolutionary Levels of Selfhood

Damasio distinguishes between a preconscious antecedent of self and two distinct notions of selfhood (Dolan 1999; Damasio 1999):

- The *proto-self*: a coherent collection of neural patterns that map, moment by moment, the physical state of the organism
- The *core self*: a transient entity that is continuously generated through encounters with objects
- The *extended self*:[1] a systematic record of the more invariant properties that the organism has discovered about itself

The basis for a conscious self is a feeling state that arises when organisms represent a largely nonconscious proto-self in the process of being modified by objects. In essence, the core sense of self is thought to depend on the creation of a second-order mapping, in certain brain regions (brainstem nuclei, hypothalamus, medial forebrain, and insular and somatosensory cortices), of how the proto-self has been altered (Dolan 1999). This gives the feeling, not just that something is happening, but that something is happening *to me*. However, it is only the extended self that generates the subjective experience of possessing a transtemporal identity (Metzinger 1999).

When we imagine, think, plan, and generally deal with information that does not only constitute our experience of things and events in the currently present external situation, we are exercising extended consciousness: "Extended consciousness has to do with making the organism aware of the largest possible compass of knowledge" (Damasio 1999, 198). It is extended consciousness that allows us to create an internal world in which we may suspend disbelief, as compared to a perceptual world experienced as outside the self. Extended consciousness relies on working memory, which can be seen as the "active scratchpad" of mental life (Baars 1998). It is in working memory that the internal world we are currently experiencing is largely created. Its main function is to allow us to consider possibilities not present in the current external situation. In contrast, core consciousness is directed exclusively to the here and now.

Extended consciousness gives us obvious advantages over organisms without it, such as the ability to plan and generally enact in the imagination possible scenarios of the future, as well as to increase the sophistication of learning from the past. Language depends on it, because we must retain linear sequences of symbols in working memory if we are to understand utterances, whether spoken or written, and then build an internal model of their meaning. But the advantages of extended consciousness depend on the fact that we can distinguish between the experience of the external word and the experience of internal worlds, both remembered and imagined. Confusion of the two indicate serious psychological problems, problems that, until recent times, would have prevented survival and the passing on of this condition.

As noted elsewhere (Waterworth and Waterworth 2003, 2), "if we react as if the external world is only imaginary we will not survive long (think of this the next time you cross a busy street). And if we think that what we are merely imagining is actually happening, we may omit to carry out basic activities on which our survival depends." How then do human beings distinguish perceptions of the external world (perceptions that are themselves largely hypothetical mental predictions) from the purely mental constructions that constitute imagined situations and events? How, in other words, do people separate the internal from the external in our experiences? This chapter suggests that presence is the feeling that evolution has given us to make this vital distinction; this is the biological purpose of presence.

Three Layers of Presence

We associate a specific layer of presence (see figure 12.1) with both the three levels of self identified by Damasio (1999, 2010) and the three intentional levels described by the

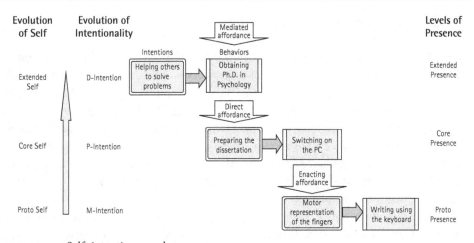

FIGURE 12.1 Self, intentions, and presence

Dynamic Theory of Intentions presented by Pacherie (2006; 2008). Further, since each layer of presence solves a particular facet of the problem of internal/external world separation (which is the purpose of the sense of presence), it is characterized by specific properties. In the following subsections, we outline the characteristics of each layer in more detail, by focusing on its particular characteristics (Riva, Waterworth, and Waterworth 2004).

The First Layer: Proto-presence (Proprioceptive)

As already noted, the main activity of the proto-self is a largely nonconscious mapping of the physical state of the organism. The evolutionary goal of the proto-self is to predict the characteristics of the external world as it is experienced through sensorial inputs.

In this process, movement plays a key role. An adaptive movement is the evolutionary goal of the proto-self, and it is only through movements that the proto-self can embed properties of the external world into its proprioceptive representation.[2] These properties are the constraints generated by the coordinate systems that describe the body. In an evolutionary process that took millions of years, the proto-self has developed to experience these constraints and use them to model the external world experienced through movement.

We consider *proto-presence* to be *embodied presence related to the level of proprioception-action coupling* (self vs. nonself as other). The more the organism is able to couple correctly perceptions and movements, the more it differentiates itself from the external world, thus increasing its probability of surviving, thus driving the evolutionary development of proto-presence. At this stage the self has only a specific intentional ability: *motor intentions*. Motor intentions are responsible for low-level (unconscious and intuitive) forms of guidance and monitoring: we may not be aware of them and have only partial access to their content. Further, their contents are not propositional.

The Second Layer: Core (Perceptual) Presence

According to Damasio (1999), the evolutionary goal of the core self is the integration of specific sensory occurrences into coherent percepts. This is done through a coherent real-time world-model with its own internal logic (Gregory 1998). Such perception depends very largely on knowledge derived from past experiences of the individual and from evolutionary history. At this stage the self has also a second intentional ability: *present-directed intentions.* These intentions are responsible for high-level (conscious) forms of guidance and monitoring directed to a specific object in the surrounding environment. They have to ensure that the imagined actions become current through situational control of their unfolding.

What is the role of core presence (the presence experienced by the core self) in this process? As we have indicated, distinguishing the *present* from the *imaginary* is essential for survival in the here and now. Core presence is a product of *the activity of selective conscious attention made by the self on perceptions.* The more the organism is able to identify the external world and its current tasks in that world as separate from the self, the greater its probability of surviving (self vs. present external world).

In general, there are two elements that allow this distinction to be made: *vividity* and *multisensoriality.* In fact, mental images are much less vivid than perceptions, and are also characterized by the predominant visual component.

The Third Layer: Extended (Reflective) Presence

The possibility of defining internal goals—not related to the here and now—and tracking their achievement is the element that allows the final shift in the evolution of the self: from meaning-as-comprehensibility to meaning-as-significance. In fact, the main feature of the autobiographical self is a new intentional ability: *future-directed intentions.* These intentions act both as intra- and interpersonal coordinators, and as prompters of practical reasoning about means and plans. In this vision, the role of *extended presence is to verify the significance to the self of experienced events in the external world.* The better the organism is able to separate itself from the present and *identify within its own representations those most relevant,* the greater are its chances of survival (self vs. possible external world).

Imagine yourself about to take the final penalty kick in a football match, the outcome of which will determine not only the match but a major international championship. This is the most important kick of your entire career as a footballer, one that will affect your future and that of your club for years to come. If you succeed in not being distracted by *thinking about* these aspects, you will focus on your own intention—winning the championship—and the significance of the event will result in an enhanced degree of extended presence.

Extended presence is also the element that allows for the subject's "*absence*," that is, *its presence in an exclusively mental activity.* During an experience of absence, such as thinking, daydreaming, or meditating, the subject tries to separate itself as much as possible from the outside world and to concentrate exclusively on its own mental processes (self vs. external world). In general, the more the subject believes that mental activity is important for its "internality," the greater its attempts will be to isolate itself from the outside world.

Presence is maximized when all three layers are integrated around the same external situation. When the layers are stimulated by conflicting content, however, presence will be reduced. As recently demonstrated by Villani and colleagues (2012), it is possible to experience more presence in doing the same thing in virtual reality than in reality. In their study they used a sample of 20 university students to evaluate the level of presence experienced in two different settings: an immersive virtual reality job simulation and a real-world simulation that was identical to its VR counterpart (same interviewer, same questions) but without technological mediation and without any social and cultural cues in the environment that may give a better meaning to both the task and its social context. Self-report data, and in particular the scores in the Spatial Presence and the Ecological Validity ITC-SOPI scales, suggest that experienced presence was higher during the virtual interview than in the real-world simulation. This interpretation was confirmed by subjective (higher in VR) but not by objective (skin conductance) anxiety scores.

In an awake, healthy animal in the physical world, proto-presence and core presence will rarely if ever be in conflict. This is an aspect of presence in the physical world that is very hard to duplicate with interactive media such as VR. In fact, in VR there is always some degree of conflict between these two layers and, when it is severe or the participant is particularly sensitive, so-called "cybersickness" (essentially a form of motion sickness) is a common result.

Presence and Action

In the previous paragraphs we described presence as a process critical for the development of the self that allows us to distinguish between "internal" and "external." But an open problem related to the research about presence is its role in cognitive science: what is its foundation in terms of the cognitive processes involved in it?

In this paragraph we suggest that presence is an intuitive metacognitive judgment that monitors our actions (Riva and Mantovani 2012). This process monitors prereflexively our activity by using an embodied intuitive simulation of the intended action developed through practice (implicit learning). In other words, we are present during an action, direct or mediated, when the simulation of the intended action (the intention of taking an apple) corresponds to the data perceived during the action (I got the apple). In this vision, the main difference between a direct action (I take the apple using my hand), a first-order mediated action (I take the apple using a stick), and a second-order mediated action (I use a joystick to move the hand of a robot taking the apple) is related to the different learning needed to simulate intuitively the intended action (Riva and Mantovani 2012).

Presence Is an Intuitive Process

As noted by Stanovich and West (2000), in the last 40 years, different authors from different disciplines suggested a two-process theory of reasoning. Even if the details and specific features of these theories do not always match perfectly, nevertheless they share the following properties (see table 12.2).

In sum, intuitive operations are faster, automatic, effortless, associative, and difficult to control or modify. Rational operations, instead, are slower, serial, effortful, and consciously controlled. As underlined by Koriat (2007, 301), this distinction "implies a separation between two components or states of consciousness—on the one hand, sheer subjective feelings and intuitions that have a perceptual-like quality and, on the other hand, reasoned cognitions that are grounded in a network of beliefs and explicit memories. It is a distinction between what one feels and senses and what one knows or thinks." For instance, we may feel that we have encountered a person before, even if we don't have an explicit memory of him or her.

Contrary to common thought, however, intuition is not solely innate. Research on perceptual-cognitive and motor skills shows that they are automated through experience and thus rendered intuitive (Kihlstrom 1987). In the case of motor skill learning, the process is initially rational and controlled by consciousness, as shown, for example, by the novice driver's rehearsal of the steps involved in parking a car: check the mirrors and blind spots; signal to the side of the space; position the car beside the vehicle I'm parking behind, and so on. However, later the skill becomes intuitive and consciously inaccessible by virtue of practice, as shown, for example, by the difficulty expert drivers have in describing how to perform a complex maneuver, and by the fact that conscious attention to it actually interferes with their driving performance.

In sum, perceptual-motor skills that are not innate—for example, driving a car—may become automatic through practice, and their operations thereby rendered intuitive. Using a metaphor derived from computer science, this process can be described as *knowledge compilation* (Kihlstrom 1987; Selman and Kautz 1996): a knowledge given in

Table 12.2 Intuition versus Reasoning

	Intuition	Reasoning
Process	Relatively fast, parallel, automatic, cognitively effortless, associative; acquisition by biology, exposure, and personal experience	Relatively slow, serial, controlled, cognitively effortful, rule-based; acquisition by cultural and formal tuition
Content	Percepts, imagery, and motor representations	Conceptual/linguistic representations
Outcome	Impressions	Judgments

a general representation format (linguistic-semantic) is translated into a different one, more usable and less computationally demanding (perceptual-motor).

Are presence and telepresence intuitive or rational cognitive processes? On one side, it is evident that presence is the *outcome* of an intuitive cognitive process: no rational effort is required to experience a feeling of presence. On the other side, however, presence is *different* from an acquired motor skill or a behavioral disposition.

A possible path to find a better answer comes from the concept of metacognition. Koriat (2007, 289) defines "metacognition" as "the processes by which people self-reflect on their own cognitive and memory processes (monitoring) and how they put their metaknowledge to use in regulating their information processing and behavior (control)." Following the distinction between intuition and reasoning, researchers in this area distinguish between *information-based* (or theory-based) and *experience-based* metacognitive judgments (Koriat 2007; Koriat and Levy-Sadot 1999). Information-based metacognitive judgments are based on a deliberate use of one's beliefs and theories to reach an evaluation about one's competence and cognitions: they are deliberate and largely conscious, and draw on the contents of declarative information in long-term memory.

By contrast, experience-based metacognitive judgments are subjective feelings that are products of an inferential intuitive process: they operate unconsciously and give rise to a "sheer subjective experience." Examples of these metacognitive judgments are (Price and Norman 2008) the "feeling of knowing" (knowing that we are able to recognize the correct answer to a question that we cannot currently recall), or the "feeling of familiarity" (knowing that we have encountered a given situation before, even if we don't have an explicit memory of it).

As Koriat and Levy-Sadot (1999, 496) argue: "The cues [for these metacognitive judgments] lie in structural aspects of the information processing system. This system, so to speak, engages in a self-reflective inspection of its own operation and uses the ensuing information as a basis for metacognitive judgments."

In other words, we can try to describe presence as the sheer subjective experience of being in a given environment (the feeling of "being there"), that is the product of an intuitive experience-based metacognitive judgment.

Intuition as Simulation

At this point, a critical question is "What is intuitively judged by presence?" Different authors have suggested a role of presence in the monitoring of action. For example, Zahoric and Jenison (1998, 87) underline that "presence is tantamount to successfully supported action in the environment"; Riva and colleagues (2011, 24) suggest that "the evolutionary role of presence is the control of agency"; finally, Slater and colleagues (2009, 208) argue that "humans have a propensity to find correlations between their activity and internal state and their sense perceptions of what is going on out there."

But how may this work? And how this process is related to intuition? As suggested by Reber (1989, 233): "To have an intuitive sense of what is right and proper, to have a vague feeling of the goal of an extended process of thought, to 'get the point' without really being able to verbalize what it is that one has gotten, is to have gone through an implicit learning experience and have built up the requisite representative knowledge base to allow for such judgment."

In simpler words, through implicit learning the subject is able to represent complex actions using perceptual-motor data and enact or monitor them intuitively. As suggested by the covert imitation theory (Wilson and Knoblich 2005; Knoblich et al. 2005), the brain instantiates a sophisticated simulation, based on motor codes, of the outcome of an action and uses this to evaluate its course. This can be achieved through a simulative forward model (Blackemore and Decety 2001; Riva 2009): during the enaction of a learned skill, a sensory prediction of the outcome of the action (simulation) is produced along with the actual motor command. The results of the comparison (which occurs intuitively) between the sensory prediction and the sensory consequences of the act can then be utilized to determine both the agent of the action and to track any possible variation in its course (see figure 12.2). If no variations are perceived, the subject is able to concentrate on the action and not on its monitoring.

In this view, presence is unconscious in the sense that we do not have detailed conscious access to its processing antecedents. It is conscious, too, in that it is a distinct phenomenology—something it feels like to have the feeling. And it is metacognitive since it conveys information about our spatial experience that permits us to monitor and eventually regulate our action. In summary, presence is an intuitive, experience-based metacognitive judgment:

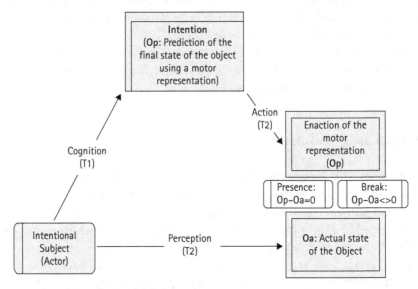

FIGURE 12.2 Simulative Forward Model

- It monitors prereflexively our activity processes.
- It is achieved using an embodied intuitive simulation of the intended action.
- Only when the subject acquires a motor skill is he or she able to simulate its outcome intuitively (implicit learning).
- A break in presence is a violation of our intuitive simulation. As a consequence, the subject is forced to shift to reasoning to understand and cope with the causes of the violation.

PRESENCE IN VIRTUAL WORLDS

As Sanchez-Vives and Slater (2005, 335) suggest, "[mediated] presence is a phenomenon worthy of study by neuroscientists and may help towards the study of consciousness, since it may be regarded as consciousness within a restricted domain." In a fully immersive virtual reality, offering aural, visual, and haptic feedbacks, many aspects affecting the experience can be controlled, manipulated, and replicated precisely, and because of this virtual realities (and to a lesser extent, other interactive media) provide a powerful paradigm for experimentation, with presence measures serving as dependent variables. The ability to design specific interactive environments with predictable effects on the sense of presence follows from this.

Designing and Measuring Mediated Presence

Often an interaction designer's aim is to design for as much presence as possible. The first suggestion this framework offers to the developers of virtual worlds is that for presence *action is more important than perception* (Riva 2008): I'm more present in a perceptually poor virtual environment (e.g., a textual MUD) where I can act in many different ways than in a lifelike virtual environment where I cannot do anything.

More, our theoretical position suggests that a typical, unexceptional level of presence arises from an intuitive split of attentional resources between layers with differing content, with some attention being directed to the current external situation and some to a different internal concern. Minimal presence results from an almost complete lack of integration of the three layers discussed above, such as is the case when attention is mostly directed toward contents of extended consciousness that are unrelated to the present external environment. By the same reasoning, maximal presence arises when proto-consciousness, core consciousness, and extended consciousness are focused on the same external situation or activity. Maximal presence thus results from the combination of all three layers with an abnormally tight focus on the same content. This will arise in a mediated experience from an optimal combination of form and content, able to support the activity of the user.

If our model can predict the conditions for maximal presence, it should also predict when and why mediated presence may be experienced at a relatively low level. This can be the case in many, indeed most, interactive situations, reflecting that the different layers of presence are less than perfectly integrated. For example, if a virtual reality is experienced without an accurate and responsive body-tracking system, there might be a high level of core presence (vividness) and a high level of extended presence (engagement), but this will not be integrated with proto-presence. Similarly, when one is engaged in reading a compelling book while sitting comfortably in a safe place, extended consciousness may be occupied by the medium, but the other layers of presence will not be involved. Even if placed in a highly immersive VR, a participant may be preoccupied with other concerns, perhaps because the mediated content is not very engaging. In this case, proto-presence and core presence may have been invoked by the medium, but not extended presence.

We foresee a program of research to test these and other predictions from our model. A particular focus for the interpretation of results would be quantum shifts in presence levels in response to manipulations of the situational conditions of activity.

CONCLUSIONS

We have presented the sense of presence as a neuropsychological phenomenon, evolved from the interplay of our biological and cultural inheritance, the function of which is the enaction of the volition of the subject: *the feeling of presence is the prereflexive perception that the agent's intentions are successfully enacted.*

In our view presence is not the same thing as consciousness—for example, in *hemispatial neglect*, a neurological disease characterized by a deficit in attention to and awareness of one side of space, the patient is conscious but is not present in a specific space. We can be conscious without feeling presence, but we cannot feel presence if we are not conscious. Presence has three critical features that cannot be explained by other cognitive processes (Riva and Mantovani 2012):

- First, *presence is an intuitive process*: only when we are able to use our body or a tool intuitively can we be present in it or in the space surrounding it. In other words, "intuition" can be the psychological translation of the concept of "transparency" that is behind a significant part of the theoretical reflection on presence.
- Second, *presence provides feedback to the self about the status of its activity*: the self perceives the variations in presence and tunes its activity accordingly.
- Third, *presence allows the evolution of the Self through the incorporation of tools*: tools do not enable us only to extend our reaching space, but when successfully mastered become part of a plastic neural representation of our body that allows their use without further cognitive effort (intuitively). In this way we can focus our cognitive resources on actions that are not only related to the here and now, improving the complexity of our goals (Damasio 2010; Riva and Waterworth 2003; Riva, Waterworth, and Waterworth 2004).

In this view, a high feeling of presence is experienced by the self as a better quality of action and experience (Zahoric and Jenison 1998). In fact, the subject perceives consciously only *significant variations* in the feeling of presence: *breakdowns* and *optimal experiences* (Riva 2006).

Why do we consciously track presence variations? In our view presence can be considered as a sophisticated evolutionary tool used to control the quality of behavior. Specifically, the subject tries to overcome any breakdown in its activity and searches for engaging and rewarding activities (optimal experiences). It provides both the motivation and the guiding principle for successful action.

Although presence is a unitary feeling, on the process side it can be divided into three different layers or subprocesses, phylogenetically different and strictly related to the evolution of self.

Presence mediated by information technology is the feeling of being in an external world, in the realization of which that technology plays a direct role. To arise and persist, it requires adequate form to be directly perceived, conscious attention to that form, and content that will sustain such attention. When we experience strong mediated presence, our experience is that the technology has become part of the self, and the mediated reality to which we are attending has become an integrated part of the other. When this happens, there is no additional conscious *effort of access* to information, nor *effort of action* to carry out overt responses in the mediated environment. We perceive and act directly, as if unmediated. The extent to which we experience presence through a medium thus provides a measure of the extent to which that technology has become an integrated part of the self. Maximal presence in a mediated experience arises from an optimal combination of form and content, able to support the intentions of the user.

NOTES

1. Damasio refers to this as the "autobiographical self." But because of its intrinsic dependence on extended consciousness, and because it consists of more than autobiographical memories and the self-conscious *idea* of self, we prefer to call this third layer the "extended self."
2. In this, we echo Sheets-Johnstone's perspective (Sheets-Johnstone 1998) on the role of movement in the evolutionary origins and development of consciousness. We consider that as movement implies consciousness, so does it further imply the need for an ability to distinguish in consciousness between self and other.

REFERENCES

Baars, B. J. 1998. *A Cognitive Theory of Consciousness.* New York: Cambridge University Press.

Baños, R. M., C. Botella, A. García-Palacios, H. Villa, C. Perpiñá, and M. Alcañiz. 2000. Presence and Reality Judgment in Virtual Environments: A Unitary Construct? *Cyberpsychology and Behavior* 3 (3): 327–355.

Baños, R. M., C. Botella, and C. Perpiña. 1999. Virtual Reality and Psychopathology. *CyberPsychology and Behavior* 2 (4): 283–292.

Biocca, F. 1997. The Cyborg's Dilemma: Progressive Embodiment in Virtual Environments. *Journal of Computer Mediated-Communication* 3 (2). http://jcmc.indiana.edu/vol3/issue2/biocca2.html. Accessed June 17, 2013.

Blackemore, S. J., and J. Decety. 2001. From the Perception of Action to the Understanding of Intention. *Nature Reviews Neuroscience* 2: 561–567.

Coelho, C., J. Tichon, T. J. Hine, G. Wallis, and G. Riva. 2006. Media Presence and Inner Presence: The Sense of Presence in Virtual Reality Technologies. In *From Communication to Presence: Cognition, Emotions and Culture towards the Ultimate Communicative Experience. Festschrift in Honor of Luigi Anolli*, edited by G. Riva, M. T. Anguera, B. K. Wiederhold, and F. Mantovani, 25–45. Amsterdam: IOS Press. http://www.emergingcommunication.com/volume8.html. Accessed June 17, 2013.

Damasio, A. 1999. *The Feeling of What Happens: Body, Emotion and the Making of Consciousness*. San Diego, CA: Harcourt Brace.

Damasio, A. 2010. *Self Comes to Mind: Constructing the Conscious Brain*. New York: Pantheon Books.

Dolan, R. J. 1999. Feeling the Neurobiological Self. *Nature* 401: 847–848.

Gregory, R. L. 1998. *Eye and Brain: The Psychology of Seeing*. Vol. 1. Oxford: Oxford University Press.

IJsselsteijn, W. A., H. de Ridder, J. Freeman, and S. E. Avons. 2000. Presence: Concept, Determinants and Measurement. Paper read at "Human Vision and Electronic Imaging V," San Jose, CA.

Kihlstrom, J. F. 1987. The Cognitive Unconscious. *Science* 237 (4821): 1445–1452.

Knoblich, G., I. Thornton, M. Grosjean, and M. Shiffrar, eds. 2005. *Human Body Perception from the Inside Out*. New York: Oxford University Press.

Koriat, A. 2007. Metacognition and Consciousness. In *Cambridge Handbook of Consciousness*, edited by P. D. Zelaso, M. Moscovitch, and E. Thompson, 289–325. New York: Cambridge University Press.

Koriat, A., and R. Levy-Sadot. 1999. Processes Underlying Metacognitive Judgments: Information-Based and Experience-Based Monitoring of One's Own Knowledge. In *Dual-Process Theories in Social Psychology*, edited by C. Shelly and T. Yaacov, 483–502. New York: Guilford Press.

Lee, K. M. 2004a. Presence, Explicated. *Communication Theory* 14: 27–50.

Lee, K. M. 2004b. Why Presence Occurs: Evolutionary Psychology, Media Equation, and Presence. *Presence* 13 (4): 494–505.

Lombard, M., and T. Ditton. 1997. At the Heart of It All: The Concept of Presence. *Journal of Computer Mediated-Communication* 3 (2). http://www.ascusc.org/jcmc/vol3/issue2/lombard.html. Accessed July 15, 2013.

Lombard, M., and M. T. Jones. 2006. Defining Presence. Paper presented to "Presence 2006: The 9th International Workshop on Presence," Cleveland, OH.

Loomis, J. M. 1992. Distal Attribution and Presence. *Presence, Teleoperators, and Virtual Environments* 1 (1): 113–118.

Mantovani, G., and G. Riva. 1999. "Real" Presence: How Different Ontologies Generate Different Criteria For presence, Telepresence, and Virtual Presence. *Presence, Teleoperators, and Virtual Environments* 8: 538–548.

Mantovani, G., and G. Riva. 2001. Building a Bridge between Different Scientific Communities: On Sheridan's Eclectic Ontology of Presence. *Presence: Teleoperators and Virtual Environments* 8: 538–548.

Mantovani, G., and A. Spagnolli. 2000. Imagination and Culture: What Is It Like Being in the Cyberspace? *Mind, Culture, and Activity* 7 (3): 217–226.

Marsh, T. 2003. Staying There: An Activity-Based Approach to Narrative Design and Evaluation as an Antidote to Virtual Corpsing. In *Being There: Concepts, Effects and Measurements of User Presence in Synthetic Environments*, edited by G. Riva, F. Davide and W. A. IJsselsteijn, 85–96. Amsterdam: IOS Press.

Marsh, T., P. Wright, and S. Smith. 2001. Evaluation for the Design of Experience in Virtual Environments: Modeling Breakdown of Interaction and Illusion. *Cyberpsychology and Behavior* 4 (2): 225–238.

Metzinger, T. 1999. The Hint Half Guessed. *Scientific American* 11: 184–189.

Metzinger, T. 2009. *The Ego Tunnel: The Science of the Mind and the Myth of the Self.* New York: Basic Books.

Moore, K., B. K. Wiederhold, M. D. Wiederhold, and G. Riva. 2002. Panic and Agoraphobia in a Virtual World. *Cyberpsychology and Behavior* 5 (3): 197–202.

Pacherie, E. 2006. Toward a Dynamic Theory of Intentions. In *Does Consciousness Cause Behavior?* edited by S. Pockett, W. P. Banks. and S. Gallagher, 145–167. Cambridge, MA: MIT Press.

Pacherie, E. 2008. The Phenomenology of Action: A Conceptual Framework. *Cognition* 107 (1): 179–217.

Price, M. C., and E. Norman. 2008. Intuitive Decisions on the Fringes of Consciousness: Are They Conscious and Does It Matter? *Judgment and Decision Making* 3 (1): 28–41.

Reber, A. S. 1989. Implicit Learning and Tacit Knowledge. *Journal of Experimental Psychology: General* 118 (3): 219–235.

Revonsuo, A. 2006. *Inner Presence: Consciousness as a Biological Phenomenon.* Cambridge, MA: MIT Press.

Riva, G. 2006. Being-in-the-World-With: Presence Meets Social and Cognitive Neuroscience. In *From Communication to Presence: Cognition, Emotions and Culture towards the Ultimate Communicative Experience. Festschrift in honor of Luigi Anolli*, edited by G. Riva, M. T. Anguera, B. K. Wiederhold, and F. Mantovani, 47–80. Amsterdam: IOS Press. http://www. emergingcommunication.com/volume8.html. Accessed July 14, 2013.

Riva, G. 2008. From Virtual to Real Body: Virtual Reality as Embodied Technology. *Journal of Cybertherapy and Rehabiliation* 1 (1): 7–22.

Riva, G. 2009. Is Presence a Technology Issue? Some Insights from Cognitive Sciences. *Virtual Reality* 13 (3): 59–69.

Riva, G. 2011. Presence, Actions and Emotions: A Theoretical Framework. *Annual Review of CyberTherapy and Telemedicine* 9: 2–5.

Riva, G., and F. Davide, eds. 2001. Communications through Virtual Technologies: Identity, Community and Technology in the Communication Age. In *Emerging Communication: Studies on New Technologies and Practices in Communication*, edited by G. Riva and F. Davide. Amsterdam: Ios Press. http://www.emergingcommunication.com/volume1.html. Accessed July 14, 2013.

Riva, G., F. Davide, and W. A. IJsselsteijn, eds. 2003. Being There: Concepts, Effects and Measurements of User Presence in Synthetic Environments. In *Emerging Communication: Studies on New Technologies and Practices in Communication*, edited by G. Riva and F. Davide. Amsterdam: Ios Press. http://www.emergingcommunication.com/volume5.html. Accessed July 14, 2013.

Riva, G., P. Loreti, M. Lunghi, F. Vatalaro, and F. Davide. 2003. Presence in 2010: The Emergence of Ambient Intelligence. In *Being There: Concepts, Effects and Measurements of User Presence in Synthetic Environments*, edited by G. Riva, F. Davide, and W. A. IJsselsteijn. Amsterdam: IOS Press. 59–82.

Riva, G., and F. Mantovani. 2012. From the Body to the Tools and Back: A General Framework for Presence in Mediated Interactions. *Interacting with Computers* 24 (4): 203–210.

Riva, G., and J. A. Waterworth. 2003. Presence and the Self: A Cognitive Neuroscience Approach. *Presence-Connect* 3 (1). http://presence.cs.ucl.ac.uk/presenceconnect/articles/ Apr2003/jwworthApr72003114532/jwworthApr72003114532.html. Accessed July 14, 2013.

Riva, G., J. A. Waterworth, and E. L. Waterworth. 2004. The Layers of Presence: A Bio-cultural Approach to Understanding Presence in Natural and Mediated Environments. *Cyberpsychology and Behavior* 7 (4): 405–419.

Riva, G., J. A. Waterworth, E. L. Waterworth, and F. Mantovani. 2011. From Intention to Action: The Role of Presence. *New Ideas in Psychology* 29 (1): 24–37.

Sadowski, W. J., and K. M. Stanney. 2002. Measuring and Managing Presence in Virtual Environments. In *Handbook of Virtual Environments Technology*, edited by K. M. Stanney, 791–806. Mahwah, NJ: Lawrence Erlbaum Associates.

Sanchez-Vives, M. V., and M. Slater. 2005. From Presence to Consciousness through Virtual Reality. *Nature Review Neuroscience* 6 (4): 332–339.

Schloerb, D. 1995. A Quantitative Measure of Telepresence. *Presence: Teleoperators, and Virtual Environments* 4 (1): 64–80.

Schubert, T., F. Friedman, and H. Regenbrecht. 2001. The Experience of Presence: Factor Analytic Insights. *Presence: Teleoperators, and Virtual Environments* 10 (3): 266–281.

Selman, B., and H. Kautz. 1996. Knowledge Compilation and Theory Approximation. *Journal of the ACM* 43 (2): 193–224.

Sheets-Johnstone, M. 1998. Consciousness: A natural history. *Journal of Consciousness Studies* 5 (3): 260–924.

Sheridan, T. B. 1992. Musing on Telepresence and Virtual Presence. *Presence, Teleoperators, and Virtual Environments* 1: 120–125.

Sheridan, T. B. 1996. Further Musing on the Psychophysics of Presence. *Presence, Teleoperators, and Virtual Environments* 5: 241–246.

Slater, M., B. Lotto, M. M. Arnold, and M. V. Sanchez-Vives. 2009. How We Experience Immersive Virtual Environments: The Concept of Presence and Its Measurement. *Anuario de Psicología* 40 (2): 193–210.

Spagnolli, A., and L. Gamberini. 2002. Immersion/Emersion: Presence in Hybrid Environments. Paper presented to "Presence 2002: Fifth Annual International Workshop," October 9–11, Porto, Portugal.

Spagnolli, A., L. Gamberini, and D. Gasparini. 2003. Situated Breakdown Analysis for the Evaluation of a Virtual Environment. *PsychNology Journal* 1 (1). http://www.psychnology. org/File/PSYCHNOLOGY_JOURNAL_1_1_SPAGNOLLI.pdf. Accessed July 14, 2013.

Stanovich, K. E., and R. F. West. 2000. Individual Differences in Reasoning: Implications for the Rationality Debate? *Behavior and Brain Sciences* 23 (5): 645–665; discussion 665–726.

Villani, D., C. Repetto, P. Cipresso, and G. Riva. 2012. May I Experience More Presence in Doing the Same Thing in Virtual Reality Than in Reality? An Answer from a Simulated Job Interview. *Interacting with Computers* 24 (4): 265–272.

Waterworth, J. A., and E. L. Waterworth. 2001. Focus, Locus, and Sensus: The Three Dimensions of Virtual Experience. *Cyberpsychology and Behavior* 4 (2): 203–213.

Waterworth, J. A., and E. L. Waterworth. 2003. The Meaning of Presence. *Presence-Connect* 3 (2). http://presence.cs.ucl.ac.uk/presenceconnect/articles/Feb2003/jwworthFeb1020031217/ jwworthFeb1020031217.html. Accessed July 14, 2013.

Waterworth, J. A., E. L. Waterworth, F. Mantovani, and G. Riva. 2010. On Feeling (the) Present: An Evolutionary Account of the Sense of Presence in Physical and Electronically-Mediated Environments. *Journal of Consciousness Studies* 17 (1–2): 167–178.

Waterworth, J. A., E. L. Waterworth, F. Mantovani, and G. Riva, eds. 2012. Special Issue: Presence and Interaction. *Interacting with Computers* 24 (4): 190–192.

Wilson, M., and G. Knoblich. 2005. The Case for Motor Involvement in Perceiving Conspecifics. *Psychological Bulletin* 131 (3): 460–473.

Zahoric, P., and R. L. Jenison. 1998. Presence as Being-in-the-World. *Presence, Teleoperators, and Virtual Environments* 7 (1): 78–89.

CHAPTER 13

··

IMMERSION IN
VIRTUAL WORLDS

··

GORDON CALLEJA

VIRTUAL worlds are enabling experiences that were not previously available through other media. One such experience is the potential to have a sense of inhabiting the simulated spaces they offer, not just through the use of the player's imaginative faculty, but also through the cybernetic circuit between player and machine. This phenomenon has been described by the terms "presence" and "immersion." Although the two terms are used in various fields and have been discussed for three decades, there seems to be a lack of consensus as to what either of them actually refers to (Ermi and Mäyrä 2005; King and Krzywinska 2006; Tamborini and Skalski 2006; Brown and Cairns 2004; Jennett et al. 2008). The term "immersion" is particularly problematic because it is used so widely when discussing experiential facets of anything from digital games to painting (Grau 2003), literature (Nell 1988), and cinema (Bazin 1967). Nevertheless the phenomenon these two terms have been enlisted to describe is crucial to our understanding of the relationship between user and virtual world, as it represents one end of a continuum of intensity of involvement with virtual worlds and addresses the very notion of being in the context of such simulated environments.

In this chapter I claim that the confusion and apprehension surrounding the use of these two terms is based on a number of challenges they pose to a clear understanding of the phenomenon they have been employed to describe. The chapter takes digital games as the most popular and experientially powerful forms of virtual worlds and thus uses them as its primary exemplar. The radical stance taken here will be to claim that this confusion arises because neither metaphor adequately describes the relationship between player and game. Both assume a unidirectional dive of human subjectivity into a containing vessel, a split between the physical "here" and the virtual "there" that is overcome temporarily when the phenomenon is experienced.

I will further argue for a more precise and conceptually productive approach that views the virtual world assimilated into the user's consciousness as a space that affords the exertion of agency and expression of sociality in a manner coextensive with our everyday reality. The metaphors of presence and immersion are therefore replaced with the notion of incorporation: an experiential phenomenon that accounts for the simultaneous assimilation into consciousness of the virtual world *and* the systemic acknowledgment of the player's location and existence therein. This turns the concept of a unidirectional plunge into the virtual on its head, and instead posits the virtual as a productive aspect of contemporary reality that is having a profound impact on notions of identity and sociality exactly because of this more seamless integration of simulated worlds and globally connected minds.

We will now consider the genesis and development of both these terms, outlining some of the major debates that have centered around their use.

Presence History and Terminology

The term "presence" originates from a paper in the field of telerobotics written by Marvin Minsky in 1980 titled "Telepresence." Although emerging from telerobotics, the experiential phenomenon Minsky writes about was already being discussed in relation to virtual reality technology. Indeed, the concern with creating systems that would foster a strong sense of being in a visually represented and cybernetically reactive system has been around since Ivan Sutherland's prototype of "The Ultimate Display," a more cumbersome version of today's head-mounted displays (Sutherland 1965; 1968). Minsky's labeling and defining the experiential sense of being in an environment where one is not actually present led a community of researchers to form the field of presence theory, dedicated to the study of the phenomenon. The research of this new field sought to define the phenomenon and then find ways of measure it in order to inform the design of virtual reality environments and the corresponding hardware.

Presence research has come across a series of definitional conflicts that have slowed its progress. The first terminological difference came in 1992 with the launch of the journal *Presence*. In the first issue, Thomas Sheridan (1992) made an argument for restricting telepresence to instances of teleoperation and using "virtual presence" to refer to presence in virtual environments. Richard Held and Nathaniel Durlach (1992), on the other hand, argued that telepresence could be used for both phenomena. Later, papers in the field dropped "telepresence" altogether and used "presence" to refer to experiences in both virtual and physical environments.

Another contentious terminological issue is the distinction between immersion and presence. The disagreement in the use of these terms has been particularly problematic for the field. The difficulties here are not merely of labeling but, as we shall discuss below, also evidence ontological divides within the field. The two terms are sometimes used interchangeably, while at other times they are given complementary meanings (IJsselsteijn and Riva 2003). More problematically, the terms have been sometimes given conflicting meanings. Mel Slater and Sylvia Wilbur define immersion as

> A description of a technology…that describes the extent to which the computer displays are capable of delivering an inclusive, extensive, surrounding and vivid illusion of reality to the sense of a human participant. (Slater and Wilbur 1997, 606)

They further contrast immersion with presence, which is defined as "a state of consciousness, the (psychological) sense of being in the virtual environment" (607). Slater later qualifies the latter distinction, describing immersion as "simply what the technology delivers from an objective point of view" and presence as "a human reaction to immersion" (Slater 2003, 1). Thus the label "immersion" is being used to describe the affective properties of the hardware, while presence is the psychological response to this technology. Bob Witmer and Michael Singer, on the other hand, view immersion as

> A psychological state characterized by perceiving oneself to be enveloped by, included in, and interacting with an environment that provides a continuous stream of stimuli and experiences. (Witmer and Singer 1998, 227)

The above use of immersion conflicts with Slater and Wilbur's definition. In fact Witmer and Singer''s use of "immersion" is very similar to Slater and Wilbur's use of "presence." More contemporary presence research (Van Den Hoogen, IJsselsteijn, and Kort 2009; IJsselsteijn 2004; Rettie 2004) follows Slater and Wilbur's conceptualization of immersion as an objective property of the technology, and presence as a psychological reaction to this technological property.

PRESENCE AND TECHNOLOGICAL DETERMINISM

By proposing immersion as a property of a technology Slater problematically implies that a technology can determine the experience of the users interacting with it. In a later paper he expands on this argument, claiming that a high-fidelity sound system makes listeners feel as though they were listening to a live orchestra, whether or not they find the music itself engaging:

> Suppose you shut your eyes and try out someone's quadraphonic sound system which is playing some music. "Wow!" you say "that's just like being in the theatre where the orchestra is playing." That statement is a sign of presence. You then go on to say "But the music is really uninteresting and after a few moments my mind started to drift and I lost interest." That second statement has *nothing to do with presence* [italics in original]. You would not conclude, because the music is uninteresting that you did not have the illusion of being in the theatre listening to the orchestra. The first statement is about form. The second statement is about content. (Slater 2003, 607)

Slater is claiming that the quality of the technology, in and of itself, can induce a particular experience whatever the content being transmitted. Aside from being problematically deterministic in its underpinnings, the claim is particularly challenging to sustain when such a complex experiential phenomenon as the sense of inhabiting a virtual environment is concerned. This conception of presence stems from Slater and Wilbur's definition cited above (Slater and Wilbur 1997, 606), where presence is claimed to have an objective component that is observable in the user's behavior. This formulation of presence has been criticized by Mantovani and Riva (1999), who find it suffers from both a contradiction in its attempt to sustain a separation between subjective and objective natures of presence, and the nature of the deterministic model of communication found in Slater and Wilbur's work that has been extensively criticized and replaced in communication and media studies.

Slater goes on to argue that content and form can be separated conceptually:

> Presence is about form, the extent to which the unification of simulated sensory data and perceptual processing produces a coherent "place" that you are "in" and in which there may be the potential for you to act. The second statement is about content. A [virtual environment] system can be highly presence inducing, and yet have a really uninteresting, uninvolving content (just like many aspects of real life!). (Slater 2003, 607)

This conceptualization does not give enough importance to the key role that interpretation and agency play in creating a sense of presence. Interpretation does not need to be a conscious action. Interactions with an environment, physical or virtual, draw heavily on our learned knowledge of that or similar environments. When this process of interpretation breaks down because the environment we come across does not fit a known mode of interpretation, we automatically become more critically removed from the environment (Heidegger 1993; Zahoric and Jenison 1998). Our attention becomes invested in interpreting the environment, an experiential mode that is antithetical to feeling present in the environment. As has been argued elsewhere (Calleja 2011), the sense of inhabiting an environment comes from the internalization and consequent blending of a number of dimensions of involvement. In this process, our prior experience, expectations, and knowledge of the environment in question form a crucial part of this interpretative relation (Zahoric and Jenison 1998). Returning to Slater's example: if you have never attended a classical music concert, nor even seen a video of one, it is not clear you could feel "present" in the way Slater describes when listening to the sound system. The nature of the content in relation to the participant's interpretative apparatus and prior lived experience is crucial for a sense of presence. The argument I am making here is thus that while high-fidelity systems are an important part of enhancing the intensity of an experience, they do not themselves create a sense of presence.

PRESENCE/IMMERSION AND MEDIA SPECIFICITY

Another problematic issue that is too often found both in presence theory and in wider discussions on immersion in related fields is the lack of distinction between involvement and presence in ergodic (Aarseth 1997) media-like games and non-ergodic media like film and literature. The idea that one can experience presence in both ergodic and non-ergodic media is now common enough in presence research that it is generally taken as a given (Witmer and Singer 1998; Schubert and Crusius 2002; Gysbers et al. 2004; Marsh 2003; Lee 2004). This wider application of the term stretches the concept of presence to account for what is essentially an entirely mental phenomenon that ignores the difference between media that connect user and environment through a cybernetic system and those that do not. Even if we claim that properties of non-ergodic media afford the experience of inhabiting an environment, that habitation is solely an imaginary one, which is not the case in the context of ergodic media. The scientific community adopted terms like presence or immersion because a new experience afforded by a novel technology came into being, leaving a lexical gap that needed plugging. Extending the terms to cover imagined presence in works of literature, film, or free-roaming imagination sidelines the core concern: the description and exploration of a phenomenon enabled by a specific technology.

It is important that a precise understanding of the phenomenon of virtual-world habitation, whatever we end up labeling that phenomenon, makes a distinction between simply imagining one is present in a scene and the considerably different phenomenon of having one's specific location and presence within a virtual world acknowledged by the system itself. When we imagine a particular scene, the action that goes on therein is willed into existence, consciously or unconsciously, by the experient. When considering virtual environments, however, the user is anchored in its domain through her avatar, which roots her to a specific location in the world that the environment, its native entities, and other users acknowledge and can react to. This aspect of virtual worlds fundamentally alters how the player perceives herself within the world that is radically different than a sense of entirely imagined presence in literary works, movies, or personal flights of fantasy. When we identify with a character in a movie or book, or imagine we are in the same room as the protagonist, we have no way of altering the course of events, no way of exerting agency. Likewise, the environments and characters represented in these media have no way of reacting to our presence, no matter how strongly we identify with them.

This tendency to ignore the specific qualities of different media when discussing presence/immersion is also rife in fields like media studies and game studies. Jane Douglas and Andrew Hargadon (2001), for example, rightly attempt to distinguish between immersion and engagement based on the critical stance of the reader or player. They explain that with immersion, "perceptions, reactions and interactions all take place within the text's frame, which itself usually suggests a single schema and a few definite scripts for highly directed interaction" (152). They contrast this with a more critical, and hence distanced, stance taken by the player or reader in the case of more complex texts. Engagement requires a more conscious and interpretative effort that results in a discontinuous interaction with the text:

> Conversely, in what we might term the "engaged affective experience," contradictory schemas or elements that defy conventional schemas tend to disrupt readers' immersion in a text, obliging them to assume an extra-textual perspective on the text itself, as well as on the schemas that have shaped it and the scripts operating within it. (152)

Douglas and Hargadon rightly recognize a continuum of experience moving from conscious attention to unconscious involvement that is important in understanding the process of engagement with games. The problem with the model they propose is their sidelining of the considerably different qualities of literary works and games and therefore the experiences they afford:

> Ironically the reader paging through Balzac, Dickens or for that matter, Judith Krantz, has entered into the same immersive state, enjoying the same high continuous cognitive load as the runty kid firing fixedly away at *Space Invaders*. (157)

Book readers might place themselves within the space world described by a literary work by exercising their imagination, but the world does not recognize their existence. The whole experience is enacted and sustained by the reader, even if the literary text guides its creation through the description. Game environments afford habitation of a virtual world that extends beyond the imagination by recognizing and reacting to the location of the player within the world, thus giving a sense of the player being anchored in a specific location in the world. Although not in itself a sufficient condition for a sense of presence to be experienced, it is a crucial part of this experience. Books do not provide readers with the possibility of actually acting within the worlds they describe outside the confines of the reader's head. Thus, Douglas and Hargadon's conceptualization of immersion remains limited to different forms of involvement without capturing the distinctive qualities of the phenomenon that immersion as transportation points to.

MIXING METAPHORS

As the previous example shows, the conceptual difficulties that permeate immersion and presence are also rife outside of presence theory. Within media studies and game studies the term is often used to refer to experiential states as diverse as engagement, perception of realism, addiction, suspension of disbelief, identification with game characters, and others. In game studies the term is frequently used but suffers from a looseness of meaning and vagueness of application, which has made theorists weary of the term. Katie Salen and Eric Zimmerman, in their *Rules of Play* (2003), have even argued that the experiential phenomenon the term has been recruited to describe does not even exist. Salen and Zimmerman's opposition to the term stems from an understandable weariness toward applications of the term that exaggerate both the impact and pervasiveness of the experience of virtual-world habitation. An example of such overromanticization of the phenomenon that Salen and Zimmerman discuss in *Rules of Play* is Francois Laramee's take: "All forms of entertainment strive to create suspension of disbelief, a state in which the player's mind forgets that it is being subjected to entertainment and instead accepts what it perceives as reality" (Laramee, quoted in Salen and Zimmerman 2003, 450). Salen and Zimmerman strongly oppose this fetishization of immersion, particularly within game design circles, and label this tendency with the term "immersive fallacy." For Salen and Zimmerman there are more important aspects to game engagement and enjoyment than immersion. They instead emphasize the importance of innovative game design. Within a design context this makes a lot of sense, not only at the time when Salen and Zimmerman wrote *Rules of Play*, but also, and probably more so, today. With soaring production budgets for mainstream, commercial games, the risk involved in innovative design is not backed up by publishers and financing parties, leading to increasingly derivative games that prioritize attractive graphics and realistic physics over novel design. The problem with Salen and Zimmerman's argument here is that they do not acknowledge that the concerns of design and those of theoretical analysis are distinct. Design theories aim to be primarily generative, while a solid analytical toolkit requires precision of concepts and solidity of argument. Salen and Zimmerman thus make a valid design claim, but a problematic analytical one. Informing design should not be confused with analyzing a particular phenomenon with the precision required of academic analysis. We can agree that good game design does not necessarily imply fostering a sense of inhabiting a game world, but that does not mean that such an experience is not important for players (or designers inclined to build such worlds) or more problematically, that such a phenomenon does not even exist. Salen and Zimmerman confuse the issue further when they cite Elena Gorfinkel's views on immersion:

> The confusion in this conversation has emerged because representational strategies are conflated with the effect of immersion. Immersion itself is not tied to a replication or mimesis of reality. For example, one can get immersed in Tetris. Therefore, immersion into gameplay seems at least as important as immersion in a game's representational space. (Gorfinkel, quoted in Salen and Zimmerman 2003, 452)

Although Gorfinkel is correct to claim that the sense of inhabiting a virtual environment does not require a replication of physical, everyday reality (as can be attested from the widespread experience of the phenomenon in fictional worlds of various kinds), she is here confusing two related, but lexically divergent terms. When Gorfinkel states that one can become immersed in *Tetris'* (Pajitnov 1985) gameplay, she is referring to the more general, previrtual environment sense of the word as defined by the *Oxford English Dictionary*: "Absorption in some condition, action, interest, etc." (Soanes and Stevenson

2003). In this sense, one can be just as immersed in solving a crossword puzzle as in clambering the 7,000 steps leading to the temple in High Hrothgar in *The Elder Scrolls V: Skyrim* (Bethesda Game Studios 2011). For ease of reference, we will label this form of immersion *immersion as absorption.*

This use of the *absorption* sense of immersion ignores a history of application in the context of virtual environments within both the humanities (Murray 1998; Ryan 2001; Laurel 1991) and presence theory (Steuer 1992; Tamborini and Skalski 2006; IJsselsteijn 2004; IJsselsteijn and Riva 2003; Waterworth and Waterworth 2003; Slater 2003). In order to avoid confusion we will label the second use of *immersion*, that is, the application of the terms that refers to the sense of inhabiting a virtual environment, with the term *immersion as transportation.* Thus, a game like *Skyrim* presents the player not just with an engaging activity, but also with a world to be navigated. A player who assimilates this game world into the gaming experience as a metaphorically habitable environment can be thought of as being *transported* to that world. This experience is made possible by locating the player in a specific location in the game world via the avatar, which the game world and its inhabitants, including other players, react to.

But this experience is not sustained by all digital games. Games like *Tetris* (Pajitnov 1985), *Bejeweled* (PopCap Games 2001), and *Eliss* (Thirion 2009) do not afford a sense of spatial habitation that is a requirement of immersion as transportation. There are at least two reasons for this. First, none of these games recognize the presence of the player within a single location in their environments. In each case the player controls objects (blocks, gems, planets) without being embodied in any single in-game entity. Second, the game environment is represented in its totality on one screen. These environments do not allow for continuous spatial navigation in an extended geographical space. Another example where immersion and transportation does not hold is strategy games in which the player controls multiple miniatures or a collective unit such as a nation without being digitally embodied in the world through an avatar. By engaging with the game world as a *map* rather than as a spatial environment, the player remains in conceptual rather than inhabited space.

By focusing on the importance of immersion as absorption in a game like *Tetris* (Pajitnov 1985), Gorfinkel, Salen, and Zimmerman ignore the importance of spatiality as a defining feature of the phenomenon to which immersion has been used to refer in the context of virtual environments. Marie-Laure Ryan (2001) has argued for the importance for the representation of the spatial qualities of a text as a crucial feature of immersion:

> For a text to be immersive then it must create a space to which the reader, spectator, or player can relate and it must populate this space with individuated objects.... For immersion to take place, the text must offer an expanse to be immersed within, and this expanse, in a blatantly mixed metaphor, is not an ocean but a textual world. (Ryan 2001, 90)

If we want to make progress in understanding this (or any) experiential phenomenon, we need to be conscious of the implications a particular term, or set of terms, has gathered in the field. This does not apply to the issue of immersion only but to any other term or metaphor that has accrued a more specialized meaning or nuance in a relevant field. Critical stances on a particular inflection of a term are often a productive means for sharpening the concept. Analysts should not ignore such accrued specificities of meaning and revert to a nominal or dictionary definition of a term. The issue becomes even more problematic when, as is the case in discussions about immersion, theorists do not explain whether they are using the dictionary definition or the more specific one.

Although we have here focused on Gorfinkel, Salen, and Zimmerman, the obstacles to understanding immersion are pervasive in the literature and discussions accumulating within game studies. Because of limitations of space and the scope of this chapter, we won't be able to give an extensive list of cases that evidence problematic formulations of immersion, but we can explore one further case for the sake of variety. Jon Dovey and Helen Kennedy (2006) use the terms "immersion" and "engagement" interchangeably to refer to the absorbing qualities of digital games:

> This quality of immersion or engagement within the game world may account for the ways in which a sense of time or physical discomfort may recede as the player's skill develops. This is a critical aspect of the unique time economy that characterizes computer gameplay. It is entirely commonplace that gameplay experience seems to lie outside of day-to-day clock time—we sit down to play and discover that hours have passed in what seemed like minutes. (8)

The engaging qualities mentioned by Dovey and Kennedy are neither specific to nor guaranteed by game environments. This sense of immersion as absorption makes the term as readily applicable to gardening or cooking as it does to game environments. While there is nothing wrong with this use of the term in itself, it undermines the more specific sense of transportation that is crucial when discussing game environments.

The Four Challenges

This chapter has so far given an overview of central discussions and points of contention in the conceptualization and analysis of the phenomenon of virtual-world habitation, that is, of presence/immersion in virtual worlds. The confusion that exists both in the field of presence research and in game research (as well as related fields) regarding this phenomenon can be summarized in four principal challenges to our understanding and conceptualization of the phenomenon:

1. *Immersion as absorption* versus *immersion as transportation*. There is a lack of consensus on the use of immersion to refer to either general involvement (Salen and Zimmerman 2003; Jennett et al. 2008; Ermi and Mäyrä 2005) in a medium or the sense of being transported to another reality (Murray 1998; Laurel 1991; Carr 2006). This is particularly problematic when researchers do not clarify

which one of these terms they are using or when they oscillate between the two within the same study (Brown and Cairns 2004; Cairns 2006).

2. *Immersion in non-ergodic media.* For a precise formulation of both immersion as absorption and immersion as transportation we need to acknowledge the specificities of the medium in question. In this case, immersion in ergodic and non-ergodic media is simply not the same thing. The challenge of addressing a complex and preconscious phenomenon such as immersion as transportation is increased considerably if we try to extend the concept to multiple media with considerably varied qualities and affordances for engagement.

3. *Technological determinism.* Although specificities of the medium are crucial for our understanding of the experiences they afford, we should avoid seeing such experiences as being determined by the qualities of the technology. A bigger screen and a higher fidelity of representation, for example, might make it easier to focus and to retain one's attention on the representation, but this does not necessarily mean that users will feel more present in the environment portrayed.

4. *Monolithic perspectives on immersion.* The principal reason for challenge 3 is that both immersion as absorption and immersion as transportation are made up of a number of experiential phenomena rather than being a single experience we can discover and measure. The various forms of experience that make up involvement need to be considered on a continuum of attentional intensity rather than as a binary, on/off switch.

INCORPORATION

Along with the challenges outlined above, the terms presence and immersion are further problematized by the fact that they imply some form of *unidirectional plunge* into a virtual world. As we will argue below, this is not the best theoretical foundation for understanding these phenomena. In particular, the assumption of *excluding* the external world so completely as the participant is submerged *into* the virtual environment is problematic. The user is not merely a subjective consciousness being poured into the containing vessel of the virtual environment. Our awareness of the virtual world, much like our awareness of our everyday surroundings, is better understood as an absorption into mind of external stimuli that are organized according to existing experiential gestalts (Lakoff and Johnson 2003; Damasio 2000). If we feel like we exist in the game world, it is because the metaphor of habitation it provides is of a sufficient fit with the experiential gestalts that inform being in everyday life.

As Lakoff and Johnson (2003) argue, meaning results from the interaction that takes place between language and lived experience, each of which modifies the other in a dialectic process. Metaphor is not simply a transformation of a literal reality; it is created by and, in turn, creates our sense of reality (Richards 1936; Lakoff and Johnson 2003). This process of mutual validation is particularly relevant in the case of more abstract

experiences, where figurative expressions facilitate the structuring necessary for the relevant experiences to be internalized.

In light of this it would make sense to adopt a metaphor to account for the sense of
virtual-world habitation that is compatible with our (as yet incomplete) knowledge
of our experience of everyday surroundings. Throughout this chapter I have avoided
contrasting virtual worlds with the real world as too often happens in such discussions,
because this distinction often leads to misleading assumptions about the nature of the
real and its relationship to the virtual (Lévy 1998). Virtual environments are an important part of our everyday life and are more productively seen as deeply interwoven with
our sense of reality. A metaphor that accounts for the sense of virtual-world habitation,
therefore, should draw upon the experiential gestalts of everyday habitation, that is, a
view of consciousness as an internally generated construct based on the organization
of external stimuli according to existing experiential gestalts (Dennett 1991; Damasio
2000; Lakoff and Johnson 2003).

The metaphors of immersion and presence are defined by their discontinuity from
the real, physical world and thus do not comfortably enable such a perspective on the
phenomenon. I thus believe that we are better served replacing these metaphors with
one that more accurately captures the nature of the experience in question. I therefore
propose the metaphor of *incorporation* to account for the sense of virtual environment
habitation on two, simultaneous, levels: first, the virtual environment is incorporated
into the player's mind as part of his or her immediate surroundings, within which the
person can navigate and interact. Second, the player is incorporated (in the sense of
embodiment) in a single, systemically upheld location in the virtual environment at any
single point in time.

Incorporation thus requires two conditions to be met for an experience to be considered such: the player incorporates, in the sense of internalizing or assimilating, the game
environment into consciousness while *simultaneously* being incorporated through the
avatar into that environment. The simultaneous occurrence of these two processes is
a necessary condition for the experience of incorporation. Put in another way, incorporation occurs when the game world is present to the player while simultaneously the
player is present, via an avatar, to the virtual environment.

Incorporation can thus be defined as *the absorption of a virtual environment into consciousness, yielding a sense of habitation, which is supported by the systemically upheld
embodiment of the player in a single location represented by the avatar.* This conception
retains the two nominal interpretations of the term incorporation: incorporation as a
sense of assimilation to mind, and that of embodiment. While I am aware that the latter
is the sense that has received more attention in the humanities and social sciences, the
work to which the term is being put here treats both senses as being essential.

Incorporation does not require sensory stimuli to arise solely from the game environment. It also accounts for input arising from outside the game environment, which
the player can integrate into the game experience. For example, if you are playing *Left 4
Dead 2* (Valve Corporation 2009) with friends in the same room and one of them cries
out for help, this does not necessarily slip you out of a state of incorporation, since that

call can be readily integrated into what is going on in the game environment. In fact, it will most likely intensify the sense of incorporation because it fosters the absorption of the game environment into the player's consciousness more decisively by blending stimuli from the game world and the immediate surroundings. Since incorporation is being conceived as an absorption into the immediate surroundings, rather than a dive into *another* space, it readily accounts for such instances of blending of stimuli from different environments. With incorporation, we do not need to view the game environment as a special, other-space that requires protection from *real* world intrusion, as long as that intrusion can be integrated into the game experience.

The definition and description of incorporation just presented precludes its application to any non-ergodic media, such as movies or books. Incorporation, as we have seen, requires that a medium specifically acknowledge the player's presence and agency within the virtual world. It is only in ergodic media that we find this kind of agency, and only in virtual environments of the sort we have discussed, that such a location and presence in the virtual world is possible. As we have discussed, a book or movie is unable to acknowledge readers' or viewers' presence, nor offer them agency, and so necessarily cannot afford incorporation.

We must not forget, however, that the systemic acknowledgment of an avatar's presence in the environment is not a sufficient criterion for incorporation to be experienced; the player's subjective disposition must also be taken into account. It is not merely a technical challenge to create incorporation; the player's role in shaping the experience is essential.

CONCLUSION

The metaphor of incorporation is part of a larger body of work (Calleja 2007a, 2007b; 2011) that explores engagement with digital games and virtual worlds starting from offline involvement to the moment-by-moment engagement with the world during interaction. The offline involvement covers issues such as general motivations for starting to engage with the world in question, desires to return to it, and all forms of thinking, planning, and communication that a player undertakes while not actually connected to the world. The moment-by-moment engagement describes experiential facets describing involvement while the user is connected to the world in question. This process is described through the player involvement model that has been covered in a number of other works. An aspect of the player involvement model, and in a sense, its culmination, is the experience of incorporation. The research that went into the model was fueled by the gaps that were described in the four challenges. After a review of the presence and immersion literature in various fields along with popular and industry uses of the terms, it became clear that a more grounded investigation of involvement was needed in order to build a more solid foundation for describing the phenomenon of virtual-world habitation. This is not to say that all instances of digital game and virtual-world involvement lead to incorporation, or that incorporation is a more or less desirable state of affairs. The term is reserved for certain experiences in virtual worlds so as to make it more theoretically solid and avoid the confusion that arises when such metaphors, particularly ones accounting for complex, hybrid phenomena get overstretched in their application, thus losing their analytical utility.

The metaphor of incorporation thus offers a more precise conceptualization of virtual-world habitation that is media specific and multifaceted, while at the same time providing a fresh perspective on the issue that is not weighed down in the confusion arising from the exclusionary logic that underpins the immersion and presence metaphors. It is also built on a robust conception of experiential phenomena that precede it in experience: attention and involvement (as expressed in the player involvement model). Finally, the concept does not need to draw a strict line of demarcation between stimuli emerging from the virtual world and the physical world by placing the focus on the internally constructed consciousness of the individual. Although it is never easy for a new concept to take root and grow, especially when landing in a field already overgrown with conflicting concepts, it is important for us to work with concepts that provide the best possible foundation for the phenomenon they attempt to describe, measure, and, eventually, design for.

References

Aarseth, E. 1997. *Cybertext: Perspectives on Ergodic Literature.* Baltimore, MD: Johns Hopkins University Press.

Bazin, A. 1967. *What Is Cinema? Essays.* Translated by Hugh Gray. Berkeley: University of California Press.

Bethesda Game Studios. 2011. *The Elder Scrolls V: Skyrim.* PC: Bethesda Softworks.

Brown, E., and P. Cairns. 2004. A Grounded Investigation of Immersion in Games. Paper presented to CHI 2004, Vienna.

Cairns, P., A. Cox, N. Berthouze, S. Dhoparee, and C. Jennett. 2006. Quantifying the experience of immersion in games. Paper read at *Cognitive Science of Games and Gameplay workshop,* Vancouver.

Calleja, G. 2007a. Digital Game Involvement. *Games and Culture* 2: 236–260.

Calleja, G. 2007b. *Digital Games as Designed Experience: Reframing the Concept of Immersion.* Unpublished Doctoral Thesis, Victoria University of Wellington, Wellington.

Calleja, G. 2011. *In-Game: From Immersion to Incorporation.* Cambridge, MA; London: MIT Press.

Carr, D. 2006. Play and Pleasure. In Computer Games. In *Text, Narrative and Play,* edited by D. Carr, A. Burn, D. Buckingham, and G. Schott, 45–58. Cambridge: Polity Press.

Damasio, A. 2000. *The Feeling of What Happens: Body, Emotion and the Making of Consciousness.* New ed. London: Vintage.

Dennett, D. C. 1991. *Consciousness Explained.* Boston: Little Brown.

Douglas, J. Y., and A. Hargadon. 2001. The Pleasures of Immersion and Engagement: Schemas, Scripts and the Fifth Business. *Digital Creativity* 12 (3): 153–166.

Dovey, J., and H. W. Kennedy. 2006. *Game Cultures: Computer Games as New Media.* Berkshire: Open University Press.

Ermi, L., and F. Mäyrä. 2005. Fundamental Components of the Gameplay Experience: Analysing Immersion. Paper presented to DIGRA 2005, "Changing Views: Worlds in Play," Vancouver.

Grau, O. 2003. *Virtual Art: From Illusion to Immersion*. Cambridge, MA: MIT Press.

Gysbers, A., C. Klimmt, T. Hartmann, A. Nosper, and P. Vorderer. 2004. Exploring the Book Problem: Text, Design, Mental Representations of Space and Spatial Presence. Paper presented to the Seventh Annual International Workshop on Presence, Valencia.

Held, R. and N. Durlach. 1992. "Telepresence." *Presence* 1 (1): 109–112.

Heidegger, M. 1993. *The Question Concerning Technology and Other Essays*. Translated by William Lovitt. New York: Harper and Row.

IJsselsteijn, W. 2004. Presence in Depth. PhD diss., Eindhoven University of Technology.

IJsselsteijn, W., and G. Riva. 2003. Being There: The Experience of Presence in Mediated Environments. In *Being There: Concepts, Effects and Measurements of User Presence in Synthetic Environments*, edited by Wijnand IJsselsteijn and Giuseppe Riva, 3–16. Amsterdam: Ios Press.

Jennett, C., A. Cox, P. Cairns, S. Dhoparee, A. Epps, T. Tijs, and A. Walton. 2008. Measuring and Defining the Experience of Immersion in Games. *International Journal of Human Computer Studies* 66 (9): 641–661.

King, G., and T. Krzywinska. 2006. *Tomb Raiders and Space Invaders: Videogame Forms and Contexts*. London: I. B. Tauris.

Lakoff, G., and M. Johnson. 2003. *Metaphors We Live By*. Chicago: University of Chicago Press.

Laurel, B. 1991. *Computers as Theatre*. Reading: Addison-Wesley.

Lee, K. M. 2004. Presence Explicated. *Communication Theory* 14 (1): 27–50.

Lévy, P. 1998. *Becoming Virtual: Reality in the Digital Age*. New York: Plenum.

Mantovani, G., and G. Riva. 1999. "Real" Presence: How Different Ontologies Generate Different Criteria for Presence, Telepresence, and Virtual Presence. *Presence: Teleoperators and Virtual Environments* 8 (5): 538–548.

Marsh, T. 2003. Presence as Experience: Film Informing Ways of Staying There. *Presence* 12 (5): 538–540.

Minsky, M. June 1980. Telepresence. *Omni Magazine*, 45–51.

Murray, J. H. 1998. *Hamlet on the Holodeck: The Future of Narrative in Cyberspace*. Cambridge, MA: MIT Press.

Nell, V. 1988. *Lost in A Book: The Psychology of Reading for Pleasure*. New Haven: Yale University Press.

Pajitnov, A. 1985. *Tetris*. PC: Spectrum Holobyte.

PopCap Games. 2001. *Bejeweled*. PC: PopCap Games.

Rettie, R. 2004. Using Goffman's Frameworks to Explain Presence and Reality. Paper presented to the Seventh Annual International Workshop on Presence, Valencia, Spain.

Richards, I. A. 1936. *The Philosophy of Rhetoric*. New York: Oxford University Press.

Ryan, M.-L. 2001. *Narrative as Virtual Reality: Immersion and Interactivity in Literature and Electronic Media*. Baltimore: Johns Hopkins University Press.

Salen, K., and E. Zimmerman. 2003. *Rules of Play: Game Design Fundamentals*. Cambridge, MA: MIT Press.

Schubert, T., and J. Crusius. 2002. Five Theses on the Book Problem. http://www.igroup.org/projects/porto2002/SchubertCrusiusPorto2002.pdf. Accessed July 15, 2006.

Sheridan, T. B. 1992. Musings on Telepresence and Virtual Presence. *Presence: Teleoperators and Virtual Environments* 1 (1): 120 –126.

Slater, M. 2003. A Note on Presence Terminology. http://presence.cs.ucl.ac.uk/presenceconnect. Accessed October 15, 2008.

Slater, M., and S. Wilbur. 1997. A Framework for Immersive Virtual Environments (Five): Speculations on the Role of Presence in Virtual Environments. *Presence: Teleoperators and Virtual Environments* 6 (6): 603–616.

Steuer, J. 1992. Defining Virtual Reality - Dimensions Determining Telepresence. *Journal of Communication* 42 (4): 73–93.

Sutherland, I. 1965. The Ultimate Display. Paper presented to the International Federation for Information Processing Congress, New York.

Sutherland, I. 1968. Head Mounted 3-Dimensional Display. Paper presented to Fall Joint Computer Conference, San Francisco, CA.

Tamborini, R., and P. Skalski. 2006. The Role of Presence in the Experience of Electronic Games. In *Playing Video Games: Motives, Responses, and Consequences*, edited by P. Vorderer and J. Bryant, 225–240. Mahwah, NJ: Lawrence Erlbaum Associates.

Thirion, S. 2009. *Eliss*. iPhone: Apple.

Valve Corporation. 2009. *Left 4 Dead 2*. PC: Valve Corporation,.

Van Den Hoogen, W., W. IJsselsteijn, and Y. Kort. 2009. Effects of Sensory Immersion on Behavioural Indicators of Player Experience: Movement Synchrony and Controller Pressure. Paper read at DIGRA 2009, "Breaking New Ground: Innovations in Games, Play, Practice and Theory," Brunel, UK.

Waterworth, J. A., and E. Waterworth, L. 2003. The Core of Presence: Presence as Perceptual Illusion. *Presence Connect*, http://presence.cs.ucl.ac.uk/presenceconnect/index.html. Accessed November 12, 2008.

Witmer, B. G., and M. J. Singer. 1998. Measuring Presence in Virtual Environments: A Presence Questionnaire. *Presence: Teleoperators and Virtual Environments* 7 (3): 225–240.

Zahoric, P., and R. L. Jenison. 1998. Presence as Being-in-the-World. *Presence: Teleoperators and Virtual Environments* 7 (1): 78–89.

PART III

···

CULTURE AND SOCIETY

···

CHAPTER 14

....

COMMUNICATION IN VIRTUAL WORLDS

....

PAUL C. ADAMS

COMMUNICATION IN VIRTUAL WORLDS

....

WHAT is the virtual? I would offer three complementary definitions. First, the term indicates an immaterial context of interaction, a kind of intangible architecture that supports and organizes interactions. In some cases a human user interacts with the context itself, while in other cases the interaction occurs between people who share the immaterial context. Second, the virtual evokes an organized field of relations that people navigate using one or two senses while suspending or separating the other senses, bracketing them in a different stream of awareness. This implies a splitting of consciousness or a sensory fragmentation such that one's focus is on mediated rather than unmediated sensations and their corresponding sensory modes. Third, the virtual can be understood as a system that permits spatially dispersed participants to interact in a way that would otherwise require proximity and face-to-face interaction. This third type of virtuality is closely tied to what the sociologist Anthony Giddens calls "distanciation" (1984) and the communication scholar Jack Goody calls "distancing" (1987, 144). Individually or in combination, these three definitions—intangible architecture, sensory fragmentation, and distanciation—encompass a large portion of what people mean by "virtual" when they are speaking of new media.[1] Here the three concepts provide a set of points to triangulate an encounter with the virtuality of "old" media.

For most authors virtuality is a recent creation or condition. For a few, however, virtuality has a genealogy some decades long. Callisen and Adkins argue: "Having a conversation with someone using a webcam or via e-mail is fundamentally no different from having a conversation using a telephone or via hand-written letter. The same information can be shared, the same assumptions made, and techniques of virtuality can be employed to compensate for a lack of audile, visual, or tactile connection" (2011, 69). What is indicated here is not that communication is the same in all of these cases, but rather that the concept of virtuality is instructive and useful for understanding any of these cases. Their argument echoes the arguments of Standage (1998) and Shields (2003), who have shown that old media merit a reappraisal in light of new conceptual frameworks. The proponents of this continuity thesis include Jay David Bolter, for whom a "writing space" is generated through the interaction of material properties of a medium with various cultural practices, and "each space depends for its meaning on previous spaces or on contemporary spaces against which it competes. Each fosters a particular understanding both of the act of writing and of the product, the written text... [while] communities of readers help to define the properties of the writing space by the demands they place on the text and the technology" (Bolter 2001, 12). These interpretations of media history suggest that instead of a historical rupture between the actual and the virtual, we should be attentive to a continuous process of virtualization and revirtualization.

In making such a claim, however, it is necessary to go a bit further and note that what we call "old" media, like the spoken word and the techniques of writing and printing, have not in fact been displaced. Old media remain essential to communication with new media. Rather than being passé, they are part of the panoply of contemporary media and are recreated anew every day. The virtuality of the Internet, even its novel sense of "presence" or "distributed embodiment" (see also Heim, chapter 6; Riva and Waterworth, chapter 12; Calleja, chapter 13; and Waterworth and Waterworth, chapter 35, all in this volume) depends on the use of words and on techniques developed for handwriting and printing (Bolter 2001). This observation is not meant to minimize the importance of digital communication as a new source of virtualization, still less to minimize the importance of telecommunication. When the telegraph permitted the separation of communication from transportation, this was a crucial break that made it possible to study "communication" per se (Briggs and Burke 2005, 21; Carey 1988, 204). But if the advent of computer-mediated communication has brought highly justified attention to virtuality, this is a revirtualization that depends in part on this earlier infusion of distanciation and sensory fragmentation via the intangible architecture of telegraph lines and switches (Marvin 1988). In premodern and even in prehistoric times intangible architecture and sensory fragmentation played important roles in communication, while distanciation was present in forms that merit investigation.

To demonstrate these points this chapter will consider virtual spaces of the word, of writing, and of printing. It could be argued that the prehistoric and classical virtual spaces were not as immersive or immediate as current forms of virtuality (see also Calleja, chapter 13 in this volume). But immersivity and immediacy are subjectively experienced, and it is possible that our impression of old media as less supportive of virtualization than new media is a comparison we make by reflecting on our own lives, in particular the contrasting experiences we have with what we have labeled "old" and "new" media. Earlier communicators, lacking encounters with high-tech forms of virtualization, attest to powerful forms of virtualization in and through their contemporaneous media.

VIRTUAL SPACES OF THE WORD

A form of virtuality is as old as the spoken word. The modes of virtuality supported by speech converge in a distinct way, as the spoken word draws together all three forms of virtualization. Most simply, the placing of people and actions in space and time is achieved by grammatical rules regarding temporal and spatial relationships. English speakers must choose, for example, whether to use "saw," "was seeing," "have seen," or "have been seeing" to describe an act of seeing that occurred at least partly in the past. Somewhat different temporal distinctions are made by the *imparfait* and *passé compose* in French. Each language's grammar constitutes a virtual temporality in which events, phenomena, and processes are inserted according to a certain logic that governs the sequencing of words. Though quite varied in their rules, languages share the use of rule-governed sequences as a way to position represented actions and events in time.

There are various forms of tacit spatiality in language, as well. The word "out" is not as simple as it seems: "The cat ran out of the house," "I ran out of money," "We ate take-out" (food), "He took her out" (on a date), and "They viewed the outtakes" (from a film) demonstrate how a single word can activate varying spatial and temporal associations according to rules that go beyond formal grammar, constituting an invisible architecture of conceptual relations. The virtual space-time of verbal communication is described in part by Saussure's (1983) dichotomous notions of syntagmatic and associative relationships, but also by the multiplicity of embodied relations captured, for example, in Massumi's (2002) concept of intensity or Lefebvre's (1991) "representations of space" and "representational spaces." Speech follows corridors, passageways, and trapdoors through which we move as we construct utterances. Speech competence comes of having internalized a way of *inhabiting* one's language. Just as the city is a product of prior and ongoing speech (Tuan 1994), speech navigates a kind of virtual city with its distinct districts, vantage points, thoroughfares, and shortcuts. The "real world" known by each community is therefore a kind of projection of its virtual world of verbal symbols onto a terrain of shared experience (for further discussion, see Rudd, chapter 15 in this volume). Language is the original form of intangible architecture surviving into the present day and mixing with all of the others that have been developed subsequently.

Oral communication also involves a subtle form of distanciation. It conveys knowledge from accumulated experiences, collected and internalized in particular moments and locations, then externalized at other times and places. This is the subtle distanciation of the word: symbolic extraction of experience from the immediacy of physical experience. Through this same process, words fragment the senses. Speech is the first of many techniques separating and recombining the senses: as we listen to a storyteller speak of "a glittering jewel," "the fragrant night," and "stinging thorns," the ear becomes an eye, a nose, and a hand. We gaze into the coals of the campfire, hearing a story while the mind's eye, ear, nose, tongue, and skin translate the story into virtual sensations of distant times and places. Distanciation via words depends on sensory fragmentation and reassembly. The coexistence of virtual architecture, distanciation, and sensory fragmentation via the word is multiplicative; together these aspects of virtuality loosen the grip of the here and now and permit word-borne excursions of sensation and thought. This is what it means to be "lost in a story." While perhaps it now requires 3D glasses and quadraphonic sound to immerse developed-world audiences, accustomed as they are to sensory barrage, the verbal elsewhere was once a potent form of virtuality. Before there was history, let alone the Internet, myths and legends took us into virtual worlds (see also Bittarello, chapter 5 in this volume).

Considering language a bit more closely, certain statements are necessarily parasitic on the space-time of the sender and receiver. If I say "Come here," you understand "here" by reference to extralinguistic information—the locational evidence of your eyes. *Deictic* statements such as "Come here," "Wait there," and "Look at that" are rooted in direct experience, in a physical, material context, employing what linguists call a *relative* frame of reference. Deictic verbalization depends on the body and its gestures in order to make sense—a body defining "here" or a pointing finger indicating "that." This is clearly *non*virtual verbalization. In contrast, many verbal communications employ an *absolute* frame of reference (Levinson 2003). For example, the statement "There is a tree east of the house" calls into being the compass points, or even a virtual lattice of latitude and longitude lines wrapped around the globe. In linguistic terms, such references are called *intrinsic* descriptions. What needs to be recognized here is that intrinsic descriptions depend on, and help perpetuate, yet another kind of virtual space. These statements fragment the senses since they draw on imagined, ideal, or hypothetical spatialities as a way of ordering the observable and tangible world. Here the intangible architecture of spatiotemporal relations embedded in language makes itself navigationally useful.

In some cases the spatiotemporal frameworks of language may be strikingly similar across cultures. In English, for example, what is good is "high," just as in the Romance and Germanic languages, north Indian languages, and even Chinese. The Hindi/Urdu term *bada* means both large and important, paralleling the figurative uses of "large" in English. Likewise, there is no problem translating "Central Committee" from Chinese to English when referring to the Chinese Communist Party, because "central" has similar connotations of power and importance in both languages.[2]

In other cases, the linguistic architecture of space and time may be strikingly different across languages. Understanding a landscape requires attention to the local language (Pred 1990). The untrained eye of a visitor, lacking the local terminology, fails to see properly. Walking through the countryside of the Faroe Islands, a visitor sees various lumps of soil without realizing that one is a pile of peat, another is material cast aside when gathering peat, and yet another is a platform used to elevate peat for drying (Edwards et al. 2010). They all look the same until one learns the local landscape vocabulary and the accompanying perceptual scheme. A similar process maps the social landscape. The German term *Heimat* has no perfect equivalent in English, nor do the French *patrie* or the Russian *Rodina* and *Otechestvo*; although related to "nation," "homeland,"

"fatherland," and "motherland," these foreign terms carry a range of unfamiliar connotations that say much about what it means to be German, French, or Russian (Müller
2007; Herb 2004).

The same is true of time: "language systematically reuses established (spatial) concepts in metaphorical ways to express more abstract (temporal) relationships" (Tenbrink
2011, 704). It is common in English, for example, to say "I'm behind on my work" or "I
got to the airport ahead of time," using the spatial concepts "behind" and "ahead" to
describe temporal relations. This does not merely conflate time and space in addition
it involves a third, more primitive set of relations centered on the body (Karmakar and
Kasturirangan 2011). In English, something that happens later is understood as "after" or
"behind" (July comes after June), while some languages place the later event "ahead" or
"in front." It is difficult for an English speaker to understand how this would work since
we are trained by our language to see or virtually inhabit time in a particular way. We
view time like a train track, whereas some other languages use the train itself as the reference frame. Just as the engine is *in front* and the rest of the cars are *behind*, July would
be "in front of" or "before" June (Shinohara and Pardeshi 2011). These linguistic differences point to the constructedness of spatial and temporal schemata.

As one learns a language, one is programmed to understand space and time in a certain way because verbal operations naturalize a particular structure of space-time. It is
not surprising that the trickiest part of learning a foreign language is mastering the use
of prepositions and verb tenses. Spatiotemporal translations are achieved in different
ways in different languages but in all cases "reference is the lesser part of meaning, pat-
ternment the greater" (Whorf 1956, 261). What this means is that phenomena and the
spatiotemporal structures organizing them simultaneously come into being as one uses
a language. In short, a language is a system of virtual spaces, associated with objects,
phenomena, terrains, territories, times, places, and values. In all of these ways, language constitutes virtual worlds, but deictic speech and relative spatiotemporal references anchor the word in the physical world, in nonverbal, embodied being-in-place.
Conversely, absolute and intrinsic forms of expression, in particular, draw on and support virtuality.

VIRTUAL SPACES OF WRITING

During "primary orality," the era before writing, signification was solidly grounded
in nonverbal information conveyed by all of the sensory modes along with the virtual
space-times of certain aspects of speech. Writing broke with this reality by *fixing* the
word, and deictic expressions lost purchase. "The spoken message depends on the mes-
senger, the written does not" (Coulmas 1989, 7). The place of the sender is split apart from
the place of the receiver. The sender can "speak" as if from nowhere, and the time and
tempo of writing does not match the time and tempo of reading. Writing therefore lib-
erates language "from the spatio-temporal constraints of its ephemeral materialization

in speech" (Coulmas 1989, 7). Stated differently, prior to the invention of writing, every verbal construct was a performance, a fleeting event, and virtual space-times of the spoken word had to be re-enacted, so the material space-time of the storyteller and audience were part of the total communication. As Coulmas argues, written communication is "detached from the 'here', 'now' and 'I' of its production" (1989, 13). The word became durable and portable, a fixed spatial pattern of symbols that could in turn speak across time and space.

This leads to an ironic shift: fixing the word mobilized it. On papyrus, bark, wood tablets, wax-coated boards, cloth, or even cumbersome clay tablets, words could be transported from place to place. Prior to writing, the scale of social integration could only reach as far as the unaided voice, but written communications were portable, extending the reach of economic and political integration and facilitating the textual construction of an "imagined community." Benedict Anderson (1983) coined this term in connection with the nation under print-capitalism, but prior to the printing press the written word allowed a sense of community the scale of a city or even an empire.

In contrast to earlier symbols like the designs on pots and textiles, or systems of counters and mnemonic devices, like quipu, writing corresponded directly to speech, but a sensory shift was required to substitute an eye for an ear (McLuhan 1995, 240). Some early writing systems consisted of basic elements representing words (logograms), while other systems represented speech sounds (phonograms), and some were hybrids combining word-symbols and sound-symbols (Adams 2009, 18–28). In addition, the sound-based systems included alphabets, syllabaries, consonant alphabets, and mixtures of the above (Gnanadesikan 2009; Coulmas 1989). In any case the position of one symbol relative to its neighbors on the writing surface encoded a difference in meaning, so writing enacted a new virtual architecture based on a two-dimensional space, rather than the three-dimensional space of face-to-face encounter, or the one-dimensional timeline of the utterance as a string of words.

This two-dimensional space where the word was fixed referenced another space in which texts circulated with mobile bodies between increasingly far-flung literati. The separation of speech from the here and now led people not only to envision empires uniting the near and the far but also the crossing of a metaphysical threshold between life and death. Thus early writing, as a cultural practice, seamlessly mixed allusions to secular and sacred power, spatial and temporal extension, conquest of territory and the "journey" to the underworld (Michalowski 1993; Rochberg 2004). In practice, the expansiveness of the fixed word was limited by the affordances of different substrates: stone versus clay, versus papyrus, versus paper, and so on. Heavy media were limited in their portability, while lighter media were more portable but deteriorated over time. The particular characteristics of the various writing surfaces supported societal extension in either space or time (Innis 1951), two contrasting types of virtual space and divergent types of societies. But this distinction must not be exaggerated; all writing achieved some measure of spatial *and* temporal extension.

The oldest extant examples of Chinese writing were on turtle shells and the shoulder blades of various animals. Apparently this writing was used for pyromantic rituals in which priests would tell the future on the basis of cracks that formed when the bone or shell was heated (Allan 1991; Keightley 1978). Elsewhere, word magic took other forms. Hieroglyphs were carved inside of burial chambers, on ceremonial objects and on stelae marking tombs in order to assist nobility on their way to the kingdom of the dead, while runes and other written spells were thought to effect cures (Adams 2010). In fact, those no longer alive *can* speak to those not yet alive through writing, so the liminal, boundary-crossing character of the word is clearly evident. The idea of a link to virtual realms drove the practice of "magically reducing," that is, dismembering, the animals appearing in hieroglyphs; the scorpion and the horned viper appeared headless so that they would not pose a hazard in or between the spaces of the living and the dead (Betrò 1996, 86). Far from simple delusion, such understandings of the word reflected the real power of the word in extending the agency of priests and ruling elites (see also Kreps, chapter 43 in this volume). Belief in metaphysical powers of the word supported physical, political power over actual dominions. Written words were instrumental in constructing what Massey (1993) calls a "power-geometry," that is, a set of connections through space that both define and differentiate places in terms of power and authority. Through early writing, the virtual structured the real and vice versa in a seamless interplay.

The virtual space of the writing surface was not a neutral, meaningless space, but rather a powerful space of incipient relations, whose intangible architecture one entered via reading and writing. Goody (1987, 188) indicates how such spatial arrangements alter the word's relation to time: "Writing provides, *inter alia*, a spatial coordinate of language, giving it an atemporal dimension which makes it possible to subject a speech act, a sentence, a chronological record, a list, to greater, more context-free, manipulations." Reading and writing required prioritization of vision over the other senses, and the resulting sensory fragmentation in turn facilitated distanciation via the ability to command, request, inform, and otherwise interact at a distance (albeit with inconvenient delays or latency that drove the process of revirtualization clear to the Internet). From its inception, however, the virtual space of the writing surface mediated between various spaces of embodied action and all three aspects of virtuality.

We can expand a bit more on what is meant by "virtuality" in this case. Societies with writing generate "a large number of lexical lists, of trees, roles, classes of various kinds, which possess several characteristics that...differ from the categories that usually emerge in oral communication" (Goody 1987, 275). Readers and writers cognitively move through lists, tables, and charts—mentally occupying them. Intriguingly, those who first acquired this cognitive capacity were more able to move around through space in a literal, embodied way as well, since literacy conferred social status and scribes often traveled with their products in order to ensure their correct reading and facilitate response. Scribal mobility constituted the growing tendrils of political and economic networks, supporting the early city and making cities the hubs of expanding empires (Schmandt-Besserat 1996). Social strata and linguistic strata were mutually reinforcing, and as Lefebvre argues, "The city of the ancient world cannot be understood as a collection of people and things in space" for the reason that "it forged its own—*appropriated*—space" involving written symbolic representations supporting both production and reproduction activities (1991, 31–32).

The training undertaken to become a scribe was a key source of social stratification, which led in turn to yet another virtual space—the layered space of literary strata. A split between high and low linguistic registers, called *diglossia*, is a mark of literate societies. People position themselves in this layered space each time they speak, depending on whether they speak in ways more closely linked to oral or written communication. This layering of language and society accentuated over time since linguistic drift was faster for speech than for writing. The written variants of a language were "standardized," inhibiting their evolution relative to local dialects. The high and low registers of language were coordinates in a virtual vertical space where certain communicators enjoyed the special status of *literati* whether they were speaking or writing. The elevated language of the scribe became a vehicle for upward social mobility.

The changes introduced by writing were so profound that it is tempting to credit the written word with the emergence of civilization itself (see, e.g., Coulmas 1989; Logan 1986; Schmandt-Besserat 1996). Government, labor specialization, agricultural innovation, long-distance commerce, and the elaboration of religious rituals appeared at roughly the same time as writing. All of them involved forms of virtualization, and these virtualizations took a new turn as they accentuated, but also partly reversed with, the diffusion of printing.

VIRTUAL SPACES OF PRINTING

Printing has been described as the first human activity that depended on standardized and interchangeable mechanical components as a means of mass-producing identical products—"truly a revolutionary invention in every department" (Mumford 1963, 135). In many ways the potentials inherent in writing were finally realized with the advent of printing. The availability of printed books rapidly surpassed that of manuscripts, and a substantial minority (and eventually a majority) of the population could finally be immersed in virtual spaces of the fixed word. There were some 27,000 editions, and over 10 million printed volumes by 1500 (Briggs and Burke 2005, 13). Superficially, printing added nothing to the types of virtualization already afforded by writing. However, the massive increase in books led to a qualitative transformation in the social and cultural significance of the fixed word. As Marshall McLuhan has observed, a quantitative change in the availability or use of a particular technology can lead to an inversion in its apparent "effects" (McLuhan and McLuhan 1988).

The virtual worlds of the printing press depended on repetitive, precise routines and likewise suggested a world of infinitely reproducible elements, analyzable and reducible to mechanism whether viewed through the lenses of biology, astronomy, agronomy, accounting, or democratic theory. But this did not translate into a regimented social landscape. Whereas writing solidified both religious and political authority, printing was

instrumental in spreading Protestantism and political insurgency. While writing facilitated empire-building, printing exposed imperial subjects to nonlocal and translocal
ideas, prompting free thought and thoughts of freedom. New centralizations of power
were certainly deployed via the printed word, but printing was also appropriated again
and again in ways that questioned and destabilized power. The fixed word catalyzed a certain "mass" of readers, though readers were anything but mass-like in their responses. One
could ruminate over a text, turn it over in one's head, internally debate it, and consider
how one felt about it. There was now the foundation of a space in which to question, critique, and reformulate anything and everything. This suggests a pair of new, interlocked,
and opposing virtual spaces—one of centralized and increasingly anonymous authority
with means of mass-producing its views, confronted by the decentralized reading public.

To take a step back, perhaps the first virtual place one associates with the printed word
is the literary place image—the finely turned phrase in a novel, serial, or short story that
captures a sense of place (Tuan 1991, 690; Pocock 1981). Printing led to mass production of books and the consequent drop in the price of the book, which led in turn to
more writers and more writing, which brought greater art to the description of places. In
the seventeenth and eighteenth centuries the flood of "chapbooks" multiplied the varied
and thrilling virtual worlds of the printed word:

> Successive generations of skillful narrators learned to simulate the colorful, odorous,
> noisy, thick-textured stuff of life; to imitate the voices of different generations and
> convey the passage of time as old bards never had. Many diverse milieux would be
> vicariously inhabited, many different lifetimes vicariously lived by generations of
> novel-readers—with somewhat paradoxical consequences. (Eisenstein 1979, 152)

The paradox was that as real life was "captured" in so many glowing descriptions, it
started to pale by comparison with the descriptions. Encounters with such a rich virtual
world led to descriptions of ordinary everyday life as boring and drab. At the same time,
as Kenneth Olwig argues: "Perhaps it is, in fact, the creation of an alternative reality,
in the form of art, which enables [the author] to become aware of patterns in his *own*
experience that he had not known before" (1981, 63). Print-based literature offered an
abundance of virtual literary worlds even as it exhausted at least some readers' capacities
to appreciate unmediated experience.

Reading as a practice evolved with the medium. Then, as now, miniaturization led
to increased encounters with virtuality. Smaller, lighter books permitted the place of
reading to become a nonplace, an anyplace, since it might move with the reader while
traveling and occupy any nook or cranny in which a reader could sequester him- or herself. This situation intensified sensory fragmentation, as well as promoting distanciated
interaction between readers. Moving through the virtual space of the text, employing
"advances and retreats, tactics and games played with the text" (de Certeau 1984, 175),
the reader enjoyed sensory fragmentation as a form of liberation.

> Because the body withdraws itself from the text in order henceforth to come into
> contact with it only through the mobility of the eye, the geographical configuration

of the text organizes the activity of the reader less and less. Reading frees itself from
the soil that determined it. (de Certeau 1984, 176)

The invisible architecture of the text was challenged by the bricolage of the
reader: "poetic ruses," "erotic, hunting, and initiatory modes of reading" (de Certeau
1984, 176), and the reader's inhabitation of the text became active and contestational.
Over time, such liberatory reading practices greatly assisted in constituting a "public"
(Habermas 1989) in place of feudal subjects.

The virtual spaces occupied by the new reading public included two-dimensional
classificatory spaces. By the seventeenth century words were being coined to fill this
space, and thereby arrange animals, plants, minerals, people, and diverse phenomena
according to taxonomic characteristics such that "the designation of each being indicates clearly the place it occupies in the general arrangement of the whole" (Foucault
1970, 159). Virtual occupation of the printed page via such tabular spaces redefined
knowledge itself. Hierarchies and taxonomies became the taken-for-granted environments of thought among literate communities, in place of narrative order and the
sequential thought-space of primary orality (Ong 1982). A table or chart exemplifies
the imprint of certain thought patterns; its cells do not simply create a box for every
thing, they demand a thing for every box. The tree diagram had been used as early as
the sixteenth century, but the early versions like the Ramist epitome or the Porphyrian
tree were not far removed from the linear organization of narrative (Briggs and Burke
2005, 17). With the emergence of more modern, elaborately branching tree diagrams
in early printed works—equivalent in all respects to what is used today to show hierarchies, genetic relationships, family trees, computer programs, flow charts, and the
dynamics of systems theory—and with the simultaneous appearance of timetables,
astronomical tables, and tables of logarithms, the page showed phenomenal versatility
as a two-dimensional virtual space.

This is not to say that such spaces were unprecedented. Game boards, city plans,
textile patterns, and temple layouts had already worked in their various ways to create spatialized orderings, taxonomies of meaning, and structured fields of interaction.
But the printed diagram popularized and generalized the habit of thinking analytically.
Although similarly structured spaces existed before the printing press, the dissemination of diagrams in thousands of identical copies facilitated critique and revision, and
therefore drew attention to the grid, the tree, and the geometrical pattern as virtual
spaces for creative, exploratory, and collaborative thought—*environments* of a rarefied
new type, Lefebvrian "representations of space" and "representational spaces" divorcing
vision from the other senses (Lefebvre 1991). That this specialization and *spatialization*
of knowledge occurred after the dissemination of the printed page suggests in addition a
new social environment, inhabited virtually by an itinerant band of scholars, scientists,
creative spirits, and political gadflies.

A key aspect of what Habermas (1989) calls the bourgeois public sphere can be traced
to the "Republic of Letters." The term, translated from the Latin *respublica literaria*,
was meant to capture the spirit of "a somewhat elusive, often deliberately mysterious,

domain" of writers and readers that formed long-distance social networks from the fifteenth to the seventeenth centuries (Eisenstein 1979, 137). This virtual republic was a space of written exchange, dependent not only on printed books but also on letters and manuscripts conveyed by private courier, travelers, paid messengers, and diplomatic pouch (Callisen and Adkins 2011, 63–64). The resulting space of interaction was a network, a web, although it conducted messages and information much more slowly than today's Web. The placeless qualities of this print and writing-based web were conveyed to readers by the use of "Cosmopolis" or "Utopia" as the place of publication on the colophon (Eisenstein 1979). Political and intellectual freedom could be implied as well by a fictitious place like "Freetown," "Villefranche," "Vrijstadt," or "Eleutheropolis" (Briggs and Burke 2005, 44). Print-culture self-consciously promoted itself as inhabiting or occupying a virtual space.

Nonetheless, the Republic of Letters had a geography. French and Latin provided lingua francas for the dispersed participants, although the multitude of expatriates and traveling scholars associated with the various print shops were more welcome in Antwerp, Rotterdam, or The Hague than in Paris or Geneva. Some controversial works were printed in private dwellings, while other printing facilities were moved from place to place (Briggs and Burke 2005, 44). Virtual place metaphors employed by inhabitants of the Republic of Letters attest to the emergence of an illicit production and trade network: "real foundries, workshops and offices were built to serve the needs of this presumably fictitious realm; real profits were made by tapping the talents which gravitated to it" (Eisenstein 1979, 139). Then as today, virtual spaces depended on at least semifixed infrastructure.

In short, printing brought an explosion of the virtual spaces of the fixed word. Mass production of printed material spawned a reading public, which did not simply ingest written material but actively and self-consciously inhabited a slippery fluid space. The space of this public confronted the space of authority, and the latter was gradually forced to adapt to the former. The printed page constituted a space for new kinds of rational, analytical thought in areas as diverse as bureaucracy, science, economics, politics, and the arts. The Republic of Letters is one root of the territorially defined democratic republics, religious sects, and scientific communities that began to emerge more explosively in the eighteenth century.

CONCLUSION

"The virtual" has deep and tangled roots. First, when humans began to develop spoken language, they began to construct a system encoding four-dimensional space-time in one-dimensional sequences of sound. Words indicated spatiotemporal structures and permitted events to be associated with near and far places, and with various times in the past, present, and future. The verbal manipulation of objects, phenomena, terrains, territories, times, places, and values, through deictic but even more through absolute references, constitutes an ancient kind of virtuality.

Second, as writing fixed the word, new kinds of virtuality developed. Words now occupied the two-dimensional space of the writing surface, where they could be organized in meaningful ways relative to other words, not just before and after other words but above and below, or in reference to figures and diagrams. Written documents, commands, records, and accounts could be stored, providing continuity through time, or moved from place to place, providing continuity through space. The fixed word therefore permitted the practical development of longer-lived and wider-flung social entities, and these spaces became part of the human experience, adding new layers of virtual presence, power, and experience. Both secular and spiritual forms of power were buttressed by pragmatic texts such as records and edicts but also through mythical and magical texts.

Third, the technique of printing did not simply increase the number of copies of books and other texts, it permitted the fixed word to be incorporated into social life in a radically different way than it had been thus far. Diffusion of written material led to the diffusion of ideas across political borders and the vastly increased potential for ideas to escape the control of ecclesiastical and political authorities. It popularized tabular and diagrammatic thought patterns. One result was the emergence of social actors such as scholars, scientists, visionaries, and radicals who self-consciously occupied a utopian space outside of the control of the main authorities of the time.

Virtual place metaphors are important and useful tools to understand what was distinct and different about old media when they were new, just as they have helped us to understand the new media of the twenty-first century. As Standage demonstrates (1998), insights about new media can be stretched back to reengage with older media, adding to the understanding that previous theorists have brought to the interplay between social formations and technologies (e.g., McLuhan 1962; 1964; Carey 1988; Marvin 1988). Rather than initiating a radical break in our relations to space, new media accentuate and multiply virtual spaces, continuing a virtualization process initiated by speech and intensified by writing and printing.

My argument points toward continuity and similarity rather than discontinuity and difference over time. On this account the newest media do not initiate but merely continue the construction of intangible architectures. By employing words, new media build onto a scaffolding of verbal space-time set up over thousands of years. If new technologies are called "virtual" because they evoke multisensory experience through vision or hearing or both, presenting an illusion of embodiment in a space that cannot be touched, tasted, or smelled, we must remember that the word pioneered this kind of sensory fragmentation by translating sights, smells, and tactile sensations into acoustical signs. We must also recall that the book subsequently diffused a radically different sensory translation, translating words from sounds to sights. If digital and electronic media are called "virtual" because they let us introduce distance into familiar social situations, we must remember that the process of distanciation was already underway as soon as hominids employed speech, and was magnified when upper social echelons developed "high" language as the province of the fixed word, with its intrinsic rather than deictic references, and its elaborate imaginary worlds.

None of the foregoing argument is meant to deny the importance of new communication technologies for the process of virtualization. Virtual architecture is *different* now, since it depends on digital codes, fiber optics, computers, and a host of other devices that make up a converging global network of networks (Kitchin and Dodge 2011). Sensory fragmentation is *different* now, as audiovisual representations seem poised to overwhelm the remaining place-based sensations of the nose, tongue, skin, and vestibular system. Distanciation is *different* as well, since the in-place interactions we virtualize no longer need to be slowed down as they were when correspondence depended on "snail mail" and publication depended on the printing press. There are new virtualities, even if virtualization is not especially new.

Part of the power of new media rests on the old. Therefore the new-old distinction must be interrogated. What we brand as "old" remains in use and is therefore current. What is new is not as innovative as it seems. To encapsulate the argument, then, the discovery of virtuality associated with new media should send us back to look again at the history of communication and explore the gradual deepening and development of virtuality.

NOTES

1. Each of these concepts has its limitations; for example, the "intangibility" of online virtual worlds may be questioned in light of the fact that computers and peripherals can be touched and manipulated, but this is not the same as actually feeling the cold, rough surface of a stone wall in a virtual dungeon. "Fully immersive" virtual environments may seem to avoid the splitting of the senses, but thus far they offer quite rudimentary tactile, olfactory, gustatory, and proprioceptive sensory modalities.
2. I am indebted to Dr. Daniel Sui and Dr. Waquar Ahmed for these examples.

REFERENCES

Adams, P. 2009. *Geographies of Media and Communication*. Malden, MA: Wiley-Blackwell.

Adams, P. 2010. Networks of Early Writing. *Historical Geography* 38: 70–89.

Allan, S. 1991. *The Shape of the Turtle: Myth, Art and Cosmos in Early China*. Albany: State University of New York Press.

Anderson, B. 1983. *Imagined Communities: Reflections on the Origin and Spread of Nationalism*. Rev. ed. New York: Verso.

Betrò, M. C. 1996. *Hieroglyphics: The Writings of Ancient Egypt*. Translated by S. A. George. New York: Abbeville Press.

Bolter, J. D. 2001. *Writing Space: Computers, Hypertext, and the Remediation of Print*. 2nd ed. Mahwah, NJ: Lawrence Erlbaum Associates.

Briggs, A., and P. Burke. 2005. *A Social History of the Media: from Gutenberg to the Internet*. 2nd ed. Malden, MA: Polity Press.

Callisen, C. T., and B. Adkins. 2011. Pre-digital Virtuality: Early Modern Scholars. In *The Long History of New Media: Technology, Historiography, and Contextualizing Newness*, edited by D. W. Park, N. W. Jankowski, and S. Jones, 55–72. New York: Peter Lang.

Carey, J. 1988. *Communication as Culture: Essays on Media and Society*. Boston: Unwin Hyman.

Coulmas, F. 1989. *The Writing Systems of the World*. Oxford: Basil Blackwell.

de Certeau, M. 1984. *The Practice of Everyday Life*. Translated by S. Rendall. Berkeley: University of California Press.

Edwards, K., R. Guttesen, P. J. Sigvardsen, and S. S. Hansen. 2010. Language, Overseas Research and a Stack of Problems in the Faroe Islands. *Scottish Geographical Journal* 126 (1): 1–8.

Eisenstein, E. L. 1979. *The Printing Press as an Agent of Change: Communications and Cultural Transformations in Early-Modern Europe*. 2 vols. Cambridge: Cambridge University Press.

Foucault, M. 1970. *The Order of Things: An Archaeology of the Human Sciences*. New York: Random House / Vintage Books.

Giddens, A. 1984. *The Constitution of Society: Outline of the Theory of Structuration*. Berkeley: University of California Press.

Gnanadesikan, A. E. 2009. *The Writing Revolution: Cuneiform to the Internet*. Malden, MA: Wiley-Blackwell.

Goody, J. 1987. *The Interface between the Written and the Oral*. Cambridge: Cambridge University Press.

Habermas, J. 1989. *The Structural Transformation of the Public Sphere: An Inquiry into a Category of Bourgeois Society*. Translated by T. Burger with the assistance of F. Lawrence. Cambridge, MA: MIT Press.

Herb, G. H. 2004. Double Vision: Territorial Strategies in the Construction of National Identities in Germany, 1949–1979. *Annals of the Association of American Geographers* 94: 140–164.

Innis, H. A. 1951. *The Bias of Communication*. Toronto: University of Toronto Press.

Karmakar, S., and R. Kasturirangan 2011. Space and Time in Language as a Pattern in General Fictivity. *Current Science* 100 (5): 627–628.

Keightley, D. N. 1978. *Sources of Shang History: The Oracle-Bone Inscriptions of Bronze Age China*. Berkeley: University of California Press.

Kitchin, R., and M. Dodge. 2011. *Code/Space: Software and Everyday Life*. Cambridge, MA: MIT Press.

Lefebvre, H. 1991. *The Production of Space*. Translated by D. Nicholson-Smith. Oxford: Blackwell.

Levinson, S. C. 2003. *Space in Language and Cognition: Explorations in Cognitive Diversity*. Cambridge: Cambridge University Press.

Logan, R. K. 1986. *The Alphabet Effect: The Impact of the Phonetic Alphabet on the Development of Western Civilization*. New York: St. Martin's Press.

Marvin, C. 1988. *When Old Technologies Were New: Thinking about Electric Communication in the Late Nineteenth Century*. New York: Oxford University Press.

Massey, D. 1993. Power-Geometry and a Progressive Sense of Place. In *Mapping the Futures: Local Cultures, Global Change*, edited by J. Bird, B. Curtis, T. Putnam, G. Robertson, and L. Tickner, 59–69. New York: Routledge.

Massumi, B. 2002. *Parables for the Virtual: Movement, Affect, Sensation*. Durham, NC: Duke University Press.

McLuhan, M. 1962. *The Gutenberg Galaxy: The Making of Typographic Man*. Toronto: University of Toronto Press.

McLuhan, M. 1964. *Understanding Media: The Extensions of Man*. New York: McGraw-Hill.

McLuhan, M. 1995. Playboy interview. In *The Essential McLuhan*, edited by E. McLuhan and F. Zingrone, 233–269. London: Routledge.

McLuhan, M., and E. McLuhan. 1988. *Laws of Media: The New Science*. Toronto: University of Toronto Press.

Michalowski, P. 1993. *Letters from Early Mesopotamia*. Edited by E. Reiner. Atlanta, GA: Scholar's Press.

Müller, M. 2007. What's in a Word? Problematizing Translation between Languages. *Area* 39 (2): 206–213.

Mumford, L. 1963. *Technics and Civilization*. New York: Harcourt, Brace and World.

Olwig, K. R. 1981. Literature and "Reality": The Transformation of the Jutland Heath. In *Humanistic Geography and Literature: Essays on the Experience of Place*, edited by C. D. Pocock, 47–65. London: Croom Helm; Totowa, NJ: Barnes and Noble Books.

Ong, W. J. 1982. *Orality and Literacy: The Technologizing of the Word*. New York: Methuen.

Pocock, D. C. D., ed. 1981. *Humanistic Geography and Literature: Essays on the Experience of Place*. London: Croom Helm; Totowa, NJ: Barnes and Noble Books.

Pred, A. 1990. *Lost Words and Lost Worlds: Modernity and the Language of Everyday Life in Late Nineteenth-Century Stockholm*. Cambridge: Cambridge University Press.

Rochberg, F. 2004. *The Heavenly Writing: Divination, Horoscopy, and Astronomy in Mesopotamian Culture*. New York: Cambridge University Press.

Saussure, F. de 1983. *Course in General Linguistics*. Edited by C. Bally and A. Sechehaye with the collaboration of A. Riedlinger. Translated by R. Harris. LaSalle, IL: Open Court.

Schmandt-Besserat, D. 1996. *How Writing Came About*. Abridged edition of *Before Writing*, vol. 1: *From Counting to Cuneiform*. Austin: University of Texas Press.

Shields, R. 2003. *The Virtual*. New York: Routledge.

Shinohara, K., and P. Pardeshi. 2011. The More in Front, the Later: The Role of Positional Terms in Time Metaphors. *Journal of Pragmatics* 43: 749–758.

Standage, T. 1998. *The Victorian Internet: The Remarkable Story of the Telegraph and the Nineteenth Century's On-line Pioneers*. New York: Walker.

Tenbrink, T. 2011. Reference Frames of Space and Time in Language. *Journal of Pragmatics* 43: 704–722.

Tuan, Y.-F. 1991. Language and the Making of Place: A Narrative-Descriptive Approach. *Annals of the American Association of Geographers* 81: 684–696.

Tuan, Y.-F. 1994. The City and Human Speech. *Geographical Review* 84 (2): 144–156.

Whorf, B. L. 1956. *Language, Thought and Reality: Selected Writings of Benjamin Lee Whorf*. Edited by J. B. Carroll. Cambridge, MA: MIT Press.

CHAPTER 15

....

SO GOOD, THEY NAMED IT TWICE? A LACANIAN PERSPECTIVE ON VIRTUAL REALITY FROM LITERATURE AND THE OTHER ARTS

....

DAVID RUDD

My title derives from the well-known song "New York, New York," referring to the fact that both the city and the state bear the same name. However, there is also the fact that the city was itself named twice, its earlier name, "New Amsterdam," coming from the Dutch (although, way before this, the indigenous Algonquin Indians, the Lenape, probably had another name for the area). In relation to virtual reality, my point is that "newness" can easily be overrated, and I shall argue that VR has actually been around far longer than some pundits suggest—in fact, since we, as a species, first began using language to name things. This will be the point of departure for my case, from which I will go on to suggest that part of the appeal of artistic works (and literature in particular) is in the way that they play around with this state of affairs: this disjunction between things and their naming.

My argument, however, will require a shift in mindset (or, perhaps, headset): away from seeing the VR age as commencing with HMDs, or head-mounted displays, to a realization that our actual heads, with their built-in sensory devices and on-board computers (i.e., brains), already do this; in other words, that they too are "systems that create a real-time visual/audio/haptic experience," to adopt John Vince's (2004, 150) definition of VR. Let me begin, then, by examining each of the phrase's constituent parts, "virtual" and "reality." I will spend more time on the latter, as this is where most confusion reigns; but, before that, some words about the "virtual" are in order.

Though both words have been stretched way beyond their semantic capacity, naming a variety of things twice (at the very least), the word "virtual" has been particularly abused. As early as 1992, Benjamin Woolley commented that the term was "a huge vessel of semantic vacuity waiting to have meaning poured into it" (1992, 58)—although this is not quite true: there was some debris left in the container prior to its recent renovation, and this material continues to color the word. Thus semantic traces from the noun "virtue," associated with that which is good—and its own etymological ties to the power of a god—live on, as we shall later see. However, for present purposes I shall use the word "virtual" to imply that something is "intangible" as opposed to "actual." My reservations about hooking this term up with "reality" will follow, but first let me make one further distinction that will help clarify the discussion: the phrase "virtual reality" will be used in full when I am talking about what I suggest might be a more embracing conceptualization of the area, reserving the abbreviation "VR" for the more restricted, cyberspace notion.

To return to my opening remarks, then—and to my title—the problem with yoking these two terms is not that they are oxymoronic (though one can see why this might be); rather, it is that they are tautological: the same thing seems to be named twice in that, as I shall argue, our dealings with reality are always already virtual. Such a claim, however, depends on an understanding of Jacques Lacan's conception of our relation to reality, and to the way we name things, to which I shall now turn.

VIRTUAL REALITY: LACAN STYLE

For Lacan, the term "reality" does not signify some bedrock that we can unproblematically access; indeed, human beings—unlike other creatures—quickly find the raw "stuff" of the universe—what Lacan terms the "Real"—inaccessible. This is because, for Lacan, humans exist primarily within two other orders through which the Real is always mediated; these are, respectively, the Imaginary and the Symbolic. In general terms, this shift away from the Real is most easily described as a move from *being* (a state of existence that all sentient creatures share) to *meaning* (which always involves the Real being framed in some way, as I shall elaborate below).

In the simplest terms, the Imaginary is conceptualized as a more visual, gestalt-like way of framing the world, whereas the Symbolic is understood to be a preeminently verbal form of signification. This shift away from the Real is seen to occur in two stages in the course of a child's development, such that, thereafter, the Real becomes generally inaccessible to us (i.e., it falls outside some form of mediation—but see below).

The Imaginary is the initial form of mediation a child experiences. It is most famously associated with what Lacan termed the "mirror stage," when a child first comes to see itself as an entity, a whole being, despite the fact that it might still lack motor control and coordination; this falsely unified image, moreover, is frequently underwritten by a child's carers, often in idealized terms ("Who's a beautiful girl, then?"). Lacan's point is that the Imaginary not only establishes our sense of identity, our ego, but, more contro-versially, that this provides a false sense of unity that initiates our development in what he calls a "fictional direction" (Lacan 1977, 2). In other words, this idealized image does not capture the "actual" person outside the frame of the mirror—not simply because the image is merely that (i.e., an image, two-dimensional, left-right reversed), but also because it exists outside the individual. Yet, despite its falsity, we find ourselves capti-vated by such representations, defending these idealized portraits of ourselves ever after, and seeking accoutrements that bolster our "image" in the form of clothes, cars, part-ners, and so forth. We are, thereby, already caught up in the realm of the virtual.

But this process is complete only when we enter the Symbolic; that is, when we become users of language. Lacan ingeniously reworks Freud's notion of the Oedipus complex to explain this, stripping it of its biological trappings (involving actual body parts and the threat of knives) and reframing it figuratively. In this scenario, each of us is forced to move away from a state where all our needs and demands are automatically ful-filled (by a mother figure), as we come to realize that there are other significant beings in our world (a paternal presence in particular). One is, therefore, not all and everything to this mother figure; however hard one tries, her attention is often elsewhere. The shadow of the father figure (what Lacan terms the Name-of-the-Father, or *Nom-du-Père*) dis-rupts the dyadic relation of mother and child, negating any simple, one-to-one relation between the child's cry (a signifier) and the succor of milk (a signified). His "No!" sun-ders this dyadic unity (hence the father is also punningly known as the *Non-du-Père*).

The Oedipal link is clear here, but it has been recast in linguistic and structural terms, such that it applies to all children (not just boys and their mothers); for all of us have to move from a state of unity with our primary carer (from an infant [literally, "speech-less"] state of *being*), where communication is a more intuitive and corporeal process, into a world of language (*meaning*), where our wants have to be framed using something that, once again, comes from outside us: the currency of language; that is, a common code, one that is in no way special to the individual but shared by all, such that even the personal pronoun "I," designed to capture our individuality, belies this notion with each usage, being passed round like a communal bottle at a party. Likewise, a personally charged term like "Mummy" not only designates all mother figures, regardless, but is in itself a fairly empty phonic replacement for the sensory immersion that this real figure offers: tactile, olfactory, audible, visible, interactive, rhythmic, pulsing, and so on.

In Lacanian terms, a gap has opened up between signifier and signified as we enter lan-guage, the Symbolic order. The fullness of being is emptied out by these linguistic signifi-ers, which are themselves also arbitrary (i.e., they differ from language to language), such that, for Lacan, we are forever after striving, through our verbal expressions, to regain that former sense of plenitude we think we once possessed. Within language, then, we are always in a state of lack; hence, he argues, running alongside these communal visual and phonic counters by way of which we converse, there is always an unsaid desire that we can never quite articulate. (We want milk, certainly, but beyond that, what we really want is full attention, to have all our desires fulfilled!) The final thing to note about this process of signification is that our own special sense of being has itself become overlain by a signifier, such that we "go under" a particular name, which also means conforming to a particular gender, ethnicity, color, nationality, condition of (dis)ability—let alone a whole future of other "normalizing" assessments. One can see how the notion of symbolic castration is effective here, as one is codified into certain preexisting categories regardless of the fact that people might not feel that these labels fully represent them. In fact, the binary configuration of gender makes the point: male/female—that is all that is on offer, take it or . . . take it: it's a nonchoice. An individual thus gains a place in society, but always with a sense of loss (which is what all the myths about paradise, about moving away from innocent, carefree childhoods relate). In Lacan's model, "subjects" (which is what we become, being able to say "I," but only because we have been subjected) are therefore in a state of ontological lack, which is what simultaneously gives rise to desire, humans' existential pact in this shift from *being* to *meaning*.

To summarize, then: as social beings we exist simultaneously within three orders. We are biological beings that eat, drink, sleep, and reproduce (in the Real), but we do so with a sense of norms about where and how it is appropriate to engage in these activities (the Symbolic), and, simultaneously, we have an idealized (and exaggerated) sense, perhaps, of our prowess as a lover, or as a chef (in the Imaginary). As the Real always stands outside symbolization, we only rarely experience it directly, but there are instances where it becomes manifest. For example, in Monty Python's *The Meaning of Life* (Terry Jones 1983), there is a scene where Mr Creosote, a grotesquely obese man whom we see eating a voluminous meal in a restaurant, subsequently throws up (or more precisely, explodes), covering all the other diners with his vomit, and precipitating their own, half-digested contributions. Here, we might say, is an eruption of the Real—although, of course, it is only a fleeting disruption, rapidly being reconceptualized in symbolic terms (as I have just described it).

It should now be more clear, after what might seem a long detour, why the phrase "virtual reality" is, at least in some senses, tautological. For, as beings within the Symbolic, where our existence is represented in terms of signifiers, we have already left behind the Real, the material "stuff" of the universe; our reality is thus, itself, virtual: we are creatures of *meaning*, not just *being*.

Let me now move on to consider the implications of this for a broader, more inclusive notion of virtual reality (accepting that we are saddled with this term).

ARTISTIC AND LITERARY CONTEXTS

In the previous section it was argued that, though embodied in the Real, we live in a reality distinct from it, largely manufactured out of symbols and images. Technically, then, we should use the plural and speak of "realities," as there are many different ways in which cultures accommodate the Real, involving religious practices, mythological schemes, philosophies, economic, political and legal systems, gender arrangements, and, of course, countless stories. Here I want to concentrate on the latter, on the ways that we seek to narrate our existence in artistic works that, of course, not only rehearse our state of virtual reality (being as much a part of it as simulators and computer games, in fact), but which also often contrive to do more. In broad terms, they either draw attention to their status as artifacts, as works that explore and comment on our human condition as lacking, desiring creatures, or they try to overcome this split, the gap between representation and the real: to reinstantiate, in short, a notion of plenitude, of wholeness, often drawing on Imaginary idealizations.

One might point to works like Dante's *Divine Comedy* and Beethoven's Ninth Symphony (incorporating Schiller's poem, evocatively entitled "Ode to Joy") as works that seek to overcome our status as fractured beings by evoking a sense of plenitude, of the sublime. On the other hand, works such as Milton's *Paradise Lost* and Shakespeare's tragedies point more directly to the fractures themselves, albeit using artistic forms that simultaneously seek to give the reader or audience some solace. A number of artistic works, especially modernist and postmodernist ones, often go further than this, deliberately playing up this gap between the Symbolic and the Real, between signifier and signified. These standard semiotic terms, introduced by Ferdinand de Saussure as the two constitutive elements of a sign, have been deployed above, but it is perhaps a good idea to be clear about their meaning, as the division between them is often overlooked. The signifier is the sensory carrier of the sign: it can comprise words, pictures, symbols, or even bodily gestures (as in sign language); the signified, in contrast, is far more difficult to determine, for one can only really use more signifiers when attempting to pin it down: it is the concept, designating the thing itself. But, as has already been made clear, it can never be the thing itself, for, as noted, when we enter the Symbolic we lose touch with actual "things": their essence slips away and we are left with empty signifiers only.

A good example of a work that demonstrates this, and exploits the gap between signifier and signified, is the frequently cited painting by René Magritte entitled *La trahison des images* (1928–1929) (e.g., Foucault 1983). This work depicts a pipe, beneath which is written, in French, *Ceci n'est pas une pipe* ("This is not a pipe"). Our immediate, mimetic reaction might be, "Of course it is. Something wrong with your eyes?" However, a moment's reflection should make us "see" that it is not: it is simply a painting of a pipe, a representation. And then there's that title—"The treason (or treachery) of images"— which might also seem to point toward the unreliability of the pipe (as people say, you wouldn't want to try to smoke it). But, if we consider the matter more dispassionately, we might then ask ourselves why we automatically privilege the authority of words over pictures. After all, the French sentence about the word "pipe" is also contained within the picture plane; in which case, its title should apply equally to these extra, painted renderings of the words: aren't these, too, "treacherous"? And yet, why grant the title such privileged status? Isn't it, also, part of Magritte's composition? It has no de facto truth value: it simply comprises more signifiers, with no more grounding in the Real than other elements. So, why not entitle the work "The Treachery of Words"?—albeit, of course, we might end up reading the painting in exactly the same way. But the main point stands, regardless: that our social world is constructed out of signifiers—both verbal and visual—such that we often forget the fact that, like money, they have currency within the realm of culture only, where we too have our habitation. The Real (wherein we are embodied) is at one remove, the place where there is simply "stuff," which we might describe more objectively (in the case of Magritte's picture) as oil-based pigment on stretched canvas.

Having given examples of artistic works that *either* draw attention to the gap between signifier and signified (between our virtual representation of something and the thing itself) *or* seek to provide some sense of overcoming that split (by ending harmoniously, or suggesting this through artistic form), let me now look more closely at how artistic works might be viewed as exemplifying virtual reality. To do this, let me return to Vince's generic definition, quoted earlier, concerning complex sensory systems and symbolic aptitudes; however, Vince then adds some important adjuncts, namely that VR systems are immersive and interactive (Vince 2004, 4–5). Initially, these facets might seem more exclusive, but, once again, I would suggest that we are too easily influenced by contemporary inflections of these words, and neglect the arguments proffered by a number of cultural critics who contend that artistic works function in just such a manner, causing readers to be "lost in a book" (Nell 1988), for instance (i.e., immersed), or engaged in a dialogue with a character or idea (i.e., interactive). Many literary critics, in fact, would argue that it is impossible to read a text passively, in that one is always anticipating, filling in gaps, and, generally, going beyond the black-and-white signifiers on the page (Gerrig 1993; Esrock 1994). Beyond this, there is much evidence for readers (beginners and experienced) engaging in more extensive interactivity: skipping passages, rereading favorite parts, looking at the end of a story first, and so on. Some readers take this further still, rewriting whole works, whether as amateurs (e.g., the phenomenon of "textual poaching," or fan fiction—e.g., Certeau 1984; Jenkins 1992; Fanfiction 2012) or as professional writers (e.g., Jean Rhys's *Wide Sargasso Sea* out of Charlotte Brontë's *Jane Eyre*, or *Foe* [Coetzee 1986] out of *Robinson Crusoe* [Defoe 1719]).

Though perhaps counterintuitive, the key point that I'd like to make is that it is precisely as a result of readers filling in the gaps that exist in texts (and thereby creating further gaps, of course), that the experience of immersion and interaction occurs. Moreover, to flag up my subsequent argument, I shall suggest that it is, perhaps ironically, works of fantasy (themselves more readily connected to notions of VR) that often make greater claims about closing the gap between signifier and signified; in other words, about being more in touch with the Real.

While my main argument concerns the ways that literary texts create a sense of virtual reality, I do want, briefly, to consider other arts, returning once again to the visual, where attempts to approximate the Real are often more startlingly deceptive, particularly in what are known as "trompe l'oeil" (i.e., "deceive the eye") works, where onlookers reach out into nonexistent spaces for illusory objects (just as cinema viewers do today in 3D films). Though trompe l'oeil effects are often limited to sections of buildings (most famously, domed ceilings that seem to open out onto the heavens), our ancestors might have experienced more profound feelings of immersion in these spaces. Thus Woolley (1992, 139) discusses churches as mnemonic spaces, with their paintings (especially the stations of the cross) and their "strategically placed objects—the font near the entrance, the memorials of past bishops surrounding the altar"—that could make an "entire cathedral a metaphorical representation of the pilgrim's progress from birth through to death and salvation." Although Woolley doesn't mention it, other senses might have further assisted this atmospheric feeling of immersion and involvement: heavenly music, singing, and chanting, for instance; the use of incense, the taste of bread and wine, and the experiences of the body itself, genuflecting, kneeling, undergoing pain, and its relief, through its movements.

There is also an auditory equivalent to trompe l'oeil, known as "trompe l'oreille," achieved by instruments imitating natural sounds, such as the cuckoo and nightingale that feature in Beethoven's *Pastoral Symphony*. And, moving on to verbal signifiers, onomatopoeia gives us the lexical counterpart of this phonic mimicry: "woof," "bang," "splat" or, in literary texts, attempts like the buzzing evoked in a phrase such as the "murmuring of innumerable bees" from Keats's "Ode to a Nightingale." However, as linguists have frequently pointed out, the way we audit these sounds differs radically from language to language, suggesting that our very senses accommodate our linguistic homeland: "bark," "woof," "bow-wow," and "ruff" (themselves quite varied) thus become "wan-wan" (Japanese), "gong" (Malay), "guk" (Indonesian), "ham" (Romanian), "haf" (Armenian), or "vov" (Danish), to name but a few variants.[1]

The key point about all these forms of mimicry, however, is precisely that: they are not the "real thing." The gap persists, just as it does in our everyday dealings with the world, which—however mundane—are almost always mediated (even our bowel movements—post potty-training—are socially regulated). Of course, such matters need not concern us in our everyday activities (any more than we need worry about the facticity of tobacco pipes). But once reflected upon, the problem of the Real, and of real-*ism*, won't dematerialize (although the main problem with the Real is, in fact, precisely the opposite: it won't materialize!). These ontological and epistemological questions persist right down to the level of subatomic particles, where one has only traces in bubble chambers, or, perhaps, predictions from mathematical models—yet more signifiers, of course.

Returning to onomatopoeia (and its equivalents in trompe l'oeil and l'oreille), although it is an evocative way of imitating the Real, it is ultimately seen as a rather gimmicky, minor player in artistic works. More convincing and sustained attempts to evoke a sense of reality through the written word are to be found elsewhere, and, perhaps preeminently, in the novel, itself closely interlinked with conceptions of realism and, concurrently, with the huge physical and sensory impact of the Industrial Revolution in the eighteenth century.

What is especially interesting about the early novel is the way that authors attempted to efface its fictional status by pretending that their works were about real events: biographies (Defoe's *The Life and Adventures of Robinson Crusoe* [1719]), accounts of travel (e.g., Jonathan Swift's *Gulliver's Travels* [1726]), exchanges of letters (Samuel Richardson's *Clarissa* [1748]), confessions (James Hogg's *The Private Memoirs and Confessions of a Justified Sinner* [1824]), and so forth. It is certainly pertinent that these fictions appeared during this period of intense capitalist growth, with its attendant increase in the manufacture of goods; moreover, members of the emergent "middling classes" themselves featured prominently, their sense of reality bolstered by the meticulous enumeration of their possessions and artifacts (novels themselves being key examples of such manufactured goods). Once again, though, despite their evocation of reality, I would want to emphasize that it is the gap, or framing of these works, that remains all-important.

This can be most clearly seen in the growth in popularity of narratives that could not possibly be real, despite using the emerging conventions of realism in their construction. These are collectively known as "It" or "Thing" narratives, where everyday objects are allowed to tell their own stories, as in "The Adventures of a Halfpenny" (1753), "The Adventures of a Silk Petticoat" (1773), *The Adventures of a Hackney Coach* (1781), or, albeit less everyday, Tobias Smollett's *Adventures of an Atom* (1769) (Blackwell et al. 2012; cf. Blackwell 2007). The framework of realism thus gave novelists considerable latitude to look at the world from unusual perspectives—but always with an awareness that these were illusory views, *constructed* from particular vantage points that would be impossible for humans to inhabit in any other way but "virtually."

As the novel became a more accepted art form during the Victorian period, realism came to be viewed in more expansive terms, moving away from a focus on individual characters. Omniscient narrators expanded their canvases to range across barriers of class, gender, and age, taking us into the minds of a whole spectrum of society (George Eliot's *Middlemarch* [1874] often being seen as the quintessential exemplar). Once again, though, it needs emphasizing that this version of the real was simply that: another construction, and one using relatively arbitrary conventions. Thus we witness few, actual everyday activities in these books, and there are relatively few working-class or lumpenproletariat characters in evidence. The latter would come into their own later in the nineteenth century with the development of a more gritty realism, termed Naturalism, as pursued by writers such as Émile Zola and George Gissing.

Moreover, at this period we see another split in the representation of reality, with many Naturalistic writers also striving for a more objective, anthropological depiction of character. This approach was partly a reaction to the artifice of the omniscient narrator who could enter anyone's head, as though possessing telepathic abilities. In contrast, another group of writers, intrigued by new explorations into the nature of the mind—especially with the arrival of psychoanalysis in the 1890s—tried to create what they saw as a more realistic fiction *precisely* by going inside and following the divagations of characters' thought processes. The novels of the American author Henry James are perhaps the most celebrated here, leading on to modernist experiments by writers like Virginia Woolf and James Joyce, following the "streams of consciousness" as they meandered through characters' minds. Joyce, one might say, united these two streams, also striving for greater Naturalism in *Ulysses* (1922), one of the most celebrated novels ever, and one where characters are finally permitted (post potty-training) to be excused. One final feature of modernism worth mentioning was the abandonment of attempts to construct neat, linear plots, where the destinies of all the characters are tidied up at the end. Instead, modernist novels tend to have sudden jumps and ellipses, often with relatively unresolved, downbeat endings.

However, alongside these different ways of representing reality, one more aspect needs mentioning, which the French *nouveau roman* of the 1950s also points toward at times. This is the "alienation effect," developed by early twentieth-century Russian Formalists and exploited by Bertolt Brecht in the theater. With this, the very *illusion* of character and plot is drawn to the reader's or audience's attention. In drama this is commonly referred to as "breaking the fourth wall," where any notion of reality held by the people seated beyond the three walls of staged action is confounded. It was thought that this ploy would actually lead to a more "realistic" appreciation of events, not only by drawing attention to their fictionality but also by demonstrating the part played by the viewer/reader in constructing that reality—that is, the virtual reality—of the text. Once again, the key point about all these works is that they are effective precisely because, in the words of the London Underground, they do indeed "mind the gap" between actuality and its artistic depiction.

Having briefly rehearsed the history of the novel and indicated how varied are its attempts at depicting reality, though always with an eye on its "virtual" status, I now want to contrast these attempts at verisimilitude, at mimicking reality, with depictions of fantasy, which, presumably because of its supposed distance from the world of the everyday, is often seen to be closer in the popular mind to notions of the virtual. Certainly, in studies of literature, it is the realistic pole that has been privileged as the more important, being associated with works of recognized classic status (for example, F. R. Leavis's highly influential work *The Great Tradition* [1948], which outlines canonical literary works written in English, limits itself to Jane Austen, George Eliot, Henry James, and Joseph Conrad).

It's the Real Thing: Fantasy, Secondary Worlds, and the Virtuously Real

On reflection, it might seem strange to privilege the realistic given that most literary works over the centuries and across cultures are what we would have to call "fantasy" in that they depart from consensus reality in some way (consider Homer's epics, classical drama, many of Shakespeare's plays, let alone countless romances, legends, myths, and so on). Of course, all this depends on one's definition of "fantasy," which a number of experts in the area like to delimit to works that depict a separate, imagined world (e.g., Nikolajeva 1988), often termed a "Secondary World" after J. R. R. Tolkien's use of that term (Tolkien 1964). This terminology, of separate worlds, certainly sounds more conducive to modern notions of VR, and, without doubt, many games are redolent of Tolkien in their themes and settings (though one seldom hears the original *Lord of the Rings* trilogy described in terms of "virtual reality"). In order to move this argument on, then, let me consider how Tolkien himself defines this special realm, and how he and others seem to gesture not merely toward the virtual, but to a more virtuous reality—if not toward the Real itself.

Rather than fantasy, Tolkien prefers to talk about *"Faërie,"* "Magic," or the "Perilous Realm" (1964, 16), privileging stories that satisfy "certain primordial human desires": our wish "to survey the depths of space and time... to hold communion with other living things" (1964, 18), and our "oldest and deepest desire, the Great Escape: the Escape from Death" (1964, 59). He sees those writing successful fantasy as being "sub-creators" (1964, 25) in that their worlds need to be fully imagined; otherwise a reader's belief is lost, and he or she is "then out in the Primary [everyday] World again... looking at the little abortive Secondary World from outside" (1964, 36). I would certainly support Tolkien's notion that a successfully realized world depends less on a "suspension of disbelief" than on creating *"literary belief,"* the latter requiring only that "the story-maker's art" be "good enough" (1964, 36). But I would then ask why Tolkien feels that there is some norm of belief that fantasy is in danger of contravening (hence the necessity for belief's "suspension"). This question is particularly poignant when one considers how embedded are our ideological, religious, and mythological ideas, and the fact that most of us were probably raised on material that went far beyond the factual, including nursery rhyme, nonsense verse, and fairy tale (and their visual equivalents); and, if I might lump it in the same category, a holy book of some sort. Why, for instance, would secondary worlds like Middle Earth require more belief than the gritty satire of *American Psycho* (Ellis 1991)? In short, I would argue that both realistic and fantasy modes of writing depend chiefly on *literary* belief; that is, on the need to maintain a sense of credibility—although it might be fashioned from the most outlandish premises (of invisibility, an antigravity material, time travel, invasion by Martians—to run exclusively with just a few of H. G. Wells's imaginative conceits). As Thomas Pavel (1986, 11) neatly expresses it, "once... fictionality is acknowledged, happenings inside the novel are vividly felt as possessing some sort of reality of their own" (cf. Gerrig 1993).

So, going back to my earlier point about us being creatures alienated from ourselves by language (and, equally, by our idealized images), we will forever strive to achieve some sort of consistency in our lives, just as we seek to sustain belief in our cultural products, and we will draw fairly freely on a variety of ideological sources, from religious creeds and icons to consumer artifacts, in order to do so. In terms of fiction, then, literary texts will always utilize a mixture of fantastic and realistic elements. Kathryn Hume is one of the few theorists of the fantastic in literature to take this more eclectic approach, arguing that "fantasy is not a separate or indeed a separable strain, but rather an impulse as significant as the mimetic impulse"; thus, she suggests, we need to "recognize that both are involved in the creation of most literature" (Hume 1984, xii). This is not to argue for eliding fantasy and realism as categories—undoubtedly they are not synonymous—merely to object to the way that so many writers seek to separate the two, often seeing the fantastic as being, somehow, more virtual, or, as is sometimes the case, more virtuous, harping back to the word's religious roots. In other words, this version of virtual reality is often seen to be attempting to come closer to a notion of the Real (particularly so in fantastic works like myths, which seek to explain ontological issues).

Tolkien is especially interesting in this regard, and it is of note that Hume commends him for conceptualizing fantasy in terms wider than the literary, for seeing fantasy as a natural human activity. Indisputably, Tolkien does presume that this is the case, but only by redefining the natural, in effect, in terms that many might see as supernatural. Of course, one could argue that, being a devout Catholic, Tolkien needed to restrict his discussion—and, indeed, his art—to the realm of *Faërie* because only in this way would he avoid being seen to tread on the toes of God's creation, or, indeed, be accused of trying to imitate it; hence his preference for the term "sub-creators." However, Tolkien then elevates the best of these sub-creators for recognizing that "the Consolation of the Happy Ending" comprises the essence of fantasy ("all complete fairy-stories must have it"), wherein there is a "*Eucatastrophe*," or "good catastrophe, the sudden joyous 'turn,'" and a concomitant sense of "joy beyond the walls of the world" (1964, 60). He finally likens this experience to the Christian's at the coming of Christ, whence "the desire and aspiration of sub-creation has been raised to the fulfillment of Creation...this story is supreme; and it is true. Art has been verified. God is the Lord, of angels, and of men—and of elves" (1964, 62–63). In this way, the secondary world becomes anything but "abortive"; rather, it gains us access to a more Real world, one where the virtual (or, indeed, the virtuous) is seen as next to the godly.

In many ways, Tolkien's fellow writer C. S. Lewis is even more interesting in the way that he conflates these two realms (everyday reality and the fantastic Real). As Lewis expresses it: "Supposing that there really was a world like Narnia and supposing it had (like our world) gone wrong and supposing Christ wanted to go into that world and save it (as He did ours) what might have happened? The stories are my answers" (Lewis, quoted in Hooper 1966, 426).

Rather than leaving the reader to experience emotional parallels with the story of Christ, as Tolkien suggests might happen, Lewis is keen that the Christian story and its message "appear in their real potency" in his tales. Thus we have Christ appear as a lion, overseeing his chosen, Narnian people before undergoing public humiliation and death on their behalf, and then, a resurrection. Unlike the early attempts at realism demonstrated by the novel, where a cloak of facticity was thrown over a fiction in order to cast the latter into relief, here—once again—the pretense of fantasy is adopted in order to convey what Lewis saw as deeper truths. As he famously declared, by casting these things "into an imaginary world, stripping them of their stained-glass and Sunday school associations," he thought he could "steal past those watchful dragons" and make Christian concerns "about God or...the sufferings of Christ...for the first time appear in their real potency" (Lewis 1966, 37). The somewhat heavy hints about Aslan's real status, however, at times seem to render Lewis's secondary world precariously "abortive" in Tolkien's terms; it is a "Perilous Realm," one might venture, but not quite in the way that Tolkien envisaged:

> "But you shall meet me, dear one," said Aslan.
> "Are—are you there [in England] too, Sir?" said Edmund.
> "I am," said Aslan. "But there I have another name. You must learn to know me by that name. This was the very reason why you were brought to Narnia, that by knowing me here for a little, you may know me better there." (Lewis 1952, 222)

In effect, these remarks seem to be more for the benefit of the reader than Edmund, who does indeed come to know Aslan better in the final novel of the series, *The Last Battle* (Lewis 1956), following a train crash that kills Edmund along with most of the other young human protagonists. Then the true Narnia—which appears to be another version of the Real—is revealed to us: a Platonic realm of ideal forms.

As I remarked earlier, there's a certain irony here, in that, while many of the writers of realistic fiction were overtly marking the fictional status of the everyday, these fantasy writers—ostensibly less concerned with the world of consensual reality—repeatedly gesture toward some underlying notion of the Real within their works: some place where signified and signifier are finally seen to be as one.

Tolkien and Lewis have not been selected because they are prototypical of fantasy writing, but because they are two of the most celebrated practitioners of this form (e.g., Manlove 1975; Gray 2009). It is certainly a mode that seems to lend itself to evocations of plenitude, of wholeness—and critics are often complicit in celebrating its power to heal social division. Here, for instance, is the children's novelist and critic Jane Yolen arguing for the privileged power of fantasy, initially drawing on Tolkien and Lewis before she moves on to consider the creation of a more recent writer, Ursula Le Guin: "A child who can love the oddities of a fantasy book cannot possibly be xenophobic as an adult," she claims. "What is a different color, a different culture, a different tongue for a child who has already mastered Elvish, respected Puddleglums [*sic*], or fallen under the spell of dark-skinned Ged, the greatest wizard Earthsea has ever known" (Yolen 2000, 54). She concludes: "So the fantasy book, like the fairy tale, may not be Life Actual but it *is* Life in Truth" (2000, 55).

Once again, we see a nod toward the Real (that which lies beyond mere appearance)— something that we also find in Bruno Bettelheim's (1976) classic work on the fairy tale. But, leaving aside this gesture, there is a particular irony in Yolen's comment in that the *Earthsea* series was to strongly change direction when Le Guin herself balked at her own myopia in originally conceiving almost everyone in the wizarding world, including her own hero, as male ("You're a wizard, Harry," as opposed to "Harriet," as J. K. Rowling— far later—has had it repeatedly drawn to her attention). In other words, I would suggest that these fantastic "virtual" worlds (like all others) are always and everywhere underwritten by "Life Actual"; that is, by our ideological mindsets, which can blinker readers as effectively as any VR headsets. So the reason that there is no problem for us in colonizing these secondary worlds is that we never really leave behind the coordinates of our own. We are still, as I've suggested all along, trapped within the confines of the Symbolic.

Perhaps one of the most chilling, and challenging, images that gives the lie to this claim of Yolen's comes in the pictures of Rudolf Hess, the Nazi war criminal, conspicuously reading Grimm's *Fairy Tales* during the Nuremberg war trials. Arguably, this is the most disturbing feature of what are often seen as harmless—because they are "fantasy"—creations: that they affect to talk of different worlds, strange lands, and, more generally, outcomes that proffer a tidy sense of "happily ever after," but which achieve this only by ignoring concrete social divisions; such fictions are, in effect, often powerfully trapped within the idealizations of the Imaginary.

Fantasy, therefore, is the mode of writing that seems, ostensibly, most allied to the artificial worlds of VR, both in its landscapes and characters, but it is also the mode that, perhaps ironically, has a tendency to hint at deeper truths than those represented within the "realistic" tradition, where the inclination is more toward the accurate delineation of appearance, to an effective mimesis. And yet, as I have suggested all along, virtual reality is always already part of our everyday existence in the world.

Perhaps one shouldn't be too surprised at this finding. Jack Zipes, for instance, one of the leading scholars of fairy tales and the fantastic, has persistently argued, since the 1970s, that the impulse of the fairy tale and the fantastic is utopian, gesturing toward a better society—although the development of capitalism, patriarchy, and industrialization might have darkened and distorted such visions (e.g. Zipes 1979; 1983). Likewise, some champions of VR see their work leading to ever better approximations of reality and, in the process, overcoming many of the problems that compromise our actual world (around skin color, class, gender, and abled-ness, for instance). VR offers realms where anything is possible, where, despite its name, or perhaps in full recognition of it, "reality" does not hold one back. Just as Magritte's canvas can declare "This is not a pipe," while the image hangs playfully before us, VR offers to do the same but more so: not only can its pipe be smoked, but one can even inhale without fear of cancer.

CONCLUSION: CLOSING THE GAP, SO MIND THE DOORS

I have accepted that we are saddled with the term "virtual reality," despite problems inherent in its etymology. However, at the least, I have suggested, we should see the phrase in wider terms, as incorporating much that artworks have traditionally encompassed—and, perhaps especially, that distancing, framing effect which artistic works produce. Beyond that, I have argued that art's ability to frame reality is particularly important because that is our lot: we are beings who live predominantly in a mediated world, and, as a result, hark back to notions of regaining some form of plenitude, of harmony. Lacan's main point, though, is that we still have a foot in the Real. Like his most famous follower, Slavoj Žižek, he rejects those poststructuralist thinkers who see everything as socially constructed; who see, in other words, the Symbolic as all that there is.

This points to a danger that is evident in some VR thinking, just as it is in some of the fantasy writing mentioned above: that for all the "virtuality" of these spaces, they aspire to provide the participant with the feeling of total immersion in another realm, ignoring our actual, more incomplete state. In simpler terms, they attempt to close the gap I have so often referred to, such that we become "at one" with ourselves. However, Lacan's point would be that our entire sense of subjectivity would then collapse: we would be reduced to an insensible stasis ("being-ful" rather than "meaning-ful" entities). Total immersion, in other words, would mean precisely the loss of any sense of selfhood. As Žižek (1997,

156) puts it, cyberspace offers "a frictionless flow of images and messages—when I am immersed in it, I, as it were, return to a symbiotic relationship with an Other in which the deluge of semblances seems to abolish the dimension of the Real."

The worry of cyberspace, then, "is not its emptiness (the fact that it is lacking with respect to the fullness of the real presence) but, on the contrary, its very excessive full-ness (the potential abolition of the dimension of the symbolic virtuality)" (Žižek 1997, 155). We can thus enjoy temporary immersion in VR, as in other alternative realities, without worry: it rehearses the same relation as that between reality and the Real, where the gap sustains our subjectivity. However, were this gap to close, as depicted in M. T. Anderson's dystopian young adult novel, *Feed* (2002), the outcome might be different. Here we see the characters flounder in the endless "feedcasts" that they receive from the "feednet," having had transmitters implanted in their brains from birth. Desire in this novel has been fully commodified by mega-corporations that turn subjects into consumer-holics. The only character to resist (because she did not receive an implant at birth) is, effectively, condemned to social exclusion—and, ultimately, to death.

The message, then, as with all our cultural products (which are expressions of this dis-junction at our core), is to keep one foot in the door. To borrow from William Blake, the doors of perception must not be allowed to shut. As long as virtual reality is recognized in these wider terms, there is no problem, nor is there one with VR itself, but if this were to become VR™ (in *Feed* the teenagers attend, disturbingly, "School™"), then we might start to worry. Then, in fact, things might become so mediocre that, like the baby's cry for milk, they name them only once.

NOTE

1. See "Bark (utterance)," http://en.wikipedia.org/wiki/Bark (utterance), accessed April 19, 2012.

REFERENCES

Anderson, M. T. 2002. *Feed*. Cambridge, MA: Candlewick Press.

Bettelheim, B. 1976. *The Uses of Enchantment: The Meaning and Importance of Fairy Tales*. London: Thames and Hudson.

Blackwell, M, ed. 2007. *The Secret Life of Things: Animals, Objects, and It-narratives in Eighteenth-Century England*. Lewisburg, PA: Bucknell University Press.

Blackwell, M., L. Bellamy, C. Lupton, and H. Keenleyside, eds. 2012. *British It-Narratives, 1750–1830*. 4 vols. London: Pickering & Chatto.

Certeau, M. de. 1984. *The Practice of Everyday Life*. Translated by S. Rendall. Berkeley: University of California Press.

Ellis, B. E. 1991. *American Psycho*. New York: Vintage.

Esrock, E. J. 1994. *The Reader's Eye: Visual Imaging as Reader Response*. Baltimore, MA: Johns Hopkins University Press.

Fanfiction Directory Links. 2012. http://fanfiction-directory.com/. Accessed April 30, 2012.

Foucault, M. 1983. *This Is Not a Pipe*. Translated and edited by J. Harkness. Berkeley: University of California Press.

Gerrig, R. J. 1993. *Experiencing Narrative Worlds: On the Psychological Activities of Reading*. New Haven, CT: Yale University Press.

Gray, W. 2009. *Fantasy, Myth and the Measure of Truth: Tales of Pullman, Lewis, Tolkien, MacDonald and Hoffmann*. Basingstoke: Palgrave Macmillan.

Hooper, W. 1966. *C.S. Lewis: A Companion and Guide*. London: HarperCollins.

Hume, K. 1984. *Fantasy and Mimesis: Responses to Reality in Western Literature*. New York: Methuen.

Jenkins, H. 1992. *Textual Poachers: Television Fans and Participatory Culture*. London: Routledge.

Jones, T, dir. 1983. *The Meaning of Life*. London: Celandine Films / Monty Python Partnership.

Lacan, J. 1977. *Écrits: A Selection*. Translated by A. Sheridan. London: Tavistock/Routledge.

Leavis, F. R. 1948. *The Great Tradition*. London: Chatto & Windus.

Lewis, C. S. 1952. *The Voyage of the "Dawn Treader."* London: Geoffrey Bles.

Lewis, C. S. 1956. *The Last Battle*. London: Bodley Head.

Lewis, C. S. 1966. Sometimes Fairy Stories May Say Best What's to Be Said. In *Of Other Worlds: Essays and Stories*, edited by Walter Hooper, 35–38. London: Geoffrey Bles.

Manlove, C. N. 1975. *Modern Fantasy: Five Studies*. Cambridge: Cambridge University Press.

Nell, V. 1988. *Lost in a Book: The Psychology of Reading for Pleasure*. New Haven, CT: Yale University Press

Nikolajeva, M. 1988. *The Magic Code: The Use of Magical Patterns in Fantasy for Children*. Stockholm: Almqvist & Wiksell.

Pavel, T. 1986. *Fictional Worlds*. Cambridge, MA: Harvard University Press.

Tolkien, J. R. R. 1964. On Fairy-Stories. In *Tree and Leaf*, 11–70. London: Allen & Unwin.

Vince, J. 2004. *Introduction to Virtual Reality*. London: Springer.

Woolley, B. 1992. *Virtual Worlds: A Journey in Hype and Hyperreality*. Oxford: Blackwell.

Yolen, J. 2000. *Touch Magic: Fantasy, Faerie & Folklore in the Literature of Childhood*. Rev. ed. Atlanta, GA: August House.

Zipes, J. 1979. *Breaking the Magic Spell: Radical Theories of Folk and Fairy Tales*. London: Heinemann Educational.

Zipes, J. 1983. *Fairy Tales and the Art of Subversion: The Classical Genre for Children and the Process of Civilization*. London: Heinemann.

Žižek, S. 1997. Cyberspace, or, The Unbearable Closure of Being. In *The Plague of Fantasies*, 127–167. New York: Verso.

CHAPTER 16

HISTORY AND CULTURAL HERITAGE IN VIRTUAL ENVIRONMENTS

ERIK CHAMPION

THE potential of virtual reality technology applied to history and to cultural heritage appears to be rich and promising. Teaching history through digitally simulated "learning by doing" is an incredibly understudied research area and is of vital importance to a richer understanding of culture and place. However, many issues await to confront us: potential confusion between what is the past and what is history; the issue of realism when applied to the simulated portrayal of history and heritage; effective and meaningful interaction; how to maintain long-term usefulness; the ownership of cultural knowledge before, during, and after it is digitally transmitted across the world; and how we can evaluate the successes and failures of this field.

BACKGROUND

Virtual heritage is considered by many to be a fusion of virtual reality technology with cultural heritage content (see Addison 2000; Addison, Refsland, and Stone 2006; Roussou 2002). Interestingly, the earliest examples of virtual heritage do not appear to be virtual reality per se, but 3D models available either as a museum exhibit, a web-based showcase of technology, or an academic test of augmented reality.

Although there have been earlier examples of digital archaeology (Reilly 1990; Sylaiou and Patias 2004), the Wikipedia lists Dudley Castle as the first example of virtual heritage in a museum, opened by Queen Elizabeth II in 1994 (Wikipedia 2013; Johnson 1996). The user could move either one of two circular buttons to navigate the laser disc-stored computer model "reconstruction" of the castle. The website describes this project as a "Virtual Tour" or as a "Virtual Reality Tour," but there is no head-mounted display, nor a wall projection that changes in viewpoint when users change their position or gaze.

The University of Columbia's Computer Graphics and User Interfaces Lab is credited with the first "mobile augmented reality" (Feiner et al. 1997); it developed augmented reality equipment for "exploring the urban environment" (i.e., heritage tours around their university). Walkers carrying the portable computer as backpack, and wearing a bulky head-tracked, optical see-through, head-worn display, would see a 3D virtual model of the main building of Bloomingdale Asylum, recreated at its original location, imposed over the real and existing campus. GPS tracked the user and updated the image as best it could; an interesting ghosting image resulted from the flickering and latency of the system. Later developments saw an augmented Pompeii developed by the MIRA Lab (Papagiannakis and Magnenat-Thalmann 2007), and ARCHEOGUIDE (Dähne and Karigiannis 2002).

One of the first web-based examples of virtual heritage was both a model of a cultural heritage site and the showcase of new technology; the Virtual Reality Modeling Language (VRML). With its offering of the second version (VRML 2.0) of this declared new 3D standard for web models, Silicon Graphics provided a VRML model of the ancient Aztec city of Tenochtitlán (Harman and Wernecke 1996). VRML was single-user only; browser software was typically buggy, and the models large and very slow.

Perhaps because of these limitations, the VRML model of the Mexican city was also slow and buggy, and there was no external landscape. The city depended on its aquatic surrounds (the original Aztec temple-city was actually a floating island in the middle of a giant lake); and Aztec culture was a vigorous fusion and distillation of earlier Mesoamerican cultures. Neither of these two important cultural and geographic aspects was communicated in the model.

Yet this was a breakthrough as an example of the latest technology offering a view of the past to those who could not travel to Mexico or visualize from drawings (the real Aztec site is now underneath the concrete of Mexico City). The potential of virtual heritage to reveal to the public through the Internet both the established science and reasoned conjectures of archaeologists and anthropologists was now upon us.

There were also computer-based virtual heritage projects in the early 1990s. Learning Sites has described its work on the Egyptian site of Buhen (Learning Sites 2011; Sanders 2008). Later that decade, the Federation of American Scientists (2011) released its educational "Discover Babylon" project, a free downloadable project, but difficult to run on modern computers. Also in America, the historian Roy Rosenweig distributed interactive CDs on American history, which led to the formation in 1994 of the Centre for New Media and History at George Mason University (now the Roy Rosenwald Center for History and New Media).

DEFINING VIRTUAL HERITAGE

Fast-forwarding to the second decade of the twenty-first century, we find virtual heritage projects are still scattered and liable to disappear. While social media has exploded, the technological projects on which many virtual models of cultural heritage sites are based are still single-user, limited in interaction, and often confuse the visitor with either a minimum of navigation cues or far too much overlapping of textual and spatial information (Tost and Economou 2007). Game engines are increasingly used to create digital environments (Anderson et al. 2010), but their genre-related affordances are seldom used, a point I wish to expand on later in this chapter. There are also interesting installation-based virtual heritage sites such as iCinema, the Panoscope of Laval University Quebec, the web-based and downloadable Virtual Museum of the Via Flaminia, and huge planetarium displays such as at the Foundation of the Hellenic World, in Athens, the curved wall of the Earth Theatre at the Carnegie Mellon Museum of Natural History, or the large VR theater at the University of California, Los Angeles. Yet virtual heritage projects dependent on the traditional examples of virtual reality technology, head-mounted displays and CAVEs, are few and far between.

And this is perplexing, for head mounted displays (HMDs) and CAVEs (Cave Automatic Virtual Environments) are arguably integral to the conventional definition of virtual reality as requiring spatial presence and head tracking (there are several such examples in this book). For example, Bryson (1996) defined virtual reality in an article in *Communications of the ACM*.

> Virtual reality is the use of computers and human-computer interfaces to create the effect of a three-dimensional world containing interactive objects with a strong sense of three-dimensional presence.

He also stressed the importance of using HMDs or CAVEs, for VR apparently requires "a head-tracked, usually stereoscopic, display that presents the virtual world from the user's current head position, including the visual cues required so the virtual scene is perceived as independent of the user, that is, has 'object constancy,' while the user moves about."

I have three issues with the above definition in regards to virtual heritage. Famous examples of virtual heritage tend to be desktop-based or fixed wall installations, and do not change according to the "user's current head position." There are many such examples of game engines and desktop-based digital worlds that can be labeled as "virtual heritage." For example, the *Forbidden City: Beyond Space & Time* (IBM's modification of the Torque game engine to showcase The Forbidden City of China); the *Discover Babylon* free and downloadable PC game; *Ancient Rome 3D* runs in Google Earth (see also the Rome Reborn project); the Building Virtual Rome case studies; downloadable Unreal Tournament ancient history models;[1] Google Warehouse models; or *Playing the Past*, the commercial serious learning game for children about the Black Plague that ravaged Europe.

Second, there appears to be an ocular-centric bias to early notions of virtual reality, (nonsighted people surely perceive a form of reality), and even augmented reality experts are now moving away from a visual-only definition of virtual reality and mixed reality (Azuma 2004; May 2004), but there are specific implications of this traditional definition of virtual reality when employed in the services of cultural heritage.

Third, virtual heritage is concerned with culture, which is not directly a question of "spatial presence." For example, UNESCO (2003) definitions of cultural heritage have widened in recent years to include the notion of intangible cultural heritage, the "practices, representations, expressions, as well as the knowledge and skills, that communities, groups and, in some cases, individuals recognize as part of their cultural heritage." This new and more inclusive viewpoint necessitates that virtual heritage considers the nonmaterial and even the nonscientific.

In line with this more generous interpretation of virtual heritage, Stone and Ojika (2000) published a definition of virtual heritage that offers a point of difference to scientific virtual reality environments:

> [Virtual heritage is] the use of computer-based interactive technologies to record, preserve, or recreate artefacts, sites and actors of historic, artistic, religious, of cultural significance and to deliver the results openly to a global audience in such a way as to provide formative educational experiences through electronic manipulations of time and space.

Unfortunately, virtual heritage projects may not appear to be computer-based, and some authors have even argued that noncomputer displays such as nineteenth-century cycloramas are a form or at least a forerunner of virtual heritage (Jacobson 2008). Sometimes the knowledge is not appropriate for consumption by global audiences, and the issue of recreation, reconstruction, or simulation is a vexing one. For despite its name, does a virtual heritage model really preserve? These considerations lead me to suggest an alternative definition: virtual heritage is the attempt to convey not just the appearance but also the meaning and significance of cultural artifacts and the associated social agency that designed and used them, through the use of interactive and immersive digital media.

ISSUES AND OBJECTIVES

In a publication cowritten with the archeologist Laia Tost (Tost and Champion 2011), I proposed six objectives to improve research into and development of virtual heritage environments. First, we should meticulously and comprehensively capture objects and processes of scientific, social, or spiritual value. Second, we should present this information as accurately, authentically, and engagingly as possible. Third, we should distribute the project in a sensitive, safe, and durable manner to as wide and long-term an audience as possible. Fourth, we should provide an effective and inspirational learning environment appropriate to the content and to the audience. Fifth, we should allow the possibility to participate in its construction. Finally, we should attempt to carefully evaluate the project's effectiveness with regards to the above aims in order to improve both the project in particular and virtual heritage in general.

The Capture and Display of Data

There is an important link between the capture of data and the display of data. First, increasing computational power, increasing ability to record and project a digital version of reality, is irrelevant if the data to be simulated existed in the past. It may even be dangerous, implying by its certainty a concrete reality (Eiteljorg 1998), which we are in fact only extrapolating from unreliable sources, our imagination, or the memory of others.

In popular usage there seems to be a conflation between the word "virtual" meaning to have the effect of the "real" without actually having material or form and as a synonym for the word "digital." Further, "appears to be real" could mean "An object looks like something that really exists," or "I can believe that it exists." Designers can use this conflation to persuade the viewer that high-resolution images imply a high degree of archaeological certainty when this is not the case (Eiteljorg 1998). An emphasis on visual representation and realism is thus not always of primary interest to archaeologists (Kensek, Dodd, and Cipolla 2002), social scientists such as Gillings and Goodrick (1996) and Anderson (2004), or to virtual heritage specialists such as Roussou and Drettakis (2005).

Authenticity and Realism

The term "virtual" implies an object that is indistinguishable from an object that physically exists, apart from its lack of physicality, or ability to affect the physical world. The comparatively recent depiction of virtual reality in popular culture, films, television, and science fiction novels emphasizes the notion of the virtual as digital simulacra, a complete and indistinguishable mirroring of physical reality created and maintained by vast data and computational power. Such a popular concept is dangerous in the area of virtual heritage for a multitude of reasons.

A representation of current reality may induce the untrained eye of the general public to believe that the original inhabitants perceived as we do. Such an inducement may diminish the understood cultural significance of the original site. According to some archaeological theorists (Renfrew 1994), an attempt at realism may conflict with interpretation.

The issue is also a problem for the designer; many designers aim for levels of detail that are never noticed, or perhaps even considered important, by general members of the public. The user requirement for a degree of realism may also vary between say, an archaeologist and a member of the general public. "Heritage always has been about people, but the challenge today is to make it relevant to a much wider section of people, and that emphasis will not necessarily be on the conservation of concrete objects" (Howard 2003, 50, 157). So while mythology and the use or implied inhabitation may not be scientifically accurate, it can afford more of a sense of place to members of the general public.

As Shackley (2001, 27) has noted, public expectation and the journey may be as important as the visit itself. If content designers view virtual heritage environments as stand-alone recreations of objects, visitors may be short-changed in terms of the learning experience. They will not have the background contextual knowledge of the archaeologist; nor can they be relied on to possess a well-trained deductive logic or a scientifically honed ability to create and test hypotheses.

Long-Term Usage, Technology, Content, and Research Data

There has been an explosion in virtual heritage conferences this century. In the last year alone, there have been calls for digital cultural heritage or virtual heritage papers by Virtual Systems and Multimedia (VSMM), ACM Virtual Reality Software and Technology (VRST), VAST (International Symposium on Virtual Reality, Archaeology and Cultural Heritage), DIME (Digital Interactive Media Entertainment and Arts Conference), Archäologie & Computer Games Learning Society, and more singular events, such as "High-Tech Heritage: How Are Digital Technologies Changing Our Views of the Past?" New Heritage Forum, and the Serious Games Summit, just to name a few. Museums and the Web and iCHIM (International Cultural Heritage Informatics Meetings) have published related work, and there is also the Digital Humanities series of conferences.

So an outside observer may believe that such academic interest, coupled with recent advances in virtual reality (VR), specifically in virtual environment technology and evaluation, would prepare one for designing a successful virtual heritage environment. Ironically (for a heritage-related field), these papers are not always archived, freely accessible to the public, and seldom if ever contain direct links to the projects being discussed. As virtual heritage projects are often one-off projects, criticism may not help improve them.

However, we can hold out hope for recent developments in Digital Humanities such as DHCommons and the Open Library of Humanities, as well as the planned cohosting and collaboration of many of theses conferences. A fully archived, publicly accessible archive, with links between projects, tools, methods, and publications, would be a great step forward for the field.

Effectiveness and Educational Value Requires Interaction

History is not a blueprint but an intersubjectively inscribed mass of interpretations, actions, intentions, and beliefs. Yet most digital simulations lack change, or interaction, or the ability to store interaction history. For example, many virtual heritage sites have brilliantly detailed temples, but no people, and no tasks to solve.

Conversely, for activity-based virtual environments, (such as games), user-based tasks are required. Participants are really visitors rather than actors or role-players; they do not learn more about themselves or the world through activity; they solve puzzles and complete tasks but do not reflect or learn more about the uniqueness of the world or themselves.

It could be counterargued that computer games featuring history and heritage can be used and interacted with in a meaningful way by teachers and students (which is the argument of McCall 2011). While I mostly agree, it also depends on the interrelation of teacher and student, and does not fully immerse the student in the *there* of virtual heritage environments. For example, Gaver and colleagues (2004, 888) write that the difference between ludic systems and typical computer systems is the following: "If a system can easily be used to achieve practical tasks, this will distract from the possibilities it offers for more playful engagement." This is a continual issue with learning environments in general.

Hein (1991) also argues that interactivity in exhibits creates more engagement by allowing users to apply the tool directly to their own life. Yet activity per se is not cultural; the visitors are not individually recognized and remembered. Allowing multiple participants to enter a virtual environment together may increase the chance of social presence, and Lave and Wenger (1991) agree; for them learning is transmitted, discovered, or "experienced in interaction with others." Unfortunately, the presence of others may actually impede or distort our understanding of different cultures.

We also seem to have inside our heads an inclination to situate through rituals and through habits of going about our daily lives. Tilley notes (1999, 29): "Rituals not only say something, they do something." Hodder attempts to show how hermeneutics (the study of interpretation, originally of historic texts) could be used in archaeology, and he explains that "ritual regulates the relationship between people and environment" (1986, 23) and artifacts indicate the shared intentions of their creators (25). Place-making is not the capturing of an evocative image of a mysterious temple, but it is more the triggering of *placeholders*, symbols that aid and define our daily activities. A place can also carry cultural indications of inhabitation driven by a cultural perspective similar to or different from our own. So a virtual heritage environment should allow us to see through the eyes of the original inhabitants, or at least feel that this place once belonged to someone else.

Yet how does one design for a cultural ritual taking place in a particular cultural place in virtual heritage environments? Digital environments typically lack an in-world social authority or audience to ensure rituals are practiced correctly; participants are not fully physiologically immersed in the digital space; they lack the means to fully teach ritualistic practice; they also lack reasons and incentives to develop and refine rituals through long-term practice.

In 2007 Bharat Dave and I proposed a new categorization of virtual environments in response to an ACADIA 2001 paper by Kalay and Marx (2001) that described eight types of virtual places, but these notions were descriptive rather than prescriptive. In the Champion and Dave (2007) paper, virtual environments are instead classified by overall design goal. The first is visualization-based, the second is activity-based, and the third covers "inscriptive" (hermeneutic) environments.

The first type of virtual environment is visual (sometimes with sound). You can walk around, zoom in and out of objects (say buildings), and that is about it. Your orientation and view can be manipulated, but the environment is not really interactive, as it does not affect your actions, and you cannot modify it. A three-dimensional fly-through of a building is one example. The advantage and disadvantage is that the environment is really a finished product; the inhabitants do not affect it, and so the model manages to be definitive, immutable, and appears consistent in appearance, which, however, is at odds with objects that change over time through fashion, fate, or neglect.

As Meister (1998) writes in his discussion of temples, in order to understand the value of a building to the culture that builds and maintains it, we need to understand how people interact with it. For early virtual heritage projects (see, for example, the case studies in Barceló, Forte, and Sanders 2000), static computer models may prove suitable for education purposes when an archaeologist or local expert is a guide; yet the information and the discursive content becomes entrenched when viewed by a solitary audience.

Game designers may also be led to believe that games using historical characters, events, or settings are readily adaptable and immediately appropriate to virtual heritage, but there are fundamental conceptual issues still to be addressed. For example, to what extent is the past more or less important or retrievable than history, and how is it attainable through interaction (as otherwise there is little point to using virtual environments)? One answer may be adopting virtual reality to represent the past or online digital worlds to represent the future, but it is still too easy to be taken in by the lure of technology and forget to concentrate on enhancing the user experience. For example, many have made the case for using game engines for virtual heritage projects (Stone 2005; Lucey-Roper 2006; Bottino and Martina 2010).

Much easier to upgrade, install, and replace, the most popular form of virtual environment is now arguably the computer game (Smith 2008). Current game consoles and desktop computers rival supercomputers of just a decade ago in power and performance. Games have context (user-based tasks), navigation reminders, inventories, records of interaction history (i.e., damage to surroundings), social agency, and levels of personalization. Games are a familiar medium to users (Petty, n.d.; Cuenca López and Martín Cáceres 2010), and, when in game mode, abstraction can be just as engaging to users as a sense of realism.

Games also form part of cultural learning and how to follow social rules, or learn about physical rules of the world, without risking personal injury (Schank 1990; Miller 1991; Petty, n.d.). We socially learn (by stories, and commands), we learn by observation (observing cause and effect, emulation, and by imitation), and we learn by play (puzzles, toys, and games).

There are indisputably certain pedagogical techniques that virtual heritage environments can learn from game design. Yet, despite the rich detailing of environments, agents, and artifacts, three-dimensional adventure games do not have a rich sense of cultural immersion. While not true for all games, the typical goal in adventure games is for collecting artifacts for the vanquishing of others, social interaction is limited to violence, time spent on reflection is punished, and we do not develop any feeling for the perspectives of the local inhabitants as their actions are typically "fight or flight."

Without a huge amount of time spent in a virtual environment, it is also doubtful that our cultural and social view of the environment will change very much. To learn another language, we can attend class, but to think in another language and to be accepted by others without thinking we have to immerse ourselves in the actual context over a long period of time, long enough to learn from trial and error. So there are significant design challenges for virtual heritage environments: to portray accurate yet believable content; to provide appropriate yet meaningful interaction; and to link both content and interaction leading to significant and useful knowledge in an abridged time period.

Participation Requires Ownership

Sardar (1996) has attacked cyberspace directly, and virtual heritage indirectly, as a form of "museumization":

> Cyberspace is particularly geared toward the erasure of all non-Western histories. Once a culture has been "stored" and "preserved" in digital forms, opened up to anybody who wants to explore it from the comfort of their armchair, then it becomes more real than the real thing. Who needs the arcane and esoteric real thing anyway? In the postmodern world where things have systematically become monuments, nature has been transformed into "reserve," and knowledge is giving way to information and data, it is only a matter of time before other people and their cultures become "models," so many zeros and ones in cyberspace, exotic examples for scholars, voyeurs and other interested parties to load on their machines and look at. Cyberspace is a giant step forward towards museumization of the world: for anything remotely different from Western culture will exist only in digital form.

The above paragraph is no doubt well intentioned, but it may persuade the reader that non-Western cultures are not interested in virtual heritage when that is clearly not the case. Perhaps the most pressing danger about the above paragraph is that it gives no clear alternative to digital environments; nor does it provide convincing proof that Western culture and only Western culture is strictly museum-fixated (and museum here seems to be used in the narrowest of senses). For example, archaeology itself is not a Western profession; there are historical accounts of two Babylonian kings who were archaeologists, Nebuchadnezzar II and Nabonidus (Spears 1996; Johnston 2010). Apart from the above attack on the West (and an overly strong conflation between tourism as convenience and digital media as mindless edutainment), the issue of ownership of virtual heritage equipment, data, and the overall intellectual property is indeed a perplexing problem that has not yet been fully resolved (Skeates 2000).

Evaluation

Do we have concrete examples of meaningful interaction in virtual heritage environments? According to the few existing user studies, so far this area is still too undeveloped (Mosaker 2001; Roussou 2005; Tost and Economou 2007; Rodriguez-Echavarria et al. 2007). While even archaeologists and technical experts have warned against an overemphasis on technical achievements, we still lack solid test cases that attempt to both build and test virtual history projects for the end user (who perhaps should not just be involved at the end of the project).

The ethnographic techniques used by researchers may be effective in recording activity, but they do not directly indicate the potential mental transformations of perspective that result from being subjectively immersed in a different type of cultural environment. How can users learn via interaction the meanings and values of others—do we need to interact as the original inhabitants did? How can we find out how they interacted and, through the limited and constraining nature of current technology, ensure interaction is meaningful, educational, and enjoyable? How do we know when meaningful learning is reached?

Insko (2003) argues that because of the many definitions of presence, one should try to evaluate it with as many measures as possible. Insko adds that a good metatest of questionnaires is to see if they distinguish between virtual presence and real presence. In other words, for many of the presence researchers, evaluation of virtual presence is based on an approximation toward real-world presence.

Interesting as this may be, real-world tests will not necessarily be of help in assessing heritage reconstructions, unless the virtual experience is supposed to tally as accurately as possible with a given and accessible real-world experience of that culture. This is a problem if the real culture being simulated no longer exists in one place or at the current time, or if the cultural knowledge is fragmented or only circulated among experts and not the general public.

In a widely cited paper, Lessiter and colleagues (2001) list four criteria they believe determine presence and immersion in virtual environments. The four criteria are physical space, engagement, naturalism or realism, and negative feelings (such as phobia, motion sickness etc.). We could add the concept of cultural presence, the sense that a cultural viewpoint *inhabited* the site.

This leads us to the thorny issue of how to evaluate such a concept. We could use questionnaires; we could test the ability of participants to extrapolate general cultural rules or other information and apply them to other heritage sites; we could test whether participants could detect other players or nonplaying characters that appeared to belong to or not belong to the resident culture. We could also test for engagement using questionnaires, by recording physiological data, or by testing the memory recall of the participants. A further option is to give users tasks to complete, and record their performance. However such testing only records their technical proficiency, and not necessarily their cultural understanding.

CONCLUSION

The above chapter has listed six major issues. I have argued that the way data is captured does not always convey the processes, decisions, and values inherent in the act itself. And how this information is to be presented raises issues of what is authentic and also how to convey the accuracy or assumptions without losing or misguiding the public. We also need to improve the accessibility of these projects to the general public. This means we need to consider the ways in which different audiences learn. If possible we should invite the audience to debate, participate, and contribute to the ongoing project in order both to educate the public and to maintain the project and to ensure both its usefulness and its longevity. However, how we evaluate these projects raises a myriad of interesting challenges.

Archaeological and architectural digital simulations have traditionally been concerned with exact replication of facts rather than with understanding, for the latter raises the annoying dilemma of how to present scientific uncertainty. For a computer model almost invariably implies certitude and replication of the "facts." Until recently, accurate digital simulations of historically uncertain or controversial findings have been left unquestioned. Yet there are educational and scientific dangers in many current computer simulations that are based on *apparent* mimetic certainty and not on the cultural agency that informs understanding.

To clarify these issues, I suggested a simple classification of virtual heritage environments. The first type of environment surrounds and orientates us (spatial presence), the second functions (allows us to do things), and the third identifies and embodies us or allows us to interpret the cultural perspective of others (is hermeneutic). Ideally, the third type of environment allows us to recognize, understand, and become (transform our worldview), but it is hard to see how it can work in practice, especially if informed guides are not available.

There is also the option of classifying by game mechanics, by platform, by content, or by audience. Unfortunately, the range of data, potential audience, and supporting technology is dynamic, vast, and highly content-specific. I have also briefly mentioned issues in the use of game engines and game genres; engagement versus learning and interaction versus historical accuracy are key concerns.

For various reasons, evaluation of the learning inside virtual heritage environments has been relatively context-free, not designed for user understanding of other cultures. Technology can overwhelm the content, especially when the knowledge driving the virtual simulation is incomplete, complex, or contradictory; and the continual need for research funding can actually impede research rather than develop it.

If virtual heritage has as its aim to educate and engage the general public on the culture of the original site, cultural artifacts, oral traditions, and artworks, then the field needs to advance not only in technological advances but also in philosophical and creative ways, especially in regards to the issues of realism, interaction, evaluation, and ownership.

NOTE

1. From http://publicvr.org, accessed June 18, 2013.

REFERENCES

Addison, A. C. 2000. Emerging Trends in Virtual Heritage. *Multimedia, IEEE* 7 (2): 22–25.

Addison, A. C., S. Refsland, and R. Stone. 2006. Virtual Heritage Guest Editors' Introduction. *Presence: Teleoperators and Virtual Environments* 15 (3): iii–iv.

Anderson, E., L. McLoughlin, F. Liarokapis, C. Peters, P. Petridis, and S. de Freitas. 2010. Developing Serious Games for Cultural Heritage: A State-of-the-Art Review. *Virtual Reality* 14 (4): 255–275.

Anderson, M. 2004. Computer Games and Archaeological Reconstruction: The Low Cost VR. In *CAA 2003—Enter the Past + Workshop 8—Archäologie und Computer Conference*, edited by Karin Ausserer, Wolfgang Börner, Maximilian Goriany, and Lisa Karlhuber-Vöckl, 521–524. Vienna: BAR.

Azuma, R. 2004. Overview of Augmented Reality. In *ACM SIGGRAPH 2004 Conference: Course Notes*. Los Angeles, CA: ACM. http://doi.acm.org/10.1145/1103900.1103926. Accessed August 8, 2013.

Barceló, J. A., M. Forte, and D. H. Sanders. 2000. *Virtual Reality in Archaeology Computer Applications and Quantitative Methods in Archaeology*. BAR S843. Oxford: Archaeopress.

Boland, P., and C. Johnson. 1996. Archaeology as Computer Visualization: "Virtual Tours" of Dudley Castle c. 1550. In *Imaging the Past: Electronic Imaging and Computer Graphics in Museums and Archaeology*, edited by Tony Higgins, Peter Main, and Janet Lang, 227–234. London: British Museum Press.

Bottino, A., and A. Martina. 2010. The Role of Computer Games Industry and Open Source Philosophy in the Creation of Affordable Virtual Heritage Solutions. In *New Trends in Technologies: Devices, Computer, Communication and Industrial Systems*, edited by Meng Joo Er. Rijeka: Sciyo. doi: 10.5772/10424.

Bryson, S. 1996. Virtual Reality in Scientific Visualization. *Communications of the ACM* 39 (5): 63–71. http://www.intechopen.com/books/new-trends-in-technologies—devices—computer—communication-and-industrial-systems/the-role-of-computer-games-industry-and-open-source-philosophy-in-the-creation-of-affordable-virtual. Accessed August 8, 2013.

Champion, E., and B. Dave. 2007. Dialing Up the Past. In *Theorizing Digital Cultural Heritage: A Critical Discourse*, edited by Fiona Cameron and Sarah Kenderdine, 333–348. Cambridge, MA: MIT Press.

Cuenca López, J. M., and M. C. Martín. 2010. Virtual Games in Social Science Education. *Computers and Education* 55 (3): 1336–1345.

Dähne, P., and J. N. Karigiannis. 2002. Archeoguide: System Architecture of a Mobile Outdoor Augmented Reality System. In *Proceedings of the International Symposium on Mixed and Augmented Reality (ISMAR'02)*, 263–264. Darmstadt, Germany: IEE Computer Society.

Eiteljorg, H. 1998. Photorealistic Visualizations May Be Too Good. *CSA Newsletter* 11 (2). http://www.csanet.org/newsletter/fall98/nlf9804.html. Accessed June 19, 2013.

Federation of American Scientists. 2011. *Discover Babylon*. http://www.discoverbabylon.org/. Accessed June 19, 2013.

Feiner, S., B. MacIntyre, T. Hollerer, and A. Webster. 1997. A Touring Machine: Prototyping 3D Mobile Augmented Reality Systems for Exploring the Urban Environment. Paper presented to the First International Symposium on Wearable Computers, October 13–14, Washington, DC.

Gaver, W. W., J. Bowers, A. Boucher, H. Gellerson, S. Pennington, A. Schmidt, A. Steed, N. Villars, and B. Walker. 2004. The Drift Table: Designing for Ludic Engagement. In *CHI '04 Extended Abstracts on Human Factors in Computing Systems*, 885–900. Vienna: ACM.

Gillings, M., and G. T. Goodrick. 1996. Sensuous and Reflexive GIS: Exploring Visualisation and VRML. *Internet Archaeology* 1. http://intarch.ac.uk/journal/issue1/. Accessed June 19, 2013.

Harman, J., and J. Wernecke. 1996. *The VRML 2.0 Handbook: Building Moving Worlds on the Web*. Reading, MA: Addison-Wesley Professional.

Hein, G. E. 1991. Constructivist Learning Theory. In The Museum and the Needs of People. Paper presented to the CECA (International Committee of Museum Educators) Conference, Jerusalem.   http://www.exploratorium.edu/ifi/resources/constructivistlearning.html. Accessed June 19, 2013.

Hodder, I. 1986. *Reading the Past: Current Approaches to Interpretation in Archaeology*. Cambridge: Cambridge University Press.

Howard, P. 2003. *Heritage: Management, Interpretation, Identity*. New York: Continuum.

Insko, B. E. 2003. Measuring Presence: Subjective, Behavioral and Physiological Methods. In *Being There: Concepts, Effects and Measurement of User Presence in Synthetic Environments*, edited by Giuseppe Riva, Fabrizio David, and Winjand A. IJsselsteijn, 109–119. Amsterdam: IOS Press.

Jacobson, J. 2008. Ancient Architecture in Virtual Reality; Does Immersion Really Aid Learning? Ph.D. diss., University of Pittsburgh.

Johnston, G. 2010. Nabodinus, Last Great King of Babylon. *Archaeology Expert*. http://www.archaeologyexpert.co.uk/nabodinus.html. Accessed August 8, 2013.

Kalay, Y., and J. J. Marx. 2001. Architecture and the Internet: Designing Places in Cyberspace. In *Proceedings of ACADIA 2001: Reinventing the Discourse*, 230–240. Pomona, California.

Kensek, K. M., L. S. Dodd, and N. Cipolla. 2002. Fantastic Reconstructions or Reconstructions of the Fantastic? Tracking and Presenting Ambiguity, Alternatives, and Documentation in Virtual Worlds. Paper presented to "Thresholds between Physical and Virtual," ACADIA 2002 Conference, Pomona, CA.

Lave, J., and E. Wenger. 1991. *Situated Learning: Legitimate Peripheral Participation*. Cambridge: Cambridge University Press.

Learning Sites. 2011. The Transition to VR: The Fortress of Buhen, Egypt. *Learning Sites*. February 11. http://www.learningsites.com/EarlyWork/buhen-2.htm. Accessed June 19, 2013.

Lessiter, J., J. Freeman, E. Keogh, and J. Davidoff. 2001. A Cross-Media Presence Questionnaire: The ITC-Sense of Presence Inventory. *Presence: Teleoperators and Virtual Environments* 10 (3): 282–297.

Lucey-Roper, M. 2006. Discover Babylon: Creating a Vivid User Experience by Exploiting Features of Video Games and Uniting Museum and Library Collections. In *Museums and the Web 2006: Proceedings*, edited by J. Trant and D. Bearman. Toronto: Archives and Museum Informatics.   http://www.archimuse.com/mw2006/papers/lucey-roper/lucey-roper.html. Accessed August 8, 2013.

May, M. 2004. Wayfinding, Ships and Augmented Reality. In *Virtual Applications: Applications with Virtual Inhabited 3d Worlds*, edited by P. B. Anderson and L. Qvortrup, 212–233. London: Springer-Verlag.

McCall, J. 2011. *Gaming the Past: Using Video Games to Teach Secondary History.* New York: Routledge.

Meister, M. W. 1998. The Getty Project: Self-Preservation and the Life of Temples. Paper presented to ACSAA Symposium, Charleston, SC, November. http://www.arthistory. upenn.edu/meister/acsaa.html. Accessed June 19, 2013.

Miller, G. L. 1991. *Approaches to Material Culture Research for Historical Archaeologists: A Reader from Historical Archaeology.* N.p.: Society for Historical Archaeology.

Mosaker, L. 2001. Visualising Historical Knowledge Using Virtual Reality Technology. *Digital Creativity* 12 (1): 15–25.

Papagiannakis, G., and N. Magnenat-Thalmann. 2007. Mobile Augmented Heritage: Enabling Human Life in Ancient Pompeii. *International Journal of Architectural Computing* 2 (5): 395–415.

Petty, A. n.d. Discovering Babylon: The Opportunities, Challenges and Irresistible Potential of Video Games as an Educational Medium. *Society of Biblical Literature.* http://sbl-site.org/ Article.aspx?ArticleID=672. Accessed June 19, 2013.

Reilly, P. 1990. Towards a Virtual Archaeology. In *Computer Applications in Archaeology 1990,* edited by K. Lockyear and S. Rahtz, 133–139. Oxford: British Archaeological Reports.

Renfrew, C. 1994. Towards a Cognitive Archaeology. In *The Ancient Mind: Elements of Cognitive Archaeology,* edited by C. Renfrew and Ezra B. W. Zubrow, 3–12. Cambridge: Cambridge University Press.

Rodriguez-Echavarria, K., D. Morris, C. Moore, D. Arnold, J. Glauert, and V. Jennings. 2007. Developing Effective Interfaces for Cultural Heritage 3D Immersive Environments. In *The 8th International Symposium on Virtual Reality, Archaeology and Cultural Heritage VAST (2007),* edited by D. Arnold, F. Niccolucci and A. Chalmers, 93–99. Brighton: Eurographics.

Roussou, M. 2002. Virtual Heritage: From the Research Lab to the Broad Public. In *Virtual Archaeology: Proc. of the VAST 2000 Euroconference,* edited by F. Niccolucci, 93–100. Arezzo, Italy: ACM Press.

Roussou, M. 2005. Can Interactivity in Virtual Environments Enable Conceptual Learning? Paper presented to the Seventh Virtual Reality International Conference (VRIC) and First International VR-Learning Seminar, Laval, Paris.

Roussou, M., and G. Drettakis. 2005. Can VR Be Useful and Usable in Real-World Contexts? Observations from the Application and Evaluation of VR in Realistic Usage Conditions. Paper presented to the HCI International 2005 Conference, First International Conference on Virtual Reality, Las Vegas, NV.

Sanders, D. 2008. Why Do Virtual Heritage? *Archaeology.* March 13. http://www.archaeology. org/online/features/virtualheritage/. Accessed June 19, 2013.

Sardar, Z. 1996. alt.civilizations.faq: Cyberspace as the Darker Side of the West. In *Cyberfutures: Culture and Politics on the Information Superhighway,* edited by Z. Sardar and J. Ravetz, 14–41. London: Pluto Press.

Schank, R. C. 1990. *Tell Me a Story: A New Look at Real and Artificial Memory.* New York: Scribner.

Shackley, M. 2001. *Managing Sacred Sites: Service Provision and Visitor Experience.* New York: Continuum.

Skeates, R. 2000. *Debating the Archaeological Heritage.* London: Duckworth.

Smith, S. P., and D. Trenholme. 2008. Computer Game Engines for Developing First-Person Virtual Environments. *Virtual Reality* 12 (3): 181–187.

Spears, A. 1996. Evolution in Context: "Deep Time," Archaeology and the Post-Romantic Paradigm. *Comparative Literature* 48 (4): 343–358.

Stone, R. J. 2005. Serious Gaming—Virtual Reality's Saviour? Paper presented to VSMM 2005 Conference, Belgium.

Stone, R. J., and T. Ojika. 2000. Virtual Heritage: What Next? *Multimedia, IEEE* 7 (2): 73–74.

Sylaiou, S., and P. Patias. 2004. Virtual Reconstructions in Archaeology and Some Issues for Consideration. *IMEROS: An Annual Journal for Culture and Technology* (4) 1. http://www.ime.gr/publications/print/imeros/en/04/article01.html. Accessed August 8, 2013.

Tilley, C. Y. 1999. *Metaphor and Material Culture*. Oxford: Blackwell.

Tost, L. P., and E. Champion. 2011. Evaluating Presence in Cultural Heritage Projects. In *International Journal of Heritage Studies* 18 (1). doi:10.1080/13527258.2011.577796.

Tost, L. P., and M. Economou. 2007. Evaluating the Impact of New Technologies on Cultural Heritage Visitors. In *Technology Strategy, Management and Socio-Economic Impact*, edited by J. Kaminski, J. McLoughlin, and B. Sodagar, 109–121. Budapest: Archaeolingua.

UNESCO. 2003. Text of the Convention for the Safeguarding of Intangible Cultural Heritage. In *The General Conference of the United Nations Educational, Scientific and Cultural Organization (UNESCO)*, edited by UNESCO World Heritage, 1–15. Paris: UNESCO.

Wikipedia. 2013. Virtual Heritage. June 9. http://en.wikipedia.org/wiki/Virtual_Heritage. Accessed June 19, 2013.

CHAPTER 17

....

FLIRTING, CHEATING, DATING, AND MATING IN A VIRTUAL WORLD

....

JULIE M. ALBRIGHT AND EDDIE
SIMMENS

EARLY theorists in the field of computer-mediated communication studies thought it unlikely if not impossible to form "normal" relationships over computer networks. Despite these dire predictions, since the advent of the Internet increasing numbers of people have used computers as a means to find and communicate with friends, lovers, and family. From seeking sex partners for casual "hookups" to finding dating relationships and marital partners, online dating has exploded, recently surpassing meeting through friends to become the third most common way people meet their spouses in the United States and Europe. Online matchmaking has evolved along with digital technology, targeting increasingly specialized audiences, from Jewish daters to those seeking a married partner for consensual cheating, to "sugar daddy" sites where young women seek older men for financial support in exchange for sex. This chapter addresses the rise of Internet-fueled romance from its initial beginnings in the 1990s, and will examine the research in this area ranging from initial relationship formation to infidelity and relationship dissolution. Questions to be explored include these: Which type of online relationship has grown the most/fastest? Which has grown least? Who is successful in online love? Given the digital divide, is there any demographic that has resolutely stayed "offline?" What has been the impact of the proliferation of smartphones? This chapter will begin by surveying the research on online dating and matchmaking, including the technologies that made it possible, then examining the directions it has taken in recent years as digital communications technologies have become faster, cheaper, more ubiquitous, and mobile, and will close by looking at future directions.

FROM BOMBS TO BOMBSHELLS: THE EVOLUTION OF ONLINE RELATIONSHIPS

Young adults—those "Gen Y" or "millennials" born in the 1980s to 1994—grew up as "digital natives" in a world where they could take the Internet and digital social connectivity for granted (Howe and Strauss 2000; Prensky 2001). Seventy-five percent of them have created a social media profile, and a third visit a social media site "several times a day" to keep in touch with friends, family, and romantic relationships (Morejon 2011). Such unremarkable behaviors enacted every day were unthinkable in the early days of the Internet, and indeed, online matchmaking may still seem impersonal, strange, or even frightening to those who haven't spent as much time online, like some baby boomers or those from the "Silent Generation" (pre–World War II) (Anderson 2005). Yet mediated matchmaking and courtship are not actually products of a brave new digital world, but instead are extensions of previous (albeit slower) mediated communications of romantic love. Historical examples of these include letter-writing by those separated by distance (Decker 2002), or prison walls (Maybin 2000), or "picture brides" in the late 1800s and early 1900s: Unable to marry across racial lines because of miscegenation laws in the United States, lonely male Asian workers facing a paucity of eligible women to marry viewed photos of potential brides, hoping to import one from overseas (Chow 1987). Some of these men misrepresented themselves to their potential brides by sending old photos or ones that inflated their social status or wealth, similar to the deceptions practiced by modern online daters (Whitty and Joinson 2009). Some have even compared online dating to the courtly love of the knights and their "ladies," the foundation of many of our modern Western notions of romantic love (Whitty and Carr 2003). Though mediated courtship is not new, computer communication as the newest form of mediated communication can be viewed as a disruptive technology in terms of altering the "stages" of interaction, the speed of intimacy, and self-disclosure, while (sometimes exponentially) increasing the pool of availables (Lea and Spears 1995).

The Internet was not designed as a venue for online love: Rather, it was created as a stable and reliable means by which academics and defense department workers could carry on wartime digital communications. The advent of the personal computer and the introduction of commercial Internet service providers (ISPs) in the early 1990s changed that, allowing average citizens to go online and communicate. Early computer communication adopters used "dial-up" connections with a modem attached to their phone line to connect to BBSs, or bulletin board systems, hosted on servers usually maintained by Internet hobbyists, a systems operator or SysOp. Since BBS systems were typically local, BBS meets or get-togethers for users to meet one another at a local restaurants or bars became common (BBS Corner 1996). BBS systems largely died out in the mid-1990s, with the advent of large commercial Internet service providers: The first of these was Delphi, which was soon followed by others, including CompuServe, Genie, and America Online (AOL) (Abbate 1999). Although the large commercial services were designed for public use, the nascent online world of cyberspace was intimidating, requiring users to type out tedious and (for many) confusing strings of Unix-based code, to navigate and communicate with other users (Abbate 1999). Typing code created a barrier to access for many of those less technologically inclined, and in the early 1990s, less than 3 percent of those in the United States were online (Wikipedia 2012). Because of the small number of users online at the time, many early online relationships were long-distance affairs, which, as a result, contained a large fantasy element; many early users never even met their online lover face to face (Cooper and Sportolari 1997). By the mid-1990s, America Online introduced the graphical user interface (or GUI) on its commercial service; this technological innovation, combined with millions of disks sent in the mail and given away at supermarkets, drugstores, and other locations for free, promised users who installed the program free hours on the service, encouraging millions of nontechnical people to get online, providing the "tipping point" the Internet needed to move online dating one step closer to the mainstream. As a result of these efforts, by the mid-1990s, AOL had surpassed 10 million users (Wikipedia 2012). AOL was also the first ISP to emphasize user interaction, providing chat rooms that people accessed by clicking large, graphical, intuitive "buttons." It is important to note, however, that AOL's chat rooms were not the first text-based form of computer-mediated romantic interaction. While the Internet was in its infancy in the 1980s, France Télécom was developing its own information "superhighway," known as Minitel. Although different from the Internet in several ways, it did offer many of the same services and information, such as weather forecasts, long-distance banking, and messaging between users. Minitel's chat services (*messageries*) were originally intended to fulfill the social function of putting lonely, shy, and elderly people in contact with each other (Kirmann 1990). However, these chat services eventually evolved into the wildly popular "Pink Minitel," or *messageries roses*, wherein users would exchange erotic messages and form sexual contacts (Dauncey 1997), causing some critics to say the French government was tacitly underwriting sexual crimes (Tempest 1989). The erotic chat services have since disappeared, and recently France Télécom announced that it would be shutting down Minitel (Colchester 2011).

AOL's chat rooms and Minitel's *messageries* foreshadowed the niche dating sites available today, which have titles like *Big Beautiful Women* and *Married but Looking*. Songs like *Computer Love* in 1994 and movies like *You've Got Mail* (1998), starring Tom Hanks and Meg Ryan, popularized online dating, helping move it along into the mainstream, encouraging even more people to try it. Yet paradoxically, as more went online, it became more difficult to connect: Servers quickly overloaded, resulting in a slow and frustrating experience. Users often encountered busy signals, and connection speeds were slow (some called AOL "America Off Line" as a result), making things like exchanging photos difficult if not impossible. To deal with this impediment, many online lovers sent photos via postal mail, while still others met sight unseen—adding to the mystery and excitement of a budding romance, yet just as often leading to disappointment when the person didn't measure up to online expectations (IRL, or "In Real Life," as it was referred to then). One early user described the first time seeing his online lover at the airport by saying, "It was like a door, slamming shut" (Albright 1995).

Technology has improved to the point that both the cost of computers and Internet connectivity has dropped while connection speeds and bandwidth have risen, bringing more users than ever online. As of March 2011, an estimated 2.095 billion people—approximately 30 percent of the world's population—accessed the Internet (Miniwatts 2011). With the growth of the Internet, online dating and matchmaking have burgeoned into a sophisticated, multi-billion-dollar-a-year business. Following the terrorist attacks of September 11, 2001, on the World Trade Center in New York City, Online matchmaking sites experiencing a notable growth spurt: Post 9/11, many people went online seeking the comfort of a relationship, resulting in an 150 percent increase in subscribers on some dating sites (Reagan 2002). Growth in this area has continued: Online matchmaking and dating sites now represent approximately $2.1 billion in yearly revenue in the United States, with over 1,500 active sites (Marketdata Enterprises 2012). The largest dating company, Match, which owns both Match.com and Chemistry.com, generated $343 million in revenue in 2010 and has a reported 1.4 million active subscribers (Boorstin 2010). Recent estimates say users online spend an average of 22 minutes each time they visit an online dating site (Mitchell 2009), totaling approximately 12 hours per week (Frost et al. 2008). With this growing popularity, large matchmaking companies are looking to expand their market: Match is buying online dating companies in the EU to expand its footprint there, and eHarmony is following suit, recently purchasing a 30 percent stake in German firm eDarling.de as well as expanding its eHarmony brand from the United States into Britain, Australia, and China (Brooks 2010).

Early online dating carried with it a "stigma," since the early Internet was largely populated by "computer nerds" (Finkel et al. 2012), so many online daters hid where they actually met, telling friends or family members they met in a bar, club, or other more "typical" place. Yet as more "average" users populate the Internet, this stigma is waning, as online dating moves into the mainstream (Finkel et al. 2012). Large online dating sites like Match and eHarmony show "average" people meeting on TV ads, to help "normalize" online dating, and more people now know someone who has dated online: By 2006, nearly a third of American adults reported knowing someone who had used a dating website, and 15 percent, or 30 million people, said they knew someone who either began a long-term relationship or married someone he or she had met online (Madden and Lenhart 2006). As opposed to just casual "hookups," many are going online seeking a "serious" relationship: sites like eHarmony encourage this, with advertisements promising to help online daters "Meet Your Soulmate." Many are successful at doing so: One recent study found that twice as many marriages occurred between people who met on an online dating site as between those who met in bars, at clubs, and other social events combined (Match.com 2010). Online dating introductions now account for 20 percent of all marriages in the United States, and meeting online has surpassed meeting through friends or meeting at work to become the third most common way that people meet romantic partners (Match.com 2010).

A survey of the online matchmaking genre has revealed the existence of several different types of dating sites:

- Search/sort/match systems, such as RSVP.com.au and Lavalife.com, which allow users to search for prospective partners based on particular characteristics
- Personality-matching systems, such as EHarmony.com, where control over matching people is retained by the site providers and based on personality testing
- Social network systems, such as Frindster.com, which encourages users to introduce people they know to the site and suggest matches between members of the same social networks (Fiore and Donath 2004; Barraket and Henry-Waring 2008)

A fourth category of online matchmaking has emerged recently in conjunction with the proliferation of "smart" devices including Internet-enabled portable smartphones and tablet devices: "apps" that are either linked to one of these three matchmaking site types or act as stand-alone applications. These will be discussed in more detail later on in the chapter.

With the boom in Internet dating, interesting patterns are emerging in terms of who is most likely to seek relationships online: Significantly and notably, though both Gen X and Gen Y have grown up with the Internet, it is now older adults who are most likely to seek (and find) relationships online (Stephure et al. 2009): Baby boomers represent the biggest growth demographic in online dating (*USA Today* 2011), and in the UK, there was a 460 percent increase in people visiting dating sites targeting "mature" daters over 50 between January 2010 and January 2011 (Experian Hitwise 2011). Most online dating and matchmaking sites display a broad sex ratio disparity between women and men: Some industry estimates place it as high as a 2.5 to 1 (Web Personals Online.com). One of the top sites for those seeking "serious" relationships, eHarmony, is said to be 56 percent female and 44 percent male (Quantcast 2012). Sites targeting more "mature" daters may have an even greater sex disparity: During the week of February 10, 2007, Experian Hitwise found that 70 percent of the visitors to SeniorPeopleMeet.com were female (Online Personals Watch, 2007). Notably, the sites within the top 100 dating sites tracked by Experian Hitwise that tipped their sex ratios in favor of males were the ones that target homosexuals, including ManHunt.net, Adam4Adam, and Gay.com personals (Experian Hitwise 2007). The typical online dater now is a woman in her midthirties, with older women in their thirties and forties being more successful at meeting matches than younger women in their twenties (Albright 2008).

TRUTH AND FICTION IN THE FUNHOUSE MIRROR OF ONLINE: THEORETICAL DISCUSSIONS

Researchers have said that online matchmaking and relationship formation has changed the "dance" of courtship and intimacy, by providing an instantly accessible, large pool of availables in an environment that enhances romantic projections (Albright and Conran 2003) and speeds up intimacy and self-disclosure relative to face-to-face interactions, a process Walther (1996) termed "hyperpersonal" communication. Early computer-mediated communication (CMC) research in the 1990s took on a decidedly pessimistic tone, saying that forming intimate relationships online was not possible, because the reduced bandwidth of computer communication resulted in few discernable social cues (Kiesler, Siegel, and McGuire 1984; Siegel et al. 1986; Sproull and Kiesler 1986). Citing social presence theory, researchers posited that fewer social cues would mean that online communicators would be less aware of the social presence of others (Short, Williams, and Christie 1976), leading to messages being more impersonal (Hiltz, Johnson, and Turoff 1986; Rice 1984). Later called the "cues filtered out" approach, it included three main tenets: (1) Computer communication filters out or transmits different cues; (2) Various media filter out or transmit different cues; and (3) Substituting technologically mediated messages for face-to-face communication will result in predictable changes in interpersonal variables (Culnan and Markus 1987). Because of this, online communication came to be viewed as lacking in social cues, as inhibiting a shared social context and reducing the social presence of communicators, and as more impersonal and less intimate than face-to-face communication (Cooper and Sportolari 1997; Sproull and Kiesler 1986; Kiesler, Siegel, and McGuire 1984). Concerns about communication technology's impact on relationships are not new: Experts voiced concerns about "impersonality" and "decreased social presence" when discussing the telephone and telegraph in the 1890s in popular science magazines (Lea and Spears 1995). Anecdotal stories of betrayal, fraud, and abuse were told at the time, serving as a "warning" narrative to those who might have viewed talking on the telephone as the equivalent of face-to-face communication.

Despite the early cynicism, some researchers saw the positives of the Internet for intimate relationship formation, and began to counter the dystopian perspective: Walther (1994) argued that forming personal relationships via computer-mediated communication is not only possible, but that relationships formed online should be considered as "real" and personal as those initiated offline (Walther 1994). Walther and Burgoon (1992) argued that the notion that interpersonal relationships were not possible in CMC because of "cues filtered out" may apply to initial interactions only, positing that CMC relationships may in fact exceed face-to-face relationships in intimacy over time. Walther stated that even with reduced social cues, communicators via CMC do form impressions, though they may form at a slower speed compared to their face-to-face counterparts (Walther 1993). Walther suggested an alternative to the "cues filtered out" approach, one he calls the "social information processing" approach, which assumes people communicating via CMC are driven to form social relationships, and that they do this by forming simple initial impressions, and then test those impressions over time (Walther 1996). Lea and Spears (1995) saw another positive aspect of CMC for intimate relationship formation, in that it expanded people beyond the limits of physical proximity by increasing the "field of availables"; yet recently, some researchers have seen this as a negative, saying that the enlarged pool may in fact lead people to commoditize potential partners and reduce people's willingness to commit to any one person (Albright 2007; Finkel et al. 2012).

Over time, as more people met online and the research literature matured, the findings on online relationships began to challenge many of the traditional ways that researchers had conceptualized initial attraction and relationship formation. Accepted notions of "stage theories" of relationship that had lovers moving from outer physical attraction to getting to know the "inner" self, and concepts related to "love at first sight," were challenged, since communicators could now decide when and how to reveal various aspects of themselves, including their physical appearance (Lea and Spears 1995). Lea and Spears were among the first to point out that the emphasis on physical attraction between two bodies as a critical initial stage for attraction was a bias within the personal relationships literature. Walther (1993) also argued that CMC may change the way that impressions are formed online, saying it allows communicators to "selectively self-present" in ways that are "stereotypically desirable." Driving these processes is the perceived anonymity of online communicators (Cooper et al. 2000; Putnam 2000; Carvalheira and Gomes 2003). Following on this line of thinking, Sherry Turkle took the psychoanalytic perspective to explain impressions formed online, saying that the online environment encourages "projection" and the development of "transference" (Turkle 1996). Both anonymity and the lack of physical proximity of online communicators can enhance projection, both through the ability to create a carefully crafted and edited "persona" to attract an online lover, and by encouraging the fantasies and desires of the online Other to proceed unchecked, extending the projection process beyond the bounds possible in a face-to-face interaction (Albright and Conran 2003). Both projection and transference leverage the fantasies and subconscious desires of people seeking love online, leading them at times to create either a false or "idealized" impression, rather than one accurately reflective of the "truth" of the online Other (Turkle 1996).

The projection process of mutual supplementation of an optimized self and an idealized other online has been termed the "virtual mirror" where the screen of the computer becomes a kind of mirror, where one projects a best self and sees in the reflection an "Other" shaped to one's own desires (Albright and Conran 2003). This occurs to some extent naturally in any social construction, where a good dialogue with a friend or lover makes us feel understood and appreciated (Gergen 1991). Huston and Levinger (1978) have said about this process:

> When the lover closes his eyes and daydreams, he can summon up a flawless partner—a partner who instantaneously satisfies all his unspoken, conflicting and fleeting desires....Compared to our grandiose fantasies, the level of reward we receive in our real interactions is severely circumscribed. As a consequence, sometimes the most extreme passion is aroused by partners who exist only in imagination or partners who are barely known.

In a study of impressions made online, followed up with "second impressions" in a face-to-face meeting, in cases where the second impression of the online lover did not match the first, the most commonly cited reason was due to the person "filling in the blanks incorrectly" (or projecting) as opposed to deception by the target of their attraction (Albright 2001), showing the commonality of projection and idealization within online impression formation.

In addition to leading to disappointment when lovers ultimately meet face to face, projection and idealization online may be playing an increasing role in "real life" divorce, as the fantasy elements of an idealized partner who "exists only in imagination" overshadows the mundane everyday reality of offline, preexisting spouses or partners. One researcher described computer communication as a kind of liminal space, as "an intermediate area of experiencing" whose fantasy elements may "degrade the institution of marriage" (Ben-Ze'ev 2004, 129). Atwood and Schwartz (2002) have also pointed to projection as a key issue to be addressed in couples counseling for those dealing with cyber affairs. Cooper, Delmonico, and Burg identified the "engine" that drives projection and fantasy online, elements that they say "combine to turbocharge, that is accelerate and intensify online sexual activity" (Cooper and Griffin-Shelley 2002, 5). These elements are anonymity, accessibility (to the Internet and to willing others), and affordability, or the "cost" of carrying on an affair online (Cooper, Delmonico, and Burg 2000). Other researchers have proposed adding a fourth "A" element: Approximation, or the ability to experiment—particularly with sexual identities and behaviors not typical to people's offline lives (Ross and Kauth 2002). Researchers have also said that in addition to projection and idealization, online affairs may also contain a strong emotional element that may make them seem particularly addictive or compelling, compared to offline relationships (Underwood and Findlay 2004).

In an effort perhaps to diminish the projection or fantasy elements and approximate more the "real life" encounters one experiences when meeting face to face, some online services have turned to 3D "avatars" in virtual environments in an effort to bring the physical and nonverbal communication elements into online matchmaking. Sites like Second Life, OmniDate, AvMatch, and RED Virtual Date allow users to virtually eat or drink in restaurants, and stroll exotic beaches while allowing users to nonverbally interact with their animated mate (Krawczyk-Wasilewska and Ross 2011). Rather than lowering the fantasy element, however, these avatars may enhance it, by allowing users to "selectively self-present" by choosing an avatar that is much more attractive than the person is in real life, and by living a lifestyle that exceeds their socioeconomic capabilities, including rides in limousines and walks in idyllic beach settings (Krawczyk-Wasilewska and Ross 2011). These sites seem to have been met with limited success, requiring fast processor and Internet connection speeds, and are often difficult to navigate for the casual user; easier-to-use social networking sites like Facebook appear to have usurped the attention of users of these sites. As an example, although Second Life has 24 million registered users, according to CEO Rod Humble, only 1 million of those users log on in a month in 2012 (Reahard 2012).

LYING TO GET A LOVER

A famous *New Yorker* cartoon came out a few years ago depicting a dog seated in front of a computer screen, with the tag line "On the Internet, no one knows you're a dog."

Though humorous, it summarizes a common fear many people have about online dating: Being deceived (Gibbs, Ellison, and Heino 2006; Lawson and Leck 2006). An online dating profile does allow one to curate and present an idealized "self" to the world that is optimized to make the most positive impression possible, leaving out unattractive or less desirable qualities. In spite of these fears, only a few studies have examined deception and infidelity online, and its impact on sincere communicators (Cornwell and Lundgren 2001; Whitty 2002; 2003; 2005). Extant research reveals that fears of deception online may be largely unfounded—or at least overblown: Several large-scale studies on online dating in the United States have found that the majority of Internet users do not lie online (Albright 2002; 2008), while another found that 80 percent of online daters lied, though those lies were typically small, like adjusting one's weight by approximately 5 percent (Toma, Hancock, and Ellison 2008). Lies online fall across clear gendered patterns, with men lying about personal assets, relationship goals, personal interests, and personal attributes, and women most likely to lie about weight (Hall et al. 2010; Toma, Hancock, and Ellison 2008), appealing to typical gendered patterns of attraction. Even older gentlemen beyond their reproductive years expressed a preference for more attractive women, incentivizing women to lie about things like weight and age (Hitsch, Hortaçsu, and Ariely 2010).

Some studies have found that the number one lie men tell online is in regard to their marital status, stating they are single when they are in fact married (Hitsch, Hortaçsu, and Ariely 2010), though this lie may soon be a thing of the past: The website Ashley Madison has cropped up as a matchmaking site targeting those married but seeking an extramarital affair. Ashley Madison claims to have over 12.5 million registered users, billing itself as "the largest online married dating site," with the slogan "Life is Short—Have an Affair" (AshleyMadison.com). Members can keep their photos private, sending interested others "keys" to view their photos if the interest is mutual. Users make no effort to hide their marital status. Though the site has attracted a large user base, it has not been without controversy: Ads for the site were rejected by both the Super Bowl and the City of Toronto, as were various proposed naming grants, such as one rejected by a stadium in New Jersey and another rejected by an airport in Phoenix, Arizona—even though the offers were for more than US$10 million (Wong 2010; Fisher 2010).

FUTURE DIRECTIONS: "SUGAR DADDIES," SOCIAL MEDIA, AND LOCATION BASED DATING

Several key trends have recently emerged in the genre of online dating. They are (1) the rise of niche dating sites, (2) location-based dating, and (3) the use of social media sites like Facebook for initiating romantic relationships.

Initially, large dating sites like those hosted by Yahoo, Match.com, and eHarmony targeted a wide swath of users who varied in terms of age, race, and other demographic variables. In recent years, niche dating sites have appeared that have attempted to "narrow the playing field" by appealing to daters seeking partners based on specific demographic factors such as religion, age, socioeconomic status, or shared values and interests. One example is sites that cater to users' religious orientations and values, such as JDate (for Jewish daters), ChristianMingle and CatholicMatch; another site, Christian Singles, displays the tagline "Find God's Match For You" when users log in.

A second category of niche dating sites is that targeting particular racial and ethnic groups, including Black People Meet and ChnLove, aimed toward Asian daters. Another example, Shaadi, combines features of old and new matchmaking by "digitizing" traditional Indian matchmaking. The site has met with success, claiming to have over 20 million members and to have matched over 2 million marriages worldwide. Additionally, the company advertises 250 "Shaadi Centers" that offer wedding and other matchmaking-related services (Shaadi.com). In addition to religious and racial/ethnic dating sites, there are sites specifically related to age, with some appealing to the growing demographic of aging baby boomers, such as the site *Senior People Meet*. Similarly, there are "intergenerational dating" sites like Cougar Life and It's Just a Number; Cougar Life specifically appeals to older women, sometimes referred to as "cougars," who seek younger men, likewise referred to as "cubs." The site claimed to have over 2,272,000 members as of January 2012.

Though mainstream sites like Match.com can match gay users, niche sites specifically targeting gay users have emerged, including Adam4Adam, Outpersonals, Men4Ken. com, and Manhunt. Some of these sites use words drawn from gay culture in their descriptors, including offering "bear" as a body type choice (Fiore and Donath 2004). Much of the research literature in this area has focused on serostatus (e.g., HIV) and health-related issues around risk and sex-seeking behaviors online for this population (see Bull and McFarlane 2000; Bolding et al. 2005).

Last, one particularly interesting development in recent years has been sites appealing to married men who are seeking affairs or financial "arrangements"—targeting "sugar daddies" and "sugar babies." According to the website SeekingArrangement.com, a sugar daddy is "a successful and generous man who is willing to pamper and offer financial help or gifts to a young person in return for friendship and companionship," while a "sugar baby" is "an attractive, ambitious and goal oriented individual who has a lot to offer. He or she is generally younger and is looking to meet wealthy, successful and generous people who are willing to pamper and offer financial assistance or gifts in return for their friendship or companionship." Sites in this genre include SeekingArrangement. com and SugarDaddie.com. On the periphery of this genre are sites where women seek "contributors" to pay for their breast implants, like myfreeimplants.com. Framing itself as a "social networking site," women on the site post personal ads featuring their photos, with ads seeking men to sponsor breast implant surgery in exchange for "fun, friendship—and free breast implants!" The site claims 750 "success" stories, with before and after photos of the surgery recipients.

Mobility

Mobility is another significant trend impacting meeting and mating online. In 2009, sales of smartphones reached 172.4 million units worldwide, up 23.8 percent from 2008 (Gartner 2010). In the UK, according to the Office for National Statistics, 45 percent of Internet users used a mobile phone to connect to the Internet in 2011, and 6 million people accessed the Internet over their mobile phone for the first time in the previous 12 months (Office for National Statistics 2011). Smartphones will enable both voice and video to be introduced to online matchmaking, as well as location-based dating via cell phone GPS capabilities.

Large online dating sites like Plenty of Fish, Match.com, and eHarmony and smaller niche sites like Millionaire Match are recognizing this trend, and have created mobile apps to address the growing demand. Plenty of Fish, said to be the largest online dating site with 39 million registered users, reported more than 300 million monthly visits to its free iPhone and Android apps in January 2012 (PR Newswire 2012). Of key significance is the fact that many mobile devices contain a Global Positioning System (GPS), which can track, log, and upload the user's location to the Internet. Sites like OkCupid are taking advantage of this capability by introducing apps that include new ways to connect for densely located urban daters. Referred to as "geosocial dating," new, location-based apps like Meet Moi NOW, Skout, Grindr, and Streetspark enable users to sort through list of potential mates based upon their geographic location, which mainly target short-term relationships or "hookups" as opposed to longer term relationships. An *Adweek* article on these new dating apps described them as offering users "the ability to order up sex on demand" (Anderson 2011). These apps are proving popular with a younger demographic of users, typically those in their twenties (House 2012). One of the aps in this genre is Grindr: Launched in 2009, it represents both niche and location-based apps by targeting the gay community, providing sexual hookups for users that may find it difficult to meet a partner. Geosocial apps have proven popular: Skout claims 1 million users, yet women seem to be slower to adopt them than men, apparently fearing they may attract stalkers (Sutter 2010).

An unintended consequence of geolocation and online dating has recently been uncovered: Many online dating sites fail to remove metadata from photos of online daters, leaving users who snap photos and upload photos with their cell phones vulnerable to revealing their geographic location (Novini 2012). In the study, 23 percent of sites failed to remove geolocation data (Novini 2012). Notably, all of the sites that failed to remove metadata on user's photos were smaller, niche dating sites, based on age, ethnicity, hobbies, and so on, showing that some of the newer online dating site owners have not yet thought through the privacy implications of online matchmaking to protect their users.

SOCIAL MEDIA AND ITS IMPACT ON ONLINE DATING

Last, social networking sites have surged in popularity in recent years, led by Facebook that launched in 2004 and reached the figure of one billion registered users in mid-2012 (Facebook 2012). Facebook was the number one social networking site as of May 2011 with 157.2 million visitors per month, followed by MySpace (34.9 million visitors per month), LinkedIn (33.4 million visitors per month), and Twitter (27.0 million visitors per month) (Lipsman 2011). Use of social media sites is almost ubiquitous among youth, particularly those college aged: One nationally representative survey of US youth by the Pew Internet and American Life Project found that 41 percent of 12- to 13-year-olds and 61 percent of 14- to 17-year-olds use social networking sites (Lenhart and Madden 2007), while another found that 91 percent of college students surveyed use Facebook. com (Wiley and Sisson 2006). Although the youth demographic is large on social networking sites, the biggest growth demographic has been among older users, particularly baby boomers. Though Facebook has met with huge success, research has shown that users typically are not using it to meet new people, but instead are connecting or reconnecting with people they already know (Ellison, Steinfield, and Lampe 2007). Users are also more likely to "search" for people they know or have already been acquainted with, as opposed to seeking out new relationships (Lampe, Ellison, and Steinfield 2006). However, since opening its site to the wider public in 2006, Facebook has fostered new romantic relationships—not through users seeking out "new" loves, but rather, via people reconnecting with long lost loves and former school mates, possibly contributing to the dissolution of preexisting relationships: A 2010 survey in the United States conducted by the American Academy of Matrimonial Lawyers (AAML) found that 81 percent of lawyers surveyed said they have seen an increase in Facebook as a contributor to divorce in recent years, with 66 percent claiming it as a primary source for divorce evidence, followed by MySpace at 15 percent, Twitter at 5 percent, and other choices listed at 14 percent (AAML 2010). British divorce firm Divorce Online cites Facebook as a factor in 20 percent of all divorce petitions in the UK in 2009 (Telegraph 2009).

Because of its huge customer reach, efforts have been made to tap into Facebook by online dating entrepreneurs: In 2007, Zoosk was launched as a third-party application that runs within Facebook. Tying together matchmaking with social media, users can meet those connected to their social network, chat, and set updates. This approach has met with some success, particularly among younger users. By 2010, Zoosk was among the top-rated Internet dating sites, with over 5 million unique users (Datingsitesreviews. com 2012).

The future of social media and online matchmaking may not lie only in apps, but also in datamining. In 2012, a new dating site attempted to differentiate itself from traditional matchmaking services by incorporating user activity and preferences mined from sites like Netflix and Amazon.com, in an effort to create a more nuanced, richer profile of daters. The site, theComplete.me, has been discussed as moving away from a norm of "privacy" (the hallmark of most other dating sites like eHarmony) toward one of "transparency" to match the perceived evolving values of the millennial generation who grew up sharing the minutia of their everyday lives online. While theComplete.me eventually folded, it is likely that many similar services will emerge over the coming years. One similar site already underway is Tastebuds (www.tastebuds.fm), a website that matches users based upon their mutually shared tastes in music. Similar to theComplete.me, Tastebuds imports a user's music listening history and favorite bands from Facebook and popular music streaming services like Last.fm and Spotify. Tastebuds also collects data about upcoming concerts and notifies users when other subscribers are also planning to attend, providing them the opportunity to "break the ice" with potential dates. Using social media data to predict and recommend real-world dating activities, sometimes in real time, is just one example of how online dating sites are beginning to bridge the real and virtual worlds.

CONCLUSION

The world of online dating has grown and matured since the early days of online communication, when fewer than 3 percent of the American public were online, to now, when online dating has become the third most common way that people meet their spouses in the United States and Europe. New developments such as the rise of social media have impacted who meets and where, and the massive penetration of smartphones and other gps-enabled mobile devices provide new opportunities for location-based dating, enabling both positive experiences of meeting someone with potentially common interests due to proximity, to unintended outcomes like cyberstalking. The increase of baby boomers online who may be less likely to go to places like bars and clubs to meet a match ensures that online dating will continue to grow, particularly sites that appeal to this demographic, like Senior People Meet and other age-targeted niche sites.

The research has largely assuaged the common fear that "everyone lies online"— the majority of online daters do not lie about basic information about themselves, or the lies told are small. Instead, when first and second impressions (from online to offline) don't match, it is more the fault of projection of the dater's desires onto the online lovers, rather than their being the victim of deceit. The online dating world may be "self-correcting" for deceit both through social networking, where users have access to other's social networks to verify identity, and through the emergence of sites like Ashley Madison (for married daters overtly looking to have an affair) and "sugar daddy" sites, where (often) married men seeking an "arrangement" can safely do so without hiding their marital status. While these sites have drawn the ire of religious leaders and others, they are indicative of the segmentation of the online dating market into smaller, more segmented, targeted options for users. Such niche dating sites, or "microsegmentation" will no doubt continue as a notable trend in the future, with the convergence of disparate databases and more powerful data-mining techniques enabling even more nuanced and comprehensive profiling. What remains to be seen are the new ways that users will be microtargeted, and the new services that will become available as the socio-technical systems evolve, particularly in the mobile and data-mining arenas, as well as the unintended consequences of these developments such as an erosion of privacy or an inability to escape an undesirable past, since "the Internet never forgets."

References

Abbate, J. 1999. *Inventing the Internet*. Cambridge, MA: MIT Press.

Albright, J. M. 1995. Online Love: Sex, Gender and Relationships in Text-Based Virtual Reality. Unpublished paper presented at the Pacific Sociological Association, Seattle, Washington.

Albright, J. M. 2001. Impression Formation and Attraction in Computer Mediated Communication. (Unpublished doctoral dissertation), University of Southern California.

Albright, J. M. 2007. How Do I Love Thee and Thee and Thee: Impression Management, Deception and Multiple Relationships Online. In *Online Matching*, edited by M. Whitty, A. J. Baker, and J. A. Inman, 81–93. London: Palgrave.

Albright, J. M. 2008. Sex in America Online: Sex, Gender, Sexual Identity, Marital Status and Sex-Seeking on the Internet. *Journal of Sex Research* 45 (2): 175–186.

Albright, J. M., and T. Conran. 2003. Constructing and Deconstructing Intimacy Online. *Journal of Systemic Therapies* 22 (3): 42–53.

American Academy of Matrimonial Lawyers. 2010. Big Surge in Social Networking Evidence Says Survey of Nation's Top Divorce Lawyers. February 10. http://www.aaml.org/about-the-academy/press/press-releases/e-discovery/big-surge-social-n etworking-evidence-says-survey-. Accessed June 19, 2013.

Anderson, A. 2011. A New Kind of Love Story. Adweek, May. http://www.adweek.com/hephzibah-anderson/new-kind-love-story-131195. Accessed June 19, 2013.

Anderson, T. L. 2005. Relationships among Internet Attitudes, Internet Use, Romantic Beliefs, and Perceptions of Online Romantic Relationships. *Cyberpsychology and Behavior: The Impact of the Internet, Multimedia and Virtual Reality on Behavior and Society* 8 (6): 521–531.

Atwood, J. D., and L. Schwartz. 2002. Cyber-Sex: The New Affair Treatment Considerations. *Journal of Couple and Relationship Therapy* 1 (3): 37–56.

Barraket, J., and M. S. Henry-Waring. 2008. Getting It On(line) Sociological Perspectives on E-dating. *Journal of Sociology* 44 (2): 149–165.

BBS Corner. 1996. BBSUser FAQ. http://www.bbscorner.com/usersinfo/userfaq.htm. Accessed August 9, 2013.

Ben-Ze'ev, A. 2004. *Love Online: Emotions on the Internet*. Cambridge: Cambridge University Press.

Bolding, G., M. Davis, G. Hart, L. Sherr, and J. Elford. 2005. Gay Men Who Look for sex On the Internet: Is There More HIV/STI Risk with Online Partners? *AIDS* 19 (9): 961–968.

Boorstin, J. 2010. The Big Business of Online Dating. *CNBC*, February 12. http://www.cnbc.com/id/35370922/The_Big_Business_of_Online_Dating. Accessed June 19, 2013.

Brooks, C. 2010. Online Personals Watch. http://www.onlinepersonalswatch.com/news/2010/03/eharmony-invested-in-edarlingde.html. Accessed June 19, 2013.

Bull, S. S., and M. McFarlane. 2000. Soliciting Sex on the Internet: What Are the Risks for Sexually Transmitted Diseases and HIV? *Sexually Transmitted Diseases* 27 (9): 545–550.

Carvalheira, A., and Gomes, F. A. 2003. Cybersex in Portuguese chat rooms: A study of sexual behaviors related to online sex. *Journal of Sex & Marital Therapy* 29: 345–360.

Chow, E. N. 1987. The Development of Feminist Consciousness among Asian American Women. *Gender and Society* 1 (3): 284—299.

Colchester, M. 2011. France Télécom to Bid Adieu to Minitel. *WSJ.com*, July 25. http://online.wsj.com/article/SB10001424053111904772304576465573343018168.html. Accessed June 19, 2013.

Cornwell, B., and Lundgren, D. 2001. Love on the Internet: Involvement and misrepresentation in romantic relationships in cyberspace versus realspace.*Computers in Human Behavior* 17: 197–211.

Cooper, A., and L. Sportolari. 1997. Romance in Cyberspace: Understanding Online Attraction. *Journal of Sex Education and Therapy* 22 (1): 7–14.

Cooper, A., S. Boies, M. Maheu, and D. Greenfield. 2000. Sexuality and the Internet: The Next Sexual Revolution. In *Psychological Perspectives on Human Sexuality*, 519–545. Hoboken, NJ: John Wiley and Sons.

Cooper, A., D. L. Delmonico, and R. Burg. 2000. Cybersex Users, Abusers, and Compulsives: New Findings and Implications. *Sexual Addiction and Compulsivity* 7 (1–2): 5–29.

Cooper, A., and E. Griffin-Shelley. 2002. Introduction. The Internet: The Next Sexual Revolution. In *Sex and the Internet: A Guidebook for Clinicians*, edited by A. Cooper, 1–15. New York: Brunner-Routledge.

Culnan, M. J., and Markus, M. L. 1987. Information technologies. In *Handbook of organizational communication: An interdisciplinary perspective*, edited by F. M. Jablin, L. L. Putnam, K. H. Roberts, and L. W. Porter, 420–443. Newbury Park, CA: Sage Publications.

Datingsitesreviews.com. 2012. Zoosk.com Information, Statistics, Facts and History. http://www.datingsitesreviews.com/staticpages/index.php?page=Zoosk-com-Statistics-Facts-History. Accessed August 9, 2013.

Dauncey, H. 1997. A Cultural Battle: French Minitel, the Internet and the Superhighway. *Convergence: The International Journal of Research into New Media Technologies* 3 (3): 72–89.

Decker, W. M. D. 2002. Epistolary Practices: Letter Writing in America before Telecommunications. *Modern Philology* 99 (3): 440–443.

eHarmony.com. 2009. Dating Tips. http://advice.eharmony.com. Accessed January 12, 2012.

Ellison, N., C. Steinfield, and C. Lampe. 2007. The Benefits of Facebook "Friends": Social Capital and College Students' Use of Online Social Network Sites. *Journal of Computer-Mediated Communication* 12 (4): 1143–1168.

Experian Hitwise. 2007. http://www.experian.com/hitwise/. Accessed August 9, 2013.

Experian Hitwise. 2011. Love Is in the Air for Over 50s. February 14. http://weblogs.hitwise.com/robin-goad/2011/02/love_is_in_the_air_for_over_50.html. Accessed June 19, 2013.

Facebook. 2012. One Billion People on Facebook. October 4. https://newsroom.fb.com/News/457/One-Billion-People-on-Facebook. Accessed August 10, 2013.

Finkel, E. J., P. W. Eastwick, B. R. Karney, H. T. Reis, and S. Sprecher. 2012. Online Dating: A Critical Analysis from the Perspective of Psychological Science. *Psychological Science in the Public Interest* 13 (1): 3–66.

Fiore, A. T., and J. S. Donath. 2004. Online Personals: An Overview. In *CHI '04 Extended Abstracts on Human Factors in Computing Systems*, 1395–1398. New York: ACM.

Fisher, K. 2010. Risque Website Offers $10 Million for Sky Harbor Name Change. *ABC15*. http://www.onlinepersonalswatch.com/news/2010/02/ashley- madison-offers-10-million-for-sky-harbor-name-change.html. Accessed August 9, 2013.

Frost, J. H., Z. Chance, M. I. Norton, and D. Ariely. 2008. People Are Experience Goods: Improving Online Dating with Virtual Dates. *Journal of Interactive Marketing* 22 (1): 51–61.

Gartner. 2010. Gartner Says Mobile Worldwide Mobile Phone Sales to End Users Grew 8 Per Cent in Fourth Quarter 2009; Market Remained Flat in 2009. Press release, February 23. *Gartner Group.* http://www.gartner.com/it/page.jsp?id=1306513. Accessed June 19, 2013.

Gergen, K. 1991. *The Saturated Self.* New York: Basic Books.

Gibbs, J. L., N. B. Ellison, and R. D. Heino. 2006. Self-Presentation in Online Personals: The Role of Anticipated Future Interaction, Self-Disclosure, and Perceived Success in Internet Dating. *Communication Research* 33 (2): 1–26.

Hall, J. A., N. Park, H. Song, and M. J. Cody. 2010. Strategic Misrepresentation in On-line Dating: The Effects of Gender, Self-Monitoring, and Personality Traits. *Journal of Social and Personal Relationships* 27 (1): 117–135.

Hiltz, S. R., K. Johnson, and M. Turoff. 1986. Experiments in Group Decision Making Communication Process and Outcome in Face-to-Face vs. Computerized Conferences. *Human Communication Research* 13 (2): 225–252.

Hitsch, G., Hortacsu, A., and Ariely, D. 2010. What makes you click: Mate Preferences in Online Dating. 2005 Meeting Papers*Quantitative Marketing and Economics* 8 (4): 393–427.

House, K. 2012. As 20-somethings Take to Online Dating, Entrepreneurs Respond. *Oregon Live*, February 12. http://www.oregonlive.com/living/index.ssf/2012/02/as_20-somethings_take_to_onlin.html. Accessed June 20, 2013.

Howe, N., and W. Strauss. 2000. *Millennials Rising: The Next Great Generation.* New York: Vintage.

Huston, T. L., and G. Levinger. 1978. Interpersonal Attraction and Relationships. *Annual Review of Psychology* 29 (1): 115–156.

Kiesler, S., J. Siegel, and T. W. McGuire. 1984. Social Psychological Aspects of Computer-Mediated Communication. *American Psychologist* 39 (10): 1123–1134.

Kirmann, H. 1990. Minitel: The French Love Affair with Telematics. *IEEE Micro* 10 (2): 88–90.

Krawczyk-Wasilewska, V., and A. Ross. 2011. Matchmaking through Avatars: Social Aspects of Online Dating. Paper presented on the panel "Shaping Virtual Lives: Identities on the Internet," 10th Congress of the Société International d'Ethnologie et de Folklore (SIEF), Lisbon, April 17–21.

Lampe, C., N. Ellison, and C. Steinfield. 2006. A Face(book) in the Crowd: Social Searching vs. Social Browsing. In *Proceedings of the 2006 20th Anniversary Conference on Computer Supported Cooperative Work*, 167–170. New York: ACM.

Lawson, H. M., and K. Leck. 2006. Dynamics of Internet Dating. *Social Science Computer Review* 24 (2): 189–208.

Lea, M., and R. Spears. 1995. Love at First Byte? Building Personal Relationships over Computer Networks. In *Understudied Relationships: Off the Beaten Track*, edited by Julia T. Wood and Steve Duck, 197–233. Newbury Park, CA: Sage.

Lenhart, A., and M. Madden. 2007. Teens, Privacy and Online Social Networks: How Teens Manage Their Online Identities and Personal Information in the Age of MySpace. Pew Internet and American Life Project, Washington, DC.

Lipsman, A. 2011. The Network Effect: Facebook, Linkedin, Twitter, and Tumblr Reach New Heights in May. ComScore. June 15. http://www.comscore.com/Insights/Blog/The_Network_Effect_Facebook_Linkedin_Twitter_Tumblr_Reach_New_Heights_in_May. Accessed June 20, 2013.

Madden, M., and A. Lenhart. 2006. Online Dating. Pew Internet and American Life Project. March 5. http://www.pewinternet.org/Reports/2006/Online-Dating.aspx. Accessed June 20, 2013.

Marketdata Enterprises. 2012. The US Dating Services Market. *Market Research.com*. January 1. http://www.marketresearch.com/Marketdata-Enterprises-Inc-v416/Dating-Services-6773764. Accessed June 20, 2013.

Match.com. 2010. Match.com and Chadwick Martin Bailey 2009–2010 Studies: Recent Trends: Online Dating. http://cp.match.com/cppp/media/CMB_Study.pdf. Accessed June 20, 2013.

Maybin, J. 2000. Death Row Penfriends: Some Effects of Letter Writing on Identity and Relationships. In *Letter Writing as a Social Practice*, edited by D. Barton and N. Hall, 151–177. Amsterdam: John Benjamins.

Miniwatts. 2011. Internet World Usage. http://www.internetworldstats.com/stats.htm. Accessed August 9, 2013.

Mitchell, R. L. 2009. Online Dating: Analyzing the Algorithms of Attraction. *PCWorld*. February 19. http://www.pcworld.com/article/159884-2/online_dating_analyzing_the_algorithms_of_attraction.html. Accessed June 20, 2013.

Morejon, R. 2011. Social Media Age Demographics for Facebook and Twitter. August 30. http://roymorejon.com/social-media-age-demographics-for-facebook-and-twitter/. Accessed June 20, 2013.

Novini, R. 2012. CU-Boulder Study: Some Websites Don't Remove GPS Data from Photos. *KRDO.com*. January 12. http://www.krdo.com/news/30200842/detail.html. June 20, 2013.

Office for National Statistics. 2011. Internet Access: Households and Individuals 2011. August 31. http://www.ons.gov.uk/ons/rel/rdit2/internet-access---households-and-individuals/2011/stb-internet-access-2011.html. Accessed June 20, 2013.

Online Personals Watch. 2007. http://onlinepersonalswatch.typepad.com/news/2007/02/where_the_women.html. Accessed August 7, 2013.

PR Newswire. 2012. Plenty of Fish Emerges as Most Visited Mobile Dating Application. http://www.prnewswire.com/news-releases/love-on-the-run-plentyoffish-emerges-as-most-visited-mobile-dating-application-138999434.html. Accessed August 10, 2013.

Prensky, M. 2001. Digital Natives, Digital Immigrants. *On the Horizon* 9 (5): 1–6.

Putnam, D. E. 2000. Initiation and Maintenance of Online Sexual Compulsivity: Implications for Assessment and Treatment. *CyberPsychology and Behavior* 3 (4): 553–564.

Quantcast. 2012. eHarmony.com Traffic and Demographic Statistics. http://www.quantcast.com/eharmony.com/geo/countries#!demo. Accessed August 9, 2013.

Reagan, B. 2002. Bored of the Rings. *Wall Street Journal*, August 15, section R4.

Reahard, R. 2012. Linden Lab's *Second Life* Extremely Profitable, Company Looking to Expand. *Massively*. March 15. http://massively.joystiq.com/2012/03/15/linden-labs-second-life-extremely-profitable-company-looking. Accessed June 20, 2013.

Rice, R. 1984. Mediated Communication. In *The New Media*, edited by R. Rice and Associates, 133–136. Beverly Hills, CA: Sage Publications.

Ross, M. W., and M. R. Kauth. 2002. Men Who Have Sex With Men, and the Internet: Emerging Clinical Issues and Their Management. In *Sex and the Internet: A Guidebook for Clinicians*, edited by A. Cooper, 47–69. New York: Brunner-Routledge.

Shaadi.com. 2012. About Us. http://www.shaadi.com/introduction/about-us.php. Accessed August 9, 2013.

Short, J. A., E. Williams, and B. Christie. 1976. *The Social Psychology of Telecommunications*. New York: John Wiley and Sons.

Siegel, J., V. Dubrovsky, S. Kiesler, and T. W. McGuire. 1986. Group Processes in Computer-Mediated Communication. *Organizational Behavior and Human Decision Processes* 37 (2): 157–187.

Sproull, L., and S. Kiesler. 1986. Reducing Social Context Cues: Electronic Mail in Organizational Communication. *Management Science* 32 (11): 1492–1512.

Stephure, R. J., S. D. Boon, S. L. MacKinnon, and V. L. Deveau. 2009. Internet Initiated Relationships: Associations between Age and Involvement in Online Dating. *Journal of Computer-Mediated Communication* 14 (3): 658–681.

Sutter, R. 2010. With New GPS Dating Apps, It's Love the One You're Near. *CNN*. August 6. http://edition.cnn.com/2010/TECH/innovation/08/06/gps.dating.apps/#fbid=3UApRU jvYZt&wom=false. Accessed June 20, 2013.

Telegraph. 2009. Facebook Fuelling Divorce, Research Claims. December 21. http://www.telegraph. co.uk/technology/facebook/6857918/Facebook-fuelling-divorce-research-claims.html. Accessed June 20, 2013.

Tempest, R. 1989. Minitel: Miracle or Monster? Erotic Message Services Have Become the Dirty Little Secret of France's Videotext Network. Critics Say the Government May Be Profiting from Crime. *Los Angeles Times*. October 21. http://articles.latimes.com/1989-10-24/news/ mn-718_1_france-telecom. Accessed June 20, 2013.

Toma, C., J. T. Hancock, and N. Ellison. 2008. Separating Fact from Fiction: An Examination of Deceptive Self-Presentation in Online Dating Profiles. *Personality and Social Psychology Bulletin* 34 (8): 1023–1036.

Turkle, S. 1996. *Life on the Screen: Identity in the Age of the Internet*. London: Weidenfeld and Nicholson.

Underwood, H., and B. Findlay. 2004. Internet Relationships and Their Impact on Primary Relationships. *Behaviour Change* 21 (2): 127–140.

USA Today. 2011. Boomers Swelling the Ranks of Online Dating Sites. June 3. http:// yourlife.usatoday.com/sex-relationships/dating/story/2011/06/Boomers-swelling-the-ra nks-of-online-dating-sites---/48018456/1. Accessed June 19, 2013.

Walther, J. B. 1993. Impression Development in Computer-mediated Interaction. *Western Journal of Communication* 57: 381–398.

Walther, J. B. 1994. Anticipated Ongoing Interaction versus Channel Effects on Relational Communication in Computer-Mediated Interaction. *Human Communication Research* 20 (4): 473–501.

Walther, J. B. 1996. ComputerMediated Communication: Impersonal, Interpersonal, and Hyperpersonal Interaction. *Communication Research* 23 (1): 3–43.

Walther, J. B., and J. K. Burgoon. 1992. Relational Communication in Computer-Mediated Interaction. *Human Communication Research* 19 (1): 50–88.

Wikipedia. 2012. Internet. http://en.wikipedia.org/wiki/Internet. Accessed August 9, 2013.

Whitty, M. T. 2002. Liar, Liar! An Examination of How Open, Supportive and Honest People Are in Chat Rooms. *Computers in Human Behavior* 18 (4): 343–352.

Whitty, M. T. 2003. Pushing the Wrong Buttons: Men's and women's Attitudes towards Online and Offline Infidelity. *CyberPsychology and Behavior* 6 (6): 569–579.

Whitty, M. T. 2005. The "Realness" of Cyber-cheating: Men's and Women's Representations of Unfaithful Internet Relationships. *Social Science Computer Review* 23 (1): 57–67.

Whitty, M. T., and A. N. Carr. 2003. Cyberspace as Potential Space: Considering the Web as a Playground to Cyber-flirt. *Human Relations* 56 (7): 869–891.

Whitty, M. T., and A. N. Joinson. 2009. *Truth, Lies and Trust on the Internet*. New York: Psychology Press.

Wiley, C., and M. Sisson. 2006. Ethics, Accuracy and Assumption: The Use of Facebook by Students and Employers. Paper presented at the Southwestern Ohio Council for Higher Education Special Topics Forum, Dayton, OH, November.

Wong, S. 2010. Phoenix Rejects $10M Offer from Infidelity Web Site. *Arizona Republic*. http://infidelity-investigations.blogspot.com/2010/02/phoenix-rejects-10m-offer-from.html. Accessed August 9, 2013.

CHAPTER 18

....

CYBERSEX

....

STÅLE STENSLIE

MILLIONS of people practice it every day. It has become a common, if not natural part of human sexuality. But what is cybersex? How do we do it? And why?

The chapter aims to give an outline of cybersex from its historic origins, via current practice and technologies, toward experimental, future-oriented possibilities. Central to this overview are also the various critical commentaries that both color and channel cybersexual practice, societal acceptance, and technological developments. Important questions treated throughout include, Is cybersex "real"? (Lenhard 2011, 1). Or just the virtual counterpart of sex? A fake kind of sex? And perhaps the most challenging question: What is the future of sexuality?

Cybersex describes erotic and sexual pleasure experienced through cybernetic,[1] digital, and computer-based technologies and communication (Glyn Jones 1996, xv; Waskul 2004, 36). As a concept, it covers a wide range of sexual activities and experiences ranging from flirtatious e-mails and text-based chats to mechanically advanced telehaptic communication systems. The broadest definition of cybersex therefore covers all sexual activities and experiences encountered in "cyberspace"—the global and complex network of computers and humans. Cybersex is consequently also a product of technology. Technology is never neutral, but channels our libido in ways specific to its various constructions. It "catalyzes changes not only in what we do but in how we think" (Turkle 1985, 13). Yet what if we possessed a magic technology that could give us anything we wanted? At anytime? What sex would we then think of? Or practice? The combination of our strong human sexual drive with our dreams of technology spawns sexual imagination, linking technology, and sex closer than we often like to think. Technologies ranging from the digital, robotics, and synthetic biology have an embedded promise to satisfy all our needs and desires, leading to an inclination to sexualize technologies. From real product descriptions like Apple's sexy devices to fictitious sci-fi gadgets, they all trigger our imagination, stimulating us to imagine ourselves being in control of all-powerful prosthetics, rendering the impossible real. One such dream is represented in Ovid's story of Pygmalion and Galatea (Hardie 2002, 190). The technologically skilled sculptor Pygmalion works so hard and persistently on the female sculpture of Galatea that the goddess of love, Venus, seeing how much in love he is, breathes life into the sculpture. Galatea is shaped from inanimate, dull matter to become our perfect love partner who—potentially—satisfies all our needs and desires. Sculpted as she is perfectly to our individual and unique desires, Galatea represents a kind of holy grail of cybersex; an ideal, exclusive, personal, and ultimately unattainable love partner.

Ivan E. Sutherland's (1965) description of "The Ultimate Display" is another example of how we eroticize technology. It is a "display" or interface that can materialize any need or fantasy. If you imagine a chair, you will materialize a chair you can sit in. If you fire a bullet, it will be lethal. "With appropriate programming such a display could literally be the Wonderland into which Alice walked," Sutherland wrote in 1964 (506). It is foreseeable that many Internet users would like to swap current screen-based interfaces with such a vital and causal fantasy world and spend quite some time there. Appropriating and programming oneself to become one with the ultimate and fantastical identity handle Alice is likely at some point to trigger the wish to have sex as Alice. Or even with her. Our future cyberbodies as well as our sex partners can be traded in, redesigned, and made available at any time (Kramarae in Jones 1998, 115). Cyberspace thus promises us a new kind of sex with and within a new kind of body, the technologically enhanced telematic body.

Technological fantasies such as "The Ultimate Display" represent what Michael Heim calls our marriage to technology. It is also a Neoplatonic expression of Eros and our erotic relationship to computers and digital networks: "The world rendered as pure information not only fascinates our eyes and minds, but also captures our hearts. We feel augmented and empowered. Our hearts beat in the machines. This is Eros" (Heim 1993, 85).

Cybersex: The First Steps

Our love for the machine has, since the beginning, spun off into a loving through the machine. Historically, electronic cybersex originates with the dots- and dashed-based communication via the telegraph. As early as 1880 the book *Wired Love*, written by Ella C. Thayer, describes how lovers meet "online," wired via the telegraph (Joinson 2007, 34).

Despite the slow speed and minimal length of messages, the telegraph not only caused several controversies as to whether it was a medium for indecent behavior or not, but it also reportedly brought several couples together. The telegraph is another example of how we sexualize technologies to experience mediated sexual pleasures.

Electromechanically, the first step toward induced sex came with the introduction of the first commercial vibrators in the 1880s. Although disguised as treatment against "female disorders" such as the unspecific diagnosis "hysteria," the actual effect of these devices was renewing of "sexual vigour" (for men) and "restoring (women's) bright eyes and pink cheeks" by massaging female patients to orgasm (Maines 2001, 15–19).

Even though cybersex today is a product of digital technologies, it is by no means new, and "porn is its oldest device" (Cramer and Home 2005). So is the debate around mediated and therefore "artificial" sexuality. Discussions about the pros and cons of sexuality have been reinvoked with every major technological innovation, from the erotic images found on Greek vases (Posner 1994, 355), love letters, and explicit images to the telegraph and on toward photography, film, telephone, home video, Internet (Waskul 2004, 3), virtual realities, and biotechnology.

CYBERSEX IN LITERATURE AND THE MOVIES

Psychology is the physics of virtual reality (William Bricken 1990)

Visions of cybersex have a long history in fiction and fantasy. Several of the significant images and visions of cybersex within popular culture, literature, and film impact the way we think and sexually utilize technology today.

In the book *Brave New World* (1932), Aldous Huxley described the *Feelies*—a future movie format that gives you a sense of touch in addition to seeing and hearing (Benyon, Turner, and Turner 2005, 404). In the feelies, people would feel they were a part of the action. When watching a couple on screen making love, they would feel the lovers' exchange of cutaneous strokes, sense their heat and sweat, feel their heartbeats, and hear through their ears. It remains unclear how this was to be technologically achieved, but the feelies represent a strong conceptual development in terms of expanding audiovisual representations with haptic sensations to create and tell a corporeally convincing story (Paterson 2007, 133).

The *Excessive Machine* appears in the fantasy-sci-fi film *Barbarella* (1968), starring Jane Fonda. Shaped like a piano-like organ for the body, the Excessive Machine is made to pleasantly torture the genitalia of the user until she or he dies through overstimulation and all-powerful orgasms. So the movie presents a criticism of our love for the machine with all its artificial pleasures and unforeseeable consequences.

William Gibson describes simulated sexual experience, the so-called SimStim (Simulated Stimulation), in his book *Neuromancer* (1984). The technology wires your brain and body directly to a prerecording of another person's full neural and sensory experience, enabling a form of body swapping. Instead of seeing Madonna in concert you would, for example, experience being her, in her body, singing her songs, on stage, live while you sensed the audience' excitement and smell. Or swap to recordings of Elvis and have sex as him with Madonna. In Gibson's cyberpunk universe, the SimStim has become *the* entertainment medium and has replaced television. SimStim sex is also considered a "pure" form of sexual experience since it is devoid of venereal diseases and health risks, quite in opposition to the "meat puppets" that are still forced to have sex with their real bodies.

The SQUID device (Superconducting Quantum Interference Device) appears in the film *Strange Days* (1995). Inspired by the SimStim, it is a hairnet like device to be put on the subject/user's head. The minidisc-based system can record the wearer's entire sensory experience for later playback. As music can be shared via CD and MP3 players, so SQUID can project you into the sensory body of others. Similar to the SimStim, the SQUID technology makes you feel as if you really are the other person. It is a "switchboard of souls" as well as bodies.

A popularized version of Sutherland's vision of "The Ultimate Display" is the *Holodeck* of the *Star Trek* TV series. It is a simulated reality facility located on the starship *Enterprise*. In several episodes, its holographic technology is used to materialize any fantasy a crew member would have of an ideal and willing partner (Roberts 1999).

However, experiential recording and transfer technology (mental-corporeal induction technology) like SimStim, SQUID and the Holodeck has not yet been realized. The closest metaphor for future cybersex similar to contemporary virtual and nonphysical online sex was perhaps in the 1993 movie *Demolition Man*, featuring Sylvester Stallone. Here cybersex has transformed into a form of telepathic, corporally detached, and "pure" sex that this future society considers ideal as it avoids repercussions such as sexually transmittable diseases and pregnancy. These "ideal" aspects mirror issues relevant to current online cybersex.

Cybersex Today: Cyberchat Sex

The current cybersexual (r)evolution started almost instantly when online chat and text communication were introduced at the outset of the Internet early in the seventies. Early chat systems such as *Talkomatic*[2] connected users via the computer screen to see the same messages and stories appearing character-by-character as they were typed. Although a generic system, *Talkomatic* users soon started using it for romances and intimate forms of communication (Crumlish and Malone 2009, 4). Here the first steps were taken toward present chat-based cybersex that relies on textual communication, writing skills, and verbal communication. Interaction is here about hot stories and semiotics, and not dependent on real-life characteristics such as external appearance, gender, race, religion, or social status (Ben-Zeev 2004, 17).

Sex-based chat, exchanging sexually explicit messages describing or simulating a sexual experience, quickly became popular in the early days of the Internet online services such as CompuServe and America Online. On Internet Relay Chat (IRC), Multi User Dungeons (MUDs), and MOOs (Mud Object Oriented) sex chat developed into a form of role-playing where the participants pretend they are having and performing actual sexual relations (Soble and Power 2008). It is a form of fantasy sex where participants describe their actions and environment in written form and in turn respond to their chat partners. Cybersex chat relies on stimulating the erotic imaginations of the users and by triggering consensual hallucinations that lead the users toward—eventually—the written story of a climax. The communication is designed for autoerotic stimulation of the user's own sexual feelings and fantasies. As described in Hahn:

> The goal of MUD sex is the same as the goal of regular sex (without the babies): to bond temporarily in a way that is physically and emotionally satisfying. To do so, two people will exchange messages so as to lead one another into a high level of sexual arousal, culminating in a well-defined resolution. (1996, 570)

SEXY ME'S

One of the most important functions in chat-based cybersex is the ease of assuming and changing between personal (real world) and virtual identities, the so-called "handles" or "avatars."[3] Users can design and present their virtual identity and looks as only limited by their language and profile picture. One can literally project into any identity, action, and look, anything that text and stories can describe. Grabbing the attention of others through one's sexy, "beautiful" appearance is as rewarding in virtuality as in real life. As the protagonist in the movie *Circuitry Man* (Lovy 1990) says: "Why jack off (in real life) when you can jack in?"

Although chat is almost explicitly nonvisual, chat users graphically depict in words and word-paint their encounters. An illustrative example of how cybersex and cyber-sexual descriptions can function through real-time, text-based chat in IRC, MOOs, and MUDs is the following transcript:

WELLHUNG: Hello, Sweetheart. What do you look like?

SWEETHEART: I am wearing an expensive red silk blouse, a black leather mini skirt and high-heeled boots. I am tanned and very buffed. I work out everyday. My measurements are 36-24-36. What do you look like?

WELLHUNG: I'm 6'3 and about 250 lb. I wear glasses and have on a pair of blue sweat pants I just bought at Wal-Mart. I'm also wearing an old T-shirt, it's got some barbecue sauce stains on it and it smells kind of funny.

SWEETHEART: I want you. Would you like to screw me?

wellhung: OK

SWEETHEART: We're in my bedroom. There's soft music playing on the stereo and candles on my nightstand. I look up into your eyes and I'm smiling. My hand works its way down to your crotch and I begin to feel your huge swelling bulge.[4]

Chat rooms allow users to develop different personalities according to different environments. Users can simultaneously live different lives through characters in separate chat rooms or "realities," all while continuing their day job (Turkle 1985). As a consensual and text-based fantasy, cybersex is both available and portable to various contexts and technologies. Text allows for fast designs as well as re-designs of online personalities and stories. Real-time exchange of text is therefore still much used in connection with other technologies such as online virtual reality (VR) communities (e.g. *Second Life*) as well as video chat.

A common phenomenon encountered in sex chat is gender swapping, where users pretend to be of the opposite sex. One reason for this is the fact that fewer women than men practice cybersex (Waskul 2003). Swapping from real-life man to virtual, online woman will therefore possibly attract more attention. And does it really matter who one really is?

FANTASY SEX IN FANTASY BODIES

Online, everyone can be anyone (Waskul 2004, 9), turning our virtual identity into a discursive performance that spawns extraordinary sexual imaginations and encounters. On the online chat forum and MUD *FurryMuck*, users communicate as anthropomorphic animals with human personalities and desires. Sexual encounters are frequent and, because of the handles' descriptions, it takes on strange, fantastical dimensions when, for example, a "female, green-skinned, naked skunk" engages "a sweet, cuddly panda with multiple penises." The following is a transcript of a pornographic exchange from a *FurryMuck*:

> "You're, just, a, fucking, cock, slut." the dog panted as he fucked the writhing rabbit wildly.
> "YESSS YESSS A SLUT!! MOOOREEEE!" Cindy dug her paws into his shoulders and shrieked as she felt his cock swell.
> "HHUGGAHHHAHAA!!!" he howled as he thrust extra deep, then his cock jerked as he started to fire hot gushes of cum into the crazed bunny beneath him.[5]

Although this chat excerpt is explicitly pornographic, there are clear differences between an offline porn story and furry sex in that the latter represents a story written and happening in real time as an online dialogue between two consenting participants. It also takes time to learn, as chat is a verbal interaction that needs careful scripting to be exciting and to compensate for the lack of physical interaction (Ben-Ze'ev 2004).

One important question is whether this can be described as real sex or not. As Arthur and Marilouise Kroker (1987, 21) comment: "In technological society, the body has achieved a purely rhetorical existence." You are who you write yourself to be. However, in phenomenological terms, as long as the participants experience the sex as real, it becomes real sex. Even if you masturbate your way to orgasm during online cybersex, it still indicates a real sexual experience. In effect, text-based cybersex can be just as real as normal sex through the strong and reportedly physical responses it induces. The realness of cybersex is also confirmed in the many offline depictions, imaginations, and debates in popular media.

EXPANDED CHAT: CYBERSEX IN
VIRTUAL REALITY

Faster Internet connections rapidly expanded cybersex chat first by adding porn video and, soon after, the live-cam with synchronous video communication between participants. Now it is consumed in a great variety ranging from flirting instant messages, contact adverts for offline sex, text-based sex chat, video porn, and various forms of chat in combination with video- and VR communication. Popular and free forms of video-based cybersex include having audiovisual sex on Skype (Skype Sex [Bruce, Steward, and Corinna 2010, 70]) and Chatroulette,[6] the latter randomly connecting its 1.5 million worldwide users (Turkle 2011, 225). An emerging form of cybersex is *sexting*—a portmanteau of sex and texting—which primarily involves mobile phones to exchange explicit messages and images. Users of sexting are called sexters. New apps such as SnapChat and Facebook's Poke messaging app allow users to send images with a lifespan of up to 10 seconds. This has triggered a new viral wave of smartphone sexters to send sexually explicit sexting images. As the image disappears it can be sent and viewed seemingly without risk of trackback. However, this does not protect the images from screenshots.[7]

In virtual worlds such as *IMVU*[8] and *Second Life*,[9] users' 3D avatars can engage in graphically represented sex through advanced preprogrammed animation and custom scripting of movements (Rymaszewski 2006, 75).

Cybersexual interaction between graphic 3D avatars in VR has been common for some time, most notably in *Second Life*. User-controlled avatars interact sexually on-screen by mouse and keyboard commands or through automated, scripted movements. In effect, cybersex in VR has much in common with both chatting and live video chat in that its cybersexual practice is built on an on-screen consensual fantasy arousing sexual emotions leading to autoeroticism and masturbatory behavior.

Within the *Second Life* online community there is a "booming cybersex economy including brothels and avatar prostitutes controlled by real people" (Siegel 2005). One reason for this might be that *Second Life* has a real-world and functional economy through its Linden Dollar system. As the *Second Life* character "Murphy" says:

> It's a 3D chat room and it in no way infringes on our lives…I'm running clubs, I have slave girls, I have loves and adventures. And it's all a fun adventure to him (her real life husband) and me. (Wagner in Johnson, 2010, 211)

Combining sexual and legal fun with the possibility of earning money is not likely to dampen cybersexual activities.

It is much discussed how much cybersex is really going on. Exact numbers and statistics are hard to get, and commercial surveys rarely disclose their sources. How big is cybersex and how many practice it? It is estimated that cybersex in the form of viewing online porn is a $5 billion a year[10] business, earning the Internet its reputation as the largest pornography store in the history of mankind. This substantial, online market mirrors the complexity and diversity of human sexuality. As Internet "Rule 34" puts it: if you can imagine it, it exists as Internet porn (Paasonen 2011, 1). While most humans display sexual curiosity, it is to be anticipated that most Internet users sooner or later try cybersex in some form or another. Yet there are no consistent numbers as to how many people regularly practice cybersex. One indication is the number of cybersexual searches, which is between 10 and 15 percent of all search engine traffic (Ogas and Gaddam 2011). Another is the number of porn sites; estimates range from 260 million to just 4 percent of all active websites. This could indicate fewer than 100,000 active porn sites (Ruvolo 2011). This does not cover cybersex in social media or sexting on mobile phones. If 4 percent of Facebook's soon-to-be one billion users regularly practice cybersex, this could indicate 40 million daily users; a significant number, but far from everybody. If we estimate a range from 10 percent to 4 percent of all current 2.3 billion Internet users (2012),[11] there would be from 230 million to less than 100 million cybersex practitioners. Emerging technologies will influence both the numbers and demography of users. The advent of sexting on smartphones is likely to increase the numbers of eWhores who do eWhoring through selling explicit pictures.[12]

How real is the experience of cybersex in VR today? Despite our techno-erotic fantasies, Ben-Ze'ev (2004) describes cybersex as straightforward social interaction where "people send provocative and erotic messages to each other, with the purpose of bringing each other to orgasm as they masturbate in real time." Here the sex is as real as your orgasm. In technological terms, cybersex is still remote from the cybersexual visions as described in the aforementioned literature and movies. Although practice-based cybersex has impacted on the boundaries of human sexuality, it is still some way from realizing its full potential. Yet it has significantly impacted how we connect and communicate. How, then, does the virtual dimension really function as sex? Is not sex without a body a kind of fake sex? As the next section will show, sensing a physical form of sex does not always need to involve a real body.

Phantom Sex

Why does cybersex work when it is so obviously distant, noncorporeal, and mediated through wires? A phenomenon that makes cybersex not just believable, but appearing real, is the combination of our sexual imagination with our discursive online identities. First of all, we have a "natural tendency to fantasize and close gaps in subjectively important information in ambiguous situations" (Joinson 2007, 316). This, in combination with users' extensive use of made-up, freely editable profiles (handles), triggers psychophysical experiences that can be described as phantom emotions, that is, feeling something as real although it is not at hand (Joinson 2007, 316). In online communication, users thus form consensual fantasies that are experienced as if they are physically real. These fantasies, so to speak, become real: users report feeling sexually aroused as if they actually had corporally intimate sex. The (real) sex between two (real) bodies is not there, but the ghostlike feeling of the other partner is strong. Just as amputees report experiencing real pain in a missing body part, cybersex users feel as if they are having real (phantom) sex. They are "sex-cited"[13] into feeling "sex-sations."[14] This has a parallel in the *phantom vibration syndrome* known to cell phone users, where "you come armed with this template that leads you to be attentive to sensations that represent a cell phone vibrating," Jeffrey Janata says, "and it leads you to over-incorporate non-vibratory sensations and attribute them to the idea that you're receiving a phone call."[15] This is a phenomenon of neuroplasticity—the brain's ability to form new connections in response to changes in the environment (Shaw and McEachern 2001). Likewise, we seem to come armed with templates for sensing sex, even if it is "only" virtual.

There is neurological evidence that we are born to love. Our "near-desperate need for love" literally lives in the brain in the subset of brain cells called mirror neurons (Horstman 2011, 1). They are specialized to respond to what we see, hear, and sense. The behavior and emotions that others display are effectively reflected, mimicked, and mirrored in our brains (Voland and Grammer 2003, 319). We thus understand others by feeling, not by thinking alone. In part, this explains the causal self-strengthening of cybersexual communication. When we read, listen, and see during cybersex, these neurons help us identify and become one with others. We literally project ourselves into the body of others, feeling what they feel, becoming erotized by others' arousal and readiness. As in normal sex, such an awareness of the other's arousal is a key element in getting excited (Soble 2006, 213). A curious example of this is the so-called "panda porn," where panda bears are shown video "porn" of other pandas copulating. Seeing these explicit images make them reproduce better (Rhatigan 2010, 29). How does this mirroring affect the profound deceptions we encounter in cyberspace such as the invented personalities, bodies, and fantastical identities encountered in *FurryMuck* (Collins in Soble and Power 2008, 128)? The physiological effects produced by mirror neurons turns cyberspace into an extension of our bodies, affecting our senses and emotions in real time. Mirror neurons thus explain how our cybersexual fantasies can be experienced as real physiological sensations. Although we meet imaginary people online, they are still somewhat real to us. Yet there is no actual bodily touch happening, leaving us wishful for dildonic and material technologies to let that come about.

Teledildonics: Dressing Up for Cybersex

One of the most influential recipes for sex in virtual reality has been Howard Rheingold's vision of teledildonics as a sexual communication device. Rheingold got the word "dildonics" from the computer visionary Ted Nelson, who coined it in 1974.[16] The following excerpt describes teledildonics as a future, ultimate form of "tactile telepresence":

> Picture yourself...getting dressed for a hot night in the virtual village. Before you climb into a suitably padded chamber and put on your headmounted display, you slip into a lightweight...bodysuit....Embedded in the inner surface of the suit...is an array of intelligent effectors...ultra-tiny vibrators of varying degrees of hardness, hundreds of them per square inch, that can receive and transmit a realistic sense of tactile presence....You can reach out your virtual hand, pick up a virtual block, and by running your fingers over the object, feel the surfaces and edges....You can run your cheek over (virtual) satin and feel the difference when you encounter (virtual) human flesh. Or you can gently squeeze something soft and pliable and feel it stiffen and rigidify under your touch. (Rheingold 1992, 346)

This description was inspired by the excitement about VR technologies that marked the early nineties, sparked by VPL Research and the National Aeronautics and Space Administration's (NASA) research on bodysuits and head-mounted displays (HMDs). For the first time in history, and almost three decades after Sutherland first demonstrated real-time 3D graphics with his 1966 "Sword of Damocles" system (Pimentel and Teixeira 1995), users could access a similar experience on a commercially available system. The cultural craze and thinking surrounding VR served as an inspiration for the sci-fi horror movie *Lawnmower Man* (Leonard and Everett 1992), which depicted participants wearing HMDs and bodysuits to engage in hardcore VR cybersex. In the movie, the sex goes horribly wrong, traumatizing the female sex partner into insanity, thus providing a strong image for the potentially negative consequences of future cybersex.

The "cyberSM" project (Stenslie 2010) demonstrated in 1993 the first haptic, full-body, person-to-person communication system between Cologne and Paris (fig. 18.1). It created a multisensory cybersexual experience based on real-time, visual, auditory, and tactile communication through a computer environment. Through wearing bodysuits with built-in vibrotactile, heat- and electric-current-based stimuli, participants were enabled to physically "touch" each other over distances. The bodysuit stimulated eight larger zones on the body, thus inducing an immersive sense of being touched. Initially, participants choose their own visual identity, or avatar, from a large 3D "bodybank" of scanned and digitized human bodies. Users can mix pieces from any gender, creating transgendered avatars. At the outset of communication, the personal avatars are exchanged and, from then on, function as an interface both to be touched and to transfer touch back to its originator. Altogether, therefore, cyberSM represents a rough, but functioning version of Rheingold's teledildonic vision, capable of forming strong emotional and sensual ties between its participants. One of the ironies of technologically mediated sex is exemplified through the use of bodysuits. You have to dress to have sex.

Another pleasure suit where users could copulate without physical contact (Jütte 2005, 334) was Vivid Entertainment's Cyber Sex Suit (1999). Shaped as a tight wetsuit and attached to a desktop computer, it was conceived for the commercial sex market, but never made it through safety tests. Other related bodysuit-based and haptic interactive

FIGURE 18.1 The cyberSM (Stenslie 2010) teletactile communication experiment from 1993, connecting multiple participants dressed in haptic bodysuits.

projects based on vibrotactile effectors are found in both the military and the commercial sectors. Examples are the TactaVest haptic feedback system, the Philips "emotions jacket" and the Hug Shirt by the CuteCircuit company (Seymour 2008, 40). The Hug Shirt is a Bluetooth and Java-enabled telephone device in the shape of a shirt that lets users exchange vibrotactile stimuli over distance. Although these are not made specifically for cybersex, there is little doubt that users in a future mass market will cross the fine line dividing everyday contact and sex.

Cybersex Machines

Cybersex is not just about virtual and nonphysical sex online, but is also a term covering experiencing corporeal sex with and through various mechanical interfaces and machines. This includes both on- and offline interaction with devices such as computer-controlled dildos and "fuck machines." These devices have in common that they more often than not try to mimic the moves and touch of a human sexual partner.

Sex machines are built in a wide range of models both for sale and as home kits. One example is the Thrillhammer, which lets its users set speed, stroke length, stroke depth, and time of a mechanically moving dildo (Archibald 2005).[17] The RealTouch device[18] is an artificial and mechanical vagina that allows users to "feel the action." Connecting the RealTouch device to the computer is described as a "gateway to non-stop action with...willing partners, who are always ready when you are. As the videos play (on the computer screen), *RealTouch* synchronizes the movements of its interior, heating elements, lube mechanism, and orifice to match the onscreen events in real-time."[19]

In relation to virtual, online sex, these sex machines can be described as sexual prosthetics in terms of extending the body functionality if connected online, thus letting users mechanically and teledildonically copulate with each other while watching the sexual encounter on screen, but also through utilizing the body of the user similar to Gibson's description of the abject "meat puppets" in *Neuromancer*. Users can thus exercise active control over the sexual experience of their online partner, but in turn also be subject to control themselves.

One example of extraordinary sex machines supposed to function virtually through invisible forces is the "sex boxes" by Wilhelm Reich. In 1940 he constructed small, human-sized chambers that supposedly functioned as "orgone" and sexual energy accumulator chambers. Reich explained orgone as a primordial cosmic energy necessary to release the orgiastic potency in life. The chambers were built in relation to sexual therapeutics, but the core idea is simple: experiencing orgasms is a healthy and necessary part of life. This "definite sexual effect" of the orgone accumulator is also described by William S. Burroughs, who built one himself (Burroughs 1993, 164). A similar technology is described in the movie *Sleeper* (1973) by Woody Allen, featuring orgasmatron booths.

CYBERSEXUAL TECHNOLOGIES AND PROJECTS

Is cybersex really sex? Some argue that if it is less real, then it is also less sex (Soble and Power 2008, 211). If you are after real sex, then you will not be satisfied by the phantom feeling; you want the actual in-body, cutaneous experience. A range of experimental projects give an indication of how digital technology might influence and shape our sexual and intimate future.

Cybersexual computer games have been around since 1980. One of the best-known historical games is *Virtual Valerie* by Michael Saenz, released in 1990. Here penetration fantasies reached new depths (Price and Shildrick 1999, 141). The goal of the game is to make the virtual character Valerie achieve orgasm by moving a dildo-icon in and out of her vagina. A meter measures the on-screen activity, eventually making Valerie come. The high number of sales[20] indicates users' curiosity for visual sex-based games as a source of pleasure.

Experimental audio has also been used to produce cybersexual pleasures. *Cyborgasm* (1993) by Lisa Palac, the editor of the former *Future Sex* magazine, is a highly explicit audio CD with a collection of erotic fantasies "so real you're not just hearing sex, you're having it" (Weiss 1996, 201). Using binaural, so-called 3D audio recording technology live on (real) location, *Cyborgasm* features sounds ranging from "sweet nothing whispers to no-holds-barred lust." *Cyborgasm* reveals the romantic, surreal, voyeuristic and dark sides of sexual fantasy and the importance of sound in such experiences (Weiss 1996, 201). Here the audio becomes a sensory substitute for the lack of touch, indicating that sound also is useful "to convert any kind of sensory information to touch" (Danilov, Tyler, and Kaczmarek in Grunwald 2008, 479) or at least an impression thereof.

How cyberintimacy can produce a sense of touch through cross-modal manipulation of sight and touch is demonstrated in the media art installation *Telematic Dreaming* (1992) by Paul Sermon.[21] The installation connects two double beds, each with one participant, in separate locations via a real-time videoconferencing network. The participants see the projection of each other on the bed, thus giving a visual impression of sharing the same bed. The video-based interaction contains no direct tactile stimulation, but users report a strong sense of physicality both when touching the projection of the other and when being virtually touched (Kozel in Classen 2005, 439). One of the main aims of the art installation is to critically show how the user's telepresent body is controlled by a voyeurism of its self. At the same time, it is a prime demonstration of how haptic vision produces a mental impression of touch through live imagery, indicating how and why we find telematic embraces intimate, personal, and possibly sexual.

Another experimental cybersex domain is found in augmented reality, where, for instance, virtual manga dolls like the cyber figurine Alice[22] can be controlled and manipulated by visual markers. The doll can be undressed and talks and reacts to every "touch," showing how augmented, visual interaction can induce haptic sensing (Paterson 2007).

Human-robot relations are also an active area for cybersexual explorations, ranging from the inanimate "Real Doll" sex puppets to Japanese sex robots to Geminoids (geminoid.dk) (Lévy 2008) (see also Billinghurst et al., chapter 37 in this volume).

A stranger vision of cybersex is found in Bjørk's video "All Is Full of Love," directed by Chris Cunningham (1999), where two robots engage in sex. This raises the question when and if computers can have "sex" too, whether in the form of genetic algorithms breeding new computers and programs or some form of asexual reproductions in an attempt to reproduce natural reproduction (see Taylor, chapter 32 in this volume, on digital evolution and asexual reproduction).

One missing link in cybersexual simulation is smell. As important as it is for sex, there exists no sufficiently advanced or sensorially convincing technology to produce this vital sensorial ingredient (Jütte 2005, 333). Several unsuccessful attempts have been made, such as the Smell-O-Rama movies from the fifties and DigiScents *iSmell* (Marks 2002, 113). Without a complete sensory immersion, how can we experience cybersex as good as, or even better than, normal sex?

Taxonomy of Cybersexual Immersion

The subjective sense of immersion is a good measure of how real a cybersexual experience might feel. Immersion is the "suspension of disbelief" (Laurel 1993, 113), making our online, consensual fantasies come alive (see also Calleja, chapter 13 in this volume). From a phenomenological point of view, immersion is "the sense of presence through which the user feels corporeally connected to the world" (Ryan 2001, 14). Sherman and Craig (2003, 381) point to two kinds of immersion: the mental and the physical (sensory). Mental immersion is what makes current nonphysical cybersex environments (chat, live video, VR, etc.) feel real, supported through mechanisms such as mirror neurons and neuroplasticity. Haptic physical immersion is still uncommon. It results as the experience of haptic impressions involving the user's physical body, often caused by some form of mechanical and computer controlled technology like the cyberSM project. Physical, somatic, and corporeal immersion relevant for cybersexual experiences can be subdivided into *visual*, *aural*, and *tactile* immersion.

Visual immersion is found in Sermon's *Telematic Dreaming* (1992). As users have reported, it creates sensations of presence with others, immersion in the story, and phantom sensations of touch (Classen 2005, 439), all of which influence our sense of having corporeal sex. Vision can in itself create sensations of touch (Paterson 2007, 56). Vision-touch synesthesia, a mental sensation of haptic immersion, can be caused by visual impressions similar to the haptic imagery of cinema (Marks 2002, 13) and cross-modal transfers from vision to touch are found both in movies and *Telematic Dreaming*. Given the right combination, haptic vision without real physical stimuli can enhance the somatic sensations and sense of immersion. So-called *haptic images* encourage a bodily relationship between the image and the viewer (Marks 2002, 3; 2000, 129). Visual stimulation can thus cause sensory impressions of both touch and smell. This partly explains why users find cybersexual imagery real.

Aural immersion is experienced in *Cyborgasm* (1993), based on binaural sound, recorded and reproduced as it is heard stereophonically by the ear. Although a rough averaging out of human aural physiology, binaural recording can give the sound of "being there" as auditory sensory substitution provides an impression of space and presence (Dodsworth 1998).

Tactile immersion, as in Rheingold's teledildonics, is difficult to produce (Stenslie 2010, 124). Cybertouch in immersive environments is usually caused by cross-modal synesthesia or a specific vibrotactile stimulation of the users through bodysuits (cyberSM) or teledildonics (RealTouch). Common difficulties to overcome are wearability problems, such as fitting problems of interface/suit, restriction of movement, and vibrotactile stimuli with a poor range/resolution/expressivity and, currently, costs.

These are some of the technologies and approaches that give cybersex a physical dimension, but do they make the sex better? Or at least instantaneous?

INSTANT SEX

Cybersex is highly attractive to many because of its assurance of instant sexual gratification. It promises you what you want, when you want it, at low cost, minus the "messiness and hassles" of a person-to-person relationship, and with complete anonymity (Gula 2010, 169). What if we could have instant sex and cyborgasms at the push of a button? If possible, then it would most likely have been produced a long time ago; the human sexual apparatus and interplay appear far too complex. And yet there are neurological and physiological shortcuts to induce orgasms in males within minutes. For example, applying the medical FertiCare vibrator, with the right combination of vibratory amplitude and frequency to the male "G-spot" on the shaft of the penis, can produce physiological ejaculation within the shortest time. However, this technique comes with a warning. Unless the user is also psychologically erotized he or she might experience harmful problems with the heart. The *Artgasm* project (Stenslie 2010, 133) successfully used this technology to make participants involuntarily come, thus verifying the possibility of a future Orgasmatron. There are complex ethical and psychological dimensions to consider when producing instant sex with little or no foreplay, such as users' reports of ejaculations with lessened feeling of pleasure. Instant sex appears, therefore, at its best to be considered an extension of current online cybersexual communication and foreplay with other human participants through words, video, and voice. After all, it takes time to be erotized.

CRITIQUE AND ETHICAL ISSUES

Cybersex has been the subject of much critique, from gender-based issues and concerns commented on in postmodern cyberfeminism (Haraway 2004, 112; Plant 1998; Stone 1996, 17; Turkle 2011, 211) to law enforcement's control of cybersexual crime (Waskul 2003, 52) to health issues (Cooper 2002, 63). The critique can be generalized in two approaches: (1) replacement theory—how it degenerates and replaces human sexuality; and (2) addition theory—how cybersex adds to human sexuality.

The replacement theory focus on the dark side of cybersex, calling it "the crack cocaine of sexual addiction" (Cooper 2002, 63), leading to negative aspects such as: cybersexual dependency; compulsory, out-of-control sexual behavior; and sexual isolation. Since it apparently demands a lower level of social skills and intimacy than in real life, cybersex is here seen as an escape in need of therapy. Referring to hard-core, violent, sexist, and racist cybersex, Dines (2010) argues that porn desensitizes and actually limits our sexual freedom, making its omnipresence a public health concern we can no longer ignore.

Cybersex can create sexual problems such as Internet sexual compulsion and behavior. These users fall into three categories: (1) a discovery group; (2) a predisposed group who have experienced "out-of-control sexual behavior on the Internet while obsessing over unacted-on sexual fantasies and urges"; and (3) a lifelong sexually compulsive group with "ongoing and severe sexual behavior problems" (Edwards et al. 2011). The question arises: who is to define when a sexual behavior problem exists? Furthermore, is it a problem based on moral or material issues? One evident material issue relates to users spending too much money on online porn. Solutions to this can be quite practical and related to users understanding, assessing, and managing their Internet use. Moral issues are complex and manifold, but often relate to how our online anonymity makes our sense of moral freedom greater. In turn this seems to lessen our sense of moral emotions such as shame and guilt when being unfaithful to real-life partners and expressing controversial emotions such as hate and intense sexual desires (Ben-Ze'ev 2004, 115). This makes it a challenge to achieve a balance of healthy online with healthy offline sexuality.

On the Internet, we are together, yet corporeally alone (Turkle 2011). This lonely and physical fact turns cybersex into a form of masturbatory autoeroticism. This goes against religiously correct conduct such as the catechism of the Roman Catholic Church. Here masturbation is seen as a "gravely disordered action" since it violates the purpose of sex as the "total meaning of mutual self-giving and human procreation in the context of true love."[23] The range of serious and complex issues goes on. Online, your avatar can have sex with anyone and anything (*FurryMuck*). If it is only simulated sex, how to argue that it is morally wrong? What about pedophilia and having sex with avatars looking like children (see also Ess, chapter 41 in this volume)? *Second Life* has forbidden any form of "ageplay," describing it as the sexual act between a child and adult avatar despite both users being over 18 in real life (Johnson 2010, 211).[24] Who is to police this within a multidimensional cyberspace? The movie *Strange Days* portraits cybersexual acts of rape. In an online analogy, what if your avatar kills its virtual lover afterward? These are surely extreme questions compared to the more mundane and sexually normal interests most people show online (Ogas and Gaddam 2011), but other real-life consequences are starting to have an impact. Many, and in particular Asian and East European women, are now engaged in the cybersex industry as porn professionals and workers (Ogas and Gaddam 2011). Without Gibson's SimStim technology, their future status remain uncertain, but likely comparable to "meat puppets."

On the other side, cybersex can solve sexual problems. The addition theory argues that cybersex is "a healthy way to explore sexuality in a safe environment" (Delmonico and Griffin in Gula 2010, 169), enabling humans to get out of isolation and into contact with others. Cybersex practitioners in *Second Life* credit cybersex with helping them to overcome sexual repression and sense of shame (Wagner 2007). Despite the numerous potentially negative aspects, there are perhaps more positive aspects that may even increase our happiness (Ben-Ze'ev 2004, 129).

The ethics of cybersex are as complex as the cybersexual diversity found online. It is therefore also "as much about discourse as about intercourse" (Thomas in Waskul 2004, 106). Cybersex represent a continuing, existentially important discussion. What happens to our sexuality with the commoditization of cybersexual desires? Is cybersex only harmless fantasy? Will we forget how to touch in real life? What about our everyday, normal contact with other people? Will touch be sexualized when even the simplest handshake is remapped to teledildonic sensations? (Rheingold in Waskul 2004, 321). Also, since "sex is perfectly natural, but not naturally perfect" (Johanson 1992), it has to start somewhere, and sexual behavior has also to be learned. Cybersex is here, both a starting point and a playground.

In Wiener's publication on the cybernetic theory (1954, 1
only be understood through a study of the messages
which belong to it." New technologies and increasing cyl
many questions open concerning how our society might dev.
approach the dystopic visions of the move *Blade Runner*, where (the
Pygmalion myth) you can grow your own living, sexual pets—or even your ow.
thereby turning sex into factual autoeroticism? As globalization swells and the matrix
of computer networks shrink distance, this will amplify the multicultural, multisexual
aspects of the world. Such a scenario will affect the sexual preferences and needs of the
"sexiest primate," making them exponentially grow and diversify. What will this do to
us? The day cybersex becomes better than real sex, humanity will slowly die out. Or will
human nurture and care win? It seems clear, though, that cybersex is here with us and
challenging our notions of sex as an epidermal, skin-to-skin activity.

Notes

1. "Cybernetic" refers to Norbert Wiener's cybernetic theory describing control and communication through machinic systems.
2. Designed by Doug Brown in 1973, built upon the PLATO architecture (Woolley 1994).
3. Although "avatar" is commonly used to describe visual representations.
4. http://pastebin.com/kXquBrZu, accessed August 8, 2013.
5. http://www.garethsden.com/adult_furry_stories/garethsden.com_adventuresofcindy_1slumberparty.html, accessed August 8, 2013.
6. http://chatroulette.com/.
7. http://reviews.cnet.com/8301-19512_7-57429513-233/sexters-who-are-all-about-caution-this-apps-for-you/, accessed August 8, 2013.
8. http://www.imvu.com.
9. http://secondlife.com/.
10. http://www.businessinsider.com/14-amazing-facts-about-internet-porn-2010-6#us-consumers-account-for-over-half-of-all-online-porn-revenue-4, August 8, 2013.
11. http://www.howmanyarethere.org/how-many-internet-users-are-there-in-the-world-2012/, accessed August 8, 2013.
12. http://www.imperva.com/docs/HII_Monitoring_Hacker_Forums_2012.pdf, accessed January 31, 2013.
13. Portmanteau from "sexually" and "excited."
14. Portmanteau from "sexual" and "sensations."
15. http://www.usatoday.com/news/health/2007-06-12-cellphones_N.htm, accessed August 8, 2013.
16. http://wiki.opendildonics.org/, established to document the development and history of sex technology in all forms.
17. http://www.thethrillhammer.com.

//www.realtouch.com.
tp://www.realtouch.com/device, accessed August 8, 2013.
http://articles.sun-sentinel.com/1993-07-12/business/9301230734_1_software-publishers-association-software-makers-member- software, accessed August 8, 2013.
21. http://creativetechnology.salford.ac.uk/paulsermon/dream/, accessed January 31, 2013.
22. http://www.geishatokyo.com/jp/ar-figure/figure.html, accessed April 10, 2012.
23. Catechism 2352, http://www.vatican.va/archive/ccc_css/archive/catechism/p3s2c2a6.htm, accessed August 8, 2013.
24. http://secondlifeproject.wordpress.com/2011/03/04/let%E2%80%99s-not-be-heteronormative-here-my-experience-with-virtual-sexuality-experimentation/, accessed August 8, 2013.

REFERENCES

Allen, W., dir. 1973. *Sleeper*. Written by W. Allen and M. Brickman. United Artists.
Archibald, T. 2005. *Sex Machines: Photographs and Interviews*. Los Angeles: Process.
Benyon, D., P. Turner, and S. Turner. 2005. *Designing Interactive Systems: People, Activities, Contexts, Technologies*. Essex (UK): Pearson Education.
Ben-Ze'ev, A. 2004. *Love Online: Emotions on the Internet*. New York: Cambridge University Press.
Bigelow, K., dir. 1995. *Strange Days*. Story by J. Cameron and J. Cocks. Twentieth Century Fox.
Bricken, W. 1990. Virtual Reality: Directions of Growth. September 10. *SIGGRAPH Proceedings, 1990*. http://www.hitl.washington.edu/publications/m-90-1/. Accessed August 8, 2013.
Bright, S., and L. Palac. 1993. *Cyborgasm*. Audio CD.
Bruce, M., and R. M. Stewart, eds. 2010. *College Sex—Philosophy for Everyone: Philosophers with Benefits*. Oxford: John Wiley and Sons.
Burroughs, W. S. 1993. *The Adding Machine: Selected Essays*. New York: Arcade Publishing.
Classen, C. 2005. *The Book of Touch*. New York: Berg.
Cooper, A. 2002. *Sex and the Internet: A Guidebook for Clinicians*. New York: Brunner-Routledge.
Cramer, F., and Stewart Home. 2005. Pornographic Coding. http://www.netzliteratur.net/cramer/pornography/london-2005/pornographic-coding.html. Accessed August 8, 2012.
Crumlish, C., and E. Malone. 2009. *Designing Social Interfaces*. Cambridge: O'Reilly Media.
Dines, G. 2010. *Pornland: How Porn Has Hijacked Our Sexuality*. Boston: Beacon Press.
Dodsworth, C. 1998. *Digital Illusion: Entertaining the Future with High Technology*. New York: ACM Press.
Edwards, W. M., D. Delmonico, and E. Griffin. 2011. *Cybersex Unplugged*. N.p.: Createspace.
Glyn Jones, R. 1996. *Cybersex*. New York: Carroll & Graf.
Grunwald, M. 2008. *Human Haptic Perception: Basics and Applications*. Boston: Birkhäuser.
Gula, R. M. 2010. *Just Ministry: Professional Ethics for Pastoral Ministers*. Mahwah, NJ: Paulist Press.
Hahn, H. 1996. *The Internet Complete Reference*. 2nd ed. Berkeley, CA: Osborne McGraw-Hill.
Haraway, D. J. 2004. *The Haraway Reader*. New York: Routledge.
Hardie, P. R. 2002. *Ovid's Poetics of Illusion*. New York: Cambridge University Press.
Heim, M. 1993. *The Metaphysics of Virtual Reality*. New York: Oxford University Press.
Horstman, J. 2011. *The Scientific American Book of Love, Sex and the Brain: The Neuroscience of How, When, Why and Who We Love*. Oxford: John Wiley and Sons.
Johanson, S. 1992. *Sex Is Perfectly Natural but Not Naturally Perfect*. New York: Viking.

Johnson, P. 2010. *Second Life, Media, and the Other Society*. New York: Peter Lang.

Joinson, A. N. 2007. *The Oxford Handbook of Internet Psychology*. New York: Oxford University Press.

Jones, S. 1998. *CyberSociety 2.0: Revisiting Computer-Mediated Communication and Community*. Thousand Oaks, CA: Sage.

Jütte, R. 2005. *A History of the Senses: From Antiquity to Cyberspace*. Cambridge: Polity Press.

Kroker, A., and M. Kroker. 1987. *Body Invaders: Panic Sex in America*. Montreal: New World Perspectives.

Laurel, B. 1993. *Computers as Theatre*. Reading, MA: Addison-Wesley.

Leonard, B., dir. 1992. *Lawnmower Man*. New Line Cinema.

Lenhard, J. 2011. *Hyperreal Obscenities: Baudrillard on Cybersex*. Norderstedt, Germany: GRIN Verlag.

Lévy, D. 2008. *Love + Sex with Robots: The Evolution of Human-Robot Relations*. New York: Harper Collins.

Lovy, S., dir. 1990. *Circuitry Man*. DVD. Sony Pictures Home Entertainment.

Maines, R. P. 2001. *The Technology of Orgasm: "Hysteria," the Vibrator, and Women's Sexual Satisfaction*. Baltimore, MD: Johns Hopkins University Press.

Marks, L. U. 2000. *The Skin of the Film: Intercultural Cinema, Embodiment, and the Senses*. Durham, NC: Duke University Press.

Marks, L. U. 2002. *Touch: Sensuous Theory and Multisensory Media*. Minneapolis: University of Minnesota Press.

Ogas, O., and S. Gaddam. 2011. *A Billion Wicked Thoughts: What the World's Largest Experiment Reveals about Human Desire*. New York: Dutton.

Paasonen, S. 2011. *Carnal Resonance: Affect and Online Pornography*. Cambridge, MA: MIT Press.

Paterson, M. 2007. *The Senses of Touch: Haptics, Affects, and Technologies*. Oxford: Berg.

Pimentel, K., and K. Teixeira. 1995. *Virtual Reality: Through the New Looking Glass*. New York: Intel/McGraw-Hill.

Plant, S. 1998. *Zeros + Ones: Digital Women + the New Technoculture*. London: Fourth Estate.

Posner, R. A. 1994. *Sex and Reason*. Cambridge, MA: Harvard University Press.

Price, J., and M. Shildrick. 1999. *Feminist Theory and the Body: A Reader*. New York: Routledge.

Rhatigan, J. 2010. *Book of Science Stuff*. New York: Imagine.

Rheingold, H. 1992. *Virtual Reality*. New York: Simon and Schuster.

Roberts, R. 1999. *Sexual Generations: "Star Trek, the Next Generation" and Gender*. Urbana: University of Illinois Press.

Ruvolo, J. 2011. How Much of the Internet is Actually for Porn? *Forbes Online*. http://www.forbes.com/sites/julieruvolo/2011/09/07/how-much-of-the-internet-is-actually-for-porn/. Accessed August 8, 2013.

Ryan, M.-L. 2001. *Narrative as Virtual Reality: Immersion and Interactivity in Literature and Electronic Media*. Baltimore, MD: John Hopkins University Press.

Rymaszewski, M. 2006. *Second Life: The Official Guide*. Oxford: John Wiley and Sons.

Seymour, S. 2008. *Fashionable Technology*. Vienna: Springer-Verlag.

Shaw, C. A., and J. C. McEachern. 2001. *Toward a Theory of Neuroplasticity*. Philadelphia: Psychology Press.

Sherman, W. R., and A. B. Craig. 2003. *Understanding Virtual Reality: Interface, Application, and Design*. San Francisco: Morgan Kaufmann Publishers.

Siegel, A. 2005. Sexual Evolution. www.datadreamer.com/teledildonics.pdf. Accessed August 8, 2013.

Soble, A. 2006. *Sex from Plato to Paglia: A Philosophical Encyclopedia*. Vol. 1. Westport, CT: Greenwood.

Soble, A., and N. P. Power. 2008. *The Philosophy of Sex: Contemporary Readings*. London: Rowman and Littlefield.

Stone, A. R. 1996. *The War of Desire and Technology at the Close of the Mechanical Age*. Cambridge, MA: MIT Press.

Stenslie, S. 2010. *Virtual Touch*. Oslo: Oslo School of Architecture and Design.

Sutherland, I. E. 1965. The Ultimate Display. In *Information Processing: Proceedings of the IFIP Congress*, 506–508. Amsterdam: North-Holland.

Turkle, S. 1985. *The Second Self: Computers and the Human Spirit*. New York: Simon and Schuster.

Turkle, S. 2011. *Alone Together: Why We Expect More from Technology and Less from Each Other*. New York: Basic Books.

Vadim, R., dir. 1968. *Barbarella*. Distributed by Paramount Pictures.

Voland, E., and K. Grammer. 2003. *Evolutionary Aesthetics*. New York: Springer.

Wagner, M. May 26, 2007. *InformationWeek*. http://www.informationweek.com/news/199701944? pgno=1. Accessed April 1, 2012.

Waskul, D. D. 2003. *Self-Games and Body-Play: Personhood in Online Chat and Cybersex*. New York: Peter Lang.

Waskul, D. D. 2004. *Net.seXXX: Readings on Sex, Pornography, and the Internet*. New York: Peter Lang.

Weiss, A. S. 1996. *Experimental Sound and Radio*. Cambridge, MA: MIT Press.

Wiener, N. 1954. *The Human Use of Human Beings: Cybernetics and Society*. Boston: Houghton Mifflin.

Woolley, D. R. 1994. *PLATO: The Emergence of Online Community*. http://www.thinkofit.com/plato/dwplato.htm. Accessed August 8, 2013.

CHAPTER 19

A VIRTUAL ASSEMBLY: CONSTRUCTING RELIGION OUT OF ZEROS AND ONES

ROBERT M. GERACI

DOWN ON THE VIRTUAL ANT FARM

THANKS to technological progress in and rapid deployment of artificial intelligence and virtual reality worlds, we have an opportunity to reimagine our religious lives. Instead of sacrificing religion at a technoscientific altar, in our secular age we have new ways of creating meaning and experiencing transcendence. The portability, decreasing costs, and vast reach of digital technologies ensure that they will be among the most powerful ways in which to create a world replete with both religious meaning and technological sophistication. While the consensus on this is not yet unanimous, both technical experts and the consuming public see many possibilities for re-enchanting the world through virtual reality; as a result, scholars must employ a method competent to address virtual worlds and their place in religious life. By borrowing actor-network theory (ANT) from the sociology of science, scholars of religion and virtual worlds can appreciate how the residents of virtual worlds employ those worlds and their contents to perform a variety of religious tasks.

As the population increasingly avails itself of virtual technologies, many religious practices and beliefs will necessarily change; so to follow these changes and provide an accurate account of them we need a new method for their study. Virtual worlds are sophisticated technical apparatuses; they are, themselves, the products of profound academic, economic, mechanical, and leisure collaboration. A virtual world is a "synchronous, persistent network of people, represented as avatars, facilitated by networked computers" (Bell 2008, 2). In keeping with this definition, this chapter will primarily address gaming and digital platforms that create worlds that can be simultaneously occupied by many residents. While exploring and acting within games such as *Skyrim* or *Spore* can have meaningful results, this chapter engages the specific effects of virtual worlds upon religious life. Although there is profound continuity from prior technologies, virtual worlds are not simply glorified books, and they do permit new ways of socializing. To track the social bonds they afford, we must delve into the nature and contents of the worlds.

According to ANT theorists, social relationships are encoded and solidified primarily through durable physical objects. Merely agreeing to support one another is insufficient, so we build group cohesion into the landscape. "It's the power exerted through entities that don't sleep and associations that don't break down that allows power to last longer and expand further—and, to achieve such a feat, many more materials than social compacts have to be devised" (Latour 2005, 70). That is, to maintain social arrangements, we solidify them, literally, in objects. The Torah does not just create mutual obligations between ancient Hebrews and their God, it connects modern Jews to one another in a system of mutual recognition and support. Its divine contract is subordinate to its social contract—its restriction of how people will act toward and among one another. The power of religious objects can be quite strong in this regard.

Typically, sociologists study social groups by focusing upon human actors and institutions, but frequently these are impossible to fully understand without appreciating how natural objects participate in our social groups. To appreciate how physical objects redirect human actions, consider the "polling place priming effect." Multiple studies have confirmed that where an individual votes can produce predictable outcomes; that is, if you want voters to decide one way rather than another, you would be well off restricting their polling options to specific places that will produce the desired results. Voting in schools, for example, inclines voters toward proeducation voting, while voting in churches can encourage socially conservative voting about issues such as abortion or birth control (see Blumenthal and Turnipseed 2011). Even *imagining* that one is in a church—as opposed to a collegiate student center, for example—impacts the voter, inclining him or her toward a politically conservative stance (Heflick 2009). It is clear, then, that the polling place is an actor; it acts upon the voter, redirecting him or her from one outcome toward another. Building an actor-network requires that we identify the natural objects that participate in our society; it requires that we find all of the actors, be they human or not.

Because both humans and nonhumans are actors, sociologists, theologians, and others must appreciate the complex ways in which the "natural" and the "artificial" intertwine in the religious use of virtual worlds. Religions are both natural and social artifacts; they exist as a consequence of the people, places, and communities that compose them and, increasingly, the technologies through which they are mediated, be these texts, arts, or television shows. Virtual worlds are, of course, also assemblages of the natural and the social. As we look deeply into the constituents of modern life, we will find that every one of them is likewise both natural and social. It is turtles all the way down. But while many assemblages may be taken as understood and, therefore, resist further interrogation, the brave new world of modern religion and its virtual components may not be. To understand how religion will work in the twenty-first century demands that we take apart the virtual assembly and follow the influence of every actor ("real" or "virtual," human or nonhuman) that helps produce it. In part, virtual worlds reveal that religions have always been constructed out of both "social" and "natural" objects; however, the depth to which this is the case in a time of revolutionary technology demands that we interrogate who and what contributes to our religious lives. In the twenty-first century, a true and helpful sociology of religion must account for new constituents of the religious world; these new participants in our sacred economy include many humans but also nonhumans (especially virtual worlds and their content).

A web of social relations is vast, with many points where one person, group, or thing connects to others; appreciating this process does not become simpler when one examines virtual worlds. As a consequence, we need a sociological method strong enough to account for the many elements of our virtual societies, which are never cleanly severed from conventional reality. In order to see which objects can be used to tie knots at the points of intersection in our virtual networks, we can employ ANT. Actor-network theory posits that many actors, both human and nonhuman, compose every society, and that some of those actors employ others precisely for the purpose of maintaining social groups. The users, residents, and occupants of virtual worlds use the worlds and their contents to stabilize religious and quasi-religious communities. As we press forward into the virtual age, ANT will be crucial if we wish to appreciate the role of virtuality in religious practice and belief.

RELIGIOUS ARTIFACTS

Religions are complicated institutions. We often simplify them, hiding their histories, their controversies, their schisms, and their richness; we do this through the magic of the word—by naming them. As Adam mastered divine creation by giving names to all of God's creations in Genesis, we name a convoluted mix of practices, beliefs, texts, traditions, doctrines, symbols, and so on, and thereby gain a certain power over it. Of course, it has been widely recognized that to speak of "Judaism" or "Hinduism" or any other tradition as though it were some monolithic entity across space and time is to assert little more than our own ignorance; nearly all religions are composed of many sociohistorical traditions (see Holdrege 2000; Smith 1983). At times, however, it helps to use shorthand, and certainly it is not without meaning to speak, for example, of Hinduism as a religion practiced in India and elsewhere. As long as we pay meticulous attention to the ways (material, discursive, and social) in which identity is imagined, explored, and established, it is possible to make intelligible taxonomic claims (Smith 1983, 18). Nevertheless, religions are difficult to capture, and such taxonomic systems as we might envision will never succeed in doing it completely. Sometimes—especially in times of change or novelty—we must unpack those names, tracing the many elements that compose a religious system, tradition, or practice.

Specifically, a fully developed sociology of religion will attempt to account for individual persons, institutions over the course of time, material objects like temples, texts, or landscapes, and immaterial objects like beliefs or traditions, especially as they are made real through practices and physical objects like icons and catechisms. Even bodies can be religious objects, as we habituate behaviors in them, and those behaviors subsequently reinforce particular social groupings and ideas (see Bourdieu [1980] 1990). All of these things are actors; all of them influence one another, changing the course of history. A sociology that speaks only of the human and omits the nonhuman has simply not recognized the true nature of a society or the forces that bring one together (see Latour 2005).

Religious groups, like other communities, must work hard to maintain their stability over time; one of their chief assets is the plethora of symbols and structures they construct to uphold social relations. Actor-network theory recognizes that power relations and cultural meta-discourses could not exist without objectification, without instantiation in actual objects. Applied to religion, this means that hierarchies, beliefs, and even whole theologies must remain attached to the empirical realm. The richness of religious iconography and architecture is a testament to this fact. At one time, Christians perhaps required passwords or secret signs to recognize one another, but such "objects" are themselves ephemeral; a crucifix worn about the neck suffices much more readily to define group membership, express a theology of atonement through Jesus of Nazareth, and even encourage adherence to one moral code or another. Without Bibles, crosses, churches, and other such objects in circulation, Christian communities would flounder and their theologies dissolve. Naturally, this is not just a characteristic of Christian life, but of all religious communities.

Religious societies are thus collaborations of things we ordinarily call social (e.g., theories of atonement) and things we ordinarily call natural (e.g., crucifixes). In ANT, the things that bear the burden of such convolution are actors every bit as important as the intentionally acting human beings. The layering of social and natural in each object is important to their roles in society. A holy text is clearly a natural object constructed out of pigment and page, and yet it is also a social object constructed out of reading and writing practices, influential ideas, and patterns of dissemination. Even the precise nature of the construction matters: a Bible printed on human flesh will affect a reader differently than will one made out of pulped wood.

To speak, to name, is to delimit, and it is vital to our intellectual endeavor if we want to understand what religion is and, more importantly for our present cause, what virtual religion is. It is—to repeat—turtles all the way down; so at some point we must name names and proceed. But let us try to name only those names whose identities are as uncontroversial as we can manage. Where the controversies and complexities are, let us proceed cautiously and with a willingness to think about what might be at stake. To call a book the Bible hides more than it illuminates, and yet the Bible is the Bible and sometimes we must accept it at that. When a controversy arises, however, then it is time to start unpacking the relations.

The creation and use of virtual objects means that the sociology of religion has an entirely new catalog for analysis. Of course, this is precisely because religious people now have a vast array of new objects to employ in stabilizing their groups, ideas, and practices. Likewise, it is the case that with recourse to such objects, religious practitioners have devised new social systems and theological perspectives. While the total number of virtual objects that can do religious work is almost infinite, and the categorization of them is fuzzy at best, there are a few clear types of virtual actors: the things in virtual worlds, the grouping mechanisms of virtual worlds, and the virtual worlds themselves. Within each of these groups, we find new actors that stabilize social relations, from the borders around communities to the ideas, hopes, and practices that users advocate, appreciate, and aspire toward.

The Circulation of Virtual Objects

Bibles are generally—though not always—uncontroversial, but other religious artifacts are not. When groups take up residence online, the social and natural objects constitutive of their existence multiply in fascinating and important ways. While objects online sometimes lack the permanence of their conventional counterparts, they are no less real for that, and no less able to give form and shape to ideas, traditions, and interpersonal connections. In virtual worlds, objects become powerful actors in a religious society, knitting a community together (or creating schisms within it), sustaining a community over time, and even representing and transmitting the group's beliefs and expectations. Virtual objects act upon human actors, and it this power to shape individual beliefs and practices that makes them so important.

To theorize regarding virtual worlds demands rigorous attention to the landscapes and their contents. A futuristic landscape obviously encourages different behaviors from a fantasy landscape, or one that resembles a church or schoolyard. Objects in game worlds also encourage new behaviors; these are especially apparent when the player must create the character whom he or she will play in the game. For example, the presence of mineral veins in the online game *World of Warcraft* encourages the player to choose mining as one of his or her character's professions. At the same time, the presence of herbs encourages players to choose herbalism, and the presence of defeated animal foes encourages skinning. In fact, many players will spend enormous amounts of time at their gathering professions, such as by traveling in preordained circles to mine all of the same mineral veins for hours on end (see also Yee 2006, 69). To further complicate matters, the availability of all these raw materials encourages crafting professions such as alchemy, engineering, or leatherworking. As each character can have only two professions, the competition produced subsequently affects how players travel through the game. The division of labor forges economic and social connections among individuals and imbues a player's behavior with significance not only to him or her, but to others as well.

The presence of virtual objects can be a hindrance to virtual worlds as well as a boon. For example, *City of Heroes* lead designer Matthew Miller notes that some storylines are difficult to use because if an object is there for all users but relevant to only a few, then it will be disruptive for many players. As an example, Miller points to a world where players encounter a dead body in the street: "this works great in a single-player game where you can guarantee that the only person finding the body is the person who needs to find it. But in a multiplayer game like *City of Heroes*, we couldn't have a dead body only show up on one person's screen and not another, and if it showed up for you, yet it wasn't important for a mission you were doing, you would be confused by its presence" (Miller 2009, 127). As technology improves, however, virtual-world designers are getting around this concern. In *World of Warcraft*, for example, "phasing" allows different players to be in different phases of the game; thus the body could be there for someone who has not completed a particular series of events, and absent for those who have (or vice versa).

We can see how virtual objects affect players in game worlds such as *World of Warcraft* and *City of Heroes*, but these do not generally do specifically religious work. Many virtual worlds, however, do have specifically religious objects, such as the *kippot* worn by some Jews in *Second Life*. By wearing a virtual *kippah* or a virtual Christian T-shirt, SL residents can provoke conversation, represent their communities, and remind other residents of religious perspectives, morals, and practices. Such objects can thus have meaningful effects in the world. One creative example of this is the fascinating diversity of objects created for the Aslan's How ministry in *Second Life*. The region, which is built to include key locations in C. S. Lewis's *The Lion, The Witch, and the Wardrobe*, provides "notecards" that explain the theological significance of objects such as the Stone Table upon which Aslan was sacrificed and also incorporates "books" that—when clicked by the visitor—either provide notecards on complex Christian concepts such as its relationship to science or launch recorded sermons on the topics. The presence of both the obvious Christian teaching objects, such as books on theology, and those objects that only implicitly teach about Christianity, such as the Stone Table, gives visitors something to do (i.e., click on them to see what will happen), and subsequently those objects can act in the virtual world upon a person in the conventional world.

Thanks to progress in artificial intelligence (AI), the influence of virtual objects is increasing. As artificial intelligence improves—either by producing more dastardly opponents or by enabling more communicative allies—the virtual landscape will increasingly shape how players interact with it and what goals those players pursue. Already, users of social worlds like *Second Life* have used the scripting languages to produce artificially intelligent agents, including chatterbots that carry on simple conversations with visitors. Rensselaer Polytechnic Institute researcher Selmer Bringsjord and his collaborators, for example, have produced an AI in *Second Life* that they claim has the reasoning powers of a four-year-old child (*Inside Rensselaer* 2008). Likewise, *Second Life*'s founder, Philip Rosedale, desires to produce an AI in that world (Au 2010). People, in general, often form emotional attachments with machines (see Reeves and Nass 1996), and in virtual worlds they can become profoundly attached to artificially intelligent nonplayer characters, such as the "companions" that Bioware includes in its games (e.g., *Star Wars: The Old Republic*).[1] Such AIs could potentially be—and almost certainly will be—employed to specifically religious ends. Just as Christians have long visualized their own inner struggles as the reflection of whispering from a devil on one shoulder and an angel on the other, they may one day have a virtual angel walking through virtual worlds with them, encouraging them to "do the right thing." Already, the Bioware companions leverage players to make particular decisions: the companion's relationship to the player improves or deteriorates based upon moral decisions taken by the player. While this is grounded in a computation of morality and a tree of possibilities rather than artificial intelligence, it remains the case that the companion's presence affects the moral choices of the player. Likewise, other aspects of the virtual environment can reshape a player's mental states and game decisions.

THE TIES THAT BIND

Communities, including religious communities, are in constant danger of dissolution. While it would be absurd to apply the laws of thermodynamics to group behaviors, it remains the case that something akin to entropy increases: individuals differentiate, opinions diverge, and collectives collapse. This is particularly true as more members join the group. To keep the group functional, to ensure that individuals remain a part of the group, requires work. Objects can help with this task: every Jew who dons a *kippah* reinforces his own identification with the group and the mutual bonds that hold all members together. The very act of grouping can be made substantial as well, as when one receives a certificate of completion or membership after joining a religious group. In virtual worlds, groups are not maintained by verbal or typewritten agreement; rather, they are made real through mechanisms provided by the worlds' designers. There are actual group affiliations, generally visible by others, which help contain and affirm membership.

A virtual group is a special kind of object. While in some sense less tangible than other kinds of objects (such as virtual copper or silver), they can nevertheless produce even more powerful results. Every virtual world includes tools to promote social bonds among particular users. Many virtual worlds, for example, allow players to create and join "guilds," form alliances, or otherwise enroll in a community. Though in some sense virtual—for they are largely restricted to the virtual world[2]—these grouping technologies are decidedly real; they exert influence upon residents. Many gamers, for example, will structure their daily lives around a guild calendar that indicates when and where guild members appear online (Jakobsson and Taylor 2003). In *Second Life*, residents may establish groups for a nominal cost, after which the founder can dictate whether enrollment is open or by invite, free or at cost, and establish a hierarchy among members, some of whom will have prerogatives to send messages to the group or administer land owned by the group. Similarly, players in online games can create guilds, whose membership and resources they administer. Virtual-world group affiliations tie members together, enable communication, and even lend groups a permanence belied by the ease with which virtual-world residents can drift in and out of new communities. Prospective members can find groups through *Second Life*'s search features, and a *Second Life* group does not go away even if the members stop using it; the group can thus be resurrected and can reconnect individuals who have otherwise lost contact with one another. This actually means that virtual grouping strategies can be *more* permanent than conventional ones, as the latter are hard to reconstitute several years after a group stops spending time together.

Virtual groups can remain viable over considerable periods of time and even across the gulfs between virtual worlds. After the makers of *Uru: Ages beyond Myst* closed the world in 2004, for example, thousands of *Uru* players migrated together into other virtual worlds, such as *Second Life* and *There* (Pearce and Artemesia 2009; 2010). Their migrations, and their efforts to reestablish the *Uru* communities in several virtual worlds, including a renewal of *Uru* itself, demonstrate the profound commitments that players can have to virtual worlds and the communities they produce therein. At a smaller level, guild groups can also migrate from one world to the next, retaining their hierarchies and divisions of labor even as they move into new games (see Mandelkow 2011).

The study of religion in virtual worlds must account for the actual ways in which virtual groups get formed and maintained. The technologies of grouping, and the opportunities they do or do not afford in those worlds, are important, as are the game design choices that make grouping desirable or not. By including the grouping mechanisms themselves in our analysis, we greatly improve our understanding of how virtual worlds can be used religiously.

Digital Pilgrimage

Just as objects in virtual worlds act upon users, the worlds themselves are objects that act. A virtual world is a conglomerate of designer choices, end-user practices, and technological apparatus; this means that as sociologists of the virtual, we can unpack some of these and see how the worlds act upon their users, providing new goals and enabling new practices. It is a necessary tautology to state at the outset that different virtual worlds affect different people differently, but the variety of such powers can be tremendous. Some virtual worlds incline users to transport their religious practices online, while others encourage quasi-religious practices that might lure users entirely away from traditional religious practice. In either case, the world itself is part of the social practice of religion; it cannot be ignored as a neutral intermediary for religious thought, but instead must be seen as mediating ideas, changing them, and shaping those who receive them.

Virtual worlds enable a wide array of religious experiences and practices, and as a consequence religious people are traveling to them, bringing their faith with them. Several virtual worlds directly support the importation of traditional religions, though they—as is the tendency of all empirical objects—reconfigure those traditions. For example, after Linden Lab allowed free accounts for *Second Life*, a host of religious individuals, from Hari Krishnas to conservative Christians, set up shop in-world. They built temples, churches, meditation gardens, meeting halls, and other sacred spaces. Participants joined groups and came to worship together. But such virtual practice could not be the same as practice on earth. What to make of the Christian Eucharist, for example? Protestant theologian Douglas Estes argues that Christians *must* find a way to provide the Eucharist in virtual worlds (Estes 2009, 123), but that is not the sort of thing other Christians, such as the Catholic Church, with its doctrine of transubstantiation, will find easy to accomplish. Without question, religious individuals will continue to create and participate in online rituals, but we should expect that their transfer to this new medium will produce changes in their internal logic, symbolism, materials, or practices (Heidbrink 2007; Miczek 2008; Radde-Antweiler 2007).

It is important that virtual worlds can encourage religious work. Worlds like *Second Life* and the now-defunct *There.com* provide tools for creation and thereby encourage the creative acts themselves. This leads to users re-envisioning their religious lives, building new ways of believing and practicing. Beliefs, for example, can be written into the landscape and the objects of a virtual church. Some theologians (e.g., Knight 2009; 2010) find that *Second Life* provides an effective site for human beings to experience divine love. By seating congregants in a circle of comfortable-looking chairs, Knight affirms the divine embrace at her Koinonia church in SL. But many who find such love in *Second Life* do so precisely because they were denied it in earthly churches (Knight 2010); as a consequence, the inscription of one kind of belief in SL may well come at the cost of a commensurate criticism of other churches.

Even as virtual worlds reshape the internal politics of religious groups, they will also intervene in the external relations among varying religions. Although hopes that the Internet might produce a beatific union of humankind seem Pollyannaish, some users do hope that virtual worlds can help advance ecumenical work. There are Christians, Jews, and Muslims, for example, who use SL as a site for sharing their faiths with outsiders and hope that the environment can be part of a peace-building process. Some SL residents, for example, actively hold conversations that will produce positive relationships among the different faiths (Geraci 2014).

Even as traditionally religious individuals rush to fill the virtual void, virtual worlds enable meaningful action or transcendent experiences for other—less obviously religious—users. They believe that virtual reality could provide heavenly realms for experiences of transcendence and even salvation. Computer scientists, video game designers, and even sociologists have collaborated in such soteriological visions, each in their own way offering religious visions of cyberspace (e.g., Geraci 2010; Helmreich [1998] 2000; Kelly 1999; Kurzweil 2005; Moravec 1988; Turner 2006).

Human beings who enter virtual worlds can find quasi-religious solace in their virtual lives. Virtual worlds can provide experiences akin to those of religion, especially opportunities to transcend the limits of human existence. Even early virtual-world experiments enabled such powerful feelings. For example, one commentator described *Osmose* as a "virtual kundalini, an expression of philosophy without any words, a state of holy being which reminds us that, indeed, we are all angels" (Davis 1996). More recently, Tracy Fullerton and her colleagues have sought to produce a "game mechanic of enlightenment" in their game *Night Journey*. Fullerton acknowledges that enlightenment is "almost an impossible experience to model in a game . . . but perhaps playing it can serve as an evocative cue, like a metaphor, to bring to mind a memory or form a pathway for a future experience."[3] Neither *Osmose* nor *Night Journey* is a full-fledged virtual world, as both are/were single-player, but they provide the template for how we might think through the religious potential of a virtual world.

Virtual worlds offer us an opportunity to become—if only in limited ways—divine; this power, in fact, explains a great deal of the cultural enthusiasm for online video gaming. Gamers who enter the magical worlds of Azeroth (*World of Warcraft*), Norrath (*EverQuest*), Middle Earth (*Lord of the Rings Online*), or other games may begin their virtual lives weak and unimportant, but their progress through the games' quest sequences virtually assures them they will become respected champions, wielders of tremendous power, and, ultimately, world-saving heroes. In *World of Warcraft*, players "enter a smaller, more perfect universe in which satisfaction is not guaranteed, but we gain a pretty good chance of achieving moments of limited perfection" (Nardi 2010, 120).

The sanctity granted to divine programmers, angelic players, or virtual craftsmen through virtual worlds means that those worlds are inextricably intertwined with contemporary religious life. Virtual worlds provide a wide array of religious opportunities, enabling experiences of the divine, feelings of transcendence, establishment of ethical guidelines, and more (Geraci 2014). Sometimes they do so in collaboration with traditional religious groups, as when a conventional church establishes a presence in *Second Life*, but sometimes they do so in parallel to conventional religious practices.

The emergence of virtual worlds implies several challenges for traditional religious groups. Insofar as religious groups can form in virtual worlds, then brick-and-mortar temples on earth will face competition from them. Of course, some religious people and groups will find this to be an opportunity rather than a difficulty, but unquestionably others will vigorously resist virtualization. At the same time, because virtual worlds can provide their inhabitants with transcendent opportunities that rival those of religion, they could potentially begin to replace traditional religious groups and affiliations (see Bainbridge 2010, 62; Bainbridge and Bainbridge 2007). As a consequence, virtual worlds are new and potentially powerful actors in a complete sociology of religion.

Conclusion

The features of virtual worlds throw into relief the ways in which people produce and maintain religious groups. They help us to see that individuals sustain religious networks by stabilizing them in various objects: symbols, buildings, texts, rituals, even bodies. The study of religion must increasingly account for the ways in which people use the long-term solidity of objects to sustain social relations that would otherwise dissolve, and must recognize that virtual worlds and their objects are now part of the religious economy of modern life.

While the influence of many religious objects is relatively straightforward (e.g., wearing a cross identifies one as a Christian and enmeshes one in a number of social relations), others are considerably more controversial. Even a cross, after all, can be controversial. In some churches, wearing a crucifix would mark one as a theological and social outsider. How much more so, then, can a virtual cross act? It is important to reveal controversy rather than mask it in simple terms. The religious activity resulting from or taking place within virtual worlds is new and dynamic; it demands that we multiply the many actors in the networks. While it would be impossible to do so within this chapter, which does not investigate any particular religious view, behavior, or institution, it is clear from the examples above that studying religion in virtual worlds means letting the actors proliferate.

Virtual worlds are actors, but so are many of their constituent elements. We might, for example, think of *Second Life* as an actor under the large umbrella of Christianity: it provides a shapeable landscape, it enables experimental theologies, and it reveals institutional insecurities. *Second Life* changes Christian practice for some people and thus acts within Christian history while also affecting many other communities. At the same time, particular objects within virtual worlds (such as grouping mechanisms, virtual buildings, and "tip jars" for tithing to churches or charities, etc.) are genuine actors. The presence of a tip jar can change a person's intended behavior—either through guilt or inspiration.

Many virtual objects affect new, rather than traditional, religious groups. *World of Warcraft* can serve as stand-in for heaven, providing an opportunity for players to feel like heroes. Game designers can experience their own apotheosis in the production of virtual worlds (see Bartle [2003] 2004; Bartle 2011; Koster 2011). New churches can form and operate entirely online. While we cannot know if virtual objects will prove as successful as earthly objects in concretizing social relations and stabilizing religion, shifts in behavior that tend to emphasize online activity may give them considerable force.

As religious practitioners increasingly produce and maintain their communities through digital mediation, there will be both challenges and opportunities for religious life. Unquestionably, the world of religion is changing. Both theologians and scholars of religion must note the ways in which virtual worlds exert influence over both individuals and traditional religious communities. Religious communities emerge out of relationships that must be stabilized by objects; whether virtual objects will suffice over many years remains to be seen but, at present, they help form the religious assemblies of modern life.

Notes

1. I am grateful to Nat Recine, of my research project (NSF EAGER—Virtually Meaningful: The Power and Presence of Meaning in Virtual Worlds), for informing me of the Bioware

companions and demonstrating to me their significance in virtual worlds. Interested readers could, for example, see the wealth of comments on how players of *Mass Effect 2* could not bear to ignore a companion in her distress, and comment upon a video of what happens if you do not hug her (http://www.youtube.com/watch?v=yk8_iHLSwMA&feature=related).

2. Many online communities have offline meetings (weekly, annually, etc.), and so they are not strictly limited to virtual activity.

3. Tracy Fullerton, personal e-mail interview with the author, January 1, 2012.

References

Au, W. J. 2010. Philip Rosedale Attempting to Create Sentient Artificial Intelligence that Thinks and Dreams in Second Life! *New World Notes* weblog. February 3. http://nwn.blogs.com/nwn/2010/02/philip-rosedale-ai.html. Accessed June 16, 2011.

Bainbridge, W. S. 2010. *The Warcraft Civilization: Social Science in a Virtual World.* Cambridge, MA: MIT Press.

Bainbridge, W. S., and W. Bainbridge. 2007. Electronic Game Research Methodologies: Studying Religious Implications. *Review of Religious Research* 49 (1): 35–53.

Bartle, R. (2003) 2004. *Designing Virtual Worlds.* Berkeley, CA: New Riders.

Bartle, R. 2011. Gods and Games. Presentation presented to the University of Bristol AASS Conference, March 17. http://www.youhaventlived.com/qblog/2011/QBlog220311A.html. Accessed July 3, 2011.

Bell, M. W. 2008. Toward a Definition of "Virtual Worlds." *Journal of Virtual Worlds Research* 1 (1): 1–5.

Blumenthal, J. A., and T. L. Turnipseed. 2011. The Polling Place Priming (PPP) Effect: Is Voting in Churches (Or Anywhere Else) Unconstitutional? *Boston University Law Review* 91 (2): 563–599.

Bourdieu, P. (1980) 1990. *The Logic of Practice.* Translated by R. Nice. Stanford, CA: Stanford University Press. http://jcmc.indiana.edu/vol12/issue3/campbell.html. Accessed August 8, 2008.

Davis, E. 1996. Osmose. *Wired* 4.08, August. http://www.wired.com/wired/archive/4.08/osmose.html. Accessed February 20, 2008.

Estes, D. 2009. *SimChurch: Being the Church in the Virtual Age.* Grand Rapids, MI: Zondervan.

Geraci, R M. 2010. *Apocalyptic AI: Visions of Heaven in Robotics, Artificial Intelligence, and Virtual Reality.* New York: Oxford University Press.

Geraci, R. M. 2014. *Virtually Sacred: Myth and Meaning in World of Warcraft and Second Life.* New York: Oxford University Press.

Heflick, N. 2009. Voting in Churches Increases Conservative Voting Choices. The Big Questions blog in *Psychology Today.* http://www.psychologytoday.com/blog/the-big-questions/200912/voting-in-churches-increases-conservative-voting-choices. Accessed June 10, 2011.

Heidbrink, S. 2007. Exploring the Religious Frameworks of the Digital Realm: Offline-Online-Offline Transfers of Ritual Performance. *Masaryk University Journal of Law and Technology* 1 (2): 175–184.

Helmreich, S. (1998) 2000. *Silicon Second Nature: Culturing Artificial Life in a Digital World.* Berkeley: University of California Press.

Holdrege, B. 2000. What's Beyond the Post? Comparative Analysis as Critical Method. In *A Magic Still Dwells: Comparative Religion in the Postmodern Age*, edited by K. C. Patton and B. C. Ray, 77–91. Berkeley: University of California Press.

Inside Rensselaer. 2008. Bringing "*Second Life*" to Life: Researchers Create Character with Reasoning Abilities of a Child. *Inside Rensselaer* 2 (5). http://www.rpi.edu/about/inside/issue/v2n5/second.html. Accessed June 16, 2011.

Jakobsson, M., and T. L. Taylor. 2003. *The Sopranos* Meets *EverQuest*: Social Networking in Massively Multiplayer Online Games. Paper presented to MelbourneDAC, the Fifth International Digital Arts and Culture Conference. hypertext.rmit.edu.au/dac/papers/Jakobsson.pdf. Accessed July 12, 2010.

Kelly, K. 1999. Nerd Theology. *Technology in Society* 21 (4): 387–392.

Knight, K. 2009. Sacred Space in Cyberspace. *Reflections* 96 (2): 43–46.

Knight, K. 2010. Interview by the author, conducted in *Second Life*. August 22.

Koster, R. 2011. Bartle Talks (Virtual) Religion. Blog post on Raph Koster's personal web page, March 28. http://www.raphkoster.com/2011/03/28/bartle-talks-virtual-religion/. Accessed July 2, 2011.

Kurzweil, R. 2005. *The Singularity Is Near: When Humans Transcend Biology*. New York: Viking.

Latour, B. 2005. *Reassembling the Social: An Introduction to Actor-Network-Theory*. New York: Oxford University Press.

Mandelkow, D. 2011. *Leveling Up into a Community: An Analysis of Authentic Fakery in Videogames*. Undergraduate honors thesis, Manhattan College, Riverdale, NY.

Miczek, N. 2008. Online Rituals in Virtual Worlds: Christian Online Services between Dynamics and Stability. *Online—Heidelberg Journal of Religions on the Internet* 3 (1): 144–173.

Miller, M. P. 2009. Storytelling in a Multiplayer Environment. In *Third Person: Authoring and Exploring Vast Narratives*, edited by P. Harrigan and N. Wardrip-Fruin, 125–130. Cambridge, MA: MIT Press.

Moravec, H. 1988. *Mind Children: The Future of Robot and Human Intelligence*. Cambridge, MA: Harvard University Press.

Nardi, B. 2010. *My Life as a Night Elf Priest: An Anthropological Account of World of Warcraft*. Ann Arbor: Michigan University Press.

Pearce, C., and Artemesia. 2009. The Diasporic Game Community: Trans-ludic Cultures and Latitudinal Research across Multiple Games and Virtual Worlds. In *Online Worlds: Convergence of the Real and the Virtual*, edited by William S. Bainbridge, 43–56. New York: Springer.

Pearce, C., and Artemesia. 2010. *Communities of Play: Emergent Cultures in Multiplayer Games and Virtual Worlds*. Foreword by T. Boellstorff and B. A. Nardi. Cambridge, MA: MIT Press.

Radde-Antweiler, K. 2007. Cyber-rituals in Virtual Worlds, Wedding-Online in Second Life. *Online—Heidelberg Journal of Religions on the Internmet* 3 (1): 174–211.

Reeves, B., and C. Nass. 1996. *The Media Equation: How People Treat Computers, Television, and New Media Like Real People and Places*. New York: Cambridge University Press.

Smith, J. Z. 1983. *Imagining Religion: From Babylon To Jonestown*. Chicago: University of Chicago Press.

Turner, F. 2006. *From Counterculture to Cyberculture: Stewart Brand, the Whole Earth Network, and the Rise of Digital Utopianism*. Chicago: University of Chicago Press.

Yee, N. 2006. "The Labor of Fun: How Video Games Blur the Boundaries of Work and Play." *Games and Culture* 1 (1): 68–71.

GAMES

Elder Scrolls V: Skyrim. Bruce Nesmith (lead designer). Bethesda Softworks, 2011.

EverQuest. Ryan Barker (lead designer). Sony Online Entertainment, 1999.

Lord of the Rings Online. Nik Davidson (lead designer). Turbine and Midway Games, 2007.

Mass Effect 2. Preston Watamaniuk (lead designer). Electronic Arts, 2010.

Night Journey, The. Tracy Fullerton and Bill Viola (designers). University of Southern California Electronic Arts Game Lab, 2010.

Osmose. Char Davies (designer). Immersence, 1995.

Second Life. Linden Research, 2003.

Spore. Will Wright (lead designer). Electronic Arts, 2008.

Star Wars: The Old Republic. Gabe Amantangelo (lead designer). Electronic Arts and LucasArts, 2011.

Uru: Ages beyond Myst. Lee Sheldon (designer/lead writer). Ubisoft, 2003.

World of Warcraft. Rob Pardo, Jeff Kaplan, and Tom Chilton (lead designers). Blizzard Entertainment, 2004.

CHAPTER 20

....

ACOUSTEMOLOGIES OF
THE CLOSET

....

WILLIAM CHENG

ONLINE video games in recent years have increasingly supported voice-chat functions that enable players to speak with one another using microphones connected to computers and consoles. Vocal communications greatly assist collaborative and competitive gaming by offering a quick and hands-free means of verbal exchange. But even with its obvious utility, voice-chat has been denounced by some players and critics as an unwelcome development in game design. As media researcher and designer Richard Bartle puts it:

> If you introduce reality into a virtual world, it's no longer a virtual world: it's just an adjunct to the real world. It ceases to be a place, and reverts to being a medium. Adding reality to a virtual world robs it of what makes it compelling—it takes away that which is different between virtual worlds and the real world: the fact that they are not the real world. Voice is reality. (2003)

In August 2007, the introduction of voice-chat into the online communities of *Second Life* incited protests from various residents who worried that the sounds of live human voices would undermine the pseudonymity of this virtual world. Anthropologist Tom Boellstorff explains that what "made debates about voice [in *Second Life*] particularly impassioned were questions of presence and immersion that implicated the boundary between virtual and actual. Some residents felt voice would facilitate greater intimacy, [but] other residents felt that voice would damage a border between the virtual and actual that they wished to maintain" (2008, 114; see also Wadley and Gibbs 2010, 192). Detractors of voice-chat pined for *Second Life*'s prelapsarian days, for an era when it had not yet been possible for the grits and grains of human voices to fold excessive reality into their online world. Many inhabitants feared that the implementation of voice-chat would lead to a mass exodus of disillusioned individuals from *Second Life*, or, at the very least, create an irreparable schism between populations willing to embrace voice and those refusing to do so. Among the outcries were predictions that voice-chat would bring about the end of this virtual world by violating what made the world *virtual* in the first place.

At stake in disputes over voice-chat in *Second Life* were concerns about the power of voices to carry identifying information that one might wish neither to divulge (as a speaker) nor apprehend (as a listener). Journalist Clive Thompson, for example, describes an instance of rude awakening he once experienced while playing the online game *World of Warcraft*:

> Recently I logged into *World of Warcraft* and I wound up questing alongside a mage and two dwarf warriors. I was the lowest-level newbie in the group, and the mage was the de-facto leader. . . . He [the mage] seemed like your classic virtual-world group leader: confident, bold and streetsmart. But after a few hours he said he was getting tired of using text chat—and asked me to switch over to Ventrilo, an app that lets gamers chat using microphones and voice. I downloaded Ventrilo, logged in, dialed him up and . . . realized he was an 11-year-old boy, complete with squeaky, prepubescent vocal chords. When he laughed, his voice shot up abruptly into an octave range that induced headaches. . . . Oh, and he used "motherfucker" about four times a sentence, except when his mother came into his bedroom to check on him. (2007)

The wizard (or mage) behind the curtain revealed himself, in this case, as a potty-mouthed child whose prior demonstration of gaming expertise made him seem older than he actually was. Thompson goes on to explain: "There's no doubt that hearing each other's voices abruptly changed our social milieu. He seemed equally weirded out by me—a 38-year-old guy who undoubtedly sounds more like his father than anyone he recognizes as a 'gamer.' After an hour of this, we politely logged off and never hooked up again." The ability of disembodied voices to betray bodily identities—however vaguely—gave rise here to an exchange that was apparently too close for comfort. "With voice," concludes Thompson, "the real world is honking in your ear." In virtual worlds, this awkward tale suggests, we speak, and therefore, we suddenly are.

Yet questions of who we *are* in virtual worlds—and what it means to (co)exist in these spaces—are confounded by popular conceptions of video games as playgrounds where performativity and plural identities prevail. Our avatars, ourselves: where do we draw the line? The pseudonymous nature of online interactions promotes and authorizes role-playing and polyvocality. It is in this authorization that gamers, griefers, and Internet users in general can take refuge. As Ken Hillis argues, online communications constitute a mode of "ventriloquism [that] can serve as a defensive strategy, one that seems to project the source of the message to somewhere or something else other than the sender" (2009, 147). To *say* that one *was speaking* in a different voice comprises a double speech act, a manner of free indirect discourse that skirts liability via slippages between impersonation and authentic expression. Players qua ventriloquists who displace voices onto alternate entities—avatars, trolling personae, and so forth—retain the flexibility to disavow what they say (when under critical fire), and then to take credit for what they *have said* (as soon as it is opportune to do so). Offenders in online games find safe haven precisely in the ease with which transgressive acts can *pass* as ostensible forms of role-play.

The extent to which disembodied voices evoke human bodies necessarily depends on the varying capabilities of individuals to deploy and to decode these voices as timbral, registral, and phonetic indices of appearance, age, sex, sexuality, ethnicity, nationality, class, (dis)ability, and other physiological and cultural identity categories. This chapter explores the social ramifications and critical conversations that have emerged from the coming (out) of voice in online gamespaces. What happens when players of online games drop their masks and introduce their own voices into a virtual space? How do the sounds of these voices influence players' actions and relations? What factors bear on the differing proclivities of players to speak out? And what new masks—new fictions of identity—might materialize when voices of players conjure ambiguous, multiplicitous, or duplicitous identities? By extending metaphors of the prosthesis and the closet, I show how technologies of voice-chat in video games foster practices of assimilation, repression, deception, and revelation. In doing so, I interrogate traditional characterizations of voice as a site of authentic, agentic expression. I conclude with insights into the sexual politics of voice-chat in the audibly male-dominated communities of online first-person-shooter games.

BEHIND THE CURTAIN

What's in a voice? For neo-Barthesians, self-proclaimed opera queens, and theorists of corporeal feminism, there's one answer that says a lot: the *body* is in the voice.[1] As an oral signature, the voice is, as Emily Wilbourne writes, "[c]onditioned by and yet fragmented from semantic meaning...the sonorous remnant of speech, an unwieldy synecdoche for the body" (2010, 5). The voice, in other (or its own) words, can already say much even when its speaker is not trying to say anything at all. In online gameworlds, voices of players accentuate the porousness of the real-virtual divide by registering as objects of phenomenological and somatic excess. These voices, in short, can ring false by telegraphing too many truths about the speaking body.

Unlike the animated gestures and canned sounds that players of games can perform with their avatars—say, a wave of the hand, a gunshot, a taunt—a player's own voice is in no way restricted by a game's preprogrammed audiovisual palette. As noted by telecommunications scholar Edward Castronova:

> Much of the immersive effect of the [virtual] world occurs because everything you see and *hear* in the worlds conforms to the designer's theme. If it is a medieval world, all the buildings look medieval, the music is medieval-sounding, and the animals and trees look like they were taken from fourteenth-century France.... The failure of user communication to conform to the world's atmosphere is not much of a problem when it is confined to a small chat box. With a voice system, however, everyone will hear the modern-day babbling of others all the time. (2005, 89, emphasis in original)

The very performability of an avataric gesture or sound underscores it as a technically sanctioned behavior within a game. The fact that an action is *possible* (and can be executed by all players) mitigates, to an extent, its deviant potential. It is for this reason that live voices—with their spontaneous, unscripted expressive capabilities—are so often highlighted by players as palpable embodiments of human difference in otherwise disembodied environments.

Sounds of players speaking through avatars render these simulated bodies legible as surrogate living entities. An avatar is a prosthesis, serving as a "bodily appendage-cum-psychic extension and therefore as an actual (if not material) part of the person" (Hillis 2009, 132). But a player's voice in a game also inversely functions like a prosthesis *for* an avatar by fulfilling a purpose that is at once compensatory (enhancing the perceived aliveness of the spoken-for avatar) and intrusive (submitting a *too*-human sound into a virtual space).[2] Insofar as prostheses are meant to fill correctional roles, they simultaneously normalize bodies—(re)making them whole (read: wholly human)—while pointing up the contrivances of human normalcy. The standardizing agenda of a visible prosthesis implicitly reproduces its own ambivalence by virtue of the appended body that is perceived as almost normal, but not quite.[3] Prostheses unsettle holistic ideals of corporeality and facile distinctions between nature and technology. They not only draw attention to their own artificial status, but also expose human identity as a mutable cultural invention—an arbitrary assemblage of signifying parts prone to physiological as well as epistemic alteration, extension, fracture, and substitution.[4]

Scholars in recent years have come to treat voice as a kind of discursive prosthesis. As Vivian Sobchack observes, the "theoretical use of the prosthetic metaphor tends to transfer *agency* . . . from human actors to human artifacts. . . . The animate and volitional human beings who use prosthetic technology disappear into the background—passive, if not completely invisible—and the prosthetic is seen to have a will and life of its own" (2006, 23, emphasis in original; see also Kurzman 2001, 378–382). Characterizations of voice as an autonomous, subversive force appear perhaps nowhere more prominently than in feminist and queer scholarship on opera and song. Writers have insisted on the power of the lyric voice with relation to the erotic cult of diva-worship, the sonic interstitialities of castrati and cross-dressed performers, and extralinguistic utterances such as the scream (Friedheim 1983, 63–70), the cry (Poizat 1992), and laughter (Bronfen 1996; Huebner 2006). Questioning Catherine Clément's ([1979] 1988) emphasis on women's victimized roles in opera, Carolyn Abbate offers a counter-narrative wherein singing heroines could be heard to exist "as sonority and sheer physical volume, asserting themselves outside spectacle and escaping murderous fates" (1993, 254). Voice is salvaged here, (so) to *speak*, as a way of affirming a virtuosic female presence that rages against opera's pandemic of undone prima donnas. She sings; therefore, she survives, transcending corporeal fate and living on through the vibrations of her miraculous voice. The catch with this hermeneutics of material vocal triumph is how it's enabled precisely by voice's relative *immateriality* and definitional promiscuity. Just as music is often cited for its nonrepresentational and ineffable qualities, so voice is frequently invoked, in the words of Michelle Duncan, as "a place-marker for something unarticulated or inarticulable, taking on a rhetorical task in the service of a theoretical argument" (2006, 284). As a chameleonic poster-child of subjectivist critique, voice has traditionally been harnessed to say whatever we—as students of music, poetry, and the humanities—have aimed to make it say.

A strain of romantic idealism runs through the arguments of writers who privilege voice as an acoustic window into the soul. This mindset posits, on the one hand, an inviolable bond between voice and human subjectivity. On the other hand, it displaces agency from the individual onto the reified, prosthetic voice. To conceive of voice as somewhere *out there*—whether as a diva's postmortem echo or as an autograph of a player's body in a gameworld—is to call into question the naturalness of voice and its relationship to the human subject. In a study of speech politics, Adriana Cavarero stresses a "vocal ontology of uniqueness," the idea that "the voice manifests the *unique being* of each human being, and his or her spontaneous self-communication according to the rhythms of a sonorous relation" (2005, 173, emphasis in original). To this point, Jonathan Sterne cautions against "[idealizing] hearing (and by extension, speech) as manifesting a kind of pure interiority" (2003, 15). Questions of uniqueness and humanness aside, what needs to be resisted are blanket understandings of voice (and the speech it may carry) as somehow capable of conveying a degree of agency or sincerity that lies beyond the alternative expressive potential of text, gesture, and other forms of communication. As declared by a *Second Life* resident in an online forum: "I hate voice. I hate it with a passion. I'm a woman and I'm shy. I am a nerdy bookish person and I'm more at home with text. It's a place where my nasal voice and softness disappear and my ability to write lets my personality *really* come out" (Kathy, March 1, 2007).

Especially with online interactions, it would be presumptuous, even ableist, to think that the articulation of a so-called real, complete, or sincere identity cannot occur without vocal communication. Practices of role-play in online games complicate what it means to speak one's identity and, consequently, what it means for any disembodied voice to be or to sound authentic to begin with. In daily life, people who speak do so, as a matter of course, in multiple voices—voices that vary in speech content, timbre, register, inflection, affectation, loudness, rhythm, and pacing according to the pressures and affordances of different social situations. Denaturalizing voice—stripping away its association with true identity—opens up conceptual possibilities akin to those extended by notions of gender performativity. One such possibility might involve understanding voice *as* performance, as a socially adaptable construct that acquires the *guise* of coherent, authentic expression (solely) via the repetition of stylized speech acts and learned vocal qualities.

Beneath the Mask

On Internet forums devoted to debates about the respective merits of voice-chat and text-chat in online games, a proponent of the latter remarked: "If you introduce [voice into a virtual space] the whole ambience changes: the shy are revealed as shy, and the noisy start to dominate. [But] it is hard to type LOUDER than everyone else in the room" (Owen Kelly, 2007). A concurring forum participant stated: "Text may get messy, but it's pretty demo-cratic—everyone gets a say eventually" (Ace Albion, 2007). Those who took issue with these views pointed to the online first-person shooter (online FPS) game as a genre that greatly benefits from voice-chat. As one player put it: "Text (and democracy) are slow. In games with tactical situations, speech is the only way to give orders while fighting" (anonymous, 2007). Characterized by graphic simulations of gunplay and team-based combat, online FPS games require players to cultivate quick reflexes and strategic maneuvers. Voice-chat allows players to relay orders to teammates, call for help, and divulge enemy positions in the heat of battle. A team's chances for victory can hinge largely on the consistency with which players are able and willing to impart pertinent information to allies during a match.

Vocal transmissions tend to be considerably quicker and less cumbersome than typ-ing. Since text messages in most online games appear in miniscule chat boxes near the edges of a screen, they can easily go unread amid a wealth of visual stimuli competing for the player's attention. The proper use of voice in online shooters therefore carries sig-nificant ludic capital, testifying to the speaker's dedication to teamwork and competitive gameplay. Yet as noted above by one of the forum respondents, voice communications seem most useful when they are used *un*-democratically—that is, when not everyone on a team opts to speak at once, or when certain players seize leadership roles by speaking more loudly and authoritatively than others.

In this hierarchy of audibility, female players don't fare so well. Many women report a reluctance to use voice-chat in online FPS games out of a fear that the sonic revelation of their real-world sex might prompt male players to respond in an undesirable man-ner. One player says she abstains from speaking "because some of us are afraid we'll get [hit] on by sketchy nerds or yelled at by 12-year-olds who don't want to play a girl online" (Xkc20d, 2007). Another player states: "Throw up a vent [Ventrilo] server, the girls stop talking completely, the shy people shut up mostly, and all that is left are the 12–18 year old guys, and it becomes a locker room. Not so much fun, really" (Judson, 2007). Players who speak in this locker room are, by default, the ones setting the tone of the gamespace. The prevalence of adult male voices in online FPS games, as such, contributes to for-mations of homosocial soundscapes in which all players are assumed to be men unless one vocally outs oneself as otherwise. Female players who participate in mute play will thus automatically pass as men and escape direct sexual harassment, but such behavior entails the bargaining of silence for immunity.

Women who speak in online FPS games rarely fail to garner attention and excited commentary not least because of how uncommon it is to hear female voices in these environments. Sounds of female voices that are discerned as such can impact a match's social dynamics in a number of ways: it might lead (mostly) male players to inquire into and obsess over the identity of the (supposedly) female speaker; it might instigate an explosion of misogynist jokes and expletives; or it might have a domesticating effect, causing swearing to drop to a minimum and the communications between players to become unusually chivalrous and polite.

Players of online games rarely inquire into one another's appearance, class, race, nationality, education, or occupation. The real-life identities of teammates and rivals are understood to be privileged information that is irrelevant to the technical goals of a match. Respect for mutual anonymity, however, often goes out the window when female (or sexually ambiguous) voices are heard on a server. It is not uncommon for a speaking woman to get bombarded with invasive questions about her height, weight, hair color, ethnicity, sexual experience, state of dress, and even bra size. Among the most popular inquiries tend to be those concerning age, relationship status, and physical attractiveness—all of which are posed presumably with the intention of confirming a female speaker as an admissible and worthwhile object of desire.

One might be tempted to rescue the agency of nonspeaking women in online games by imagining them as gleefully passing through the ranks of more outspoken players, reveling in role-play as silent soldiers. Peggy Phelan, writing about the politics of visibility, remarks on the "real power in remaining unmarked" in her attempts to expose the "[falsifying] binary between the power of visibility and the impotency of invisibility" (1993, 6). Similarly, Linda Schlossberg states that even though the act of passing "generally holds larger social hierarchies firmly in place," it can nonetheless be "a uniquely pleasurable experience, one that trades on the erotics of secrecy and revelation" (2001, 3). The construal of passing as pleasurable is no doubt appealing for its empowering political orientation. Yet—like many outlooks grounded in standpoint epistemology—this runs the risk of reinscribing the very power gradients that a deminoritizing discourse purports to undermine. A danger in valorizing the passing of the oppressed is that it casts subjugated individuals as somehow appeasable by their putative occupation of a moral or intellectual high ground. As Barbara Hillyer notes, passing "involves adopting the values of the privileged group; it causes 'emotive dissonance'; it is harmful to mental and physical health; it makes the secret the central focus of the passer's life…and it maintains the very repressive system that causes it" (1993, 150). Trading silence for impunity comprises a social contract not unlike that which underpinned the former American military policy of Don't Ask, Don't Tell. Such arrangements permit discrimination to pass as paranoid indifference (oxymoronically so) as a way of bringing prejudicial ideologies back within the pale of a supposedly greater good.

In the case of most online FPS games, players who engage in matches are dispersed across hundreds (if not thousands) of different servers, each of which can accommodate only a limited number of players at a given time. Any player can join a server as long as it has an available slot and is not password-protected. It is standard for players to hop quickly from one server to another (maybe after playing a match or two on each one) so as to experience different maps and game modes. Rapid, unpredictable turnovers in server populations constantly bring together new communities of players who may not be acquainted with one another at the outset of a match. Closets in online FPS games hence lie on perpetually shifting ground: a female player who decides to speak and to come out as a woman would have to do so continuously lest she's mistaken again for a (silent) man by incoming players who haven't yet heard her speak. In an online FPS game, falling silent results in reabsorption into its male homosocial fabric. The only way to *stay* out is to keep talking. So whereas a policy such as Don't Ask, Don't Tell did not permit outed individuals to return to the closet (and to remain in military service), the closets in online FPS games are nothing if not a point of magnetic return. It is by now a truism, in the views of feminist, queer, and disability scholars, that coming out entails not a single or temporally delimitable act, but rather an exercise in repetition, a cyclical routine of always coming out *again*.[5] Fitted with revolving doors, the closet is a heuristic home base at best, its ins and outs hopelessly blurred in the everyday imagination.

Complicating the politics of voice-chat in online games are instances in which voices fail to yield definitively sexed bodies. A common question that outspoken women first get asked is *whether* they are women at all. On an Internet forum, one player explains: "Whenever I play the game [*Team Fortress 2*] and use voice-chat, all I get is: 'Are you 12 or a girl?' And then starts the 'You should be in bed' / 'This is a big boy game' / 'You should be playing hello kitty instead' kind of stuff, until I quit" (Karma Guard, 2008). Inquiries into whether a player is a woman *or* a boy indiscriminately infantilize and feminize women and younger men in one fell swoop, conflating their perceived amateurism as a way of denying the prerogative of either group to partake in what some would maintain as a grown man's game. Boys themselves, granted, often participate in the harassment of women; they are, however, also occasionally mistaken *for* women and harassed accordingly by adult male players (as well as by other young boys, who themselves could be mistaken for women—and on it goes). A boy who takes the initiative to harass might thus do so as a means of disavowing boyhood, of preemptively asserting that he *is* a (soon-to-be) man and that he can dish out the abuse just as effectively as the grown-ups can. A similar self-disavowal may likewise inform the bullying actions of older players who, by openly mocking youths and adolescents, become better positioned to detach themselves from the juvenile image that society still associates with gamers of all ages.

Beyond the Pale

Back in 2010, the topic of this chapter came up while I was having a round of late-night drinks with a friend. I summarized my plans for the case study as best as I could, explaining players' anxieties about voice-chat, the sexual politics of passing and coming out in online games, and so on. My friend, after listening to this spiel, chimed in with a solution to problems of sexual harassment in online games. His suggestion had to do with voice-changing devices, which, he reasoned, could eliminate bigotry and social hierarchies if the technology were integrated into games and made available to all players. The ubiquitous use of voice-changers, in his view, would muddy the crosshairs of potential harassers and give heart to shy players who might otherwise hesitate to speak. The argument seemed to be that the widespread (and ideally obligatory) use of voice-changers could lead to a paradise regained, a cyber-utopia where wizards may return behind the curtain, where *Second Life* residents would have no more cause to protest, and where closets could effectively be everywhere—and, consequently, nowhere.

These measures are technically possible, but chances are that adding vocal camouflage would not be enough to prevent discrimination from seeping into online spaces. For while it is true that someone using a voice-changer in an online FPS game might be able to escape harassment by passing as a normatively voiced adult male (whatever one imagines this to sound like), deeper problems lie in the structures of repression that compel women, children, individuals with speech impediments, nonnative English speakers (on English-speaking servers), and other voice-adverse players to pass in the first place, whether via silence or voice-changers. In any event, among the FPS players whom I have interviewed, few reported ever having used a voice-changer. Several players in fact responded defensively, stating they would never go for such a technology because they didn't feel like they had anything to hide. One player additionally said he found it "silly to go the extra mile to be anonymous on the Internet" when the medium already offers a layer of concealment and security (interview, Sepharite, May 31, 2010). For some players, the ability to speak with one's own voice provides a happy compromise between total obscurity and excessive disclosures of identity—a means of reclaiming a sonorous glimmer of the purportedly real self amid online interactions.

Vocal exchanges among players in games are no doubt more than just idle chatter. These conversations are integral to modern multiplayer games, and indeed, to any online platform that encourages the adoption of alternative, contrarian, and pluralist personae. Possibilities for different kinds of games—games predicated on aural fascination, lewd inquiry, and harassment—can all of a sudden erupt upon the introduction of voices that, in whatever capacity, sound like they do not belong. In gameworlds, players' voices carry considerable powers of communication, imprinting prosthetic stamps of selves into realms of prerendered sprites and sounds. Accompanying these voices are practices of oppression and passing that should be addressed precisely because they are inscribed in silence. To penetrate this silence is to venture behind the curtain, beneath the mask, and beyond the pale of definitive identities. It means struggling with knowing nothing about those who do not speak, while bracing for the possibility of finding out too much—or sometimes, still not quite enough—about those who do.

Acknowledgments

I would like to thank Karen Collins, Mark Grimshaw, Brandon Masterman, Kiri Miller, Ingrid Monson, Alexander Rehding, Sindhumathi Revuluri, Kay Kaufman Shelemay, Jack Vishneski, and the reviewers of this volume for their insightful comments on earlier drafts. Parts of this chapter were presented at meetings of the Modern Language Association (January 4, 2013), the Society for Ethnomusicology (November 19, 2011), Music and the Moving Image (May 22, 2011), and the American Musicological Society (November 5, 2010).

Notes

1. See respectively Barthes (1977, 179–189), Koestenbaum (1993), and Grosz (1994).
2. Literary theorists, sociologists, philosophers, linguists, and scholars of disability in recent years have increasingly applied biomedical conceptions of prostheses to critical explorations of identity and agency in poststructuralist perspectives. As Vivian Sobchack explains: "Sometime, fairly recently, after 'the cyborg' became somewhat tired and tiresome from academic overuse, we started to hear and read about 'the prosthetic'—less as a specific material replacement of a missing limb or body part than as a sexy, new metaphor that, whether noun or (more frequently) adjective, has become tropological currency for describing a vague and shifting constellation of relationships among bodies, technologies, and subjectivities" (2006, 19). For studies on prostheses' cultural and discursive valencies, see Nelson (2001, 304–305), Mitchell and Snyder (2000), Jain (1999, 31–54), Lury (1998), and Wills (1995).
3. Theories of posthumanism posit "the body as the original prosthesis we all learn to manipulate, so that extending or replacing the body with other prostheses becomes a continuation of a process that began before we were born" (Hayles 1999, 3). For additional discussions of prostheses and identity ambivalence, see Garland-Thomson (2009, 128–129), Wilson (1995, 239–259), and Tanenbaum (1986, 63–65).
4. The concept of the prosthesis has been invoked in a small number of musical studies to date. Tia DeNora likens music to a "prosthetic device [that] provide[s] organizing properties for a range of... embodied experiences and in ways that involve varying degrees of deliberation and conscious awareness on the part of music's conscripts" (2000, 103). Raiford Guins and Omayra Cruz describe turntablism as "an instance of media as technological extension/prosthetic" (2006, 225). Jennifer Iverson frames elements of electronica in Björk's music as "a prosthesis, a mechanical supplement that draws attention to the lack latent in the natural voice" (2006, 65).
5. On "coming out" as an exercise in repetition, see Halberstam (2005, 52–53), Samuels (2003, 237), Kleege (2002), Butler (1997, 302), and Tyler (1994, 222).

References

Abbate, C. 1993. Opera; or, the Envoicing of Women. In *Musicology and Difference: Gender and Sexuality in Music Scholarship*, edited by Ruth A. Solie, 225–258. Berkeley: University of California Press.

Barthes, R. 1977. *Image, Music, Text*. Translated by Stephen Heath. London: Fontana.

Bartle, R. A. 2003. Not Yet, You Fools! *Game Girl Advance*. http://www.gamegirladvance.com/archives/2003/07/28/not_yet_you_fools.html. Accessed February 16, 2009.

Boellstorff, T. 2008. *Coming of Age in Second Life: An Anthropologist Explores the Virtually Human*. Princeton, NJ: Princeton University Press.

Bronfen, E. 1996. Kundry's Laughter. *New German Critique* 69: 147–161.

Butler, J. 1997. Imitation and Gender Insubordination. In *The Second Wave: A Reader in Feminist Theory*, edited by Linda Nicholson, 300–15. New York: Routledge.

Castronova, E. 2005. *Synthetic Worlds: The Business and Culture of Online Games*. Chicago: University of Chicago Press.

Cavarero, A. 2005. *For More Than One Voice: Toward a Philosophy of Vocal Expression*. Translated by Paul A. Kottman. Stanford, CA: Stanford University Press.

Clément, C. (1979) 1988. *Opera, or the Undoing of Women*. Translated by Betsy Wing. Minneapolis: University of Minnesota Press.

DeNora , T. 2000. *Music in Everyday Life*. Cambridge: Cambridge University Press.

Duncan, M. 2006. The Operatic Scandal of the Singing Body: Voice, Presence, Performativity. *Cambridge Opera Journal* 16 (3): 283–306.

Friedheim, P. 1983. Wagner and the Aesthetics of the Scream. *19th-Century Music* 7 (1): 63–70.

Garland-Thomson, R. 2009. *Staring: How We Look*. Oxford: Oxford University Press.

Grosz, E. 1994. *Volatile Bodies: Toward a Corporeal Feminism*. Bloomington: Indiana University Press.

Guins, R., and O. Z. Cruz. 2006. Prosthetists at $33^1/_3$. In *The Prosthetic Impulse: From a Posthuman Present to a Biocultural Future*, edited by Marquard Smith and Joanne Morra, 221–236. Cambridge, MA: MIT Press.

Halberstam, J. 2005. *In a Queer Time and Place: Transgender Bodies, Subcultural Lives*. New York: New York University Press.

Hillis, K. 2009. *Online a Lot of the Time: Ritual, Fetish, Sign*. Durham, NC: Duke University Press.

Hillyer, B. 1993. *Feminism and Disability*. Norman: University of Oklahoma Press.

Huebner, S. 2006. Laughter: In Ravel's Time. *Cambridge Opera Journal* 18 (3): 225–246.

Iverson, J. 2006. Dancing out of the Dark: How Music Refutes Disability Stereotypes in *Dancer in the Dark*. In *Sounding Off: Theorizing Disability in Music*, edited by Neil Lerner and Joseph N. Straus, 57–74. New York: Routledge.

Jain, S. S. 1999. The Prosthetic Imagination: Enabling and Disabling the Prosthesis Trope. *Science, Technology, and Human Values* 24 (1): 31–54.

Kleege, G. 2002. Disabled Students Come Out: Questions about Answers. In *Disability Studies: Enabling the Humanities*, edited by Sharon Snyder, Brenda Brueggemann, and Rosemarie Garland-Thomson, 308–16. New York: Modern Language Association of America.

Koestenbaum, W. 1993. *The Queen's Throat: Opera, Homosexuality, and the Mystery of Desire*. New York: Poseidon Press.

Kurzman, S. L. 2001. Presence and Prosthesis: A Response to Nelson and Wright. *Cultural Anthropology* 16 (3): 378–382.

Lury, C. 1998. *Prosthetic Culture: Photography, Memory and Identity*. New York: Routledge.

Mitchell, D. T., and S. L. Snyder. 2000. *Narrative Prosthesis: Disability and the Dependencies of Discourse*. Ann Arbor: University of Michigan Press.

Nelson, D. M. 2001. Phantom Limbs and Invisible Hands: Bodies, Prosthetics, and Late Capitalist Identifications. *Cultural Anthropology* 16 (3): 303–313.

Phelan, P. 1993. *Unmarked: The Politics of Performance*. New York: Routledge.

Poizat, M. 1992. *The Angel's Cry: Beyond the Pleasure Principle in Opera*. Translated by Arthur Denner. Ithaca, NY: Cornell University Press.

Samuels, E. 2003. My Body, My Closet: Invisible Disability and the Limits of Coming-Out Discourse. *GLQ: A Journal of Gay and Lesbian Studies* 9 (1/2): 233–55.

Schlossberg, L. 2001. Introduction. In *Passing: Identity and Interpretation in Sexuality, Race, and Religion*, edited by María Carla Sánchez and Linda Schlossberg, 1–12. New York: New York University Press.

Sobchack, V. 2006. A Leg to Stand On: Prosthetics, Metaphor, and Materiality. In *The Prosthetic Impulse: From a Posthuman Present to a Biocultural Future*, edited by Marquard Smith and Joanne Morra, 43–72. Cambridge, MA: MIT Press.

Sterne, J. 2003. *The Audible Past: Cultural Origins of Sound Reproduction*. Durham, NC: Duke University Press.

Tanenbaum, S. J. 1986. *Engineering Disability: Public Policy and Compensatory Technology*. Philadelphia: Temple University Press.

Thompson, C. 2007. Voice Chat Can Really Kill the Mood on *WoW*. *Wired.com*. http://www.wired.com/gaming/virtualworlds/commentary/games/2007/06/games_frontiers_0617. Accessed February 16, 2009.

Tyler, C.-A. 1994. Passing: Narcissism, Identity, and Difference. *differences: A Journal of Feminist Cultural Studies* 6 (2/3): 212–248.

Wadley, G., and M. R. Gibbs. 2010. Speaking in Character: Voice Communication in Virtual Worlds. In *Online Worlds: Convergence of the Real and the Virtual*, edited by William Sims Bainbridge, 187–200. New York: Springer.

Wilbourne, E. 2010. *Lo Schiavetto* (1612): Travestied Sound, Ethnic Performance, and the Eloquence of the Body. *Journal of the American Musicological Society* 63 (1): 1–43.

Wills, D. 1995. *Prosthesis*. Stanford: Stanford University Press.

Wilson, R. R. 1995. Cyber(body)parts: Prosthetic Consciousness. *Body and Society* 1 (3–4): 239–259.

PART IV

SOUND

CHAPTER 21

BREAKING THE FOURTH WALL? USER-GENERATED SONIC CONTENT IN VIRTUAL WORLDS

KAREN COLLINS

In the 1960s, Allan Kaprow described the art practice of Happenings as "A game, an adventure, a number of activities engaged in by participants for the sake of playing" (in Higgins 1976). Kaprow, like others of his time, sought to break down the *fourth wall* of artistic practice by exposing the constructed nature of the artistic practice and theatrical space. The fourth wall is a term borrowed from dramatic theory that considers the theatrical stage as having three walls (two sides and a rear) and an invisible fourth-wall boundary between the actors and audience. Breaking the fourth wall, then, has been a euphemism for eliminating the divide between creator and audience. In theater, for instance, breaking the fourth wall included exposing the production values that went into creating the set design, lighting, and so on. Today, the concept is also used to describe the blurred "boundaries between the fictional and real world, either drawing something *into* the fictional world from outside, or expelling something *out* of the fictional into the non-fictional" (Conway 2009). In simple terms, the fourth wall divides the space between the "real" world and contrived, virtual worlds. Kaprow saw Happenings as a way of democratizing and distributing artistic practice, whereby a performative space could be created temporarily through collective play and the self-reflexive, subtle awareness of its own constructed nature. In much the same manner, we might consider online virtual worlds as such a "self-aware" distributed artistic practice: a telepresent Happening.

In this chapter, I consider the experience of user-generated sonic content in virtual worlds in terms of the concept of the fourth wall, situating this content in regards to this dynamic between audience and virtual space. Although virtual worlds don't necessarily rely on user-generated content, the scale and scope of virtual worlds certainly lend themselves to a crowd-sourced approach, and user-generated content is responsible for significant portions of some worlds. This crowd-sourcing of content has led to some criticism of the game industry as taking advantage of the free labor of fans to extend shelf life and reduce research and development costs (Sotamaa 2007). While much of the work on user-generated content in games has focused on this relationship between developers and players, there are many interesting aspects of user-generated content that have been neglected, particularly when it comes to sound. Here, I argue that user-generated sound is in a unique position with regards to breaking the fourth wall. First, I present a brief overview of user-generated content in virtual worlds, and explore how user-generated content in general contributes to the social interactions that occur and to the breakdown of the fourth wall. Then I focus specifically on the types of auditory content that are generated and shared between players. Finally, I explore the use of sound as a mediator between the virtual- and the real-world spaces.

USER-GENERATED CONTENT IN VIRTUAL WORLDS

Schroeder (2008) defines virtual worlds as persistent online "virtual environments in which people experience others as being there with them—and where they can interact with them." This definition, however, places the emphasis of virtual worlds on presence ("being there with them") rather than the multitudes of creative performative practice that occur. In virtual worlds players perform, create, and share meanings in a cocreative, self-reflexive, and fluctuating impermanence. The majority of popular virtual worlds have been *game oriented*, in which there is a series of goals or objectives and in which the players work in cooperation or competition with each other, including role-playing games (e.g., *World of Warcraft*), real-time strategy (e.g., *Age of Empires*), first-person shooters (e.g., *Hitman: Blood Money*), and more casual-oriented game worlds like *Glitch*. On the other hand, not all virtual worlds have specific game-like tasks for a player: *Second Life*, for instance, is a virtual world that is not game oriented, since there is no series of objectives for the user—these types of virtual worlds are, rather, sandboxes in which players can explore, interact with others, and build virtual-world objects and spaces. In both game-oriented and sandbox-style virtual worlds, players create objects and avatars and engage in a variety of interactive social acts. For many multiplayer games, the structure of the games forces players to interact, since players rely on each other to progress in some cases, making cooperative relationships integral to success (Caplan, Williams, and Yee 2009, 1313).

As a component of social interaction, *user-generated content* is one of the driving factors of virtual worlds. User-generated content in this context can be defined as the objects, actions, and sounds that occur in a virtual space that are contributed by players and were not predefined (i.e., preprogrammed or prescribed) by the space. For example, players can create objects and upload them so that other users can use them in their own virtual space. In *The Wealth of Networks*, Benkler describes the function of massively multiplayer games (and by extension, all virtual worlds) as places "to build tools with which users collaborate to tell a story... [players] produce a discrete element of 'content' that was in the past dominated by centralized professional production... this function is produced by using the appropriate software platform to allow the story to be written by the many users as they experience it" (2006, 74). It is this distributed authorship that distinguishes virtual worlds from most other types of video game play: the story is not scripted or created by developers in advance, but rather unfolds over time through the creative and performative practices of the players. This is not a *choose*-your-own adventure, but a *create*-your-own adventure. Axel Bruns argues that in the context of virtual worlds the creative component is so integral to play that the current terminology is inadequate: "The very idea of content *production* may need to be challenged: the description of a new hybrid form of simultaneous production and usage, or *produsage*, may provide a more workable model" (2007). An equally accurate way to describe such media is *cocreative* (Morris 2003), in which neither the developers nor the players are the sole creators and mediators of a game, but that through the personalized act of play, players bring their own content, meanings, and ideas into the game. The meanings that are created in the virtual space are shared meanings, stories coconstructed and told between groups of people who are all contributing content.

In addition to the cocreative aspect as breaking down the barrier between audience (player) and the performance/text (virtual world), self-reflexivity is also critical to breaking down the fourth wall, through commenting on itself and signifying its own constructed nature. In television and theater, the fourth wall is broken by a character speaking to the audience directly, for instance, thus immediately signifying the artificial nature of the production and yet at the same time allowing the audience into the character's space through that corecognition of artifice. The actors are "in on the same joke" as the audience, and through that shared meaning and acknowledgment of artifice, the fourth wall is broken down. In the case of virtual worlds, the players similarly know that they are populating the space with objects and characters, and producing the story with their own creations and performances. Players understand the artifice of the space, and I would argue that, rather than breaking engagement, the involvement of the player-audience in the performance-creation act allows the player into that space in ways that contradict the normal player-character divide. Nowhere is this breakdown of the fourth wall more apparent than in the user-generated *auditory* content of virtual worlds, including sound effects, voice, and music. Although early virtual worlds lacked such sonic interactions between players, today these interactions are a critical part of the social dynamic that takes place.

Auditory User-Generated Content

Sound is in a particularly unique position when it comes to the fourth wall: sound exists not behind a wall (virtual or otherwise), but penetrates our physical space: it is simultaneously in the diegesis of the world, but also in our own space. In this way, it always serves as a mediator between the virtual and the real. In terms of user-generated content, then, sound should be a particularly strong force in breaking the fourth wall. User-generated audio, in other words, does not just extend the virtual into the real, but also extends the player's world into the virtual space. A few examples will illustrate this point.

EverQuest, launched in March 1999, was one of the most popular early online virtual worlds, with nearly half a million subscribers at a time when the Internet was far less ubiquitous. Although auditory latency was common in those days, *EverQuest* cleverly combated both latency issues and repetitiveness by introducing the concept of allowing users to tie custom sound effects from their own computer to events whenever a specific phrase appeared in the text-based chat window, a function that was part of an update called "Audio Triggers" in late 2005. Since text messages would scroll fairly quickly at times across screens, and players needed to be able to quickly react to certain phrases, by playing an auditory warning tied to keywords they could be alerted to any important phrase. For example, players might want to know that they had just been kicked, so they could set an alert for "kicks YOU," and if the phrase "A frost giant savage kicks YOU for 30 points of damage," appeared, players would immediately know that they had been attacked, before they could even read the phrase. Sound files were stored on the player's server, and only the player heard the sound, unless players were using voice-chat, in which case the sound may have played back loudly enough to be heard through the player's microphone. In such cases—or in cases where players told another player what triggers they were using—it was common for other players to sonically "spam" the player, by repeatedly typing in that phrase to trigger the audio file. For example, on an *EverQuest* forum, a player explains, "Never tell guild mates your audio triggers or you will get spammed. . . . A warrior in my last guild had 'enrage' set as his audio trigger and the audio was of a gong sound. Several of us found this out and in between fights we would /tell Vortimer enrage and listen to his bongs whenever he spoke on Ventrilo."[1] Despite the risks of sharing the trigger keywords with other players, players liked to discuss their unique approaches to using sound effects on websites and in-game chat, often sharing their ideas and trying to outsmart others by attempting the most witty or creative uses of sound effects. Another example of allowing user-generated sound effects to be tied to objects or events in the virtual world can be found in *Second Life*, in which players can tie sound effects samples to objects that they have created. For example, a user-generated motorcycle can play sound effects of a motorcycle (or other sound) selected or produced by the creator. When creating the object, creators set permissions that allow others to modify that object, and thus they can enable others to adjust the sounds, create new sounds, and so on (see Marcus 2007). Players can in this way sonically customize objects in the world, and can add humor or their own style to the overall soundscape of the space. In this way, players bring the real world into the virtual (and vice versa), by acknowledging the artifice of the creative practice and intentionally bringing that artifice into the game. The sound effects may be completely unrealistic or unconnected to the object or phrase involved, yet the *act* of tying them to each other, and of sharing them with others, extends the real world into the virtual space, breaking that fourth wall. By allowing players to select their own sounds and tie these sounds to particular events or objects, designers are beginning to allow players to sonically own their own personal virtual space, a further step toward seeing the virtual space as an extension of the real.

More common than customizing sound effects, however, is the customization of musical content in virtual worlds. In most cases, music in virtual worlds is typically pre-composed pieces triggered by the player (see Collins 2008), although increased varia-tion is possible: *Glitch*, for instance, allows players to collect musical blocks and then use whatever blocks the player has collected to compose a song. In this way, the overall music is produced according to the player's individual experience of the game, even though the sequences themselves are pregenerated. In other cases, specific interactions between certain characters could lead to spontaneous jam sessions between characters, as in a game like *Asheron's Call 2: Fallen Kings*, in which different species of characters played different types of instruments, and the interaction between players caused changes to the music (see Fay, Selfon, and Fay 2004, 473–499). There are also cases where players can press music-mapped keys or input an ABC Notation file to create and perform their own music in virtual worlds, such as in *The Lord of the Rings Online: Shadows of Angmar (LoTRO)* or *Mabinogi.*[2] *LoTRO*, for example, allows players, once they have obtained a musical instrument, to enter a "music mode" that uses the ASCII keyboard to play songs in real time. While many players like to explore the musical option themselves, it can prove to be annoying to other players in the game: "That is the one system about lotro I dearly hate. Nothing like standing in 21st hall and having soom [*sic*] moron pull out a set of bagpies [*sic*] and start playing freebird or something else. That is enough to make your ears blead [*sic*]." On the other hand, many players like the system's innovation and enjoy the ambiance it gives to the game: "I love the music system in LoTRO. I enjoy hearing people standing around playing instruments. It makes the towns more interest-ing and alive. LoTRO is the only game I've played where people sometimes sit around in a tavern, talk, play music, and smoke pipes for fun" (Webb 2010). The important idea here is that even with mistakes (or perhaps because of the mistakes), player-generated music "makes the towns more interesting and alive." Player-generated music, in other words, even though it recognizes its own artifice and may break with the context of the virtual space, creates a different type of engaging experience for players.

Music may also be entirely streamed into the virtual world from outside, as in *Second Life*, which can stream in MP3 or other music formats. Performances are created by streaming music live from the performer's computer through software like SHOUTcast or Icecast, and are then tied to a specific locale. What is interesting about some of the *Second Life* concerts is the audience participation at the events, often tying the lyrics to avatar actions. Craig Lyons, for instance, performed a song called "Winter" and the audience made it snow, and Maxx Sabretooth's song "You Can Leave Your Hat On" sent fans searching their inventory for hats to wear (Ferreiro 2010). Similarly, *Habbo* allows players to design their own guest room, which can be customized with their own objects, furniture, wall patterns, virtual pets, and so on. What interests our discussion here is the introduction of version 13 of the game in 2007, which launched the Traxmachine. *Habbo* advertised "from out of the silence, we bring you HabboTrax, putting the power in your hands to fill the hotel with sound! Let the beat...drop when you start mixing and making music!" (Habbo 2007). Players can load up to four "Traxpacks" of nine samples each to create a soundscape or musical background to their personal virtual space. Songs created on the sequencer are known as Traxtunes and are composed by players, who can save them to a virtual CD, play them on a jukebox, and trade them with other players. Blogs, social networking sites, and forums have grown up around the Trax, sharing and selling songs to other players. In other words, some virtual spaces have afforded the opportunity to players to integrate their own selected music—to DJ their own space—without compromising the character of the overall space. Players discuss at length the music they listen to while they play: a simple search for music in *World of Warcraft* will reveal hundreds of forum discussions about what music fits "best" with the game.

The sharing of preexisting music also occurs as players use their voice over IP (VoIP) microphones to input sound and music into a game. While the original idea of VoIP was to communicate and share tactical information during the gameplay, many players use VoIP to socialize, and one particularly interesting trend has been for players to stream music (over the headset) into the game, sharing songs with other players. In fact, this became so popular that VoIP software company Teamspeak designed the idea into the third version of the software to make it easier for players to share music over the network through an artificially intelligent agent (sometimes much to the dismay of others). VoIP software Ventrilo, for instance, warns users "it can be annoying for people who don't want to hear it, especially if your server is for a guild that raids or works together in a massive multi-player online game. For these purposes, one option is to create a channel for music that others can access and play in" (Darrington 2011). The desire to set up one's own streaming channel has led to in-game VoIP radio systems where players can broadcast their own music, effectively becoming virtual-world DJs.

As noted, the average player is not a professional sound designer or music supervisor and may pick contextually inappropriate sounds or music to populate the virtual space. It is very common for players to choose very literal examples of sounds and music to tie to particular events—the literal following of lyrics in the *Second Life* example discussed above, for instance, illustrates this effect. This is particularly common in the selection of music—that is to say, players attempt to find lyrics to match an event, rather than music to capture an emotion, mood, or general feeling of an area. Indeed, there are many aesthetic consequences to allowing user-generated content. The music composed for virtual worlds is designed to "fit" with the aesthetic and framework of the world. By allowing players to customize music, this fit can be disrupted, and new meanings and emotional relationships generated (see Wharton and Collins 2011). While customization might be a desired trait for the consumer, the designers of the game (along with the composers) must relinquish control over the musical soundtrack to the game. Wharton and Collins (2011) found that players consciously or subconsciously attempted to make connections between the music that they chose and a game's narrative, events, imagery, and playing tactics. Sometimes the music influenced the game, and sometimes the game influenced the music. One player of *World of Warcraft*, for instance, recalls how he or she always associates particular bands with the game, after listening to the albums while playing the game: "I vividly remember riding with my dwarf hunter around Stranglethorn, listening to The All-American Rejects. Those were the 'good old' days when I was part of a proper guild and I even managed to get into some raiding action regularly. Whenever I hear songs by The All-American Rejects, it reminds me of those times. . . . So yeah, whenever I [hear] these two bands, I'm instantly transported to WoW" (Solo 2011).

As described above, allowing user-generated musical content may interfere with the feelings of presence or realism of the virtual space. In particular, tying music to content literally might draw attention to the artificial nature of the construction. Players may choose inappropriate music that contradicts rather than reinforces actions or events, thus also drawing attention to the artifice. Nevertheless, players as mentioned are actively engaged in selecting and sharing musical ideas with other players: there is clearly an equally compelling if different type of experience that occurs with the ability to select and share music: the fourth wall of the experience is broken down by the activity.

Finally, of course, there is also vocal sonic content that is shared between players in the virtual space. Voice channels in virtual worlds are typically configured like a telephone conference call, with all members of a team connected to each other but not to other teams in the virtual world. In this way, teams of players can conspire and discuss tactics, share information, talk about the game or about things external to the game (Drachen and Smith 2008). In their work on the online version of *Counter-Strike*, Wright, Boria, and Breidenbach (2002) go so far as to argue that "The meaning of playing *Counter-Strike* is not merely embodied in the graphics or even the violent gameplay, but in the social mediations that go on between players through their talk with each other and by their performance within the game. Participants, then, actively create the meaning of the game through their virtual talk and behavior." Voice is clearly faster than typing, and generally voice is seen as an advance over text. Text requires players to type, which means that their hands must be free to type, and so they cannot type and move their character simultaneously. With voice the player's hands are freed and coordination between players can happen more quickly, a critical point in ensuring a team's success in some games. Voice can also pick up the nuances of speaking that can be misinterpreted in text. Emotion, personality, and mood can be more easily conveyed through voice. In some sense, the use of VoIP reduces the feeling of mediated interaction between players, since the voices are real and the responses instant, creating a real sense of social presence (Ducheneaut et al. 2006).

There are also problems with VoIP in virtual worlds, however. Some players feel that voice adds little to genres that are not based on collaborative play, and that the use of the voice channel in those cases degenerates primarily into trash talking other players (Wadley, Gibbs, and Benda 2005). This is somewhat dependent on genre, however: in role-playing games, for example, the practice of *grinding* means that players have time to engage in social conversation as a means of reducing the boredom of these parts of large multiplayer games.[3] In other genres, voice is not as helpful, and there are reasons that voice is sometimes maligned. Confusion can be caused by an inability to know if one's own voice was heard. Not hearing a response to a question or comment, for instance, with a lack of visual cues, means players are sometimes left repeating themselves (Gibbs, Hew, and Wadley 2004).

Furthermore, if players don't know the person to whom they are speaking (virtually or in reality) and there are many characters on-screen, it may be difficult to match the voice to the avatar (Wadley et al. 2005). Likewise, when there are too many players on-screen or some particularly vocal players, there may be a lot of simultaneous conversations, which are harder to track in voice than with text. In *Unreal Championship*, for instance, the voice channel was designed so that all players were mixed at the same volume, which had the effect of disembodying the voice by eliminating proximity effects (Gibbs et al. 2004). However, Gibbs, Hew, and Wadley (2004) found that a poorly designed proximity algorithm means that a voice may suddenly appear midsentence "with no sense of a person approaching or receding. Participants found these voices just as disembodied as those in *Unreal Championship*." The Dolby company describes the problem with existing systems: "there are lots of stress-points in the system. You have players using mono headsets and low quality microphones, the codecs aren't very good, and there is also the issue of people who have their microphones settings too low or too high. The results even on relatively controlled services such as Xbox Live are clipping, distortion, and microphones picking up echoes: essentially an audio mush" (Arnold and Langsman 2009, 18). If the voice is spatially placed and the sound level is set according to distance, the "audio mush" becomes much easier to separate into perceptually meaningful sound information.

One of the most significant sound problems with VoIP is the "ludic leakages" that occur, that is, the game sounds leaking into the real world—and vice versa—which disrupt the immersion (Pearce, Boellstorff, and Nardi 2009, 177). Having family members speaking to or near the player may be picked up by the microphone and enter the game. Players in one study reported "breathing, eating, household noise, speech from family members, TV, and music were accidentally transmitted into the voice channel" (Wadley, Gibbs, and Benda 2005; cf. Hew, Gibbs, and Wadley 2004). Such sound, of course, dispels the illusion of the virtual world, allowing the everyday into the realm of the virtual. The most significant criticism—and most difficult to overcome—of VoIP in virtual worlds is that the illusionary aspects of role-play can be destroyed when speakers are clearly of different age, gender, or ethnicity than that of their avatar. Although, recently, microphone equipment has been designed to disguise the voice, the unnaturalness of the voice through modulators can itself be a distraction, and many players prefer not to tweak their voice (Wadley, Gibbs, and Benda, 2007). But this inability to disguise the self destroys the suspension of disbelief, argues Richard Bartle (2003):

> If you introduce reality into a virtual world, it's no longer a virtual world: it's just an adjunct to the real world. It ceases to be a place, and reverts to being a medium. Immersion is enhanced by closeness to reality, but thwarted by isomorphism with it: the act of will required to suspend disbelief is what sustains a player's drive to be,

but it disappears when there is no disbelief required....Adding reality to a virtual world robs it of what makes it compelling—it takes away that which is different between virtual worlds and the real world: the fact that they are not the real world.

This incorporation of the real into the virtual may be particularly jarring when the virtual world is not representative of reality (e.g., more like *World of Warcraft*, rather than like *Second Life*). The fact that some of the talk that occurs is "out of character" (such as asking for technical or help related to game mechanics), or that ludic leakages might interfere with the game means that role-play can be disrupted by voice. However, given that we are already "breaking the fourth wall" by allowing user-generated content into the space, is the incorporation of the real world really so intrusive to the immersive experience? Are there instances where breaking the wall increases immersion rather than disrupts that experience?

CONCLUSIONS: A FOURTH WALL OF SOUND

"Immersion" as a concept of gameplay is often discussed in terms of "presence," the feeling of "being there," with the player being immersed "in the game." But, rather than view the game strictly as a separate space into which we may become immersed, we may more accurately speak of the player being immersed "in the game*play*." It is the *act* of play, including content creation, that leads to the immersive experience. Therefore, we may do better to focus on distinguishing types of immersion that occur in gameplay, specifically, immersion in the narrative—what we might refer to as "presence"—and immersion in the experience—what we might refer to as "engagement." While we may feel less present in virtual worlds in which we partake in user-generated content sharing, the act of creation within that space may lead to a more engaging experience. Moreover, it may be the case that if we create something (objects, sounds) in the virtual space, we can extend our sense of self into that world, increasing that sense of presence. Rather than viewing engagement as one step on the way to immersion (see, e.g., Brown and Cairns 2004), engagement should be viewed as a different *type* of immersive experience, equally important and as meaningful to the player.

User-generated content is typically created outside of the fictional world (that is, the player makes the object or content outside the diegesis of the game), but is then incorporated into the virtual space—much as someone may create a chair for a dollhouse, which then becomes part of the story that a child may make up about that space. The player, then, is not in a position of either audience or actor in a virtual world, but rather holds a position in between, simultaneously being both actor and audience. The fourth wall that divides the virtual world from the real, as shown, is broken in this space as the actor/audience, virtual/real dichotomies are destroyed. User-generated content need not *break* immersion, in other words, because we are not ever wholly outside the space, and therefore we cannot ever be wholly in the space. Rather, we may become immersed in the *experience* of cocreation and play. Just as the audience participation and fourth-wall breaking of Brecht's theater meant that "not only is artifice no obstacle to entertainment but [it] allows additional levels of engagement to occur" (Pinchbeck 2006, 406), virtual worlds allow us to engage in the gamespace in new ways not afforded by offline games.

Conway (2009) describes several cases in video games where the fourth wall is intentionally broken down by the designers—for example, the game character addresses its player, or dirt spray is left on the screen, implying that we are witnessing the scene through a camera—in such instances, argues Conway, the wall may become broken but the space of the "magic circle" is extended to include the player. The theory of the "magic circle" first proposed by Huizinga (1955), and later taken up by Salen and Zimmerman (2003, 95-96), is "shorthand for the idea of a special place in time and space created by a game....As a closed circle, the space it circumscribes is enclosed and separate from the real world." In other words, the magic circle is a kind of psychological space in which the game exists.[4] Conway (2009) argues that the fourth wall in games, rather than delineating the space in a manner that breaks the suspension of disbelief (as it may in theater or film), allows an increased suspension of disbelief by being inclusive of the player—by expanding the magic circle to incorporate those outside elements of play.

Perhaps most importantly, as mentioned above, sound *always* transcends the fourth wall, and thus sound always extends the virtual space into the real space. The view of the magic circle as a physical space, that is "quite well defined since a video game only takes place on the screen and using the input devices (mouse, keyboard, controllers), rather than in the rest of the world" (Juul 2008) is overtly ocularcentric. The game does not only take place on the screen: it simultaneously takes place in the auditory space around us. The magic circle of the game always extends beyond the screen into our own physical space because sound emanates from speakers (or headphones) into that space. If we can accept that the magic circle of the game, or the fourth wall between the virtual and real, is extended into the player's space through the use of sound and through player-generated content (among other techniques), the combination of these two phenomena—player-generated sonic content, in other words—suggests that we are missing—or at least, downplaying—some key elements in our current conceptions of immersion.

Returning to Benkler's concept that creators of virtual worlds "build tools with which users collaborate to tell a story," we see that the shared authorship of virtual worlds not only takes place in terms of storytelling and object-building, but the overall soundscape is very much created by the "audience" of players. The fourth wall that divides the imaginary virtual world from the real world is broken down by the self-reflexive cocreative practices of the players and by the extension of the sonic virtual world into the real-world space. Indeed, it is not the believability of the virtual-world space that makes these worlds attractive to players: it is the engagement with content creation and the performative, social interactions that are an important component of that practice.

A common recent question in the game world is: "Are videogames art?" Film critic Roger Ebert repeatedly stoked the fires by declaring that games cannot be art. But what Ebert misses is the shift in art in the twentieth century from objects to practice, a shift that has been referred to as a change of focus on *doing*, rather than on objects: a shift to an aesthetics of relationships (Green 2010, 2). Bourriaud has called this shift "relational aesthetics," echoing Benkler in stating that such art sets the environment—provides the tools—for collaborative creation and shared activity (Bourriaud 1998, 113). Gell likewise redefines art as the "social relations in the vicinity of objects mediating social agency…between persons and things, and persons and persons via things" (1998, 5). Considered in this way, by providing the tools of creation and breaking down the fourth wall between audience and actors, and between virtual and real, virtual worlds can be viewed as an important phase in redefining video games as participatory, engaging, performative art spaces.

NOTES

1. *EverQuest* forums. *Station.com.* http://forums.station.sony.com/eq/posts/list.m?topic_id=114012, accessed January 15, 2011.
2. ABC Notation is a text-based shorthand music notation system in which text editors can be used to write music.
3. Grinding refers to the fact that in order to increase a character's experience points, financial situation, and so on, a certain amount of work is undertaken on the part of the player in killing off weaker enemies, searching for items, and so on in a very repetitive and time-consuming manner.
4. Arguments have developed within game studies as to the nature of—and indeed the existence of—the magic circle. It has been noted that the magic circle is not as definitive as might be presumed: public performance of game playing and the notion of spectatorship suggests that an exclusive magic circle cannot exist. Moreover, in games such as *World of Warcraft*, the concept of a magic circle becomes problematic because demarcations become more soft and fluid when players role-play their character offline at fairs or conventions (Lamnes 2008).

REFERENCES

Arnold, S., and M. Langsman. 2009. He's Behind You. *Audio Media* 37: 18. http://www.mediafire.com/?ogieaun2goy6xoc. Accessed May 16, 2011.

Bartle, R. A. 2003. Not Yet You Fools! *Game Girl Advance.* http://www.gamegirladvance.com/2003/07/not-yet-you-fools.html. Accessed May 16, 2011.

Benkler, Y. 2006. *The Wealth of Networks: How Social Production Transforms Markets and Freedom.* New Haven, CT: Yale University Press.

Bourriaud, N. 1998. *Esthétique relationnelle.* Dijon: Les presses du réel.

Brown, E., and P. Cairns. 2004. A Grounded Investigation of Game Immersion. Paper presented to CHI 2004, April 24–29, Vienna.

Bruns, A. 2007. Produsage: Towards a Broader Framework for User-Led Content Creation. In *Creativity and Cognition: Proceedings of the 6th ACM SIGCHI Conference on Creativity and Cognition*. Washington, DC: ACM. 13–15.

Caplan, S., D. Williams, and N. Yee. 2009. Problematic Internet Use and Psychosocial Well-being among MMO Players. *Computers in Human Behavior* 25 (6): 1312–1319.

Collins, K. 2008. *Game Sound: An Introduction to the History, Theory and Practice of Video Game Music and Sound Design*. Cambridge, MA: MIT Press.

Conway, S. 2009. A Circular Wall? Reformulating the Fourth Wall for Video Games. *Gamasutra*. July 22. http://www.gamasutra.com/view/feature/4086/a_circular_wall_reformulating_the_.php. Accessed June 21, 2013.

Darrington, J. 2011. How to Set Up Ventrilo Music Channel. *eHow*. January 20. http://www.ehow.com/how_7822682_set-up-ventrilo-music-channel.html. Accessed May 16, 2011.

Drachen, A., and J. H. Smith. 2008. Player Talk: The Functions of Communication in Multi-player Role-Playing Games. *Computers in Entertainment* 6 (4): 1–36.

Ducheneaut, N., N. Yee, E. Nickell, and R. J. Moore. 2006. Alone Together? Exploring the Social Dynamics of Massively Multiplayer Online Games. In *Proceedings of CHI 2006, Conference on Human Factors in Computing Systems*. New York: ACM Press. 407–416

Fay, T. M., S. Selfon, and T. J. Fay. 2004. *DirectX 9 Audio Exposed: Interactive Audio Development*. Plano, TX: Wordware Publishing.

Ferreiro, L. 2010. *Second Life*'s Thriving Music Scene. *Los Angeles Times*, June 9. http://articles.latimes.com/2010/jun/09/entertainment/la-et-secondlife-concerts-20100609. Accessed May 16, 2011.

Gell, A. 1998. *Art and Agency: An Anthropological Theory of Art*. New York: Oxford University Press.

Green, J.-A. 2010. Interactivity and Agency in Real Time Systems. In *Soft Borders Conference and Festival Proceedings: Papers*, 84–88.. http://softborders.art.br/downloads/ebook.pdf. Accessed June 21, 2013.

Gibbs, M. R., K. Hew, and G. Wadley. 2004. Social Translucence of the Xbox Live Voice Channel. In *Entertainment Computing—ICEC 2004: Third International Conference, Eindhoven, the Netherlands, September 1–3, 2004: Proceedings*, edited by M. Rauterberg, 377–385. New York: Springer.

Habbo. 2007. Trax-Machine. *Habbo*. http://www.habbo.com/groups/Trax-Machine. Accessed June 3, 2011.

Hew, K., M. R. Gibbs, and G. Wadley. 2004. Usability and Sociability of the Xbox Live Voice Channel. In *Proceedings of IEEE 2004, Australian Workshop on Interactive Entertainment*, February 13, Sydney, Australia, 50–58.

Higgins, D. 1976. The Origin of Happening. *American Speech* 51 (3–4): 268.

Huizinga, J. 1955. *Homo Ludens: A Study of Play Element in Culture*. Boston, MA: Beacon Press.

Juul, J. 2008. The Magic Circle and the Puzzle Piece. Paper presented to "Philosophy of Computer Games" conference, August 13–15, Oslo, Norway, 56–65.

Lammes, S. 2008. Spatial Regimes of the Digital Playground: Cultural Functions of Spatial Practices in Computer Games. *Space and Culture* 11 (3): 260–272.

Marcus, T. D. 2007. Fostering Creativity in Virtual Worlds: Easing the Restrictiveness of Copyright for User-Created Content. *New York Law School Review* 52: 67–92.

Morris, S. 2003. WADs, Bots and Mods: Multiplayer FPS Games as Co-creative Media. *Level Up Conference Proceedings*. Utrecht: University of Utrecht, November (CD-ROM)

Pearce, C., T. Boellstorff, and B. A. Nardi. 2009. *Communities of Play: Emergent Cultures in Multiplayer Games and Virtual Worlds.* Cambridge, MA: MIT Press.

Pinchbeck, D. 2006. A Theatre of Ethics and Interaction? Bertolt Brecht and Learning to Behave in First-Person Shooter Environments. In *Technologies for E-Learning and Digital Entertainment: First International Conference, Edutainment 2006, Hangzhou, China, April 16–19, 2006*, edited by Z. Pan et al., 399–408. Berlin: Springer-Verlag.

Salen, K., and E. Zimmerman. 2003. *Rules of Play.* Cambridge, MA: MIT Press.

Schroeder, R. 2008. Defining Virtual Worlds and Virtual Environments. *Journal of Virtual Worlds Research* 1 (1), July. https://journals.tdl.org/jvwr/article/view/294/248. Accessed June 21, 2013.

Solo, D. 2011. The Music of WoW. *Wow Alone*, May 16. http://wowalone.blogspot.com/2011/05/music-of-wow.html. Accessed November 21, 2011.

Sotamaa, O. 2007. On Modder Labour, Commodification of Play, and Mod Competitions. *First Monday* 12 (9)3. Accessed June 21, 2013.http://frodo.lib.uic.edu/ojsjournals/index.php/fm/rt/printerFriendly/2006/1881.

Wadley, G., M. Gibbs, and P. Benda. 2007. Speaking in Character: Using Voice-over-IP to Communicate within MMORPGs. *Proceedings of the 4th Australasian Conference on Interactive Entertainment.* Melbourne, Australia.

Wadley, G., M. R. Gibbs, and P. Benda. 2005. "Towards a framework for designing speech-based player interaction in multiplayer online games." In *Proceedings of the Second Australasian Conference on interactive Entertainment* (Sydney, Australia, November 23–25, 2005). ACM International Conference Proceeding Series, vol. 123. Creativity & Cognition Studios Press, Sydney, Australia, 223–226.

Webb, J. 2010. Lord of the Rings Online Column: Freebird! *MMORPG.com.* January 19. http://www.mmorpg.com/gamelist.cfm/game/45/feature/3936/Freebird-.html. Accessed November 21, 2011.

Wharton, A., and K. Collins. 2011. Subjective Measures of the Influence of Music Personalization on Video Game Play: A Pilot Study. *Game Studies* 11 (2), May. http://gamestudies.org/1102/articles/wharton_collins. Accessed June 21, 2013.

Wright, T., E. Boria, and P. Breidenbach. 2002. Creative Player Actions in FPS Online Video Games: Playing Counter-Strike. *Game Studies* 2 (2). http://www.gamestudies.org/0202/wright/. Accessed May 23, 2011.

Audiovisual Materials

Age of Empires. Ensemble Studios, 1997.
Asheron's Call 2: Fallen Kings. Turbine, 2002.
Counter-Strike. Vivendi, 1999.
EverQuest. Sony, 1999.
Glitch. Tiny Speck, 2011.
Habbo Hotel. Sulake, 2000.
Hitman: Blood Money. IO Interactive, 2006.
The Lord of the Rings Online: Shadows of Angmar. Turbine, 2007.
Mabinogi. devCat, 2004.
Second Life. Linden Lab, 2003.
World of Warcraft. Blizzard, 2004.

CHAPTER 22

....

SONIC VIRTUALITY: UNDERSTANDING AUDIO IN A VIRTUAL WORLD

....

TOM A. GARNER AND MARK GRIMSHAW

A precise understanding of virtuality is hindered by disagreements concerning its exact definition. From a perspective of popular usage, the word *virtual* is synonymous with *near* and *almost*, which when applied to our understanding of virtual reality (VR) describes a near-perfect recreation of reality, placing virtuality a single notch below reality at the top of a continuum, with unreal at the base. The term *virtual* is also echoed in words such as *essential* and *fundamental*, a reflection that could describe VR as an approximation of actuality that achieves the most significant aspects of the reality it imitates while being distinguishable in the minor details. We differentiate between virtuality and virtual reality, identifying the former as a more general term for describing an entity as less than real. In contrast, virtual reality can refer to both a technological development implementing computer generated sensory information, and an individual's subjective perception of reality. This chapter explores acoustic ecology (AE) theory within the domain of digital games and examines the variables and measurements of acoustic virtuality. Also discussed are the various concepts connected with embodied cognition (EC) and knowledge theory, and the associative notion that reality is an illusion and all existence is inherently virtual. The term *digital games* refers to modern computer video games and more specifically the first-person shooter (FPS) genre, which places the user within a three-dimensional virtuality.

John Leslie King (2007, 13) identifies the inherent meaning of virtuality as the opposing counterpart to what is real, suggesting that without the virtual, reality could not exist. Logical deduction develops this notion to posit that virtuality has existed for as long as we have been able to comprehend reality. The difficulty with this definition lies in our limited and abstract understanding of *real*. King (14) cites research identifying cognitive perception of the unreal as real (referencing actual improved audio quality affecting perceived visual quality of a multimodal stimulus). What we perceive is unequal to what *is*. This notion could be extended to suggest that each individual possesses a unique reality containing various *perceived truths* that are accepted within that reality with a conviction comparable to that felt toward objective truths. This calls into question the existence of so-called objective truths and asks: is all existence inherently virtual? Does the very nature of our thought processing distill all knowledge and certainties to beliefs and opinions? Could the oxymoronic signifier *virtual reality* in fact be the single concrete truth?

Accepting virtuality as simply the antithesis of reality would classify the term as anything unreal, (unnatural, inauthentic, false, etc.). From a philosophical perspective, such a definition is valid at a theoretical level, but ultimately limits our opportunity for development, in terms of both conceptual understanding and technological advancement. A more detailed understanding of virtuality would support creative design choices within various industries, developing the immersive qualities of various media to ultimately generate a better user experience for innumerable products.

The associations between virtuality as a concept and virtual reality as a technology advocate digital games as a prime medium for virtuality research. While visual information from a game exists on a two-dimensional plane, game audio exists within the same 3D environment as the listener (Grimshaw 2008), revealing greater complexity and blurring the lines that separate reality from virtuality, and consequently promoting audio as the preferred sensory modality for this research.

CONCEPTS OF VIRTUALITY

> There has never been a totally secure view of reality, certainly not in the industrial era of history. People say that the world is not as real [as] it used to be. (Woolley 1993, 6).

From a highly theoretical perspective, it is appropriate to suggest that should a digital game successfully generate a virtual world indistinguishable from that of reality, then potentially any dream from within the imagination could be fully experienced in both body and mind; with a further opportunity for such dreams to be shared, exchanged, and experienced alongside other people. Such possibilities reveal a substantial potential value for virtuality research, whereby a comprehensive understanding of human perception could facilitate technology capable of placing a user within a total immersion environment that is perceivable as reality but with the limitless freedoms that virtuality could afford.

Chalmers, Howard, and Moir (2009) argue that although human beings perceive the world with five senses, cross-modal effects can have substantial impact upon perception "even to the extent that large amounts of detail of one sense may be ignored when in the presence of other more dominant sensory inputs." This may go some distance to explaining the immersive capacity of a digital game. While information received during gameplay may typically be limited to visual, audio, and haptic data, the way in which the information is presented generates an illusion of full sensory input (a concept that is more fully explored later in the section on embodied cognition). Hughes and Stapleton (2005) support this notion, arguing that "the goal of VR is to dominate the senses, taking its users to a place totally disconnected from the real world."

In her book *The Rational Imagination*, Ruth Byrne (2005, 3) identifies counterfactual imagination as a component of creative thought in which an impossibility, related to reality, can be experienced within the mind's eye. Reality is transformed through manipulation of facts into an alternate world of fiction, a world that could arguably be described as virtual. Imagining an alternate reality in this way is not a passive "dreamlike" experience but rather an (inter)active one, directed by the creator in real time. This differentiates the alternative reality of counterfactual imagination from film, theater, and fiction novels. Digital games, however, share with imagination the opportunity for real-time user interaction within an impossible environment.

For Michael Heim (1998, 4) virtual reality is technological, an "emerging field of applied science." This focus differentiates between terms associated with *unreal*, separating virtuality from *artificial reality*, a phrase that Woolley (1993, 5) defines as a circumstance in which a fiction has become fact through creation of a product that originally only existed within a fictional world. In utilizing a technological perspective, it is best to avoid more abstract theoretical notions; a clear distinction between reality and virtuality, alongside a practical method for measuring virtuality, is required. Heim (1998) distinguishes between *hard* and *soft* virtual reality (VR). Soft VR is described as essentially a diluted form, that is, anything based in computers or that can be argued as *other than real* (Heim illustrates by way of advertising techniques that state their product or service as *the real thing*, suggesting that their competitors are less than real and, in essence, virtual). Heim argues that such a definition is counterproductive to the progression of virtual reality development and presents the standards, or "three I's," of virtual reality (1998, 7): immersion, interactivity, and information intensity.

In the book *Architecture Depends* (2009, 87), Jeremy Till asserts that an established statement by Laurie Anderson (that virtual reality will never be fully accepted as truth until developers "learn how to put in dirt") is not to be literally translated and subsequently posits that "dirt" refers to temporality. Within a digital game context, such a concept is being considered, particularly within the genre of role-playing and real-time strategy games. Weapons may deteriorate, buildings may fall into disrepair, plants and animals may starve, and relationships may lose closeness; these are but a few examples of gameplay mechanics simulating the "dirt" of reality, with consequences and interrelations that relate directly to the player. However, the association between virtual reality and time documented by Till suggests that such efforts remain distinctly unreal because such temporal elements are autonomous and most commonly relate to an internal clock as opposed to the globally shared system of time.

Hughes and Stapleton (2005) consolidate relevant literature to elucidate various conceptual positions on the reality/virtuality continuum. In this framework, reality and virtual reality exist on polar extremes with mixed reality (MR—a relatively even distribution of actual and virtual elements within an environment) occupying the center point, augmented reality (synthetic objects added into a real landscape) positioned between MR and reality, and augmented virtuality (real objects, situated within a virtual landscape) located between MR and VR. In addition, Hughes and Stapleton note that MR also refers to the entire spectrum of reality/virtuality and that the reality types are points on a continuum rather than discrete classes of reality.

THE VIRTUALITY OF AUDIO

A player is situated in the living room, seated comfortably, and initiating a game experience. As the player commences by progressing through the game setup menus, a variety of feedback beeps confirm actions within the interface. As the player enters the game, a transcendent voice counting down to match-start is heard, followed by verbal orders from a nonplayer character (NPC) heard over a short-wave radio. The player hears the sound of the plasma rifle charging, footsteps in the snow, and the rattle of equipment. As an enemy is observed and engaged, the sound of plasma weapon firing dominates the soundscape, followed by a visceral impact expressed by the sound of screams and melting flesh. As the enemy lies sprawled across the battlefield, a voice (originating from a live player via voice over Internet Protocol [VoIP]) is heard loud and clear, "Whatever! Lucky shot!" as a chorus of cheers confirms the player's righteous kill.

The above scenario elucidates the complexities that arise when attempting to classify and measure sonic virtuality. Feedback sounds supporting menu/interface navigation have no physical relationship between action and sound, with the chosen audio sample retaining only a semantic association. Transcendent voice-overs are prerecorded material with no identifiable (real or virtual) source, while NPC radio messages originate from a clearly identifiable source but are not propagated via a natural physical source. The sound of a fictional entity such as a plasma rifle (a symbolic auditory icon [Grimshaw and Schott 2008]) does not possess physical causality and can only be created by way of synthesis or sampling (recording) of an alternative sound (again, with only a semantic link between sound and source/action). Footsteps in the snow may utilize a sample taken from a genuine source, but often a recording of walking on cornstarch is implemented. This represents a common example of hyperreal sound, in which designers have consistently utilized an alternative audio sample to the extent that a listener is likely to recognize the false sample as more genuine than the actual physical sound.

All of these sounds originate from the game engine, but they still exist within reality, propagated by artificial (but nonetheless physical) equipment, traveling and reflecting through actual spaces (Grimshaw 2008). In a similar vein, Natkin (2000) documents a practical implementation of virtual soundscapes within actual spaces, in which the sound waves are propagated via headphones and utilize postproduction processing to create an artificial representation of the physical space. In this circumstance it is not the actual sound that is virtual, but instead the method with which the sound is broadcast.

For Natkin, this propagation of audio is virtual, though the audio samples themselves are highly likely to be classified by many as real. Bronkhorst (1995) provides a correlating argument, identifying a differentiation of audio virtuality between sounds that originate from a natural and from an artificial propagation source.

This notion is complicated further when considering VoIP audio. Although VoIP transmitted audio originates from a live speaker, the information is digitized, then re-encoded as sound wave data before it reaches the listener, and commonly a delay exists between speaking into the headset and receiving the sound from the audio output. While the audio input possesses a stronger temporal and semantic association with the received output, the propagation is nonetheless artificial. This can be expanded to question the *reality* of electronically amplified live sound, and further complexity arises when considering the difference between analogue and digital signal processing (an issue that has garnered significant debate in recent years). If we were to define virtual audio as any sound propagated by an artificial projection medium, then a significant proportion of academic experimentation into sound deals exclusively with virtual audio. This highlights the following questions: Is the nature of recording/playback/amplification of a sound originally emitted from the natural world enough to make that recording virtual? Is there a distinct separation between virtual and artificial?

At present, mainstream digital games generate sensory data in visual, audio, and tactile modalities. As a result, even game developers that strive to achieve realistic soundscapes must expand the purpose of audio to perpetuate a simulated sensation of olfactory, tactile, and gustatory input via representational inference. A visually rendered corpse alone may not trigger an olfactory sensation of decay, but the sound of buzzing flies and wriggling maggots around it has a much greater potential to do so. This issue establishes a clear divide between reality and the virtuality of current digital games. Audio designers are often required to compromise between playability (a sound design that supports player action via extradiegetic audio feedback, representative of other sense data) and realism (a soundscape more akin to reality, focused upon diegetic sounds). The notion of realism is questionable, however, when observing a game experience as a whole. Although a *realistic* virtual soundscape may (virtually) reflect its reality counterpart, the lack of audio input compensating for other sensory modalities creates an incomplete experience, lacking immersion and, ironically, appearing unrealistic. Extended exposure to fictitious *Hollywood-esque* Foley sounds has determined that genuine source recordings of many dynamic sounds (shotgun blasts, footsteps in the snow, etc.) are often perceived to be unrealistic. As the lines separating the virtual and the real become increasingly blurred, the audience is becoming more likely to be immersed by the hyperreal than the actual. Games are not simply simulations of real events; they are unique constructs that are better perceived as real-life activities (Shinkle 2005).

Several questions concerning virtuality are hereby raised: How can we better understand sonic virtuality? Where does reality end and virtuality begin? Can virtuality in relation to sound be classified and measured and, if so, how? The remainder of this chapter addresses these questions and concludes with a conceptual framework to facilitate clearer classification of sounds and support future development of a workable measurement system for sonic virtuality. Here the various concepts of virtuality (as they relate to audio) form a framework that distinguishes between real and virtual audio, while allowing space for incremental points between the polar extremes. Understanding the complex interrelations between human and environment (be it real or virtual) is fundamentally shaped by the psychological approach adhered to when theorizing the processes of the human mind. This chapter advocates EC theory to explore the way in which we define, perceive, and interact with sound. Virtual and real acoustic ecologies are also explored within the context of affective response to digital game play.

EMBODIED COGNITION AND VIRTUALITY

The following is a hypothetical thought process designed to elucidate a central concept of embodied cognition. During an abstract contemplation of defying gravity and leaping upward into space (a notion that, on reflection, originated from a brief glance at the sky), various additional simulations of stimuli are recalled. A visual representation of James Bond on a jetpack, the simulated physical sensation of leaping ever higher and John Williams's iconic Superman theme all manifest themselves. A single conceptual construct has been characterized by both virtual sensory stimuli and simulated motor actions. Here a general concept that many may experience is personalized by the immediate environment and our unique memory.

The concept that cognition is a biological process grounded by bodily experience and the environment has garnered increasing support in recent years (Garbarini and Adenzato 2004). Shinkle (2005) posits that memories of past events are not limited to stored knowledge of external proceedings; emotional responses (characterized by physiological states and discrete response behaviors) play a crucial role in defining these perceptions and experiences. This notion describes a system that processes objective and affective data initially at an autonomic level, producing physiological changes that are *felt* by the individual and fed back into the system for cognitive processing. Such a system challenges Cartesian dualism, arguing against a centralized mind within the brain that is capable of detached processing, instead proposing an integrated system that incorporates long-term memory, current physiology, and the surrounding environment.

Andy Clark's 1997 book *Being There: Putting Brain, Body and World Together Again* advocates the concept of integrated cognition, stating that "minds are *not* disembodied logical reasoning devices" (1) and that rejection of the centralized processor concept in favor of an embodied perspective is an increasingly popular attitude in the fields of robotics and artificial intelligence. The concept of integrated cognition bears some similarity to the notion of *autopoiesis*, especially in the autopoietic concept of a *consensual domain*. This domain is brought about by the structural coupling (the interplay) between mind, body, and environment (see Winograd and Flores 1986, 46, 49). Clark

(21) further questions classical cognitive theory by means of the *representational bottleneck* concept, which states that for a central processing unit to function, all sensory data must be converted into a single symbolic code for comprehension, then translated into various data formats to carry out the different motor responses. Such a process is theorized to be time consuming and expensive, leading to the conclusion that a centralized system could not possibly respond adequately to real-time pressures of everyday life. Sensory filters, such as attention, reduce the processing load by "sensitizing the system to particular aspects of the world—aspects that have special significance because of the environmental niche the system inhabits" (Clark 1997, 24), a system that Clark relates to Jakob Von Uexkull's (1957) concept of the *Umwelt* (a reduced perception of the actual environment as defined by the individual's needs, desire, and lifestyle).

Construal level theory (CLT) argues that increasing psychological distance (space-time-relevance) promotes more abstract thought (Lieberman and Trope 2008); however psychological distance (PD) can only be measured in relation to the here and now and is consequently dependent on the current environment. The *here and now* notion that constitutes part of the EC theory is detailed in Margaret Wilson's *Six Views of Embodied Cognition* (2002). This text argues that a cognitive model must be established in a real-world environment context (*situated cognition*—the *here*); recognize temporal and real-time effects (*time-pressured cognition*—the *now*); acknowledge the environment as an integral part of the model (an ecological framework); and accept that the function of all cognitive thought is ultimately to guide action whether in the immediate circumstance or in planning for a future event. A futurity can be related to virtuality in that it cannot be directly interacted with and exists as an insubstantial entity. If we accept that contextualization determines a significant proportion of a sound's perceptual makeup, then any attachment of PD may severely affect the perceived reality of a sound (for example, the sound of a distant car alarm may be less *real* than an individual's home fire alarm, as the latter is more firmly rooted within one's personal reality).

The concept of EC posits that thought cannot exist outside the here and now and that conscious appraisal of an object or situation cannot be detached from sensory input, a notion not dissimilar from that of *thrownness*. First established by Martin Heidegger in the 1927 publication *Sein und Zeit* (*Being and Time*), the concept of thrownness is succinctly communicated within the contexts of computer science and cognition by Winograd and Flores (1986, 33–35). Within this text, thrownness supports the principles of EC, in that it refers to existence within the world as fundamentally inseparable from the environment in which we exist. Winograd and Flores document that to have *no* impact upon the environment is essentially impossible, as even doing nothing has consequences. They also state that individuals cannot separate themselves from a situation to reflect upon it, as it is not a static entity but rather a continuous movement, and accurate prediction of outcomes (outside of a laboratory) is, consequently, unachievable. This constant fluctuation and evolution of existence makes a stable representation of the environment (or a situation within it) unattainable; Winograd and Flores argue that "every representation is an interpretation" (35), and postevent analysis remains fraught with subjective bias.

If we are to agree that all thought is under the continuous and forceful influence of the surrounding environment, current personal physiology, and long-term memory, and also that such circumstances dictate that no perception can reflect reality entirely, then we could further posit that all experience is virtual. We are the sole population of our own virtual realities. Our universe supports countless parallel worlds, each with many consistencies, but many with striking differences. In developing a continuum of sonic virtuality, the above theory argues that *real sound* is impossible, and the polar extremes cannot be absolute real and absolute virtual.

Garbarini and Adenzato (2004) argue that cognitive representation relies on *virtual activation* of autonomic and somatic processes as opposed to a duplicate reality based in symbols. For example, the sound of hissing is likely to have an acute physiological impact upon an individual with an anxiety about snakes. Although establishing threat connotations (*there is a snake nearby, snakes are poisonous, snakes could bite me*) with the object requires cognitive signification, a history of ophidiophobia would support a conditioned subroutine, bypassing lengthier cognitive processing to connect the object (hiss sound) directly to the autonomic nervous system. An embodied theory would not accept pure behavioral conditioning, however, and instead would suggest that the object would first stimulate virtual sensory data (a snake's image, movement, etc.) that characterize the actual stimulus and generate a threat interpretation. The entire process remains fundamentally cognitive, but only a fraction of the input data needs full appraisal, as the simulated data is already directly linked to the human autonomic nervous system (ANS—a primarily subconscious system, chiefly controlling involuntary physical actions) through conditioning, supporting an efficiently responsive process achieved via reduced cognitive load.

This suggests that the embodied cognitive processing of a sound can be significantly affected by the presence (or absence) of cognitive shortcuts. Özcan and Egmond (2009) discuss the way in which ambivalent audio can have dramatically different meanings depending upon associated visual stimuli. Without such contextualization support, the listener's perception of the sound would be greatly dependent upon long-term memory (established conventions, passed experiences, etc.), current environment (temperature, space, etc.), and physiology (including established neuro-pathways such as cognitive bypass routines). Essentially, listeners are immersed within their own exclusive virtual reality, where the embodied perception of the received sound is as unique as the individual.

Recollection of memories to deduce and arrange future plans is also embodied in sensory data. Existing research has argued that memory retrieval can cause a re-experiencing of the sensory-motor systems activated in the original experience, the physiological changes creating a partial re-enactment (Niedenthal 2007). This notion strongly relates to the auditory concept of *phonomnesis* (an imagined sound that can be unintentionally perceived as real [Augoyard and Torgue 2005]). In this scenario, the mind (in response to an initial stimulus) generates a re-experiencing of a sound that can be classified as virtual.

The experiencing of sound stimuli can be differentiated from the other sensory modalities by way of the specific neural geography through which auditory processing occurs (see Kaas et al. 1999). This series of neural structures includes both the modality specific (such as the primary auditory cortex and cochlear nucleus) and the general (temporal lobe). This suggests that, while information gathered regarding the virtuality of perceived sound can be applied to general sensory experience, research with a specific focal point upon sound stimuli is critical to obtaining a comprehensive understanding of virtuality across the senses.

Augoyard and Torgue provide an invaluable reference guide to various acoustic and psychoacoustic events in their work *Sonic Landscapes* (2005), within which various phenomena are documented that relate (in varying ways) to both EC and virtuality. As individuals experience numerous and complex soundscapes throughout their lives, such phenomena are potentially commonplace. Sound may bring forth a past memory by way of anamnesis; it may force a person's attention upon a specified place through hyperlocalization, or even provoke a sensation that the space within which the listener is positioned is shrinking (narrowing [Augoyard and Torgue 2005]). As listeners, we have the perceptual capacity to focus our attention upon an individual speaker within a room of thousands by disregarding all irrelevant audio information (known as the *cocktail party effect*). Psychoacoustic entities can manipulate listener behavior and dictate future action via incursion (alarm, phone ringing, etc.), dictate the listener's level of vigilance (the *Lombard effect*), and even incite a euphoric state (*phonotonie*). With regards to virtuality, three perceptual phenomena of particular interest are *phonomnesis*, *remenance* (a perceptual continuation of a sound that is no longer being propagated) and the *Tartini effect* (a sound that is physiologically audible but that has no physical existence); here a combination of tones will provoke the sensation of an additional frequency that is not physically present (an occurrence that has been implemented in military and crowd-control applications [Augoyard and Torgue 2005]). Such auditory phenomena arguably relate heavily to EC theory; if the listener were capable of detached and objective audio perception, then such sonic illusions and auditory holograms would not exist.

ACOUSTIC ECOLOGY AND SONIC VIRTUALITY

Originating in the 1960s within R. Murray Schafer's seminal work, *acoustic ecology* refers to "how organisms interpret and are affected by natural and artificial sounds" (Esbjörn-Hargens and Zimmerman 2009, 491). This ecology incorporates the auditioning organism as an integral component of the soundscape, in which separate individuals may receive widely different audio information from the same acoustic space. This elucidates the connection between AE and EC, in that the embodied nature of listening creates a personalized virtual auditory experience; and because the individual is a foundation of ecology theory, AE is, therefore, virtual. Within this chapter we have explored general conceptual notions relating to virtuality and suggested ways in which EC theory may determine all sound (indeed all existence) to be inherently virtual. Progressing from these ideas, the following section details human hearing (incorporating modes of listening, psychoacoustic theory, and contextual conventions), alongside virtual AE models.

The concept of a virtual sonic ecosystem within a first-person shooter (FPS) environment resonates with the notions of EC and AE in that it embraces an amalgamation approach, as outlined by Grimshaw and Schott (2008), classifying listener, soundscape, and environment as inseparable components in an integrated system. Their *virtual acoustic ecology* (VAE) asserts that game sound exists as part of an intricate relationship between the player, the audio engine (virtual soundscape), and the resonating space (real acoustic environment). First-person-perspective digital game sound utilizes a substantial number of sounds with the explicit purpose of representing a virtual environment that players will find immersive, irrespective of the fact that they are not physically situated within that world. Such audio is intrinsically associated with virtual actions and entities, but the sound waves physically exist purely within the domain of reality, each sound resonating within actual spaces and interacting with real surfaces before reaching the listener's ear.

The foundational belief underpinning this construct is that our biology, the enveloping sensory input of the present, and the long-term memory data representing our history are all crucial factors in thought processing and behavior determination, essentially an intricate matrix of causality. Emotion directs attention toward specific current stimuli and filters out sensory data that possess a low emotional relevance. Long-term memory (LTM) retrieval and memory transfer function between short-term memory and LTM can depend upon the emotional value of the content (Friestad and Thorson 1986) and, therefore, could manipulate how individuals' history impacts upon their current cognition and behavior. During audition, the intensity of the emotional experience and the conscious desire of the listener will influence the listening modes, determining the nature of the sonified data that will be extracted from the audio. That information may in turn determine the reappraisal and characterization of the audio, subsequent auditory data perception, attention focus, emotional state changes, and so on.

The following consolidates the associated theoretical concepts of VAE, EC, and virtuality to establish a framework of variables relative to sonic virtuality (figure 22.1). Creating a sound from component waveforms by way of synthesis could be asserted as a more virtual sound class when compared to a sound with a natural origin. Although the framework also classifies recorded and artificially propagated audio as virtual, unless the sound is synthesized, the ultimate origin is arguably real. Propagation differentiates between natural resonance and electronic amplification, classifying the latter as more virtual. Several variables connected to semantic association are presented, the rationale stating that a sound with several relevant semantic attachments to entities perceived as genuine will support the *reality* of the sound (for example, a voice with semantic attachments to an NPC will resonate with more truth than a transcendent *voice of god*).

Reality	Virtuality
Natural Origin	Synthetic Origin
Casual Representation	Symbolic Representation
Natural Propagation	Artificial Propagation
Immediate Temporality	Delayed Temporality
Visible Source	Acousmatic
Natural Acoustic Reflections	Artificial Acoustic Reflections
High number of Semantic Associations	Low number/absence of Semantic Associations
High Perceived Realism of Source/Action	Low Perceived Realism of Source/Action
Analogue Signal Processing	Digital Signal Processing
High Quality Sound	Low Quality/Distorted Sound
Live Presentation of Audio	Presentation of Recorded Audio
Speaker as Artificial Source	Headphones as Artificial Source

FIGURE 22.1 The sonic virtuality framework of variables.

Audio Functionality and Modes of Listening

The previous section outlined a set of (relatively) objective acoustic variables that determine the virtuality of a sound. Here we explore contextualization and listening function, asserting that such effects further enable the personal virtual realities documented earlier.

A sound without context is effectively a shell that can have little significance for listeners and may potentially be classified as virtual because listeners cannot attach the sound to an entity that exists within their reality. The contextualization of sound is a process central to AE, where assumption and expectation originating from individuals' perception of their current environment establishes a context frame that supports associations made between the sound and information regarding the source (Özcan and Van Egmond 2009). Contextualization has the capacity to alter completely a listener's perception of audio information and, consequently, research has identified several *modes* of listening that attempt to account for such effects.

Gaver (1993) states that nonspecific, or everyday, listening refers to hearing events within the environment rather than the sounds themselves. Gaver elaborates, positing that during everyday listening, audio perception bypasses conscious semantic translation. The sound of a car's engine accelerating is not consciously perceived as such, instead simply as *a car*. Cusack and Carlyon (2004) expand upon the above concepts in their exploration of attention processes in audio perception. They describe a "hierarchical decomposition of the soundscape" wherein attention is focused on ever increasing levels of specificity. This concept reflects the notion of *reduced listening* (Chion 1994), which describes conscious attention toward the sounds themselves. In their conceptual framework of listening modes, Tuuri, Mustonen, and Pirhonen (2007) indirectly

support EC theory, stating that as listeners we "do not perceive sounds as abstract qualities, rather, we denote sound sources and events taking place in a particular environment" (13). Their work identifies eight discrete modes of listening that can be positioned
along the construal level theory continuum. The act of separating an individual sound
from a composite (hi-hats from a drum loop, for example) is that of clearly distinguishing the received audio information from the actual soundscape. In this circumstance, our mode of listening is generating a virtual representation of the actual sound
environment.

Tuuri, Mustonen, and Pirhonen (2007) also argue that "some sounds encourage the
use of certain modes more strongly than others" (13). In "A Climate of Fear" (Garner
and Grimshaw 2011) we argue that the modes of listening are largely determined by the
perceived intensity of the sound, as determined by psychological distance, physiological
reflex, and immediate affective response. Let us use a fire alarm as an example. When
listening to such a significantly intense sound, a high-level listening mode (e.g., reduced
listening—evaluating the frequency and temporal difference between the component
tones) is highly improbable, and the listener is effectively forced to respond by way of
reflexive (break current behavior, immediate new action) and connotative (imminent
danger, must evacuate!) listening. The sound itself was intentionally designed to evoke
such a response, supporting the acceptance of this theory within general product design
industries. A continuous, unchanging sound may fluctuate in terms of the listening
mode it encourages because of the complexities of the audio ecology. Returning to our
fire alarm, while the immediate listening mode demands a reflexive function, prolonged
exposure to the sound affords the listener time to appraise the sound with higher-level
cognition. At this point a listener may begin to evaluate the causality (*Where is that
alarm coming from?*) or the functionality (*Is that actually the fire alarm, or is it the bur-
glar alarm?*) of the sound. Such changes in perceptual listening modes are primarily
instinctive, and although conscious control is possible, the notion of choice is essentially
an illusion, as the embodied nature of the listener's personal virtuality manipulates the
outcomes of the choice.

Within a complex soundscape we are capable of attenuating sonic input to focus on
increasing levels of specificity. A city soundscape may be reduced to the compound
sounds of a motorbike, which can then be concentrated to the individual sound of tires
treading asphalt. We may reflexively recoil from these sounds to avert the vehicle, or
evaluate the qualities of the sound to cross the street without visually confirming the
location of the bike. In such a circumstance, individuals placed within the same acoustic
space may provide dramatically different descriptions of the sonic environment even if
they are required to provide an objective account of their experience. Through hearing
alone, we may even mistake the vehicle for a taxi or van through misinterpretation of
semantic associations. John Greco (2010) argues that "our causal explanations typically
cite only one part of a broader causal condition" (74). This may explain how such an
audio misinterpretation may occur, as the listener perceives an engine sound, establishes
a causal syllogism (motorbikes have engines, I hear an engine, therefore a motorbike
is present), and makes a false assumption that is accepted as reality unless conflicting

information is provided. The well-established *Gettier problem* (Gettier 1963) highlights issues with justified true belief theory, proposing various scenarios (similar to that above) that argue an individual may (justifiably) accept a truth as knowledge from a misinterpretation of information. Here truth is accepted as reality despite the fact that the justification is virtual, and it could further be asserted that (in many scenarios) an individual is capable of accepting a fallacy as knowledge (and feeling justified in doing so) because of the nature of the virtuality of the causal explanation.

This chapter has utilized concepts of EC theory to help explain why both reality and virtuality remain deeply subjective and personal concepts. A review of relevant literature and logical deduction has provided a theoretical differentiation between real and virtual digital game audio that could precipitate a great deal of future empirical research. At this stage it would be inappropriate to describe these variables as concrete determiners of virtuality. Instead, the intention is to highlight the potential factors that could have an impact upon perceived virtuality. It is also suggested that virtuality can only be perceptual and is always sensitive to the nature of the individual's personal reality. That such individual virtual existences are truth is a bold but compelling statement; the notion that a higher level of being may have control over our lives in the same way that we control our digital game avatars is one best left for another day.

References

Augoyard, J., and H. Torgue. 2005. *Sonic Experience: A Guide to Everyday Sounds.* Montreal: McGill-Queens University Press.

Bronkhorst, A. W. 1995. Localization of Real and Virtual Sound Sources. *Journal of the Acoustical Society of America* 98: 2542–2553.

Byrne, R. M. J. 2005. *The Rational Imagination: How People Create Alternatives to Reality.* Cambridge, MA: MIT Press.

Chalmers, A., H. Howard, and C. Moir. 2009. Real Virtuality: A Step Change from Virtual Reality. *Proceedings of the 2009 Spring Conference on Computer Graphics*, New York, 9–16.

Chion, M. 1994. *Audio-vision: Sound on Screen.* New York: Columbia University Press.

Clark, A. 1997. *Being There: Putting Brain, Body and World Together Again.* Boston, MA: MIT Press.

Cusack, R., and R. P. Carlyon. 2004. Auditory Perceptual Organization inside and outside the Laboratory. In *Ecological Psychoacoustics*, edited by J. Neuhoff. Boston, MA: Elsevier Academic Press, 16–48.

Esbjörn-Hargens, S., and M. E. Zimmerman. 2009. *Integral Ecology: Uniting Multiple Perspectives on the Natural World.* Boston, MA: Integral Books.

Friestad, M., and E. Thorson. 1986. Emotion Eliciting Advertising: Effects on Long-Term Memory and Judgement. *Advances in Consumer Research* 13: 111–116.

Garbarini, F., and M. Adenzato. 2004. At the Root of Embodied Cognition: Cognitive Science Meets Neurophysiology. *Brain and Cognition* 56: 100–106.

Garner, T. A., and M. Grimshaw. 2011. A Climate of Fear: Considerations for Designing a Virtual Acoustic Ecology of Fear. In *Proceedings of the 6th Audio Mostly Conference*, Coimbra, Portugal. New York: ACM, 31–38.

Gaver, W. 1993. What in the World Do We Hear? An Ecological Approach to Auditory Event Perception. *Ecological Psychology* 5 (1): 1–29.

Gettier, E. L. 1963. Is Justified True Belief Knowledge? *Analysis* 23: 121–123.

Greco, J. 2010. *Achieving Knowledge: A Virtue-Theoretic Account of Epistemic Normativity.* New York: Cambridge University Press.

Grimshaw, M. 2008. Autopoiesis and Sonic Immersion Modeling Sound-Based Player Relationships as a Self-Organizing System. Paper presented to the Sixth Annual International Conference in Computer Game Design and Technology, November 12–13, Liverpool, UK.

Grimshaw, M., and G. Schott. 2008. A Conceptual Framework for the Analysis of First-Person Shooter Audio and Its Potential Use for Game Engines. *International Journal of Computer Games Technology 2008*, http://www.hindawi.com/journals/ijcgt/2008/720280/. Accessed July 31, 2013.

Heidegger, M. (1927) 1962. *Being and Time.* Translated by J. Macquarrie and E. Robinson. New York: Harper.

Heim, M. 1998. *Virtual Realism.* New York: Oxford University Press.

Hughes, C. E., and C. B. Stapleton. 2005. The Shared Imagination: Creative Collaboration in Augmented Virtuality. In *Proceedings of Human Computer Interaction International 2005 (HCII2005)*, Las Vegas, http://citeseerx.ist.psu.edu/viewdoc/download?doi=10.1.1.76.2246&rep=rep1&type=pdf. Accessed July 31, 2013.

Kaas, J. H., T. A. Hackett, and M. J. Tramo. 1999. Auditory Processing in Primate Cerebral Cortex. *Current Opinions in Neurobiology* 9: 154–170.

King, J. L. 2007. Dig the Dirt: Hashing over Hygiene in the Artifice of the Real. In *Virtuality and Virtualization,* edited by K. Crowston, S. Sieber, and E. Wynn, 13–18. Boston, MA: Springer.

Lieberman, N., and T. Trope. 2008. The Psychology of Transcending the Here and Now. *Science* 322: 1201–1205.

Natkin, S. 2000. Mapping a Virtual Sound Space into a Real Visual Space. Paper presented to International Computer Music Conference, Berlin, Germany.

Niedenthal, P. M. 2007. Embodying Emotion. *Science* 316: 1002–1005.

Özcan, E., and R. Van Egmond. 2009. The Effect of Visual Context on the Identification of Ambiguous Environmental Sounds. *Acta Psychologica* 131: 110–119.

Shinkle, E. 2005. Feel It, Don't Think: The Significance of Affect in the Study of Digital Games. In *Proceedings of DiGRA 2005: Changing Views—Worlds in Play,* http://www.digra.org/dl/db/06276.00216.pdf. Accessed July 1, 2013.

Till, J. 2009. *Architecture Depends.* Cambridge, MA: MIT Press.

Tuuri, K., M. Mustonen, and A. Pirhonen. 2007. Same Sound—Different Meanings: A Novel Scheme Form of Listening. *Proceedings of Audio Mostly 2007,* Ilmenau, Germany, 13–18.

Von Uexkull, J. 1957. A Stroll through the World of Animals and Men. In *Instinctive Behaviour,* edited by C. Schiller. New York: International Universities Press, 5–80.

Wilson, M. 2002. Six Views of Embodied Cognition. *Psychonomic Bulletin and Review* 9: 625–636.

Winograd, T., and F. Flores. 1986. *Understanding Computers and Cognition: A New Foundation for Design.* Norwood, NJ: Ablex Publishing.

Woolley, B. 1993. *Virtual Worlds: A Journey in Hype and Hyperreality.* Oxford: Blackwell.

CHAPTER 23

....

VIRTUAL WORLDS: AN ETHNOMUSICOLOGICAL PERSPECTIVE

....

TREVOR S. HARVEY

ONE Wednesday night, while searching for live music performances in the virtual world of *Second Life*, I walked into MJ's Blues and Dance Club, a live music venue that billed itself as a "Classic Rock-n-Roll, Blues, Jazz, and All Around Good Time Entertainment Establishment." Looking around the digitally constructed room from the perspective of my avatar—my computer-rendered, human-like body that indicates my presence and place within the virtual world—I observed the club was a spacious hall boasting a large dance floor and two stages. One stage, outfitted with turntables and other equipment for DJs, was empty, but on the other stage stood Ictus Belford, a thirty-something male avatar, who was wearing blue jeans, a long-sleeve T-shirt, and sneakers (see figure 23.1). As Ictus sang Bob Dylan's "Knockin' on Heaven's Door," accompanying himself on his acoustic Takamine guitar, the audience of about 20 avatars chatted (via text messages) and danced, occasionally adding Linden Dollars (*Second Life* currency) to Ictus's tip jar, which sat conspicuously at the front of the stage. Covering the wall behind Ictus were pictures of other virtual-world musicians who have performed at MJ's, a testament to the club's prominence in the live music scene of *Second Life*. After singing several cover tunes, Ictus introduced one of his own original compositions:

> I'm going to do a song I wrote. It's about *Second Life* and my first few days' experience in this wild, wild world. This song is called "No More Real Life."

There was an immediacy to Ictus's voice, similar to the intimate sound of a closely miked radio DJ, that suggested a closer proximity between our avatars in the digitally constructed space than was visually evident and that did not at all match the cavernous appearance of the club. This discrepancy between what I was *seeing* and what I was *hearing* was perhaps even more pronounced because of the artificial reverb that was

FIGURE 23.1 Ictus Belford performing at MJ's Blues and Dance Club.

added to Ictus's vocals. As with his voice, there was a clarity and presence to the acoustic, steel-string guitar, suggesting the utilization of a piezoelectric pickup device that allows a guitar to be plugged directly into a personal computer. Indeed, as I sat in my bedroom in Florida, controlling my avatar with my mouse and keyboard while peering into my computer screen, Ictus was more than a thousand miles away in Oklahoma, singing into a microphone connected to his computer, which projected his voice and guitar in real time through an Internet-based audio-streaming channel into the virtual club where our avatars stood separated only by the short rise of the virtual stage upon which his avatar was performing.

Live music performances, such as the one described above, are common events within *Second Life*; multiple clubs and venues feature live musicians or DJs at any hour of the day (or night), any day of the week. Within these venues, participants dance, sing, and converse, mirroring "real-world" music-oriented sociality. To an ethnomusicologist like me, interested in lived musical experiences, live music concerts in *Second Life* present a compelling environment for investigating how musical phenomena play an important part of meaning-making in the social life of virtual-world participants. The temporality of music and the physical nature of sound (concepts further discussed in Knakkergaard, chapter 24 in this volume) are critical issues in understanding the vital role of musical activities in virtual worlds. By exploring the manifestation of "virtual" concerts within an avatar-based virtual world, I seek to understand how musicians and audiences experience "liveness" in the context of computer-mediated, digital environments. I posit that the value placed on live performances within *Second Life* suggests a particular efficacy to aurality in actualizing social relationships within virtual space such that real-time musical performances serve to bridge "virtual" and "actual" experiences in so-called "virtual worlds."

MUSIC IN VIRTUAL WORLDS

Second Life is a graphically rich, user-designed environment within which human participants interact via avatars. To even the most casual observer, music plays a central role in the social life of *Second Life* participants. The immense importance of music to the design, marketing, and user experiences in virtual worlds is evident from the proliferation of music-themed virtual worlds throughout the first decade of the twenty-first century. From massively multiplayer online social games (e.g., *Popmundo*) to 3D digital spaces for social listening (e.g. *3DJay* and *MixM8*), music-oriented virtual worlds attract users into online environments through attempts to draw out meaningful sociomusical participatory action.

Participants in virtual worlds such as *Second Life* tend to divide musical sounds into two broad categories: (1) "live" music, meaning music that is controlled in real time by human actors and streamed into the digital space with minimal latency; and (2) nonlive, preprogrammed music. Live music events, as defined by *Second Life* participants, include not only live musicians, whose offline performances are simultaneously streamed into the virtual world, but also DJs, who generally play commercially released, prerecorded music, but socially interact with their virtual-world audience in real time as they select, introduce, and play back recordings. Nonlive musical sounds include constant music streams established by owners of land parcels as a soundtrack for their virtual space. The employment of such ambient music provides soundscapes to the user-constructed landscapes of *Second Life*, much the way that background music is used in shopping malls, elevators, and other public and commercial spaces. While the sources of both live and ambient music are located outside of *Second Life* and streamed into the virtual world via third-party audio streaming services such as SHOUTcast, users have also created virtual musical instruments, allowing avatars to simulate musical performance not only through the animation of the avatar, but also by scripting the automatic playback of musical sound associated with that instrument (see figure 23.2). While these various categories of musical experience within virtual worlds utilize different technologies for enacting musical performances, they each articulate ways in which musical behavior affects perceptions of being "in" the virtual world. Of these categories, however, only live music performances are conceived of as social events—circumscribed times and spaces defined as socially interactive gathering places for participant avatars.

As with the many text-based virtual worlds, or Multi-User Dungeons (MUDs), that preceded it (see Curtis 1996; 2001), *Second Life* stands apart from other graphically rich virtual worlds in that the software developers endowed *Second Life* with no specific purpose or meaning for the users. While *World of Warcraft*, *Entropia Universe* (which includes the music-themed *Rocktropia*), and many other 3D-rendered, avatar-based

FIGURE 23.2 The author (known as Collyier Heberle in *Second Life*) playing a Bach prelude on the virtual pipe organ at Balboa Park, San Diego.

virtual worlds were conceived and developed as games with predetermined goals and achievement-based rewards, *Second Life* offers no such goal-oriented purpose for its users. This distinction is clearly articulated in both personal conversations and published reports, where *Second Life* participants repeatedly and adamantly reject the suggestion that they are playing a "game" (see, for example, Boellstorff 2008; Kirkpatrick 2007). Thus, *Second Life* participants create meaning for their own existence by engaging in social practices connected to or extending from their "real life" interests. Live music concerts, which are among the most popular attractions in *Second Life*, often serve to draw participants toward, and provide an environment for social engagement, leading to the development of a rich and active musical culture within the virtual world.

Ethnomusicology and Digital Culture

The founding of ethnomusicology as a discipline in the middle of the twentieth century brought a "new emphasis upon the relationship of music to culture" and institutionalized a branch of musicological research whose focus was not so much on the "definition of music styles... [but on] an understanding of music as a human phenomenon" (Merriam 1960, 107–108). In pursuit of this goal, Alan Merriam, a founding member of the discipline of ethnomusicology, sought to distinguish the existing humanistic focus on musical works (product) from the social-scientific concern of human behavior and social activity (process) (1964). The process of music-making by human actors, rather than the resulting art-object of musical production, continues to be a central focus for ethnomusicological research today.

As Merriam and others sought to establish ethnomusicology as an academic discipline in the 1950s, they saw their efforts as an evolution of cross-cultural musicological research that had been going on for more than half of a century. The emergence of ethnomusicology as a social-scientific practice around the turn of the twentieth century was a response to new research in acoustics, developments in audio engineering, and the evolution of recording technology (for example, see Ellis 1885; Gilman and Fewkes 1891; Hornbostel and Sachs 1914). Throughout the twentieth century, these areas of techno-scientific knowledge—and the musical machines developed therefrom—became increasingly vital in defining and determining the research activities of Western ethnomusicologists who continued to focus on traditional (i.e., technologically "primitive"), non-Western cultures. Criticizing what he identified as colonial practices and attitudes related to the technologically privileged position of ethnomusicologists, René Lysloff (1997) called for an "ethnomusicology of technoculture" to expand critical engagement with music-cultural practices in relation to media and information technology. Still, the study of new technologies pertaining to sociomusical life within emergent digital cultures has only recently received some attention within the field of ethnomusicology (see Miller 2012). By applying an ethnographic lens to musical activity in *Second Life*, I hope to raise awareness of the relationship between sociomusical life and Internet-oriented digital technology within virtual worlds and, on a more general level, foreground important ways of conceptualizing musical performance and participation within our twenty-first-century, digitally mediated experiences.

EXPERIENCING THE "VIRTUAL" IN VIRTUAL WORLDS

After introducing his song "No More Real Life" during his set at MJ's Blues and Dance Club, Ictus began to strum his guitar in a medium-slow tempo. Starting on a D-major chord and then moving to a D-minor chord, Ictus produced an unexpected shift in tonality that, together with the relatively slow pacing of the song, presented a sense of ambiguity to the listener. The unsettled harmonic quality of the guitar part seemed fitting, an appropriate accompaniment to his descriptive lyrical retelling of his initial experiences in the disembodied realm of *Second Life* and the complex relationship between online experiences and offline perceptions of virtual worlds (see Weblink: Audio 23.1):

> I was sitting at my desktop looking at this cartoon girl
> She was telling me she wants to give this Second Life a whirl

> Wondering what the hell I was doing here
> Oh my God, I'm flying somewhere
> No more real life
> I want my second life
> No more real life
> Gotta have my second life

Initiation narratives that communicate the difficulties and wonderment that new participants experience when entering a virtual world for the first time are commonly shared both within and outside of *Second Life*. In the opening paragraph of his monograph, *Coming of Age in "Second Life,"* anthropologist Tom Boellstorff compared his initial experience with *Second Life* to the classic Malinowskian ethnographic description of entering the field:

> Imagine yourself suddenly set down surrounded by all your gear, alone on a tropical beach close to a native village while the launch or dinghy which has brought you sails away out of sight. You have nothing to do, but to start at once on your ethnographic work. ... This exactly describes my first initiation into field work in Second Life. (Boellstorff 2008, 3)

Indeed, entering *Second Life* for the first time is a strange and disorienting experience. After choosing a name (which also serves as a username for logging in to the *Second Life* servers), a new resident must then create her avatar, the digitally rendered body that represents the participant's being within the virtual space and the agent through which she interacts with that world. Special computer code, known as a physics engine, establishes the laws and constraints by which the movement and interaction of digital bodies within virtual space must abide. This visually based simulation of physicality underlies the conceptualization of virtual worlds as "immersive" environments. Such immersion, however, is often disrupted as a new resident develops an understanding of the "physical" presence of her own body (or avatar) in reference to other digital objects. Learning to control the avatar's movement in space, through the arrow keys on the computer keyboard, can be a difficult and frustrating process. The shortcomings of the computer keyboard as a fluid human-computer interface are readily apparent as the new resident struggles to orient herself within the virtual space, creating a rupture between self and physical environment, and avatar and virtual environment. The disorienting experience described by Boellstorff is reaffirmed by Ictus in the second verse to "No More Real Life":

> And then she said I needed hair
> Well, I was thinking: who cares
> I hadn't been here just a day or two
> Since I got into this room I can't find my way out of here

In both of these examples, Boellstorff and Ictus focus on the ocularcentric manifestations of being within *Second Life*—they perceive and interpret their virtual experience as a visually simulated world. Indeed, it is this visual representation of intended actions (or perhaps even more so, unintended actions) that accentuates the disembodied nature of living in a digital environment and distinguishes virtual worlds like *Second Life* from other socially oriented networked spaces (Krotoski et al. 2009). This ocularcentric environment accentuates the sense of disembodiment within virtual worlds, where computer-generated objects, including one's very own avatar, always remain exterior to one's bio-physical body. Thus, the term "virtuality," generally understood to mean "almost" or a "simulation," is commonly used to describe social life and interaction in "virtual worlds."

These common discourses of virtual reality suggest an experience that is separate and distinct from our "real lives," a space in which fantastical desires may be played out in ways impossible or improbable in the "real world." There are certainly elements to *Second Life* that support this perspective of the virtual: as Ictus sings in the first verse of his song, "Oh my God, I'm flying somewhere." Further investigation, however, reveals that the virtual is not separate from, but rather embedded within, "real life" experiences, and musical performance can play a vital role in actualizing virtual-world experiences. As I endeavor to articulate the relationship between the virtual and the actual within live music performances in *Second Life*, I follow Steve Woolgar in his call for developing "a much more sophisticated appreciation of the relations between online and offline" (2002b, 8). In the introductory chapter to his edited volume, *Virtual Society?* (2002a), Woolgar offers "five rules of virtuality" as analytic tools for investigating the relationship between virtuality and actuality. One of these rules, in particular, deserves mention in relation to *Second Life* live music events, namely that virtual technologies supplement rather than substitute for real activities.

LIVE MUSIC CONCERTS IN *SECOND LIFE*

Ictus was initially drawn to *Second Life* for social, not musical, reasons. "I hated it," Ictus said to me when describing his initial experience with *Second Life*. Controlling his avatar, his virtual body, was frustrating, as was the increased demand on computing power and Internet bandwidth, causing lag (temporal delays) inherent in such graphically rich, but geographically distributed, environments.

> I couldn't move too quick, just like a walking stick
> She called it lag, I thought, "It's more like a drag"
> And then she crashed and left me standing there
> All alone holding her bag
> No more real life
> I want my second life.

Soon, however, Ictus discovered the live music scene and began playing concerts. Five years later, despite his initial frustrations, Ictus maintains a permanent residence in a contemporary house on a private island, all paid for by his earnings (mostly from tips) as a musician in *Second Life*. While none of the songs in his repertoire are as reflexive of the *Second Life* experience as his song "No More Real Life," this song is indicative of Ictus's attempt to bridge the "virtual" and "actual" through musical expression in *Second Life*. Through this song—or more specifically, through live performances of this song for audiences of avatars—Ictus expresses not only the disjuncture of disembodied experiences in virtual worlds but a desire to actualize his virtual-world experiences.

According to anthropologist Marilyn Strathern, the term "virtual" has undergone "an intriguing metamorphosis from the concrete to the abstract" (Strathern 2002, 305). The root word from which "virtual" descends, "virtue," which references the qualities and essence of a thing, has been overshadowed by emphasizing the visual simulations of virtual worlds. Unlike the physical separation experienced through digitally based visual simulation, the materiality of digitally processed and distributed sound via performances by musicians such as Ictus is reconstructed "live" and literally embodied through the process of hearing. Thus, the sonic aspect of live music concerts is one of several actualizing mechanisms for *Second Life* audiences.

Within the context of virtuality, we may understand actuality as two closely related concepts: the first, informed by the French word *actualité*, implies that actuality is something that exists now, something that is current; and the second indicates that that which is actual emerges through action—suggesting an active process to actualization. Thus, while *Second Life* participants may experience disembodied distantiation from the virtual world in which their avatar resides, musical participation can serve to transcend this separation by actualizing the social experience—an active practice of making technologically mediated sociomusical processes current and more immediate. The issue of immediacy in establishing privileged modes of communication (e.g., face-to-face speech versus written communication versus computer-mediated electronic messaging) has a long history in communication studies (see Sterne 2003). More recently, however, scholars have challenged assumptions that communication involving a lower degree of technical complexity is any less mediated than communication within networks of digital devices (see Inoue 2003).

For *Second Life* participants, live concerts offer a certain amount of temporal immediacy between performers and audience members. The simultaneity of social action allows musicians to simulate familiar experiences of playing for audiences in "real life." The musicians I have met in *Second Life* did not perform first in a virtual world, but rather had offline experience performing on stage in front of audiences before discovering the possibility of live concerts in virtual worlds. Accustomed to conventional behaviors of audiences in relation to their performances (e.g., clapping), the natural inclination for these musicians was to expect certain responses from the avatars attending virtual-world performances, leading to a comparison of their online performances to offline experiences.

In an interview by Slim Warrior on the Metaverse TV show *Amped Up*, Damien Carbonell discussed the mental shift musicians encounter when moving from offline performance venues to computer-mediated virtual worlds.[1] Slim Warrior (aka

SlimGirlFat), herself an active musician in virtual worlds and other online spaces, asked Damien to relate how the "buzz" musicians get from performing in front of "real life" audiences compares to live performances in virtual worlds. For Damien, the lack of aural feedback from the audience was perhaps the biggest barrier to perceiving temporal immediacy between himself and the audience:

> It takes some getting used to—going from a real stage and then going to the virtual world where you can't really read the audience because you don't hear the clapping, you don't hear if they're holding full-length conversations with each other mid-song and not listening to you, you know, you don't really hear all of that. So, at first it kind of feels like nobody's paying attention because you can't hear anything and you're so used to hearing the crowd. But after you adjust and kind of figure out how to tell if people are enjoying themselves and things like that then, yeah, you can really get a buzz off of it.

The "buzz" sought by musicians in live performance situations cannot be simulated in virtual worlds; it must arise from actual sociality within that space. For musicians, such as Damien, developing modes of sociomusical interaction between audience members and performers in virtual worlds is crucial to the viability of "live" performances in digital space. Understanding and manipulating multimodal communicative action in virtual worlds—the aural, visual, and textual—is crucial to successful live performances. As Damien explained to Slim Warrior in the same interview:

> And it is that multi-tasking thing where, you know, perhaps in a live performance you're not listening to what they're talking about, but with *Second Life* you're actually reading what people are saying and it gets you a chance to be . . . you know, it becomes a little more personal because you're recognizing people's names.
>
> You know, what I think it does also, it gets your fans and your support a chance to get to know you through your music on a far more personal level than if you were doing a [real-life] gig.
>
> That's something I've enjoyed a lot about *Second Life* is the more personal feel to it. That's why when I started doing it I kept saying, over and over again, that I'm not putting on a concert, you know, I'm doing a show. There's a whole different atmosphere to it. It's more like I want people to feel like we're sitting around a campfire jamming. You know, I don't want people to feel like they're looking at me on an untouchable stage 20 feet away. It's a whole different atmosphere.

The desire to create social settings aimed at enhancing or enabling the development of intimate social interactions within virtual worlds is frequently expressed by musicians in *Second Life*. Just as in mainstream popular music, virtual-world songs often serve as a vehicle for relating romantic encounters and exploring the meaning of such relationships, as demonstrated in Ictus's "No More Real Life." Having watched friends engage in online romance, another *Second Life* musician, Rich Desoto, wrote "Avatar Girl," a song in which he remarks upon the development of romantically inclined intimate relationships that sometimes follow the "hyperpersonal" (Walther 1996) social interaction possible within virtual worlds (see Weblink Audio 23.2):

> I'm in love with an avatar girl
> She looks so good in this virtual world
> I watch her dance, I watch her talk with her friends
> And when she can she cuddles up with me again
> I'm in love with an avatar girl
> Doo n' doo, doo n' doo doo doo
> I'm in love with an avatar girl
> What is this place I have fallen in to?
> So many things here that I can do...
> When I arrived it seemed oh so strange
> But something kept me coming back again
> Doo n' doo, doo n' doo doo doo
> I'm in love with an avatar girl

My point here is not to sensationalize social interaction within virtual worlds by focusing on romantic affairs, but rather to establish the actuality of intimacy experienced in virtual worlds. Like Damien, Rich believes that live music performances in virtual worlds can provide an opportunity for close interaction among performers and audiences. In a personal interview I conducted with Rich, he explained how playing for offline audiences differs from virtual-world audiences and the benefits he finds as a performer to the modes of social engagement offered in the digital realm:

> As you can tell probably from my show this morning, I like to really interact [with the audience]. And there's maybe times where I want to just go into a musical vamp so I can do that interaction and respond to the chat or talk about specific event items or ... the hostesses or the people in the audience ... And there's a lot to be said about how your audiences and the people that interact with you understand you as a performer and you as a person ... What I don't get ... I don't get the facial expressions and the nuances from body language, but I do get the comments and ... I think we don't often as musicians get that in real time. By the time the feedback comes, it's in the event of, you know, a letter or an e-mail or a lack of sales or ... it's always a residual feedback, but this is an immediate ... like you said, more intimate.

Rich's statement on immediacy here is not merely an observation of the temporal compression made available via communication technology, but also speaks to a social intimacy that challenges our assumptions of virtuality as a highly mediated, technical process. Damien expressed it this way:

> I get touched a lot when I'm playing shows, especially when I'm playing an original [song] and there's people out there typing the lyrics to a song that I wrote in local chat. It's very touching.

Actualizing Online Sociality through Virtual Musical Participation

Back at MJ's Blues and Dance Club, where I first encountered Ictus, he was not the only one performing on stage during his set. He was accompanied by Carrie Laysan, his then *Second Life* wife and manager—and the inspiration of the song "No More Real Life." In her performances with Ictus, Carrie did not produce audible music; rather she would "sing" in (text) chat, while her avatar strummed her psychedelic "spork"—a multicolored, guitar-shaped instrument modeled after the hybrid spoon-fork utensil (see figure 23.3).

As an audience member at concerts featuring Ictus accompanied by Carrie, only Ictus's guitar and voice were streamed into the virtual-world music venue and relayed by my computer speakers. But both Ictus's and Carrie's avatars stood on stage, strumming their associated virtual instruments. Despite not producing actual sound, Carrie played an active and important role in actualizing the social experience at Ictus's live concerts, typing the lyrics to the songs in the chat as Ictus sang them. At times, Carrie's "backup vocals" enticed audience members to participate, and they, too, would "sing" along with the song in chat. When I asked Carrie how she started this process of virtual "musicking" (Small 1998) she explained:

FIGURE 23.3 Ictus Belford, guitar, and Carrie Laysan, spork, performing at Crystal Sands.

It started with me typing lyrics. I've always kinda just sung in chat along with him, just not all of the words. [Ictus] had several fans who were Korean…well, Korean and [from] other countries…but a couple of the Koreans thanked me [after the show] because they said they could understand better when I typed the lyrics.

So, I dunno, I just hopped on stage one day and said I was gonna play backup…and sing backup, and then when people started asking me to type the lyrics—more and more people asked me to type lyrics—I did. More and more. And then people started expecting me to get on stage and type. It feels weird to be "singing" from the audience. So then I asked [a friend] to make my spork pretty since I was using it so much.

Carrie's participation within the context of Ictus's concerts again raises questions about liveness, virtuality, and the nature of musical performance. The "virtual musicking" of Carrie's avatar, however—what we may perceive as a representation of musical performance—is hardly different from the simulated musical movements of Ictus's avatar. The actions of both avatars fall within what Kiri Miller calls "schizophonic performances" (Miller 2009). Building upon R. Murray Schafer's concept of "schizophonia," a "nervous" term he employed to emphasize "the split between an original sound and its electroacoustical transmission or reproduction" (Schafer 1977, 90), Miller utilizes "schizophonic performances" to characterize what Philip Auslander describes as musical practices "in which the visual evidence of performance [has] no relation to the production of sound" (Auslander 1999, 86). As a technologically mediated musical experience, schizophonia arises in response to the "socially and historically produced…categories of the live and the recorded [that] are defined in a mutually exclusive relationship" (Wurtzler 1992, 89). Generally accepted conceptions of "liveness," Steve Wurtzler explains, depend upon both temporal simultaneity and spatial copresence, as opposed to the temporal anteriority and spatial absence of recordings.

Liveness within *Second Life*, however, is not only conceptualized along conditions of spatial and temporal relationships between musician and audience, but is also understood as a socially interactive process of musical—not necessarily sonic—communication that may be extended to Carrie's performative practices. Through her performances, Carrie mediated social interaction among audience members and between the audience and Ictus. Carrie's role as a *Second Life* musician reveals not an "almost" musician nor the "simulation" of musical behavior, but rather the exhibition of virtual musicianship as an extension of the virtue of sociomusical activity into live music settings in *Second Life*.

Within the virtual world of *Second Life*, the animated actions of digital bodies can have an actualizing effect. Drawing upon Deleuze's ideas of virtuality and actuality, William Echard argues that there are multiple activities of musical practice that offer "devices for building sensitivity to [and perhaps actualize] the virtual" (Echard 2006, 10). Just as Ictus's real-life guitar serves to "actualize music as sound" (2006, 11), Carrie's spork and textual "singing" are technological apparatuses that provide a means of actualizing the avatar as a musician. Similarly, the textual chatting and animated dance moves of the audience's avatars help to actualize their participatory role in this sociomusical event.

"I *love* the audience participation!" Carrie told me.
"Do you [ever] find it intrusive?" I asked.

"Nooooo. Noooo, I love it! I love being a part of the show and getting [the audience] into it."

"You see in real life, bands stop playing and let the audience sing," Ictus added. "Do you know what a thrill that is for that band?"

Carrie continued, "Sometimes he plays a chord and I type the lyrics to the first line of the song and ... *Bam*, they go nuts!"

Conclusion

Virtual worlds such as *Second Life* function as important environments for Internet-based social interaction. As our daily lives, both personal and professional, become increasingly enmeshed in digitally mediated sociality, virtual worlds, I believe, can provide insight for understanding how music and aurality fit into our contemporary musical world. Linden Lab, the developer and owner of *Second Life*, established a relatively open platform that not only allowed users to create the simulated, 3D environment in which they interact, but also empowered *Second Life* residents to derive meaning from their own participatory practices—a digitally rendered analog to so-called "real life." Lacking a predetermined, goal-oriented purpose, *Second Life* participants derive significance for their virtual existence through social interaction.

Second Life residents are not living in a parallel world separate from the "real world" in which we have actual experiences, but rather, as suggested by Woolgar, physical and virtual activities are integrally connected. For *Second Life* avatars, sociomusical participation is embedded in "real life" as much as it is a part of the virtual world in which the live music event is taking place. As one audience member at a concert I attended said: "Nothing like listening to Ictus and doing the laundry."

Live music events in *Second Life* are a social space in which interpersonal relationships are actualized and individual avatars negotiate the simultaneity of their social identity as both online and offline social actors. The embodied nature of musical experience creates an immediacy for social interaction that transcends typical assumptions about the virtuality of computer-mediated communication through the realization of meaningful social participation.

Note

1. Slim Warrior's interview with Damien Carbonell was broadcast on Episode 4 of *Amped Up* and is available at http://vimeo.com/22274629.

References

Auslander, P. 1999. *Liveness: Performance in a Mediatized Culture*. New York: Routledge.
Boellstorff, T. 2008. *Coming of Age in "Second Life": An Anthropologist Explores the Virtually Human*. Princeton, NJ: Princeton University Press.

Curtis, P. 1996. Mudding: Social Phenomena in Text-Based Virtual Realities. In *High Noon on the Electronic Frontier: Conceptual Issues in Cyberspace*, edited by Peter Ludlow, 347–373. Cambridge, MA: MIT Press.

Curtis, P. 2001. Not Just a Game: How Lambdamoo Came to Exist and What It Did to Get Back At Me. In *High Wired: On the Design, Use, and Theory of Educational MOOs*, edited by Cynthia Haynes and Jan Rune Holmevik, 25–42. Ann Arbor: University of Michigan Press.

Echard, W. 2006. Sensible Virtual Selves: Bodies, Instruments and the Becoming-Concrete of Music. *Contemporary Music Review* 25 (1–2): 7–16.

Ellis, A. J. 1885. On the Musical Scales of Various Nations. *Journal of the Society of Arts* 33: 484–527.

Gilman, B. I., and J. W. Fewkes. 1891. *Zuni Melodies*. Boston: Houghton, Mifflin.

Hornbostel, E. M. von, and C. Sachs. 1914. Systematik Der Musikinstrumente. *Zeitschrift für Ethnologie* 46: 553–590.

Inoue, M. 2003. Speech without a Speaking Body: "Japanese Women's Language" in Translation. *Language and Communication* 23 (3–4): 315–330.

Kirkpatrick, D. 2007. *Second Life*: It's Not a Game. *Fortune Magazine*, January 23. http://money.cnn.com/2007/01/22/magazines/fortune/whatsnext_secondlife.fortune/index.htm. Accessed March 21, 2012.

Krotoski, A. K., E. Lyons, and J. Barnett. 2009. The Social Life of Second Life: An Analysis of the Social Networks of a Virtual World. In *Living Virtually: Researching New Worlds*, edited by Don Heider, 47–65. New York: Peter Lang.

Lysloff, R. T. A. 1997. Mozart in Mirrorshades: Ethnomusicology, Technology, and the Politics of Representation. *Ethnomusicology* 41 (2): 206–219.

Merriam, A. P. 1960. Ethnomusicology Discussion and Definition of the Field. *Ethnomusicology* 4 (3): 107–114.

Merriam, A. P. 1964. *The Anthropology of Music*. Evanston, IL: Northwestern University Press.

Miller, K. 2009. Schizophonic Performance: Guitar Hero, Rock Band, and Virtual Virtuosity. *Journal of the Society for American Music* 3 (4): 395–429.

Miller, K. 2012. *Playing Along: Digital Games, Youtube, and Virtual Performance*. New York: Oxford University Press.

Schafer, R. M. 1977. *The Tuning of the World*. New York: Knopf.

Small, C. 1998. *Musicking: The Meanings of Performing and Listening*. Hanover, NH: University Press of New England.

Sterne, J. 2003. *The Audible Past: Cultural Origins of Sound Reproduction*. Durham, NC: Duke University Press.

Strathern, M. 2002. Abstraction and Decontextualization. In *Virtual Society? Technology, Cyberbole, Reality*, edited by Steve Woolgar, 302–313. New York: Oxford University Press.

Walther, J. B. 1996. Computer-Mediated Communication. *Communication Research* 23 (1): 3–43.

Woolgar, S., ed. 2002a. *Virtual Society? Technology, Cyberbole, Reality*. New York: Oxford University Press.

Woolgar, S. 2002b. Five Rules of Virtuality. In *Virtual Society? Technology, Cyberbole, Reality*, edited by Steve Woolgar, 1–22. New York: Oxford University Press.

Wurtzler, S. 1992. "She Sang Live, But the Microphone Was Turned Off": The Live, the Recorded and the Subject of Representation. In *Sound Theory, Sound Practice*, edited by Rick Altman, 87–104. New York: Routledge.

CHAPTER 24

....

THE MUSIC THAT'S
NOT THERE

....

MARTIN KNAKKERGAARD

Den abstrakteste Idee, der lader sig tænke, er den sandselige Genialitet.
Men igjennem hvilket Medium lader den sig fremstille ene og alene—ved
Musik.[1]

Søren Kierkegaard, *Enten-Eller* (Kierkegaard 1975, 55–56)

PERHAPS the most magical thing about music is the fact that strictly speaking it is not
there. Whereas almost all other artifacts—aesthetically purposed or not—are at least to a
certain extent physically present, in the sense that they can be touched, held, or felt, music
is simply not. Music is transitory. It is an art of time and it is reasonable to claim that
its primary domain actually is time and only secondarily sound, thus leaving room for
not only rests, pauses, and breaks, which are as important in music as they are in spoken
and written language, but also leaving room for and underlining the importance of the
actual performance, the articulation, or the embodiment of the music. Music is always
passing and is not there to reach out for and hold back. Music is only present in its transition, and the minute it is brought to a stop, it is gone. Furthermore, music is transitory
in the sense that its primary resource, its building material, is air, and music's expressive
articulation of time is not just carried by the air, it is also molded, structured, and shaped
in air. The air is, though, more than just a transmitter of sound or sound information: it is
the only physical manifestation of what is heard as sound, the agent that not only transmits but also allows for the sounding of any initiator's movement and resonance. Without
air, a musical instrument, which is "just" a typically adjustable medium that is brought
into oscillation by the exertion of some sort of action upon it, would make no sound at all
(Taylor 1992, 4–5). With sound, the air is the central medium; what other mediums do—
like the musical instrument—only influences the way the air moves or "sounds."

Sounds that are recognized as musical are normally referred to as tones, and, in general, music is considered an art of tones. In other words, not all sounds have the quality
to be recognized or acknowledged as tones, and it is common to distinguish between
harmonic and inharmonic sounds of which only the first—at least until recently—aspire
to be accepted as tones. This distinction between harmonic and inharmonic sounds,

which is constantly challenged and negotiated in Western cultures, and has been for at least the last thousand years, implicitly points to a more fundamental element in the transitory nature of music: the distinction between tone and frequency carried out by human perception.

The perception of frequencies as tones is a psychological phenomenon that is probably unique to humans. It is interesting to note that in order to be recognized as a tone there typically have to be more frequencies present. A single sine wave is usually not perceived as a musical tone although it has distinct pitch and certainly cannot be inharmonic. Instead, a tone almost always consists of a bundle of frequencies, of sine waves (and this gives rise to its distinguishing timbre) even though it is perceived as only one particular tone whose pitch can be decided upon.

At the same time, music is not restricted to the use of tones. Even traditional music allows the inclusion of sounding signals that are inharmonic. These sounds, like the ones produced by nonpitched percussion such as snare drums and cymbals, are obviously used widely in many styles and genres; they are, however, typically not referred to as tones but as beats. Even sound events that are entirely without the presence of tones can be processed as musical insofar as they are acknowledged as intentional—organized—musical expressions. This notion of intentionality is generally important, reflecting the premise that "music is sound that is organized into socially accepted patterns" (Blacking [1973] 2000, 25), and it also allows for the inclusion of music that is solely utilizing nonpitched signals—like pieces for rhythm ensemble and, for instance, pieces that lean toward the concepts of modern sound art (see later). Music of this type includes musique concrète and even futurist music along with more or less hybrid forms of music of the first half of the twentieth century.

These short introductory notes all point in the same direction. Sound and music are a function of the human perceptual response to pressure shifts in the air caused by outbursts of energy as a result of some kind of physical activity intended to form some kind of sound structure for its own sake. Music as such can be approached—and appreciated—in three forms: as a physical phenomenon, as a perceptual phenomenon, and as an aesthetic artifact or phenomenon (an idea) (Moylan 2007). It is through an understanding of these three forms, in particular the aesthetic form, that one can comprehend music's lack of corporeal presence and thus appreciate the virtuality of music.

MUSICAL SOUND

Approaching musical sound as a physical phenomenon is generally attributed to natural science. Thus, the given preunderstanding is that the phenomenon is quantifiable and can be measured relatively precisely. Natural science understands sound as differences of pressure—vibrations—in plastic matters, first and foremost, as stated, in air. It is primarily measured in frequency, amplitude, and time and can secondarily be described with reference to timbre (composite frequencies) and to space (characteristics and reverberation of the physical environment in which the sound is sounding). As a physical phenomenon, musical sound is "just sound," and, as such, is initially not accessible for human hearing, as humans are prone to involuntarily—perceptually—process and—cognitively—interpret any heard sound. Approaching musical sound as a solely physical phenomenon without "analyzing" what the sound is the sound of and why it is sounding implies what Pierre Schaeffer termed "écoute réduite," "a listening mode that focuses on the traits of the sound itself, independent of its cause and meaning" (Chion 1994, 28)—an almost impossible task that only is possible when the sound in question is not known in advance and its source cannot be identified in the environment.

Instead, almost all musical sounds are appreciated as perceptual phenomena and are thus tied to neuropsychological processes that, in the case of music, give rise to the notion of pitch, loudness, duration, timbre (qualitative), space (location environment), and so on. In this sense musical sound—as well as all other sound—acts as an indexical sign referring to cause and context; for example, what vehicle and where or which instrument and what situation. This kind of appreciation of sound is dependent upon human sensing of sounds as objects, sounds of things (Ihde 2007, 60), and in this way expresses a phenomenological understanding that is based on experience, situation, and body.

As an—artistic—idea, musical sound is tied to levels of, and relationships between, pitches, leading to a notion of motives, figures, harmony, and scales, for instance. Dynamic implications include articulation, accentuation, and shaping, just as duration nurtures the sense of movement, tempo, and time, for example. Different sound sources such as instruments and various processors contribute to the palette of expressive means that is specific to the artistic work, while the actual perceived space that is generated and constituted as the interrelations between sound sources leads to the forming of the abstract "soundscape," the particular artifact, which is understood as the musical piece, the autonomous gestalt, or, as Ferrara puts it, sound in form (1984, 359).

The musical artifact is thus equipped with (navigational) information, direction, and movement inside a perceived yet completely abstract auditory "room," a sound mirage. Not only that, the room itself is typically experienced as a specific situation with implications of emotion, temperament, and other elements of psychological "sense" and "matter."

Making Music Sound

Historically, music has been produced by means of the human voice along with a great variety of specially designed musical instruments. These acoustical sources are the main components in generating music's fundamental virtuality, the abstract auditory room, as described above. However, this situation shifted gradually during the twentieth century.

In the modern world most music is produced and mediated by means of media that are dependent upon electricity. Electricity is essential to all segments of mass media related to music and sound production. The recording, processing—and very often also the generation—of sound is totally dependent upon electricity, as is its final reproduction by the loudspeakers. Although sound recording started out as a purely mechanical phenomenon, electricity soon became a central element. The invention of the valve in 1906 (Chanan 1995, 38), and its integration into the production process, in particular turned out to be a decisive contribution that eventually allowed the producer to break the conditions of natural acoustics and achieve a reproduced sound image that to a certain extent corresponds to the psychoacoustic experience of sounding music—or other sounds—in natural surroundings.[2] Placing microphones in a given location, for instance a concert hall or a recording studio, to pick up the sound signals that are emitted by sound sources will—unprocessed—hardly ever produce a sound image that matches what a human would experience when exposed to those signals in the same room. Human hearing takes an active part in the hearing process. This is not just a psychoacoustic fact but also a fundamental precondition, a premise, in Husserlian phenomenology that is taken to be true in the context of any kind of human sensing of the world. This process of hearing alters what is "actually" sounding and is measurable scientifically. The integration of electrical means in the recording process has made it possible to continuously adjust sound levels, filter frequencies, and so on so that the reproduction of the recording more accurately resembles what is "heard" or rather perceived by a human ear, in situ: the producer's ear. What comes out of the entire process is a production of a dynamic sound image that actually is a reorganization of all sound elements that were (per)formed in the recording studio and registered electronically. For many years, sound production was almost entirely aimed at reproducing what was performed in a way that came as close as possible to what was experienced by a listener who was present in the location where the sound was performed or generated. This effort gave rise to the notion of high fidelity (or just hi-fi) especially within the field of consumer audio equipment. However, this struggle to reproduce the sound of performance as accurately and authentically as possible does not exclude the fact that, even in the early days of sound and especially music recording, the sound image that was produced was really a virtual image. Not merely because sound waves are transformed into electric currents that cannot be unaltered by the process that later reintroduces them as sound waves but even more so because the reproduced sound waves are optimized to sound as if they are not altered and manipulated. The produced sound image is intentionally designed to reproduce the experienced sound image "originally" heard, a process that in a way combines the object correlates, the noema of the heard sound, with the subject correlates, the noetic element. However, the actual result is a technology-based construction, the sound image of "analytic clarity and almost tactile proximity" (Chanan 1995, 133). What the consumer hears is not an unmediated reproduction of the performance as it was at that point in time and in that particular space but is, rather, a technological creation of both recorded and new sonic fragments assembled within a virtual acoustic space—an abstract auditory room.

From the middle of the 1930s, more and more of the sounds that went into the recording were themselves generated by means of electricity; electrophones like the electric guitar and the Hammond organ, and later—although it was among the very first electrophones—the synthesizer gradually began to be used. Although electrophones were included in many music compositions of the classical tradition from around 1920 onward, they never came to dominate the contemporary music genre except within the electroacoustical scene in the latter half of the century. This domination, however, became the case within popular music, where the electric guitar and its cousin the electric bass in many genres gradually came to replace their acoustic counterparts almost entirely. Insofar as these new instruments can be seen as electrified versions of the original acoustic instruments, they could bespeak a sort of low-level virtuality, but strictly speaking this was hardly ever the case. Both instruments were acknowledged as new instruments right from the start and gave rise to the construction of new designs like the solid-body versions of the electric guitar and the electric bass that left out the acoustic resonance case entirely and which both gradually became the dominating variants.

Since the 1950s, the music of the recording studio increasingly has been the primary musical reference to the general public—maybe even before because the jukebox accounted for three-quarters of record sales in the 1940s (Cowen 1998, 164) when it, besides radio, was the major distributor of popular music—rapidly leading to a situation where music productions have come to refer to other music productions and only sporadically to live performances. Although music productions initially could be said to correspond to live performances—especially those that were broadcast from concert halls and dancing palaces to radio listeners (although, of course, they were also altered and optimized as described above)—this gradually changed by the end of the 1950s as the music that was produced in recording studios started living a life of its own and "recordings...began to gain a counterfeit perfection that live performances could not match" (Griffiths 1998). The types of production methods that at the same time were introduced by leading producers such as Sam Phillips, Leiber and Stoller, and Phil Spector (Moorefield [2005] 2010, 5–6) quickly led to new concepts of sounding music that distanced itself more and more from live acoustics and reached a state of sound imaging by the mid-1960s that generally did not correspond to real-life performances at all. More importantly, it did not strive to. The reference for music productions was an acoustic abstraction taking the realm of music further into the purely imaginative, adding an overnatural presence and an almost tactile sense of surroundings that cannot exist.

Although the recording studio involves a number of manipulations that lead to the construction of sonorous phantoms whose components may be altered in ways that make them "supernatural," the relation or reference to real-life sound generation is maintained as long as there is talk of the analog studio. No matter how "unrealistic" and contradictory the actual combination of sound sources, their amplitudes and individual environments, and common otherworldly surroundings are, they can still be understood and perceived as referential to—or anchored in—real-life acoustics that are somehow familiar.

Building composite sound-images, as the result of the intervention of the mixing console, layering, tape editing, and multitrack recording, to organize inputs of analog sound signals, became a major feature of the era of electronic recordings. With the introduction of the digital recoding studio, however, most if not all of the premises of the analog sources and technologies are altered or overruled. As everywhere where digitalization makes its entrance, the conditions are completely changed once and for all. It matters little that the implementation of digital technology is carried out by mimicking—or remediating—analog technological means and principles; the possibilities, premises, and the constructive reaches have not just been radically changed, they are new. Through digitalization, music production enters a kind of double virtuality. The virtualization through digital means of the analog studio—whose products themselves build a kind of virtuality—implies virtuality is lifted up to another degree.

In order to exemplify the transition, the following section will produce a short analysis approximating an understanding of "what" is thought to be experienced: what sound images are perceptually and noematically formed, so to speak, what horizons sounds and sound images call upon to be acknowledged noetically, how they are conceptualized, and how these mental elements can be processed hermeneutically.

MIRAGES

From her eponymous debut album from 1985, Suzanne Vega stood out as a guitar-playing singer-songwriter with roots in the modern American folk tradition and with a clear tendency to a rock music expression. Not unusual for the singer-songwriter genre, the lyrics are a critical observance, evaluating social and sociopsychological factors often with a sense of the humoristic and grotesque.

At the same time there are features that bring emotion and emotional implications into quiet and meek reflexive psychological illumination, generating a kind of vulnerable nakedness. These features are reinforced by Vega's ability to convey all her songs with a subcompressed voice, which gives the impression of self-inquiry and reflection. Her expressiveness seems altogether understated and transparent, which—along with a distinctive touch of the pantomimic and novelistic—gives the impression that her musical alter ego stands exposed in a fragile and intimate atmosphere.

In a sense, these characteristics become especially evident in the complex and stylistically relatively broad fourth album *99.9 F°* (1992). Many of the tracks on the album appear musically carefree and cheerful regardless of textual content. This hallmark endows the album with a touch of funfair entertainment and celebration, but at the same time of humiliation and destruction. The impression is counterbalanced by the fact that the cover is decorated with photographs that are mostly black and white, in which Vega appears in different poses alone and with the musicians (presumably) dressed in attire reminiscent of variety shows and carnivals of the past. Something tricky and unpredictable is suggested, with strongmen, prostitutes, and pickpockets. As such, it corresponds to the illustration of the cover of the Doors' *Strange Days* (1966), which also draws heavily on the circus metaphor, and especially the entertainer as freak, the deviant, maladjusted, by virtue of or in spite of his social, mental, or physical disabilities—or whatever it may be—who exists in a second, parallel, reality.

The impression of the complex and stylistically branched in Vega's *99.9. F°* is supported and amplified by an unconventional instrumentation, where concrete and often indefinable sounds and sound sources appear on an equal footing with the common instruments of popular music.

The indeterminacy of certain sounds—are they samples of the sound of machines, sounds recorded in stairwells or streets, or are they synthetic sounds created in the studio or lab, or mixtures or hybrid forms thereof?—contributes to a situation, where the phonogram's acoustic illusion, its reliance upon and reference to sounds outside the control of the technology (i.e., the implicit assertion that the media is anchored in an original), is degraded and threatened from within. The lapse or absence of similarity with sounds from the "real world" of some of the sounds employed in the sound image leads to a questioning of the authenticity of the image in general. What is it the sound image depicts? The presence of acousmatic[3] sound seems to reveal that the location, which is folded out in the sonic space of the sound studio, is only original and valid inside the studio, not outside. The stage that Vega seems to appear on thus becomes virtual in another sense than that which characterizes the popular musical standard production and its cult of the concert stage podium. The presence of extraneous sounds—or unprocessed instruments—seems to rebound on the production of the other instruments and sounds and reveals these themselves as constructions.

Already from the beginning of the song "In Liverpool" it is clear that it comprises an ambiguous acoustic environment in the aforementioned sense. And it later turns out that the ambiguity is also reflected on a formal level.

On the vertical plane—in the A section—sounds quite openly belong to different acoustic environments, while the B section, in contrast, unfolds within a standard sound image, a particular aesthetic that is characteristic of the production of popular music. The contrast thus obtained is hardly accidental. The listener is moved from one kind of listening position to another.

A closer examination shows that even the rhythm of the A section, with its smooth, but at the same time somewhat heavy character, introduces an ambiguity: a light, dreamy, "flapping" six-quaver rhythm, which at the same time can be seen as an old-fashioned 4/4 rhythm based on eighth-note triplets. Although it as such seems natural to transcribe the piece in 4/4, 6/8 would be more proper, as several factors promote the time signature's dreamy and scattered feeling. This applies first and foremost to the instrumentation and production.

Traditionally, listeners are accustomed to the sound of the grand piano recorded with the microphones placed relatively close to the instrument, producing a sensation that the listener is almost playing the instrument himself. Here, the recording of the piano is done in such a way that it produces the sound—and image—of an upright piano placed in a gymnasium or similar. The fat, warm sonority, which we know from the standard production of the well-tuned grand piano, is absent. Instead, the sonorous quality is thin, a little sharp and shrill, yielding an almost unattractive sound, which does not quite sound newly tuned. Where the sound of the piano, both the sound of an upright piano itself and the particular acoustics, seems to signal a specific kind of location—the empty gymnasium, the abandoned village hall—its musical content, the F-minor chord in the corny, old-fashioned triplets, can be seen as a naive element, a collage, that signals a childish universe designating the dreamy amateur or the contemplative, cogitating artist.

The piano is accompanied by a continuously repeated percussion figure, a loop that is made up of percussion sounds that might as well have come from a workshop machine or from hand drums or foot stomps or empty cardboard boxes in a warehouse. The location is indeterminate. The acoustic environment of the percussion loop is different from the piano's environment as well as from the rest of the sound sources in the A section. Thus, the loop gains the character of a documentary recording, a sound recorded on location in its normal environment, or rather as a "paraphrase" on the documentary that uncovers the principle of selection, sampling, as a constructive engagement, an interpretation. The loop induces a monotonous cyclic element, which is supported by the piano's persistent repetition of the high-pitched F-minor chord.

The bass holds a role as interpreter of the F-minor chord leading it from Fm into Dbmaj7 and Dm7b5 and, as such, also plays the part of an outsider. The bass stands out as the only electric instrument of the A section, and it also manages to elude spatial determination and location. The bass seems to belong to the environment of the production in the same manner as credits in a film belong to the filmstrip level. For the bass, this is not an unusual situation partly because of purely acoustical implications, as deep tones are characterized by a ubiquity, an omnipresence. In "In Liverpool," however, this acoustical feature of the bass is exaggerated and retouched; there is a certain dryness and proximity, a deficiency of reverberation, which places the instrument in an imaginary point. The bass does not negotiate an identity or position in the dramatic sound space of the production; instead it acts as a mediator between the acoustic and harmonic space.

Prominently placed in the sound image, but in a position where the shaded tone universe of the piano and the percussion seems embedded in the background and the bass's dry, almost effectless presence is in front, is the sound of Vega's vocal in an intimate, but because of the reverberation, spatially realistic presence. Virtually in the same perspective layer, but less strongly marked, is also an acoustic guitar, and this brings to mind the notion of Suzanne Vega singing and playing her guitar in a specific point in an otherwise indeterminate space.

The listener is caught in this really fantastical universe. The gray background seems to express a point somewhere between a sparse accompaniment and a tone painting. As if the listener, from a position that virtually coincides with the space of the bass (a nowhere), is watching Suzanne Vega in a particular room where the background is generated at the same time, virtually as a film that is rolled up on a screen behind the soloist, as a function and an illustration of her introspective and thoughtful song and play. It almost makes sense to refer to a built-in seating position, to a stage and the live sets, even though the three acoustic spaces cannot exist simultaneously outside the production's virtualization.

Where the abstract, the purely structural, difference between the A and B sections is restricted (strictly speaking, there is a simple and straightforward strophic progression in interrelation between the sections, a balance equivalent to a traditional question-answer relation) the dramatic contrast is significant because of the instrumentation and the production of the piece.

Unlike the A section, there is nothing fantastical to the B section—or chorus—except perhaps that it precisely does not have any similar fantastical implications and, as such, gets an alternative perceptual effect. It appears as a traditional sound image regarding both the instrumentation and its production, a popular musical cliché, the pure sound-box that appears to enjoy wide dissemination in all branches of popular music from the late 1960s onward.

Apart from the technical implications of historical leanings, the B section could just as well have been produced in 1970 as in 1992. The same applies for the structure of the music; the harmony is anchored in repetitive alternation between VI, VII, V, and I, and the extensive use of common note affinity, as well as the affinity of fifths strictly observing the Aeolian scale, speaks its own emblematic language. Neither here nor in the melody does there occur a single tribute to functional harmony; no dominants, no resolution signs. It is only the repetition, the steady flow of a four-bar pattern with only a few accidental deviations, and a melodically profiled motif, that—together with an unambiguous sense of 6/8—characterizes the section. In isolation, the character of the B section comes perilously close to the trivial, but the formal staging, the previous A section, seems to ensure that the B section still gains a dramatic force that overshadows its unmistakable *Schein des Bekannten*.[4]

In addition to this, the B section is profiled—and qualified—by its evident and convincing interaction with the lyrics. The B section—and the instrumental C section— appears sweeping and rotating, almost carousel-like in its evocation of the mad boy who throws himself off the tower's top. Through this tone painting, the cyclic structure obtains relevance and impact seen both in relation to the musical-formal interaction with the A section and with respect to the dramatization of the lyrics. The musical triviality of the B section is, on the one hand, a haven in an otherwise ambiguous audio sequence staged by the A section, but proves, on the other hand, precisely by dint of its triviality to stand out as the alienating postponement of a tragic riot directed against the emptiness of late modernity. With its unadulterated popular musical expressiveness, the B section is produced in a conventional standard that has been around since the 1960s, deprived of any relation to other sites than that of the recording studio and can as such be perceived as Vega's empathy for the boy's fatal protest against his loss.

Many of the same traits are found in "Blood Makes Noise" from the same album. The scenario is certainly another. The text evidently represents one party in a conversation; a patient who speaks with, or rather to, his doctor. As listeners, we seem to be situated in the doctor's office, but there are features of the production that indicate that we really are one with the patient; the voice is recorded in such a way that the sound of the space— the reflections of the room—is cut away. This kind of production technique is normally associated with the seductive crooner, but since Vega's voice is reproduced entirely without reverb, one gains a sense of density of supernatural proximity that is further supported by undisguised overdubs—producing a notion of double exposure—with two different filtrations and timbres causing it to differ significantly from the crooner voice. Instead, a special effect is achieved in that Vega's voice seems to transcend the boundary between performer and listener.

The impression of being one with or trapped inside a performer who suffers from severe tinnitus allegedly caused by roaring blood in the vessels is reinforced by the heavily filtered voice timbres, as well as by the distorted and filtered perspective the other instruments appear in.

The musical impression is much more homogeneous than that which characterized "In Liverpool." There is a clear and uncompromising polarization of certain musical, relatively homogeneous structures. The song's alternation between A and B sections is not supported by changes in the acoustic scenarios, but is at all times carried by a specific ideal, close to that which characterizes the A section of "In Liverpool." Yet the perceptual difference is significant. Whereas the listener is located in an artificial, virtual, and nondramatized listening position when listening to "In Liverpool," namely the neutral viewing point of the studio from which it can be observed from the outside, the listener is pulled into the very midst of things in "Blood Makes Noise," surrounded by the instrumental—and industrial—sound sources that make up the tonal texture.

Besides the sample-like percussion, a careless bass figure penetrates the setting as an almost manifest paraphrase on entertainment and amusement. It identifies a fresh and lively sound image, which, however, is contrasted by the enclosed and distorted guitar and by the dry vocals establishing a narrow, almost respiring room that inspires a sense of the trapped and squeezed. We neither look at the performer nor above her shoulder; instead we are trapped inside a performer's self-experience.

LATE REFLECTIONS

When listening to these tunes—and interpreting them as exemplified above—it is necessary to keep in mind that none of the characteristics that lead to the interpretation—the perceived artifact—are real. Even if the sound sources were recorded in the different environments, as they appear to be, they are put together to produce the artifact that only can exist as a perceptual phenomenon, a mirage. When evaluated noetically, the components contradict each other, and yet what is experienced is in a psychological sense coherent aesthetic pieces of artistic articulation. They are virtual "nowheres" building virtual "somewheres" as a function of the listener's perception.

The apparent use of concrete sound is of course not tied to the realm of the digital recording. Real-world sound that goes beyond the curious (exotic), as for instance the inclusion of cannons in Tchaikovsky's *1812 Overture*, was integrated in music by Eric Satie and George Antheil in the 1920s, for instance, and it was the primary sonorous material for the musique concrète movement of the late 1940s and onward. In the case of

Vega, however, the real-world components work both as dramatic signs giving evidence of extramusical content and as structural elements on a par with traditional musical instruments. At the same time, the sounds of the musical instruments of the artifact are, as demonstrated here, treated very much like semiotic documentary too and not just as structural elements. By means of the digital technology, every element, concrete or, for instance, sung notes, can be processed identically; that is, as digital samples of sound. Thus, every note, played or sung, as well as every beat and every breath, is at hand like Lego bricks that can be put together at will.

Thus the aesthetic object, the artifact, is a result of separate elements brought together on the premises of the production and the electronic equipment, but, at the same time, it is also an object that is brought into existence as a unified gestalt by virtue of the listener's perception, an object whose apparently coherent totality is as impossible as the constructions found in drawings and paintings by the Dutch artist M. C. Escher. Much in the same way as the latter relies on "optical illusions," these objects are acoustical illusions that make up an apparently trustworthy sound image, which, however, just like Escher's artwork, does not stand up to closer examination.

Phonograms that originally aimed at direct analogue reproduction (repetition) of (concert) transmissions or recordings gradually turned into modeled idealizations of the concert situation, leading to a sound imaging that is more or less relieved of any obligation toward real-life acoustics but that is still inseparable from the limits of analogue recording equipment. In the very same process, the sound of recorded music—and recorded musical sound sources—has become the primary reference to the public, overruling the live sound of the acoustic and electric instruments, as the loudspeaker has taken the position as the general distributor of music. To the majority of listeners, the sound of music today is the sound of loudspeakers. And the stage that dominates all stages on which music is performed is that of the electrified sound even when the sounding signals stem from the vibrating bodies of the acoustic instruments of the symphony orchestra.

In the age of digital sound, there are musical trajectories that temporarily exceed the physical phenomena that are the boundaries of sound, leading to a situation where the virtuality, which is produced by means of analogue technology in the sound studio, itself becomes the model for a new form of virtualization. In the digital production, the tools and processes of the traditional nondigital studio are mimicked—typically in the form of remediation—and the virtuality of the product is elevated to the next, or highest, degree, forming a situation where any relation to acoustic sound sources has to be understood as a construction, or reconstruction, not a reproduction. In this way, the artifact to a certain extent draws upon the listener's familiarity with the phonogram as a particular genre that is independent of the performed musical work.

In the digital realm, nothing nonnumerical is reproduced; it is, instead, constructed. As soon as an analog input—insofar as there is talk of input at all—is converted into numeric data, these data obviously have to be converted back into analog form again in order to be phenomenologically appreciated as sound. Although it can be claimed that the shift from atoms to bits (Negroponte 1995, 11–12) covers a shift from a given materiality—from air, transitory or not—to a representation of this very materiality, the resulting representation, the numeric tables, can be read or rematerialized in completely different ways that have nothing in common with whatever was originally digitized. This implies that what initially was generated as a numeric index of, for instance, the registration of a sound wave can be read out as a drawing or a text on paper, a film, or even a three-dimensional object. What is materialized is entirely dependent on which kind of decoder is chosen.

Thus, music's determination as a transitory sensory phenomenon that generates a notion of a virtual physical form and structure, but which is just a product of our perception, is twisted into a secondary virtuality, as the bits are not anything but bits—which is the same as virtually nothing.

NOTES

1. The most abstract idea conceivable is the sensuous genius. But through which medium is this solely expressible? By music.
2. The so-called cocktail party phenomenon that allows us to understand one talker relatively easily when others are talking at the same time (Bronkhorst 2000, 117).
3. Acousmatic sounds are "sounds one hears without seeing their originating cause" (Schaeffer 1967 quoted in Chion 1992, 71).
4. Famous expression by the German composer J. A. P. Schulz (1747–1800) stating that a piece of music that is meant to appeal to a broader public needs to have a "flavor of the well known" in order to succeed.

REFERENCES

Blacking, J. (1973) 2000. *How Musical Is Man?* Seattle: University of Washington Press.

Bronkhorst, A. W. 2000. The Cocktail Party Phenomenon: A Review of Research on Speech Intelligibility in Multiple-Talker Conditions. *Acta Acustica United with Acustica* 86 (2000): 117–128.

Chanan, M. 1995. *Repeated Takes: A Short History of Recording and Its Effects on Music.* London: Verso.

Chion, M. 1994. *Audio-Vision: Sound on Screen.* New York: Columbia University Press.

Cowen, T. 1998. *In Praise of Commercial Culture.* Cambridge, MA: Harvard University Press.

Ferrara, L. 1984. Phenomenology as a Tool for Musical Analysis. *Musical Quarterly* 70 (3): 355–373.

Griffiths, P. 1998. Callas Sings Bob Dylan? Could Be. *New York Times*, January 11, http://www.nytimes.com/1998/01/11/arts/classical-view-callas-sings-bob-dylan-could-be.html.

Ihde, D. 2007. *Listening and Voice: Phenomenologies of Sound.* Albany: State University of New York Press.

Kierkegaard, S. (1843) 1975. *Enten-Eller.* Odense: Gyldendal.

Moorefield, V. (2005) 2010. *The Producer as Composer. Shaping the Sounds of Popular Music.* Cambridge MA: MIT Press.

Moylan, W. 2007. *Understanding and Crafting the Mix: The Art of Recording.* Boston, MA: Elsevier.

Negroponte, N. 1995. *Being Digital.* London: Hodder & Slaughton.

Taylor, C. 1992. *Exploring Music: The Science and Technology of Tones and Tunes.* Philadelphia: Institute of Physics Publishing.

PART V

....

IMAGE

....

CHAPTER 25

....

THROUGH THE LOOKING GLASS: PHILOSOPHICAL REFLECTIONS ON THE ART OF VIRTUAL WORLDS

....

GARY ZABEL

IN 1967 Guy Debord wrote, in *Society of the Spectacle*: "In societies where modern conditions of production prevail, all of life presents itself as an immense accumulation of spectacles. Everything that was directly lived has moved away into a representation" (Debord 1967 [1977], 1). An English translation of the book was published in paperback ten years later. On its cover, there is a photograph of a movie audience wearing 3D spectacles. The book designer understood that "the society of the spectacle" would not reach full development until images became immersive. Computerization made possible what the 3D cinema of the 1950s and 1960s could only imperfectly anticipate, first in the form of computer games, and then as full-blown virtual worlds. Artists have been drawn to both media, but especially to virtual worlds such as *Second Life* and *OpenSim*. The appeal is understandable. What painter, for example, has not entertained the fantasy of the canvas as a portal permitting physical entry into the world of the painted image? Virtual worlds bring that fantasy closer to realization. This chapter attempts to shed philosophical light on this new development in the realm of images.[1]

In order to understand art made in virtual worlds, it is necessary to locate it within three thematic contexts. Proceeding from the general to the specific, the art of virtual worlds is a form of new media art; its medium is computer-generated virtuality; and its virtuality has the form of worldhood. In what follows, we will consider each of these themes in order, as well as the specific "dimensional" characteristics (in a sense to be clarified) that make virtual worlds a unique medium of aesthetic expression.

New Media Art

There is no word in any language that distinguishes what we now call "art" from other forms of making prior to about 400 years ago. The emergence of the word follows epochal changes in the institutions and practices of making that occurred during that initial salvo of modernity, the Renaissance. At the heart of these changes is the successful bid of painters and sculptors to free themselves from the medieval guild system, and to achieve a status equivalent to that of the scholar-practitioners of what was then referred to as "the arts." Traditionally the arts included both the seven liberal arts of the medieval curriculum (grammar, logic, rhetoric, arithmetic, geometry, music, and astronomy), and an alternative grouping under the seven Muses, more appropriate to Renaissance humanism (history, poetry, comedy, tragedy, music, dancing, and astronomy). The arts occupied the mental side of the division between mental and manual activity, the side of the learned professions as opposed to the crafts organized by guilds, the side of the life of the mind in contrast with that of the body as an instrument of physical work. Over the course of the Renaissance, the visual arts of painting and sculpture migrated from the manual to the mental side of the social division of labor. "Art" in the modern sense of the word, with the visual arts at its center, established itself as a learned profession rather than a craft activity, and thereby shed its association with the traditional devaluation of manual work in the eyes of the upper classes. The elite patronage system that supported the arts in this period was both partial cause and result of this bid to liberate art from the laboring body.

Still, the basis of the artist's claim to elevated status was proficiency in technique. Technique is mastery of artistic material. Artistic technique remains a form of *techne*, in the ancient Greek sense of knowledge that guides the process of making. Art, therefore, remained stubbornly connected with manual skill, in spite of its Renaissance claim to high status. But the material upon which artistic technique works is more than sheer physical material—the wood, stone, metal, and so on—of the guild-based crafts. While never losing its physical qualities, the material of "art," in the new sense of the word, is primarily historical and expressive in character. In analogy with the Renaissance arts of history, literature, and music, artistic material is matter as the historical deposit of past acts of meaningful shaping. As a historical sedimentation, the expressive possibilities of artistic material change over time. The artist's ability to understand, shape, and expand these possibilities constitutes the essence of artistic technique (Adorno 1984, 300–308).

The development of modern technology as a radically new form of *techne*, transforms the nature of artistic technique. Modern technology makes its appearance in the first phase of the Industrial Revolution. As Marx points out in the first volume of *Capital*, the reconfiguration of bodily labor into a series of discrete, repetitive movements that characterizes the transition from guild to industrial production prepares the way for the substitution of machinery, such as the power loom, for the human body in the labor process (Marx 1976, 490–491). In its second phase, however, one that Marx barely lived to see, industrial technology breaks even more radical ground. It proceeds to apply machinery to forms of making that have no bodily model, such as chemical and electrical processes. The second kind of modern technology, shaping without bodily precedent, leads to the creation of new media, and the emergence of new media art. Here even the residual attachment of the arts to manual skill burns away.

The earliest forms of new media art are photography and cinema, each of which depends upon the development of chemical processes, optical devices, and finally electrical machines. Walter Benjamin refers to both of these arts in his enormously influential essay "The Work of Art in the Age of Its Technological Reproducibility." But we need to be careful here. Benjamin's treatment equivocates on the question of whether reproducibility is reproduction of an original. Although he recognizes that photography, for example, has no single authentic print, his paradigmatic example of reproducibility is that of a photograph of an artwork, a statue or painting, that possesses what Benjamin calls an aura, a mark of its authenticity and authority, derived from its original place in magical or religious practices (Benjamin 2008, 21–22). In his description, the aura of the original is lost through its photographic reproduction. It would seem, on this account, that the photograph is a degraded reproduction of the original thing, namely, the original minus its aura. But this fails to recognize the fact that, while photography and cinema may produce multiple copies, these "copies" are sui generis, and not subordinated to a model to be replicated. The light reflected by the surface of a physical thing and focused by the lens of the camera initiates a series of physical and chemical events that results in a fundamentally new image, even when that series is steered by the photographer's desire to "capture the subject." If the digital image has now made the problem of the authenticity and truth of the photographic image intractable, this is merely because it has made apparent what was already the case with analogue imagery, that is, that the photographic image is something fundamentally different from an ordinary percept caught on film. In spite of the apparent realism of photography and cinema, these two forms of new media art are not essentially reproductive at all. Their innovative character involves instead new forms of productivity beyond bodily production.

The emergence of new media art breaks the link tying artistic technique to manual skill, but it does not complete the process of assimilating art to the learned professions. The new media artist is a sibling of neither craftsman nor scholar. Rather he or she is an organizer and operator. For example, the photographer organizes camera, chemical bath, negative, enlarger, paper, and so on into an ensemble of processes resulting in the photo. The photographer also operates the camera, enlarger, and print drier, all of which are machines interposed between his or her body and the artwork. In cinema, the director is organizer of a crew that makes the film—cameramen, sound engineers, editors, and so on—who in turn operate the machines that shape the cinematic material. Organization and operation certainly belong to the life of the mind, but not as it was understood by Renaissance humanism. That is to say, they do not belong to that dimension of human existence that elevates it above the material world and the problem of its mastery. Instead, organizing and operating are concerned precisely with the mastery of matter, but through the manipulation of intermediary machines, especially those involving chemical and electrical processes. Since organization and operation take over the functions of manual technique, new media art is "conceptual" from the beginning. Its conceptuality, however, is more akin to that of applied science and technology than to the high-culture-creating intellect of Renaissance humanism. In this very specific sense, photographers and directors are the first "conceptual artists."

The conceptualism of photography and film reaches its culminating expression in the formalized symbolic languages of computerized new media art. The earlier phases of modern technology interposed physical machine processes between maker and material. The current phase interposes symbols. It is true that digital symbols are usually connected to such physical machines as computer screens, printers, and speakers. The point, however, is that by operating with any one of a nested hierarchy of formalized languages—machine language, programming language, or application—the artist directly faces symbols, but not the machines they operate. In working on formal symbols, computer art differs from older new media art.

VIRTUALITY

The concept of the virtual has a long history in Western thought, going back to the ontological distinction Aristotle makes in his *Metaphysics* between substance in a state of latency (*dynamis*) and substance in a state of full and active presence (*energeia*) (Aristotle 1968, Book Theta). Being is said in many ways, Aristotle tells us, but one of the ways in which it is said is primary, and all of the others are parasitic upon that primary sense. We distinguish, for example, between a quality, such as being snub-nosed, and the underlying substance (*ousia*) that possesses the quality, say, Socrates; or between a location, such as being above the moon, and a substance, such as one of the fixed stars, that is in this location. The various ways in which being is said are what Aristotle calls the categories, and substance is the primary category. Latency and presence are not categories, however, but the ways in which substance itself has being prior to any of its qualities, locations, or other categorial specifications. Aristotle gives the examples of a seed and the full-grown tree into which the seed develops, and an unworked block of marble and the statue that emerges from it. The seed may be rough or smooth, and the tree may be gnarled or straight, but none of these qualities concerns the relation between *dynamis* and *energeia*. That relation involves the development of the tree from the seed, that is, the full unfolding of the underlying substance. Similarly, the marble may be white or pink, and the final statue painted or not, but the relation between *dynamis* and *energeia* pertains, not to these categorial specifications, but rather to the emergence of the statue from the marble under the sculptor's hand.

For Aristotle, *dynamis* is just as much a form of being as *energeia*. Still, *energeia* has an ontological priority over *dynamis* that derives from its ability to account for processes of change. Every natural or artificial process of change is a transition from latency to full presence. But such transitions can be initiated only by something that is already fully present. This is why Aristotle postulates the existence of a prime Unmoved Mover, a fully present being who is the final cause of change by acting as the lure or perfect exemplar to which all things seek approximation. This is also at the root of the medieval conception of God as *actus purus*, as the ultimate object of desire who keeps the whole universe in motion, the cosmic pole of Love who, as Dante says in the incomparably beautiful final canto of *The Divine Comedy*, "steers the sun and the other stars."

The Romans translated *energeia* with the single word, *actus*, but they used two words they regarded as synonyms as translations of *dynamis*: *virtus* and *potentia*. This lack of distinction in meaning is appropriate, since Aristotle had not distinguished between two senses of *dynamis*. But medieval thinkers who followed the Romans made the distinction that Aristotle and his Roman translators had not. In particular, Duns Scotus and Thomas Aquinas introduced the technical term *virtualiter* to signify that which has being in a virtual, though not a potential manner.

Aquinas applied the concept of having being *virtualiter* to the existence of elements in a mixture (Aquinas 1948, Ia, 76, 4 ad 4). He made the point that elements exist virtually, not because of a potential to separate from the mixture, but rather because they contribute their special powers to the mixture, without appearing as distinct substances. Earth is *virtualiter* in marble, for example, because it is what makes marble heavy, not because it is potentially the independent element, earth. In this sense, being is virtual when it does not fully and explicitly appear, and yet is the locus of a real power, or efficacy.

Scotus's conception of being *virtualiter* is related to his anti-Aristotelian thesis that being is univocal, not analogical in meaning (Scotus 1978, 3–9). For Scotus, Aristotle was wrong when he claimed that being is said in many ways, and achieves unity only when each meaning is analogically related to the primary sense in which it is said, namely being as substance. Aquinas had followed Aristotle by arguing that our talk of God is based on an analogical extension of our talk about the only entities we encounter in direct experience, namely God's creatures. But Scotus argues against this Thomistic-Aristotelian position by claiming that being means precisely the same thing whether it is attributed to God or to creatures. His argument is that God is infinite in character. But this means that God possesses in an unlimited degree all the positive attributes possessed by finite things. However, in order for this assertion to be meaningful, God must possess the same attributes as finite entities, differing only in the way in which he possesses them. Whether we are speaking of the attributes of God or of creatures, our language has a univocal sense. Scotus introduces the concept of virtual being in the context of his theory of univocity.

If being is always said in the same way, Scotus asks, then what is the status of the "transcendentals"? The transcendentals are expressions such as truth, unity, and goodness that lie above any genus because they must be predicated of whatever has being. For Scotus, unity, truth, and goodness are coextensive with being, and yet they add something to the concept of being. Being is always said in the same way, but there is more to say about being than is contained within its concept. This means that the transcendentals are present within being, not as real parts of its essence (*in quid*), but in a virtual manner (*virtualiter*).

Both Aquinas's and Scotus's ideas of virtuality lie opposite to what the word "virtual" later came to mean in English: the sort of, but not quite real. For the two medieval thinkers, virtuality is augmentation rather than impoverishment. Virtual being adds something to actual being, so that the sum of the two is more than either regarded separately. The virtual and the actual are equal and irreducibly distinct aspects of reality.

Henri Bergson renewed this medieval conception of virtuality as augmentation in the late nineteenth century. In his early masterwork, *Matter and Memory*, Bergson contrasts what he calls the "pure past" with the actual memory-image that makes the past available to our living present (Bergson 1962, 171). Say I meet someone on the street whom I know, but cannot remember from where. Was it my freshman year in college, or my stint in the army, or ... ? Bergson says that I am searching in the pure past for the stratum of memory where the person is located. The person must belong to my pure past as something real, or I would never be able to assign him a memory-image in a successful act of recollection. The pure past is real but virtual, in that it is not part of my actual present. Common to Aquinas, Scotus, and Bergson is the fact that each of these thinkers contrasts virtuality with actuality, but not with reality. The virtual and the actual are both real. This means that the concept of virtual reality has been with us for at least 800 years, 2,300 years if we trace it back to its progenitor, Aristotle.

Jaron Lanier was probably the first to use the expression "virtual reality" to refer to computer-generated immersive environments in the 1980s. But Ivan Sutherland had already vetted the idea in a three-page paper published in 1965, titled "The Ultimate Display." Sutherland focuses on the ability of graphical displays to make the mathematical processes involved in computation available to the human senses (Sutherland 1965, 506–508). By simulating sensory objects, the task of the display "is to serve as a looking-glass into the mathematical wonderland constructed in computer memory." The display is not limited, however, to simulating ordinary objects and processes. Since the rules of programming are not constrained by the laws of physics, Wonderland can be populated with strange denizens such as negative masses, opaque objects that suddenly become transparent, and triangles whose edges become rounded as soon as someone looks at them. Sutherland envisions the Ultimate Display as a room where the computer directly controls matter, like the Holodeck that would later be made famous by the *Star Trek, Next Generation* television series: "A chair displayed in such a room would be good enough to sit in ... and a bullet displayed in such a room would be fatal." Properly programmed, "such a display could literally be the Wonderland into which Alice walked." In 1968, Sutherland took the first step toward realizing his vision of a digital Wonderland when he implemented the earliest form of virtual reality with wire-frame graphics and a stereoscopic head-mounted display.

At the same time Sutherland was implementing his early version of virtual reality, Gilles Deleuze was finishing *Logic of Sense*, an important philosophical work that includes an extended discussion of Wonderland (Deleuze 1990, 1–35). The world Alice enters when she falls through the rabbit hole or passes through the mirror subverts not only the laws of physics, but those of ordinary logic as well. According to Deleuze, Alice is caught up in a paradoxical logic of events. After reaching the bottom of the rabbit hole, for example, Alice recognizes that she is becoming bigger (than her earlier size), and smaller (than her later size) at one and the same moment. The events in Alice's world have no trouble exhibiting normally incompatible properties. The Stoics were the first to recognize that events are not things, but play on the surfaces of things. In a famous Stoic example, a knife, my arm, and the movement of the knife along my arm are all physical. But "having been cut" is not a physical property of my arm. It is a "sense," a surface effect of the underlying state of physical things. While physical being is actual, the realm of senses, or events, is virtual. The logician-storyteller Lewis Carroll is the second great explorer, after the Stoics, of the virtual realm of sense and its paradoxes.

For Deleuze, though virtuality is an aspect of reality rather than a linguistic artifact, it is nevertheless inherently expressible in language as the sense, or ideal content, of propositions. This is a major theme in twentieth-century philosophy, especially in the work of Frege, Meinong, and Husserl. Between the proposition as a linguistic entity and the state of affairs it denotes, there is the meaning of the proposition, the way in which it denotes. Meanings are ways of "seeing as," varying "slants" on things. For example, I can see and refer to the pen as lying on the table, or as a gift from my friend, or as having been made in France. Husserl calls meanings *noemata*, literally, "thought objects." In a celebrated turn of phase, he says that the tree burns, but the noema of the tree does not.

Lewis Carroll's books reflect on the nature of sense, not philosophically, but by humor, pun, and paradox. Wonderland and the looking-glass world are places where sense runs rampant, where it replaces things and states of affairs. (A great deal of Alice's confusion stems from the fact that she often takes senses to be things.) What links senses with events is the significance of the verb and its derivatives: a burning tree, a shrinking child, a grinning cat. We understand something *as* something when we grasp the verb that characterizes it, and so the manner in which it appears. The Cheshire Cat's grin survives the disappearance of the cat because it is not a physical being, but rather a grinning way of being a cat, in other words, a cat-event.

Contrary, even contradictory, meanings can coexist when regarded as meanings, rather than as belonging to things and states of affairs. In an example from Meinong, the round square has a perfectly definite sense, even though it is impossible for such a thing to exist. Or in another feline example from Carroll, Alice recognizes in a moment of lucidity that it doesn't make any difference whether cats eat bats, or bats eat cats, as long as we do not know which is true (as long as we regard both as pure senses). Paradoxically, nonsense is a part of the logic of sense as contrasted with the logic of things.

Although Deleuze does not discuss computers in his book, his insights nevertheless illuminate the nature of computer-generated virtual reality. Just as the virtual domain of sense is a surface effect of underlying physical states, computer-generated virtual reality is a surface effect of the underlying state of hardware. Computer hardware is able to assume any number of possible physical states. Each state is a differential, and normally changing, distribution of electrical charges. Programming code constrains the plasticity of the physical machine by determining the way the charges may be distributed. The machine distributes charges in such a fashion as to simulate the operation of a typewriter, or a camera, or a sound studio, and so on. This was Turing's discovery (Turing

2004, 58–90). A universal Turing machine (universal because it has a notionally infinite memory) can simulate any finite machine. The real machine has virtual effects on the surface level, the level where the user interacts with the machine. This is the so-called "user illusion." Physical processes occurring in depth give rise to surface virtual effects. But this is just the point the Stoics, Lewis Carroll, and Deleuze make.

Worldhood

Shortly after the development of head-mounted displays and associated devices, artists began making virtual art. But because of the equipment involved, including fast computers with enormous memories, this was a very expensive proposition, sometimes requiring the investment of hundreds of thousands of dollars, and therefore corporate or government sponsorship. When virtual worlds resident on the Internet began to develop over the last two decades, the monetary barrier to creating virtual art was broken. The opening of *Second Life* in 2002 was especially important in this regard, since SL makes its content-creation tools available to users.

The fact that virtuality takes the specific form of a world or plurality of worlds has important consequences for the practice of virtual art. But what exactly is a world? Kant tackles this question in his *Inaugural Dissertation*:

> In a substantial composite, just as analysis does not end until a part is reached which is not a whole ... so likewise synthesis does not come to an end until we reach a whole which is not a part, that is to say, a world. (Kant 1968, 47)

The problem both analysis and synthesis presented to Kant is that of completing an infinite task in a finite time. Neither the simple part nor the world as a whole can be given in sense experience, because analysis in the first case and synthesis in the second cannot be carried to a conclusion. Simple part and ultimate whole are what Kant calls "Ideas of Reason." In the *Critique of Pure Reason*, he tells us their only legitimate function is regulative in character. The Idea of a world gives us, not knowledge, but a rule that tells us to carry on with synthesis no matter how far we have gone (Kant 1978, 449–458).

What for Kant is a regulative Idea is for Husserl something we directly experience (Husserl 1970, 142–143, 161–164). For Husserl, we experience the world, but not in the same way we experience discrete objects. We experience objects as standing out against the ground of a world that surrounds them, a world that can be explored but not exhausted. The object presents itself as something that invites us to surpass it, something that refers to other things, and ultimately to the totality of things. But this totality can never be given as something over and done with. The world-totality always remains radically open. We are in the midst of a world that draws us into itself, a world that is perpetually excessive, and so cannot be represented as a completed whole.

Our incarnation in a living body is the correlate of the infinite openness of the world. For Husserl, the world gives itself as arrayed around a living body that is mobile and exploratory, a body that can move beyond every finite object in the act of probing the world that is that object's ground. The experience of being in a world through a living body is that of immersion. To be immersed means to be in the midst of things (*in media res*) rather than holding them at a distance. The French phenomenologist Merleau-Ponty would later say that there is no bird's-eye view of the world, no "high altitude thinking" that could provide us with a comprehensive conceptual grasp. Or as his friend Jean-Paul Sartre was to paraphrase him: "We are grounded from birth" (Sartre 1965, 158).

Virtual worlds are immersive because immersion is a necessary condition of any world we are capable of experiencing perceptually. In the case of virtual worlds, however, immersion is mediated through the user-controlled avatar as a digital surrogate of the perceiving, mobile body. New visitors to virtual worlds are often astonished to find just how powerful the experience is of being lodged in an avatar body. Avatars, for example, keep appropriate distances from one another, getting close enough to make face-to-face communication effective, but not so close as to infringe on each other's "personal space." Perhaps even more surprisingly, when a user's physical body is tired, he or she often experiences the desire to have the avatar sit or lie down. Of course, the more intense such palpably somatic sensations are, the more powerful the experience of immersion.

However, immersion is not only perceptual in character. It also involves such psychological phenomena as the fixation of attention and the willing suspension of disbelief, both of which are involved, for example, when we are immersed in the imaginary world of a play or novel. In the collaborative work, *4 Jetpacks 4*, the virtual artists Bryn Oh, Nonnatus Korhonen, and Glyph Graves explore both perceptual and narrative forms of immersion in a self-enclosed installation that hosts a narratively structured performance piece (see Weblink: Zabel 1 immersion 1-30).

Like immersion, interaction is a necessary condition of worldhood. If we were incapable of interacting with other things, then we would not share with them a common world-context. Husserl insists that, before causality is a category of the exact natural sciences, the world of ordinary experience connects objects with one another and with embodied subjects in a common "causal style." Heidegger makes a similar point when he says that being-in-the-world involves "dwelling" along with other beings (Heidegger 1962, 105). We share a world with other things only when things matter to our bodies, when they have an actual or potential impact upon us, and when, conversely, our bodies matter to things. In virtual worlds, the avatar is able to manipulate objects, to move them from place to place, to sit or stand or lie upon them, to make them crash into one another, and so on. And just as importantly, objects may block the avatar's movements and so must be circumvented by varying bodily strategies, just as we must walk around some obstacles in the actual world, or jump over others. In other words, causal efficacy runs in both directions: from avatar to object, and from object to avatar. This reciprocal, interactive connection is a form of engagement, an encompassing inclusion of the avatar and its user in a surrounding world of real things (see Weblink: Zabel 2 interactive 1-19).

The use of the word "real" here is a conscious choice on the part of the author. One of the unfortunate linguistic habits of participants in *Second Life* is to contrast *Second Life* with Real Life (SL with RL, in the online shorthand of the initiated). But SL is RL, in one of its virtual expressions. Virtual worlds are not fake, or even imaginary worlds. They are computer-generated augmentations of reality.

The Six Dimensions of Virtual Art

In the history of new media, artists have tended initially to treat the new on the model of the familiar. Most media theorists are familiar with this principle from Marshall McLuhan's work, through it is also present in more sophisticated form in the philosophical hermeneutics of Hans Gadamer, as well the aesthetics of reception of Hans Robert Jauss. The basic idea is that our encounter with something new always occurs within an horizon of expectations that we carry with us from the past, and that shapes our acts of interpretation. Understanding occurs through the gradual modification of prejudices (prejudgments) in the light of ongoing experience. With respect to the history of new media, the earliest photographers shot historical and mythical scenes in studios in emulation of academic painting, and the first filmmakers kept their movie cameras stationary in accordance with older photographic practices. It takes considerable time and experimentation to discover the unique dimensions of the material made available by a new medium, and hence the artistic technique required for its mastery. The art of virtual worlds (at most two or three decades old) has followed this pattern, tending to fall back in its initial stages on earlier filmic, photographic, painterly, sculptural, and architectural models. But this phase is coming to an end as virtual artists begin to explore the unique dimensions of their medium.

Let us stipulate a definition of "dimension" as a parameter or matrix along which data changes in accordance with a rule. Given this definition, time and space are specific examples of dimensionality, but not the only ones. Temperature and air pressure, for instance, are dimensional in that they change in a rule-governed way when we move from the surface of the earth to the sky. Color has differing forms of dimensionality depending upon the color wheel an artist employs. Programmable computer operations are also dimensional in this usage of the word, since programs are comprised of algorithms, which are so strictly rule-governed that they can be implemented by machines.

At their current stage of development, virtual worlds posses six dimensions that collectively distinguish art made there from that of other forms of new media art. These dimensions are

1. Immersion
2. Interaction
3. Ambiguity of identity
4. Environmental fluidity

5. Artificial agency
6. Networked collaboration

We have seen that immersion and interaction are necessary conditions of world-hood. Without them, virtual worlds would not be worlds at all. These two ontological conditions of worldhood are, at the same time, aesthetic dimensions of art created in virtual worlds. The other four dimensions result from particular, contingent decisions concerning design and implementation. They apply specifically, though not exclusively, to *Second Life* as well as other virtual worlds that permit user-created content, and hence artistic activity. (*World of Warcraft* exhibits these four dimensions, although it does not permit user-created content.)

Ambiguity of identity results from the fact that our bodily presence in the virtual world is mediated by a variable digital representation (an avatar). Dwelling within a world involves being present in a body. The body both constitutes our perspective on things and makes us present to other embodied experiencers. Though personal identity can be a very complex construction, its ultimate foundation is continuity of bodily presence. But in SL and similar worlds, digital bodies and the names that uniquely identify them can be altered, multiplied, discarded, or exchanged at the will of the user. Since bodily presence is open to such radical discontinuity, the identity of the virtual person is protean and ambiguous, including indicators of age, gender, race, and even biological species. In a globalized age of fluid identities, this is an especially rich area for artists to explore (see Weblink: Zabel 3 ambiguity of identity 1-17).

Environmental fluidity is to the external virtual world what the protean character of identity is to the internal sphere. Since the virtual environment is constructed from graphical primitives and scripts that can be altered very rapidly, constancy is the exception rather than the norm. It is in the virtual world that Marx's famous observation about capitalist modernity reaches fruition: "All that is solid melts into air" (see Weblink: Zabel 4 environmental fluidity 1-10).

Artificial agency refers to the facility with which software agents can be embedded in virtual worlds. Since the virtual world is itself a complex program, it is relatively easy to introduce into it artificial life and intelligence as responsive and even evolving forms of aesthetic expression. Here the artwork sheds its character as an object, becoming an actor instead (see Weblink: Zabel 5 artificial agency 1-8).

Because virtual worlds reside on servers connected to the Internet, they offer unprecedented opportunities for collaboration across national and linguistic boundaries. Such networked collaboration between artists, as well as artists and audiences, can involve formidable organizational and aesthetic difficulties. But never before has art been capable of such globalized collectivity (see Weblink: Zabel 6 networked collaboration 1-15). It is true, of course, that virtual worlds share some of these dimensions with other forms of new media, but no other medium exhibits the entire group of six. The whole cluster is what makes the art of virtual worlds something unique.

In 2009–2010, through the nonprofit organization Virtual Art Initiative, I initiated collaborative explorations of each of the six dimensions discussed above in *Second Life*.

Each collaborative team included between 2 and 12 artists charged with producing a single work or an integrated group of works exploring one of the six dimensions in an attempt to discover some of its inherent expressive possibilities. The whole effort was conceived as an experiment in the reflective mastery of the material that is unique to the art of virtual worlds. More than 40 artists from 14 countries participated in the project, and their work was exhibited in six virtual exhibitions in *Second Life*, as well as in the physical space of the Harbor Gallery of the University of Massachusetts at Boston in April 2010.

Although I have already made Weblink references to this work above, the short space of the present chapter does not permit a discussion of the results of the project in the actual pages of this book. For that, the interested reader will have to travel to the book's virtual augmentation by going to its associated website. There we will discuss the collaborative works while illustrating them with digital images and videos.

NOTE

1. The are important political questions of Debordian inspiration that need to be raised concerning the images that populate virtual worlds, but that is a theme for another discussion.

REFERENCES

Adorno, T. 1984. *Aesthetic Theory*. Translated by C. Lenhardt. London: Routledge and Kegan Paul.

Aquinas, T. 1948. *Summa Theologica*, Vol. 1. Translated by Fathers of the English Dominican Province. New York: Benziger Brothers.

Aristotle. 1968. *Metaphysics*. Translated by Richard Hope. Michigan: University of Michigan Press.

Benjamin, W. 2008. The Work of Art in the Age of Its Technological Reproducibility. In *The Work of Art in the Age of Its Technological Reproducibility and Other Writings on Media*, edited by Michael W. Jennings, Brigid Doherty, and Thomas Y. Levin, translated by Edmund Jephcott, Rodney Livingstone, Howard Eiland, et al., 19–55. Cambridge, MA: Harvard University Press.

Bergson, H. 1962. *Matter and Memory*. Translated by Nancy Margaret Paul and W. Scott Palmer. London: George Allen and Unwin.

Debord, G. (1967) 1977. *Society of the Spectacle*. Detroit: Red and Black.

Deleuze, G. 1990. *The Logic of Sense*. Translated by Mark Lester. New York: Columbia University Press.

Heidegger, M. 1962. *Being and Time*. Translated by John Macquarrie and Edward Robinson. New York: Harper and Row.

Husserl, E. 1970. *The Crisis of European Sciences and Transcendental Phenomenology*. Translated by David Carr. Evanston, IL: Northwestern University Press.

Kant, I. 1968. On the Form and Principles of the Sensible and Intelligible Worlds. In *Selected Pre-Critical Writings*, translated by G. B. Kerferd and D. E. Walford, 45–92. Manchester: Manchester University Press.

Kant, I. 1978. *Critique of Pure Reason*. Translated by Norman Kemp Smith. London: Macmillan.

Marx, K. 1976. *Capital*. Vol. 1. Translated by Ben Fowkes. London: Penguin.

Sartre, J.-Paul. 1965. Merleau-Ponty. In *Situations*, translated by Benita Eisler, 156–226. Greenwich, CT: Fawcett.

Scotus, D. 1978. *Philosophical Writings*. Translated by Allan Wolter. Indianapolis: Bobbs-Merrill.

Sutherland, I. E. 1965. The Ultimate Display. In *Information Processing: Proceedings of the IFIP Congress*, 506–508. Amsterdam: North-Holland

Turing, A. 2004. On Computable Numbers with an Application to the Entscheidungsproblem. In *The Essential Allan Turing*, ed. B. Jack Copeland, 5–90. Oxford: Oxford University Press.

CHAPTER 26

RECREATING VISUAL REALITY IN VIRTUALITY

ANTHONY STEED

A virtual environment (VE) is a 3D model that can be displayed in various media. VEs can be simulations of imagined places, or they can represent real environments. Currently, most modeling of VEs is done by offline processes; that is, various 2D and 3D content elements are created in editing programs prior to the VE being experienced by a user. To generate the experience for the user, a separate control system loads a set of content elements and does a real-time rendering of them in different media. An example would be a typical modern console game where, although the game players control elements of the content through their interactions, most of the content and assets were created beforehand. Forms of mixed reality or virtuality are emerging where some elements of the VE models are created in real time as the user experiences the VE. This could be as simple as including live video in a game, or as complex as simulating a remote place in detailed 3D. In this chapter we will look at the technologies that create the visual media of the broad range of mixed reality systems, from virtual reality systems through to augmented reality systems.

Mixed reality systems cover a very wide range of display system types, but at their core is a computer system that contains some form of 3D model of an environment (VE model) that is then rendered by computer software and hardware to create one or more images that can be displayed on display panels or display surfaces alongside appropriate audio and perhaps haptic outputs. As we discuss the different types of virtuality system, the main distinguishing factor will be whether the systems use offline, preprepared assets, or are sampling and interpreting data from the real world in real time. In the second section we will focus on more detail on VR systems. In the third section we will revisit Milgram and Kishino's virtuality continuum (Milgram and Kishino 1994). We critique and update Milgram's discussion by analyzing in more technical detail how virtual and real spaces can be mixed. We point out that certain decisions, such as how to model people or places, force step-changes in technology and thus lead to different possibilities of mixed reality; thus the continuum isn't necessarily very contiguous. In the fourth section we will pick up the themes of registration and configuration that are involved in mixed reality systems. We discuss the processes by which mixed reality systems are constructed from different data inputs. In the fifth section we will describe real-time systems that reconstruct environments and their contents in real time. We will conclude with a discussion of the limitations of current technologies and some avenues for future research.

RECREATING VISUAL REALITY IN VIRTUAL REALITY

Overview

When we talk about VR we must distinguish between two different characteristics of the experience. The first characteristic is the type of media that is presented. While sometimes referred to as VR in the associated academic literature, the media itself and the computer model that generates it are more commonly called a virtual environment (VE). A VE is a representation (a model) inside a computer that can be experienced by a user through the use of various display devices. The main component of a VE consists of visual descriptions of objects and their properties; these descriptions will be in 3D. The VE will usually include audio descriptions of objects. Less commonly it includes tactile (touch), haptic (force), and other descriptions of objects. The second characteristic of VR is the technology that is used to experience a VE. The popular image of VR from the 1990s was the head-mounted display (HMD) where the user's senses were surrounded by the visual (and audio) displays. This type of system was often described as an immersive display because wherever users looked they could see and hear the VE environment. That is, it surrounded and included the user. Because the display could be head-tracked, the display could be updated so that it appeared that the VE was stationary and it was user that was moving. Today, surround-screen displays (SSDs) are more common in deployment because they are more suitable for group use. We describe the architecture of an SSD in the following section.

The types of object or place that might be simulated in a VE cover a vast range of scales from simulations of microscopic structures through to simulations of galaxies, and they cover variety representation styles from abstract through to photorealistic. The VE might be animated or interactive. It might include behaviors of mechanical systems or natural phenomena. The VE might represent existing objects or environments, speculative environments such as design plans for new buildings or consumer products, or fantasy environments.

A Typical System Architecture

To illustrate the processes involved in realizing a VE, figure 26.1 gives a high-level over-view of the process for creating the visual displays of a type of SSD system that is com-monly known as a CAVE-like display (Cruz-Neira, Sandin, and DeFanti 1993). The figure shows the different types of software and systems that are involved in the cre-ation of a visual display that wraps around the user. Users will stand inside this display and will have the impression from a first-person point of view that they are "immersed within" the display. In the figure we can see that a piece of modeling software (*content production software*) creates *content*: 2D and 3D media that we will explain later, which can then be loaded into a *control system*. The control system then passes the 2D and 3D media to multiple *image generator* systems that generate changing 2D media (i.e., real-time video) that are routed to display devices, in this case projectors. The control system also generates audio via an *audio generator* that drives speakers. The control sys-tem also receives input from various *interface devices*.

A diagram of an example of such a display, the ReaCTor display at University College London, is shown in figure 26.2. The ReaCTor consists of four display screens: three walls and a floor. The three walls are 3 m by 2.2 m and the floor is 3 m by 3 m. Each of the three walls is back-projected and the floor is front-projected. Each surface is illuminated by a Christie Mirage projector that shows images at 1,400 by 1,050 pixels image resolu-tion. The projector frame rate is 120 frames per second (120Hz). Each projector shows alternating left and right eye images, and the users wear glasses that flicker and mask out the image that is intended for the other eye. The users thus see stereo imagery at 60Hz. For one user inside this display system, head movements can be tracked and the images

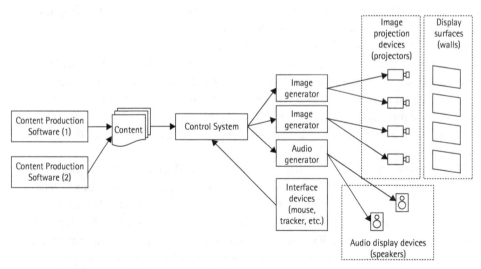

FIGURE 26.1 Overview of systems involved in constructing an immersive VR on an SSD. Light-colored lines are real-time processes, dark are offline.

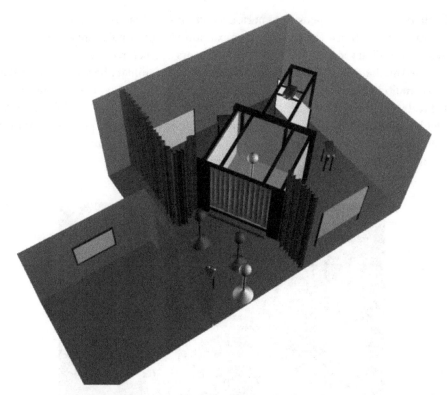

FIGURE 26.2 A 3D model representation of the ReaCTor display at University College London. The display has three walls and a floor. It is shown with a curtain over the empty wall.

on the walls can be drawn with a near correct perspective for each of the user's eyes. As that user walks around inside the display, he or she sees a stereo image with correct motion parallax for their movement.

With SSDs, the illusion of solidity and size of the content displayed can be very compelling. But what could the user see on these walls? Figure 26.3 shows four very different simulations that can be run. These have very different visual qualities, from an abstract visualization (figure 26.3a, a visualization of brain structure), through representing collaborative tasks (figure 26.3b, a puzzle-solving task), to representing speculative design (figure 26.3c, a previsualization of a yacht). Figure 26.3d is a 3D reconstruction of a real environment into which a reconstruction of a person is inserted. The reconstruction is done in real time, and it is a form of augmented virtuality as discussed in the third section of this chapter.

Image Generation

In the early 1990s progress in real-time computer graphics was driven by the simulator industry. The concern of the simulator industry was in training operators of complex machinery or those who might be involved in complex operations. Such training was difficult, dangerous, or expensive to perform and thus simulators were used to replace some training situations. The most obvious example is flight simulation: pilots for commercial and military aircraft can train on simulators and can receive certain certifications based on their simulator performance. Similarly, the military have long used VR to simulate multiple participants in theater of war scenarios. This can involve some operational training, but also tactical training. A modern example is the VIRTSIM simulator, which provides an immersive VR simulation for a squad of 12 personnel. Within this simulation they can practice tactical maneuvers in urban environments. A review of other industrial application of VR can be found in Brooks (1999).

(a)

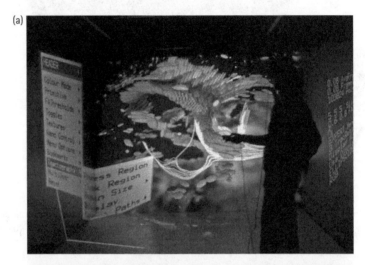

(b)

FIGURE 26.3 Four very different types of visual representation that can be supported on VR systems.

(c)

(d)

FIGURE 26.3 (Continued)

More recently, the driving force behind the development of image generation has been computer and video games. Initially PC games, then games consoles drove the development of more and more complex graphics processing units (GPUs). Recently there is a new push for GPUs on mobile devices, and at the time of writing (early 2012), the iOS and Android systems were supporting image generators nearing the capabilities of the last generation of games consoles (Sony PS3 and Microsoft Xbox 360). At this time, most of these GPUs follow a rendering architecture that is based around a *graphics pipeline* that has been widely used for over two decades. However, there are signs that this pipeline architecture might be replaced, or at least complemented, by new architectures in the next few years.

The graphics pipeline is illustrated in figure 26.4. This is the pipeline that would be found in each of the "image generators" in figure 26.1. In the graphics pipeline there

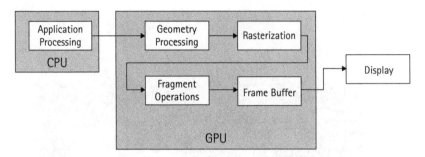

FIGURE 26.4 A high-level overview of the graphics pipeline in modern image generators.

is a split between a central processing unit (CPU) process and the various processes that take place on the GPU. The CPU is responsible, at least, for submitting content to the GPU to be displayed. It is thus responsible for deciding what content is going to be drawn. It must also make decisions about how the scene should be configured, such as how it will be lit. The CPU thus sends to the GPU the following types of information:

- 3D geometric descriptions of the objects within the scene
- 2D image data to use to describe the surfaces of the objects
- A description of a virtual lighting situation for the objects
- A description of a virtual camera to draw the scene
- Rendering state and (in modern GPUs) *shader programs* that specify procedures to operate on the geometry and image data sent to the GPU

A complete description of the capabilities of the system is beyond the scope of this chapter; the interested reader is referred to textbooks on graphics, of which there are many (e.g., Slater et al. 2001; Shreiner and Angel 2011; Akenine-Moller et al. 2008). However, most important for this chapter are the descriptions of 3D geometry and 2D imagery.

Modern GPUs and the associated content production pipelines that drive them use a type of 3D geometry called a boundary representation, and of the various types of boundary representation, the most common is a geometric mesh. The mesh is formed of polygons, where each polygon is defined by a sequence of 3D points or vertices. In the model shown in figure 26.5a we can see a wireframe representation that emphasizes that the 3D model was made from a set of triangles. These triangles modeled walls, floor, and furniture. In this case, a lighting solution was run on the model so that every vertex had a brightness indicating how much light it received (this was calculated using a radiosity process [e.g., see Slater et al. 2001, ch. 15]. Every vertex also had a texture coordinate, which indicated how to drape the texture maps, the image maps shown in figure 26.5b, onto the model. These texture maps defined the diffuse color for the triangles.

In order to produce the final image in figure 26.5c, in addition to the 3D model and 2D image maps, we had to tell the GPU about a camera from which to render the model,

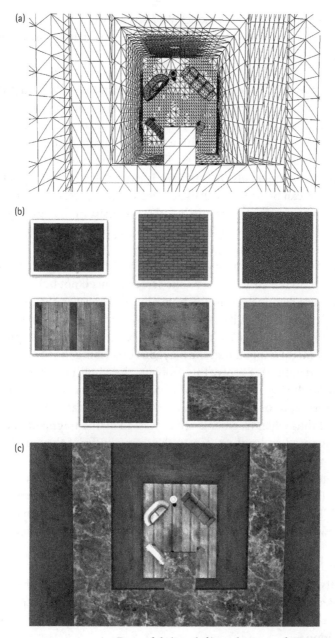

FIGURE 26.5A, 26.5B, AND 26.5C A 3D model (top left) and a set of 2D image maps (top
-right) are composed together to create a lit model of a pit (bottom). Based on the virtual
pit from University of North Carolina at Chapel Hill and University College London (Usoh
et al. 1999).

and a set of lights to illuminate the model. We also had to configure the graphics pipeline by giving some details of how data sent to the GPU was structured, and which shader programs should be used.

Returning to the pipeline in shown in figure 26.4, we can describe some important features about the GPU's internal processing. The first to note is that there are two configurable stages (geometry processing, fragment operations), and one fixed function stage (rasterization). Geometry processing is responsible for taking the camera and lighting specifications, applying these to the mesh, and then outputting the geometry in a screen-based coordinate system. Following this, the fixed function stage converts polygons into *fragments*. A fragment is essentially a "proto-pixel": it contains information that can be used to calculate the color of a pixel on the screen. The next stage is fragment operations, essentially a 2D composite of the newly produced fragment with other data sources such as image maps, previously created images, and so on. The fragment operations stage then possibly outputs a colored pixel to the frame buffer. The first thing to note about this process is that it is polygon driven: every time a polygon is sent to the GPU, if it is on the screen (it need not be), fragments are created, and they are composed into the frame buffer. However, the polygons are in no particular order, and thus on its own this process cannot resolve issues such as occlusion and ordering of depth (e.g., in the figures the furniture should appear in front of the floor, but it might happen that the polygons describing the floor come after those describing the furniture). To solve this problem, the whole pipeline supports 3D, with rasterization producing fragments that have a depth associated with them that corresponds to the depth of the polygon at that point. The frame buffer stores depth in a *z-buffer*, and thus when fragments are processed by the fragment operations stage, they can be ignored and not written to the frame buffer if they are behind what is already drawn.

This very quick introduction to the GPU cannot convey the flexibility and power of modern GPUs. Indeed, they have become so powerful that there are communities exploiting GPUs for other purposes such as medical imaging or encryption. We would highlight a few features that should be borne in mind for later discussion:

- The GPU deals with a 3D scene.
- 2D assets can be loaded and placed within a scene by placing them on a polygon mesh. Because 2D images can be loaded, it follows that video can be loaded.
- The GPU will deal with occlusion and depth information by storing z (depth) information.

Control Systems and Content Production

There is a vast range of control system software available for VR. Examples include commercial packages such as 3DVia Virtools from Dassault Systems, Vizard from WorldViz, and a variety of open source packages such as VRJuggler or Diverse. These packages support a range of different VR configurations, and can be adapted to support the broader range of mixed reality systems. The roles of the control system include

- Driving the image generators, audio generators, etc.
- Loading data assets from storage such as disk or web services
- Managing the simulation of the VE, including any interactive elements in the scene. This might include running some form of physics simulation, or artificial intelligence simulation to control representations of people in the scene
- Describing the configuration of the VR system
- Reading interaction devices such as tracking devices, button devices, etc.
- Dealing with any real-time networking (e.g., for games or distributed simulation)

Some of these roles will be defined by the physical infrastructure of the VR display (e.g., number of image generators, interaction devices, etc.). Some will be defined by software that is designed for a specific application. Others will be defined by the content that describes a particular scene. Each of the aforementioned control systems utilizes a different programming language and/or a different set of libraries and interfaces for the functionality it provides. There is very little standardization at this level, except at the level of interfacing to the media generators, where there are standards such as OpenGL (for the graphics pipeline) and OpenAL (for audio) that isolate the programmer from the specifics of the hardware. VRJuggler, for example, mainly provides a set of C++ classes and a framework within which applications can be built and managed. Virtools provides its own scripting language (the Virtools Scripting Language) and a schematic editor for managing different parts of the code. Virtual Reality Modeling Language and its successor X3D provide a file format in which interactive scenes can be described. They support animation, interactive elements such as buttons and sliders, scripting in Java and ECMAScript (JavaScript), geometry, texture, lights, and so on. However, they are not very widely supported in modern platforms, except for static 3D content. This is partly because the simulation model they describe is relatively hard to implement, and it might fit badly with a control system's other functionality.

Fortunately for 3D content and 2D content there are good standards for creation and sharing of assets. For 2D content, most control systems support a wide range of common file formats such as PNG and JPEG. Thus the full range of 2D image content production tools can be used to generate these. As in other domains, the creation of a 2D image might start from a digital image, from a simulation of some sort (e.g., an experimental simulation), or by being drawn by hand. It might also be video imagery from a camera or other source. There are few restrictions on the types of imagery that can be used in VR systems.

Similarly, 3D content can be sourced from the real world by scanning a real object using a variety of processes, or it can be simulated (e.g., a fractal) or created by hand. The range of software and systems here is very diverse. A general-purpose 3D editing package is Autodesk 3ds Max, but this is complex to learn. A simpler program is Google Sketchup. Programs such as Autodesk 123D Catch can make 3D models from photographs. The model shown in figure 26.5 was created by hand in Autodesk 3ds Max 2012 using free furniture models that were downloaded from the TurboSquid website. Within 3ds Max, the scene was assembled and then texture mapped (i.e., textures were applied to the surfaces), and then a simple lighting calculation was done to give the appearance of the room being lit by area light sources (e.g., note that the shadows on the walls and floors are soft shadows rather than hard shadows).

The Virtuality Continuum Revisited

As we have seen, VR can be used to simulate a wide variety of different situations. The modeling pipeline discussed above indicates that assets are created offline before the session, but already we can note a couple of interesting aspects of typical VEs. First, creating an immersive VE involves tracking the user so that the correct images can be created on the displays. Second, the VE might be a representation of a real place or include representations of real objects or people. Thus even within a "standard" VR, there are links to the real world, and what one sees in the VE might reflect some aspects of the current state of the real world. There is one very important way that this can be true: in an HMD, when one looks down, one might see a representation of a body, and that body might look like your own. Further, if you were holding an object when you donned the HMD, you might see the same object within the HMD. Further still, perhaps the VE mimics the place where you were when you donned the HMD (Slater et al. 1998; Steed et al. 2002).

This blend between real and virtual has long been studied within the real-time graphics communities. An important set of framing concepts was provided by Milgram and Kishino (1994) in their description of the virtuality continuum. This continuum is shown in figure 26.6.

Milgram and Kishino have placed real environments and VEs at the opposite ends of a spectrum that includes various levels of "mixing" of realities, hence the generic term mixed reality (MR). This is a rough description that shows that one can add VE elements to a real scene to create an "augmented reality" (AR), or real elements to a VE to create an "augmented virtuality" (AV). Some authors just use the term AR, without using

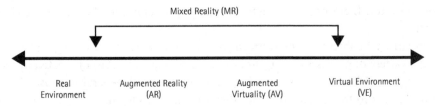

FIGURE 26.6 Milgram and Kishino's simplified representation of a "virtuality continuum".

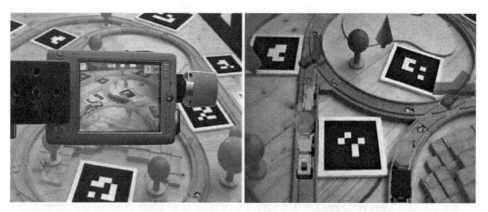

FIGURE 26.7 An AR showing a virtual train overlaid onto a real train set. From Wagner et al. 2005. Images courtesy of Daniel Wagner.

augmented virtuality, but Milgram and Kishino were specifically noting that one can have more or fewer real and virtual objects in different systems.

The field of AR is large with many variants and situations of use (Azuma et al. 2001; Bimber and Raskar 2005). An AR demonstration is shown in figure 26.7. This demonstration shows virtual trains shown running over a real toy train track. Although this particular demonstration is running on a mobile device, the system is similar in many ways to the VR system discussed in the second section of this chapter in that there is virtual content (the train), and there is tracking (in this case effected by camera-based tracking). The motion of the trains is simulated, so as users look at the screen, they see the trains moving as if they were on the rails in the real world. As the user moves the mobile device, the camera is able to detect the large black and white images that are known as *markers*. From the 2D position and shape of the markers on the camera image, the device is able to estimate the camera's position, and thus it can calculate where the virtual objects are on the screen. It can then use the camera image as the background in a rendering, and render the virtual train so it appears to be in front of the real toy track.

AR can be achieved in a number of different modes. The train example is a "through device" mode, where AR is only seen on a screen. An alternative would be to make the AR immersive, in the same way that VR was immersive, by making it completely surround the user. This can be achieved with head-worn glasses, where users see the real world through the glasses, but with objects inserted into their view. There are various other modes for display AR, such as projecting onto real objects. See Azuma et al. 2001 and Bimber and Raskar 2005 for excellent reviews.

AR systems thus attempt to give the impression that the real world is changed somehow. Returning to the demonstrations in figure 26.7, the black and white markers do two things: they tell us where the objects are in the real world in a local coordinate system defined by the markers, and they also tell us about the identity of the objects that one would expect to see here. Thus they define how the virtual and real are linked, something that we will return to look at shortly.

FIGURE 26.8 Cloning a real object virtually (Freeman 2010).

In contrast, an AV is primarily a VR, but with real-time integration of data from the real world. Figure 26.3d, is an example of an AV. There was a virtual model of a real room, which was captured using photographs of the walls and a tape measure. The person that was seen in the room was a live insert from a real camera, a Microsoft Kinect, which captures depth and color. The two were mixed together in the GPU to give the impression that the person in the ReaCTor was seeing a room with that person in. Note that this model is itself interesting because the virtual room model is a real room. In fact it is the same room where the person shown in the snapshot is standing. The room was captured offline beforehand because this particular camera doesn't deal well with capture of whole environments. This should hopefully suggest that there are some interesting variants of mixing real objects and virtual objects. Figure 26.8 shows an example from Freeman (2010) (see also Freeman et al., 2005; Freeman and Steed, 2006). In a sequence of four panels, the figure shows the process of creating a virtual clone of an object. In the top left, we see the original scene with a marker to locate the camera. The user creates a virtual cylinder with which the user will clone the real object, a tin of lip balm that is on the right. In the top-right image and bottom-left image, the cylinder is moved by the user to fit the same shape as the tin. In the bottom-right image a second virtual tin is created. However, it is not obvious in this screenshot which is the virtual one or the real one. This should show us that AR mixes virtual content, but that virtual content might itself be modeled on the real scene.

We can return to the taxonomy of Milgram and Kishino to start to clarify the options here (see fig. 26.9). They describe three axes of comparison of different mixed reality systems:

- *Extent of world knowledge*: this axis describes what is known about the real world that is being monitored. At the very least, this means that some location in the world is known (e.g., the marker, or the position of the tracker as known from some other calibration) or that some VE model of a real object is known. Note that, for example, in the examples in figure 26.7 we needed to know where the real track was in order to place the train upon it. In figure 26.8 we knew where the real tin was because the cylinder was manipulated to fit the tin. Then we created a VE model of the tin. We thus knew where and what the object was, so we could create a copy.
- *Reproduction fidelity*: this axis describes the detail with which a display can reproduce the virtual elements of the display. In an AR this would refer to any

Extent of World Knowledge

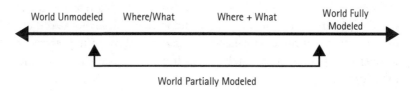

Reproduction Fidelity

Extent of Presence Metaphor

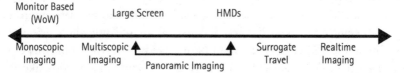

FIGURE 26.9 The three axes of the taxonomy of Milgram and Kishino: extent of world knowledge, reproduction fidelity, and extent of presence metaphor.

object that is inserted into the display. In an AV this would refer to the inserted elements. It might also refer to the VE in a VR. This dimension thus covers a complex topic, but the important aspect is that we distinguish different systems by the fidelity of reproduction of the object. This is especially important in certain applications where visual quality is important. An example is a virtual television studio, which can be seen as a type of augmented virtuality: in this case it is important for visual consistency that the quality of reproduction of the actors that are filmed is similar to the virtual set that they are inserted into (see Gibbs et al. 1998 for an overview of this area). The most obvious aspect is the visual quality with which a 3D model is created (cf. the image in figure 26.8, in which it is hard to detect the difference between the virtual and real tins in this screenshot), or the quality of any live video insert. We could extend that dimension with the various types of depth camera and real-time capture systems that have become common (see the fifth section of this chapter).

- *Extent of presence metaphor*: this axis covers the type of experience that the user has and whether this is first person or a limited window on the world (WoW). In the extreme, the VR or mixed reality might be seen from a static position with a limited field of view, but more commonly it is seen in some form of surround display (e.g. an SSD) or a mobile display. This axis again simplifies a complex area. The example in figure 26.7 is a moving WoW, so you can effect virtual travel around the mixed reality (i.e., you can move around the train set), but you only see a mono image. In this dimension real-time imaging refers to the fact that one could experience a remote place as if one were physically located there. This style of interaction is sometimes called *telepresence*, and the term *presence* is often used to refer to experiencing a purely VR as if it were a real place that one could visit (Sheridan 1992).

The taxonomy of Milgram and Kishino thus provides us with a way of contrasting different types of mixed reality. To complement their taxonomy we can highlight two further considerations that distinguish between different systems: *primary environment* and *immediacy of representation*. The notion of a primary environment complements the main virtuality continuum. While it is quite clear that the intention of plotting this axis was not to claim that it was actually a continuum between real and virtual, it is nevertheless clear that the main "environment" could be one of three things: a pure virtual environment, the local environment, or a remote real environment. One can think about what the background of the environment that users see is: even in a HMD they might be seeing a video of their immediate environment, they might be seeing a video or dynamic reconstruction of somewhere else, or they might be seeing a VR. Other objects might be inserted or overlaid into this environment. There are situations where a virtual environment is intended to look like an extension of the real environment (e.g., Gibbs et al. 1999; Raskar et al. 1998, see figure 26.15), but in general it doesn't make sense to attempt to overlay two backgrounds, given that the backgrounds completely surround the user. Once the background is set, one can then think about how media from different environments are integrated. All forms of combination are possible here. This is not to say that background is literally just what is behind everything else; in mixed reality the background can be a full 3D model into which different objects can be mixed and properly depth occluded (e.g., see the discussion of figure 26.11).

Immediacy of representation is a simple concept: it refers to the age of the content that is represented in the mixed reality and thus its veracity. A 3D model that is constructed in real time (see the fifth section) is by its nature "true" in that it is a capture from sensors, and while it might be manipulated by processing and filters, it represents something that is occurring now. If the model was made previously, by, say, an offline process, then there is immediately a question of whether the model is up to date, or whether it is even a faithful representation of the objects that it represents. In Figure 26.3b, the avatars are modeled, and somewhat visually similar to one of the authors of the associated work and papers. However, it is not animated, and it's not clear if he still looked like that at the time (maybe he grew a beard?). Furthermore, there are two very similar-looking avatars, so one of them is unlikely to be true! This is somewhat covered by the axis of extent of world knowledge, but even the most detailed model might be out of date. This is particularly true for models of humans. In contrast, the human in figure 26.3d, is obviously "live" in that it looks like a human and moves in ways consistent with human motion. However the image is very low detail and contains a lot of distracting artifacts. It is very easy to capture 2D video, and it is relatively easy to capture 3D motion of objects, even articulated objects such as humans, but it is currently hard to capture dynamic 3D models (though see the fifth section). Immediacy of representation is very important in at least two ways. First, it may be that in a collaborative environment, one user is seeing the object directly and another is seeing some form of virtual representation, in which case it is important that there be no important discrepancies between their views. Second, specifically for human communication, immediacy of representation supports successful communication because it means that body language, gestures, eye-gaze, and so on, are preserved and faithful to the users' emotional state and communication intent.

A final observation to make about mixed reality systems is that they can be flexible in that any one user might switch modes of presentation during the experience. The MagicBook system (Billinghurst et al. 2001) allows users to switch from AR mode to VR mode during the experience. Initially users are looking at a book with markers on the page, but they can fly down into the pages and experience the content from a first-person point of view on a HMD. Another interesting aspect is that different users of a collaborative mixed reality do not need to be using the same mode of interaction. For further discussion of these issues see Benford and colleagues (1998), Brown and colleagues (2003), and Steed and colleagues (2002).

Tracking and Configuration for Mixed Reality

As we have seen, one main difference between a VR model and a more general model for a mixed reality is that the mixed reality must maintain information models about the real environment(s) that are being mixed with. We may need to track a real object in order to place an augmentation on it, or we may want to insert a virtual model of something that is remote. The main roles of a control system for a mixed reality system are visualized in figure 26.10. In this figure we can note that the control system must monitor the remote and local environments. Monitoring involves one or more of the following:

- One or more videos of the scene
- Tracking or localizing the video in the scene
- Tracking or localizing objects
- Identifying objects in the scene
- Creating 3D models

The most important aspect of this type of control system is that it must merge data from several sources. In particular, it must be able to synthesize a consistent image that combines the data sources. An example shown in figure 26.11 illustrates this (Freeman et al. 2005). In this example there are two data sources: a VE consisting of simulations of two people (two avatars) and a video of a real environment consisting of a meeting room with two tables and three chairs. In figure 26.11, right, we see the final mixed reality that we want to create: the avatars appear to be seated at the tables in the real environment. This is more complex than it might first appear: note that the avatars appear to sit in the chairs that are in the real environment. Further, note that the avatars are occluded properly by the real environment, that is, the avatars' legs are obscured by the table. To accomplish this, we can't just treat the virtual graphics as an overlay on the video, we

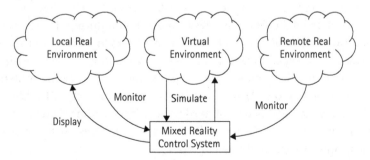

FIGURE 26.10 The main roles of a control system for a mixed reality system.

FIGURE 26.11 Configuring a mixed reality model of a meeting room.

must model more information about the scene. In particular we need to know the positions of the tables and chairs in the video image: the tables in order that they can be used to obscure parts of the scene, and the chairs because this is where the avatars will be positioned to sit. Figure 26.11, left, shows the scene without any configuration: this is the same video, but nothing is known about the registration of the video with respect to the scene, and the avatars are not positioned on chairs. Once the chairs and tables have been calibrated to the video, there is no need to draw them to the screen, as they would overlap the real video. However, recall that the GPU models the visual scene with depth, so the geometry of the table can be used to mask out the virtual scene. Specifically the tables and chairs can be drawn into the z-buffer only, so that when the avatars are drawn, any part of them that is behind the table (i.e., further away in depth) can be ignored.

This ability to layer objects in depth is an important one for mixed reality. This principle is used in virtual sets for television production so that presenters can be behind or in front of the VE (see Gibbs et al. 1998). It is sufficient in many situations to simply provide a depth ordering: for example, virtual assets and video might be mixed in layers as might happen in a 2D video composite. Figure 26.12 shows that in many situations this isn't sufficient because in this example, the avatar is in front of some parts of the video, but behind others. If the scene can be modeled more accurately, then other effects are possible. In particular, if one cannot only determine the geometry, but how it is lit, then the virtual objects can be illuminated by the same lighting. Figure 26.12 shows an example where a laptop is tracked within a camera image (Jacobs et al. 2005). Because the geometry of the laptop is known (i.e., the shape of the laptop, angle of its screen, and where the marker is on the laptop), we can position a virtual laptop in the video image in the same place. This virtual laptop is not shown, but because we know where the light is (in this example the light source position was estimated from the video, but the light source could just be tracked or in a known position), we can cast a shadow from the virtual laptop. This virtual shadow is cast on the virtual object that is drawn: the virtual human that walks around the laptop.

To create a mixed reality, a certain amount of modeling of the real environment is needed. 3D models might be made of objects or places, and then some aspects of the

FIGURE 26.12 A virtual avatar walks into the shadow cast by a real object. It also casts a shadow on the real environment (Jacobs et al. 2005).

FIGURE 26.13 Two types of marker used in AR demonstrations. Left: the Hiro marker from the ARToolkit (Kato and Billinghurst 1999). Right: a QRCode.

world are tracked. The process of modeling objects is often done offline in the manner described in the second section in this chapter. In the next section we describe emerging methods of real-time reconstruction. Tracking can be done with the types of marker already described. Two common marker types are shown in figure 26.13. The left is perhaps the most common marker seen in AR demonstrations because it is one of the default markers with the ARToolkit system (Kato and Billinghurst 1999). It is easy to track this marker because of the large border. The marker on the right is a QRCode, of the type that is commonly found on packaging and in print material currently. It can be tracked less easily, but it holds much more data. ARToolkit can only identify a limited number of markers, so it must be known what these are attached to; thus the meaning of the marker is bound to the application that observes the marker; different applications will treat the marker differently. The QRCode can be self-describing, as there is enough data to encode a URL and thus fetch a web resource that describes application-specific data.

The state of the art now in AR is moving away from explicit markers to image-based targets and general object tracking. Modern AR toolkits such as Vuforia from

Qualcomm provide a variety of marker types but also image-based tracking. The image does need to have sufficient amounts of suitable structure in order for the tracking to be successful. Lepetit and colleagues (2003) present a system that can track 3D objects based on their visual properties. They demonstrate an AR application of augmenting such objects. Implicit in such systems is the identification of the object in question.

Aside from visual tracking, there are many other tracking systems that can be used to track cameras, users, or objects in the environment. They range from other types of optical system that would otherwise be used for motion capture, through to magnetic tracking systems of the type long used for VR systems; see Welch and Foxlin (2002) for a review.

MODELING IN REAL TIME

Figure 26.14 represents the interaction between offline and online phases of a mixed reality. In the offline phase we see that the objects in the world are modeled, and some configuration of them is made in order to relate them to each other and to coordinate systems that are tracked. In the online phase a mixed reality system processes the images it receives and the tracking information it has, calculates a new status for the mixed reality state, and renders this. This obviously limits the expressive power of the mixed reality in that the 3D models for objects must be known beforehand.

Current research is attempting to tackle this problem by moving more of the modeling of the scene to the run-time system. The first approach to this is to add tools to configure the mixed reality models online by user editing. A seminal system in this area is the Tinmith system (Piekarski and Thomas 2001). Tinmith was an outdoor, wide-area mobile AR system. A 3D model editing system was built on this system so that mobile

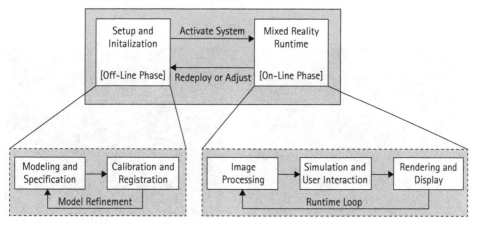

FIGURE 26.14 The interaction between offline and online phases of a mixed reality control system. From Freeman (2010).

users could edit a 3D model of their locality. A similar motivation inspired the work shown in figure 26.8 (Freeman 2010).

Aside from user editing, there has been a lot of research on the application of novel sensor hardware and computer vision techniques to reconstruct scenes in real time. This is a very broad area, so we highlight a few novel systems in complementary areas. The first area is the reconstruction of human motion. Two seminal systems are the Office of the Future system shown in figure 26.15 and the Blue-C system shown in figure 26.16. The Office of the Future simulated a cross-table collaboration (Raskar et al. 1998). The remote participant was captured by an array of cameras that were used to approximate that participant's 3D shape. In figure 26.15 we can see further virtual content: the background was a virtual model and the local and remote participants had virtual tools to collaborate with the model in front of them. The Blue-C system achieved a similar aim but for a person who is immersed in an SSD (Gross et al. 2003). In figure 26.16, left, we

FIGURE 26.15 Office of the Future system. Image courtesy of Department of Computer Science, University of North Carolina at Chapel Hill.

FIGURE 26.16 Left, the walls of the Blue-C system. Right, a user standing in front of her own reconstruction. Images courtesy of Markus Gross, ETH Zurich.

see the SSD that was constructed with walls that can be switched between transparent and translucent. By filming through these walls, researchers were able to reconstruct the person moving inside the system. Figure 26.16, right, shows a person inside the Blue-C who was standing in front of her own reconstruction.

These two systems use sets of cameras pointing at the user, but an alternative is to capture the environment from the user's own point of view, or from something that the user can aim into the world. An example of the first is the reconstruction of the hands of the user from head-mounted cameras. By using stereo computer vision techniques, Gordon and colleagues (2002) were able to track the user's hands from a pair of head-mounted cameras. These stereo video views were also presented inside the HMD, an example of a video see-through AR system. The use of hand tracking allowed the relative depth of the hand and any virtual content to be judged, thus making such content potentially interactive. A technology that has gained some mass exposure recently is depth cameras similar to the Microsoft Kinect. As mentioned previously, this camera, and similar cameras, can produce a color map and a depth range to the scene. The potential uses of these for mixed reality are only just being explored. A very promising direction is demonstrated in the KinectFusion system (Izadi et al. 2011), which can capture a 3D scene by having a user sweep a Kinect camera around. While this cannot capture moving shapes in real time as did the Blue-C and Office of the Future systems, KinectFusion has immediate application in constructing the static or infrequently moving parts of the scene to allow correct registration of virtual content.

CONCLUSION

The term virtuality covers a range of technologies, from VR through to AR. Although the types of media and experience created by VR and AR are very diverse, we have seen that at their core, VR and AR systems can model 3D spaces and mix media that represent those spaces to form a consistent, novel mixed reality. In this chapter we have seen some of the basic technologies that go into recreating the visual aspects of mixed reality. We started from the capabilities of modern GPUs that are able to process 3D models and 2D models to create real-time images. We then discussed the need to integrate different types of 3D model and to track elements of the real world in order to mix real and virtual content. As illustrated by discussion of the Milgram and Kishino virtuality continuum, there are many ways in which knowledge from the real world can be integrated into the virtual world.

The field of mixed reality is moving quickly, and new types of demonstration emerge every year. While technology will continue to develop, especially in the area of smarter camera technologies and computer vision techniques that can reconstruct the scene in 3D, there is unfortunately a lack of common software frameworks and tools. Thus we can hope that over the next few years, a few more of the technologies become available in easy-to-use tools that make the full power of virtuality available to more content producers and more users.

References

Akenine-Moller, T., E. Haines, and N. Hoffman. 2008. *Real-Time Rendering.* 3rd edition. Natick, MA: A. K. Peters.

Azuma, R., Y. Baillot, R. Behringer, S. Feiner, S. Julier, and B. MacIntyre. 2001. Recent Advances in Augmented Reality. *IEEE Computer Graphics Applications* 21 (6): 34–47.

Benford, S., C. Greenhalgh, G. Reynard, C. Brown, and B. Koleva. 1998. Understanding and Constructing Shared Spaces with Mixed Reality Boundaries. *ACM Transactions on Computer–Human Interaction* 5 (3): 185–223.

Billinghurst, M., H. Kato, and I. Poupyrev. 2001. The MagicBook: A Transitional AR Interface. *Computers and Graphics* 25 (5): 745–753.

Bimber, O., and R. Raskar. 2005. Spatial Augmented Reality: Merging Real and Virtual Worlds. Natick, MA: A. K. Peters.

Brooks, F. P. 1999. What's Real about Virtual Reality? *IEEE Computer Graphics Applications* 19 (6): 16–27.

Brown, B., I. MacColl, M. Chalmers, A. Galani, C. Randell, and A. Steed. 2003. Lessons from the Lighthouse: Collaboration in a Shared Mixed Reality System. In *Proceedings of the SIGCHI Conference on Human Factors in Computing Systems (CHI '03)*, 577–584. New York: ACM.

Cruz-Neira, C., D. J. Sandin, and T. A. DeFanti. 1993. Surround-Screen Projection-Based Virtual Reality: The Design and Implementation of the CAVE. In *Proceedings of the 20th Annual Conference on Computer Graphics and Interactive Techniques (SIGGRAPH '93)*, 135–142. New York: ACM.

Freeman, R. 2010. Rapid Interactive Modelling and Tracking for Mixed and Augmented Reality. PhD diss., University College London.

Freeman, R., and A. Steed. 2006. Interactive Modelling and Tracking for Mixed and Augmented Reality. In *Proceedings of the ACM Symposium on Virtual Reality Software and Technology (VRST '06)*, 61–64. New York: ACM.

Freeman, R., A. Steed, and B. Zhou. 2005. Rapid Scene Modelling, Registration and Specification for Mixed Reality Systems. In *Proceedings of the ACM Symposium on Virtual Reality Software and Technology (VRST '05)*, 147–150. New York: ACM.

Gibbs, S. J., C. Arapis, and C. J. Breiteneder. 1999. Teleport—towards Immersive Copresence. *Multimedia Systems* 7 (3): 214–221.

Gibbs, S., C. Arapis, C. Breiteneder, V. Lalioti, S. Mostafawy, and J. Speier. 1998. Virtual Studios: An Overview. *IEEE MultiMedia* 5 (1): 18–35.

Gordon, G., M. Billinghurst, M. Bell, J. Woodfill, B. Kowalik, A. Erendi, and J. Tilander. 2002. The Use of Dense Stereo Range Data in Augmented Reality. In *Proceedings of the 1st International Symposium on Mixed and Augmented Reality (ISMAR '02)*, 14–23. Washington, DC: IEEE Computer Society.

Gross, M., S. Würmlin, M. Naef, E. Lamboray, C. Spagno, A. Kunz, E. Koller-Meier, et al. 2003. Blue-C: A Spatially Immersive Display and 3D Video Portal for Telepresence. In *ACM SIGGRAPH 2003 Papers (SIGGRAPH '03)*, 819–827. New York: ACM.

Izadi, S., D. Kim, O. Hilliges, D. Molyneaux, R. Newcombe, P. Kohli, J. Shotton, S. Hodges, D. Freeman, A. Davison, and A. Fitzgibbon. 2011. KinectFusion: Real-Time 3D Reconstruction and Interaction Using a Moving Depth Camera. In *Proceedings of the 24th Annual ACM Symposium on User Interface Software and Technology (UIST '11)*, 559–568. New York: ACM.

Jacobs, K., J.-D. Nahmias, C. Angus, A. Reche, C. Loscos, and A. Steed. 2005. Automatic Generation of Consistent Shadows for Augmented Reality. In *Proceedings of Graphics Interface*

2005 (GI '05), 113–120. Waterloo, ON: Canadian Human-Computer Communications Society, School of Computer Science, University of Waterloo.

Kato, H., and M. Billinghurst. 1999. Marker Tracking and HMD Calibration for a Video-Based Augmented Reality Conferencing System. In *Proceedings of the 2nd IEEE and ACM International Workshop on Augmented Reality (IWAR '99)*, 85–94. Washington, DC: IEEE Computer Society.

Lepetit, V., L. Vacchetti, D. Thalmann, and P. Fua. 2003. Fully Automated and Stable Registration for Augmented Reality Applications. In *Proceedings of the 2nd IEEE and ACM International Symposium on Mixed and Augmented Reality*, 93–102. New York: ACM.

Milgram, P., and F. Kishino. 1994. A Taxonomy of Mixed Reality Visual Displays. *IEICE Transactions on Information Systems* E77-D (12): 1321–1329.

Piekarski, W., and B. H. Thomas. 2001. Tinmith-Metro: New Outdoor Techniques for Creating City Models with an Augmented Reality Wearable Computer. In *Proceedings of the 5th IEEE International Symposium on Wearable Computers (ISWC '01)*, 31–38. Washington, DC: IEEE Computer Society.

Raskar, R., G. Welch, M. Cutts, A. Lake, L. Stesin, and H. Fuchs. 1998. The ofFice of the Future: A Unified Approach to Image-Based Modeling and Spatially Immersive Displays. In *Proceedings of the 25th Annual Conference on Computer Graphics and Interactive Techniques (SIGGRAPH '98)*, 179–188. New York: ACM.

Sheridan, T. B. 1992. Musings on Telepresence and Virtual Presence. *Presence: Teleoperators and Virtual Environments* 1 (1): 120–126.

Shreiner, D., and E. Angel. 2011. *Interactive Computer Graphics: A Top-Down Approach with Shader-Based OpenGL*. 6th edition. Boston, MA: Pearson Education.

Slater, M., A. Steed, and Y. Chrysanthou. 2001. *Computer Graphics and Virtual Environments: From Realism to Real-Time*. Boston, MA: Addison-Wesley Longman.

Slater, M., A. Steed, J. McCarthy, and F. Maringelli. 1998. The Virtual Ante-Room: Assessing Presence through Expectation and Surprise. In *Virtual Environments '98: Proceedings of the Eurographics Workshop in Stuttgart, Germany, June 16–18, 1998*, edited by M. Goebel, U. Lang, J. Landauer, and M. Wapler, 41–48. New York: Springer.

Steed, A., S. Benford, N. Dalton, C. Greenhalgh, I. MacColl, C. Randell, and H. Schnädelbach. 2002. Mixed Reality Interfaces to Immersive Projection Systems. Paper presented to the Immersive Projection Technology Workshop, March, Orlando, FL.

Usoh, M., K. Arthur, M. C. Whitton, R. Bastos, A. Steed, M. Slater, and F. P. Brooks Jr. 1999. Walking > Walking-in-Place > Flying, in Virtual Environments. In *Proceedings of the 26th Annual Conference on Computer Graphics and Interactive Techniques (SIGGRAPH '99)*, 359–364. New York: ACM Press / Addison-Wesley.

Wagner, D., T. Pintaric, F. Ledermann, and D. Schmalstieg. 2005. Towards Massively Multi-user Augmented Reality on Handheld Devices. In *Proceedings of the Third International Conference on Pervasive Computing (PERVASIVE'05)*, edited by H.-W. Gellersen, R. Want, and A. Schmidt, 208–219. Berlin: Springer.

Welch, G., and E. Foxlin. 2002. Motion Tracking: No Silver Bullet, but a Respectable Arsenal. *IEEE Computer Graphics and Applications* 22 (6): 24–38.

CHAPTER 27

....

THE TRANSLATION
OF ART IN
VIRTUAL WORLDS

....

PATRICK LICHTY

WITHIN the past decade, virtual worlds have emerged as a prominent factor in technological culture. Virtual economies such as those of games like *Everquest* have rivaled
gross domestic products of small nations (King and Borland 2003, 221–228), and record
numbers of users are participating in online games and environments. Another aspect
of emergent technoculture, that is, the culture that emerges from the confluence of society and high technology, is the formation of virtual artists' communities in corresponding online worlds including *World of Warcraft* (WoW) and *Second Life* (SL). The works
generated by these virtual communities include virtual galleries of 2D works translated
into 3D galleries, *machinima* (video works created from the capture of live action in virtual worlds), performance, and interactive in-world works. From these practices and
modes of representation there arise questions of modality, audience, context, and formalism. This text will examine New Media art practices in virtual worlds, and the online
virtual environment SL in particular, and consider the context and translation of these
works from the tangible to the virtual, the "mixed/cybrid," the formal work of virtual art
to discern its function between modes of existence, and its location within culture.

This discussion needs to be more closely defined, as the word "virtual" alludes
to nearly anything operating through computer digital mediation, including networks, cellular nets, the Internet, and virtual environments. The discussion herein is
limited to real-time 3D platforms, including multiplayer online role-playing games
(MMORPGs) like WoW and multi user virtual environments (MUVEs) like SL. Even
this level of specificity leaves a problematically large set of examples; thus this study will
focus on practices within SL. While we may elide some aspects of social functions of
3D online environments such as differences between multiplayer online gaming and
non-goal-oriented world platforms, the issues of form, audience, and engagement
remain consistent. It is by examining the specific effects of art in virtual worlds that, as

Grau states, an analysis can be made in terms not only of comparison to history, but in relation to it as well as contemporary practice in terms of phenomenology, aesthetics, and origination (Grau 2004, 8–10).

ASPECTS OF PRACTICE

Four aspects of artistic practice in virtual worlds relate to the representational modality and the permeability of the boundary between worlds, associated problems of audience, context of the virtual or transmediated, and questions of form. Modality refers to the location and vector direction of the work's relation between worlds, such as importing physical work into *Second Life*, or the realization of SL-based works in the physical (directly or via interpretation). Audiences for virtual work are often small, as servers can only manage limited numbers of avatars (usually 50–75 per region), and presuppose certain educational and technical resources, as well as one's familiarity with online/technoculture. It can be said that context is cultural as well as technical, as virtual worlds have their own specific cultures, and art created for one milieu may not translate well to another. Last, is there a virtual formalism in online worlds? Before looking at works in SL, let us examine these four attributes (modality, audience, context, and formalism), then consider a series of artists' works that fall under this framework.

Considering representational modalities in virtual-world-based art, the nature of communication is dependent upon its location and vector. What I mean by vector is a gesture of direction, simultaneity, concurrence, or stasis in regards to its movement between worlds. For example, execution of a virtual project exhibits a gesture defined by formal, cultural, and conceptual contexts. Is it a purely virtual installation, meant to be experienced from inside the world only, akin to Char Davies's early VR work *Ephemere* (Wands 2006)? In *Ephemere*, users donned traditional glove and goggles for a first-person VR experience, and navigated using a vest that controlled their movement in the environment by sensing their breathing and translating that to buoyancy in the virtual world. Aside from the simulated world, are there different levels of representation of work outside of the online experience, either as edited media, or realized virtual structures in physical form? Or, is the work in question basically two-dimensional work translated into a virtual construct? This epistemological "movement" within and between worlds has four basic structures: work that is essentially traditional physical art translated to the virtual, "evergent" work that is physically realized from virtual origins, the virtual itself, designed entirely for the client/browser experience, and "cybrids" (as we will discuss subsequently) that exist concurrently between various modalities.

The semiotics of the reiteration of tangible works in virtual space is straightforward, as is work meant to be experienced entirely in-world. However, movement from the virtual to the tangible, which includes consideration of works existing with simultaneous physical and virtual components, presents complex models. Artist Marcos Novak has used the term "evergence" to refer to the physicalization of structures that have their origin in the virtual. While evergent technologies and artworks have been realized through haptic devices and sensor arrays, other technologies like rapid prototyping and computerized fabrication are more direct examples of processes illustrating properties of evergence. However, the idea of evergence only addresses the "original" work of virtual art whose vector everges it into the physical, but does not account for simultaneous modes of representation, which is the subject of the cybrid.

Peter Anders, in his book *Envisioning Cyberspace* (1998, 193–196), explored the "cybrid" environment existing simultaneously in virtual and physical modes. Examples of cybridity are augmented reality, physical computing, and telepresence. In SL, cybridity is limited as it utilizes only the physical interfaces of screen, keyboard, and mouse, and does not integrate the physical environment as part of the interface to the virtual. There are works that clearly illustrate the cybrid, an example being Perry Hoberman's *Systems Maintenance* (1998),[1] in which a room's layout is reiterated in virtual, miniature, and full-scale forms. The interactor is challenged to consider the (in)consistencies between worlds by aligning, composing, or resolving these juxtapositions. Contrasted with Hoberman, SL is far more virtual, though artists in this discussion attempt to problematize this platonic duality. Additionally, a metaphor in relation to the cybrid is that Linden Lab's (the maker of SL) product name itself is proxy as an existential overlay to the physical. Linden Lab's invocation of this metaphor raises questions about the intent of the creation of such worlds and how (or if) artists engage with virtual environments. Virtual/physical concurrence can be passive/multimodal (i.e., Second Front performances) or direct (physical computing), representing a developing arena for mixed-mode virtual works. However, modality is related to the question of form through the use of medium and development of context, and is our next topic.

How an artist communicates through a medium (context, mode) is also relative to what the artist says (form, content). The previous two artists covered here fulfill the content portion in the first half of the chapter, leading us to form. The problem of formalism leads us to the criticism of Greenberg and Antin. Greenberg, in essays such as "The New Sculpture" and "American-Type Painting" (Greenberg 1961), developed the aesthetics of high modernist formalism that stress the essence of the medium, foregrounding artists such as Rothko and Judd. Greenberg solidifies the link between the "medium and the message," paralleling other thinkers such as McLuhan.

The problem with invoking Greenberg stems from his foundations in material formalism taken in context with the formalism of virtual worlds, where there is only a simulation of it. One could say that there is formalism in code, or in clients like SL as defined by their methods of representation, such as through 3D hardware/graphics cards and software drivers, as well as the tools themselves. Methods of modeling, texturing of objects, and virtual projection define formalism for virtual worlds, if one can remap from modernism to postmodernism by substituting the object for the Baudrillardian simulacrum. Verisimilitude of form is what becomes essential in virtual worlds and in subsequent layers/protocols, such as the client, code, and constructors.

While Greenberg provides some answers regarding virtual formalism, David Antin offers the added dimension of distinctive qualities of a medium. In *Video: The Distinctive Features of the Medium* (1986), Antin defines formal qualities of video as being distinct from TV as being created bottom up, rather than hegemonically/institutionally (top-down). This could distinguish open environments like SL versus video games like WoW, in that in games, the objects are "mostly" defined, or are at least not easily modified. The perceived problem may be that the SL software is made by a corporation, the art-structures created by the users, much like the Portapak "portable" video recorder as created by Sony. However, in WoW, *EverQuest, Eve Online*, and so on, the universe, characters, and modalities are tightly defined, thus creating a more limited context for expression.

Also related to audience engagement through works in virtual worlds is the cultural context of the milieu, as virtual worlds have specific cultures. This is proportional to the degree of user involvement and community coherence. Evidence of cultural specificity in SL is illustrated by words like "griefing" (social disruption), "Ruthing" (the fact that all avatars materialize as females, or "Ruths"), and "Goreans" (the community of role players using John Norman's *Gor* pulp fantasy book series). Specific terms also exist for worlds like WoW, and these linguistic traces illustrate cultural peculiarities of online worlds, but this is not limited to the virtual. There are numerous semiotic differences from culture to culture, such as the gesture for "OK" in the West possible being interpreted for money (*okane*) in Japanese culture or the signification of white as representing purity or death. Therefore, the virtual artist has tremendous communication challenges, not only in regards to bridging misperceptions between contemporary and New Media art cultures, but also the particular environment that the artist is working in.

This is evident in a 2007 ban on what is termed as ageplay, or depiction of child avatars in what might be considered erotic or sexual situations. The issue, as reported by Reuters's SL office (Reuters 2007) is that the ability to modify avatars, or virtual bodies, into childlike forms has resulted in "childplay," or simulated sexual acts with childlike avatars. The sim-sex practice created controversy in the Netherlands, Italy, and other countries in which child pornography laws are far more stringent than in the United States, and was banned by Linden Lab in 2007. This writer does not contest the illegality of child pornography, but what is more interesting is a strange parallel to American controversy over child nudity in the arts (see also Ess, chapter 41 in this volume).

In 2007, artists Zoe Hartnell and Sysperia Poppy created artworks for their *The King Has Fallen* gallery, which are mostly offline due to in-world controversy (Hartnell and Poppy 2007). These depicted Hartnell's dolls in Victorian "gothic lolita" style, a fashion style popular in Japan in the first decade of the century, in various erotic configurations. Hartnell's works echo Hans Bellmer's *La Poupee* (Lichtenstein 2001) in their manipulation of anatomically correct dolls, as well as commonly available Japanese makes of dolls. In August 2007, Hartnell and Poppy's gallery was taken offline by the artists because of community controversy regarding their work and its relation to the child-play ban instituted by Linden Lab. While this sort of controversy has its precedents in the representation of child-forms such as the 1989 Mapplethorpe exhibition at the Cincinnati CAC, the general ban on erotic depictions of childlike avatars shows the challenges the artist faces in terms of representational practice and cultural context in a given environment.

Another issue specific to the creation of work in virtual worlds is that of audience. Audience engagement can be problematic as there are limitations of server technology. A region in SL has a maximum avatar capacity of 100 concurrent users, and areas begin to fail at fewer than 80 visitors at a time because of server and network workloads. The SL client (as well as most MMORPG games) requires a high-performance computer system. These two requirements limit the audience in terms of actual number of people who can experience a work at one time, as well as establishing socioeconomic barriers for the patron. This is due to the relatively high system and network connection requirements and requisite technical proficiencies, including figuring out different interface paradigms and learning 3D modeling tools and programming, creating assumptions of privilege in online worlds. Therefore, universal access to virtual work cannot be assumed to be viable, but questions remain as to the sociocultural impact of art residing in virtual worlds.

The social effects of representational practices in virtual worlds and how they reach audiences are mixed, and their reactions are unpredictable. The incident of the "nuclear bomb" on the Australian ABC Island (Canning 2007) drew widespread attention more as a novelty than as threat, and there are questions as to its being a media fabrication for publicity by ABC itself. Regardless, it is emblematic of a practice called "griefing," a form of in-world aggravation that seldom results in more than bemused news stories or, in extreme cases, restoration of an SL region to a previous state. Although griefing is merely an extreme case of an in-world agitprop practice, interventions of art would not gain much attention except for the efforts of external media bloggers, interventionists' sites, and the occasional news organization. In the case of the virtual work of art, in most cases, it is the metaphorical case of the tree falling in the woods needing a witness to experience the sound of its toppling.

Intermezzo: From Pataphysics to Practice

I have discussed some of the concerns that I have experienced in the creation of art in virtual worlds as an artist and critic. Form, audience, context, and modality frame many of the issues of praxis intrinsic to the creation of work in these spaces. The following is an explication of artists' practices in SL that illustrates different configurations of the four qualities that I have discussed. In addition, the reader may notice the direction that my narrative takes from the "imported" physical work, to the evergent/cybrid, to the wholly virtual. It is through this movement from the largely physical to the wholly virtual that I hope to create an epistemic continuum from which we derive understanding of the different ways artists engage with virtual worlds.

REPRESENTATIONAL VECTORS IN VIRTUAL ART

The Problem of Transmediation

According to the definition in *Webster's Revised Unabridged Dictionary*, transliteration is "The act or product of transliterating, or of expressing words of a language by means of the characters of another alphabet."

Thus, one of the first steps artists take in integrating their work into virtual worlds is the practice of transmediation, or the translation between environments/milieus, that is, physical work moved into virtual spaces. This, paraphrased from the Second Life Community Conference presentation by the MacArthur Foundation's Connie Yowell, is the recreation of the physical in the virtual, and a method of orienting oneself in unfamiliar terrain. This, says Yowell, is the first step in the engagement with virtual worlds, as transmediation of the physical is a gesture of recreating the familiar in alien milieus in order to orient oneself in terms of space, identity, community, culture, and history. Transmediation of traditional media (2D art) into the virtual is reminiscent of the contextual incongruities as mentioned regarding Hoberman's *Systems Maintenance*. Using this piece as a metaphor, we can see that the transmediator tries to align tangible and virtual, but then cybrid and virtual formalists are less concerned with continuity, being more interested in the differences and distinctions between worlds and scales.

It is problematic to appear critical of artists re-presenting print, painting, and photography in virtual worlds as merely making an analogy to a 3D website or direct remodeling of a conventional white box gallery into a virtual world. A conversation with Warhol Factory superstar Bibbe Hansen in her SL gallery, built with son Channing, encapsulates the issues of remediation clearly. For her, making virtual galleries was "difficult" for a number of reasons, including presence and issues of scale on different screen sizes. These issues necessitate formal adjustments of the work to compensate for perception via client-based experience, such as ensuring different sizing of work, different placement to ensure proper viewing angles, and avatar ergonomics. But, conversely, community and real-time social interaction through avatar embodiment-by-proxy within the virtual gallery do make it more than merely a 3D website. However, other issues come into play, including attendance and synchronic time—which are issues for all 3D installations and vibrant sites for conversation that fall outside the scope of this chapter.

The issue of what my colleague Gregory Little and I have called "attendance" or "attended work" is a problem with so much computational/New Media art. This relates to the matter of an artist or other docent needing to attend to the work for many reasons—perhaps the work is not intuitive in its operation. Or perhaps software or hardware requires nursing in that it fails occasionally and the gallery/museum personnel lack the technical training or time to demonstrate the work or reboot the machinery. SL is particularly problematic in this respect in that its interface is so complex that it often requires a docent to lead the nonenthusiast through the environment.

Synchronic time under my definition can have two meanings. First, it has to do with events in real-time mediated environments, for example MUVEs like SL, being accessible, more or less, worldwide *at the same time.* That is, a performance that is enacted at noon "Second Life Time" (or Pacific Standard Time, as SL computer servers reside in California) happens in the late evening in Istanbul. For example, when I collaborated with Beijing-based artist Cao Fei for the Yokohama Biennial, I had to keep in mind that she was often online synchronically in exact opposition to my clock, twelve hours ahead.

The other issue of asynchronicity is that SL is a real-time environment, and the preservation of work is often kept through "machinima" or machine-cinema edited from captures of live action from inside the environment. Asynchronicity is introduced when the machinima separates viewers in time from the live events, therefore taking them out of context with live events. Simply put—the recorded/edited event in SL, or any other virtual world, operates in a time separate from that of the moment of its occurrence, and this difference in synchronicity changes the context of the experience of the work.

Transmediation and the Collision of Cultures

Adding to the challenges of translation of embodiment and representation between mediums, there are the challenges of cultural heterogeneity in online worlds and their respective aesthetics. It is no surprise that commercialism and high culture, wrapped inside the integral role that commerce plays in SL, would clash. Clement Greenberg, in *Avant-Garde and Kitsch,* problematizes the avant-garde's disconnection with patronage and the rise of mass production commodity culture. Combined with the rise of a mass digital imaging/video culture through inexpensive tools and distribution networks, two social strata appear.

First, the ubiquity of commerce fosters creation of a commodity decor art economy that, Greenberg says, "demands nothing of its customers except money—not even their time" (Greenberg 1961, 7). Greenberg also posits the commodity art scene as not entirely devoid of content, but being more akin to folk art than the high arts of the Western tradition that were supported by patronage before the rise of the twentieth-century avant-garde. The linkage of populist art to capitalism is a logical association in SL culture, bearing cultural similarities to Greenberg's analogy to avant-garde disconnection from capital, and the commercial and decor art market belonging to mass culture.

Cultural stratification was evident at the Second Life Community Conference in 2007, where the event's Art Expo featured artists from the online community. In line with Greenberg's expectations of kitsch's "appearance" of culture, the exhibitors presented abstract art that either drew heavy influences from popular fin-de-siècle artists like Kandinsky and Matisse, or abstract cyberart similar to that of the mid-1990s. The numerous online shops in SL that offer virtual decor art for virtual homes mirrors the multi-million-dollar tangible decor market. The issue is that in the early days of mass virtual cultures, contexts and audiences emerge that seem to reflect the tangible. As with the tangible world, the issue of art and reproduction tends to center on the function of the work, including issues of intent, content, context, and audience; analogies being Maxfield Parrish versus Titian, or even Kinkaide versus Bierstadt.

The Problem Children: Remediation/Reiteration

While transmediation of works into virtual worlds centers its issues on problems of representation and culture, including commerce's convergence with culture in the case of SL, the next shift toward the virtual deals with the representation of performance-based works in virtual worlds. A work that informs this strategy is Marina Abramovic's 2005 Guggenheim work *Seven Easy Pieces* (Abramovic 2005), where she recreated seven performance artworks in new contexts. Many of these works, the most striking of which was Vito Acconci's *Seedbed*, both reiterate and recontextualize the texts. This set of performances, stated Abramovic, was intended to refresh the history of performance art by recreating these experiences through virtual embodiment. The issue that Abramovic foregrounds in her recreation is the relation of context to the subtlety of meaning in performance. In the case of Acconci's work, the onanistic element of *Seedbed* is fundamentally reformulated by the change in gender. In this way, Abramovic, through this work and the six others, questions the specificity of the pieces' context in terms of time, place, and embodiment. But then one may ask, does reiteration of a work preserve its meaning in a different context by remediating from the tangible to the virtual? If one can learn from Marina Abramovic's performance of classic performance artworks in her 2005 *Seven Easy Pieces* exhibition, and then Eva and Franco Mattes's remediation of other classic performances into SL, the lesson would be that context is an essential part of any art. Context and environment are as essential to a work as a frame is to a painting.

I use the term *remediated* performance (the whole notion of remediation and translation between media being dealt with at length in an excellent volume by Bolter and Grusin [2000]) as used by artists including Scott Kildall and Eva/Franco Mattes (Mattes 2010) to describe practices that recreate works in performance art in virtually "embodied" media. With both artists, the recreation/remediation of performance artworks serves two purposes. It subverts the visceral immediacy that performance art creates by eliminating the body. Conversely, these remediation artists playfully ask the question of affect in virtual performance through the viewer's connection to the avatar. This tension between subverting the immediacy of the body and invoking our identification with the virtual doppelganger illustrates the difficulty in being in the liminal space of being present in two worlds.

In *Paradise Ahead* (2006), Kildall recreates 12 performance pieces, exploiting the virtual "zone of ambiguity" that simulated worlds present while referencing the familiarity of the body and iconic art performances.[2] In this series, Kildall recreates works by Abramovic (*Rest Energy*), Burden (*Shoot*), Ono (*Cut Piece*, fig. 27.1), Klein (*Leap Into the Void*), and Tan (*Lift*) that center discourse at the vicarious site of the body, but the embodied threat becomes ironic through the virtualization of the site. Burden's *Shoot*

FIGURE 27.1 *Paradise Ahead—Yoko Ono's Cut Piece.* Copyright 2007 by Scott Kildall. http://www.kildall.com/artwork/2007/paradise_ahead/images/05_diptych.jpg, Accessed August 16, 2013.

becomes a referent to the familiar work, but also resembles a first-person shooter game mise en scène. By confronting the (virtual) body, Kildall leaves us torn between Dionysian visceral engagement of danger, abandon, flight, pain, and epiphany and the Apollonian rationalization of the throwaway avatar. Each work hovers between oblivion and the eternally respawnable in the uncomfortable space between the virtual "toy" body and flesh and blood.

On the other hand, the Mattes' *Thirteen Most Beautiful Avatars,* as seen in figure 27.2 (2006) references Warhol's series of film portraiture from 1964 to 1965, including *Thirteen Most Wanted Men, Thirteen Most Beautiful Boys,* and *50 Personalities.*[3] In *Avatars,* the Mattes create close-ups of avatars from SL, including avatar celebrities of the time. Where Warhol created rather abject, mugshot-like vignettes of his subjects, each avatar portrait is coquettish and dramatic, illustrating the techno-utopian dream of eternal youth and beauty, and the YouTube promise of everyone having their 15,000 website hits of fame. The irony is in the ideal of fame and beauty in SL, which is an astute read by the artists, first in that fame in a microcosmic environment is analogous to fame in any online community (often that of visibility), and second in that beauty is an exercise of fashion shopping for clothes, skins, and bodies. When a community that has generated as much media attention as that of SL, and where anyone is as beautiful as patience to shop for accoutrements and pocketbooks allows, who are the famous? More importantly, in the land where everyone is potentially beautiful, who are the "most" beautiful? The irony of this is that in a world where beauty is universally attainable, the concept itself becomes rhetorical, and in essence, more a matter of fetish and fashion.

Another ironic piece is the Mattes' remediation of Joseph Beuys's *7000 Oaks,*[4] originally sponsored by New York City's Dia Foundation as a project for Documenta 7. Designed as a mission for social and environmental change, *7000 Oaks* took five years

FIGURE 27.2 *Thirteen Most Beautiful Avatars*. Source: Eva and Franco Mattes, aka 0100101110101101.ORG.http://www.0100101110101101.org/home/portraits/, Accessed August 16, 2013.

to complete, with 7,000 trees with corresponding columnar basalt stones, the last of which were planted at Documenta 8 in 1987. The Mattes' remediation, created in SL on the twenty-fifth anniversary of the 1982 inauguration, and with locations in at least two regions, reiterates the Beuys work as "part of a global mission to effect environmental and social change."[5] The "stones" are evident throughout the virtual world, which obviously either has participatory effects or fosters awareness of the original's intent or both. The remediation of Beuys's work in the virtual is problematized by Julian Bleecker's missive "When 1st Life Meets 2nd Life: The 1685 Pound Avatar and the 99 Ton Acre" (Bleecker 2007), where he does some calculations and posits that an avatar emits the same amount of CO_2 as driving an SUV 1,293 miles, or an acre of virtual land emitting 99 tons of greenhouse gases. Perhaps this is the logical function of placing *7000 Oaks* in SL, but it illustrates the difficulties of reconciling the vector of recontextualizing conceptual works from the tangible into the virtual, in terms of pragmatism and performativity.

The Evergents: Extruding Physicality from the Virtual

For our discussion, we have been describing gestures and translations between the virtual and the tangible worlds. In the case of transmediated work, conventional/

traditional artwork is directly translated into the virtual with little formal modification. As mentioned, there is little augmentation to the work, and in many cases, the work meets challenges of the necessity for re-presentation in virtual worlds because of altered issues of perspective and scale. Or the transmediated work is reduced to Greenbergian commodity kitsch or a form of digital folk/populist art. In our third case study, the remediators tackle the challenges of recontextualization of performative works and the contradictions and tensions they create between the body and the avatar. The first represents a direct translation from the tangible to the virtual, and the second represents a vector pointing to the virtual from the tangible. The next logical point of departure is the inversion of the remediation vector, or the gesture from the virtual to the tangible, or the gesture of evergence, or the emergence into the physical from the virtual where no physical referent had previously existed.

A pop culture reference illustrating the concept is the emergence of the character Flynn from the computer world in the movie *Tron* (Lisberger et al. 1982). The flaw in this argument is that Flynn had been digitized into the ENTCOM mainframe, and a better metaphor would be that the anthropomorphic program-construct Tron had materialized into the physical world himself. From a metaphorical perspective, there are a number of artists who have practices that center around constructed identities that are re-presented in the physical, like Mariko Mori's *Pop Idol* action figure edition for Parkett. But, since this discussion deals specifically with representational practices in virtual worlds, a prime example would be the development of work of Lynn Hershman-Leeson.

For years, Hershmann has explored the practice of constructed, mediated, and manipulated identities, a seminal work being her series of Roberta Breitmore works of the 1970s. In these works, Roberta is described as a constructed person interacting with real people. For four years, Hershman-Leeson "performed" Roberta's life in various contexts in San Francisco, documenting her "life" in installation and photography. For *Life to the Second Power*,[6] she created a mixed reality archive in SL based on her 1972 work, *Dante Hotel*. Her various fictive personas, including Breitmore, reborn as Roberta Ware, join software constructs DiNA and Agent Ruby in the Life Squared archive in "NeWare Island" maintained by Stanford University. What is more interesting is Hershman-Leeson's evergence of the virtual Roberta with rapid prototyping company Fabjectory as an extension of her metaphor of realizing the conceptual Roberta in the streets of San Francisco. However, the Roberta (Ware) who is the denizen of the *Life to the Second Power* installation in figure 27.3, now exists as a miniature statue, is perhaps the "real" Roberta Ware, as opposed to the "dramatization" of Roberta Breitmore. The Stanford project is a logical extension of Hershman-Leeson's work in mediated identity, and brings it to the wholly virtual.

The Simulacrum as Root Node: SL-Based Works

In *Simulacra and Simulation* (1994), Jean Baudrillard wrote of simulated culture, or one that exists without a referent to the real, but expresses itself in terms superseding

FIGURE 27.3 *Life Squared*, 2007. Courtesy Lynn Hershman-Leeson. http://presence.stanford. edu:3455/collaboratory/346, Accessed August 16, 2013.

the real. While it might be possible to create works that exist in the virtual that do not express themselves in terms of references to the tangible, they are likely also extremely subtle or outside the embodied paradigm of human experience. The previous example of Breitmore/Ware is problematic in that one could argue Breitmore is a hybrid identity, and that Ware is a cybrid, existing in multiple worlds. While this may be true, the function of using Ware as exemplar is that of William Gibson's repeating trope of extrusion of the virtual into the tangible; my categorization of works may define cultural "functions" of key aspects of the artists' installations more concisely than the whole of a given piece. Therefore, for the discussion of art that acts as simulacra of craft and proxies of identity, tangible referents here are seen as merely representative or "theaters" for the simulacrum. This is the case of Cao Fei's *iMirror* installation at the 2007 Venice Bienniale.

A three-part documentary about her time as a "cosplayer" (person who dresses in genre costumes, such as fetish, anime, and so on) in SL (Cao 2007), *iMirror* (fig. 27.4) continues the ongoing dialogue about mediated identity including artists like Hershman-Leeson, but much more specifically the impact of Asian pop media. This international conversation includes work by Huyghe et al. (*No Ghost, Just a Shell*), Mori (*Idol Singer*), and Murakami (*Hiropon, Little Boy* exhibition), and questions the relationship in defining cultural identity. Fei takes this one step further, extrapolating the obfuscation of abstracted identity by representing a virtual anime character flaneur piloted

FIGURE 27.4 A Second Life Machinima, 28 min. Cao Fei/China Tracy, *I•Mirror*, 2007. Courtesy of Artist and Vitamin Creative Space. Image provided directly by Vitamin Creative, 2009.

by a Chinese woman in a rapidly changing world navigating through a wholly mediated milieu.

In *iMirror*, Cao Fei represents three aspects of SL, the commercial/popular perspective, the affective/narrative (through her virtual love story), and a series of avatar portraits to describe it as a place, another of being, and as a community. The Venice Biennale installation consisted of a dome-like structure where the various components of *iMirror* are mirrored in SL. According to critic Domenico Quaranta, the installation represents the melancholic quality of online worlds, and gives the viewer a real flavor of virtual existence (Quaranta 2007). But on the other hand, Quaranta also states that the more "genuine" Fei tries to make the work, the more distortions between realities emerge, making both "theaters" in the (in)tangible problematic. However, it is this problematic nature that reifies *iMirror*, like *No Ghost, Just a Shell*, as a purely virtual work that is difficult to frame.

The last of the "purely virtual" artists under consideration here is the Italian avatar artist Gazira Babeli.[7] Gazira, which is another word for transient, admits to no physical existence, except vague admissions to being a "pirate signal" beamed out of Milan. This is where Babeli meshes her practice with other New Media "code artists" like Mez Breeze. Gazira is like the *Neuromancer* AI who interacts ironically with her native platform; observing, injecting noise (*Grey Goo*), suffering temptation (*Gaz of the Desert* [after Bunuel, a frame of which is seen in fig. 27.5]). The traces of her existence as SL scripts, text, and video are on her site, but little of her seems to everge into the tangible, except for web traces. The rest of her interventions are wholly online, with persistent installations of attacking Warhol soup cans, singing pizzas, and collapsing monoliths

FIGURE 27.5 *Gaz of the Desert*. Image courtesy Gazira Babeli. Image provided directly by Gazira Babeli, 2009.

on Locusolus Island. Gazira is probably one of the most frustrating artists for her opacity between worlds (more so even than Hershman-Leeson/Breitmore), but also one of the more entertaining, as Gaz is a fractious autonomous spirit who threatens to everge from the virtual, but is a winking signifier of chaos in an otherwise highly ordered world.

The Cybrids: Concurrent Practices and Virtual Worlds

The last representational strategy left is where artists occupy several spaces simultaneously. The closest yet may be Hershman-Leeson or Cao Fei, but in their respective bodies of work the "center of gravity," or focus, is firmly in the tangible or the virtual. In the case of the cybrid artist, there is the gesture of concurrence, that is, praxis that is designed to operate simultaneously in the virtual (in-world), online (Internet-based), and tangible spaces. The formal issues for simultaneous representation in mixed worlds are similar to those encountered by Kit Galloway in the 1980 conceptual work *Hole in Space*,[8] in which a life-sized video "hole" collapsed the space between New York and Los Angeles. Although Galloway's metaphor for punching through physical space with mediated space is very direct, it still speaks strongly enough that exhibitions have taken place that explore the boundaries between worlds.

Turbulence.org's *Mixed Realities* commissions (2007) address paradoxes of works stretching across multiple worlds.[9] Works by John Craig Freeman, Usman Haque et al., Kildall and Scott, Magruder et al., and Pierre Proske were selected for their engagement with SL, online/Internet, and physical interactions. These include constructing works in virtual worlds, everging/controlling them and creating multiple interactions. A work that takes the Galloway metaphor and expands it into interactions as signals reverberate between worlds is Proske's *Caterwaul*.[10] Far from the utopian messages of human connection in *Hole in Space,* the Proske piece features the line, "When someone screams in real life, do they hear us in virtual reality? Do they want to?" A 12-foot by 15-foot wall is embedded with five microphones and a series of speakers linked to SL through a Max/MSP patch. In *Caterwaul,* the gallery sounds are transmitted to the Turbulence server and to the SL space, but through the translation to the virtual, the sounds reverberate, degrade, and feed back to create a howl of lamentation. Drawing parallels to Quaranta's comments regarding the distortions between multiple realities, *Caterwaul* takes Galloway's connective portal and injects the self-reflexivity of the semiotic gap to illustrate the imperfect translation between worlds.

Another group using the Galloway metaphor to explore linkages between spaces is the virtual performance art group Second Front. Consisting of nine members from Vancouver to Milan, Second Front probes the social issues of virtual worlds through critical and playful situations. Their October 4 performance for the opening of the IMAL New Media Center in Brussels, entitled *The Gate* (2007),[11] was a trompe l'oeil of Rodin's *The Gates of Hell* that looked out upon a portal that fed live bidirectional video between the Odyssey Island art server and IMAL. In tangible space, *The Gate* is a life-sized projection of the writhing tableau vivant avatar sculpture and reception area created by Yannick Antoine and Yves Bernard, while a similar area is evident in the virtual, illustrated in figures 27.6 and 27.7. Even though the metaphor to Galloway is evident, the distortions remain, as Rodin's vision erupted with hails of pontoon boats and anvils from a faucet at its top, reiterating the irruptions between the virtual and the tangible.

One other aspect of Second Front's praxis that illustrates their self-reflexivity regarding performance across multiple worlds is the dissemination of their interventions as media performance itself. Paying attention to the question how many people can constitute an online audience at one time, Second Front recontextualizes its performances as edited performance videos and narrative blog. The goal is that multiple audiences from the viral/machinima, blogosphere, and SL art cultures are addressed through dissemination of information in manners/gestures tailored for the given audience. Where this representation of performance through different media channels, adjusting the message to fit the medium and mode of delivery, becomes problematic is at the boundary of performance it questions. Given this question, are Second Front's different media interventions merely different forms of documentation or media performance, with differing time scales of audience feedback? It is at this fundamental questioning of time, space, performance, and representation that virtual art challenges traditional and Internet New Media.

FIGURE 27.6 *The Gate (or Hole in Space, Reloaded)*. Image courtesy Yannick Antoine / Yves Bernard and Second Front. http://www.imal.org/TheGate/img/hi/hires3.jpg, Accessed August 16 2013.

Conclusion

Throughout this chapter, we have traversed between the tangible and virtual while combining possibilities of moving from one to the other, as well as artists operating in simultaneity in multiple worlds. In musing upon movement from one to the other, this essay attempts to propose some formal, modal, and contextual issues as grist for the ongoing conversation on the development of art created within virtual social worlds. The range of praxis that artists engage with is multivalent, from the relatively direct transmediated oeuvres to the enigmatic liminal works that live between worlds, and the wholly virtual; works that illustrate a form of embodied conceptualism. Although the works we have explored are extensive, there are others such as Alan Sondheim / Sandy Baldwin, Adam Nash, Annabeth Robinson, Nathaniel Stern, Avatar Orchestra Metaverse, and many others whose SL-based works engage in other performative, formal, and conceptual practices. While this early analysis suggests that artists may initially engage in recreating the tangible as a process of orienteering in virtual worlds, or even a Greenbergian reiteration of marketing/kitsch, practices diverge broadly after making the initial step into the

FIGURE 27.7 *The Gate (or Hole in Space, Reloaded)*. Image courtesy Yannick Antoine / Yves Bernard. From http://flickriver.com/groups/the_gate/pool/interesting/, Accessed August 16, 2013.

virtual. Ironically, while much of popular focus is centered on the transmediation, the most widely recognized works are in almost all the other representational modes: the remediated (Mattes), evergent (Hershman-Leeson), virtual (Cao Fei, Babeli), and cybrid (Second Front). Each addresses their modality, context, and audience outside of the virtual, even outside the New Media community, and therefore makes an argument for their apparent acceptance. The engagement with elements of virtual worlds within contemporary art presents challenges for artists and audiences alike. What is obvious from work of the mid-2000s is that it represents a site of intense inquiry and cultural activity, and it is hoped that this chapter will contribute to the conversation regarding art from virtual environments, its distinctive qualities, and its evolution.

NOTES

1. A video archive is at http://framework.v2.nl/archive/archive/leaf/other/.xslt/nodenr-142973, Dutch Electronic Arts Festival, Accessed January 23, 2009.
2. Documentation for Scott Kildall's *Paradise Ahead*, http://www.kildall.com/artwork/2007/paradise_ahead/paradise_ahead_description.html, Accessed January 16, 2009.
3. Eva Mattes and Franco Mattes, *Thirteen Most Beautiful Avatars*, installation, Postmasters Gallery, New York. For documentation see http://www.postmastersart.com/archive/010rg_07/010rg_07_window1.html, Accessed August 16, 2013.

4. Online documentation is at http://www.diacenter.org/ltproj/7000/1982, Accessed August 16, 2013.
5. Documentation for the Mattes' *7000 Oaks* (2008) is at http://www.0100101110101101.org/home/performances/performance-beuys.html, Accessed January 24, 2009.
6. Lynn Hershman-Leeson, *Life to the Second Power*, 2006–2007, online archive, http://presence.stanford.edu:3455/LynnHershman/261, Accessed January 25, 2009.
7. Her website is http://www.gazirababeli.com, Accessed January 12, 2009.
8. See Kit Galloway and Sherrie Rabinowitz, *Hole-In-Space*, online documentation, http://www.ecafe.com/getty/HIS/, Accessed January 15, 2009.
9. *Mixed Realities* commissions, http://transition.turbulence.org/comp_07/awards.html, Accessed January 12, 2009.
10. Pierre Proske, *Caterwaul*, 2007, online proposal, http://transition.turbulence.org/comp_07/proposals/proske/index.html, Accessed January 19, 2009.
11. IMAL Interactive Media Arts Laboratory, Brussels, Belgium, October 4, 2007. Documentation at http://www.we-make-money-not-art.com/archives/009770.php, Accessed January 16, 2009.

REFERENCES

Abramovic, M. 2005. *Seven Easy Pieces*. Guggenheim Museum, New York, November 9–15. http://www.guggenheim.org/exhibitions/abramovic/. Accessed January 16, 2009.

Anders, P. 1998. *Envisioning Cyberspace*. San Francisco: McGraw Hill.

Antin, D. 1986. Video: The Distinctive Features of the Medium. In Video Culture: *A Critical Investigation*, 147–166, edited by John G. Hanhardt. Layton, UT: G. M. Smith, Peregrine Smith Books, in association with Visual Studies Workshop Press.

Baudrillard, J. 1994. *Simulacra and Simulation*. Translated by Sheila Faria Glaser. Ann Arbor: University of Michigan Press.

Bleecker, J. 2007. When 1st Life Meets 2nd Life: The 1685 Pound Avatar and the 99 Ton Acre. *NearFutureLaboratory.com*. February 9. http://www.nearfuturelaboratory.com/index.php?p=297. Accessed January 22, 2009.

Bolter, J., and R. Grusin. 2000. *Remediation: Understanding New Media*, Cambridge, MA: MIT Press.

Canning, S. 2007. ABC's Virtual Site "Griefed." *News.com.au*, May 23. http://www.news.com.au/entertainment/story/0,23663,21780235-7486,00.html. Accessed January 12, 2009.

C. Fei. 2007. Interview by Paddy Johnson. *Art Fag City*, August 3, http://www.artfagcity.com/2007/08/03/1005/. Accessed January 12, 2009.

Grau, O. 2004. *Virtual Art*. Cambridge, MA: MIT Press.

Greenberg, C. 1961. Avant Garde and Kitsch. *Art and Culture: Critical Essays*. Boston, MA: Beacon Press.

Hartnell, Z., and Poppy, S. *Censorship is No Bueno*, http://archive.org/details/CensorshipIsNoBueno, Accessed January 11, 2009

King, B., and J. Borland. 2003. *Dungeons and Dreamers: The Rise of Computer Game Culture, from Geek to Chic*. San Francisco, CA: McGraw Hill.

Lichtenstein, T. 2001. *Behind Closed Doors: The Art of Hans Bellmer*. Berkeley: University of California Press.

Lisberger, S., dir. 1982. *Tron*. DVD. Los Angeles: Walt Disney / Buena Vista Productions.

Quaranta, D. 2007. Semiotic Phantoms. *Videoludica.com*. July 30. http://www.videoludica. com/news.php?news=706&lang=en. Accessed January 12, 2009.

Reuters, A. 2007. Virtual Porn Illegal in Italy. Reuters Second Life online news, February 23. http://secondlife.reuters.com/stories/2007/02/23/virtual-child-porn-illegal-in-italy/. Accessed January 17, 2009.

Wands, B. 2006. *Art of the Digital Age*. New York: Thames and Hudson.

CHAPTER 28

....

PAINTING, THE VIRTUAL, AND THE CELLULOID FRAME

....

SIMON J. HARRIS

THE discussion within this chapter originates from my inherent desire to understand how paintings are looked at. As a painter, I find the relationship between the viewer and the painting always remains paramount. Consequently, this concern remains throughout the process of construction. It remains from the initial conceptualization to the hanging on the wall. It remains and is the question: how is the painted surface viewed in duration? Indeed, it was Clement Greenberg (1993, 81) who famously stated that the true virtue of modernist painting was its "at onceness." Greenberg claimed this was repeatable with each new encounter; he compares this to the mouth continuously repeating the same word. However, the breaking of this notion into one of fragmented encounters or events has the potential for change (to use Greenberg's analogy and, as the philosopher Gilles Deleuze would suggest, turn it on its head): the mouth continuously stuttering words.

It is in the virtual and actual of the surface of painting that the basis of this chapter is formed. For the purpose of this investigation the virtual, in its most basic philosophical structure, can be understood as an extension to the actual. In this sense, the virtual brings the actual into being and thus extends the potential of the actual beyond itself.

This chapter engages in the analysis and application to painting of the Deleuzian concepts of the "virtual image," the "actual image," and the "crystal image" within the cinematic. As this process emerges, it will be further examined and explored through specific paintings I produced in 2008 and 2011–2012:

- *The Curious Pigmentation of the Pearl*, 2008 (fig. 28.1]
- *Is It a Was*, 2008 (fig. 28.2)
- *Celluloid Suicide*, 2011 (fig. 28.3)
- *Celluloid Noir*, 2012 (fig. 28.4)

FIGURE 28.1 Simon J. Harris, *The Curious Pigmentation of the Pearl*. Oil on canvas. 132 × 116.8 cm. Private collection.

FIGURE 28.2 Simon J. Harris, *Is It a Was*. Oil on canvas. 132 × 116.8 cm. Private collection.

FIGURE 28.3 Simon J. Harris, *Celluloid Suicide*. Oil on linen, 116.8 × 132 cm. Private collection.

FIGURE 28.4 Simon J. Harris, *Celluloid Noir*. Oil on linen, 116.8 x 132 cm. Private collection.

Furthermore, it is through the discussion, contextualization, and understanding of these paintings that the convention of the terms "painter" and "viewer" will be interrogated. This is in order to discuss the encounter from both the viewer's and the painter's perspectives—and discuss a point at which they merge, without a single-sided authorial dominance.

I shall refer to this as the *viewer encounter circuit*. The term "circuit" is used to suggest that the encounter can be reciprocal or circular in its relationship. It is the specific encounter between the viewer and the painting that becomes problematic: the paintings are the antithesis of a prescriptive encounter. The situation is as with the cinematic; films that allow vagueness or divert from a prescriptive story arc in their narrative allow a degree of self-interpretation. These films are eminently rewatchable and discussable and remain exemplary, with each new visit giving a greater understanding or potential of reinterpretation or even misinterpretation. However, the films that depend on strict linear narrative structure can only remain merely illustrative of their devices and often remain in the domain of entertainment and are rarely discussed outside of this premise. Thus, the general functions of my paintings will be discussed through the assumptions of the painter as viewer.

The viewer encounter circuit is an encounter, first, with the dimensions of the physical artifact, that is, the object and then subsequently the surface. In effect, the viewer negotiates the objecthood encounter. In its most basic structure, objecthood is taken as the perceived object, an object in the world with no content or meaning. Therefore, as the viewer moves through the first objecthood encounter, the object is dismissed, through either a conscious dismissal or an unconscious endeavor. Following this encounter with objecthood, a second encounter emerges, the negotiation of the surface. Interestingly, at this particular stage the surface could be considered as the physical artifact. However, a danger lies in the second encounter, when all the elements remain fixed and framed. Through the unfixing or delimiting of the individual elements, the movement of the eye becomes only the first step in the relationships formed through the act of viewing. Albeit there is an undeniable physicality of the eye, within the relationship of the eye acting as agent to the mind, the eye can act in a purely visual manner and inform the mind objectively of what is perceived. Alternatively, the eye can act in a haptic capacity and relay a physicality that has a subjective touch within it or activates more than a single sense receptor and creates a plurality between the actual and the virtual.

The transverse of this encounter is the *painter encounter circuit* in which the surface is not fixed and is initiated as primarily subjective.

In addition, through the development of the virtual as a method of making and viewing, painting's surface becomes the hinge with which to explore the expansion of both the painter encounter circuit and the viewer encounter circuit. The pivotal role of the "surface as hinge" for both the painter and the viewer acknowledges the space where the virtual and actual can oscillate. It could be argued that at the point of oscillation, one is in the painting looking out.

Plundering, Virtuality, and Formalism

The genesis of this enquiry is a longstanding personal angst about, not what painting is, but what the implications for the process of making and viewing painting are. In essence, what is painting doing? What changed/altered subjectivity can be brought forth, in, upon, and of the surface of painting? The core, and subsequent implications, of these questions comes from the translator's notes to *A Thousand Plateaus* by Giles Deleuze and Félix Guattari. Brian Massumi notes that the reader is encouraged to steal at will:

> Most of all, the reader is invited to lift a dynamism out of the book entirely, and incarnate it in a foreign medium, whether it be painting or politics. The authors steal from other disciplines with glee, but they are more than happy to return the favor. Deleuze's own image for a concept is not a brick, but a "tool box." The question is not: is it true? But: does it work? What new thoughts does it make it possible to feel? What new sensations and perceptions does it open in the body? (Massumi in Deleuze and Guattari 2004, xv–xvi)

It is the idea of the plundering of dynamisms or concepts from one discipline and moving them into another medium that has allowed the history of painting to become a treasure chest to plunder rather than a style or movement to better...modernism, post-modernism, minimalism, and so on. Thus, the wholesale theft has begun, which in turn has enabled a changed reading of the formalisms in painting that previously denoted its limits. In this instance, formalism is taken as an aesthetic judgment that interrogates the structural and technical components of the picture plane, which contains all there is to know about the artwork. Thus, formalism has no regard for its concept, content, or context. In this changed reading, the idea of "new sensations and perceptions" makes it difficult in the aesthetic judgment to discount concept, content, and context. However, as previously stated, this is not the prescriptive content of the painter or viewer but rather the oscillation of the potential sensation released as the virtual, actualized in the surface of painting.

The notion of the virtual in painting may at first be considered not as implanting dynamism in a "foreign medium" but as already inherent. However, it is through the plundering of Deleuze's specific interpretation of the virtual, and his employment of this interpretation to the formalisms of cinema in his book *Cinema 2*, that the concept of the virtual as a space is to be replanted in painting, and in it an understanding of duration. Deleuze in *Cinema 2* is himself indebted to Bergson through the plundering of his notions of duration and time, as discussed in *Memory and Matter*. It is through the development of the concept of the "recollection-image" by Bergson and advanced by Deleuze that the nexus of the emerging method of the virtual is formed—a concept that, when explored, establishes the virtual as a space that expands and challenges formalisms in both painting and cinema and confronts the limits of both.

OPERATING THROUGH THE FORMAL

The concept of the virtual as a space is best explored through the paintings: *The Curious Pigmentation of the Pearl* (2008) and *Is It a Was* (2008) (figs. 28.1 and 28.2). Both these paintings derived from a period of examination and drawing of Johannes Vermeer's *Girl with a Pearl Earring* (ca. 1667). The origin derived from the concept of advancing from a figurative given—the signified. The enquiry originated not in the observation of subject as object but from the observation of the subject as subjective. It is important to note that this was not an act of deconstructive inquest or a quest for an abstracted image, but as an act of construction. As noted by John Rajchman in *Constructions* when discussing Deleuze: "He makes construction the secret of empiricism, the originality of pragmatism" (Rajchman 1998, 2–3). The notion of empiricism is the theory of attaining knowledge through experience; the act of painting thus becomes a way of thinking—of operating—through the formal constraints and within the results—of responding to the surface of painting and subsequently the questioning and answering within, upon, and of the material concerns. In its fundamental nature: what new pictorial spaces could be discovered from an established pictorial order derived in the Renaissance world that could have any relevance in the digital era?

The start of the constructive enquiry was conservative and completely in the domain of the painter: with an exact-sized facsimile of Vermeer's *Girl with a Pearl Earring* obtained and an equally scaled paper on which to draw, the image was constructed. However, while mimesis might have been at play, it certainly was not the goal. The image was drawn to a point of completion and then erased. This was repeated on the same piece of paper until, on its final erasure, the paper tore. The object lesson to be learned through this endeavor was muscle memory. Could the image be drawn sufficiently to be able to mimetically enact the image without the referent and from pure recollection? (See fig. 28.5.) With this enabled, canvases were prepared at an increased scale of 3:1. The intention now was not to mimetically present this image to the viewer but to discover the discrete spaces and folds in the memory obtained through the drawings—to find the figural (figs. 28.1–28.2).

The Figural

It is important to state that through this chapter, a concept of "the image" will be discussed in a variety of forms. The initial conception of the "image" is, in this case, to be thought of outside of figurative and/or purely abstract terms, that is, a conception in which the former figurative image acts as description and the latter abstract image as appearance. Thus, when "the image" is discussed, the concept of the "figural" will be employed. The figural can be considered as a further method of thought—the figural does not denote the object of its representation—it does not describe an object as a figurative representation, nor is it an ethereal abstraction.

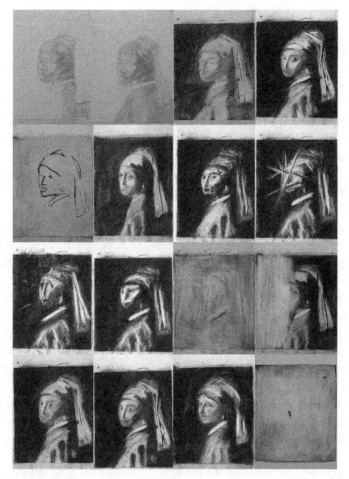

FIGURE 28.5 Simon J. Harris, *Multiple Drawings* (16 of 48). Pencil and charcoal on paper, 39 x 44.5 cm (each). Courtesy of the artist.

As a concept, the figural acting as the signifier significantly alters its signified, which is no longer a representation of reality and of the signified as the reality itself. This is a signifier not of an actuality but of a virtual. The figural acts as a "will to art," in essence, impact, and sensation, and has the potential to unite the objective and the subjective. Deleuze explores this concept extensively in *Francis Bacon: The Logic of Sensation* (2005b).

It is Simon O'Sullivan (2009, 252–253) who contextualizes this when he notes that, for Deleuze, through the paintings of Francis Bacon, the figural does a kind of violence to the figurative. However, the figural divorces the figurative from the narrative and isolates it. Through isolation and ultimate disruption, the figural enables a point of departure. The figural therefore fills the space or, at least, is between the figurative and the nonfigurative. This is significant because the figural is not preemptive to the figurative, yet as a system of random marks it can allow the figurative to emerge.

The Possibility of Fact

The figural is vital, as it isolates or disrupts the figurative and its relationship to its object. The figurative is a statement of fact or "matter of fact." In addition, it is important to note that as a type of isolation or disruption the figural is significantly different from the notion of abstracting information from its object; this particular type of abstraction can be sourced and is very evident, as an example, in Piet Mondrian's tree series: *Avond, Red Tree* (1908) or *Grey Tree* (1911). In addition, O'Sullivan notes the figural is employed as a point of departure in Bacon's paintings, in essence a moving beyond the figure, further exemplifying the in-between operation of the figural as neither figurative or nonfigurative: "the figural involves a *becoming* of the figure...a zone of indiscernability" (O'Sullivan 2009, 252–253).

Hence, through "a zone of indiscernability," the figural moves "the image" from a statement or "matter of fact"—the actually seen—to a "possibility of fact"—the virtual. The development of the "possibility of fact" derives from Deleuze discussing "the diagram": "The diagram is thus the operative set of asignifying and nonrepresentative lines and zones...and the operation of the diagram, its function, says Bacon, is to be 'suggestive.' Or, more rigorously, to use language similar to Wittgenstein's, it is to introduce 'possibilities of fact'" (Deleuze 2005b, 71). It is the suggestive or the "possibility of fact" that provides a potential for the interiority of painting that is not to achieve a figurative line of representation or a pure abstract line. As an example of a pure abstract line Deleuze uses Jackson Pollock's abstract action paintings.

It is important to note that the potential of the "possibility of fact" is not less or reduced from the actual. In fact, the correlation between the virtual and the actual is the important premise. Indeed, as Bergson notes when discussing the possible and the real:

> There is especially the idea that the possible is *less* than the real, and that, for this reason, the possibility of things precedes their existence. They would thus be capable of representation beforehand; they could be thought of being realised. But it is the reverse that is true. If we leave aside the closed systems, subjected to purely mathematical laws, isolable because duration does not act upon them, if we consider the totality of concrete reality or simply the world of life, and still more that of consciousness, we find there is more and not less in the possibility of each successive state than in their reality. For the possible is only the real with the addition of an act of mind which throws its image back into the past, once it has been enacted. But that is what our intellectual habits prevent us from seeing. (Bergson 1992, 99–100)

It is, then, through Bergson's enactment of the possible that the "surface as hinge" becomes both doubled and strangely coupled with the emerging notion of a "possibility of fact," in which the signifiers become sufficiently disrupted, thus allowing and even encouraging a *failure* to read that in turn brings its own subjectivity. This leads to an encounter circuit that is activated for both viewer and painter. Bergson's "act of the mind" constitutes the painting as subjectivity. The figural as a changed subjectivity delimits the "surface as hinge" from the surface as present to the painter and as past to the viewer through the "possibility of fact." The delicate core of the "surface as hinge" creates a past and present that are in fact contemporaries and in a temporal duration for both painter and viewer. Thus, to employ Bergson: "The possible is therefore the mirage of the present in the past" (1992, 101). As David Rodowick notes, the figural is also virtual:

> The figural énoncé is virtual; it does not necessarily derive from any prior existence. Split from within by the noncoincidence of figuration, affirmation, and designation, signs proliferate in an endless temporal stream. The figural is electronic and digital era par excellence. (Rodowick 2001, 72)

It is precisely the proliferation of signs within the digital era that allows the advancement of Deleuze's celluloid framing of images into a mutated understanding of these paintings. Initially, the subjectivity of the signs painting presents is effected by the highly finished and shiny-in-the-extreme surface of the artifact. In this, the viewer had to decide or assume a mode of engagement with either the reflection-image or the image behind the surface. Intriguingly, neither could quite exist in the same *milieu*. The term *milieu* is taken from *A Thousand Plateaus*, meaning "surroundings," "medium," and "middle," and is employed philosophically by Deleuze and Guattari to mean all three (2004, xvii).

Through the *viewer encounter circuit* when facing the shiny-in-the-extreme surface, the transition from the reflection image to the beyond would, for the viewer, have the potential to confirm an active participation, in essence, creating active viewers who have already discovered their own subjectivity within the encounter circuit and created a type of visual leap from one virtual to another, each with its own actual and virtual located within the surface as the image. As Deleuze notes: "The actual is always objective, but the virtual is subjective: it was initially the affect, that which divides itself in two as affecter and affected, 'affection of self by self' as definition of time" (2005a, 80).

Visual Leaps

The leap acts as a leap through an interval or from two distinct planes of temporality. Each encounter brings with it a new encounter circuit as if it were the first with no connection to the previous or the next. The virtual image in the reflection image does not exist once the eye has moved into the image behind the surface where the viewer is in another incarnation of the virtual. The reflection image remains in the first movement and can only be active in that milieu, and the eye has to refocus to activate the second movement, that of the image behind the surface.

The active component within this encounter is the eliciting of sensation and could be described as "an enrichment of the present" through the discovery of the discrete play of paint or that combination of gestalts which forms a relationship to the perception-image

Deleuze employs to discuss the movement-image in cinema. In its simplest conception, the perception-image acts as the mobility of the eye within the image. All is new and delineating; therefore time is activated; a temporality could be identified, but as a plane of temporality and thus closely divisible by time. Both images retain their own distinct relationship to a very different actual. Through this movement, Bergson notes:

> Art enables us, no doubt, to discover in things more qualities and more shades than we naturally perceive. It dilates our perception, but on the surface rather than in depth. It enriches our present, but it scarcely enables us to go beyond it. Through philosophy we can accustom ourselves never to isolate the present from the past which it pulls along with it. Thanks to philosophy, all things acquire depth—more than depth, something like a forth dimension which permits anterior perceptions to remain bound up with present perception, and the immediate future itself to become outlined in the present. Reality no longer appears in the static state, in its manner of being; it affirms itself dynamically, in the continuity and variability of its tendency. What was immobile and frozen in our perception is warmed and set in motion. (1992, 157)

Through the analysis of this distinct type of viewing emerged the implication of a Deleuzian concept of the virtual in cinema that could be planted in the "foreign material" of painting. In essence these paintings became significant in developing a mode of thought that could address the potential of the virtual image and its relationship to an actual image.

THE FORMAL FRAME AND IMAGES OF THE FLOATING WORLD

The formal frame frames the objecthood of painting, that of its surface, thus enabling the material structure to act as a mount would in the construction of picture frames. Through the acknowledgment of its own objecthood, the painting in effect creates two distinct actual planes from which to progress. As Deleuze notes: "The frame teaches us that the image is not just given to be seen. It is legible as well as visible" (2009, 14). It is through this legibility that aesthetic composition can be derived, yet this is a changed notion of composition, changed through the concept that the frame is not enclosing the image but has the potential to allude to an out-of-shot, or a half-remembered history or sensation. Within the compound of sensation, and by the action, the frame allows to be perceived an organization of the eye.

This is best discussed through painting, specifically *Celluloid Suicide* and *Celluloid Noir* (figs. 28.3–28.4]. As can be observed, the material support of the painting becomes implicit in its construction, acting as a mount would in a picture frame. Indeed, it is through the frame that the virtual is identified and that the flux between the virtual and actual starts to present itself in a durative event. Thus the relationship these paintings have to their original referents bears no meaning for the exploits of the viewer. It is not necessary for the viewer to know, for example in the case of *Celluloid Suicide*, that the image is derived from a photograph taken looking out of the back windscreen of a moving car on a rainy day or that *Celluloid Noir* is taken from a book on night photography. These are merely the starting points at which the viewer becomes complicit in the formulation of the narrative.

Neither the frame nor the emerging sensation can exclusively endure the duration needed in an evoking of the cinematic. However, through advancement within the digital era of the eye as a haptic agent of the mind, a multiplicity of planes can be created in which to support it, in whatever way it maybe fragmented.

As a motif, this can be explored though the conjoining of the Japanese concept of *Ukiyo-e*—"images of the floating world" in which beauty and sublime are divorced from the reality of the everyday world and the relationship between the dream-image and the recollection-image.

A quintessential example is Christopher Nolan's *Inception* (2010), which proves a case point. In particular, through the opening sequence, where the Japanese screen paintings that envelop the room have been echoed in the richness of the color saturation of the film itself and within the concept of the extended dream, it would appear as if the characters have become figures in the screen paintings. As the paintings envelop the room, almost placing the characters in the midst of the painted landscape, the mimic of this is presented for the viewer in the enveloping of the images presented as perception-image leading to recollection-image within the function of dream-image. It is acknowledged that, in cinematic duration, there is a discrete connection between the previous image and the next image as it contributes to the unfurling of the film. However, these connections exist in a circuit larger than that of the physicality of images framed side by side. The relationship this has to the painted image becomes complex, but it is through the breaking of Greenberg's "at onceness" into the fragmented encounter and the frame of the recollection-image that the relationship can emerge. In acknowledging the discrete elements in the objecthood and surface, the recollection-image is not of a whole composition but of fragmented zones. In much the same way the recollection of a film is not of a linear portrayal. Rather, the recollection jumps and weaves through the zones of the film. Through the conjoining of the recollection-image as fragmented and the recollection of jumping and weaving through the zones of the painting, perception of it as static recollection or "at once" is unattainable. Thus the painting bears a closer relationship to cinema than once thought.

The Dream-Image

The dream-image has its own relationship to the virtual. Again, the relationship within the virtual of *Inception* as the dream-image is interesting as an example: The dream-image of Nolan's *Inception* has its own direct connection to the virtual and the actual images, in which the central characters have to enable devices in order to identify the actual and the dream, as they become indistinguishable from each other—not as an oscillation but as a stasis of the moment. Confirmation is needed of the actual as the plane of the real; the indiscernability becomes that distinct. The actual becomes virtual, which in turn becomes an extended virtual, and so on infinitely. With each extended plane in opposition to the previous, each presenting itself as actual, each tries to assert its dominance as the actual when lived in.

As the dream extends to further planes of complexity, time is displaced and extends, one minute becomes an hour in the previous plane of the dream. As each plane extends into the next, the temporality of the previous advances through to the next plane but does not merge with the previous one; each is different and distinct. However, it is the development of the perception-image to recollection-image outside of the dream-image, the interplay between the virtual and actual as an oscillation, rather than a progression, that becomes the nexus for the interiority of painting outside of the dream-image that remains worthy of note.

> What, more precisely, is the difference between a recollection-image and dream image? We start from a perception-image, the nature of which is to the actual. The recollection, in contrast—what Bergson calls "pure recollection"—is necessarily a virtual image. But, in the first case, it becomes actual in so far as it is summoned by the perception-image. It is actualized in the recollection-image which corresponds to the perception-image. (Deleuze 2005a, 54)

Indeed, images react or act differently in painting to this specific type of infinity, which expands in linear progression. Painting presents its image as an internality that is singular in a way that doesn't allude to the cinematic previous and next. However, the function of the durative qualities of these images warrants a closer examination, chiefly, the function and employment of the recollection-image. The concept of the recollection-image first appears with Bergson, as previously stated, as he discusses time and duration. However, it is important how Deleuze appropriates the recollection-image to discuss a distinct function of duration in cinema. It is the resulting duration or specifically the levels of connecting temporality that support duration that becomes the key concept for the "possibility of fact" within the interiority of painting. This has the potential to allow greater understanding of, and to expand the role of, the figural in painting.

The Recollection-Image

Deleuze develops the notion of the recollection-image within cinema as a device that is employed in the conventions of flashback or montage. However, it is in the direct correlation Deleuze makes through the definition of the "recollection-image," or "mnemosign," that the virtual image enters a relationship with the actual image and furthers it. It is the furthering of the actual that presents the image as image through the affection of self by self with the half-remembered. It is this specific relevance, through painting, in which the painter/viewer encounter circuit can change to an active duration within and of it.

Historically, this has been observed in the paintings of James McNeill Whistler, specifically, *Cremorne Gardens, No. 2* (1872–1877): "As the master not of actuality observed, but of the half-seen, of the recollected, he seems to have trusted a fragile expanse of a single hue to trigger specific memories of place and time of day" (Wilkin 1994, 28). In essence, this is how the flashback or montage can be utilized within the painter encounter circuit through the employment of the seen in the half seen and half remembered.

However when the half seen and half remembered merge, an oscillation occurs that develops from a univocal subjectivity of the object as subject. As subject and object merge yet remain distinct in their difference, the "surface as hinge" can become an active agent in the encounter, moving outside of the subject/object binary opposition encounter into a wider circuit of connections. Through this development, which endorses a pictorial advancement, the fragmented images emerge. Through the expansion of the half remembered, the half-truths, and the almost seen pictorial advancements, reality is constructed. This is a reality born of the virtual—this is a signifier not of an actuality but of a virtual. With each new encounter to the surface this virtual is succinctly expanded upon, as more of the *reality* is discovered. Yet it is in its absolute failure to communicate the actual of the seen that the virtual actualizes its own seen, thus extending the actual and creating more potentiality within the "possibility of fact." For example, in *Celluloid Suicide* the mimesis of the image is not taken from a photograph looking out of the back windscreen of a moving car on a rainy day but rather from an emerging space that has the half remembered at play. Certainly, *Is It a Was* is not the mimesis of *The Girl with a Pearl Earring*. Rather they are implicit and emerging spaces created through both the painter and the viewer, with the surface acting as hinge.

It is through the very failure to communicate the seen—the actual—that abstract painting thus transmutes from formal reduction—the abstracted—into a pictorial/abstract figural hybrid that is in the realm neither of the figurative nor of pure abstract appearance. The fixed moment or stasis of painting—the motionless state—significantly changes, potentially uniting both painter and viewer through the affirmation of being. A metamorphosing from the "matter of fact" to a "possibility of fact" occurs that sets in motion an active duration through the act of the recollection-image, an image that remains divorced and isolated from constructed narrative and is yet more complicit than that of pure singular sensation. The image ceases to be descriptive of this or that object; indeed, it fails in the task. It is an image that activates an attentive recognition that comes through the recollection image. To quote Deleuze again:

> Attentive recognition informs us to a much greater degree when it fails than when it succeeds. When we cannot remember, sensory-motor extension remains suspended, and the actual image, the present optical perception, does not link up with either the motor image or a recollection-image which would re-establish contact. It rather enters into relation with genuinely virtual elements, feelings of *déjà vu* or past "in general" (I must have seen that man somewhere...). (2005a, 52)

Conclusion: The Blurred, Déjà Vu, Oscillation, and the Crystal Image

It is proposed that interiority within painting does not have to be sustained absolutely, nor is it an attempt to constitute the parts to the whole or make visible the manual space of the painter. On the contrary, it is the suggestive space or the allusion to—or the illusion of—the possibilities of fact that is the point of reference. Through the "possibility of fact" an interiority in painting is rendered that is not subjected through the authorial seen of the painter but becomes a source of déjà vu for both the viewer and the painter, a surface that holds its own discrete moments for both, who do not sit in opposition to each other or in a relation of dominance.

It is essential that the image delimit the exteriority of both objecthood and frame. This correlates the virtual to the actual, the imaginary to the seen, action and stasis as an oscillation. This is not a simultaneous act of object absorbing subject or vice versa. This is sustained oscillation of both object and image: an oscillation between the point of *the blurred*, which is a perceptually given—déjà vu—and a mutated pictorial fact. In fact, it is imperative that this oscillation occurs; it is through the oscillation between the actual image and the virtual image that the zone of indiscernability can occur.

The distinction between pictorial fact and *the blurred*, which is perceptually given, holds further potential. This can be tracked through Deleuze's discussion of Bacon: "Thus follows a third path, which is neither optical like abstract painting, nor manual like action painting" (2005b, 77). The third path of Bacon as established through the figural would seems to suggest that the figural could be employed as a signifier, albeit a mutated signifier. Significantly, then, it is the action of the signifier for the viewer as it becomes signified that creates a direct correlation between the recollection image in cinema and the rhythm of the "surface as hinge" in painting. This potential allows a mutual virtual space in painting to emerge that has a flow of duration and retains its figural—its given. The image is no longer consigned to the romantic idealism of expressionism or the monochromaticity of reductionism: not "information from things... but rather... finding within things the delicate, complicated abstract virtualities of other things" (Rajchman 1998, 73–74).

It is as the virtual and the actual oscillate to a point of indiscernability presenting the possibility of fact—the blurred and the pictorial, the seen and the unseen, the real and the imaginary—that the image becomes a crystal image. It is in achieving the crystal image that the goal of the paintings discussed here lies. The crystal image presents itself as the unseen image brought forth through the surface.

What we see in the crystal is no longer the empirical progression of time as succession of presents, nor its indirect representation as interval or as whole; it is its direct presentation, its constitutive dividing in two into a present which is passing into a past which is preserved, the strict contemporaneity of the present with the past that it will be, of the past with the present that it has been. It is time itself which arises in the crystal, and which is constantly recommending its dividing in two without completing it, since the indiscernible exchange is always renewed and reproduced. (Deleuze 2005a, 262)

It is important to note that for Deleuze the moment of abstraction is when the material support exceeds the "message of the medium and us as senders and receivers of them." The medium is not the "message," a view in which the medium is a type of "self-referential literalness," but when the message begins to stutter "and…and…and" (Rajchman 1998, 73–74). It is essential, then, that abstraction is viewed outside of a reductive scheme of "not" but within, upon, and of the relations to "and." It is this type of abstraction that is correlated in the figural and envelops it in larger circuits that create their own temporalities. It is thus through the subsequent planes of temporality within the paintings discussed that the "possibility of fact" and the direct oscillation between the virtual and the actual become edifying within the relationship to the crystal image. As the crystal is able to withstand the divisible, the figural in the paintings is able to withstand the divisible of the virtual and actual and even mutates and recodes the signifiers and signified presented into asignifying lines and zones. It is as the image moves through the perceptually given—from the recollection, to the crystal—that the duration in the static image generates its dynamism.

REFERENCES

Bergson, H. 1992. *The Creative Mind: An Introduction to Metaphysics*. New York: Carol Publishing.

Deleuze, G., and F. Guattari. 2004. *A Thousand Plateaus*. Translated by Brian Massumi. London: Continuum.

Deleuze, G. 2005a. *Cinema 2*. Translated by Hugh Tomlinson and Robert Galeta. London: Continuum Books.

Deleuze, G. 2005b. *Francis Bacon: The Logic of Sensation*. Translated by Daniel Smith. London: Continuum Books.

Deleuze, G. 2009. *Cinema 1*. Translated by Hugh Tomlinson and Barbara Habberjam. London: Continuum Books.

Greenberg, C. 1993. *The Collected Essays and Criticism*. Vol. 4: *Modernism with a Vengeance*. Edited by John O'Brien. Chicago: University of Chicago Press.

Nolan, C., dir. 2010. *Inception*. DVD. Warner Bros. Pictures.

O'Sullivan, S. 2009. From Stuttering and Stammering to the Diagram: Deleuze, Bacon and Contemporary Art Practice. *Deleuze Studies* 3 (2): 247–58.

Rajchman, J. 1998. *Constructions*. Cambridge, MA: MIT Press.

Rodowick, D. 2001. *Reading the Figural, or Philosophy after the New Media*. Durham, NC: Duke University Press.

Wilkin, K. 1994. Surprised by Whistler. *Modern Painters* 7 (4): 26–29.

PART VI

....

ECONOMY AND LAW

....

CHAPTER 29

VIRTUAL LAW

GREG LASTOWKA

DEFINING THE VIRTUAL

How we understand the intersection of the legal and the virtual depends largely on how we define both terms. The virtual is certainly the more ambiguous term. In its most ancient usage, the virtual was derivative of the personal characteristic of virtue, yet we rarely use the word in that sense today. The more modern adjective describes a thing that mimics the essence, but not the actuality, of the word it modifies. For instance, an action can be virtually complete, which means that it is complete for all practical purposes, but not formally complete.

The most popular usage today of virtual derives from this modern meaning: we use the term virtual to broadly reference digital technologies and simulations that replicate the surface appearances and interactive behaviors of tangible objects. As a result, almost anything involving technologies of digital simulation can colloquially be described as virtual. In this chapter, I focus on the intersection of law with this broad category of virtual technologies.

My primary focus will be on the intersection of the law with video games and virtual worlds. Avatars in video games can described as virtual bodies because they are designed to simulate the appearance and active behaviors of physical bodies. However, avatars are not physical bodies. Digital representations of gold coins in online games are called currencies because they have economic value within the context of the game and often outside that context. They are virtual currencies primarily because they are intangible and nonofficial forms of currency. Recently popular virtual worlds such as *Second Life* and *World of Warcraft* may be the contemporary cutting edge of virtual technologies. These popular virtual worlds are platforms that often take the form of games and allow users, represented as avatars, to exchange virtual currencies and communicate with each other within virtual landscapes populated with virtual objects (Lastowka 2010). Though they do not represent the contemporary limit of virtual technologies, they do constitute large-scale virtual systems where users are psychologically absorbed in very complex virtual environments (Boellstorff 2008).

Philosophically and aesthetically, the modern technological virtual does not represent a radical break with the past. The technological virtual should properly be partnered, analytically, with a long history of mimetic practices. Prior technologies—costumes, puppetry, painting, photography, film, and robotics—provide essentially the same sorts of pleasures and anxieties we derive from more recent virtual technologies (Grau 2004; Dibbell 1998). Our concerns about virtual technologies today echo older concerns found in the myth of Pygmalion or Plato's allegory of the cave. The shock and thrill we experience watching a three-dimensional film like *Avatar* is just the latest way in which we find pleasure in the confusion between reality and artifice. This is not to say that virtual technologies are not novel, but simply that they have clear historical predecessors that created analogous anxieties.

Video games, the core creative genre of the technological virtual today, are largely based on forms of pleasurable mimetic confusion. The primary new feature of video games is algorithmic interactivity. The digital puppetry of games is accomplished through feats of programming that create highly complex simulations of objects and environments. Even a simple game like *Tetris* is a marvel of modern technology. More complex interactivity provides more pleasurable and more persistent forms of playful confusion.

Mimetic representations of humans and animals have existed, in the form of dolls and statues, from the earliest human civilizations. But virtual technologies extend the pleasures provided by interacting with representations of living things. For instance, when one cares for a virtual dog in a video game, the pleasure of that caretaking experience derives in part from how well the simulation models interactions with a real dog (Turkle 2011). If we were to strip the user's technological interaction with the program of its canine fiction, presenting it as a mathematical process of user inputs and algorithmic analysis, the game of tending a virtual pet (at least for many users) would quickly lose its appeal. As Jesper Juul notes, the pleasure of video games flows from the fact that they are half-real (Juul 2005).

But while this mimetic confusion is central to the appeal of many games, the unreality of the game is equally important. Virtual dogs would probably be less fun to play with if their suffering carried moral consequences. Virtual pets sometimes die through a player's neglect, and this may stir some feelings of sadness and guilt, but that emotional reaction can be understood as a form of play itself, just as a child might play at mourning for a "dead" doll (Turkle 2011).

The statement that virtual dogs are not real, however, is formally wrong. Virtual dogs are quite real. They are made of electromagnetic machinery that has a true physical (digital) reality. Our interactions with them are real interactions. When we emphasize that virtual dogs are not real, we clarify the difference between a real dog and a virtual dog: the gap of simulation. We also emphasize that the simulated death or abuse of a virtual dog should not be confused with the abuse or death of a real dog, even if the permitting a certain level of confusion may be enticing as a form of play.

The opposition of the real and the virtual is primarily a shorthand that highlights a particular shift in semantic context. When we speak of the dogs in a painting, we call them dogs, rather than searching for some other word to emphasize the fact that the dogs at issue are represented by oil on canvas. The virtual/real distinction provides for linguistic efficiency when we are speaking colloquially—with a syllable or two, we can quickly separate the universe of representations from the universe of "real" things represented. When we speak of simulations, we need not look for a new vocabulary of "painted dogs" that are "simulating movement" across "painted fields." Once the listener understands the representational context, the conventional words can be used to describe the virtual landscape. We use the virtual/real distinction to stress the fact that language can bridge between two very different realms.

For this reason, one might argue that virtual law, strictly speaking, should be confined to the law that is represented in simulations and depictions. Such representations of law do exist, both in television's courtroom dramas and even in virtual environments where law is performed as play (Mnookin 1996). However, the fact that people represent law and play at law is largely unremarkable, given that all that exists in the real is subject to depiction and reenactment in the virtual.

The more interesting question, for both law and the virtual, is how law that is real applies to things that are virtual, such as virtual dogs and virtual worlds. The virtual/real distinction does not keep "real" law from exerting its power over virtual objects. Law—property law and copyright at a minimum—can and does sometimes apply to objects depicted in simulations. So the most interesting question of virtual law is not if the real law applies to virtual things, but exactly how our existing law applies to realms of representation and simulation—and, ultimately, exactly how far the real law should extend in its efforts to regulate the virtual realm.

The Reality of Virtual Law

Although the entertainment appeal of the virtual is often premised on pleasurable confusions, the law is premised on categorical clarity. Neglecting a virtual dog may create curious feelings of guilt, but in the eyes of the law, while abusing a real dog can be illegal, to neglect a virtual dog is not to violate the law—it is simply to interact with a simulation. When a dog dies in an online game, the law does not deny that an event has occurred. It simply describes that event as a representation accomplished through technology that, while it may be interesting socially, has rather few legal implications (Lessig 1999).

However, some virtual events do invoke legal consequences. Legal practitioners today sometimes use the term "virtual law" to describe the range of laws that regulate virtual worlds and social interactions within them (Duranske 2008). While the future of the term is not clear at the present moment, for the sake of clarity, the term "virtual law" should probably be distinguished from terms like "cyberlaw" or "Internet law," which encompass the legal issues raised more generally by computer and Internet technologies

(Bellia et al. 2010). Virtual law is a very recent term used specifically to describe the legal regulation of social software that entails avatars, intangible objects, virtual currencies, and simulated places (Lastowka 2010).

Certain laws are more likely to have purchase when applied to virtual worlds and related technologies. Intellectual property laws, information privacy laws, electronic trespass laws, and online contracting laws all have particular importance. These laws applied to virtual things may differ substantially from the laws governing "real" counterparts. For instance, a robotic dog is not a legal dog, so any laws that prevent abuse to dogs would not prevent the abuse and destruction of a robotic dog. Yet when Sony Electronics once manufactured a particular robotic dog, the AIBO, it asserted that owners in the United States who installed customized software on that robotic dog were violating Sony's intellectual property rights under the Digital Millennium Copyright Act (Lessig 2005). These same laws might be employed to prohibit tampering with entirely intangible virtual dogs, such as simulated dogs on a commercial website. "Real" dogs, by contrast, have no significant intersections with the laws of copyright, intellectual property, and computer hacking, and are generally viewed by the law as the chattel property of their owners.

The same claims regarding copyright ownership and interactions with simulations have extended to all user interactions with virtual worlds. An example from the United States is the 2010 decision in the case of *Blizzard v. MDY* (2010). Blizzard is the creator of a very popular virtual world, *World of Warcraft* (WoW), which at the time hosted over ten million players worldwide. MDY created and sold WoWGlider, a piece of software used by players of WoW to automate their avatars. MDY had no license from Blizzard to make WoWGlider and did not share its profits with Blizzard. Blizzard objected to the sale of the software, and the dispute was litigated in federal court.

WoWGlider was a tool that allowed WoW players to walk away from the game while their avatars performed automated actions. WoW is a multiplayer game, so automation provided those players with competitive advantages. Like robots, automated avatars can operate around the clock without rest, more rapidly accomplishing in-game objectives and acquiring virtual currency. WoWGlider was hardly the first form of avatar automation software. Indeed, there is a common term for using avatar automation software: "botting," which suggests how one's avatar is turned into a (virtual) robot.

Many players of games like WoW object to the practice of botting. They believe that all active avatars in a virtual world should be controlled by active players. They believe accomplishments in virtual worlds should be earned by players who are physically present at their keyboard. And so they frown upon botting as a form of cheating (Consalvo 2007). Despite this norm, MDY's WoWGlider proved to be a very popular piece of software. Approximately 100,000 copies of WoWGlider were sold to players, earning substantial profits for MDY.

Players who used WoWGlider, however, were required to consent to the terms and conditions of WoW in order to run the game's software. Without this license, players were legally forbidden to access the virtual world via Blizzard's computer servers. Though initially it was not entirely clear whether botting was prohibited by Blizzard, the game's terms of service eventually made this prohibition explicit. In addition, Blizzard took technological steps to prevent players from botting. It created a software program called Warden that worked to detect players who were running unauthorized software such as WoWGlider. When Warden detected such software, it shut down access to the game's servers.

Despite the contractual prohibition and the technological efforts of Warden, MDY continued to sell WoWGlider. It rewrote the program to avoid detection by Blizzard, making millions of dollars in the process of frustrating Blizzard's efforts. It should be noted that the commercial popularity of WoWGlider was likely tied to its utility as a tool for gold farming, a term that refers to the harvesting and resale of virtual currency from virtual worlds (Dibbell 2006). The virtual gold currency of WoW was commonly sold by players at the time for (real) money through a variety of third-party websites. The WoWGlider software replicated the technological vector of automated labor—just as robotic factories can be profitable offline, so can botted avatars be profitable in the context of the virtual economies of virtual worlds.

The dispute between Blizzard and MDY resulted in a trial court ruling in favor of Blizzard that prohibited the sale of WoWGlider on the basis that it violated both copyright and unfair competition laws. This ruling was appealed by MDY to a panel of the federal Court of Appeals for the Ninth Circuit. On appeal, Blizzard argued, as it had before the trial court, that players who violated the prohibition on botting were guilty of copyright infringement. It is worth noting that the players directly accused of infringement were not before the court, but determining the legality of their actions was essential to determining the liability of MDY. If the players had infringed copyright, MDY did not dispute that it aided and profited from the activity, and therefore would incur contributory liability for the infringements pursuant to US law.

Blizzard had two separate arguments that players who used Glider for botting were guilty of copyright infringement. First, Blizzard argued that when players played the game, they copied certain portions of the game's software code into their computers' random-access memory. Because this copying occurred while players were violating the antibotting terms of the software license, Blizzard claimed that the RAM copying amounted to copyright infringement. With regard to this first argument, the Ninth Circuit ultimately disagreed, reversing the lower court that had sided with Blizzard. It ruled that the violation of the license term was insufficiently related to Blizzard's copyright interests to give rise to a claim for copyright infringement. Thus, WoW players using the automated botting program were not guilty of copyright infringement by virtue of making unauthorized copies of portions of the game's software code.

Blizzard's second copyright-based argument proved more successful with the appellate court. It noted that the makers of the WoWGlider software had designed the program to avoid detection by Blizzard's Warden software. The Warden software prevented access to Blizzard's game servers, which, like the game program itself, were also software protected by copyright law. The Ninth Circuit ruled that, pursuant to the statutory language of the Digital Millennium Copyright Act ("DMCA"), WoWGlider illegally operated to circumvent the protection system of the Warden program and grant players access to the (copyright-protected) "dynamic non-literal elements" of the game. So, ultimately, while the players using the software did not violate traditional copyright laws by virtue of botting, they did violate the technologically specific law of the DMCA by using WoWGlider to evade Warden. Hence, MDY was liable for selling a program that enabled a form of copyright infringement.

The preceding analysis may seem complex, but it actually simplifies some of the complexity of the copyright law and technology that were at issue in the case. Much more might be said about whether the court properly understood the operation of the technology and whether it properly interpreted prior judicial precedent and the DMCA. It would be a mistake to suggest that the result in the MDY case was preordained. Doctrinally and technologically, the case presented the court with some very complex and novel issues.

Virtual law is characterized by this sort of complexity and novelty. The intersection of law and new technology often features similar doctrinal and technological complexities. Lengthy statutory enactments and complex common-law doctrines are applied to equally complex technologies, often making the ultimate legal outcomes in any case (although rationally produced within the framework of legal reasoning) unascertainable at the outset. Legally, the terrain of the virtual, like the terrain of any new technology, seems to be perpetually fraught with ambiguity and unanswered questions. For businesses operating in this landscape, navigating law is often primarily about ascertaining and managing legal risk.

In the WoWGlider case, the ultimate result was that MDY was required to pay over three million dollars in damages to Blizzard. This effectively bankrupted MDY and killed the software tool it had created. With respect to future technologies, the opinion creates a strong presumption that game companies possess the legal right to set binding rules concerning the use of avatar automation software. The ruling is therefore important to the public because it speaks to the legal viability of a new technology. From now on, if the opinion is correct, players who use botting software that is targeted by a program like Warden are engaged, according to the law of the United States, in an activity that violates copyright law.

While this prohibition may seem to be, in the context of the WoWGlider case, a rule that only penalizes cheaters and undermines the profits of gold farmers, it has much broader consequences. Imagine, for instance, a similar prohibition against avatar automation in the context of a virtual world that operates not as a game, but as a public forum. Granting platform owners the private right to prohibit users from carrying customized software tools into virtual spaces could surely limit the expressive freedoms of the public and award greater social control to private businesses. Offline, we have become accustomed to a status quo where privately owned copyrights have little influence over what technologies we may use in conjunction with our physical bodies. By analogy, we are a society used to the law of dogs, not the law of virtual dogs.

As we move in avatar spaces, however, the law that regulates our society shifts in unanticipated ways. In virtual worlds, it turns out that copyright law is a means by which private owners can legally prohibit the coupling of user avatars with specific technological controls. In the long term, this sort of power in the hands of private companies could have a substantial effect on the balance of power between corporations and individuals.

THE LANDSCAPE OF VIRTUAL LAW

As previously stated, virtual law is composed of particular fields of law that apply to virtual technologies. In this section, I will describe some of the particular legal structures and doctrines that apply to virtual technologies.

As a threshold matter, it is important to see that virtual technologies are not simply sites upon which existing law acts impartially and predictably. Despite the way it tends to imagine itself, the institution of law is not fixed and immutable. When law applies to new technologies, law inevitably changes as a result. The technological virtual, like any culturally significant technology, has made and will continue to make new law (Cardozo 1921).

This is in part because law, at the margins, is incurably ambiguous. Perhaps the most famous illustration of this fact involves H. L. A. Hart's prohibition: "no vehicles in the park." That rule may seem clear, unambiguous, and easy to enforce. Most of the time, it is. We know what a vehicle is and what a park is. We know that a virtual vehicle, such as an illustration of a truck or a virtual truck on the screen of a handheld game, is also not a legal truck. However, the rule does have some fuzzy edges. As Professor Lon Fuller asked many years ago: what if an army truck were mounted in a park on a pedestal as a memorial to war veterans? (Fuller 1958). Would that sculpture violate the rule in question?

Fuller's hypothetical sculpture was a bridge between the virtual and the real. It was a real truck operating in a simulative manner. Because it was a real truck, the prohibition should have applied. But because it functioned as a representation, the prohibition should not have applied. The guiding goal of the H. L. A. Hart hypothetical prohibition was to eliminate noise, fumes, and the risk of physical harm to pedestrians in the park, so it made no sense to prohibit this particular vehicle from entering into the park, given that it would pose none of those risks. The literal phrasing of the hypothetical law conflicted with the law's purpose, suggesting to thoughtful jurists that an exception to the literal rule was warranted in the case of the pedestal truck.

Like Fuller's truck on the pedestal, many new technologies challenge the application of existing laws simply by virtue of presenting courts with unprecedented artifacts. Courts confronting new technologies must decide how existing laws apply to them. The US Supreme Court, like courts in all jurisdictions, regularly confronts claims involving objections to the use of new technologies.

For instance, does scanning the outside of a building with a thermal imaging device amount to a search of the building's interior? (How can one search an interior while standing outside and "looking" at an exterior wall?) Does reading a police officer's text messages sent by a department-issued paging device invade that officer's reasonable expectation of privacy in his communications? (Who can reasonably expect privacy in messages that travel "in the open" through state computers?) All of these situations, and many others, have forced courts to ask what is essentially the "no vehicles in the park" question with respect to old laws and new technology. Even if a law does or does not explicitly prohibit a particular activity made possible by a new technology, courts may question whether permitting or not permitting that activity accords with the deeper justifications of the existing legal rules. Accordingly, it happens quite often that when claimants bring novel technologies to courts, courts make what is essentially new law concerning those technologies.

The WoWGlider case illustrated one instance of this with regard to virtual technologies. That case applied the rules of copyright to the technology of avatar automation software. But virtual technologies are challenging legal rules in other fields as well. The scope of these challenges is potentially as broad as the scope of law itself, but some particular fields deserve specific mention.

Jurisdiction

It is common for virtual technologies, such as virtual worlds, to enable cross-border personal interactions within virtual environments. Avatars in WoW may stand together in a simulated space despite the fact that their controllers are thousands of miles distant from each other in the real world. Some virtual technologies do not give rise to significant jurisdictional concerns, but many online games offer users the possibility of interacting with strangers from around the world. While there are certainly benefits to these sorts of interactions, they also raise new puzzles concerning legal jurisdiction.

For instance, imagine that two malefactors, A and B, jointly scam another party, C, within the context of a virtual world hosted on the servers of Company D. Now imagine that A, B, C, and D are all physically located in separate countries. Each of these countries has its own particular criminal and civil rules concerning the fraudulent activity that occurred. Which legal rules should apply to this situation? There are several choices, obviously. The rules applied might be those understood by the perpetrators subject to punishment: A and B. We could also apply the rules that protect the victim, C. Since the action took place on the servers of Company D, we might apply the rules of that jurisdiction, even though none of the affected parties are normally governed by those rules. Or perhaps there should be some other set of rules that apply to actors who have disputes in international spaces, something like the rules of admiralty law.

The jurisdiction question is a vexing matter for online interactions generally. It is not specific to virtual technologies (Zittrain 2005). However, the immersive nature of virtual technologies makes the problem more troublesome in that context. In a more standard online situation, when C is in Singapore and is contracting online with A, it is likely that C knows that A is in England and is aware that Singapore's local laws may not protect C's rights. However, when multiple parties are interacting via avatars within the context of a virtual world, the pleasurable illusion that they are participating in the guise of avatars in a virtual society may color their expectations regarding what rules will apply to their behavior. The prospect of a separate legal order, an order specific to the virtual world, may seem more appealing in that context.

However, there is no separate jurisdiction of virtual law. The contemporary legal rule with respect to online jurisdictional confusion is that each jurisdiction with a potential stake in the matter has the option to enforce its own rules as far as it desires to do so. As David Post has explained, this rule is not new and it poses no insurmountable practical difficulties. The true difficulties with the rule are theoretical. The contemporary legal response to the problem of Internet jurisdiction is inconsistent with the notion that governments enforce laws with the consent of the governed (Post 2009). In virtual environments, this consent may be an illusion. Person A may have no idea that interactions with C will invoke the laws of Singapore, and even if A realizes this, A may not know exactly what the law of Singapore entails. So while Singapore may have the right to punish A for harms that C suffered due to A's actions, this result seems problematic from the standpoint of legal theory.

Contract

The above description of the WoWGlider case explained how Blizzard enforces its anti-botting rules in WoW by a combination of technological power, copyright entitlements, and contractual prohibitions. The last of these, contract law, is perhaps the primary means by which the creators of virtual worlds and other consumer-directed virtual technologies attempt to structure their legal rights vis-à-vis the public. Most companies that offer online services or software require that those who use their service consent to lengthy terms of service via so-called clickwrap agreements. These agreements are rarely read by those who agree to them and are often written in legal jargon that is difficult to decipher and that is primarily designed to benefit the companies that draft the agreements (Lastowka 2010).

To the extent that these agreements are enforceable, they may effectively institute a separate sort of virtual jurisdiction, supplanting standard expectations with the particular expectations set forth in the contracts. States that enforce these contracts effectively replace their own laws with private laws. Where variance from the background laws reflects a desirable agreement between virtual technology companies and their users, this may be desirable. But where the majority of those using virtual technologies are unaware of the legal consequences of the contractual terms, the state enforcement of such terms may ultimately operate against the public interest.

Some jurisdictions may limit the legal enforcement of online contracts where terms are deemed unfair to consumers. Even in the United States, where courts are generally inclined to support these agreements, there have been cases involving virtual worlds where particular contractual terms have been deemed unenforceable. One of the most publicized of these cases, *Bragg v. Linden Research* (2007), involved the virtual world of *Second Life*. Marc Bragg was a lawyer from Pennsylvania who was banned from *Second Life* by Linden Lab, the owner of that virtual world. Bragg protested that he owned several thousand dollars of virtual land and property within Second Life and that Linden Lab had failed to compensate him for the loss of his property when it unfairly terminated his account. Bragg brought suit against Linden Lab for value of his lost property (Feinman 2010).

Linden Lab did not deny that it had taken Bragg's virtual property, but it denied that Bragg had any legal rights to that property. As the lawyer for *Second Life* explained: "The term 'virtual' may not have a strict legal interpretation, but if anything it means that the thing being described is NOT whatever comes after the word 'virtual'" (Lastowka 2010, 17). In addition, Linden Lab claimed that before Bragg could file suit, he was required to subject his claim to arbitration in California. Bragg claimed that this arbitration provision was so lopsided that it could not be enforced against him. The federal district court agreed. It ruled that Bragg was not required to travel to California to submit to arbitration proceedings that would likely be more expensive than the amount in controversy. Because the arbitration clause was deemed unconscionable (it was deemed unfair and in violation of public policies), the court held that the case could proceed in federal court. Soon afterward, the Bragg dispute was settled.

The Bragg case has been the subject of extensive legal commentary, but it illustrates a simple point: the effort to use contractual terms to create separate rules for virtual jurisdiction has limitations as a strategy. Courts in the United States and elsewhere may give private parties broad freedoms to use contracts to create separate legal regimes. However, when the rules fashioned by businesses are viewed as substantially harmful to consumers and the public, some courts and legislatures will create legal exceptions that invalidate contractual terms that are deemed oppressive or unjust.

Contract is perhaps the most powerful legal tool that creators of virtual technologies can use to protect themselves from legal risks. As the Bragg case illustrates, however, the tool is not a perfect solution as a matter of protecting companies or consumers. As virtual technologies proliferate, the enforceability of clickwrap contracts will likely be tested repeatedly requiring courts and legislatures to make specific rulings with respect to virtual technologies. These rules will determine whether particular rules violate standards of fairness in consumer-oriented contracts.

Property

Virtual property—including virtual dogs—can have real monetary value. In the game of *EverQuest II*, for instance, a player named Noah Burns reportedly made a considerable sum selling virtual dogs known as Halasian Maulers (Lastowka 2010). Burns found that by exploiting an error in the software code of *EverQuest II*, he could duplicate the virtual dogs and sell them to other players for platinum, the game's virtual currency. He could then sell the platinum to a wholesaler for real money. Though selling platinum for real money violated the contractual terms of *EverQuest II*, the owner of the game, Sony Online Entertainment, was not always effective in policing against the practice. Though Burns was eventually discovered, he reportedly made about $100,000 in profits before his account was terminated (Guest 2008).

The story of the Halasian Maulers was just a small affair in a much larger virtual economic picture. Around the world, many thousands of individuals, like Burns, are engaged in the commercial acquisition and sale of virtual property. As noted before, this sort of activity is commonly called gold farming. Perhaps the most well known company to have operated in the gold-farming industry is the Hong Kong–based Internet Gaming Entertainment, or IGE for short (Dibbell 2006). Reportedly, as early as 2006, IGE made over $250 million buying and selling virtual property (Lastowka 2010).

Richard Heeks, a researcher at the University of Manchester, estimates that, in 2007, the revenues from professional gold farming exceeded one billion dollars (Heeks 2009). In 2011, researchers Vili Lehdonvirta and Mirko Ernkvist estimated that the market for virtual property had expanded to roughly $10 billion, consisting of both direct sales of virtual items by companies to consumers and independent exchanges on virtual platforms, such as the sale of Halasian Maulers (Lehdonvirta and Ernkvist 2010). Given the growing size of virtual economies, the law has been increasingly involved with disputes concerning the value and ownership of virtual property.

The litigation over WoWGlider was indirectly a dispute over virtual property rights, given that the software was known to be an effective tool for gold farming. Likewise, the Bragg case was a dispute over virtual property, since Bragg's primary complaint was that the loss of his account in *Second Life* deprived him of the ability to profit from the sale of his virtual property. Other cases in other jurisdictions have also raised the question of the legal status of virtual property.

In November 2007, for instance, a 17-year-old in the Netherlands was charged with the theft of virtual property within the virtual world of *Habbo Hotel*. The value of the stolen property was roughly five thousand dollars and the thief had obtained it by stealing the account passwords of other players. At roughly the same time, two other Dutch teenagers were prosecuted for stealing virtual property from another teen. However, these two boys had physically threatened the victim with a knife offline and forced him to hand over, within the virtual world, a (virtual) amulet and a mask (Lodder 2010). Ultimately, the Supreme Court of the Netherlands found that the virtual property at issue in the latter case could be the subject of criminal theft. The Republic of Korea has already heard hundreds of cases involving crime and virtual property (Yoon 2004).

While some courts may struggle with the theft of intangible value, it is a fact that many forms of wealth today are divorced from tangible embodiments. As the Dutch Supreme Court observed, intangible property interests are not unprecedented. A bank account today is not a pile of coins that sits in a locked vault. Rather, it exists primarily as a line of code in a system of financial software. Our economy today is increasingly bound up with technologies of digital representation, making much of e-commerce just as intangible as virtual worlds.

A growing volume of legal literature debates whether and how the law might sort out rights in virtual property. Joshua Fairfield, a prominent commentator on the subject, argues that economic theory supports the recognition of markets in virtual property (Fairfield 2005). Others, like Barton Beebe, have questioned this claim on the basis that virtual property is only artificially scarce and its protection only serves to perpetuate class distinctions (Beebe 2010). In theory, in the world of *EverQuest II*, there could be an unlimited number of Halasian Maulers and everyone could have one. A virtual dog may be worth a hundred dollars today, but if the owner of the platform were to change the software code, it might be worth only pennies tomorrow.

However, it is also true that artificial scarcity creates value in other corners of society, and law does not simply disregard valuable property because the value is based on artificial scarcity. Given the real economic stakes in virtual worlds, it seems increasingly unlikely that the law will be unable to ignore the real value of virtual property. Eventually, some compromise must be obtained as courts or legislatures will need to grapple with the reality of virtual property. At present, however, there is no clear legal consensus on the future path of virtual property.

Copyright, jurisdiction, contract, and property hardly exhaust the variety of legal fields that touch upon virtual technologies. Future courts may be asked to decide, for instance: Does an avatar have a right of privacy? Can an avatar be defamed? Should participants in virtual worlds enjoy rights of free speech and free association? What laws should govern the hacking of virtual technologies and who should have the power to enforce those laws?

There is no clear answer to many of these questions, but it seems inevitable that they will be posed to courts.

Conclusion: The Trajectory of Virtual Law

The prior sections of this chapter have offered a variety of perspectives on virtual law as a matter of the real law applied to real technologies. From this perspective, the trajectory of virtual law seems to be one in which the power of the state is eroding in favor of the power of private parties. The WoWGlider case, for instance, shows that copyright can be used as a tool to enforce private rules in virtual environments that might not be enforced in analogous ways offline. The ubiquity of clickwrap agreements (contracts formed by clicking on an "I accept" button) suggests that those who operate consumer-facing virtual technologies are using contract law as a means to set separate terms that govern user rights and responsibilities in the online context. The ambiguities around virtual property may allow some forms of crime and profit that occur in the context of virtual economies to fall outside the ambit of existing laws.

However, in addition to these developments in positive law, we should recognize that virtual technologies challenge the law in two additional ways, namely by operating in ways that allow mimetic and technological powers to shape society and by allowing technology to supplant legal rules.

As I noted previously, the entertainment pleasures of virtual technologies come in part from the extent to which they produce confusion in the mind of the audience.

Though the death of a virtual dog is not understood, logically, as equivalent to the death of a real dog, it may nevertheless produce significant emotional reactions. Plato, speaking through Socrates in the *Republic*, famously feared that playwrights and poets wielded a dangerous social power and should be subject to careful state supervision. Plato's recommendation of a tightly regulated artistic culture is often viewed as fundamentally incompatible with modern tenets of liberal democracy. However, it is clear that Plato identified a troublesome problem—those with the power to manipulate the virtual do have power to sway the behavior of the public.

Modern advertising techniques do not merely respond to consumer preferences, but also shape consumer desire and popular culture. Despite this fact, marketing and popular media are generally subject to minimal regulation. In the United States, advertising, like entertainment software and virtual technologies, is viewed legally as a form of protected speech, a move that gives substantial leeway to the parties who employ them. Postmodern critics of simulation like Jean Baudrillard echo Plato's concerns when they lament the extent of our popular susceptibility to media imagery and narrative. And legal scholars like Julie Cohen, Ian Kerr, and Ryan Calo have raised resonating policy concerns about the capacities of virtual technologies, when used commercially, to shape our behavior and our perceptions.

A second and related observation is that the private power to control social software can be more effective, in many cases, than the right to call upon the state to enforce particular legal rules. Owners of virtual technologies enjoy both private property ownership of their machinery and the associated right to exercise creative control over their virtual environments. Few governments enjoy this kind of power.

Returning to the cases discussed above, it is important to note that most of them turned on the exercise of technological power. In the WoWGlider case, if Blizzard had effectively blocked the operation of the botting software with the Warden program, it would not have needed to litigate its copyright claims in federal court. In its efforts to combat gold farming directly, Blizzard has generally chosen to rely on technology, banning accounts of suspected gold farmers. The Bragg case provides a rare example of a banned player who challenged a virtual-world owner's exercise of technological power, but at considerable expense and only after that power was exercised to his detriment. And the story of the Halasian Maulers shows a rare example of a virtual entrepreneur who, by finding a flaw in the platform's software, managed to profit from his own (unauthorized) technological power, though ultimately his account was banned as well. And those who hack the accounts of gamers and steal virtual property are certainly profiting from a form of technological wrongdoing—but the law in many jurisdictions has still not decided whether they are thieves.

In conclusion, the intersection of the virtual and the legal is a very real and very dynamic region of modern law. It is characterized by complexity and ambiguity, but it exhibits a clear trajectory, one largely consistent with the legal trajectory of other institutions in the modern neoliberal order. As virtual law expands, so do private powers based on private ownership and rulemaking. If we limit the domain of virtual law to the work of legal institutions, we can see it as a realm where legal doctrines of intellectual property, contract, and property work to expand the powers of those who provide and maintain virtual technologies. If we broaden our notion of the legal to include forms of social regulation enacted by technological power, this only amplifies the conclusion that the rise of virtual law corresponds with the decline of traditional legal institutions.

REFERENCES

Beebe, B. 2010. Intellectual Property Law and the Sumptuary Code. *Harvard Law Review* 123 (2010): 809–889.

Bellia, P. L., Paul S. B., Brett M. F., and David G. Post. 2010. *Cyberlaw: Problems of Policy and Jurisprudence in the Information Age*. St. Paul: West Group.

Boellstorff, T. 2008. *Coming of Age in "Second Life": An Anthropologist Explores the Virtually Human*. Princeton, NJ: Princeton University Press.

Cardozo, B. 1921. *The Nature of the Judicial Process*. New Haven, CT: Yale University Press.

Consalvo, M. 2007. *Cheating: Gaining Advantage in Videogames*. Cambridge, MA: MIT Press.

Dibbell, J. 1998. *My Tiny Life*. New York: Henry Holt.

Dibbell, J. 2006. *Play Money: Or, How I Quit my Day Job and Made Millions Trading Virtual Loot*. New York: Basic Books.

Duranske, B. 2008. *Virtual Law: Navigating the Legal Landscape of Virtual Worlds*. Chicago: American Bar Association.

Fairfield, J. A. T. 2005. Virtual Property. *Boston University Law Review* 85: 1047–1102.

Feinman, J. M. 2010. *Law 101*. New York: Oxford University Press.

Fuller, L. L. 1958. Positivism and Fidelity to Law—a Reply to Professor Hart. *Harvard Law Review* 71: 630–672.

Grau, O. 2004. *Virtual Art: From Illusion to Immersion*. Cambridge, MA: MIT Press.

Guest, T. 2008. *Second Lives: A Journey through Virtual Worlds*. London: Random House Digital.

Heeks, R. 2009. Understanding "Gold Farming": Developing Country Production for Virtual Gameworlds. Information Technologies & International Development 5 (3). http://itidjournal.org/itid/article/view/383/179. Accessed June 24, 2013.

Juul, J. 2005. *Half-Real: Video Games between Real Rules and Fictional Worlds*. Cambridge, MA: MIT Press.

Lastowka, G. 2010. *Virtual Justice: The New Laws of Online Worlds*. New Haven, CT: Yale University Press.

Lehdonvirta, V., and M. Ernkvist. 2010. Knowledge Map of the Virtual Economy: Converting the Virtual Economy into Development Potential. In *InfoDev, Information for Development Program*. Washington, DC: infoDev / World Bank. http://www.infodev.org/infodev-files/resource/InfodevDocuments_1076.pdf. Accessed June 24, 2013.

Lessig, L. 1999. *Code and Other Laws of Cyberspace*. New York: Basic Books.

Lessig, L. 2005. *Free Culture: The Nature and Future of Creativity*. New York: Penguin.

Lodder, A. R. 2010. The 2009 Dutch Convictions on Virtual Theft Conflict Resolution in Virtual Worlds: General Characteristics. SSRN eLibrary. http://papers.ssrn.com/sol3/papers.cfm?abstract_id=1590144. Accessed June 24, 2013.

Mnookin, J. L. 1996. Virtual(ly) Law: The Emergence of Law in LambdaMOO: Mnookin. *Journal of Computer-Mediated Communication* 2 (1), June. http://onlinelibrary.wiley.com/doi/10.1111/j.1083-6101.1996.tb00185.x/abstract Accessed October 14, 2013.

Post, D. G. 2009. *In Search of Jefferson's Moose: Notes on the State of Cyberspace*. New York: Oxford University Press.

Turkle, S. 2011. *Alone Together: Why We Expect More from Technology and Less from Each Other*. New York: Basic Books.

Yoon, U.-G. 2004. Real Money Trading in MMORPG Items from a Legal and Policy Perspective. *SSRN eLibrary.* http://papers.ssrn.com/sol3/papers.cfm?abstract_id=1113327. Accessed June 24, 2013.

Zittrain, J. L. 2005. *Internet Law Jurisdiction*. New York: Foundation Press.

Cases

Bragg v. Linden Research. 487 F.Supp.2d 593 (E.D. Pa. 2007).

MDY Indus., LLC v. Blizzard Entm't, Inc. 629 F.3d 928 (9th Cir. 2010).

CHAPTER 30

....

VIRTUALITY IN THE
SPHERE OF ECONOMICS

....

VILI LEHDONVIRTA

THIS chapter examines virtuality and reality in the context of economic affairs. Digital objects and currencies found in game worlds and other online hangouts are considered play and make-believe, and branded as "virtual" to distinguish them from the serious world of "real" consumption and economy. However, virtual goods are increasingly bought and sold for real money, and the value of such trade has now reached several billion US dollars per year. This encroachment of the "virtual" into the "real" serves as an occasion for a critical reevaluation of supposed economic realities.

INTRODUCTION: RUSSIA'S POST-SOVIET
VIRTUAL ECONOMY

....

In 1990s post-Soviet Russia, enterprises, government branches, and households were engaged in a curious system of commerce that was different from the Soviet planned economy, but also unlike the Western free-market system that reformers wanted to instate (Gaddy and Ickes 1998; 2002). Its characterizing feature was that enterprises paid much of their dues to each other, to their workers, and to the tax collectors in kind, and that everyone who received such payments accepted them at a higher face value than what the market price of such goods would have been. In particular, manufacturing companies were able to tap into Russia's massive natural resources at rates far below world market prices by paying with their own overpriced products instead of currency. This effective subsidy allowed Russia's unreformed manufacturing sector to survive the sudden exposure to global competition. But to those who looked at accounting books as if they represented world market prices, it created an illusion that Russia's economy was much larger than it in reality was. When Western economists understood what was happening, they branded the system a "virtual economy" of "virtual revenues" generated through "virtual prices" (Gaddy and Ickes 2002).

The most common use of the term "virtual" in economic literature is technical: it is used in models to indicate a theoretical construct that is not intended to have an empirical counterpart. But in those rare cases where it is used to describe an empirical concept, I argue that it has three important characteristics that the case of Russia's post-Soviet economy illustrates well. First, calling something a "virtual" entity is intended to indicate that the entity in question has the appearance or some of the usual characteristics of its kind, but is nevertheless not the real thing. In other words, a virtual thing is an illusion, a pretense, or even an outright fraud. Second, the "virtuality" of an entity is always established in relation to something else that represents the "real." In the case of Russia's post-Soviet economy, the "real" prices that Western economists had in mind were world market prices, and the "real" economy was a Western-style market economy. These two characteristics of the term lead to a third and arguably the most important characteristic, which I will illustrate below.

Although Russia's post-Soviet system was notoriously inefficient and it is not my intention to defend it here, the system also had its proponents. The in-kind payments in effect meant that national gas and oil income was being distributed to the people as a form of social welfare, through wages in the enterprise sector. This type of social welfare was not part of the free-market reformers' agenda, as they wanted to privatize Russia's natural resources. By calling the prevailing system a "virtual" economy, the reformers could promote the notion that the system was inferior and had to be replaced by one that qualified as a "real" economy. For some, the "real" system would be better, but for others, it would be worse—it was a political struggle, and "virtual" was a political word. In other words, the third characteristic of the term "virtual" is that it is a loaded word that tends to be used as a rhetorical device to persuade readers toward a particular viewpoint.

The sphere of economics extends from scholarly economic debates to public discourse concerning economic affairs. In the recent years of economic tumult, this distinction has become increasingly permeable. In the remainder of this chapter, I examine virtuality in the sphere of economics through two contemporary phenomena: virtual consumption and virtual money. Both originally earned the addition "virtual" to their name through associations with information technology and virtual worlds, which are multiuser environments that in turn probably owe their label to the concept of virtual reality. According to the *New Oxford American Dictionary*, the adjective "virtual" in computing means "not physically existing as such but made by software to appear to do so." Mundane examples include virtual memory and virtual computer. In information technology, this adjective is almost purely descriptive with little value content. But it will be seen that in discourse on economic affairs, it acquires the three characteristics that were identified above in connection with Russia's virtual economy. In the concluding section, I consider what the "marginalization by virtualization" of the two phenomena under scrutiny suggests about the realities of our economy.

Virtual Consumption of Digital Goods

Digital games and online communities have for a long time included features that simulate economic activity. For example, *Habitat*, opened in 1985, was an early pioneer of digital environments. It used two-dimensional graphics to represent spaces such as home, hotel, and arcade, where cartoon-style characters controlled by users could talk and interact. The landscape was scattered with vending machines from which users could purchase virtual items ranging from weapons to furniture. Purchases were paid with a currency called Tokens, which was distributed to the users for free (Dibbell 1998, 172). This was a kind of "consumption play": an activity that mimics actual consumption without really being so (Lehdonvirta, Wilska, and Johnson 2009). So-called massively multiplayer online games (MMOs) have since taken consumption play much further: they feature simulations of whole economies, complete with processes of extraction, manufacturing, trade, and consumption. Such simulations are clearly "virtual economies" in the sense of "not physically existing as such but made by software to appear to do so," and that is indeed the name applied to them in popular as well as academic literature (Castronova 2006). The simulated goods that circulate in these economies are called "virtual goods."

The status of virtual economies as simulations began to be questioned, however, when players started to exchange virtual goods for real money. Around 1999, some MMO players started to put their game goods on auction in the recently launched e-commerce sites like eBay (Castronova 2006; Huhh 2008). Perhaps surprisingly, they soon received bids from other players. When an auction was completed, payment was carried out using ordinary means, such as check or money order. The two players then met up in the game and the seller handed the auctioned object to the buyer. This way, an exchange value measured in US dollars or Korean won could soon be observed for virtual goods ranging from characters to gold nuggets. The biggest publicly reported player-to-player trade is the 2007 sale of a character in the online game *World of Warcraft* for approximately 7,000 euros (Jimenez 2007).

As trade volumes increased, what started as a player-to-player phenomenon soon attracted commercial interest. Professional players, known as "gold farmers," began to play the games for profit rather than pleasure, harvesting massive amounts of game assets and selling them to wealthier players on online markets. By mid-2000s, this activity had grown into a whole industry that was estimated to employ as many as 100,000 game laborers in digitally connected low-income countries such as China (Lehdonvirta and Ernkvist 2011). Virtual goods are now also among the most sought-after commodities among cybercriminals (Krebs 2009). Criminals hack into players' game accounts, steal the enclosed virtual items and currencies, and sell them on electronic marketplaces for a profit.

Before long, game publishers and online community operators took note of this phenomenon. Instead of charging users a subscription fee or showing advertisements, they realized that they could generate revenues by selling virtual items to their users. This business model first became popular in Korea, China, and Japan (Nojima 2008; Wi 2009; So and Westland 2010), and around 2009, broke into mainstream Western online business (Lehdonvirta and Ernkvist 2011). For example, American game developer Zynga makes relatively simple simulation and nurturing games that anyone can play for free on Facebook. Their hit game *Farmville* at best claimed over 90 million active players. Those players who wish to advance faster in the game's virtual economy can buy items such as virtual tractors and tractor fuel. So many players do that Zynga earned $1.14 billion from its games in 2011. In total, approximately $7 billion worth of virtual items and currencies were estimated sold by publishers in 2010 (Lehdonvirta and Ernkvist 2011). More virtual tractors were sold in a day than real tractors in a year. Most recently, virtual goods have become a highly popular way to spend money in mobile and tablet games.

Some people reacted with hostility toward this new type of consumption. In Finland, opinions in the media and public discourse concerning spending on game goods were rather negative during most of the 2000s (Lehdonvirta 2009a). Many parents of children and teenagers who were purchasing game items saw it as another unnecessary expense and fought actively against it. Consider the following quotes, taken from readers' comments on an article related to virtual consumption published in the online version of the newspaper *Helsingin Sanomat* on March 23, 2008 (quoted in Lehdonvirta 2009a, 11–12):

> It is completely insane to pay for something that in reality does not exist.
>   Consider what better and real reality you could have gotten for that money.
>   It's pointless to pay for virtual stuff when it could just as well be free.
>   [Selling virtual goods] represents taking advantage of children both economically and psychologically.
>   Previously you couldn't abuse children in business like this. It's incredible that Finland is a major player in this immoral practice. I wonder how many Finns' income depends on getting children to consume the most foolish things!

The comments above exemplify a number of common views held toward virtual consumption that question the rationality of spending money on virtual goods. Virtual goods are typically seen as illusory, imaginary, unreal, or even nonexistent. They are contrasted with "real" goods, which are rational, useful, and valuable. Something real is better than something virtual. According to this view, virtual goods are not worth anything, either because of their ephemeral nature, or because they are digital, and digital image flows are reproducible without cost. Spending real money on virtual goods is therefore considered irrational.

It is probably safe to say that the above views, highly critical of virtual consumption, are often arrived at without substantial study or experience of the actual practices of virtual consumption. They are outsider impressions. The insiders, the virtual consumers themselves, obviously have substantial experience and embodied knowledge regarding the actual practices as well as the meanings and motivations behind virtual consumption. But they lack the motivation and perhaps also the capability and analytical distance to express these in a form that could be digested by parents, regulators, and mainstream media, and thus fail to contribute to a debate on virtual consumption.

What is at stake in this debate? From a societal perspective, the spending of real money on virtual goods, as an emerging phenomenon, does not have an established position in society. It could be characterized as "gaming," which carries with it certain meanings and places it in a certain ethical frame: recreational spending, leisure, but also frivolousness, distraction, and even addiction. It could also be characterized as a form of "online shopping": economic activity, conventional, legal, but also hedonistic and subject to a different set of ethical concerns. And it could also be characterized as "exploitation," as above.

The way in which parents, regulators, and other authorities conceptualize (or fail to conceptualize) virtual consumption has very practical implications for the people involved, individuals as well as companies (Lehdonvirta 2009a). For example, whether society sees virtual consumption as something legitimate and desirable or something irrational and subversive will greatly shape its uptake as an economic activity. In Korea, the National Assembly has passed a law that makes certain types of real-money trading of virtual goods illegal (Lehdonvirta and Virtanen 2010). In Finland, complaints from parents led the consumer ombudsman, a public official, to call for negotiations with Sulake, a company operating an online hangout popular among teenagers (Lehdonvirta and Virtanen 2010). Consequently, Sulake now imposes a weekly limit on the amount of money its customers can spend on virtual goods. The limit varies from country to country. According to Sulake, the spending cap is set to correspond approximately with the local price of a cinema ticket (Lehdonvirta and Virtanen 2010). Purchases of cinema tickets, sweets, clothes, or indeed anything else that young people spend their money on are not capped in this way—the spending cap is unprecedented. Greg Lastowka's chapter in this book (chapter 29) contains more examples of legal struggles related to virtual goods.

Research on virtual consumption does not support most of the negative interpretations put forward in the public discourse. First, the position that spending real money on virtual goods is insane because the goods "do not really exist" is untenable (Lehdonvirta 2009a). Virtual goods are not figments of imagination: they are physically stored in database servers and are visible and can be manipulated through computer interfaces. In this sense, they are even more tangible than many of the more conventional ways of spending money, like watching a movie or listening to music. Virtual goods clearly do exist, and in this sense are quite "real."

Second, virtual goods are not useless as goods, even though they are "virtual" in the sense of being implemented in software. Empirical studies suggest that consumers use virtual goods in digital media for many of the same purposes as they use material goods in physical environments: to seek fulfillment of needs, real or imagined (Martin 2008; Lehdonvirta 2009a; 2009b), to construct and communicate social distinctions, bonds, and identity positions (Martin 2008; Lehdonvirta 2009a; Lehdonvirta, Wilska, and Johnson 2009), and to stimulate and pursue hedonistic fantasies (Denegri-Knott and

Molesworth 2010). In other words, although virtual goods obviously cannot offer nutrition or shelter to the body, they are quite capable of being used in the majority of roles that commodities are used in a consumer society. Chapters 17, 18, and 19 of this book (Albright and Simmens; Stenslie; Geraci) show how behaviors like dating, sex, and religion are acted out over digital media; it should come as no surprise that consumerism can be acted out over digital media also.

Still, those who assert that virtual goods are not "real" are probably not meaning it in the ontological sense, but rather in a more practical and colloquial sense. Virtual goods are digital and limited to digital spaces only. Even if we accept that virtual goods are technically part of the same reality as everything else, it can be argued that in practice they are not present in most situations or their impact is so insubstantial that they are more like fantasy than actual goods. Turn the computer off, and their thin link to reality disappears. Thus virtual goods "do not really exist" in the way the living room sofa does (Lehdonvirta 2009a).

Studies of media use show that the proportion of time spent with digital media continues to increase even in countries where it is already high (e.g., Räsänen 2008). For people who interact mostly in the digital world, it is the living room sofa that lacks presence and impact in most situations. If those are the measures of reality, it is the sofa that must be termed "unreal" in such a case. Furthermore, the digital world is increasingly penetrating into face-to-face social situations. Mobile devices, public display screens, and, in the near future, wearable computing and augmented reality applications make it possible for virtual objects to have presence and impact in social situations of the material world (Montola and Stenros 2009; Nojima 2008). For example, location-based service Foursquare creates a virtual layer of collectible badges on top of urban gathering places, and millions of participants compete to obtain them. A particular virtual badge might afford its owner not only social status among peers, but tangible economic benefits at the restaurant or establishment in question.

From an economic perspective, the strongest argument in support of the "reality" of virtual consumption is that businesses based on selling virtual goods contribute to the gross domestic product (GDP) in the very same way as their more material counterparts. The more people spend on virtual goods, the more virtual goods business will contribute value to the economy. The same applies to any goods, from furniture to cinema tickets. Virtual goods are perhaps more ephemeral than many material goods, because they might, for example, disappear suddenly if the operator goes out of business. But in today's economy, economic prosperity is not measured by the amount of durable goods hoarded in vaults, but by GDP: the total spending on final goods and services produced in a country (Burda and Wyplosz 1997, 21). Thus lack of durability can even be a virtue to the national economy, if it leads to repeated spending.

Given that virtual goods are in practice "real"—they are used for largely the same purposes as other consumer goods, and they contribute to the national economy just like any other goods—what is at the root of the assertions to the contrary? Why are the people quoted in the examples above attempting to marginalize digital item sales by positing a strong boundary between "real" and "virtual" consumption? In part, this is probably explained by the inertia of consumption-related social norms. The categories of consumption that are considered necessary and permissible, and those that are considered a luxury and a vice, change slowly over time (Belk 2004, 71–72). For example, over the past two decades, computers and mobile phones have undergone a classificatory shift in rich countries, from unnecessary or pretentious luxury to basic necessity. This suggests that more recently emerged forms of technology consumption, such as virtual items, simply take time to become acceptable, regardless of their harms or benefits.

There may also be a deeper reason for the "marginalization by virtualization" of digital item sales. Critical thinkers such as Baudrillard (2002) and Lury (1996) suggest that we live in a consumer culture where the primary means through which people pursue meaning in their lives is through the purchase and accumulation of goods. Virtual consumption is such a strikingly naked example of this culture that it perhaps provokes people to realize the futility of their own pursuits. Decorating a physical home with the latest interior design is after all little more than an expensive and environmentally destructive sibling of decorating a virtual playhouse with which to impress friends. Consumers unwilling to let go of the fantasy that their material consumption games are somehow more meaningful and serious may thus find it necessary to marginalize virtual consumption lest it cause uncomfortable cognitive dissonance.

VIRTUAL MONEY, REAL MONEY?

Besides virtual goods, the Internet has also seen a huge proliferation of so-called "virtual currencies" during the past decade (Lehdonvirta and Ernkvist 2011; Lehdonvirta 2009a). Many of these currencies are simply play money that is used in online games to trade game items. Others are used in the manner of arcade tokens to facilitate purchases of digital goods: the consumer buys the currency from the vendor and then spends it on the vendor's or the vendor's partners' products. Facebook Credits are an example of such token money. Still others are digital currencies intended to be used in general online commerce between any willing parties. Bitcoin is the most prominent example of such a currency. In some cases, the distinctions are blurred, and a currency that was originally intended for a more limited purpose becomes a general online currency. An example of this is Q Coin, a token money issued by a company called Tencent that became an almost general online payment system in China, until the People's Bank of China issued a proclamation prohibiting the use of virtual currencies in the trade of physical goods.

What all of these currencies have in common is that they are termed "virtual money" in media and popular discourse. The "real money" implied by this terminology is national currencies like the US dollar and the euro. So what is the essential difference between "virtual money" and "real money"? The difference is not that one is digital and the other is not. Some virtual currencies come in the form of physical cards or tokens, and most dollars and euros today exist only in the form of digital records in banks' accounting systems. To analyze the real difference, it is necessary to first clarify what real money is. In the midst of economic crises, fluctuating exchange rates, and unpredictable interest rates, we hear a lot of talk about money and finance in the media, yet very few people today could say what money actually is.

Economists generally identify three purposes for money: it is (1) a medium of exchange, (2) a store of value, and (3) a unit of account (Mankiw 2009, 80–81). Money is defined through these purposes: any object or record that is used for these purposes is and can be called money (80–81). Let us clarify these purposes below.

If two people wish to exchange goods via barter, the problem is that they both have to have something that the other party desires for the exchange to be possible. Failing that, they have to find a third person that is willing to accept something from the first person in exchange for something desired by the second person. Needless to say, this makes trade difficult. The problem can be avoided by using a medium of exchange: a universal commodity that everyone accepts as payment, either because they need it directly, or because they know that they can always later exchange it to something that they need. In ancient Egypt, gold was used for this purpose, whereas in Babylonia, silver and grain were used. In Iron Age Finland, squirrel pelts were the favored medium of exchange.

A store of value is simply something that is used to preserve value across time. An apple farmer is rich in apples after harvest, but the apples will perish in a few months. To have something to pay with even months after harvest, the farmer must exchange the apples to something more durable. Historically, precious metals have been popular stores of value.

A unit of account is a measuring stick in which value is measured. For example, prices and debts can be expressed in euros or ounces of gold. Sometimes the currency used as the medium of exchange is different from the unit of account. For example, the euro was adopted as an accounting unit in governments and banks before actual euro coins and notes were released into circulation. But in general, one region tends to have one main money that is used for all the three purposes.

Now that we have defined real money, how does virtual money differ from it? Consider the most frivolous example: virtual gold coins used inside an online game. They are used as a medium of exchange to facilitate transactions between players. If the game has perishable goods, players will certainly also use the gold coins as a store of value. And it goes without saying that the gold coins are used as a measure of value when expressing prices of goods and debts between players. The perhaps surprising conclusion seems to be that virtual money does not differ in any way from "real" money. There is simply money.

In practice, the difference between those currencies that tend to be called "virtual money" and those that are afforded the status of "real money" is in the size of their currency areas. Economists usually understand a currency area as a geographic area within which a particular currency can be used to pay for goods and services (Mankiw 2009, 362–363). But an equivalent and more flexible definition is that a currency area is the total set of goods and services payable with a given currency. Virtual gold coins in an online game can for the most part only pay for virtual goods inside the game, and perhaps also for some services provided by dedicated players of the game. A national currency can usually pay for a much larger variety of goods and services, although it probably cannot be used to pay for the aforementioned virtual goods. Differences in the sizes of the currency areas are only differences of degree, not of any fundamental quality. In some cases a virtual currency may even have a currency area that rivals small national currencies in size, as perhaps was the case with China's Q Coin. When the People's Bank took action against this digital currency, it was not because of its virtuality, but because of its reality, its real economic influence. Still, in its rhetoric, the bank emphasized that virtual currencies should not be confused with real economic affairs, marginalizing the Q Coin.

A reader might intuitively suggest that there is nevertheless one fundamental difference between real and virtual money: that real money is more trustworthy than virtual money. After all, real money is issued by governments and banks, whereas virtual currencies are typically issued by Internet companies and other smaller private organizations. To analyze this claim, it is useful to understand how money obtains its value in the first place. So-called commodity money, such as grain or coins made from a precious metal, is valuable thanks to being made from a valuable substance. Another main type of money is fiat money, which is valuable thanks to being generally accepted as payments for goods and services somewhere, usually because of a government mandate (a fiat) requiring so (Mankiw 2009, 81–83). Other variations include representative money, which represents a claim to something valuable (e.g., gold deposit certificate), and token money, which is valuable thanks to someone pledging to redeem it for something of value.

Some virtual currencies are fiat money (e.g., virtual gold coins in a game), some are token money (e.g., Facebook Credits), and there are also virtual commodity currencies—for example, users of online hangout *Habbo Hotel* used virtual chairs and sofas as a currency, as these objects also had use value. The trustworthiness of all these currencies is limited by the fact that the records that make up the money are controlled by private organizations. The records might be destroyed, or the organization might recklessly issue so much new money that the value of the currency is destroyed. In contrast, material commodity currencies like actual gold coins are safer in this respect, although the value of commodities does fluctuate significantly, which hampers their use as money. Most national currencies today are fiat money. Fiat currencies like dollars and euros have enjoyed very stable values in the past decades, thanks to active adjustment of the money supply by central banks.

What does this mean for trustworthiness? Overall, it is probably true that virtual currencies are in practice less trustworthy today than national currencies. But this is by no means an absolute rule. Just as with digital currencies, the materials from which national fiat currencies are made of (i.e., bits, paper and metal) are almost worthless. National currencies used to be backed up by precious metals, that is, a dollar used to represent a claim to a quantity of gold, but this is no longer the case. National currencies thus have the same potential to completely lose their value as virtual currencies have. And this does happen: most recently, the Zimbabwe dollar, a "real money" according to conventional understanding, began to experience rapid inflation in 2005. The inflation exceeded 200 million percent in 2008. The whole currency was abandoned in 2009. During these four years, almost any "virtual" currency would have been a more reliable store of value—even virtual gold coins in an online game! In other words, virtual money does not fundamentally differ from real money—there is only money.

Conclusions: Marginalization by Virtualization

Through Russia's virtual economy as well as more recent examples of virtuality in the digital world, I sought to show that in the sphere of economics, the notion of virtuality tends to be associated with illusion, pretense, and even fraud. To be virtual is to be non-existent, whereas the economy is a sphere of material provision. Thus virtuality is a vice, not a virtue. Virtuality is always established in relation to something else that represents the "real." In the case of virtual consumption, the implied real is the whole set of more established consumption practices, especially the consumption of material goods. In the case of virtual money, the quite explicitly stated real is the set of national currencies, no matter how unstable.

As the analyses in this chapter have demonstrated, when such dichotomous language is subjected to scrutiny, it turns out that the dichotomy is delusory. Virtual consumption is no less real than more conventional forms of consumption; it is arguably more tangible than the consumption of film or other media. Virtual goods are used for social signification and identity games in the same way as other goods in a consumer culture. Sales of virtual goods contribute to the national economy in the same way as their more conventional counterparts. As for virtual money, no fundamental difference can be found from highly respected national currencies, only differences of degree. Elsewhere similar real-virtual dichotomies have been argued to be equally misleading (Lehdonvirta 2010). The fact that we are nevertheless so apt to see such dichotomies around us perhaps reflects the prominence of dichotomies in the history of Western thought, from Plato's theory of forms to Cartesian mind-matter dualism. But an error is made when these metaphysical categories are imposed on the ontological reality around us.

In the introduction to this chapter, it was argued that in the sphere of economics, "virtual" is a loaded word that can be used in politics. In the previous sections, we saw that this "marginalization by virtualization" can occur for several reasons. Recognizing such a frivolous pursuit as virtual consumption as a valid economic activity places in question the meaningfulness of the whole consumption-centered economy. In effect, it shows that in a consumer society, *all* consumption is virtual. Marginalizing digital virtual consumption by placing it in an ontologically distinct category of "fake" things avoids this challenge to prevailing norms and values. Marginalization by virtualization may thus be a spontaneous reaction arising from the need to avoid cognitive dissonance.

In the case of virtual money, there is an even stronger need to maintain prevailing conceptions. As I write this, serious doubts about the viability of the common European currency, the euro, are being expressed by French president Nicolas Sarkozy. Central banks around the world are looking for alternatives to the US dollar as a reserve currency. Digital networks have made it practical to create private currencies that are used for the very same purposes as national currencies, but as of yet in much smaller scale. Despite their troubles, national currencies are still recognized as the "real money" and are therefore seen as the safest and most legitimate choice. But next-generation private digital currencies, which the distributed currency Bitcoin heralds, might in many ways turn out to be safer for the user than national currencies that risk falling prey to politics and special interests. If this turns out to be the case, then the trust placed in national currencies would hang largely on the mere idea of them being "real" money. Upholding the fictional real-virtual dichotomy would become a matter of national importance.

References

Baudrillard, J. 2002. Consumer Society. In *Selected Writings*, 2nd edition, edited by M. Poster, 32–59. Stanford, CA: Stanford University Press.

Belk, R. W. 2004. The Human Consequences of Consumer Culture. In *Elusive Consumption*, edited by K. M. Ekström and H. Brembeck, 67–86. Oxford: Berg.

Burda, M., and C. Wyplosz. 1997. *Macroeconomics: A European Text*. 2nd edition. New York: Oxford University Press.

Castronova, E. 2006. Virtual Worlds: A First-Hand Account of Market and Society on the Cyberian Frontier. In *The Game Design Reader: A Rules of Play Anthology*, edited by K. Salen and E. Zimmerman, 814–863.. Cambridge, MA: MIT Press.

Denegri-Knott, J. and M. Molesworth. 2010. Concepts and Practices of Digital Virtual Consumption. *Consumption Markets and Culture* 13 (2): 109–132.

Dibbell, J. 1998. *My Tiny Life: Crime and Passion in a Virtual World*. New York: Henry Holt.

Gaddy, C., and B. Ickes. 1998. Russia's Virtual Economy. *Foreign Affairs* 77: 53–67.

Gaddy, C., and B. Ickes. 2002. *Russia's Virtual Economy*. Washington, DC: Brookings Institution Press.

Huhh, J. S. 2008. Culture and Business of PC Bangs in Korea. *Games and Culture* 3 (1): 26–37.

Jimenez, C. 2007. The High Cost of Playing *Warcraft*. BBC News Online, September 24. http://news.bbc.co.uk/2/hi/technology/7007026.stm. Accessed on July 28, 2010.

Krebs, B. 2009. The Scrap Value of a Hacked PC. *Washington Post Security Fix*. http://voices.washingtonpost.com/securityfix/2009/05/the_scrap_value_of_a_hacked_pc.html. Accessed March 15, 2011.

Lehdonvirta, V. 2009a. *Virtual Consumption*. Publications of the Turku School of Economics A-11:2009. Turku School of Economics: Turku. http://info.tse.fi/julkaisut/vk/Ae11_2009.pdf. Accessed on June 1, 2011.

Lehdonvirta, V. 2009b. Virtual Item Sales as a Revenue Model: Identifying Attributes That Drive Purchase Decisions. *Electronic Commerce Research* 9 (1): 97–113.

Lehdonvirta, V. 2010. Virtual Worlds Don't Exist: Questioning the Dichotomous Approach in MMO Studies. *Game Studies* 10 (1). http://gamestudies.org/1001/articles/lehdonvirta. Accessed June 1, 2011.

Lehdonvirta, V., and M. Ernkvist. 2011. Knowledge Map of the Virtual Economy. World Bank: Washington DC. http://www.infodev.org/en/Document.1076.pdf. Accessed June 1, 2011.

Lehdonvirta, V., and P. Virtanen. 2010. A New Frontier in Digital Content Policy: Case Studies in the Regulation of Virtual Goods and Artificial Scarcity. *Policy and Internet* 2 (3): 7–29.

Lehdonvirta, V., T.-A. Wilska, and M. Johnson. 2009. Virtual Consumerism: Case *Habbo Hotel*. *Information, Communication and Society* 12 (7): 1059–1079.

Lury, C. 1996. *Consumer Culture*. New Brunswick, NJ: Rutgers University Press.

Mankiw, N. G. 2009. *Macroeconomics*. 7th edition. New York: Worth Publishers.

Martin, J. 2008. Consuming Code: Use-Value, Exchange-Value, and the Role of Virtual Goods in *Second Life*. *Journal of Virtual Worlds Research* 1 (2). https://journals.tdl.org/jvwr/article/view/300/262. Accessed on May 1, 2010.

Montola, M., and J. Stenros. 2009. *Pervasive Games: Theory and Design*. Boston, MA: Morgan Kaufmann.

Nojima, M. 2008. 人はなぜ形のないものを買のか　仮想世界のビジネスモデル [Why do people buy immaterial goods: Virtual world business models]. Tokyo: NTT Publishing.

Räsänen, P. 2008. The Aftermath of the ICT Revolution? Media and Communication Technology Preferences in Finland in 1999 and 2004. *New Media and Society* 10 (2): 225–245.

So, S., and J. C. Westland. 2010. *Red Wired: China's Internet Revolution*. London: Marshall Cavendish.

Wi, J.-H. 2009. *Innovation and Strategy of Online Games*. London: Imperial College Press.

PART VII

A-LIFE AND ARTIFICIAL
INTELLIGENCE

CHAPTER 31

··

ON THE ROLE OF "DIGITAL ACTORS" IN ENTERTAINMENT-BASED VIRTUAL WORLDS

··

PHIL CARLISLE

MODERN video games bear little resemblance to the original paddle and ball games that were their digital origins. They offer virtual worlds of ever increasing fidelity and experiences where natural user interface techniques are increasingly used to interact with the virtual environment. Game developers have spent a considerable amount of time developing techniques for creating engaging characters both visually and behaviorally; however the continuing trend in most video games is to develop the emotional connection between players and characters using noninteractive methods.

As our understanding of the interactive medium develops, it becomes clearer that this is not the only approach available, and designers are beginning to explore the potential of the development of interactive characters and how they respond to player interactions within the video game medium. The motivation for exploring these interactions lies in the emotional connection between the player and the virtual character. The major goal of many game designers is to create worlds and characters that have an emotional impact on the player, and this requires that the player believes in the illusion of the world and its inhabitants. Because video games are an interactive form, it is often obvious when interactivity is removed during portions of the game where narrative is delivered. This poses a question about the applicability of the passive narrative form used in traditional media, where participants are expected to engage with the characters of a story by forming an empathic bond with them. With interactive worlds like video games, the player is not simply a voyeur but instead is an active participant in the ongoing narrative, and this opens up many new opportunities and asks fundamental questions about the design of the narrative experience.

Video game designs that merge the interactive nature of gameplay with the narrative forms of storytelling in a new interactive way are slowly developing. Researchers from Carnegie Mellon University's Oz Project research group used the term "interactive story worlds" to describe such designs (Mateas 1997). Story worlds offer the player interactions with virtual characters and worlds, but have an overarching narrative context for the interactions. Users are fundamentally embedded within the narrative and form the narrative through their actions, and, ultimately, the world and its inhabitants must be behaviorally believable and responsive to these actions in order to engage the player.

In this chapter I will discuss the potential for new experiences offered by the further development of interactive virtual characters and their expressive behaviors. The term "digital actor" is used in this chapter, because I believe that for video games, the primary goal is to evoke an emotional response from the player during the act of interacting with the character, as well as to drive a central narrative. This goal is very similar to the purpose of actors in theater, animation, and cinema.

I will begin by surveying other uses of virtual characters and how this relates to the use of virtual characters in entertainment. I will describe how many of the techniques used in other media to create compelling characters can be applied to digital actors and the nature of "acting" and how it relates to the development of expressive behaviors. I will consider the technical and design challenges surrounding the creation of believable characters for interactive story worlds. Although I must acknowledge that sound is an important aspect of such characters, I will limit myself to the visual and behavioral aspects of these characters. I will discuss how digital actors can be "directed" to perform their desired role, how these roles change dynamically throughout an interactive play session, and how techniques are used to control the narrative experience.

Finally, I aim to address the nature of human emotional attachment to virtual characters, what they mean to players, what interactions are possible and desirable, and how they may fundamentally challenge our perception of what it means to be a "living" being.

OTHER FORMS OF VIRTUAL CHARACTERS

Outside of the entertainment area, virtual characters have been the subjects of considerable research. Applications for training, education, human computer interaction, and social simulation have all been developed, and yet the application of virtual characters for entertainment has seen relatively little research. While this chapter has an overall focus on the use of digital actors within entertainment, it will attempt to consider alternative uses of such rich emotional interactions.

Embodied conversational agents (Cassell 2000) have many similarities to characters in video games. They are virtual agents, often with humanoid characteristics and virtual representations, which interact with human participants. The fact that these conversational agents are "embodied" as virtual characters situated within a three-dimensional world differentiates them from simple knowledge delivery agents; however, the central purpose of these embodied agents is usually either to transfer knowledge or to study the effectiveness of communicative acts.

Another area that currently employs embodied virtual agents is the field of simulation and training, where there are typically characters to interact with in the training scenario. This is used, for example, to train soldiers to deal with situations when in unfamiliar localities (Dill 2011). Similarly, virtual agents are often employed in the research and simulation of crowds, particularly for the purposes of modeling crowd movement and flow for purposes such as evacuation (Pelechano, Allbeck, and Norman 2008).

In the early 1990s, as personal computers became more powerful, interactive agent research in a form that closely resembles that of video game characters was undertaken under the name "believable agents," with groups such as CMU's Oz Project and MIT's synthetic characters lab developing new models and techniques that are among the most directly applicable academic approaches to virtual agents for use in video games. Works such as *Facade* (Mateas and Stern 2003) and *Improv* (Perlin and Goldberg 1996) and similar work by Blumberg and Galyean (1995) have a great deal of similarity to, and affinity with, works within video games.

Finally, works within the field of interactive storytelling such as Cavazza, Charles, and Mead (2002; 2004) have a strong similarity to the field of virtual characters used by video games. However, there are differences in that interactive storytelling places greater importance on the generation of "story" as a means to drive the character actions. In essence the difference is that video game characters often are simply beings used to create a richer experience, rather than characters in a plot. Hence, video game characters may have more autonomy than the traditional character in an interactive story.

The Goal of Entertainment

The fundamental goal for the majority of video games is to provide entertainment. This goal is an important factor when considering believable agents from a research perspective, as we attempt to develop technologies and approaches to deliver that goal of entertainment. Rather than scientific exactitude, we are instead attempting to achieve player engagement and appropriate agent behavior that can be considered entertaining. This is problematic as currently there is no method of determining the entertainment qualities of video game characters. However, we can learn much from the techniques developed for similar entertainment mediums.

To quote Mateas:

> The success of a believable agent is determined by audience perception. If the audience finds the agent believable, the agent is a success. AI tries to measure success objectively. How many problems could the program solve? How long did the robot run around before it got into trouble? How similar is the system's solution to a human's solution? Such audience independent evaluations of research don't make sense for characters. (1997)

This is a very strange notion for technology-minded researchers. The concept that it is the perception of the approach that holds value, rather than the approach itself, is quite challenging. Yet it makes perfect sense to think this way if the goal is to create entertaining and memorable experiences.

Especially suitable for video game characters is the application of techniques developed for stop-motion animation typified by the multiple works of Disney. Indeed, many training materials used to develop video game characters refer to principles developed at Disney (Thomas and Johnston 1995).

The appropriate use of techniques from other entertainment mediums is helpful; however, the nature of the interactive medium of video games is fundamentally different, and it is this difference, the ability of the user to interact with the medium, that causes a number of significant challenges. In a stop-motion animation context, the creator is able to fully describe all aspects of the viewer experience. Each individual frame of animation is hand-edited and shot individually and then later composited into a running animation, thus allowing the creator to employ techniques that can rely on the knowledge of how any given frame fits in with the overall story structure. However, an interactive medium by its nature must allow for interaction. In a typical video game 3D world, that interactivity causes challenges in dealing with the viewpoint of the user. In essence, the experience of the game changes as the user (player) of the game interacts with the game. Thus, any character interactions may also be interpreted differently depending on changes of the players' viewpoint.

In order to counteract this lack of viewpoint control, current video games employ techniques that temporarily lock the player viewpoint at points in the game, typically during narrative exposition. This technique is most commonly seen in the use of cutscenes. These are predefined scenes that are triggered by player interactions where the viewpoint is locked out from player control and is instead controlled by designer direction much as in stop-motion animation and film. This shift between interactive and noninteractive scenes is problematic because it causes abrupt shifts in the perception of the player and changes the nature of the interaction between the player and the game.

One of the primary aims of much of the work involved in video game character development is to create characters that can interact with players in meaningful ways and to eventually overcome the reliance on cutscenes to drive the narrative, instead relying on the characters through their behavior to create a more emergent narrative that can include dynamic interactions with the player.

The Techniques of Video Game Characters as Digital Actors

If we accept that video game characters are primarily employed to engage and interact with the player and are designed to try to make the player feel a certain way about any interactions, then we can consider the more important question, which is the nature of these interactions and how they can enrich the interactive experience for players.

There is a very specific set of problems when we consider interactions in the virtual world, as we cannot "stage" the interactions in quite the same manner as we might be able to in the real world. The nature of interactive entertainment suggests that new techniques must be employed in order to try to evoke an emotional response. However, it is useful to discuss those techniques that have been used successfully to evoke the required emotional response in other media and to consider how applicable such techniques would be in an interactive form.

Appeal

"Appeal" is the term described in *The Illusion of Life* (Thomas and Johnston 1995) to denote the "design" of a character such that it has attributes that make it fundamentally interesting or endearing to an audience. In the world of traditional animation typically employed by Disney, this was reduced to a number of core attributes that were considered appealing to a mass-market audience: for example, the use of larger than realistically proportioned eyes, smaller body proportions, and rounded faces to make the characters more childlike and thus more emotionally engaging. We can see that even in theater and cinema the notion of appeal still has value, as we typically consider more fully realized characters more interesting. This suggests that appeal is a universal trait of characters that we find worthwhile, and thus we should be seeking to adopt similar concepts for the interactive medium. Specifically for video game characters, we can employ many of the aspects from characters designed for traditional stop-motion animation, with the caveat that there are certain technical limitations that would currently restrict the designs for use in an interactive context. For example, there is currently not enough processing power to produce a real-time interactive version of Rapunzel[1] because the costs of simulating her hair would be too great.

Movement and Animation

Many of the principles of animation described in *The Illusion of Life* and very well detailed in *The Animator's Survival Kit* (Williams 2001) are also directly relevant to adoption for digital actors. Given that the fundamentals of motion are the same in the interactive form, the use of anticipation (predicting an important event by motioning one part of the body toward it before fully responding with the whole body), follow-through, secondary action, and overlapping action are reasonable techniques to apply to an interactive form. Based as they are on the dynamics of motion observed through the study of human and animal motion, these techniques are commonly applied to animations to help convince the viewer to believe the character is actually alive.

Modern video game technologies, such as motion capture (the capturing of joint orientations and positions using various hardware approaches), allow many of the features of stop-motion animation to be easily recreated. However, outside of relatively realistic human movements, it still requires a skilled animator to use the digital tools in much the same way as a stop-motion animator would, using key frames to describe significant poses and using in-betweens to interpolate the key poses. The difference in perceived qualities of "realistic" motion capture-based animation and "expressive" key-frame animation is an area that requires further study, but observation suggests that there are some significant psychological effects occurring and that these effects should not be discounted if the goal is an emotional response from the player.

Simulation

Computational models used in simulation are often directly applicable to video game characters. For example, a crowd-modeling simulation was used in the video game *Heavy Rain* to simulate the movement of a large crowd of shoppers in a shopping mall for one interactive scene in the game. Other games have used dynamics simulations for elements such as balance control and hit reactions. For example, the game *Grand Theft Auto IV* used techniques for balance control similar to work by Wrotek, Jenkins, and McGuire (2006) in order to create a character locomotion model that could react to dynamic objects, stand with some stability on a moving platform, and grasp for a handhold on an unstable platform. The incorporation of simulation elements within the video game character can enhance the ability of the character to react appropriately in more dynamic contexts, avoiding obvious behavioral errors that highlight to the player that the character is not "alive"—such as running into easily visible obstacles. One of the most significant challenges faced by developers of video game characters is the increasing fidelity of the environmental representation. Techniques such as physically correct destruction of environments provide many challenges for aspects of character locomotion, such as knowing when a structure is safe to walk on or when an obstacle may be blocking movement and may be moved out of the way. It is clear that the visual and simulation fidelity of video game worlds has improved and will continue to improve over time, adding to the complexity of any character development effort.

Nonverbal Behavior and Social Cues

An important aspect of human behavior that is currently lacking in many video game virtual worlds is the ability for characters to communicate nonverbally through the use of body language, gaze, gesture, and posture. This, along with many social cues that are absent within interactions between characters, is an area where video game characters can be considerably improved. Although research in this area suggests that appropriate behaviors are possible (for instance see Peters, Pelachaud, and Bevacqua 2006; García-Rojas, Gutiérrez, and Thalmann, 2008; Egges, Zhang, and Kshirsagar 2003), the application of such research has only just begun to be incorporated into commercial video games. For example, work on the social distances used within social interactions described by (Kendon 1990) are incorporated into a framework suitable for use within a video game by Pedica and Vilhjálmsson (2008).

As video game characters are developed further, the fidelity of nonverbal cues is likely to improve. Technologies such as the MotionScan system used in the video game *L.A. Noire* allow full facial motion capture and replay, adding to the fidelity of the facial representation, but still suffer from problems with actor body movement registration issues where the facial performance may not exactly coincide with the body performance because the two performances have been captured in isolation from one another.

There is, however, the problem of evaluating such nonverbal cues within the video game medium. While Bailenson and colleagues (2005) offer some useful work when studying interactions between players in the real world and avatars (three-dimensional characters controlled by other players) in the virtual world, a systematic study of player interactions with non-player-controlled characters does not exist at present. Unfortunately, the typical virtual-world avatar representation is less expressive than would be desirable for autonomous video game characters, and we have yet to be able to study any virtual character that has the autonomy and expressive range required for digital actors.

On the Nature of Acting

One of the primary reasons we believe the fiction of a piece of cinema is that we believe in the performance of the actors. We are able to empathize with their character, or at least understand the motivations for the actions they engage in. With the best performances we can become attached to the character in a way that engrosses us and transports us to the point where we forget that the actor is merely playing a role, giving us a performance. Instead we start to believe actors are the characters they are playing (see also Martin, chapter 9 in this volume). For all of the visual and behavioral fidelity we can engender in virtual characters, they have a fundamental limitation in that they are not alive. It may seem like an obvious statement, but actors' capacity to perform as a human character must stem from their own life. Of course, it is generally possible to study the techniques of acting described in *An Actor Prepares* (Stanislavski 1989, 313) and *Games for Actors and Non-actors* (Boal 1992), but the limitation remains that living beings are too complex to fully simulate, especially when it comes to aspects of intelligence. In essence we must accept that our goal is not to be able to create a perfect digital reproduction of a human actor, but simply to emulate those aspects of the acting craft that allow an audience to connect emotionally with a performance. We are, in fact, not only trying to create the illusion of life, but also trying to create the illusion of a live performance.

A major difficulty in this area is the lack of any scientific approach to evaluating actor performance. We may study individual aspects of a performance, such as how actors move within the scene, or how they control their own body, but we do not have a full understanding of how an actor's performance maps to changes in an audience's emotional state. It may be that evaluating the psychology of any given performance is impossible because of the complexity of the interactions involved. However, we can apply observational techniques to the qualities of both live actor performances and those of virtual actors in an effort to gain some insight into what constitutes an effective performance.

The Staging Problem, AI "Directors," and the Automatic Creation of Content

Perhaps the biggest challenge faced by video game developers is the cost of production when authoring content. In a video game virtual world, every aspect must be designed and programmed, and it is frequently the cost of production that determines the quality of the final artifact. For the aspects involved with digital actors, the main cost of production beyond the animation and locomotion of the character is the design cost involved in the direction of the actor. A great deal of effort is expended on coordinating digital actor performances. For instance, Isla (2008) describes the design effort involved in creating an engaging battle scenario. As an alternative to expensive designer-scripted scenarios, Booth (2009) describes a system that balances the creation of enemies (in this case, hordes of zombies) by estimating the level of player stress from their actions in the game world and adjusting the timing and composition of enemy forces as stress levels change.

In many ways, this system is similar to an interactive storytelling system, in that it provides designers with a method of controlling the intensity of the experience at a more abstract level, rather than directly controlling individual agents.

While algorithmic generation of game content is reasonably common, for example the use of procedural generation of the world in the game *Minecraft* (Persson 2010), recent experiments in procedural methods have shown interesting results in other areas. For example, Smith and Whitehead (2010) generate the two-dimensional grid of the world using procedural methods similar to those found in *Minecraft*. However, the properties of the generated content are then evaluated using a number of design criteria (for example, how often there are reachable platforms) and are selected for use in the final game world. The interesting aspect here is that the criteria used for selection are determined from a number of designer-created worlds using data-mining techniques often used in machine learning. It seems likely that similar techniques may be used to automatically author gameplay, stories, and characters by mining existing designer-authored experiences to determine preferable qualities. Indeed Smith, Nelson, and Mateas (2010) demonstrate how to algorithmically generate game designs themselves, although it is likely to be some time before full automation of the design process is achieved.

One of the emerging trends in video games is the ability to capture data, normally in the form of interaction metrics, which are then used to improve the mechanics of the game. Similar data can be used for other purposes, with one particularly interesting use put forth by Sunshine-Hill (2010), where simulations of larger populations are captured and distilled into statistical models that are then used to create plausible behaviors for characters who are created dynamically as the player moves around the environment. This "alibi" method relies on the player's inability to perceive the intentions of many characters, allowing the system to segue believable behavior into an entirely simulation-based scenario such that new characters feel as though they have had prior purpose.

This notion that players have limited attention resources is commonly used in the behavior design of video game characters; with most games employing a level-of-detail algorithm that controls the fidelity of the virtual characters both visually and behaviorally as players shift the focus of their attention. In essence, many games simply remove characters from the game if they are far enough away from the viewpoint of the player. Many implementations also reduce the frequency of behavior calculations for agents that are outside of some designer-created bounding volume. In this way, processing resources can be shared among the agents where performance is focused, and the fidelity of the characters that are being simulated can be increased.

An interesting aspect of this approach is that it bears some resemblance to the staging principle used in traditional animation, repurposed as an optimization technique. However, there have been proposals (such as Stocker et al. 2010 and Carlisle, Manning, and Grimshaw 2011) that suggest that this staging aspect can be used to enhance the fidelity of behavior inside the focus, rather than to optimize and reduce behavior outside the focus.

More work is required in order to understand the nature of what constitutes the better aspects of games, be it in design, aesthetics, or functionality. The ability of computers to use exemplars and to construct new structures using those examples suggests that we may one day see worlds both populated and controlled by procedural methods. Worlds that have been generated by algorithms that have learned to consider what makes for a good game experience.

Real Emotions, Virtual Characters

One of the most exciting aspects of video game characters is their ability to elicit emotional responses from the player. Yet this area of video games is both underresearched and underdeveloped.

An example of research that has been developed for commercial video games is the work by Bruce Blumberg at MIT. Blumberg has a deep love of dogs, to the extent that he has been working on virtual dogs and the recreation of doglike behavior for many years, including his Ph.D. thesis, "Old Dogs, New Tricks: Ethology and Interactive Characters" (1997). More recently he has worked with a video game company to produce a title called *World of Zoo* (Blue Fang Games and Blumberg 2009), which demonstrates many of the aspects of animal behavior he developed during his research. Animal-like behaviors can also be seen in the video games *Kinectimals* and *Black & White*.

Similarly, Perlin offers an alternative approach to developing characters that are life-like, often preferring to simply work on a small subset of motions rather than considering all motion for a given character. In his work *Sid and the Penguins* (Perlin 1998), Perlin animates a set of dancing penguins to a musical backing. Using principles from traditional cartoon animation such as squash and stretch, these relatively simplistic penguin characters perform a dance that feels emotionally resonant. As a piece of entertainment these characters can be viewed as "digital dancers."

One of the primary reasons that animals are often portrayed as characters in video games is that their behavior is viewed as emotionally driven. This may be because we generally perceive animal state of mind from nonverbal cues alone, so we do not require verbal feedback to perceive the intent of an animal "actor." To quote Blumberg (1997):

> Part of the fun of pets such as dogs is that we attribute clear motivational states to them on the basis of their motion, posture, direction of gaze, etc. That is, we feel as if we "know" when they are happy or sad, aggressive or submissive. (14)

This brings up a real problem for most video game creators, who often want to create human-like characters such that they can be set in an environment that the player can identify with. The depth of behavior expressed (and subsequently understood) by humans is vast and computationally impossible to reproduce, even if we understood all of the processes of human behavior completely enough to simulate them. Therefore, a great deal of care has to be taken when choosing a space for the characters to inhabit. Many creators choose to use more abstract worlds in order to preserve the character performance while still providing some familiarity for the player. This is a technique that has been used to great effect in other media, perhaps the greatest example being cartoons where abstractions of reality are used to represent both the worlds and the characters within them.

It is easy for video game creators to focus on developing an understanding of the technology required to manipulate the character for gameplay purposes. Animations, locomotion, and different approaches to logic, perception, and memory are all required before digital actors can truly perform their role, and yet the fundamental role of player perception has to remain foremost in the developer's mind. Otherwise, the player will consider the virtual character a game token that is simply in the game to perform a functional role, rather than a living character in its own right.

How Do We Create These Engaging and Expressive Characters?

Emotional and social engagement happens when two or more parties engage in a commonly understood pattern of actions and reactions. Without the notion of commonly understood patterns, we simply cannot understand the intent of the action. Ekman's (1978) work on the universality of emotional expressions suggests an evolutionary basis for our ability to process emotion. Specifically, he studied facial expressions throughout different populations, including tribes who have had little contact with the Western world, and found that there are several universal emotional expressions. This suggests that we have evolved some core emotional reactions and expressions. However, this notion of universal expression is complicated by the fact that many cultures do have unique emotional expressions, suggesting that culture also has an effect on emotional portrayal at least. This is important because, by seeking to create characters that engage players in both social and emotional ways, great care must be taken when considering the context of these interactions and the culture that the player is from. If a social interaction is performed out of context, it is likely to break the illusion of life.

In academia, the OCC (Ortony, Clore, and Collins 1988) model of emotion is predominant, although many do not use a complete implementation of the model. Similarly, the personality model of Costa and McCrae (1985) is often used. Commonly, these models are contained within a BDI (belief, desire, intention) architecture as described by Rao and Georgeff (1995). In video games, a BDI-like system is often implemented, with needs-based desires used in games such as *The Sims*. No matter the implementation aspects, the key factor is the development of appropriate responses to social and emotional interactions, both between virtual characters and with the player.

Just as observation is key to the development of traditional cartoon animation, it is likely that the correct observation and reproduction of emotional and social behaviors will play a significant part in the development of video game characters. Although a great deal of useful research is available from social psychology, such as concepts of personal space (Hall 1963), social group formation (Kendon 1990), and physical social interactions (Argyle 1988), it must remain part of the character developers' task to observe and understand actual human behavior if they are to ever achieve the illusion of life in their characters.

The development of vision-based user input systems such as the Kinect offers a more natural user input experience, and their use in video games opens up new possibilities, in that players are faced with a new interface with which to interact with characters. This new interface allows developers to explore the semantics of interaction, and it may be that new social gestures are actually more powerful than simply extending into the virtual world the real-world gesture set that each player currently uses. An example of this is in the video game *Kinectimals*, which uses the Kinect full-body tracking system to allow players to play with virtual pets by performing physical "petting" actions. Another example is the video game *Johann Sebastian Joust*, which uses a Playstation Move motion controller to track players in a real-world space as they seek to disturb each other, offering an experience that is part augmented reality, part video game, and part social activity.

We have yet to fully understand the potential for such interfaces, but it may be that with a more natural form of interaction, we can more easily feel that virtual characters are "alive" and thus more easily form emotional attachments to them.

Player Perception and Its Effect on the Experience of Interactions with Digital Actors

This issue of how players of video games interact with the characters within the virtual world is key to our understanding the qualities required in digital actors. The limited viewpoint of a virtual world obviously has an impact on our perception, as reduced peripheral awareness, difficulties in judging depth, and limited resolution all introduce artifacts that may hinder our understanding. This is especially true of the more subtle cues required for us to judge the emotional content of nonverbal interactions. Situations in which we are normally able to read the emotional state of another human using visual nonverbal cues are described by Parunak and colleagues (2005).

A difficulty in relating the qualities of virtual character interactions to specific research areas is that of measuring the perception of the player regarding the emotional content of the interactions with the characters in the virtual world. Although there is some research in this area, such as that by Nacke (2009), Bailenson and colleagues (2005), and Louchart and Aylett (2007), significant research is still required before we are able to fully explore the relationship between player interactions with virtual characters used in video games and how these interactions affect the emotional state of the player.

CONCLUSION

A question that arises when studying player interactions with virtual characters for the purposes of entertainment is "What does this form of interaction mean?" The relatively poor behavioral fidelity of character behaviors in current video games suggests that we are at an early stage in the medium and that substantial development and research work is needed before we can fully explore the medium. The ability to spend time being entertained in a virtual world filled with interesting virtual characters has not yet been fully realized, but anyone practiced in developing such characters understands that, as we gain a better understanding of the possibilities for new forms of interaction, new types of gameplay will emerge. It is reasonable to assume that new forms of interactive story worlds will allow us to embrace new narrative forms and explore new concepts in an interactive way. Perhaps one of the most interesting possibilities is posed by Frasca (2001), who describes a scenario where virtual characters within the video game *The Sims* are used in a manner similar to Boal's "theatre of the oppressed" (307). Using virtual characters to enact such a scene may challenge players' view of their own participation and existence within it.

Whatever shape this new form of interactivity takes, the ability of video game characters to offer deeper and more emotional interactions in dynamic situations is clearly a desirable goal. Video game creators are constantly trying to improve the behavioral fidelity of their worlds and characters in order to engage more fully with their audience. There remain considerable research opportunities across a range of areas such as evaluation of emotional interactions, development of interaction models, interface tools used to direct character performances, and problems relating to the narrative experience within the interactive form.

Note

1. Rapunzel—A classic Grimm Brothers fairytale in which a girl with long hair is forced by an evil enchantress to live in a tower. Rapunzel is required to let down her hair to allow access to the tower.

References

Argyle, M. 1988. *Bodily Communication*. London: Taylor & Francis.

Bailenson, J. N., A. C. Beall, J. Blascovich, J. Loomis, and M. Turk. 2005. Transformed Social Interaction, Augmented Gaze, and Social Influence in Immersive Virtual Environments. *Human Communication Research* 31 (4): 511–537.

Blumberg, B. M. 1997. Old Tricks, New Dogs: Ethology and Interactive Creatures. Ph.D. diss., Massachusetts Institute of Technology.

Blumberg, B. M., and T. A. Galyean. 1995. Multi-level Direction of Autonomous Creatures for Real-Time Virtual Environments. *Proceedings of the 22nd Annual Conference on Computer Graphics and Interactive Techniques—SIGGRAPH '95*, 47–54. New York: ACM Press.

Boal, A. 1992. *Games for Actors and Non-actors*. New York: Routledge.

Booth, M. 2009. The AI systems of Left 4 Dead. *Game Developers Conference*. http://www.valvesoftware.com/publications/2009/ai_systems_of_l4d_mike_booth.pdf.   Accessed March 19, 2012.

Carlisle, P., S. Manning, and M. Grimshaw. 2011. Social Objects: A Framework for Social Interactions between Videogame Characters. *Artificial Intelligence and Simulation of*

Behaviour 50–55. http://www.aisb.org.uk/publications/proceedings/aisb2011.zip. Accessed August 13, 2013.

Cassell, J. 2000. Embodied Conversational Agents. *Social Psychology* 40 (1): 26–36.

Cavazza, M., F. Charles, and S. J. Mead. 2002. Interacting with Virtual Characters in Interactive Storytelling. In *Proceedings of the First International Joint Conference on Autonomous Agents and MultiAgent Systems*, 318–325. New York: ACM Press.

Cavazza, M., F. Charles, and S. J. Mead. 2004. Developing Re-usable Interactive Storytelling Technologies. *Building the Information Society* 156: 39–44.

Costa, P. T., and R. R. McCrae. 1985. *The NEO Personality Inventory Manual*. Odessa, FL: Psychological Assessment Resources.

Dill, K. 2011. A Game AI Approach to Autonomous Control of Virtual Characters. Paper No. 11136, Interservice/Industry Training, Simulation, and Education Conference. http://www.iitsec.org/about/PublicationsProceedings/Documents/11136_Paper.pdf. Accessed June 25, 2013.

Egges, A., X. Zhang, and S. Kshirsagar. 2003. Emotional Communication with Virtual Humans. In *Intelligent Virtual Agents (Lecture Notes in Artificial Intelligence)*, 3661: 243–263. Berlin: Springer.

Ekman, P. 1978. Facial Expression. In *Nonverbal Behavior and Communication*, edited by A. Siegman and S. Feldstein, 97–117. Oxford: Lawrence Erlbaum.

Frasca, G. 2001. Rethinking Agency and Immersion: Video Games as a Means of Consciousness-Raising. *Digital Creativity* 12 (3): 167–174.

García-Rojas, A., Gutiérrez, M. and Thalmann, D. 2008. Simulation of individual spontaneous reactive behavior. In *Proceedings of the 7th International Joint Conference on Autonomous Agents and Multiagent Systems* 1: 143–150. New York: ACM Press.

Hall, E. T. 1963. Proxemics: The Study of Man's Spatial Relations and Boundaries. *Mans Image in Medicine and Anthropology*, 422–445. New York: International Universities Press.

Isla, D. 2008. Building a Better Battle: HALO 3 AI Objectives. http://www.bungie.net/inside/publications.aspx. Accessed March 7, 2011.

Kendon, A. 1990. *Conducting Interaction: Patterns of Behavior in Focused Encounters.* Cambridge: Cambridge University Press.

Louchart, S., and R. Aylett. 2007. Evaluating Synthetic Actors. In *Proceedings, Artificial Intelligence and the Simulation of Behavior Symposia*, 439–445. http://www.aisb.org.uk/publications/proceedings/aisb2007/aisb07-body.pdf . Accessed August 13, 2013.

Mateas, M. 1997. An Oz-Centric Review of Interactive Drama and Believable Agents Technical Report CMU-CS-97-156, Carnegie Mellon University. http://www.cs.cmu.edu/~michaelm/publications/CMU-CS-97-156.pdf. Accessed March 7, 2011.

Mateas, M., and A. Stern. 2003. Integrating Plot, Character and Natural Language Processing in the Interactive Drama Façade. In *Proceedings of International Conference on Technologies for Interactive Digital Storytelling and Entertainment (TIDSE 03)*, 9: 139–151. Stuttgart: Fraunhofer IRB Verlag.

Nacke, L. E. 2009. Affective Ludology: Scientific Measurement of User Experience in Interactive Entertainment. Ph.D. diss., Blekinge Institute of Technology, Blekinge, Sweden.

Ortony, A., G. L. Clore, and A. Collins. 1988. *The Cognitive Structure of Emotions*. New York: Cambridge University Press.

Parunak, H. V. D., R. Bisson, S. Brueckner, R. Matthews, and J. Sauter. 2005. Representing Dispositions and Emotions in Simulated Combat. Paper presented to "Defence Applications of Multi-Agent Systems," July 25, Utrecht, Netherlands.

Pedica, C., and H. Vilhjálmsson. 2008. Social Perception and Steering for Online Avatars. In *Proceedings of the Eighth International Conference on Intelligent Virtual Agents*, 104–116. Berlin: Springer.

Pelechano, N., J. Allbeck, and B. Norman. 2008. *Virtual Crowds: Methods, Simulation and Control*. San Francisco, CA: Morgan & Claypool.

Perlin, K., and A. Goldberg. 1996. Improv. In *Proceedings of the 23rd Annual Conference on Computer Graphics and Interactive Techniques—SIGGRAPH '96*, 205–216. New York: ACM Press.

Perlin, K. 1998. *Sid and the Penguins*. http://mrl.nyu.edu/~perlin/experiments/sid/. Accessed March 9, 2012.

Peters, C., C. Pelachaud, and E. Bevacqua. 2006. Social Capabilities for Autonomous Virtual Characters. *Proc. International Digital Games Conference*, 37–48. http://nestor.coventry.ac.uk/~cpeters/pubs/GAMES2006.pdf. Accessed August 13, 2013.

Rao, A. S., and M. P. Georgeff. 1995. BDI Agents: From Theory to Practice. *Proceedings of the International Conference on Multi-Agent Systems* 95: 312–319. Cambridge: MIT Press.

Smith, G., and J. Whitehead. 2010. Analysing the Expressive Range of a Level Generator. *PCGames '10: Proceedings of the 2010 Workshop on Procedural Content Generation in Games*, Article 4. New York: ACM.

Smith, A. M., M. Nelson, and M. Mateas. 2010. Ludocore: A Logical Game Engine for Modeling Videogames. *Proc. IEEE Conference on Computational Intelligence and Games (CIG 2010)*, 91–98. http://game.itu.dk/cig2010/proceedings/papers/cig10_012_086.pdf. Accessed August 13, 2013.

Stanislavski, C. 1989. *An Actor Prepares*. New York: Routledge.

Stocker, C., L. Sun, P. Huang, W. Qin, and J. Allbeck. 2010. Smart Events and Primed Agents. *Intelligent Virtual Agents (Lecture Notes in Computer Science)* 6356: 15–27. Berlin: Springer.

Sunshine-Hill, B. 2010. Perceptually Realistic Behavior through Alibi Generation. *Proceedings of the Sixth AAAI Conference on Artificial Intelligence and Interactive Digital Entertainment*, 83–88. Palo Alto: AAAI Press.

Thomas, F., and O. Johnston. 1995. *The Illusion of Life: Disney Animation*. New York: Hyperion.

Williams, R. 2001. *The Animator's Survival Kit: A Manual of Methods, Principles and Formulas for Classical, Computer, Games, Stop Motion and Internet Animators*. London: Faber & Faber.

Wrotek, P., O. C. Jenkins, and M. McGuire. 2006. Dynamo: Dynamic, Data-Driven Character Control with Adjustable Balance. In *Proceedings of the 2006 ACM SIGGRAPH Symposium on Videogames*, 61–70. New York: ACM Press.

Games

Black & White. Lionhead, Electronic Arts, 2001.

Grand Theft Auto IV. Rockstar Games, Take Two Interactive, 2008.

Heavy Rain. Quantic Dream, Sony Computer Entertainment, 2010.

Kinectimals. Frontier Developments, Microsoft, 2010.

Johann Sebastian Joust. Die Gute Fabrik, 2011.

L.A. Noire. Rockstar Games, Take Two Interactive, 2011.

Minecraft. M. Persson, 2010.

The Sims. W. Wright (lead developer). Maxis, Electronic Arts, 2000.

World of Zoo. B. Blumberg (lead developer). B. F. Games, THQ, 2009.

CHAPTER 32

....

EVOLUTION IN
VIRTUAL WORLDS

....

TIM TAYLOR

ACCORDING to the neo-Darwinist theory of evolution, the richness and complexity of biological life can be explained in terms of three fundamental processes: reproduction, heritable variation, and competition for limited resources leading to natural selection. The beautiful simplicity of this picture raises the intriguing question: might it be possible to instill these processes in a virtual world, and, in so doing, unleash an ongoing evolutionary process that populates that world with a rich ecosystem of complex virtual organisms?

Attempts to do precisely this have a history as long as that of the modern digital computer itself. This chapter starts with a brief review of past work and the current state of the art; although much of this work is remarkable, the quest for open-ended evolution remains elusive; after an initial burst of activity, these systems tend to quickly reach a quasi-stable state beyond which no further qualitative changes are observed.

These results raise a nagging question: just how far can evolution progress in such worlds beyond what is easily discoverable by virtue of the specific way in which the world has been designed? The nature of these systems is examined in order to address this question. It turns out that such an analysis can tell us much, not just about evolution in virtual worlds, but also about the very nature of virtual worlds and the similarities and differences that exist between the virtual and the real.

In the latter part of the chapter, I pull together these ideas in order to map out the main components of a more comprehensive framework in which to study evolution in virtual worlds. This involves careful consideration of the desirable properties and representation of organisms and environment; a central issue here is how to design worlds in which the reproductive success of an organism depends upon its local environment, thereby promoting continual evolution. Considering the low-level design requirements to build a virtual world in which organisms and environment are richly interconnected could be described as a "bottom-up holistic" approach.

PREVIOUS WORK

In the late 1940s, von Neumann became interested in the question of how complicated machines could evolve from simpler ones (von Neumann 1966).[1] He wished to develop a formal theory of self-reproducing machines—machines that could build copies of themselves. Specifically, he was interested in self-reproducing machines that were robust in the sense that they could withstand some types of mutation and pass these mutations on to their offspring; such machines could therefore participate in a process of evolution (Taylor 1999, 46–48). Looking for a suitable formalism that was both simple and enlightening, von Neumann developed a two-dimensional cellular automaton framework in which to demonstrate his ideas.

Although the design was not implemented on a computer before his untimely death in 1957, von Neumann's work can be regarded as the first attempt to instantiate an evolutionary process in the context of a modern, digital computational framework.[2] The work was seminal in setting out the logic of self-reproduction for evolving complex machines. A fundamental aspect of the design, which circumvented a potential infinite regress of description, was the dual use of information both to be interpreted as instructions for building a duplicate machine, and to be copied uninterpreted for use in the duplicate.[3]

Nevertheless, because of his focus on the logic of self-reproduction, von Neumann did not specifically deal with various other biological concerns, most notably regarding energy and the collection of raw materials.[4] Furthermore, he did not consider *interactions* between machines as a driving force for increased complexity. Rather, the little mention he did give to such interactions concerned their potential harmful effect in disrupting the functioning of self-reproduction within an individual machine. Von Neumann considered a system that had the *potential* for an evolutionary increase in complexity, but did not address the question of where the *drive* for such an increase may arise from within an evolutionary system itself.

However, some early implementations of computational evolutionary systems did consider interorganism interactions. Barricelli (1962; 1963), and Conrad and Pattee (1970) designed systems where mutualistic associations could arise between organisms. Although both systems exhibited some interesting ecological and evolutionary dynamics, attempts to evolve complex behaviors met with limited success. Conrad and Pattee remarked: "It is evident that the richness of possible interactions among organisms and the realism of the environment must be increased if the model is to be improved." They continued: "One point is clear, that the processes of variation and natural selection alone, even when embedded in the context of an ecosystem, are not necessarily sufficient to produce an evolution process" (407–408).

More recently, one of the most notable attempts to create a computational system in which natural selection leads to an open-ended evolutionary process has been Ray's *Tierra* (Ray 1991). This work studied the evolution of a population of self-reproducing computer programs, where the programs were written in a language based upon modern assembly code. The Tierran environment was a block of initially blank computer memory into which a single seed program, written by Ray, was placed. The program copied itself, one instruction at a time, into a new location in memory, and therefore created a new copy of itself; both copies then proceeded to reproduce, and so on until the memory filled up. When the memory was full, older programs were removed by the operating system to make room for new ones. Random mutations were sometimes introduced in the copying operations, such that variations emerged in the offspring programs. Ray observed that the programs evolved to reproduce more quickly, by optimizing their ancestral self-reproduction algorithm.[5] Furthermore, some of the most interesting results were due to ecological interactions; in particular, parasitism was seen to evolve, where short programs emerged that could only reproduce with the help of longer "host" programs. Resistance to parasites, "hyperparasites" (programs that subvert parasites for their own reproduction), and other related phenomena were also observed.

Tierra generated great interest within the nascent artificial life community in the early 1990s. However, as impressive as the results were, each particular run of the system would eventually reach a state of stasis in which only selectively neutral variations were seen to emerge (Ray 1992; 2011).

In 1993, inspired by *Tierra*, Ofria, Brown, and Adami developed a related system called *Avida*—for a recent overview, see Ofria, Bryson, and Wilke (2009). Unlike *Tierra*, where reproductive success ultimately boils down to how quickly a program can produce a copy of itself, programs in *Avida* can increase their rate of reproduction by performing specific, user-defined computational problems. *Avida* has been used to study the evolution of complex features (Lenski et al. 2003), but the drive for increased complexity was engineered into the environment by the authors via the provision of nine progressively more complex reward functions. Similarly, most of the other published studies with *Avida* have addressed specific topics either by making suitable adjustments to the reward functions (e.g., Elsberry et al. 2009) or by making targeted changes to the mechanisms for inter-program interaction (e.g., Beckmann and McKinley 2009). Thus, this work tends to be focused on evolving particular behaviors rather than addressing the question of how intrinsic drives for diversity and complexity can arise from within the system itself.

Taking a somewhat different approach, Holland developed a model called *Echo* that emphasizes the role of ecological interactions and exchange of resources in the evolution of complex adaptive systems (Holland 1995; Hraber, Jones, and Forrest 1997). *Echo* has been used for various studies involving ecological modeling (e.g., Schmitz and Booth 1996; Hraber and Milne 1997). However, its design is still restricted in terms of the evolvability of agents; the fact that the *Echo* operating system implicitly interprets the agents' behavioral specifications means that they can never come to encode anything more than the fixed range of actions (e.g., offense, defense, trade, and mating) predefined by the designer.

At around the same time as the original development of *Echo*, Yaeger created a complex virtual ecology of evolving agents called *Polyworld* (Yaeger 1994). In Yaeger's system, agents controlled by genetically determined neural networks move around a two-dimensional environment, collecting energy, fighting, and mating. The agents are capable of a simple form of learning, and possess a relatively sophisticated vision system where visual input is determined by a rendering of the scene from an individual agent's point of view. In addition, physical obstacles and barriers can be placed in the environment to restrict the agents' movements. Yaeger presented a qualitative description of results, in which it appeared that distinct species of organisms evolved and coexisted. However, evolvability is still restricted by the fact that interagent interactions are drawn from a small set of primitive behaviors (move, turn, eat, mate, attack, light, and focus).

Perhaps the most visually impressive work on evolution in virtual worlds to have been conducted to date has been that of Sims, together with more recent related work by other authors (Sims 1994b; 1994a; Ventrella 1999; Taylor and Massey 2001; Lassabe, Luga, and Duthen 2007; de Margerie et al. 2007; Miconi 2008). Sims allowed the body shape and movements of three-dimensional creatures to evolve at the same time, in a virtual world featuring simulated Newtonian mechanics. Each creature is built up from a genetic description that describes both its morphology and its control architecture. This representation provides modularity to the mapping from genotype to phenotype, and naturally leads to features such as duplication and recursion of body parts. In some runs, the creatures lived in a simulated fluid medium, and, in others, they lived in a terrestrial environment with gravity and a ground plane. In contrast to most of the previously discussed work, Sims used a traditional genetic algorithm with fitness functions designed to reward specific behaviors (such as moving forward, or following a target) rather than employing self-reproduction and open-ended evolution. Some example creatures evolved by Taylor and Massey (2001), inspired by Sims's original system, are shown in figure 32.1 (see Weblink: Video 32.swimmer.1-6 and Video 32.crawler.1-2).

One of the reasons that Sims's system produced such good results was that he modeled the physics of a three-dimensional environment accurately enough that objects moved realistically when subjected to forces and torques. Hence the beautiful movements produced by many of his evolved creatures were due just as much to the accurately modeled physical environments as they were to the creatures' individual controllers. In some of his later work, Sims (1994a) looked at evolving pairs of opponents to compete in simple games (involving fighting for possession of a free moving cube); work that graphically demonstrated how coevolutionary arms races (Dawkins and Krebs 1979) can lead to complex morphology and behavior.

Several other authors have attempted to move away from explicitly defined fitness functions to create virtual worlds with simulated physics where creatures may evolve in a more open-ended fashion. Earlier work was performed in two-dimensional worlds (e.g., Ventrella 1999) and more recent work in three dimensions (e.g., Miconi 2008). However, the computational complexity of the simulations only allowed for populations of a couple of hundred creatures, and the evolutionary results reported so far have been fairly restricted.

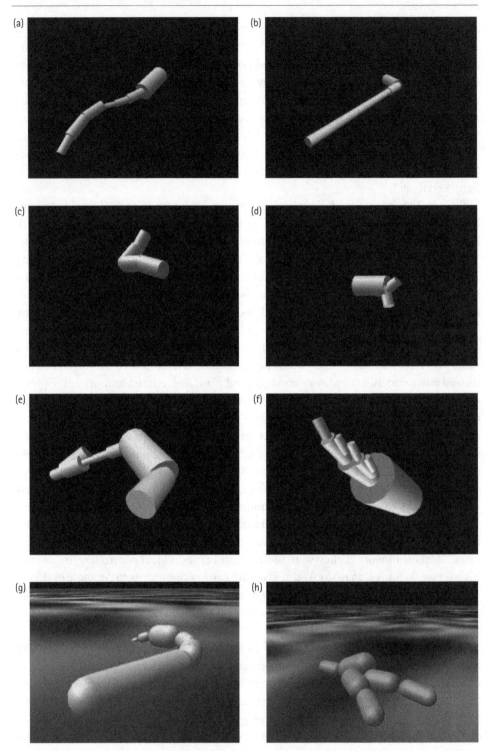

FIGURE 32.1 Some virtual creatures evolved by Taylor and Massey (2001). (a) Swimmer 1; (b) Swimmer 2; (c) Swimmer 3; (d) Swimmer 4; (e) Swimmer 5; (f) Swimmer 6; (g) Crawler 1; (h) Crawler 2.

OPEN PROBLEMS

It is clear from the preceding review that work on evolution in virtual worlds has not yet succeeded in reproducing the long-term evolutionary dynamics observed in the biological world. Although much of this work is remarkable, none has achieved an open-ended, evolutionary dynamic involving a long-term, intrinsic drive for increased diversity and complexity of the virtual organisms. One conceivable explanation is that the scale of these systems, both in terms of population sizes and durations of runs, has simply not been large enough to date; if a much larger system were run for a much longer time, perhaps we would see more interesting evolutionary phenomena emerge. However, there are a number of reasons to believe that the poor evolvability is due not just to issues of scale, but also to some more fundamental problems with the way in which these systems have been designed. Some of the most apparent of these issues are highlighted below. Consideration of the results of work to date, in the light of such issues, suggests that the processes of self-reproduction with heritable mutation and selection, by themselves, are insufficient to explain the open-ended evolution of diversity and complexity.

Fitness

In much of the work described above, there was a conscious attempt to avoid defining an explicit rule—a "fitness function"—to determine which individuals were allowed to reproduce. It has often been argued that avoiding an explicit fitness function is a key ingredient for achieving open-ended evolution (e.g., Packard 1988; Miconi 2008). A common way to accomplish this has been through self-reproduction—requiring organisms to build their own offspring rather than employing an extrinsic mechanism to decide which organisms can reproduce. Describing the design of *Tierra*, Ray explained:

> [Self-reproduction] is critical to synthetic life because without it, the mechanisms of selection must also be predetermined by the simulator. Such artificial selection can never be as creative as natural selection. The organisms are not free to invent their own fitness functions. Freely evolving creatures will discover means of mutual exploitation and associated implicit fitness functions that we would never think of. Simulations constrained to evolve with predefined genes, alleles, and fitness functions are dead-ended, not alive. (Ray 1991, 372)

However, the situation is somewhat more complicated, because in order to "discover means of mutual exploitation," the system must allow the evolution of new forms of *interaction*, and the requirement of self-reproduction by itself is not sufficient to ensure this. The question of evolving new forms of interaction is discussed in the following section. Furthermore, some authors have argued that even in virtual worlds with self-reproducing organisms, there will always be some aspects of the reproduction process that have to be designed a priori by the programmer (e.g., Miconi 2008). However, I argue later in the chapter that the degree to which this is true depends on how the distinction between organisms and environment is represented in the virtual world.

Restricted Ecological Interactions

The most interesting evolutionary innovations to emerge in *Tierra* were those that involved interactions between different programs, such as parasitism, immunity to parasites, hyper-parasites, and so on. However, the range of interactions that could emerge was restricted to those that were possible given the specific "interaction enabling" features of the language in which the programs were written; these allowed a program to search for a particular location in a neighboring program, and to read or execute code from that location. These facilities enabled certain types of interaction (mostly related to parasitism and related phenomena), but did not allow for the appearance of many other conceivable interactions.

Interorganism interactions in most of the other work discussed above were even more restricted. An interesting exception was the work of Sims on evolving pairs of opponents to compete in games in a three-dimensional virtual world. Here the interactions between the opponents were mediated through the creatures' bodies, modeled as physical structures in an environment with simulated Newtonian mechanics. These environmental dynamics afforded the potential for a rich variety of possible interactions. The resulting coevolutionary arms races produced some of the most impressive results for virtual evolution yet observed.

Another aspect of opening up the potential range of interactions between organisms is allowing for the evolution of new sensors and effectors.[6] These provide the two directions of influence between environment and organism across the organism's boundary, and the evolution of these capacities is difficult in a computational medium because the representation of this boundary is usually hard-coded and immutable. However, without such evolution, these systems are confined to evolving complex computational processing on the sensory information provided by the system designer—they are unable to evolve new forms of input and output in order to exploit other properties of the environment. This topic will be returned to below.

In some of the other work previously discussed, such as *Echo* and *Polyworld*, the environments contained material resources that organisms had to find and collect in order to survive and reproduce. This introduced the possibility of indirect interactions between organisms, where the availability of resources in the environment for one organism could be affected by the behavior of other organisms. The evolutionary potential of these systems still suffered from the organisms having a fixed set of actions available to them. In the biological world, organisms have to collect the materials and energy required to create their offspring, as well as to maintain their own structure. This direct link between uptake, transformation, storage, and excretion of resources, on the one hand, and survival and reproduction on the other hand, is missing in all of the systems described above, and I return to these issues below.

Fixed Representation and Structure

An issue common to the majority of systems discussed above is that the basic structure of an organism is fixed. For example, a Tierran organism always consists of a string of code (the program) together with various elements that together define the state of its "virtual CPU" (namely, four registers, a stack, and an instruction pointer); in *Echo*, an organism consists of a chromosome that defines its behavior, and a reservoir in which it stores any resources it has acquired from the environment. In the biosphere, the most dramatic moments in evolutionary history have been the so-called major transitions (Maynard Smith and Szathmáry 1995), in which the very structure of an organism has radically changed (e.g., the transition from unicellular to multicellular life). Such changes are not possible in virtual worlds in which the scheme for representing an organism is not itself mutable.

A related issue is the very direct, and fixed, relationship between "genotype" (an organism's hereditary material) and "phenotype" (an organism's physical presence and behavior in its environment) in some of these systems. This issue arises when the machinery that processes the genotype (e.g., the virtual CPU in *Tierra*) is not itself evolvable. Without the possibility of evolving new ways to decode the genotype into a working phenotype, there is no chance of evolving different, and potentially better, ways of representing complex phenotypes.

Lack of Complex Dynamics in Environment

One of the key aspects missing from all of the previously described work, with the exception of that of Sims and related studies, is an environment possessing its own complex dynamics. In most of these systems, the environment is essentially an inert medium that provides a space in which organisms can exist, in some cases with resources and other items. As already noted, the lifelike movements displayed by Sims's evolved creatures were a result of the interaction of the creatures' limb movements and the simulated Newtonian dynamics of the environment.

An environment can potentially provide many different functions, such as force fields that determine how objects move, various mechanisms for the transmission of information, determining how objects interact, and so on. To date, very little attention has been given to how the properties of the environment affect the evolution of complex organisms. These issues will be further discussed below.

Furthermore, it is widely accepted that at least some of the mass extinction events in the history of biological life were caused by external shocks such as meteor impacts (Raup 1986), and yet few virtual worlds model such catastrophes induced by the abiotic environment. However, it has been argued that most extinction events, and the continual turnover of species that result from them, may be caused by the intrinsic dynamics of the evolutionary process itself (Solé et al. 1997). Whether or not external shocks are required to promote continued large-scale evolutionary change remains an open question.

Restricted Population Size and Structure

Most of the work reported above could cope with population sizes of a few hundred individuals, or a few thousand at most; *Avida* is capable of running the largest populations, up to around 12,000 individuals in recent work (Elsberry et al. 2009). It is likely that the evolutionary potential of these systems is significantly restricted because of these small population sizes. In the biological literature, the concept of "minimal viable population" (MVP) refers to the lower bound on population size such that a species can survive in the wild. Recent surveys suggest a median MVP value of approximately 5,000 individuals (Traill, Bradshaw, and Brook 2007).[7]

Theoretical reasons for a minimum viable population size include inbreeding and lack of genetic diversity, and demographic and environmental stochasticity. Furthermore, if a system is to accommodate food chains of species at different trophic levels, many individuals of the species at the lower levels are required to provide sufficient food for species at higher levels. While it can be dangerous to apply empirical results from the biological world directly to virtual worlds, these factors do serve as a warning that the limited capacity of many virtual worlds to support large population sizes may be a problem.

It should also be noted that, in much of the existing work, organisms reproduce asexually—there is no mixing of genetic material between individuals either "vertically" (through sexual reproduction) or "horizontally" (the exchange of genetic material between unrelated organisms). Although some attempts have been made to introduce sexually reproducing organisms into these worlds (e.g., Taylor 1999), evolution of such populations tends to result in the emergence of simpler, asexually reproducing variants that eventually replace the sexually reproducing individuals. Both vertical and horizontal gene transfer are common in biological life and have significant, if not fully understood, consequences (e.g., Hurst and Peck 1996; Doolittle 2000). The omission of such processes in current work on virtual evolution is therefore likely to be a substantial source of divergence from the dynamics of biological evolution.

COMPONENTS OF A MORE COMPREHENSIVE FRAMEWORK

One reason for the limited results of past work is often an overemphasis on the requirements for a Darwinian evolution process to the exclusion of other aspects of biological theory. In particular, much of the work pays very little attention to ecological processes such as food webs and resource cycles. As will be discussed later, it is likely that such processes play an important role in promoting the open-ended evolution of diversity and complexity.

However, it is also apparent from the analysis above that there are other important issues to be addressed, beyond those traditionally tackled in the fields of theoretical biology and ecology. These include the design of the environment and the representational relationship between organisms and environment. Such questions seldom arise in traditional biological theory because the nature of the physical and chemical world can be taken as a given. However, when designing virtual worlds, we must explicitly design all aspects of the world; careful thought must go into this design if we wish to produce a world in which an open-ended evolutionary process may unfold. Here, I pull together these ideas in order to map out the main components of a more comprehensive theoretical virtual biology.

Design Goals

It should be emphasized that the following sections describe many different aspects of the design of a virtual world that might support an open-ended evolutionary process. A substantial research effort is required to make progress in these areas. In reality, at least in the near future, the design goals of specific virtual worlds are likely to be more narrowly defined; hence, some aspects of the following will be more immediately relevant than others.

Some examples of possible objects of study include the following:

- A focus on the origin of living systems and the evolution of basic autonomy versus a focus on agents with "higher-level" intelligent behavior involving processes such as learning, memory, communication, and language
- Evolution in "native" digital environments with discrete memory locations and discrete execution of instructions (e.g., Internet agents) versus evolution in simulated physical environments with (simulated) continuous time and space
- Guided evolution to produce agents for specific purposes versus open-ended evolution of diverse, complex organisms

In the following sections, I discuss the relevance of each topic in relation to each of these goals. Much of this concerns the design of virtual worlds that can support open-ended evolutionary processes with as few restrictions as possible as to what can evolve. This necessarily requires us to focus for the most part on basic, low-level design features. If the design goal of the system is to evolve organisms with higher-level, more human-like intelligence, then it may make sense to forgo some of the complete freedom in evolvability of organism structure, and concentrate on specific mechanisms designed to aid the evolution of features such as learning, memory, and communication. However, further discussion of such issues is beyond the scope of this chapter.

Nature of the Individual

What constitutes an appropriate representation for an individual organism will depend upon the design goals of the virtual world. In the biological world, organisms are continually engaged in the procurement of matter and energy, not just to reproduce, but also simply to survive and maintain their own structure. Thus, organisms are the connecting tissue of twin hierarchies—an evolutionary hierarchy (involving levels such as genes, organisms, and species) and an ecological hierarchy (involving levels such as organisms, ecosystems, and the global biosphere) (Eldredge 2008).

In the context of the design of a virtual world, the notion of an organism as an ecological actor presents a variety of issues, particularly the modeling of food chains (and associated processes of capture, storage, transformation, use, and exchange of resources), and the representation of the organism's structure.

The concepts of food chains and webs, as used in the biological literature, only make sense in virtual worlds in which organisms are composed of atomic elements that are subject to a law of conservation. In von Neumann's cellular automata model, for example, and in *Tierra* and *Avida*, organisms could create copies of themselves "out of thin air," without having to collect the individual components required to build the copy from elsewhere in the environment. Hence, in these worlds, there is no requirement for, or possibility of, the emergence of food chains. The consequences of this will be discussed in the following section.

Some of the other systems discussed previously, such as the work of Conrad and Pattee and of Holland, did require the organisms to collect resources in order to reproduce. However, in these systems the requirement to collect resources was not directly connected to the composition of the organism itself but was essentially arbitrary. This arbitrariness arises because the organisms are not fully embodied in their virtual worlds—their representation is distinct from that of the environment. I discuss later the consequences of this lack of embodiment, in terms of the evolution of ecosystems and of the evolution of an organism's own structure.

Whether or not the organisms are fully embodied in the virtual world, the nature of their genetic information—the inherited information passed from parent to offspring—must be carefully considered. Von Neumann's work on self-reproducing automata addressed the issue of how to ensure the availability of pathways in the space of possible genomes to allow evolution to move from simple to complicated organisms. His proposed architecture, upon which his self-reproducing automata are based, is a solution to the problem, and gives the automata the potential to evolve into progressively more complicated forms. However, the design of systems such as *Tierra*—in which programs reproduce simply by copying themselves one instruction at a time, with no strict genotype-phenotype distinction—suggests that von Neumann's full architecture is not always required for the evolution of complexity. In the case of *Tierra*, programs can reproduce in this manner because they are one-dimensional structures where each element can be easily accessed in order to be read and copied. In the two-dimensional environments considered by von Neumann, such a strategy would not be possible in general. We can therefore say that the self-reproduction architecture required in order to allow for the evolution of complex organisms will depend on the nature of the medium—in particular, on its dimensionality and dynamics. More work is required to fully understand these dependencies.

In addition, the mechanisms for replication and mixing of genetic information, both vertically and horizontally, must also be considered. Ideally, it should be possible for new mechanisms for genetic mixing to evolve, and this again points to the desirability of allowing an organism's structure to be subject to evolution; I deal with this point below.

Finally, any virtual evolutionary system must be seeded with some designed structure—an ancestral organism—to start the evolutionary process. The choice of a suitable seed structure will depend upon the design goals of the system. To recreate the origin and early evolution of life, imposing few assumptions on what might emerge, an appropriate seed might be a simple self-replicating structure with the ability to initiate other dynamics in the world.[8] If, however, the focus of the system is on the evolution of higher-level intelligence, then it may be desirable to start with a more complex ancestor that already has some assumptions and capacities for information processing, communication, and learning.

Nature of the Ecosystem

The general lack of support for complex ecosystems in existing virtual worlds has already been highlighted. Organisms in systems such as *Tierra* and *Avida* compete for CPU time to execute their instructions (which the authors of these systems regard as a metaphor for competition for energy), and they also compete for limited space in memory in which to build their offspring. However, as already noted, the matter from which they are composed can be created out of thin air (it is not conserved), and is therefore not something for which organisms compete.

There are several consequences that arise from this lack of competition for building blocks. First, in addition to a lack of competition between organisms for resources in the environment, organisms are not themselves resources of matter for other organisms; a program in *Tierra* can read an instruction from a neighboring program, but it does not need to (and indeed is unable to) actually *remove* instructions from the neighbor in order to build its offspring. Although a program can read and execute useful code from a neighboring program (we might say that the neighbor is acting as a resource of *information*),[9] there is no life-or-death struggle between organisms over the very building blocks from which they are composed. Hence the coevolutionary pressures on the organisms to develop increasingly elaborate defenses and weapons are much weakened, if not totally absent.

Second, in the biosphere, the conservation of matter, and the resultant cycle of resources that this necessitates throughout an ecosystem, creates an underlying *interconnectedness* between all members of the ecosystem. Organisms are consumers and producers of resources, and the existence of one species creates opportunities for other species to exist (e.g., ones that feed on it, or which decompose its waste). Furthermore, the interconnectedness of ecosystems means that the loss of one species may have significant ecological and evolutionary consequences for many other species in the system. Hence, the lack of competition for material resources in virtual evolution systems is probably a significant contributory factor to their lack of continued evolutionary activity and their low diversity of species.

In addition to considering material resources, the role of energy, or its equivalent in virtual worlds, must also be considered. Above, it was suggested that CPU time in *Tierra* and *Avida* might be regarded as an analogy to energy in biological systems. But energy in the physical world is, of course, a much richer concept; at the chemical level, it determines which chemical reactions can happen and when and, at the physical level, it allows organisms to deploy stored energy as useful work, acting against an external physical force and thereby exhibiting a degree of autonomy. Whether or not it is appropriate to model such properties in a virtual world will depend on the design goals for the system.

When designing a virtual world, decisions must be taken about how to model energy and material resources, and the rules that govern the reaction, transformation, capture, storage, and transmission of materials. These decisions will depend on whether one is trying to simulate physical systems or to work in a more native computational domain (or somewhere in between these two extremes). As explained above, the decisions taken will have significant consequences for the evolutionary behavior of the system—although the precise nature of these consequences remains to be elucidated. It is therefore important that the decisions are carefully considered and related to explicit motivations derived from the design goals, rather than being treated as a mere implementation detail.

Nature of the Medium

Perhaps more than any other aspect, the nature of the medium in which the evolving virtual organisms live has received very little explicit discussion in previous work. The medium is the shared area in which organisms and abiotic objects act and interact. It defines the concepts of space and neighborhood. In addition, it defines any global dynamic processes that act on all objects contained within it (the "laws of physics"), and hence also defines a global concept of time. As I discuss in this section, many of the virtual evolutionary systems we have considered also have predefined areas of space specifically associated with individual organisms; these do not exist in the shared medium and are therefore not subject to the global laws of physics. Similarly, many systems also have local update procedures specifically associated with individual organisms rather than applying to all (biotic and abiotic) objects in the medium. Indeed, some systems *only* support these local update procedures for organisms, which therefore exist in an inert medium possessing no global laws of physics.

The nature of the medium is generally not discussed in traditional theoretical biology, as the properties of the physical world can be taken for granted. But the evolutionary phenomena that might be expected to arise in a system are intimately related to the properties of the medium in which the evolutionary process is unfolding, as will be highlighted in this section. Hence, it is vital that these properties are carefully considered when designing a virtual world.

Discrete and Continuous Media

In some of the preceding discussion, a distinction has been drawn between "native computational" environments (such as those provided in *Tierra* and *Avida*), and simulated physical environments (such as those provided in the work of Sims and related studies). One component of this distinction is whether the space in which organisms live is discrete or continuous. In practice, assuming the world is implemented on a digital computer, the space must be discrete at some level, as the position of an object cannot be specified to an infinitely fine level of detail. Thus, in practice, this component is in fact a continuum of "granularity of discreteness" rather than a discrete-continuous dichotomy. The same comments also apply to the representation of time in the virtual world.

Embodiment and Evolvability

A more relevant distinction in the current context is the algorithm by which the state of the world is updated. This may operate at the level of the smallest elements of the world (e.g., an update rule for an individual cell in a cellular automaton) or it might operate on higher-level constructs. For example, in *Tierra*, the state of the world is updated by the "virtual CPU" possessed by each live program. Each program's virtual CPU decides which instruction to execute at the current time step. In Sims's virtual creatures, there is a multistage update algorithm, in which a creature's controller is first updated to determine the forces to be applied by each of its joint actuators at that moment; then the simulation of Newtonian mechanics is updated to determine the resultant movement of the creature.

The important point is that, in any virtual world in which the update algorithm operates on anything other than the smallest elements of the world, a design decision has to be made about which higher-level constructs to act upon. This then "hardwires" the notion of these higher-level constructs into the design of the system itself. In work on evolution in virtual worlds, these higher-level constructs are, of course, usually the organisms themselves. If the state of the world is being updated at the level of the organism rather than lower-level elements, the system must be able to identify and keep track of the organisms. This necessarily requires a predefined representational distinction between organism and environment and means that some aspects of the organism's structure are not embodied in the medium.

For example, in *Tierra*, an organism is defined as a string of instructions together with the various elements associated with its virtual CPU (i.e., its registers, stack, and instruction pointer). But only the string of instructions is embodied in the shared medium of the world—the Tierran memory space—and thus only this is potentially accessible to other organisms. Furthermore, although Tierran organisms have to copy their instructions into a new spot in the environment in order to reproduce, they do not have to copy their registers, stack, and so on; these items are automatically replicated by the system when an organism reproduces rather than having to be explicitly copied by the organism itself.

Similarly, in Sims's work, only a creature's limbs exist in the environment as simulated physical bodies. Its controller, actuators, sensors, and genetic description and decoding mechanism are not represented as physical entities in the environment. Instead, they are composed of predefined components that are not themselves evolvable. As a consequence, a creature could never evolve a new method of producing itself from its genetic description (a new genotype-phenotype mapping), nor could it evolve new types of sensors or actuators.

Such a predefined representational distinction between organism and environment therefore introduces serious consequences for the evolvability of the system. Because the basic design of an organism has been predefined, it is not itself able to evolve; a program in *Tierra* could not experience a major evolutionary transition in its architecture to become a multiprocess parallel program—unless such a capacity was explicitly programmed into the system by the designer, as was the case in Thearling and Ray (1994). And yet, as mentioned earlier, these kinds of major transitions in the organization of individual organisms have marked key moments in the evolution of complex biological life (Maynard Smith and Szathmáry 1995).

Certainly, those components of an organism that are not represented within the shared medium (such as a Tierran organism's registers or a creature's actuators in Sims's system) *could* evolve if the system was so designed. The point, however, is that these components are not constructed by the organism itself when it is building its offspring; the mechanism for their reproduction, and the potential ways in which they could evolve, must therefore be predefined by the designer. Hence, such components could still only evolve in certain predefined ways.

Furthermore, a predefined representational distinction between organism and environment implies the existence of a boundary between the two to demarcate what does, and does not, belong to an organism. If the organism is to do anything in the world, this further entails predefined mechanisms for specific cross-boundary processes, possibly involving the transport of resources or the transmission of forces or information. But, again, if these must be predefined, then the ability to evolve new cross-boundary processes (e.g., new sensors or effectors) will be absent or, at best, only evolvable in certain predefined ways. I will return to this topic shortly.

Interconnectedness through the Properties of the Medium

Returning to the nature of the algorithm that updates the state of the world, there are other aspects of its implementation that also have important consequences for the evolutionary potential of the system. In a "computational-like" medium like

Tierra, the elements are discrete memory locations containing state information that is treated as instructions or data or both. Memory locations are inert unless specifically acted upon by an instruction; the modes of interaction in such systems, mediated by specific instructions, therefore have to be explicitly designed into the system.

In contrast, in worlds with simulated physics, the medium supports dynamics that act upon all elements, such as gravity and fluid drag forces (in Sims's work), and the transmission of visual information (in *Polyworld*). Hence, objects in simulated physical worlds are continuously affected by the presence of other objects in the world, without having to actively initiate interactions. They are bathed in a sea of information providing a potentially rich Umwelt and representing another form of interconnectedness between organisms in addition to that provided by the existence of an ecosystem of resources.[10] Such dynamics provide rich possibilities for interorganism interactions, as discussed above. In contrast, objects in a computational medium are blind to their surroundings unless they utilize specific mechanisms for communication that have been predefined by the designer.

Evolution of New Sensors and Effectors

Simulated physical worlds may support phenomena in one or multiple domains; the domains of Newtonian dynamics and transmission of light have already been mentioned, but any number of other domains of physical phenomena could also be implemented, in addition to phenomena that have no analogues in the real world. In virtual worlds with simulated physics, the medium of the environment therefore inherently exhibits complex phenomena, and an important aspect of the evolution of complexity concerns the question of how organisms can evolve to capture and exploit these phenomena for their own benefit. The designer of a virtual world must provide the organisms with some tools with which they can sense and influence their surroundings—that is, with some sensors and effectors. In Sims's work, for example, a fixed set of different actuators is available for use in an organism's joints. Each sensor or actuator will work with a particular domain of phenomena (e.g., the joint actuators work in the domain of Newtonian dynamics, and light sensors work in a very simplified version of the domain of electromagnetic radiation).

An important aspect of open-ended evolution is how organisms can evolve to do things beyond what has been "programmed in" to the system by the designer. This relates not just to evolving complex information processing tasks, but also to evolving new ways of interacting with the world—new sensors and effectors. Within a single domain, new forms of action might arise if an organism evolves to initiate progressively more complex chain reactions of dynamics in the environment. However, if the environment has multiple domains of phenomena, we face the additional problem of how organisms might evolve to capture phenomena in a new domain in which no sensors or effectors have been predefined by the designer. Ultimately, this must come down to (at least some) components in the system having multiple properties across different domains, which can act as bridges from one domain to another. In an evolutionary context, an organism might have evolved to make use of a component because of its properties in one domain (e.g., its ability to act as an actuator), but other properties of the same component may subsequently become useful and be selected for (e.g., the same component may also be sensitive to light, and therefore act as a rudimentary eye). Hence, in worlds in which components exist that can act as bridging technologies across multiple domains of phenomena, organisms can evolve new forms of sensors and effectors beyond those programmed into the system by the designer.

Physical Ecosystem Engineering and Niche Construction

The capture and use of food and energy by organisms was considered in a previous section. However, biological organisms utilize many aspects of their environment beyond those that provide food and energy. Nontrophic resources may be useful to an organism in a multitude of ways, by making its life easier or less dangerous in some way. Examples include resources that help regulate the environment (e.g., providing shelter or protection); tools to help with the capture, preprocessing, storage, and transport of other resources; tools for offense and defense against other organisms; tools to extend an organism's capabilities for signaling and communication, and so on.

By using resources in the environment in this way (a process known in the literature as "physical ecosystem engineering" or "niche construction"),[11] an organism's behavior can have significant ecological and evolutionary consequences for other organisms of the same or different species (Jones, Lawton, and Shachak 1997; Odling-Smee, Laland, and Feldman 2003). For example, species that build nests for their offspring reduce the selection pressure on the offspring's ability to withstand harsh environments by buffering environmental variation. Another example is provided by the dam-building activity of beavers that drastically alters the local environment experienced by the beavers and many other species in a way that can last for many generations (Naiman, Johnston, and Kelley 1988). In this situation, there is a "reciprocal causation" in the relationship between organism and environment; changes to the environment caused by the action of a species can alter the selective environment acting upon the same or other species and therefore affect how they evolve (introducing a form of "ecological inheritance" in addition to genetic inheritance).

If the medium of a virtual world is endowed with nontrophic resources that can help organisms survive in some way, similar processes of physical ecosystem engineering and niche construction can be expected to emerge. These processes provide another level of interconnectedness between organisms in the environment, such that changes in the behavior of one organism will affect other organisms and thereby potentially promote continued evolutionary activity. In addition, heterogeneity in the environment, which could result from processes such as niche construction, can lead to spatial segregation of organisms. In time, this can lead to isolated populations, thus promoting speciation and diversity within the system.

Bringing It All Together:
Embodiment, Self-Reproduction,
Interconnectedness, and Open-Ended
Evolution

The considerations in the previous section help elucidate the relationship between the concepts of fitness, self-reproduction, and open-ended evolution. If some parts of the organism are reproduced automatically according to a predefined mechanism (i.e., not embodied in the medium), there must be a predefined procedure to decide *when and how* such a mechanism operates. Such parts will therefore not be subject to variation and evolution or, at best, only subject to evolve in certain predefined ways. That is, in order to avoid any hardwired restrictions on evolvability, the organisms must be *fully embodied* in the shared medium of the world. Full embodiment entails an organism being composed solely of components that are subject to the general laws of physics of the medium and are not subject to any special higher-level update rules. Full embodiment therefore *necessitates self-reproduction*, as it entails that there are no special ancillary processes to aid in the identification and reproduction of organisms. Of course, depending on the design goals of the system, one might forgo total evolvability to more easily achieve particular outcomes.

The concept of a fitness function can be viewed as the determination of whether, and when, an organism can reach a state where it can reproduce. Hence, for a community of organisms, it defines a driving force that influences the current state and direction of change of the composition of the community. For open-ended evolution, we wish to avoid fitness functions that define static fitness landscapes, as these imply optimal states beyond which no further evolution is possible. The way to avoid static fitness functions is to make the fitness of an organism dependent not just on the organism itself but also on its local environment (which may include other organisms). This can be achieved if the medium creates interconnectedness between organisms, through the creation of food webs, through dynamic processes supported by the medium such as the transmission of forces or information, or through niche construction. Such a dependency will introduce coevolutionary drives and dynamic, shifting fitness landscapes.

To summarize, the degree of embodiment of an organism in the medium dictates which aspects of the organism are evolvable rather than hard-coded. By definition, those parts that are embodied must be constructed by the organism itself when it is building its offspring. Hence, there is a close relationship between embodiment and self-reproduction, and the degree to which these are present determines the extent to which an organism can freely evolve without predefined constraints. For self-reproducing organisms, the variety of possible forms is also clearly determined by the properties of the medium and its capacity to support complex arrangements of components and dynamic processes of action and interaction between components. These aspects define the set of potential organisms, but even with a large set of possibilities, the ability of the evolutionary process to traverse the genetic space from one to another may still be restricted. This is precisely the problem that von Neumann tackled, and for which his genetic architecture is a solution (but perhaps not the only solution). Having considered the diversity and connectivity of the space of potential organisms, the drive for evolution must also be considered. This comes from the decision on which organisms can reproduce and when (i.e., the concept of fitness). If this depends solely on the organism itself, it will lead to a static fitness landscape and the likelihood of eventual stasis in the population. If, however, fitness depends on the organism and its local environment, a dynamic fitness landscape will arise, with opportunities for continual evolution. This can come about through the interconnectedness between organisms provided by food webs involving abiotic or biotic resources, by dynamic processes of interaction and communication supported by the shared medium, or by physical ecosystem engineering and niche construction.

The organisms in *Tierra* are self-reproducing, but they are not fully embodied, so the structure of organisms that can evolve is restricted. A limited, unidirectional connectedness is allowed by organisms being able to read (but not write) the code of neighboring organisms. Of the systems discussed earlier, only those of von Neumann and Barricelli are fully embodied. However, neither of these worlds support laws of conservation of matter, and hence they lack the notion of food webs and the associated interconnectedness between organisms and coevolutionary dynamics that arise from them. Although Barricelli observed many interesting results, his virtual world is also hampered by the fact that the evolutionary process unfolds in an inert computational medium.[12]

The organisms in both Barricelli's and von Neumann's systems turned out to be very sensitive to perturbations from the environment. This is a particular problem with von Neumann's organisms, which are vastly more complicated than those studied by Barricelli. This raises the caveat that if an organism is fully embodied in the shared medium of the world, it must *engage in maintaining its own structure* so that it can survive perturbations from the environment for long enough to enable it to reproduce. Thus, a major challenge in future work is to create a system in which fully embodied organisms actively maintain their own structure[13] while still fulfilling the other requirements for open-ended evolution discussed throughout this chapter.

As demonstrated in the preceding discussions, the pursuit of open-ended evolution in virtual worlds requires synthesizing knowledge not just from a narrowly defined view of neo-Darwinism, but also from the wider literature on theoretical biology, in addition to addressing more technical concerns. By making advances in the various areas outlined here, in the near future we can expect to see significant improvements in the evolutionary potential of virtual worlds to produce diverse ecosystems of complex virtual organisms.

Notes

1. This chapter focuses on the technical challenges of instantiating evolution in virtual worlds. For cultural and philosophical perspectives on the history of artificial life, see Riskin (2007) and Johnston (2008). Discussion is omitted of popular computer games such as *Spore* (Electronic Arts, 2008), as these generally model evolution at a very superficial level (Bohannon 2008).

2. A working implementation, based upon von Neumann's design with some minor changes, was developed more recently by Umberto Pesavento and Renato Nobili (Pesavento 1995).

3. Von Neumann's description of the logical design of a self-reproducing machine can equally be applied to the reproductive apparatus of biological cells. However, although his work predated the unraveling of the details of DNA replication by some years, it had little impact on developments in genetics and molecular biology (Brenner 2001, 32–36).

4. Von Neumann had originally intended to return to these issues later on (von Neumann 1966, 83, 93–99).

5. The optimizations came about by the natural selection of variant programs, introduced by random mutations, which required less CPU time to effect their replication. This could be achieved by finding ways to reproduce with fewer instructions (as fewer instructions to copy meant a faster replication rate); Ray observed the evolution of self-replicating programs that were barely one-third of the length of his original handwritten ancestor. Alternatively, in other runs he observed programs that had evolved more sophisticated copying algorithms that could copy a given size of program using fewer CPU cycles than the original ancestor (Ray 1994).

6. The terms *effector* and *actuator* are both used in this chapter, and have slightly different meanings. An effector is a device that causes a change in the environment (e.g., a wing can cause flight when suitably controlled). An actuator is a device that actually provides motive power (e.g., a muscle). An effector will therefore contain at least one actuator as a subcomponent.

7. Although see Garnett and Zander (2011) and Brook et al. (2011) for further debate on this topic.

8. For a full discussion, see Taylor (1999, §7.2) and and Taylor (2001).

9. This feature was exploited by the evolved parasites discussed earlier.

10. Hoffmeyer (2007) provides an interesting elaboration of these issues from the perspective of biosemiotics.

11. The term "niche construction" actually refers to a broader category of phenomena whereby organisms modify the environment that they experience. This includes changes to trophic, as well as nontrophic, aspects of the environment, and also cases such as dispersal and migration (Odling-Smee, Laland, and Feldman 2003).

12. Although in later work he did allow organisms to compete in games and thereby develop more interesting behaviors (e.g., Reed, Toombs, and Barricelli 1967).

13. Examples of initial work in this area include McMullin and Varela 1997 and Hutton 2007.

References

Barricelli, N. A. 1962. Numerical Testing of Evolution Theories. Part I. Theoretical Introduction and Basic Tests. *Acta Biotheoretica* 16 (1–2): 69–98.

Barricelli, N. A. 1963. Numerical Testing of Evolution Theories. Part II. Preliminary Tests of Performance. Symbiogenesis and Terrestrial Life. *Acta Biotheoretica* 16 (3–4): 99–126.

Beckmann, B. E., and P. K. McKinley. 2009. Evolving Quorum Sensing in Digital Organisms. In *Proceedings of the 11th Annual Conference on Genetic and Evolutionary Computation (GECCO 2009)*, 97–104. New York: ACM.

Bohannon, J. 2008. Flunking Spore. *Science* 322 (5901): 531.

Brenner, S. 2001. *A Life in Science*. As told to Lewis Wolpert. Edited by Errol C. Friedberg and Eleanor Lawrence. London: BioMed Central.

Brook, B. W., C. J. Bradshaw, L. W. Traill, and R. Frankham. 2011. Minimum Viable Population Size: Not Magic, but Necessary. *Trends in Ecology and Evolution* 26 (12): 619–620.

Conrad, M., and H. Pattee. 1970. Evolution Experiments with an Artificial Ecosystem. *Journal of Theoretical Biology* 28: 393–409.

Dawkins, R., and J. R. Krebs. 1979. Arms Races between and within Species. *Proceedings of the Royal Society of London* B 205 (1161): 489–511.

de Margerie, E., J. B. Mouret, S. Doncieux, and J.-A. Meyer. 2007. Artificial Evolution of the Morphology and Kinematics in a Flapping-Wing Mini-UAV. *Bioinspiration and Biomimetics* 2 (4): 65–82.

Doolittle, W. F. 2000. Uprooting the Tree of Life. *Scientific American*, February: 90–95 .

Eldredge, N. 2008. Hierarchies and the Sloshing Bucket: Toward a Unification of Evolutionary Biology. *Evolution: Education and Outreach* 1: 10–15.

Elsberry, W. R., L. M. Grabowski, C. Ofria, and R. T. Pennock. 2009. Cockroaches, Drunkards, and Climbers: Modeling the Evolution of Simple Movement Strategies Using Digital Organisms. In *Proceedings of the IEEE Symposium on Artificial Life 2009*, March, 92–99. Nashville, TN: IEEE.

Garnett, S. T., and K. K. Zander. 2011. Minimum Viable Population Limitations Ignore http://www.cell.com/trends/ecology-evolution/issue?pii=S0169-5347%2811%29X0012-5 Evolutionary History. *Trends in Ecology and Evolution* 26 (12): 618–619.

Hoffmeyer, J. 2007. Semiotic Scaffolding of Living Systems. In *Introduction to Biosemiotics: The New Biological Synthesis*, edited by M. Barbieri 49–166. Dordrecht: Springer.

Holland, J. H. 1995. *Hidden Order: How Adaptation Builds Complexity*. Reading, MA: Addison-Wesley / Helix Books.

Hraber, P. T., T. Jones, and S. Forrest. 1997. The Ecology of Echo. *Artificial Life* 3 (3): 165–190.

Hraber, P. T., and B. T. Milne. 1997. Community Assembly in a Model Ecosystem. *Ecological Modelling* 103: 267–285.

Hurst, L. D., and J. R. Peck. 1996. Recent Advances in Understanding of the Evolution and Maintenance of Sex. *Trends in Ecology and Evolution* 11 (2): 46–52.

Hutton, T. J. 2007. Evolvable Self-Reproducing Cells in a Two-Dimensional Artificial Chemistry. *Artificial Life* 13 (1): 11–30.

Johnston, J. 2008. *The Allure of Machinic Life: Cybernetics, Artificial Life, and the New AI*. Cambridge, MA: MIT Press.

Jones, C. G., J. H. Lawton, and M. Shachak. 1997. Positive and Negative Effects of Organisms as Physical Ecosystem Engineers. *Ecology* 78 (7): 1946–1957.

Lassabe, N., H. Luga, and Y. Duthen. 2007. A New Step for Artificial Creatures. In *IEEE Symposium on Artificial Life (ALIFE'07)*, 243–250. Piscataway, NJ: IEEE Xplore.

Lenski, R. E., C. Ofria, R. T. Pennock, and C. Adami. 2003. The Evolutionary Origin of Complex Features. *Nature* 423: 139–144.

Maynard S., J., and E. Szathmáry. 1995. *The Major Transitions in Evolution*. Oxford: W. H. Freeman.

McMullin, B., and F. J. Varela. 1997. Rediscovering Computational Autopoiesis. In *Proceedings of the Fourth European Conference on Artificial Life (ECAL97)*, edited by P. Husbands and I. Harvey, 38–47. Cambridge, MA: MIT Press/Bradford Books.

Miconi, T. 2008. Evosphere: Evolutionary Dynamics in a Population of Fighting Virtual Creatures. In *IEEE World Congress on Computational Intelligence (CEC2008)* June: 3066–3073. http://ieeexplore.ieee.org/stamp/stamp.jsp?tp=&arnumber=4631212&isnumber=4630767. Accessed August 3, 2013.

Naiman, R. J., C. A. Johnston, and J. C. Kelley. 1988. Alteration of North-American Streams by Beaver. *Bioscience* 38 (11): 753–762.

Odling-Smee, F., K. Laland, and M. Feldman. 2003. *Niche Construction: The Neglected Process in Evolution*. Princeton, NJ: Princeton University Press.

Ofria, C., D. Bryson, and C. Wilke. 2009. Avida: A Software Platform for Research in Computational Evolutionary Biology. In *Artificial Life Models in Software*, 2nd edition, edited by A. Adamatzky and M. Komosinski, 3–36. London: Springer Verlag.

Packard, N. H. 1988. Intrinsic Adaptation in a Simple Model for Evolution. In *Artificial Life*, vol. 6 of *Santa Fe Institute Studies in the Sciences of Complexity*, edited by C. Langton, 141–155. Reading, MA: Addison-Wesley.

Pesavento, U. 1995. An Implementation of von Neumann's Self-Reproducing Machine. *Artificial Life* 2 (4): 337–354.

Raup, D. M. 1986. Biological Extinction in Earth History. *Science* 231 (4745): 1528–1533.

Ray, T. S. 1991. An Approach to the Synthesis of Life. In *Artificial Life II*, volume 10 of *Santa Fe Institute Studies in the Sciences of Complexity*, edited by C. Langton, C. Taylor, J. Farmer, and S. Rasmussen, 371–408. Reading, MA: Addison-Wesley.

Ray, T. S. 1992. Evolution, Ecology and Optimization of Digital Organisms. Technical Report 92-08-942, Santa Fe Institute.

Ray, T. S. 1994. Evolution, Complexity, Entropy and Artificial Reality. *Physica D* 75: 239–263.

Ray, T. S. 2011. November. Personal e-mail communication.

Reed, J., R. Toombs, and N. A. Barricelli. 1967. Simulation of Biological Evolution and Machine Learning. *Journal of Theoretical Biology* 17: 319–342.

Riskin, J., ed. 2007. *Genesis Redux: Essays in the History and Philosophy of Artificial Life*. Chicago: University of Chicago Press.

Schmitz, O. J., and G. Booth. 1996. Modeling Food Web Complexity: The Consequence of Individual-Based Spatially Explicit Behavioral Ecology on Trophic Interactions. *Evolutionary Ecology* 11: 379–398.

Sims, K. 1994a. Evolving 3D Morphology and Behavior by Competition. In *Proceedings of Artificial Life IV*, edited by R. Brooks and P. Maes, 28–39. Cambridge, MA: MIT Press.

Sims, K. 1994b. Evolving Virtual Creatures. In *Computer Graphics, Annual Conference Series (SIGGRAPH'94)*, July, 15–22. New York: ACM.

Solé, R. V., S. C. Manrubia, M. Benton, and P. Bak. 1997. Self-Similarity of Extinction Statistics in the Fossil Record. *Nature* 388: 764–767.

Taylor, T. 1999. From Artificial Evolution to Artificial Life. Ph.D. diss., Division of Informatics, University of Edinburgh. http://www.tim-taylor.com/papers/thesis/. Accessed August 3, 2013.

Taylor, T. 2001. Creativity in Evolution: Individuals, Interactions and Environments. In *Creative Evolutionary Systems*, edited by P. J. Bentley and D. W. Corne, 79–108. San Francisco, CA: Morgan Kaufman.

Taylor, T., and C. Massey. 2001. Recent Developments in the Evolution of Morphologies and Controllers for Physically Simulated Creatures. *Artificial Life* 7 (1): 77–87.

Thearling, K., and T. S. Ray. 1994. Evolving Multi-cellular Artificial Life. In *Artificial Life IV*, edited by R. Brooks and P. Maes, 283–288. Cambridge, MA: MIT Press.

Traill, L. W., C. J. Bradshaw, and B. W. Brook. 2007. Minimum Viable Population Size: A Meta-analysis of 30 Years of Published Estimates. *Biological conservation* 139: 159–166.

Ventrella, J. 1999. Animated Artificial Life. In *Virtual Worlds: Synthetic Universes, Digital Life, and Complexity*, edited by J.-C. Heudin, 67–94. Reading, MA: Perseus Books.

von Neumann, J. 1966. *The Theory of Self-Reproducing Automata*. Edited by A. W. Burks. Urbana: University of Illinois Press.

Yaeger, L. 1994. Computational Genetics, Physiology, Metabolism, Neural Systems, Learning, Vision and Behavior, or PolyWorld: Life in a New Context. In *Proceedings of Artificial Life III*, edited by C. Langton, 263–298. Reading, MA: Addison-Wesley.

CHAPTER 33

··

VIRTUAL ECOLOGIES AND ENVIRONMENTS

··

DAVID G. GREEN AND TOM CHANDLER

A VISION OF THE FUTURE

IMAGINE a future in which you could visit any corner of the world in virtual reality, even places you could never visit in person. And not just the world as it is, but as it was in the past, as it will be in the future, and even as it could never be. Such a future offers many benefits. Environmental planners could try out management scenarios and the public could see for themselves the impact that humans have on the natural environment.

Many elements of the above vision already exist. Ecology, conservation, and environmental science make increasing use of simulation and 3D models. The entire world is mapped and monitored remotely. Global circulation models even capture processes that affect the entire globe. Online services allow virtual tours of many cities. Virtual worlds are standard in digital games and raise the prospect of virtual tourism to global destinations (and even other worlds) that tourists could never visit in real life.

As we shall see, simulation has already led to many new insights in ecology. Building upon these foundations, virtual reality has the potential to change ecology and environmental science radically. By integrating many different factors, it offers an ability to deal with the real complexities of ecosystems. In doing so, it would make it possible to address important issues that could not easily be studied previously.

Virtual representation of the natural world, as presented here, is the combination of two distinct technologies: simulation modeling and 3D models. Historically, these two traditions came to be applied to environments by very different routes: simulation as a tool in scientific research and 3D graphics as a core technology of the entertainment and computer games industries. Only after the turn of the new millennium did it really become practical to combine the two technologies, but applications that combine them do not yet include the seamless interactivity seen in computer games. Therefore, we will argue for the benefits of 3D models in later sections. Certainly, different applications require different representations, and some might require more sophisticated representation than others. Oversimplified models can wipe out a great deal of the processes involved. For example, even a 2D model includes a lot more detail than a nonspatial model, and, as we shall show later, higher dimensional models embody much more detail and therefore reveal more about the ecosystems being modeled.

Taken together, simulation and 3D graphics amount to a new paradigm, which we refer to here as the virtual model. In this overview of the virtual model in ecology and environments, we first explore the origins and achievements of the two individual strands, and then discuss the paradigm of the virtual model as it applies to the natural world. This discussion includes some of the issues involved in applying virtual models to ecology, as well as new dimensions it opens up. In particular, we describe some challenges that arise in the application of virtual modeling to environmental problems, including integration, complexity, and scale.

SIMULATION: FROM CLUB OF ROME TO ARTIFICIAL LIFE

In environmental research, simulation helped to bridge the barriers between disciplines by combining many different features in a single model. Reconstructing past civilizations, for instance, requires inputs from archaeologists, historians, ecologists, climatologists, geographers, computer scientists, and many others. The resulting models make it possible to ask questions that cannot be answered in any other way. In doing so, they yield new insights that are often unsuspected and crucial.

In ecology, simulation makes it possible to investigate the complex interplay between populations and the environment. In the real world, there are some experiments you could never do, but in a virtual world you can grow a forest back over hundreds of years, or release a deadly virus into the wild without destroying the very thing you are trying to save.

Simulation began contributing to the environmental debate from the very first. In 1972, a group of scientists calling themselves the Club of Rome released results of a study in which they used simulation models to project current global processes forward based on a variety of scenarios (Meadows et al. 1972). Their *Limits to Growth* model attempted to reconstruct the main driving processes in several domains, including environment, agriculture, economics, education, and human population. Its projections for the future included runaway pollution and a crash in world population. These startling predictions of global cataclysms caused a sensation when they were published. A critical backlash followed, but despite its flaws, the study made two important points: first, environmental issues need to be taken seriously; second, simulation has the ability to address major environmental issues.

Much of the criticism of *Limits to Growth* involved picking apart details of the model. In retrospect, the criticisms highlight general problems that are faced by all environmental simulation models. First, there is the problem of "garbage in, garbage out": if the inputs are wrong, then the outputs will be wrong too. A second problem is calibration. With literally hundreds of variables and relationships, it is difficult even to get reasonable values for all the parameter values. Third, complex systems are often highly sensitive to initial conditions, so even slight inaccuracies can lead to erroneous results. Fourth, local variations can be important. The *Limits to Growth* model treated entire regions as a uniform whole. Subsequent developments have shown that marked regional differences occur in response to environmental challenges. Finally, it is easy to omit important relationships. By its very nature, no model is ever a complete representation of the world. Models always omit details. And these details sometimes have important effects.

Without doubt, the most successful environmental models have been those used in weather forecasting. The crucial importance of accurate weather forecasts has made weather one of the most intensively studied of all natural systems. It was while using an early weather simulation that Lorenz (1963) detected the phenomenon of sensitivity to initial conditions, which characterizes chaotic behavior in complex systems. This sensitivity limits the ability to make reliable forecasts. For many years even forecasts 24 hours ahead were notoriously unreliable. However, by the turn of the millennium, faster computers and the establishment of worldwide data-monitoring networks made seven-day outlooks possible.

Virtual Experiments

Environmental science, and especially ecology, faces two problems that make real-life experimentation difficult, and often impossible. First, as we mentioned above, there are some experiments you cannot do in the real world. Burn down a forest to watch it regenerate and the forest may never recover. Or it may take longer to recover than the observer's lifetime. In a virtual world, on the other hand, you can torch a forest repeatedly and observe it regenerating over virtual decades or centuries.

Second, the time scale of ecological change makes many experiments impractical. Some trees can live for hundreds of years. So a single experiment on forest succession may not be completed within the lifetime of an individual scientist. There is also the problem that forest clearing and other human-induced environmental changes are happening so quickly that ecologists try to cope by using "natural experiments," such as observing the state of forests subjected to fire at different times in the past. However, there is a real need to test hypotheses in a single system.

Another advantage of simulation in ecology is its ability to deal with the complexity of nature. Traditional science is reductionist. It seeks to understand nature by a divide-and-conquer approach: reduce a large system into smaller pieces that you can study. Once you understand all the pieces, you understand the whole. In ecology, this approach works only up to a point. Carrying out experiments on a plant's physiology in a growth chamber gives precise, repeatable results, but they are never an accurate guide to how the plant will perform under field conditions, where it interacts with the thousands of other trees that surround it.

Unexpected results often emerge when you bring the pieces together, and simulation provides a practical way to detect and study these surprises. In a simulation model you bring together all the knowledge you may gain about all the pieces, allowing you to carry out virtual experiments on the whole. It also forces researchers to state their assumptions, all their assumptions, explicitly and precisely.

The above issues highlight the differences between the simple systems studied by traditional science and the complex systems that abound in environmental science. Engineers, for instance, can control artificial systems by constraining key variables so that they remain within desired limits. One method is to use negative feedback to automatically dampen fluctuations. In environmental systems, however, constraining variables (e.g., rainfall) is often impossible. More importantly, in complex systems, positive feedback magnifies small local irregularities into global patterns.

Dealing with Geography

Early simulations of ecosystems were essentially just extensions of mathematical modeling. They used formulas to calculate population changes, but also included rules to account for particular events or conditions. For a long time simulations ignored geography. The assumption was that local changes in environmental parameters (e.g., soil moisture, elevation) explained all the geographic variation in populations. But by the late 1980s increasing computing power made it practical to test this assumption in spatially explicit models.

One success of ecological simulation modeling was to demonstrate the huge effects wrought by interactions within a landscape. Take seed dispersal for example (fig. 33.1). In a forest, most seeds fall close to the parent tree. So when a gap opens in the forest, the nearby trees are local seed sources and have the best chance of reproducing at that

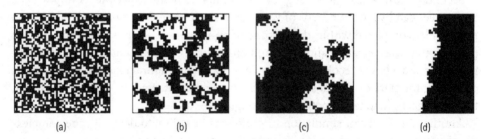

(a)   (b)   (c)   (d)

FIGURE 33.1 Virtual experiments into the effects of spatial interactions on plant distributions (after Green 1994). These simulations show scenarios involving two plant species (shaded black and white) competing in a landscape. (a) Seeds disperse anywhere; (b) Localized seed dispersal around parent plants produces clumps; (c) Fires make clumps coalesce into patches; (d) Environmental gradients sort the species into zones.

site. This process leads to plants having clumped distributions. Combined with environmental variation and other spatial processes (e.g., fire), dispersal plays a key role in the formation of zones (both in space and time) and in the maintenance of ecological diversity.

Multiagent Simulation

As we saw earlier, simulations face many problems when they try to replicate the behavior of a particular system in the real world. In environmental simulation, there is typically a huge cost in time and effort to gather accurate data and to validate, test, and refine the model. To take an example, if you model an ecosystem comprising (say) 100 species, then the model needs to take into account some 10,000 possible interactions! This is difficult enough. But if you try to simulate the ecosystem at the level of individual plants and animals, then there may be literally millions of "agents" whose behavior needs to be modeled precisely. The number of unknown parameter values therefore grows exponentially.

Problems such as these have limited the use of simulation as a routine tool in environmental research and management. However, simulation has proved much more successful in theoretical studies, where the problems of calibration and validation are simpler. Instead of trying to forecast what will happen in a real system, simulation can carry out virtual experiments in which they reveal what *could* happen under given scenarios (sets of assumptions). For this reason, multiagent models have found direct applications to real environmental and ecological problems.

To avoid the problem of garbage in, garbage out mentioned earlier, virtual experiments need to work from simple to complex. That is, instead of throwing everything into the mix to see what happens, they need to work systematically, starting with the fewest assumptions so that outcomes can be understood.

Artificial Life

In the early 1990s, the use of multiagent simulation in ecology and other fields gave rise to a new field of research, now known as *artificial life* (often shortened to *A-life*). This uses simulation to investigate a wide range of theoretical issues in ecology and biology (Langton 1989). One of the great successes of A-life has been to demonstrate ways in which global phenomena in the living world emerge out of local interactions. Perhaps its chief insight is that although living systems may be very different from one another, identical processes often underlie the way they self-organize. For instance, A-life models showed that similar patterns of interactions between individuals allow schools of fish and flocks of birds to form and move without any central control (Reynolds 1987). Likewise, environment processes such as the spread of fire, disease, and exotic plants are all cases of percolation and related to physical processes such as nuclear chain reactions.

Among its other achievements, A-life proved the value of simulation as a means to study complex issues in theoretical biology and ecology. It also helped to promote the new paradigm of *natural computation*, which interprets processes in nature as information processing. This paradigm is reflected in the increasingly widespread use of simulation to study living and environmental problems. It is also evident in the principle of turning to living systems when seeking solutions to complex computational problems.

In the 1970s, the game *Life* excited much attention by showing that simple, life-like rules could produce order from initially random patterns. This game sparked off research into an entire class of systems called cellular automata (CAs). These are arrays of cells, each having a state that is programmed to change in response to its neighbors.

Applied to ecology, CA models are used to model virtual landscapes in which each cell denotes an area of the earth's surface. Models of seed dispersal and competition reveal how large-scale plant distributions form (Green 1989; 1994) and how they influence long-term trends in forest change. CA models of fire spread are used to experiment with strategies to contain the spread of wildfires.

Abstracting the idea of interactions into other virtual systems, A-life studies showed how simple rules governing local interactions underlie many complex processes in biology and environmental science. Seminal results came from a study by Hogeweg and Hesper (1983), who showed that simple rules of social interaction sufficed to explain the formation of bumblebee colonies. Later studies extended this insight to many other cases.

The spatial arrangement of items in an ant colony, for instance, arises from the combined effects of individual behavior and positive feedback. Ants create clumps by picking up scattered items and drop them where they find other, similar items. Feedback allows large clumps to grow at the expense of small ones (fig. 33.2).

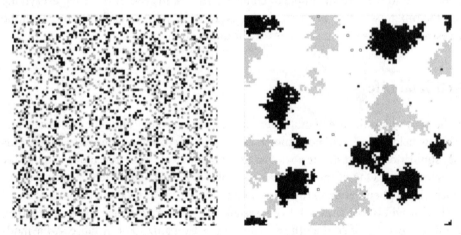

FIGURE 33.2 Self-organization in a virtual ant colony. At left a newly formed colony has objects (shaded) scattered at random throughout. Ants pick up these objects as they wander around and drop them when they find a similar object. This process forms clumps of similar objects. Positive feedback makes the large clumps grow at the expense of small ones. At right is the end result, with the objects sorted into large piles.

Other simulations have also influenced perceptions of the global environment. Daisy World (Lovelock and Margulis 1974; Lovelock 1988) was a simple simulation model that showed how organisms can influence, and to some degree stabilize, the planet's environment. Shifting distributions of black and white daisies altered the balance of reflected versus absorbed heat in the atmosphere, so dampening fluctuations in global temperature.

As mentioned earlier in this section, the paradigm of natural computation influenced computer science. Just as virtual experiments reveal (say) how an ant colony organizes itself, so too they reveal ways that nature has evolved to solve complex problems. One result is that biological ideas now abound in computing. The general principle is to abstract the essential computational idea embodied in a model of some process in nature, then generalize it and apply it elsewhere. So examples like the virtual ant colony lead to an *ant sort algorithm*, which in turn belongs to an entire field of research known as *swarm intelligence*.

Generalizing from other kinds of models of nature has likewise led to hybrid fields of research. We have already seen how simulation of landscapes is associated with the study of cellular automata and other multiagent computation. Simulating evolution led to genetic algorithms (Holland 1975), which are widely used to solve complex optimization problems, and to the more general field of evolutionary computation.

Ecologies of the Past and Present in Virtual Reality

Today the word "virtual" has come to mean almost anything on or mediated by a computer, but the concept of "virtual reality" is much more specific. In the 1980s, the computer scientist Jaron Lanier (Conn et al. 1989) described a specific set of three-dimensional graphics coupled with intense simulation. Ever since then, his term "virtual reality" has always maintained a strong association with geometric 3D models.

The endeavor of "modeling" virtual ecologies with 3D geometry means that the complexity of the model is concerned not only with processes and agent interaction but also with representation of the virtual world in varying degrees of realism. The necessity of dealing with 3D space shifts the definition of what it is to "model" an ecosystem from the abstract to the concrete. Like an architect's scale model of a building concept, an ecological system constructed in virtual reality seeks to convey an environment that is at once artificial and familiar. While the geometrical and Cartesian space of 3D modeling software programs such as *AutoDesk Maya* (AutoDesk 2011) has deep roots in computer science, the worlds that they are used to create draw their inspiration not only from mathematical simulation but from disciplines as photography, sculpture, and cinema.

Although the much-hyped "goggles and gloves" virtual reality of the 1990s remains largely unknown in the public domain, a virtual reality accessed through standard personal computers is arguably very much in evidence in computer games. Recent computer games boast ever richer and more realistic environments, but where landscape elements and vegetation are brought into play, their purpose is usually just to provide scene and setting. The point of the simulation in these games is, after all, to engage the human player in the game world, where the player is the center of the simulated universe; ecology is often an incidental green backdrop to action and adventure.

Even in games with an ecological or evolutionary theme, such as Will Wright's early *SimEarth: The Living Planet* (Maxis 1990) and Wright's more recent title *Spore* (Maxis 2008), the goals of designing "sentient" beings or "higher life forms" ensure that game play consistently overrides scientific details.

While there are large-scale representations of time and space in strategy games, the most immersive and detailed environments are usually focused on the immediacy of the present tense. What we can question next is what might happen if we removed both the "goal" and the "player" from these worlds and switched the ecology from the background to the foreground. Perhaps if we can substitute the urgency of dodging bullets or designing our way toward a "winning" result, to be an observer instead of a participant, we can take the time to consider what approximation of virtual reality ecology might offer us.

When we compare virtual reality ecology with a cellular automata simulation of ecology, the very different factors of representation are key considerations. For example, in creating a 3D model of a forest, the designer of a virtual reality model needs to consider how the models of trees can be crafted into identifiable species. Whether for games or animations, much of the crafting of 3D-modeled vegetation in virtual worlds is assisted by specialized plug-ins running variations of L-system growth algorithms (fig. 33.3).

FIGURE 33.3 Developmental growth in tree models using seed algorithms. L-systems (Lindenmayer 1968) can generate realistic-looking models of trees by capturing the rules that govern branching, leaf patterns, and other aspects of growth.

Modeling vegetation to fill and frame the virtual landscape in a virtual world is only part of the picture. The modeler also needs to consider how the terrain beneath the trees undulates in subtle grades and textures and how the shafts of virtual sunlight filter through the canopy. Taking it a step further, finer grades in the dimension of time might deal with the motion, and sound, of the leafy branches swaying in the virtual breeze. Such possibilities, clearly, offer the premise of a more tangible and experiential vision of a virtual ecology, but to what end?

Perhaps the opportunity offered by virtual ecologies is not only to experiment with them, but also to visit them. Though time may be rendered in explicitly detailed moments, we can still jump forward or backward through vast swathes of time. The popular television documentary *Life After People* (de Vries 2008) used 3D modeling and animation technologies to visually imagine how the human ecologies of agriculture and urban spaces would revert to a natural state in the decades and centuries following humanity's hypothetical disappearance. Moving much further in time, but instead into the deep past, we could bring to life the prehistoric ecologies of Permian or Carboniferous swamps in museum diorama displays.

Within the cinematic space of virtual reality, the scale of landscape being envisaged is complicated not just by the detail of the models but also by the familiar associations that meet the human eye. The most important transition here is the difference between merely viewing a visualization of the landscape on the one hand and (virtually) visiting it on the other. For example, larger scale virtual reality models can be regarded somewhat dispassionately, as one would examine a map or the passing view glimpsed from a plane window (see fig. 33.4). However, when we are brought to ground level (see fig. 33.5), we are offered a vision that equates to walking through the landscape, albeit on a computer screen.

FIGURE 33.4 A virtual model of the interior of South West Island, Northern Territory.

FIGURE 33.5 A virtual view of the interior of South West Island, at the experiential level.

If we were to descend from a high view (fig. 33.4) toward the ground (fig. 33.5), then the trees dotting the landscape would transform from generalized green forms to particular species of eucalypts and acacias. Compelling clues as to the location of the ecology we are visiting can be offered as soon as we glimpse the animated 3D forms of kangaroos bounding through the waist-high grass. There is no need to resort to sub-headings or map key symbols. Since so much of the environment is highly visual, it would make sense to enhance what we can hear around us as well: and again, what you would hear as you stood still on the ground would be different from what you could hear from far up in the sky. Virtual reality can deal with ecosystems on scales ranging from the miniscule worlds of microorganisms right up to continent-sized expanses. But as soon as we leave the space of everyday experience, the chance of offering intuitive cues and clues (via light, shade, motion, and sound) in a virtual ecosystem becomes increasingly difficult.

While a virtual reality ecosystem model might be driven by the same invisible vari-ables as a two-dimensional diagrammatic ecosystem model, it also brings other more nuanced variables to the fore. Explicitly visual simulations can take into account the pos-sible or probable constitution of the landscape in reference to the impact of fire regimes, invasive species, stocking rates, or climate change. While the close approximation of the simulation image to an actual photograph presents perils in implicit acceptance and believability, it also neatly conveys qualities of a dynamic landscape that might be clum-sily communicated in a more abstract visualization. For example, in figure 33.5, intuitive cues in light and shade indicate that the landscape is baked by a tropical sun and suggest the representation of a season other than the monsoon. Though the landscape we see is based upon the cartographic layers of a geographic information system (GIS) data set, views of such immersive, cinematic "virtual realities" make for an entirely different kind of "map" in which spatial simulations of ecology play out.

Another consideration for a 3D ecological simulation is sound. While the significance of sound design in the crafting of an immersive player experience in digital games is well known (Grimshaw 2007; 2010), the use of sound in three-dimensional ecological or biological simulations is only beginning to be explored. In a three-dimensional ecological simulation sounds can convey information about the virtual environment by inference and suggest ecological phenomena even though they are never included as discreet models themselves. As an ornithologist can identify the presence of furtive bird species by their calls alone, in a virtual ecology, a birdcall can imply that a certain species of bird is present without any requirement for a 3D model of the bird to be seen (or created). Again, just as the color and texture of the ground in a virtual ecological model can convey a parched landscape instead of a waterlogged one, subtle sound signals can allow readers of the visualization to deduce other cues about the virtual ecology they are both seeing and hearing. While the total mix of ecological sounds undoubtedly adds to the atmospheric richness of the virtual ecology being experienced, decoding the significance of certain environmental sound cues might depend on ecological expertise. For example, animal sounds that are territorial or for courtship might imply seasonality, and the sound signature of specific insects such as crickets or cicadas might depend upon the presence of certain vegetation types with which they are associated.

Such considerations for scale, visual consistency, geometric models, color, and sound all played a part in the endeavor of visualizing the ecology of the medieval Cambodian city of Angkor (Chandler 2009). Much of the challenge in reconstructing scenes from Angkor's history involved visualizing the cultural landscape of early tropical urbanism: the human ecology of Angkor. With the world population surpassing seven billion at the time of writing, the scope for the study of ecologies without regard for human impact is severely compromised. Where once human interaction and ecologies were seen as separate issues, they are now understood as intimately interlinked. Similarly interlinked is the range of disciplines upon which a 3D visualizer must draw to realize a scene from centuries ago.

In the image in figure 33.6 we see a still frame from an animation of part of Angkor's settlement pattern. The virtual camera is angled from a high vantage point. Here many data sources are drawn together from a range of disparate academic studies. For example, the visual suggestion for the composition and variance of the vegetation is based on pollen cores taken at Angkor (Penny et al. 2006) and floristic species mentioned in stone inscriptions (Jacob 1978); the layout of the roads and ponds is derived from archaeological surveys (Evans et al. 2007); and the style of the houses is drawn from studies on South East Asian architectural studies (Dumarçay and Smithies 2003). In figure 33.7, we delve deeper into the virtual model and view it at eye level: here all the dynamics change. The elements that would be classed as "agents" in an ecological simulation here become distinct. The essential units in the human ecological system, people, have changed from abstractions to identifiable "characters." We can witness in microcosm the quotidian activities that, multiplied many times over, shape the form and space of

FIGURE 33.6 A view over the landscape of medieval Angkor, Cambodia, showing the settlement.

FIGURE 33.7 A reconstructed view of medieval Angkor at road level, showing the trees, sky, and terrain from an eyewitness perspective.

an extensive preindustrial capital. Moving the model several centuries ahead, we can examine the gradual depopulation of Angkor and visualize forsaken village shrines and shrub-infested rice fields. Here too, sounds could feature as indicators of the transformation from a human-engineered agrarian ecology to a dense tropical forest. Instead of agricultural animals and human activity we would begin to hear species that eschew the space of humans but dwell happily in tall dipterocarp forests. Visualizations of the abandonment of Angkor might be accompanied by the searching, long-ranging whoops of gibbons.

Combining Eco-simulation and 3D Modeled Environments

What we are here calling *virtuality* is the union of the two technologies discussed in the previous sections. As we saw, both simulation and 3D graphics of natural landscapes became popular only when computer technology became powerful enough to provide sufficient speed and memory to make them feasible. This applied even more to their combination. Not until the year 2000 did it become feasible for simulations to incorporate immersive 3D in more than a superficial fashion.

One motivation for combining simulation and 3D is the need to make research results understandable for the general public, especially where the results have a bearing on issues that are politically or socially sensitive. At this point, early in the third millennium, increasing public awareness of "green" issues made this motivation particularly strong for environmental research.

An example of this motivation is the need of the forestry industry to address public concern about clear-felling and logging in native forests. The industry had good simulation models that allowed companies to project tree growth and landscape change over time. Combining these models with 3D graphics led to packages, such as *SmartForest* (Orland, Radja, and Su 1998), that employed virtual reality to allow users to see and explore forests in a region as they changed over time.

Ecological Virtuality in Practice

Working examples that demonstrate a cohesive integration of 3D virtual worlds and simulated ecosystems (Deussen et al. 2002; Zamuda et al. 2007), though present in the literature, remain rather thinly spread. Where simulation and 3D graphics meet in the games industry, computer game engines can offer high levels of realism in rendering natural environments; but these are geared toward visual aesthetics and atmosphere rather than ecological verisimilitude. One of the reasons for the relative dearth of applications that combine ecological simulation and virtual reality is that this combination is not always necessary. Given the circumstances, often either a simple, interactive simulation or a noninteractive visualization will suffice. However, there are examples where both the rendering of ecological processes and 3D graphics are interdependent, such as the role of visions of future landscapes in influencing a community's perception. Studies

FIGURE 33.8 Two contrasting visualizations of the same scene, showing the relative projected condition of River Red Gum trees (*E. camaldulensis*) with sustaining (left) and inadequate (right) water availability.

by Lange (2010) and Sheppard (2005) underscore the utility of realistic landscape visualizations in communicating visions of deliberately planned or climate change-impacted future landscapes to nonexperts. Sharing these views of the future in a graphically familiar and compelling manner is foremost a communicative tool, but it can also influence future change in people's awareness and affect behavior and policy. For example, figure 33.8 depicts a virtual view of trees on the Murray River floodplain derived from a GIS database. In a two-dimensional map, stands of trees at risk of dying if water management regimes went unchanged were merely marked as red, but in a three-dimensional view, the ecological implications of a forest under threat are more effectively realized without resort to cartographical abstractions. Given that so many of the predictions made in the complex science of climate change have been obfuscated by political and special interest groups, perhaps 3D visions based on ecological simulation will find their most imminent application in communicating and influencing the public's awareness of likely scenarios where maps, graphs, tables, and reports fail. And here, after demonstrating ways in which virtual ecologies can reach into the past and address the present, we can next consider how they might be used to look ahead into the future.

VIRTUALITY AS A TOOL

Is it possible to create a technology by which we could put together simulations or virtual reality models to address any problem, anywhere, at very short notice? Governments, for example, often need to address very difficult questions in a short time with limited information. How will a proposed pulp mill affect the environment around it? Can genetically modified organisms be contained?

Major practical hurdles must be overcome before the above vision can be realized. No model truly recreates the real world; there are always limits and gaps. Also, acquiring up-to-date data is a practical impossibility: even the best fire spread model, for instance, can be rendered invalid by minute-to-minute changes in fuel moisture and local wind eddies.

We now look briefly at each of the main problems we encounter when trying to use virtual models as practical tools.

Problem 1: Integration

Perhaps the greatest practical challenge for the virtual model is the integration problem. This is the need to combine four elements: model definition, structure and processing, user interface, and adequate data. Simulation packages provide environments that simplify the development of models. Most packages have incorporated the first three elements, especially in specialized domains such as environmental modeling. However, even with user-friendly development environments, defining and implementing simulations of natural environments still requires a major effort.

There also remains a massive coordination problem to integrate modeling environments with real data that are valid, timely, and appropriate.

Problem 2: Calibration

A complex model may have many variables. As we saw earlier, a complex model can have literally thousands of parameters. All of these interactions have parameters whose values need to be determined for the model!

Calibrating models becomes an even greater problem when the features involved are changing continuously. In the case of fire spread again, environmental properties such as humidity, fuel moisture, and wind velocity can vary from minute to minute.

The only way to model such a system with a reasonable chance of prediction is to update the key parameters as they change. The solution is real-time monitoring of a real system to maintain its virtual image. Advances in microminiaturization and communications have made this possible. Wireless sensor networks can consist of hundreds or even thousands of small sensors that feed back data to a base station.

Problem 3: Emergence

Another problem is that sheer complexity renders many ecosystems inherently unpredictable (Green et al. 2006). But simulation allows us to explore crucial scenarios and to test the sensitivity of ecosystems to changes of many kinds. As we have seen, whole new fields of research, such as artificial life, use computer simulation to explore life as it could be, so providing valuable insights about the real world.

One of the characteristics of complex systems is that local variations and disturbances can grow into global features. As we saw earlier, many features of ecosystems (such as patchy distributions) emerge as the results of interactions within a landscape. The exact patterns can be unpredictable and unexpected. Only simulation reveals them.

Emergent properties and behavior can make complex systems literally unpredictable. Take a relatively straightforward problem such as simulating the pattern of spread in a wildfire. A fire is an emergent phenomenon. It emerges from interactions in which burning fuel ignites other fuel nearby. The way a fire spreads depends on many factors including temperature, humidity, and wind speed and direction, but most importantly, it depends on the distribution of fuel. If fuel is sparse, then the pattern of spread can be unpredictable.

Problem 4: Context

Virtual reality may give the appearance of reality, but it is not. VR models are limited by what is programmed into them. And no model can include everything. The real world is not limited in this way. A common source of difficulty in trying to prevent accidents is the phenomenon of cascading contexts (Green 2013).

The very realism of virtual reality simulation models is in itself a danger. If you see what looks like reality, it is easy to believe it is reality. This is dangerous because even the best virtual reality simulation is still just a model, and not reality inside a computer. And just as important as what is in a model, is what it leaves out. In one sense or another, models treat their subject as a closed system. But in the real world, ecosystems are open systems; they are richly connected to everything around them. You can simulate the ecosystem within a lake, for instance, but not every detail of the ecosystems that surround it, not the geomorphology that shapes the earth beneath it, nor the global weather patterns that affect its water. At best you can only approximate its surroundings under certain conditions. But if those surroundings change, then connections left out of a model can radically alter the system.

Problem 5: Real-Time Interactivity

Once integration, calibration, emergence, and context have been addressed, we need to ask how the scientist, student, or general public would interact with a computer-mediated vision of ecology. Clearly, the ability to alter courses of forest succession or desertification in a simulation, and observe the 3D modeled results in real time, is an attractive prospect. But from what vantage point would the computer user view these events, and how should the passage of time over decades, centuries, or millennia be conveyed?

As we have discussed, the prospect of "visiting" a 3D virtual landscape implies walking through and among its geometry, and this is quite different from viewing the same landscape cartographically from far above. But if the user is to experiment with, for example, a 70-year period and a 700 square-kilometer expanse, then observing the simulation one tree at a time would be severely limiting. If, for example, we wanted to simulate theories of planetary scale ecological change such as the catastrophe that marked the end of the Cretaceous, we would require both a good deal of scale (an entire planet) and time (millennia to millions of years) to review it properly.

This problem of real-time interactivity is a complex one because interfaces and modes of experience in ecological simulations remain unfixed, and there are as many conceivable interfaces for simulations as there are possible topics for simulation. Simply mimicking the zoom-in and zoom-out functionality of GoogleEarth and adding "time sliders" is one approach, but hardly an imaginative or innovative one. While the repurposing of computer game technologies may assist, the premise of the simulation user's intent may complicate matters: we must be careful not to transform the simulation from an open-ended experiment into a game with goals, objectives, and strategies.

A New Paradigm

To meet the challenge of complexity, studies in virtual modeling have evolved an approach different from traditional mathematical modeling (Green and Leishman 2011). This new, *virtual model paradigm* is rapidly developing alternatives to the methods evolved by traditional science over hundreds of years (table 33.1).

Table 33.1 summarizes some of the differences between two modeling paradigms in ecology. What we refer to here as "traditional" models are typically mathematical models that express processes purely as relationships between variables.

Table 33.1 Differences between Modeling Paradigms

Issue	Traditional	The virtual model
Model representation	Formulas	Simulation
Model development	Curve fitting	Network analysis
Model presentation	Graphical plots	Virtual reality
Data resources	Rare and expensive	Abundant and cheap
Planning	Forecasting	Scenarios
Control	Optimization	Adaptation
Interpretation	Algebraic	Sensitivity, resilience

Instead of mathematical formulas, the virtual model paradigm implements models as simulations or virtual reality (table 33.1). Because complex systems are often unpredictable, virtual models use scenarios to examine cases of importance. Unlike mathematical models, which can be analyzed by algebraic manipulation, virtual models are investigated using sensitivity analysis, which traces changes in the outcome as values of variables are changed systematically. Such models are possible because on-the-ground data, which for centuries were rare and expensive to obtain, have rapidly become abundant and cheap.

A Virtual Future

Why virtual ecologies? In environmental research, VR and simulation help bridge the barriers between different disciplines. Reconstructing past civilizations, for instance, requires inputs from archaeologists, historians, ecologists, climatologists, geographers, computer scientists, and many others. The resulting models make it possible to ask questions that cannot be answered in any other way, and yield insights that are often unsuspected but crucial.

To take just one example, virtual models may help to address the important problem of scale. Because of its reductionist nature, traditional science tends to ignore interactions that occur across different scales. One problem that arises this way is the need to bridge the gulf from genes to growth to geography, which we will refer to as the *3G problem*. The ways in which plants and animals perform in a landscape depend on the way they grow. And the way they grow depends on their genetic makeup. Related species often have similar genetic makeup, but occupy very different ecological roles in different environments.

The introduction of L-system models to biology (Lindenmayer 1968; Prusinkiewicz and Lindenmayer 1990) have made it possible to create extremely realistic models of growing plants in an environment (Deussen et al. 2002; Zamuda et al. 2007). The ability of L-systems to capture the organization of growth as sets of syntactic rules hints at the possibility of mapping these rules to underlying genetic regulatory networks and hence to a plant's genotype. At the other extreme, a plant's growth determines where it will grow, how it will respond to the prevailing environment, and how it will interact with competing species. A virtual model offers the prospect of capturing processes across all of the different scales involved in the 3G problem. Meeting this challenge would open the prospect of predicting the likely ecological effects of genetic manipulation.

Great though the contributions of simulation and VR have been to our understanding of the natural world, their chief uses so far have been in entertainment. The most advanced simulation and imaging technology is devoted to building better games. This raises the question whether virtual reconstruction of the natural world will prove a means to conserve the reality, or will prove to be merely another way to exploit it.

Ultimately, however, the above question may be immaterial. How we choose to manage the environment depends on our perceptions of nature. So perception becomes the reality. But in virtual reality, reconstructions of nature can be anything we choose to make them. The most important question is how we choose to represent that reality.

REFERENCES

Chandler, T. 2009. Animations of Angkor. *National Geographic Online.* http://ngm. nationalgeographic.com/2009/07/angkor/angkor-animation. Accessed October 27, 2009.

Conn, C., J. Lanier, M. Minsky, S. Fisher, and A. Druin. 1989. Virtual Environments and Interactivity: Windows to the Future. In *ACM SIGGRAPH 89 Panel Proceedings,* 7–18. New York: ACM.

Deussen, O., C. Colditz, M. Stamminger, and G. Drettakis. 2002. Interactive Visualization of Complex Plant Ecosystems. In *Vis 2002: IEEE Visualization 2002, Proceedings,* 219–226. New York: ACM.

de Vries, D., dir. 2008. *Life after People: The Series.* Flight 33 Productions.

Dumarçay, J., and M. Smithies. 2003. *Architecture and Its Models in South-East Asia.* Bangkok: Orchid Press.

Evans, D., C. Pottier, R. Fletcher, S. Hensley, I. Tapley, A. Milne, and M. Barbetti. 2007. A Comprehensive Archaeological Map of the World's Largest Preindustrial Settlement Complex at Angkor, Cambodia. *Proceedings of the National Academy of Sciences of the United States of America* 104: 14277–14282.

Green, D. G. 1989. Simulated Effects of Fire, Dispersal and Spatial Pattern on Competition within Vegetation Mosaics. *Vegetatio* 82: 139–153.

Green, D. G. 1994. Connectivity and Complexity in Ecological Systems. *Pacific Conservation Biology* 1 (3): 194–200.

Green, D.G. (2013). *Of Ants and Men.* Springer, Berlin.

Green, D. G., and T. G. Leishman. 2011. Computing and Complexity: Networks, Nature and Virtual Worlds. In *Philosophy of Complex Systems,* edited by C. A. Hooker and J. Collier, 151–175. *Handbook of the Philosophy of Science,* vol. 10. Amsterdam: Elsevier BV.

Grimshaw, M. 2007. Sound and Immersion in the First-Person Shooter. *Proceedings of CGames* 2007: 119–124.

Grimshaw, M. 2010. Player Relationships as Mediated through Sound in Immersive Multi-player Computer Games *Comunicar* 34: 73–81.

Hogeweg, P., and B. Hesper. 1983. The Ontogeny of the Interaction Structure in Bumblebee Colonies: A Mirror Model. *Behavioral Ecology and Sociobiology* 12: 271–283.

Holland, J. 1975. *Adaptation in Natural and Artificial Systems.* Ann Arbor: University of Michigan Press.

Jacob, J. 1978. The Ecology of Angkor: Evidence from the Khmer Inscriptions. In *Nature and Man in South East Asia,* edited by E. P. Stott, 109–127. London: School of Oriental and African Studies.

Lange, E., and S. Hehl-Lange. 2010. Making Visions Visible for Long-Term Landscape Management. *Futures* 42 (7): 693–699.

Langton, C. G., ed. 1989. *Artificial Life.* Reading, MA: Addison-Wesley.

Lindenmayer, A. 1968. Mathematical Models for Cellular Interaction in Development I. Filaments with One-Sided Inputs. *Journal of Theoretical Biology* 18: 280–289.

Lorenz, E. N. 1963. Deterministic Nonperiodic Flow. *Journal of Atmospheric Science* 20 (2): 130–141.

Lovelock, J. E., and L. Margulis. 1974. Atmospheric Homeostasis by and for the Biosphere: The Gaia Hypothesis. *Tellus* 26: 2–10.

Lovelock, J. E. 1988. *The Ages of Gaia*. New York: Norton.

Meadows, D. H., D. L. Meadows, J. Randers, and W. W. Behrens. 1972. *The Limits to Growth*. New York: Universe Books.

Orland, B., P. Radja, and W. Su. 1998. SmartForest: An Interactive Forest Data Modeling and Visualization Tool. In *Remote Sensing and Ecosystem Management: Proceedings of the Fifth Forest Service Remote Sensing Applications Conference*, 283–292. Portland: DIANE Publishing.

Penny, D., C. Pottier, R. Fletcher, M. Barbetti, D. Fink, and Q. Hua. 2006. Vegetation and Land-Use at Angkor, Cambodia: A Dated Pollen Sequence from the Bakong Temple Moat. *Antiquity* 80: 599–614.

Prusinkiewicz, P., and A. Lindenmayer. 1990. *The Algorithmic Beauty of Plants*. New York: Springer-Verlag.

Reynolds, C. W. 1987. Flocks, Herds, and Schools: A Distributed Behavioral Model. *Computer Graphics* 21: 25–34.

Sheppard, S. R. J. 2005. Landscape Visualisation and Climate Change: The Potential for Influencing Perceptions and Behaviour. *Environmental Science and Policy* 8 (6): 637–654.

Zamuda, A., J. Brest, N. Guid, and V. Zurner. 2007. Modelling, Simulation, and Visualization of Forest Ecosystems. In *Eurocon 2007: The International Conference on Computer as a Tool*, 2600–2606. New York: IEEE.

Games and Software

Autodesk Maya. Autodesk, 2011. http://usa.autodesk.com/maya/. Accessed October 26. 2011.

Sim Earth. Microprose, Maxis, 1990.

Spore. Maxis / Electronic Arts, 2008.

CHAPTER 34

COMPUTATIONAL MODELING OF BRAIN FUNCTION AND THE HUMAN HAPTIC SYSTEM AT THE NEURAL SPIKE LEVEL: LEARNING THE DYNAMICS OF A SIMULATED BODY

GABRIEL ROBLES-DE-LA-TORRE

THE human sense of touch and related haptic capabilities such as kinesthesia are essential to interact with our environment (Robles-De-La-Torre 2006). If we suddenly lost our haptic capabilities, we would immediately fall to the floor. We would be unable to walk and to manipulate objects. We could not properly articulate speech, nor chew and swallow our food. Further, neither visual nor aural information would be enough to compensate for major haptic capability loss. Yet human haptic capabilities have been much less studied than other senses such as vision and hearing. This is perhaps understandable, given the complexity, yet subtlety of these capabilities. Haptic capabilities involve motor actions, perception, cognition, and other major brain functions acting together. It is not difficult to see that the study of haptic capabilities offers a unique window into the workings of skilled human performance and related brain functions during interaction with real or virtual environments.

A major open problem is how to understand haptic capabilities and their related brain functions in terms of computations based on the neural spike signals that the brain uses. Such fundamental understanding would shed light on how the brain works and produces behaviors. This in turn would also help understand how the computational properties of brain function shape skilled interaction with real and virtual environments. For example, the brain's computational features determine what can and cannot be learned about a virtual or real environment, how fast this can be achieved, how this knowledge can be applied and extended to new situations, what level of fidelity is needed in a virtual environment so its features can be adequately learned, and so on. This chapter proposes a possible way in which human haptic capabilities could be understood in terms of computation at the level of neural spike signals. In brief, a computational model is proposed to understand one of the most basic haptic capabilities: how the brain learns the dynamics of the body, and how this knowledge is used to predict the result of a motor action. Such acquired knowledge constitutes the brain's *internal model* (e.g., Davidson and Wolpert 2005; Wolpert, Diedrichsen, and Flanagan 2011) of the body. Although this chapter concentrates on how an internal model of a body is learned, this is just a special case of a much broader situation: how does the brain learn internal models of body and environments, either real or virtual? How is this information used to interact with real and virtual environments? Or, how do the computational features of the brain influence the "realism" of a virtual environment? It is discussed how the "realism" of virtual environments might be defined mainly in terms of the computational framework presented here.

In the brain it is common to find neural spike activity that follows a Poisson point process (Shadlen and Newsome 1998; Faisal, Selen, and Wolpert 2008). The relationship, if any, of such Poisson processes to brain function is unknown at the present time. Here it is shown that Poisson-point-process neural spikes can be used to learn the internal model of a simulated body and, more generally, of a category of nonlinear systems. The learned internal model accurately predicts the simulated body's sensory spiking response to motor commands. As described here, such Poisson-spike computations allow using overall statistical properties of spiking signals to extract millisecond-level, time-dependent, dynamical information about the body and, more generally, the environment. These results are readily generalizable to cases with multiple sensory modalities (e.g., haptic, visual, auditory), involving multidimensional sensorimotor spiking signals, and to some cases with non-Poisson statistics. The paradigm naturally integrates mean firing rate and temporal computations (Stein, Gossen, and Jones 2005; Johansson and Birznieks 2004), and can be implemented with parallel, neural-like architectures. The Poisson paradigm also allows, in principle, to model processes such as recalibration of limb function during growth, as well as other brain functions such as neural plasticity after injury. All these processes can be modeled and simulated at the level of neural spike processing. In this manner, the paradigm contributes to an area that has been little explored: the modeling of haptic functions (e.g., Klatzky and Lederman 1993; Johnsson and Balkenius 2007; Debats et al. 2010; Hayward 2011), in addition to its contributions to brain function modeling in general.

The Human Haptic System and Its Importance as a Model of Skilled Action

We actively explore and manipulate our environment, typically with our hands, as when gauging the shape of an object by sliding a finger over it, or when using tools to perform a task. When we perform such activities, we are *haptically* exploring or interacting with our environment (e.g., Robles-De-La-Torre 2008). Unlike vision or hearing, haptic interaction is heavily bidirectional. That is, during haptic interaction, the environment typically reacts to actions. This in turn modifies/modulates the interaction process itself. For example, let us consider a person exploring the shape of a small, flexible rubber ball by enclosing and squeezing it with his or her hand. For this, the person's brain needs to plan and execute complex motor actions (hand/finger movements). The ball deforms as the person squeezes it, and the resulting change in shape is haptically perceived by the person. This information helps the person to plan and execute subsequent hand/finger movements (e.g., to avoid dropping or breaking the ball). Therefore, haptic interaction involves learning information about the environment and using this information to immediately plan and execute motor actions to gather further information. In many cases, haptically acquired information is learned and then employed to enable future actions, for example, learning tool use and then applying this information many times in the future. We may not commonly realize that it is necessary also to learn how to use our own body in some situations. For example, as children develop and physically grow, the brain needs to relearn how to control the changing body. As another example, a convalescent person needs to relearn how to walk after months of bed rest. These and other cases rely heavily on haptic capabilities, that is, sensing and learning the characteristics of our bodies and environment and using this information to plan and perform complex, skilled actions.

The study of haptic interaction offers a window into the workings of the brain in general, and on how the brain generates behavior. The many aspects of haptic interaction in humans involve multiple brain functions such as perception, memory, learning, cognition, and motor control. It also involves the person's body, especially the skin, muscular system, and related kinesthetic sources of information (Robles-De-La-Torre 2008). Throughout this chapter, the term *human haptic system* will refer to all these functions and components working together during haptic interaction.

Internal Model Learning as a System Identification Problem

System identification is an engineering technique that allows modeling the input-output behavior of an unknown system (Marmarelis and Marmarelis 1978). Multiple, known input signals are applied to the system, the corresponding outputs are observed, and this information is used to obtain the model of the system through an algorithm (Marmarelis and Marmarelis 1978). The model can be used to compute a prediction of how the system reacts to a given input signal. It can be readily seen that this identification process is an analog of how an organism learns about its environment. Here it is proposed that the learning of internal models can be seen as a system identification process carried out by the brain.

One system identification technique is of special interest here. This technique uses a spiking signal that follows a Poisson point process as the input to identify a system. The spiking signal is typically represented by a train of Dirac delta functions (Krausz 1975). This Poisson identification technique has been typically used to model neural systems (Krausz 1975; Marmarelis and Marmarelis 1978; Marmarelis and Berger 2005). In such applications, the spiking input signal (fig. 34.1a) and the corresponding neural system response (also a spiking signal) are used by the Poisson identification technique to obtain an estimated function that models the neural system. Poisson identification is a very powerful technique that allows identifying a subset of all finite-memory (in the dynamical-system sense), analytic,

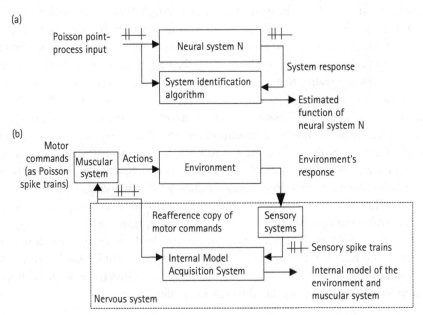

FIGURE 34.1 Using Poisson system identification to model internal model learning through neural spikes. (a) Neural systems' response to Poisson-distributed spike trains and Poisson system identification have been used before to experimentally probe and characterize neural function. (b) It is proposed here that the same system identification procedure can model the nervous system's capability to learn internal models of nonlinear body/environment dynamics. A system identification algorithm computes internals models from the reafference copy of motor commands and the sensory neural signals related to the commands, both in spike train form.

time-invariant nonlinear systems (Krausz 1975; Marmarelis and Berger 2005). Note how Poisson identification uses a statistical input to obtain dynamical information about the system. Poisson identification allows to characterize the function of the neural system in terms of kernel functions (Krausz 1975; Marmarelis and Berger 2005; see also "Internal Model Computation" below). These kernels encapsulate the behavior of the neural system and can be used to estimate the system's output to an arbitrary spiking input signal.

Here it is proposed that the brain's internal model learning capability can be modeled by Poisson identification algorithms (fig. 34.1b). In this proposal, by analogy with the typical Poisson identification application in figure 34.1a, the brain would be probing the body and environment through spiking signals (motor commands, fig. 34.1b). The motor commands are applied to the body's muscular system to execute actions and allow interaction with a real or virtual environment. The environment's response to the actions in turn stimulate the body's sensory systems (e.g., the sense of touch, vision, etc.). This results in sensory spiking signals (fig. 34.1b). Such signals, together with a copy of the motor command spiking signals (the reafference copy, fig. 34.1b), are used by the brain to learn internal models of the muscular system and the environment. Again, note the close analogy of each corresponding step in figures 34.1a and 34.1b. By applying Poisson identification to these spiking signals (see "Internal Model Computation" below), the corresponding kernel functions are computed. These kernels are the internal model of the nonlinear body and environment. Kernel computations model those performed by the brain to build the internal model of the body and environment. Throughout this chapter, this application of Poisson system identification to internal model learning is called *Poisson learning*.

To illustrate this approach, the learning of the internal model of a simple, nonlinear body is simulated. The nonlinear body consists of a muscle and a Golgi tendon organ. The muscle contracts when stimulated by a motor command. The motor command is simulated by a Poisson-point-process spike train. The Golgi tendon organ senses muscle contraction force and encodes it into a frequency-modulated spiking signal. The motor command and Golgi tendon signals are used to compute the body's internal model. In the sections that follow, the internal model computation and the features of the simulated body are described.

INTERNAL MODEL COMPUTATION

A discrete, nonlinear system $y(n)$ can be expressed (Krausz 1975; Marmarelis and Berger 2005) as the summation of a series of mutually orthogonal functionals $Q_i[z(n);h_i]$, which depend on the functions h_i (the system's Poisson kernels of order i), and on $z(n)$ (a zero mean, Poisson-point-process train of Dirac delta functions that model neural spikes); $z(n)$ is the input signal applied to $y(n)$. In this chapter, the set of Poisson kernels h_i constitutes the internal model of the nonlinear system $y(n)$. For simplicity, only the first two kernels are used and estimated as follows (Krausz 1975; Marmarelis and Berger 2005): $h_o = E[y(n)]$ and $h_1(m) = E[y(n) z(n - m)]/\mu_2$. The operator $E[]$ denotes expected value, and $\mu_2 = \lambda (1 - \lambda)$. λ is the mean spiking rate of the Poisson input signal z(n). $\lambda=5$ spikes/s is used for computing the kernels in the simulations discussed here. The internal model kernels are used to predict the response of the muscle-Golgi organ system to motor commands. For this, the first-order kernel h_1 is used as the impulse response function of the muscle-Golgi tendon organ system. The predicted response is the sum of h_0 plus the convolution of h_1 and a given spike train signal. To speed up the calculations, and without loss of generality, Dirac delta functions are substituted with Kronecker delta functions. The spikes z(n) have magnitude 1.

CHARACTERISTICS OF THE SIMULATED MUSCLE AND GOLGI TENDON ORGAN

The simulated muscle is an array of muscle fibers that contract/relax synchronously and isometrically and whose forces add up linearly following a well-known (Herbert and Gandevia 1999) twitch model $mt(n) = F\, n\, \exp(1 - n/T)/T$. $F = 0.85$ N is the muscle's twitch force, and $T = 40$ ms is the twitch contraction time. The total force exerted by the simulated muscle, $F_m(n)$, is a linear combination of twitches $mt(n - t_i)$, generated by motor command spikes appearing at time t_i.

Golgi tendon organ models relate the mean firing rate of the organ to muscle force (Prochazka 1999). To my knowledge, there are no Golgi tendon models that produce an organ's actual output spikes from force information. The simulations used here require such a realistic model. For this reason, the simulated Golgi tendon organ used here is based on an sinusoidal oscillator $O(n) = \sin(4\pi F_m(n))$, whose instantaneous frequency is proportional to $F_m(n)$, the simulated muscle force. The Golgi tendon organ's spiking train output consists of Kronecker delta functions that are obtained by generating a delta function whenever the sinusoidal oscillator's output $O(n) > 0.5$ and $dO(n)/dn > 0$. The delta functions have magnitude 1, which is chosen to speed up kernel computation. Again, this does not imply a loss of generality. The time resolution used in all computations is 1 millisecond.

SIMULATING INTERNAL MODEL LEARNING THROUGH NEURAL SPIKE SIGNALS

A series of Poisson motor commands is applied to the simulated body (fig. 34.2a), and the resulting Golgi tendon organ output is recorded. Both signals are used to compute the internal model of the simulated body as described above.

Figure 34.2 shows a representative sample of the signals used to compute the internal model. Here a motor command (fig. 34.2a, $\lambda = 5$ spikes/s) is applied to the simulated muscle, whose resulting contraction force (fig. 34.2b) is encoded by the Golgi organ's spike train (fig. 34.2c). Zero- and first-order Poisson kernels are computed from these data. The first-order kernel is shown in figure 34.2e. The zero-order kernel is $h_0 = 0.0167$ (both kernels have arbitrary units). These kernels are the simulated body's internal model. The Golgi organ's response in figure 34.2c is now predicted using the internal model and the motor command in figure 34.2a. The predicted Golgi organ response is shown in figure 34.2d. As can be seen from figures 34.2c and 34.2d, the prediction substantially reproduces the timing of the actual Golgi organ response (fig. 34.2c), although not its magnitude. This is not a major drawback, as the Golgi organ signal information is contained in the timing of the spikes. If needed, spike magnitude can be easily corrected through a simple filter. The actual and predicted spike signals also differ in other ways. The actual spikes are noise free, while the predicted spikes have some background noise. The actual spikes are Kronecker delta functions with magnitude of 1, while the predicted spikes rise and decay in a finite time.

Spike timing is the major feature of the actual and predicted signals, and the following analysis concentrates on this aspect. To compare the timing of these signals it is necessary to eliminate or minimize signal differences that are unrelated to signal timing. To achieve this, the predicted spikes are preprocessed before analysis. Background noise is removed. Predicted spikes are converted into Kronecker delta functions with a magnitude of 1. The timing of these delta functions corresponds to the timing at which peak magnitude occurs in the original, predicted spikes.

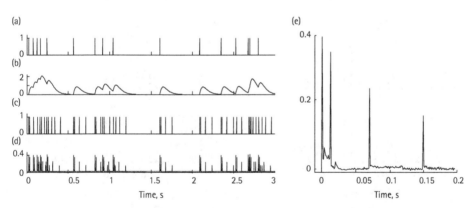

FIGURE 34.2 An internal model obtained through Poisson learning predicts the behavior of a simulated, nonlinear muscle-Golgi-tendon-organ body. In this typical simulation result, a motor command (a, $\lambda = 5$ spikes/s) is applied to the simulated muscle, whose resulting force (b) is sensed and encoded by the Golgi organ's spike signal (c). The internal model of the muscle-Golgi organ system (e), obtained through Poisson learning, is used to compute a prediction (d) of the Golgi organ's response to the motor command in (a). Force units are in Newtons; all other magnitudes have arbitrary units.

Actual Golgi organ spikes and preprocessed, predicted spikes are compared through their cross-correlation. Ideally, this cross-correlation should be equal to the autocorrelation of the actual Golgi organ spikes. Cross-correlations were computed over 3,000 simulated, 10-second trials, involving over one million spikes per cross-correlation. For simplicity, Poisson motor commands with different spike rates are used to assess the internal model's predictive capability. Any other spiking motor signals could be used instead.

When a Poisson motor command with $\lambda = 0.5$ spikes/s is used to predict Golgi organ spikes, the cross-correlation of actual and preprocessed, predicted spikes (fig. 34.3a, top panel, peak value of 17.2) closely resembles the ideal autocorrelation of the actual spikes (fig. 34.3a, bottom panel, peak value of 19.2). This means that the number of spikes and their overall timing are very similar in both signals.

Now let us examine what happens with the prediction when the firing rate of the motor command increases. For this, the same internal model is used to compute a new series of predicted Golgi organ spikes, now using a motor command with $\lambda = 6$ spikes/s. To perform the analysis, the predicted spikes are preprocessed in the same way described above. The cross-correlation of actual spikes and preprocessed, predicted spikes results in a function with a peak of 44.0 (fig. 34.3b, top panel), while the ideal autocorrelation's peak was 168.7 (not shown). This indicates that the timing of actual and predicted signals differed more here than in the prior example. Further analysis indicates that about 30 percent of the preprocessed, predicted spikes do coincide in timing with the actual spikes (within the maximum time resolution of 1 millisecond). To assess the effect of timing errors on the cross-correlation, the errors of the predicted spikes are simulated. For this, the timing of the actual Golgi organ spikes is degraded with Gaussian noise

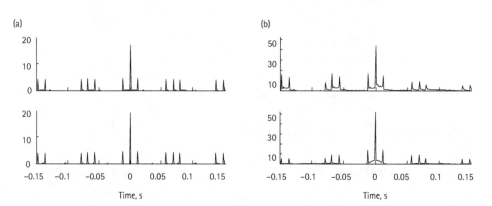

FIGURE 34.3 Cross-correlations confirm the timing accuracy of internal-model-predicted Golgi organ spikes. The cross-correlation of actual and preprocessed, predicted spikes (a, top panel, motor command with $\lambda = 0.5$ spikes/s) closely approaches the ideal function, the autocorrelation of actual spikes (a, bottom panel). For a higher motor command rate ($\lambda = 6$ spikes/s), the cross-correlation of actual and preprocessed, predicted spikes (b, top panel) was approximated by the cross-correlation of actual spikes with spikes whose timing was degraded with Gaussian noise (b, bottom panel, $\sigma = 8$ ms).

(zero mean, σ = 8 ms). Gaussian noise shifts these actual spikes in time by a random, Gaussian amount. Only some actual spikes are time-degraded: the spikes whose timing does not coincide with that of preprocessed, predicted spikes. This timing-degraded version of the actual spikes is cross-correlated with the original, actual spikes. The result is shown in figure 34.3b, bottom panel. This cross-correlation function has a peak value of 51.7. Compare this to the cross-correlation of actual and predicted spikes (fig. 34.3b, top panel). These cross-correlations have comparable peak magnitudes (44.0 vs. 51.7), as well as similar periodicities and overall shape. When the Gaussian noise σ is either smaller or larger than 8 milliseconds, the similarity of the cross-correlations in figure 34.3b is not improved (data not shown). This analysis suggests that the timing error of predicted spikes can be modeled by Gaussian noise with a moderate σ = 8 milliseconds. Given the properties of the Gaussian distribution, this analysis means that about 68 percent of the inaccurate, predicted spikes are still within 8 milliseconds of the actual spikes. As mentioned above, about 30 percent of the predicted spikes coincided in time with the actual spikes. Together with the Gaussian analysis of spike error, this means that about 98 percent of the predicted spikes are within a reasonable 8 milliseconds of the actual spikes. This, while not perfect, still constitutes a respectable result for such a basic prediction. While a simple, first-order internal model estimate is used here for the prediction, improvements can be expected from higher-order internal model kernels.

SPECIAL ADVANTAGES OF POISSON LEARNING

The simulations above show that Poisson learning can obtain the internal model of a nonlinear, simulated body from neural spike information. Remarkably, Poisson learning allows using overall statistical properties of spiking signals to extract millisecond-level, time-dependent, dynamical information about a system. In the example presented above, Poisson learning characterizes a simulated body by processing a single motor command and a single sensory spike signal. However, Poisson identification readily generalizes to handle systems with multidimensional inputs/outputs (Krausz 1975; Marmarelis and Marmarelis 1978). This means that Poisson learning of internal models can be used in principle in situations involving multidimensional motor commands and multidimensional sensory signals. Such multidimensional signals would model the multiple spike signals traveling in different axons of one or more motor or sensory nerves. Note that multidimensional sensory signals could represent kinesthetic signals, as in the example presented here, but also include signals from other sensory modalities such as vision, hearing, vestibular sense, taste, or smell. The use of multidimensional motor and sensory signals would allow modeling situations in which multiple senses guide complex skilled behaviors to learn internal models of nonlinear environments with multidimensional features. This would allow modeling important aspects of behavior in real-world situations. These contributions add to current models of neural spike computation, which commonly concentrate on learning spike sequences (e.g., Yusoff and Grüning 2010; Mohemmed et al. 2011).

Some readers may wonder about the meaningfulness of a Poisson point process to represent the motor commands involved in internal model learning. It could appear that a statistical motor command is incompatible with the kind of fine, skilled actions normally used to learn internal models. This is not so. Clearly, even though skilled action is so finely planned and executed, its underlying neural motor commands can be statistically characterized. Statistical characterization of neural signals is not incompatible with the deterministic motor actions they underlie. In this context, the Poisson learning paradigm offers a new interpretation of neural statistics: if neural motor commands can be characterized by Poisson point processes, then important aspects about the dynamics of body and environment can be learned. In this regard, it must be stressed that Poisson point processes actually constitute an important part of the known statistics of neural signals in the brain (Shadlen and Newsome 1998; Faisal, Selen, and Wolpert 2008). Poisson learning assigns a computational role to these statistics.

Poisson learning can also shed light on a related, more general question. It has been very difficult to relate behavior, which happens in a time scale of seconds or longer, to its corresponding neural spike activity in the brain, which occurs at a time scale of milliseconds. This is a key open problem not only in the context of the human haptic system, but also in that of skilled actions and in behavior in general (Drew and Abbott 2006). Internal model learning is an important behavior that typically requires practice over seconds or longer. The Poisson learning paradigm presented here allows relating neural spike computations to internal model learning in a precise, powerful computational sense. Therefore, Poisson learning has the potential to help understand other important aspects of behavior in terms of neural spike computation.

Poisson learning is able to identify a subset of all finite-memory (in the dynamical-system sense), analytic, time-invariant nonlinear systems (Krausz 1975; Marmarelis and Berger 2005). This means that Poisson learning is able to deal with a wide variety of real-world situations. However, the brain deals with situations that are not formally covered by such nonlinear systems. This includes dealing with systems that approach infinite memory (such as a missing limb or an irreparably broken tool), or time-varying systems (such as a growing, developing muscular system and body). However, Poisson learning might be able to deal with some of these situations. For example, applying Poisson learning to deal with a changing, growing muscular system might be possible by continuously recomputing the relevant internal model kernels to reflect muscular changes over time. This strategy to recompute kernels to deal with time-varying systems has been suggested for typical Poisson identification applications (Marmarelis and Berger 2005). Poisson identification can also be extended to non-Poisson cases (Krausz 1975; Marmarelis and Marmarelis 1978; Marmarelis and Berger 2005), which applies also to Poisson learning as presented here.

POISSON LEARNING, MEAN FIRING RATES, AND TEMPORAL NEURAL CODES

Poisson learning suggests a new role for random variability and seeming "noise" in neural codes: that of allowing the extraction of the nonlinear dynamics of body and environment (for current ideas on noise roles in the brain see Stein, Gossen, and Jones 2005; Deco, Rolls, and Romo 2009; McDonnell and Ward 2011). The Poisson learning paradigm also fits naturally with other concepts used to model brain function, such as mean neural firing rates (e.g., Drew and Abbott 2006; Deneve, Latham, and Pouget 1999). Poisson learning incorporates a mean firing rate as an important parameter of spike computation in the form of λ, the mean spiking rate of the motor commands used in Poisson learning (see "Internal Model Computation" above). Further, in Poisson learning, λ has important roles. It is used to (1) compute internal model kernels, (2) estimate the rate of convergence of this computation (Krausz 1975), and (3) estimate the order of the nonlinearity of the system to be identified (Marmarelis and Berger 2005). This suggests new, similar computational roles for mean firing rates in the brain in the context of Poisson learning. For example, the brain may probe the complexity involved in learning internal models by using different firing rates to gauge the relevant nonlinearities, and then adjusting accordingly, perhaps by choosing an optimum firing rate.

In addition to mean firing rates, another important concept in current models of brain function is that of a temporal neural code. In this concept, the timing of spike signals in single neurons and in neural populations is proposed as a key element in neural computations (Johansson and Birznieks 2004; Stein, Gossen, and Jones 2005). In Poisson learning, the timing of neural spikes also plays an important role in internal model computation. In general terms, Poisson internal model computation involves cross-correlations between motor commands and sensory signals. Spike timing explicitly occurs in these computations. For example, the internal model's first order kernel, h_1, is given by $h_1(m) = E[y(n) \, z(n - m)]/\mu_2$, where $y(n)$ is the output spike train occurring in response to the input Poisson process spike train $z(n)$. In this kernel computation, the timing of spikes in $y(n)$ and $z(n - m)$ helps determine the value of the kernel. For example, if a spike in $y(n)$ occurs at time n, then $y(n)$ contributes to kernel computation. If a spike does not appear in $y(n)$ at time n (i.e., $y(n) = 0$), then $y(n)$ does not contribute to kernel computation as the product $y(n) \, z(n - m) = 0$. The same applies to the spike signal $z(n - m)$. Therefore, the timing of spikes in Poisson learning contributes decisively to internal model computation (see also "Neural Implementation of Poisson Learning" below).

All the above indicates that Poisson learning naturally integrates temporal and mean rate computations, two concepts that are commonly considered as mutually exclusive

(Stein, Gossen, and Jones 2005). In addition, Poisson learning offers new insights into possible roles of these concepts, as described above.

COMPUTATIONAL REQUIREMENTS AND POSSIBLE NEURAL IMPLEMENTATION OF POISSON LEARNING

The use of higher-order kernels introduces substantial computational requirements. In systems with one input and one output, such as the one exemplified in this chapter, a discrete version of a first-order kernel can be stored as a one-dimensional vector, a second-order kernel requires a matrix, and a third-order kernel needs a three-dimensional array. Each additional kernel order requires an extra dimension. The computational requirements grow accordingly. However, in practice several factors help alleviate these requirements. Many nonlinear systems may be represented with lower-order kernels. The kernels themselves tend to be very sparse. Alternative kernel computation methods, such as Montecarlo integration (Marmarelis and Marmarelis 1978) could be used, or massively parallel computing options may be used, as described below.

This brief discussion on the computational requirements of Poisson learning leads naturally to considering possible implementations of internal model kernel calculation in the brain.

A simple possibility is the following. Poisson kernel computation is based on cross-correlations, such as the operations used to compute the first-order kernel used here (see "Internal Model Computation" above). With the discrete domain signals used here, involving only Kronecker delta functions, the multiplications in cross-correlations can be posed instead as a series of AND operations between a system's output, $y(n)$, and time-delayed versions of the system's input, $z(n)$, followed by a summation (Marmarelis and Marmarelis 1978). These AND operations are analogous to spike coincidence detections involving the time-shifted versions of $z(n)$. This and the related summation mimic basic features of temporal processing in real neurons and neural circuits. Many of these Poisson learning computations can be performed in parallel with an architecture based on these analogies. This and other network approaches for Poisson identification (Alataris, Berger, and Marmarelis 2000) may be able to implement Poisson learning in the brain and take advantage of the brain's massively parallel architecture. As a final note, using AND operations instead of floating point multiplications to compute Poisson learning kernels considerably decreases the computational load. This is possible because of the on-off character of the signals used. It is suggestive to speculate that perhaps analogous operations are used by neurons to obtain similar advantages, and that perhaps this is a reason why neurons communicate mainly in spike form.

The Realism or Virtuality of Environments and Poisson Learning

It is clear that brain function shapes how we perceive and interact with our environment. When perceiving and interacting with computer-created virtual environments, brain function also defines how realistic the virtual environment appears to be. How can we meaningfully define the realism or virtuality of computer-created or real environments?

From the point of view of the nervous system, most, if not all, features of the body and environment are experienced through neural spike signals. Motor spike signals probe the body and environment, and sensory spike signals retrieve the results of motor commands or the state of the body. Using these signals, the brain constructs our remarkable sensory and motor experience of the world.

Let us consider the case of a nervous system that is totally detached from its body. Let us assume that this nervous system is not damaged as a result of its excision, and that its physiology can continue normally. Let us assume also that all motor nerves are intact, and that the sensory nerves lack only their sensory receptors, but have no other damage. Let us assume that, in this state, all the neural signals entering or exiting the nervous system are neural spikes.

Let us imagine that we can read and understand all the excised brain's motor signals, and that we can use them to computationally simulate a body and how this body reacts to motor signals. Let us also imagine that we can use this simulation to generate adequate, relevant sensory signals, which are in turn fed back into the excised nervous system. As a result, the excised nervous system experiences some sort of "environment."

We can use this thought experiment to explore the concepts of realism and virtuality of the "environment" that the excised nervous system experiences. Clearly, such "environment" is totally virtual. Yet does it appear "realistic" to the excised nervous system? Not necessarily, as its realism depends on the quality of the simulation that is fed back to the nervous system. For example, the simulation may produce only a "cartoon" environment instead of a more naturalistic one. From this, we can see that the *virtuality* of the environment would depend only on the degree in which the environment is synthetic, that is, computer-generated. In the case of the excised brain, we have an almost completely computational environment. We would still need hardware to read motor spikes, to generate sensory spikes, and to run the simulation, but not much else.

Going into the other extreme, let us imagine that we can reinsert the excised brain into the normal person from which it was taken so the person becomes normal again. The environment that the person experiences now is not virtual at all. It is the person's normal, everyday environment, defined by the physics of the world. By definition, the environment now seems totally realistic to this normal person.

Let us imagine now that the person becomes psychotic and experiences hallucinations. His or her perception of the environment differs considerably from that of another, normal person. The psychotic person would still experience his or her environment, including hallucinations, as realistic, while to the normal person it would not seem realistic at all. That is, the normal person does not experience the hallucinations of the psychotic person.

From these examples we can see that the realism of a virtual environment may depend on the quality of the computer simulations that create it, as in the case of the excised brain, but also on the features of the brain functions that process and experience the simulation. Further, the realism of an environment may depend on the workings of more than one brain, as happened with the psychotic and normal persons: what may be realistic to one person may not be so to another. Ultimately, the quality of a simulated environment depends on measures of fidelity of the simulation (frequently related to the physics of an environment), but also on the features of brain functions. This is because the quality of a simulated environment is frequently defined in terms of how a person experiences it, which involves a measure of subjectivity. The fidelity of the simulation can be computationally defined. How can we also computationally characterize a person's subjective perception of a simulated environment? Clearly, the person's subjective perception would depend on how his or her brain processes neural spike information related to interaction with the simulated environment. Therefore, a first step to define an environment's realism in purely computational terms could use the concepts and features of Poisson learning. For example, let us assume that a person interacts with a real, nonlinear environment E that can be entirely described by Poisson kernels $P(n)$ of order n. Let us suppose that E' is a computer simulation of the real environment E, and that E' can be described by a set of Poisson kernels $P'(m)$, of order m. Let us assume that the person's brain uses Poisson computations to learn both $P(n)$ and $P'(m)$, and has the neural machinery to compare them after they are learned. Then, the realism of E' relative to E could be expressed in terms of the respective Poisson kernels, as a function $r(E',E) = f(P(n), P'(m))$. This "realism" function would be expected to decrease as m became lower than n, and to increase otherwise, and peak in value when m = n. This would be because a nonlinear system that is described by Poisson kernels up to order n may not be accurately described by kernels with lower order, and the person's brain would detect this. In other words, if we know that the brain can learn a nonlinear system of order n, then a simulation of this system with a lower order nonlinear system will be unrealistic. In this manner, the fidelity of the simulation would be directly related to the computational features of a user's brain.

FUTURE RESEARCH DIRECTIONS

Poisson learning concepts allow thinking about brain functions in powerful, abstract terms that can be precisely expressed as spike signal computations. This allows using these concepts to think about the myriad open questions that relate to the spiking signals used by the brain. What can and cannot be learned through such spike-processing mechanisms? How is neural plasticity related to spiking signals? What is the role, if any, of seemingly noisy patterns of neural spike firing? Why are spiking signals used at all? Poisson learning concepts offer possible mechanisms to help answer these and other questions, as briefly discussed as follows.

As we have seen, Poisson learning assigns a powerful computational role to seemingly random neural spike signals following a Poisson process. It is possible that non-Poisson spiking patterns in the brain have similar computational properties, perhaps complementing or assisting Poisson spiking computations.

Poisson learning may help understand some aspects of neural plasticity. For example, after a person suffers a stroke, he or she may not be able to normally control his or her body. However, as time goes on, there is frequently some recovery, which sometimes may be quite complete. How does this happen in terms of the brain's computational capabilities? Poisson learning suggests a possible way. As mentioned above (see "Internal Model Learning as a System Identification Problem"), Poisson system identification has been used to characterize the behavior of neural circuits. Therefore, it is possible to speculate that a brain module possessing Poisson learning capabilities could learn the function(s) of a different brain module. If major injury affects one of these brain modules, the other, intact module may eventually take over the functions of the injured one.

Poisson learning may also help determine the computational limitations of the brain. For example, neural spiking in the brain has a maximum firing rate in the order of hundreds of Hz. Although using a maximum firing rate would not theoretically limit Poisson learning of nonlinear systems (those described by Poisson kernels), in practice a maximum firing rate would mean that the time to learn some nonlinear systems may be unrealistically long. This is because the Poisson mean firing rate λ affects the rate in which the Poisson learning converges (Krausz 1975). Higher firing rates mean faster learning. From experience acquired by performing Poisson kernel computations, it would seem that convergence may proceed more slowly as the order of the kernels describing a nonlinear system increases. From this, it is reasonable to presume that, when a given firing rate λ is used, Poisson kernels can be learned in a reasonable amount of time only up to a certain kernel order. This would help define categories of nonlinear systems whose internal models can or cannot be learned in practical terms. This in turn would illuminate related limitations in brain functions relying on internal models, such as motor control.

Ultimately, the question of whether the brain actually uses Poisson learning can be answered only by experimental work. Interaction with haptic virtual objects might be the natural experimental approach to help determine whether Poisson learning constitutes part of the brain's learning arsenal. Today, haptic technology allows creating virtual environments consisting of computer-generated haptic virtual objects that can be touched and manipulated in real-time (Robles-De-La-Torre 2008). The features of haptic virtual objects are defined through detailed computational models. During haptic interaction with virtual objects, it might be possible to relate the computational characteristics of objects to the computations that the human haptic system should perform to allow effective interaction. These computations include the processing of perceptual information, the learning of virtual object characteristics, and the planning and execution of actions. Such computations may be understood in terms of the Poisson paradigm presented here. To achieve this, sensory and motor neural signal activity would be recorded during virtual object interaction, and its patterns analyzed in terms of Poisson learning.

Poisson learning also suggests new methods to help design and analyze experiments involving simultaneous motor and sensory neural recordings during complex behaviors, especially in combination with paradigms involving internal model learning during visuomotor tasks (e.g., Robles-De-La-Torre and Sekuler 2004; Wolpert, Diedrichsen, and Flanagan 2011), and interaction with haptic virtual objects (e.g., Robles-De-La-Torre and Hayward 2001). Poisson kernels could be used to characterize the information that the brain can extract from the experimentally observed motor and sensory spike signals arising during behavior. If the observed motor spikes follow a Poisson process, such analysis would directly use the ideas presented in previous sections. If the observed motor spikes do not follow a Poisson process, then there are possible alternatives. For example, the statistics of the motor spikes may be represented as a combination of a Poisson process and one or more different processes. If so, at least part of the spiking activity might be described by Poisson learning. The related brain capabilities might be understood in terms of the computational qualities of the relevant Poisson kernels. Further, possible extensions of Poisson learning to cases with non-Poisson statistics may also be used here.

Finally, the ideas presented here could also be used in areas such as machine learning to help design intelligent systems that learn and adapt to their environment. In particular, Poisson learning may be used as the basis for new learning algorithms in artificial neural networks.

ACKNOWLEDGMENT

I thank Vincent Hayward for helpful comments on a previous version of this manuscript.

REFERENCES

Alataris, K., T. W. Berger, and V. Z. Marmarelis. 2000. A Novel Network for Nonlinear Modeling of Neural Systems with Arbitrary Point-Process Inputs. *Neural Networks* 13: 255–266.

Davidson, P. R., and D. M. Wolpert. 2005. Widespread Access to Predictive Models in the Motor System: A Short Review. *Journal of Neural Engineering* 2: 8313–8319.

Debats, N. B., R. W. van de Langenberg, I. Kingma, J. B. J. Smeets, and P. J. Beek. 2010. Exploratory Movements Determine Cue Weighting in Haptic Length Perception of Handheld Rods. *Journal of Neurophysiology* 104: 2821–2830.

Deco, G., E. T. Rolls, and R. Romo. 2009. Stochastic Dynamics as a Principle of Brain Function. *Progress in Neurobiology* 88: 1–16.

Deneve, S., P. E. Latham, and A. Pouget. 1999. Reading Population Codes: A Neural Implementation of Ideal Observers. *Nature Neuroscience* 2: 740–745.

Drew, P. J., and L. F. Abbott. 2006. Extending the Effects of Spike-Timing-Dependent Plasticity to Behavioral Timescales. *Proceedings of the National Academy of Sciences* 103: 8876–8881.

Faisal A. A., L. P. J. Selen, and D. M. Wolpert. 2008. Noise in the Nervous System. *Nature Reviews Neuroscience* 9: 292–303.

Hayward, V. 2011. Is There a "Plenhaptic" Function? *Philosophical Transactions of the Royal Society B* 366: 3115–3312.

Herbert, R. D., and S. C. Gandevia. 1999. Twitch Interpolation in Human Muscles: Mechanisms and Implications for Measurement of Voluntary Activation. *Journal of Neurophysiology* 82: 2271–2283.

Johansson, R. S., and I. Birznieks. 2004. First Spikes in Ensembles of Human Tactile Afferents Code Complex Spatial Fingertip Events. *Nature Neuroscience* 7: 170–177.

Johnsson M., and C. Balkenius. 2007. Neural Network Models of Haptic Shape Perception. *Journal of Robotics and Autonomous Systems* 55: 720–727.

Klatzky, R. L., and S. J. Lederman. 1993. Toward a Computational Model of Constraint-Driven Exploration and Haptic Object Identification. *Perception* 22: 597–621.

Krausz, H. I. 1975. Identification of Nonlinear Systems Using Random Impulse Train Inputs. *Biological Cybernetics* 19: 217–230

Marmarelis, P. Z., and V. Z. Marmarelis. 1978. *Analysis of Physiological Systems: The White-Noise Approach*. New York: Plenum.

Marmarelis, V. Z., and T. W. Berger. 2005. General Methodology for Nonlinear Modeling of Neural Systems with Poisson Point-Process Inputs. *Mathematical Biosciences* 196: 1–13.

McDonnell, M. D., and L. M. Ward. 2011. The Benefits of Noise in Neural Systems: Bridging Theory and Experiment. *Nature Reviews Neuroscience* 12: 415–426.

Mohemmed, A., S. Schliebs, S. Matsuda, and N. Kasabov. 2011. Method for Training a Spiking Neuron to Associate Input–Output Spike Trains. *IFIP Advances in Information and Communication Technology* 363: 219–228.

Prochazka, A. 1999. Quantifying Proprioception. *Progress in Brain Research* 123: 133–142.

Robles-De-La-Torre, G., and V. Hayward. 2001 Force Can Overcome Object Geometry in the Perception of Shape through Active Touch. *Nature* 412: 445–448.

Robles-De-La-Torre, G., and R. Sekuler. 2004. Numerically Estimating Internal Models of Dynamic Virtual Objects. *ACM Transactions on Applied Perception* 1: 102–117.

Robles-De-La-Torre, G. 2006. The Importance of the Sense of Touch in Virtual and Real Environments. *IEEE Multimededia* 13: 24–30.

Robles-De-La-Torre, G. 2008. Principles of Haptic Perception in Virtual Environments. In *Human Haptic Perception: Basics and Applications*, edited by Martin Grunwald, 363–379. Boston, MA: Birkhauser.

Shadlen, M. N., and W. T. Newsome. 1998. The Variable Discharge of Cortical Neurons: Implications for Connectivity, Computation, and Information Coding. *Journal of Neuroscience* 18: 3870–3896.

Stein, R. B, E. R. Gossen, and K. E. Jones. 2005. Neuronal Variability: Noise or Part of the Signal? *Nature Reviews Neuroscience* 6: 389–397.

Wolpert, D. M., J. Diedrichsen, and J. R. Flanagan. 2011. Principles of Sensorimotor Learning. *Nature Reviews Neuroscience* 12: 739–751.

Yusoff, N., and A. Grüning. 2010. Supervised Associative Learning in Spiking Neural Network. *Lecture Notes in Computer Science* 6352: 224–229.

PART VIII

....

TECHNOLOGY AND
APPLICATIONS

....

....

CHAPTER 35

DISTRIBUTED EMBODIMENT: REAL PRESENCE IN VIRTUAL BODIES

....

JOHN A. WATERWORTH AND EVA L. WATERWORTH

In this chapter, we discuss the notion of mediated presence, the familiar feeling of being experientially present to a greater or lesser extent in a virtual or mixed reality, and describe how this form of virtuality is developing into something new that we call "distributed embodiment." Distributed embodiment describes how our sense of being present in the world is becoming separated from our sense of ownership of a particular body, through the development of new approaches to deploying the technologies of virtualization that give rise to what is known as "mediated presence," or "telepresence" (Bracken and Skalski 2010). The possibility for distributed embodiment comes from the physical-virtual nature of familiar, first-person embodiment. We move from a sense of presence in the physical world, through a mediated sense of presence in virtuality, to the mediated sense of being in the physical-virtual world in another body than our own.

Presence is the *feeling* of being in an external world (Waterworth et al. 2010). As discussed in chapter 12 in this volume, by Riva and Waterworth, human consciousness of being present in an external environment has its roots in the animal feeling of something happening from outside the self rather than from within. In other words, the sense of presence distinguishes the self from the nonself. This suggests two key principles. First, the feeling of presence is an embodied phenomenon, a source of information (analogous to emotional engagement) through which we monitor and adjust our reactions and level of attention to our surroundings. Second, mediated presence is fundamentally the same phenomenon as natural presence; it concerns the extent to which we feel ourselves to be in our present surroundings, at the present time. Mediated presence is the feeling of being present through virtuality experienced as a convincing perceptual "illusion of non-mediation" (Lombard and Ditton 1997). As in natural presence, this varies moment by moment according to what is presently happening in our surroundings (see Waterworth et al. 2010 for a fuller account). We may feel hardly present at all in the physical world (a state we call *absence*; Waterworth and Waterworth 2001) if nothing is happening there that is of interest or that impacts on our well-being, and so it is with mediated presence. Presence arises from active awareness of our embodiment in a present world around us. Presence is not consciousness, and we may be highly conscious while feeling absent, at those times when we are relatively unaware of our own embodiment.

Our earlier publications suggest that presence is the means by which an organism knows when something is happening in the present world at the present time, and is the manifestation of an encoded ability to know when consciousness is occupied with situations in the immediate, outside world. For organisms in a natural environment, it is obviously vital for survival to pay conscious attention and respond rapidly to present threats and opportunities. This need is a key driver for development, both within the developing organism and when viewed as evolutionary change. Through evolution, this fundamental ability of all conscious organisms has developed in humans into the ability to distinguish external, physical events and situations from events and situations realized mentally, as internal reflections in thought and imagination. This is a necessary distinction that cannot be made on the basis of emotional appraisal or reality judgments, because imagined situations trigger the same emotional responses as physical situations (Russell 2003)—and may also be judged real or unreal (as may physical events). To do this, people need to be able to *feel directly* when they are attending to the current external world; this is the feeling of presence. It is closely bound up with the intention to act, of mental and bodily readiness for action in the physical or in a virtual world (see Riva et al. 2011).

We see the development of increasing virtuality as part and parcel of the evolution of the human sense of presence, but also suggest that not all forms of virtualization play a similar role in this. We argue that only when the boundary of the self is experientially altered by technology can we say that presence has evolved into new forms, that the sense of presence and the virtual forms are *coevolving*. This perspective provides the grounding for understanding how our sense of presence could shift from our own bodies to other, virtual, bodies. Recent experiments with the sense of presence, as well as new gaming and communication innovations that are starting to appear on the market, already point to a new way of being conscious, a way of feeling real presence in a virtual body, that we suggest is the next step in the evolution of presence. This implies that the virtual other body is incorporated (literally) into our sense of self.

CAN YOU TICKLE YOURSELF?

René Descartes gets a bad press these days, along with any other suggestions that smack of dualism. Almost no one takes seriously the view that we form a representation of the world in our brains, which we then somehow "view" mentally to know what the world is like. The very idea is widely ridiculed as suggesting some sort of private internal cinema where a projection of the external world is watched by a homunculus (in whose head sits another mini-observer, and so on, in infinite regress)—the so-called Cartesian theater (Dennett 1991). And we also all know that how we experience the external world does depend on what goes on in our heads, specifically our brains. We know that drugs, sickness, aging, and trauma, to name but a few, change the way our brains process information and so alter our perception of what is "out there" in the world. We need to have a body, too, with its capacities for sensing and for action, to be able to have any impression of the world around us. Some theorists talk of "enacting a world" out there through action (Varela et al. 1999). By this view, it is not that there is a world out there, at least not an objectively definable one, it is rather that we bring one into being through our actions.

And yet we claim that, in a sense, the world we experience *is* a Cartesian theater, but it is one that we experience as existing *outside* our heads. This is the world in which we feel ourselves to be, bodily, at the present time and place. It is a Cartesian theater because it exists for us by virtue of what is happening, electrically and chemically, in our brains; and we are experiencing it, though not as merely a passive member of the audience but as an actor in the show.

Some thoroughgoing antidualists (for example Dennett 1991, in the process of explaining consciousness away) conveniently ignore the fact that there *is* a world that we do experience as being *inside* our heads, because it exists nowhere else. When we read a book, or fantasize about the future, or fret about the past, the world in which we are absorbed is not experienced as being out there, in the present. We divide our mental and especially our very limited attentional resources between these two worlds: one we experience as internal, which is not tied to the present time and place, and the other that we experience as external, which is. Media such as novels or fairy stories, represented on the page with the abstract symbols of written language, create a vivid and believable world (fictional or factual, or usually a bit of both) *inside* our heads. But we do not experience presence in this way, since there is no perceptual illusion of nonmediation.

Fact or fiction can be represented in both abstract and concrete forms of media, and the increasing development of virtuality brings with it a shift toward concrete representations—forms that look, sound, and even feel like the things they are experienced as being. In cinemas and homes throughout the developed world, movie and especially game devices seek to evoke ever-stronger impressions of reality in virtuality (see Bracken and Skalski 2010). This involves closely matching the Cartesian coordinates of reality with appropriate, body-position-sensitive sights, sounds, and tactile stimulation. Our perceptual-motor systems then project their "findings" about what is happening onto whatever really does exist "out there." Information technology thus fools the mind-body by matching its expectations of how a three-dimensional world of physical objects looks, sounds, feels, and behaves. This is not necessarily always what is thought of as increased "realism" or exactly related to the level of technological immersion. High realism may magnify the impact of whatever mismatches are perceived, as in the Uncanny Valley effect (Misselhorn 2009). And while experienced presence tends to increase with immersion, the use of high-end immersive technology does not guarantee a convincing experience of presence.

So, can you tickle yourself? The point of this question is that it brings forth a quick-and-dirty appraisal of where the boundary between self and other lies. Normally, the self is roughly collocated with the physical body. In other words, self-image and body image are mentally collocated. Even though we can conceive of the body as an object, it does not have the same status as other objects in the world. We (again, normally) only see this particular object from the inside, with what we call a first-person perspective.

We know that some technology can change the boundary of the body, by becoming part of the self—the blind man's stick is the classic example from phenomenology (Merleau-Ponty 1962), the constantly worn spectacles, even the car we drive daily. Most people cannot tickle themselves (at least, not with amusing effect), but a tickling machine can do the job. For most people, only something other, the nonself, can successfully tickle them. By our view, the feeling of presence tells us what is other and what is ourselves. When we mistake our own thoughts or actions for those of another, it is an indication that the presence mechanism has broken down.

PRESENCE AND DISTRIBUTED COGNITION

The relation between self and other is reflected in prevalent arguments about the impact of information and communication technology on consciousness, and on the relationship between the mind and the body. One is the common observation that since the world of digital communications is increasingly part of our bodies—not only embedded or attached devices such as sensors or electrodes on the brain, but also carried devices such as mobile phones or laptops—it is becoming clear that we are basically and even naturally cyborgs, blends of animal and machine with "extended minds" (e.g., Clark 2003). Another view is that tangible interaction characterizes the future of virtualization—this is "where the action is" (Dourish 2001). Yet another is that the mind exists as a result of the whole range of interactions between people and artifacts in the pursuit of activities (e.g., Kaptelinin and Nardi 2006). Related themes have also been made in the literature of distributed and extended cognition (e.g., Perry 2003). All of these views have merit, but we can put their claims into a new perspective when we consider the sense of mediated presence, stressing the significance of presence in distinguishing self from other.

When we are deprived of the electronic tools we have become used to and depend on in everyday activities, we naturally feel somewhat lost and confused. This is one of the stronger arguments for viewing new information technology as part of the extended self. The loss may feel as if a part of memory has been erased, as when the address book on one's mobile phone suddenly disappears through an electrical fault. But it may also feel as if some aspect of one's world no longer exists, for example when the Internet connection is down and one's normal interactions there are not possible. These are quite different psychological effects that reflect the sense of presence in operation. We do feel strong presence in some kinds of mediated environments, such as videoconferences and VR, and relatively strong presence in cinemas and even some websites. But we do not feel present within an electronic address book; nor would we want to.

We use the general term of "distributed cognition" to cover these views that neglect the role of presence. The common theme of such views is a perspective that suggests that the mind is not located in and is not only a function of the brain, but it is also distributed among the information artifacts we encounter in the world, and including those we carry with us (Clark 2003; Perry 2003). This may seem surprising, but is it really? The mind evolved to deal with objects and events in the world through our own movements and actions. If I perceive a tree, for example, physically located in my immediate surroundings (among other trees, and many other things that I also perceive), it is not experienced by me as residing in my head—that would not be helpful for survival. It is out there, while I, myself am in here, in my head. If I am able to think about the tree, it is because my cognition is in a sense distributed to include the tree. The mind does not build a detailed internal representation of the tree because it does not need to; the tree is there in all its glory to be inspected at any moment. It is not such a conceptual leap to suggest that the same applies to information artifacts in the surroundings, which in themselves also function as processors of information (see also Hutchins 1996). But recent developments in virtual technology take us beyond the extended mind and toward the initially more surprising idea of what we call *distributed embodiment*.

The strength of the feeling of presence experienced is a potentially powerful factor in understanding the extent to which technology has become experientially internalized as part of the self. Information can be seen as "realized," that is, given concrete form, either internally in the mind, or externally, in the physical world. When information must be realized internally to be given form and understood, such as that expressed in the abstract symbols of language, any information technology involved in its expression is experienced as part of the other. A character in a novel, for example, is in this sense realized in the mind of the reader and not on the page; the technology involved—the book—remains external. In contrast, when information is realized externally, as concrete forms in or as a surrounding environment in which one can act directly, the technology may become part of the self. An action-based computer game is one common example. The expert player acts directly in a virtual world that has been realized externally, while the technology creating the world effectively disappears from view—in what we have termed *perceptually seductive technology* (Waterworth 2001). To be part of the self, information technology must create or modify an external other of which it is not perceived to be a part; this will be another in which, or with which, we can feel consciously present in virtuality.

We suggest that rather than focusing on notions such as "distributed cognition," by which artifacts perceived as situated in the external environment contribute to the problem-solving work of the singular and body-centered mind, it is time for a new focus on distributed embodiment.

DEVELOPING FIRST-PERSON PRESENCE AND SOCIAL PERSONAS

As with simpler organisms, the sense of self of the newborn infant is underdeveloped, but we believe the feeling of presence is already there when the newborn is conscious. The newborn infant is either present or unconscious, since the capacity for mental reflection has not yet emerged. Mental reflection is conscious mental activity that does not elicit a sense of presence; it also underlies the development of the self. The self develops largely through social interaction, and as this increases through development, so does the capacity for varying degrees of presence. As the child becomes increasingly mobile and also capable of reflective thought, a calibrated sense of presence supports action on and in the external world (Riva et al. 2011), in parallel with increased capacity for internal thought, imagination, and planning.

The developed adult draws continuously on a sophisticated sense of presence to support successful actions in the world, actions that embody both long- and short-term intentional strategies for carrying out activities. In old age, capacities for action decline as the sense of presence diminishes. Attention is increasingly directed toward the self and away from the external world. The common dementias of old age are accompanied by a partial breakdown in the sense of presence. This is reflected in the familiar problems experienced by the demented elderly in distinguishing internal worlds of reflection from the external world around them and in completing planned activities. Without a conscious sense of presence, we can no longer act successfully on our intentions.

The phenomenon of mediated presence, the compelling experience of being perceptually located in a computer-generated three-dimensional world surrounding the self, is already well recognized and documented, although no single theoretical perspective to explain presence has yet been agreed upon (Lombard and Jones 2006). We are also all familiar with the notion of social presence in virtuality, and millions have experienced the sharing of a virtual space with other people, and of the potential to be represented in that space in a wide variety of ways, such as a cartoon character in a social virtual world or a persona illustrated on a social network page. The first is closely analogous to the feeling of "natural" presence in the physical world around us, but the world in which we are immersed is not the physical world in which our body is located. Our perspective is a first-person one; the world surrounds the self who is experiencing it. The second demonstrates that our social personas can be numerous and do not necessarily reflect our embodied physical reality. Our avatars may represent beings quite unlike our physical bodies or our everyday social characters. We experience them from a third-person perspective.

A first-person view on the world has been the norm throughout human development, both in the physical world and in classic VR (virtual reality). Both are experiences in which we view the virtual or physical world from within our own body, looking out and acting on the world around it. In such VR, we move our physical head and the virtual view changes accordingly; we move our physical arms and hands and we see a representation of these body parts depicted as if they were collocated with our internal image of our physical body. Such body-eye coordination is essential, but we are very adept at dealing with mappings of bodily actions onto the behavior of tools, as long as the behavior of the tool is closely coordinated with movements of the body. This is how we can use a computer mouse, drive a car, or fly a remote control model airplane.

Increasingly often, we see ourselves represented in the third person in social virtual spaces—look, that's me over there. But this is generally not in a realistic way, and with minimal coordination between body and virtual image—as when mouse actions or arrow buttons control gross movements and preprogrammed gestures of our avatar. (There are examples of first-person perspective social spaces [distributed VRs] too, but these tend to be restricted to a limited, projected own-body [e.g., just an arm or a gun].) In these social spaces we can usually choose the appearance of our virtual persona from a selection of avatars or avatar parts. And these social spaces do give us a degree of copresence, even though we are looking at ourselves from the outside, as a third-person self among the third-person selves of one or more other people (Turkle 2005).

Changing our experiences of our own body is a key aspect of the future development of presence, not least the potential to experience events from a wide variety of observational perspectives. Standard perceptual effects such as "the rubber hand illusion" (Botvinick and Cohen 1998) have been successfully reproduced in virtual reality and, with reduced vividness, mixed reality situations (IJsselsteijn et al. 2006: Holmes and Spence 2007). The body image can be remarkably flexible, and may be "stretched" well beyond the confines of the biological body. It has been known for some time that it is possible for virtual reality to achieve a kind of "sensory rearrangement" resulting in modified experiences of one's own body (Biocca and Rolland 1998; Castiello et al. 2004; Normand et al. 2011; Riva 1998; Riva et al. 2011).

DISTRIBUTED EMBODIMENT: THIS MIND IN THAT BODY

Technologically induced "out-of-body experiences," using relatively simple technology, have been reported for several years (e.g., Ehrsson 2007; Lenggenhager et al. 2007). In these cases, it is as if we observe media representations of ourselves from the outside while simultaneously experiencing *individual presence as the observed person*. This is a truly novel mode of consciousness for people in normal mental states, and opens up a wealth of new possibilities for entertainment experiences, in areas such as game playing, sports broadcasts, and many other types of TV show.

> Manipulation of the visual perspective, in combination with the receipt of correlated multisensory information from the body was sufficient to trigger the illusion that another person's body or an artificial body was one's own. This effect was so strong that people could experience being in another person's body when facing their own body and shaking hands with it. Our results are of fundamental importance because they identify the perceptual processes that produce the feeling of ownership of one's body. (Petkova and Ehrsson 2008)

We can already, at least to some extent, produce the feeling of being in a virtual body that is also experienced as remotely located, separated from our own body. This is the feeling that "that is me over there, and I am present in that body." That body might look like this body, or not. If not, then it is as if I have different selves. If the other self looks like someone else, I might think that I have the experience of having that person's body—and I might have that experience, at least to some extent, as revealed in physiologic responses indicating appropriate emotional change (see New Scientist 2010; Slater et al. 2010).

New, cheap gaming technologies (at the time of writing, most obviously, Microsoft's Kinect system) open these possibilities and more for everyday use. The most significant aspect of these new systems, apart from their affordability and "hackability," is that they can readily and quite accurately locate and track several individual bodies, voices, and faces in three-dimensional physical space. This means that, for example, an avatar or a robot can relatively easily be programmed to mirror the movements and facial expressions of a person, either locally or at a distance. This leads to developments such as the following (among many others):

- Teleconferencing applications, where the participants are represented as avatars that move their bodies and faces in exact accord with those of the distributed participants
- Wall-sized responsive displays, controlled by the body and in almost any location
- Interactive "fitting rooms" for trying on new clothes before buying
- Remote control of (as) robots
- Interactive "workbenches" and other surfaces for close, highly dexterous interaction (architecture, inspecting medical imagery)
- Physiotherapeutic application and sports training

The other is not confined to human bodies. With the right visual and tactile stimulation, one could in principle feel present in an animal body, or even an inanimate object. If I see myself as that creature or thing, and feel myself to be present in that body, might I come to know what it feels like to be, for example, a bat (Nagel 1974) or a box? This is more than virtualization, more than the representation of things and their behavior, and my ability to identify with them. It is the feeling that I am present as them—not metaphorically, but literally.

Presence transference to another body—distributed embodiment—need not involve much simulation. All of this can be accomplished through virtual reality, where every pixel and all behavioral and physical responses must be specified precisely to cover all possible events. But it can also, and more easily and flexibly, be done in the augmented reality we increasingly inhabit. This includes sensors in objects, people, and even animals, and distributed large and small displays that respond to sensed events nearby or at a distance. This reality mixes the real and the virtual in a blended world of almost unimaginable possibilities.

DIRECT BRAIN-COMPUTER INTERACTION: CAN WE SIDESTEP PERCEPTION?

At its core, presence—in physical or virtual environments—is perceptual. The perception of an environment is not the same thing as imagining the environment, and the point of a sense of presence is to allow us to distinguish between what we imagine and where we really are right now (Waterworth et al. 2010). It is sometimes said that VR works because the world is virtual. In some sense, this is true, in that we do not perceive everything about what is out there in the world, and often we misperceive. As Gregory suggested, our perception presents us with hypotheses of what exists (Gregory 1997). But it does not follow from this that the imagined is the same as the virtual. Presence in virtuality is significant not because reality is virtual, but because—for the organism if not the intellect—VR is real, in a way that mental imagery is not.

But there is a way to go other than simulating the physical world and presenting the results for perception via the senses. Why not use technology to stimulate the brain directly? Placing a few electrodes in the correct places allows us to track the changing electrical activity corresponding to perception. And by applying electrical fields in the right places, we should be able to produce electrical activity corresponding to whatever perceptions we would like to produce in a head. The expanding field of brain-computer interaction (BCI) focuses on the potential of the first approach—detecting electrical brain activity and using it to interact with a device or virtual environment, whether this is a physical wheelchair or a computer-based game or other virtual world. The approach has been successful (e.g., Leeb et al. 2007), but the experience is not that of presence, but of absence, with a significant effort of action in the world. Through biofeedback, we can learn when we are producing certain electrical patterns and how to control them, to some extent, especially if highly motivated by disability (Hochberg et al. 2006). But this is a far cry from experiencing a convincing illusion of acting directly in a virtual world.

On the other side, direct brain stimulation—transcranial magnetic stimulation (TMS)—has been applied in psychotherapy, for example in the treatment of neurological and psychiatric disorders, such as depression and auditory hallucinations, although there is little reliable evidence of its effectiveness (Slotema et al. 2010). It is perhaps best known for producing extraordinary experiences, some producing feelings of being in the presence of the divine. The so-called God Helmet (see Persinger et al. 2010), invented by Stanley Koren, applies weak, fluctuating magnetic fields to the right hemisphere parietal and temporal lobes. Typically, this is said to produce a sense of the presence of another in the room, and quite often this has been experienced as a divine other. With some individuals, however, there is no effect, and other kinds of presence are common, sometimes these are experienced as malign or threatening. But other groups (e.g., Larsson et al. 2005) have failed to replicate these findings, and the evidence for specific effects remains sparse. The unanswered question, then, is can specific information be realized by TMS? This would be a direct computer-mind interface and would be experienced as other, although the perceptual channels are not involved.

Conclusions: The Future of Distributed Embodiment

When we experience strong mediated presence, our experience is that the technology has become part of the self, and the mediated reality to which we are attending has become an integrated part of the other. When this happens, there is no conscious *effort of access* to presented information (the simulated reality), nor *effort of action* to carry out overt responses. We can perceive and act directly, as if unmediated. The extent to which we experience presence through a medium thus provides a measure of the extent to which that technology has become part of the self. This is not simply a matter of "sensory replacement" as addressed in classical virtual reality research—the personal significance of the mediated situation and other factors relating to content are known to cut across technological sophistication in inducing presence. It is a matter of how and where we experience the boundary between self and other. We predict that presence will increasingly be experienced and studied in *blended realities* of the physical and virtual. Our changing experiences of presence reflect the changing virtual/physical world in which we live.

The virtual world can replace the sense of presence in the physical world, or enhance it. The former case comprises the definition of virtual reality (VR); the latter is the aim of augmented or mixed reality (AR). Distributed embodiment, real presence in *another* virtual body, is something else. It depends on and confirms the surprising ease with which our body image can be manipulated and transferred in relation to our sense of self. We know that it is possible to transfer ourselves to other bodies (or body parts, or objects), to have a real sense of presence in them, or as them. This can be done with rubber arms, with manikins or other people, and also in VR. That it works in VR is not surprising, since in VR we always have the illusion of being embodied in a virtual body—though conventionally this is collocated with our own physical body.

Future research on distributed embodiment should systematically implement and experiment with different viewpoints of media experience, involving singular and multiple first-, second-, and third-person virtual representations of self and others. To date, the evidence is both limited and weak. Factors such as the degree of coordination between body and virtual image, sensory-motor coupling, and visual similarity (among others) will need to be varied and the impact on the sense of presence assessed (by means of triangulations of introspective, behavioral, and neuropsychological data). A search for quantum shifts in the nature and quality of presence in response to specific manipulations of perceived embodiment should be the focus. This work has already started (e.g., Ehrsson 2007; Lenggenhager et al. 2007; Slater et al. 2008; 2010), but many questions remain open at this time. We still don't know with any precision: To what extent does collocation of body and virtual image affect our sense of presence? What are the limits of out-of-the-body experiences? Can direct brain stimulation match or even exceed the potential of virtual body image manipulation for vivid re-embodied experiences?

The results of this ongoing research will open up new possibilities. New knowledge will lead to techniques that will result in products that manipulate our sense of self—of when, where, who, and even what we feel ourselves to be. The future applications of real presence in virtual bodies will be numerous, including psychotherapy to restore body image distortions (such as anorexia), entertainment (imagine watching a movie and feeling really present in the body of a main character), mediation (experiencing situations as if one were the other party), and mental and physical rehabilitation, among many others. An understanding of how and to what extent we can experience real presence in other virtual bodies will be enormously important in these and other fields.

But we should remember that many people already demonstrate that they want to be in both the physical world and in virtuality at the same time. Distributed embodiment in the real world may be what will have mass appeal. The major challenge for the future will be effectively and cheaply to shift the sense of presence from one's own body to another, without replacing or excluding the physical world in which we all exist.

References

Biocca, F. A., and J. P. Rolland. 1998. Virtual Eyes Can Rearrange Your Body: Adaptation to Visual Displacement in See-Through, Head-Mounted Displays. *Presence* 7: 262–277.

Botvinick, M., and J. Cohen. 1998. Rubber Hands "Feel" Touch That the Eye Sees. *Nature* 391: 756.

Bracken, C. C., and P. Skalski. 2010. *Immersed in Media: Telepresence in Everyday Life.* New York: Routledge.

Castiello, U., D. Lusher, C. Burton, Glover, S., and P. Disler. 2004. Improving Left Hemispatial Neglect Using Virtual Reality. *Neurology* 62: 1958–1962.

Clark, A. 2003. *Natural Born Cyborgs: Minds, Technologies, and the Future of Human Intelligence.* Oxford: Oxford University Press.

Dennett, D. 1991. *Consciousness Explained.* London: Allen Lane.

Dourish, P. 2001. *Where the Action Is: The Foundations of Embodied Interaction*. Cambridge, MA: MIT Press.

Ehrsson, H. H. 2007. The Experimental Induction of Out-of-Body Experiences. *Science* 317 (5841): 1048.

Gregory, R. L. 1997. *Eye and Brain*. 5th edition. Oxford: Oxford University Press.

Hochberg, L. R., M. D. Serruya, G. M. Friehs, J. A. Mukand, M. Saleh, A. H. Caplan, A. Branner, D. Chen, D. Penn, and J. P. Donoghue. 2006. Neuronal Ensemble Control of Prosthetic Devices by a Human with Tetraplegia. *Nature* 442 (7099): 164–171.

Holmes N., and C. Spence. 2007. Dissociating Body Image and Body Schema with Rubber Hands. *Behavioral and Brain Sciences* 30: 211–212.

Hutchins, E. 1996. *Cognition in the Wild*. Cambridge, MA: Bradford Books, MIT Press.

IJsselsteijn, W. A., Y. A. W. de Kort, and A. Haans. 2006. Is This My Hand I See before Me? The Rubber Hand Illusion in Reality, Virtual Reality, and Mixed Reality. *Presence: Teleoperators and Virtual Environments* 15: 455–464.

Kaptelinin, V., and B. Nardi. 2006. *Acting with Technology: Activity Theory and Interaction Design*. Cambridge, MA: MIT Press.

Larsson, M., D. Larhammarb, M. Fredrikson, and P. Granqvist. 2005. Reply to M. A. Persinger and S. A. Koren's Response to Granqvist et al. Sensed Presence and Mystical Experiences Are Predicted by Suggestibility, Not by the Application Of Transcranial Weak Magnetic Fields. *Neuroscience Letters* 380 (3): 348–350.

Leeb, R., D. Friedman, G. R. Müller-Putz, R. Scherer, M. Slater, and G. Pfurtscheller. 2007. Self-Paced (Asynchronous) BCI Control of a Wheelchair in Virtual Environments: A Case Study with a Tetraplegic. *Computational Intelligence and Neuroscience* 20 (April 2007): Article 7.

Lenggenhager, B., T. Tadi, T. Metzinger, and O. Blanke. 2007. Video Ergo Sum: Manipulating Bodily Self-Consciousness. *Science* 317 (5841): 1096–1099.

Lombard, M., and T. Ditton. 1997. At the Heart of It All: The Concept of Presence. *Journal of Computer Mediated-Communication* 3 (2). http://jcmc.indiana.edu/vol3/issue2/lombard.html. Accessed July 29, 2013.

Lombard, M., and M. T. Jones. 2006. Defining Presence. Paper presented to Presence 2006: The 9th International Workshop on Presence, Cleveland, OH.

Merleau-Ponty, M. 1962. *Phenomenology of Perception*. London: Routledge & Kegan Paul.

Misselhorn, C. 2009. Empathy with Inanimate Objects and the Uncanny Valley. *Minds and Machines* 19 (3): 345–359.

Nagel, T. 1974. What Is It Like to Be a Bat? *Philosophical Review* 83 (4): 435–450.

New Scientist. 2010. The Real Avatar: Body Transfer Turns Men into Girls. May 13. http://www.newscientist.com/article/dn18896-the-real-avatar-body-transfer-turns-men-into-girls.html. Accessed June 27, 2013.

Normand, J.-M., E. Giannopoulos, B. Spanlang, and M. Slater. 2011. Multisensory Stimulation Can Induce an Illusion of Larger Belly Size in Immersive Virtual Reality. *PLoS ONE* 6 (1): e16128.

Perry, M. 2003. Distributed Cognition. In *HCI Models, Theories, and Frameworks: Toward an Interdisciplinary Science*, edited by J. M. Carroll, 193–223. San Francisco, CA: Morgan Kaufmann.

Persinger, M. A., K. Saroka, S. A. Koren, and L. S. St-Pierre. 2010. The Electromagnetic Induction of Mystical and Altered States within the Laboratory. *Journal of Consciousness Exploration & Research* 1 (7): 808–830.

Petkova V. I., and H. H. Ehrsson. 2008. If I Were You: Perceptual Illusion of Body Swapping. *PLoS ONE* 3(12): e3832. doi: 10.1371/journal.pone.0003832.

Riva, G. 1998. Modifications of Body-Image Induced by Virtual Reality. *Perceptual & Motor Skills* 86 (1): 163–170.

Riva, G., J. A. Waterworth, E. L. Waterworth, and F. Mantovani. 2011. From Intention to Action: The Role of Presence. *New Ideas in Psychology* 29 (1): 24–37.

Russell, J. A. 2003. Core Affect and the Psychological Construction of Emotion. *Psychological Review* 110 (1): 145–172.

Slater M., D. Perez-Marcos, H. H. Ehrsson, and M. Sanchez-Vives. 2008. Towards a Digital Body: The Virtual Arm Illusion. *Frontiers in Human Neuroscience* 2, Article 6: 1–8, August 20, doi: 10.3389/neuro.09.006.2008.

Slater, M., B. Spanlang, M. V. Sanchez-Vives, and O. Blanke. 2010. First Person Experience of Body Transfer in Virtual Reality. *PLoS ONE* 5 (5): e10564.

Slotema, C. W., J. D. Blom, H. W. Hoek, and I. E. C. Sommer. 2010. Should We Expand the Toolbox of Psychiatric Treatment Methods to Include Repetitive Transcranial Magnetic Stimulation (rTMS)? *Journal of Clinical Psychiatry* 71 (7): 873–884.

Turkle, S. 2005. *The Second Self: Computers and the Human Spirit*. Twentieth Anniversary Edition. Cambridge, MA: MIT Press.

Varela, F. J., T. Thompson, and E. Rosch. 1999. *The Embodied Mind: Cognitive Science and Human Experience*. Cambridge, MA: MIT Press.

Waterworth, E. L. 2001. *Perceptually-Seductive Technology: Designing Computer Support for Everyday Creativity*. Umeå: Umeå University, Department of Informatics. http://urn.kb.se/resolve?urn=urn:nbn:se:umu:diva-65867. Accessed June 27, 2013.

Waterworth, E. L., and J. A. Waterworth. 2001. Focus, Locus and Sensus: The Three Dimensions of Virtual Experience. *Cyberpsychology and Behavior* 4 (2): 203–214.

Waterworth, J. A., E. L. Waterworth, F. Mantovani, and G. Riva. 2010. On Feeling (the) Present: An Evolutionary Account of the Sense of Presence in Physical and Electronically-Mediated Environments. *Journal of Consciousness Studies* 17 (1–2): 167–189.

CHAPTER 36

....

LEVEL OF REALISM: FEEL, SMELL, AND TASTE IN VIRTUAL ENVIRONMENTS

....

ALAN CHALMERS

THE real world is multisensory. Humans perceive this world with all sensory organs concurrently. The interaction between the senses can be significant, including large amounts of detail of one sense being ignored when in the presence of other more dominant sensory inputs. For example, in ventriloquism, the sound appears to be coming from the lips of the dummy. Such cross-modal effects can substantially alter the way in which an object or scene is perceived.

It is crucial, therefore, that virtual environments (VEs) that are attempting to create the same perceptual response from a user as if he or she were actually "there" in the real scene being depicted, include all necessary sensory stimuli that are present in the real world. Failure to do so may mean that some real-world phenomena are missing in the VE, leading to different knowledge acquisition in the VE than is required in reality. For example, not including the smell of a burning cable behind a control panel may provide the user in the VE with a false sense of well-being, which would most certainly not be the case in the real world.

Although feel (and in particular touch) is increasingly being used in VEs, smell and taste are rarely included. A human has about 20 different types of "feel senses," the most common of which are heat, cold, pain, and pressure or touch receptors. Some areas of the body contain more sensors than others, making these areas more sensitive to feel. Haptics in virtual environments is a large, active, multidisciplinary field. However, current haptic devices suffer from a number of limitations. In particular, they have limited feedback capabilities compared to the human's tactile sensory system. For example, the human hand consists of millions of specialized tactile sensors all working in parallel, whereas current haptic interfaces typically have less than 10 tactile feedback motors.

The sense of smell is one of the primal chemical senses in humans. Smell adds richness to our lives, for example, the smell of coffee in the morning or freshly baked bread

FIGURE 36.1 The smell process for virtual environments from source, to capture, to delivery.

in the supermarket. In fact we may never forget an important smell. Humans perceive taste by the smell of the food via the nose, its texture and its temperature detected. Smell and taste combine to form flavor.

This chapter considers the level of realism that can be achieved in VEs through the inclusion of feel, smell, and taste. It is currently not possible to simulate feel, smell, and touch with full physical accuracy in VEs. Selective delivery methods are thus also discussed. Such techniques exploit cross-modal interactions to provide "perceptual equivalence" between a real world and a VE experience.

REAL VIRTUALITY

VEs offer the possibility of simulating potentially complex, dangerous, or threatening real-world experiences in a safe and controlled manner. They can provide a powerful and fully customizable tool for *personalized* training and allow attributes of human behavior in such environments to be examined. Such virtual reality (VR) systems attempt to deliver two key features: *realism* and *real time*. In particular, the real-time element is essential to provide an interactive experience to the user. Despite many advances in hardware and software over the decades, VR systems still reduce realism in order to achieve the desired real-time performance (Chalmers and Ferko 2008). While real-time performance in VEs is typically accepted as 25 frames per second (fps) and above (computer games typically demand 60 fps), the definition of realism is more elusive. Many applications do not in fact need any physically based realism in order for the user to accomplish a task successfully (Ferwerda 2003). Such systems are capable of delivering "mission familiarity" rather than actual world experience. This may mean, however, that some real-world phenomena are missing in VR, leading to different knowledge acquisition in VR than is required in reality. For example, in pilot safety training, inaccurate representation of glare on a screen may make the screen contents visible in VR, when in the real aircraft, the angle of the sun coming through the cockpit canopy and shining on the screen may make the contents completely invisible.

To accurately simulate reality, virtual environments need to be based on physical simulations and stimulate multiple senses (visuals, audio, smell, touch, etc.) in a natural manner. Such environments are known as *real virtuality* (Chalmers et al. 2009). Natural delivery of multiple senses is especially important, as a human's perception may be significantly affected by interactions between all these senses (Stein and Meredith 1993). In particular, cross-modalities (the influence of one sense on another) can substantially alter the way in which a scene is perceived and the way the user behaves (Calvert et al. 2004). At present there is no simulator available that can offer such a full sensory real-world experience. A key reason is that today's computers are not yet powerful enough to simulate the full physical accuracy of a real scene for multiple senses in real time. However, there is the potential to achieve real virtuality *now*, because of the brain's inability to process all the sensory input received at any given moment. Rather, based on an individual's identity and self-perception, including any previous experience, they initially attend to those stimuli that are most salient or important for the task being undertaken (James 1890; Yarbus 1967).

LEVEL OF REALISM

Level of realism (LoR) is defined as a fidelity measure of how perceptually close a virtual scene is to the real multisensory scene it is attempting to depict (Chalmers and Ferko 2008). In the real world, there is an intimate linkage between the dominant and minor senses (Calvert et al. 2004). The dominant senses are typically visuals, audio, and kinesthetic (tactile, visceral, and sense of self sensations of the body), however, in an emergency situation, the most persuasive sensory cue, for example the smell of burning, may dominate (Welch and Warren 1980). The key to an authentic model of perception is the combination and integration of multiple sources of sensory information. To deliver a perceptually equivalent "real-world experience" to the user in a VE, it is necessary to deliver the "appropriate" level of sensory stimulation to the user for each sense. As long as the sensory stimuli are delivered in a natural manner and their fidelity is above the threshold of what the user would be attending to in the real world, it is not necessary to integrate these senses in any way during delivery, as the brain will do this exactly as it would in the real world.

There have been a considerable number of studies reporting individual differences in the degree and nature of multisensory integration. For example, not everyone is sensitive to cross-modal fusion illusions such as the McGurk and illusory flash effects and their strength varies widely across observers (Calvert et al. 2004). In addition, motivation and personality (Giolas et al. 1974), linguistic experience (Sekiyama and Tohkura 1991), gender (Irwin and Whalen 2006), attention (Alsius et al. 2005), and the aging process (Townsend et al. 2006) have all been shown to modulate the level of multisensory integration. However, inter-individual differences in cross-modal binding do appear to be consistent within individuals across different multisensory interactions (Tremblay et al. 2007). Furthermore, individuals appear to differ with respect to the rules used for cross-modal fusion (e.g. averaging, linear summation, or power law summation models) (Guest and Spence 2003). These aspects of variance across individuals are small in factors that matter for the purposes of judging whether "appropriate" levels across users differ widely (Calvert et al. 2004). Nevertheless these factors need to be taken into account in a real-virtuality environment.

In multisensory integration, one modality often dominates the other at a specific point in time. Depending on the type of information, different combination and integration strategies are used, and prior knowledge is often required for interpreting the sensory signals (Ernst and Bülthoff 2004). Several hypotheses exist in cognitive neuroscience advocating a condition for modality dominance (Andersen et al. 2004). For example, Lederman and Klatzky (2004) show that when considering a surface texture, visuals, audio, or touch many dominate depending on how the task is approached. Although a growing body of work is considering the interaction of senses in the real world, to the best of my knowledge, there is little work on considering this problem in the context of complex virtual environments.

The perception of an environment, P, may be described as a function over time (t) and preconditioning (ρ) of task (τ) (Chalmers and Ferko 2008):

$$P_\tau(t, \rho) = \omega_v V(t, \rho) + \omega_a A(t, \rho) + \omega_s S(t, \rho) + \omega_t T(t, \rho) + \omega_f F(t, \rho) + \omega_\delta \Delta(t, \rho)$$

where V = visuals, A = audio, S = smell, T = taste, and F = feel. These correspond to the proportion of human attention being paid to each of the senses. Δ is a "distraction factor" indicating how focused the user is on the environment. For example, the user may be distracted by thinking about a pretraining briefing, a phone call from a family member, and so on. Although other methods of how the senses combine have been proposed (e.g., Ernst and Bülthoff 2004), the perception equation provides a straightforward starting point for determining at what precision to deliver each sense in a virtual environment. ω_i is the particular perceptual weighting that each of the senses, and any distraction, has for the perception of that particular moment, with $\Sigma\omega_i \leq 1$. Each of these weightings is the threshold value below which the perception of the environment would be different from the perception if one were "there" in reality. Above this threshold there is no perceptual difference, and thus in the equation, the value of each ω_i is capped at this threshold (Chalmers and Ferko 2008).

A key point is that it is not necessary for a VE to determine precise thresholds for cross-modal effects. A VE will deliver an authentic experience as long as "above threshold" of just noticeable differences (JNDs) of the senses can be achieved. The ω_i can thus determine the *precision* of the simulation and delivery of each of the senses that needs to be achieved to ensure the user has a high-quality experience. This enables computational resources within the VE to be applied with the maximum efficiency.

SMELL AND TASTE

Senses such as visual, audio, temperature, and motion can be encoded as digital streams in a straightforward manner, and for the most part their capture and delivery are very well understood. Smell and taste, on the other hand, are substantially more difficult to manage. This is simply a result of the medium that smell and taste use, that of molecules. Smell and taste is the result of a biochemical reaction between human receptor and a binding site on a molecule, though in truth it is far more complex than this. When humans identify an aroma, it is unlikely that it is due to one single molecule, but the interaction of tens (if not hundreds or thousands) of molecules and many millions of biochemical reactions. For example, the smell of coffee is composed of many hundreds of "smelly" molecules, but we simply recognize it as coffee.

Natural odor molecules (for humans), with the notable exception of a few molecules such as hydrogen sulphide (the characteristic smell of decayed eggs), are carbon-based molecules. Such molecules are small, which enables them to float in the air and form an invisible plume of odor; known as volatility. Odor molecules' surface area relative to the volume is large. It is not yet known precisely how an odor molecule is detected. One theory is that it is the shape of the molecules that allows it to be correctly identified by the nose. Another more recent idea is that it is the "vibrational modes" of an odorant that are its signature (Francoa et al. 2011). This idea suggests an odor molecule may be viewed as a collection of atoms on springs, and it is the quantum effect, that is, the energy of just the right frequency, that causes the spring to vibrate and thus the molecule to be identified (Francoa et al. 2011).

A human's ability to smell occurs in the 2–4 cm^2 tissue of the olfactory epithelium of the nose. This area contains 500–1,000 different types of olfactory receptors that only last for 60 days, but are continually renewed. These receptors encode information about the chemical composition of odor molecules into neural signals, with each type of olfactory receptor tuned to different odor molecules (Ressler et al. 1994). Smell in an environment may be captured manually by sucking the air across an automated thermal desorption (ATD) tube, figure 36.1 (middle). The odor molecules stick to the fine granular material in the tube. The trapped molecules can then be determined by first passing them through a gas-liquid chromatography (GLC) instrument, which separates the complex mixture of odorants (many natural odorant mixtures have between 10 and 600 individual odorant molecules) into constituent molecules. From the GLC, the molecules pass into a mass-spectrometer, which produces a resultant histogram of the molecules present. Current mass-spectrometer devices are not precise, and many molecules may be missed. A human nose, that of a trained molecular scientist, is often used to identify any odor molecules that the device may not have detected (G. Dodd, personal communication, 2009).

In order to recreate smell in a VE, the captured and analyzed chemical components need to be resynthesized within a laboratory and then released to the user at the correct time (and removed once no longer needed). Though this task appears difficult, the human system aids us. First, humans are very poor at telling smell concentration gradients (because smell initially developed as a warning mechanism). Furthermore, many smells are composed of key odorant markers (KOMs), which are a small number of single molecules that when mixed can produce a close approximation to the desired smell. It is possible to capture and analyze samples in close to real time (for example, using SIFT-MS, or Soft Ionization MS), but the cost of the instrumentation, its bulky nature, and the time for the human operator to interpret the results make it unrealistic. Instruments that replicate the human olfactory system (so-called electronic noses) could be used, but are designed to identify smells, not the chemical components within them.

SMELL IN VES

Despite the importance of scent in our everyday life, little work has been done to include smell in virtual environments. Real exhibits, on the other hand, such as the Jorvik Viking Museum in York, have had smells piped to parts of the exhibit for many years, which has been shown to aid visitors in remembering information (Aggleton and Waskett 1999). One of the earliest attempts to include smell in a virtual setting was Morton Heilig's Sensorama (Rheingold 1992). Developed in the early 1960s, this mechanical device was capable of displaying stereoscopic 3D images and included user movement, stereo sound, wind, and aromas that could be triggered during the film. Unfortunately, Heilig was unable to find financial backing for his device and nothing further was developed. Only much more recently has smell been introduced into virtual environments, for training (e.g., Washburn et al. 2003), and therapy (e.g., Barfield and Danas 1995; Chen 2006). Results from preliminary studies have shown that the introduction of smell does indeed increase the user's sense of "presence" in the virtual environment (Dinh et al. 1999; Zybura and Eskeland 1999). In particular, the introduction of realistic smells, including the smells of burning rubber and flesh, have been used effectively to treat soldiers returning from Iraq with post-traumatic stress disorder (Pair et al. 2006). Most recently an interactive olfactory display was also developed for a "cooking game," in which the duration and strength of a number of predefined smells was controlled and blended in real time into a number of recipes by the game (Nakamoto et al. 2008).

In 2009, Ramic-Brkic and colleagues showed that the presence of smell in an environment can have a major effect on the perceived quality of computer graphics. In particular they exploited the cross-modal effect between the strong smell of cut grass and real-time rendered animation of grass blades. The smell of cut grass, cis-3-hexenol, is a single odor molecule, easy to produce, and it can be delivered in a straightforward manner using an off-the-shelf atomizer. Two animations of grass terrain were used in their study. One was rendered in high quality (HQ—fig. 36.2a) with eight times antialiasing for grass and with shadows. The other one was rendered at low quality (LQ—fig. 36.2b) with no antialiasing and no shadows. Both videos were rendered at 1,280 × 800 pixel resolution using a GeForce 8600M graphic card. Their results, figure 36.2c showed that 80 percent of subjects were able to tell the quality difference between the two animations when no smell was present, but only 50 percent could tell the difference when the smell was present, which is equivalent to chance.

TASTE IN VES

Taste is very closely related to smell, with smell contributing as much as 75 to 95 percent of taste. Taste buds on the human tongue and a few on the roof of the mouth detect the

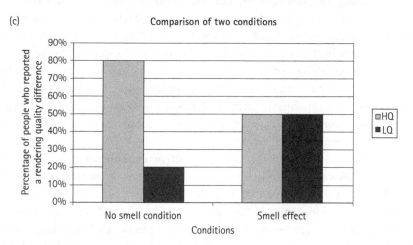

FIGURES 36.2 High-quality frame (a), low-quality frame (b), comparison of results (c) (Ramic-Brkic et al. 2009). Images courtesy of Belma Ramic-Brkic and Kevin Boulanger.

chemical molecules of food. In addition, the smell of the food is determined by the nose, while its texture and temperature are distinguished by mechanoreceptors and thermo-receptors respectively.

There are five primary tastes: salty, sour, bitter, sweet, and umami (from the Japanese "tasty," and corresponding roughly to the taste of glutamate) (Abdi 2002). Recent brain-imaging studies have shown that there is a difference in the way in which professional tasters and amateurs appreciate flavor. Sommeliers of wine tasting have a more analytical approach, with stronger activations in the dorso-lateral prefrontal cortex, while the nonprofessionals showed much stronger activations in emotion-related areas such as hippocampus and amygdala (Castriota-Scanderberg et al. 2005). Smell and taste combine to form flavor, which may also be influenced by other cross-modal interactions (Verhagen and Engelen 2006). For example, Woods and colleagues (2011) showed that background noise unrelated to food being eaten reduces its saltiness and sweetness while increasing its perceived crunchiness.

Although research on the perception of taste started as long ago as the late 1500s, very little work has been done on virtual taste. A notable exception is the work of Iwata and colleagues (2003). In 2003 at the SIGGRAPH Emerging Technologies exhibition, they-presented their food simulator: a haptic interface to mimic the taste, sound and feeling of chewing real food. A device in the mouth simulated the force of the type of food, a bone vibration microphone provided the sound of biting, while the chemical simulation of taste was achieved via a micro-injector.

Feel

A human's sense of feel originates in the dermis layer of our skin. The dermis is filled with nerve endings of many sensory neurons. When a subject touches, or is touched by, an object, a force is imposed on the sensors of the skin. Details of this force are then conveyed to the brain. There are about 20 different types of "feel sensations," the most common of which are heat, cold, pain, and pressure or touch receptors. Some areas of the body contain more sensors than others, making these areas more sensitive to feel. For example, the tongue has a high concentration of nerve endings of pain and fewer nerve endings of heat. This explains why it hurts so much if we bite our tongue and why we can easily burn our mouths if we eat something hot. Other most sensitive areas are hands, lips, face, neck, fingertips, and feet.

Haptics in virtual environments is a large, active, multidisciplinary field. However, current haptic devices suffer from a number of limitations. In particular, they have limited feedback capabilities compared to the human's tactile sensory system. Limitations of current haptic devices include high price, high weight and size, bandwidth limitation, latency between a human operator and the force feedback, being designed for very specific purpose, and instability if the update rate is much less than 1 kHz (Robles-De-La-Torre 2006; Saddik 2007).

DISCUSSION

Current state-of-the-art virtual reality systems compromise the realism of the environments they are simulating in order to achieve the required interactivity of the system. This is because even modern computer hardware is simply not capable of simulating, to a full degree of physical accuracy, in real time, the complexities of the real world. Furthermore, virtual reality seldom provides more than two sensory stimuli (typically visuals and audio, or visuals and touch). A real-virtuality system, on the other hand, provides perceptual realism by delivering many multisensory stimuli (visuals, audio, feel, smell, and taste) in a natural manner. That is, it achieves a level of realism in the virtual world that is perceptually equivalent to that of the real world. It achieves this high level of authenticity by selectively delivering real-world stimuli, exploiting the fact that the human perceptual system is simply not capable of attending to all stimuli at the highest precision all the time (Debattista et al. 2007; Chalmers et al. 2009). Rather, we selectively attend to objects within the scene, perhaps resulting in large amounts of detail from one sense going unnoticed when in the presence of competing sensory inputs from another modality (Mack and Rock 1998), or subtle signals in one modality being strongly enhanced by congruent information in another sense.

Indeed, the senses can significantly influence each other. For example, several researchers have shown that high-quality sounds coupled with visual stimuli increase the perceived quality of the visual displays (Storms 1998; Winkler and Faller 2005). Mastoropoulou and Chalmers (2004) showed that the combination of tempo and emotional suggestiveness of music affects users' visual perception of temporal rate and duration. Motion has a similar perceptual effect. Ellis and Chalmers (2006) showed that a perceptually aware selective renderer could exploit the cross-modal interference between a human's visual and vestibular system to substantially reduce the quality of parts of an image without the viewer being aware of any difference. Even our sense of taste can be affected by other dominant sensory stimuli. For example, Zampini and Spence (2004) showed that stale potato crisps tasted fresher when they were accompanied by an electronically generated "crispy" sound. For this work, Zampini and Spence won the 2008 Ig Nobel Prize in Nutrition.

The ability to deliver full real-world experiences in a safe and controlled manner using high-fidelity VE has long been a "holy grail" for a wide range of applications, including defense, firefighting, building design, archaeology, sports, and surgery. A recurrent problem is that training in VEs often encourages a set of responses and abilities that fail to mimic sufficiently accurately real-world situations. High fidelity and flexibility of the virtual platform with respect to the user's changing motivations and goals is of the essence.

A key to the success of VEs is thus to understand thoroughly the level of realism (LoR) that will be required in order to achieve the necessary perceptual equivalence between the real-world scenario and its virtual simulation. This minimum LoR is the lowest quality level of delivered multisensory stimuli in order to achieve a one-to-one mapping of an experience in the virtual environment with the same experience in the real environment. Failure to achieve this level by omitting key sensory stimuli, such as high-fidelity smell, feel, or even taste, may result in users adopting a different task strategy in the virtual world than in the real world.

REFERENCES

Abdi, H. 2002. What Can Cognitive Psychology and Sensory Evaluation Learn from Each Other? *Food Quality and Preference* 13: 445–451.

Aggleton, J., and L. Waskett. 1999. The Ability of Odors to Serve as State-Dependent Cues for Real-World Memories: Can Viking Smells Aid the Recall of Viking Experiences? *British Journal of Psychology* 90: 1–7.

Alsius, A., J. Navarra, R. Campbell, and S. Soto-Faraco. 2005. Audiovisual Integration of Speech Falters under High Attention Demands. *Current Biology* 15: 839–843.

Andersen, T. S., K. Tiipanna, and M. Sams. 2004. Factors Influencing Audiovisual Fission and Fusion Illusions. *Cognitive Brain Research* 21: 301–308.

Barfield, W., and E. Danas. 1995. Comments on the Use of Olfactory Displays for Virtual Environments. *Presence* 5 (1): 109–121.

Calvert, G., C. Spence, and B. Stein, eds. 2004. *The Handbook of Multisensory Processes*. Cambridge, MA: MIT Press.

Castriota-Scanderberg, A., G. Hagberg, A. Cerasa, G. Committieri, G. Galati, F. Patria, S. Pitzalis, C. Caltagirone, and R. Frackowiak. 2005. The Appreciation of Wine by Sommeliers: A Functional Magnetic Resonance Study of Sensory Integration. *Neuroimage* 25: 570–578.

Chalmers, A. G., and A. Ferko. 2008. Levels of Realism: From Virtual Reality to Real Virtuality. In *SCCG '08: Proceedings of the 24th Spring Conference on Computer Graphics*, 27–33. New York: ACM Press.

Chalmers, A. G., D. Howard, and C. Moir. 2009. Real Virtuality: A Step Change From Virtual Reality. In *SCCG '09: Proceedings of the 25th Spring Conference on Computer Graphics*, 9–16. New York: ACM Press.

Chen, Y. 2006. Olfactory Display: Development and Application in Virtual Reality Therapy. In *Advances in Artificial Reality and Tele-existence: Proceedings of the 16th International Conference on Artificial Reality and Telexistence, ICAT '06*, 580–584. Berlin: Springer.

Debattista, K., A. G. Chalmers, R. Gillibrand, P. Longhurst, G. Mastoropoulou, and V. Sundstedt. 2007. Parallel Selective Rendering of High-Fidelity Virtual Environments. *Parallel Computing* 33 (6): 361–376.

Dinh, H. Q., N. Walker, C. Song, A. Kobayashi, and L. Hodges. 1999. Evaluating the Importance of Multi-sensory Input on Memory and the Sense of Presence in Virtual Environments. In *Virtual Reality, 1999: Proceedings, IEEE*, 222–228. Los Alamitos, CA: IEEE Press.

Ellis, G., and A. G. Chalmers. 2006. The Effect of Translational Ego-Motion on the Perception of High Fidelity Animations. In *SCCG 2006*. New York: ACM Press.

Ernst, M. O., and H. Bülthoff. 2004. Merging the Senses into a Robust Percept. *Trends in Cognitive Sciences* 8 (4): 162–169.

Ferwerda, J. 2003. Three Varieties of Realism in Computer Graphics. In *Proceedings SPIE Human Vision and Electronic Imaging*, 290–297. Bellingham, WA: SPIE.

Francoa, M. I., L. Luca Turina, A. Mershinb, and E. M. C. Skoulakisa. 2011. Molecular Vibration-Sensing Component in *Drosophila melanogaster* Olfaction. *Proceedings of the National Academy of Sciences of the United States of America* 108 (9): 3797–3802.

Giolas, T. G., E. C. Butterfield, and S. J. Weaver. 1974. Some Motivational Correlates of Lipreading. *Journal of Speech and Hearing Research* 17: 18–24.

Guest, S., and C. Spence. 2003. What Role Does Multisensory Integration Play in the Visuotactile Perception of Texture? *International Journal of Psychophysiology* 50: 63–80.

Irwin, J., and D. Whalen. 2006. A Sex Difference in Visual Influence on Heard Speech. *Perception & Psychophysics* 68 (4): 582–592.

Iwata, H., H. Yano, T. Uemura, and T. Moriya. 2003. Food Simulator. In *ICAT '03: Proceedings of the 13th International Conference on Artificial Reality and Telexistence*. New York: IEEE Press.

James, W. 1890. A saliency-based search mechanism for overt and covert shifts of visual attention. *Principles of Psychology*. New York: H. Holt.

Lederman, S. J., and R. L. Klatzky. 2004. Multisensory Texture Perception. In *The Handbook of Multisensory Processes*, edited by G. Calvert, and C. Spence, 107–122. Cambridge, MA: MIT Press.

Mack, A., and I. Rock. 1998. *Inattentional Blindness*. Cambridge, MA: MIT Press.

Mastoropoulou, G., and A. G. Chalmers. 2004. The Effect of Music on the Perception of Display Rate and Duration of Animated Sequences: An Experimental Study. In *TPCG '04: Theory and Practice of Computer Graphics 2004*, 128–134. Los Alamitos, CA: IEEE Press.

Nakamoto, T., S. Otaguro, M. Kinoshita, M. Nagahama, K. Ohinishi, and T. Ishida. 2008. Cooking Up an Interactive Olfactory Game Display. In *IEEE Computer Graphics and Applications*, 75–78. Los Alamitos: IEEE Press.

Pair, J., B. Allen, M. Dautricourt, A. Trekunov, M. Liewer, K. Graap, G. Reger, and A. Rizzo. 2006. A Virtual Reality Exposure Therapy Application for Iraq War Post-traumatic Stress Disorder. In *IEEE Virtual Reality 2006*, 67–72. Piscataway, NJ: IEEE Press.

Ramic-Brkic, B., A. G. Chalmers, K. Boulanger, S. Patttanaik, and J. Covington. 2009. Cross-Modal Effects of Smell on Real-Time Rendering of Grass. In *SCCG'09: Proceedings of the 25th Spring Conference on Computer Graphics*, 175–179. New York: ACM Press.

Ressler, K., S. Sullivan, and L. Buck. 1994. A Molecular Dissection of Spatial Patterning in the Olfactory System. *Current Opinion in Neurobiology* 4: 588–596.

Rheingold, H. 1992. *Virtual Reality*. New York: Simon and Schuster.

Robles-De-La-Torre, G. 2006. The Importance of the Sense of Touch in Virtual and Real Environments. In *"Haptic User Interfaces for Multimedia Systems,"* special issue of *IEEE Multimedia* 13 (3): 24–30.

Saddik, A. 2007. The Potential of Haptic Technologies. *IEEE Instrumentation & Measurement Magazine* 10 (31): 10–17.

Sekiyama, K., and Y. J. Tohkura. 1991. McGurk Effect in Non-English Listeners: Few Visual Effects for Japanese Subjects Hearing Japanese syllables of High Auditory Intelligibility. *The Journal of the Acoustical Society of America* 90 (4 Pt 1): 1797–1805.

Stein, B., and M. Meredith. 1993. *The Merging of the Senses*. Cambridge, MA: MIT Press.

Storms, R. 1998. Auditory-Visual Crossmodal Perception Phenomena. PhD diss., Naval Postgraduate School, Monterey, CA.

Townsend, J., M. Adamo, and F. Haist. 2006. Changing Channels: An fMRI Study of Aging and Cross-Modal Attention Shifts. *NeuroImage* 31 (4): 1682–1692.

Tremblay, C., F. Champoux, P. Voss, B. A. Baconn, F. Lepore, and H. Théoret. 2007. Speech and Non-speech Audio-visual Illusions: A Developmental Study. *PLoS ONE* 8: e742.

Verhagen, J., and L. Engelen. 2006. The Neurocognitive Bases of Human Multimodal Food Perception: Sensory Integration. *Neuroscience and Biobehavioral Reviews* 30: 613–650.

Washburn, D., L. M. Jones, R. Satya, C. Bowers, and A. Cortes. 2003. Olfactory Use in Virtual Environment Training. *Modelling and Simulation Magazine* 2 (3): 19–25.

Welch, R. B., and D. H. Warren. 1980. Immediate Perceptual Response to Intersensory Discrepancy. *Psychological Bulletin* 3: 638–667.

Winkler, S., and C. Faller. 2005. Audiovisual Quality Evaluation of Low-Bitrate Video. In *SPIE/IS&T Human Vision and Electronic Imaging,* 139–148. Bellingham, WA: SPIE.

Woods, A. T., E. Poliakoff, D. M. Lloyd, J. Kuenzela, R. Hodson, H. Gonda, J. Batchelora, G. B. Dijksterhuisa, and A. Thomas. 2011. Effect of Background Noise on Food Perception. *Food Quality and Preference* 22 (1): 42–47.

Yarbus, A. L. 1967. Eye Movements during Perception of Complex Objects. In *Eye Movements and Vision*, edited by L. A. Riggs, 171–196. New York: Plenum Press.

Zampini, M., and C. Spence. 2004. The Role of Auditory Cues in Modulating the Perceived Crispness and Staleness of Potato Chips. *Journal of Sensory Studies* 15 (9): 347–363.

Zybura, M., and A. Eskeland. 1999. Olfaction for Virtual Reality. Quarter Project, Industrial Engineering 543, University of Washington.

CHAPTER 37

....

DEVELOPING HANDHELD AUGMENTED REALITY INTERFACES

....

MARK BILLINGHURST, HUIDONG BAI, GUN LEE, AND ROBERT LINDEMAN

AUGMENTED reality (AR) allows users to see virtual imagery overlaid on their surrounding real environment. Using Azuma's definition, AR interfaces have three key characteristics: (1) the virtual and real imagery are combined together, (2) the virtual content is interactive in real time, and (3) the virtual content can be fixed in space relative to the real world (Azuma 1997). These qualities provide an idea of the display, interaction, and tracking technologies needed for a good AR experience. For example, there must be a display capable of showing real and virtual content together, and tracking technology to find the user's viewing position.

From Sutherland's early work (Sutherland 1965), most AR systems have traditionally used a head-mounted display (HMD) to view the virtual content. However, many people do not want to wear HMDs because of social factors, and they can be difficult to use because of their weight, limited resolution, connecting cables, and additional tracking hardware.

In recent years AR applications have migrated to other devices, including tablet PCs (Vuforia AR SDK),[1] PDAs (Wagner and Schmalstieg 2003), mobile phones (Moehring, Lessig, and Bimber 2004), and other handheld platforms (fig. 37.1). The modern smartphone is ideal for AR because it combines a full color display, fast CPU and graphics processors, networking, integrated cameras, and GPS and compass sensors. Hundreds of millions of AR-capable smartphones are now sold every year, making this one of the most widely used platforms for augmented reality. By the end of 2012, the iPhone and Android app stores had over eight hundred AR applications, and some, like the Layar AR browser (Layar 2012), have tens of millions of users.

However, although handheld AR (HHAR) applications are widely available, there have been few guidelines for designing their user interface. When using a handheld

FIGURE 37.1 Typical handheld AR application.

AR application, the user looks at the screen of the device to view the AR scene and needs at least one hand to hold the device. So the user interface is very different from HMD-based AR applications and design guidelines, such as those provided by Höllerer (2004), where the user is looking through the display and has both hands free. In this chapter we review research in HHAR to produce a set of design guidelines. We also provide a series of case studies showing how these guidelines can be applied in practice.

Related Research

The first handheld AR systems date back to Fitzmaurice's Chameleon interface (1993) and Rekimoto's Transvision system (1996). Both used LCD displays that were connected to desktop computers and a magnetic tracking system to find the position and orientation of the LCD displays. The Chameleon system allowed people to move an LCD display around a room and to see virtual information on the screen related to objects in the room. For example, holding the display over a map caused names of cities to appear. It was not a true handheld AR system because the user did not see a video view of the real world on the handheld display, but it still showed the concept of anchoring virtual content in space.

The Transvision application used handheld LCD displays to allow two people to see a shared virtual object in the space between them, appearing as an AR overlay on a live video view of the real world. The users could move the handheld display around in a very natural way to see the virtual content from different positions. Both Transvision and Chameleon used the spatial position of the display to retrieve virtual information in space. However, in these cases the main interaction was largely limited to changing the view of the virtual content based on the position of the LCD panel. There was no direct interaction with the content itself.

As significant handheld computing and graphics became available, researchers explored the use of PDAs for AR applications. First there was work such as the AR-PDA project (Geiger et al. 2001) and BatPortal (Ingram and Newman 2001) in which the PDA was used as a thin client for showing AR content generated on a remote PC server. The PDA would be used to capture a picture that was then sent to the PC for remote processing and adding virtual content onto the image. The final result was sent back to the PDA for viewing, which was necessary as early PDAs did not have enough capability for stand-alone AR applications. However, in 2003 the first self-contained PDA AR application appeared (Wagner and Schmalstieg 2003), and then collaborative AR applications based on PDAs (Wagner et al. 2005). As AR became available on handheld devices, interaction methods expanded to include the use of stylus and touch screen input, or tracked physical objects.

Mobile phone-based AR followed a similar development path. Early phones did not have enough processing power, so researchers explored thin client approaches. The AR-Phone project (Cutting, Assad, and Hudson 2003) used Bluetooth to send phone camera images to a remote server for processing and graphics overlay, taking several seconds per image. Then Henrysson and Ollila (2004) and Moehring et al. (2004) independently developed mobile phone computer vision libraries capable of AR tracking. This allows consumer smartphones to provide a HHAR experience. Currently there are many different marker-based and markerless computer vision-tracking techniques running in real time on mobile phones (such as the Vuforia AR SDK). These allow mobile AR tracking from almost any surface, and facilitate a wide variety of interaction methods, such as using keypad or touch screen input.

In addition to computer vision-based mobile AR, many mobile phones have GPS and compass sensors in them that can provide an outdoor AR experience. Commercial AR browsers such as Layar, Wikitude, and Junaio show virtual tags on real-world points of interest.[2] Interaction in these applications is mostly limited to touching virtual tags to show more information about the point of interest, or using on-screen buttons. There is also ongoing research on how to improve outdoor AR experiences. For example, Langlotz and colleagues (2012) have developed a system that uses orientation tracking based on computer vision motion flow detection, which is initialized using data from a GPS sensor, and provides significantly improved tracking.

There has been ongoing research on suitable interaction methods for HHAR, but few guidelines for using these methods. In systems based around tethered LCD displays or PDAs, it is natural to use stylus or touch input, but there are other possibilities as well. In the AR-PAD project (Mogilev et al. 2002), buttons and a trackball are used as input in a face-to-face AR game. In Wagner's indoor navigation tool (Wagner and Schmalstieg

2003) user input is a combination of stylus interaction and visual tracking of markers in the environment.

Handheld AR applications also support interaction with AR content by interacting directly with the real world. In the *Invisible Train* (Wagner et al. 2005), the user moves a virtual train around a model of real train tracks, touching the PDA screen with a stylus to change the position of the tracks. In the AR-Kanji game (Wagner and Barakonyi 2003) the user looks through the PDA screen to view real cards that have Japanese language symbols on them. These can be manipulated by hand, and when the cards are seen, virtual models appear corresponding to the English translation of the characters.

The movement of the HHAR display itself can be used for input. In *Mosquito Hunt*, virtual mosquitoes are superimposed over a live camera image and simple motion flow techniques allow the user to shoot the mosquitoes by moving the phone.[3] Similarly, in the *Marble Revolution* game the player can steer a virtual marble through an on-screen graphical maze by moving the phone and using computer vision techniques for detecting the phone tilt.[4]

Effective interaction can also be performed by combining several methods together. Wither, DiVerdi, and Höllerer (2009) developed a system for in situ content creation in unprepared environments. Camera tracking and stylus input were used together to create new 2D and 3D content as well as manipulating existing content. Similarly, Kim, Gerhard, and Woo (2011) presented a method for modeling rooms and annotating locations on a phone. A user stood in a fixed position and measured the dimensions of a room by selecting edges of walls visible through the touch screen, and the system would quickly capture it using camera input.

As shown, there has been an evolution of HHAR systems from tethered displays to self-contained mobile phones with various on-board sensors. These systems support a variety of different interaction methods, from touch screen input, to using real-world objects. In the next section we discuss appropriate interface metaphors for handheld devices.

INTERFACE METHODS

There are several key differences between using a handheld AR interface and using a traditional HMD-based AR system:

- The HHAR display is handheld rather than headworn.
- The HHAR device affords a much greater peripheral view than an HMD.
- With a HHAR system, the display and input areas are connected and, with a touch screen device (e.g. iPhone), the display and input areas can be the same.
- HHAR applications are typically used for short periods of time, compared to HMD AR applications, where the AR view is always visible.

This means that interface metaphors developed for HMD based systems may not be appropriate for HHAR systems. For example, desktop AR applications often use a Tangible AR (TAR) metaphor (Kato et al. 2001) in which physical objects are used to manipulate virtual content. This works very well for HMD-based AR applications where the user can reach out and directly move the physical objects. However, TAR interfaces assume that the user has both hands free to manipulate physical input devices, which will not be the case with handheld systems. Appropriate handheld interface techniques would have to be used one-handed and rely on touch screen, keypad input, or device motion.

We have been exploring two interaction metaphors for handheld AR: handheld viewing and handheld manipulation. In handheld viewing (fig. 37.2) the device is used as a "Magic Lens" into the AR scene. Virtual content viewed on the display can be interacted with by touching the display with a stylus or finger. Interaction with the virtual content requires interacting with the handheld screen. This is the approach used in the *Invisible Train* and AR browser applications such as Layar. Touch screen resolution is high enough to support fine-scaled manipulation, and a variety of 3D user interface methods can be used to provide 3D object manipulation, although such methods are difficult to use while moving and sometimes fingers can hide part of the user interface.

Handheld manipulation techniques involve using the handheld device itself as a tangible input object, and its motion to interact with the AR content. First, the AR scene is viewed on the device screen and touch input used to select an object. Once a virtual object is selected, it is attached to the device and moved as the user moves the device (fig. 37.3). The position of the virtual object is fixed relative to the handheld screen. The small form factor of handheld devices allows an object-based approach to be used where input techniques are based around motion of the phone itself. In order to interact, the device can be moved relative to the real world instead of touching a screen. For

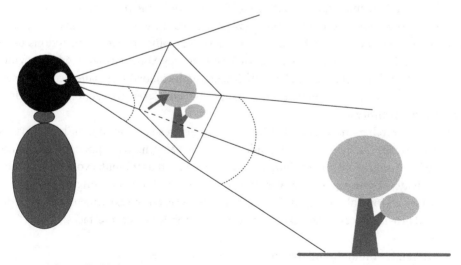

FIGURE 37.2 Handheld viewing metaphor.

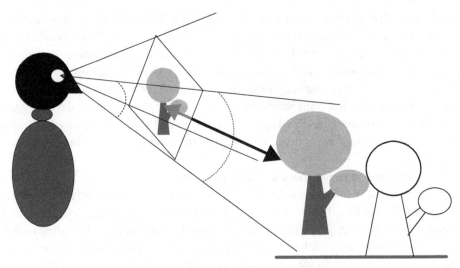

FIGURE 37.3 Handheld manipulation metaphor.

example, in the AR-PAD interface, a virtual object can be fixed relative to the screen and then positioned in the real world by moving the screen (Mogilev et al. 2002). Computer vision tracking is used to track the position of the device relative to the real world.

HANDHELD AR INTERFACE GUIDELINES

A number of human computer interaction (HCI) guidelines have been developed for non-AR handheld interfaces and interfaces in general. These are also useful for designing HHAR interfaces. Norman (1988) describes four principles of good practice: (1) ensure a high degree of visibility, (2) provide continuous clear feedback, (3) present a good conceptual model, and (4) offer good mappings between the actions users perform and the results they achieve. In a similar way Shneiderman (1997) provides "Eight Golden Rules of Interface Design," including the following: enable frequent users to use shortcuts, offer informative feedback, permit easy reversal of actions, and reduce short-term memory load.

Other researchers have provided interface guidelines specific to handheld devices. Apple produces Human Interface Guidelines for developing iOS applications, including the following: avoid screen clutter, minimize required user input, avoid unnecessary interactivity, express essential information succinctly, and provide a fingertip-sized target area for all controls.[5] Gong and Tarasewich (2004) examine existing interface guidelines and provide a set of practical design rules for mobile device interfaces:

- Design for multiple and dynamic contexts
- Design for small devices

- Design for limited and split attention
- Design for speed and recovery
- Allow for personalization
- Design for enjoyment

Researchers exploring interaction with 3D graphics and virtual reality scenes on mobile devices have also provided useful interface guidelines. For example, Mountain and colleagues (2005) use handheld devices for showing 3D city models and recommend using physical motion of the device itself to allow people to pan around the 3D virtual model. Users can hold their mobile phone in front of them and turn around to see the virtual reality content from different perspectives. It is also important that the virtual scene content is registered accurately with the user's location in the real world (Mountain and Liarokapis 2005).

People developing HHAR interfaces should follow these general interface guidelines, but there are also more specific guidelines that are useful. From the research presented in the related work section and our own experience with building handheld AR prototypes we apply the following guidelines:

1. *Provide an uncluttered AR view*: The handheld device can be used to provide an AR view of the real world, with virtual objects being attached to real-world locations. However, for this to be effective the AR view should be uncluttered, and most of it should be used to show a live camera view of the real world.
2. *Indicate the quality of sensor input*: HHAR typically involves computer vision-based tracking, or use of on-board sensors such as GPS and inertial compass to track the user's viewpoint. However, these sensors often have some errors, and showing how accurate the tracking is can improve the user experience.
3. *Match interface requirements to device ergonomics and the task at hand*: It is important to appropriately match how users are required to hold the handheld device with the task they are being asked to perform.
4. *Use natural physical motion as an input mechanism*: Handheld devices can be easily manipulated, so the device motion itself is a natural input mechanism. Turning the handheld screen to view AR content surrounding a user is very natural, as is having the interface automatically react to different device orientations.
5. *Combine AR and non-AR views in appropriate ways*: Use non-AR views to show information that is not 3D and doesn't need to be tagged to a real-world location or object. For example, a 2D text view can show more detailed information about a virtual object shown in the AR view.
6. *Use simple input*: Any required input should be usable when the user is moving with the device, and possibly engaged in other tasks. So simple touch input, or viewpoint-based interaction, is ideal.
7. *Minimize application delays*: Handheld devices typically have slower processors and simpler graphics hardware, while at the same time AR applications require

interactivity. Thus the application content should be optimized for real-time performance.

The way these guidelines could be applied can vary dramatically from application to application. In the next three sections we present several case studies of handheld AR interfaces showing how these guidelines are used in practice. The following case studies will be presented:

1. *AR Lego*: An example of using tangible AR interaction and device motion to interact with the virtual content.
2. *GeoBoids*: An outdoor AR game showing how several different interaction methods can be used at the same time in a handheld AR application.
3. *CityViewAR*: An outdoor AR application showing how AR and non-AR views can be combined in appropriate ways.

Table 37.1 shows which AR guidelines are followed in each of the applications.

Table 37.1 The AR Interface Guidelines Used in the Sample Applications

	AR Lego	GeoBoids	CityViewAR
1. Provide an uncluttered AR view	✓		✓
2. Indicate the quality of sensor input		✓	✓
3. Match interface to device ergonomics	✓	✓	✓
4. Use natural physical motion for input	✓	✓	✓
5. Combine AR and non-AR views appropriately		✓	✓
6. Use simple input	✓		✓
7. Minimize application delays	✓	✓	✓

CASE STUDY 1. *AR LEGO*: TANGIBLE AR INTERACTION

AR Lego was a mobile phone AR application designed to explore interaction techniques based around motion of the phone itself (Henrysson, Billinghurst, and Ollila 2005). It used a Symbian port of the *ARToolKit* computer vision library that allowed the position and orientation of the phone to be tracked relative to printed markers.[6] Nokia 6630 phones were used, and the application was able to run at 15 frames per second.

FIGURE 37.4 *AR Lego* application on the mobile phone.

A simple scene of virtual Lego bricks was shown on a set of AR tracking markers (fig. 37.4). Bricks were selected by positioning virtual crosshairs over them and then pressing the joypad button on the phone keyboard. Once selected, bricks could then be moved using a range of different positioning and rotation methods.

The following positioning methods were implemented:

- *A/Tangible:* When selected, the virtual object is held at a fixed position relative to the phone and moves when the user moves the phone.
- *B/Keypad:* The selected object is continuously translated in the X, Y, or Z directions depending on the phone keypad buttons pressed.

The following object rotation methods were implemented:

- *A/ArcBall:* When the phone moves, the relative motion of the phone is used as input into the arcball technique (Chen, Mountford, and Sellen 1988) to rotate the currently selected object.
- *B/Keypad:* The object rotates about its own axis according to phone keypad input. Left and right button input causes rotation left and right about the vertical axis, and so on.
- *C/Tangible:* The object is fixed relative to the phone and rotates when the user moves the phone.

As can be seen, the tangible input methods follow AR interface guidelines 1, 3, and 4 from the previous section: providing an uncluttered view, matching interface

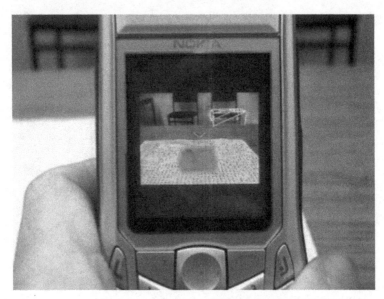

FIGURE 37.5 Moving a virtual object to a target wireframe on the mobile phone.

requirements to device ergonomics, and using natural physical motion as an input mechanism. Once the application was developed we conducted a simple experiment to explore how effective the handheld manipulation techniques were compared to other methods. We used a task in which a single block needed to be rotated or translated to fit into a wireframe target (fig. 37.5). Two user studies were conducted, one for different translation methods, and one for rotation methods, both using the same set of nine subjects (seven male and two female). For complete details see Henrysson, Billinghurst, and Ollila (2005).

In the translation task there was a significant difference in the time to position objects, with the tangible input method being the quickest. Positioning the object when fixed to the phone was almost twice as fast on average as using keypad input. Users thought that when the object was fixed to the phone it was easier to position the object correctly, but they could position the model more accurately with the keypad input.

For the rotation user study, there was also a significant difference in the time it took users to orient objects. However, this time, the arcball and keypad input conditions were on average twice as fast as using the tangible rotation condition. However, the subjects thought that the conditions were equally easy to use and enjoyable.

This result showed the importance of matching the AR interaction technique to the affordance of the handheld device (guideline 3). In this case the tangible manipulation method worked well for positioning virtual objects compared to keypad input, but not for rotating them. This is because once users start rotating the phone, they soon move it to the point where they can no longer see the screen, forcing them to repeatedly rotate it to get a large object rotation. In contrast, with keypad input they can just hold the device still while pressing a key to cause object rotation.

CASE STUDY
2. *GEOBOIDS*: SURROUND GAMING

GeoBoids is an Android game that illustrates how several interaction methods can be used at the same time in a mobile AR application. The game is designed to combine fast-paced, arcade-style action with large-scale physical user movement for exergaming. Virtual geometric creatures, GeoBoids (see fig. 37.6), can be seen on the player's phone, appearing around the player's physical location. The player's goal is to travel to those places identified on a map, and collect the GeoBoids.

Two main gameplay modes have been implemented: Field Mode and Arcade Mode. Field Mode play assumes the player is standing in a large open space. In this mode, the player sees a digital map of the local area, with locations of GeoBoid flocks displayed as overlays (fig. 37.7a). The player position is denoted by an oriented arrow, which is updated dynamically as the player moves around the physical world. An audible sonar "ping" is played using spatialized audio according to the distance and direction toward a GeoBoid flock, helping the player to find the nearest GeoBoid. Once the player is within range of a flock, play switches to the Arcade Mode.

As the player approaches a flock, the device changes to an AR view (fig. 37.7b), and the player enters the Arcade Mode. In this mode, the player is faced with waves of GeoBoids that they must capture within a set amount of time. Capturing a GeoBoid

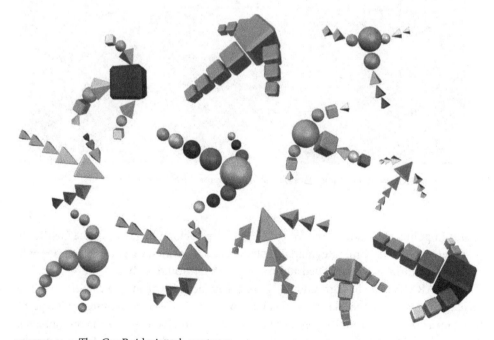

FIGURE 37.6 The GeoBoid virtual creatures.

(a)

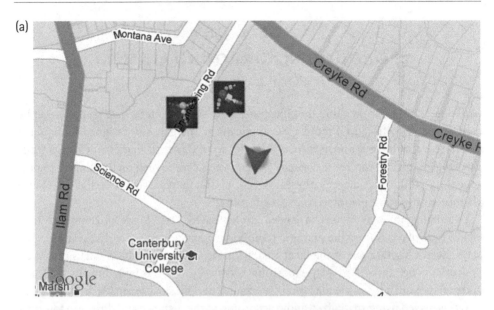

(b)

FIGURE 37.7A AND 37.7B (a) Field Mode map; (b) Arcade Mode view.

results in points and added time for the player. The flocking behavior of the GeoBoids is implemented from Craig Reynolds's OpenSteer code,[7] which we ported to the Google Android platform, and spatialized audio is supported through FMOD.[8]

In the AR view, the background image of the game is fed from the camera, and the virtual viewpoint of the player is matched to motion of the real camera viewpoint using measurements from the device sensors (accelerometer + gyro + magnetometer). As a result, the GeoBoids appear as if they are situated in the real world. Interestingly, although no image-based registration is done, feedback from user testing showed that players thought the GeoBoids were interacting with the environment.

The motion sensors are used to allow "point and shoot" interaction, with a swipe gesture used to capture the GeoBoid within the on-screen crosshairs. A continuously updating radar display shows the location of GeoBoids around the player, and an on-screen countdown timer is used to provide motivation for the player to capture all the GeoBoids as quickly as possible.

One of the unique game mechanics we incorporated in *GeoBoids* is the use of whistle input (fig. 37.8). Within the AR view, if the player whistles into the phone at the correct pitch and for longer than a minimum duration, the GeoBoids get scared. As a result, they flock more tightly, thereby making them easier to capture. A tracking bar at the right side of the AR view lets the players know if they are at the correct pitch.

The *GeoBoids* design followed several of the guidelines introduced above. We attempted to appropriately match how users would be required to hold the phone with the estimated duration of the task they were being asked to perform (guideline 3). For example, map view mode had the player hold the phone horizontal, matching its orientation with the 2D layout of the map. In AR view mode, however, we chose a handheld looking-glass approach, to better situate the GeoBoids in the real world. In addition, the AR view interaction was sporadic, with pauses after each level, allowing the player to rest his or her arms.

The AR view had a radar display showing the compass feedback (guideline 2) and the game also combined the AR view and a non-AR map view in an appropriate way (guideline 5). It is very natural to use a map view to guide users to a location and then switch

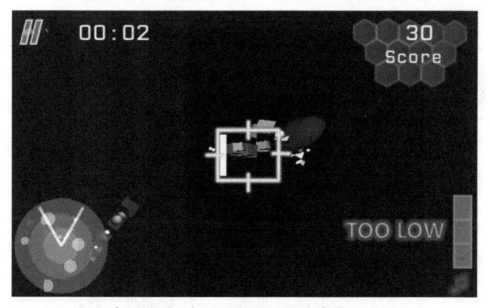

FIGURE 37.8 GeoBoids AR display elements showing whistle feedback.

Table 37.2 Results of Questionnaire (1 = fully disagree, 5 = fully agree)

Question	Rating response	
	Mean	Std. Dev.
I learned how to play the game pretty quickly.	4.75	0.463
Capturing GeoBoids was pretty easy.	4.38	0.916
The "swipe" gesture for capturing worked well for me.	4.13	1.126
The radar display was helpful for doing well in the game.	4.13	1.356
The graphical elements were attractive.	4.13	0.641
The "whistle" input was fun.	2.63	1.061
It was easy to understand the whistle meter.	2.50	0.756
Overall, I thought this game was fun.	4.13	0.641

to an AR view in the arcade mode. Finally, natural physical motion was used for input in the AR view, allowing players to move the display around themselves to search for GeoBoids (guideline 4). However, the visual interface was not as uncluttered as the *AR Lego* application, and also using a whistle input with swipe gestures is not as simple as it could have been.

In order to explore the usability of the interface we conducted a pilot test with eight participants. They were asked to play the game for 10–20 minutes, and to give feedback through a questionnaire on the design of the interface, input methods, and overall gameplay. The questionnaire included questions asking users to respond using a five-point scale (from 1 = fully disagree to 5 = fully agree), as well as those asking for free-form text about features they liked and improvements needed. Table 37.2 summarizes the results of the questionnaire rating questions.

The feedback from users was mostly positive on overall gameplay and the design of the user interface, while the results also revealed improvements that were needed for whistle interaction. In terms of the game features that they most liked, the participants mentioned the game being integrated with the real world, providing an AR-style gameplay environment, active movement involved in the gameplay to move and search for GeoBoids, and including new types of interaction such as whistle detection. The participants said that the features that needed improvement included the whistling not working well and making them tired, the GeoBoids not actively engaging with the player, and the visual appearance of *GeoBoids*. Some participants appeared unable to whistle, suggesting other types of input should be considered, such as blowing or shouting.

These results show how following good design principles can produce a HHAR experience that is easy to learn and enjoyable to use. The main area for improvement is in the use of whistling input, but this is also the area that the interface design departs most from the suggested guidelines by not providing simple input or matching the interface requirements to the task at hand.

Case Study 3. *CityViewAR*: Outdoor AR with POI

One of the main application areas in handheld AR is geographic information browsing. The *CityViewAR* application (fig. 37.9) is designed as an outdoor AR information browsing application for providing information related to buildings in Christchurch, New Zealand (Lee et al. 2012). Many buildings in the city were affected by earthquakes in September 2010 and February 2011, and over 900 of them have since been demolished. The goal of this application was to show the city as it was before the earthquakes hit and so enable people to remember the city as it was.

The application takes advantage of built-in phone sensors (e.g., GPS, electronic compass, and accelerometer) to provide information about the user's current location and viewing direction. *CityViewAR* shows geolocated information using different methods, including AR, a digital map, and a list view. Following guideline 5, each of the methods was used to show information in the most appropriate way.

In the AR view, virtual information is overlaid on a live camera background, so a virtual three-dimensional (3D) model of a demolished building can be shown on-site, as if it were still standing there. The application uses GPS sensor information for tracking geographical position of the device, and a compass for measuring the camera viewing direction. Sensor feedback is provided through a radar display that shows information around the user as small dots on concentric circles, so that the user can understand the relative locations of the points of interest (POI) in the real world.

FIGURE 37.9 *CityViewAR* application.

Users can tap on the virtual buildings in the AR scene, and a popup dialog will show a brief description of the selected building with some icons that link to more detailed image and text content (fig. 37.10). The popup dialog is shown at the bottom of the screen in a display-fixed manner, which makes it easier to read the text information, and prevents the AR view from becoming cluttered.

The same set of information can be viewed either on an interactive map view or in a list (see fig. 37.11). The user can interact with the map using touch gestures, such as swiping for translating and pinching for zooming. In addition to the user's location and orientation, the map view shows POI as icons on the map, which can be selected to access further text and picture content. The map view shares the same dialog as the AR view, providing a consistent user experience. The list view shows the POIs sorted in order of

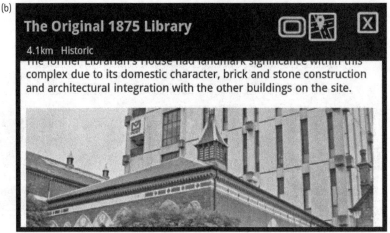

FIGURE 37.10A AND 37.10B Popup dialog showing the description of a selected virtual building (a) and detailed content of a building (b).

(a)

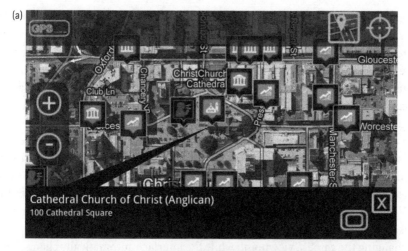

(b)

FIGURE 37.11A AND 37.11B Interactive map view (a) and list view (b).

distance from the user's current location. It provides an efficient way to search for a specific POI by name or by browsing the whole set of information.

While most of the user interaction is done with the touch screen interface, *CityViewAR* also changes the view based on the orientation of the device. In the map view, the user can change to the AR view by holding the device up for a couple of seconds with the camera looking above the horizon. In the AR view, if the user holds the device facing down for some duration, the application switches into map view. This allows users to easily change between views, even with one hand.

The *CityViewAR* application has information and 3D models of more than 110 buildings. Loading the whole set of models not only takes time at startup, but also results in low frame rate performance on the mobile device. To overcome this, *CityViewAR* only loads the 3D models closest to the user's location, ensuring the application runs at a high frame rate, and avoiding cluttering the AR view.

The *CityViewAR* application was developed based on the Google Android operating system, and it is executable on devices running Android 2.2 or later with the required sensors (camera, GPS, compass, and accelerometer). The map data is based on the Google Map service, and the 3D buildings are modeled and registered to the map using Google Sketch-up software. The POI information is stored in an SQLite database included in the application, and the 3D buildings are rendered using an in-house-developed outdoor AR library based on Android and OpenGL ES.

The *CityViewAR* application follows the interface guidelines provided earlier. The AR view is shown to provide 3D information, while map and list views are used to provide more detailed text and pictures. The AR view is uncluttered, with a radar view showing the location of all the virtual content, and requires only simple touch input for interaction. Visual cues are provided as to the accuracy of the GPS and where the user is facing. The user's motion in the real world is naturally mapped onto the virtual view information, changing the camera viewpoint; while the interface automatically changes between the AR view and map view depending on how the user holds the device. Finally, the content has been optimized to ensure no delays when running.

In order to evaluate how effective the AR component of the *CityViewAR* application was we conducted a small user study. Forty people used the software, 20 with the AR view enabled (AR group), and 20 with the AR interface being disabled (just using the map and list views). Subjects used the application on Android tablets in a city street where most of the buildings had been demolished. They were free to walk around the street exploring the building content. The time they took using each of the viewing modes was measured. We asked general usability questions, and used the Game Experience Questionnaire (GEQ) (IJsselsteijn, de Kort, and Poels n.d.), a tool developed to measure overall game experience, to capture feedback about the experience.

Overall, people found the application very easy to use in both AR and non-AR conditions. In the AR case, users on average gave a score of 7.8 on a Likert scale of 1 to 9, (where 1 = not very easy to use and 9 = very easy to use) while, in the non-AR case, people gave an average score of 7.3. See figure 37.12 for responses to the general usability questions. When specifically asked if they had any problem using the application, less than half of the participants reported any issues, and only 10 percent of the AR users said that they had trouble with the AR technology.

There was no significant difference between conditions in the distance traveled and time using the application. However, from the GEQ survey we found a small, though statistically significant difference in the overall experience between the people who used the *CityViewAR* application with and without the AR interface. The AR group judged their overall experience to be better than the non-AR users, showing that the AR components added to the user experience. In the condition with the AR view enabled, people used it more than half the time, and spent a quarter of their time with the map view and another quarter with the various information and picture views. The non-AR group spent a little bit more than half their time in the map view.

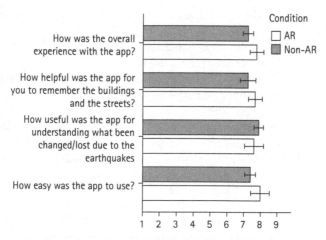

FIGURE 37.12 User feedback for the *CityViewAR* application, comparing AR and non-AR conditions.

Overall these results show that a well-designed HHAR interface can indeed improve the user experience. Full details of the user study and the application can be found in Lee et al. (2012).

Conclusion

In this chapter we have provided some suggested interface guidelines for handheld augmented reality applications and shown how these can be applied through several example case studies. As handheld AR becomes more and more common, it is important for researchers to share lessons learned in developing effective interfaces. This is an effort to provide some guidelines drawn from earlier related work and our own research and development. Handheld AR applications that follow these guidelines, such as the *GeoBoids* game or *CityViewAR* application, have been found to be easy to use. However more research needs to be done. As new devices are developed and alternative input methods arise, there will be an opportunity to explore new interaction metaphors and interface guidelines.

Notes

1. Vuforia AR SDK: http://www.qualcomm.com/solutions/augmented-reality/, accessed June 27, 2013.
2. Layer website, http://www.layar.com/, accessed January 2, 2012; Wikitude website, http://www.wikitude.com/, accessed January 2, 2012; Junaio website, http://www.junaio.com/, accessed January 2, 2012.

3. *Mosquito Hunt* website, https://www.icg.tugraz.at/~daniel/HistoryOfMobileAR/, accessed June 15, 2012.
4. *Marble Revolution* website, http://handheld.softpedia.com/get/Games/Arcade/Marble-Revolution-21182.shtml, accessed June 15, 2012.
5. Apple developer website, "iOS Developer Library," http://developer.apple.com/library/ios/#documentation/UserExperience/Conceptual/MobileHIG/Introduction/Introduction.html, accessed January 2, 2012.
6. ARToolKit website: http://www.hitl.washington.edu/artoolkit/, accessed June 27, 2013.
7. OpenSteer code, http://opensteer.sourceforge.net/, accessed January 2, 2012.
8. FMOD sound library website, http://www.fmod.org/, accessed June 15, 2012.

References

Azuma, Ron. 1997. A Survey of Augmented Reality. *Presence* 6 (4): 355–385.

Chen, M., S. Mountford, and A. Sellen. 1988. A Study in Interactive 3-D Rotation Using 2-D Control Devices. *Computer Graphics* 22 (4): 121–129.

Cutting, D., M. Assad, and A. Hudson. 2003. AR Phone: Accessible Augmented Reality in the Intelligent Environment. Paper presented at the Annual Conference of the Australian Computer-Human Interaction Special Interest Group (OZCHI 2003), November 26–28.

Fitzmaurice, G. 1993. Situated Information Spaces and Spatially Aware Palmtop Computers. *Communications of the ACM* 36 (7): 39–49.

Geiger, C., B. Kleinjohann, C. Reimann, and D. Stichling. 2001. Mobile AR4ALL. Paper presented to the Second IEEE and ACM International Symposium on Augmented Reality (ISAR 2001), October 29–30.

Gong, J., and P. Tarasewich. 2004. Guidelines for Handheld Mobile Device Interface Design. Paper presented to the Decision Sciences Institute Annual Meeting, 2004.

Henrysson, A., M. Billinghurst, and M. Ollila. 2005. Virtual Object Manipulation Using a Mobile Phone. Paper presented to the 2005 International Conference on Augmented Tele-existence (ICAT '05), December 5–8.

Henrysson, A., and M. Ollila. 2004. UMAR—Ubiquitous Mobile Augmented Reality. Paper presented to the Third International Conference on Mobile and Ubiquitous Multimedia (MUM2004), October 27–29.

Höllerer, T. 2004. User Interfaces for Mobile Augmented Reality Systems. Ph.D. diss., Columbia University.

IJsselsteijn, W. A., Y. A. W. de Kort, and K. Poels. n.d. The Game Experience Questionnaire: Development of a Self-Report Measure to Assess the Psychological Impact of Digital Games. http://www.citeulike.org/user/mjparnell/article/4934050. Accessed July 15, 2013.

Ingram, D., and J. Newman. 2001. Augmented Reality in a Wide Area Sentient Environment. Paper presented to the Second IEEE and ACM International Symposium on Augmented Reality (ISAR 2001), October 29–30.

Kato, H., M. Billinghurst, I. Poupyrev, N. Tetsutani, and K. Tachibana. 2001. Tangible Augmented Reality for Human Computer Interaction. Paper presented to Nicograph 2001.

Kim, H., R. Gerhard, and W. Woo. 2011. Interactive Annotation on Mobile Phones for Real and Virtual Space Registration. Paper presented to the IEEE and ACM International Symposium on Mixed and Augmented Reality (ISMAR 2011), October 26–29.

Langlotz, T., D. Wagner, A. Mulloni, and D. Schmalstieg. 2012. Online Creation of Panoramic Augmented Reality Annotations on Mobile Phones. *IEEE Pervasive Computing* 11 (2): 56–63.

Lee, G. A., A. Dunser, S. Kin, and M. Billinghurst. 2012. *CityViewAR*: A Mobile Outdoor AR Application for City Visualization. Paper presented to the International Symposium on Mixed and Augmented Reality (ISMAR 2012), November 5–8.

Moehring, M., C. Lessig, and O. Bimber. 2004. Video See-through AR on Consumer Cell Phones. Paper presented to the International Symposium on Augmented and Mixed Reality (ISMAR'04), November 5–8.

Mogilev, D., K. Kiyokawa, M. Billinghurst, and J. Pair. 2002. AR Pad: An Interface for Face-to-Face AR Collaboration. Paper presented to the ACM Conference on Human Factors in Computing Systems 2002 (CHI '02), April 20–25, 2002.

Mountain, D., and F. Liarokapis. 2005. Interacting with Virtual Reality Scenes on Mobile Devices. In *Proceedings of the 7th International Conference on Human Computer Interaction with Mobile Devices & Services (MobileHCI '05)*, 331–332. New York: ACM.

Mountain, D., F. Liarokapis, J. Raper, and V. Brujic-Okretic. 2005. Interacting with Virtual Reality Models on Mobile Devices. In *4th International Workshop on HCI in Mobile Guides*, Salzburg, September 19. New York: ACM.

Norman, D. 1988. *The Psychology of Everyday Things*. New York: Basic Books.

Rekimoto, J. 1996. TransVision: A Hand-Held Augmented Reality System for Collaborative Design. Paper presented to the Virtual Systems and Multi-Media (VSMM '96) conference, September 18–20.

Shneiderman, B. 1997. *Designing the User Interface*. Reading, MA: Addison Wesley.

Sutherland, I. 1965. The Ultimate Display. In *Information Processing: Proceedings of IFIP Congress*, 506–508. Amsterdam: North-Holland.

Wagner, D., and I. Barakonyi. 2003. Augmented Reality Kanji Learning. Paper presented to the IEEE and ACM International Symposium on Mixed and Augmented Reality (ISMAR 2003), October 7–10.

Wagner, D., T. Pintaric, F. Ledermann, and D. Schmalstieg. 2005. Towards Massively Multi-User Augmented Reality on Handheld Devices. Paper presented to the Third International Conference on Pervasive Computing, May 8–13.

Wagner, D., and D. Schmalstieg. 2003. First Steps towards Handheld Augmented Reality. Paper presented to the Seventh International Symposium on Wearable Computers (ISWC2003), October 21–23.

Wither, J., S. DiVerdi, and Tobias Höllerer. 2009. Annotation in Outdoor Augmented reality. *Computers & Graphics* 33 (6): 679–689.

CHAPTER 38

··

AVOIDABLE PITFALLS
IN VIRTUAL-WORLD
LEARNING DESIGN

··

KEYSHA I. GAMOR

A virtual world is a graphically rich, 3D immersive environment inhabited by avatars. Avatars are representations of the users who are interacting in the space. A virtual world inherently has the potential to provide a memorable experience for the users because of its characteristics and attributes, such as contextually authentic representations of events, places, spaces, objects, and experiences, as well as its social media capabilities, such as its chat and sharing tools; all necessary components for experiential learning. Virtual worlds are, therefore, ideal for training, education, meetings, conferences, workshops, and entertainment. They can also be used as analytical spaces, performance-based work environments, telework platforms, collaborative workspaces, and even sensory rich environments for simulations and what-if scenarios.

In the not so distant past, it was nearly impossible for most to conceive of a time when people across the globe would transcend space and time through social media tools like Facebook, Twitter, Flickr, and YouTube. Social media have been revolutionary in the way that we communicate, and in real time, share information, ideas, and points of view. Virtual worlds have the same "game changing" potential to transform the way in which social media connect us and the way work happens because they offer built-in social media and much more. In order for virtual-world projects to be successful, however, more purposeful thought should be invested into initial planning and design. This chapter discusses observations about common pitfalls to avoid when embarking upon a virtual-world design and implementation project.

Learning from the past, should, if nothing else, help us to avoid similar pitfalls already experienced. In the context of learning, there appear to be some common pitfalls between e-learning and virtual learning environments, such that some of the lessons learned in e-learning are directly applicable to immersive, virtual learning environments, like virtual worlds. In the early days of e-learning, proponents touted its many benefits: it could reduce training costs, provide convenient anytime/anywhere access, and offer engaging and repeatable learning opportunities, more efficient learning programs, reusable learning objects, superior and individualized learning content, and more. There have been mixed results over the years about the effectiveness of e-learning and the platforms used to deliver the content. From institutional to ethical issues, there are many lessons that could be gleaned from the growing history of this medium (Expertus, Inc. and Training Industry, Inc. 2010; Shachar and Neumann 2010; US Department of Education 2009). The continued evolution of virtual worlds, having the primary similarity of being online applications that can be used for informal and formal learning, could leapfrog some of the challenges seen in e-learning's past, if the lessons are recognized and applied. While virtual worlds, at a much earlier state in its evolution as MUDs (originally Multi User Dungeons, latterly Multi User Domains), have been around at least since 1978 (Jackson 2007), the most recent rush to jump on the virtual-world bandwagon without sufficient planning and research may result in more failed pilots, bankruptcy of vendor businesses, retarded adoption cycles, and possibly resignation to the notion that virtual worlds are fad technologies that will soon fade away. A 2008 press release, issued by the Gartner research firm, indicated that 9 out of 10 virtual-world programs are not successful within 18 months of launch because of the *failure to plan*. Planning is something we can all do, and the lack of planning should not be the primary reason for the failure of any project. The discussion in this chapter highlights the need for those in the industry to identify concrete requirements, discover and implement useful lessons learned, and select meaningful applications that will lead to an increase in successful implementations. The observation that virtual worlds have continued to survive and evolve, even when hardware and network limitations were among the most serious factors in its slow adoption, suggests that it is worth the planning efforts necessary to help ensure project success, and to continue to validate, not undermine this as a critical phase in the evolution of learning technology and pedagogy.

As alluded to earlier, there are some lessons from the e-learning life cycle and early discoveries in virtual-world implementation projects that may enable organizations to make better decisions about everything from procurement to maintenance, thus increasing the potential for more favorable outcomes. This chapter is not intended to be a step-by-step solution guide, but an outline of suggestions for an organization to take into account when considering a virtual-world project. Leveraging lessons gleaned from decades of experience with this technology, as well as some formal and informal research, this chapter highlights four common pitfalls relative to planning. This chapter should be read as a colleague's sidebar conversation with another colleague about similarities observed between the evolution of e-learning platforms and virtual-world platforms and common pitfalls to be aware of before embarking on a virtual-world project.

It is my position that a traditional instructional systems design model, with some modifications at the tactical level, can be relevant to designing learning experiences for virtual worlds. It would be difficult to argue that there is no need to conduct some type of Analysis; create some kind of overall Design; do some actual Development; start and complete the Implementation or delivery of a project or product; and Evaluate the process, outcomes, or other intended goal of a project or product (ADDIE). ADDIE is a systematic, traditional instructional systems design process model by definition, but it is also useful if thought of as a high-level construct through which to approach a particular problem or challenge. As the discussion in this chapter centers on extracting lessons learned from e-learning and applying them to virtual worlds, the phases of the ADDIE model will serve as an appropriate component of a virtual-world learning design framework. Even though ADDIE is also often referred to as a "production process" model, it is best applied as a high-level guide, with the substeps modified to suit a particular modality. ADDIE is a useful framework that (known by a variety of names across many domains) has been proven in many industries (architecture, software development, engineering, training design, etc.). Leveraging lessons learned and best practices obtained through research and experience in other learning contexts offers a different way of viewing and using ADDIE in virtual worlds. As this chapter focuses on the issue of the lack of planning—the reported reason that 90 percent of virtual-world projects fail—the common pitfalls that threaten the analysis phase of the ADDIE model is the scope of this chapter.

This chapter is written from the perspective of a question: "What were the shortcomings in planning that may have contributed to such an alarming failure rate of virtual-world learning design projects?" In attempting to answer this question, observations seem to suggest problems with initial analyses and assessments. With this awareness, a pattern emerges that resembles something familiar; some of these same problems were perceived in the early days of e-learning too. Since there appear to be similarities in the problems, could there be similarities in the solutions?

Indeed, the instructional value of virtual worlds is still in debate, more than likely pending outcomes of further empirical research and empirical indications of return on investment (ROI). However, early reports indicate that learners assert major shifts in the way they think, learn, and work when engaging in immersive virtual worlds (Bartle 2004; Dede 2007; Ketelhut 2007). Given the immersive nature of virtual worlds for interaction, experiential learning theory is ideal as a foundation for understanding the affordances of the immersive learning that happens in a virtual world. From John Dewey (1938) to David Kolb (1984), theorists have described experiential learning as educational events in which the participant's subjective experience is fundamental to the learning process. In this sense, it is not just about "what is presented," but about "how a learner interacts with the what." Equally important, it is also about how the learner applies the newly acquired knowledge to other experiences (Gamor 2011a; 2011b). When I used the term 'virtuality' in my pre-doctoral work and doctoral dissertation (2001, Gamor), I was struggling to find a meaningful expression to describe how and where I had been spending time applying my ideas and conducting my research. Using the popular jargon of the time did not seem to capture the qualitative *essence* of my experience. Somehow, using "computer-aided learning" or "computer-based learning" didn't encompass all that the virtual experience afforded me. I realized that I had been to *and in* a place that was as real to me as the cushioned, black mesh chair I sat on inside my home office, and I quickly came to realize that this virtual experience was more than computer-aided; it was a type or extension of reality—hence, like Sherry Turkle (1996), I began to call this state 'virtuality'. Moreover, virtuality, to me, is a type of synthetic, digital, liquid reality that I believe could, should, and will become part of our every day physical reality for any extension of our day-to-day tasks, including meaningful work. Virtuality provides a level of personal experience that is encoded in the memory and can be called upon as needed, just like those experienced in physical life. Whereas physical access can often be a formidable impediment, virtuality can be a very real and powerful means to overcoming such obstacles in order to create experiences that are just as tangible.

Personal experience is memorable, meaningful, and unique to the individual. An individual constructs meaning and knowledge from experiences; the meaning and knowledge gained are accessible for reflection, sharing, or transfer to other situations, contexts, or experiences (Jonassen et al. 1991; Kolb 1984). Virtual worlds enable this sort of interaction and cognition no matter the intended purpose—activities, courses, meetings, conferences, or other. In the final analysis, it is imperative that virtual worlds be used to solve communication, training, or education problems that could benefit from experiential learning and constructivist learning theories.

This chapter, organized in terms of "pitfalls," discusses four common mistakes to avoid during phase 1, the analysis phase of a virtual-world project. The pitfalls to watch out for begin with the front-end analysis. It is imperative to understand what types of challenges or motivations are behind any virtual-world project; therefore, project planners should avoid the temptation of omitting the front-end analysis. While this might be seen as a costly task, a common misconception in the early days of e-learning, a solid front-end analysis can save exponentially more money in the long run. Examining pitfall 1 more closely will help us extract the lesson learned from the older technology and apply it to the new.

PITFALL 1: OMITTING THE FRONT-END ANALYSIS

The temptation with virtual worlds, as with their predecessors and other learning technologies, is to be so enamored and preoccupied with the technology itself that focus is diverted from the criticality of identifying the instructional strategy requirement(s) that the technology must support. Being distracted and overly consumed with the virtual worlds' user interfaces, attributes of objects, or other features has also impeded growth in the development of pedagogically sound and unique (tool-specific) applications of this technology. While these practices are important from a user-interaction/experience perspective in order to understand the affordances of the tool set, the way in which the learning experience is constructed and organized must move to the forefront of our focus. The technology is the enabler, just as it was with e-learning applications (compact discs [CDs], web-based training [WBT], learning management systems [LMSs], learning content management systems [LCMSs], content management systems [CMSs], etc.), and a virtual world, after all, is a technology that "should" enhance, improve, extend, transform, and transfer the learning "intervention" from a unique event to a persistent experience with implications that impact upon the way in which users learn and work (Holden et al. 2010). This may seem a large task for this technology; however, if this tool does not fill a gap in our existing toolkit, then these questions have to be asked: "Why use it? What niche can virtual worlds fill?"

Digging deeper, we should examine pedagogies that are appropriate for this 3D immersive tool, rather than simply apply the same strategies from e-learning to immersive learning. The early days of e-learning, when people simply dumped instructor-led training content onto compact discs, courseware screens, or web pages, are well documented in the literature. We had what the industry calls "glorified page turners," and learners were bored and disengaged. Student completion rates were abysmal. A virtual world, as an immersive learning environment, has attributes that foster collaboration through experience—that is, experience with the environment (interactive), experience with other people (collaborative), and experience with authentic contexts (immersive). Thankfully, none of these concepts applied in a learning context are new; therefore, as discussed earlier, sound learning theory is available to consult for understanding how best to begin applying and testing the efficacy of this tool, and how best to effectively plan before embarking on an implementation project.

In addition to being experiential learning environments, it is evident that virtual worlds, as multimedia learning tools, also embody the elements of constructivist learning environments. Many researchers note that constructivist learning environments offer experiences and interactions with which learners create their own interpretations and perceptions (Dabbagh 2008; Dede 2005; Delwiche 2003; Nelson et al. 2007; Walker 2009). Experiences and interactions are embedded within authentic contexts that provide learners the opportunity to construct knowledge from multiple perspectives and authentic situations (Dabbagh 2008; Jonassen et al. 1991; Rheingold 1991). David Jonassen and colleagues (1994), leaders in constructivist theory and methods, point out that social and cognitive constructivism have significant implications for instructional design that can be applied to virtual worlds as constructivist learning environments. It is, therefore, logical to consult constructivist learning theory when considering virtual worlds. If parallels between the tenets of this theory and identified project goals exist, a closer look at virtual worlds as a potential addition to one's technology toolkit makes sense.

Given that the primary reason for the failure of most virtual-world implementations is directly attributable to a failure to plan, it is important to start with a thorough analysis of the requirements, relevant theories, and sound strategies that would ensure that a virtual-world project will have a chance at being successful. Part of this thorough analysis should also include an examination of the solutions that may address the needs that are identified during the analysis phase. In other words, if a virtual world appears to be part of a potential solution, then the analysis conducted during the initial planning phase should indicate and reinforce that. It is best for the requirements to drive tool selection, rather than the other way around.

Omitting the front-end analysis should not be an option. The front-end analysis yields critical information that will affect a project on through to its success or failure. When the project succeeds, it will be clear what information led to good decisions and good outcomes, and if the project fails, the gaps in the analysis will be evident. Understanding the unique benefits of the tool is one benefit of a thorough front-end analysis. It is during a survey of the potential solutions and their affordances that sound decisions are made about tool selection. This is also the subject of another common pitfall to avoid.

PITFALL 2: FAILING TO RECOGNIZE THE UNIQUE AFFORDANCES OF VIRTUAL LEARNING ENVIRONMENTS (VLES)

In the e-learning arena, we can observe that some design approaches are better than others for specific learning, communication, or training purposes. Using an online textbook as part of an e-learning implementation may provide the desired information, for example, but may not offer the desired experience. Similarly, rote memorization activities or lectures could be applied in a virtual world and could communicate the desired information, but it is not the best use of the tool and will not yield the desired experience. Failing to recognize the unique affordances of potential instructional technologies will result in disappointing design strategies that do not exploit the benefits of those technologies.

Virtual-world applications are particularly useful "when learners need to gain high-level skills (e.g., in Bloom's taxonomy: application, analysis, synthesis, and evaluation) in order to perform critical job functions (e.g., develop sales strategies to meet clients' unique requirements)" (Whiteside 2002, 9). Virtual worlds, by design, are immersive and constructivist; therefore, they are intrinsically challenging, realistic, authentic, meaningful, and motivating (Affiliated Computer Services 2009; Calongne 2008; Dede 2007; Gamor 2001; Gao et al. 2008).

There are six features most virtual worlds have in common (O'Driscoll 2009; Federation of American Scientists 2009; Virtual World Review 2009). The benefits of virtual worlds as a teaching and learning medium are valuable for both the individual learner and groups, as illustrated in table 38.1 (Gamor 2010).

Understanding the attributes is just a start. It is also important to be aware of the various manifestations of the attributes in-world. As shown in table 38.2, "the concept of immersion in virtual worlds is achieved through the six common characteristics which have different in-world representations" (Gamor 2010, 182).

Table 38.1 Virtual-World Affordances and Their Benefits for Individuals and Groups

O'Driscoll's affordances of virtual worlds	Individual-focused benefit	Group-focused benefit
Cocreation	Fosters peer-to-peer support and tutoring	Fosters multiuser content development or modification
Coexistence	Enlivens communication and interaction; blurs the line of distance	Enables multiuser simultaneous interaction in a shared environment
Collaboration	Enables users to self-select groups based upon goals or needs	Encourages users to develop peer, affinity, skill, interest, and/or groups
Graphic user interface (GUI)	Offers visual context of environment and other inhabitants	Offers visual context of environment and other inhabitants
Persistence	Maintains 24/7 existence; provides convenient access	Enables progress and change to take place regardless of individual log-in status; helps close the distance/time gap
Presence	Defines distance; provides situated context	Minimizes feelings of "disconnectedness"

Table 38.2 Affordances of Virtual Worlds and Their In-World Representations

O'Driscoll's affordances of virtual worlds	Representation of affordances in virtual worlds
Cocreation	Materializes through building concepts, objects, and other creations together
Coexistence	Emerges through occupying space with other participants at the same time
Collaboration	Exists through sharing ideas, thoughts, and work products synchronously and asynchronously, constructing a potentially endless feedback/interaction loop
Graphic user interface (GUI)	Appears through a representation that illustrates the key elements of the authentic context(s) necessary to create a feeling of "being there"
Persistence	Manifests through preservation of ideas, thoughts, work products, and other objects
Presence	Appears as the capability to engage in real-time interaction with others who are in world

Awareness of these characteristics is critical in analyzing the value of virtual worlds relative to project requirements and, subsequently, in determining how best to incorporate virtual worlds into your organization's toolkit.

In addition to offering the basic affordances of virtual worlds, most platforms are designed for a particular target audience or offer enhanced capabilities of the basic, common features. Thoroughly examining the characteristics of potential solutions sets is critical, for selecting the wrong tool for given requirements could result in undesired outcomes. It is this assessment that must take place during the initial planning phase and that is so often excluded.

Being aware of a technology's strengths is essential, but knowing its weaknesses is equally significant. The awareness of strengths and weaknesses paves the way toward meaningful applications, which leads to yet another pitfall to avoid.

PITFALL 3: REPURPOSING VERSUS RE-ENGINEERING CONTENT

There is likely plenty of thought and discussion about repurposing e-learning course content in the newly acquired virtual worlds. Many applications are using the evolution of the virtual world as a new way to do the same activities. In other words, a good number of current implementations are using a 3D environment to do what could be done in a 2D environment, leaving the question: Why bother?

Early lessons learned in designing learning for virtual worlds indicate outcomes similar to that of transitioning instructor-led content to e-learning platforms. Industry experience has proved that it is not useful merely to post content from a face-to-face course into an e-learning interface. Likewise, early lessons continue to underscore that it is not the best use of a virtual world to do only things that can be done in a 2D environment, such as posting lectures, presentation slides, and audio clips.

While the unidirectional content need not be discarded, it must be re-engineered to fit within the new environment. This means that, instead of asking participants to view a collection of photos, they could be asked to participate in a 3D guided tour or map out a guided tour based on their own research. Rather than merely look at a diagram, participants could build a map, model, or other graphical representation instead. In place of a lecture-based experience, participants could engage in a hands-on, experiential, narrative experience, like a 3D quest.

In order to plan such experiences, it is necessary to know what instructional strategies are appropriate for virtual worlds. Re-engineering existing instructional strategies for an immersive environment begins with modifying them into active, creative, collaborative strategies. Doing stimulating, unique things in virtual worlds is exactly the selling point. They offer us a way to do things we could otherwise not do as easily, or could not do at all. While this is, indeed, an exciting conundrum to have, it also leads to another potential pitfall: the tendency to oversell.

PITFALL 4: NOT CONTAINING EXPECTATIONS ON WHAT VLES CAN ACCOMPLISH

One of the most critical errors in the early days of e-learning was overselling what e-learning could do. It was commonly believed that someday e-learning would replace all training and would yield tremendous cost savings to organizations. Closer to reality, e-learning has supplemented instructor-led training and provided some cost savings. E-learning is not appropriate for all learning needs, and e-learning has its own costs— from conception through maintenance. Likewise, especially in instances of economic downturns, virtual worlds have been pinpointed as *the* way we will communicate and collaborate in the future. It is doubtful that virtual worlds will supplant either face-to-face or e-learning constructs, but rather augment them when the unique affordances of virtual worlds can be of worthwhile benefit. Virtual worlds are great for specific needs and have their own life-cycle costs that must also be considered.

In keeping with constructivist theory, virtual worlds facilitate a learner-centered approach instead of an instructor-centered approach. Participants maintain a good deal of control over how to navigate through the graphically and contextually rich learning experience. Participants may also report a sense of comfort that many, if not all, the same collaboration tools they have become accustomed to in the real world are available in-world. This, however, does not suggest that the virtual world be void of guidance. While there are many paths to the goal, a clear goal must be communicated to participants, and there should always be in-world objects that, as needed, help the participant to reach the goal.

That being said, a virtual world's value comprises a combination of how it is designed and the efforts of the participants. By their nature, virtual worlds foster higher-order thinking skills, but the in-world objects have to support the desired skill level. Observations of failed virtual-world implementations reveal that many virtual-world designers have posted traditional, static content in-world and wondered why it fell flat. The environments were built, but no one came, or they came once and did not return. The attributes of a virtual world are all about possibilities. Virtual worlds offer the *possibility* of improved collaboration, enhanced opportunities for cocreation, heightened awareness of coexistence, a strong sense of presence, empowerment through persistence, and engagement through rich GUI. This is all true for virtual worlds only if they are specifically designed to exploit the possibilities.

The bottom line is this: a virtual world, as a technology, can be customized to challenge participants with anything from concept familiarization to procedural practice, and many other applications in between. Virtual worlds can be used for assessment pur-poses as well. In this case, performance-based assessments should be designed with a peer-support aspect (Chin and Williams 2006; Jonassen 2000; Merrill 2007). Indeed, "problem finding is central to problem solving" (Dede 2007), and virtual worlds provide a multisensory, immersive, graphically rich way to communicate, collaborate, coexist, and cocreate (Gamor 2011c).

While most projects remain in their pilot phases, virtual worlds are still being explored in education, business, and military settings (for the latter, see Smith, chapter 40 this volume). Given the added benefit of cost savings, virtual worlds are being considered for semiregular use for events, such as conferences or meetings. Such requirements may usher in new pricing structures beyond those that are currently avail-able. Since procurement of a virtual world is not a cheap proposition when you take into account the full life cycle of the technology and the requirements associated with it, it is clear that cost savings alone may not be a sufficient justification for investing in virtual worlds for an organization. However, when coupling cost avoidance with other benefits of virtual worlds, a long-term, strategic vision for the potential of this technol-ogy emerges, one that enables educators and trainers to foster the development of more agile participants and employees, more intuitive interactions, and more effective com-munication—whether in business or education. It is these carefully developed benefits that must be clearly and succinctly presented during the initial planning phase, and with pros and cons, couched in such a way that they adequately contain the expectations of the virtual-world stakeholders.

Conclusion

Virtual worlds are not the answer to *all* training, education, business, collaboration, and analytical problems. They simply offer another dimension to the way we could possibly work. There are some early indications of benefits, but the research is yet incomplete. What we can say is this: based upon what we know about e-learning, experiential learn-ing, and constructivist learning theories, we have reasonable expectations for what vir-tual worlds will afford us. This must also be tempered by the notion that cultural and social shifts are also required in order for virtual-world projects to meet with success.

Embarking on a virtual-world implementation project is not something to jump into without careful planning. It is important to align projects' goals with the strategic plan of the organization or course curriculum. The tool itself should never be put ahead of the requirements, in the same way that the proverbial cart should not come before the horse. A well-conceived virtual-world implementation plan could result in a long-term return on investment, as virtual worlds are scalable to grow with an organization's needs at a manageable pace.

The four pitfalls presented in this chapter provide but a few common mistakes to avoid and identify some critical issues organizations should investigate before starting a

procurement process to obtain a virtual world. If a thorough analysis indicates a requirement for this technology, then immersive learning environments have the ability to provide a whole new dimension, indeed, to open a whole new world to an organization.

References

Affiliated Computer Services. 2009. *3D Learning and Virtual Worlds*. Dallas: Author.

Bartle, R. R. 2004. *Designing Virtual Worlds*. Indianapolis, IN: New Riders Publishing.

Calongne, C. M. 2008. Educational Frontiers: Learning in a Virtual World. *Educause Review*
43 (5). http://www.educause.edu/EDUCAUSE+ReviewEDUCAUSEReviewMagazineVol
ume43/EducationalFrontiersLearningin/163163. Accessed April 2, 2009.

Chin, S. T., and J. B. Williams. 2006. A Theoretical Framework for Effective Online Course
Design. *Journal of Online Learning and Teaching* 2 (1). http://jolt.merlot.org/05007.htm.
Accessed January 3, 2009.

Dabbagh, N. 2008. Select Instructional Models/Theories to Develop Instructional Prototypes.
Instructional Design Knowledge Base, Graduate School of Education, George Mason
University, Fairfax, VA. http://classweb.gmu.edu/ndabbagh/Resources/IDKB/models_
theories.htm. Accessed December 3, 2008.

Dede, C. J. 2005. Planning for "Neomillennial" Learning Styles: Implications for Investments
in Technology and Faculty. In *Educating the Net Generation*, edited by J. Oblinger and D.
Oblinger, 226–247. Boulder, CO: Educause Publishers. http://net.educause.edu/ir/library/
pdf/pub71010.pdf. Accessed March 2, 2012.

Dede, C. J. 2007. Reinventing the Role of Information and Communications Technologies in
Education. *Yearbook of the National Society for the Study of Education* 106: 11–38.

Delwiche, A. 2003. MMORPG's in the college classroom. The state of play: Law, games and
virtual worlds. New York Law School. http://www.nyls.edu/user_files/1/3/4/17/49/Delwiche.
pdf. Accessed November 2, 2009.

Dewey, J. 1938. *Experience and Education*. New York: Macmillan.

Expertus, Inc. and Training Industry, Inc. 2010. The State of LMS Report. http://www.
trainingindustry.com/media/3314559/the%20state%20of%20lms%20report.pdf. Accessed
April 3, 2011.

Federation of American Scientists. FAS Virtual Worlds Whitepaper. http://vworld.fas.org/
wiki/FAS_Virtual_Worlds_Whitepaper. Accessed March 20, 2009.

Gartner, Inc. 2008. Gartner Says 90 Per Cent of Corporate Virtual World Projects Fail within
18 Months. Press release. http://www.gartner.com/it/page.jsp?id=670507. Accessed March
20, 2009.

Gamor, K. I. 2001. *Moving virtuality into reality: A comparison study of the effectiveness of
traditional and alternative assessments of learning in a multisensory, fully immersive VR
physics program*. Unpublished Doctoral dissertation, George Mason University, Fairfax, VA.

Gamor, K. I. 2010. Adopting Virtual Worlds in ADL: The Criticality of Analysis. In *Learning
on Demand: ADL and the Future of E-Learning*, edited by Bob Wisher and Badrul Khan,
177–194. Alexandria, VA: ADL.

Gamor, K. I. 2011a. Exploiting the Power of Persistence in Virtual Worlds. In *User Interface
Design for Virtual Environments: Challenges and Advances*, edited by Badrul Khan, 142–155.
Washington, DC: IGI Global.

Gamor, K. I. 2011b. Signs and Guideposts: Expanding the Course Paradigm with Virtual Worlds. In *Multi-user Virtual Environments for the Classroom: Practical Approaches to Teaching in Virtual Worlds*, edited by Giovanni Vincenti and James Braman, 86–99. Hershey, PA: IGI Global.

Gamor, K. I. 2011c. What's in an Avatar? Identity, Behavior, and Integrity in Virtual Worlds for Educational and Business Communication. In *Handbook of Human Factors in Web Design*, 2nd edition, edited by Robert Proctor and Kim Vu, 739–749. New York: CRC Press.

Gao, F. J. M. N., and M. J. Koehler. 2008. Comparing Student Interactions in *Second Life* and Face-to-Face Role-Playing Activities. In *Proceedings of Society for Information Technology and Teacher Education International Conference*, edited by K. McFerrin, R. Weber, R. Carlsen, and D. A. Willis, 2033–2035. Chesapeake, MD: AACE.

Holden, J. T., P. J. L. Westfall, and K. I. Gamor. 2010. *An Instructional Media Selection Guide for Distance Learning: Implications for Blended Learning and Virtual Worlds*. 6th edition. Boston: USDLA.

Jackson, P. 2007. The Real Business of Virtual Worlds: Firms Creating New Virtual Worlds Must Balance Real Revenues with High Risks. March 23. Forrester Research, Cambridge, MA. http://www.forrester.com/Research/PDF/0,,44748,00.pdf. Accessed May 3, 2009.

Jonassen, D. H. 2000. Toward a Meta-theory of Problem Solving. *Educational Technology: Research and Development* 48 (4): 63–85.

Jonassen, D. H., J. Campbell, and M. Davidson. 1994. Learning with Media: Restructuring the Debate. *Educational Technology Research and Development* 42: 31–39.

Jonassen, D. H., R. S. Grabinger, and N. D. C. Harris, 1991. Instructional Strategies and Tactics. *Performance Improvement Quarterly* 3: 29–47.

Ketelhut, D. J. 2007. The Impact of Student Self-Efficacy on Scientific Inquiry Skills: An Exploratory Investigation in *River City*, a Multi-user Virtual Environment. *Journal of Science Education and Technology* 16 (1): 99–111.

Kolb, D. A. 1984. *Experiential Learning: Experience as the Source of Learning and Development*. Englewood Cliffs, NJ: Prentice Hall.

Merrill, M. D. 2007. A Task-Centered Instructional Strategy. *Journal of Research on Technology in Education* 40 (1): 5–22.

Nelson, B. C., D. J. Ketelhut, J. Clarke, E. Dieterle, C. J. Dede, and B. E. Erlandson. 2007. Robust Design Strategies for Scaling Educational Innovations: The *River City* MUVE Case Study. In *The Educational Design and Use of Simulation Computer Games in Education*, edited by B. E. Shelton and D. A. Wiley, 209–231. Rotterdam: Sense Press.

O'Driscoll, T. 2009. Attributes of Virtual Worlds. *Wadda Tripp Blog*. http://wadatripp. wordpress.com/2009/03/. Accessed March 15, 2009.

Rheingold, H. 1991. *Virtual Reality*. New York: Summit Books.

Shachar, M., and Y. Neumann. 2010. Twenty Years of Research on the Academic Performance Differences between Traditional and Distance Learning: Summative Meta-analysis and Trend Examination. *Merlot Journal of Online Learning and Teaching* 6 (2). http://jolt.merlot. org/vol6no2/shachar_0610.pdf. Accessed March 12, 2012.

Turkle, S. 1996. Virtuality and Its Discontents. *The American Prospect*. http://web.mit. edu/sturkle/www/pdfsforstwebpage/ST_Virtuality%20and%20its%20discontents.pdf. Accessed January 24, 2012.

US Department of Education, Office of Planning, Evaluation, and Policy Development. 2009. Evaluation of Evidence-Based Practices in Online Learning: A Meta-analysis and Review of Online LEARNING studies. http://www.ed.gov/rschstat/eval/tech/evidence-based-practices/finalreport.pdf. Accessed on July 12, 2010.

Virtual World Review. *What Is a Virtual World?* http://www.virtualworldsreview.com/info/whatis.shtml. Accessed April 6, 2009.

Walker, V. L. 2009. 3D Virtual Learning in Counselor Education: Using *Second Life* in Counselor Skill Development. *Journal of Virtual Worlds Research* 2: 13–14.

Whiteside, A. 2002. Beyond Interactivity: Immersive Web-Based Learning Experiences. *eLearning Developers' Journal* 3, September 4. http://www.elearningguild.com/pdf/2/090402des-h.pdf. Accessed April 6, 2009.

Further Reading

Bransford, John D., Ann L. Brown, and Rodney C. Cocking. 1999. *How People Learn: Brain, Mind, Experience, and School.* Washington, DC: National Academy Press.

Castronova, Edward. 2007. *Exodus to the Virtual World: How Online Fun Is Changing Reality.* New York: Palgrave McMillan.

Clarke, Jody, Christopher J. Dede, and Edward Dieterle. 2008. Emerging Technologies for Collaborative, Mediated, Immersive Learning. In *The International Handbook of Technology in Education* edited by J. Voogtand and G. Knezek, 901–909. New York: Springer-Verlag.

Khan, Badrul H. 2005. *Managing e-Learning: Design, Delivery, Implementation and Evaluation.* London: Information Science Publishing.

Kolb, David A., Richard E. Boyatzis, and Charalampos Mainemelis. 2000. Experiential Learning Theory: Previous Research and New Directions. In *Perspectives on Cognitive, Learning, and Thinking Styles*, edited by R. J. Sternberg and L. F. Zhang. Mahwah, NJ: Lawrence Erlbaum. http://science5.net/e/experiential-learning-theory-w1629.html. Accessed November 8, 2013.

CHAPTER 39

MEDICAL CLINICAL USES OF VIRTUAL WORLDS

GIUSEPPE RIVA

As noted by Satava and Jones more than a decade ago (Satava and Jones 2002), the advantages of virtuality to healthcare can be summarized in a single word: revolutionary. Since the development of methods of electronic communication, clinicians have been using information and communication technologies in healthcare: telegraphy, telephony, radio, and television have been used for distance medicine since the mid-nineteenth century (Wootton 1999). However, the possible impact of virtual reality (VR) on healthcare is even higher than the one offered by the new communication technologies (Gorini et al. 2008). In fact, VR is at the same time a technology, a communication interface, and an experience (Riva 2002).

This is why the research in the virtual reality field is moving fast. If we check the two leading clinical databases—MEDLINE and PSYCINFO—using the "virtual reality" keyword we can find 4,442 papers listed in MEDLINE and 5,120 in PSYCINFO (all fields query, accessed July 29, 2013).

From the analysis of the retrieved papers we can find that the first healthcare applications of VR started in the early 1990s because of the need of medical staff to visualize complex medical data, particularly for surgery planning and during surgery itself. Actually, surgery-related applications of VR fall mainly into three classes: surgery training, surgery planning, and augmented reality for surgery sessions in open surgery, endoscopy, and radiosurgery. A couple of years later, the scope of VR applications in medicine has broadened to include neuropsychological assessment and rehabilitation (Riva, Wiederhold, and Molinari 1998; Riva 1997b).

In this chapter I outline the current state of research and technology that is relevant to the development of VR applications in medicine. Moreover, I discuss the clinical principles, technological devices, and safety issues associated with the use of VWs in medicine.

VIRTUAL WORLDS IN HEALTHCARE

The Two Faces of VR in Healthcare

For many healthcare professionals, VR is first of all a technology. Since 1986, when Jaron Lanier used the term for the first time, VR has been usually described as a collection of technological devices: a computer capable of interactive 3D visualization, a head-mounted display, and data gloves equipped with one or more position trackers. The trackers sense the position and orientation of the user and report that information to the computer that updates (in real time) the images for display.

However, the analysis of different VR applications clearly shows that the focus on technological devices is different according to the goals of the healthcare provider.

For instance, Rubino and colleagues (2002), McCloy and Stone (2001), and Székely and Satava (1999, 1305) in their reviews share the same vision of VR: "a collection of technologies that allow people to interact efficiently with 3D computerized databases in real time using their natural senses and skills" (McCloy and Stone 2001, 913). This definition lacks any reference to head-mounted displays and instrumented clothing such as gloves or suits. In fact, less than 20 percent of VR healthcare applications in medicine are actually using any such immersive equipment.

However, if we shift our attention to behavioral sciences, where immersive devices are used by more than 50 percent of the applications, VR is described as "an advanced form of human-computer interface that allows the user to interact with and become immersed in a computer-generated environment in a naturalistic fashion" (Schultheis and Rizzo 2001, 82). In fact, to achieve the feeling of "being there" the VR applications use specialized devices such as head-mounted displays, tracking systems, earphones, gloves, and sometimes haptic-feedback devices (Riva 2005).

These two definitions underline two different visions of VR. For physicians and surgeons, the ultimate goal of VR is the presentation of virtual objects to all of the human senses in a way identical to their natural counterpart (Székely and Satava 1999). As noted by Satava and Jones (2002), as more and more of the medical technologies become information-based, it will be possible to represent a patient with higher fidelity to a point that the image may become a surrogate for the patient—the *medical avatar*. In this sense, an effective VR system should offer real-like body parts or avatars that interact with external devices such as surgical instruments as near as possible to their real models. From a practical viewpoint, this medical avatar could be used both for learning and training, and for improving the assessment and treatment of actual patients.

For clinical psychologists and rehabilitation specialists the ultimate goal is radically different (Rizzo et al. 1998). They use VR to provide a new human-computer interaction paradigm in which users are no longer simply external observers of images on a computer screen but are active participants within a computer-generated three-dimensional virtual world. Within the virtual environment (VE) the patient has the possibility of learning to manage a problematic situation related to his or her disturbance (see below). The key characteristics of VEs for these professionals are both the high level of control of interaction with the tool without the constraints usually found in computer systems, and the enriched experience provided to the patient (Parsons and Rizzo 2008). VEs are highly flexible and programmable. They enable the therapist to present a wide variety of controlled stimuli, such as a fearful situation, and to measure and monitor a wide variety of responses made by the user (Repetto and Riva 2011). This flexibility can be used to provide systematic restorative training that optimizes the degree of transfer of training or generalization of learning to the person's real-world environment (Saposnik and Levin 2011).

Moreover, virtual reality systems open the input channel to the full range of human gestures: in rehabilitation it is possible to monitor movements or actions from any body part or many body parts at the same time. On the other side, with disabled patients, feedback and prompts can be translated into alternate and multiple senses.

APPLICATIONS OF VIRTUAL REALITY IN MEDICINE

Medical Education

The teaching of anatomy is mainly illustrative, and the application of VR to such teaching has great potential (Ellaway 2010). Through 3-D visualization of massive volumes of information and databases, clinicians and students can understand important physiological principles or basic anatomy. For instance, VR can be used to explore the organs by "flying" around, behind, or even inside them. In this sense VR can be used as both a didactic and an experiential educational tool, allowing a deeper understanding of the interrelationship of anatomical structures that cannot be achieved by any other means, including cadaveric dissection.

A significant step toward the creation of VR anatomy textbooks was the acquisition of the Visible Human male and female data made in August 1991 by the University of Colorado School of Medicine (Ackerman 1991). The Visible Human female data set contains 5,189 digital anatomical images obtained at 0.33-mm intervals (39 Gbyte). The male data set contains 1,971 digital axial anatomical images obtained at 1.0-mm intervals (15 Gbyte). Since 2000, the US National Library of Medicine in partnership with other US government research agencies has begun the development of a toolkit of computational programs capable of automatically performing many of the basic data-handling functions required for using Visible Human data in applications (Ackerman, Yoo, and Jenkins 2001).

The National Library of Medicine made the data sets available under a no-cost license agreement over the Internet, and this allowed the creation of a huge number of educational VEs.

In the future we can expect the development of different VR dynamic models illustrating how various organs and systems move during normal or diseased states, and how they respond to various externally applied forces (e.g., the touch of a scalpel).

Apart from anatomical training, VR has been used for the training of specific medical operations. For example, using VR it is possible to simulate the activity required for performing a 12-lead ECG (Jeffries, Woolf, and Linde 2003) or an endotracheal intubation in an emergency care setting (Mayrose and Myers 2007). In both cases, VR simulators allowed the acquisition of necessary technical skills required for the procedure (Roy et al. 2006).

Virtual Endoscopy

Every year the screening for cancer requires the performance of over 2 million video colonoscopic procedures. However, these procedures are not ideal:

- All endoscopic procedures are invasive.
- The patients are subject to complications such as perforation and bleeding.
- The cost for a typical colonoscopy is significant.

To overcome these problems, different researchers are implementing virtual endoscopy (Rubino et al. 2002). Virtual endoscopy is a new procedure that fuses computed tomography with advanced techniques for rendering three-dimensional images to produce views of the organ similar to those obtained during "real" endoscopy. Moreover, intelligent color-enhancement technology may even emphasize the vascular morphology, allowing better targeted endoscopic treatment and improving patient outcome (Rimbas, Haidar, and Voiosu 2011).

A virtual endoscopy is performed by using a standard CT scan or MRI scan (Satava and Jones 2002), reconstructing the organ of interest into a 3-D model, and then performing a fly through it. Typical examples include the colon, stomach, esophagus, tracheo-bronchial tree (bronchoscopy), sinus, bladder, ureter and kidneys (cystoscopy), pancreas, or biliary tree (Moorthy et al. 2003).

Virtual endoscopy is completely noninvasive and thus without known complications (Wang et al. 2011). The cost is less than traditional endoscopy, since it is performed in the same place and manner as all imaging modalities, utilizes the same staff, and has no consumable materials.

Surgical Simulation and Planning

Surgeons know well that in training there is no alternative to hands-on practice. However, students wishing to learn laparoscopic procedures faced a tough path (Durlach and Mavor 1995): they start by using laparoscopic trainers consisting of a black box in which endoscopic instruments are passed through rubber gaskets. Later, the students begin practicing these techniques on inanimate tissues, when allowed by their cost and availability. Obviously, there is a substantial difference for students between training with artificial or inanimate tissues and supervised procedures on real patients. This is why, in the early 1990s, different research teams tried to develop VE simulators. The science of virtual reality provides an entirely new opportunity in the area of simulation of surgical skills using computers for training, evaluation, and eventually certification. However, the first simulators were limited by low-resolution graphics, the lack of tactile input and force feedback, and the lack of realistic deformation of organs. In the last years a new generation of simulator has appeared that has shown improved training efficacy over traditional methods (Scott et al. 2008; Jones 2007). These simulators now combine registered patient data with anatomical information from an atlas for a case-by-case visualization of known structures and offer the same method of interaction as in the real case (Alaraj et al. 2011).

Another typical use of visualization applications is the planning of surgical and neurosurgical procedures (Alaraj et al. 2011). The planning of these procedures usually relies on the studies of series of two-dimensional MR (magnetic resonance) and/or CT (computer tomography) images, which have to be mentally integrated by surgeons into a three-dimensional concept. This mental transformation is difficult, since complex anatomy is represented in different scanning modalities, on separate image series, usually found in different sites/departments. A VR-based system is capable of incorporating different scanning modalities coming from different sites, providing a simple-to-use interactive, three-dimensional view.

VR in Neuropsychological Assessment and Rehabilitation

The use of VR in clinical psychology has become more widespread (Riva 2005). The key characteristics of virtual environments for most clinical applications are the high level of control of the interaction with the tool, and the enriched experience provided to the patient (Schultheis and Rizzo 2001).

On one side, it can be described as an advanced form of human-computer interface that allows the user to interact with and become immersed in a computer-generated environment in a naturalistic fashion. On the other side VR can also be considered as an experiential form of imagery that is as effective as reality in inducing emotional responses.

These features transform VR into an "empowering environment," a special, sheltered setting where patients can start to explore and act without feeling threatened (Botella et al. 1998). Nothing patients fear can "really" happen to them in VR. With such assurance, they can freely explore, experiment, feel, live, and experience feelings and thoughts. VR thus becomes a very useful intermediate step between the therapist's office and the real world (Botella et al. 2004).

Typically, in VR the patient learns to cope with problematic situations related to his or her problem. For this reason, the most common application of VR in this area is the treatment of phobias—that is, fear of heights, fear of flying, and fear of public speaking (Wiederhold and Wiederhold 2003; Emmelkamp 2005; Opris et al. 2012; Parsons and Rizzo 2008) and other anxiety disorders—that is, panic disorders, post-traumatic stress disorders, generalized anxiety disorders, and stress management (McLay et al. 2011; Reger and Gahm 2008; Gorini, Pallavicini, et al. 2010; Villani and Riva 2012; Villani et al. 2012; Gorini, Schruers, et al. 2010; Repetto and Riva 2011; Stetz et al. 2011).

Indeed, VR exposure therapy (VRE) has been proposed as a new medium for exposure therapy (Gorini, Pallavicini, et al. 2010) that is safer, less embarrassing, and less costly than reproducing the real-world situations. The rationale is simple: in VR the patient is intentionally confronted with the feared stimuli while allowing the anxiety to attenuate. Avoiding a dreaded situation reinforces a phobia, but each successive exposure to it reduces the anxiety through the processes of habituation and extinction.

VRE offers a number of advantages over in vivo or imaginal exposure. First, VRE can be administered in traditional therapeutic settings. This makes VRE more convenient, controlled, and cost-effective than in vivo exposure. Second, it can also isolate fear components more efficiently than in vivo exposure. For instance, in treating fear of flying, if landing is the most fearful part of the experience, landing can be repeated as often as necessary without having to wait for the airplane to take off. Finally, the immersive nature of VRE provides an almost real experience that may be more emotionally engaging than imaginal exposure.

A possible criticism of this approach is the lack of connection with the real life of the patient: the behavior of the patient in VR has no direct effects on the real-life experience, and the emotions and problems experienced by the patient in the real world are not directly addressed in VR exposure (Repetto and Riva 2011). To address this issue, Riva suggested a new approach, defined "interreality" (Riva 2009; Riva et al. 2010) that extends the clinical setting to a hybrid environment, bridging the physical and virtual world. In interreality the technology allows a bidirectional connection between the virtual and real worlds without removing the boundaries that define them. In other words, the behavior in the real world influences the virtual environment—for example, if emotional regulation is poor during the day, then some exercises in the virtual environment are unlocked in order to train this ability—and behavior in the virtual world influences real life—for example, if individuals participate in a virtual support group, they can interact with other participants during the day via SMS.

However, it seems likely that VR can be more than a tool to provide exposure and desensitization (Riva 2005). As noted by Glantz and colleagues (1997), "VR technology may create enough capabilities to profoundly influence the shape of therapy" (92). Emerging applications of VR in psychotherapy include post-traumatic stress disorder (Rothbaum et al. 2001; McLay et al. 2011), sexual disorders (Optale 2003), pain management (Hoffman 2004; Li et al. 2011), and eating disorders and obesity (Riva et al. 2006).

For example, according to the "allocentric lock hypothesis—ALH" eating disorders and obesity may be the outcome of a primary disturbance in the way the body is experienced and remembered (Riva 2012; Riva and Gaudio 2012): individuals with these disturbances may be locked to an allocentric (observer view) negative memory of the body that is no longer updated by contrasting egocentric representations driven by perception. Using immersive VR, it is possible to induce a controlled sensory rearrangement that facilitates the update of the biased body image. This allows the differentiation and integration of new information, leading to a new sense of cohesiveness and consistency in how the self represents the body. In fact, immersive VR can be considered an "embodied technology" for its effects on body perceptions (Vidal, Amorim, and Berthoz 2004; Lambrey and Berthoz 2003; Riva 1997a). VR users become aware of their bodies during navigation (Riva 2011): their head movements alter what they see. The sensorimotor coordination of the moving head with visual displays produces a much higher level of sensorimotor feedback and first-person perspective (egocentric reference frame).

The results of this approach are very promising. Riva and his group (Riva et al. 2012) have recently tested it in a randomized controlled trial to date with 163 morbidly obese patients (fig. 39.1). This trial compared experiential cognitive therapy (ECT)—the VR-based treatment for obesity—with nutritional (NT) and cognitive-behavioral (CBT) approaches along with waiting list controls. At the 12-month follow-up, experiential CT was significantly better in maintaining the results of the treatment than both CBT (percentage of subjects who maintained or improved the weight reduction: ECT [22/46, 48 percent] vs. CBT [11/38, 29 percent], odds ratio: 2.25) and NT (percentage of

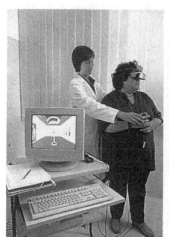

FIGURE 39.1 The use of VR in the treatment of obesity: A phase of the therapy (*left*) and a screenshot of the virtual environment (*right*).

subjects who maintained or improved the weight reduction: ECT [22/46, 48 percent] vs. NT [3/26, 29 percent], odds ratio: 7.03). Riva and colleagues use experiential CT also in the treatment of anorexia, bulimia, and binge eating (Riva et al. 1999; Riva et al. 2002). A similar approach was presented and tested by Perpiñá, Botella, and Baños (2003) in the treatment of eating disorders.

The embodied effects of VR may be used in other pathologies too. Lambrey and Berthoz (2003) showed that subjects use conflicting visual and nonvisual information differently according to individual "perceptive styles" (bottom-up processes) and that these "perceptive styles" are made more observable by the subjects changing their perceptive strategy, that is, reweighting (top-down processes).

Viaud-Delmon, Berthoz, and Jouvent (2002) showed that subjects with high trait anxiety, for example, subjects with symptoms of panic and agoraphobia, have a strong dependence on a particular reference frame in which the sensory information is interpreted and in which the subject remains anchored. A VR experience aimed at modifying the sensory reference frame may be useful in speeding up the process of change. Future studies are needed both to identify specific perceptive styles in different pathologies and to define the best protocols for changing them.

Another medical field in which VR has been fruitfully applied is neuropsychological testing and rehabilitation. Actual applications range from rehabilitation of people with intellectual disabilities (Standen and Brown 2005), to motor assessment and rehabilitation (Holden 2005), to brain damage assessment and rehabilitation (Saposnik and Levin 2011; Rose, Brooks, and Rizzo 2005). Here the advantage of VR on traditional assessment and intervention is provided by three key features: the capacity to deliver interactive 3D stimuli within an immersive environment in a variety of forms and sensory modalities; the possibility of designing safe testing and training environments; and the provision of "cueing" stimuli or visualization strategies designed to help guide successful performance in support of an error-free learning approach (Morganti 2004; Schultheis, Himelstein, and Rizzo 2002).

Beyond clinical applications, VR has been revealed to be a powerful tool for behavioral neuroscience research (Bohil, Alicea, and Biocca 2011). Using VR, researchers can carry out experiments in an ecologically valid situation, while still maintaining control over all potential intervening variables. Moreover, VR allows us to measure and monitor a wide variety of responses made by the subject.

VR HARDWARE AND SOFTWARE

For many years one of the main obstacles to the development of VR applications was the price of the equipment: a typical VR system required a costly, fridge-size Silicon

Graphic workstation in the range of US$250,000 and up. Even if high-end applications still require powerful workstations, during the last five years about 65 percent of the VR applications for healthcare were developed for use on PC platforms.

The significant advances in PC hardware that have been made over the last 15 years are transforming PC-based VR into a reality. The cost of a basic desktop VR system has gone down by many thousand of dollars since that time, and the functionality has improved dramatically in terms of graphics processing power. A simple immersive VR system now may cost less than US$6,000.

On the software side, an interesting low-cost solution is the use of 3D engines included in commercial 3D games for developing simple virtual environments. Many 3D games (US$50 each) include level editors that allow the user to customize the environments and the avatars.

Obviously, level editing does not allow full control of the environment. In particular, the user interaction with the 3D objects is usually very limited. To overcome this limitation, now there are different VR development toolkits available for PCs, ranging from high-end authoring toolkits that require significant programming experience to simple "hobbyist" packages. Despite the differences in the types of virtual worlds these products can deliver, the various tools are based on the same VR development model: they allow users to create or import 3D objects, to apply behavioral attributes such as weight and gravity to the objects, and to program the objects to respond to the user via visual and or audio events. Ranging in prices from free[1] to US$5,000 (3DVia Studio Pro or Unity Pro), the toolkits are the most functional of the available VR software options. While some of them rely exclusively on C or C++ programming to build a virtual world, others offer simpler point-and-click operations to develop a simulation (see fig. 39.2).

FIGURE 39.2 The free NeuroVR 2 editor (http://www.neurovr.org).

Using VR toolkits, it is also possible to bring in files from a wide array of 3D and animation packages,

This trend is also parallel to the development of online VR worlds, such as *Second Life*.[2] Compared to the traditional VR worlds, the online worlds appear to have much to offer to exposure-based therapy (Repetto and Riva 2011). Since they allow multiplayer interactions, the therapist and the patient can share the same online virtual space. This means that the therapist can accompany the patient through a particularly threatening experience just by logging onto a specific website and adopting a preferred avatar. The way of interaction as well as the surrounding environment can be easily modified on the basis of therapeutic needs. In the case of social phobia, for example, after practicing with the therapist within a closed environment (i.e., the therapist's virtual office), the patient can be taken to a virtual world populated by other avatars and asked to initiate a conversation and obtain feedback from them in real-time audio through the use of a microphone. Similarly, patients with agoraphobia can be exposed to a variety of unfamiliar worlds different from those the clinician can provide in an office setting.

Challenges and Issues

Technical Challenges

Even if the significant advances in computer and graphics technology have drastically improved the characteristics of a typical VE, VR is still limited by the maturity of the systems available. Even today, no off-the-shelf solutions are available. So, the setup of a VR system usually requires a lot of patience for dealing with conflicting hardware or missing software drivers. Nearly every VR system requires a dedicated staff or at least computer technician to keep the system running smoothly. Moreover, much VR technology is still uncomfortable or unpleasant to use. In particular, below are listed some current VR technology limitations for users (Gross 2002):

- Virtual acoustic displays that require a great deal of computational resources in order to simulate a small number of sound sources
- Force feedback and tactile displays, still in their infancy, with limited functionality
- Image generators that cannot provide low-latency rendering of head-tracked complex scenes, requiring severe trade-offs between performance and scene quality
- Position trackers with small working volumes, inadequate robustness, and problems of latency and poor registration
- HMDs with limited field of view, and encumbering form factor

As we have seen, a typical area for VR applications is surgery. However, there have been few developments in the area of tactile feedback. The ability to feel tissue is important. Procedures that require palpitation, such as artery localization and tumor detection, are extremely difficult when the only form of haptic exploration is in the form of forces transmitted through long, clumsy instruments.

Safety Issues

The introduction of patients and clinicians to VEs raises particular safety issues (Durlach and Mavor 1995). In fact, despite developments in VR technology, some users still experience health and safety problems associated with VR use (Nichols and Patel 2002). The key concern from the literature is VR-induced sickness, which could lead to problems (Lewis and Griffin 1997) including the following:

- Symptoms of motion sickness
- Strain on the ocular system
- Degraded limb and postural control
- Reduced sense of presence
- The development of responses inappropriate for the real world, which might lead to negative training

The improved quality of VR systems is drastically reducing the occurrence of simulation sickness. For instance, a recent review of clinical applications of VR reported few instances of simulation sickness, and nearly all were transient and minor (Riva, Wiederhold, and Molinari 1998). In general, for a large proportion of VR users these effects are mild and subside quickly.

Nonetheless, patients exposed to VR environments may have disabilities that increase their susceptibility to side effects. Precautions should be taken to ensure the safety and well-being of patients, including establishing protocols for monitoring and controlling exposure to VR environments.

Strategies are needed to detect any adverse effects of exposure, some of which may be difficult to anticipate, at an early stage. According to Lewis and Griffin (1997) exposure management protocols for patients in virtual environments should include the following:

- Screening procedures to detect individuals who may present particular risks
- Procedures for managing patient exposure to VR applications to ensure rapid adaptation with minimum symptoms
- Procedures for monitoring unexpected side effects and for ensuring that the system meets its design objectives

Finally, the effect of VEs on cognition is not fully understood. In a report, the US National Advisory Mental Health Council (1995) suggested that "Research is needed to understand both the positive and the negative effects [of VEs]...on children's and adult's perceptual and cognitive skills." Even if the report was published over two decades ago, finding an answer still requires the merging of knowledge from a variety of disciplines including (but not limited to) neuropsychology, neuroimaging, educational theory and technology, human factors, medicine, and computer science (Bohil, Alicea, and Biocca 2011).

Research and Clinical Issues

In the last five years there has been a steady growth in the use of VR in healthcare because of advances in information technology and a decline in costs. As we have seen, using the "virtual reality" keyword, we can find 4,442 papers listed in MEDLINE and 5,120 in PSYCINFO (all fields query, accessed July 29, 2013). Much of this growth, however, has been in the form of feasibility studies and pilot trials.

The "best" evidence in evaluating the efficacy of a therapy/approach is the results of randomized, controlled clinical trials. However, if we check the available literature we can find only a limited number of controlled trials.

Why are there so few controlled trials in VR research? The possible answers are three. The first is the lack of standardization in VR devices and software. To date, very few of the various VR systems available are interoperable. This renders difficult their use in contexts other than those in which they were developed. The second is the lack of standardized protocols that can be shared by the community of researchers. The third is the costs required for the setup trials. As we have just seen, the lack of interoperable systems added to the lack of clinical protocols forces most researchers to spend a lot of time and money in designing and developing their own VR application: many of them can be considered "one-off" creations tied to a proprietary hardware and software, which have been tuned by a process of trial and error. According to the European-funded project VEPSY Updated, the cost required for designing a clinical VR application from scratch and testing it on clinical patients using controlled trials may range between US$150,000 and US$200,000. As noted by the US National Research Council (Hughes et al. 1999):

> the government support has been the single most important source of sustained funding for innovative research in both computer graphics and VR. Beginning in the 1960s with its investments in computer modeling, flight simulators, and visualization techniques, and continuing through current developments in virtual worlds, the federal government has made significant investments in military, civilian, and university research that laid the groundwork for one of today's most dynamic technologies. The commercial payoffs have included numerous companies formed around federally funded research in graphics and VR. (227)

In Europe the most important source of funding for healthcare VR applications was the European Commission through its Information and Communication Technologies program.[3] However, in the last five years the funds for VR research coming from the

European Commission have been between one-third and one-fifth of the total amount distributed by the US government.

Conclusions

In general, the presented overview of current applications shows that VR can be considered a useful tool in diagnosis, therapy, education, and training. However, several barriers still remain. The PC-based systems, while inexpensive and easy to use, still suffer from a lack of flexibility and capabilities necessary to individualize environments for each patient (Riva 2005). On the other hand, in most circumstances the clinical skills of the therapist remain the most important factor in the successful use of VR systems. It is clear that building new and additional virtual environments is important so that therapists will continue to investigate applying these tools in their day-to-day clinical practice. Further, many of the actual VR applications are in the clinical investigation or laboratory stage, as clearly showed by the lack of controlled trials.

Significant efforts are still required to move VWs into commercial success and therefore routine clinical use. Possible future scenarios will involve multidisciplinary teams of engineers, computer programmers, and therapists working in concert to treat specific clinical problems. Finally, communication networks are transforming VWs into shared worlds in which individuals, objects, and processes interact without regard to their location. In the future, such networks will probably merge VR and telemedicine applications, allowing us to use VE for such purposes as distance learning, distributed training, and e-therapy.

It is hoped that by bringing together this community of experts, further stimulation of interest from granting agencies will be accelerated. Information on advances in VR technology must be made available to the healthcare community in a format that is easy to understand and invites participation. Future potential applications of VR are really only limited by the imaginations of talented individuals.

Notes

1. http://www.neurovr.org, accessed June 29, 2013.
2. http://www.secondlife.com, accessed June 29, 2013.
3. http://cordis.europa.eu/fp7/ict/programme/home_en.html, accessed June 29, 2013.

References

Ackerman, M. J. 1991. The Visible Human Project. *The Journal of Biocommunication* 18 (2): 14.

Ackerman, M. J., T. Yoo, and D. Jenkins. 2001. From Data to Knowledge: The Visible Human Project Continues. *Medinfo* 10 (2): 887–890.

Alaraj, A., M. G. Lemole, J. H. Finkle, R. Yudkowsky, A. Wallace, C. Luciano, P. P. Banerjee, S. H. Rizzi, and F. T. Charbel. 2011. Virtual Reality Training in Neurosurgery: Review of Current Status and Future Applications. *Surgical Neurology International* 2: 52.

Bohil, C. J., B. Alicea, and F. A. Biocca. 2011. Virtual Reality in Neuroscience Research and Therapy. *Nature Reviews Neuroscience* 12 (12): 752–762.

Botella, C., C. Perpiña, R. M. Baños, and A. Garcia-Palacios. 1998. Virtual Reality: A New Clinical Setting Lab. *Studies in Health Technology and Informatics* 58: 73–81.

Botella, C., S. Quero, R. M. Banos, C. Perpina, A. Garcia Palacios, and G. Riva. 2004. Virtual Reality and Psychotherapy. *Studies in Health Technology and Informatics* 99: 37–54.

Durlach, N. I., and A. S. Mavor, eds. 1995. *Virtual Reality: Scientific and Technological Challenges.* Washington, DC: National Academy Press. http://www.nap.edu/books/0309051355/html/index.html. Accessed June 29, 2013.

Ellaway, R. 2010. Virtual Reality in Medical Education. *Medical Teacher* 32 (9): 791–793.

Emmelkamp, P. M. (2005). Technological innovations in clinical assessment and psychotherapy. *Psychotherapy and Psychosomatics* 74 (6): 336–43.

Glantz, K., N. I. Durlach, R. C. Barnett, and W. A. Aviles. 1997. Virtual Reality (VR) and Psychotherapy: Opportunities and Challenges. *Presence, Teleoperators, and Virtual Environments* 6 (1): 87–105.

Gorini, A., A. Gaggioli, C. Vigna, and G. Riva. 2008. A Second Life for eHealth: Prospects for the Use of 3-D Virtual Worlds in Clinical Psychology. *Journal of Medical Internet Research* 10 (3): e21.

Gorini, A., F. Pallavicini, D. Algeri, C. Repetto, A. Gaggioli, and G. Riva. 2010. Virtual Reality in the Treatment of Generalized Anxiety Disorders. *Studies in Health Technology and Informatics* 154: 39–43.

Gorini, A., K. Schruers, G. Riva, and E. Griez. 2010. Nonhomogeneous Results in Place Learning among Panic Disorder Patients with Agoraphobia. *Psychiatry Research* 179 (3): 297–305.

Gross, D. 2002. Technology Management and User Acceptance of VE Technology. In *Handbook of Virtual Environments: Design, Implementation, and Applications*, edited by K. M. Stanney, 533–542. Mahwah, NJ: Lawrence Erlbaum Associates.

Hoffman, H. G. 2004. Virtual-Reality Therapy: Patients Can Get Relief from Pain or Overcome Their Phobias by Immersing Themselves in Computer-Generated Worlds. *Scientific American* 8: 58–65.

Holden, M. K. 2005. Virtual Environments for Motor Rehabilitation: Review. *CyberPsychology & Behavior* 8 (3): 187–211; discussion 212–219.

Hughes, T., D. D. Clark, P. M. Banks, and W. C. Lineberger, eds. 1999. *Funding a Revolution: Government Support for Computing Research.* Washington, DC: National Academy Press. http://stills.nap.edu/html/far/contents.html. Accessed June 29, 2013.

Jeffries, P. R., S. Woolf, and B. Linde. 2003. Technology-Based vs. Traditional Instruction: A Comparison of Two Methods for Teaching the Skill of Performing a 12-Lead ECG. *Nurs Educ Perspect* 24 (2): 70–74.

Jones, D. B. 2007. Video Trainers, Simulation and Virtual Reality: A New Paradigm for Surgical Training. *Asian Journal of Surgery* 30 (1): 6–12.

Lambrey, S., and A. Berthoz. 2003. Combination of Conflicting Visual and Non-visual Information for Estimating Actively Performed Body Turns in Virtual Reality. *International Journal of Psychophysiology* 50 (1–2): 101–115.

Lewis, C. H., and M. J. Griffin. 1997. Human Factors Consideration in Clinical Applications of Virtual Reality. In *Virtual Reality in Neuro-psycho-physiology: Cognitive, Clinical and Methodological Issues in Assessment and Rehabilitation*, edited by G. Riva, 35–56. Amsterdam: IOS Press.

Li, A., Z. Montano, V. J. Chen, and J. I. Gold. 2011. Virtual Reality and Pain Management: Current Trends and Future Directions. *Pain Management* 1 (2): 147–157.

Mayrose, J., and J. W. Myers. 2007. Endotracheal Intubation: Application of Virtual Reality to Emergency Medical Services Education. *Simulation in Healthcare* 2 (4): 231–234.

McCloy, R., and R. Stone. 2001. Science, Medicine, and the Future: Virtual Reality in Surgery. *British Medical Journal* 323 (7318): 912–915.

McLay, R. N., D. P. Wood, J. A. Webb-Murphy, J. L. Spira, M. D. Wiederhold, J. M. Pyne, and B. K. Wiederhold. 2011. A Randomized, Controlled Trial of Virtual Reality-Graded Exposure Therapy for Post-traumatic Stress Disorder in Active Duty Service Members with Combat-Related Post-traumatic Stress Disorder. *Cyberpsychology, Behavior, and Social Networking* 14 (4): 223–229.

Moorthy, K., S. Smith, T. Brown, S. Bann, and A. Darzi. 2003. Evaluation of Virtual Reality Bronchoscopy as a Learning and Assessment Tool. *Respiration* 70 (2): 195–199.

Morganti, F. 2004. Virtual Interaction in Cognitive Neuropsychology. In *Cybertherapy: Internet and Virtual Reality as Assessment and Rehabilitation Tools for Clinical Psychology and Neuroscience*, edited by G. Riva, C. Botella, P. Legéron, and G. Optale. Amsterdam: Ios Press. http://www.cybertherapy.info/pages/book3.htm. Accessed June 29, 2013.

Nichols, S., and H. Patel. 2002. Health and Safety Implications of Virtual Reality: A Review of Empirical Evidence. *Applied Ergonomics* 33 (3): 251–271.

Opris, D., S. Pintea, A. Garcia-Palacios, C. Botella, S. Szamoskozi, and D. David. 2012. Virtual Reality Exposure Therapy in Anxiety Disorders: A Quantitative Meta-analysis. *Depression and Anxiety* 29 (2): 85–93.

Optale, G. 2003. Male Sexual Dysfunctions and Multimedia Immersion Therapy. *CyberPsychology & Behavior* 6 (3): 289–294.

Parsons, T. D., and A. A. Rizzo. 2008. Affective Outcomes of Virtual Reality Exposure Therapy for Anxiety and Specific Phobias: A Meta-analysis. *Journal of Behavior Therapy and Experimental Psychiatry* 39 (3): 250–261.

Perpiña, C., C. Botella, and R. M. Baños. 2003. Virtual Reality in Eating Disorders. *European Eating Disorders Review* 11 (3): 261–278.

Reger, G. M., and G. A. Gahm. 2008. Virtual Reality Exposure Therapy for Active Duty Soldiers. *Journal of Clinical Psychology* 64 (8): 940–946.

Repetto, C., and G. Riva. 2011. From Virtual Reality to Interreality in the Treatment of Anxiety Disorders. *Neuropsychiatry* 1 (1): 31–43.

Rimbas, M., A. Haidar, and M. R. Voiosu. 2011. Computed Virtual Chromoendoscopy: Enhanced Videocapsule Endoscopy Is of Potential Benefit in Gastric Antral Vascular Ectasia Syndrome Refractory to Endoscopic Treatment. *Journal of Gastrointestinal and Liver Diseases* 20 (3): 307–310.

Riva, G. 1997a. The Virtual Environment for Body-Image Modification (VEBIM): Development and Preliminary Evaluation. *Presence, Teleoperators, and Virtual Environments* 6 (1): 106–117.

Riva, G., ed. 1997b. *Virtual Reality in Neuro-psycho-physiology: Cognitive, Clinical and Methodological Issues in Assessment and Rehabilitation*. Amsterdam: IOS Press. http://www.cybertherapy.info/pages/book1.htm. Accessed June 29, 2013.

Riva, G. 2002. Virtual Reality for Health Care: The Status of Research. *Cyberpsychology & Behavior* 5 (3): 219–225.

Riva, G. 2005. Virtual Reality in Psychotherapy: Review. *CyberPsychology & Behavior* 8 (3): 220–230; discussion 231–240.

Riva, G. 2009. Interreality: A New Paradigm for e-Health. *Studies in Health Technology and Informatics* 144: 3–7.

Riva, G. 2011. The Key to Unlocking the Virtual Body: Virtual Reality in the Treatment of Obesity and Eating Disorders. *Journal of Diabetes Science and Technology* 5 (2): 283–292.

Riva, G. 2012. Neuroscience and Eating Disorders: The Allocentric Lock Hypothesis. *Medical Hypotheses* 78: 254–257.

Riva, G., M. Bacchetta, M. Baruffi, and E. Molinari. 2002. Virtual-Reality-Based Multidimensional Therapy for the Treatment of Body Image Disturbances in Binge Eating Disorders: A Preliminary Controlled Study. *IEEE Transactions on Information Technology in Biomedicine* 6 (3): 224–234.

Riva, G., M. Bacchetta, M. Baruffi, S. Rinaldi, and E. Molinari. 1999. Virtual Reality Based Experiential Cognitive Treatment of Anorexia Nervosa. *Journal of Behavioral Therapy and Experimental Psychiatry* 30 (3): 221–230.

Riva, G., M. Bacchetta, G. Cesa, S. Conti, G. Castelnuovo, F. Mantovani, and E. Molinari. 2006. Is Severe Obesity a Form of Addiction? Rationale, Clinical Approach, and Controlled Clinical Trial. *CyberPsychology and Behavior* 9 (4): 457–479.

Riva, G., G. Castelnuovo, G. Cesa, A. Gaggioli, F. Mantovani, and E. Molinari. 2012. Virtual Reality for Enhancing the Cognitive Behavioral Treatment of Obesity: A Controlled Study with One-Year Follow-up. Paper presented to Medicine 2.0'12 at Boston.

Riva, G., and S. Gaudio. 2012. Allocentric Lock in Anorexia Nervosa: New Evidence from Neuroimaging Studies. *Medical Hypotheses* 79 (1): 113–117.

Riva, G., S. Raspelli, D. Algeri, F. Pallavicini, A. Gorini, B. K. Wiederhold, and A. Gaggioli. 2010. Interreality in Practice: Bridging Virtual and Real Worlds in the Treatment of Posttraumatic Stress Disorders. *Cyberpsychology, Behavior and Social Networks* 13 (1): 55–65.

Riva, G., B. Wiederhold, and E. Molinari, eds. 1998. *Virtual Environments in Clinical Psychology and Neuroscience: Methods and Techniques in Advanced Patient-Therapist Interaction.* Amsterdam: IOS Press. http://www.cybertherapy.info/pages/book2.htm. Accessed June 29, 2013.

Rizzo, A. A., B. Wiederhold, G. Riva, and C. Van Der Zaag. 1998. A Bibliography of Articles Relevant to the Application of Virtual Reality in the Mental Health Field. *CyberPsychology & Behavior* 1 (4): 411–425.

Rose, F. D., B. M. Brooks, and A. A. Rizzo. 2005. Virtual Reality in Brain Damage Rehabilitation: Review. *CyberPsychology & Behavior* 8 (3): 241–262; discussion 263–271.

Rothbaum, B. O., L. F. Hodges, D. Ready, K. Graap, and R. D. Alarcon. 2001. Virtual Reality Exposure Therapy for Vietnam Veterans with Posttraumatic Stress Disorder. *Journal of Clinical Psychiatry* 62 (8): 617–622.

Roy, M. J., D. L. Sticha, P. L. Kraus, and D. E. Olsen. 2006. Simulation and Virtual Reality in Medical Education and Therapy: A Protocol. *CyberPsychology & Behavior* 9 (2): 245–247.

Rubino, F., L. Soler, J. Marescaux, and H. Maisonneuve. 2002. Advances in Virtual Reality Are Wide Ranging. *Bmj* 324 (7337): 612.

Saposnik, G., and M. Levin. 2011. Virtual Reality in Stroke Rehabilitation: A Meta-analysis and Implications for Clinicians. *Stroke* 42 (5): 1380–1386.

Satava , R. M, and S. B. Jones. 2002. Medical Applications of Virtual Reality. In *Handbook of Virtual Environments: Design, Implementation, and Applications,* edited by K. M. Stanney. Mahwah, NJ: Lawrence Erlbaum Associates, Inc. 368–391.

Schultheis, M. T., J. Himelstein, and A. A. Rizzo. 2002. Virtual Reality and Neuropsychology: Upgrading the Current Tools. *Journal of Head Trauma Rehabilitation* 17 (5): 378–394.

Schultheis, M. T., and A. A. Rizzo. 2001. The Application of Virtual Reality Technology in Rehabilitation. *Rehabilitation Psychology* 46 (3): 296–311.

Scott, D. J., J. C. Cendan, C. M. Pugh, R. M. Minter, G. L. Dunnington, and R. A. Kozar. 2008. The Changing Face of Surgical Education: Simulation as the New Paradigm. *Journal of Surgical Research: Clinical and Laboratory Investigation* 147 (2): 189–193.

Standen, P. J., and D. J. Brown. 2005. Virtual Reality in the Rehabilitation of People with Intellectual Disabilities: Review. *CyberPsychology & Behavior* 8 (3): 272–282; discussion 283–288.

Stetz, M. C., J. Y. Kaloi-Chen, D. D. Turner, S. Bouchard, G. Riva, and B. K. Wiederhold. 2011. The Effectiveness of Technology-Enhanced Relaxation Techniques for Military Medical Warriors. *Military Medicine* 176 (9): 1065–1070.

Székely, G., and R. M. Satava. 1999. Virtual Reality in Medicine. *BMJ* 319 (7220): 1305.

Viaud-Delmon, I., A. Berthoz, and R. Jouvent. 2002. Multisensory Integration for Spatial Orientation in Trait Anxiety Subjects: Absence of Visual Dependence. *European Psychiatry* 17 (4): 194–199.

Vidal, M., M. A. Amorim, and A. Berthoz. 2004. Navigating in a Virtual Three-Dimensional Maze: How Do Egocentric and Allocentric Reference Frames Interact? *Cognitive Brain Research* 19 (3): 244–258.

Villani, D., A. Grassi, C. Cognetta, P. Cipresso, D. Toniolo, and G. Riva. 2012. The Effects of a Mobile Stress Management Protocol on Nurses Working with Cancer Patients: A Preliminary Controlled Study. *Studies in Health Technology and Informatics* 173: 524–528.

Villani, D., and G. Riva. 2012. Does Interactive Media Enhance the Management of Stress? Suggestions from a Controlled Study. *Cyberpsychology, Behavior and Social Networking* 15 (1): 24–30.

Wang, D., X. E. Wei, L. Yan, Y. Z. Zhang, and W. B. Li. 2011. Enhanced CT and CT Virtual Endoscopy in Diagnosis of Heterotopic Pancreas. *World Journal of Gastroenterology* 17 (33): 3850–3855.

Wiederhold, B. K., and M. D. Wiederhold. 2003. Three-Year Follow-up for Virtual Reality Exposure for Fear of Flying. *Cyberpsychology & Behavior* 6 (4): 441–446.

Wootton, R. 1999. Telemedicine: An Introduction. In *European Telemedicine 1998/99*, edited by R. Wootton, 10–12. London: Kensington Publications.

CHAPTER 40

....

MILITARY SIMULATIONS
USING VIRTUAL WORLDS

....

ROGER SMITH

THE military has always worked to fight battles in a synthetic or artificial environment before fighting them in the real world. There are so many variables that getting everything right is extremely difficult. Planning and rehearsal are primary tools for accomplishing this in simulation. Sand tables with wooden and stone markers that allowed commanders to explain their plan to dozens of soldiers were some of the earliest virtual worlds. Board war games replaced the sand with paper and added rules so a player could actually do some predictions in a crude virtual space. New technologies like movies, electronics, hydraulics, computers, and networks have all changed the face and usefulness of these military tools.

In this chapter we will explore the important and empowering role that virtual worlds can play in future military planning, training, and operations. From the seeds of simple sand tables, military scientists have created sophisticated simulations and games for predicting, reacting to, and thinking about the future. This field is constantly growing and changing as it adopts new ideas and new technologies that become available from a wide variety of parallel disciplines. Computer game technologies are some of the most recent tools to significantly impact military planning and training. Virtual worlds are potentially the next big step in making military simulations more expansive, persistent, and accessible for training. We explore the potential that these offer for a training capability that is constantly available in the networked cloud to any solder, sailor, airman, or marine in the world. Virtual worlds could further extend the military university classroom by bringing to life ancient battles currently confined to static maps in books and by connecting to live operations or exercises occurring in any location around the world. Finally, we discuss the importance of cybersecurity around these virtual spaces. As they become mirrors of real operations, they become some of the most valuable information spaces on the global network. Penetrating one could potentially reveal the plans and capabilities of another country's entire military force and political hierarchy. They become much more than just a "game space," but are a digital mirror that accurately reflects everything that exists in the real world. When this occurs, they become equal in importance to all of the physical assets that they reflect. The future military potential for virtual worlds is almost without bounds.

A Brief History of Simulation for Military Training

In preparation for sending soldiers to Europe during World War II, the US Army created extensive field maneuvers in the forests and hills of the state of Louisiana (Bolger 1986). Tens of thousands of soldiers rehearsed their roles and used their new radios to report their actions to commanders who were miles away. This allowed these commanders to rehearse their strategies for positioning and moving large units, as well as the protocols for transmitting that information accurately to the units in the field. These Louisiana Maneuvers planted the seeds for large-scale, live rehearsal that would become the primary mission for the world's largest training range, the National Training Center located in the desert of eastern California.

But live-action war games are expensive to execute and require months of planning. Replicating them with paper or a computer can make the experience much more accessible and repeatable. Weiner believed that ancient Oriental generals may have planned their battles using icons on a map or scribbles in the sand (Weiner 1959). As far back as the Roman Empire, military leaders used sand tables with abstract icons to represent soldiers and units in battle. These allowed the leaders to visualize and manipulate a small physical copy of the battlefield. It provided a window for them to see information in geographic perspective and enabled multiple players to pit their own ideas against one another. Though the visual representation was the initial value of the practice, the map or playing board upon which multiple options could be compared proved to be even more powerful. These tools allowed leaders and their staff members to compete against each other or against historical records in an attempt to determine which ideas would be the most effective (Perla 1990).

Sand tables were turned into board war games using wooden and cardboard maps and markers. One of the most famous was Koenigspiel, or the "King's Game," created by Christopher Weikhmann of Ulam, Germany, in 1664 (Perla 1990). It consisted of a checkered board, borrowed from the game of chess, and 30 pieces that represented the King, Marshall, Colonel, and lower ranks down to Private. Some critics dismissed this as simply a "fancified" version of chess, but it began a thought process for creating accurate representations of the battlefield that has carried through four centuries. In 1780, Dr. C. L. Helwig created "War Chess," in which he significantly expanded the checkered board to 1,666 squares, coloring each to represent a different type of terrain (Perla 1990). He created 120 pieces for the game to increase the complexity of actions that could be modeled. Finally, he introduced the idea of aggregate units, so that a single piece could represent an entire infantry, cavalry, or artillery unit. Helwig's ideas significantly shaped the direction of war-gaming over the next three hundred years. His concepts are clearly present in the board games produced in the late twentieth century (Perla 1990).

Shortly after the first computers were invented, they were applied to war-gaming. In 1948, the Army Operations Research Office created the "Air Defense Simulation" that ran on one of the earliest Univac computers (Davis 1995). It only represented enemy aircraft, anti-aircraft guns, and naval guided missiles in a generic three-dimensional Cartesian space. But it was quickly followed by Carmonette, which began development in 1953 and was used operationally from 1956 to 1970. Carmonette offered a much richer virtual space that included tanks, antitank weapons, infantry, helicopters, and radio communications (Davis 1995). It also made use of the relatively new "Monte Carlo Method" of statistical modeling that had been invented by Stanislaw Ulam and John von Neumann during their work on the Manhattan Project. From those simple roots, computer war games became a staple in military training, the analysis of atomic weapon effectiveness, and prediction of conventional battle outcomes. Most modern military forces now possess a number of computer war games for use in training, combat analysis, and weapon design.

Most recently, the military has developed virtual simulators of aircraft, helicopters, tanks, ships, and even squads of infantry. Crude systems of this type began to appear shortly after the commercialization of the first aircraft at the beginning of the twentieth century. These devices allowed an aspiring pilot to learn the basic principles behind controlling an aircraft in flight. The most famous of these was Edwin Link's "Blue Box," which he created in 1930 and sold to the budding US Army Air Corps (fig. 40.1). This machine offered a mechanical and electronic replica of an aircraft that could be used to

FIGURE 40.1 Link "Blue Box" trainer, 1942. Source: Wikipedia.

test a pilot's ability to control an aircraft. Later models included a mechanical "mouse" that sat on a desktop and traced the path of the aircraft by driving across a map, showing the instructor exactly how well the pilot was able to follow directions (Rolfe and Staples 1988).

In 1990, Air Force Col. Jack Thorpe began work on a new kind of simulator, one that could be linked to others in the same facility or at bases around the world. The result was the Simulator Networking project (SIMNET), which delivered a standardized tank simulator and a network protocol that allowed the device to send essential information about the location and actions of the tank to other simulators across the computer network (Hapgood 2004). This allowed dozens of devices to participate in the same virtual environment as teammates or opponents. Crews in simulators no longer had to be satisfied with shooting static targets or simple drone objects that were preprogrammed. For the first time, they could pit their skills against a live and unpredictable opponent, forcing all participants to raise their level of competence to remain alive in on the virtual battlefield (Miller and Thorpe 1995).

Virtual Worlds Dawning

Virtual worlds are a natural extension of the diverse and evolving family of simulators. These raise interesting questions that must be dealt with if this technology is to be used to support actual warfare. For example, in the real world each soldier has a distinct rank, organizational assignment, skill set, code of ethics, legal restrictions, and life-supporting relationships. Must a military virtual world identically match all of these in order to provide useful functionality? To what degree do the soldier's real-world experiences need to be mimicked in the virtual world? If a soldier is promoted, reprimanded, transferred, or deployed, does that same change occur to his or her VW avatar as well? Can actions in the virtual world be the basis for a promotion or commendation in the real world? Does the larger military organizational structure exist within the VW? Is it populated by avatars of the same people that populate it in the real world? Does this structure adapt automatically as the real structure changes? Are real-world IT systems linked to the VW so that real-world information is automatically reflected in the state of the virtual world?

A virtual world that links soldiers together could potentially reach out to their families as well, allowing them to "phone home" by rendezvousing at a shared virtual island to converse with the avatars of family, exchange pictures, and share videos. Should this be allowed? Does it present a security hole through which our enemies could access real battlefield information? Will we ever create systems that are secure enough to allow this kind of dual use?

The answers to these kinds of questions will significantly affect the form and functionality of any virtual world that is widely adopted by the military.

When the data in the virtual world are drawn directly from the state and actions of real-world objects, it becomes much more than a training and communication space—it is a mirror of the real world with a number of additional uses. It becomes a tool for understanding and making decisions about the real world. Orson Scott Card's 1985 novel *Ender's Game* depicted a world in which the training exercises of Ender Wiggins were actually part of a galactic struggle to the death between two species vying for control of a planet (Card 1985). Everything that happened in the virtual world was actually carried out in the real world. Was this a flight of fancy, or will the next generation of virtual worlds enable this kind of warfare? For decades we have fired weapons at targets beyond visual range. These weapons are guided to a specific point in space using digital maps inside the weapon's computer brain. More recently, we have learned to use remotely piloted drone aircraft to fire lethal munitions at targets seen on a video screen. Several national air forces are aggressively creating unmanned combat aircraft that use a digital map of the world and the enemy threat locations to navigate to a target, identify it, and release weapons—potentially without the need for human intervention. There are already multiple ground robots equipped with rifles that can be fired by a human operator looking at the target through the robot's camera eyes. These systems use a digital map of the world either on the combat vehicle or in the manned control system. A military virtual world takes this one step further by displaying all of that data with 3D avatars and models. This visualization makes the VW an extremely accessible and useful tool for perceiving what the combat platforms see, understanding the opportunities that surround them, and making a decision to take action. As we enable the tracking of every vehicle and every soldier on the battlefield, we can inject that information into a VW in real time. Combining that with surveillance equipment that has near-perfect awareness of enemy movements will allow us to populate a VW with all of the essential information that exists in the real world. Commanders and computer algorithms can evaluate the VW rather than the real world, make lethal decisions, and route orders through the VW to real combat platforms. These kinds of virtual worlds have the potential to reduce friendly fire, more accurately assess battle damage, simulate an action just moments before committing it to real-world execution, and support legal reviews of combat activities.

Future military virtual worlds will not just be a playground for rehearsal, but rather an integrated picture of real-world data and real-world actions. They will be an inseparable blend of the real and the virtual.

ADOPTING GAME TECHNOLOGY

Virtual-world technology has come to the military from its roots in entertainment. Early concepts on the use of games were being demonstrated as early as 1996. The Marine Corps modified the extremely popular 3D shooter DOOM and simply labeled it "Marine DOOM" (McLeroy 2008; Newman 1995). Though it generated a great deal of interest, the game was so primitive that it was very hard to imagine any real value in using these systems for a serious military purpose (fig. 40.2). Looking

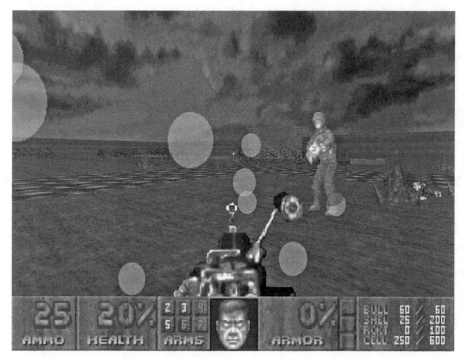

FIGURE 40.2 US Marine Corps modification of DOOM. Source: Lebigh's DOOM Blog, http://doom.starehry.eu/?p=407, accessed June 29, 2013.

forward from 1996, it was almost impossible to imagine the computational and visualization power that would exist in a common desktop computer just 10 years later. As a result, the concept of a military training system based on game technologies was delayed for almost a decade as computer technology advanced the power of the desktop systems to a level much closer to that found in the traditional, large-scale simulators.

The serious use of game technologies has evolved from niche applications that appear clever, but not particularly useful, to something that is now part of mainstream military training. These tools are currently becoming certified applications where the representations within the games are validated just as any other simulation. Games have taken their place alongside big simulators as accepted training tools (Aldrich 2009; Bergeron 2006; Michael 2005). This adoption pattern from fringe users to the core body of trainers has been driven by at least five major forces (fig. 40.3).

Advances in game technology to a level acceptable to military users are based firmly upon advances in computer hardware and software. As computer chips and graphics cards became more powerful, the amount of work that could be done in a very small and affordable package became increasingly impressive. This made it possible to create simulation models on a standard desktop computer that are sufficiently accurate to represent the physical and behavioral characteristics of the real world. As these technologies

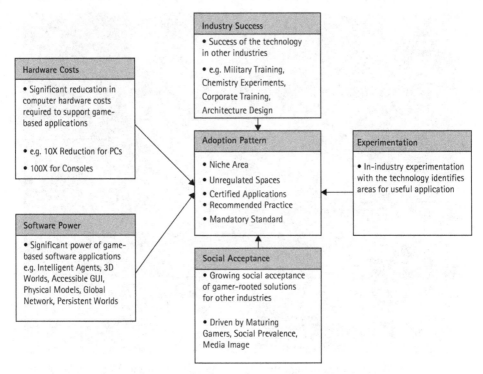

Hardware Costs

• Significant reducation in computer hardware costs required to support game-based applications

• e.g. 10X Reduction for PCs
• 100X for Consoles

Industry Success

• Success of the technology in other industries

• e.g. Military Training, Chemistry Experiments, Corporate Training, Architecture Design

Adoption Pattern

• Niche Area
• Unregulated Spaces
• Certified Applications
• Recommended Practice
• Mandatory Standard

Experimentation

• In-industry experimentation with the technology identifies areas for useful application

Software Power

• Significant power of game-based software applications e.g. Intelligent Agents, 3D Worlds, Accessible GUI, Physical Models, Global Network, Persistent Worlds

Social Acceptance

• Growing social acceptance of gamer-rooted solutions for other industries

• Driven by Maturing Gamers, Social Prevalence, Media Image

FIGURE 40.3 Five forces of game technology adoption. Source: Smith 2008.

were discovered by other industries, they began to show up in new systems for conducting science, designing buildings, delivering teleconferences, providing psychological counseling, and hundreds of other applications. The constant coverage of these systems by the media led to significant social acceptance of computer games. They grew from toys used by a small demographic of teenage boys to something that is now part of almost everyone's casual entertainment. This level of social acceptance opened the doors for their acceptance by the military as well. Finally, within the military research and experimentation communities, there were literally hundreds of independent experiments going on with game technologies, each of which identified a unique and valuable application. These five forces seemed to surround and drive the adoption of the technology to a point where it is now accepted on a par with the traditional live, virtual, and constructive training systems (Smith 2008).

Virtual worlds can potentially follow this same path.

Though slightly different from game technologies, VWs are similar enough that they can benefit from the same five forces. If a 3D shooter game with a small play area and a short time focus can provide useful training, then a virtual world for a much larger space and longer time horizon should be applicable to even larger military problems. The most compelling feature of virtual worlds is the fact that the worlds they create are constantly active regardless of the participation of any individual player or group. These worlds are alive and changing 24 hours a day, seven days a week (Smith 2009). This allows them to become an integrator of thousands of real-world data sources, creating an up-to-date mirror of the real world.

"Always On" Training

Soldiers need a training space that is "always on" and within which they have the power to design custom content and schedule collective training. Our current simulators and war games require a large number of support staff and specialized facilities. A military virtual world would move the complex server-side operations into a professionally managed IT center, while allowing soldiers to access it from a simple client on their desktops. This would enable 24/7 training operations that are focused on the needs of the soldier, rather than limiting them to a single week at a specific training center. With such a system soldiers and units could create the scenario that they want to train against and coordinate the event with other units to provide support functions and enemy role-playing. The real power of such a system is in putting training within the immediate reach of each soldier and unit.

The twenty-first century is a time of constant planning, preparation, decision-making, and action for the military. The missions that our soldiers are asked to perform are unconventional and constantly changing. To prepare for this, they need training tools that are flexible and always available. They need access to a 24/7 training range that can be configured by the soldiers to match their next mission. For such a range to be "always on," globally accessible, and integrated, it must be an online digital space, not a traditional physical space.

This shift to 24/7 availability has not yet been applied in military training. Training facilities are still difficult for military units to get access to, and they rely on a very limited staff of specialists to use them. A globally accessible virtual world in which training can be designed and conducted without the help of a dedicated staff is the only way to provide 24/7 access to training. This would create a training space that is located within reach of every soldier and every unit. It would allow planning and preparation to be conducted immediately after the conception of a new mission. It would also allow soldiers to refresh their skills and build their knowledge at any time. When they are ready to learn, the tools to support them would be at their fingertips.

The technical support for this is the desktop computer that has evolved into a supercomputer in your home. A typical desktop computer today has more computing power than resided in an entire simulation center just a decade ago. With this kind of affordable and available power, each soldier's computer can become a personal training range. Once connected to the Internet, it becomes a powerful node in a global training network. There would no longer be a need for soldiers to travel to a specially configured training center to conduct virtual training. These old central training hubs could be transitioned into a training service available within a military cloud-computing environment.

Military units should be able to enter this virtual space, coordinate with other users, and create scenarios that address their training needs. This kind of ad hoc, just-in-time gameplay is currently available to high school students in online games that support thousands of simultaneous users. A similar, but more realistic world can certainly be created for military training. These virtual worlds would include the tools necessary for users to create objects from scratch, arrange them into a customized training vignette, and script behaviors for computer-controlled avatars.

Imagine ten thousand soldiers securely logging into a virtual world from computers inside of the military's protected Internet domain. Soldier are identified by their official credentials and assigned an avatar, unit association, and virtual location to match their real-world identity. Using virtual radios like voice over IP, virtual C4I systems like map applications, and virtual vehicles, they are connected to each other just as they would be in a physical formation and physical training event. Leaders within the group use in-world editing tools to create a specific lay down of the enemy, friendly, and neutral forces across a 100-square-mile area. The terrain for this play box is imported directly from military terrain databases and is an exact match to its real counterpart. Finally, the behaviors of thousands of automated avatars are activated based on their identities, intentions, and past experiences. Selected from a toolbox of custom pieces, this scenario would allow units to come together according to their own schedules to train against a customized, but still validated, set of enemy behaviors.

The soldiers in these units might be viewed as a "flash mob" coming together when needed for a specific purpose and then dissipating just as quickly once the training event was finished. This model is significantly different from what is possible today. Our current training capabilities are dominated by systems and databases that require dedicated experts to prepare an event, that are available for a short period, and that must be scheduled months or even years in advance. The power of an "always on" virtual world, patterned from "always on" online games like *World of Warcraft*, is within reach for military training.

The military has a long history of posing the same question every time a new technology for training is introduced—"Will this totally replace older forms of training?" Looking back over many hundreds of years of sand tables, board war games, computer games, and virtual simulators, it is clear that the answer has always been "no". New technologies allow us to train in new ways. Sometimes those improvements replace older, less effective methods. But they have never completely replaced an existing method. Even with the near-perfect computer and electronic technology in a flight simulator, there are aspects of operating an aircraft and flying a mission that have to be done in the real equipment. Also, no matter how good an infantry rifle simulator is, it cannot completely replace the experience of marching through rough terrain with a 100-pound pack and having to bring your weapon to bear on a threat within a few seconds. Military training began as purely live training, to which we have added sand tables, war games, computer games, and virtual simulators over the centuries. Virtual worlds will join this family, offering new capabilities, replacing some previously ineffective methods, and becoming part of an integrated fabric for preparing soldiers for the dangers of war.

VIRTUAL-WORLD EDUCATION THEATER

"Always on" virtual worlds offer many more powerful capabilities than just training the soldiers in a shared environment. They also create a virtual education theater in which students in classrooms can observe real operations. These can be viewed in real time as they happen or delayed to match the teaching schedule at the school. Connecting as a passive viewer without an avatar in the world, individual students or instructor-led classrooms can navigate the world and watch any event that has occurred, whether it was a few hours ago or a few seconds ago. The data stream can also be edited automatically and in real time to eliminate sensitive information and to provide anonymity to the units who are actually under training.

Unlike a television program, this data stream is not fixed and permanent. It represents orders for specific avatars to take specific actions within a virtual world. As that data stream is recorded, it becomes a script in which every object and every event is recorded. This can be modified and replayed with variations. This creates the opportunity for a classroom of students to use the data as a basis for planning and creating their own versions of the events. Instructors can make assignments for groups of students to begin with a small vignette in the virtual world and incorporate the knowledge they have gained in class to see how it would play out within a larger scenario drawn from real-world training. The multiple outcomes that result would provide a rich set of data to consider, compare, judge, grade, and learn from in a classroom setting.

For centuries, military schools and courses have studied historical battles and analyzed the brilliant and fatal decisions that were made. An always-on virtual world would take this one step further, allowing students to direct these battles and insert their own solutions.

Robert Putnam argued that humans seek a number of different spaces in their lives where they can express different aspects of their personalities. Specifically, he looked at the impact that the Internet was having on traditional social activities, like a bowling league. He found that Internet social groups were meeting a number of needs that previously required face-to-face interaction. As a result of this new form of socialization, physical participation in a number of traditional activities was declining because the social need was being satisfied more conveniently in online communities (Putnam 2001). Virtual worlds for military education, training, and rehearsal will have a similar effect. The space and the activities will be distinctly different, just as bowling and attacking virtual trolls are very different, but will satisfy the underlying need to learn and understand a challenging situation. The degree to which a virtual world accomplishes this is only partly driven by its ability to create a realistic space. It may present a familiar, but unique and different, environment and still accomplish the same objective or meet the same need. Scott McCloud explained a similar trait in comics. They do not have to exactly imitate the real world to effectively communicate their message. In fact, in most cases, there is a better way to tell a story when you can take artistic license with the environment, emphasizing what is most important and minimizing the surrounding noise (McCloud 1994). Massively multiplayer online games and virtual worlds create "realistic" spaces, but they also retain a unique rendition of that reality and combine it with features that are intentionally fantastic. This modification of the real is not necessarily a negative trait when using that world for training. Applying the works of Putnam and McCloud, we can make these unique renderings more effective at communicating a message and conveying new skills than a perfect replication of the real world. With realism comes unnecessary detail, complexity, and confusion. A military virtual world is trying to do a better job of training than can be accomplished in the real world, and being better may require being different by reducing the exactness of the real world (Holland 1999; Waldrop 1993).

VISUAL INTEGRATION SPACE

This type of virtual space is also a natural integration medium for data collected from the real world. As we instrument every soldier and vehicle in the military, we have the means to track their movements and actions in real time. When combined with near perfect surveillance of enemy assets, this gives us all of the data necessary to create a window into real-world operations. It will no longer be science fiction to imagine actions in a virtual world being tied directly to outcomes in the real world, à la *Ender's Game* (Card 1985). The virtual world will become a medium for transferring information and orders to and from the real battlefield. We have become comfortable with a UAV pilot flying a drone from thousands of miles away and releasing deadly weapons based on the video images from remote cameras. A really robust virtual world would give us the ability to apply this kind of warfare to almost every platform on the battlefield. A military virtual world could become the global command-and-control system of the future. When this does happen, these virtual worlds become the most important computer applications in our arsenal—and attractive targets for our cyber enemies.

Virtual worlds can provide an integration space for data of all kinds. In the late 1990s Col. Jack Thorpe and others envisioned a global network of training simulators (Neyland 1997; Hapgood 2004; Miller and Thorpe 1995). These would be able to share data between widely distributed sites and significantly different systems. At that time, scientists and military thinkers expected all data to reside in and be managed by the training system at the end of the network. Today, we have expanded on that concept and have introduced intermediary computer servers where this data can be translated, integrated, redirected, and stored. The complete virtual world now resides in a cloud of networked computer services and is available to anyone who needs it.

This middle tier of computers means that integrated data can be directed to any node on the network. More recently, computer scientists have also moved all calculations within the virtual world to these middle servers, delivering only the finished results of computation and visualization to the end nodes. When this happens, the user's computer need not be a high-powered computer, but can be any device with the ability to render images and pass user commands back to a cloud-based server. Suddenly, every computer, no matter how powerful, becomes a potential node in the global training network. Suddenly a cell phone can present a rich virtual world for soldier participation because all of the heavy computation is being done on a server in the cloud, not on the device in the palm of his hand.

As networks become faster, the servers residing in the Internet cloud are no longer remote storage devices, but become personal computing resources that appear to be almost as close as the device in your hand. This effectively places a complete training system in the palm of every soldier who has the need to use it.

CYBERSECURITY

Today, "cybersecurity" and "cyberwarfare" refer to the protection, injury, and death of digital bits in communication messages, databases, and stored files (Clarke 2010). When a military virtual world becomes an exact replica of the real world, our cyberdefenses will need to protect the virtual world much more rigorously because it has the power to directly trigger real-world actions. Breaking into a VW database could mean the death of real people and the destruction of real objects (Smith 2010). This potential has been identified in science fiction for at least three decades (Stross 2007; Vinge 1981). We are finally reaching the point where those visions can be realized.

In a future where virtual worlds mirror the positions and actions of real-world objects, there is a one-to-one correlation between the cyberworld and the real world, with little need for complex analysis to understand what the data mean. Anyone who can access and manipulate the virtual world has a window into real-world plans, actions, and objects, and can potentially influence those by changing data in the virtual world.

This direct correlation makes the virtual world one of the most attractive and valuable targets for cyberattack and cyberdefense. This includes protecting training data, which is actually a map of the future plans and future capabilities of a country's military. These rich virtual worlds will attract the most talented hackers once they understand the real nature of the data contained within them. Cybersecurity needs to be applied to the virtual world with the same diligence that it has been applied to classified real-world data.

When the cyberworld/virtual world is so tightly knit with the real world, it becomes a valuable pressure point in conflicts between two nations that use this technology. Currently, disagreements are addressed first with diplomacy. When that does not solve the problem, actions might escalate to economic sanctions and military blockades. These could be followed by Special Forces intervention and finally full-scale war. A cyberattack could fit into this escalation of conflict. Spying upon, manipulating, and destroying cyber/virtual data may become a form of persuasion following diplomacy, but preceding intervention or warfare. The impact of cyber/virtual actions may sway one side or the other to turn to negotiation, rather than continuing to escalate. Or, conversely, cyberattacks could push a nation into escalation because it hopes to be more competitive and effective with its Special Forces than it would be as a digital adversary (Kramer 2009).

Could warfare in virtual space take on the leverage that currently resides in diplomatic, economic, terrorist, and combat actions? Such leverage would require that the virtual world be inseparable from the operations of a country's military or economy. The loss of the virtual world would have to significantly weaken the country itself. Today's electronic banking systems have become just such an essential digital dimension of society. Their loss would significantly weaken and even destroy important parts of our country. One could imagine a virtual world becoming so useful and so widely adopted that it held a similar status, at which point its defense would be just as important as defending the physical borders of the country.

Conclusion

A virtual world is an information space that has been rendered in three dimensions. It is not just a training space or an entertainment space. The virtual world can be a playground, a training range, or a command-and-control space depending upon the information that is being rendered. It can be a visually literal mirror of the world, or contain modifications that make the real information even more valuable. Realism and value are not measured visually; they are measured by the degree of understanding that is achieved by their representation.

Creating virtual worlds for training is an excellent first step for introducing them to a national military and demonstrating the power of an integrated world in 3D. This can potentially stimulate the spread of the technology into other important military functions like command and control, logistics management, and intelligence. Over time, virtual worlds could become a standard tool for all types of military operations that deal with the actions and locations of real objects of interest.

References

Aldrich, C. 2009. *The Complete Guide to Simulations and Serious Games: How the Most Valuable Content Will Be Created in the Age beyond Gutenberg and Google*. New York: Pfeifer Books.

Bergeron, B. 2006. *Developing Serious Games*. Boston, MA: Charles River Media.

Bolger, D. 1986. *Dragons at War: Land Battle in the Desert*. New York: Ivy Books.

Card, O. S. 1985. *Ender's Game*. New York: Tor Books.

Clarke, R. A. 2010. *Cyberwar: The Next Threat to National Security and What to Do about It*. New York: Ecco HarperCollins.

Davis, P. 1995. Distributed Interactive Simulation in the Evolution of DoD Warfare Modeling and Simulation. *Proceedings of the IEEE* 83 (8): 1138–1155.

Hapgood, F. 2004. Simnet. *Wired Magazine*, May. http://www.wired.com/wired/archive/5.04/ ff_simnet_pr.html. Accessed March 28, 2011.

Holland, J. 1999. *Emergence: From Chaos to Order*. New York: Basic Books.

Kramer, F. D., S. H. Starr, and L. Wentz, eds. 2009. *Cyberpower and National Security*. Washington DC: Potomac Books.

McCloud, S. 1994. *Understanding Comics: The Invisible Art*. New York: Harper Paperbacks.

McLeroy, C. 2008. History of Military Gaming. *Soldiers Magazine*, August 27. http://www.army. mil/-news/2008/08/27/11936-history-of-military-gaming/. Accessed March 28, 2011,

Michael, D., and S. Chen. 2005. *Serious Games: Games That Educate, Train, and Inform*. Boston, MA: Course Technology PTR / Cengage Learning.

Miller, D., and J. Thorpe. 1995. SIMNET: The Advent of Simulator Networking. *Proceedings of the IEEE* 83 (8): 1114–1123.

Newman, R. J. 1996. Warfare 2020. *US News and World Report*, August 5: 34–41.

Neyland, D. 1997. *Virtual Combat: A Guide to Distributed Interactive Simulation*. Mechanicsburg, PA: Stackpole Books.

Perla, P. 1990. *The Art of Wargaming*. Annapolis, MD: Naval Institute Press.

Putnam, R. 2001. *Bowling Alone: The Collapse and Revival of American Community*. New York: Touchstone Books.

Rolfe, J. M., and K. J. Staples, eds. 1988. *Flight Simulation*. Cambridge: Cambridge University Press.

Smith, R. 2008. Five Forces Driving Game Technology Adoption. *Proceedings of the Interservice/ Industry Training, Simulation, and Education Conference*, November. Fairfax, VA: National Training Systems Association.

Smith, R. 2009. *Games: The Virtual Frontier*. National Research Council, Committee on Modeling, Simulation, and Gaming. http://www.modelbenders.com/papers/RSmith_ NRC_MSG.pdf. Accessed March 28, 2011.

Smith, R. 2010. Computing beyond the Firewall. *Research Technology Management*, May–June. http://www.iriweb.org/Public_Site/RTM/RTM_Journal_Online.aspx.

Stross, C. 2007. *Halting State*. New York: Ace Books.

Vinge, V. 2001. *True Names and the Opening of the Cyberspace Frontier*, edited by James Frenkel, 239–230. New York: TOR Books.

Waldrop, M. M. 1993. *Complexity: The Emerging Science at the Edge of Order and Chaos*. New York: Basic Books.

Weiner, M. 1959. *An Introduction to War Games*. RAND Publication P-1773. http://www.rand. org/pubs/papers/P1773/. Accessed June 1, 2011.

PART IX

UTOPIA AND DYSTOPIA

CHAPTER 41

ETHICS AT THE BOUNDARIES OF THE VIRTUAL

CHARLES M. ESS

OUR love of play and fiction argues that our fascination with "the virtual"—including virtual worlds, virtual communities, virtual reality, and so on—is as old as human imagination itself. This reminder of the long history of our engagements with "the virtual" is crucial to a more contemporary focus on computer-mediated forms of "the virtual." Specifically, how we understand the virtual vis-à-vis our larger frameworks of reality and experience is decisive for our ethical reflections. Most simply, if we highlight the virtual as radically disparate from our ordinary understandings, practices, and experiences, then the virtual will thereby require (relatively) novel ethical reflection and (at least in part) new ethical frameworks. If, however, the virtual is more continuous than discontinuous with our historical sensibilities and frameworks, then our ethical reflections and frameworks appropriate thereto may likewise remain (largely) continuous with earlier frameworks and reflections.

This starting point, moreover, broadly describes the two phases of our thinking about the virtual as facilitated and enabled by computer technologies over the last several decades; this starting point further describes the larger collection of issues examined in information and computer ethics (ICE) more generally, as well as in the research and literatures of computer-mediated communication (CMC). The first phase, in parallel with larger enthusiasms in the early 1990s, hailed new virtual spaces (perhaps most notably, virtual communities) as places of unprecedented freedom and liberation. By contrast, in what now appears to be the second phase—marked by Pierre Lévy's influential critique of such dualism (1998)—our understanding of the relationships between "the virtual" and "the real" has become more complex, but in general, less dualistic. Broadly, the technologies and applications of virtuality used most widely—for example, text-based and later 2D and 3D virtual communities and worlds—have become increasingly suffused within the everyday experiences of the primary users of these technologies.

Certainly, stand-alone virtual environments such as CAVEs (Cave Automatic Virtual Environments) continue to develop, but these environments remain relatively exotic ones, unavailable to most people outside of dedicated research labs and installations. At the same time, various forms of *continuities* between our online and offline experiences have been increasingly emphasized, for example, within game research and scholarship (as highlighting, for example, the historical continuities between the fictive worlds of precomputation games and their computational analogues) and in the literatures of computer-mediated communication (CMC) more broadly (Ess and Consalvo 2011). For example, as mobile computing devices—primarily smartphones, tablet computers, and the growing "Internet of things" (e.g., GPS-enabled cameras and GPS-enabled computers for tracking one's daily run or bicycle ride)—increasingly dominate our use of and attention to networked computers as our access to the virtual, we grow increasingly familiar with uses of these devices to *augment* rather than replace our experience of our physical surroundings. Further developments of direct brain-computer interfaces can certainly offer ever greater possibilities of the "virtual only" experiences envisioned since at least the 1950s by both science fiction writers and philosophers. At the same time, however, it is equally realistic to suggest that such interfaces are likely to be as embedded in everyday life—such as sensor and computing devices worn in our clothing—and thereby used to augment rather than replace our direct experience of the world around us. And, as we will see below, this trajectory of embedding computer-enabled virtuality within the everyday is supported most fundamentally by a philosophical anthropology rooted especially in phenomenology that highlights how far we ineluctably bring our embodied sense of self into our experiences of virtual worlds (Ess and Thorseth 2011).

To explore these matters, I first review the history of our understandings of the diverse possible relationships between the real and the virtual. Second, I examine our usage of these terms, including a working definition of "the virtual" and affiliated examples (virtual communities, virtual worlds, etc.). This is conjoined with an emerging philosophical anthropology that provides us with a set of working assumptions for how we understand what it means to be ethical human beings as embodied and engaged in virtual domains. Two examples will illustrate how this philosophical anthropology foregrounds *virtue ethics* and *deontology* as primary ethical frameworks in contemporary analyses and resolutions of ethical challenges in virtual domains. (Briefly: virtue ethics seeks to identify the habits and practices (virtues) of excellence necessary for individual contentment and community harmony. *Deontology* highlights human autonomy and the (near-) absolute rights such autonomy entails.)

My aim here is to thus articulate the historical backgrounds and philosophical developments that provide us with both a robust understanding of human beings and a correlative ethical framework: this understanding and framework demonstrably enable us to come to grips with important ethical issues at the boundaries of the virtual. In doing so, we discover that this phenomenologically rooted deontology and virtue ethics directly challenge early dualisms that privileged the virtual, and reassert the priority of real-world practices and harms as the touchstone of ethical reflection.

FROM THE REAL TO THE VIRTUAL—AND BACK AGAIN

William Gibson's *Neuromancer* has profoundly influenced the emerging conceptions of the then-new "cyberspace" from the 1980s through the mid-1990s. To begin with, Gibson is credited with coining the term "cyberspace," to refer to what he calls a "consensual illusion" created by the interactions between billions of human beings as facilitated by computer networks and databases (Gibson 1984, 51). Surprisingly, however, in his characterization of how minds may experience such a cyberspace, Gibson draws upon an explicitly *theological* dualism. Specifically, Gibson takes up St. Augustine's notions of the eternal soul as radically distinct from a mortal body. Such a soul may hope for an eternity of bliss, at least once separated from the body, where the body is understood through Augustine's conception of original sin. This doctrine identifies the body in terms of a (male) sexuality that stubbornly resists rational control and the drive toward the Good. The upshot is a demonization of body and sexuality—and with them, women—as both radically different from and incorrigibly opposed to the soul. Indeed, Gibson directly echoes Augustine's language of "the Fall" when he describes how his hero, Case, loses his virtuoso abilities to maneuver through cyberspace; Gibson further echoes Augustine's account of original sin as occasioned by the woman who ostensibly tempts the otherwise virtuous man from his original and unproblematic communion with God (see Gibson 1984, 6, 239; cf. Ess 2010, 5ff.)

Such a dualistic understanding of the real-virtual dichotomy has other sources as well. Katherine Hayles, for example, uncovers dualistic modes of thinking in the foundational conceptions of cybernetics as developed by its founding father, Norbert Wiener, in the 1940s and 1950s (Hayles 1999). Moreover, Howard Rheingold helped popularize early 1990s virtual communities as disembodied meeting spaces open to all regardless of physical location and other limitations (1993). And in his famous "Declaration of Independence of Cyberspace," John Perry Barlow characterized cyberspace as "a world that is both everywhere and nowhere, but it is not where bodies live" (1996). At the extreme, finally, the originally Augustinian dualisms imported by Gibson into prevailing notions of cyberspace—and with it, the virtual—manifested themselves as religious all over again in what Stephen D. O'Leary and Brenda Brasher characterize as a "cybergnosticism" (1996). Cybergnosticism echoes the Gnostic belief that a soul, as radically separate from the body, can achieve immortality through acquiring a secret knowledge (*gnosis*): for cybergnostics, this secret knowledge and correlative immortality will emerge online.

Certainly, much of the impulse behind these dualisms was salutary: among other things, "liberation in cyberspace" was to free those otherwise systemically oppressed and exploited in a material and largely patriarchal world—beginning with women and children. More broadly, as virtual realities and virtual communities were documented and characterized—most notably, by Sherry Turkle (e.g., 1995)—their radical divorce from material realities allowed them to serve as ideal sandboxes for a postmodern identity play, that is, the exploration of multiple, ephemeral, and fragmented identities afforded by multiple and anonymous (or pseudonymous) identities in diverse online spaces.

In ethical terms, however, such dualisms were deeply problematic. As James Moor pointed out in 1985, the growing field of computer ethics was spawned in part by what he called "policy vacuums"—that is, new possibilities of interaction enabled by computers and computer networks to which no existing policy directly applied, beginning with issues of privacy (Moor 1985). Within the field of computer ethics, then, the "uniqueness debate" emerged as to how far such policy vacuums could be resolved using existing ethical frameworks—and how far such vacuums might require more or less novel ethical approaches (cf. Bynum 2010, 32). More specifically, such dualisms in our approach to virtual realities can issue, for example, in defenses of behaviors and expressions in the online environment that can only be understood as evil in the material world. So, for example, a common response to those critical of, say, the acts of rape and killing necessary to succeed in a game such as *Grand Theft Auto* is to say "It's only a game"—by which defenders ostensibly mean: there is no significant connection between our online and offline behaviors and acts—and hence, the ethical rules and social norms of the offline world simply do not apply to the online/virtual world.

These ontological dualisms between the virtual and the real—and thus the dualistic approach to ethics that resulted—were challenged very early on, however, both by way of case examples as well as on theoretical grounds. Perhaps most famously, Julian Dibbell's account of a "Rape in Cyberspace" (1993) helped catalyze critical reflection on how far our acts and norms in cyberspace could be meaningfully sundered from those in the material world (cf. Van Gelder [1985] 1991). That is, what for some appeared to be "just words" in a virtual space could nonetheless conjure up a very close sense of the profound violation of real-world rape. Moreover, within CMC research, critical feminist reflection recognized and warned against these early dualisms as risky for women (Stone 1991, 113). At the same time, empirical findings (e.g., Baym 1995; Kolko and Reid 1998) began to show that the presumptively hard lines between the virtual and the real were—with few exceptions—consistently blurred in praxis: this included specifically the "virtual communities" earlier celebrated by Rheingold (Kendall 2002). For her part, Katherine Hayles rejected these dualisms in favor of a "posthuman" conception, in which (among other things) "embodiment replaces a body seen as a support system for the mind" (1999, 288). By 2002, Barry Wellman and Caroline Haythornthwaite could characterize our online engagements in terms of *The Internet in Everyday Life*, the title of their coedited volume. In most domains of contemporary Internet studies, finally, we begin with the presumption that the online is largely continuous with our offline identities, norms, practices, and so on (cf. Ess and Consalvo, 2011).

Indeed, this turn away from dualistic modes of thinking is powerfully reinforced with regard to the particular assumption of a strong divide between mind and body: a rapidly growing literature in neuroscience highlights precisely the role of the body in our knowing and navigating the world around us. Especially as collected in the views of "enactivism," "the embodied mind," and "embodied cognition," the stress here is on a range of mind-body mechanisms that operate at a tacit, prereflective level, providing us with a continuous multisensory awareness of our surroundings and our place and possibilities therein. As Susan Stuart summarizes these views, "there is an inseparability of mind and world, and it is *embodied practice* rather than *cognitive deliberation* that marks the agent's *engagement* with its world" (2008, 256). For Stuart, this antidualism means, however, that now is the time for us to consider the ethics of the virtual.

REAL, VIRTUAL, ACTUAL: POSSIBLE MEANINGS, WORKING DEFINITIONS

Before doing so, however, we can take advantage of recent work that clarifies and makes more precise the meanings of such key terms as "virtual," "real," and "actual." To begin with, Marianne Richter points out a core distinction:

> Generic terms [are] super-ordinate concepts that allow for the distinction between sub-concepts (e.g., "elephant" and "dolphin" can be subsumed under the generic term "animal"). Modal terms refer to a different usage of terms in the way that they denote modalities of facts or propositions. Basic modal terms are "necessary," "possible" and "actual." (2011, 42)

Conceptual and philosophical clarity require that we use a given term either as a generic or modal one—but not both. Many common uses of the term "virtual," however, often fall into this confusion. That is, we often use "virtual" to refer to examples that amount to subcategories of the virtual as a *generic* term—including virtual communities, virtual romances, or virtual memory (cf. Søraker 2011, 44). But this is different in kind from uses of "virtual" as a *modal* term, as in the examples of "virtual reality" and "virtual actuality," which refer to given modes of being (cf. Ess and Thorseth 2011, xi and following).

Johnny Søraker helpfully builds on this point. So he distinguishes between (*a*) virtual *communities*, such as chat rooms, discussion forums, social networking sites, and the MUDs (Multi-User Dungeons) and MOOs (MUD object oriented) so central to 1990s CMC research and emphases on *postmodern* identities, and (*b*) virtual *worlds* (e.g., *World of Warcraft*, *Second Life*), virtual *reality*, and virtual *environments*, including offline video games (Søraker 2011, 65). As we are about to see, this distinction helps clarify whether our ethical considerations apply to virtual communities or to a virtual world or to both. Specifically, a *text*-based virtual community of the 1990s style might well allow for a greater gap between the offline and the online. But particularly on phenomenological grounds, as we move into ever-more *visual* environments such as virtual worlds, this gap will almost always be closed.

To begin with, virtual worlds, realities, and environments more fully replicate the body online—for example, through still or moving pictures and audio (think YouTube and Skype). In addition, in at least some virtual communities—for example, Facebook—the weight is laid on a strong coherency between your online presence and your offline identity (as would also be true, for example, if you want to do online banking or shopping). In doing so, they thereby soften the 1990s' hard duality between "the virtual" and "the real."

Moreover, Søraker uses "indexicality" to refer to our sense of presence in a three-dimensional space, including *a first-person view* that is rooted in Husserl's phenomenological account of how we know and navigate the world as *embodied* human beings (Søraker 2011, 63). In Søraker's taxonomy, indexicality is definitive of virtual environments generally and virtual worlds specifically. By contrast—and in part as they rely primarily on *text-based* self-representations—only "the virtual" in the generic sense and virtual communities as such do not necessarily entail indexicality (2011, 85). This means that as human beings, we have an ineluctable tendency to bring a unitary sense of self with us, so to speak, wherever we go—certainly as we enter online environments that include reasonably strong representations of our body, but also the otherwise non-indexical domains of virtual communities per se.

What this means in ethical terms: on the one hand, such 1990s dualisms and correlative defenses of the "It's only a game" sort may still hold for specific sorts of online environments—especially if they are more text-based, designed to foster anonymity or pseudonymity, or are devoted to sensitive or marginalized identities and practices (e.g., GLBTQ discussion boards, as especially useful for such persons otherwise isolated by geography and culture). On the other hand, indexicality—along with both the CMC research noted above, and, as we are about to see, a phenomenologically rooted philosophical anthropology more specifically—rather emphasize how far our online sense of selfhood, identity, and thus of moral agency and responsibility are inextricably interwoven with our offline sensibilities, practices, and so on.

A Philosophical Anthropology: What Does It Mean to Be an Ethical—and Embodied—Human Being Engaged in Virtual Environments?

Some of the earliest critiques of dualistic assumptions at work in earlier conceptions of cyberspace and virtual environments were rooted in phenomenological analyses of how we come to know and learn to navigate in our world(s) as embodied human beings (Borgmann 1999). As Hubert Dreyfus (2001) argues, for example, insofar as education includes attention to the mastery of embodied skills—for example, playing music, making medical diagnoses and offering treatment, even playing chess—it thereby requires the *embodied* copresence of an experienced teacher. This is especially true with regard to a specific form of *ethical* judgment—what Socrates and Aristotle characterized as *phronesis*, a kind of reflective (rather than determinative or deductive) judgment that works "from the ground up," that is, from within the multiple, specific, and concrete details of a given context in order to first discern what more general principles, norms, codes, and so on, may apply to that context. In part, embodied copresence is required for such learning insofar as much of this knowledge and understanding is *tacit*, rather than something that even experts can articulate and make explicit in language (e.g., in a lecture or article).

As well, such knowledge is always acquired and applied from our own first-person perspective (cf. Ess 2011, 21f.) In particular, Johnny Søraker's account of indexicality builds on both the phenomenologies of Albert Borgmann and Edmund Husserl. In this light, the most successful virtual environments succeed in part because they most closely imitate our embodied, first-person perspective. As Søraker observes:

> Being in a reality requires having a first-person view, and it is impossible to have more than one first-person view. That is, you cannot participate in multiple virtual realities simultaneously any more than you can be in more than one spatiotemporal place simultaneously in physical reality. You can have as many avatars in as many virtual worlds or environments as you like, but as soon as you experience the virtual reality "through your own eyes" you can only be in one virtual reality at a time. (2011, 63)

The resulting conception of selfhood and identity thus weighs more in the direction of a unitary rather than a multiple and fragmented postmodern understanding.

This emerging philosophical anthropology is especially crucial with regard to the *ethical* frameworks we may take up in considering our acts and behaviors in virtual environments. That is: this anthropology leads most frequently to an emphasis on *virtue ethics*, an ethical framework that has enjoyed a significant renaissance over the past several decades in Western philosophy, alongside more familiar *utilitarianisms* and *deontologies*. This is in part as this anthropology takes up a Kantian understanding of human being as a rational *autonomy*, one whose first characteristic is thereby the capacity to give oneself one's own law. In Kantian ethics, this leads to the foundational duty of mutual *respect* for one another as human beings: in the second formulation of the categorical imperative, we are always to treat others as ends in themselves, never as a means (to our own ends or goals) only (Kant 1965, 52). That is, if we regard other human beings as merely means to our own goals, we thereby deny them of their fundamental autonomy as precisely the capacity to determine and pursue their own goals. This is, to be sure, a core tenet of modern *deontology* (Ess 2013, 206–212; Alexander and Moore 2007). As the same time, Bjørn Myskja has argued that Kant's account of the importance of deception in the development of social trust thereby leads to a "virtuous circle." That is, the more we practice *being* trustworthy agents with one another (a deception, at least at first, insofar as we may be less than fully trustworthy persons), the more we thereby *become* such trustworthy persons. Myskja argues this is specifically true of virtual worlds online (Myskja 2011).

Such virtuous circles point to a central emphasis of virtue ethics—that is, that the habits and capacities requisite for individual contentment and community harmony are not "given" but only acquired—and that over the period of a lifetime, as such habits and capacities are *practiced*. This is most especially the case for the critical virtues of trust, empathy, patience, perseverance, and, most importantly, *phronesis* itself as the core capacity for ethical judgment.

Moreover, this philosophical anthropology stresses a nondual relationship between self and body—that is, selves who experience our worlds, both virtual and nonvirtual, from the irreducibly unique first-person perspective of an embodied being. This means, as a number of philosophers and theorists have now observed, not only that, in effect, we by and large bring our virtues (along with our sense of identity and selfhood) with us as we enter into new virtual spaces: it further means that these virtual spaces may offer new opportunities precisely for practicing and improving upon traditional virtues—in contrast with an earlier dualistic approach that stressed instead the effective abandonment of real-world, embodied ethical norms and practices. So, for example, Miguel Sicart argues that the virtual environments at work in a wide range of computer-based games can serve as distinctively significant places for the development of a range of ethical virtues, most centrally including *phronesis* (2009). Similarly, Shannon Vallor has powerfully argued that virtual environments such as social networking sites may foster—but also limit in important ways—friendship and its affiliated virtues (2012).

In particular, we can see how virtue ethics is at work in specific ethical issues evoked by virtuality.

The Virtual and the Real in Ethics: Recent Case Studies

Virtual Adultery in Cyberspace?

We begin with a thought experiment offered by Susan Stuart in the context of her own contribution to this philosophical anthropology—what she calls a "softer enactivist ontology" that takes on board both phenomenological analyses (including those of Merleau-Ponty) and an extensive array of neurologically based findings that emphasize that "There is an inseparability of mind and world, and it is embodied practice rather than cognitive deliberation that marks the agent's engagement with its world" (Stuart 2008, 256).

Stuart's ontology is developed precisely in order to consider how far especially fully immersive forms of virtual reality might succeed in persuading us that in such realities, we are indeed fully engaged with a *real* world. Stuart recognizes the many benefits of what she calls experiential technologies, for example, flight and medical simulators that allow pilots and physicians to practice and improve their skills (virtues), but without risking either their own lives or those of patients (2008, 257ff.).

The ethical concerns begin to emerge for Stuart with the use of video games such as *Halo 2*. Stuart cites the example of a soldier from the 276th Engineer Battalion of the US Army, who described his real experience of warfare in Iraq: "It felt like I was in a big video game.... I couldn't believe I was seeing this. It was like 'Halo.' It didn't even seem real, but it was real" (Vargas 2006, cited in Stuart 2008, 259). Stuart highlights here the key ethical difficulty: what are the real-world consequences of our more or less completely blurring formerly clear boundaries between the real and the virtual? That is, most crudely, we can understand much of ethics as the concern to avoid real-world harms, most certainly including killing. Recall the defense, "It's only a game": insofar as a clear boundary holds between the real and the virtual, and given that our acts in the virtual do not issue in real-world harms, then such acts may be ethically unproblematic. By contrast, what might have been an "ethics-free" virtual game now fully blurs with real-world death— but it is not *experienced* as real by the agents involved. An ostensibly ethics-free virtuality, as no longer distinguishable from material reality, thus threatens, worst case, to erase the ethics of the real world altogether, with literally fatal consequences. But if real-world harms are the touchstone of ethics, then, in the face of the blurring of the real-virtual boundary, most especially insofar as this blurring risks extinguishing our ability to fully experience such harms directly, then real-world harms must regain priority.

To be clear: Stuart intends not to condemn violent video games but rather to dramatically make the point that with current technologies—and certainly those in development—we are already at the point where the once reasonably clear boundary between virtual and real is all but erased. Given the historical significance of this boundary for our ethical reflections, Stuart's argument is that now is the time to consider how we may be required to revise and reshape our ethical frameworks and sensibilities in order for them to be of use.

Stuart makes this point a second way with the example of a "virtual reality adultery suit" (2008, 259ff.). The sensors and receptors of such a suit are designed to control and respond to the actions and experiences of one's avatar in a virtual world. The user of such a suit will be able to interact with another suit-user via their avatars or AI-driven avatars representing, for example, famously attractive persons or perhaps more homely ones, depending on one's pocketbook. Previously, we might have been able to ethically distinguish between real-world adultery and, say, identifying with the adulterous hero or heroine in a novel: again, we presume that as long as such fantasies do not issue in real-world betrayal, such fantasies are (largely) harmless. But as with the soldier's experience—what happens when the virtual-real boundary is more or less completely blurred? As Stuart asks, "are you being unfaithful to your partner or spouse?" (2008, 260). Whatever our responses may be, again the point for Stuart is "The morality of the one [the virtual world] is not easily separable from the other [the real world] as we understand from the fact that—with an ever increasing frequency—action in the virtual world spills over and affects our lives in the real world." Given this blurring, in particular, Stuart concludes: "If the experience is, as far as it can be imagined, indistinguishable from the real thing, even down to the subterfuge of not revealing it to your loved one, then it smacks of infidelity."

So far, then, it would seem that the blurring between our experiences of the virtual and the real increasingly implies that our ethical sensibilities regarding the virtual must *increasingly* import, so to speak, our more familiar ethics from the material world of embodied, human beings; but this is precisely *contrary* to especially earlier justifications for their radical separation and thus irrelevance to one another. This same point is made in a second way, and with regard to the "real world" example of virtual child pornography.

Virtual Child Pornography

Litska Strikwerda points out that child pornography is one of the few ethical bright lines in contemporary information ethics and law (2011, 141ff.). That is, child pornography is criminalized more or less everywhere. But what about *virtual* child pornography, that is, pornographic materials in which the "children" are entirely the result of digital production processes that involve no real children? Do we have any ethical reasons to critique such materials—much less legal grounds for criminalizing them?

To examine this question, Strikwerda takes up three legal and ethical frameworks, beginning with John Stuart Mill's harm principle, as definitive of modern liberalism. As Mill's utilitarianism insists, those acts that result in more harm than pleasure are wrong as they counter utilitarian efforts to maximize pleasure. But the harm principle means that "victimless" crimes—most notably, prostitution—cannot be consistently rejected. Rather, if no real, material, *bodily* harm results from such acts, but only pleasure, then society has no ethical grounds for criminalizing such acts. Analogously, if the production of virtual child pornography causes no direct, real, bodily harm to real children, but only pleasure for those who consume it, then likewise, there are no ethical grounds for condemning it (Strikwerda 2011, 144ff.).

A second approach here is paternalism. On this view, society has an interest in prohibiting acts that may lead to harm of others. So contemporary societies prohibit smoking in enclosed public spaces, for example: while individuals are left free to harm themselves, such societies seek to prohibit doing so in ways that will harm others. Analogously, if the production, distribution, or consumption of virtual child pornography leads to harm—for example, as it inspires or aids pedophiles in encouraging real children to engage in sexual acts—then we would have ethical grounds for criminalizing such material. But the available evidence does not show a clear link between the production and consumption of virtual child pornography and real-world sexual acts toward children. Hence, at least in light of current evidence, the paternalism principle cannot justify criminalizing virtual child pornography (Strikwerda 2011, 146–151).

Strikwerda then takes up virtue ethics as conjoined with the phenomenological analyses of what Sara Ruddick has characterized as "complete sex" (Ruddick 1975). Ruddick first of all critiques more dualistic understandings of sexuality—that is, as something that occurs solely between "bodies" as somehow radically separated from their "owner's" sense of selfhood and identity. Rather, a phenomenological account of our most intense experiences (such as experiences of playing sports) foregrounds how in such experiences, there is no felt mind-body dualism, but rather an immediate unity of self and body. Not all sexual experiences count (or need to count) for Ruddick as involving such direct unity: but she argues that those that do are morally preferable first of all because in such experiences, our own personhood and autonomy cannot be separated from our bodies, and hence these experiences foster the Kantian duty of respect for the Other as a person. Ruddick further argues that such sexual experiences thereby foster two additional virtues—namely, the norm of equality and the virtue of loving (Ruddick 1975, 98ff.).

In contrast, then, with paternalistic or liberal approaches, this phenomenological background first of all means that "it is not necessary to prove a causal link between virtual child pornographic images and actual instances of abuse to consider them as harmful" (Strikwerda 2011, 151). Second, empirical evidence suggests that the production, distribution, and consumption of virtual child pornography *are* affiliated with a view of children (and women) as inferior objects to be dominated: in Strikwerda's phrase, such materials *eroticize* inequality (2011, 155). If we endorse, following Kant, Ruddick, and Strikwerda, equality between persons as a vital ethical norm and virtue, that is, one that must be *practiced* in our attitudes and behaviors toward others, then it seems clear that the production, distribution, and consumption of virtual child pornography fundamentally violate this norm. For Strikwerda, this violation justifies criminalizing virtual child pornography alongside its real-world counterpart (2011, 155–158).

Strikwerda's analysis demonstrates how a phenomenologically rooted virtue ethics provides a robust ethical framework for grappling with ethical issues at the boundaries of the virtue and the real. In particular, if our moral intuitions tell us that virtual child pornography is ethically suspect, this framework helps us articulate a basis for those intuitions, whereas the more familiar utilitarianism and deontology seem unable to come to grips with the issue. But whatever our intuitions on this issue may be, the larger point is to see a distinct advantage of phenomenology and virtue ethics over utilitarian approaches in our efforts to grapple with ethical challenges at the virtual-real boundary. That is, insofar as this boundary still holds, and insofar as this boundary is used to defend acts that otherwise fail to issue in real-world, material harm, both phenomenology and virtue ethics challenge such defenses in ways beyond the limits of earlier utilitarianisms. To begin with, whatever the states of our technologies, from both phenomenological and virtue ethics perspectives, the real (body) and the virtual (selfhood, mind) are not as easily distinguishable as such a defense would presume. Specifically, as Stuart has emphasized, virtue ethics endorses the pursuit of habit and practices that become literally in-corporated within our bodies (Stuart, personal communication to CE). In some ways and some cases, as the analogy of the solitary smoker suggests, it may well be true that we can somehow indulge in intentions and attitudes (i.e., built on objectification and inequality) in a mental domain somehow separate from our physical acts. But insofar as our phenomenological anthropology holds, and insofar as we take on board both the Kantian and virtue ethics trajectories of that anthropology—minimally, we will be wary of any such dualism and the intentionalities and sensibilities of inequality and objectification it defends. Especially in the face of the threat Stuart highlights—that is, a blurring of the real-virtual boundary that threatens to extinguish our ability to experience real-world harms as *real*—phenomenology and virtue ethics provide a much-needed complement to a utilitarianism that presumes such an ability as foundational to the maximization of the good.

The Virtual and the Real in Ethics: Future Directions?

As Stuart presciently warned, the boundary between computer-enabled virtuality and our experiences of the material world surrounding us continues to blur as technologies continue to develop. As the example of virtual child pornography suggests, the resulting ethical issues may well seem, at least on first glance, to be genuinely novel. But as the history of ethics in general, and as the history of information and computing ethics more specifically—including, as I have tried to show here, ethics at the boundaries of the virtual—suggest, we generally find ways to apply established ethical frameworks to such ethical challenges and with at least reasonable success.

This by no means demonstrates that no significantly new challenges will emerge that will escape more established ethical frames. If anything, multiple advances in both our understanding of how the brain(-body) works and in our technological abilities to exploit that understanding continue to fuel the development of brain-computer interfaces that approach the wildest dreams of earlier science-fictions (e.g., Nicolelis 2011). The "brain in a vat" scenario—namely, the capacity to sustain human consciousness upon either an organic or nonorganic "platform" no longer connected to one's body—seems increasingly possible; and, in certain cases, such a possibility seems obviously desirable and ethically unproblematic. Those whose awareness of and control over their own bodies have been destroyed by war, accident, or disease would likely rejoice at having a real-world robot body linked to their brain that would allow them to experience and enjoy the world as an embodied being. And certainly there will be those, following the dreams of Hans Moravec (1990) and Ray Kurzweil (2001), who will pursue some sort of computer-mediated immortality, however virtual and disembodied it may be. Whether or not such immortality is ultimately satisfying, a first ethical question will be one of access: who will be able to enjoy such immortality as a presumptively scarce resource, at least in its first iterations?

At the same time, however, some of the most recent work in philosophy of mind reiterates the stubborn resistance of embodied knowledge and identity to erasure in virtual environments, a resistance increasingly apparent over the last decade (and more). That is, to begin with, *despite* the increasing sophistication, accessibility, and uses of virtual environments, contemporary philosophical exploration of our experiences of personal identity online expand earlier critiques of the dualisms undergirding 1990s conceptions of "liberation in cyberspace." Briefly, a number of applicable theories of identity (psychological, narrative, and so on) make clear that if the human body is lost, our most important sensibilities of personal identity go with it. Moreover, new technologies are increasingly used for the sake of liberating real-world human beings in real-world contexts—most famously, the Arab Spring of 2011 (e.g., Bakardjieva and Gaden 2012; Ess 2012).

These developments point to an ongoing dialectic between technological developments and usages that continuously enhance our capacities to experience and explore "the virtual" in ways largely disconnected from embodiment vis-à-vis our (so far) ineluctable insistence on understanding human identity—and thereby ethics—as a primarily embodied matter. This dialectic is in keeping with the larger history of ethics in the face of diverse forms of development, including technological development. This larger history further shows the trend I have sought to illustrate here—namely, that despite an initial and often overwhelming sense of a novelty that escapes earlier ethical frameworks and analyses, we gradually learn to develop ethical approaches to new technologies that include both the familiar and the more novel.

Of course, it remains perfectly possible that these patterns will be obliterated by some overwhelming technological (and/or social and/or political and/or environmental...) development that eliminates all possibility of such a dialectic. But in the meantime, I hope that this chapter may provide some useful history and examples for those who come along to take up these new technologies and their ethics.

References

Alexander, L. and M. Moore. 2007. Deontological Ethics. *The Stanford Encyclopedia of Philosophy*, Fall 2008 edition, edited by E. N. Zalta. http://plato.stanford.edu/archives/fall2008/entries/ethics-deontological/. Accessed June 29, 2013.

Bakardjieva, M., and G. Gaden. 2012. Web 2.0 Technologies of the Self. *Philosophy and Technology* 25 (3): 399–413. doi:10.1007/s13347-011-0032-9.

Barlow, J. P. 1996. A Declaration of the Independence of Cyberspace. February 9. http://w2.eff.org/Censorship/Internet_censorship_bills/barlow_0296.declaration. Accessed June 29, 2013.

Baym, N. 1995. The Emergence of Community in Computer-Mediated Communication. In *CyberSociety: Computer-Mediated Communication and Community*, edited by S. G. Jones, 138–163. Thousand Oaks, CA: Sage.

Borgmann, A. 1999. *Holding onto Reality: The Nature of Information at the Turn of the Millennium*. Chicago: University of Chicago Press.

Bynum, T. W. 2010. The Historical Roots of Information and Computer Ethics. In *The Cambridge Handbook of Information and Computer Ethics*, edited by L. Floridi, 20–38. Cambridge: Cambridge University Press.

Dibbell, J. 1993. A Rape in Cyberspace or How an Evil Clown, a Haitian Trickster Spirit, Two Wizards, and a Cast of Dozens Turned a Database into a Society. *Village Voice*, December 21, 36–42.

Dreyfus, H. 2001. *On the Internet*. New York: Routledge.

Ess, C. 2010. Trust and New Communication Technologies: Vicious Circles, Virtuous Circles, Possible Futures. Knowledge, *Technology, and Policy* 23 (3–4): 287–305.

Ess, C. 2011. Self, Community, and Ethics in Digital Mediatized Worlds. In *Trust and Virtual Worlds: Contemporary Perspectives*, edited by C. Ess and M. Thorseth, 3–30. Oxford: Peter Lang.

Ess, C. 2012. At the Intersections between Internet Studies and Philosophy: "Who Am I Online?" Introduction to special issue, *Philosophy & Technology* 25 (3): 275–284. doi:10.1007/s13347-012-0085-4.

Ess, C. 2013. *Digital Media Ethics. Second edition*. Cambridge: Polity.

Ess, C., and M. Consalvo. 2011. What Is "Internet Studies"? In *The Handbook of Internet Studies*, edited by M. Consalvo and C. Ess, 1–7. Oxford: Wiley-Blackwell.

Ess, C. and M. Thorseth. 2011. Introduction. In *Trust and Virtual Worlds: Contemporary Perspectives*, edited by C. Ess and M. Thorseth, vii–xxix. Oxford: Peter Lang.

Gibson, W. 1984. *Neuromancer*. New York: Ace Books.

Hayles, K. 1999. *How We Became Posthuman: Virtual Bodies in Cybernetics, Literature, and Informatics*. Chicago: University of Chicago Press.

Kant, I. 1965. *Grundlegung zur Metaphysik der Sitten* [Groundwork of the Metaphysics of Morals]. Hamburg: Felix Meiner Verlag.

Kendall, L. 2002. *Hanging Out in the Virtual Pub*. Berkeley: University of California Press.

Kolko, B., and E. Reid. 1998. Dissolution and Fragmentation: Problems in Online Communities. In *Cybersociety 2.0*, edited by S. Jones, 212–231. Thousand Oaks, CA: Sage.

Kurzweil, R. 2001. The Web within Us: Minds and Machines Become One. *Kurzweil Accelerating Intelligence*. http://www.kurzweilai.net/the-web-within-us-minds-and-machines-become-one. Accessed June 29, 2013.

Lévy, P. 1998. *Becoming Virtual*. New York. Basic Books.

Moor, J. 1985. What Is Computer Ethics? *Metaphilosophy* 16 (4): 266–275.

Moravec, H. 1990. *Mind Children: The Future of Robot and Human Intelligence*. Cambridge, MA: Harvard University Press.

Myskja, B. 2011. Trust, Lies, and Virtuality. In *Trust and Virtual Worlds: Contemporary Perspectives*, edited by C. Ess and M. Thorseth, 120–136. Oxford: Peter Lang.

Nicolelis, M. 2011. *Beyond Boundaries: The New Neuroscience of Connecting Brains with Machines–and How It Will Change Our Lives*. New York: Times Books.

O'Leary, S. D., and B. Brasher. 1996. The Unknown God of the Internet. In *Philosophical Perspectives on Computer-Mediated Communication*, edited by C. Ess, 233–269. Albany: SUNY Press.

Rheingold, H. 1993. *Virtual Community: Homesteading on the Electronic Frontier*. Reading, MA: Addison-Wesley.

Richter, M. 2011. "Virtual Reality" and "Virtual Actuality": Remarks on the Use of Technical Terms in Philosophy of Virtuality. In *Trust and Virtual Worlds: Contemporary Perspectives*, edited by C. Ess and M. Thorseth, 31–43. Oxford: Peter Lang.

Ruddick, S. 1975. Better Sex. In *Philosophy and Sex*, edited by R. Baker and F. Elliston, 280–299. Amherst, NY: Prometheus Books.

Sicart, M. 2009. *The Ethics of Computer Games*. Cambridge, MA: MIT Press.

Søraker, J. 2011. Virtual Entities, Environments, Worlds and Reality: Suggested Definitions and Taxonomy. In *Trust and Virtual Worlds: Contemporary Perspectives*, edited by C. Ess and M. Thorseth, 44–72. Oxford: Peter Lang.

Stone, A. R. 1991. Will the Real Body Please Stand Up? Boundary Stories about Virtual Cultures. In *Cyberspace: First Steps*, edited by M. Benedikt, 81–118. Cambridge, MA: MIT Press.

Strikwerda, L. 2011. Virtual Child Pornography: Why Images Do Harm from a Moral Perspective. In *Trust and Virtual Worlds: Contemporary Perspectives*, edited by C. Ess and M. Thorseth, 139–161. Oxford: Peter Lang.

Stuart, S. 2008. From Agency to Apperception: Through Kinaesthesia to Cognition and Creation. *Ethics and Information Technology* 10 (4): 255–264.

Turkle, S. 1995. *Life on the Screen. Identity in the Age of the Internet*. New York: Simon & Schuster.

Vallor, S. 2012. Flourishing on Facebook: Virtue Friendship and New Social Media. *Ethics and Information Technology* 14 (3): 185–199. doi:10.1007/s10676-010-9262-2.

Van Gelder, L. (1985) 1991. The Strange Case of the Electronic Lover. In *Computerization and Controversy*, edited by C. Dunlop and R. Kling, 364–375. San Diego, CA: Academic Press, 1991.

Vargas, J. A. 2006. Virtual Reality Prepares Soldiers for Real War: Young Warriors Say Video Shooter Games Helped Hone Their Skills. *Washington Post*, February 14. http://www.washingtonpost.com/wp-dyn/content/article/2006/02/13/AR2006021302437.html. Accessed June 29, 2013.

Wellman, B., and C. Haythornthwaite. 2002. *The Internet in Everyday Life*. Malden, MA: Blackwell.

CHAPTER 42

THE SOCIAL IMAGINARY OF VIRTUAL WORLDS

PATRICE FLICHY

IN research on the discourse accompanying technology, scholars in the field of science and technology studies have paid particular attention to the promises made to the public by the promoters of a science or technique. Nuclear technology, genetically modified organisms (GMOs), and nanotechnologies, for example, have by no means fulfilled the promises made by their designers; in fact these promises have often proved to be illusions. The comparative analysis of promises and fears is part of the long tradition of the study of controversies and the governance of science (Wynne 2008).

The theoretical orientation of this chapter is different, for it focuses on the technical imaginary (Flichy 2007a; 2007b). The aim is not to see how different representations of the same technology clash, or how the promoters of a device seek to appeal to or even to fool the public, but to understand how common representations take shape between different stakeholders concerned with a technology. Initially, these discourses may of course vary widely or even contradict one another, but they end up converging. Our focus is not the public debate surrounding a technology (should it be launched or prohibited), but rather the study of the imaginatively created common world required to invent and develop a technical device such as virtual reality.

Let us start by considering social scientists who have studied social imaginaries and utopias (Appadurai 1996; Taylor 2004; Ricoeur 1986).[1] Note, first, that the notion of a social imaginary is not a set of disembodied ideas of reality; "rather it is what enables through making sense of the practices of a society" (Taylor 2004, 2). Arjun Appadurai sees this imaginary not as something resembling a dream, but as an essential element of social practices:

> No longer mere fantasy (opium for the masses whose real work is somewhere else), no longer simple escape (from a world defined principally by more concrete purposes and structures), no longer elite pastime (thus not relevant to the lives of ordinary people), and no longer mere contemplation (irrelevant for new forms of desire and subjectivity), the imagination has become an organized field of social practices (1996, 31).

The mediums conveying this imaginary have taken on new forms: neither philosoph-ical or theoretical discourses, nor legends or old myths, but everyday mass culture man-ifested in the media in the form of narratives or images (science fiction novels, films, TV programs). Appadurai sees this mass culture as "a new force to the imagination in social life today" (53)—an analysis echoed in that of Dahlgren (2009) on the "popular public sphere."

Contrary to the romantic model in which the imaginary is the result of the individual creation of a talented artist, the contemporary social imaginary is collective, the result of a shared understanding that is negotiated and accepted by all, and that seems sufficiently evident to be explicated. Charles Taylor describes it as

> the ways in which people imagine their social existence, how they fit together with others, how things go on between them and their fellows, the expectations that are normally met, and the deeper normative notions and images that underlie these expectations ... that common understanding that makes possible common practices and a widely shared sense of legitimacy. (2004, 23)

Clearly, the imaginary concerns thought patterns, for example our position in time and space, as well as our normative background.

This social imaginary that makes social practices meaningful is not essentially lim-ited to the elite; it is shared by society as a whole and especially by ordinary individuals. Imagination "has now become a part of the quotidian mental work of ordinary peo-ple.... [They] have begun to deploy their imaginations in the practice of their everyday lives" (Appadurai 1996, 5).

Finally, imagination is an important cultural resource that enables new forms of inno-vation and ways of using them to exist. Imagination is necessary to produce a collective meaning, negotiated and then accepted by all. In fact, humans need to imagine collec-tively if they are to be able to interact, to give meaning to their practices, and then to engage in them.

But to further our insight into how the social imaginary enables individuals to engage in action, we need to draw on the work of another philosopher, Paul Ricoeur, and his comparative analysis of utopia and ideology in the political imaginary of the nineteenth century.

In contrast with characteristic Marxist and Marxian understandings, Ricoeur argues that ideology is not the opposite of reality, for reality is symbolically mediated. Hence, the current perspective that opposes utopia and reality overlooks the fact that reality is not a state but a process. In fact, ideology and utopia are the two opposite extremes of the social imaginary. While the former seeks to preserve the social order, the latter aims to overturn it. As a result, there is constant tension between stability and change. Utopia enables us to explore new avenues; it presents an alternative to existing models, but always contains the risk of escaping reality. On the other hand, ideology can be content with masking reality, but it also offers legitimacy to choices made, and provides an identity for social collectives.

In the final analysis, Ricoeur's conviction is "that we are always caught in this oscilla-tion between ideology and utopia ... we must try to cure the illnesses of utopia by what is wholesome in ideology—by its element of identity—...the petrifications of ideologies by the utopian element" (Ricoeur 1986, 312). The philosopher is aware of the risk of remaining in a circular flow of thought that constantly returns to one concept or another. Instead, he says, we should imagine a spiral. It is precisely this dynamic perspective that we ought to adopt to become aware of the imaginary of virtual worlds. It allows us to distinguish three forms of utopia (Flichy 2007a):

1. The *watershed utopia* in which the schemes conceived are widely diverse, often opposed. Actors discover the projects of others. These improbable encounters can be passing occurrences or profoundly fertile events.
2. The *project utopia* in which a real alternative to existing technical devices is constructed as the models roughed out in the preceding phase become full-blown projects.
3. The *phantasmogoric utopia* in which no technical incarnation of the utopia is built. It is a refusal to face the technical reality.

We can, moreover, identify two forms of ideology: the *mask ideology*, in which aspects of reality are readily concealed in order to promote the new technique; and the *mobilization ideology*, in which the positive function is to mobilize the actors concerned—both the producers of the technology and its users.[2]

On this basis, two salient characteristics of the socio-technical imaginary emerge:

1. The imaginary proposes alternatives, offers elements to explore possibilities and then to create an innovation by mobilizing different forms of utopia and ideology.
2. The imaginary is a constituent element of identity and of the coherence of a human group; it is visible in popular mass culture; it is shared; it gives meaning to and organizes a variety of social practices.

It is this aspect of the social imaginary that we will study first, by examining the role of science fiction in the imaginary of virtual worlds. We will then examine the utopias and ideologies involved in the construction of imaginary worlds. Using the cases of *Second Life, Habitat,* and massively multiplayer online games (MMOs), we will focus on three themes: the creation of worlds; circulation within these spaces; and the body.

A Shared Culture: Science Fiction

Many observers have pointed out the links between virtual worlds and science fiction. In *Computers as Theatre,* where she theorizes virtual reality, Brenda Laurel explains that "the notion of virtual reality has been enhanced by the fiction of William Gibson and other writers in the Cyberpunk genre, as well as the Holodeck construct developed by the creators of Star Trek" (Laurel 1992, 185). But Laurel's wording ("to enhance") needs clarification. Science fiction has been mobilized by multiple actors of virtual reality: from designers, to computer scientists, to users with diverse objectives. Innovators first saw it as an element of utopian thinking. In a famous article, "The Ultimate Display," Ivan Sutherland (1965), who used Sketchpad to create one of the first graphic software packages, defined his view of how computer technology could be used to manipulate objects. He concluded with a seminal text in the literature of the imaginary: "With appropriate programming such a display could literally be the Wonderland into which Alice walked" (Sutherland 1965, 507). Literature thus fulfills a utopian function; it enables us to imagine a different world where computers could be used to create a virtual space in which we could circulate. Other computer scientists, on the other hand, have used the science fiction literature as a tool for utopian thinking, not for themselves but for others. Science fiction thus becomes an educational tool. This is the case of Marvin Minsky, one of the most significant pioneers and developers of artificial intelligence, who wrote a novel with science fiction author Harry Harrison, to make his theories known to the general public (Harrison and Minsky 1992).

Novelists and filmmakers do not have scientific or technical projects. Even though they do sometimes popularize computer technology and virtual reality, most of them imagine daily life in the cyberspace age, and more widely in high-tech worlds. They create technological utopias that present the functioning of new societies in which these new technical devices are at the center of people's lives. In *Neuromancer*, William Gibson hesitates between these two perspectives (popularization and imagined fiction) when he defines cyberspace as a "graphic representation of data abstracted from the banks of every computer in the human system" and as a "consensual hallucination" (Gibson 1984, 67).

This hallucination is presented in detail. As Bruce Sterling puts it, "we see future from the belly up, as it is lived, not merely as dry speculation" (Sterling 1986, 3). Novelists thus flesh out the technical utopias of engineers and futurologists, but do not merely illustrate technical innovations; they produce literature. They design fictional worlds in which technology is applied in daily life. These virtual worlds provide a particularly attractive field for this type of science fiction.

Novels, films, and TV series are mass culture products that are not primarily aimed at taking a stand in the debate surrounding computer technology. Unlike other technical utopias written in either rosy or gloomy terms,[3] contemporary science fiction on computer technology, and especially the cyberpunk movement (Gibson, Sterling, etc.), takes on a greyer tone. Technology is at the heart of a world in which digital simulation replaces sensorial experience, where one can live a different life, but this is also above all a world of eccentrics and pirates—the dregs of cyberspace. There are furthermore powers that are hidden to a greater or lesser degree, and that seek to control this new world. Hence, cyberpunk novelists want to both imagine the multiple possibilities of the virtual worlds and denounce a disquieting world of generalized control.

Cyberpunk science fiction was so successful that it has often been thought to be at the origin of the creation of virtual worlds. This was the case with the notion of metaverse, invented by Neal Stephenson in his novel *Snow Crash* (1992). For instance, the Wikipedia article on metaverse contains a paragraph proposing "a timeline of virtual environments inspired by the Metaverse concept" with, notably, *There* and *Second Life* (SL). It presents a chronology that could suggest that Metaverse is at the origin of virtual worlds. This is obviously a highly questionable view of the concept of inspiration. As historian of art Michael Baxandall so aptly puts it: "if one says that X influenced Y, it does seem that one is saying that X did something to Y rather than Y did something to X. But in the consideration of good pictures and painters the second is always the more lively reality" (Baxandall 1985, 59). Thus, it is not Stephenson who inspired the creators of SL, but the latter who found in him a source of inspiration or even a prestigious reference likely to lend more of an aura to their project. That is exactly what Thomas Malaby said in his lengthy interview with Philip Rosedale, the creator of SL: he "pointed to science fiction and the work of Neal Stephenson... as providing the inspiration for this virtual environment. Stephenson's term for it, *metaverse*, was the term Lindens used most frequently when reaching *for a literary label* for Second Life" (Malaby 2009, 51; my emphasis). According to another source, the other core founders of Linden Lab (the firm that designed SL) found their source of inspiration elsewhere. Andrew Meadows commented: "so some of the inspiration wasn't so much the Metaverse as described by Stephenson" (Au 2008, 24) as 3D computer-generated imagery. As for Cory Ondrejka, Linden's chief technology officer, he had never even read *Snow Crash* when he joined the company! (Au 2008, 24).

Thus, science fiction is not at the origin of computer networks or virtual reality, but it is part of the social imaginary of computer scientists, and they readily borrow expressions from it that are part of the geeks' common culture. When John Quarterman wrote one of the first comprehensive books on the Internet and computer networks (1990), he very naturally called it *The Matrix*, and in his preface thanked Gibson, from whom he had borrowed this title. That was nine years before the title served again for an immensely successful film that popularized the term "matrix." The notion of metaverse was likewise adopted by computer specialists. It describes a future Internet of persistent, shared, 3D virtual spaces. Projects surrounding the definition of common standards or interfaces thus emerged within the various working groups in the computing world. In this case, "metaverse" became a showcase-word capable of mobilizing engineers and scientists around a project such as the Metaverse Roadmap.[4]

Science fiction therefore offers the various promoters of a new technology a symbolic universe in which they can meet and communicate around the same imaginary. Many computer enthusiasts who lived in complete isolation found in *Neuromancer* or *Snow Crash* and in the film *Matrix* a common culture, a community of debate, a framework structuring their desires and intuitions. As Gibson so neatly put it: "I gave computer nerds the permission to wear black leather" (qtd. in Dery 1996, 107). They also found a repertoire of fictional situations enabling them to give meaning to new computer projects such as virtual reality.

One of the first users of SL recalls: "I think most of us were sci-fi fans and we saw what looked like the beginning of the metaverse" (Au 2008, 41). And the collective to which he belonged was to give Gibson's name to the "sim" they built in honor of the cyberpunk novelist (42).

This computer culture spread beyond the hackers to a wider public and the media. The leading computing culture magazine, *Wired*, urged science fiction novelists to do reports on the most remarkable new practices of the digital age.[5] Thus, at the interface between fiction and reality, the technical imaginary of science fiction novels participated in this mobilization of the actors of technical innovation: scientists and engineers, amateurs wildly enthusiastic about the subject, journalists, and early users. As soon as the first Arpanet mailing lists were created in 1975, a science fiction list, SF-Lovers, became the most popular unofficial list, and a similar group appeared on Usenet the year it was launched (1979). Science fiction was thus at the core of scientists, and computer specialists' passions.

As for lay users in the first virtual communities such as the Well, they invented new episodes for *Star Trek* 10 years later (Winter 1994). Novels and films enabled these different stakeholders to create a common social imaginary that made their computer activities meaningful. For instance, technological fictions did not simply accompany a technical innovation, they participated in its definition and constructed, via *Wired*, a mobilization and imagined new uses.

This common social imaginary is also found in other forms that allow for festive gatherings in "real life," such as Burning Man, the carnival held every summer for the past two decades in the Nevada desert. Sterling noted that it "may be something like a physical version of the Internet" (Sterling 1996). The creator of this festival, Larry Harvey, who came from the world of artistic events, commented several years later: "I gradually realized that this environment that we've created is a physical analog of the Internet.... It allows people to conjure up entire worlds—like websites—voila! out of nothing" (Turner 2009, 83). The Burning Man festival makes it possible to physically construct a utopian world in the middle of the desert for a few days. The participants "provide a shared language for gathering in online social networks, meeting in parties" (89). Philip Rosedale, among others, was seduced by this improvisational community, in which he found "an intuition he'd pursue in building Second Life into a full-fledged online world" (Au 2008, 21). Burning Man is thus effectively a *watershed utopia* (that is, a widely diverse utopia where everyone can discover others' projects).

How to Create a Virtual World

While Burning Man is a "physical analog" of the Internet, SL gives it a virtual space, a body. The spatial metaphor of network had already played a key part in the development of the Internet. With this network, data can be circulated and distant communities called virtual communities created. But this circulation and interaction remain abstract; online communication via the Internet is largely disembodied. As early as 1991, Allucquere Rosanne Stone noted: "it is important to remember that virtual community originates in, and must return to, the physical.... Even in the age of the technosocial subject, life is lived through bodies" (Stone 1991, 113). Virtual reality makes it possible to flesh out the Internet in a represented space, to give substance to cybernauts.

But how can this type of world be built? The construction of a virtual world raises complex computing questions. How do the designers see their activity? First, they can consider themselves as all-seeing and omnipotent novelists who create their own world, at will. This situation seemed to stand to reason for the designers of one of the first virtual worlds, *Habitat*. They perceived their role as "omniscient central planners." But that soon proved to be impossible. *Habitat* had been designed for 20,000 avatars, so there was a need for "20,000 houses organized into towns and cities with associated traffic arteries and shopping and recreational areas. We needed wilderness areas between the towns so that everyone would not be jammed together into the same place. Most of all, we needed things for 20,000 people to do" (Morningstar and Farmer 1991, 286–287). It was therefore toward a different imaginary of the construction of the world that they were to turn. They believed that they should leave the actors of this world to do what they wanted to, and to focus on a spontaneous order, or the self-organized system described by Hayek. "It was clear that we were not in control. The more people we involved in something, the less in control we were" (288). The designers were thus seen essentially as facilitators.

Fifteen years later, the designers of SL considered building their world in a similar way, based on an antiauthority model with regard to relations both with the employees and with the residents. The idea was to set up a self-governance model reflecting the neoliberal tradition of the invisible hand of the market and one of the essential management principles put forward in The Tao of Linden: "Your choice is your responsibility" (Malaby 2009, 136). As for the residents, they were mobilized to provide "user-created contents" according to a process that one of them called "a 3D wiki" (Au 2008, 44).

Ondrejka sees this as a necessity.

> Residents of digital worlds consume content at an incredible rate. With the rising costs of content development, developers have turned to several options to reduce these costs. Massively multiplayer online role-playing games solve this problem by limiting the rate of progress through the game.... Second Life, on the other hand, utilizes the incredible energy and creativity of its residents by making creation a fun and integrated part of the experience. This constant generation of new content keeps the world dynamic and fresh and helps to retain residents over long periods of time (Ondrejka 2004, 3).

As in the counterculture tradition (Flichy 2007a; Turner 2006), this is a combination of unbridled passion and lucrative professionalization (Flichy 2010), expressed so well by one of the pioneers of SL: "I had ideals that we were going to forge the free idealistic Utopia.... But... money makes things happen; it's in some ways an undesirable reality, but the benefit it has had to SL is immeasurable" (Au 2008, 48). The open and large watershed utopia of a medium created by the people (it is no coincidence that Surowiecki's book, *The Wisdom of Crowds*, is one of Linden Lab's references) turned into a mask ideology that concealed aspects of reality to better promote SL. The residents had the impression of working for their pleasure, but in fact they were working for Linden Lab! There is, however, another element that should not be overlooked: the imaginary of user-created content constituted a mobilization ideology capable of drawing toward this virtual space a host of cybernauts. SL thus became the place one had to be in.[6]

TRAFFIC IN THE CITY

This space created by cybernauts was first conceived of as a 3D city in which avatars could move around. It could be a real city like Paris, which constituted the decor of the *Deuxième Monde*, a virtual universe created by the French TV channel Canal Plus, in 1997. Or, on the contrary, as we have seen with *Habitat* and SL, it could be a space created haphazardly by the residents. Circulation within these cities, especially when they are unknown spaces such as SL, is a key element of life in these virtual worlds. SL is too large and complex for inhabitants to walk or even fly through: hence, a teleportation system was introduced, allowing for direct access to any point in space. But the Linden Lab team wanted to apply to the virtual world the urban planning perspective of Jane Jacob (1961), in which urban life is based on chance encounters. It therefore limited the use of teleportation to distances between intermediary points called telehubs. Beyond these hubs, residents had to walk and thus to make themselves open to random opportunities. This system was, however, challenged by the residents, who preferred a point-to-point system that would take them directly to their destination. The result was a shift from an urban poaching perspective to one of efficient circulation designed to draw attention away from the vastness of the space, so that, from 2005, residents could move as quickly as possible from one activity to another.

We thus see that the imaginary of a project must be negotiated with the other stakeholders and particularly the users. This is when a *project utopia* (an alternative to previous virtual transportation devices) is constituted, that is, a shared imaginary, negotiated with the different actors.

GIVING INTERNAUTS A BODY

The other key feature of virtual worlds is the richness and complexity of the actors circulating and taking part in them. Just as Burning Man is a "physical analog" of the Internet, so an observer of SL considers that this virtual world is "the physical Internet" (Scola 2007). Like the first virtual reality projects summed up by Laurel, this physical Internet constitutes a watershed utopia[7] compared to the preceding developments in computer technology and Internet. The idea is to involve not only minds but also bodies. It is, however, not enough just to put these bodies in this virtual world; they also have to be able to act, and the avatar is the embodiment of the cybernaut's intelligence.

This watershed utopia has fueled many projects. In the mythical history of Linden Lab, as related by the members of the firm, during one of the first meetings with the investors, residents were given access to existing software bricks, and several of them started to build characters. Ondrejka, who had rather had in mind building a game world with robots, realized that "people are going to have human artifacts. And if you're going to need to have people...[that] means avatars" (Au 2008, 30). Linden Lab consequently built a *project utopia* consisting of a virtual world in which virtual characters played an essential part. This virtual world is not a decor like the "deuxième monde" in which avatars could walk, but a world built by the avatars themselves.

In addition to this imaginary of the designers, it is particularly interesting to look at the imaginary of the internauts because, as we have seen, they are extremely active. Internauts and designers are both stakeholders in the collective social imaginary. The book by journalist-photographer Robbie Cooper enables us to study this internaut imaginary. In *Alter Ego* (2007), he presents photo portraits of sixty internauts who had created their own avatar in an MMO or in SL, and next to each portrait a photo of their avatar, with a short interview. From this very rich material two main themes emerge: identity and otherness; and anonymity and social life.

Identity and Otherness

Some players see their avatar as their alter ego. "He looks like me, he thinks like me and he acts like me because he is me and I am him. His past is my past" commented one of them (Loukakis).[8] Others, in contrast, create an avatar very different from themselves. For instance, a seriously handicapped player who spends over 10 hours a day on online games explained, with regard to his avatar, that the other players "treated me an equal...we were all just gamers" (Rowe). Likewise, a gamer who loved medieval fantasy said that he "would have liked to have lived in that period" (Ki-Jang), and a male student chose to have a different life through a female avatar who bore "a strong resemblance to [his] feminine side" (Te Dunne). Changing one's sex also allows for different types of social relations. Rebecca Glasure noted that "by playing as a guy, I found that people treated me differently."

But between these extreme cases, we find that most internauts combine these two approaches in one way or another. A 24-year-old woman created an avatar that looked exactly like her but was 20 years older. She commented that her avatar "looks the way that I aspire to be when I'm older" (Brown). Another woman's avatar wore the same clothes as she did, but was 20 years younger: "My avatar looks like my real self, but about twenty years younger....She's just an extension of myself in this virtual space" (Rufer-Bach).

Thus, an avatar that is identical to its creator can also be different since it's an extension of his or her being: "a bit of me and a bit of the person that I'd like to be" (Jorden).

While the avatar is a combination of the real self and the ideal self, it may also appear as an alter ego (I'm him, he's me), a kind of partner (we can't be without each other).

This avatar is everything that Creola wants to be: strong, famous, respected, and so on: "Together we make one complete person" (Creola). Harisu, in contrast, describes her avatar as a boyfriend: "it's more like your partner." Quin sees his avatar as having a public role: it "is not an extension of my real-world personality. Rather it's the public role I adopt, much like Madonna...adopts an outward public persona."

This duplication of the individual is not only situated in a fantasy world, it also affords an opportunity to revive a former life. For example, a young mother carried on her career as a dancer...online. Other internauts prefer to play as couples; they create two avatars that play together in the virtual world. "Our characters are a couple, as are we" (Capdecomme).

This imaginary of cyberselfing is not peculiar to MMO gamers or SL residents; we likewise find it in the work of scholars like Sherry Turkle (1995), who considers that virtual worlds allow for the development of multiple selves freed from the corporeal bonds of the offline self.[9] We also find disdain for the "meat" of embodiment, preached by Gibson and other science fiction novelists. But while this common outlook appears to be a mobilization ideology that rallies the actors of this new activity, some see it as a mask ideology concealing reality. Laura Robinson, for instance, refutes the perspectives of such postmodern theorists as Stone and Turkle, arguing that the construction of self is the same online and offline. "The cyberself is the emergent product of social interaction" (Robinson 2007, 104).

Anonymity and Social Life

Social interactions are another salient feature of the world of avatars and their creators. Some players appreciate the fact that cyberspace allows them to be anonymous, without social markers, and thus to develop interactions at will, unrestricted by social control. Avatars are not bound by rules, and some gamers see this as an opportunity to rest and to be free of the social roles that we have to play in the real world. Others enjoy the freedom that these new worlds offer, and set challenges for themselves, for instance to adopt a particular behavior in a virtual world for a season or for longer.

Cybernauts see these new worlds as a new sphere of sociability suited to their own constraints and desires. They can overcome their shyness or an image of themselves that they dislike, to become more authentic and develop new social relations. In this way they try to create a new social life. Mothers of young children, who are unable to go out, experience it as a new space for sociability: "Second Life allows me to go places and hang out with other people without the fuss of having to find a baby-sitter" (Hance). The online world also enables gamers to meet very different types of people. For instance, Miller, a young Californian, considers that "through virtual worlds many people will be exposed to other cultures." In these different cases, it is less the virtual universe that appeals to people than the opportunities it affords for social interaction.

With regard to identity and otherness, there is no direct clash between anonymity and the strengthening of social ties. It is by severing their ordinary social relations that internauts can build new ones. The virtual world thus enables them to live a fiction intensely. But it can also enable them to learn and to experiment with social relations: for a shy teenager, learning to be attractive and to seduce; for an adult, learning to define his or her social role. After this experimental phase, the residents of SL, for example, use their avatar to give a real image of themselves or, more exactly, the image of themselves that they would like to have—in a sense their ideal self.

This freedom of the virtual body that enables MMO gamers and SL residents to have different experiences that are not unrelated to their own identity constitutes a powerful imaginary of virtual modes shared by almost everyone: designers, cybernauts, science fiction writers, and some academic scholars alike. They all have the same fascination for the ability to defy the limits of the lived body and the constraints of the coherence of the self, characteristic of the offline world. But the utopia can sometimes get out of control, moving out of the framework of the project and becoming a *phantasmogoric utopia* that has no technical incarnation. Instead of playing, as the avatar did, on the real body and the simulated body, virtual reality is perceived as a way of attaining immortality. For instance, the Extropians, a New Age group linked to the cyber culture that appealed to well-known names like roboticist Hans Moravec and AI researcher Marvin Minsky, have a phantas-magorical view of the virtual body. They imagine uploading the brain and perhaps other body parts into an artificial substrate. But you can go further than this uploading and

> choose what emotions and moods to experience, inhabit artificial bodies of either sex... invent new emotions, spawn sub-processes and merge them back into 'yourself', incorporate parts of other people's minds.... Are you still you? Even in the present day, one comes across people fixed in a way of life, who refuse to develop. Would clinging to one's original personality be just as unskilful a behaviour in a world with uploading? If you don't open this Pandora's box, someone else will (Kennaway 1992, 2).

Thus, with the Extropians we find the same themes as those imagined by the partici-pants of virtual worlds, but in a phantasmagorical mode, since the idea is to upload one's body and then to change it. Here we see a utopia of a very different nature, since it has not participated in the elaboration of a technological device, as it focuses more on an imaginary world than on designing innovation.

Conclusion

Virtual worlds are a fine example of the role of the imaginary in the development of a family of innovations. This imaginary constitutes the foundations of a common world that brings together different actors in a society (designers, users, science fiction writ-ers, intellectuals, etc.) so that they can produce and use the same technique. Utopias and dreams play an important role in shaping innovation. They are not only a pecu-liarity of inventors; they concern much larger social groups that develop different rep-resentations of the same technology. At the root of a sociotechnical context we find a whole range of imagined technological possibilities that seem to warrant investigation, not as the initial matrix of a new technology but rather as one of the resources mobilized by the actors to construct the frame of reference of their activities. But the social imaginary of virtual worlds is not only a common world accepted by all; it has various forms, with tensions between them. Whereas at the outset we find an open and confused watershed utopia, like the idea of a "physical analog" of the Internet in Burning Man and the initiators of SL, later on the utopia has tended to slide into a phantasmogorical form, like the Extropians, or to stabilize in a common project requiring multiple adaptations, like teleportation in SL. This utopia quickly becomes a mobilization ideology that serves to bring designers and users together, but it may also take on the form of a mask ideology that hides the illusions of life in the virtual world. Hence, the social imaginary constitutes a dynamic, constantly moving spiral that the observer must follow attentively.

Yet the existence of a common, motivating, and mobilizing technical imaginary at the origin of a technology does not necessarily mean that this technology has positive effects for society. This is an entirely different issue that warrants analysis. The evaluation of technologies is an important element of policies that the public authorities have to implement with regard to techniques. This evaluation must be based not on discourses but on real practices, and take into account the impact on the environment and on society. The study of imaginaries also raises another question as well: why and how do a society and its members adopt a technology? That is the value of such research.

Notes

1. The proximity between Appadurai and Taylor is clearly apparent in an issue of *Public Culture* 14 (1) (2002) entitled "New Imaginaries."
2. See Flichy 2007a for further discussion and examples.
3. In the current definition, different from the one used here, we call these optimistic fictions utopias and these pessimistic fictions dystopias.
4. http://metaverseroadmap.org/overview/, accessed June 29, 2013.
5. From 1993 to 1996, *Wired* published articles by William Gibson, Neal Stephenson, and Bruce Sterling.
6. Nearly 800,000 people logged onto *Second Life* more than once every month (*Metaverse Journal*, May 12, 2011).
7. A widely diverse utopia where everyone can discover others' projects.
8. Robbie Cooper gives the name of the players he photographed and interviewed. In his book, there are no page numbers.
9. Turkle's theses were widely disseminated throughout cyber culture, mainly by *Wired* (Turkle 1996).

References

Appadurai, A. 1996. *Modernity at Large: Cultural Dimensions of Globalization.* Minneapolis: University of Minnesota Press.

Au, W. J. 2008. *The Making of "Second Life": Notes from the New World.* New York: Collins.

Baxandall, M. 1985. *Patterns of Intention.* New Haven, CT: Yale University Press.

Cooper, R. 2007. *Alter Ego: Avatars and Their Creators.* London: Chris Boot.

Dahlgren, P. 2009. *Media and Political Engagement. Citizens, Communication and Democracy.* New York: Cambridge University Press.

Dery, M. 1996. *Escape Velocity: Cyber culture at the End of the Century.* New York: Grove Press.

Flichy, P. 2007a. *The Internet Imaginaire.* Cambridge, MA: MIT Press.

Flichy, P. 2007b. *Understanding Technological Innovation: A Socio-technical Approach.* Cheltenham, UK: Edward Elgar.

Flichy, P. 2010. *Le sacre de l'amateur: Sociologie des passions ordinaires à l'ère numérique.* Paris: Le Seuil.

Gibson, W. 1984. *Neuromancer.* New York: Ace Books.

Harrison, H., and M. Minsky. 1992. *The Turing Option.* New York: Warner Books.

Jacob, J., 1961. *The Death and Life of Great American Cities.* New York: Random House.

Kennaway, R. 1992. Methods of Uploading. Extopians mailing list URL. http://www.aleph.se/Trans/Global/Uploading/kennaway.121692.txt. Accessed June 29, 2013.

Laurel, B. 1992. *Computers as Theatre.* Menlo Park, CA: Addison-Wesley.

Malaby, T. 2009. *Making Virtual Worlds: Linden Lab and "Second Life".* Ithaca, NY: Cornell University Press

Morningstar, C., and R. Farmer. 1991. The Lessons of Lucasfilm's *Habitat.* In *Cyberspace: First Steps,* edited by Michael Benedikt, 273–301. Cambridge, MA: MIT Press.

Ondrejka, C. R. 2004. A Piece of Place: Modeling the Digital on the Real in *Second Life.* June 7. http://ssrn.com/abstract=555883. Accessed June 29, 2013.

Quarterman, J. 1990. *The Matrix: Computer Networks and Conferencing Systems Worldwide.* Bedford, MA: Digital Press.

Ricoeur, P. 1986. *Lectures on Ideology and Utopia.* New York: Columbia University Press.

Robinson, L. 2007. The Cyberself: The Self-ing Project Goes Online. Symbolic Interaction in the Digital Age. *New Media & Society* 9 (1): 93–110.

Scola, N. 2007. Avatars Politics: The Social Applications of *Second Life.* Institute for Politics, Democracy & the Internet. http://www.knightdigitalmediacenter.org/resources./2007Election08-Avatar%20Politcs.pdf. Accessed January 2012.

Stephenson, N. 1992. *Snow Crash.* New York: Bantam Books.

Sterling, B. 1986. Foreword to *Burning Chrome,* by William Gibson. New York: Arbor House.

Sterling, B. 1996. Greetings from Burning Man. *Wired,* November. http://www.wired.com/wired/archive/4.11/burningman.html. Accessed June 29, 2013

Stone, A. R. 1991. Will the Real Body Please Stand Up? Boundary Stories about Virtual Cultures. In *Cyberspace: First Steps,* edited by Michael Benedikt, 81–88. Cambridge, MA: MIT Press.

Sutherland, I. 1965. The Ultimate Display. In *Information Processing 1965: Proceedings of IFIPS Congress* 2: 506–508. Amsterdam: North-Holland.

Taylor, C. 2004. *Modern Social Imaginaries.* Durham, NC: Duke University Press.

Turkle, S. 1995. *Life on the Screen: Identity in the Age of the Internet.* New York: Simon &Schuster.

Turkle, S. 1996. Who Am We? *Wired,* January. http://www.wired.com/wired/archive/4.01/turkle.html. Accessed June 29, 2013.

Turner, F. 2006. *From Counterculture to Cyber culture.* Chicago: University of Chicago Press.

Turner, F. 2009. Burning Man at Google: A Cultural Infrastructure for New Media Production. *New Media & Society* 11 (1–2): 73–94.

Winter, M. 1994. The Complete Guide to the Well (Whole Earth Lectronic Link). http://www.skeptictank.org/files/cowtext/wellmanh.htm. Accessed June 29, 2013.

Wynne, B, and European Expert Group. 2008. *Science and Governance: Taking European Knowledge Society Seriously*. Milan: EPOC.

CHAPTER 43

··

VIRTUALITY AND
HUMANITY

··

DAVID KREPS

As our lives become increasingly encroached upon by the digital virtuality of our exponentially advancing twenty-first-century information society, will this be at the cost of
our humanity? Writers such as Sherry Turkle (2010) seem to believe this transformation has already begun with circles of people sitting together in silence engaging with
their smartphones. When our senses are surrounded by interactive exposure to telepresent realities—the faces of those we are speaking to across the world overlaid upon
the world before our eyes, streams of data passing across the pavements and shopfronts
as we pass, electronic voices calling our name and tantalizing us with goods they know
we want—when the worlds around us are both real and virtual, does this grant us additional scope to express our humanity, or constitute such an overload that engagement
fatigue exhausts our faculties?

At our off-grid holiday resorts in rugged mountainous territory or remote wilderness encampments, luxuriating in isolation-downtime, delighting in the simplicities
of one-to-one, face-to-face conversation with no distractions, are we savoring a richer,
more traditional humanity? Resting in natural landscape with no overlaid streams of
historical and commercial data, out beyond the boundaries of location-aware personal
shopping avatars telling us where to get what they already know we would "Like," do
we feel the high-tech virtuality-soaked everyday of our lives is missing something we
have gone on vacation to recoup? Or does this vision of a virtu-reality that beckons in
the coming decades mistake digital virtuality for something other than simply the latest manifestation of the—very human—dreams our ingenuity and inventiveness have
managed to make manifest?

The answer to these questions, of course, awaits the course of history, but if an author
in the early part of this century is to guess at what may transpire, I would suggest
that it depends on what one understands by the terms virtuality, humanity, and reality. It can be cogently argued that virtuality is something humanity has been playing

with for a very long time—that our very selfhoods and societies are in fact a virtual layer over the physical realities of our bodily existence. Similarly, the more physical side of such virtualities envisaged in the digital, with all its hardware and antennas and the rare earth mining, is but the latest, and arguably more lightweight version of the physical sides of our civic societies that once dealt in huge blocks of stone, and more recently industrial reshapings of entire landscapes. Looked at in this light, virtuality becomes, in truth, a mark of our humanity, that which in itself sets us apart from the rest of nature (at least in our eyes.)

This chapter sets out to explore these questions with reference to the work of philosophers such as Henri Bergson ([1908] 2004; [1911] 1944; [1935] 2006), and his concepts of perception and moral obligation, and Michel Foucault (1977; 1988; 1990; 1992; 1995a; 1995b; 1997; 1998), and his concepts of discourse, power, and epistemic shifts in history. These philosophical backgrounds then underpin the more recent theorizing of thinkers such as Karen Barad (2007), Stephen Gill (2003), and Michael Hardt and Antonio Negri (2000), whose agential realism and neo-Gramscianism together constitute a broad picture within which the material manifestation of our dreams can be better understood. Through this discussion we will explore the key questions of this chapter: what should we understand by the terms virtuality, humanity, and reality?

What Is Virtuality?

Virtuality Is Consciousness

Henri Bergson's groundbreaking work of the first decade of the twentieth century, *Matter and Memory* ([1908] 2004), "affirms the reality of spirit and the reality of matter, and tries to determine the relation of the one to the other by the study of a definite example, that of memory" (vii). Although propounding what is on the face of it a dualistic philosophy, Bergson nonetheless succeeds in providing us with a monistic philosophy where matter and spirit (the latter understood as *consciousness*) are two sides of one coin. Bergson pioneered what later the French poststructuralist Jacques Derrida would term a "deconstructive" approach (Derrida 1974). Deconstruction aims to espy any binaries, for example, subject/object, male/female, symbolic/imaginary, rational/emotional, and to contest the normative dominant in such pairs, preferring to show the dependency of the dominant upon the supposedly subservient half of the pair, and through the deconstruction of the assumptions and knowledge systems that set up such binaries to show the fluidity between them, how one becomes the other from particular perspectives. Bergson achieves this in *Matter and Memory* with nothing less than realism and idealism, between the belief that our reality is ontologically independent of our experience, and the belief that human experience providing us with the only window we have upon the world, cannot tell us if anything external to that experience exists.

Bergson first establishes the truth of both consciousness and of external reality: if the nerves that convey perception to one's consciousness are cut, it is perception that vanishes, not one's consciousness or the object being perceived. He then defines matter as "an aggregate of images." By "image" he means "a certain existence which is more than that which the idealist calls a *representation,* but less than that which the realist calls a *thing,*—an existence placed half-way between the 'thing' and the 'representation'" (Bergson [1908] 2004, 7). Importantly, the most significant image of all is our own body, which we perceive both from the outside—looking at our hands—and from the inside— our "affections." He takes issue with the Enlightenment conception (see Warburton 1998 on Locke and Hume) that representations of the outside world exist within our minds. For this to be the case the entire material universe would have to exist in our heads, which it plainly does not. The brain is part of the material universe, not the other way around. Matter thus becomes "the aggregate of images, and perception of matter these same images referred to the eventual action of one particular image, my body" (Bergson [1908] 2004, 7). The body is the "privileged" image that is both perceived, and perceives.

He then states the problem of the realist position on matter, and the idealist position that counters it, in the following terms: "How is it that the same images can belong at the same time to two different systems, the one in which each image varies for itself and in the well-defined measure that it is patient of the real action of surrounding images, the other in which all change for a single image, and in the varying measure that they reflect action of the privileged image?" (Bergson [1908] 2004, 12). He takes these two opposites, finds what they have in common, and turns both of them inside out and upside down. What realism and idealism have in common is that they both assume "perception has a wholly speculative interest; it is pure knowledge." This is posited as different from scientific knowledge. "The one doctrine starts from the order required by science, and sees in perception only a confused and provisional science. The other puts perception in the first place, erects it into an absolute, and then holds science to be a symbolic expression of the real. But, for both parties, to perceive means above all to know." Bergson disputes this. For him perception is an integral part of how conscious beings are situated in the material world, and this has nothing to do with knowing (17).

Consciousness—the ability to know—must, on the contrary, be quite separate from perception, which Bergson asserts is an entirely physical, biological series of stimuli and electrical signals moving centrifugally and centripetally between the brain and the nerve endings. Consciousness, on the contrary, must not be physical at all. Bergson maintains that the nervous system and the brain—the entire body in fact—is merely a "centre of action" (Bergson [1908] 2004, 5), where perceptions trigger reactions that in turn trigger movement. It is this purely physical, biological perception-action flow that is interrupted by consciousness, to enable comparison between several different options, and choice between them, before either proceeding or shelving a reaction. This is, for Bergson, uniquely human.

Neuroscientific studies in the first decade of the twenty-first century would seem to offer further proof of this conception of the body as an action center, beyond the late nineteenth-century examples Bergson gives in his book. Mirror neurons (Kilner et al. 2007; 2009; Rizzolatti and Craighero 2004) turn out to behave in just such a manner: "In humans, in addition to action understanding, the mirror-neuron system plays a funda-mental role in action imitation" (Rizzolatti and Craighero 2004, 169). In other words, perception triggers responses in the brain, not only when something is actually per-ceived, but also when it is only consciously conceived: the same neural activity is wit-nessed when something is perceived as when it is remembered or imagined. The brain is thus the action center, ready to proceed or shelve a reaction to perceptions—whether from the external world or from consciousness.

Consciousness is then neither the "epiphenomenon" of matter, as the scientific realist would have it, nor the foundation of reality, as the idealist would have it. For Bergson, it finds its true locus in another of his deconstructive new conceptions. This latest deconstruction is nothing less than a reconception of the nature of time and space. Here he moves entirely beyond the reach of science into the realm of philosophy. As Adamson puts it,

> the epistemological foundations of science, as much as the ontological grounds of the object of any scientific point of view, draw a clearly definable line between that which science is capable of describing and that which philosophy has the potential to express. This distinction is drawn by the difference between the discrete and the continuous. Science is, unavoidably, constrained within and by, the ontological limitations of the discrete, for the simple reason that it is the necessary condition of both information and objectivity. The objective can only be determined when, as Bergson puts it, we take a 'snapshot' of duration (Adamson 2000, 54).

Bergson's conception of continuous reality is tempero-spatial, in direct contrast to the scientific conception of the spatiotemporal discrete moment it casts as the real. It is in duration, the *durée reélle* as Bergson terms it ([1911] 1944), that consciousness resides, as the human corollary of that continuity, that movement, which science can only express as a series of stops, and fails to conceive in its ongoing indivisibility: something that common sense of course grasps intuitively. Conscious living matter, understood in this way, becomes a center of what Bergson terms "indetermination"—the ability to choose—and therefore establishes a point where what is otherwise determined by scientific laws may be interrupted and new directions taken. "Let us posit that system of closely-linked images which we call the material world, and imagine here and there, within the system, centers of real action, represented by living matter" (Bergson [1908] 2004, 21). Real action is undertaken by conscious beings.

Virtuality, then, following Bergson, I will conceive of as being consciousness itself: cer-tainly something that is not material, but not merely a mysterious epiphenomenon that science cannot explain, rather the source, and location, in a tempero-spatial under-standing of a continuous reality, of that precious quality that makes us human: *choice*—the "indetermination" by which consciousness is distinguished from mere perception.

Discourse and Epistemes

But human choice is not so simple a faculty as to be granted solely and exclusively to independent human subjects observing external reality, as the realist would assert, nor immune from the codetermination of reality the nonhuman exerts upon the human, as the idealist would have it. Choice is about knowing, and to choose is to exert power.

Consciousness and choice, coupled with the fundamentally social nature of human beings, begets language. Language is by definition a shared, structural phenomenon (Williams 1999, 37). Language, as a shared phenomenon, consists in discourse. The notion of discourse is thus key to understanding virtuality as I have conceived it. Michel Foucault has given us the finest description of the nature of discourse. I shall here move on from Bergson to outline, briefly, how Foucault conceives discourse and the matrix of knowledge and power it has determined in recent centuries.

Foucault's units of discourse, "statements," are performances that could be described as "serious speech acts" (Foucault 1995b, 48). The statement is therefore like something that can be cited—it carries weight, like the proper formula to open a meeting, but is not distinct from the status of its speaker. To use a rather gendered metaphor, when the chairman of the board declares the meeting open, the meeting is open. When the tea-lady utters it, everyone laughs. This is because the "truth game," or "enunciative field" (Foucault 1995b, 109), in which the formula is placed requires that it be uttered only by an authorized subject for it to be "true." Most importantly, it is their place in the network of other serious speech acts, and nothing more, that gives speech acts their seriousness, and thus makes them statements. The so-called unity of the group figures such as psychology, economics, grammar, medicine, and so on, which have grown up since the Enlightenment, Foucault questions at this level, preferring to label them as groups of statements he calls "discursive formations." It is the discursive formation in which a statement, as a serious speech act, gains its seriousness. These discursive formations are held together by discursive relations that, rather than connecting concepts or words with one another, "determine the group of relations that discourse must establish in order to speak of this or that object, in order to deal with them, analyse them, classify them, explain them etc. These relations characterise … discourse itself as a practice" (46). Discursive practices, then, become the glue that holds all that is social together.

Thus discourse is inseparable from the nature and exercise of power in modern societies, which is in fact positive, and immanent, being exercised at all times and from all points in any relation. What may seem like "repression" is in fact more usually a forceful enjoinder to behave in a specific way, rather than any other. Nor is power applied externally upon our relations with one another, but internally within and between them, and in idiosyncratic configurations at all levels of society, rather than in some simple top-down hierarchy. There are no individuals who are singly or collectively exercising power within society, whom the rest ultimately obey; all individuals are caught up in the nexus—this discursive field—of power relations. Resistance to power is therefore part of the power relationship, and not external to it, and takes different forms in different contexts (Foucault 1998).

Foucault gathered all these discursive practices into epistemes, periods of time covering centuries, and described the possibility of huge epistemic shifts in history. The matrix of knowledge and power suffusing discursive practices he terms "disciplinary" power and locates within the modern episteme, a shift from the former sovereign power of the previous epistemic period. Neither a form of knowledge, nor a type of rationality, the "episteme" is nothing less than the total set of relations that unite the discursive practices of a given period.

Virtuality: Summary

To summarize, then, we find in Bergson a description of consciousness as a virtual layer that is a temporal counterpoint to matter understood scientifically as a fixed, spatial stop, providing reality with real action in the manner of choice, as opposed to the mere action-reaction of scientific laws. Consciousness, moreover, as a part of this temporal continuity, is inevitably a shared, and thereby social, experience through the formation and use of language, which gives it expression, and which forms itself into discourse. In the modern episteme, this discourse constitutes a matrix of knowledge and power, and creates for itself, through the performative utterance of statements, discursive formations and relations played out in discursive practices.

But there is a crucial element here that suggests to us an epistemic shift in the course of "human" history, from a past wherein the statements of the family, clan, tribal, or even national leader determined the path of discourse, to a crucial break from such discursive hierarchy to a notion of "humanity" beyond tribal or national groupings: a notion of humanity as a *species*. We must return to Bergson for more on this.

WHAT IS HUMANITY?

"Christ died for all our sins..."

Bergson, in his last work, *The Two Sources of Morality and Religion* ([1935] 2006), defined humanity in relation to a further, characteristic deconstruction of opposites: between the notion of societies and the notion of society; between that which is closed and that which is open. Prefiguring, in some ways, elements of the later Foucauldian disciplinarity, Bergson offers a description of the social as a system of obligation. The free choice that consciousness grants us is all too soon overlaid by the necessary coordination required of social grouping. "While his consciousness, delving downwards, reveals to him, the deeper he goes, an ever more original personality, incommensurable with the others and indeed indefinable in words, on the surface of life we are in continuous contact with other men whom we resemble, and united to them by a discipline which creates between them and us a relation of interdependence" (Bergson [1935] 2006, 14). This discipline and interdependence comprise a foundational moral obligation to one another that forms the glue of social grouping. But these groupings are always, by definition, ultimately, closed. Any individual grouping, be it family, clan, tribe, nation, or even a grouping of nations such Europe, or "the West," is "to include at any moment a certain number of individuals, and exclude others" (30). For Bergson this is a "natural" state, akin to the societies created by that other most social of Earth's creatures, the ant. Yet this is no simple biodeterminism, for Bergson is clear on the essential point that consciousness marks a fundamental distinction between the ant and us. It is in the distinction between the closed and the open that Bergson finds *choice* at its most powerful, and its most *human*. "Between the society in which we live and humanity in general there is...the same contrast as between the closed and the open; the difference between the two objects is one of kind and not simply one of degree" (32).

This is not the place to enter into the detailed philosophical and metaphysical arguments concerning the nature of morality and religion Bergson undertakes in this work. It is Bergson's contention that the urge to expand one's horizons beyond closed societies to an apprehension of the open society is one invariably undertaken by inspired individuals whom others then follow. There are ample signs of his own belonging to the somewhat triumphalist white, male European elite of the 1930s peppered through his ideas in this work, which no doubt contributed to the demise of his reputation in the postwar period, and in the final section of the work it is clear that he speaks from a profound and exclusive faith in Christian mysticism—as opposed to several other creeds he openly criticizes for not being sufficiently developed in their thought (Bergson [1935] 2006, 222–227)—things that many readers (including myself) find difficult to accept. Indeed, in the eighteenth, nineteenth, and early twentieth centuries the category "human" we use today as a leveling concept to include all people was a racially contested term in the hands of many scholars, used to exclude as much as to define a particular segment of what we understand today as "humanity" (Hall 1997).

Nonetheless, the fundamental point Bergson makes is one that stands up to scrutiny. Whether spurred by Christian mysticism or some other urge, the fundamental distinction between a notion of "our society" and that of "human society"—in the modern understanding of the term, "human"—is one that lies at the root of the highest ideals. A Foucauldian genealogy of such thinking would—I argue—reveal not just Christian, but a whole range of comparable historical developments, perhaps remembered as the achievements of individuals, but more likely better understood as the evidence of a "critical ontology of ourselves," a "historico-practical test of the limits we may go beyond," and thus "work carried out by ourselves upon ourselves as free beings" (Foucault 1988, 47).

Liberty, Equality, Fraternity

This "critical ontology of ourselves," moreover, can be seen beyond the realm of both mysticism and religion, in the search begun in northwestern Europe in the Middle Ages from the demise of feudalism toward a more "universal suffrage" (e.g., John Bull and the English Peasant's Revolt of 1391), and then the decentralization of power to a parliamentary elite (e.g., the English Civil War of the mid-seventeenth century, and the later

Glorious Revolution of 1688 enshrining parliamentary control of the restored monarchy). These movements found their great expression in the revolutions (a century later) in America and in France. Democracy—not the "false democracies, those cities of antiquity, based on slavery" (Bergson [1935] 2006, 281)—is perhaps indeed, of all political systems, the "only one to transcend, at least in intention, the conditions of the 'closed society'" (281).

In the years following the revolutions in America and France, Thomas Paine, in his *Rights of Man* ([1791] 1995) asserted that: "Conquest and tyranny, at some early period, dispossessed man of his rights, and he is now recovering them" (213). With characteristic fervor and optimism, he continues, "Government founded on a moral theory, on a system of universal peace, on the indefeasible hereditary Rights of Man, is now revolving from west to east, by a stronger impulse than the government of the sword revolved from east to west. It interests not particular individuals, but nations, in its progress, and promises a new era to the human race." Humanity, in this reading, is gathered into nations, but not confined by them: this is Bergson's "open society" just as much as the Christian mystics of which he was so fond. Paine was an abolitionist, too, unlike some of his white supremacist contemporaries such as Thomas Jefferson (Selfa 2002). Importantly, Paine makes the fundamental distinction between a constitution and a government—that a constitution "is not the act of a government, but of a people constituting a government" (238).

This principle of the people's right to constitute their own government, as the march of these new ideas progressed, itself saw moves toward decentralization in the ideas of those opposed to centralized parliamentary and autocratic power in the rapidly industrializing nations of the nineteenth century. By the 1860s, suspicion of all extant forms of government had reached new heights, and those engaged in the promotion of freedom from tyranny were of the fervent belief that widespread social revolution was imminent. Two camps, libertarian and authoritarian—epitomized by the towering figures of Mikhail Bakunin and Karl Marx, respectively—championed these two versions of socialism. "Marx and most authoritarian socialists did not give much thought to the forms of organization that might concretize or translate into reality the ideal of a free, stateless society. They naively assumed that the 'Worker's State' would in some natural, spontaneous fashion eventually evolve into the ideal" (Dolgoff 1980, 7). History has indeed shown Bakunin and the libertarian socialists' counterarguments to be well founded. "Proudhon, Bakunin, Kropotkin, and their successors—the collectivist, communist, and syndicalist anarchists—understood that freedom (paradoxical as this may seem) must be organized, must systematically permeate every cell of the social body" (7). Foucault's power/knowledge matrix, indeed, must be suffused with enjoinders and balances that promote liberty and equality, rather than domination and opposition; simply removing the latter and hoping for the best cannot suffice. "Freedom is inseparable from local autonomy, workers' control, community control; but such self-governing local units and groups can function, survive, and prosper only by coordinating their activities. A vast network of free associations, federated at every level and preserving the maximum degree of local autonomy, was therefore envisaged as the only feasible alternative to the suffocating centralized State" (Dolgoff 1980, 7). As Bakunin put it, "Liberty without socialism is privilege, injustice; socialism without liberty is slavery and brutality" (Bakunin 1980, 127).

Humanity: Summary

So our notion of humanity is one that religious and political idealists have—in both similar and divergent ways—promoted as something that is profoundly *international*, even *transnational*; an idea that unites us all in striving for the greatest freedom of the individual to be him- or herself, a freedom that is curtailed only insofar as it is situated in an equality that ensures we are not free to oppress others—a curtailment, moreover, that we gladly accept by dint of our fraternal affection for our fellow men and women. Liberty situated in an equality guaranteed by fraternity. This freedom is an ideal far beyond the power/knowledge matrix of domination and opposition described by Foucault, which has encroached upon us since the Enlightenment.

But—as we saw earlier—human choice is not just about our relations with one another: it is not immune from the codetermination of reality the nonhuman exerts upon the human. External reality—including the disciplinated body we perceive and with which we perceive it—is constantly and (to use a word of Paine's) indefeasibly implicated in our choices and determinations.

What Is Reality?

The Material-Discursive

To understand the codetermination of both our conscious choice and the impact of external reality, we must adopt Barad's notion of the material-discursive and grasp how practices manifest in apparatuses. Echoing Bergson's deconstruction of the positions of the realist and the idealist, Barad argues that "quantum theory leads us out of the morass that takes absolutism and relativism to be the only two possibilities" (2007, 18). Turning to Neils Bohr for support, she presents her notion of "agential realism" as an "epistemological-ontological-ethical framework that provides an understanding of the role of human and nonhuman, material and discursive, and natural and cultural factors in scientific and other social-material practices" (26). For Barad, "the heart of the lesson of quantum physics" is that "we are a part of that nature that we seek to understand" (26).

Having thus harnessed quantum physics to her cause, Barad then explores the implications for philosophy. She quotes Donna Haraway to the effect that "What counts as an object is precisely what world history turns out to be about" (qtd. in Barad 2007, 470). Rather than objects, Barad asserts, with Bohr, it is *phenomena* that we should concentrate upon. Phenomena, significantly, differ crucially from objects, in that while an object is something that *is*, a phenomenon is something that *happens*. In this ontological focus upon what *happens* in the real, the notion of diffraction becomes central. Barad indeed announces it as "an apt overarching trope" for her book (27). Diffraction describes the behavior of waves when they overlap or meet an obstruction. The wave-particle-duality paradox in quantum physics also uses diffraction: both light and matter itself display both wave-like and particle-like properties. "What lies at the heart of the paradox is the very nature of nature" (27). Barad points out that visual metaphors are common in epistemology—especially reflection. Again she uses Haraway to support her argument, reminding us that "Haraway proposes diffraction as an alternative to the well-worn metaphor of reflection.... Whereas reflection is about mirroring and sameness, diffraction attends to patterns of difference" (27). Diffraction, moreover, includes agency: "Our knowledge-making practices, including the use and testing of scientific concepts, are material enactments that contribute to, and are a part of, the phenomena that we describe" (32).

Addressing the leaning of some antirealist positions toward relativism, for Barad, "agential realism", though staunchly nonrelativist, "rejects the notion of a correspondence relation between words and things and offers in its stead a causal explanation of how discursive practices are related to material phenomena" (Barad 2007, 45). She again attacks the realist position by destabilizing the notion of fixity. Quoting Hacking (1999), she relates how the notion of representationalism goes back to Democritus and the first distinction between the "real" and its "appearance"—caused by the concept of atomism: "Is the table a solid mass made of wood or an aggregate of discrete entities moving in the void?... The problem of realism in philosophy is a product of the atomistic worldview" (48). Barad summarizes: "The asymmetrical faith we place in our access to representations over things is a historically and culturally contingent belief that is part of Western philosophy's legacy and not a logical necessity" (49). Ultimately, "The assumption of thingness remains in place at the base of Hacking's entity realism," and Barad argues that "Realness does not necessarily imply thingness" (56).

Barad offers *performativity* as a way out of this conundrum. "Butler draws on Foucault's suggestion that the repetition of regulatory practices produces a specific materialization of bodies," (63) she tells us, giving rise to Butler's well-known theory of iterative citationality—that the roles we perform preexist us, and that we cite them in the knowledge that they will be understood because they are as known to those to whom we perform them as they are to us. Butler gives an account of matter as "a process of materialization that stabilizes over time to produce the effect of boundary, fixity, and surface we call matter" (Butler 1993, 9), which for Barad means "an unsettling of nature's presumed fixity" (2007, 64).

What we have thus far conceived (for convenience) as the virtual, conscious, "layer" of human society, in short, indivisibly expresses itself through—and is codetermined by—the performative practices that instantiate physical infrastructure and technologies: realities that are conceived *durationally* rather than as "fixed things." This infrastructure and these technologies have, in turn, direct bearing upon who we are and the choices that we make. Reality, as we know it, is codetermined by the human and the nonhuman in a "mangle" (Pickering 1995) of interrelated influence and agency.

It is clear that not just prior to, but throughout both the Christian and the modern era, those individuals in our society who wield a controlling influence on the physical infrastructure and technologies of society have been the rulers and leaders of society (for all that their rule may be determined by Foucauldian matrices of power relations). Clearly, the ideal of "humanity" as a great leveler apportioning to all the "rights of man" has not translated well into our social structures, where—contrary to this ideal—huge disparities in wealth exist, and the apparatuses of our technological society materialize practices that are suffused with politics—specifically with the politics of control. Lately, indeed, our leaders have become, in fact, very clever in seeming to promote the ideal while ensuring they retain that control.

Empire

Antonio Gramsci re-evaluated in his *Prison Notebooks* the traditional Marxist under-standings of modern capitalist societies, by arguing that rather than being determined by underlying economic necessities, culture and politics formed a web of relations with the economy in which there is a continual shift of emphasis and influence. For this process he coined the term *hegemony*. Although somewhat fluid in meaning, in his *Notebooks* Gramsci best defines this term as "The 'spontaneous' consent given by the great masses of the population to the general direction imposed on social life by the dominant fundamental group; this consent is 'historically' caused by the prestige (and consequent confidence) which the dominant group enjoys because of its position and function in the world of production" (Gramsci [1971] 2007, 12). Importantly, as Jones points out in his study of Gramsci's work, "the maintenance of that consent is dependent upon an incessant repositioning of the relationship between rulers and ruled" (2006, 3).

Following Roosevelt's New Deal of the 1930s, the Second World War tightened the relationship between government and economy through mandatory "mobilization" of industrial units and workforce for the production of arms. This mobilization was not "stood down" in 1945, as the Second World War became the Cold War, but evolved into what has since been termed the military-industrial complex—the combination of a nation's armed forces, its suppliers of weapons systems, supplies and services, and its civil government. This military-industrial complex, moreover, through European and transatlantic treaties, special relationships, and political settlements under American leadership, soon established what Gill terms an international military-industrial com-plex, in which many countries' armed forces, weapons manufacturers, and government agencies are knitted together in codependent alliances (Gill 2003, 58).

Moreover, the futuristic, impersonal machines that served as "the defining devices of cold war technology" (Turner 2006, 2)—the early, mainframe computer—belied a collaborative culture among the computer programmers. This community comput-ing culture, in the 1960s and 1970s, through the efforts of New Communalists such as

Stewart Brand, formed a crucial alliance with part of the hippie counterculture of the time. This, when spliced with a resurgent Republican entrepreneurialism spearheaded by philosopher and author Ayn Rand (Curtis 2011a; 2011b), brought about the personal computer revolution, and the promise of "a countercultural dream of empowered individualism" (Turner 2006, 2). All this took place as part of the rise of a physics- and mathematics-centered research culture, from the Second World War through to the 1990s, leading ultimately to the contemporary phenomenon of Internet billionaires (Mirowski 2002).

The Internet, originally a Cold War command-and-control structure, significantly, becomes in the twenty-first century not only the medium of multinational power relations, but the realm of a transnationalism that hegemonically appropriates the supranational ideal of humanity and sells it to us wrapped up in shiny gadgets (Dean 2009).

In Hardt and Negri's post-Gramscian vision of the world order, *Empire* (2000), the apparent "decline in sovereignty of nation-states...does not mean that sovereignty as such has declined...sovereignty has taken a new form, composed of a series of national and supranational organisms united under a single logic of rule" (xi–xii). They call this new global form of sovereignty "Empire," which is to be understood very differently from imperialism. The earlier "imperialist" form was centered, while the current "Empire" is decentered. The earlier form focused upon the boundaries of the nation-state, making those within superior to those without, controlling the flow of goods and people across those boundaries to maintain that relation. The current form focuses upon boundaryless flow of goods and people and is thus "a *decentered* and *deterritorializing* apparatus of rule that progressively incorporates the entire global realm within its open, expanding frontiers" (xii). Empire is thus more a Foucauldian discursive formation than an old European imperialist power. "The United States does not," Hardt and Negri assert, "and indeed no nation-state can today, form the center of an imperialist project" (xiv). Witness the rise of the BRIC countries (Brazil, Russia, India, and China) and the relative decline in US power. Indeed it could be argued that the global financial crash of 2008 created a fourth phase New World Order, in Gill's terms—a furthering in the development of Hardt and Negri's Empire—a much more multipolar world.

Reality: Summary—the Spectacle

So what we understand as "reality" proves itself to be rather more slippery than might at first appear, open to tempero-spatial interpretations that reject the notion of "thingness" in favor of material-discursive practices in which we are all entwined, and which codetermine our experience and our choices. Worse, those who hold more reins than the rest in the marshaling of resources and determination of practices turn out to be very adept at maintaining their controlling positions with our unwitting collusion.

Perhaps, indeed, focusing once more upon the digital virtuality at the heart of this book, it would be truer to say that the real leaders of the early twenty-first-century world—of the world many of us inhabit daily—are Mark Zuckerberg of Facebook, the inheritors of the late Steve Jobs of Apple, and Sergey Brin of Google (Kreps 2011). Half a billion people daily were logging onto Facebook by late 2011 (Svetlik 2011), freely providing their information for data mining (Andrejevic 2010), many using smartphones either made or inspired by Apple, and all engaging in the free play of multiple masks of selfhood social networking provides (Kreps 2010).

Although these names and digital spaces will inevitably change as the century unfolds, their strategies are transparent: appealing hegemonically to our ideal of transnational humanity and fellowship, they ensure our continued engagement in the transnational capitalism that makes them rich and keeps us working to maintain their wealth.

In a disciplinated matrix of power/knowledge relations, surrounded by material-discursive nonhuman influences upon our agency, and subject to the hegemonic leadership of elites continually remodeling the way in which they lead us, *choice* is something our consciousness is perhaps not always best placed to make our own. Critical theory has long focused upon this, from a number of angles, leading us to question the directions in which we, as a society, are going. In truth, perhaps, we are truly living in Debord's *Society of the Spectacle* ([1967] 1994), our eyes glued to our (albeit mobile) screens at all times, our consumer society helping to maintain inequalities and elites.

Conclusion

Through this discussion I have sought to explore a key three-in-one question: what should we understand by the terms virtuality, humanity, and reality?

Virtuality, with Bergson, we have found, can be equated with consciousness, seen as integral to a temporal continuity that forms a virtual counterpoint to matter, understood as a fixed, spatial stop. This virtuality provides the universe we engage in with real action in the manner of choice, as opposed to the mere action-reaction of scientific laws. This virtuality is a shared, social experience—the world of discourse, which today takes the form of a matrix of knowledge and power, and creates for itself, through the performative utterance of statements, discursive formations, and relations played out in discursive practices.

Humanity, we have seen, is something that is profoundly *transnational*, an idea that unites us all in striving for the greatest freedom of the individual to be him- or herself, a freedom that is curtailed only insofar as it is situated in an equality that ensures we are not free to oppress others—a curtailment, moreover, that we gladly accept by dint of our fraternal affection for our fellow men and women. Liberty is situated in an equality guaranteed by fraternity.

Reality, we have seen, is open to tempero-spatial interpretations that reject the notion of "thingness" in favor of material-discursive practices in which we are all entwined, and which codetermine our experience and our choices, and proves also to be a site of contention, where elites seek to maintain hegemonic control of both resources and the rest of us.

Students and theorists of virtuality need awareness of a wide range of conditioning contexts, philosophical, political, and ontological, to ensure a critical appreciation of what virtuality is and could be doing for or to us, and in this chapter I have attempted to look at several. Humanity, we have seen, is (at least today) a species-wide and leveling ideal. Virtuality is discourse itself, as old as humanity, but it is also material-discursive: manifesting itself in infrastructure and technologies that in turn codetermine our choices.

The digital virtuality that is the focus of much of this book, I have argued in this chapter, is but a continuation of the virtuality that is human consciousness. But the political, material-discursive context within which it sits must also be a focus for critical understanding: is it leading us in the direction of our ideal, or merely supporting the power of entrenched elites? Practitioners of virtual-world design take note: the spaces you create are real enough, and the human relations are as filled with knowledge and power as in any other context. In our off-grid holiday resorts, escaping from the overlaid streams of location-aware data, we will be seeking simplicity, peace, and rest, for the virtual world is different in degree, not in kind, from the world of the everyday.

References

Adamson, G. D. 2000. Science and Philosophy: Two Sides of the Absolute. *Pli* 9: 53–85.

Andrejevic, M. 2010. Social Network Exploitation. In *A Networked Self: Identity, Community, and Culture on Social Network Sites*, edited by Z. Papacharissi, 82–101. New York: Routledge.

Bakunin, M. 1980. *Bakunin on Anarchism*. Translated and edited by S. Dolgoff. Montreal: Black Rose Books.

Barad, K. 2007. *Meeting the Universe Halfway: Quantum Physics and the Entanglement of Matter and Meaning*. Durham, NC: Duke University Press.

Bergson, H. (1911) 1944. *Creative Evolution*. Translated by A. Mitchell. New York: Random House.

Bergson, H. (1908) 2004. *Matter and Memory*. Translated by N. M. Paul and W. S. Palmer. London: Dover.

Bergson, H. (1935) 2006. *The Two Sources of Morality and Religion*. Translated by R. Ashley Audra. Notre Dame, IN: University of Notre Dame Press.

Butler, J. 1993. *Bodies That Matter: On the Discursive Limits of "Sex"*. London: Routledge.

Curtis, A., dir. 2011a. *All Watched Over by Machines of Loving Grace*. BBC.

Curtis, A. 2011b. How the "Ecosystem" Myth Has Been Used for Sinister Means. *The Observer*, May 29. http://www.guardian.co.uk/environment/2011/may/29/adam-curtis-ecosystems-tansley-smuts. Accessed August 28, 2013.

Dean, J. 2009. *Democracy and Other Neoliberal Fantasies*. Durham, NC: Duke University Press.

Debord, G. (1967) 1994. *The Society of the Spectacle*. Translated by D. Nicholson-Smith. New York: Zone Books.

Derrida, J. 1974. *Of Grammatology*. Translated by G. C. Spivak. Baltimore, MD: John Hopkins University Press.

Dolgoff, S. 1980. Introduction to *Bakunin on Anarchism*. Translated and edited by S. Dolgoff, 3–21. Montreal: Black Rose Books.

Foucault, M. 1977. *Discipline and Punish: The Birth of the Prison*. Translated by A. Sheridan. London: Penguin.

Foucault, M. 1988. *Technologies of the Self: A Seminar with Michel Foucault.* Edited by L. H. Martin, H. Gutman, and P. H. Hutton. Amherst: University of Massachusetts Press.

Foucault, M. 1990. *History of Sexuality.* Vol. 3: *The Care of the Self.* Translated by R. Hurley. London: Penguin.

Foucault, M. 1992. *History of Sexuality.* Vol. 2: *The Use of Pleasure.* Translated by R. Hurley. London: Penguin.

Foucault, M. 1995a. *Madness and Civilization: A History of Insanity in the Age of Reason.* Translated by R. Howard. London: Routledge.

Foucault, M. 1995b. *The Archaeology of Knowledge.* Translated by A. Sheridan. London: Routledge.

Foucault, M. 1997. *The Order of Things: An Archaeology of the Human Sciences.* London: Routledge.

Foucault, M. 1998. *History of Sexuality.* Vol. 1: *The Will to Knowledge.* Translated by R. Hurley. London: Penguin.

Gill, S. 2003. *Power and Resistance in the New World Order.* Basingstoke: Palgrave.

Gramsci, A. (1971) 2007. *Selections from the Prison Notebooks.* Translated by Q. Hoare and G. N. Smith. Kings Lynn: MPG Books Group.

Hacking, I. 1999. *The Social Construction of What?* Cambridge, MA: Harvard University Press.

Hall, S. 1997. *Representation: Cultural Representations and Signifying Practices.* London: Sage Publications.

Hardt, M., and A. Negri. 2000. *Empire.* Cambridge, MA: Harvard University Press.

Jones, S. 2006. *Antonio Gramsci.* London: Routledge.

Kilner, J. M., K. J. Friston, and C. D. Frith. 2007. The Mirror-Neuron System: A Bayesian Perspective. *NeuroReport* 18: 619–623.

Kilner, J. M., A. Neal, N. Weiskopf, K. J. Friston, and C. D. Frith. 2009. Evidence of Mirror Neurons in Human Inferior Frontal Gyrus. *Journal of Neuroscience* 29: 10153–10159.

Kreps, D. 2010. My Social Networking Profile: Copy, Resemblance, or Simulacrum? A Poststructuralist Interpretation of Social Information Systems. *European Journal of Information Systems* 19 (1): 104–115.

Kreps, D. 2011. Social Networking and Transnational Capitalism. *tripleC—Cognition, Communication, Co-operation* 9 (2): 689–701.

Mirowski, P. 2002. *Machine Dreams: Economics Becomes a Cyborg Science* Cambridge: Cambridge University Press.

Paine, T. (1791) 1995. *Rights of Man.* Oxford: Oxford University Press.

Pickering, A. 1995. *The Mangle of Practice: Time, Agency and Science.* Chicago: University of Chicago Press.

Rizzolatti, G., and L. Craighero. 2004. The Mirror-Neuron System. *Annual Review of Neuroscience* 27: 169–192.

Selfa, L. 2002. Slavery and the Origins of Racism. *International Socialist Review* 26. http://www.isreview.org/issues/26/roots_of_racism.shtml. Accessed June 30, 2013.

Svetlik, J. 2011. Facebook Attracts Half a Billion People in One Day. *CNET.* September 23. http://crave.cnet.co.uk/software/facebook-attracts-half-a-billion-people-in-one-day-50005304/. Accessed September 11, 2011.

Turkle, S. 2010. *Alone Together.* London: Basic Books.

Turner, F. 2006. *From Counterculture to Cyber culture.* Chicago: University of Chicago Press.

Warburton, N. 1998. *Philosophy: The Classics* London: Routledge.

Williams, G. 1999. *French Discourse Analysis: The method of Post-structuralism.* London: Routledge.

CHAPTER 44

....

VIRTUAL DYSTOPIA

....

ANDREA HUNTER AND VINCENT MOSCO

THE promise and the allure of the sublime is that it will lead to transcendence, lifting us out of the banality of everyday life. Throughout history the sublime has been most often linked to the wonders of the "natural" world, such as towering mountains and powerful storms (Battersby 2007; Burke [1757] 1990; Kant [1790] 2007; Shaw 2006). In the late nineteenth and throughout the twentieth century, the sublime became associated with technology as first the railroad, then the telegraph, electricity, and even the telephone promised to usher in peace and prosperity. The sublime has reappeared in the digitally saturated late twentieth and early twenty-first centuries, now tied to virtual worlds and visions of cyberspace. Often the promise of virtual worlds has been linked to utopian ideals. Virtual spaces have been described as places where the limits of the "real" world can be left behind. Geography will no longer matter as people come together virtually, fostering mutual understanding (Flew 2008; Turkle 1995). However, not all virtual words are utopian. In the most popular multiplayer online game, *World of Warcraft*, for instance, players enter a dystopian virtual world where they are under threat from unknown terrors (monsters, dragons, plagues, etc.). It might seem as if dystopias such as this should be repellent, rather than compelling. However, the attraction of virtual dystopias comes from their connection to the sublime. While beauty invokes pleasure and identification, the sublime is terrifying, awe-inspiring, and forces one to grapple with the unknown and with the nature of existence (Mosco 2004). Similarly, the dystopian is compelling, not only because ghoulishness and strife are ways of dealing with mortality and the presence of evil in the world, but also because it evokes terror, which is linked to the unknown, including death. Virtual dystopias offer a type of sublime transcendence that allows people to deal with horror, without "actually" having to experience it. That said, there is a complex, porous relationship between virtual dystopia and reality as the two realms intermingle and inform each other.

These themes will be explored through exemplars from three different media spanning three decades of computer-inspired virtuality. Written pre-Internet, *Mona Lisa Overdrive* (1988), part of William Gibson's cyberspace trilogy, imagines a virtual world that is terrifying and compelling. It is indeed virtual, but still intimately tied to characters' embodied forms. The film *Inception* (Nolan 2010) examines the fluid relationship between reality and virtuality, in the form of dreamworlds within dreamworlds, leading the audience to question the difference between what is real and what is virtual. In *World of Warcraft* (2004–2013), players band together in guilds to fight. Many develop strong ties and engage in this virtual world in a way that overlaps with their embodied realities. The social aspect of this game is a large part of its success, as players find community in the face of adversity and transcendence from the banality of the everyday in a virtual dystopia of war and risk that never fully threatens what Gibson (1984) would call the "meat" (6) of the embodied individual. These case studies all have a complex relationship between the virtual and the real. What unites them, however, is a sense that one is entering a world where dystopia can be experienced in relative safety.

Dystopia is inextricably linked to utopia, and is often defined as its antonym. The first recorded use is in a parliamentary speech given in 1868 by John Stuart Mill, who was looking for a name to identify the opposite of utopia (Vieira 2010). Since then, dystopia has come to be associated with a genre of literature that is both didactic and moralistic—visions of a dismal future are put forward as a warning of what should be avoided (Sargent 2006). While utopian literature has a long history, stretching back to the sixteenth century, dystopian literature is the child of the twentieth century, beginning in earnest after the two world wars. This genre tends to focus on the themes of totalitarianism and the dangers of scientific and technological progress. In addition to serving as a warning about how life might turn out if certain paths are followed, dystopias are a way to deal with terror or horror, from a safe place. As Slaughter (2004) describes, dystopias serve as a "temporary catharsis" (23). "We can experience our anxiety and fear in the safe confines of a book, a movie theatre or TV screen, where they can also be safely resolved, at least for the time being" (xxii).

The sublime's connection with dystopia derives from its connection with terror, darkness, and horror. In the eighteenth century, John Dennis ([1704] 1996), the English critic, writes that the sublime does not persuade, rather it "ravishes and transports us, and produces in us a certain admiration, mingled with astonishment and surprise" (37). For Dennis, the sublime is linked to "terrible" ideas, such as hell, witchcraft, and monsters, or natural events such as storms, earthquakes, or volcanoes. This theme of terror is taken up in Edmund Burke's inquiry into the sublime. For Burke, the sublime object (found in nature) fills the mind of the observer, causing astonishment and horror, rendering one unable to contemplate anything else. The sublime is evoked when one is faced with something that is seemingly endless, infinite, vast, powerful, obscure, and of great magnitude or difficulty. The sublime experience is ultimately not a negative one, however. As Shaw (2006) describes, "The self may delight in sublime terror as long as actual danger is kept at bay" (54).

This sense of an overwhelming, intense, terrible experience is also taken up in another influential eighteenth-century text on the sublime, Kant's *Critique of Judgment* ([1790] 2007). In Kant's sublime, the imagination is overwhelmed by an experience (either because of its size or its power) to the point where it is impossible to fully understand what one is faced with (the vastness of a mountain, the power of a storm, the expanse of the universe) (Hertz 1985; Shaw 2006). The sublime moment comes when the mind is able to grasp that it is facing an infinity it cannot fully comprehend (Crowther 1989; Shaw 2006). As with Burke, Kant's experience of the sublime is not entirely negative, but rather there is something uplifting and elevating in the revelation that the mind is grasping an infinity that is beyond full comprehension (Crowther 1989; Kirwan 2005; Shaw 2006). For both Burke and Kant, facing the unknown or the incomprehensible is part of the sublime experience, focusing on how this confrontation can elevate the soul and the mind, and bring about a sense of transcendence. Thus, while there is a connection between the sublime and horror because confronting the "unthinkable" is an essential element of the horror genre (Thacker 2011), Burke and Kant would remind us that, absent an actual confrontation with horror, the experience is ultimately transcendent.

In the twentieth century, the first use of the phrase "technological sublime" is usually attributed to Leo Marx (1964), and his description of how writers in the nineteenth century responded to the arrival of the railroad in the American pastoral landscape. The railroad became a symbol of hope, peace, and unity. It would annihilate space and bring people together, and those lucky enough to ride in one would never see the world in the same way again (Marx 1964; Nye 1994). At the same time, the railroad was also mysterious and dangerous. Most people did not understand how this technology worked, and this sort of obscurity only added to the sense of danger and terror that helped build the sublime experience. It eventually became clear, however, that the railroad was not going to live up to its sublime promises because it was also a source of labor strife and air pollution, and was plagued by frequent accidents. Furthermore, the train ride that seemed shocking and unbelievable to those first riders ceased to hold the same luster a few decades later. This is the pattern with the technological sublime—new technology begins as sublime and eventually fades into the banal. The telegraph was heralded as a harbinger of world peace (Carey 1989; Standage 1998). Electricity was going to lead to safe cities, abundance, and an end to conflict (Marvin 1988; Nye 1990, 1994). In the late twentieth and early twenty-first centuries, computers, the Internet, and all things "dot-com" seduced investors and consumers with the lure of the "digital sublime" (Mosco 2004).

In every iteration of the technological and digital sublime, however, there is a link with the dystopian. While on one hand technology is imbued with promises of peace and prosperity, it is also seen as potentially dangerous and unsettling. It is precisely this uncertainty—the feeling of terror and danger—that adds to the sublime experience.

What is common to all these treatises on the sublime is that the terror, danger, uncertainty, and insecurity one feels are only transformative and uplifting insofar as the observer is not in any genuine mortal danger. An essential aspect of the sublime is that terror is experienced from a safe distance (Burke [1757] 1990; Kant [1790] 2007; Mosco 2004; Nye 1994; Shaw 2006). Virtual dystopia affords the observer this safety, enabling the sublime experience without threatening the embodied individual.

However, the line between the virtual and the real can be murky. In common-sense, everyday language, the virtual and the real are set up as polar opposites. The real is equated with something concrete or tangible. The virtual, by contrast, signifies "absence, unreality or non-existence" (Shields 2003, 19). In practice it is extremely difficult to draw such a sharp distinction between the two. (No doubt Archbishop Thomas Cranmer would agree. His defense of the virtual had very real consequences. He was executed in the 1500s in large part because he defended the virtuality of the Eucharist, that the bread and wine taken during Mass was not *actually* the body and blood of Christ [Shields 2003].) In the twentieth and twenty-first centuries the virtual has a strong connection to digital hardware and software, and debates around what is real and what is virtual have centered around whether one enters a "new" world through computer-mediated communication, or if the virtual is simply an extension of the material world (Flew 2008). Despite the present-day connection to computing technology, the fluidity between the real and the virtual predates the Internet. Many cultures view the virtual, in the form of memories and dreams, as real. Even though they may not be tangible or actual, they are still experienced as real and as affecting the material world. Similarly, spirituality and religion have a material effect on a person's sense of self, ways of organizing, and ways of living (Shields 2003). The virtual also existed pre-Internet, through built environments such as architecture and panoramas. In the nineteenth century, commercial panoramic spectacles were created, designed to envelop paying customers in a 360-degree "virtual" environment that would transport them, temporarily, out of their regular environment (Shields 2003). Even prior to this, the interior of churches provided examples of elaborate built virtual environments. The images of heaven painted on ceilings and the architecture of the church itself were designed to "draw the viewer into a spectacle which transcends the everyday spaces of the temporal world" (Shields 2003, 8). One of the premier examples of this, as Wertheim (1999) describes, is Giotto's fresco of heaven on the back wall of the Arena Chapel in Padua (26).

Similarly, there is a long history of depicting dystopias in art and architecture, meant to momentarily transport the viewer into another world, as warnings of what could become of humanity. For instance, many medieval churches had "dooms," depictions of the Last Judgment, painted and carved in their interiors, depicting souls ascending to heaven and the unlucky descending to hell. These types of visual warnings were popular, particularly in northern Europe, where paintings were also mounted in public places such as town halls and even hospitals, to remind magistrates, judges, the sick, and others of what could befall them (Ayers 2008; Gibson 1973). Two of the most dramatic and horror-filled triptychs from that era that portray images of hell, are the Dutch painter Hieronymous Bosch's *Last Judgment* and *The Garden of Earthly Delights* (Gibson 1973). However, while these dystopian images served as warnings, dystopian virtuality takes on new, prescient meaning in an increasingly mediated and digital world, where part of the allure of the dystopian is that it can become a place of refuge and community. In the three cases that follow, the virtual is enabled by technology. In *Mona Lisa Overdrive* (1988), most people enter cyberspace by attaching electronic "trodes" to their temples. In the film *Inception* (Nolan 2010) the characters enter dreamworlds through machines that administer a chemical concoction. The passage into *World of Warcraft* (2004–2011) is through a computer console. However, in each of these cases, there is no clear divide between the real and the virtual.

In William Gibson's cyberspace trilogy—*Neuromancer* (1984), *Count Zero* (1986), and *Mona Lisa Overdrive* (1988)—cyberspace is something mysterious and alluring. It is a vast, fragile, constantly mutating space of "unthinkable complexity" (1984, 51) that contains "a graphic representation of data abstracted from the banks of every computer in the human system" (51); a "consensual hallucination" (51) that people can "jack" into and out of at will. The "real" world is a dark and unfriendly place, where nature has been replaced with urban sprawl. Cyberspace, by contrast, is a place of light and mystery. It is formless, intangible, and seemingly infinite. In *Mona Lisa Overdrive* (1988), when Angela enters cyberspace "the bright grid of the matrix ranged around her like an infinite cage" (49). Angela remembers that schoolchildren were taught to think about cyberspace this way: "There's no there, there" (48). Gibson's cyberspace deals with the infinite and the nature of existence (cyberspace is humanity pared down to data), themes that are central in the Kantian and Burkean notions of the sublime. It differs, however, in that while Kant and Burke looked to nature—such as mountains and storms—for the sublime, Gibson moves it into the realm of computer-generated data (Voller 1993). Essentially, Gibson's trilogy foreshadows the allure of the digital sublime.

The dystopian is manifest in several ways throughout this trilogy. First, the world the characters find themselves in is a dystopian landscape. The earth, transformed into a maze of industry and technology, is a dangerous, dark place. Second, cyberspace, although a place of temptation, is also dystopian in that it is unstable and dangerous. In *Mona Lisa Overdrive* (1988) a murder and kidnapping is plotted and masterminded from cyberspace by the clone Lady 3Jane. Throughout the trilogy, cyberspace is the home of "console cowboys"; hustlers who jack in, looking to steal information. However, Gibson's characters cannot ignore the siren call of cyberspace, despite the dangers they encounter within it. Part of its allure is its formlessness, its vastness, and, perhaps most importantly, because it holds the digital essence of humanity. In *Mona Lisa Overdrive* (1988), a recurring theme is whether cyberspace really is infinite, or whether it has a shape. Gentry, one of the central characters, becomes obsessed with figuring out the overall form of the matrix. It overtakes him and becomes his "grail" (76). Gentry's quest represents the Kantian notion of grappling with the ungraspable, and wrestling with the nature of human existence. At the end of the book, the matrix (cyberspace) has evolved, become a sentient being, and thus *does* in fact have a shape. However, as the matrix achieves sentience, it becomes aware of other matrixes, other forms of cyberspace that are nonhuman. Cyberspace, a metaphor for the universe, remains infinite, still unexplored. The nature of human existence and our relationship to the universe is still a question.

A key aspect of the sublime is that one experiences it without ever truly being in danger. Part of the attraction of cyberspace, although it may be an insecure, unstable place, is that one can enter it, leaving the body behind. However, the line between the virtual world of cyberspace and the "real world" is porous. First, what happens in cyberspace does have consequences in the real world. For instance, in the first book in the trilogy, *Neuromancer* (1984), we learn that Case, the protagonist, has been chemically altered for stealing from his employers; the chemicals have affected his nervous system, prohibiting him from jacking into cyberspace. This is devastating for Case, who "had lived for the bodily exhalations of cyberspace" (6). Now he is trapped in the "meat" of his own body, a prisoner "of his own flesh" (6). Second, Gibson maintains that life itself can transcend the real and exist virtually in cyberspace. In *Mona Lisa Overdrive* (1988), several of the characters end up forgoing their bodies completely. Lady 3Jane, for instance, dies in the "real" world only to "live" on in cyberspace. At the end of the book Angela and her boyfriend Bobby both die in "real life" so that they can live together in cyberspace. Death of the body is not the end. As the character Molly says: "There's dying, then there's dying" (301). Cyberspace is, ultimately, a place of escape and of refuge; it is a place where Angela and Bobby can finally be together, free from the stress and pressure of the "real" world.

Voller (1993) claims that Gibson's protagonists have a very different take on the sublime than did the Romantics. While the Romantics turned to the sublime in a search for "the eternal, the infinite" (27), the protagonists in Gibson's novels enter into cyberspace in search of the "wealth and power immanent in data" (27). They return from cyberspace not enriched from contemplating the divine or the eternal, but rather "empowered and enriched...only in the most literal sense of those words" (27). While this is certainly the case, in particular for the "hustlers" that occupy the first two books in the trilogy, it is only a partial reason why cyberspace is sublime. Cyberspace is alluring because it contains the essence of human life. When people enter cyberspace, they are awestruck by the immensity of the matrix and its seemingly infinite reach. Certainly what the characters get from their experience with cyberspace is danger, thrill, power, and a sense of control. But cyberspace represents all of human existence, and entering cyberspace is a search for the meaning of this existence.

In the film *Inception* (Nolan 2010), the virtual dystopias the characters enter are also enabled by technology, but of a different sort. The central character of the film—Dom Cobb (Leonardo DiCaprio)—is a dream "extractor" by profession. Cobb and his team are paid to enter people's dreams in order to steal their secrets. The science behind this process is never entirely clear. Dreamers are administered a chemical intravenously that first sedates them, and then allows others to enter the same dream. The premise of the film is that people keep their innermost secrets locked deep in their subconscious, which are only accessible by descending through different dream levels (dreams within dreams). The film begins with Cobb hired to plant an idea in the subconscious of the heir to the world's largest energy empire (a process known as inception—hence the film's name) that will force him to divest his company.

The dystopia in this film manifests in two ways: the general plot line and the fragility (instability) of the dreams. On one level the entire film is dystopic in that Cobb is a wanted man who lives in fear of being caught and charged with his wife's death. In order to stay out of custody he has to leave behind the people he loves most in the world, his children. Throughout the film Cobb is also pursued, or haunted, by the memory of his dead wife, Mal. (Although we never find out what her full name is, *mal* means bad or sick in French.) Mal reappears in every dream that Cobb enters, as a manifestation of his subconscious that he cannot control. In every encounter she vacillates between contrite and hostile, in the end always turning against Cobb by maiming (or killing) his friends and turning him in.

It is also apparent that the dreams themselves are not safe places. They are fragile and susceptible to collapse. Throughout the film the foundations of the dreams shake and are ultimately destroyed by action in other dreams or the real world. For instance, in the film's first scene the building Cobb is in literally falls down around him as the dream comes to an end. In the second dream an angry mob is approaching, burning buildings and tearing up the landscape. On a meta level, of course, all dreams are susceptible to collapse the moment the dreamer wakes.

As mentioned, dystopias are usually created as critiques of present-day society, or as warnings of what society could become. They are typically set in the future, even though they are clearly referring to what is happening in the now, and the consequences that could result (Booker 1994). *Inception* breaks the mold, in that it is not necessarily set in a dystopian future. (It is unclear what the exact time frame is.) As well, the dystopia created is not one of social commentary, but rather focuses on the self. The warning that repeats throughout the film is to make peace with life and especially with relationships, because we are never truly free of them. What drives Cobb is a deep feeling of regret that torments and traps him. The point of the film is that we may bury our secrets deep in our subconscious, but they will never completely disappear. Here the film draws heavily on psychology, in particular Freud's theories of the unconscious as the place where people hide their unacceptable thoughts and memories of traumatic events.

Within the film, the sublime appears through the dystopian dreamscapes. The dreams evoke astonishment and terror, yet at the same time are irresistible. This is perhaps best exemplified by the character Ariadne—who has been hired as an "architect" to construct the dreams that Cobb will enter. When she is first introduced to shared dreaming, the dream seems no different from reality. But once she becomes aware of her ability to manipulate the entire world around her, defying the laws of physics, she is shocked, astonished, and then finally terrorized, as she is attacked and killed (only to wake up in reality).

Despite this terror, shared dreaming is so seductive, so sublime, that once she has experienced it, everyday life is not enough. Initially, Ariadne walks out on Cobb. Arthur, Cobb's colleague, is very concerned, since they need her to pull off the "inception." However, Cobb reassures him that Ariadne will be back; once she has had a taste of dreaming, reality will seem pale. Sure enough Ariadne returns, saying to Arthur: "I tried not to come, but…" To which Arthur replies: "There's nothing quite like it."

The sublime, although it suggests terror, is also, at another level, nonthreatening. While one comes face to face with something incredibly large or powerful that provokes astonishment or horror, one is never really in mortal danger. This film plays with this idea on several levels. First, although dreams are fraught with danger, the "real" bodies of the dreamers are never threatened. When people are killed in a dream, they do not die, they simply wake up. The dreamer experiences these different worlds, without any real threat of becoming captured by them. (The one exception is that one can be sent into "limbo," an unstructured dream space from which one might never fully wake up. However, even this sentence is not a final death-knell; one stays alive in limbo, and one's body stays alive, although unconscious, in the real world.) Second, just as Gibson's characters never really die, but live on in cyberspace, the movie questions whether anyone really dies, or whether people simply live on in dreams and memories.

Inception plays with the real and the virtual, emphasizing the porous nature of both. The consistent theme throughout is whether one can distinguish between what is real and what is not. The audience quickly learns not to trust which is which. The film asks us to question whether reality is actually a dream and vice versa. We are also meant to question whether the distinction between reality and dreams even matters. The whole point of inception is that an idea can be planted in someone's mind in a virtual environment, which will then take root, grow, and affect reality. While one world might be real and the other virtual, they are both actual, in the sense that there is crossover between the two and subsequent material consequences. *Inception* also suggests that dreams are seductive because they are places where we can revisit what has been lost. Although Cobb's wife is a destructive force, part of the reason Cobb continues in his line of work is to continue to be close to her. The virtual dystopias he enters, although dangerous, are also sanctuaries preserving the memory of his wife.

Both *Inception* and *Mona Lisa Overdrive* allow the audience to enter a dystopian world that it can leave by pressing stop, leaving the theater, or closing the book. It allows the audience to contemplate these dystopias from a safe distance. *World of Warcraft* (2004–2013), however, differs in that the audience moves from a passive/sidelined position to become a vital participant in building and maintaining the dystopia. The audience is integrally involved, even though the experience remains virtual, not in the screen but in front of it.

World of Warcraft is a "quest" game that draws on the traditions of offline adventure and role-playing games, such as *Dungeons and Dragons* (Corneliussen and Rettberg 2008; Ducheneaut et al. 2006). It is a dystopian virtual game world, in that the fundamental aspect, as its name suggests, is war. Players create their own avatars and fight mythical creatures as well as each other. This can be done alone, but most often players band together, often in guilds, to attack and destroy "the enemy."

World of Warcraft is not just a game space but is presented as a "world," complete with a complex geography, population, culture, and history (Kryzwinska and Lowood 2006). A great deal of this game focuses on players creating personas and improving their characters by taking on quests and challenges. The game gives players the chance to escape "real life" and be reborn as someone new online. As Castronova writes: "We are no longer stuck with the Game of Life as we receive it from our ancestors. We can make a new one, almost however we like" (2005, 70). Many players use the game to reinvent themselves as something completely different. As Rettberg (2008) describes: "We have the opportunity to wipe the slate clean, to start again and choose new lives in a new world" (23).

In addition to being able to reinvent oneself, the game also offers players a place where they can engage in rewarding work. McGonigal (2011) argues that many people have day jobs that are banal and unfulfilling. *World of Warcraft*, by contrast, is all about teamwork that "emphasizes collaboration, cooperation and contributions to a larger group" (30). Indeed, the social aspect of this game is crucial for survival. A player can explore the game alone, but to complete quests players have to band together. Most guilds become very complex social entities, complete with hierarchies, customs, and internal economies (Malone 2009). Interaction is an integral part of the game, unlike most computer games that are played alone or in small groups (Kryzwinska and Lowood 2006).

While some argue that violence in games actually serves to desensitize the player to violence in "real life" (Carnagey, Anderson, and Bushman 2007), others see games such as *World of Warcraft* as offering a thrilling adventure, wherein the player can be a hero (or a villain), confronting danger without actual threat to the body (Aarseth 2008). In *World of Warcraft*, players fight and even die in the virtual game world, but their material bodies are always safely ensconced in a seat in front of a computer console. Even within the game there is the chance (and expectation) of resurrection. Players can be brought back to life by the healing powers of other players. Essentially, *World of Warcraft* allows the player to experience a romanticized version of war—and how they would act in warfare—without the messy realities of trenches, mud, bullets, bombs, and, of course, actual death (Klastrup 2008). The game gives players an escape from the everyday. Those who might feel that their "real" lives are barely under control, have the opportunity within the game to demonstrate not only control, but also heroism. There is also a strong sense of community and social ties that comes out of battles, as people work together to defeat the enemy.

World of Warcraft is sublime because it offers a reprieve from the day-to-day, a place where people come together to have fun, socialize, and escape the banality of their everyday lives (Aarseth 2008). The sense of community is one of the main attractions of the game. The drudgery of the real world can be left behind for a world of strong social bonds and heroism. However, in many ways there is not a sharp separation between the game and the so-called "real world." There are tangible connections that *World of Warcraft* plays on and exploits. Even though the game takes place in the realm of the virtual, players often act in ways that blur the boundaries between the real and the virtual. For instance, there is a trade system in the game that permits people to sell their wares through auctions. These auctions often spill out beyond the game boundaries into other websites where real money changes hands (Kryzwinska and Lowood 2006). As well, even though people have the opportunity to create avatars that are very different from whom they are in real life, players are still largely influenced by social and cultural norms. These norms shape the choices made in the virtual world, just as they do in the "real world." Players are more reluctant to play "ugly" or "bad" characters, and overwhelmingly choose avatars from races that conform to highly stereotypical canons of beauty (e.g., the tall, lean, and often scantily clad female night elves). Rettberg (2008) argues that the game has been so successful because "it offers a convincing and detailed simulacrum of the process of becoming successful in capitalist societies" (20). It offers players "a capitalistic fairy tale" (20) where the moral is hard work can pay off. While in real life one may be hampered by birthright or unlucky circumstances (be they social, economic, or physical health), in *World of Warcraft* you can choose your physical attributes, and hard work will bring wealth and status.

In all three cases, the boundary between the real and the virtual is blurry. It is practically impossible to separate the two. However, virtual dystopias are attractive, in part, because they seem to offer transcendence, an escape from the banal routine of everyday life. As media forms, William Gibson's cyberspace trilogy and the film *Inception* offer the audience a window into virtual dystopia from a safe place. In this way, they have much in common with pre-Internet versions of virtual dystopia in art and architecture. *World of Warcraft* differs, in that players are immersed in a virtual dystopia instead of experiencing it from a distance. Even still, gamers are removed, in that they can step out of the game at anytime, just as the reader can close the book, or the viewer can press stop or walk out of the theater. What all three cases exemplify, however, is that virtual dystopias are attractive, because of their connection to the sublime. The astonishment, awe, and terror that are faced in virtual dystopias transport people out of their everyday experiences and allow them to contemplate their place in the universe or existence, or, in the case of *World of Warcraft*, to experience a sense of social cohesion, community and belonging that might be lacking in "real" life.

References

Aarseth, E. 2008. A Hollow World: World of Warcraft as Spatial Practice. In *Digital Culture, Play and Identity: A World of Warcraft Reader*, edited by H. G. Corneliussen and J. W. Rettberg, 111–122. Cambridge, MA: MIT Press.

Ayers, T., ed. 2008. *The History of British Art: 600–1600*. New Haven, CT: Yale University Press.

Battersby, C. 2007. *The Sublime, Terror, and Human Difference*. London: Routledge.

Booker, M. K. 1994. *The Dystopian Impulse in Modern Literature*. Westport, CO: Greenwood Press.

Burke, E. (1757) 1990. *A Philosophical Enquiry into the Origin of our Ideas of the Sublime and Beautiful*. Oxford: Oxford University Press.

Carey, J. 1989. *Communication as Culture: Essays on Media and Society*. Boston: Unwin Hyman.

Carnagey, N., C. Anderson, and B. Bushman. 2007. The Effect of Video Game Violence on Physiological Desensitization to Real-Life Violence. *Journal of Experimental Social Psychology* 43 (3): 489–496.

Castronova, E. 2005. *Synthetic Worlds: The Business and Culture of Online Games*. Chicago: University of Chicago Press.

Corneliussen, H. G., and J. W. Rettberg. 2008. "Introduction: 'Orc Professor, LFG' or Researching in Azeroth." In *Digital Culture, Play, and Identity: A "World of Warcraft" Reader*, edited by Hilde G. Corneliussen and Jill Walker Rettberg, 1–15. Cambridge, MA: MIT Press.

Crowther, P. 1989. *The Kantian Sublime*. Oxford: Clarendon Press.

Dennis, J. (1704) 1996. The Grounds of Criticism in Poetry. In *The Sublime: A Reader in British Eighteenth-Century Aesthetic Theory*, edited by A. Ashfield and P. de Bolla, 35–39. Cambridge: Cambridge University Press.

Ducheneaut, N., N. Yee, E. Nickell, and R. Moore. 2006. Building an MMO with Mass Appeal: A Look at Gameplay in *World of Warcraft. Games and Culture* 1 (4): 281–316.

Flew, T. 2008. *New Media: An Introduction*. Oxford: Oxford University Press.

Gibson, W. 1973. *Hieronymus Bosch*. New York: Praeger.

Gibson, W. 1984. *Neuromancer*. New York: Ace Books.

Gibson, W. 1986. *Count Zero*. New York: Ace Books.

Gibson, W. 1988. *Mona Lisa Overdrive*. New York: Ace Books.

Hertz, N. 1985. *The End of the Line: Essays on Psychoanalysis and the Sublime*. New York: Columbia University Press.

Kant, I. (1790) 2007. *Critique of Judgment*. Edited by N. Walker. Translated by J. C. Meredith. Oxford: Oxford University Press.

Kirwan, J. 2005. *Sublimity: The Non-rational and the Irrational in the History of Aesthetics*. New York: Routledge.

Klastrup, L. 2008. What Makes *World of Warcraft* a World? A Note on Death and Dying. In *Digital Culture, Play, and Identity: A "World of Warcraft" Reader*, edited by H. G. Corneliussen and J. W. Rettberg, 143–166. Cambridge, MA: MIT Press.

Kryzwinska, T., and H. Lowood. 2006. Guest Editors' Introduction. *Games and Culture* 1 (4): 279–280.

Malone, K.-L. 2009. Dragon Kill Points: The Economics of Power Games. *Games and Culture* 4 (3): 296–316.

Marvin, C. 1988. *When Old Technologies Were New: Thinking about Electronic Communication in the Late Nineteenth Century*. New York: Oxford University Press.

Marx, L. 1964. *The Machine in the Garden: Technology and the Pastoral Ideal in America*. New York: Oxford University Press.

McGonigal, J. 2011. *Reality Is Broken: Why Games Make Us Better and How They Can Change the World*. New York: Penguin.

Mosco, V. 2004. *The Digital Sublime: Myth, Power, and Cyberspace*. Cambridge, MA: MIT Press.

Nolan, C. dir. 2010. *Inception*. Warner Brothers Pictures.

Nye, D. 1994. *American Technological Sublime*. Cambridge, MA: MIT Press.

Nye, D. 1990. *Electrifying America*. Cambridge, MA: MIT Press.

Rettberg, S. 2008. Corporate Ideology in *World of Warcraft*. In *Digital Culture, Play, and Identity: A "World of Warcraft" Reader*, edited by H. G. Corneliussen and J. W. Rettberg, 19–38. Cambridge, MA: MIT Press.

Sargent, L. T. 2006. In Defense of Utopia. *Diogenes* 209: 11–17.

Shaw, P. 2006. *The Sublime*. London: Routledge.

Shields, R. 2003. *The Virtual*. London: Routledge.

Slaughter, R. A. 2004. *Futures beyond Dystopia: Creating Social Foresight*. London: Routledge.

Standage, T. 1998. *The Victorian Internet: The Remarkable Story of the Telegraph and the Nineteenth Century's On-line Pioneers*. New York: Walker and Company.

Thacker, E. 2011. *In the Dust of this Planet*. Vol. 1 of *Horror of Philosophy*. Winchester, UK: Zero Books.

Turkle, S. 1995. *Life on the Screen*. New York: Simon and Schuster.

Vieira, F. 2010. The Concept of Utopia. In *The Cambridge Companion to Utopian Literature*, edited by G. Claeys, 3–27. Cambridge: Cambridge University Press.

Voller, J. G. 1993. Neuromanticism: Cyberspace and the Sublime. *Extrapolation* 34 (1): 18–29.

Wertheim, M. 1999. *The Pearly Gates of Cyberspace*. New York: Norton.

Game

World of Warcraft. 2004–2013. Blizzard Entertainment. http://us.battle.net/wow/en/. Accessed June 30, 2013.

AN AFTERWORD IN FOUR BINARISMS

....

TOM BOELLSTORFF

THE 44 chapters comprising this handbook defy easy categorization or even summation. The topics their authors address, as well as the methods and conceptual apparatuses they bring to bear, vary so greatly that any attempt at a unified conclusion would obfuscate more than it would reveal. In place of such a misguided quest I here provide an afterword in four binarisms that capture key insights and tensions running through the constituent chapters of this handbook. These resonate with my own research agendas (see Boellstorff 2008; 2011a) and the ethnographic research that has been one valuable approach to exploring these agendas (as detailed in *Ethnography and Virtual Worlds: A Handbook of Method*, Boellstorff et al. 2012, and the work of my coauthors Bonnie Nardi (2010), Celia Pearce (2006), and T.L. Taylor (2009)).

My turn to dualisms as analytical trope reflects my appreciation for the place of discreteness in the constitution of the digital, at its base a combination of 1s and 0s (Boellstorff 2012). Dualism is not the invention of René Descartes, Christianity and its opposition of Word and Flesh, Daoism and its opposition of yin and yang, or any other such historical specificity. Dualism is a foundational feature of all human languages, indeed of information as such and even the quantum mechanics whose discrete entities undergird the real. At issue is not the transcendence or dissolution of dualism but its deontologization—recognizing its contingency and emergence, and thus its vulnerability to deconstruction and reconfiguration. It is in this spirit that I proffer the following binarisms as points of entry for reconsidering virtuality.

ONE: REALITY AND WORLD

When it comes to the question of the virtual as it relates to technology, one of the most fundamental sources of confusion involves virtual reality versus virtual world. So often we are talking past each other, one interlocutor discussing virtual reality while the other expounds on virtual worlds. "Virtual reality" focuses attention on perception and the individual body. It raises questions of goggles and gloves, sight and sound, touch and taste and smell. The virtuality in question is one of immersion and presence in terms of sensory input.

The notion of "virtual world" refers to something very different. At issue here are online places that persist even as individuals enter and leave them. These online places need not require the sensory immersion of virtual reality interfaces. Early virtual worlds were based solely on text, and a few still are. Most contemporary virtual worlds have beautiful graphics and dynamic sound, but few seek to extend further into the sensorium; even with regard to vision and hearing, sensory immersion is rarely the goal. Most participants are happy with desktop, laptop, or even mobile device screens that do not surround them in terms of the senses.

The crucial kind of presence with regard to virtual worlds is social presence: the ability to be copresent with social others, not all of them necessarily human (some can be computer-controlled characters). Such copresence is linked to the place-ness of virtual worlds. This is clearly demonstrated by the fact that asynchronic sociality is important in most virtual worlds. Because virtual worlds are places, it is, for instance, possible for me to start work on a building, log off, and then for you to log in and continue working collaboratively on the building even though I am not there. Note that this kind of asynchronic social presence could take place in a text-only virtual world and has very little to do with the notion of virtual reality. Virtual reality is always about synchronic engagement: a sensory stimulus or response now, in the present moment.

Just how far the "virtual" of virtual reality is from the "virtual" of virtual worlds is illustrated by the fact that virtual reality does not even need the Internet. You can put on a set of virtual reality goggles linked by wires to a camera a volunteer carries around a room. In contrast, few scholarly or everyday understandings of "virtual world" would include a computer-generated place that existed only on one computer and ceased to be whenever that computer was turned off, even if that place had avatars. Histories of virtual worlds typically begin with text-based Multi User Domains (MUDs) that had no pretension to virtual reality whatsoever. What they had was place-ness (not just a sense of place) and social immersion made possible through an Internet connection, even at "dial-up" speeds.

Science fiction and other works of artistic imagination have often anticipated aspects of virtual reality and virtual worlds, and have even played demonstrable roles in their design. However, science fiction is not always a reliable guide to empirical reality. One way in which this has been the case has been with regard to the conflation and thus confusion of virtual reality and virtual worlds. *The Matrix* trilogy of movies is an influential exemplar. In these films, virtual reality—full sensory immersion via being "plugged in" while prone in a chair, oblivious to the physical world—is coupled with a virtual world, the "Matrix" itself, which appears as a modern urban environment. Here, virtual reality is assumed to be the method for accessing a virtual world. One does not imagine Neo holding up an iPad and swiping his fingers across the screen to engage in fisticuffs with his evil opponent.

The reality, of course, is that the domains of virtual reality and virtual world are more like a Venn diagram, with only a slight overlap. Most virtual reality devices are not about virtual worlds, and most virtual worlds do not make use of virtual reality devices. It is possible to use virtual reality technologies to access virtual worlds, but this seems to be of limited interest, for instance military and medical uses. Even in the domain of online gaming, where sensory immersion might seem attractive, there is little evidence for a significant interest in virtual reality technologies, but rather new frontiers of "augmented reality" that overlay the virtual and the actual without resolving them into one. Binarisms persist. This has significant import for any understanding of "virtuality," because it indicates that we are not talking about a single concept. We will often be making apples-and-oranges arguments when talking about the virtual if we assume that both virtual reality and virtual worlds lie within our analytical purview. In other cases we may indeed be hitting on elements of the virtual common to virtual reality and virtual worlds, but this cannot be presumed at the outset.

Two: Unreal and Real

These confusions regarding the relatively minor overlap between "virtual reality" and "virtual world"—and thus the divergent notions of virtuality in play—relate directly to the second binarism under discussion, that of "real" versus what I will provisionally term the "unreal." The deeply flawed opposition between virtual and real, with the concomitant narrative they are increasingly "blurring," remains the single biggest conceptual impediment to a more robust and accurate understanding of virtuality. The opposition between virtual and real is a normative move that a priori consigns the virtual to the domain of unreality. It undermines the legitimacy and value of research on virtuality and can imply a romantic notion of reality that has no Internet in it—or no computers in it, or even no technology in it.

What constitutes the "real" when placed in a dichotomous relationship with the virtual is rarely consistent or clear. There is of course a longstanding and vibrant interdisciplinary body of work addressing questions of the real. This work can draw from notions of ideal form in a Platonic tradition, or notions of brute physicality. It can draw from Lacanian notions of a supposedly universal stage of human development, or Marxist notions of an economic base. Philip K. Dick, one of the most astute science fiction authors, famously defined reality as "that which, when you stop believing in it, doesn't go away" (Dick 1985, 3).

The problem is that no matter what definition of "the real" you use, there is no way to exclude virtuality and particularly virtual worlds without caricaturing the virtual as always already fantastical, unproductive, and inconsequential. Yet we see aptly demonstrated a range of fascinating ways that virtuality has social consequences, online and offline. This compels us to continue the theoretical and empirical work of investigating the ontological status of the virtual, and thereby the ontological status of what is often termed the actual or physical. But all this, online or offline, is real in some fashion, and unreality—however defined—is not exclusive to the virtual.

One factor contributing to these confusions involves the category mistake of taking a subset of activities that occur within a virtual context as indicative of virtuality writ large. For instance, one of the most popular uses of virtual worlds is for gaming, as can be seen by online games like *World of Warcraft*. When the broad appeal of such games is taken to indicate unreality (often coupled with the suggestion that the gamers in question "get a life"), two levels of misconstrual result. First, as noted by Richard Bartle, a pioneer in the development of virtual worlds, "virtual worlds are not games. Even the ones written to *be* games aren't games. People can play games *in* them, sure, and they can be set up to that end, but this merely makes them venues. The Pasadena Rose Bowl is a stadium, not a game" (Bartle 2004, 475, emphasis in original). Second, using the existence of games to diagnose unreality ignores how games are consequential and very "real" aspects of all human cultures. Similarly, the fact that forms of drama, playacting, and role-playing take place in some virtual worlds does not make them unreal—first, because these activities do not take place in all virtual worlds, and second, because such activities are part of social reality. All told, then, there is a need for rethinking the relationship of the real not just to technology but also to representation, social construction, and production. Reconsidering the binarism of real and unreal will thus provide us with a better conceptual framework for apprehending the consequentiality of virtuality itself.

THREE: EMIC AND ETIC

A third binarism central to current tensions and debates over virtuality involves the distinction between what anthropologists term emic (insider) versus etic (outsider) concepts, a terminology first developed by the philosopher Kenneth Pike on the model of the linguistic distinction between phonemic and phonetic analysis (see Geertz 1983, 56–57). It often happens that an etic term will become emic over time. "Homosexual," for instance, was an etic term originating from the mid-nineteenth-century world of sexology but later became an emic term, such that individuals could say, "I am homosexual" (Boellstorff 2011b). Emic terms can also become etic: a convenient parallel example is "gay," which began as insider slang but has since become a term of psychological theory. Both these examples illustrate how some concepts can be simultaneously emic and etic.

Such multiplicity of emic and etic definition is a hallmark of "virtual." Unlike, say, "asynchronic" or "ontological," "virtual" is an everyday term. In colloquial English it can mean "almost," as in "we are virtually home." It now also can act as a synonym for "online." Everyday notions of "virtual world" are typically not informed by a Deleuzeian opposition to the actual, nor by a concern with potentiality or becoming: the reference is usually simply to a place you go to online that looks three-dimensional and where you can play a game or shop. Additionally, while many Internet-related terms globalize and become loanwords in other languages, this does not always happen, and of course a "loanword" takes on new meanings over time.

For researchers, designers, and participants, a crucial area for clarification and conversation involves ambiguities as to whether we are using "virtual" as an etic or emic term, and also the existence of multiple etic and emic definitions. Nor is this issue unique to the notion of virtuality: "real" and "game" are also examples of terms used in emic and etic senses, with multiple definitions in both cases. Even the notions of "immersion" and "presence" are not immune from these dynamics. In all these cases, the existence of multiple definitions is not necessarily a problem to be resolved. It may accurately reflect the reality of multiple cultural logics, multiple modalities and platforms for online engagement, and multiple communities of scholarly practice.

At issue here is not just matters of terminological precision, important as those are, but matters of perspectival knowledge. The study of online culture is often marked by a slippage between the descriptive and the proscriptive, from the analysis of what is, to claims regarding what someone thinks should be. Such slippages are enabled by slippages between the emic and etic. Proscriptive recommendations are certainly legitimate—they are in fact necessary to everything from design to activism. Etic analysis is valid as well, for while it is important that researchers be able to write in multiple voices and genres for multiple audiences, outsider analyses written primarily for one's research community have much to offer. To push forward the conversation on virtuality, however, it is vital to be clear as to when we are speaking in emic or etic terms, and to value descriptive, emic theorizations of the virtual before rushing to a proscriptive or normative mode. It is exciting to see the many careful lines of inquiry in formation that engage with these varied modes of apprehending virtuality.

FOUR: UTOPIA AND DYSTOPIA

The forms of prescription and normative judgment discussed above with regard to insider versus outsider perspectives are aspects of the fourth and final binarism I will discuss, that of utopia and dystopia. As an anthropologist I am trained to regard claims of human universals with suspicion, for all too often they turn out to be the thinly disguised lifeways and perspectives of those in power. Yet we cannot allow such healthy skepticism to imply we can only talk about locality, not least because localities can be predicated on hegemonies of their own. With regard to virtuality, it is worth attending to the fact that while the pattern is not a rigid universal, it is certainly the case that, throughout human history, emerging technologies have been met with simultaneous narratives of utopia and dystopia. An exemplary body of scholarship has shown how new technologies tend not to be interpreted neutrally, but rather as potentially bringing great good—even saving humanity—or as harbingers of destruction and oppression.

Indeed, the relative subsidence of such utopian and dystopian narratives often indicates that a technology is no longer seen as such, but has become a mundane tool for living.

We are on the threshold of new banalities of virtuality: the embedding of virtuality into everyday life. This banalization and new ubiquity for the virtual does not mean that everything will become augmentation, and virtual worlds will disappear. Nor does it mean that virtual worlds will become dominant and we will live our lives jacked into fantasy landscapes. Against the tendency of some thinkers and "evangelists" to posit lockstep stages and rigid timelines, reality usually moves in many directions at once. For instance, while highly immersive virtual worlds will certainly continue, we are already seeing the rise of virtual worlds that are integrated into social networking sites (as Cloud Party is integrated with Facebook). The avatarization of the self (which appears not just in avatars narrowly conceived, but in things like a Facebook homepage) will be transformed as the "personal cloud" emerges as a central form of aggregate online selfhood.

At the risk of sounding obvious, we will see continuity and change, augmentation and immersion. We will see uses of the virtual that we can deem detrimental—addictive, callous, crassly commercial, bigoted, and cruel. We will see uses of the virtual that we can deem beneficial—liberating, community-building, self-transforming, and challenging of established hierarchies and centers of power. We will continue rediscovering that these questions of benefit or detriment cannot be absolutely associated with any particular technological configuration; they are rather the products of social action—what we do with the technologies in their design, experience, and unexpected hackings and repurposings. It is thus in our engagement with technology and social action that we can better understand virtuality in its past formations and present-day dynamics—and work toward better futures.

References

Bartle, R. A. 2004. *Designing Virtual Worlds*. Indianapolis, IN: New Riders.

Boellstorff, T. 2008. *Coming of Age in Second Life: An Anthropologist Explores the Virtually Human*. Princeton, NJ: Princeton University Press.

Boellstorff, T. 2011a. Placing the Virtual Body: Avatar, Chora, Cypherg. In *A Companion to the Anthropology of the Body and Embodiment*, edited by Frances E. Mascia-Lees, 504–520. New York: Wiley-Blackwell.

Boellstorff, T. 2011b. But Do Not Identify as Gay: A Proleptic Genealogy of the MSM Category. *Cultural Anthropology* 26(2): 287–312.

Boellstorff, T. 2012. Rethinking Digital Anthropology. In *Digital Anthropology*, edited by H. A. Horst and D. Miller, 39–60. London: Berg.

Boellstorff, T., B. Nardi, C. Pearce, and T. L. Taylor. 2012. *Ethnography and Virtual Worlds: A Handbook of Method*. Princeton, NJ: Princeton University Press.

Dick, P. K. 1985. How to Build a Universe That Doesn't Fall Apart Two Days Later. In *I Hope I Shall Arrive Soon*, 1–23. Garden City, NY: Doubleday.

Geertz, C. 1983. "From the Native's Point of View": On the Nature of Anthropological Understanding. In *Local Knowledge: Further Essays in Interpretive Anthropology*, 55–72. New York: Basic Books.

Nardi, B. 2010. *My Life as a Night Elf Priest: An Anthropological Account of World of Warcraft*. Ann Arbor: University of Michigan Press.

Pearce, C. 2009. *Communities of Play: Emergent Cultures in Online Games and Virtual Worlds*. Cambridge: MIT Press.

Taylor, T. L. 2006. *Play Between Worlds: Exploring Online Game Culture*. Cambridge: MIT Press.

INDEX

....

Note: Page numbers end in "f" indicate figures; those ending in "t" indicate tables.